BOARD OF EDUCATION
OF CHARLES COUNTY
LA PLATA, MARYLAND 20646

TEXTBOOK LABEL

Book No._____

Property of

Thomas Stone High School

(Name of School)

INSTRUCTIONS: The pupil to whom this book is loaned will sign in space provided below. He or she will be required to pay to this school the cost price of this book if it is lost or damaged during the period for which it is loaned. Allowance will be made for wear caused by careful use.

Signature of Pupil	Date Loaned	Condition

Heath
BIOLOGY

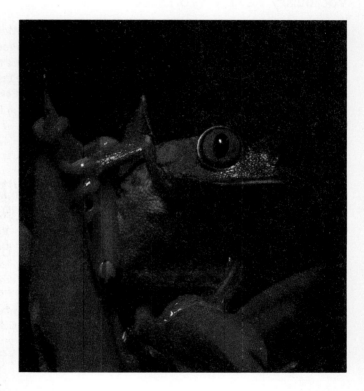

James E. McLaren
Biology Teacher
Newton South High School
Newton Centre, MA

Lissa Rotundo
Biology Teacher
Baltimore Polytechnic Institute
Baltimore, MD

'Laine Gurley-Dilger, Ph.D.
Biology Teacher
Township High School, District 214
Arlington Heights, IL

CONTRIBUTING WRITERS

Ricki Lewis, Ph.D.
Lecturer in Biology and Science Writer
State University of New York at Albany
Albany, NY

Ronnee Bernberg Yashon
Biology Teacher
Lake View High School
Chicago, IL

Hunter Havelin Adams
Researcher, Science
  Consultant
Argonne National Laboratory
Chicago, IL

D.C. Heath and Company
Lexington, Massachusetts/Toronto, Ontario

HEATH BIOLOGY PROGRAM

Pupil's Edition
Teacher's Edition
Teacher's Master Assignment Guide
Laboratory Investigations
Laboratory Investigations, Teacher's
   Edition
Study Guide
Blackline Transparency Masters
Vocabulary Review Worksheets

Biology Matters
Teacher's Resource File
Overhead Transparencies
Computer Test Bank
Computer Test Bank, Teacher's Guide
Biosolve Software: Internal Medicine,
   Infectious Disease, Toxicology
Support Sampler and Answer Book

Executive Editor: Ellen M. Lappa
Editorial Development: Marilyn J. Steele, Toby Klang,
   Tracey L. Cohen
Project, Cover Design: Jane Miron
Design Assistance: Irene Elios, Lisa Fowler, Myril
   Sheer, Nancy Smith-Evers, Richard Spencer

Marketing Manager: Richard G. Ravich
Production: Mary Hunter, Barbara Kirk
Editorial Services: Marianna Frew Palmer
Readability Testing: J & F Incorporated
Cover Photograph: Red-eyed tree frog; Kevin Schafer,
   Peter Arnold, Inc.

CONTENT REVIEWERS

Barry Bogin, Ph.D.
Department of Behavioral Sciences
University of Michigan
Dearborn, MI

Harry Haigler, Ph.D.
Associate Professor of Biophysics
   and Physiology
University of California
Irvine, CA

Robert Jurmain, Ph.D.
Professor of Anthropology
San Jose State University
San Jose, CA

Elias Lazarides, Ph.D.
Division of Biology
California Institute of Technology
Pasadena, CA

Leo Richards, Ph.D.
Associate Professor of Curriculum
   and Instruction
University of Southern California
Los Angeles, CA

Maureen Stanton, Ph.D.
Associate Professor of Botany
University of California
Davis, CA

Claude Villee, Ph.D.
Andelot Professor of Biological
   Chemistry, Emeritus
Harvard University Medical School
Boston, MA

Published simultaneously in Canada
Printed in the United States of America
International Standard Book Code Number 0-669-25710-9
   4 5 6 7 8 9 0

CONTENTS

UNIT 1 — INTRODUCTION TO BIOLOGY

Chapter 1 — SCIENCE OF LIFE   2

NATURE OF BIOLOGY   3
☐ Science, Biology, and You   ☐ Themes in Biology   ☐ Investigating a Problem   ☐ Controlled Experiments   ☐ The Research Method   ☐ Scientific Theories   ☐ Following Scientific Leads
WORKING IN BIOLOGY   12
☐ Extending the Senses   ☐ Microscopes   ☐ Electron Microscopes   ☐ Tools of a New Age
Laboratory Activity: A Controlled Experiment   17   **Chapter Review**   18

Chapter 2 — CHARACTERISTICS OF LIFE   20

BIOGENESIS: LIFE PRODUCES LIFE   21
☐ Spontaneous Generation   ☐ Where Do Microorganisms Come From?
☐ Pasteur Provides an Answer
RECOGNIZING LIFE   27
☐ Some Characteristics of Life   ☐ Discovery and Importance of Cells
☐ More Unique Characteristics of Life   ☐ Summarizing the Characteristics of Life
Laboratory Activity: Distinguishing a Living Thing from a
Nonliving Thing   33   **Chapter Review**   34

Chapter 3 — BASIC CHEMISTRY   36

COMPOSITION OF MATTER   37
☐ Elements Make Matter   ☐ Atoms Make Elements
☐ Atoms Have Energy   ☐ Compounds from Elements
CHANGES IN MATTER   41
☐ Covalent Bonding   ☐ Ions and Ionic Bonding   ☐ Chemical Reactions
☐ Mixtures and Solutions   ☐ Acids and Bases
Laboratory Activity: Observing a Chemical Reaction   47
Chapter Review   48

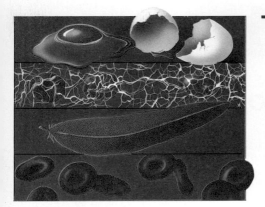

Chapter

4   BIOMOLECULES   50

CARBON AND BASIC BUILDING BLOCKS   51
☐ Organic Compounds   ☐ Carbohydrates   ☐ Lipids
PROTEINS AND ENZYMES   58
☐ Amino Acids and Proteins   ☐ Protein Shape and Function
☐ Enzymes
Laboratory Activity: Properties of an Enzyme   63
Chapter Review   64

Chapter

5   CELL STRUCTURE AND FUNCTION   66

THE CELL: THE BASIC UNIT OF LIFE   67
☐ The Work of a Cell   ☐ Structure of a Cell   ☐ The Nucleus   ☐ Cytoplasm:
Cytosol and Organelles   ☐ The Plasma Membrane   ☐ The Cell Wall
THE CELL AND ITS ENVIRONMENT   77
☐ Diffusion   ☐ Permeability   ☐ Selective Permeability
and Osmosis   ☐ Animal Cells and Osmosis
☐ Turgor Pressure and Plasmolysis
THE CELL'S LIVING BOUNDARY   83
☐ Passive vs. Active Transport   ☐ Facilitated Diffusion
☐ Active Transport
Laboratory Activity: The Response of Plant Cells
        to Environmental Change   86
Chapter Review   87

Chapter

6   ENERGY AND THE CELL   90

ENERGY FROM FOOD   91
☐ ATP: Energy Currency of the Cell   ☐ Fermentation   ☐ Cell Respiration: An Overview
☐ Cell Respiration: Chemical Steps   ☐ Fermentation in Aerobic Organisms
PHOTOSYNTHESIS: CAPTURING THE SUN'S ENERGY   99
☐ Light Reactions   ☐ Calvin Cycle and Its Products
☐ Comparing Photosynthesis and Respiration
Laboratory Activity: Role of Light in Photosynthesis   105
Chapter Review   106

Chapter

7 CELL REGULATION 108

NATURE OF DNA 109
☐ Nucleic Acids ☐ Function of DNA ☐ Structure of DNA ☐ DNA Code ☐ Replication of DNA
PROTEIN SYNTHESIS 114
☐ Structure and Function of RNA ☐ Transcription: DNA to RNA ☐ How the Code Works
☐ Translation: RNA to Protein
Laboratory Activity: Transcription and Translation 119
CUTTING EDGE: Gene Silencers 120 **Chapter Review** 122

Chapter

8 MITOSIS AND CELL DIVISION 124

DIVISION OF CELLS 125
☐ Mitosis ☐ Cytokinesis
SIGNIFICANCE OF MITOSIS AND CELL DIVISION 129
☐ Unicellular Organisms ☐ How Size Affects Cells ☐ Multicellular Organisms
☐ Tissues, Organs, and Systems ☐ Cell Replacement
REGULATION OF MITOSIS AND CELL DIVISION 134
☐ Lifespan of a Cell ☐ Growth Regulators in Healthy Cells ☐ Abnormal Cell Division ☐ Cancer
Laboratory Activity: How a Cell Is Affected by the Surface-to-Volume Ratio 139
CUTTING EDGE: New Weapons to Fight Cancer 140 **Chapter Review** 142
ISSUES IN BIOETHICS: Data Faked to Get Grant 144 **Unit Review** 145

UNIT **2** *GENETICS AND EVOLUTION*

Chapter

9 BASIS OF HEREDITY 148

PATTERNS OF INHERITANCE 149
☐ Mendel's Hybrid Peas ☐ Dominant and Recessive Traits ☐ The Principle of Segregation
☐ Genotype and Phenotype ☐ Solving Genetics Problems ☐ Testcross
☐ Principle of Independent Assortment ☐ Codominance
THE CELLULAR BASIS OF HEREDITY 157
☐ Chromosome Number ☐ Asexual and Sexual Reproduction ☐ Meiosis
☐ The Chromosome Theory of Inheritance
Laboratory Activity: Probability and Heredity 161 **Chapter Review** 162

Chapter

10 CHROMOSOMES AND GENES 164

CHROMOSOMES AND INHERITANCE 165
☐ Sex Determination ☐ Sex Linkage and Linkage Groups
☐ Sex Linkage in Humans ☐ Crossing Over
CHANGES IN GENETIC MATERIAL 170
☐ Mutagens ☐ Nondisjunction: A Chromosomal Mutation
☐ Other Chromosomal Mutations ☐ Gene Mutations
Laboratory Activity: Mapping Genes Using
       Crossover Frequency **175**
CUTTING EDGE: Somatic Gene Therapy **176**
Chapter Review 178

Chapter

11 HUMAN INHERITANCE 180

PATTERNS OF INHERITANCE 181
☐ Traits Controlled by Multiple Alleles ☐ Traits Determined by Multiple Genes
☐ Sex-Limited and Sex-Influenced Traits ☐ Genes and the Environment
HUMAN DISORDERS 184
☐ Disorders Caused by Gene Mutations ☐ Disorders Caused by Nondisjunction
DETECTING DISORDERS 189
☐ Identifying Carriers ☐ Finding Disorders Before Birth ☐ Genetic Counseling
TREATING DISORDERS 193
☐ Treatment During Pregnancy ☐ Treating Inborn Errors of Metabolism
   Laboratory Activity: Dihybrid Crosses **195**
      CUTTING EDGE: Sequencing the Human Genome **196**   **Chapter Review 198**

Chapter

12 APPLICATIONS OF GENETICS 200

CONTROLLED BREEDING 201
☐ Selection ☐ Inbreeding ☐ Hybridization
ARTIFICIAL METHODS OF GENETIC CONTROL 205
☐ Polyploidy ☐ Cloning ☐ Genetic Engineering ☐ Manipulating Nature
Laboratory Activity: Production of Genetically Identical Plants by
       Vegetative Propagation **209**
CUTTING EDGE: Deliberate Release of Genetically Engineered Microbes **210**
Chapter Review 212

Chapter

13 POPULATION GENETICS 214

VARIATION IN POPULATIONS   215
☐ Definition of Species   ☐ Clines and Subspecies   ☐ Gene Pool
☐ Hardy-Weinberg Principle
CHANGES IN POPULATIONS   221
☐ Mutation   ☐ Small Populations   ☐ Nonrandom Mating   ☐ Migration
☐ Harmful Genes
Laboratory Activity: Understanding a Gene Pool   **225**
CUTTING EDGE: Are Cheetahs on the Road to Extinction?   **226**
Chapter Review   228

Chapter

14 EVOLUTION 230

EVIDENCE OF EVOLUTION   231
☐ Evidence from Fossils   ☐ Determining the Age of Fossils
☐ Evidence from Structure   ☐ Evidence from Development
☐ Evidence from Molecular Biology
THEORY OF EVOLUTION   236
☐ Early Evolutionary Theory   ☐ Darwin and Natural Selection
PROCESS OF EVOLUTION   239
☐ Natural Selection Observed   ☐ Speciation   ☐ Adaptive Radiation
☐ Convergent Evolution   ☐ Stabilizing Selection
☐ The Pace of Evolution
Laboratory Activity: Variations Among Individuals   **245**
Chapter Review   246

Chapter

15 HISTORY OF LIFE 248

ORIGIN OF LIFE   249
☐ Chemical Evolution   ☐ First Cells   ☐ Origin of Eukaryotes
MULTICELLULAR LIFE   254
☐ Precambrian Era   ☐ Paleozoic Era   ☐ Mesozoic Era: Age of Reptiles
☐ Cenozoic Era: Age of Mammals
Laboratory Activity: Coacervates—A Model for Cell Evolution   **259**
Chapter Review   260

Chapter
16 HUMAN EVOLUTION 262

THE HUMAN AS A PRIMATE 263
☐ Primate Characteristics ☐ Apes and Humans
TRACING HUMAN EVOLUTION 267
☐ Evidence of Human Evolution ☐ Early Hominid Fossils
☐ Later Hominid Forms ☐ Culture and Human Brain Evolution ☐ Modern Humans
Laboratory Activity: Comparing Primate Hemoglobins 272
Chapter Review 274

Chapter
17 CLASSIFICATION OF LIFE 276

SYSTEMS OF CLASSIFICATION 277
☐ Binomial Nomenclature ☐ Levels of Classification ☐ Modern Techniques of Classification
☐ Three-Kingdom System ☐ Five-Kingdom System
IDENTIFYING ORGANISMS 284
☐ How a Classification Key Works ☐ How to Use a Classification Key
Laboratory Activity: Using a Classification Key to Identify Insects 287
CUTTING EDGE: The Number of Species on Earth 288
Chapter Review 290
ISSUES IN BIOETHICS: Geneticist Refuses Screening 292
Unit Review 293

UNIT **3** *MICROBIOLOGY*

Chapter
18 MONERANS AND VIRUSES 296

KINGDOM MONERA 297
☐ Moneran Cells ☐ Classification of Monerans ☐ Nutrition ☐ Reproduction in Monerans
☐ Exchange of Genetic Material ☐ Importance of Bacteria
VIRUSES 305
☐ Structure of Viruses ☐ Replication of Viruses ☐ Types of Viruses ☐ AIDS Virus
☐ Treatment of Viral Diseases ☐ Viruses and Cancer ☐ Origin of Viruses
Laboratory Activity: Growing Bacteria in the Laboratory 313
Chapter Review 314

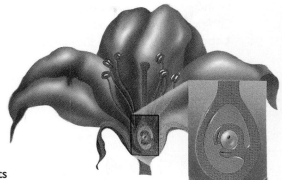

Chapter
19 PROTISTS 316

ANIMALLIKE PROTISTS 317
☐ Sarcodines ☐ Ciliates ☐ Other Animallike Protists
PLANTLIKE PROTISTS 322
☐ Unicellular Algae ☐ Multicellular Algae ☐ Reproduction in Multicellular Algae
FUNGUSLIKE PROTISTS 330
☐ Acellular Slime Molds ☐ Cellular Slime Molds ☐ Mildew and Water Molds
Laboratory Activity: Structure and Population Growth of *Blepharisma* 333
Chapter Review 334

Chapter
20 FUNGI 336

CHARACTERISTICS OF FUNGI 337
☐ Structure of Fungi ☐ Nutrition in Fungi ☐ Reproduction in Fungi
VARIETY OF FUNGI 339
☐ Zygomycota ☐ Ascomycota ☐ Basidiomycota ☐ Imperfect Fungi ☐ Lichens
Laboratory Activity: Fungi and Lichens 345
Chapter Review 346
ISSUES IN BIOETHICS: AIDS Testing Law Passed 348   **Unit Review** 349

UNIT 4 PLANTS

Chapter
21 SEED PLANTS 352

ANGIOSPERMS 353
☐ Characteristics of Angiosperms ☐ Monocots and Dicots
FLOWERS 355
☐ Flower Structure ☐ Ovule and Pollen Formation ☐ Pollination ☐ Fertilization
FRUITS AND DISPERSAL 361
☐ Fruit Development and Structure ☐ Dispersal
GYMNOSPERMS 363
☐ Conifers ☐ Life Cycle of a Pine ☐ Other Gymnosperms
Laboratory Activity: Germination of Pollen Grains 367
Chapter Review 368

Chapter
22 PLANT STRUCTURE AND DEVELOPMENT 370

DEVELOPMENT OF THE PLANT BODY 371
☐ Seed Structure ☐ Seed Dormancy ☐ Germination and Establishment
PLANT BODY ORGANIZATION 374
☐ Organs of Seed Plants ☐ Plant Tissues
VEGETATIVE REPRODUCTION 378
☐ Natural Vegetative Propagation ☐ Applied Propagation Techniques
Laboratory Activity: The Effect of Moisture on the Germination of Radish Seeds 381
Chapter Review 382

Chapter
23 ROOTS AND STEMS 384

ROOT SYSTEMS AND GROWTH 385
☐ Root Systems ☐ Primary Growth in Roots ☐ Primary Root Tissues
☐ Secondary Growth in Roots ☐ Adventitious Roots
STEM STRUCTURE AND FUNCTION 389
☐ External Features of Stems ☐ Herbaceous Stems
☐ Primary Tissues of a Woody Stem ☐ Secondary Growth
of a Woody Stem ☐ Modified Stems
CONDUCTION OF WATER AND FOOD 395
☐ Intake of Water and Nutrients ☐ Conduction through the Xylem
☐ Translocation of Food
Laboratory Activity: Examination of the
Growing Tip of a Root 399
Chapter Review 400

Chapter
24 LEAVES 402

LEAF STRUCTURE AND FUNCTION 403
☐ Leaf Shape and Arrangement ☐ Structure of the Leaf ☐ Leaf Venation
☐ Photosynthesis in the Leaf ☐ Gas Exchange ☐ Transpiration ☐ Wilting
LEAF MODIFICATIONS 409
☐ Specialized Leaves ☐ Insectivorous Plants
Laboratory Activity: The Observation of Guard Cells 411
Chapter Review 412

x

Chapter

25 PLANT GROWTH AND RESPONSE   414

PATTERNS OF PLANT GROWTH   415
☐ Time Patterns of Plants   ☐ Growth Patterns of Plants   ☐ Plant Hormones   ☐ Apical Dominance
PLANT RESPONSE   419
☐ Tropisms   ☐ Control of Flowering   ☐ Leaf Senescence   ☐ Nastic Movements
Laboratory Activity: The Effect of Gibberellic Acid on Stem Growth   **423**
Chapter Review   424

Chapter

26 PLANT DIVERSITY AND EVOLUTION   426

PLANT KINGDOM   427
☐ Evolutionary Trends in Plants   ☐ Plant Classification
BRYOPHYTES   429
☐ Characteristics of Bryophytes   ☐ Mosses   ☐ Liverworts   ☐ Adaptations to Life on Land
SPORE-BEARING VASCULAR PLANTS   433
☐ Whiskferns   ☐ Club Mosses   ☐ Horsetails   ☐ Ferns
Laboratory Activity: Characteristics That Distinguish
Different Types of Plants   **437**
Chapter Review   438
ISSUES IN BIOETHICS: Rain Forest Vandalized   **440**
Unit Review   441

UNIT **5**   *INVERTEBRATES*

Chapter

27 SPONGES AND CNIDARIANS   444

CHARACTERISTICS OF ANIMALS   445
☐ Subkingdoms Parazoa and Metazoa   ☐ Animal Development   ☐ Body Symmetry
PHYLUM PORIFERA   450
☐ A Typical Sponge   ☐ Reproduction of Sponges   ☐ Sponge Diversity
PHYLUM CNIDARIA   453
☐ Polyps and Medusae   ☐ The Hydra: A Typical Cnidarian   ☐ Jellyfish, Sea Anemones, and Corals
Laboratory Activity: Microscopic Structure of Sponges and Cnidarians   **457**
Chapter Review   458

Chapter

28 WORMS 460

PHYLUM PLATYHELMINTHES: FLATWORMS 461
☐ Flatworm Characteristics ☐ Class Turbellaria: Free-Living Flatworms
☐ Class Trematoda: Flukes ☐ Class Cestoda: Tapeworms
PHYLUM NEMATODA: ROUNDWORMS 466
☐ Nematode Characteristics ☐ Parasitic Nematodes
PHYLUM ANNELIDA: SEGMENTED WORMS 468
☐ Annelid Characteristics ☐ Class Oligochaeta: Earthworms ☐ Other Annelids
Laboratory Activity: Comparing Flatworms and Roundworms 473
Chapter Review 474

Chapter

29 MOLLUSKS AND ECHINODERMS 476

PHYLUM MOLLUSCA 477
☐ Gastropoda: Snails and Slugs ☐ Class Pelecypoda: Bivalves
☐ Class Cephalopoda: Squids and Octopuses
PHYLUM ECHINODERMATA 482
☐ Characteristics of Echinoderms ☐ Class Asteroidea: Starfish
Laboratory Activity: Structure of a Squid 485
Chapter Review 486

Chapter

30 ARTHROPODS 488

SUBPHYLUM CHELICERATA 489
☐ General Arthropod Characteristics ☐ Characteristics of Chelicerates ☐ Class Arachnida: Spiders
☐ Other Chelicerates
SUBPHYLUM MANDIBULATA 493
☐ Class Crustacea ☐ Classes Diplopoda and Chilopoda
CLASS INSECTA 496
☐ Insect Body ☐ Insect Development ☐ Grasshopper
DIVERSITY OF INSECTS 501
☐ Feeding Adaptations ☐ Adaptations in Appearance ☐ Reproductive Adaptations ☐ Social Insects
Laboratory Activity: Observing Insect Behavior 505
Chapter Review 506
ISSUES IN BIOETHICS: Biological Controls vs. Pesticides 508   **Unit Review** 509

UNIT **6** *CHORDATES*

Chapter
31 VERTEBRATES 512

PHYLUM CHORDATA 513
☐ What Is a Chordate? ☐ Chordate Subphyla
VERTEBRATES 516
☐ What Is a Vertebrate? ☐ Vertebrate Classification ☐ Fossil Vertebrates
☐ Evolutionary Trends in Vertebrates
Laboratory Activity: Structure of a Primitive Chordate 521
Chapter Review 522

Chapter
32 FISH 524

JAWLESS FISH 525
☐ Primitive Fish
CARTILAGE FISH 527
☐ Skeleton and Movement of the Shark ☐ Shark Skin and Teeth ☐ Gas Exchange
☐ Temperature Regulation ☐ Shark Reproduction ☐ Rays and Skates
BONY FISH 530
☐ External Anatomy ☐ Digestion and Excretion ☐ Circulation and Gas Exchange
☐ The Nervous System of the Perch ☐ Reproduction in the Perch
☐ Adaptations of the Bony Fish ☐ Fossil Osteichthyes
Laboratory Activity: The Respiratory Rate of a Goldfish 537
Chapter Review 538

Chapter
33 AMPHIBIANS 540

CHARACTERISTICS OF AMPHIBIANS 541
☐ Evolving from Water to Live on Land ☐ A Typical Amphibian: The Frog ☐ Frog's Skeleton
☐ Frog Digestion and Excretion ☐ Frog Circulation ☐ Frog Respiration ☐ Frog's Nervous System
☐ Frog's Senses ☐ Frog Reproduction and Development
OTHER AMPHIBIANS 550
☐ Order Urodela: Salamanders ☐ Order Apoda ☐ Fossil Amphibians
Laboratory Activity: Frog Development 553 **Chapter Review** 554

Chapter
34 REPTILES 556

CHARACTERISTICS OF REPTILES 557
☐ Adaptations to Land ☐ Reptile Eggs
MODERN REPTILES 559
☐ Anatomy of the Snake ☐ Variety of Snakes ☐ Lizards ☐ Order Chelonia: Turtles ☐ Order Crocodilia ☐ Order Rhynchocephalia: Tuataras
REPTILE EVOLUTION 564
☐ Dinosaurs ☐ Other Extinct Reptiles
Laboratory Activity: Color Change in a Chameleon 567
Chapter Review 568

Chapter
35 BIRDS 570

CHARACTERISTICS OF BIRDS 571
☐ Origin of Birds ☐ Feathers ☐ Structures of the Head ☐ Other External Features
INTERNAL FEATURES OF BIRDS 575
☐ Skeleton ☐ Feeding and Digestion ☐ Respiratory System ☐ Circulatory System
☐ Excretory System ☐ Nervous System ☐ Reproduction ☐ Embryo Development
Laboratory Activity: Density of Bones 583   **Chapter Review** 584

Chapter
36 MAMMALS 586

CHARACTERISTICS OF MAMMALS 587
☐ Common Features of Mammals ☐ Mammalian Development
MONOTREMES AND MARSUPIALS 589
☐ Characteristics of Monotremes ☐ Characteristics of Marsupials
☐ Representative Marsupials
PLACENTAL MAMMALS 592
☐ Characteristics of Placental Mammals ☐ Some Types of Placentals
MAMMAL EVOLUTION 599
☐ Origin of Mammals ☐ Rise of Modern Horses: An Example of Mammalian Evolution
Laboratory Activity: Effect of Temperature on Respiration 601
Chapter Review 602
Evolution of Life 604
Evolution of Vertebrates 606
ISSUES IN BIOETHICS: Teens Debate Animal Rights 610
Unit Review 611

UNIT **7**

THE HUMAN BODY

Chapter

37 BONES, MUSCLES, AND SKIN   **614**

HUMAN SKELETON   615
□ Bone and Cartilage   □ Joints of the Human Skeleton
MUSCLES AND SKIN   619
□ Skeletal Muscle   □ Chemistry of Contraction   □ Movement of Joints
□ Cardiac Muscle and Smooth Muscle   □ Structure and Function of Skin
Laboratory Activity: A Survey of Human Body Tissues   **625**
Chapter Review   626

Chapter

38 DIGESTION AND NUTRITION   **628**

UPPER ALIMENTARY CANAL   629
□ The Digestive Process   □ The Mouth   □ The Esophagus   □ Stomach Structure and Function
LOWER ALIMENTARY CANAL   633
□ The Pancreas and Liver   □ Small Intestine: Structure   □ Small Intestine: Function
□ The Large Intestine
NUTRITION   638
□ Measuring Energy in Food   □ Carbohydrates and Fats in the Diet   □ Proteins in the Diet
□ Vitamins, Minerals, and Water   □ The Importance of a Balanced Diet   □ Eating Disorders
Laboratory Activity: Measuring Food Energy   **645**
Chapter Review   646

Chapter

39 RESPIRATION AND EXCRETION   **648**

RESPIRATION   649
□ External and Internal Respiration   □ The Human Respiratory System
□ Gas Exchange   □ The Mechanism of Breathing
□ Control of Breathing Rate
EXCRETORY SYSTEM   656
□ The Organs of Excretion   □ The Nephron: Structure   □ The Nephron: Function
□ Homeostasis of Body Fluids   □ Kidney Failure
Laboratory Activity: Lung and Kidney Structure   **661**
Chapter Review   662

XV

Chapter

40 CIRCULATION 664

THE HEART AND BLOOD VESSELS 665

□ The Heart □ Heart Rate □ Heart Disorders □ The Pattern of Circulation □ Blood Vessels
□ Blood Pressure

BLOOD AND LYMPH 671

□ Blood Plasma and Clotting □ Red Blood Cells and Blood Types □ White Blood Cells
□ The Lymphatic System □ Circulation and the Liver

Laboratory Activity: The Structure of the Heart **677**

Chapter Review 678

Chapter

41 DISEASE AND IMMUNITY 680

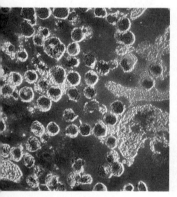

INFECTIOUS DISEASE 681

□ Agents of Disease □ Disease Transmission

THE BODY'S DEFENSES 684

□ Restricting Access □ The Immune System □ Recognizing Invaders
□ T Cells, B Cells, and Immunity □ AIDS Virus and the Immune System

TREATING DISEASE 691

□ Vaccines □ Antibacterial Drugs □ Immune System Malfunctions and Control
□ Hope for the Future: Lymphokines and Monoclonal Antibodies

Laboratory Activity: Microorganisms in the Environment **695**

CUTTING EDGE: New Diseases **696**

Chapter Review 698

Chapter

42 THE NERVOUS SYSTEM 700

TRANSMISSION OF INFORMATION 701

□ Neurons and Nerves □ The Nerve Impulse

CENTRAL AND PERIPHERAL NERVOUS SYSTEMS 704

□ The Central Nervous System □ The Cerebrum
□ Other Structures of the Brain □ The Spinal Cord
□ The Peripheral Nervous System

THE SENSES 710

□ The Skin Senses □ Taste □ Smell □ Hearing and Balance □ Vision

Laboratory Activity: Skin Sensitivity to Touch **715**

Chapter Review 716

Chapter

43 CHEMICAL REGULATORS 718

A DELICATE BALANCE 719
☐ Nervous vs. Chemical Controls   ☐ A Summary of Body Hormones
☐ Target Cells and Receptors
ENDOCRINE GLANDS AT WORK 724
☐ The Hypothalmus-Pituitary Connection   ☐ Negative Feedback Mechanisms
☐ The Sex Hormones
☐ Insulin and Glucagon: Hormones Keeping a Balance   ☐ Other Endocrine Sources
☐ New Developments in Endocrinology
Laboratory Activity: Hormones and Feedback Systems 731
Chapter Review 732

Chapter

44 SUBSTANCE ABUSE 734

DRUGS AND ABUSE 735
☐ Dependence on Drugs   ☐ Some Drugs That Are Abused   ☐ Endorphins—Natural Opiates
ALCOHOL AND TOBACCO 739
☐ Immediate Effects of Alcohol Consumption   ☐ Effects of Long-Term Drinking
☐ Effects of Smoking and Tobacco Use   ☐ Effects of Smoking on Others
☐ Using Prescription Drugs
Laboratory Activity: Effect of Drugs on the Heart Rate 745
Chapter Review 746

Chapter

45 HUMAN REPRODUCTION 748

THE STRUCTURES OF REPRODUCTION 749
☐ Male Reproductive System   ☐ Female Reproductive System   ☐ The Menstrual Cycle
THE PROCESS OF REPRODUCTION 755
☐ Fertilization   ☐ Implantation and Early Development   ☐ Differentiation
☐ Harmful Effects on the Fetus   ☐ Birth   ☐ Formation of Twins
Laboratory Activity: The Development of a Fertilized Egg 763
Chapter Review 764
ISSUES IN BIOETHICS: Early Treatment Proved Harmful 766
Unit Review 767

UNIT **8**   *ECOLOGY*

Chapter

46 BEHAVIOR   770

INSTINCT AND LEARNING   771
☐ Behavior and Natural Selection   ☐ Innate Behavior   ☐ Learning   ☐ Types of Learning
PATTERNS OF BEHAVIOR   776
☐ Orientation   ☐ Courtship   ☐ Territoriality and Aggression   ☐ Social Behavior   ☐ Communication
Laboratory Activity: Learning by Trial-and-Error   **779**
Chapter Review   **780**

Chapter

47 DISTRIBUTION OF LIFE   782

BIOMES ON LAND   783
☐ The Biosphere   ☐ Biomes and Climate
☐ Tundra   ☐ Taiga   ☐ Temperate Deciduous Forests
☐ Temperate Rain Forests   ☐ Grasslands   ☐ Deserts   ☐ Mountains
AQUATIC BIOMES   793
☐ The Marine Biome   ☐ Freshwater Biomes   ☐ Estuaries
Laboratory Activity: Soil Properties and Plant Growth   **797**
Chapter Review   **798**

Chapter

48 ECOSYSTEMS AND COMMUNITIES   800

LIVING COMMUNITIES   801
☐ Ecosystems   ☐ Organisms in the Environment   ☐ Flow of Energy   ☐ Energy Pyramids
☐ Symbiosis
CHANGES IN COMMUNITIES   807
☐ Primary Succession   ☐ Secondary Succession
CYCLES IN THE BIOSPHERE   809
☐ Water Cycle   ☐ Carbon Cycle   ☐ Nitrogen Cycle   ☐ Oxygen Cycle
Laboratory Activity: Examination of Nitrogen-Fixing Bacteria   **813**
Chapter Review   **814**

Chapter
49 POPULATION DYNAMICS   816

POPULATION GROWTH PATTERNS   817
□ Biotic Potential   □ Population Growth   □ Population Size
ENVIRONMENTAL RESISTANCE   819
□ Density-Independent Factors   □ Density-Dependent Factors
THE HUMAN POPULATION   822
□ Changes in the Human Population   □ Predictions for the Future
Laboratory Activity: Effect of Different Reproductive Patterns on Population Size   825
Chapter Review   826

Chapter
50 HUMAN IMPACT ON THE BIOSPHERE   828

NATURAL RESOURCES   829
□ Soil   □ Water   □ Wildlife   □ Forests
ENERGY RESOURCES   833
□ Nuclear Energy   □ Solar Energy   □ Biomass Energy   □ Wind, Water, and
Geothermal Energy   □ Energy Conservation
POLLUTION   836
□ Air Pollution   □ Water Pollution   □ Other Pollutants
Laboratory Activity: Effects of Acid Rain   841
Chapter Review   842
ISSUES IN BIOETHICS: Medical Wastes Pollute Beach   844
Unit Review   845

CAREERS IN TEACHING BIOLOGY   846
CAREERS IN PHARMACEUTICALS   847
CAREERS IN BOTANY   848
CAREERS IN MEDICINE   849

APPENDICES
A Measurements Used in Biology   850
  Periodic Table of the Elements   850
B Care and Use of the Microscope   851
  Laboratory Safety   852
C Five-Kingdom Classification   854

GLOSSARY   860

INDEX   883

CREDITS   902

xix

LABORATORY ACTIVITIES

1 A Controlled Experiment 17
2 Distinguishing a Living Thing from a Nonliving Thing 33
3 Observing a Chemical Reaction 47
4 Properties of an Enzyme 63
5 The Response of Plant Cells to Environmental Change 86
6 Role of Light in Photosynthesis 105
7 Transcription and Translation 119
8 How the Rate of Diffusion in a Cell Is Affected by the Surface-to-Volume Ratio 139
9 Probability and Heredity 161
10 Mapping Genes Using Crossover Frequency 175
11 Dihybrid Crosses 195
12 Production of Genetically Identical Plants by Vegetative Propagation 209
13 Understanding a Gene Pool 225
14 Variations Among Individuals 245
15 Coacervates: A Model for Cell Evolution 259
16 Comparing Primate Hemoglobins 272
17 Using a Classification Key to Identify Insects 287
18 Growing Bacteria in the Laboratory 313
19 Structure and Population Growth of *Blepharisma* 333
20 Fungi and Lichens 345
21 Germination of Pollen Grains 367
22 The Effect of Moisture on the Germination of Radish Seeds 381
23 Examination of the Growing Tip of a Root 399
24 The Observation of Guard Cells 411

25 The Effect of Gibberellic Acid on Stem Growth 423
26 Characteristics That Distinguish Different Types of Plants 437
27 Microscopic Structure of Sponges and Cnidarians 457
28 Comparing Flatworms and Roundworms 473
29 Structure of a Squid 485
30 Observing Insect Behavior 505
31 Structure of a Primitive Chordate 521
32 The Respiratory Rate of a Goldfish 537
33 Frog Development 553
34 Color Change in a Chameleon 567
35 Density of Bones 583
36 Effect of Temperature on Respiration 601
37 A Survey of Human Body Tissues 625
38 Measuring Food Energy 645
39 Lung and Kidney Structure 661
40 The Structure of the Heart 677
41 Microorganisms in the Environment 695
42 Skin Sensitivity to Touch 715
43 Hormones and Feedback Systems 731
44 Effect of Drugs on the Heart Rate 745
45 The Development of a Fertilized Egg 763
46 Learning by Trial and Error 779
47 Soil Properties and Plant Growth 797
48 Examination of Nitrogen-Fixing Bacteria 813
49 Effect of Different Reproductive Patterns on Population Size 825
50 Effects of Acid Rain 841

CONCEPT MAPPING
A Study Technique

How do you study? Do you reread a chapter over and over the night before a test, hoping you will remember all the information the next day? Do you take notes and try to memorize them? Perhaps you make flash cards of the information and quiz yourself. If your study method is one of the methods described here, you are learning by rote memorization. When you learn by rote memorization, information is stored in your short-term memory. Often this kind of learning only lasts a short time.

Learning information so that you can remember it longer and use it to solve problems involves getting that information into your long-term memory. Does your method of studying help you transfer information from short-term memory to long-term memory? Does your method of studying help you find relationships between ideas you are learning? Most methods do not. Making a concept map or idea map does.

Processing Information

Making a concept map is based on how you process or remember information. Quickly read

the sentences below. Then cover up the sentences and take the mini-quiz that immediately follows.

1. Nick walked on the roof.
2. George chopped down the tree.
3. Chris sailed the boat.
4. Ben flew the kite.

Mini-Quiz:

1. Who chopped down the tree?
2. Who walked on the roof?
3. Who flew the kite?
4. Who sailed the boat?

You probably did fairly well on the quiz because deep in your long-term memory you know about Santa "St. Nick" Claus, George Washington, Christopher Columbus, and Benjamin Franklin. Now look at this list of words. Read it over slowly for about 20 seconds, and then cover up the words. Recall as many as you can.

black	sweater	brown	shirt
cinnamon	dove	gloves	green
canary	garlic	parrot	pepper

Look at this second list of words and again memorize as many as you can in 20 seconds:

vanilla	yellow	horse	desk
chocolate	red	camel	table
strawberry	green	elephant	chair

Which list was easier to remember? The second list was easier to remember because the words are grouped.

The grouping or categories linked the words together and helped you remember them. For example, the category *flavors* helped you remember vanilla, chocolate, and strawberry. Grouping words also reduces how much information you must memorize. For example, by using what's in your long-term memory and recognizing four groups in the list, you could more easily memorize twelve concepts.

You can also look at groups of terms and give them a name that represents their main idea. For example: math, science, English, history, and art are all *school subjects*. The main idea for that group of items is *school subjects*. Try to find the main idea for these terms:

Canada, Germany, Mexico, USA, and France are _____

banjo, guitar, violin, piano, and drum are _____

Concept Mapping

Concept mapping helps you figure out the main ideas in a piece of reading material. A concept map can also help you understand that ideas have meanings because they are connected to other ideas. For example, when you define a pencil as a writing utensil, you have linked the idea or concept of a *pencil* to the ideas of *writing* and *utensil*. Look at the following words:

| car | tree | raining | thundering |
| dog | cloud | playing | thinking |

All of these words are concepts because they cause a picture to form in your mind. Are the following words concept words?

| are | when | where | then |
| the | with | is | to |

No. These are linkage words. They connect, or link, concept words together. In a concept map, words that are concepts go in circles or boxes, and words that are linking the concepts go on a line connecting the circles or boxes.

How is a concept map different from note-taking or making an outline? If you outlined pages 619–623 it might look like this:

Outline

I. Types of Muscle Tissue
  A. Smooth Muscle

1. Makes up walls of many organs
2. Makes blood vessels elastic to keep blood flowing
3. Makes upper digestive tract push food to stomach
4. Has smooth-looking cells with tapered ends
5. Works involuntarily

B. Cardiac Muscle
  1. Makes up the heart
  2. Looks striped under the microscope
  3. Contracts involuntarily
  4. Is very strong for pushing out blood
  5. Does not get tired like arms and legs

C. Skeletal Muscle
  1. Is attached to your bones
  2. Moves your skeleton
  3. Looks striped under a microscope
  4. Is voluntarily controlled since it works only when you want it to work

Now look back at pages 619 to 623. Would you want to reread those pages over again, trying to learn all of that information for a test? Would you prefer the slightly shorter outline? Or would you rather study a concept map like the one on the right, especially if you had made it yourself? If you made the map, your long-term memory would already *know* parts of that map. Reviewing the map would make studying easier.

How to Make a Concept Map

First, identify the main concepts by writing them in a list. Then put each separate concept from your list on a small piece of paper. You will not have to use this paper technique once you make a few maps, but it is helpful at first. Remember, your list shows how the concepts appeared in the reading, but this may not necessarily represent how you link the concepts.

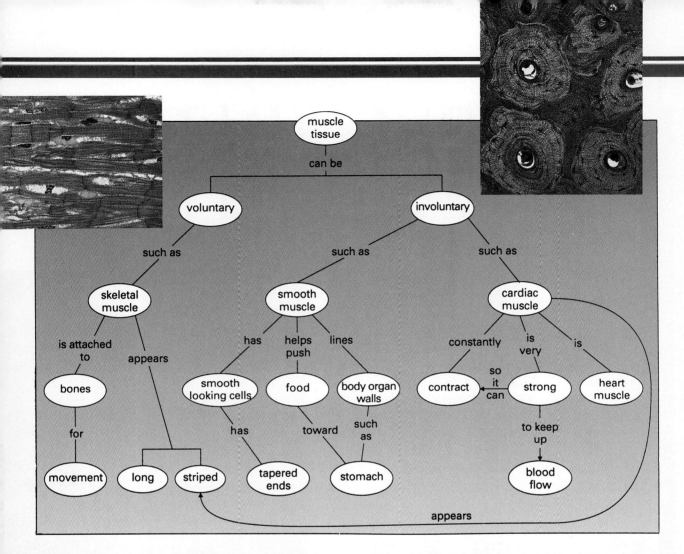

The concept map shows:

muscle tissue — can be — voluntary / involuntary

voluntary — such as — skeletal muscle
involuntary — such as — smooth muscle
involuntary — such as — cardiac muscle

skeletal muscle — is attached to — bones
skeletal muscle — appears — striped
bones — for — movement

smooth muscle — has — smooth looking cells
smooth muscle — helps push — food
smooth muscle — lines — body organ walls

smooth looking cells — has — tapered ends
food — toward — stomach
body organ walls — such as — stomach

cardiac muscle — constantly — contract
cardiac muscle — is very — strong
cardiac muscle — is — heart muscle

strong — so it can — contract
strong — to keep up — blood flow

long — striped

appears

The next step is to put the concepts in order of most general to most specific. Examples are most specific and will go at the bottom.

Now begin to rearrange the concepts you have written on the pieces of paper on a table or desktop. Start with the most general main idea. If that main idea can be broken down into two or more equal concepts, place those concepts on the same line. Continue to do this until all the concepts have been laid out.

Use lines to connect the concepts. Write a statement on the line that tells why concepts are connected. Do this for all the lines connecting the concepts.

Do not expect your map to be exactly like anyone else's map. Everyone thinks a little differently and will see different relationships between certain concepts. Practice is the key to good concept mapping. Here are some points to remember as you get started:

1. A concept map does not have to be symmetrical. It can be lopsided or have more concepts on the right side than on the left.
2. Remember that a concept map is a shortcut for representing information. Do not add anything but concepts and links.
3. There is no perfect or single correct concept map for a set of concepts. Errors in a concept map occur only if the links between concepts are incorrect.

INTRODUCTION TO BIOLOGY

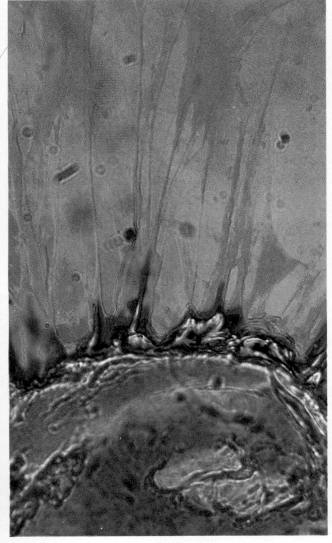

Specially stained micrograph of tumor tissue

Molecules take shape on a glass sketchboard

UNIT 1

Computer-generated molecule of DNA

Microscopic view
of pollen grains by computer

Chapter 1 Science of Life
Nature of Biology
Working in Biology

Chapter 2 Characteristics of Life
Biogenesis: Life Produces Life
Recognizing Life

Chapter 3 Basic Chemistry
Composition of Matter
Changes in Matter

Chapter 4 Biomolecules
Carbon and Basic Building Blocks
Proteins and Enzymes

Chapter 5 Cell Structure and
Function
The Cell: The Basic Unit of Life
The Cell and Its Environment
The Cell's Living Boundary

Chapter 6 Energy and the Cell
Energy from Food
Photosynthesis: Capturing the Sun's Energy

Chapter 7 Cell Regulation
Nature of DNA
Protein Synthesis

Chapter 8 Mitosis and Cell Division
Division of Cells
Significance of Mitosis and Cell Division
Regulation of Mitosis and Cell Division

1

Chapter

1

SCIENCE OF LIFE

Overview

NATURE OF BIOLOGY

1-1 Science, Biology, and You
1-2 Themes in Biology
1-3 Investigating a Problem
1-4 Controlled Experiments
1-5 The Research Method
1-6 Scientific Theories
1-7 Following Scientific Leads

WORKING IN BIOLOGY

1-8 Extending the Senses
1-9 Microscopes
1-10 Electron Microscopes
1-11 Tools of a New Age

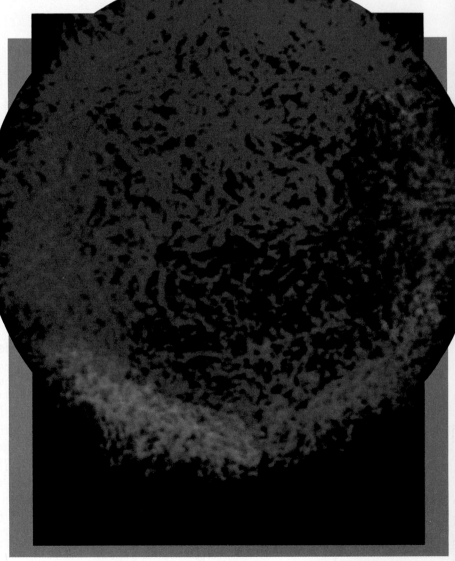

A computer was used to generate this image of a cold virus. What other tools do biologists use in studying life?

NATURE OF BIOLOGY

When you get a splinter in your finger the anticipation of its removal, as much as the immediate pain, may make you wince. The prospects of probing tweezers leave you wondering if the procedure is absolutely necessary. You may have been told that bacteria from a splinter can cause infection. Maybe this is enough of an answer for you, or perhaps you want to know more.

The first step in finding answers is making observations. However, making productive observations requires you to know a few things before you get started. The French biologist Louis Pasteur once said, "In the field of observation, chance favors only the prepared mind." In other words, being in the right place at the right time is not enough. You also need sufficient background knowledge to make sense out of observations. Studying biology will provide you with a foundation to understand your own observations about the living world.

1-1 Science, Biology, and You

Science is a way of knowing about the physical world. Anyone can be a scientist. No laboratory or advanced college degree is needed. As soon as you ask questions about the things you observe, and begin to look for answers, you are doing science.

People who work in science have certain characteristics in common. Among these characteristics are curiosity about one's environment and the willingness to try to understand it. Other characteristics of scientists include logical work strategies and a willingness to share what is learned with others.

Sharing information gives people an opportunity to have their work reviewed and doublechecked. It also informs other scientists of work in fields related to theirs.

The range of topics to study in science is so vast that no single person could ever know everything. In fact, in order to make scientific study more manageable, it is classified into different subjects. Questions that involve living things are grouped under the science of **biology**. Other areas of science, like chemistry, physics, and astronomy, focus on topics that involve nonliving events.

Branches of Biology The science of biology is divided into specific areas based on what is being studied. For example, botany is a biological science that focuses on plants, whereas zoology [zō ol′ ō jē] is the study of animals. Ecology is the study of relationships of living things to each other and to the environment. There are many more subdivisions of biology, just as there are many divisions of science. In this biology course, you will touch

Section Objectives

A **Explain** the role of observation in science.
B **List** the eight major themes that unify the study of biology.
C **Compare** a hypothesis and a theory.
D **Write** a hypothesis as an *"If . . . then"* statement.
E **Explain** how experiments are used to test hypotheses.
F **List** the steps of the research method in a correct sequence.

DO YOU KNOW?

Word Root: The word *science* derives from the Latin *scientia* which means "knowledge." Other words that come from this root are *conscience*, *conscious*, and *prescience*.

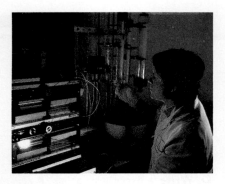

Figure 1-1 Most research in biology is now occurring on the molecular level. Scientists working on the causes, nature, and cures for diseases like cancer and AIDS are working in laboratories with the chemical nature of living things.

on several branches of biology. You will study the processes of life, how living things are constructed, and some of the changes that living things undergo.

What will you do with the knowledge you gain? You may be very interested in biology and decide to study it further. How will what you learn here be important to you? These are reasonable questions for you to ask. During your life, you will make decisions about many things related to biology. The kinds of foods you eat and the medical treatments you undergo are obvious examples. You also will have to think about the effects of pollution in your neighborhood. You will be given the opportunity to voice an opinion in this course about biological issues that could affect your life.

1-2 Themes in Biology

When you approach new information, you have probably discovered that learning is easier if you can put the information into a pattern or context. For example, can you name, in order, the colors of the rainbow spectrum? The colors are Red, Orange, Yellow, Green, Blue, Indigo, and Violet. You could simply repeat that sequence many times until it is familiar, or you could remember ROY G. BIV. The letters of this fictional person's name help to remind you of the first letters in the color sequence.

One mistake students make in learning an entirely new subject such as biology (or history, or math) is to think of the subject as a mass of facts that must be memorized. After all, you have seen in this chapter that science is a process for collecting new information and there is a great deal of information in the fifty chapters of this text. But science is not just a collection of facts. This text is not like a telephone book that presents vast amounts of unconnected information. Most of the information scientists gather fits into patterns and those patterns help to explain observations and make predictions. Knowing the patterns gives you a context for the information you will learn.

This section outlines eight basic themes of biology. These themes will occur over and over as you read through the text. Recognizing the themes will help you organize your thinking. To help you recognize the themes, the text margins contain boxes labeled **Biology Insight** that will point out how the reading illustrates one of the eight basic themes.

Theme 1: Process of Science In Chapter 1 you will be introduced to the organized manner in which scientists uncover explanations. Ideally, every statement in this text should be accompanied by supporting observations or experiments. However, if supporting information were included with each statement, it is unlikely that this text would fit into your school locker!

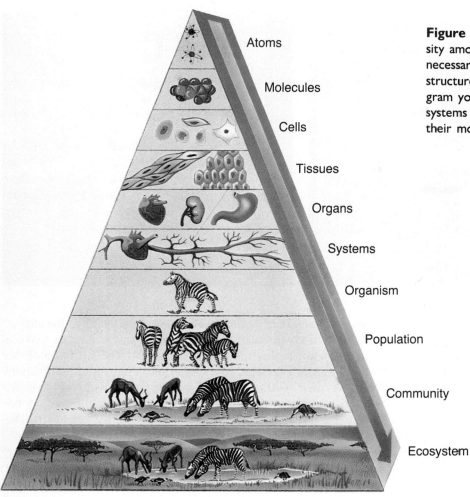

Atoms

Molecules

Cells

Tissues

Organs

Systems

Organism

Population

Community

Ecosystem

Figure 1-2 The enormous diversity among living things makes it necessary to use an organizational structure to study them. In this diagram you see how complex living systems can be broken down to their molecular components.

Theme 2: Levels of Organization Scientists tend to break down complex problems into simpler parts that are easier to study. Be aware that the natural world can be thought of as being made of increasingly complex levels of organization as shown in Figure 1-2. The elements of each level in Figure 1-2 interact to form the more complex level below. As you read through this text, it will help if you know which level you are on and how that level is related to other levels.

Theme 3: Unity And Diversity Living things are sometimes so different, or *diverse,* it is hard to imagine how they could be related to each other. What could be more diverse than a mouse, a maple tree, and a mushroom? Yet, as you learn about cells and some of the molecules of life, you will see that there is more similarity among these living things than there is diversity. All living things show remarkable similarity, or *unity,* when observed closely enough.

Figure 1-3 Though living things may be very diverse, there are certain components that they all share. In these photographs you see two very different living organisms, yet at the microscopic level they contain the same structure—the cell.

Figure 1-4 Protection from predators is an adaptation that ensures the survival of a species. In this photograph, you see that when an organism can blend into its surroundings, it is less likely to be noticed by predators.

Theme 4: Structure Is Related to Function By looking at the shape, size, and composition of a hammer or a saw, you can make a good guess about the function of each tool. The *structure* of the hammer or saw is related to its *function*. You would not imagine pounding nails with a saw or cutting wood with a hammer. Similarly, in biology, you will see that the structure of an organism (or of a cell, or a molecule) is clearly related to the function of that organism (or that cell, or molecule).

Theme 5: Adaptation And Evolution The close relationship of structure to function in biology shows that living things are generally well suited to live in their particular environment—they are well adapted. *Adaptation* is so universal, that biologists assume organisms have the ability to change slowly over time and to stay adapted to a changing environment. Such slow change over time is called *evolution*.

Theme 6: Continuity of Life While there is much evidence that organisms evolve over long time periods to meet changes in their environment, most populations of organisms are stable. Stability results because organisms resemble their parents from whom they inherit genetic information. Resemblance of offspring ensures adaptation to a given environment and allows for potential change in the long term.

Theme 7: Homeostasis. Homeostasis means staying the same. Maintaining stability for many organisms ensures survival. The ability to maintain a constant body temperature in spite of changes in the outside temperature helps some organisms survive. Living things have many mechanisms for maintaining stability in the face of changes in the environment.

Theme 8: Life Forms Are Interconnected No living thing on the planet can survive in the absence of other living things. The connections may be obvious (birds that build nests in trees) or subtle (birds and trees exchange oxygen and carbon dioxide— two substances that are essential to each organism). You will learn that human beings can exert powerful effects on other living things, such as maintaining or destroying habitats. You will also learn that other organisms can exert powerful effects on humans, as in the case of organisms that spread disease.

You may not yet understand the power of each of these ideas. But as you see the themes appear again and again throughout the text, they should become as familiar and as comfortable to you as the names of your friends.

1-3 Investigating a Problem

An important characteristic of science is using an organized approach to solve problems. You can learn the methods scientists use and later put them to use in your own studies. The first steps of investigating a problem are described in the famous example that follows.

Making Observations Accurate observations are essential in any problem-solving situation. In the late 1700s, for example, people observed that smallpox, a terrible disease, occurred far more often among city dwellers than among farmers. Death from smallpox was common and anyone who survived was left with disfiguring scars. Curiously, people who worked around cows almost never got smallpox, but they did get a much milder disease called cowpox.

Forming a Hypothesis While many people were aware of the difference between city and country smallpox rates, it was an English doctor named Edward Jenner who actually made use of the observation. Jenner wondered if cowpox somehow provided protection against smallpox. At first, his explanation was only an educated guess. Such a preliminary explanation to a problem is called a **hypothesis** [hī poth′ ə sis].

A hypothesis is an idea to work from. Often a scientist will develop several hypotheses related to a single problem. They are like the rough sketches an artist may draw before doing an oil painting. Just as the sketches change while the artist works on early ideas, a hypothesis may be revised in light of new information.

A scientific hypothesis has an important role in problem solving. It is used to make predictions that can be tested. Hypotheses are often made in a form called an *"If . . . then"* statement. For example, *if* someone recovers from cowpox, *then* that person is protected from getting smallpox. In this form, the prediction is

Figure 1-5 Bacteria can be grown in a laboratory in a petri dish. Each circular area in the photograph is a different bacterial colony.

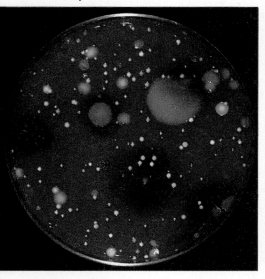

the second part of the statement. For Jenner, the next step was to test his prediction.

Testing the Hypothesis An **experiment** tests the predictions made by a hypothesis. Jenner began his experiment by infecting a young boy with cowpox. Testing the hypothesis several weeks later, Jenner deliberately exposed the boy to smallpox. The boy stayed healthy. This first test supported Jenner's hypothesis, and soon people lined up at his door to be infected with cowpox. Jenner's hypothesis was further tested on other people. The same results supported Jenner's hypothesis.

Jenner's initial observation led to an important discovery and the eventual elimination of a terrible disease. Suitably modified, Jenner's method works against a number of other diseases. But Jenner himself never knew why his procedure worked. That discovery was made long after his death.

The use of experiments is crucial to learning new information. When you work in the laboratory, you will conduct experiments. Although your experiments may not be as dramatic as Jenner's, you will be following similar procedures. Also, you will read about other interesting experiments. The next section will take you further in your knowledge of scientific methods.

1-4 Controlled Experiments

An experiment isolates a single factor that is directly responsible for an effect. Suppose, for example, you are investigating whether or not a particular medicine prevents infection. Your hypothesis might be stated as follows: "*If* the medicine prevents infection, *then* the medicine will prevent the growth of bacteria that cause the infection."

Figure 1-5 shows bacteria growing in a glass petri dish. A gelatinlike material in the dish contains food and other substances necessary for growth. When bacteria are placed on the surface of the gelatin, they grow and reproduce until millions of bacteria become visible as a cloudy film.

Controlling Variables Figure 1-6 illustrates an experiment that could be used to test your hypothesis. To prepare a petri dish you would pour a suspension of bacteria over the gelatin. If left alone for a few days, the bacteria would form an even film over the surface. After preparing a dish, however, you place two paper disks on the gelatin surface. One disk has been soaked in the medicine you are testing, the other has not. The medicine-soaked disk is called the variable. A **variable** is one condition in the experiment that differs while other conditions remain the same. The second disk is called a control. The **control** provides a standard of comparison for the one factor in the experiment that varies. Without the control you would not know whether

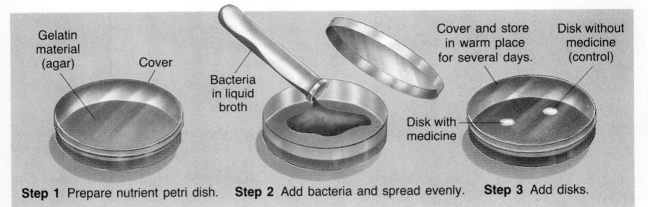

Step 1 Prepare nutrient petri dish.   Step 2 Add bacteria and spread evenly.   Step 3 Add disks.

it was the medicine, or perhaps the paper disk itself, that stopped the growth of the bacteria you tested.

The photograph in Figure 1-6 shows what the petri dish would look like after several days. Notice the clear ring around the medicine-soaked paper disk. No such ring is visible around the control disk. How do these results support your hypothesis that the medicine prevents the bacteria from growing? If there had been no clear ring around either disk, the hypothesis would be rejected.

Collecting Data When doing the experiment, you might collect and write down information. You might track the differences in bacterial growth. You might measure the size of the clear ring around the disk to compare it with the ring from another medicine. All measurements and observations from a controlled experiment are called **data** and are recorded whether or not they support the hypothesis. The data are then analyzed to form conclusions.

Experiments are usually more complex than the one described here. They may need several controls and require many more steps. They also may be less straightforward, leading researchers to many dead ends before useful information is gained. However, all well-organized experiments have similarities in structure. When you do investigations in the laboratory, look for examples of controls, variables, and data in your procedures.

1-5 The Research Method

You have been reading about a general procedure, called the **research method**. This method is frequently used to answer scientific questions. The steps of the research method are usually listed as

1. observing;
2. defining the problem or question;

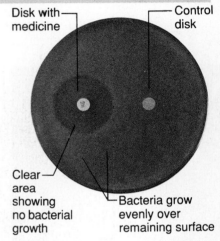

Step 4 Note growth pattern.

Figure 1-6 A controlled experiment is used to determine whether a particular medicine will be effective in stopping the growth of bacteria.

CONSUMER BIOLOGY

Parents use experimental design in introducing new foods to a baby. One new food (the variable) is introduced each week and the baby is monitored to note any digestive problems. These problems occur when the baby's digestive system is not developed enough to handle the type of food introduced.

3. forming a hypothesis;
4. testing the hypothesis with a controlled experiment;
5. observing and recording results;
6. forming conclusions by confirming or modifying the hypothesis;
7. reporting results.

A list like this may suggest that scientists follow the research method as they would a cookbook recipe. But such a view would be an oversimplification. The steps listed above are frequently modified in a scientific investigation. Sometimes there are shortcuts, detours, or dead ends. Doing research requires the ability to follow results wherever they take you. The research method is simply a useful guide.

1-6 Scientific Theories

When a hypothesis explains many observations and leads to predictions that are continually supported by experiments, it then may be called a **scientific theory**. The word *theory* is defined carefully in science. People often use the word to mean an idea that is uncertain. A scientific theory, however, is an idea that is widely accepted as a correct explanation. Theories continue to explain new observations.

In the nineteenth century, Louis Pasteur provided evidence that some diseases are caused by tiny living things called **microorganisms** [mī′ crō or gan izmz] growing inside the body. At first, Pasteur's idea was only a hypothesis. Very few people accepted it. With more experiments and more data, however, the hypothesis was accepted as a theory. Today, it is commonly accepted that many diseases are caused by microorganisms.

A scientific theory can be changed if new evidence is uncovered. But theories are rarely discarded. It is more common for theories to be modified slightly in the light of new evidence.

You also should be careful when you use the word *proof*. Evidence supports or rejects hypotheses and theories, but it cannot prove them. It is always possible that in the future a new idea will provide a better explanation.

1-7 Following Scientific Leads

The course of scientific research is not always predictable. Research may produce unexpected results that send the investigation in an entirely different direction. New equipment and technology can open up whole new areas of research.

Sometimes a hypothesis is made before there is enough information to support it. Consider the story of the Hungarian doctor, Ignaz Semmelweis. Semmelweis worked in a hospital in Vienna, Austria, some 40 years before microorganisms were

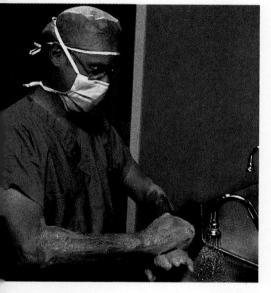

Figure 1-7 Understanding the role of microorganisms in disease led to methods of disease prevention. Surgeons and nurses must scrub their hands and arms with a special soap before surgery to prevent the spread of infection to patients.

thought to cause disease. In Semmelweis's hospital, it was common for women to die of fever shortly after giving birth.

Semmelweis noticed a connection between women who died of fever and doctors who did not wash their hands before assisting in childbirth. He hypothesized that the doctors carried the disease-causing agent on their hands. Semmelweis insisted that doctors wash their hands before delivering babies. When this was done, the number of women who developed fever dropped dramatically.

Today Semmelweis's conclusion may seem obvious, but the doctors of his day resisted it. With no theory to explain why dirty hands could cause fever, the idea was difficult to sell. Semmelweis died in 1862, a defeated man who had failed to convince more than a few that his ideas were correct.

A factor that is not listed in the research method is the role of luck. In 1928 an important discovery was made in the laboratory of the British scientist Alexander Fleming. Fleming was investigating bacterial growth and noticed that green mold interfered with the growth of the bacteria in some of the petri dishes. A clear ring was evident around the green mold. Many researchers would have simply thrown out the spoiled dish, but Fleming did not. He thought that the mold must have produced something that killed the microorganisms. He was right, the "something" he discovered was **penicillin**, a chemical that kills certain bacteria without harming the body. Today penicillin is a widely used medicine to fight bacterial infection.

As you study biology remember the facts and theories presented here represent the efforts of thousands of researchers working over hundreds of years. Biology is a constantly growing and changing body of knowledge. Some of the theories you read about today will undoubtedly change.

CHECKPOINT ◆

1. What role did observation play in Edward Jenner's discovery of a way to control smallpox?
2. A _____ is a temporary explanation that can be tested.
3. What do you call an experiment in which only one factor is allowed to vary?
4. List the steps of the research method.
▶ 5. Create your own hypothesis in *If . . . then* form.
▶ 6. Which biological themes are illustrated by the following:
   a. The white fur of the snow rabbit blends into the winter background making the animal difficult to see.
   b. Organisms tend to resemble their parents—they share similar characteristics.

▶ Denotes a question that involves *interpreting* and *applying* concepts.

WORKING IN BIOLOGY

G *Explain* the function of tools and measurement in science.

H *Compare* and *contrast* the light microscopes and the electron microscope.

I *Describe* how the scanning electron microscope differs from the transmission electron microscope.

J *List* some of the tools used in modern biological research and state the function of each one.

The fictional detective, Sherlock Holmes, was famous for his ability to observe. He was, in fact, a good example of someone who uses scientific procedures. He observed things no one else noticed and created hypotheses from clues. He then tested his hypotheses with further observation.

Holmes used other scientific methods. Like any careful observer, he made measurements. By measuring the size, shape, and depth of a footprint in the mud, Holmes could deduce the height, sex, and weight of a suspect. Holmes is often pictured holding a magnifying glass. Such a device allowed him to find clues he otherwise would miss. He used the magnifying glass to extend his vision. In science, many such tools extend the senses.

1-8 Extending the Senses

The human senses are limited. A dog easily hears sounds that you cannot, and it will detect the aroma of your dinner long before you can. Honeybees see things that are invisible to humans. Some bacteria have an internal compass that indicates direction. To study objects in a new way, you can extend your senses by the use of specialized tools. Think of how a magnifying glass or a camera lens changes the world you see!

You can use tools to measure quantities like mass, length, sound, time, and temperature. By making measurements you can describe your observations more clearly and accurately. Measurement helps you keep track of changes you might not notice if you relied only on your senses. Measurement also helps to remove personal impressions from scientific data.

A universal system of measurement allows scientists to communicate their results more effectively. For that reason, scientists use *Le Système International d'unités*, more commonly referred to as SI. SI was developed from the older metric system. SI uses units of measure such as meter (m) and kilogram (kg). SI also has the advantage of being easy to use because of its decimal base and its systematic naming of units. To give you a picture of some of the SI units you will be working with, consider that a millimeter (mm) is about the width of the wire of a paper clip. If you measured a paper clip's mass it would be about a gram (g). A centimeter (cm) is about the width of a fingernail on your little finger, and a meter is about the length of a softball bat. Appendix A summarizes the basic units and relationships of SI.

In addition to making measurements, scientific tools are used for detecting things that could not otherwise be observed. For example, telescopes help astronomers to see stars and galaxies

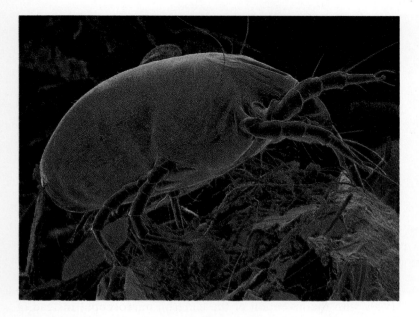

Figure 1-8 The scanning electron microscope has opened up a view of another level of living organisms. You cannot see the dust mite that lives on bedding and furniture.

not visible to the naked eye. Heat sensors are used to reveal what parts of a house need better insulation. X rays can pinpoint where a bone is broken. In the next few sections, you will read about some tools that are particularly important in biology.

1-9 Microscopes

A **microscope** is an instrument consisting of a lens or combination of lenses that produce an enlarged image of small objects. The invention of the microscope revealed a whole new world to biologists. They were able to extend the limits of what could be seen. The microscope made it possible to make observations, ask questions, and find answers like never before.

The earliest microscopes consisted of a single, strongly curved lens mounted in a metal plate. Microscopes with a single lens are called *simple microscopes*. In the late 1600s, a Dutch naturalist named Anton von Leeuwenhoek learned to make simple microscopes that could magnify objects as much as 400 times (usually written 400×). At this magnification a shoe would be longer than a football field! Leeuwenhoek was able to see forms of life so small that millions of them could occupy an area the size of your fingernail.

A better instrument soon replaced the simple microscope. The **compound microscope** uses two lenses rather than one. The two lenses are mounted at opposite ends of a tube through which an object is viewed. Such a microscope allows magnifications up to 1000 times. Refer to Appendix B for a thorough explanation of the parts and functions of a modern compound microscope.

DO YOU KNOW?

Word Root: *Micro-* means "small." Since this prefix occurs frequently in biological terms, you should memorize it. The suffix *-scope* designates an instrument used for viewing; it comes from the Greek *skopein*, "to look at."

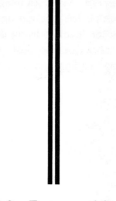

Figure 1-9 Test your ability to resolve detail. Prop up this book and then back away until the two lines seem to become a single line. As the distance you back away increases, the resolving power of your eyes increases.

Both simple and compound microscopes are called *light microscopes* because they use visible light to illuminate the object being viewed. As a result, modern microscopes have one limitation that cannot be overcome. The nature of light makes it impossible for a compound microscope to distinguish, or resolve, objects closer together than about 0.000 2 mm*, regardless of magnification. **Resolution** is the ability to distinguish between two objects next to each other. You can experience the effects of resolution. Follow the directions in the caption for Figure 1-9 to test the ability of your eyes to resolve the two lines.

At 1000 times, the compound microscope resolves as much detail as possible. Unfortunately, many of the things biologists want to see are smaller than the compound microscope can reveal.

1-10 Electron Microscopes

The problem of resolving small objects was largely solved in the 1940s with the invention of the electron microscope. Instead of directing visible light through an object, the **transmission electron microscope** (TEM) directs a beam of tiny particles called electrons.

* Various styles are used to group digits in large and small numbers to make them easier to read. In this book, a space is used in place of a comma to group digits. Thus 10,000 appears as 10 000.

Figure 1-10 Scanning electron microscopes are used to photograph surfaces of objects. The technician can view the specimen on a monitor.

The TEM uses special doughnut-shaped magnets rather than glass lenses to focus an image. Because the human eye cannot respond to electrons, the magnified image must be projected onto a television screen or photographic film. The object being viewed in the microscope must be sliced extremely thin so the electrons can pass through it and produce an image. The preparation of the object for the TEM involves freezing, slicing, and treating the object with a variety of chemicals. These processes can distort the appearance of the object.

An advantage of the TEM is its ability to distinguish very small objects. It can resolve two objects as close together as 0.000 000 5 mm or five ten-millionths of a millimeter! This detail results from magnifications near one million times. At this magnification, a sneaker would stretch from Boston to New York City.

Another instrument that shows great detail is the scanning electron microscope. The **scanning electron microscope** (SEM) takes pictures of surfaces rather than of thin slices. This means that in some cases whole organisms can be used. The pictures have an almost three-dimensional quality. Look again at the picture at the beginning of this chapter. It was taken with an SEM. (The actual images are made in black and white. Color is added later to enhance the pictures.)

The tools used in a given investigation depend on the kind of information needed. Compare the three photos in Figure 1-11,

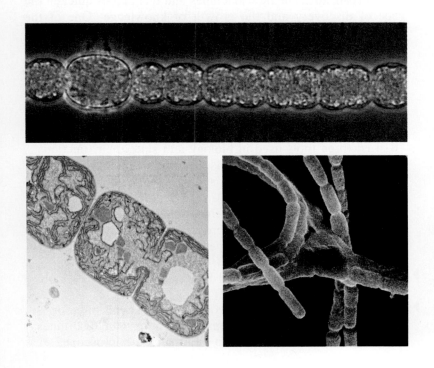

Figure 1-11 The three photographs of the same cyanobacterium as it appears through three different kinds of microscopes. *Top:* Compound light microscope. *Left:* Transmission electron microscope. *Right:* Scanning electron microscope.

one taken through a light microscope, one through a TEM, and one through an SEM. Each photo reveals different characteristics of the same subject.

1-11 Tools of a New Age

In the last forty years, new tools have been developed with increasing frequency. Some of these tools permit new kinds of work to be done. There are instruments that allow surgery on a single cell under a microscope. Other tools divide cells into their various components, a process called **microdissection**. Thus each part of a cell can be studied separately. Microdissection techniques can be used in altering the contents of a cell to study the functions of various parts.

Scientists can isolate and purify different parts of a cell mixture by using a centrifuge. A **centrifuge** is an instrument that applies very high forces to small objects by spinning them rapidly. This spinning produces a force like the one that keeps water in a bucket if it is swung rapidly in a circle. When put in a centrifuge, cell parts in a test tube settle into layers. Heavier parts settle nearer the bottom of the test tube than the lighter parts.

Computers are able to store enormous amounts of information and sort it rapidly. A computer can imitate complex biological systems and test hypotheses before experiments are done on living organisms. The new machines and techniques quicken the pace of discovery and the growth of knowledge. One of the challenges you will face in the future will be keeping up with the vast amount of new information uncovered every year.

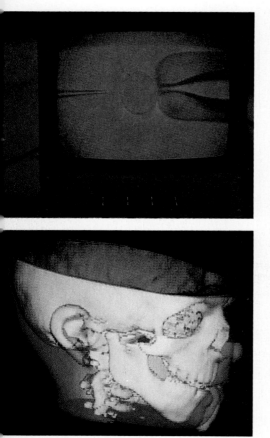

Figure I-12 *Top:* Cell surgery can be performed using microdissection techniques. You will learn later about research in altering the contents of cells. *Bottom:* Computer tomography scanners can be used to diagnose bone fractures and are used in planning reconstructive surgery.

▶ Denotes a question that involves *interpreting* and *applying* concepts.

CHECKPOINT ◆

7. What measurement system is used in science? Why aren't standard English measurements used?
8. List three tools used in biology and state their functions.
9. Give two reasons why tools are used in biology.
10. How many lenses are in a simple microscope? In a compound microscope?
11. What is the primary difference between the light microscope and the electron microscope? Between the transmission electron microscope and the scanning electron microscope?
▶ 12. Give your own example of how measurement makes observations more useful.
▶ 13. A compound microscope could be made with three or four lenses that would magnify far more than 1000 times. Why would it be useless to build such a microscope?

A CONTROLLED EXPERIMENT

Objectives and Skills

☐ *Controlling variables* in an experiment.
☐ *Observe* and *gather data* from an experiment.
☐ *Draw conclusions* based on data gathered.

Materials

Safety goggles and lab apron
150 mL 10% noniodized salt solution
150 mL of tap water
1 100-mL graduated cylinder
1 10-mL graduated cylinder
1 cm ruler
6 petri dishes
1 wax pencil
1 flat toothpick
Small vial of brine shrimp eggs

Procedure and Observations

1. Read all instructions for this laboratory activity before you begin your work.
2. Put on your safety goggles and lab apron.
3. Use a wax pencil to label the top of six petri dishes as follows: 10% on the first dish, 8% on the second, 6% on the third, 4% on the fourth, 2% on the fifth, and 0% on the sixth.
4. Using the large graduated cylinder, measure out 30 mL of salt solution and pour it into the 10% petri dish.
5. In the 8% dish pour 24 mL of salt solution and 6 mL of water. (Use the large graduated cylinder for larger amounts and the small one for small amounts. Be sure to rinse the graduated cylinder each time.)
6. In the 6% dish pour 18 mL of salt solution, 12 mL of water, and mix.
7. In the 4% dish pour 12 mL of salt solution, 18 mL of water, and mix.

8. In the 2% dish pour 6 mL of salt solution, 24 mL of water, and mix.
9. In the 0% dish pour 30 mL of water.
10. Using a toothpick as a spatula, remove the brine shrimp eggs from the vial and sprinkle them onto the water surface in each of the six petri dishes.
11. Set the dishes aside for three or four days.
12. Before leaving the laboratory, clean up all materials and wash your hands thoroughly.
13. After three or four days, count the number of living shrimp in each dish. If there are too many to count, place a square piece of paper measuring 2 cm on each side under each dish and count the number of shrimp in this area of each dish. On a separate piece of paper, draw a data table like the one shown below. Record the number of shrimp found in each solution.

SHRIMP HATCHING						
Salt %	10%	8%	6%	4%	2%	0%
Number of Shrimp						

Analysis and Conclusions

1. What factor in this experiment is allowed to vary?
2. What factors in this experiment are controlled?
3. What salt concentration did you find to be best for hatching brine shrimp eggs?
4. Do the results of this experiment support the hypothesis that there is one particular salt concentration that favors the hatching of brine shrimp eggs? Explain.

CHAPTER REVIEW

Summary

▸ Science is a way to find out how the world works by seeking answers to questions. Biology is the branch of science that studies living things. Science is objective; the results of scientific investigations can be repeated. Results of experiments are shared among people.

▸ People working in science frequently use the research method to solve problems. Hypotheses are developed to explain observations or answer questions. Controlled experiments are used to test hypotheses. The results of the experiments determine whether a hypothesis is accepted or rejected.

▸ Tools and measurements are used in science to help gather information, thereby extending the range of normal human senses. The light microscope and electron microscope are two examples of tools that permit observations that would otherwise be impossible.

▸ Scientific knowledge grows rapidly as new information becomes available through the development of new tools.

Vocabulary

biology	microscope
centrifuge	penicillin
compound	research method
microscope	resolution
control	scanning electron
data	microscope
experiment	scientific theory
hypothesis	transmission electron
microdissection	microscope
microorganisms	variable

Concept Mapping

A concept map is a diagram that summarizes relationships among ideas. For example, you have many ideas about school. They include ideas about students, teachers, the principal, lessons, homework, and tests. One type of concept map is shown here.

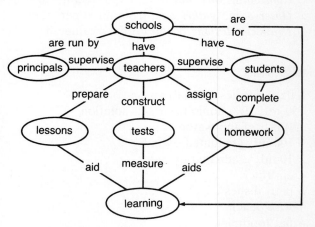

Complete a concept map for science. Copy the incomplete map below. Use the Vocabulary list in selecting words to fill in the missing terms.

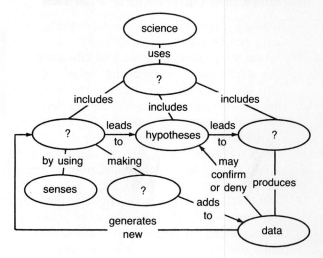

Review

1. What is the name of the procedure that is often followed in science to solve problems?

2. Why is the sharing of information between scientists important?
3. A preliminary explanation that must be tested by experiment is called a _____.
4. What disease prevented people from getting smallpox?
5. The results of an experiment are called _____.
6. What are factors that remain the same in an experiment called?
7. How did luck play a role in the discovery of penicillin?
8. What group of living things was discovered with the aid of the microscope?
9. Animals as different as fish, birds, frogs, and humans all have a substance in their blood that carries oxygen. What theme of biology does this observation illustrate?
10. The lenses of a light microscope are made of _____.
11. What is the source of illumination in the electron microscope?
12. Explain how Pasteur's hypothesis about the role of microorganisms in disease became a theory.

Interpret and Apply

13. How does learning by trial and error fit into the scientific method?
14. State Semmelweis's hypothesis in an "If . . . then" statement.
15. Give an example of a situation where a scientist may not follow the steps of the research method.
16. Why was the invention of the microscope necessary before a truly scientific explanation of disease became possible?
17. What kind of microscope would be used to study the internal structure of a white blood cell? Explain your answer.
18. Shark teeth are pointed triangles with sharp edges. Cows have many box-like teeth with rough, flattened surfaces. How is the structure of these teeth related to their function?
19. How do the teeth in question 18 illustrate adaptation?

Critical Thinking

20. Human memory tends to be selective. People often remember events that seem to fit patterns and forget events that do not fit patterns. How might this tendency create problems for someone who is trying to perform an objective experiment?
21. Suppose the experiment described in Section 1-4 gave results in which neither disk had any effect on the growth of bacteria. What would be your next step if you were the person in charge of this experiment?
22. Explain why reporting results in a journal article helps to make science objective.
23. Two plants are placed near a window. Both get the same attention, but one of them dies.
    a. State a hypothesis that you could test to find out what happened.
    b. Describe an experiment to test the hypothesis.
    c. Describe results of such an experiment that would support your hypothesis.
24. Explain how an automobile mechanic might use the research method to repair cars.

Chapter

2

CHARACTERISTICS OF LIFE

Overview

BIOGENESIS: LIFE PRODUCES LIFE

2-1 Spontaneous Generation

2-2 Where Do Microorganisms Come From?

2-3 Pasteur Provides an Answer

RECOGNIZING LIFE

2-4 Some Characteristics of Life

2-5 Discovery and Importance of Cells

2-6 More Unique Characteristics of Life

2-7 Summarizing the Characteristics of Life

Do you see living and nonliving things in this picture?

BIOGENESIS: LIFE PRODUCES LIFE

If you leave a piece of bread, cheese, or fruit out in the open long enough, mold will eventually grow on it. The mold seems to appear from nowhere. You learned in the last chapter that before the invention of the microscope, microorganisms were unknown. At that time there was no scientific explanation for the sudden appearance of molds. People believed that nonliving things produced living things. Such beliefs were common at a time when people did not understand the differences between living and nonliving things.

2-1 Spontaneous Generation

The idea that living things can arise from nonliving material is called **spontaneous generation**. Aristotle, the ancient Greek scientist, concluded that spontaneous generation was a reasonable explanation for the origin of some living things. For almost 2000 years after Aristotle, people saw no reason to doubt the idea of spontaneous generation because it was consistent with common observations. For example, wormlike maggots often appear on meat that is left out too long. After spring rains, frogs, insects, and plants seem to materialize from the dried out mud of ponds.

Until the 1600s, most people accepted the idea that animals could spring from nonliving materials. A well-known Belgian doctor of the time, Jan Baptist van Helmont, even wrote a recipe for making mice by throwing grain and old rags into the corner of a room! Spontaneous generation was a hypothesis supported by many observations. What eventually happened to the idea of spontaneous generation is an excellent example of how a hypothesis may be tested and changed to reflect new evidence.

In the 1660s, an Italian doctor named Francesco Redi challenged the idea of spontaneous generation. He wanted to know why wormlike maggots appeared on the surface of decaying meat. Redi's first step was to make careful observations. He allowed meat to decay in an open box. Within several days, maggots appeared on the surface of the meat.

Most people would have stopped watching the maggots at that point, but Redi continued. He was patient and persistent—two qualities that are valuable in scientific work. About 20 days later the maggots formed hard shells around themselves. In about another week adult flies emerged from these shells. Redi recalled seeing the same type of flies on the meat in the early part of his experiment. He concluded that the maggot was not a worm at all but an early stage in the fly's life.

After this discovery, Redi proposed an alternative hypothesis for the origin of maggots. He said that maggots were not spon-

Section Objectives

A **Evaluate** the observations, hypotheses, experimental evidence, and conclusions in the spontaneous generation controversy.

B **Compare** the experimental procedures used by Spallanzani with those used by Needham.

C **Describe** Pasteur's contribution toward answering the question of spontaneous generation.

Figure 2-1 You have probably seen molds like this one growing on spoiled food. Is the mold itself a living thing? If so, where does it come from?

Characteristics of Life   **21**

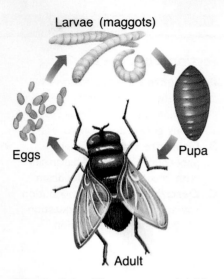

Figure 2-2 The stages in the life cycle of a fly were unknown until they were discovered by Redi. People now know that many insects—including beetles, butterflies, and bees—undergo similar changes during their lives.

taneously generated but came from eggs that flies laid on meat. As a scientific hypothesis, Redi's idea was testable. He set up a controlled experiment in which his hypothesis and the idea of spontaneous generation predict different results. Note the difference when the two ideas are put into an "*If . . . then*" statement. *If* maggots come from fly eggs, *then* maggots will appear only in open jars where flies can deposit eggs on the meat. However, *if* maggots appear by spontaneous generation, *then* they will appear whether the jar is open or closed.

Redi tested his hypothesis by putting different kinds of meat into separate containers and sealing them tightly. He put the same kinds of meat into other containers that he did not cover. Spontaneous generation predicts that maggots will appear in all containers. Redi's idea predicts that maggots will appear only in the open jars where the flies could land on the meat and lay eggs. In fact, maggots appeared only in the open containers, confirming Redi's hypothesis.

Redi used proper scientific methods. He repeated the experiment many times with different kinds of meat, different kinds of jars, and at different seasons of the year. He always got the same results. (Redi must have been a dedicated scientist to live with the awful smell of rotting meat!)

Redi even anticipated a possible objection to his experiments. Those who believed in spontaneous generation accepted the hypothesis that air must be allowed to circulate freely into the closed jars in order for life to develop. The argument was that air might carry some unknown "active principle" necessary for spontaneous generation to occur. Redi performed another experiment where jars containing meat samples were covered with a fine mesh cloth. The cloth allowed air to enter the containers but prevented flies from reaching the meat. Redi observed flies landing on the cloth and even laying eggs on it. Some of the eggs on the cloth hatched. But the meat remained free of maggots. Redi's experiments are shown in Figure 2-3. Compare the results he obtained by controlling different factors.

Redi never claimed that his experiments disproved all possible cases of spontaneous generation. He did state, however, that

Figure 2-3 Why are Redi's procedures good examples of controlled experiments?

Maggots

No maggots

Maggots on cloth, not on meat

spontaneous generation does not explain specifically the maggots appearing on decaying meat.

In the century after Redi's death, other scientists did experiments similar to his. They showed that spontaneous generation could not explain the origin of any known plant or animal. However, the idea of spontaneous generation was not yet totally rejected. It actually gained popularity with the discovery of microorganisms.

2-2 Where Do Microorganisms Come From?

Recall from Chapter 1 that Anton von Leeuwenhoek was one of the first people to make and use microscopes. With his simple microscopes he looked at pond water, rainwater, scrapings from his teeth, and hundreds of other substances. In 1675, Leeuwenhoek first observed and described microorganisms. He called these tiny creatures ''animalcules'' and ''cavorting beasties.'' Leeuwenhoek's fascination with these smallest living things was recorded in detailed drawings and notes based on observations made over a period of many years.

Spontaneous generation gained new support with Leeuwenhoek's discovery. The large numbers and rapid appearance of these tiny living things were difficult to explain. Eighteenth-century scientists studied the growth of microorganisms by making mixtures of water and food, then filtering the mixtures to form a clear broth. Soon such broths became cloudy. The cloudy mixture seen through the microscope revealed countless numbers of microorganisms. Observers concluded that the microorganisms must have come from the nonliving liquid!

In 1748, a Scottish scientist named John Needham performed an experiment similar to Redi's. Knowing that heat kills microorganisms, Needham boiled a meat broth. He then sealed the container with a cork. As a control, Needham left a container of boiled meat broth open to the air. In both containers microorganisms reappeared! Needham claimed to have evidence supporting spontaneous generation. He argued that all of the microorganisms were killed and the container was sealed, so the microorganisms had to come from the nonliving broth. Can you think of a flaw in Needham's experiment?

Several decades later an Italian scientist, Lazzaro Spallanzani, read about Needham's experiment and recognized one or two weaknesses in it. Spallanzani decided to do his own research. Recall that in science, being able to repeat the results of an experiment is important. Spallanzani performed an experiment similar to Needham's, but with two significant changes. First, Spallanzani showed from earlier experiments that boiling the

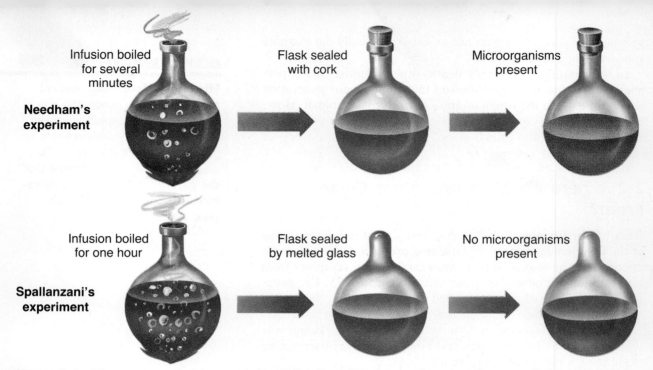

Needham's experiment

Infusion boiled for several minutes → Flask sealed with cork → Microorganisms present

Spallanzani's experiment

Infusion boiled for one hour → Flask sealed by melted glass → No microorganisms present

Figure 2-4 The experiments of Needham and Spallanzani differed in two ways—how long the flasks were heated and how tightly they were sealed.

broth for 5 or 10 minutes does not destroy all the microorganisms. So he boiled his containers for almost an hour. Second, Spallanzani used a different method to seal the flasks. He believed microorganisms are carried in the air and did not think Needham's corks sealed the flasks tightly enough.

The two experiments are compared in Figure 2-4. After extended boiling, Spallanzani closed his flasks by heating the mouths of the containers until the glass melted and sealed the openings completely. With this treatment, the broth in Spallanzani's containers stayed free of microorganisms as long as the containers remained sealed. When he broke the seals, however, he found microorganisms in the broth within hours. These results supported the idea that microorganisms are present in the air and multiply when they fall into a food supply.

Although Spallanzani's controlled experiments were carefully designed and performed, the idea of spontaneous generation did not disappear. In fact, the argument continued for another 100 years!

One major objection to Spallanzani's experiments was similar to the difficulty Redi had encountered. Critics said that by heating the broth, Spallanzani had destroyed some "active principle" in the air. Spallanzani could not refute this objection because he believed that fresh air carried microorganisms and that heating the air killed them. He could not think of an experiment in which the microorganisms could be killed without also destroying the "active principle."

2-3 Pasteur Provides an Answer

The French chemist Louis Pasteur is one of the great figures in the history of science. In 1861, Pasteur did a remarkably simple experiment that convinced many people that spontaneous generation does not produce microorganisms. The experiment is illustrated in Figure 2-5.

Pasteur placed clear broth in long-necked glass flasks. He then heated the neck of each flask and bent it into an S-shaped curve. Pasteur heated the flasks for a long time at high temperature to kill any microorganisms present. When the flasks cooled, water droplets condensed in the curved necks. Dust particles carrying microorganisms settled in the curves of the flask, becoming trapped in the liquid water. However, unlike Spallanzani's sealed containers, air could pass in and out of the flask easily. No one could object that an "active principle" in the air was kept out of the flasks.

As a control, Pasteur broke the necks of several flasks to remove the curve. In every case, dust from the air settled into the broken flask, and the broth turned cloudy and teemed with microorganisms. The same thing happened when Pasteur tipped the flasks to permit contact between the broth and the contaminated water droplets in the neck. However, Pasteur's other flasks stayed free of organisms as long as they were undisturbed.

Figure 2-5 Pasteur's experiment improved upon Spallanzani's by leaving the flasks open to the air. Microorganisms were trapped in the curved necks and did not contaminate the broth unless the flasks were disturbed as shown.

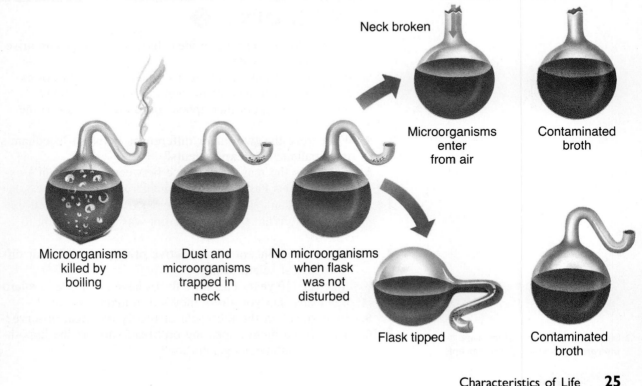

Neck broken

Microorganisms killed by boiling

Dust and microorganisms trapped in neck

No microorganisms when flask was not disturbed

Microorganisms enter from air

Contaminated broth

Flask tipped

Contaminated broth

Figure 2-6 Some of Pasteur's original flasks, over 120 years old, are still on display in Paris and are still free of microorganisms.

In fact, flasks from Pasteur's original experiments have been preserved in Paris. They are still crystal clear!

Twenty years after Pasteur's experiments, the idea of spontaneous generation had completely disappeared. In 1870, the English scientist, Thomas Henry Huxley, first used the term **biogenesis** [bī'ō jen ə sis] to describe the concept that all living things arise only from other living things of the same type. The theory of biogenesis is well accepted in biology today. In fact, biogenesis is one of the characteristics by which life is defined.

CHECKPOINT ◆

1. What is the name for the idea that living things can arise from nonliving matter?
2. Who showed that spontaneous generation could not explain the appearance of maggots on decaying meat?
3. Where do maggots that appear on decaying meat come from?
4. What were the two major differences between Needham's and Spallanzani's experiments?
5. What was the major difference between Spallanzani's experiment and Pasteur's experiment?
▶ 6. John Needham thought he was performing controlled experiments. What factor or factors was he neglecting to control?
▶ 7. Why is the concept of an "active principle" in the air difficult to test scientifically?
▶ 8. For over 120 years Pasteur's flasks have been free of microorganisms. Do you think they will remain this way?
▶ 9. What stages in the life cycle of the fly did Redi observe?
▶ 10. How would mold appearing on bread support the hypothesis of spontaneous generation?

▶ Denotes a question that involves *interpreting* and *applying* concepts.

RECOGNIZING LIFE

Once the idea of biogenesis gained acceptance, people began to look more closely at the distinction between living things, or **organisms**, and nonliving things. What do organisms require to stay alive? What makes them different from nonliving things? Both of these questions were important to the designers of the *Viking* space probes that landed on Mars in 1976. On the surface of Mars, the *Viking* probes automatically carried out experiments designed to detect signs of life. The search for life in other parts of the universe continues. How will we recognize life if we find it? What characteristics do we look for? The study of the characteristics of life here on Earth provides a basis for the search for life elsewhere in the universe.

Section Objectives

D *State* the cell theory and *name* some of the scientists who developed it.

E *Summarize* the relationships among growth, reproduction, and inheritance.

F *List* and *explain* the characteristics shared by all living things.

2-4 Some Characteristics of Life

A major challenge to the designers of the *Viking* spacecraft was to devise experiments that could recognize evidence of living things. If you were a *Viking* scientist, what would you look for? Ideally you might try to find characteristics common to all organisms that are not shown by nonliving things. Consider the following characteristics.

Movement Organisms show movement in many different ways. Animal movements include swimming, walking, crawling, hopping, and flying. Their movements enable them to obtain food, build homes, and defend themselves. Plant movements are not as obvious as those of animals. Some flowers open and close daily. The leaves of some plants bend toward the direction of sunlight, which changes throughout the day.

Response Movement is one way organisms react to events in their surroundings, or **environment**. A **stimulus** is any change in the environment that causes a reaction. An organism's reaction to a stimulus (plural: stimuli) is called a **response**. All organisms respond to certain kinds of stimuli. These responses can have forms other than movement. For example, some trees respond to the stimulus of shortened hours of sunlight by losing their leaves in autumn.

Energy Use Another characteristic of life is a need for energy. The ability to do work is called **energy**, and all organisms perform work. Organisms called **autotrophs** [ot′ ō trōfs] can manufacture their own food. Plants are autotrophs; they absorb energy from light and manufacture food from carbon dioxide and water by a process called **photosynthesis** [fō tō sin′ thə sis].

Animals do not have the ability to make their own food. These organisms are called **heterotrophs** [het′ ə rə trōfs]. They must

Figure 2-7 Although the plants shown vary in characteristics such as height, leaf shape and size, and type of root system, they are all autotrophs. Some of their cells contain the same specialized structures which trap energy from the sun and use it to produce food.

Energy

Autotroph

Heterotroph

Heterotroph

Heterotroph

Figure 2-8 Energy from the sun is used by autotrophs to make food. Heterotrophs get energy either by eating autotrophs or by eating other heterotrophs.

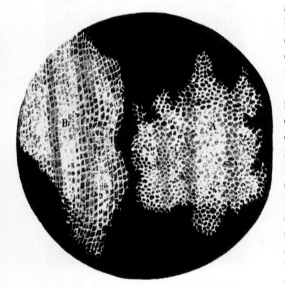

Figure 2-9 Robert Hooke's original drawings of thin slices of cork as seen under the microscope show the small compartments he called cells. The compartments reminded Hooke of rooms in prisons and monasteries called cells.

eat plants or other animals to get energy. Therefore, as shown in Figure 2-8, energy ultimately comes to most living things from the sun.

Excretion When organisms take in energy from food, some of the energy is not used and is usually released from the organism as heat. Organisms also get rid of chemical wastes from the breakdown of food by the process of **excretion**. Heterotrophs excrete many chemicals; an example is carbon dioxide. Carbon dioxide reenters the atmosphere and is used by autotrophs during photosynthesis.

All the characteristics you have just read about—movement, response to stimuli, energy use, and excretion of wastes—are common to living things but not unique to them. Think about a candle flame. What characteristics of the flame fit those just mentioned? It will flicker (movement) when you blow on it (response to stimulus). The flame requires a constant supply of fuel (wax from the candle). Flames produce a lot of energy (heat and light) and wastes (soot and carbon dioxide). Yet candle flames are not alive. Cars move, burn fuel, and produce wastes. Paper clips move in response to the stimulus of a magnet. Yet cars and paper clips are not alive. How do you distinguish these things from living organisms? It is necessary to look for other characteristics that are unique to life.

2-5 Discovery and Importance of Cells

The invention of the microscope opened up a whole new world to biologists. In 1665, the English scientist, Robert Hooke, examined thin slices of cork under a microscope. Figure 2-9 shows what he saw. Hooke named the small empty compartments cells.

The cells that Hooke observed were not alive, and he never pursued his discovery.

Almost 200 years passed before anyone recognized the importance of cells. During those years, however, investigators made countless observations of living things with improved microscopes. With more information, some generalizations began to emerge. In 1835, the French biologist, Felix Dujardin, concluded that many microorganisms consisted of a single cell.

Three years later, the German zoologist, Theodor Schwann, reported that cells are present in animal tissues. At the same time, he began working with a botanist, Matthias Schleiden. Schleiden was a plant specialist who had observed thousands of plants under the microscope. He found that cells are also present in plant tissues. Their observations led Schleiden and Schwann to suggest that all organisms are made of one or more cells. Their combined evidence gave great support to their idea.

By 1858, Rudolph Virchow, another German biologist, concluded from his observations of dividing cells that cells can arise only from other cells. He made this statement just three years before Pasteur conducted the experiments that weakened support for the idea of spontaneous generation.

Observations of these scientists and others formed the basis of the **cell theory** which states that

1. the **cell** is the basic living unit of organization for all organisms;
2. all organisms are composed of cells or cell products;
3. all cells come from other cells

Cells Based on the above accepted theory, something must be composed of cells or cell products to be classified as a living thing. Organisms consisting of a single cell are called **unicellular**. Those that are composed of more than one cell are called **multicellular**.

Biogenesis The third part of the cell theory is another way of stating the principle of biogenesis. Life is also characterized by the fact that living things come from other living things.

The candle flame discussed earlier is not composed of cells and it is the result of a chemical reaction (burning). Although it has several of the characteristics of life, the absence of cells and the nature of the origin of the flame prevent it from being classified as a living thing.

A summary of the ideas, discoveries, and experiments leading to acceptance of the theory of biogenesis and the cell theory is helpful at this point. Figure 2-11, on the next page, summarizes the contributions of the scientists you have read about in this chapter. The growth of knowledge in science often depends on the combined work of many people over long periods of time.

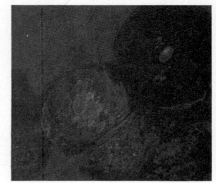

Figure 2-10 Cells come in a remarkable variety of shapes and sizes. Yet in spite of this diversity, all cells have many common features. *Top:* Plant cells. *Bottom:* Human skin cells.

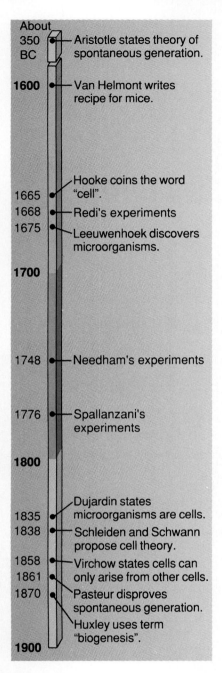

About
350 BC — Aristotle states theory of spontaneous generation.

1600 — Van Helmont writes recipe for mice.

1665 — Hooke coins the word "cell".
1668 — Redi's experiments
1675 — Leeuwenhoek discovers microorganisms.

1700

1748 — Needham's experiments

1776 — Spallanzani's experiments

1800

1835 — Dujardin states microorganisms are cells.
1838 — Schleiden and Schwann propose cell theory.
1858 — Virchow states cells can only arise from other cells.
1861
1870 — Pasteur disproves spontaneous generation.
Huxley uses term "biogenesis".
1900

Figure 2-11 A time line is useful for summarizing important dates, people, and events. This time line highlights the spontaneous generation controversy and developments in the cell theory.

2-6 More Unique Characteristics of Life

You have already seen that cells are unique to living things. However, you might argue that a dead plant or animal is also made of cells. Remember that the first cells viewed and named by Robert Hooke were not alive.

Metabolism How do living cells differ from dead cells? One difference is that living cells use energy from food to maintain internal organization. You know that unless you use some energy in your room at home, it soon becomes disorderly. The same is true for cells. They are like complex pieces of machinery that must be kept in good repair in order to continue working. The sum of the chemical and physical processes working inside a cell is called **metabolism** [mə tab'ə liz əm]. Metabolism involves obtaining energy and using it to carry out cell activities.

Water Requirement The material inside every cell is mostly water. Cell metabolism must take place in a water environment. All living things require water to survive.

Organic Compound Production The kinds of chemicals made by living things are unique and are called **organic compounds**. Many of these organic compounds are large, complex, and highly organized. You will learn more about them in Chapter 4.

Growth and Development Metabolism enables a cell to grow. During growth, a cell makes and adds substances and structures to itself. Using the same processes, multicellular organisms grow by adding more cells.

From the moment its life begins until it reaches maturity, an organism changes as it grows. The process of orderly change is called **development**. Consider the many changes that have occurred in your own body since you were born. You will continue to change as you grow older.

Reproduction with Inheritance Since no single organism lives forever, one of the most important characteristics of life is reproduction. **Reproduction** is the process by which organisms produce more organisms of the same kind. The principle of biogenesis is just a different way of saying that reproduction is a characteristic of living things.

You have probably noticed that offspring tend to look more like their parents than like other organisms of the same kind. Humans are fond of pointing out family resemblances in their children. **Inheritance**, the passing of characteristics from one generation to the next, is a feature of all living things. Inheritance plays a role in guiding the growth and development of each organism. Although a nonliving thing, such as a fire, may get larger and change, the process is not as orderly as the process of growth and development shown by living things.

Adaptation An existing structure or behavior that contributes to the survival of an organism in a particular environment is called an **adaptation**. Although adaptation is a characteristic shown by all living things, organisms adapt to their own environments in a wide variety of ways. Several examples of adaptation are shown in Figure 2-12. Adaptations that suit an organism to one environment might be harmful to an organism in a different environment. You will learn more about the importance of adaptation in later chapters.

2-7 Summarizing the Characteristics of Life

No matter how different a lion and a dandelion appear, they share many characteristics that separate them from nonliving things. While some nonliving things show a few of these characteristics, only living things show all of them. The characteristics that are used to separate living things and nonliving things are summarized in Table 2-1 on the next page.

Interfering with any one of these characteristics can prevent the survival of an organism. Food preservation techniques are based on this principle. Extreme temperatures interfere with the metabolism of microorganisms, so heating and chilling food preserves it for a while. Since living things require water, drying food will also inhibit the growth of microorganisms. Chemical preservatives added to food may interfere with the metabolism, reproduction, or growth and development of microorganisms.

Figure 2-12 Organisms show adaptations suited to their environments. *Top left:* The color and scent of the flowers attracts insects. *Top right:* The streamlined dolphin's body allows swift movement through water. *Bottom:* The fennec, a small desert fox, gets rid of excess heat through the surface area of its large ears.

COMPARING LIVING AND NONLIVING THINGS

Living	Characteristic	Nonliving
☑	Movement	☑
☑	Response	☑
☑	Energy Use	☑
☑	Excretion	☑
☑	Cells	☐
☑	Biogenesis	☐
☑	Metabolism	☐
☑	Water Requirement	☐
☑	Organic Compound Production	☐
☑	Growth and Development	☐
☑	Reproduction with Inheritance	☐
☑	Adaptation	☐

Table 2-1

CHECKPOINT ◆

11. What are the three parts to the cell theory and who were the first scientists to propose them?

12. How are the processes of growth, reproduction, and inheritance related?

13. What is the name of the process by which cells use energy to maintain organization, grow, and carry out other activities?

14. What is a structure or behavior that allows an organism to survive in its environment?

▶ 15. You have received a sample of material from Mars. You notice that something moves in the sample when you shine a light on it. Do you conclude that you have found life on Mars? Explain your answer.

▶ 16. What makes the cell theory a theory and not a hypothesis?

▶ 17. Crystals exhibit regular patterns of growth. Are crystals considered living? Explain your answer.

▶ 18. A wooden door is composed of cells. Is it considered to be a living thing? Explain your answer.

▶ Denotes a question that involves *interpreting* and *applying* concepts.

DISTINGUISHING A LIVING THING FROM A NONLIVING THING

Objectives and Skills

☐ *Make* and *record* observations of an "artificial organism."
☐ *Make* and *record* observations of living, microscopic organisms.
☐ *Compare* your observations of the living and nonliving things.

Materials

half of a petri dish	dropper
slide	forceps
coverslip	tap water
microscope	rubber cement
light source	pond water

Procedure and Observations

Part I A Nonliving Thing

1. Read all instructions for this laboratory activity before you begin your work.
2. Half fill a petri dish with water.
3. Squeeze a *small* drop of rubber cement from the tube onto the surface of the water.
4. Observe the behavior of the rubber cement. Make a chart like the one on this page to record your observations. Pay particular attention to characteristics that make the drop of glue seem as if it were alive.

Part II Observation of Organisms

1. Using the dropper, place a small sample of pond water on a clean glass slide. Most organisms are near the bottom and near plants. Obtain your drop of water from these areas. Use the forceps to lift a small amount of the stringy green material from the water and add it to your slide.
2. Place a coverslip over the drop of water.

3. Look at the slide under low power. Scan the slide for interesting organisms. If you find something particularly interesting, you may want to switch to higher magnification.
4. Draw at least three of the organisms you find. On the same chart you made in step 4 of Part I, summarize the characteristics of living things observed in your organisms.
5. Before leaving the laboratory, clean up all your materials and wash your hands.

OBSERVING CHARACTERISTICS OF LIFE		
	Glue Drop	Pond Water Organisms
1.		
2.		
3.		
4.		

Analysis and Conclusions

1. How many characteristics of a living thing did you observe in the drop of glue?
2. List several ways you could demonstrate that the drop of glue is not a living thing.
3. You did not observe the drop of glue consuming food. Does this negative observation show that the drop is not alive? Explain.
4. How many characteristics of living things did you observe in the organisms living in the pond water? What characteristics of living things did you not observe?
5. Based on your observations, can you demonstrate that the pond-water organisms are alive and the glue drop is not alive? Explain.

CHAPTER REVIEW

Summary

▶ The idea that living things can arise from non-living things once was a widely accepted idea. Redi, Spallanzani, and Pasteur used the research method to show that organisms could come only from other similar organisms.

▶ At about the time scientists demonstrated biogenesis, other scientists proposed the cell theory. Cells are the unit of structure and function in all living things, and cells arise from other cells.

▶ The characteristics of life that may sometimes be shown by nonliving things include the following:
1. Movement
2. Response
3. Energy use
4. Excretion of wastes

▶ Characteristics of life that are unique to living things are the following:
1. Cells present
2. Biogenesis
3. Metabolism
4. Water requirement
5. Production of organic compounds
6. Growth and development
7. Reproduction with inheritance
8. Adaptation to the environment

Vocabulary

adaptation	metabolism
autotroph	multicellular
biogenesis	organic compounds
cell	organism
cell theory	photosynthesis
development	reproduction
energy	response
environment	spontaneous generation
excretion	stimulus
heterotroph	unicellular
inheritance	

Concept Mapping

Using the method of concept mapping described in the front of this book complete a concept map for organisms. Copy the incomplete concept map and fill in the missing terms.

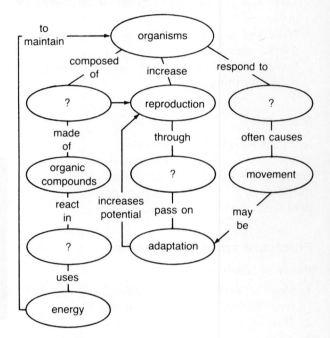

Review

1. Name one observation that was used to support the idea of spontaneous generation.
2. What Greek scientist stated that some animals arose by spontaneous generation?
3. Redi was the first scientist to observe the various life stages of what organism?
4. Why did the idea of spontaneous generation gain popularity with the discovery of microorganisms?
5. The experiments of Redi, Needham, Spallanzani, and Pasteur are described in this chapter. Which of these scientists had evidence supporting spontaneous generation? Supporting biogenesis?

6. What is the basic unit of structure and function of all living things?
7. Give an example of an adaptation.
8. What kinds of organisms carry out photosynthesis?
9. What is the original source of all the energy used by organisms?
10. What are organisms called that cannot make their own food?
11. In what form is energy usually lost by organisms?
12. List at least four characteristics found in living things but not in nonliving things.
13. In Needham's experiment, what was the control?

Interpret and Apply

14. What two observations caused Redi to suspect that flies were involved with the maggots that appeared on decaying meat?
15. In Redi's first experiment with the eight jars, what was the experimental variable?
16. What did Redi claim the results of his experiment showed?
17. What observations did Spallanzani make that caused him to suspect Needham's experiments were not carefully controlled?
18. What did Pasteur's experiments show that Spallanzani's did not?
19. How does plant movement differ from animal movement?
20. What do cells do with the energy they obtain from food?
21. Is it possible to get a candle flame to reproduce by holding the flame to the wick of another candle? How is this different from reproduction in an organism?
22. Why does freezing help to preserve food?
23. No one has ever looked at every living organism under a microscope to see if it has cells. Why are scientists so confident that the cell theory is correct?

Critical Thinking

24. How does the movement of an animal differ from the movement of a windup toy?
25. How does the energy used by a candle flame differ from energy used by a cell?
26. What is the difference between something that is dead and something that was never alive? Use your knowledge of the characteristics of life to answer this question.
27. Occasionally you find some mealworms when you open a bag of flour. Give a reasonable explanation for how these organisms might have gotten into the bag.
28. Scientists now know that many microorganisms can form spores that are very resistant to heat. How could this fact have led to the apparently contradictory results of Needham and Spallanzani?
29. Virchow made his statement about cell origins before Pasteur did his experiments. Why do you think it was necessary for Pasteur to do the experiments?
30. Explain why there must be an exception to the statement that all cells come from preexisting cells.

BASIC CHEMISTRY

Overview

COMPOSITION OF MATTER

3-1 Elements Make Matter
3-2 Atoms Make Elements
3-3 Atoms Have Energy
3-4 Compounds from
     Elements

CHANGES IN MATTER

3-5 Covalent Bonding
3-6 Ions and Ionic Bonding
3-7 Chemical Reactions
3-8 Mixtures and Solutions
3-9 Acids and Bases

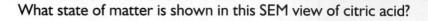

What state of matter is shown in this SEM view of citric acid?

COMPOSITION OF MATTER

Air, water, and soil around you is matter which is made of the same building blocks as the matter in your cells. Matter obviously can take a variety of forms. Three familiar forms are solids, liquids, and gases. To understand matter in its various forms, we must look further than solids, liquids, and gases. We need to look at the basic particles that make matter.

3-1 Elements Make Matter

Matter is anything that has mass and takes up space. All matter is composed of one or more elements. An **element** is a substance that cannot be broken down into simpler substances. Oxygen, copper, and gold are familiar elements, but you have probably never heard of scandium or samarium. The known elements are shown in the periodic table in the appendix. All matter is composed of one or more of these elements. Each element is represented by a **chemical symbol**.

Each element has a set of properties that distinguishes it from other elements. For example, oxygen is a colorless, odorless gas at room temperature. Copper, on the other hand, is a bronze-colored solid that conducts heat and electricity well. These properties explain why copper is used in electrical wiring and over the bottom surfaces of pots and pans.

Section Objectives

A *Distinguish* among the structural features of solids, liquids, and gases.

B *List* the characteristics of electrons, protons, and neutrons.

C *Explain* the importance of chemical energy to cell processes.

D *Use* a chemical formula to state the kinds and proportions of atoms in a compound.

E *Distinguish* between atoms, molecules, compounds, and ions.

Figure 3-1 Particles in a solid are close together and move very little. In a liquid, the particles are farther apart and free to move about each other. In a gas they are very far apart and move freely through space.

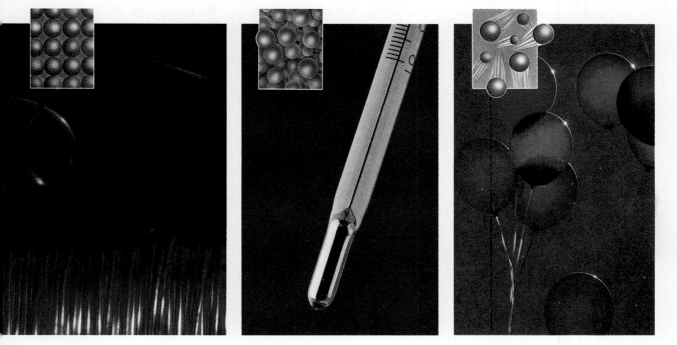

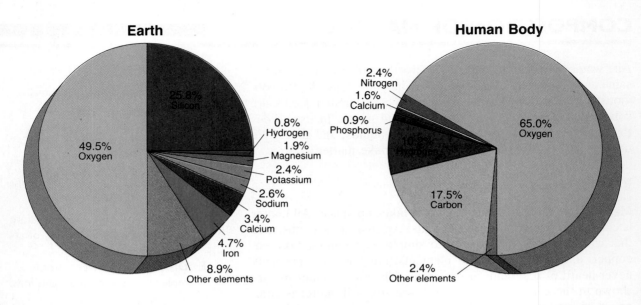

Earth

25.8% Silicon
0.8% Hydrogen
1.9% Magnesium
2.4% Potassium
2.6% Sodium
3.4% Calcium
4.7% Iron
8.9% Other elements
49.5% Oxygen

Human Body

2.4% Nitrogen
1.6% Calcium
0.9% Phosphorus
10.2% Hydrogen
65.0% Oxygen
17.5% Carbon
2.4% Other elements

Figure 3-2 A comparison of the elements found on Earth vs. the human body.

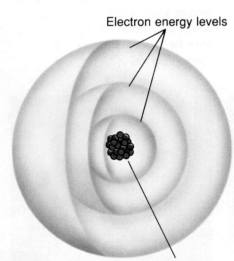

Electron energy levels

Nucleus with protons and neutrons

Figure 3-3 The nucleus of an atom contains protons and neutrons. Electrons occupy an electron cloud, which is simply a region around the nucleus where electrons are likely to be found. Hence the atom has no definite boundary or sharp edge.

The elements important to the study of biology are shown in Figure 3-2. Note the similarities and differences between the elements that make a large percentage of our Earth and those that compose the human body. From Figure 3-2, what four elements make up about 95 percent of the matter in your body?

3-2 Atoms Make Elements

All elements are made of atoms. An **atom** is the smallest particle of an element that retains the characteristics of that element. All atoms of copper have the properties of copper. Copper atoms give the element its color and conducting properties. Carbon atoms in a diamond give the diamond its hardness and light refracting properties.

Since atoms are too small to see, scientific models are used to describe how atoms might look. Experiments have shown that atoms are made of even smaller electrically charged particles.

The center of each atom contains a **nucleus** composed of two different particles called **protons** and **neutrons**. Protons are positively charged and neutrons have no charge. Moving in regions outside the nucleus are particles called **electrons**. Electrons are negatively charged.

Every atom in an element has an equal number of protons and electrons, and is electrically balanced, or neutral. In other words, the positive and negative charges are equal in number, so the atom has no net charge. Since atoms are the building blocks of matter, they have mass also. Protons and neutrons have the same mass. Electrons are much lighter. One proton has the same mass as about 1840 electrons.

3-3 Atoms Have Energy

Another important property of atoms is that they have energy. This energy in atoms comes from various sources and can be collectively described as chemical energy. What causes atoms (or matter) to be a source of energy and how is it useful to living things? Some chemical energy comes from the electrons in the atom. Electrons are in motion and occupy certain regions in space depending on their energy. Electrons closest to the nucleus have less energy than those farthest from the nucleus. The forces that hold electrons, protons, and neutrons together as an atom also contribute to the chemical energy of the atom. It is chemical energy from matter that provides the fuel for the chemical reactions necessary for life.

3-4 Compounds from Elements

You may be wondering how there can be so many different types of matter if there are only 109 different elements? For example, carbon is 17.5% of your body mass yet you don't bear any resemblance to a diamond which is pure carbon. Fortunately, elements combine to form billions of different substances with new properties. The carbon in your body is carbon combined with other elements. Substances made from elements that are combined chemically are called **compounds**.

A **chemical formula** shows the kinds and proportions of atoms in a compound. Symbols for the elements are used in writing chemical formulas. Table 3-1 shows the chemical formulas of some familiar compounds.

CONSUMER BIOLOGY

Dietary minerals are really chemical elements. Trace minerals are found in the body in amounts less than 5 grams.

Table 3-1

CHEMICAL FORMULAS OF COMMON SUBSTANCES	
Substance	Chemical Formula
Table Salt	$NaCl$
Water	H_2O
Oxygen Gas	O_2
Carbon Dioxide Gas	CO_2
Ethanol	C_2H_5OH
Acetic Acid	$HC_2H_3O_2$
Glucose	$C_6H_{12}O_6$

Water Molecule
Oxygen

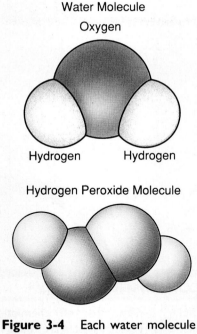

Hydrogen   Hydrogen

Hydrogen Peroxide Molecule

Figure 3-4 Each water molecule contains one oxygen atom for every two hydrogen atoms. The hydrogen peroxide molecule is also made from oxygen and hydrogen atoms. Note that in this molecule the ratio is two oxygen atoms for every two hydrogen atoms. This difference in the ratio of atoms gives hydrogen peroxide properties that differ from those of water.

▶ Denotes a question that involves *interpreting* and *applying* concepts.

The properties of a compound are often different from the properties of the elements from which it is made. Hydrogen (H) is a gas that is lighter than air, which means hydrogen in a balloon will rise as helium does. Oxygen is also a gas, which you know as an essential part of Earth's atmosphere. When hydrogen and oxygen gases are mixed, nothing happens. But if an electrical spark is used to energize the system, an explosive reaction occurs, forming water molecules.

Molecules are the smallest units of a compound that still have the properties of that compound. In a water molecule the ratio of hydrogen atoms to oxygen atoms is always 2 to 1. That is why the formula for water is written as H_2O. Hydrogen and oxygen can also combine in another ratio to form hydrogen peroxide which has the formula H_2O_2. Hydrogen peroxide is used as a bleach and an antiseptic. What is the ratio of hydrogen to oxygen atoms for this compound? From Table 3-1, how many oxygen atoms make up a molecule of oxygen? How many carbon atoms are in a molecule of carbon dioxide?

Molecules are generally *neutral* particles. Experiments show that some compounds are not made from molecules. A substance like table salt is made from electrically charged particles. Electrically charged atoms or groups of atoms are called **ions**. The ratio between sodium ions and chlorine ions in table salt is always one sodium ion for every chlorine ion as shown by the formula in Table 3-1. Sodium chloride is a compound required for cells to function properly. As you will see in Section 3-6, compounds made from ions have properties that differ from those that consist of molecules.

CHECKPOINT ◆

1. How are matter and energy related?
2. What are the four most abundant elements in the human body?
3. How are elements, atoms, and compounds related?
4. Where is most of the mass of an element located?
5. What property of an atom is utilized in making cell processes occur?
6. What is the name of a substance made of two or more elements chemically bonded together?
▶ 7. State the number of atoms for each element in the following compounds.
    a. $C_6H_{12}O_6$
    b. $HC_2H_3O_2$
    c. CH_3CHNH_2COOH
    d. $CH_3CHOHCOOH$

CHANGES IN MATTER

Living cells depend on the ability of atoms to combine in specific ways. The processes your body goes through in digesting food involves breaking food down to form simple compounds. Cells use simple compounds to form new complex compounds. The new compounds are used to make new cells to replace dying cells within your body.

3-5 Covalent Bonding

The atoms in most compounds you will learn about in biology are held together by covalent [kō vā′ lənt] bonds. A **covalent bond** results when two atoms share a pair of electrons. In a covalent bond, the shared electrons provide the "glue" that holds the atoms together.

The water molecule, for example, is held together by a covalent bond. As illustrated in Figure 3-5, each of the atoms in the water molecule (H_2O) shares its electron with another atom.

In a water molecule, the atoms share a single pair of electrons. Such covalent bonds are called **single bonds**. Covalent bonds can involve more than one pair of electrons. Sometimes atoms can share two pairs of electrons to form a **double bond**. When one carbon atom and two oxygen atoms react to form carbon dioxide (CO_2), the carbon atom forms a double bond with each oxygen atom.

Covalent bonds between atoms can be shown with a single straight line connecting the chemical symbols for the two atoms. The line represents one shared pair of electrons.

H—H
Hydrogen gas

/ O \
H   H
Water

O=C=O
Carbon dioxide

3-6 Ions and Ionic Bonding

Compounds like sodium chloride are not composed of molecules. When sodium chloride is dissolved in water, experiments show that the saltwater solution contains charged particles rather than neutral molecules.

Even though atoms are neutral, they are composed of positively charged protons and negatively charged electrons. Some compounds are formed when atoms lose or gain electrons. If an atom loses or gains an electron, it becomes an ion. If a chlorine atom gains one electron, it has 18 electrons and 17 protons for a net -1 charge. The symbol for a chloride ion is written as Cl^-.

Section Objectives

F **Compare** ions, ionic bonds, and ionic substances with covalent substances and their bonds.

G **Identify** the components and characteristics of solutions.

H **Interpret** a chemical equation.

I **Compare** the properties of polar and nonpolar solvents.

J **Relate** pH to the definitions of acids and bases and to the cellular environment.

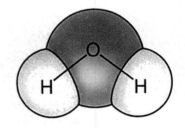

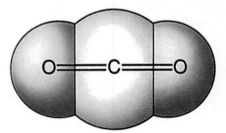

Figure 3-5 The electrons shared between atoms in water and carbon dioxide can be shown by straight lines to represent the covalent bonds. Each bond represents two shared electrons.

Figure 3-6 *Left:* The electrical nature of a saltwater solution is shown using this conductivity apparatus. The presence of charged particles in the solution completes the circuit to light the bulb. *Right:* By contrast the same apparatus is used to test a sugar solution, which is molecular.

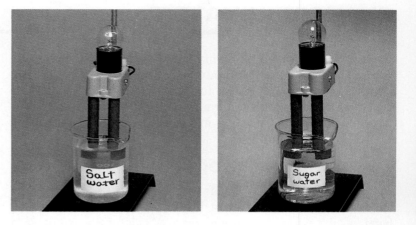

Not all ions are negatively charged. For example, sodium has 11 protons and 11 electrons. Sodium loses electrons when it forms compounds. A sodium ion has 10 electrons and 11 protons. What net charge would the sodium ion have? How would you write the symbol for the sodium ion?

In earlier science courses you learned that objects of opposite charge attract. The negative chloride ion (Cl^-) and the positive sodium ion (Na^+) are attracted to each other. This attraction between oppositely charged ions is called an **ionic bond**. An ionic bond forms when an atom such as sodium loses an electron to another atom that accepts electrons, such as chlorine.

Ions can also be groups of atoms. For example, CH_3COO^- is called the acetate ion. The charge on this group of atoms as a whole is -1. Another important ion in biology is the hydroxide ion, OH^-.

You will learn in Chapter 6 that the transfer of electrons and the formation of ions are essential to living organisms. For example, part of the photosynthesis process involves electron transport reactions. In addition your nerve and muscle cells cannot function without proper amounts of sodium, potassium, and calcium ions. These ions must be part of your diet. You will read about these ions in greater detail in Chapters 37 and 42.

Figure 3-7 An ionic bond in sodium chloride is formed when an electron from sodium is transferred to chlorine as shown by the model. This transfer results in the formation of a positive and negative ion. The attraction between oppositely charged ions is the bond.

Sodium

Atom	Ion
11 p⁺	11 p⁺
11 e⁻	10 e⁻
0 charge	+1 charge

Chlorine

Atom	Ion
17 p⁺	17 p⁺
17 e⁻	18 e⁻
0 charge	−1 charge

Sodium atom becomes a sodium ion

Chlorine atom becomes a chloride ion

3-7 Chemical Reactions

The process by which elements react to form new compounds can be described as a chemical change or chemical reaction. A chemical reaction involves the rearrangement of chemical bonds with a release or absorption of energy. For example, one chemical reaction that occurs in plants during photosynthesis is the production of sugars from carbon dioxide and water. Using symbols and formulas, the reaction can be represented as

$$3CO_2 + 3H_2O + Energy \longrightarrow C_3H_6O_3 + 3O_2$$

The numbers to the left of each molecule indicate the number of molecules involved. The arrow means, "reacts to give." Substances to the left of the arrow are called **reactants.** Substances to the right of the arrow are called **products**.

The shorthand form of this equation represents three molecules of carbon dioxide and three molecules of water plus energy reacting to give one molecule of sugar ($C_3H_6O_3$) and three molecules of oxygen. The plant uses sugar to store energy and releases oxygen into the environment.

Notice that the total number of carbon atoms on each side of the arrow is the same. Can you show that the same is true for oxygen and hydrogen? In all chemical changes, atoms can be rearranged into different combinations but they cannot vanish or appear from nowhere.

Conditions must be appropriate before a reaction can take place. You know, for example, that photosynthesis cannot occur without light which provides the energy needed to start the reaction. Nor could this reaction occur without water. In photosynthesis, water is directly involved in the chemical reaction.

In the previous sections, you saw that atoms are sources of energy. When substances react, energy is absorbed to break

Figure 3-8 The relative energy of a reactant or product can be compared by the amount of energy absorbed in breaking reactant bonds versus that released in forming product bonds. *Left:* The reactants have less energy than the products. Breaking the reactant bonds absorbs more energy than is released in forming new bonds for the products. *Right:* The reactants have greater energy than the products. The energy absorbed in breaking the reactant bonds is far less than that released in forming the product bonds. Thus for a reaction as a whole, energy is released or absorbed depending on the relative energies of the reactants and products.

Potential Energy Diagrams for Reactions

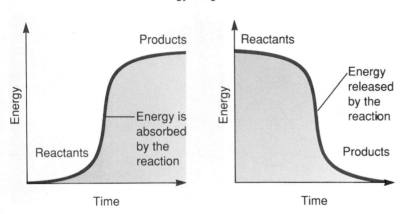

Solute Molecule ○ Solvent Molecule

Figure 3-9 In a solution, the solute molecules, or ions, are evenly distributed among the solvent molecules.

bonds. When new bonds form, energy is released. As a result, you have two types of chemical reactions. In some reactions the breaking of bonds absorbs more energy than is released during the formation of new bonds. In others the breaking of bonds absorbs less energy than is released in forming new bonds.

3-8 Mixtures and Solutions

Water is a key component of cells and provides the medium through which nutrients enter and wastes exit a living cell. Thus the ability of substances to dissolve in water is critical to life functions. Also most chemical reactions occur more easily when the reacting substances are in water solution.

When a substance dissolves in water without chemically changing the water or the substance, a mixture is formed. A **mixture** occurs when any two substances are not chemically combined. A **solution** is a class of mixtures in which individual molecules or ions of substances are uniformly distributed. The formation of a solution is a physical change. When sugar dissolves in water it does not react chemically with the water. If the water is evaporated or boiled away, the sugar remains intact.

Solutions have two parts. The **solvent** is the medium in which some substance is dissolved. The **solute** is the substance dissolved in the solvent. In a sugar and water solution, sugar is the solute and water is the solvent.

Water has unique properties that make it an excellent solvent. Notice in Figure 3-10 that the bonds between the hydrogen atoms and the oxygen atom in a water molecule are at an angle. The large positive oxygen nucleus (with eight protons) attracts the bonding electrons in the molecule more than the two small hydrogen nuclei. The electrons in the covalent bonds spend more time near the oxygen atom than near the hydrogen atoms. As a result, the oxygen side of the molecule has a slight negative charge, and the hydrogen side has a slight positive charge.

Figure 3-10 *Left:* The polarity of a water molecule is the result of an unbalanced charge distribution. The shared electrons tend to spend more time at the oxygen end of the molecule. *Right:* Vegetable oil is nonpolar. Therefore it does not dissolve (is insoluble) in a polar solvent like water.

Negative end

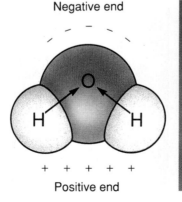

Positive end

Even though the water molecules have the same number of electrons and protons, the distribution of these charges is unbalanced. A **polar molecule** is any molecule with an unbalanced charge distribution.

Because water molecules are polar, they attract each other as well as other polar molecules and ions. This attraction causes almost any polar or ionic compound to dissolve in water. Solutes that dissolve in a solvent are **soluble**. Nonpolar substances do not dissolve in water. Substances that do not dissolve in a particular solvent are **insoluble**.

3-9 Acids and Bases

Two common groups of compounds that react in water are acids and bases. A number of acids and bases are found in your home. Lemon juice owes its sour taste to citric acid. Vinegar contains acetic acid. Baking soda and ammonia contain bases. Finally, you may be familiar with the effects of stomach acid and the occasional need to take an antacid (a base). What distinguishes an acid from a base?

An **acid** is any substance that releases hydrogen ions when mixed with water. For example, acetic acid has the formula CH_3COOH. Experiments show that when acetic acid mixes with water, the hydrogen atom that is bonded to the oxygen is released as a hydrogen ion. A negative acetate ion is a product of this reaction as shown in the following equation.

$$CH_3COOH \xrightarrow{\ H_2O\ } H^+ + CH_3COO^-$$

CONSUMER BIOLOGY

Eggs are often used in recipes as emulsifying agents to break up oil and fat molecules so they mix with other substances more readily.

CONSUMER BIOLOGY

Many household cleaners contain acids and bases. Always check the labels on cleaning products for potential hazards in using the cleaner.

Figure 3-11 If the pH of the water in this aquarium is above or below a certain range (usually 7.2 to 7.6), the fish will die.

Figure 3-12 The pH scale.

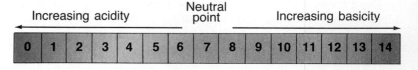

Increasing acidity | Neutral point | Increasing basicity

| 0 | 1 | 2 | 3 | 4 | 5 | 6 | 7 | 8 | 9 | 10 | 11 | 12 | 13 | 14 |

A **base** is a substance that separates in water, forming ions that react with hydrogen ions. Sodium hydroxide, NaOH, is a base. If a sodium hydroxide solution is mixed with an acetic acid solution, the hydroxide ion (OH^-) from the base combines with the hydrogen ion (H^+) from the acid to form H_2O, water.

$$NaOH + CH_3COOH \longrightarrow H_2O + CH_3COONa$$

The strength of an acid or a base is measured by the **pH scale**. The pH scale ranges from 0 to 14.

Pure water is neutral and has a pH of 7.0. The pH of acid solutions ranges from 0 to 7. Basic solutions range from a pH of 7 to 14. The farther a solution's pH is from neutral, the more acidic or basic the solution. Which is more acidic, cola with a pH of 3, or tomato juice with a pH of 4?

The pH scale is based on powers of 10. Thus cola with a pH of 3, is ten times more acidic than tomato juice, with a pH of 4, and a thousand times more acidic than a solution with a pH of 6. Living cells are very sensitive to the pH of their environment. Your cells, for example, are bathed in a fluid that has a pH of 7.2, slightly basic. If the pH of the fluid changes by only two tenths of a point in either direction (this means doubling the amount of acid or base), cells may die.

CHECKPOINT ◆

8. How many electrons are shared between atoms held together by a double bond?
9. Name the substances remaining at the completion of a chemical reaction.
10. What term describes a substance that dissolves in a solvent?
11. What is the pH range of an acid? of a base?
▶ 12. Write the symbol and charge for each of the following ions.
   a. magnesium, which has 12 protons and loses two electrons
   b. nitrogen, which has 7 protons and gains three electrons
▶ 13. State the total number of electrons for each ion described in item 12.
▶ 14. What chemical properties keep wax from mixing with water?

▶ Denotes a question that involves *interpreting* and *applying* concepts.

LABORATORY ACTIVITY

OBSERVING A CHEMICAL REACTION

In this laboratory activity, you will apply the scientific method to predict the time it takes for a chemical reaction to occur.

Objectives and Skills

☐ *Observe* and *describe* the factors affecting a specific chemical reaction.
☐ *Form a hypothesis* about the nature of the reaction based on its observed behavior.
☐ *Design an experiment* that might produce evidence for or against your hypothesis.

Materials

250-mL flask with tight rubber stopper containing unknown liquid
clock or watch with second hand
safety goggles
lab apron

Procedure and Observations

1. Read all instructions for this laboratory activity before you begin your work.
2. Wear safety goggles and lab apron.
3. ☠ Bring a flask containing an unknown liquid to your work area. *CAUTION:* **The liquid in the flask is caustic. Do not open the flask and do not allow the contents to come in contact with skin or clothing.**
4. Observe the liquid in the container very closely and record as many of its characteristics as you can on a separate piece of paper.
5. Hold the flask firmly around the neck with one hand and on the bottom with the other. Give the flask one rapid shake. *CAUTION:* **Keep your thumb over the stopper so it does not shake loose.**
6. Record your observations. Give the flask one more rapid shake. Time the reaction with a clock or watch.

7. Now give the flask two shakes and time the reaction. Time the reaction for three, four, and five shakes. On a separate sheet of paper, draw a data table like the one shown below. Record your data.

DATA TABLE		
Number of Shakes	Observations	Time for Reaction to Finish (seconds)
1		
2		
3		
4		
5		

8. Before leaving the laboratory, clean up all your materials and wash your hands thoroughly.

Analysis and Conclusions

1. Describe the relationship between the number of shakes and the time of reaction.
2. What evidence can you give that a chemical reaction occurs when you shake the flask?
3. What is the minimum number of substances that must be in the flask? What evidence can you give to support your answer?
4. What evidence do you have that something in the air above the liquid is involved in this reaction?
5. Make a hypothesis that might explain what is happening in the flask.
6. Design an experiment to test your hypothesis from the previous question.

Basic Chemistry **47**

CHAPTER REVIEW

Summary

▶ Matter can be classified as solids, liquids, and gases. All matter is made of elements which are composed of atoms. All atoms are composed of smaller particles such as protons, electrons, and neutrons. These particles vary in charge and mass.

▶ Energy is anything that is not matter but can cause a change in matter. Atoms, elements, and compounds have chemical energy which is used to fuel chemical reactions.

▶ Elements are substances made of a single kind of atom. Elements are organized by properties on the periodic table.

▶ Atoms are electrically neutral, because the number of protons is balanced by an equal number of electrons.

▶ When elements combine to form compounds, a chemical change occurs. Energy is either released or absorbed in every chemical reaction. This energy comes from the breaking and forming of new bonds.

▶ Molecules are groups of atoms held together by covalent bonds. The atoms in some compounds are held together by an ionic bond which is the attraction between oppositely-charged ions. Covalent bonds are formed when atoms share electrons. Ionic bonds are formed when atoms transfer electrons.

▶ A solution is made of a solute dissolved in a solvent. Water is a particularly good solvent because it is polar. Polar molecules have an uneven distribution of electric charge within the molecule and are soluble in water. Nonpolar solutes are insoluble in water.

▶ The pH of a solution shows whether the solution is an acid or a base. Cells must maintain a slightly basic pH within a narrow range to exist.

Vocabulary

acid	mixture
atom	molecule
base	neutron
chemical formula	nucleus
chemical symbol	pH scale
compound	polar molecule
covalent bond	product
double bond	proton
electron	reactant
element	single bond
ion	soluble
ionic bond	solute
insoluble	solution
matter	solvent

Concept Mapping

Using the concept mapping method described at the front of this book, complete the concept map for compounds. Copy the incomplete map shown below. Then fill in the missing terms.

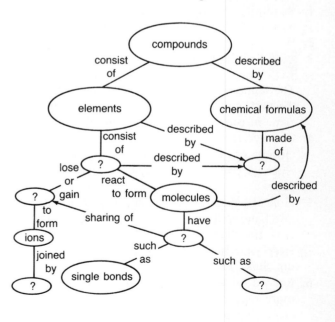

Review

1. What are the three common states of matter?
2. Energy has no mass or volume but can cause a change in _____ .
3. What four elements make up most of the human body?
4. Name the three particles that make up atoms.
5. Write the chemical symbols for each of the following elements.
   a. hydrogen   c. chlorine
   b. carbon   d. sodium
6. Write the names of the elements represented by each of the following symbols.
   a. Mg   b. K   c. Fe   d. P
7. What electric charge is found on each of the three atomic particles?
8. What is a chemical change?
9. What is a substance that is made of different elements that are chemically combined?
10. What kind of chemical bond involves sharing electrons?
11. Does sodium form a positive or negative ion? Explain your answer.
12. In many solutions, water is the _____ .
13. What is the pH of pure water?
14. What types of compounds in solution give a pH greater than 7?
15. Explain the importance of chemical energy to cell processes.

Interpret and Apply

16. Look at Figure 3-1. Which state of matter has the most rigid arrangement of atoms?
17. Analyzing the structures shown in Figure 3-1, tell why a liquid is defined as having no distinctive shape but takes on the shape of its container.
18. How do the electrons in an atom differ in relation to the nucleus?
19. What is the difference between an element and a compound?

20. Determine the number of atoms of each element in each of the following compounds.
    a. H_2CO_3 c. KCl
    b. H_3PO_4 d. $NaHCO_3$
21. How does making a solution differ from making a compound?
22. What is the difference between single bonds and double bonds?
23. Describe the essential difference between an ionic bond and a covalent bond.
24. What holds ions together in a salt crystal?
25. Why does sodium chloride dissolve in water?
26. How is the matter making up a cell similar to the matter making up a rock?

Critical Thinking

27. A uranium atom has 92 protons, 92 electrons, and 146 neutrons. Approximately what percentage of its mass is due to electrons?
28. Determine whether energy is released or absorbed in the following chemical equation. Cite a reason for your answer.

$$ATP \rightleftharpoons ADP + P + Energy$$

29. Methane (CH_4) combines with oxygen gas to form carbon dioxide (CO_2) and water. Write a chemical equation for this reaction. Include appropriate numbers in front of each molecule to ensure that the number of atoms of each type is the same on both sides of the equation.

Chapter

4

BIOMOLECULES

Overview

CARBON AND BASIC BUILDING BLOCKS

4-1 Organic Compounds

4-2 Carbohydrates

4-3 Lipids

PROTEINS AND ENZYMES

4-4 Amino Acids and Proteins

4-5 Protein Shape and Function

4-6 Enzymes

Ingredients: Water, Protein, Fats, Carbohydrates, Ions, Salt, Carbon Dioxide, Acids, Bases, Hydrogen Peroxide, Minerals, Vitamins

Which ingredients supply energy for this athlete's body?

CARBON AND BASIC BUILDING BLOCKS

Even though carbon is not the most abundant element in the human body, the chemistry of living things is organized around carbon. Complex carbon compounds related to living things are classified as biomolecules. Some important classes of biomolecules are listed on the chapter opening photo.

Scientists once thought that all carbon compounds were made by living things. Thus biomolecules were usually studied in the branch of chemistry called organic chemistry. Today, however, many thousands of organic substances like nylon and polyester are made in laboratories all over the world. Therefore the scope of organic chemistry has broadened to include all carbon compounds produced naturally or in the lab.

4-1 Organic Compounds

The chemistry of carbon is relatively simple. The complexity comes from the amazingly large number of molecules that carbon forms using very few different elements. The simplest carbon compound is formed when a single carbon atom bonds to four hydrogen atoms. The result is the methane molecule represented in Table 4-1. Methane is a major component of the natural gas used for cooking food and heating homes. Note that Table 4-1 represents methane in three different ways. Each model reveals different information. The third model shows the 3-dimensional structure of methane. It is important to remember that even though compounds are generally represented in two dimensions on paper, they exist as 3-dimensional structures. Methane belongs to a group of compounds called **hydrocarbons** [hī′ drō kär bəns]. Hydrocarbons are molecules made of hydrogen and carbon.

In addition to hydrogen, other elements, such as oxygen and nitrogen, can form covalent bonds with carbon. In this chapter, you will see diagrams of a variety of carbon compounds that

Section Objectives

A **Describe** some of the bonding properties of carbon.

B **Distinguish** between families of organic compounds.

C **Recognize** alcohols, amines, and carboxylic acids by functional groups in organic molecules.

D **Summarize** the types and functions of carbohydrates.

E **List** the major types of lipids.

F **Describe** the properties of lipids and their functions in cells.

DO YOU KNOW?

Information: The element carbon is 200 times more common in living things than it is in nonliving things.

Table 4-1

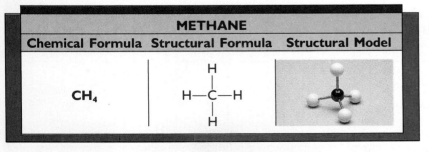

METHANE		
Chemical Formula	Structural Formula	Structural Model
CH_4	H | H—C—H | H	

Table 4-2

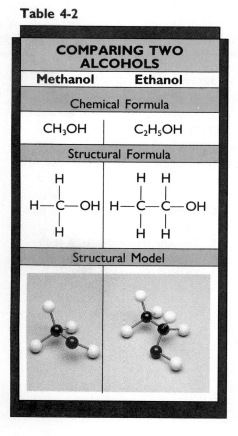

COMPARING TWO ALCOHOLS	
Methanol	**Ethanol**
Chemical Formula	
CH_3OH	C_2H_5OH
Structural Formula	
Structural Model	

contain these elements. Note that in each case, every carbon atom forms four chemical bonds. A carbon atom can form four single bonds, or combinations of single, double, and triple bonds that total no more than four. Carbon atoms can form compounds with straight chains, branched chains, and rings. Watch for these arrangements in illustrations shown later in the chapter.

Look at the first molecule drawn in Table 4-2. Compare it to the structure of methane in Table 4-1. Do you see the difference? Note that there is an oxygen atom between the carbon atom and the hydrogen atom. This compound is called methanol. You will see a similar arrangement in the second molecule of Table 4-2. This compound is called ethanol. Both methanol and ethanol belong to a class of organic compounds called alcohols. Alcohols are distinguished from other organic compounds by the presence of a functional group, $-OH$. A **functional group** gives a molecule or family of molecules distinctive properties. For example, alcohols are distinguished as a family by the presence of $-OH$. The $-OH$ group makes alcohols more soluble in water than similar molecules that are not alcohols.

Two other functional groups that occur in biomolecules are the carboxyl group, $-COOH$, and the amino group, $-NH_2$. The carboxyl group releases hydrogen ions in water so these compounds are often referred to as organic acids. Amines, on the other hand, function as organic bases in that they accept hydrogen ions from acids. Table 4-3 shows examples of three important classes of organic compounds. The symbol R is used in organic molecules to represent the hydrocarbon portion of the molecule.

Table 4-3

IMPORTANT BIOLOGICAL FUNCTIONAL GROUPS			
Class	**Functional Group**	**Structure**	**Example**
Alcohols	Hydroxyl —OH	$R—OH$	
Carboxylic Acids	Carboxyl —COOH	$R—C$ $\begin{smallmatrix} O \\ \\ OH \end{smallmatrix}$	
Amines	Amino —NH$_2$	$R—N$ $\begin{smallmatrix} H \\ \\ H \end{smallmatrix}$	

4-2 Carbohydrates

The day before a marathon race, many runners "load" their bodies with carbohydrates. Their diet includes foods like pancakes, syrup, breads, spaghetti, cakes, and cookies. Why do you think runners would select these particular foods? All these foods are rich in sugars and starches which when broken down into simpler molecules provide an energy source for cells.

Sugars and starches are carbohydrates. **Carbohydrates** are organic compounds made of carbon, hydrogen, and oxygen. Most carbohydrate molecules contain two atoms of hydrogen for every atom of oxygen.

Carbohydrates are classified by the number of sugar units in the molecule. The smallest carbohydrates are simple sugars called **monosaccharides** [mon ō sak′ ə rīds]. They consist of a single sugar unit. The most common monosaccharides, like those shown in Figure 4-1, contain five or six carbon atoms. They are usually ring-shaped molecules with several carbon atoms and one oxygen atom in the ring. **Glucose** is the most common simple sugar and is the primary cellular fuel of most organisms. Compare the chemical formula of glucose with the chemical formula of galactose. The shaded area highlights the structural differences between them. This small difference results in two entirely different compounds with different chemical properties.

Monosaccharides are small building blocks for larger carbohydrate molecules. Cells combine the small building-block molecules into large molecules by a chemical reaction called **biosynthesis**. When two monosaccharides are combined, a sugar called a **disaccharide** [dī sak′ ə rīd] is formed. The disaccharide sucrose, or table sugar, is synthesized from the monosaccharides glucose and fructose. Any two monosaccharides can combine to form a disaccharide. For example, two glucose molecules combine

DO YOU KNOW?

Information: Lactose is a sugar produced in the milk of all mammals but does not occur in any other living thing.

Figure 4-1 The structure of monosaccharides. Notice that glucose, galactose, and fructose all have the same chemical formula, yet their structural formulas are different.

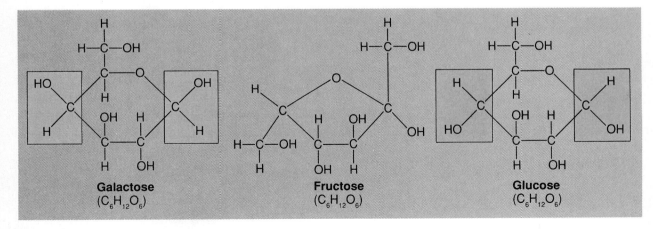

Galactose $(C_6H_{12}O_6)$

Fructose $(C_6H_{12}O_6)$

Glucose $(C_6H_{12}O_6)$

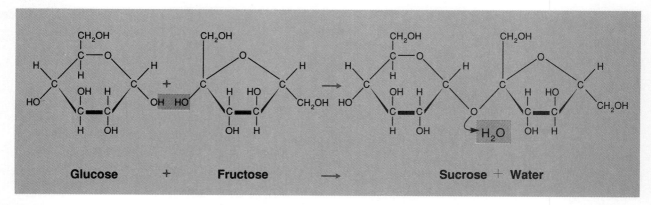

Glucose + Fructose ⟶ Sucrose + Water

Figure 4-2 The disaccharide sucrose is formed when glucose and fructose join. Notice the production of a water molecule as the bond between the monosaccharides is formed.

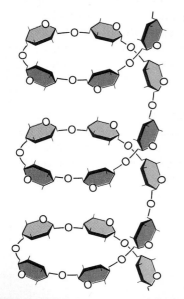

Figure 4-3 In plants, sugars are stored in the form of starch. Starch is composed of two different polysaccharides. One kind called amylose, contains 1000 or more glucose units. Starch molecules may have branched or unbranched chains.

to form the disaccharide maltose, or malt sugar. Lactose, or milk sugar, is a disaccharide made of glucose and galactose.

Large carbohydrate molecules called **polysaccharides** are built by joining three or more monosaccharides. Polysaccharides are an example of large molecules, or **macromolecules**, found in cells. Polysaccharides serve as an energy source and provide structural support for cells. Plants make *starch* which is a polysaccharide. Starch is a long chain of hundreds or even thousands of glucose molecules. Plants make starch to store energy for future use. Seeds such as rice, corn, and wheat contain starch to be used as an energy source by young plants. Potatoes are another plant structure that stores energy in the form of starch.

Cellulose [sel′ ū lōs] is another polysaccharide made by plants. It is the most abundant biomolecule on Earth. Paper, wood, and cotton all contain cellulose. Furniture, books, and clothing are made largely of cellulose. Like starch, cellulose is a long chain of thousands of glucose molecules. Starch and cellulose differ in the way the glucose molecules are bonded. Cellulose does not store energy for the plant but gives plant cells structural support.

Animals store energy in the form of the polysaccharide *glycogen* [glī′ kə gen]. Glycogen also is made of thousands of glucose molecules. It has a structure similar to plant starch. Animals that make glycogen store it in their livers and muscles.

Reactions involving carbohydrates are a major source of cell energy. When eaten, sugars enter the cells and are broken down. The energy released when the chemical bonds are broken is much greater than the energy absorbed to form new bonds. Cells then use the energy released from this process to build new cells and tissues.

Before sugars can enter cells, they must be the size of monosaccharides. Polysaccharides are broken down by a chemical reaction called **hydrolysis** [hī drol′ ə sis]. As shown in Fig-

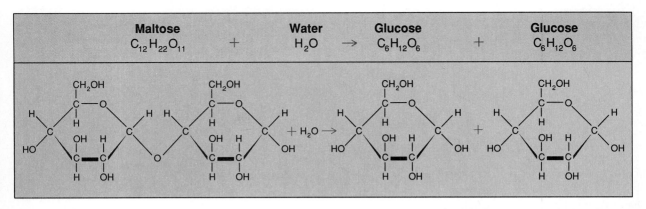

| Maltose $C_{12}H_{22}O_{11}$ | + | Water H_2O | → | Glucose $C_6H_{12}O_6$ | + | Glucose $C_6H_{12}O_6$ |

Figure 4-4 The hydrolysis of maltose.

ure 4-4, the addition of a water molecule splits a large molecule into two smaller molecules. Hydrolyzing food molecules to make them easier to absorb is called **digestion**.

Cellulose is a major part of the leafy vegetables, whole wheat, carrots, and other plant material in your diet. Cellulose often is called fiber, or roughage. Your body cannot break down cellulose into its component glucose molecules. Cellulose simply passes through your body. Thus since bonds are not broken, the energy of the cellulose molecule is not available to your cells. Nonetheless, fiber is known to be an important part of a healthy diet. A high-fiber diet seems to decrease the risk of cancer in the digestive tract.

4-3 Lipids

Bacon fat, vegetable oil, butter, margarine, and furniture wax are examples of lipids. **Lipids** are nonpolar organic molecules. Recall that water is a polar substance, and normally only polar or ionic substances will dissolve in water. Lipids, therefore, do not dissolve in water.

The insolubility of lipids in water gives them important functions in organisms. For example, lipid molecules form a barrier between a cell and its watery environment. The lipid layer of blubber in whales and walruses insulates the entire organism from the icy water. Skin oils help to repel water from the feathers of ducks.

Another important function of lipids is to store energy. The body fat of animals consists of cells containing large lipid droplets. When food is not available, these lipids can be broken down to provide energy.

The building blocks of an important group of lipids are fatty acids. **Fatty acid** molecules are long chains of carbon atoms with

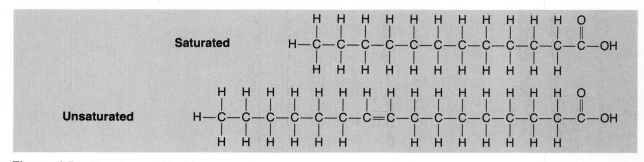

Figure 4-5 Two fatty acids. Notice that the unsaturated fatty acid has a double bond in the carbon chain. What might a polyunsaturated fatty acid look like?

a $-COOH$ (carboxyl) group at the end. If the carbon chain has the maximum possible number of hydrogen atoms attached to it, the molecule is said to be **saturated**. Molecules that have double bonds, and therefore fewer hydrogen atoms, are **unsaturated**. In both cases the carbon chain is nonpolar, so it is insoluble in water.

The majority of fat in organisms consists of molecules called **triglycerides** [trī glis′ ə rīdz]. They are composed of three fatty acid molecules combined with a three-carbon alcohol called *glycerol* [glis′ ə rol]. When triglycerides are broken down by hydrolysis, they produce the same molecules that compose them; fatty acids and glycerol. Do you think that a triglyceride would be soluble in water?

The three fatty acids in a triglyceride can be identical or can vary in length and have different numbers of double bonds. If

Figure 4-6 Forming a triglyceride involves combining three fatty acids with an alcohol called glycerol. Notice that a water molecule is formed as each of the three fatty acids is attached to the glycerol.

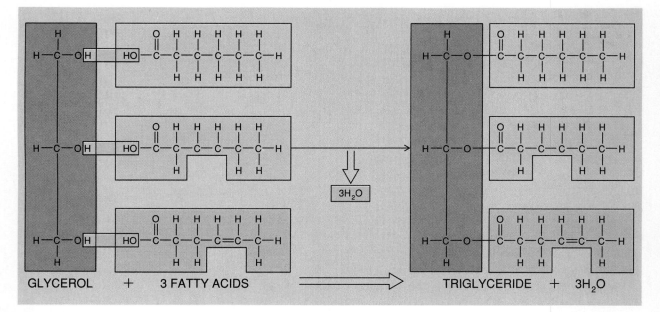

GLYCEROL + 3 FATTY ACIDS ⟶ TRIGLYCERIDE + 3H$_2$O

the fatty acids have more than two double bonds, they are **poly-unsaturated**. Triglycerides such as butter and lard are made from saturated fatty acids. They are solid at room temperature. A triglyceride that is solid at room temperature is called a **fat**. A triglyceride that is liquid at room temperature is called an **oil**. Oils usually contain unsaturated fatty acids and are more commonly made by plants than by animals. Corn oil and peanut oil are some familiar examples of oils with unsaturated fatty acids.

The energy released from a reaction involving triglycerides is more than double that released from a reaction using a similar mass of carbohydrates. The human body can store less than a day's energy supply in the form of glycogen, but it can store a three-month supply in the form of triglycerides. If you consume more carbohydrates than you need, your cells convert the excess to triglycerides. You then store the triglycerides in the fatty tissues of your body.

You may have heard that eating saturated fat is associated with increased risk of heart and blood vessel disease. What is it about saturated fats that might cause disease? In later chapters you will learn more about the role of fats and oils in your diet.

Figure 4-7 Some foods that are sources of fat in your diet. Can you tell which foods provide saturated triglycerides and which produce unsaturated triglycerides?

CHECKPOINT ◆

1. What is the name for the study of carbon compounds?
2. In compounds, how many bonds does each carbon atom share with adjacent atoms?
3. Draw the functional group for alcohols, carboxylic acids, and amines.
4. What functional groups are present in a glucose molecule?
5. Name three polysaccharides.
6. What chemical reaction converts disaccharides to monosaccharides?
7. What property do all lipids have in common?
8. What are the building blocks of triglycerides?
9. What carbohydrate is the primary source of fuel for most cells?
▶ 10. The hydroxyl group for alcohols is polar. How does this fact explain why methanol dissolves in water but methane does not?
▶ 11. What do triglycerides and polysaccharides have in common?
▶ 12. Look at Figure 4-6. What functional groups can you identify on fatty acids? on glycerol?

▶ Denotes a question that involves *interpreting* and *applying* concepts.

Section Objectives

Section Objectives

G *Describe* the structure of an amino acid.

H *Diagram* the process that joins amino acids to form polypeptides and proteins.

I *Explain* how the amino acid sequence of a protein determines the shape of the protein.

J *List* several functions of proteins in living things.

K *Discuss* how enzymes speed up chemical reactions in the cell.

Proteins perform a wide variety of tasks in living things. They are among the largest and most complex molecules in the cell. A typical protein molecule may be constructed with thousands of atoms. As a result, proteins are classified as macromolecules. Knowing about the structure and function of proteins is essential to understanding how living things work.

4-4 Amino Acids and Proteins

Proteins [prō′ tēns], like other macromolecules, consist of smaller building-block molecules bonded together. They have a greater variety of structure and function than any other group of macromolecules. For example, hair, spider webs, feathers, and turtle shells are made of protein. Some of the functions resulting from this varied structure are shown in Table 4-4.

A major function of proteins is to serve as a source of raw materials, supplying your cells with the building blocks necessary to synthesize new body parts. Animals may be the primary source of protein in your diet: meat, fish, and dairy products are rich

Table 4-4

SOME PROTEIN FUNCTIONS		
Function	**Examples**	**Illustration**
Energy Source	Egg white and yolk Meat Fish	
Fight Infection	Fibers in blood clot Antibodies	
Structural Component	Feathers Human hair Spider's web	
Assist Life Processes	Oxygen transport in red blood cells Aid in digestion	

in protein. Plant materials like soybean and beans also are excellent sources of protein. A second protein function is for cell energy, when available supplies of carbohydrates and lipids are exhausted.

Proteins are made from building blocks called **amino acids**. An amino acid has four parts, all bonded covalently to the same central carbon atom. Three of the parts—a hydrogen atom, an amino group ($-NH_2$), and a carboxyl ($-COOH$) group—are common to every amino acid.

The fourth part of the amino acid molecule is a distinct atom or group of atoms. This group is designated by the letter R. Figure 4-8 shows the parts of an amino acid. The R groups are different in different amino acids. Some R groups are ionically charged (plus or minus), some are polar, and some are nonpolar. An amino acid's R group determines its chemical properties. All organisms, from bacteria to humans, are composed of combinations of the same 20 amino acids.

Amino acids are joined by peptide bonds. A **peptide bond** is the bond that forms between an organic acid ($-COOH$) group of one amino acid and an amino group of a second amino acid. The shaded portions of Figure 4-9 show the groups involved. Are the R groups of the amino acids included in the peptide bonds?

When two amino acids join, the molecule formed is called a *dipeptide*. When more than two amino acids are bonded, a **polypeptide** chain is formed. Proteins are long polypeptides with an average length of 200 amino acids.

Proteins are distinguished from one another by the sequence of their amino acids. With 20 different amino acids to occupy any place in a chain of 200 amino acids, the number of possible proteins is enormous. The amino acids are like letters in the alphabet. Think about how many words are made with 26 letters! Thousands of different words and a countless number of sentences are made by arranging the 26 letters of the alphabet. Similarly, a protein is made by arranging the 20 different amino acids in a specific sequence.

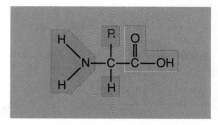

Figure 4-8 Every amino acid has an amino group, a hydrogen atom, and an organic acid group attached to a central carbon atom. The R group is different for each amino acid.

CONSUMER BIOLOGY

Protein and amino acid supplements can be dangerous. Though they can be advertised to help build muscle and provide protein to dieters, such is not the case. People have died on liquid protein diets. Amino acid supplements can cause severe imbalances and all amino acids are toxic in excess.

Figure 4-9 A peptide bond (outlined in color) joins two amino acids and forms a dipeptide.

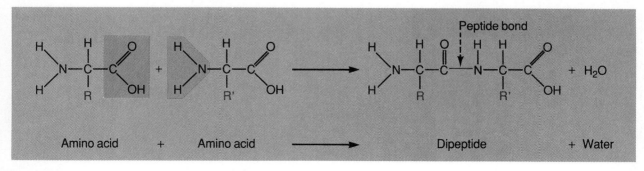

BIOLOGY INSIGHT

Structure is Related to Function: The three-dimensional shape of each protein determines its function in a living organism.

Figure 4-10 The amino acid chain (primary structure) is twisted and folded (secondary structure) as the R groups interact. The polypeptide folds back on itself, acquires a 3-dimensional shape (tertiary structure), and becomes a functional protein. Some proteins cluster in a more complex arrangement (quaternary structure).

4-5 Protein Shape and Function

As the cell combines amino acids, the R groups of the amino acids interact with each other to bend the polypeptide chain in a unique way. For example, positively-charged R groups are attracted to negatively-charged R groups of other amino acids in the protein. R groups with the same electric charge repel each other. Water-soluble R groups move toward water molecules that surround the protein in the cell. R groups that are insoluble in water move closer to each other and away from the surrounding water molecules. These forces combine to cause the polypeptide chain to twist and fold into a three-dimensional shape. Protein molecules with the same amino acid sequence have exactly the same three-dimensional shape. Figure 4-10 shows the complex folding of a polypeptide chain to form a functional protein. Many proteins may consist of more than one polypeptide chain.

Every protein made by the cell has a specific function. The function it performs is due to the protein's unique molecular shape. This molecular shape is due to the order of amino acids. If even one amino acid is out of order or changed, the entire protein can fold differently. This change may totally alter the function of the protein.

4-6 Enzymes

A cell continues to live because of its metabolism. The thousands of chemical reactions must occur continuously. At normal cell temperatures these reactions proceed too slowly for the cell to

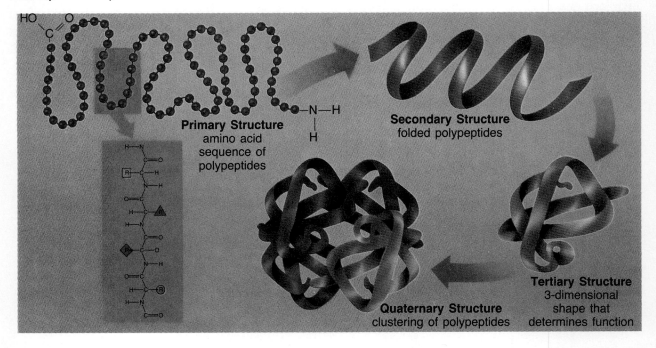

Primary Structure
amino acid sequence of polypeptides

Secondary Structure
folded polypeptides

Tertiary Structure
3-dimensional shape that determines function

Quaternary Structure
clustering of polypeptides

live. These reactions require a **catalyst**, or a molecule to increase their rate. Biochemical reaction rates are increased by substances called **enzymes** [en′ zīms]. Almost all the chemical reactions that take place in living cells require a specific enzyme. Thus, enzymes are essential to a cell's life because they regulate its metabolism.

Recall from Chapter 3 that most chemical reactions require energy to get them started. For example, for water to form from hydrogen and oxygen gas, energy must be supplied to the system to break the bonds between atoms in the two gases. A spark (energy) is used to start the reaction. The minimum energy needed to cause a particular reaction to occur is called **activation energy**.

An example of a reaction that occurs in organisms is the hydrolysis of maltose, a disaccharide, into two molecules of glucose. The hydrolysis of maltose requires an initial input of energy. In a test tube, you can supply the energy to activate the reaction by heating the tube. Using this amount of heat energy to hydrolyze maltose in a cell would kill the cell. Fortunately, cells produce enzymes which reduce the amount of activation energy required to start a chemical reaction. With an enzyme present, reactions occur quickly at normal cell temperatures. Without enzymes, reactions proceed too slowly for a cell to live.

The shape of the enzyme molecule is the key to its function. *Maltase* is the enzyme that hydrolyzes maltose. On the surface of the maltase molecule is an area called the active site. The **active site** is where the chemical reaction occurs. The shape of the active site is determined by the 3-dimensional structure of the enzyme molecule.

The active site of maltase matches the shape of the maltose molecule. Maltose fits into the active site much as your hand

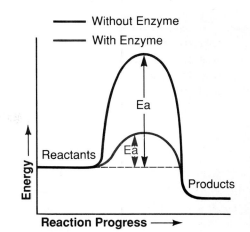

Figure 4-11 The amount of activation energy (E_a) necessary for a chemical reaction to proceed is reduced when an enzyme is involved.

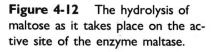

Figure 4-12 The hydrolysis of maltose as it takes place on the active site of the enzyme maltase.

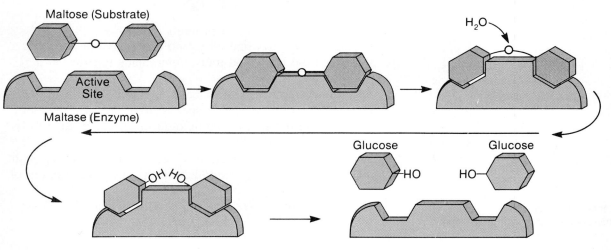

fits into a glove. Although maltose fits into the active site, the fit is not perfect. After it enters, the maltose molecule is slightly twisted or distorted. This distortion makes the bond easier to break between the two glucose portions of the molecule.

When the bond between parts of the maltose molecule breaks, two glucose molecules are released. The active site of maltase is then ready to accept another maltose molecule. Thus the enzyme speeds up the hydrolysis of maltose but is not changed by the reaction.

Due to its three-dimensional shape, an enzyme molecule has an active site that matches only a specific molecule. The molecule on which an enzyme acts is called the **substrate**. Maltose is the substrate acted on by the enzyme maltase. Amylase is an enzyme that accepts starch molecules as a substrate. Because the active site of an enzyme combines with one kind of substrate molecule, there is a different enzyme for every type of reaction in a cell. Thousands of different chemical reactions occur in every cell, so even a bacterial cell needs thousands of different enzymes to live!

Many enzymes require an additional substance called a **cofactor** to catalyze a reaction. A cofactor can be either an organic molecule called a **coenzyme** or a metal ion. Coenzymes are often the carriers of reactive functional groups. Some vitamins are part of specific coenzyme molecules that are essential to the proper functioning of the cell. Some metal ions that are cofactors are familiar elements such as iron, copper, and zinc.

A cell's structure and function are determined by the enzymes it produces. By producing a particular group of enzymes at a particular time, the cell controls its activities.

CHECKPOINT ◆

13. List four functions of proteins in cells.
14. Name the parts that all amino acids have in common.
15. Name the bond that joins amino acids together in a protein.
16. What determines the shape of a protein?
17. What kind of substance speeds up a chemical reaction?
18. What term refers to the amount of energy needed to begin a chemical reaction?
▶ 19. Explain how the function of the enzyme, maltase, might be affected if one amino acid in its structure was out of sequence.
▶ 20. How might the absence of vitamins in your diet affect your cells?

▶ Denotes a question that involves *interpreting* and *applying* concepts.

LABORATORY ACTIVITY

PROPERTIES OF AN ENZYME

In this activity, you will examine some properties of an enzyme called peroxidase. This enzyme breaks down hydrogen peroxide, which is a toxic by-product of cell metabolism, into harmless water and oxygen.

Objectives and Skills

- *Compare* the activity of peroxidase under a variety of external conditions.
- *List* the similarities and differences between an inorganic catalyst and an enzyme.
- *Explain* how different conditions affect the activity of an enzyme.

Materials

safety goggles	400-mL beaker
lab apron	3% hydrogen peroxide
5 test tubes	stock solution
test tube rack	manganese dioxide powder
forceps	fine sand
spatula	fresh liver
mortar and pestle	potato
hot plate	

Procedure and Observations

1. Read all instructions for this laboratory activity before you begin your work.
2. Put on safety goggles and lab apron for the entire experiment.
3. Set up 5 clean test tubes in a test tube rack. Pour about 2 mL of hydrogen peroxide into each test tube. Half fill a 400 mL beaker with water and put on the hot plate to boil for a later step.
4. Using the spatula, transfer a small amount of manganese dioxide powder to the first tube. Observe the amount of bubbling. Use a number scale to rate activity where 0 = no bubbles and 10 = most activity.

5. Using the spatula, transfer a small amount of sand to the second tube and observe whether any bubbles form. Rate the bubble activity.
6. In the third tube place a small cube of fresh liver. Compare the bubbling activity to the first two tubes. What number would you give to describe the activity in this tube?
7. Place a piece of liver the same size as the one used in the previous step into a mortar and pestle. Add a small amount of fine sand and grind the liver. Use a spatula to transfer the ground liver to the fourth test tube. Assign a number to describe the activity in this tube.
8. Using forceps, put a piece of liver into the boiling water bath you set up earlier. Boil the liver for about two minutes. Remove the liver with forceps and drop it into the fifth test tube. Assign a number to describe the activity in this tube.
9. If you have time, repeat steps 6 through 8 using potato instead of liver.
10. Before leaving the laboratory, clean up all your materials and wash your hands thoroughly.

Analysis and Conclusions

1. Compare the activity ratings of manganese dioxide and peroxidase.
2. What is the reason for testing sand in the second test tube?
3. How do you explain the difference in activity between whole liver and ground liver?
4. What is the effect of boiling the liver on peroxidase activity?

CHAPTER REVIEW

Summary

‣ Carbon always forms four covalent bonds with other atoms. It can bond with other carbon atoms, with other elements, or with other groups. There is an enormous variety of organic molecules based on chains and rings of carbon.

‣ Carbohydrates are made of carbon, hydrogen, and oxygen. They range in size from monosaccharides to huge polysaccharides. Simple sugars are used by cells primarily as an energy source. Starch and glycogen are used to store energy in plants and animals. Cellulose is used for structural support in plants. Most of the carbohydrate in your diet is in the form of starch.

‣ Lipids are organic compounds that are not soluble in water. Typical lipids include fats, oils, and waxes. Fats and oils are triglycerides. The principal function of triglycerides is to store energy.

‣ Proteins are macromolecules built of chains of amino acids. The sequence of the amino acids determines the identity and shape of a protein. The shape of a protein determines its function in the cell.

‣ Enzymes are proteins that catalyze chemical reactions in cells by lowering the activation energy of a reaction.

Vocabulary

activation energy	enzyme
active site	fat
amino acid	fatty acid
biosynthesis	functional group
carbohydrate	glucose
catalyst	hydrocarbon
coenzyme	hydrolysis
cofactor	lipid
digestion	macromolecule
disaccharide	monosaccharide

oil	protein
peptide bond	saturated
polypeptide	substrate
polysaccharide	triglyceride
polyunsaturated	unsaturated

Concept Mapping

Using the method of concept mapping described in the front of this book, complete a concept map for biomolecules. Copy the incomplete map and fill in the missing terms.

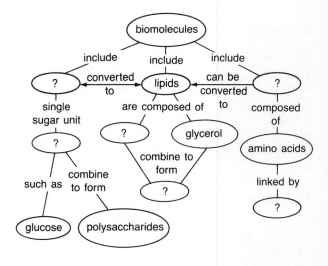

Review

1. What distinguishes organic chemistry from inorganic chemistry?
2. What two elements make all hydrocarbons?
3. In a double bond, how many pairs of electrons are shared between the two atoms?
4. Name the chemical families that contain the functional groups $-NH_2$ and $-COOH$.
5. What kind of molecules are made of many simple sugars bonded together?

6. What is the function of glycogen?
7. What important substance in your diet is found in plant seeds?
8. What is the primary function of glucose in cells?
9. Which polysaccharide cannot be used as an energy source by humans?
10. List two functions of lipids in cells.
11. What kinds of organisms tend to make saturated fatty acids?
12. What is the difference between a saturated fatty acid and an unsaturated fatty acid?
13. How do the 20 amino acids found in proteins differ from each other?
14. What kind of covalent bond joins amino acids together in proteins?
15. An enzyme reduces the _____ of a chemical reaction.
16. What is the function of a catalyst?
17. The substance acted on by an enzyme is called a _____ .
18. What is the name of the location where the substrate attaches to an enzyme?

Interpret and Apply

19. What kind of information is given by a space-filling model of a molecule that cannot be seen in the structural formula?
20. Look at the structures of glucose and fructose in Figure 4-1. Describe the one difference between these molecules.
21. What is the difference between hydrolysis and chemical synthesis?
22. Name an element that is in proteins but not found in lipids and carbohydrates.
23. Why are some amino acids soluble in water while others are not?
24. What property of proteins allows them to perform so many different functions?
25. Why are enzymes required in cells?

26. Which compound does not belong with the others on the list? (a) fiber (b) sugar (c) fat (d) starch
27. Which compound does not belong with the others on the list? (a) starch (b) fatty acids (c) cellulose (d) glycogen
28. Name the two functional groups found in amino acids.
29. Name the functional groups that can be found in carbohydrates.

Questions 30–31 are analogies. Fill in the missing word or phrase to complete each analogy.

30. Saturated is to single bond as _____ is to double bond.
31. Proteins are to amino acids as polysaccharides are to _____ .

Critical Thinking

32. Given the molecular formula C_2H_6O, draw two structural formulas for this compound.
33. List the major sources of carbohydrate in your personal diet.
34. When you eat more food than you need for energy, you store the excess food in the form of triglycerides. Why are triglycerides particularly useful for this purpose?
35. Most animals make an enzyme that hydrolyzes starch into maltose. Could this same enzyme hydrolyze cellulose into maltose? Explain.
36. How does an enzyme lower the activation energy of a reaction?
37. Adding table salt to the solution containing an enzyme generally destroys the activity of the enzyme. Remember that salt forms positive and negative ions in solution. Explain how the addition of salt could affect the function of an enzyme.

Chapter

5

CELL STRUCTURE AND FUNCTION

Overview

THE CELL: THE BASIC UNIT OF LIFE

5-1   The Work of a Cell
5-2   Structure of a Cell
5-3   The Nucleus
5-4   Cytoplasm: Cytosol and Organelles
5-5   The Plasma Membrane
5-6   The Cell Wall

THE CELL AND ITS ENVIRONMENT

5-7   Diffusion
5-8   Permeability
5-9   Selective Permeability and Osmosis
5-10   Animal Cells and Osmosis
5-11   Turgor Pressure and Plasmolysis

THE CELL'S LIVING BOUNDARY

5-12   Passive vs. Active Transport
5-13   Facilitated Diffusion
5-14   Active Transport

How many workers are employed in this cellular factory?

THE CELL: THE BASIC UNIT OF LIFE

Understanding the importance of cells begins with knowing something about cell structure. In Chapter 4, you learned about the chemicals found in living things. Now you will find out how these chemicals are used in cells. In chapters that follow, many topics you study will relate to what happens in cells. By knowing some basic information about cell structure and function, you will be in a position to understand more of what you learn later.

5-1 The Work of a Cell

The day-to-day operations within a cell are very similar to what occurs in a factory. Raw materials for the manufacture of products are delivered to the factory and distributed to the areas where they will be used. The central office makes decisions and manages the activities within the factory. Out of this office come the orders for what products will be manufactured. Finished goods are packaged and shipped to places outside the factory. In some factories, old products are recycled into new products.

Like a factory, a cell is highly organized. Inside the cell are many smaller parts, called **organelles** [ȯr gə nelz'], that carry out life processes. The organelles perform for the cell the functions that people and machines perform for the factory. Table 5-1 compares the organization of a factory to that found inside a

Section Objectives

A **Explain** how the nucleus directs cell activity.

B **Compare** and **contrast** animal and plant cells.

C **Discuss** the structure and functions of each organelle.

D **Describe** the structure of membranes.

E **Identify** the layers of the cell wall.

Table 5-1

THE CELL AS A FACTORY		
Factory Part	**Function**	**Organelle**
central office	manages activities, initiates production	nucleus
assembly line	assembles raw materials to manufacture products	ribosome
shipping	packs products for distribution	endoplasmic reticulum, Golgi apparatus
cart	transports raw materials and finished products within factory	transport vesicle
generator	provides energy for activities	mitochondrion
storage area	stores material for later use	vacuole
collection center	recycles used parts	lysosome
door	provides passage in and out	plasma membrane

Cell Structure and Function   **67**

cell. Not all the parts of a cell are listed here, but the table summarizes the most important jobs.

Most of the organelles listed in the table are probably unfamiliar to you. You will learn more details about organelles and their functions in Section 5-2. In the chapters that follow, you will learn how the various organelles work together to carry out the life processes of a cell. As you read, use the table as a quick reference, and try to identify other similarities between a cell and a factory.

Figure 5-1 The illustration below represents a typical animal cell. A cutaway view of this three-dimensional structure reveals numerous organelles.

Animal cell

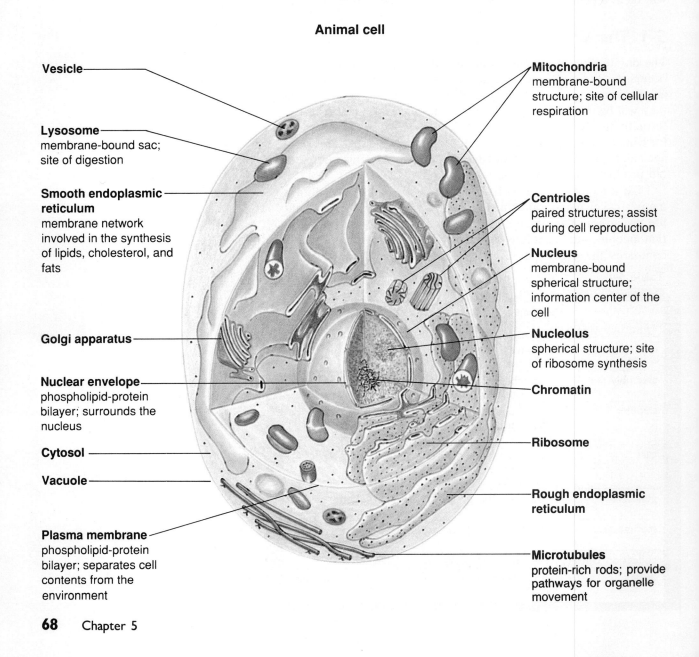

Vesicle

Lysosome
membrane-bound sac; site of digestion

Smooth endoplasmic reticulum
membrane network involved in the synthesis of lipids, cholesterol, and fats

Golgi apparatus

Nuclear envelope
phospholipid-protein bilayer; surrounds the nucleus

Cytosol

Vacuole

Plasma membrane
phospholipid-protein bilayer; separates cell contents from the environment

Mitochondria
membrane-bound structure; site of cellular respiration

Centrioles
paired structures; assist during cell reproduction

Nucleus
membrane-bound spherical structure; information center of the cell

Nucleolus
spherical structure; site of ribosome synthesis

Chromatin

Ribosome

Rough endoplasmic reticulum

Microtubules
protein-rich rods; provide pathways for organelle movement

5-2 Structure of a Cell

Recall from Chapter 2 that the study of cells began with the invention of the microscope. Viewing was limited, however, by the resolving power of the light microscope. More advanced tools, particularly the electron microscope, have led to exploration of cell structure in great detail.

Look at Figures 5-1 and 5-2. These illustrations reflect much of what is now known about the structure of animal and plant

Figure 5-2 A typical plant cell is illustrated below. Compare this plant cell with the animal cell in Figure 5-1. Study every organelle illustrated in both figures. The functions each of these cells can perform depends upon the number and kinds of organelles it contains.

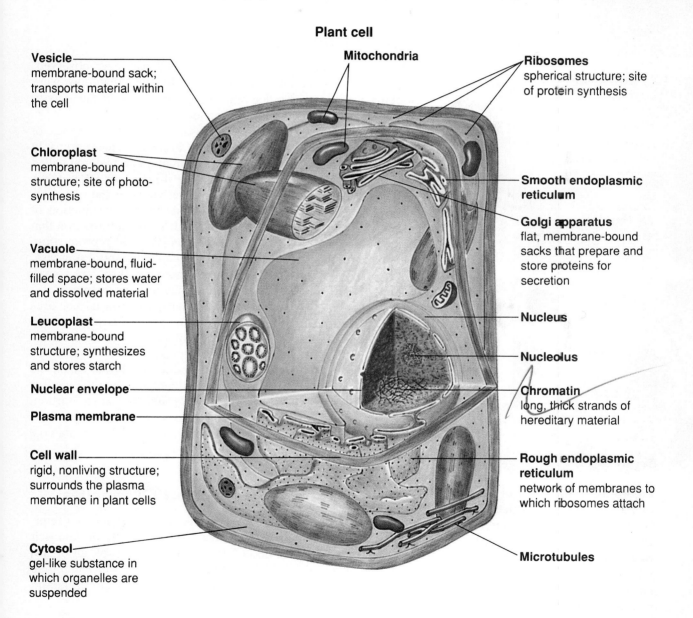

Plant cell

Vesicle—membrane-bound sack; transports material within the cell

Chloroplast—membrane-bound structure; site of photosynthesis

Vacuole—membrane-bound, fluid-filled space; stores water and dissolved material

Leucoplast—membrane-bound structure; synthesizes and stores starch

Nuclear envelope—

Plasma membrane—

Cell wall—rigid, nonliving structure; surrounds the plasma membrane in plant cells

Cytosol—gel-like substance in which organelles are suspended

Mitochondria

Ribosomes—spherical structure; site of protein synthesis

Smooth endoplasmic reticulum

Golgi apparatus—flat, membrane-bound sacks that prepare and store proteins for secretion

Nucleus

Nucleolus

Chromatin—long, thick strands of hereditary material

Rough endoplasmic reticulum—network of membranes to which ribosomes attach

Microtubules

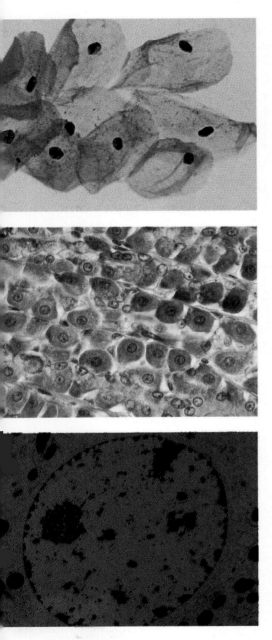

Figure 5-3 The nuclei of stained animal cells can be seen through a light microscope: *Top:* Human cheek cells. *Middle:* Stomach cells of a mammal. *Bottom:* An electron-micrograph of a mammal cell nucleus shows the tiny nucleolus (dark circular area to left).

cells. Keep in mind that not all cells contain every kind of organelle shown here. Also, the sizes of some of the organelles may be either much smaller or larger than those presented in these diagrams. Had they been drawn to scale, some organelles would appear as mere specks while others would fill the entire page!

Compare the diagrams. What similarities can you see between the two cells? How do they differ? Study the diagrams carefully. Much of what you will learn in this chapter and the next few chapters involves the structures you see in the figures.

5-3 The Nucleus

The nucleus [nü' klē əs] was the first cell part ever observed. Biologists were probably unaware at the time that they were looking at the central office of a cell factory. Most of the activity inside a cell is initiated by the nucleus.

Dispersed throughout the nucleus are long, thin strands of material called **chromatin** [krō' mə tin]. Chromatin is made primarily of protein. Another component of chromatin is a material called **deoxyribonucleic** [dē äk' sē rī bō nü klē ik] acid, or **DNA**. DNA is the chemical code that directs the activities of the cell. This macromolecule contains the instructions for the production of many of the proteins made by the cell. It is this information that is passed to the next generation of cells. Prior to reproduction, a cell's chromatin begins to thicken and coil like a spiral staircase. These coiled strands are called **chromosomes** [krō' mə sōmz]. You will learn more about chromosomes in later chapters.

One part of the chromatin is condensed into a darker area called the **nucleolus** [nü klē' ə ləs]. The nucleolus produces *ribosomes*, the organelles that are involved in making proteins. Some cells have more than one nucleolus.

The nucleus is surrounded by a double membrane called the nuclear envelope. The inner portion fits tightly around the nucleus itself. The outer portion fits loosely around the inner portion. The two fuse together in certain places, forming pores. It is thought that these pores provide a channel for the flow of material into and out of the nucleus.

5-4 Cytoplasm: Cytosol and Organelles

Most of the "workers" in a cell factory are suspended in a semi-fluid substance outside the nuclear envelope. This protein-rich material is called the **cytosol** [sīt' ə sȯl]. The cytosol, all organelles, and materials within the cell between the plasma membrane and the nuclear envelope are collectively called the **cytoplasm** [sīt' ə plaz em].

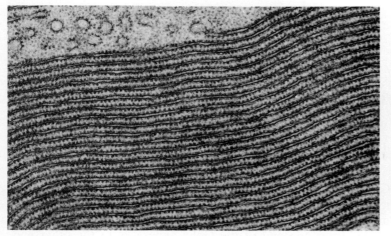

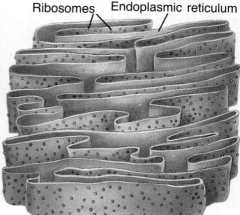

Ribosomes   Endoplasmic reticulum

Ribosomes Ribosomes [rī′ bə sōmz] are the assembly-line workers of the cell factory. These organelles are made of proteins and other macromolecules. They are found either floating freely throughout the cytoplasm or attached to the membranes of the endoplasmic reticulum (described below). Since protein synthesis occurs on ribosomes, it is easy to see how important these organelles are to a cell. In Chapter 7, you will learn about how protein synthesis occurs.

Endoplasmic reticulum The folded membranes of the endoplasmic reticulum [en də plaz′ mik ri tik′ yə ləm], or ER, are often continuous with the outer portion of the nuclear envelope. The combination of ribosomes and endoplasmic reticulum is called *rough* endoplasmic reticulum. Can you distinguish the many tiny ribosomes in Figure 5-4? Ribosomes attached to the ER synthesize proteins for **secretion**, or release, from the cell for use by other cells. Unattached ribosomes in the cytoplasm synthesize proteins that will be used within the cell.

Endoplasmic reticulum without ribosomes is called *smooth* endoplasmic reticulum. Rough and smooth ER are often continuous with each other. Proteins manufactured by the ribosomes on rough ER travel through the membrane network until they reach the smooth ER. At this point, a small portion of the smooth ER membrane forms a bubble around the protein. This bubble pinches off, forming a **vesicle**, or a membrane-bound sack. The vesicle then transports the protein to the *Golgi apparatus* for further processing. Some proteins are temporarily stored in the smooth ER and are processed or secreted later.

Golgi apparatus The Golgi apparatus [Gȯl′ jē ap ə rat′ əs] is the packaging and shipping department of the cell factory. When a vesicle carrying proteins from the ER touches the Golgi apparatus their membranes fuse. This action brings the proteins inside the

Figure 5-4   *Left:* This electron micrograph of endoplasmic reticulum shows the rough structure resulting from the presence of ribosomes (about 20 000 ×). *Right:* The three-dimensional model gives you a closer look at a typical rough ER.

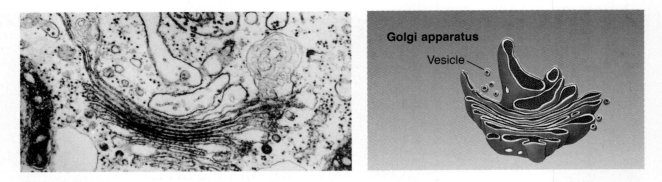

Golgi apparatus
Vesicle

Figure 5-5 *Left:* An electron micrograph shows the membranes of the Golgi apparatus. *Right:* The diagram illustrates protein-carrying vesicles as they pinch off from the Golgi apparatus.

Golgi apparatus. There, each protein molecule undergoes chemical changes, such as the addition of carbohydrates or the removal of water. As these chemical changes occur, the protein moves from one end of the Golgi apparatus to the other end. Then part of the membrane of the Golgi apparatus pinches inward and surrounds the protein. This bubble pinches off, forming a new vesicle. The vesicle carries the protein to the plasma membrane for secretion or to another organelle.

Mitochondria The mitochondria [mīt ə kon′ drē ə] are the energy suppliers of the cell. They contain enzymes that release the energy stored in food. Each mitochondrion (singular of mitochondria) is surrounded by a double membrane. The outer membrane separates the mitochondrion from the cytoplasm. The in-

DO YOU KNOW?

Historical Note: The Golgi apparatus was discovered in 1898 by the Italian microscopist, Camillo Golgi.

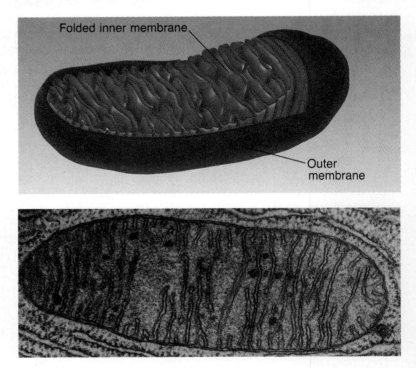

Folded inner membrane

Outer membrane

Figure 5-6 The cross sectional model of a mitochondrion (*top*) and electron micrograph (*bottom:* about 50 000×) show the double membrane and inner folding. The inner membrane would be many times longer if it were stretched out in a straight line.

ner membrane is folded into shelves that stretch across the space within the mitochondrion. The extensive folding of the inner membrane provides a larger surface area than would otherwise be possible. The folds of the membrane are covered with enzymes necessary for the complex chemical reactions that release energy.

The degree of folding of the inner membrane depends on the energy requirements of a cell. In very active cells, such as those in heart muscle or in the growing buds of plants, the inner membrane of the mitochondria is extensively folded. In less active cells, such as those that store fat, less folding occurs.

Plastids Plastids are the carbohydrate producers of the cell. They are found in plant cells and in some unicellular autotrophs. Examples of plastids include chloroplasts, chromoplasts, and leucoplasts. *Chloroplasts* [klōr′ ə plasts] contain the green pigment, chlorophyll. *Chlorophyll* [klōr′ ə fil] captures energy from sunlight for the manufacture of carbohydrates. *Chromoplasts* [krō′ mə plasts] contain the red, orange, or yellow pigments that give many flowers and fruits their distinctive color. *Leucoplasts* [lü′ kə plasts] are colorless plastids, in which starch molecules are synthesized from sugar molecules.

Vacuoles Vacuoles [vak′ yə wōlz] are the storage rooms of the cell. These organelles contain mostly water. They are most abundant in plant cells. Plant cell vacuoles may also contain food molecules, salt, or pigments.

Lysosomes Lysosomes [lī′ sə sōmz] are the recycling centers in the cell. Enzymes within the lysosomes break down large molecules from worn or damaged cell structures and make them available for reuse by the cell. The membrane surrounding the lysosome itself usually remains unaffected by the digestive enzymes it contains.

Figure 5-7 The model on the left and the electron micrograph (about 17 500×) on the right reveal the internal structure of a chloroplast. Compare this illustration to the one in Figure 5-6. Note the structural similarities between the two organelles.

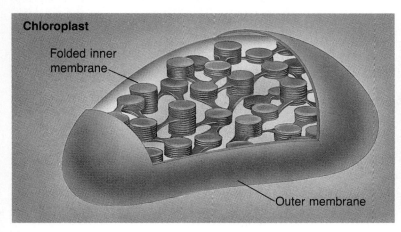

Chloroplast

Folded inner membrane

Outer membrane

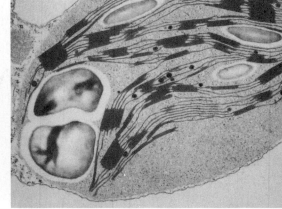

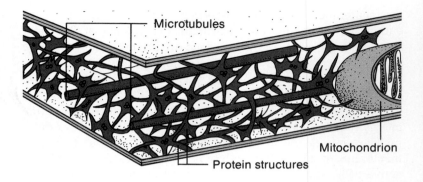

Figure 5-8 The cytoskeleton is a complex network of microtubules and protein fibers that facilitate movement and help the cell keep its shape.

Microtubules

Mitochondrion

Protein structures

A single cell can have different kinds of lysosomes. Each type contains a unique collection of enzymes. These enzymes can digest only a particular type of molecule. Lysosomes are common in animal cells, but appear less frequently in plant cells.

Cytoskeleton Until a few years ago, organelles were thought to float freely in the cytoplasm. Improved microscopic techniques, however, have revealed that the cytoplasm contains a miniature internal support system. A cell's cytoskeleton is composed of microtubules and other tiny protein structures. Together, these structural elements give the cell its shape. The cytoskeleton is like the scaffolding used to construct a building. The arrangement of microtubules within the cytoplasm can change according to the changing needs of the cell.

Microtubules also create pathways for the movement of organelles within the cell. Scientists have discovered a protein called *kinesin*, which is believed to be involved. Research suggests that the kinesin molecule attaches to the microtubule and to the organelle. The kinesin molecule moves along the microtubule, pulling the organelle with it.

Centrioles Centrioles [sen′ trē olz] occur in most animal cells and in the cells of some plants. They often lie near the nucleus. Centrioles contain microtubules, and are important in cell reproduction. You will learn more about centrioles in Chapter 8.

5-5 The Plasma Membrane

The plasma [plaz′ mə] membrane is the protective barrier that surrounds a cell. This thin membrane determines which molecules may enter or leave the cell. Because it is difficult to observe even with modern microscope techniques, the structure of the plasma membrane has been debated for many years. When examined with an electron microscope, the plasma membrane appears as a double line. According to the most widely accepted

Figure 5-9 Centrioles contain microtubules. They can be seen in this electron micrograph cross section (about 210 000 ×). These microtubules are clustered inside the centriole like wires inside a telephone cable.

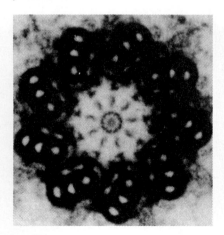

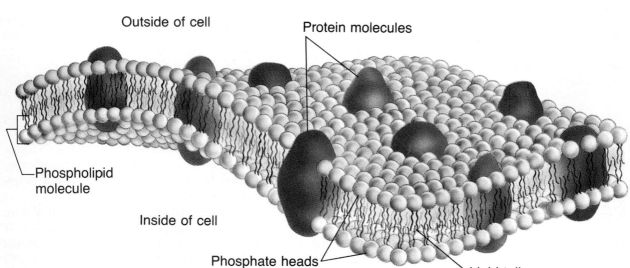

Outside of cell

Protein molecules

Phospholipid
molecule

Inside of cell

Phosphate heads

Lipid tails

Figure 5-10 Phospholipid molecules of the plasma membrane align so that the phosphate ends form the inner and outer edges of the membrane while the lipid ends are in the middle.

hypothesis, the membrane is made up primarily of a double layer of **phospholipid** [fäs fō lip′ əd] molecules and proteins. Each phospholipid is composed of a lipid and a phosphate group, as illustrated in Figure 5-10.

Notice the way the phospholipid molecules are arranged in the membrane. The lipid groups of both the inner and outer layers point toward each other. As a result, the phosphate groups of one layer point toward the inside of the cell, while the phosphates of the second layer point toward the outside of the cell.

As you learned in Chapter 4, lipids are nonpolar. The lipid ends of the phospholipids tend to "avoid" the water of the cell and of the cell's environment by pointing in toward the middle of the membrane.

Protein molecules are partially or completely embedded in the phospholipid layers. Some proteins are in contact only with the environment outside the cell. Others interact only with the cell's internal environment. Those proteins that penetrate completely through the membrane are involved in the movement of certain materials into or out of the cell.

The phospholipid molecules in the plasma membrane are not stationary. They can move sideways within the membrane. Also, certain proteins that are embedded in the membrane stay there for only a few hours. When they leave the membrane, other protein molecules take their place. Thus the components of the membrane are constantly moving, or fluid. This fluid property allows the membrane to seal itself if broken.

As you have learned, the plasma membrane is not the only membrane found in the cell. Many of the organelles described

DO YOU KNOW?

Information: The arrangement of phospholipid and protein molecules resembles the tiles in mosaic art. Because of the fluid nature of these molecules, the plasma membrane is described as a "fluid mosaic."

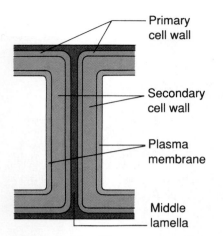

- Primary cell wall
- Secondary cell wall
- Plasma membrane
- Middle lamella

Figure 5-11   The structure of a plant cell wall

▶ Denotes a question that involves *interpreting* and *applying* concepts.

in Section 5-4 are enclosed by protein and phospholipid membranes. The plasma membrane accounts for about only one tenth of the membrane found in a cell.

5-6 The Cell Wall

The cells of plants, fungi, and some single-celled organisms are protected and supported by a cell wall. You could think of the cell walls in a multicellular plant as the plant's "skeleton." Unlike the cytoskeleton, the cell wall lies outside the plasma membrane. And unlike the plasma membrane, the cell wall does not determine what may enter or leave the cell.

The cell wall is a complex structure, illustrated in Figure 5-11. It is composed largely of the polysaccharide *cellulose*. A **primary cell wall**, laid down when the cell is formed, expands as the cell grows. In soft, flexible plants such as grasses, the cell wall does not develop further. In stiffer plants such as shrubs and trees, a **secondary cell wall** is laid down inside the primary cell wall after the cell reaches its full size. The secondary cell wall adds extra strength.

The primary cell walls of neighboring cells are not in direct contact with each other. They are separated by the **middle lamella** [lə mel′ ə], a layer composed of a jellylike polysaccharide called *pectin*.

The cell wall often remains intact after the rest of the cell has died. Most cells found in the wood of trees are no longer living. The only cell part that remains is the thickened cell walls, which continue to give the wood strength. Recall from Chapter 2 that when Robert Hooke viewed cork cells through a microscope, he saw only the outer edges of the cells. He was seeing the cell walls of the dead cork.

CHECKPOINT ◆

1. In which part of the cell is the chromatin of plant and animal cells located?
2. What kind of information is carried by the chromatin in a cell's nucleus?
3. Which organelle is the site of protein synthesis?
4. What gives plants their green color?
5. Name the two main types of molecules that make up the plasma membrane.
6. What polysaccharide composes the cell wall of plants?
▶ 7. How are lysosomes like the Golgi apparatus?
▶ 8. Why must a cell contain a full set of DNA instructions?

THE CELL AND ITS ENVIRONMENT

The concentrations of chemicals inside a cell are very different from those in the cell's surroundings. The plasma membrane separates the chemicals of the cell from those of the environment. Yet certain substances still pass through. Cells require nutrients and oxygen, which enter from the outside. This process is called **absorption**. Cells also produce waste products, such as carbon dioxide, that must be excreted. In this lesson, you will learn about the processes that govern how these substances enter and leave the cell.

5-7 Diffusion

To understand how materials move into and out of a cell, it is useful to understand the movement of molecules. As you learned in Chapter 3, molecules are not stationary. Instead, they are constantly moving about. Molecules in motion have energy of motion, known as *kinetic* energy.

As molecules move, they bump into each other. A molecule will move in a straight line until it strikes another molecule. Then, like one billiard ball hitting another, it will change its direction. The molecule will continue in the new direction until its next collision.

Collisions tend to scatter molecules apart. Molecules that are crowded together collide more often than those that are spread out. If many molecules are concentrated in a small area, their frequent collisions cause them to spread out until they are evenly distributed throughout the available space. The movement of molecules from an area of higher concentration to an area of lower concentration is called **diffusion**.

Section Objectives

F *Explain* the process of diffusion.

G *Distinguish* between permeability and selective permeability.

H *Discuss* the movement of water by osmosis.

I *Compare* the effects of osmosis on animal and plant cells.

Figure 5-12 Over time the dye molecules diffuse throughout the water.

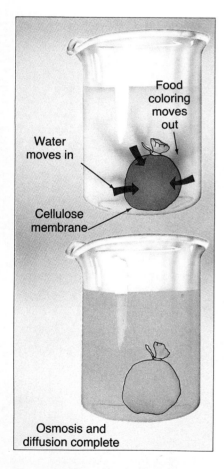

Figure 5-13 Cellulose is a permeable membrane. Food-coloring molecules and water molecules are free to move in and out of the sack.

You are probably already familiar with the effects of diffusion. If you put a spoonful of sugar in a cup of hot tea, the sugar will dissolve. At first the sugar molecules will be very concentrated at the bottom of the cup. But if you wait long enough, they will eventually diffuse throughout the entire cup of tea.

Molecules diffuse through air as well as through liquids. When you bake bread, some of the aromatic molecules bounce away from the dough. If you are sitting in the kitchen, the molecules will reach your nose rather quickly. If you are in the next room, it will take longer for the smell to reach you. Eventually, the aroma will fill the entire house.

5-8 Permeability

In addition to moving through liquids and gases, molecules can diffuse through a solid if it contains spaces large enough for molecules to pass. A material is said to be **permeable** [pər′ mē ə bəl] to certain molecules if it allows them to pass through. The plasma membrane is permeable to certain kinds of molecules.

You can demonstrate diffusion through a permeable membrane by using a sack made of cellulose. Cellulose is permeable to water and small molecules, such as the molecules of food coloring. First, fill the sack with water and blue food coloring. Then tie the open end of the sack closed and place it in a beaker of tap water. What do you predict will happen?

The molecules of blue food coloring and water can pass readily through the cellulose. The water in the beaker can also enter the sack. Because the food-coloring molecules are more concentrated inside the sack, they will tend to spread out and move out of the sack. Water molecules, which are more concentrated outside the sack, will move into the sack. Eventually the water inside and outside the sack will be uniformly pale blue.

Like the cellulose sack, the plasma membrane of a cell is permeable to most small molecules. Molecules such as water, oxygen, and carbon dioxide easily pass through the membrane. When a waste product such as carbon dioxide accumulates inside a cell, its molecules are more highly concentrated inside than outside. Therefore, carbon dioxide molecules tend to move out of the cell.

5-9 Selective Permeability and Osmosis

Sometimes a barrier allows only certain molecules to move through it. For examaple, you know that a window screen permits air to enter and leave a room, but keeps out flies. A barrier that allows only some substances to pass through it is said to be **selectively permeable**.

The plasma membrane is selectively permeable. Whether or not a molecule can pass through the plasma membrane depends on its size, charge, and solubility. Molecules that are small, nonpolar, or soluble in the phospholipid molecules of the membrane enter and leave the cell easily. There are also some large nonpolar molecules that can cross the membrane with ease.

To investigate how selective permeability affects the cell, imagine a slightly different experiment with the cellulose sack. Fill the sack with a solution of water and starch. Starch, as you learned in Chapter 4, is a large molecule. What will happen when you place this sack in a beaker of pure water? Look at Figure 5-14. Note that the starch molecules remain inside the sack. They are too big to pass through the cellulose. Since water molecules pass through, the membrane is selectively permeable.

The liquid inside the sack has a lower concentration of water than the liquid outside the sack. Water molecules will move through the sack in both directions, but more will move into the sack than out of it. This movement of water is called osmosis [äz mō′ səs]. **Osmosis** is the diffusion of water molecules through a selectively permeable membrane. In both diffusion and osmosis the molecules are moving along a gradient, or imaginary gradual slope, from higher to lower concentration. The process does not require energy from the cell because it results from the kinetic energy of the moving molecules.

As water molecules continue to enter the sack faster than they leave, pressure builds up inside the sack. The pressure caused

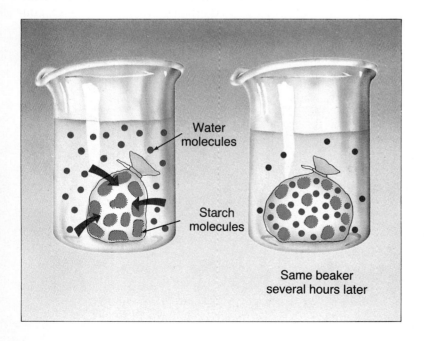

Water molecules

Starch molecules

Same beaker several hours later

Figure 5-14 Unlike water molecules, starch molecules cannot pass through the cellulose membrane. The osmotic pressure increases as water enters the sack at a faster rate than it leaves.

Cell Structure and Function **79**

CONSUMER BIOLOGY

If you like salt on your steak, add it after the meat has cooked. Salt creates a hypertonic solution on the surface of the meat. Water and other juices from the steak cells are drawn by osmosis to the surface of the steak. These liquids boil away leaving the meat dry and tasteless.

Figure 5-15 All the cellulose sacks were filled with the same proportions of starch and water. The term used to describe the solution outside each sack depends on the concentrations of dissolved substances relative to the solution inside the sack.

by osmosis is called **osmotic pressure**. The increase in osmotic pressure changes the shape of the sack in much the same way that increasing the air pressure in a bicycle tire causes the tire to change shape. As a result of osmotic pressure, the sack swells.

As the osmotic pressure increases, some of the molecules inside the sack will be pushed out. The point at which the rate of molecules leaving the sack equals the rate of molecules entering the sack is called **equilibrium**. Movement of molecules does not cease at equilibrium. But since the rate of movement in both directions is equal, there is no change in the concentration on either side of the sack.

The direction in which water molecules move during osmosis depends upon where the water molecules are more highly concentrated. The liquid surrounding the cellulose sack in Figure 5-15a is 100 percent water. The liquid in the sack is 10 percent starch and 90 percent water. When compared to the liquid inside the sack, the liquid outside the sack is said to be hypotonic. A **hypotonic solution** contains a lower concentration of dissolved substances, or solutes, than a solution to which it is being compared. As the arrows show, water molecules tend to move out of the hypotonic solution.

The sack in Figure 5-15b contains 10 percent starch and 90 percent water, but the surrounding liquid is 20 percent starch and 80 percent water. In this example, the liquid outside the sack is said to be hypertonic. A **hypertonic solution** contains a higher concentration of solutes than the solution to which it is being compared. Water molecules tend to move into a hypertonic solution.

Figure 5-15c shows a third sack containing 10 percent starch and 90 percent water. The composition of the fluid surrounding

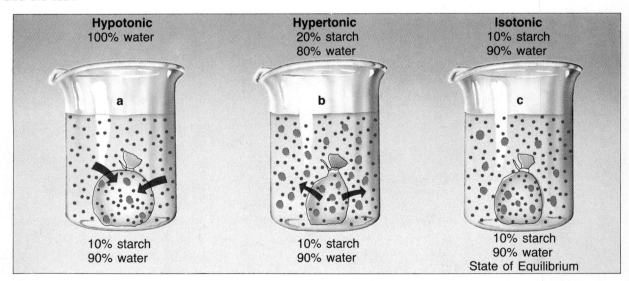

the sack is identical to the solution inside the sack. The two solutions are described as being **isotonic**. In this case, the sack and the surrounding fluid are in equilibrium. As you would expect, water molecules enter and leave the sack at the same rate.

Note that *hypertonic*, *hypotonic*, and *isotonic* are relative terms. In all three cases illustrated, the cellulose sack contains a solution that is the same concentration. The label used to describe the solution depends on the solution to which it is compared.

5-10 Animal Cells and Osmosis

Animal cells behave in much the same way as the cellulose sack. A red blood cell is about 80 percent water. If a red blood cell is placed in pure water, more water molecules will tend to enter the cell than leave it. As shown in Figure 5-17, the blood cell will swell. Eventually the increasing osmotic pressure will cause the red blood cell to burst when placed in a hypotonic solution.

If a blood cell is placed in water that is 30 percent salt and 70 percent water, more water molecules will tend to leave the cell than enter it. With fewer water molecules present, the osmotic pressure in the cell will drop. As a result of the loss of water, the blood cell will shrink when placed in a hypertonic solution.

5-11 Turgor Pressure and Plasmolysis

Unlike animal cells, the cells of plants are surrounded by a rigid cell wall. Because of this cell wall, the effect of osmotic pressure on plant cells is somewhat different from its effect on animal cells. Can you explain why this is so?

■ *BIOLOGY INSIGHT*

Adaptation and Evolution: A watery environment is essential to cells. The only organisms that are successfully adapted for living on land are those that can maintain an aqueous environment for their internal cells. Most unicellular land organisms must live in wet places, such as damp soil or decaying matter.

Figure 5-16 *Left:* Normal blood cells are disk-shaped in an isotonic solution. *Middle:* The same cells swell to the point of bursting when the surrounding solution is hypotonic. *Right:* The cells shrink when the surrounding solution is hypertonic. (all photos about 10 000 ×)

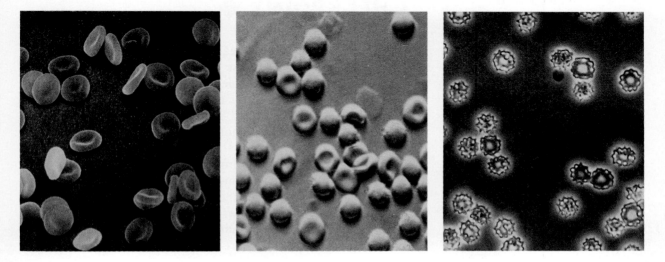

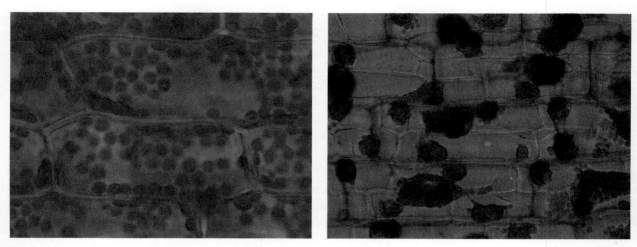

Figure 5-17 *Left: Elodea* cells are turgid in fresh water. *Right:* When these cells are placed in salt water, water leaves the cells. Do you remember the term that describes this condition?

CONSUMER BIOLOGY

If the lettuce in your refrigerator has wilted, place the lettuce in cold water. The water enters the plant cells by osmosis. Turgor pressure will build up inside the cells making the lettuce leaves crisp again.

When a plant cell is placed in a hypotonic solution, water molecules enter the cell, causing it to swell. But the cell does not burst. Instead, the cell wall resists the osmotic pressure. Osmotic pressure within a plant cell is called **turgor pressure**. Turgor pressure gives the soft tissues of plant stems and leaves their firm, rigid form. You have probably observed turgor in a crisp head of lettuce. Plant cells that are swollen with water are said to be **turgid**.

If a plant is surrounded by a hypertonic fluid, water molecules will leave the cells of the plant. As water molecules leave, the turgor pressure drops. As a result, the cytoplasm shrinks away from the cell wall. This loss of turgor pressure is called **plasmolysis** [plaz mol′ ə sis]. Plasmolysis causes plants to wilt.

CHECKPOINT ◆

9. What is diffusion?
10. What does *permeable* mean?
11. What term would you use to describe a membrane that allows only certain molecules to pass through it?
12. The point at which water molecules enter and leave a cell at the same rate is called _____ .
▶ 13. Why is turgor pressure not a characteristic of animal cells?
▶ 14. How would the rate of diffusion change if the rate of movement of molecules increases? Explain.
▶ 15. What factor determines the direction in which molecules will move during osmosis?
▶ 16. How do the effects of osmosis differ in plant and animal cells?

▶ Denotes a question that involves *interpreting* and *applying* concepts.

THE CELL'S LIVING BOUNDARY

Have you ever been sailing? It is a sport that requires great skill. A sailor must respond quickly to changes in the environment. Each time the wind changes, the sailor must adjust the position of the sail in order to remain on course.

Like a sailboat, a cell is subject to constant changes in its environment. In order to survive, a cell must adjust to each of these changes. The process of maintaining a relatively constant internal environment despite changing external conditions is called **homeostasis** [hō mē ō stā′ səs].

You have learned that particles diffuse across the plasma membrane along a concentration gradient. However, in order to maintain homeostasis, a cell sometimes must move molecules across the plasma membrane against the concentration gradient. Regulating the passage of materials is a continuous process for the plasma membrane. The cell's survival often depends on how well molecular traffic is controlled.

5-12 Passive vs. Active Transport

Permeable substances diffuse through the plasma membrane when the concentration of molecules is greater on one side of the membrane than on the other. Such action does not require the expenditure of energy by the cell. The movement of molecules without the use of cellular energy is called **passive transport**. Diffusion and osmosis are examples of passive transport.

To achieve homeostasis, however, it is often necessary for a cell to move these molecules across the plasma membrane against the direction of diffusion. This movement, which is like pushing something up a hill, requires the cell to expend energy. Movement of molecules that requires cellular energy is called **active transport**. Certain amino acids and ions, for example, are routinely moved into a cell by way of active transport.

5-13 Facilitated Diffusion

A cell is subject to constant changes in its environment. If these changes occur gradually, passive transport in the form of diffusion and osmosis is usually sufficient to meet the cell's needs. However, when changes in the environment occur rapidly, the cell must be able to respond quickly, or it will die. In some cases, the cell makes use of a special form of passive transport.

Glucose is an important source of energy for a cell. Under normal conditions, this molecule diffuses slowly across the plasma membrane. When the demand for energy inside the cell is high,

Section Objectives

J **Define** homeostasis.
K **Distinguish** between passive and active transport.
L **Explain** the process of facilitated diffusion.
M **Compare and contrast** pinocytosis and phagocytosis.

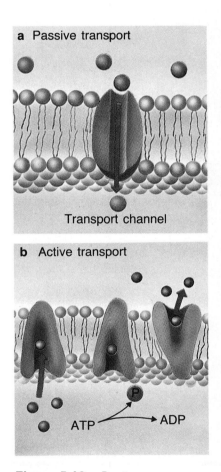

a Passive transport

Transport channel

b Active transport

ATP → P → ADP

Figure 5-18 Passive transport (a) moves molecules with the direction of diffusion. Active transport (b) uses energy to move molecules against the direction of diffusion.

Figure 5-19 The model illustrates the mechanism of facilitated diffusion. Notice how the carrier protein changes shape. This change provides an opening through which the glucose molecule enters the cell.

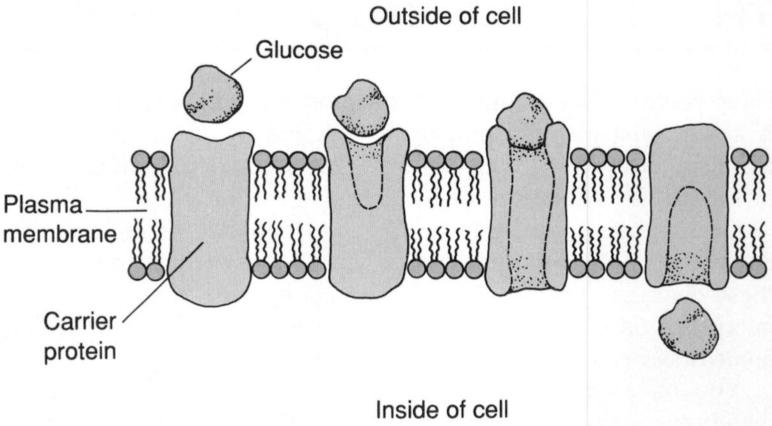

the rate of diffusion across the plasma membrane must be accelerated. This need is met by a mechanism known as facilitated diffusion. **Facilitated diffusion**, a form of passive transport, increases the rate of diffusion by the use of *carrier proteins*. Each kind of carrier protein is shaped to "recognize," or bind with, one type of molecule. When the glucose molecule binds to the surface of its carrier protein, the protein begins to change shape as illustrated in Figure 5-19. A pore starts to form at the binding site. This pore soon becomes a channel through which the glucose molecule can pass. Once the glucose molecule is inside the cell, the connection with the carrier protein is broken. The channel disappears, returning the protein to its original shape.

5-14 Active Transport

There are many instances in nature when molecules move against the direction of diffusion, that is, from an area of lesser concentration to an area of greater concentration. This situation occurs frequently at the root tips of plants. Root cells often maintain minerals in concentrations higher than those found in the environment. For this condition to occur, the cell expends energy to transport the molecule across the plasma membrane.

There are two mechanisms of active transport. The first involves carrier proteins of the sort used for facilitated diffusion. Carrier proteins, located in the plasma membrane, latch onto molecules outside the cell. As in facilitated diffusion, these molecules actually change their shape, providing the molecule with a passageway into the cell. Water-soluble molecules, such as amino acids, are taken into the cell this way. The differences between this type of active transport and facilitated diffusion are the direction of movement, which is against the diffusion gradient, and the resulting need for energy.

DO YOU KNOW?

Information: Some blood cells help prevent infection and get rid of wastes by engulfing bacteria, dead tissue, and foreign material by the process of phagocytosis.

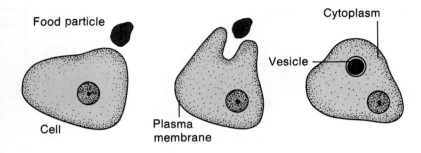

Food particle

Cytoplasm

Vesicle

Cell

Plasma
membrane

Figure 5-20 Phagocytosis occurs when the plasma membrane of a cell surrounds large particles such as food. The membrane pinches off to form a vesicle, which carries material into the cytoplasm.

The second way in which active transport may occur is by means of vesicles. **Endocytosis** [en də sī tō′ səs] is the process of transporting substances into the cell through a vesicle. Endocytosis can occur in two ways, depending on the size of what is being transported. A small particle or liquid droplet enters the cell by a process known as **pinocytosis** [pin ə sə tō′ sis]. These molecules from the environment enter indented areas of the plasma membrane. Parts of the membrane surround the molecules, forming a vesicle. When the vesicle pinches off, the remaining membrane seals itself. Once inside the cytoplasm, the vesicle releases its contents. The molecules of the membrane around the vesicle then recombine with other membranes within the cell.

When large, solid particles must be brought into the cell, another kind of endocytosis, called **phagocytosis** [fag ə sə tō′ sis] occurs. Figure 5-20 illustrates how large particles of food can be transported. A portion of the cell wraps itself around the particle. Once the food is surrounded, the plasma membrane joins together, enclosing the food particle in a vesicle. The food is then digested by special enzymes.

Pinocytosis and phagocytosis demonstrate the fluid nature of the cell membrane. When cell energy is available, the membranes of the cell can fuse or split apart, allowing the transportation of substances critical to the cell's survival.

DO YOU KNOW?

Word Root: Endocytosis is the opposite process of **exocytosis**, which is the movement of substances out of a cell. *Endo-* derives from a Greek word meaning "inside or within." *Exo-*, also from the Greek, means "outside." Other terms associated with moving materials into the cell include prefixes derived from Greek words. *Pino-* means "to drink" and *phago-* means "to eat."

CHECKPOINT ◆

17. What is the difference between active and passive transport?
18. How does facilitated diffusion benefit the cell?
19. What are the two main structures used for active transport in a cell?
20. How is pinocytosis different from phagocytosis?
21. What two mechanisms require carrier proteins?
▶ 22. How do active transport and passive transport contribute to the homeostasis of a cell?

▶ Denotes a question that involves *interpreting* and *applying* concepts.

THE RESPONSE OF PLANT CELLS TO ENVIRONMENTAL CHANGE

Objectives and Skills

☐ *Observe* the changes in a plant cell as it responds to changes in its environment.
☐ *Explain* the changes observed.

Materials

microscope slide	paper towel
coverslip	distilled water
forceps	concentrated salt water
medicine dropper	*Elodea* in aquarium
microscope	water

Procedure and Observations

1. Read all instructions for this laboratory activity before you begin work.
2. After obtaining all of your materials, prepare a wet mount slide. Using a medicine dropper, place a drop of aquarium water on your slide. Remove the tip from a leaf of *Elodea*, and use forceps to place it in the drop of water. Cover the leaf with the cover slip.
3. Observe the cells of *Elodea* under low, then high power. Draw four cells as they appear under high power. Label the cell wall, chloroplasts, cytoplasm, and any vacuoles present.
4. Place a drop or two of concentrated salt solution on one side of the coverslip. Place the edge of the paper towel on the opposite side

of the coverslip. The towel will pull liquid across the slide, and surround the *Elodea* cells in salt solution. After a few minutes, observe the cells under high power. Draw four cells. Label the parts as you did in step 3. Note any changes.
5. Using the same slide, repeat the procedure in step 4, but add distilled water instead of salt water. You may have to repeat this step several times in order to remove the salt. Again, observe under high power. Draw four cells and label the parts. Note any changes.
6. Clean up all of your materials. Before you leave the laboratory, wash your hands thoroughly with soap and water.

Analysis and Conclusions

1. What change occurred in the *Elodea* cells after you added salt water?
2. What kind of molecules left the cells? Why?
3. Could these cells live in a salt solution environment? Explain.
4. What happened when the salt water was replaced with distilled water?
5. What kind of molecules entered the cell when distilled water was added? Why?
6. Was this experiment a demonstration of active transport or passive transport? Explain.
7. Explain why using too much fertilizer can harm or kill a plant. Your explanation should include either the term *hypertonic* or *hypotonic* and the term *osmosis*.
8. Would the results of this experiment have been different if living animal cells had been used instead of plant cells? Explain.

CHAPTER REVIEW

Summary

▸ The cell is the smallest unit in which life processes can occur. A major function of a cell is to make proteins. All the parts of a cell contribute in some way to the synthesis and transport of protein molecules.

▸ In animal and plant cells, the nucleus contains the hereditary information. The nucleus also controls the activities of the cell.

▸ Between the plasma membrane and the nuclear membrane is a dense gel called cytoplasm. Within the cytoplasm are a number of organelles that have specific functions in the life of a cell.

▸ The plasma membrane is the living boundary of a cell. Because it is selectively permeable, the membrane regulates what enters and leaves the cell. The structure of the plasma membrane is a double layer of phospholipids in which proteins are embedded. All membranes within a cell are similar in structure, and can fuse with one another.

▸ The cells of plants and some other organisms are protected and supported by cell walls.

▸ Organisms exist in changing environments. However, an organism must maintain constant conditions in its internal environment in order to function properly. The cell membrane aids in homeostasis.

▸ The presence of a cell wall in plant cells and the absence of a cell wall in animal cells causes them to respond differently to changes in their environments.

▸ The direction in which a substance diffuses through a membrane depends on the relative concentrations of the substance on each side of the membrane. Hypertonic, hypotonic, and isotonic are terms that are used to describe relative concentrations of solutions.

▸ In passive transport, certain small molecules can cross the plasma membrane without the use of energy. Diffusion, osmosis, and facilitated diffusion are forms of passive transport.

▸ Active transport requires the expenditure of cellular energy. Carrier proteins and vesicles are involved in the active transport of molecules.

Vocabulary

absorption
active transport
centriole
cell wall
chlorophyll
chloroplast
chromatin
chromoplast
chromosome
cytoplasm
cytoskeleton
cytosol
deoxyribonucleic acid
  (DNA)
diffusion
endocytosis
endoplasmic reticulum
equilibrium
exocytosis
facilitated diffusion
Golgi apparatus
homeostasis
hypertonic solution
hypotonic solution
isotonic solution
leucoplast
lysosome

microtubule
middle lamella
mitochondria
nuclear envelope
nucleolus
nucleus
organelle
osmosis
osmotic pressure
passive transport
permeable
phagocytosis
phospholipid
pinocytosis
plasma membrane
plasmolysis
plastid
primary cell wall
ribosome
secondary cell wall
secretion
selectively permeable
turgid
turgor pressure
vacuole
vesicle

CHAPTER REVIEW

Concept Mapping

Using the method of concept mapping described in the front of this book, complete a concept map for membrane transport. Copy the incomplete concept map and fill in missing terms.

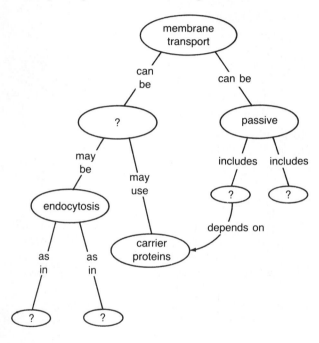

Review

1. Name three structures of the nucleus.
2. As a result of what process do molecules tend to become evenly distributed in a given space?
3. Name two types of molecules that can pass easily through the plasma membrane.
4. Why are starch molecules unable to pass through a cellulose sack?
5. When comparing two liquids, the liquid with more solute dissolved in it is (a) hypertonic, (b) hypotonic, (c) isotonic, (d) equilibrium.

6. Will a plant cell burst if placed in a hypotonic solution? Explain.
7. Name a molecule that crosses the plasma membrane with the aid of a carrier protein.
8. What is a vesicle?
9. What two types of molecular movement across membranes require vesicles?
10. What condition causes wilting?

In the following list, match the cell part to the correct description.

11. leucoplast
12. Golgi apparatus
13. plasma membrane
14. cell wall
15. ribosome
16. vacuole
17. lysosome
18. chloroplast
19. mitochondrion
20. chromatin

a. prepares chemicals for secretion
b. synthesizes proteins
c. contains hereditary information
d. stores liquids
e. releases energy from food
f. contains chlorophyll
g. contains digestive enzymes
h. supports and protects the cell parts
i. regulates which materials may enter and leave the cell
j. stores starch

Interpret and Apply

21. Name five cell parts that are bounded by membranes.
22. State two differences between the plasma membrane and the cell wall.
23. What is the difference between excretion and secretion?
24. When healthy, the human body maintains the amount of sugar in the blood at a relatively constant level. Of what principle is this an example?

25. Which of the following structures are usually found just in the cells of most plants? Which are usually found just in the cells of animals? Which are found in both?
    a. plasma membrane   f. middle lamella
    b. nucleus   g. ribosome
    c. chloroplast   h. vacuole
    d. cell wall   i. chromoplast
    e. centriole
26. What is the difference between diffusion and active transport? How are these two processes similar?
27. What principle is demonstrated when the fragrance of uncapped perfume gradually fills a room?
28. Distinguish between diffusion and osmosis.
29. Which of the following processes require the expenditure of cellular energy?
    a. osmosis   e. active transport
    b. exocytosis   f. endocytosis
    c. diffusion   g. facilitated diffusion
    d. phagocytosis
30. What would happen to a red blood cell if it were placed in a hypotonic solution?
31. What would happen if you placed a plant clipping in a solution of very salty water?
32. Why is the plasma membrane essential to the cell and its function? Why is it important for the membrane to be selectively permeable?
33. How would the response of a plant cell to a hypertonic solution differ from the response of an animal cell? Explain.
34. How might an amoeba eliminate undigestible food?

Critical Thinking

35. Most animals are heterotrophs that can move. Most plants are stationary autotrophs. Explain how the differences in the structure of plant and animal cells contribute to these characteristics.

36. Hormones are chemicals that are produced in one part of an organism, then transported to another part of the organism where they cause a response. The pancreas is an organ that secretes hormones into the bloodstream. One of these hormones is the protein insulin. What specializations would you expect to find in the cells of the pancreas?
37. Suppose that the concentration of carbon dioxide in the fluid outside a cell became higher than the concentration of carbon dioxide inside the cell. What would happen?
38. You have a sack that is not permeable to starch molecules. A sack containing 20 percent starch and 80 percent water is placed in a container of 100 percent water. (a) Is the fluid in the sack hypotonic or hypertonic compared to the surrounding solution? (b) In which direction will the water molecules tend to move?
39. During the winter, icy roads are often covered with salt. The plants that line these roads usually do not survive a hard winter. Explain why these plants do not survive.
40. If a tiny hole is made in a plasma membrane, it usually "heals" immediately, and no harm results. What property of the plasma membrane allows this?
41. The structural similarities of membranes of the ER, vesicles, Golgi apparatus, and plasma membrane allow these structures to fuse together. This in turn eases the transport of molecules from one area of the cell to another. Why is molecular transport inside the cell important?

Chapter

6

ENERGY AND THE CELL

Overview

ENERGY FROM FOOD

6-1 ATP: Energy Currency of the Cell

6-2 Fermentation

6-3 Cell Respiration: An Overview

6-4 Cell Respiration: Chemical Steps

6-5 Fermentation in Aerobic Organisms

PHOTOSYNTHESIS: CAPTURING THE SUN'S ENERGY

6-6 Light Reactions

6-7 Calvin Cycle and Its Products

6-8 Comparing Photosynthesis and Respiration

How do plants capture the sun's energy?

ENERGY FROM FOOD

The activities of all living things require energy. Swimming, flying, growing, reproducing, and even the flashing of a firefly use energy. Internal cell activities, such as active transport and making molecules, also require energy.

Energy for cells is stored in the chemical bonds of organic molecules. The lipids, proteins, and carbohydrates you studied in Chapter 4 are the fuels that power organisms. The carbohydrate glucose is a primary energy source for most cells.

Why is it important to know how cells extract energy from glucose? You will see that such knowledge can give you a basis for understanding how diet, exercise, and weight management are related to your general health. Chapter 38 deals more fully with these topics.

6-1 ATP: Energy Currency of the Cell

When glucose enters a cell it brings with it a large supply of energy stored in its chemical bonds. In order to transfer this energy from glucose to where it is required, the cell uses a carrier molecule. This energy carrier is the molecule adenosine triphosphate, or *ATP*.

To understand the function of ATP, it may help if you compare energy with money and a cell with a vending machine. Suppose you try to buy something from a vending machine, but all you have is a ten dollar bill. Most vending machines will accept only coins. You have to get change for your ten dollar bill before you can operate the machine. A similar situation exists in cells. Sugar molecules are like ten dollar bills, too large for the cell to use; while ATP is like the change you need to use the machine.

The chemical structure of ATP is shown in Figure 6-1. It is composed of a molecule of *adenine* attached to the sugar *ribose*. Attached to the ribose molecule is a chain of three *phosphate* groups.

Section Objectives

A **Diagram** the formation and **explain** the function of ATP in a cell.

B **Explain** and **locate** the fermentation process in a cell.

C **Write** the general chemical equation for respiration.

D **Describe** and **locate** the process of aerobic respiration.

E **List** the conditions under which muscles operate anaerobically.

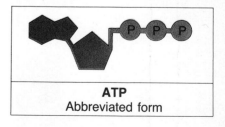

BIOLOGY INSIGHT

Unity and Diversity: ATP is one example of a molecule found universally in living things. Modified forms of this molecule are used in cells for different functions. Molecular similarity of all living things is evidence of common ancestry.

Figure 6-1 The structural formula for ATP is shown. The bond shown in red is broken when ATP forms ADP. The inset shows ATP in an abbreviated form that will be used in later diagrams.

ATP
Abbreviated form

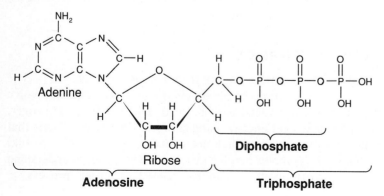

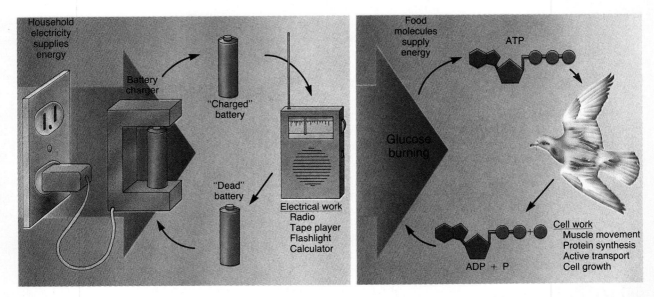

Figure 6-2 The role of ATP in a cell is to transfer energy from the breakdown of glucose to cell processes that require energy. The function of ATP can be compared to the function of a rechargeable battery.

Figure 6-3 Yeast cells shown in this scanning electron micrograph extract energy from glucose by fermentation. Note that some of the cells are reproducing by forming buds. This is one of the many energy-requiring processes carried out by these cells.

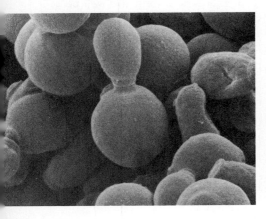

A carrier molecule like ATP must be able to absorb energy and then release it where it is needed. To release energy, a phosphate group (P) breaks off the ATP leaving adenosine *di*-phosphate (*ADP*), a molecule that has only two phosphate groups. The following equation summarizes the reaction.

$$ATP \rightleftharpoons ADP + P + Energy$$

The reverse reaction also occurs and is shown by the double arrow. ADP and P absorb energy and form ATP. By absorbing energy and then releasing it—forming ATP and then breaking it down—cells control and direct their energy usage.

ATP is an energy-carrier molecule in virtually all cells. It might help to think of ATP as a rechargeable battery as shown in Figure 6-2. The battery releases its energy to run a radio or a flashlight. Now "dead," the battery can be recharged by adding energy from household electricity. Similarly, when ATP is converted to ADP and P, energy is released to run the cell's activities. The energy needed to recharge ATP is provided from the breakdown of food molecules like glucose.

6-2 Fermentation

How does a cell extract energy from glucose to make ATP? The most common reactions to obtain energy are complex and involve oxygen. These are called **aerobic** [ə rō′ bik] reactions. However, some organisms get energy using shorter, simpler processes that do not require oxygen which are called **anaerobic** [an′ ə rō bik] reactions. The complex aerobic process will be easier to understand if you first learn about the simpler, related, anaerobic process.

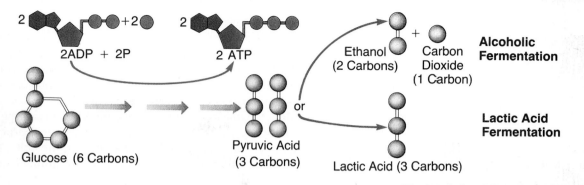

Glucose (6 Carbons)

2ADP + 2P

2 ATP

Pyruvic Acid
(3 Carbons)

or

Ethanol
(2 Carbons)

+

Carbon
Dioxide
(1 Carbon)

**Alcoholic
Fermentation**

Lactic Acid (3 Carbons)

**Lactic Acid
Fermentation**

Figure 6-4 All types of fermentation produce two molecules of ATP and pyruvic acid. Various types of fermentation convert the pyruvic acid to other waste products.

One microorganism that uses anaerobic reactions is yeast. Yeast cells obtain energy from glucose by a specific anaerobic process called **fermentation**. Fermentation begins after glucose diffuses into the yeast cell. The glucose is broken down after several chemical reactions into two, three-carbon molecules called *pyruvic acid*. The pyruvic acid is then converted to carbon dioxide and ethanol (ethyl alcohol). The energy released makes two molecules of ATP. Fermentation is summarized as:

$$\underset{\text{(glucose)}}{C_6H_{12}O_6} \longrightarrow \underset{\text{(ethanol)}}{2CH_3CH_2OH} + \underset{\text{(carbon dioxide)}}{2CO_2} + \underset{\text{(2ATP)}}{Energy}$$

Ethanol and carbon dioxide are waste products of fermentation, so they diffuse out of the cell. However, a waste product for one organism may be useful for another. People have used yeast for thousands of years. Wine, for example, is made when yeast ferments the sugar in grape juice to produce ethanol. Yeast also is used to make bread. The carbon dioxide waste forms tiny bubbles in the dough, causing the bread to rise.

Many bacteria also carry out fermentation. Instead of converting pyruvic acid to ethanol and carbon dioxide, one group of bacteria converts it to lactic acid. These are the bacteria that spoil milk. Different kinds of fermentation are identified by their waste products. **Alcoholic fermentation** and **lactic acid fermentation** are two examples. Other kinds of fermenting bacteria help to make such products as butter, yogurt, and cheese.

6-3 Cell Respiration: An Overview

Oxygen is essential to human life. You know what would happen to any person deprived of oxygen for even a short time. You may also have been surprised to learn that anaerobic organisms can live without it. But fermentation is limited to microscopic, unicellular organisms because it is inefficient. By excreting ethanol, for example, yeast cells waste energy. You may be aware that many racing cars often burn fuels with a high ethanol content. Ethanol still contains much of the energy of the original glucose molecule.

DO YOU KNOW?

Information: The bacteria that cause tetanus and gangrene in humans are anaerobic. They grow in deep wounds where there is little oxygen available.

BIOLOGY INSIGHT

Continuity of Life: Certain kinds of bacteria present today are thought to be similar to the first living cells over three billion years ago. These bacteria are all anaerobes. This finding is consistent with the theory that there was no molecular oxygen present when Earth first formed.

Figure 6-5 Cell respiration produces more energy for the cell than simple fermentation.

Aerobic organisms, on the other hand, break glucose down further into carbon dioxide and water. Pathways that use oxygen utilize more of the energy contained in the glucose molecule. The waste products have no useful energy. This total aerobic breakdown of glucose is called **cellular respiration**.

In everyday language, people often speak of breathing as respiration. However, breathing is simply a mechanical process that provides oxygen to an animal's cells. Once in the cells, this oxygen is used in cellular respiration. Although breathing is necessary for respiration, the two processes are quite different.

The chemical equation for cellular respiration is shown below.

$$C_6H_{12}O_6 + 6O_2 \longrightarrow 6CO_2 + 6H_2O + Energy$$

(1 molecule of glucose) (6 molecules of oxygen) (6 molecules of carbon dioxide) (6 molecules of water) (38 ATP)

Recall from Chapter 5 that the major site of energy generation for cells is the mitochondrion. Cell respiration produces most of the cell's ATP and these reactions occur in mitochondria. Recall that mitochondria have an inner and an outer membrane (Figure 5-6). Many enzymes controlling cell respiration are part of the folded inner membrane.

To understand the process of cellular respiration, you may want to think of the mitochondria as miniature fireplaces and the molecules of glucose as logs. When logs burn in a fireplace, they release energy as heat and light. The fire uses oxygen and gives off carbon dioxide and water as waste products. Similarly, in respiration glucose combines with oxygen to release energy and give off carbon dioxide and water.

The heat energy produced by a fire is intense. If such heat were produced in a cell, the cell would die. Cells release energy more slowly and much of the energy from glucose is shifted to the bonds of ATP using the ATP-ADP cycle.

Respiration yields far more energy than fermentation. Burning one glucose molecule with oxygen yields a maximum of 38 ATP molecules. This is 19 times the amount of ATP made by fermentation. Even at this rate, aerobic cells recover only about 40 percent of the energy in the glucose molecule. The other 60 percent is lost as heat.

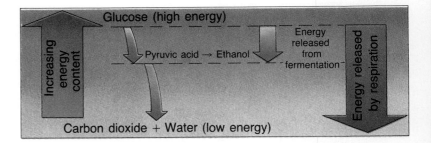

6-4 Cell Respiration: Chemical Steps

Cellular respiration occurs in two phases. The first, or anaerobic phase, occurs in the cell cytoplasm. Products of this phase enter into the second phase reactions that require oxygen. The aerobic second phase occurs within mitochondria and produces over 90 percent of the ATP made by respiration.

The anaerobic phase of cellular respiration is identical to the first steps of fermentation. Glucose is converted anaerobically into pyruvic acid producing two ATP molecules, exactly as in fermentation. In aerobic cells, however, these reactions are called **glycolysis**.

Pyruvic acid produced by glycolysis enters the mitochondrion. As you read about the steps of aerobic respiration, refer to Figure 6-7. In the mitochondrion, pyruvic acid breaks down into carbon dioxide and a two-carbon molecule called acetic acid. The carbon dioxide leaves the cell as waste, but the acetic acid attaches to a carrier molecule and goes through a series of reactions called the citric acid cycle.

Citric Acid Cycle As the word *cycle* suggests, the **citric acid cycle** is a series of reactions that begins and ends with the same compound. Citric acid is the first compound formed in this series.

Figure 6-6 Burning wood is a process similar to cell respiration. The wood is made of complex, energy-storing molecules that release energy in the form of heat and light when burned.

BIOLOGY INSIGHT

Adaptation and Evolution: The fact that all modern aerobic organisms use glycolysis as the initial phase of respiration indicates that aerobes evolved from anaerobes and utilized the chemical steps already present in fermenting anaerobes.

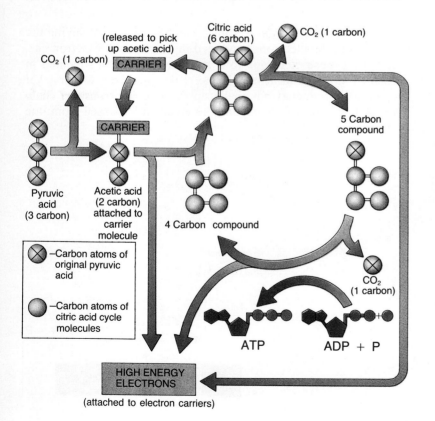

Figure 6-7 The citric acid cycle. This diagram shows what happens to the carbon atoms of a single pyruvic acid molecule. (How many pyruvic acid molecules are produced from a single glucose molecule?)

Energy and the Cell   **95**

In the beginning of the citric acid cycle, the two-carbon acetic acid attaches to a four-carbon molecule. The resulting six-carbon compound is citric acid. Citric acid is then broken down in a series of reactions. Each reaction is controlled by a separate enzyme. During these reactions, two molecules of carbon dioxide are removed, leaving the four-carbon compound at the end of each cycle. The four-carbon compound then may combine with another two-carbon acetic acid, beginning another turn of the cycle.

The overall effect of the citric acid cycle is to break a three-carbon pyruvic acid molecule into three molecules of carbon dioxide (each with one carbon). How many carbon dioxide molecules are produced from the breakdown of a single glucose molecule? (Look back at the equation on page 94.) Notice in Figure 6-7 that at one point in the cycle a molecule of ATP is produced.

More importantly, notice that during glycolysis and the citric acid cycle, many hydrogen atoms are removed. Recall that a hydrogen atom consists of a single proton and a single electron. Hydrogen atoms bring with them high energy electrons from the chemical bonds of molecules in the citric acid cycle. These high energy electrons are added to molecules in the cell called *electron carriers*.

Electron Transport Chain Aerobic cells have a way of saving the energy from the electrons produced in respiration. Electron carriers bring these electrons to a group of coenzymes located in the inner mitochondral membrane. Like members of a bucket brigade, these coenzymes make up the **electron transport chain** shown in Figure 6-8. Each time an electron is passed from one

Figure 6-8 The function of the electron transport chain is to extract useful energy from the electrons that are passed along the chain. Electrons are passed along the chain much as water is passed from one person to another in a bucket brigade. Just as water spills out of the bucket along the way, electrons in the transport chain lose some of their energy.

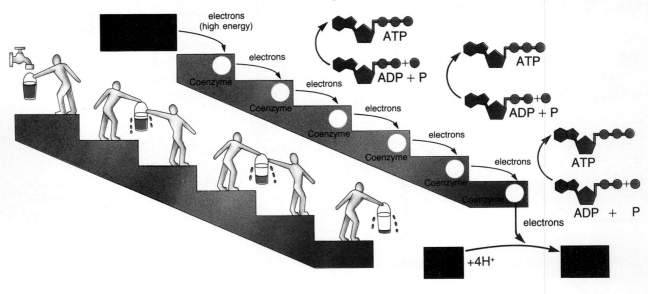

coenzyme to another, like the bucket of water, energy is released. This energy is used to form a large number of ATP molecules from ADP and P. By the time the electron reaches the end of the chain, it has lost most of its energy.

Since oxygen has not yet entered into any of the reactions, why is oxygen so essential to this process? Electrons brought in by electron carriers at the beginning of the transport chain must be removed at the end of the chain. The final acceptor of the electrons is oxygen. The hydrogen and electrons removed during the respiration reactions combine with oxygen to form water. Oxygen, then, acts like the person at the end of an automobile assembly line who drives each finished car out of the factory. If that person decides to walk off the job, the entire assembly line must shut down. Without oxygen to carry off low energy electrons, all respiration reactions come to a halt. The cell stops making ATP, and quickly dies because it no longer has an energy source.

At the completion of glycolysis and the citric acid cycle, glucose has been broken down into carbon dioxide which is released from the mitochondrion. Oxygen and hydrogen have been converted to water, and a maximum of 38 ATP's have been produced for the cell. In fact, many cells produce fewer than the maximum number of ATP molecules. The chemical reaction shown in Section 6-3 summarizes the process. Figure 6-9 shows the reactants, products, and processes in a mitochondrion. Notice that the citric acid cycle and electron transport occur at different places in the mitochondrion.

BIOLOGY INSIGHT

Structure Is Related to Function: The similarity of the internal structure of mitochondria and chloroplasts reflects their similarity of function. The electron transport chains in both respiration and photosynthesis depend upon the arrangement of the inner membranes of these organelles.

DO YOU KNOW?

Information: Cyanide is a powerful poison because it blocks the last carrier molecule in the electron transport chain. ATP production stops completely and the cell dies rapidly.

Figure 6-9 The location of respiration reactions in the mitochondria. The enzymes of the electron transport chain are attached to the folded inner membrane.

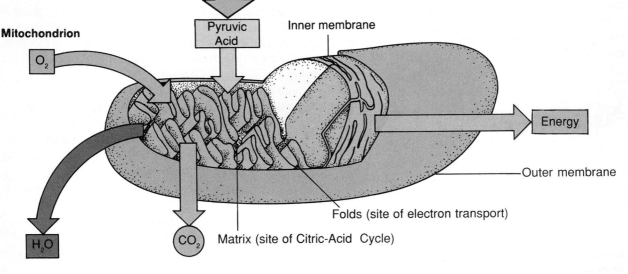

Figure 6-10 During the initial stages of a race, your muscles get energy from lactic acid fermentation.

6-5 Fermentation in Aerobic Organisms

Many kinds of cells can shift from aerobic to anaerobic processes depending on the availability of oxygen. Even in your own body, lactic acid fermentation occurs in muscle cells when there is not enough oxygen available for aerobic respiration.

When you exercise strenuously, glycolysis occurs at a high rate to supply ATP for muscle contraction. Active muscles produce a great deal of pyruvic acid. Under these conditions muscle cells may not receive enough oxygen to process all the pyruvic acid through the citric acid cycle. To continue supplying ATP for muscle contraction, your muscle cells carry out lactic acid fermentation.

When you stop strenuous exercise, you breathe deeply for a short time. The oxygen you take in as you "catch your breath" allows your cells to convert the accumulated lactic acid back to pyruvic acid. Cells vary in their ability to operate anaerobically. Nerve cells in your brain, for example, will die within minutes without oxygen. Yeast cells have mitochondria and switch to aerobic respiration when oxygen is available; otherwise they carry out alcoholic fermentation. Some kinds of bacteria are strictly anaerobic and will die in the presence of oxygen.

Anaerobic organisms are usually small and unicellular. Highly active multicellular organisms could not have evolved without the large amount of energy provided by aerobic respiration.

CHECKPOINT ◆

1. How many phosphate groups does a molecule of ATP contain?
2. What two molecules are formed when the last phosphate bond of ATP is broken?
3. What kind of fermentation do yeasts perform?
4. What are the two principal waste products of aerobic respiration?
5. Where in cells does glycolysis occur?
6. Where in cells are the enzymes of the citric acid cycle located?
7. What is the function of the electron transport chain?
8. What conditions must exist for lactic acid to form in muscles?
▶ 9. Why do almost all anaerobic organisms consist of single cells?
▶ 10. Compare the ATP production of aerobic respiration and of fermentation.
▶ 11. Why do aerobic cells die when they are cut off from oxygen?

▶ Denotes a question that involves *interpreting* and *applying* concepts.

PHOTOSYNTHESIS: CAPTURING THE SUN'S ENERGY

In the first part of this chapter you learned how organisms extract energy from the chemical bonds of glucose. However, you may wonder where glucose got its energy. With energy, after all, "there is no such thing as a free lunch."

Animals must obtain food molecules from other living things. But plants and many unicellular organisms can make their own food molecules by using the energy of sunlight. The raw materials of photosynthesis are carbon dioxide and water. The general equation for photosynthesis is shown below.

$$\underset{\text{(Light)}}{Energy} + 3CO_2 + 3H_2O \longrightarrow C_3H_6O_3 + 3O_2$$

Carbon dioxide and water combine in the presence of light to form a carbohydrate (usually sucrose and starch) and oxygen. Oxygen is a product of photosynthesis, and plants release it into the atmosphere.

You may notice some similarity between photosynthesis and cellular respiration. While they share important similarities, they are quite different in detail. In photosynthesis, two major sets of chemical reactions occur: light reactions and carbon-fixation reactions. During the **light reactions**, energy from the sun or other light source is trapped and channeled into forming ATP and high energy electrons. During the **Calvin cycle** which is a part of the carbon fixation reactions, carbon dioxide is assembled into carbohydrate molecules. ATP and electrons from the light reactions supply the energy to drive the Calvin cycle.

6-6 Light Reactions

The first phase of photosynthesis involves trapping light energy. Light travels from its source as waves of energy. As shown in Figure 6-12 on the next page, different wavelengths carry different amounts of energy. Short wavelengths carry more energy than long wavelengths.

Sunlight is a mixture of many colors, and color is determined by wavelength. If sunlight passes through a glass prism, the light is separated into the visible spectrum of colors. The colors of the visible spectrum from longest to shortest wavelength are red, orange, yellow, green, blue, and violet. Which colors carry the most energy?

When sunlight strikes a plant leaf, the energy of certain wavelengths is absorbed by special photosynthetic pigments. A **pigment** is a substance that absorbs light. Different pigments absorb different wavelengths. Wavelengths that are not absorbed are

Section Objectives

F *Write* the chemical equation for photosynthesis.

G *Describe* the process of photosynthesis.

H *Identify* the products of the light reactions and of carbon fixation.

I *Locate* on a diagram where the reactions of photosynthesis occur.

J *Compare* and *contrast* the processes of respiration and photosynthesis.

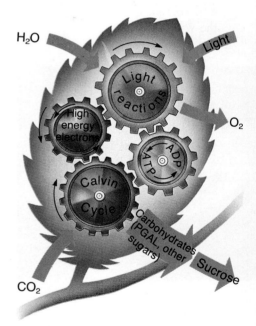

Figure 6-11 The relationship between the light reactions and the Calvin cycle. The entire photosynthetic process can be visualized as a series of interlocking gears. Energy from light drives the entire mechanism.

Energy and the Cell **99**

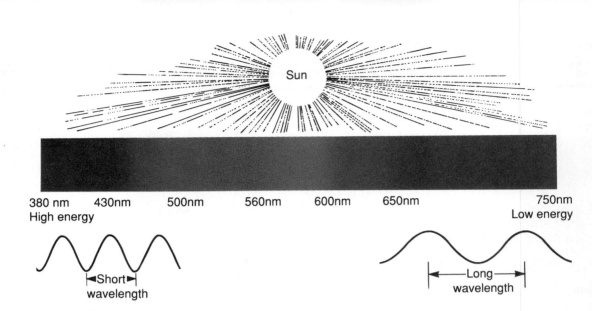

380 nm   430nm   500nm   560nm   600nm   650nm   750nm
High energy   Low energy

|◀Short▶|
wavelength

|◀——Long——▶|
wavelength

Figure 6-12 Light can be thought of as energy that travels in the form of waves. Color and energy content can be determined by the wavelength.

Figure 6-13 Chlorophyll is not the only pigment in leaves. All leaves contain other pigments which help to trap wavelengths of light missed by chlorophyll. In this leaf, some of the other pigments show up. In most leaves the other pigments are masked by the large amount of chlorophyll.

reflected. Each pigment has a characteristic color determined by the light it reflects.

Chlorophyll [klor′ ə fil] is the major photosynthetic pigment. Chlorophyll absorbs large amounts of red, orange, blue, and violet light, but very little yellow and green light. Because it reflects green and yellow light, chlorophyll appears green. In addition to chlorophyll, autotrophs contain other pigments which absorb some of the other wavelengths of light. These pigments are responsible for the yellow, red, and orange colors of some tree leaves in autumn. If pigments are essential for photosynthesis, where in the plant does photosynthesis occur? What about parts of the plant that are underground?

Photosynthetic pigments are located in chloroplasts. Like mitochondria, chloroplasts have an inner and an outer membrane. The inner chloroplast membrane folds to form stacks of disklike structures called **thylakoids** [thi′ lə koidz]. Each thylakoid contains from 200 to 400 molecules of chlorophyll. Surrounding the thylakoids is a fluid called the **stroma** [stro′ mə].

Pigments and enzymes necessary for the light reactions are embedded in the thylakoid membranes. Follow Figure 6-14 as you read. When light strikes a chlorophyll molecule, electrons absorb the energy. This energy excites the electrons and they leave the chlorophyll.

Several things can happen to these high energy electrons. In one pathway, they are passed along a series of coenzymes very similar to the electron transport chain of respiration. As in respiration, electrons lose energy from one coenzyme to another. This energy is used to make molecules of ATP from ADP and P. At the end of the chain, low energy electrons return to the original chlorophyll molecule where they can be boosted again with the absorption of light.

In a second pathway, high energy electrons are taken up by an electron carrier. These electron carriers leave the thylakoid and will be used to make carbohydrate. In this pathway, electrons cannot return to the chlorophyll and must be replaced from another source. Water molecules provide the necessary electrons. By splitting water inside the thylakoid, electrons and hydrogen ions are produced. These electrons have little energy. They enter a chlorophyll molecule and are boosted in energy, travel down the electron transport chain, and eventually replace those lost by the original chlorophyll. When water molecules are split to produce electrons, oxygen gas is produced. This oxygen is a waste product and it diffuses out of the chloroplast.

In photosynthesis, then, water is the electron *donor* and *oxygen* is created. The useful products of the light reactions are ATP and high energy electrons attached to their carrier molecules. Remember that in respiration, oxygen is the final electron *acceptor* in the electron transport chain, and *water* is formed.

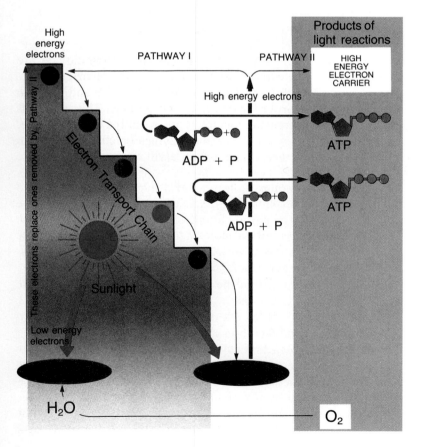

Figure 6-14 The events of the light reactions of photosynthesis. Electrons from chlorophyll either pass through the electron transport chain or are removed by electron carriers. ATP, oxygen, and high energy electrons are the products of the light reactions.

Figure 6-15 Calvin cycle—the conversion of carbon dioxide to carbohydrate molecules. Light is not necessary for the reactions to occur. The energy of ATP and high energy electrons produced by the light reactions is used to run the Calvin cycle.

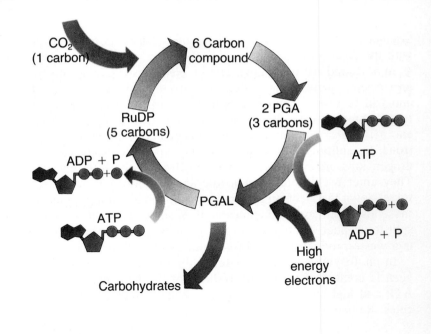

6-7 Calvin Cycle and Its Products

In the Calvin cycle, the carbon atoms in carbon dioxide are combined to form carbohydrate molecules. These reactions require energy and this energy comes from the ATP and the high energy electron carriers from the light reactions. This cycle differs from the light reactions in that light is not the energy source. The Calvin cycle is controlled by enzymes (such as rubisco) in the stroma. As you read about the Calvin cycle, refer to Figure 6-15.

The stroma contains molecules of a five-carbon sugar called *RuBP* (Ribulose bisphosphate). When carbon dioxide enters the chloroplast, its single carbon atom combines with the five-carbon RuBP to make a 6-carbon molecule. This molecule is unstable and immediately splits into two molecules of *PGA* (phosphoglyceric acid). Each PGA molecule has three carbons.

With energy input from the electron carriers and ATP of the light reactions, PGA forms a three-carbon sugar called *PGAL* (phosphoglyceraldehyde). As the cycle continues, PGAL is converted to 4-, 5-, and 6-carbon sugar phosphates. With the further input of ATP, a 5-carbon sugar phosphate is converted back to RuBP to complete the cycle. Three turns of the cycle results in the formation of six molecules of PGAL. Only one PGAL molecule can be used by the plant to form carbohydrate.

PGAL formed during the Calvin cycle diffuses out of the chloroplast. What then happens to PGAL and the other sugar phosphates formed in the plant cell? Plants use PGAL and other sugar phosphates to produce substances like sucrose and starch. Remember that plant cells have mitochondria as well as chloroplasts. But plants do not get their energy from an outside source as animals do. Some of the starch made in the chloroplasts is burned in the mitochondria of the same cell to provide ATP for the life activities of the plant cell. Sucrose is made in the cytosol and can be transported from the leaf to other parts of the plant as an energy source.

Plants do not immediately burn all the sucrose and starch that they make. Some is stored for use at night when photosynthesis is not possible. Plants that lose their leaves in winter must store starch to stay alive until the next spring.

6-8 Comparing Photosynthesis and Respiration

Although photosynthesis and respiration include many complex steps, they may seem clearer if you compare the reactions for the two processes.

Photosynthesis:

$$3CO_2 + 3H_2O \longrightarrow \underset{\text{Carbohydrate}}{C_3H_6O_3} + 3O_2$$

Respiration:

$$\underset{\text{Carbohydrate}}{C_6H_{12}O_6} + 6O_2 \longrightarrow 6CO_2 + 6H_2O$$

As you can see, the reactions are almost the reverse of each other. Photosynthesis produces a carbohydrate, while respiration involves the breakdown of a carbohydrate. One way to think of respiration is that it is an energy use process, while photosynthesis is an energy storage process.

The processes are similar in several other ways. First, both involve the conversion of energy from one form to another. In photosynthesis, light energy is changed into chemical energy. In respiration, chemical energy is changed into cellular and heat energy. Second, in both photosynthesis and respiration, an electron transport chain uses energy from electrons to form ATP.

All organisms break down food molecules to fuel life activities. Both plant and animal cells carry out respiration twenty-four hours a day. During daylight, plant cells produce enough carbohydrate to burn during the day and through the night. Organisms have the ability to store energy in biomolecules that can be broken down when energy is needed. Fat is one kind of biomolecule your body uses to store energy.

Figure 6-16 The oxygen—carbon dioxide cycle shows the relationship between autotrophs and heterotrophs. Autotrophs provide oxygen. Heterotrophs provide waste products needed for photosynthesis.

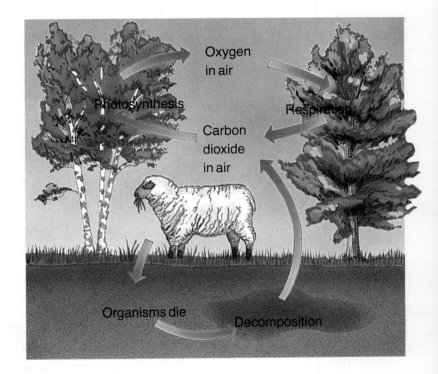

Oxygen
in air

Photosynthesis

Respiration

Carbon
dioxide
in air

Organisms die

Decomposition

Heterotrophs rely on other organisms for food; they also depend upon the oxygen produced by autotrophs. These considerations give meaning to the question, "Have you thanked a green plant today?"

Conversely, autotrophs use the waste products of heterotrophs for raw materials in photosynthesis. The interdependence of autotrophs and heterotrophs is an important relationship in biology and is shown in Figure 6-16.

CHECKPOINT ◆

12. Write the general equation for photosynthesis.
13. What is the function of chlorophyll in photosynthesis?
14. What is the final product of the Calvin cycle?
15. Where in the chloroplasts do the light reactions occur?
16. Where in the chloroplasts does the Calvin cycle occur?
17. Name one common feature of photosynthesis and respiration.
▶ 18. What is the function of the electron transport chain in photosynthesis?
▶ 19. Explain why plants would grow poorly if exposed only to green light.

▶ Denotes a question that involves *interpreting* and *applying* concepts.

ROLE OF LIGHT IN PHOTOSYNTHESIS

In this activity, you will investigate the importance of sunlight in the production of carbohydrates by plants.

Objectives and Skills

□ *Control variables* in an experiment to determine the importance of light in photosynthesis.
□ *Perform an experiment* to test for the presence of starch in the leaf of a geranium plant.
□ *Make predictions* based on experimental data.

Materials

safety goggles
lab apron
aluminum foil
paper clip
400-mL beaker
petri dish

scissors
hot plate
denatured ethanol (95%)
iodine solution
geranium plant

Procedure and Observations

1. Read all instructions for this laboratory activity before you begin your work.
2. Do this step several days before proceeding with the rest of the activity. Cut a rectangle of aluminum foil about 2 cm by 4 cm. Fold the foil in half around part of a geranium leaf and hold it in place with a paper clip. Leave the plant in a sunny window with the foil in place for about three days.
3. Wear goggles at all times during this activity.
   CAUTION: You will be using flammable organic chemicals in this exercise. Be sure there are no flames anywhere in the room.
4. Cut the foil-covered leaf off the geranium plant. Draw an outline picture of the leaf showing the position of the foil patch. Remove the aluminum foil.

5. Pour about 1 mL of alcohol into a beaker and place the beaker on a hot plate. Turn the hot plate to low heat.
   CAUTION: Do not let the alcohol boil vigorously and spatter. Adjust the heat so it boils slowly.
6. Put the leaf upside-down in the alcohol. Keep it there for a few minutes until the leaf is white in color.
7. Put about 10 drops of iodine solution into a petri dish. Remove the leaf from the alcohol and place it in the iodine solution. (Iodine is a test for starch. In the presence of iodine, starch turns blue or black.)
8. Add 20 mL of water to the alcohol in the beaker. Pour this mixture down the drain in the sink.
9. Compare the appearance of the leaf with the drawing you did in step 4. Do another drawing illustrating the results.
10. Before leaving the laboratory, clean up all materials and wash hands thoroughly.

Analysis and Conclusions

1. What is the variable and what is the control in this experiment?
2. Where is starch located in the leaf according to the iodine test?
3. What does the absence of starch in the leaf indicate?
4. What do the results of this experiment show about the importance of light in the process of photosynthesis?
5. Predict the results of a similar experiment using transparent green cellophane instead of aluminum foil. Explain your prediction.

CHAPTER REVIEW

Summary

‣ Most cellular activities require energy stored as ATP. ATP is made from ADP and P using energy from the breakdown of food molecules.

‣ Fermentation is an anaerobic, energy-producing process that leaves either carbon dioxide and alcohol or lactic acid as waste products.

‣ Cellular respiration breaks down sugar molecules in the presence of oxygen to produce carbon dioxide and water.

‣ The first stage of respiration, called glycolysis, occurs in the cytoplasm and does not require oxygen. In this stage, glucose molecules are broken down into molecules of pyruvic acid.

‣ Aerobic respiration and glycolysis occurs in the mitochondria.

‣ The citric acid cycle takes in pyruvic acid and converts it to carbon dioxide and water. Energy is extracted from glucose in the form of high energy electrons. The electron transport chain uses the energy of these electrons to make ATP.

‣ Muscle cells switch to lactic acid fermentation when there is not enough oxygen available for aerobic respiration.

‣ Photosynthesis uses light energy from the sun to make chemical energy, or food.

‣ The light reactions occur in the thylakoids of the chloroplasts. Light energy excites the electrons of chlorophyll. Excited electrons are passed along an electron transport chain, where some of the energy is used to make ATP. Other excited electrons are taken up by electron carrier molecules.

‣ The Calvin cycle occurs in the stroma of the chloroplast. During the Calvin cycle, high-energy electrons and ATP formed in the light reactions are used to power a complex cycle of reactions that produces carbohydrates from carbon dioxide.

Vocabulary

aerobic
alcoholic fermentation
anaerobic
Calvin cycle
cellular respiration
chlorophyll
citric acid cycle
electron transport chain

fermentation
glycolysis
lactic acid
  fermentation
light reactions
pigment
stroma
thylakoid

Concept Mapping

Construct a concept map for energy. Include the following terms: light energy, chemical energy, ATP, electron carrier molecules, light reactions, photosynthesis, cellular respiration, sugar, anaerobic, aerobic, glycolysis, citric acid cycle, and carbon dioxide. Use additional terms as you need them.

Review

1. Is energy taken in or released by the reaction that converts ADP + P to ATP?
2. What waste products are produced when yeast cells ferment?
3. What type of fermentation can occur in muscle cells?
4. Where in cells is the electron transport chain located?
5. What is the overall equation for respiration?
6. What are the two products of photosynthesis?
7. What is another name for the anaerobic stage of respiration?
8. What is the five-carbon compound that combines with carbon dioxide at the beginning of the Calvin cycle?
9. Chlorophyll molecules are located in structures called _____ within the chloroplast.
10. The Calvin cycle occurs in a part of the chloroplast called the _____.

11. Which of the following events takes place during the Calvin cycle of photosynthesis?
    a. Water is split.
    b. ATP is formed.
    c. Chlorophyll becomes excited.
    d. PGAL is formed.
12. Of the following events in respiration, which occurs in the cytoplasm?
    a. glycolysis
    b. electron transport chain
    c. citric acid cycle
    d. most ATP production

Interpret and Apply

13. Why must glycolysis occur before the steps of aerobic respiration can begin?
14. If yeast cells were large organisms, they could not live anaerobically. Explain.
15. Describe the role of ATP in the cell.
16. Compare alcoholic fermentation, lactic acid fermentation, and glycolysis.
17. If plant cells can make their own food, why do they have mitochondria?
18. Name two ways in which photosynthesis and respiration are alike and different.
19. Describe the role of high energy electron carriers in aerobic cells.
20. What happens to the ATP produced in mitochondria? What happens to the ATP produced in chloroplasts?
21. How close do the electron acceptor molecules have to be to the chlorophyll molecules in the light reactions? Why?
22. Which of those colors absorbed by chlorophyll contain the most energy?
23. Where do the electrons in the process of photosynthesis come from?
24. How do trees that lose their leaves for many months during the winter stay alive?
25. Why do muscle cells sometimes operate anaerobically?

Critical Thinking

26. Ethanol in sufficient quantities is a toxic substance to all organisms. Suggest a hypothesis explaining why the maximum concentration of wine is 12 percent ethanol.
27. Human heart muscle has many more mitochondria than the muscle which moves your body parts. Suggest a reason for this observation.
28. All the thylakoids in a stack are parallel to each other. The chloroplast is oriented toward the direction of light with all its thylakoids in the same direction. What function does this serve the plant?
29. When plants photosynthesize, they always make more starch than they can use for food. Why?
30. In a test tube, chloroplasts will carry out the Calvin cycle in total darkness as long as the experimenter adds several key ingredients. What would these materials be?

Chapter

7

CELL REGULATION

Overview

NATURE OF DNA

7-1 Nucleic Acids
7-2 Function of DNA
7-3 Structure of DNA
7-4 DNA Code
7-5 Replication of DNA

PROTEIN SYNTHESIS

7-6 Structure and Function of RNA
7-7 Transcription: DNA to RNA
7-8 How the Code Works
7-9 Translation: RNA to Protein

Why is DNA described as the molecular basis of life?

NATURE OF DNA

The study of biology is like putting together a puzzle. Many of the pieces—cell division, the structure of proteins, the inheritance of traits, and evolution—were found decades ago. But these areas remained isolated from each other because an important piece in the puzzle was missing. The missing piece was the structure of DNA.

Why is it so important to understand the structure of DNA? What is the role of this molecule in living cells? The answers to these and other questions are important in understanding how cells carry out life functions.

7-1 Nucleic Acids

DNA was first isolated by the Swiss biochemist Johann Friedrich Miescher in 1869. Because DNA molecules are acidic and are found in the nucleus, Miescher called them **nucleic acids**. Over 80 years passed, however, before scientists understood that DNA contains the information for carrying out the activities of the cell. For a while heredity was thought to be determined by proteins, simply because we knew much more about them than we did about DNA. How this information is coded or passed from cell to cell was unknown. To break the code, scientists had to determine the structure of DNA.

Chemical analysis had shown that DNA is made up of repeating units called **nucleotides**. A DNA nucleotide consists of a five-carbon sugar called deoxyribose, a phosphate group, and a nitrogen base. The structure of a nucleotide is shown in Figure 7-1. Each nucleotide contains one of four different nitrogen bases: **adenine** [ad' ən ēn], **thymine** [thi' mēn], **guanine** [gwan' ēn], and **cytosine** [sīt' ə sēn].

Nucleotides in DNA are joined together in a long chain, as shown in Figure 7-2. Notice that the sugar of one nucleotide is

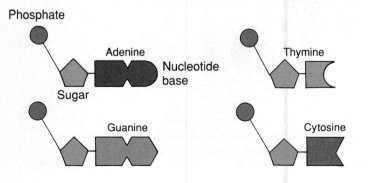

Phosphate

Adenine

Nucleotide base

Sugar

Thymine

Guanine

Cytosine

Figure 7-1 Every nucleotide in DNA has the same basic structure.

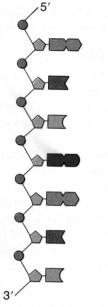

5′

3′

Figure 7-2 Nucleotides are bonded together to form a single nucleic acid chain.

Figure 7-3 Griffith injected mice with smooth and rough strains of *Pneumococcus* bacteria.

bonded to the phosphate group of the next nucleotide. Thus the sequence of a nucleotide chain has a definite direction. The end of the chain with a phosphate group exposed is called the 5′ (read as *five prime*) end. The other end, with a sugar exposed, is called the 3′ end.

7-2 Function of DNA

Frederick Griffith, a British bacteriologist, provided the first clues regarding the function of DNA. He was studying the effect that two strains of *Pneumococcus* bacteria had on mice. One of the strains caused pneumonia in mice and eventually killed them. The other strain was not harmful. The deadly strain was enclosed within a capsule, which gave the bacteria a smooth appearance. The other strain lacked a capsule and had a rough appearance. Griffith reasoned that the defense system in the mice was unable to penetrate the capsule surrounding the smooth bacteria. The smooth bacteria were able to reproduce and eventually the mice died of pneumonia.

Griffith killed the smooth bacteria with heat and injected them into the mice. The mice lived. The process Griffith used in his experiment is illustrated in Figure 7-3. He then injected mice with a mixture of live, rough bacteria and heat-killed, smooth bacteria. All of the mice died. Much to Griffith's surprise, he found live, smooth bacteria in fluid removed from the dead mice. These results were puzzling. If the mice had been injected with dead bacteria, how could live bacteria be removed?

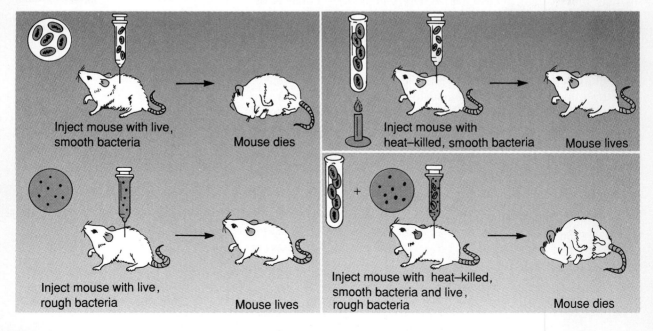

Inject mouse with live, smooth bacteria   Mouse dies

Inject mouse with heat–killed, smooth bacteria   Mouse lives

Inject mouse with live, rough bacteria   Mouse lives

Inject mouse with heat–killed, smooth bacteria and live, rough bacteria   Mouse dies

Griffith realized that there must have been something in the smooth strain that was not destroyed by heat. He suspected that this substance was transferred from the smooth bacteria to the rough bacteria. This substance caused the live, rough bacteria to form capsules and eventually kill the mice. Griffith concluded that this substance contained genetic information capable of transforming the rough bacteria into smooth bacteria. The transforming substance was later identified by other researchers as DNA.

The connection between DNA and protein production was made as a result of the work done by Sir Archibald Garrod, a physician to the English royal family. He studied a disease called alkaptonuria, in which urine turns black when exposed to air because it contains abnormally large amounts of an acid. Garrod proposed that the build-up of acid was caused by a missing enzyme in a particular biochemical reaction in metabolism. Because alkaptonuria is inherited, the absence of the enzyme must be caused by a genetic factor. Since Garrod's time, numerous other inborn errors of metabolism, each an inherited enyzme deficiency, have been described.

7-3 Structure of DNA

During the 1950s, a fierce competition to determine the three-dimensional structure of DNA took place. The race was won in 1953 by James Watson, an American biologist, and Francis Crick, a British physicist. Their success depended to a great extent on evidence collected by several biochemists.

American chemist, Erwin Chargaff, showed that in DNA, the number of adenine bases equals the number of thymine bases. The number of guanine bases equals the number of cytosine bases. Rosalind Franklin bombarded DNA with X rays, which produced a pattern on a screen. This pattern showed that DNA is made of repeating structures.

Using this information, Watson and Crick concluded that DNA is composed of two long chains of nucleotides arranged in a spiral. Their model resembles the diagram in Figure 7-4. The structure of the molecule looks like a twisted ladder and is called a **double helix**. The sides of the ladder are made of alternating sugar and phosphate molecules. The rungs of the ladder are made of nitrogen bases held together by hydrogen bonds.

The Watson and Crick model has the bases combined in a particular way. Adenine always pairs with thymine (A:T or T:A), and cytosine always pairs with guanine (C:G or G:C). A strand of DNA with the base sequence T-A-G-C-A-T must have a partner strand with the sequence A-T-C-G-T-A. This pattern of base pairing is described as being **complementary**.

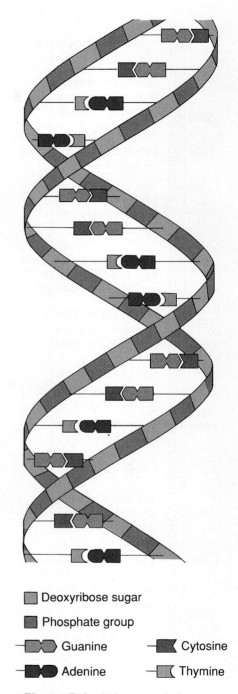

■ Deoxyribose sugar

■ Phosphate group

Guanine   Cytosine

Adenine   Thymine

Figure 7-4 Watson and Crick experimented with scale models before they found one that fit the known data on nucleic acids.

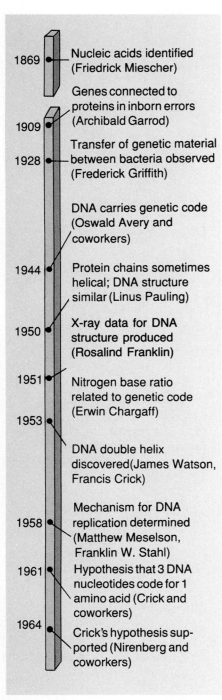

1869	Nucleic acids identified (Friedrick Miescher)
1909	Genes connected to proteins in inborn errors (Archibald Garrod)
1928	Transfer of genetic material between bacteria observed (Frederick Griffith)
1944	DNA carries genetic code (Oswald Avery and coworkers)
1950	Protein chains sometimes helical; DNA structure similar (Linus Pauling)
1951	X-ray data for DNA structure produced (Rosalind Franklin)
1953	Nitrogen base ratio related to genetic code (Erwin Chargaff)
	DNA double helix discovered(James Watson, Francis Crick)
1958	Mechanism for DNA replication determined (Matthew Meselson, Franklin W. Stahl)
1961	Hypothesis that 3 DNA nucleotides code for 1 amino acid (Crick and coworkers)
1964	Crick's hypothesis supported (Nirenberg and coworkers)

Figure 7-5 The combined efforts of many scientists have led to our current understanding of the structure and function of DNA.

7-4 DNA Code

Once the role and structure of DNA were known, the next step was to figure out how the structure carried the instructions for building proteins. Crick and his coworkers spent years trying to solve this problem. They knew that proteins play a major role in cell metabolism and are the main building blocks of the cell. They thought there must be a connection between the DNA code and the proteins produced by the cell. Recall that the sequence of amino acids in a protein chain determines which protein will be formed. Crick focused his research on trying to find what determines the sequence of amino acids in a protein.

In 1961, the group proposed a hypothesis that ultimately changed the course of biological research. They proposed that a series of three nucleotides on a DNA molecule, called a **triplet**, codes for one amino acid. If three bases code for an amino acid, 64 possibilities exist—more than enough to account for the 20 types of amino acids identified in biological proteins. From this simple hypothesis, they predicted that the sequences of bases in DNA made up the codes for the specific amino acids in a protein chain. This "alphabet" of DNA triplets specifying particular amino acids is called the genetic code. The hypothesis was supported by Marshall Nirenberg and his coworkers in 1964.

7-5 Replication of DNA

In order for a new cell to function properly, it must contain a complete set of genetic instructions. Since this information is carried on the DNA molecule, it is critical that every new cell receive an exact copy of the molecule. The DNA code is copied by the process of **replication**. In replication, new strands of DNA are synthesized from a supply of nucleotides in the nucleus.

The major steps in the replication of DNA are illustrated in Figure 7-6. Replication begins when enzymes break the hydrogen bonds between the complementary base pairs. In a sense, the DNA molecule "unzips." Separation of the strands occurs at many different places on the molecule at the same time. The sites at which separation and replication occur are called *replication forks*.

Where the DNA molecule is separated, bases are exposed. Enzymes catalyze the pairing of free-floating nucleotides to the exposed bases. Other enzymes bond the phosphate of one nucleotide to the sugar of the next. Notice in the figure that base pairing proceeds in only one direction on a particular strand. Each new strand grows from its 5′ end to its 3′ end. Separation and pairing of free nucleotides continue until the entire DNA molecule has been replicated.

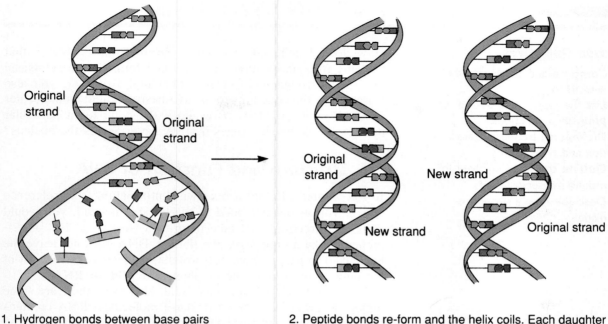

1. Hydrogen bonds between base pairs are broken. The helix opens, exposing bases. Free-floating nucleotides pair with exposed bases.

2. Peptide bonds re-form and the helix coils. Each daughter molecule consists of one parent strand and one newly formed strand.

Replication is an extremely precise process. The two original nucleotide strands serve as a mold for building the complementary strand. Each new double helix of DNA contains one strand of nucleotides from the original molecule and one newly created strand. The process of replication ensures that the exact order of bases in a molecule of DNA will be preserved and passed from one generation of cells to the next. Scientists have recently learned to replicate DNA in the laboratory. Scientists now have methods whereby they can replicate a piece of DNA a millionfold.

Figure 7-6 The action of an enzyme causes the DNA to split in various places along the strand. Because the enzyme works in one direction, bases are attached to the 5′ end in order. Bases attach to the 3′ end in segments.

CHECKPOINT ◆

1. What molecules compose a nucleotide?
2. Describe the shape of a DNA molecule.
3. What effects does base sequence in a DNA molecule have on the structures in a cell?
4. Explain the role of enzymes in DNA replication.
5. What led to the discovery of DNA structure?
▶ 6. If 27 percent of the bases in a certain segment of DNA were adenine, what would be the percentages of thymine, cytosine, and guanine?

▶ Denotes a question that involves *interpreting* and *applying* concepts.

PROTEIN SYNTHESIS

Section Objectives

F **Compare** and **contrast** DNA with RNA.

G **List** the types of RNA and **explain** their functions.

H **Distinguish** between transcription and translation.

I **Outline** the steps involved in making messenger RNA.

J **Describe** how a protein is made.

How does a cell make proteins? Recall from Chapter 5 that proteins are manufactured on ribosomes found in the cytoplasm and on the rough endoplasmic reticulum. However, you also learned that the code for protein synthesis is found on molecules of DNA in the nucleus. How does the code for a particular protein get to the ribosomes if DNA never leaves the nucleus?

7-6 Structure and Function of RNA

If you wanted to build a boat with information from reference books, you would not build in the library. Instead, you would copy the directions and take them to a workshop. Just as reference books do not leave the library, DNA does not leave the nucleus. The genetic code for protein synthesis is carried out of the nucleus on a molecule of **ribonucleic acid**, or RNA.

Like DNA, RNA is a nucleic acid. However, there are some important differences between these molecules. RNA contains the sugar ribose, whereas DNA contains deoxyribose. Instead of thymine, RNA contains the base **uracil**. Uracil forms a complementary pair with adenine. Thus the four bases in RNA are cytosine, guanine, adenine, and uracil.

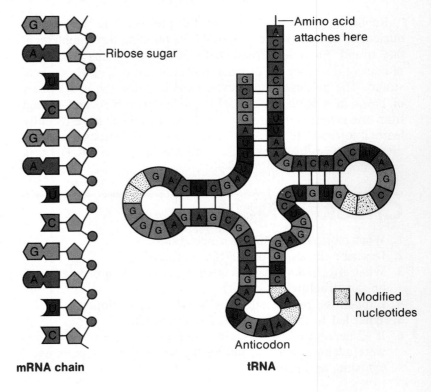

Figure 7-7 *Left:* Molecules of mRNA are made of single strands of uncoiled nucleotides. *Right:* The cloverleaf shape of tRNA results from base pairing at various points along the single strand.

Ribose sugar

Amino acid attaches here

Modified nucleotides

Anticodon

mRNA chain

tRNA

RNA differs from DNA in the molecular structure. Molecules of DNA are arranged in a double helix. As shown in Figure 7-7, molecules of RNA have different shapes.

Messenger RNA, or mRNA, carries the blueprint for a particular protein out of the nucleus to a specific site on a ribosome. **Transfer RNA**, or tRNA, in the cytoplasm attaches to a free amino acid and carries it to a ribosome. **Ribosomal RNA**, or rRNA, makes up part of the ribosomes. It is thought that rRNA is involved in the bonding of amino acids to form protein chains.

7-7 Transcription: DNA to RNA

When a protein is needed by a cell, an exact copy of the code for that protein must be made from the DNA. The process by which the DNA code is copied onto a strand of RNA is called **transcription**. Transcription is illustrated in Figure 7-8.

The process begins when enzymes open up the portion of DNA that codes for the needed protein. Only one side of the DNA double helix is transcribed, and this is called the **sense strand**. The other side, or **antisense strand**, may be involved in silencing or stopping the sense strand in some situations. The Cutting Edge on page 120 examines some interesting uses of antisense DNA.

Once the DNA locally unwinds, other enzymes then catalyze the bonding of free RNA nucleotides to the exposed bases on one of the DNA sense strands. The process is similar to DNA replication, except that adenine on the DNA pairs with uracil instead of with thymine.

Once complementary bases are paired, the phosphate end of one RNA nucleotide is bonded to the sugar end of the next.

Figure 7-8 Transcription occurs in the nucleus. A completed molecule of mRNA enters the cytoplasm through a nuclear pore. It travels through the cytoplasm until it reaches a ribosome.

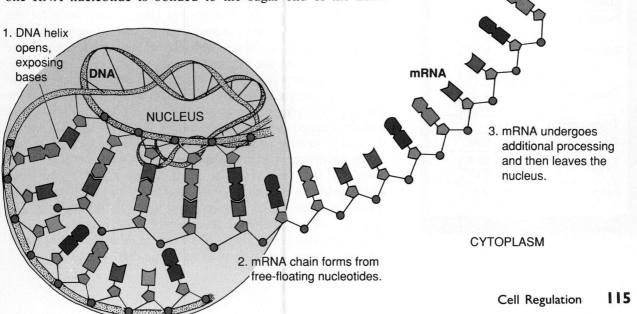

1. DNA helix opens, exposing bases

DNA

NUCLEUS

mRNA

3. mRNA undergoes additional processing and then leaves the nucleus.

2. mRNA chain forms from free-floating nucleotides.

CYTOPLASM

Cell Regulation 115

Table 7-1

AMINO ACIDS CODED BY RNA CODONS	
Amino Acid	**RNA Codon**
Alanine	GCU, GCC, GCA, GCG
Arginine	AGA, AGG, CGU, CGC, CGA, CGG
Asparagine	AAU, AAC
Aspartic Acid	GAU, GAC
Cysteine	UGU, UGC
Glutamic Acid	GAA, GAG
Glutamine	CAA, CAG
Glycine	GGU, GGC, GGA, GGG
Histidine	CAU, CAC
Isoleucine	AUU, AUC, AUA
Leucine	UUA, UUG, CUU, CUC, CUA, CUG
Lysine	AAA, AAG
Methionine (Initiation)	AUG
Phenyl- alanine	UUU, UUC
Proline	CCU, CCC, CCA, CCG
Serine	UCU, UCC, UCA, UCG, AGU, AGC
Threonine	ACU, ACC, ACA, ACG
Tryptophan	UGG
Tyrosine	UAU, UAC
Valine	GUU, GUC, GUA, GUG
Stop	UAA, UAG, UGA

This pattern of bonding continues until a terminator on the DNA strand is reached. A *terminator* indicates the end of a protein code. When transcription stops, the newly formed strand of RNA detaches from the DNA molecule.

In most cells, RNA undergoes additional processing before leaving the nucleus. A sequence of RNA usually contains extra nucleotides. These nucleotides do not code for amino acids. The function of these noncoding nucleotides, or *introns*, is not fully understood. What is known, however, is that enzymes remove some of the introns before the molecule leaves the nucleus. As the introns are removed, the coding nucleotides, or *exons*, are spliced together, forming a shorter chain. Enzymes add a string of adenine bases to one end of the molecule. A cap made of another base is added to the other end. After much preparation, mRNA leaves the nucleus.

7-8 How the Code Works

Recall that DNA carries the code for amino acids in groups of three nucleotide bases. Like DNA, mRNA carries the code for amino acids in groups of three nucleotides. The nucleotide sequence in an mRNA molecule that codes for a specific amino acid is called a **codon**. The sequence of codons in mRNA determines which protein chain will be formed during protein synthesis. A codon with the base sequence guanine-uracil-cytosine (GUC), for example, represents the amino acid valine. Thus a codon is like a three-letter word. Look at Table 7-1, which shows all the codons that can be formed from the four bases of RNA. Most of these codons code for particular amino acids. Tryptophan and methionine are the only amino acids with just one codon. Notice, though, that several codons may code for the same amino acid. For example, arginine can be represented by six different codons. Since they have the same meaning, these redundant codons are like synonyms.

Certain codons do not code for any amino acids. These codons may carry other information, such as when to begin or end the building of a protein. A codon that signals the beginning of a protein is called an *initiation codon*. A *termination codon* signals the end of protein synthesis. Look at Table 7-1.

An important property of the genetic code is that it is nearly universal. In other words, a given codon codes for the same amino acid in different organisms. The codon GCU codes for alanine in human cells, and cells of a spider or a buttercup. The idea that we each have our own genetic code is quite mistaken! There are some exceptions, however, such as the slight variations that occur in the code of mitochondrial DNA.

7-9 Translation: RNA to Protein

Once outside the nucleus, mRNA travels to a ribosome. Ribosomes can be free-floating in the cytoplasm or attached to the endoplasmic reticulum. When mRNA reaches a ribosome, the ribosome moves along the molecule until it reaches the initiation codon AUG. The initiation codon attaches to the ribosome. The codon after AUG also attaches to the ribosome. The stage is now set for protein synthesis.

The process of building a protein molecule according to the code in mRNA is called **translation**. A ribosome translates the sequence of mRNA bases into a sequence of amino acids to form a protein. Recall that ribosomal RNA is involved at this stage of protein synthesis.

How are free-floating amino acids brought to a ribosome? How do they line up in a particular sequence? Unattached molecules of transfer RNA are scattered throughout the cytoplasm. Free molecules of tRNA attach to free molecules of amino acids floating in the cytoplasm. This bonding, however, is not random. Notice the looped structure of tRNA in Figure 7-9. One loop of the molecule contains three nucleotides called an **anticodon**. The

■■ BIOLOGY INSIGHT

Structure Is Related to Function: The amino acid sequence in a protein determines how a protein will twist in assuming its three dimensional shape. It is the shape of the protein that determines its function.

Figure 7-9 Translation is an extremely complex process. However, it proceeds quite rapidly in a cell. Some bacteria can bond amino acids at a rate of 100 every 5 seconds.

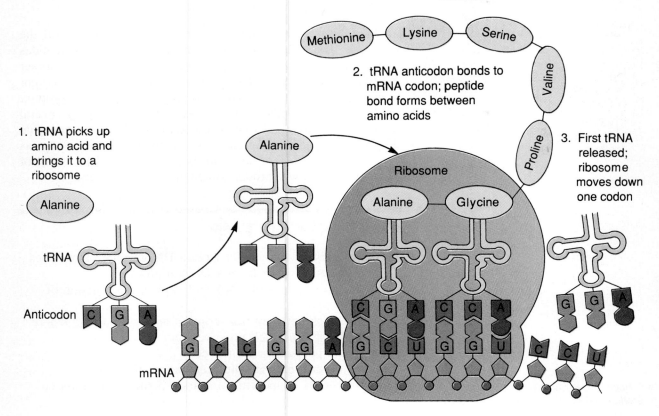

1. tRNA picks up amino acid and brings it to a ribosome

2. tRNA anticodon bonds to mRNA codon; peptide bond forms between amino acids

3. First tRNA released; ribosome moves down one codon

Methionine — Lysine — Serine — Valine — Proline

Alanine

Ribosome

Alanine — Glycine

tRNA

Anticodon

mRNA

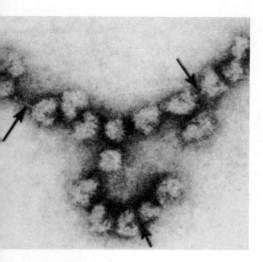

Figure 7-10 The polysome in this TEM contains 18 ribosomes. As each ribosome is translating the mRNA, 18 protein chains are being synthesized. To find the mRNA, look closely at the arrows.

anticodon determines which amino acid the tRNA will carry. Notice how a molecule of tRNA with the anticodon CGA attaches to a molecule of alanine.

Translation, which is illustrated in Figure 7-9, proceeds as follows:

1. A molecule of tRNA with a methionine amino acid attached moves toward a ribosome. There, the anticodon of the tRNA bonds to the initiation codon of the mRNA on the ribosome.
2. Another tRNA–amino acid complex bonds to the mRNA next to the first tRNA. Two amino acids are now positioned side by side. Enzymes catalyze the formation of a peptide bond between them.
3. The first tRNA is released to pick up another methionine molecule. A chain of two amino acids is now attached to the second tRNA. The ribosome moves down one codon on the mRNA molecule.
4. Transfer RNA molecules bring more amino acids to the ribosome and the bonding process is repeated.
5. Protein synthesis stops when the ribosome reaches a termination codon on the mRNA molecule. The protein chain is then released from the ribosome for use.

Once the protein is completed, messenger RNA falls off the ribosome. The mRNA breaks down into individual nucleotides that return to the nucleus. However, if the cell needs another molecule of that protein, the same mRNA can be read by another ribosome. If there is a need for multiple strands of a protein, one molecule of mRNA can be read simultaneously by several ribosomes. A group of ribosomes bound to the same molecule of mRNA is called a **polysome**. If the mRNA is very long, as many as 50 to 70 ribosomes can become attached to it. All of these ribosomes will produce identical protein chains.

CHECKPOINT ◆

7. How does a codon differ from a DNA triplet? How does an anticodon differ from a DNA triplet?
8. Name three types of RNA and explain the function of each type.
9. Distinguish between transcription and translation. Where in the cell does each process occur?
10. How do polysomes aid the cell?
11. How do enzymes aid the preparation of mRNA?
12. What would happen to translation if the termination codon on an mRNA molecule was changed?

▶ Denotes a question that involves *inter-preting* and *applying* concepts.

LABORATORY ACTIVITY

TRANSCRIPTION AND TRANSLATION

Objectives and Skills

□ *Construct a model* of a segment of DNA.
□ *Demonstrate* how free nucleotides form a strand of mRNA complementary to the DNA segment.

Materials

tracing paper
6 pieces of construction paper, different colors
pencil
tape
textbook
scissors

Procedure and Observations

1. Read all the instructions for this laboratory activity before you begin your work.
2. Use the diagram below to draw the shapes of the bases, phosphate, and sugars on a piece of tracing paper. Make a stencil by cutting out each shape.

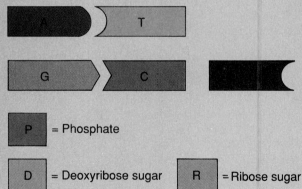

P = Phosphate

D = Deoxyribose sugar   R = Ribose sugar

3. Use the stencils to draw shapes on the construction paper. You will need the following numbers of each shape: 4 guanines, 4 cytosines, 5 adenines, 2 thymines, 3 uracils, 9 deoxyribose sugars, 9 ribose sugars, and 18 phosphates.

4. Write the letter G on each guanine outline, the letter C on each cytosine, and so on for all the shapes.
5. Cut out the guanines and place them in a stack. Do the same with the other shapes.
6. Using the appropriate pieces, construct a strand of DNA with the base code CGATTAGAC. Tape the pieces together.
7. Use the remaining pieces to construct a strand of mRNA that is complementary to the DNA strand.
8. Use the two strands to answer the questions in the Analysis and Conclusions section.
9. Clean up your materials.

Analysis and Conclusions

1. Which amino acids are coded for by the strand of DNA? By the complementary mRNA strand? Do both strands code for the same amino acids?
2. How do the shapes of bases in the strand of DNA determine the order of bases in the mRNA strand?
3. Determine the sequence of bases that would be found in the tRNA anticodons involved in translation of the mRNA strand.
4. How does the structure of DNA ensure that each protein synthesized will contain the correct amino acids?

CUTTING EDGE

Gene Silencers

When the information in a gene is transcribed into messenger RNA (mRNA), the region of the double helix locally unravels so that the RNA bases can line up with their complementary DNA bases. The half of the helix that contains the information from which RNA is transcribed is called the **sense** strand. What happens to the other side of the DNA molecule, the **antisense** strand? Scientists do not really know, but it's possible that antisense strands could prevent sense strands from being expressed. Researchers are already using this idea to turn off certain genes.

Gene silencing, or **antisense technology**, follows the base-pairing rules of adenine bonding to thymine and cytosine bonding to guanine. The silencer itself is a short piece of nucleic acid, 15 to 20 nucleotides long, that is complementary to the sequence of the mRNA transcribed from a particular gene. When the silencer meets the mRNA in the nucleus, it binds to it, preventing it from entering the cytoplasm, where it would normally be translated into protein. Gene silencing, then, shuts off production of a protein by blocking its mRNA.

Laboratory-made pieces of nucleic acid contain the nitrogenous bases found in natural RNA or DNA, but often their sugar-phosphate backbones are intentionally altered. Such changes give the nucleic acid analog (a laboratory version of the natural chemical) valuable new properties. Replacing some of the phosphates with different chemical groups can ease the silencer's passage across the cell membrane into the cell and protects it from enzymes in the cell that destroy nucleic acids.

Another way to make a gene silencer is to program a cell to make one itself. An antisense DNA sequence is stitched into a chromosome. Then the cell transcribes the sequence, producing an RNA that is complementary to the mRNA of a particular gene. The antisense RNA then binds to the mRNA, blocking its translation into protein.

APPLYING WHAT'S NEW

The great advantage of gene silencing is that it is very specific, affecting only one gene. Other methods to change gene activity, such as using chemicals

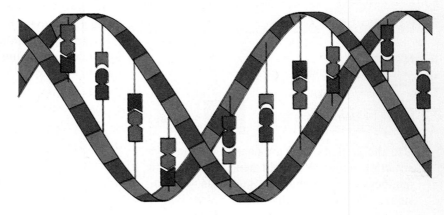

to inactivate genes, can alter several genes at a time. In human health care, the technology is used to treat viral illnesses, including AIDS, herpes simplex, chicken pox, and hepatitis (liver inflammation).

When a virus infects a human cell, it inserts its nucleic acid into a human chromosome. The human cell then manufactures the proteins encoded by the "stowaway" viral DNA. If an antisense sequence is present that is complementary to the virus's nucleic acid, it will block its replication, and the infection will be stopped. Gene silencers can also be made to block genes whose overactivity triggers cancer.

Gene silencers are also used in agriculture. One antisense sequence seeks out one of the tomato's 80 000 genes, a gene that hastens ripening. Using the gene silencer leads to fruit that stays edible longer. A silencer for a gene that confers red color to petunias produces plants with beautifully striped petals.

The most important use of gene silencers will be in basic research. The technology can silence a gene in a fertilized egg, and then—if the organism develops—you can see what happens when it lacks the protein specified by the blocked gene. Gene silencers can also be applied to cells growing outside the body to see what happens when the activity of a certain gene is masked. For example, researchers fashioned a gene silencer for a gene that normally causes immature blood cells in bone marrow to be produced in large quantities. Cells growing in the laboratory to which the gene si-lencer was added formed tiny colonies. The same types of cells grown without a gene silencer formed very large colonies. This basic research has a practical side too, because overexpression of this gene causes cancer of the blood.

DISCUSSION & RESEARCH

1. Proto-oncogenes cause certain cells to divide. When overactivated, proto-oncogenes cause cancer. How can gene silencers be used to study the normal and cancerous effects of proto-oncogenes?
2. At what stage in the expression of genetic information does a gene silencer work?
3. A fertilized egg does not actually manufacture its own mRNA until it has divided several times to form an embryo. Until that time, cellular activities are carried out using mRNA that is present in the egg, the mRNA having been passed along from the mother. How might gene silencers be used to study the roles of maternal messenger RNA?

CHAPTER REVIEW

Summary

▸ DNA was discovered in 1869, but its function remained a mystery until the mid 1940s. Researchers then realized that the genetic code of an organism was carried on DNA.

▸ DNA is composed of long chains of nucleotides. Each nucleotide contains a phosphate group, a deoxyribose sugar, and one of four different nitrogen bases. These bases are adenine, guanine, cytosine, and thymine. The structure of DNA is a double helix.

▸ DNA contains the directions for making all the proteins that a cell needs. Proteins play a major role in cell metabolism and are the building blocks of a cell. Thus the life of an organism depends on the proteins it produces.

▸ The DNA code is copied during replication. DNA replication forms two strands of DNA. Each newly created molecule contains one new strand of nucleotides and one of the original strands.

▸ The genetic information in DNA is carried out of the nucleus on a molecule of messenger RNA. Protein synthesis is carried out in the cytoplasm by mRNA and two other forms of RNA—transfer RNA and ribosomal RNA.

Vocabulary

adenine	polysome
anticodon	replication
antisense strand	ribonucleic acid
codon	ribosomal RNA
complementary	sense strand
cytosine	thymine
double helix	transcription
guanine	transfer RNA
messenger RNA	translation
nucleic acid	triplet
nucleotide	uracil

Concept Mapping

Using the method of concept mapping first described in the front of this book, complete a concept map for protein synthesis. Copy the incomplete map shown below. Fill in the missing terms.

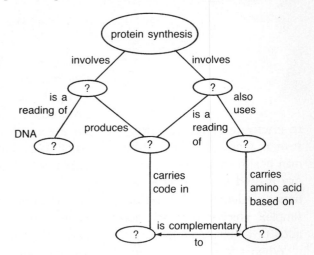

Review

1. What are nucleotides? Describe the structure of a nucleotide.
2. According to the base-pairing rule, which base pairs with guanine?
3. What bases are found in RNA?
4. How many different DNA triplets are there?
5. How are DNA and RNA similar?
6. To which two molecules does transfer RNA attach?
7. What four bases make up DNA nucleotides? RNA nucleotides?
8. What structures allow several proteins to be manufactured from a single messenger RNA at one time?
9. What is the shape of a DNA molecule?
10. Where in the cell is each type of RNA found?
11. List three differences between RNA and DNA.

Interpret and Apply

12. Compare replication and transcription. What is formed in each process?
13. What amino acid does the triplet TAG represent?
14. Explain the difference between a molecule of mRNA that leaves the nucleus and the one that was transcribed.
15. Which mRNA codons would signal the end of a protein code?
16. Write the DNA triplet, the mRNA codon, and the tRNA anticodon for the amino acid tryptophan.
17. For the DNA triplet GTA, write the complementary mRNA codon and the tRNA anticodon. What amino acid does this triplet represent?
18. How does the structure of DNA affect the way a cell functions?
19. How much of a molecule of DNA unravels during replication? During transcription? Explain your answers.

Critical Thinking

20. Why is mRNA called a messenger?
21. The bases of the two DNA strands are held together by hydrogen bonds. What property of these bonds makes them well suited for the process of replication?
22. Suppose a protein has 250 amino acids. What is the minimum number of nucleotides necessary to code for 250 amino acids? What is the minimum number of triplets?
23. The replication of DNA is usually very precise, resulting in new strands of DNA that are exactly the same as the original strand. What would happen if one of the strands was copied incorrectly? How would this affect the proteins manufactured by the cell?

24. Enzymes play a major role in DNA replication and protein synthesis. Use the line graph below and your knowledge of enzyme activity to answer the following items.

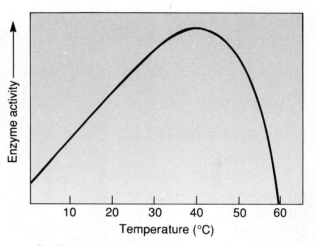

a. Compare the relative amounts of protein that will be synthesized at 10°C, 40°C, and 60°C.
b. Normal human body temperature is about 37°C. Why are changes in body temperature critical to the health of an individual?
c. People who spend a great deal of time outdoors must take steps to avoid a condition called hypothermia during winter months and heat stroke in summer months. Explain why each of these conditions is a threat to a person's health.
d. A line graph is used in science to illustrate a cause-and-effect relationship. Note that each axis in the graph has a label. What label represents the cause? The effect?

Chapter

MITOSIS AND CELL DIVISION

Overview

DIVISION OF CELLS

8-1   Mitosis
8-2   Cytokinesis

SIGNIFICANCE OF MITOSIS AND CELL DIVISION

8-3   Unicellular Organisms
8-4   How Size Affects Cells
8-5   Multicellular Organisms
8-6   Tissues, Organs, and Systems
8-7   Cell Replacement

REGULATION OF MITOSIS AND CELL DIVISION

8-8   Life span of a Cell
8-9   Growth Regulators in Healthy Cells
8-10 Abnormal Cell Division
8-11 Cancer

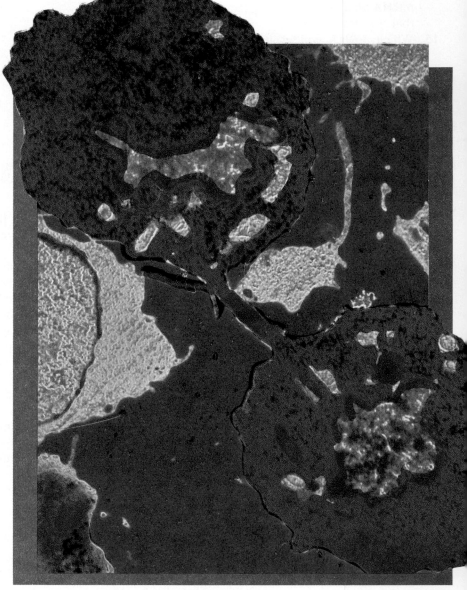

What factors control cell division?

DIVISION OF CELLS

Recall from Chapter 2 that the cell is the basic unit of structure and function in living things. The cell theory also states that all cells come from other pre-existing cells. The first statement means that each cell contains the basic "machinery" necessary to carry on essential life processes. The second statement indicates that this "machinery" is somehow passed from existing cells to new cells. The production of new, healthy cells ensures the continuation of life. In this part of the chapter, you will learn how cells reproduce.

8-1 Mitosis

In order for a cell to reproduce, the genetic information in a parent cell must be duplicated. Then the information is distributed to the new cells that are formed.

Recall from Chapter 7 that an exact copy of the DNA in a cell is made during replication. Of course, after the copies of DNA are made, the cell contains twice the normal number of chromosomes. This double set of chromosomes is then divided into two separate sets during a process called **mitosis** [mī tō′ sis]. Mitosis is a critical stage in the life cycle of a cell. Each new cell that will be produced must receive a complete copy of the original DNA in order to function normally. During mitosis, preparations are made to ensure an equal distribution of chromosomes to each new cell.

In an effort to understand how mitosis occurs, biologists have divided the process into four phases. They are called prophase, metaphase, anaphase, and telophase. The period in between these four phases is called interphase.

Interphase A cell is in interphase during most of its existence. This phase is a period of growth, when protein synthesis occurs rapidly. Toward the end of interphase, the chromosomes replicate in preparation for mitosis. At this point, the chromosomes, in the form of chromatin, are spread throughout the nucleus, much like spaghetti on a plate. The nucleolus is visible as a dark spot within the nucleus. The entire nucleus is enclosed by the nuclear envelope.

In animal cells (Figure 8-1), a pair of centrioles can be found outside the nuclear envelope. During interphase, a daughter centriole begins to form next to each of the existing centrioles. At about this point, the cell is entering prophase.

Prophase At the start of prophase, the centrioles begin to move, with their developing daughter centrioles, toward opposite ends

Section Objectives

A *Describe* the phases of mitosis.
B *Identify* the role of each cell structure involved in mitosis and cell division.
C *Compare* cytokinesis in plant and animal cells.

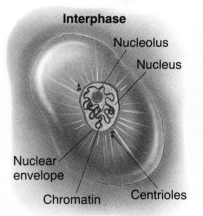

Figure 8-1 The nucleus and related structures of a cell during interphase

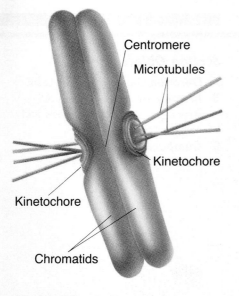

Centromere

Microtubules

Kinetochore

Kinetochore

Chromatids

Figure 8-2 Replication and equal distribution of the DNA are critical for each new cell. The centromere ensures the proper pairing of sister chromatids through metaphase. The kinetochores ensure the proper movement of chromatids during anaphase.

of the nucleus. Molecules that compose the nuclear envelope begin to disperse, and the nucleus itself becomes less sharply defined. The replicated chromosomes condense into short, thick rods that can be seen through a light microscope. The two replicas of a chromosome are now called **chromatids**. Figure 8-2 illustrates how a pair of chromatids may be arranged. They are held together at a region known as the **centromere**. This attachment ensures that the two chromatids will remain paired throughout the early phases of mitosis. Notice that a disc-shaped structure called a **kinetochore** [kə net′ ə kōr] is located on each chromatid in the centromere region. The kinetochore plays an important role in the later phases of mitosis.

As prophase progresses, the cytoskeleton breaks apart. The microtubules that make up the cytoskeleton reposition themselves. Some microtubules begin to cluster around the centrioles. This configuration resembles a starburst, or *aster*. The complete mitosis cycle is illustrated in Figure 8-3. Use the diagram as you read through the phases that follow.

Other microtubules form continuous strands that stretch between centrioles. A third group of microtubules extends from the centriole to the kinetochores of the two chromatids. The entire framework of microtubules is called the **mitotic spindle**. By the end of prophase, the nuclear envelope and the nucleolus have disappeared.

Metaphase During early metaphase, a molecule of kinesin attaches itself to each pair of chromatids. (Recall from Chapter 5 that kinesin is thought to be responsible for the movement of organelles along the microtubules.) The two chromatids begin to move towards the equator of the cell. They are pulled along the microtubule "tracks," called **spindle fibers**. Movement stops when all of the chromatid pairs reach the cell's equator.

Anaphase Anaphase begins with the separation of chromatid pairs. In response to some unknown signal, the two chromatids move in opposite directions. Once separated, each chromatid is called a chromosome. A force exerted on the kinetochore pulls the individual chromosomes toward opposite regions of the cell, called *poles*. By late anaphase, an equal number of chromosomes have reached each pole. Also, as illustrated in Figure 8-3, the plasma membrane begins to change shape. The division of genetic material that takes place during anaphase is called **karyokinesis**.

Telophase During early telophase, the chromosomes begin to uncoil, becoming a mass of chromatin once again. Fragments of the original nuclear envelope reassemble around each collection of chromatin. A nucleolus reappears inside each nucleus.

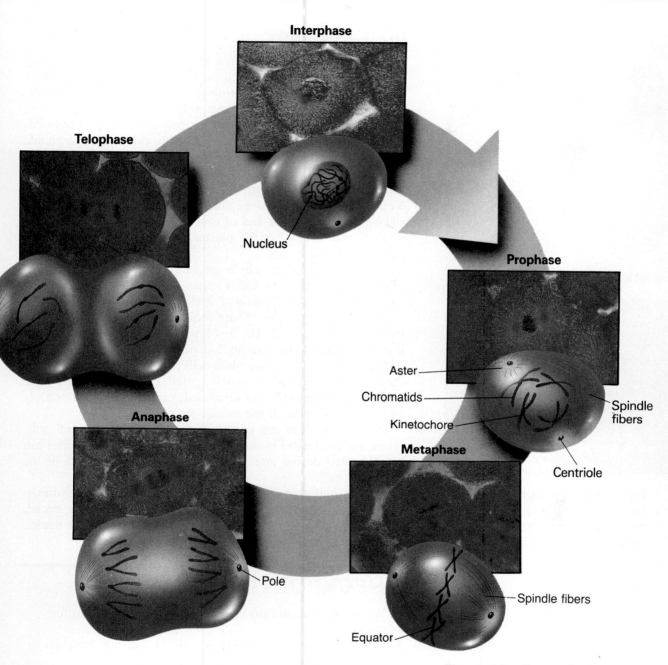

Interphase

Nucleus

Telophase

Prophase

Aster

Chromatids

Kinetochore

Spindle fibers

Centriole

Metaphase

Anaphase

Pole

Spindle fibers

Equator

Figure 8-3   Stages of mitosis.

Outside the nucleus, the spindle fibers begin to break apart. By the end of telophase, most of the microtubules have reassembled to form the cytoskeleton. Throughout the entire process of mitosis, daughter centrioles have been growing so that by the end of telophase, two mature centrioles appear at each pole.

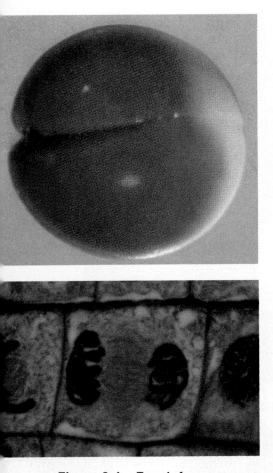

8-2 Cytokinesis

As a result of mitosis, each new nucleus contains an exact copy of the DNA from the original nucleus. But there is more to a cell than just the nucleus. How are the cytoplasm and the organelles divided up between two new cells?

Cytokinesis [sīt ō kə nē′ səs], or cell division, proceeds differently in animal and plant cells. During cytokinesis in animal cells, protein structures called **microfilaments** form a ring around the equator. When the microfilaments contract, they tighten the plasma membrane to form a curve, or **furrow**, at the equator. You can see the furrow beginning to form around the cell in Figure 8-4 *top*. By the end of cytokinesis, the furrow becomes so deep that it pinches the plasma membrane in half, forming two new, smaller cells.

Cytokinesis in plant cells involves the formation of a new cell wall. Vesicles from the Golgi apparatus gather in sheets at the equator of the cell. Contained within the vesicles are complex carbohydrate molecules. These molecules begin fusing together to form a new cell wall. The first layer of the cell wall, the middle lamella, is laid down forming a dividing plate. You can see the dividing plate between two plant cells in Figure 8-4 *bottom*. Once the wall is completed, two new, smaller plant cells have been formed. After the cells are separated, each cell builds a primary cell wall on its side of the middle lamella.

Cytokinesis does not ensure the equal distribution of cytoplasm and organelles to each new cell. Additional organelles can be replicated during interphase depending on the needs of the individual cell.

Not all cells that undergo mitosis also undergo cytokinesis. In such cases, the result is cells that have two or more nuclei. Skeletal muscle tissue is an example of cells with multiple nuclei. Skeletal muscle grows by cell fusion.

Figure 8-4 *Top:* A furrow may be clearly seen during cytokinesis in an animal cell. *Bottom:* Note the cell plate forming in the plant cell.

CHECKPOINT ◆

1. What event occurs during interphase in preparation for mitosis?
2. During which phases of mitosis are chromatids attached to each other?
3. Explain the difference between cytokinesis in animal cells and plant cells.
4. Describe the role of each of the following during mitosis: mitotic spindle, centrioles, kinetochore, centromere.
▶ 5. In what ways is telophase the opposite of prophase?
▶ 6. Why must cytokinesis occur after, rather than before, anaphase?

▶ Denotes a question that involves *interpreting* and *applying* concepts.

SIGNIFICANCE OF MITOSIS AND CELL DIVISION

Mitosis ensures that each newly created cell will contain a complete set of chromosomes. Depending on whether an organism is unicellular or multicellular, mitosis and cell division can have different effects. For unicellular organisms, the processes become a method of reproduction. In multicellular organisms, the processes aid in growth, maintenance, and the replacement of body parts.

8-3 Unicellular Organisms

A unicellular, or single-celled, organism is capable of performing almost all life processes without the benefit of mitosis and cell division. Unicellular organisms, like bacteria or amoebas, can obtain and digest food, manufacture proteins, excrete wastes, and respond to environmental changes throughout most of their lives. One process not in this list is reproduction. How do unicellular organisms produce more of themselves?

Mitosis and cell division occur when a unicellular organism divides to form two smaller cells. After a unicellular organism reproduces, the two new cells are each capable of existing independently. Eventually as they grow, one or both cells may undergo mitosis and cell division to produce other cells. Prokaryotic cells do not divide by mitosis. These cells divide by a process called binary fission which is covered in Chapter 18.

8-4 How Size Affects Cells

What happens as a single cell grows larger? In Chapter 5, you learned that the plasma membrane regulates the flow of molecules into and out of a cell. Recall that nutrients and oxygen must enter a cell, while waste products must leave. The ability of the plasma membrane to maintain the proper chemical conditions within a cell is vital. This delicate balance becomes more and more difficult to maintain as growth occurs within a cell.

To understand the problem, it is helpful to compare the cell to a sphere. The interior of the cell (the cytoplasm and organelles) is like the volume occupied by the sphere. The plasma membrane is similar to the surface of the sphere.

Figure 8-6 on the next page illustrates how the surface area and volume of a sphere (or a cell) are related. Three different size spheres are shown. The radius of the second sphere is twice the radius of the first sphere. The radius of the third sphere is three times bigger. Note the calculations for surface area and volume for each sphere.

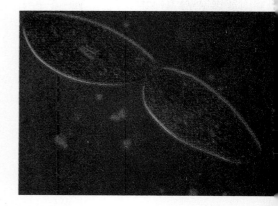

Figure 8-5 As a result of mitosis and cell division, one paramecium can reproduce and form two new ones.

	Surface area (SA) $= 4\pi r^2$	Volume (V) $= \frac{4}{3}\pi r^3$	Surface area-to-volume ratio
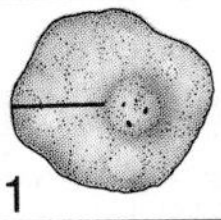 $r = 1$	$SA = 4\pi(1)^2$ $SA = 12.6$	$V = \frac{4}{3}\pi(1)^3$ $V = 4.2$	$\dfrac{12.6}{4.2} = 3$
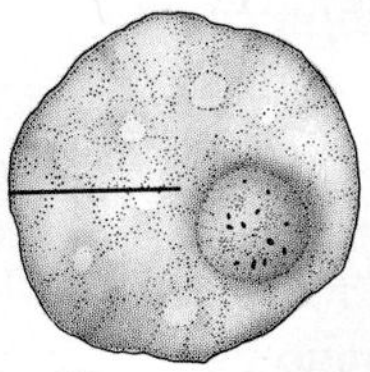 $r = 2$	$SA = 4\pi(2)^2$ $SA = 50.3$	$V = \frac{4}{3}\pi(2)^3$ $V = 33.5$	$\dfrac{50.3}{33.5} = 1.5$
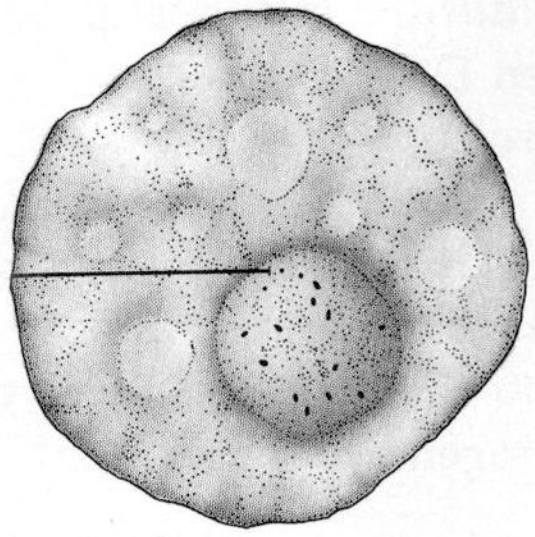 $r = 3$	$SA = 4\pi(3)^2$ $SA = 113.1$	$V = \frac{4}{3}\pi(3)^3$ $V = 113.1$	$\dfrac{113.1}{113.1} = 1$

Figure 8-6 The surface area (SA) and volume (V) have been calculated for each sphere pictured. Note that as the radius (r) in each sphere increases, so do the values of volume and surface area. However, the volume increases more quickly because volume depends on r^3 while surface area depends on r^2. The resulting surface area-to-volume ratio gets smaller.

An additional number is included in the diagram. This number gives the ratio between the surface area and the volume. Notice that as the sphere gets larger, the ratio gets smaller.

What does all this have to do with a cell? Imagine that as a cell grows in size, the amount of cytoplasm and the number of organelles increases faster than does the surface area of the plasma membrane. An increase in cell volume causes an increase in the need for nutrients and the excretion of wastes. Soon there is too little surface area to accommodate the "molecular traffic" that must cross the plasma membrane. At this point, the cell stops growing. In fact, if the cell did not stop growing, it would die. There would be more waste products produced than could be moved out through the cell membrane.

Over time, the cell divides into two smaller cells. This division provides a more manageable surface-to-volume ratio for each new cell.

8-5 Multicellular Organisms

Consider the size of a whale. If cells are limited as to how big they can grow, how can an organism become as large as a whale? The answer is for the organism to be made from many cells. You probably know that like you, the whale grew from a single fertilized egg cell. The division of cells into more cells that remain together and function together allows organisms to grow large.

Being part of a multicellular organism changes the conditions under which cells live. Cells on the inside of a multicellular organism are not in direct contact with the environment like unicellular organisms are. Therefore they are unable to obtain nutrients and excrete wastes on their own. Instead they depend on other cells. In a multicellular organism, some cells specialize in obtaining food or excreting wastes, while other cells may specialize in movement or response, and so on. The work done by one type of cell benefits all of the other cells in the organism. Most of these cells would not survive for any length of time if they were removed from the organism as a whole. Cell specialization enables a multicellular organism to perform all of the life processes that a unicellular organism can perform.

Can you think of a few examples of multicellular organisms? Somewhere in your list should be a most familiar example, *you*! The human body is one of the more complicated multicellular organisms. Each of its individual cells contributes in part to the survival of the body as a whole. Cells within the digestive system break down food, which in turn is absorbed and used by other cells in your body. The cells inside your lungs absorb oxygen from the air that you breathe. Nerve cells provide a communications link between cells. Skin cells are specialized to provide an outer protective layer for your body. Each type of cell has a specific job that affects other cells in your body.

8-6 Tissues, Organs, and Systems

As an organism grows, how do some of the new cells become specialized for particular functions? You have just learned that mitosis and cell division produce two cells that have the same DNA. If all your cells have exactly the same DNA, why do some become skin cells while others become bone cells?

Although each of your cells contains the DNA necessary for manufacturing every protein in your body, no single cell makes

Figure 8-7 There are more than 200 different types of cells in the human body. Each cell type has a specific size and shape depending on its function. Seen here (*left* to *right*) are nerve cells (50X), skin cells (400X), and skeletal muscle cells (400X).

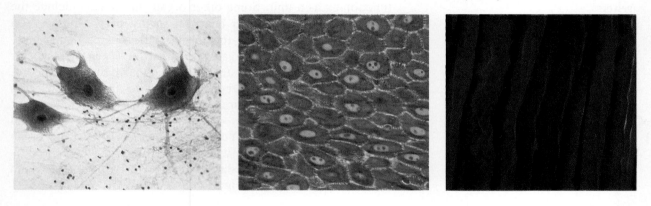

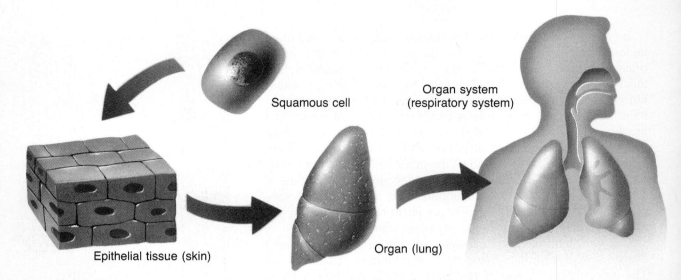

Squamous cell

Organ system
(respiratory system)

Epithelial tissue (skin)

Organ (lung)

Figure 8-8 The levels of organization for a multicellular organism are based on cells. Cells form tissues, which make up organs, which are part of an organ system. Organ systems, such as the nervous, digestive, and circulatory systems, make up the entire organism.

BIOLOGY INSIGHT

Levels of Organization: Within a cell, organelles work together to perform life functions, just as specialized functions in multicellular organisms are carried out by organ systems.

all the proteins. Each type of cell will produce only those proteins necessary for that cell to live and to do its particular job. In any cell, only certain segments of the DNA are active. As a result, only certain proteins are produced during protein synthesis.

The types of proteins present in a cell determine the kinds of activities the cell can perform and the structure that the cell will have. Cells that produce the same proteins and perform the same function frequently are found grouped together in the body. Such a cluster of cells is called a **tissue**. For example, nervous tissue is composed of many nerve cells, and muscle tissue is composed of muscle cells. Even blood is a tissue composed of groups of similar cells. You will learn about various types of white blood cells in Chapters 40 and 41.

In many organisms, several different types of tissues work together to perform a common function. The muscle, blood vessels, nerves, and other tissues that line your stomach, for example, work together to digest food. Your stomach is an example of an organ. An **organ** is composed of several different tissues functioning as a unit. Some other organs in humans include the brain, liver, kidneys, and heart. In many organisms, several different organs may work together to perform a particular function. Such a group of organs is called an **organ system**. For example, your nervous system includes your brain, spinal cord, and all the nerves that carry information to and from the parts of your body. Your respiratory system—which includes your nose, windpipe, and lungs—allows you to take in oxygen and excrete carbon dioxide. You would not survive if any organ system ceased to operate, with the exception of your reproductive system. The relationship among cells, tissue, organs, and systems is illustrated in Figure 8-8.

8-7 Cell Replacement

Cells produced as a result of mitosis and cell division do not always increase the size and complexity of an organism. When specialized cells reproduce, they produce more of the same specialized cells. Often the new cells simply replace old ones at the end of their life spans. This rate of replacement can vary. Skin cells and the cells that line your digestive tract are two types of cells that must be replaced quite frequently. However, other cells last much longer. Replacement of cells in parts of the nervous system is rare. This is why diseases or accidents that destroy nerve tissue can result in life-long paralysis or loss of sensation.

Mitosis and cell division also replace cells that have ceased to function properly. In some organisms, mitosis and cell division can result in the replacement of entire body parts, an event known as **regeneration**. This form of cell replacement is very common among plants. Many organisms feed on plants. Without the ability to regenerate leaves and stems, some plants would disappear from certain areas. Regeneration occurs in some animals as well. When a starfish loses one of its arms, a new arm will be regenerated. Humans are capable of only limited regeneration. Lost skin and blood can be replaced. Also, if a small portion of the liver is removed surgically, the organ can regenerate enough tissue to replace what is lost. Research is being conducted on how some organisms are able to regenerate body parts. It is hoped that research in this area will have applications in humans for the regeneration of nerve tissue.

Figure 8-9 Notice the small regenerating arm on the left side of this starfish.

CHECKPOINT ◆

7. What life function occurs as the result of mitosis in unicellular organisms?
8. How does the volume of a cell change in comparison to the surface area when the cell grows larger?
9. Why is surface area to volume ratio so significant for a cell?
10. If all the cells in an organism have identical DNA, why do some cells look different from others?
11. What three functions in multicellular organisms do mitosis and cell division accomplish?
12. List the levels of organization in a multicellular organism beginning with a cell.
▶ 13. What would happen to a cell if the chalone-producing segment of DNA were continuously active?

BIOLOGY INSIGHT

Adaptation and Evolution: Regeneration can save the life of an organism. If a predator holds a starfish or lizard by the tail or a limb, the appendage snaps off, enabling the animal to escape! New limbs and tails are regenerated over time.

▶ Denotes a question that involves *interpreting* and *applying* concepts.

REGULATION OF MITOSIS AND CELL DIVISION

Section Objectives

I **State** several factors that affect the life span of a cell.
J **List** some of the regulators that control growth in healthy cells.
K **List** three carcinogens and **explain** how each one affects the DNA.
L **Describe** how cancer cells overcome healthy cells.

DO YOU KNOW?

Information: In young organisms, the rate of cell production exceeds the rate at which cells die. The result is a net gain in the total number of cells, which leads to growth. In adult organisms, however, the rate of cell production is balanced by the rate of cell death. Therefore, little or no growth occurs.

Cell division is one stage in the life cycle of a cell. After division is complete, the new cells undergo a period of growth until they have approximately doubled in size. Then, if a cell is going to reproduce, its DNA will begin to replicate. When replication is finished, the cell enters another period of growth in which some of the structures needed for mitosis are produced. Finally, the cell undergoes mitosis and cell division, and the life cycle of the cell begins again.

The time between the start of interphase and the end of cytokinesis can be thought of as the life span of a cell. How rapidly this cycle of life progresses and how many times a cell divides varies. The factors that influence cell growth and rate of reproduction are only partially understood.

8-8 Life Span of a Cell

The length of time between cell divisions depends on many things. DNA influences how long any single cell in an organism will live. How often a cell divides in different species and different cell types varies. Certain types of bacteria, when grown in a petri dish, divide every 20 minutes. Some yeast cells, under the same conditions, divide every 2 hours. Cells at the root tip of certain plants divide every 14 hours. In humans, skin cells are shed continuously. Taking a shower, wearing clothes, and even clapping hands cause skin cells to shed. These cells are

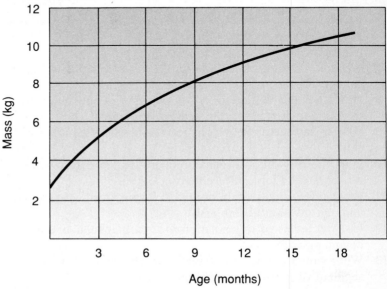

Figure 8-10 The graph represents a growth curve of an average newborn human. Can you explain the trend indicated by the curve?

replaced through mitosis and cell division. On the other hand, nerve cells probably have the longest life span. Some nerve cells stop dividing after the first few months of a baby's life! These cells can remain intact throughout life.

The age of an organism also affects how often cells divide. The younger the organism, the more often the cycle of mitosis and cell division repeats itself. Cells in some animal embryos divide every 15 minutes. Most cells in adult animals, however, live from about 8 hours to over 100 days between divisions. Cells grown in a petri dish divide only a certain number of times, which is species specific. A human cell divides about 50 times. This phenomenon, called the Hayflick limit, is like a cell's division clock. If a cell is frozen after dividing 20 times, it will continue dividing another 30 times once it is thawed. This limit will hold even if the cell has been frozen for years. In addition, cells taken from older people divide fewer times than cells from younger people.

The overall rate of growth in humans illustrates how cell division is controlled throughout the life span. A newborn will double its weight within a few months, as illustrated in the graph in Figure 8-10. However, the rate of mitosis and cell division does not continue at this pace throughout life. A human usually reaches his or her ultimate height between the ages of 14 and 21. Although weight in humans does fluctuate, an adult does not double in size under normal conditions.

8-9 Growth Regulators in Healthy Cells

What causes a cell to undergo mitosis and cell division? Recall that surface-to-volume ratio imposes a limit on the continued growth of a cell. Once that limit is reached, the cell may divide. Research suggests that chemical changes in the cell contribute to the start of mitosis. Scientists have discovered chemicals called *growth factors* that cause mitosis and cell division in some animal cells.

In addition to conditions that initiate growth of cells, other factors seem to inhibit it. For example, healthy animal cells growing in petri dishes divide normally until a single, dense layer of cells covers the bottom of the dish. Once each of the cells touches another cell, they all stop dividing. This characteristic is described as **contact inhibition** which could be one factor that controls mitosis and cell division in healthy animal cells.

8-10 Abnormal Cell Division

Occasionally, a cell loses the ability to respond to the factors that regulate its growth. Such a cell will continue to grow and

a   b   c

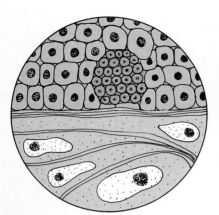 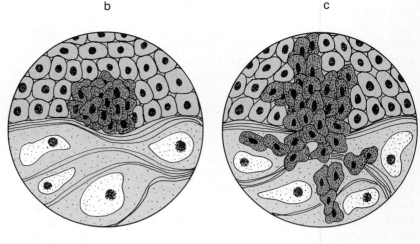

Benign tumor   Malignant tumor   Invasive malignant cells

Figure 8-11 Benign cells look very different from malignant cells when viewed through a microscope. a) Benign cells are uniform in appearance. They do not invade other body tissues. b) Malignant cells are irregular in shape and size. They grow in haphazardly shaped tumors within a tissue. c) Malignant cells migrate and invade other tissues.

divide in an uncontrolled way. The cells created by abnormal cell division likewise undergo unregulated division. Eventually a dense mass of abnormal cells, or *tumor*, is formed.

Tumors are not always life-threatening. Some tumors, called *benign tumors*, occur quite frequently. One example of a benign tumor is a wart. Warts result when a certain kind of virus invades skin cells and causes them to reproduce rapidly. Although warts are annoying, they are not dangerous. Another example is "skin tags," which are tiny nobs of raised skin cells. They too are annoying, yet harmless. Tumors also can develop inside the body. Breast tissue is a common site for tumor development. Most tumors found in breast tissue are benign.

Benign tumors do not usually threaten the life of their host. The cells in the tumor grow in one area of the body, and do not invade other tissues. Benign tumors can be surgically removed, and the affected individual usually suffers no ill-effects. If, however, a benign tumor is not removed, it will continue to grow. Large benign tumors can be very painful or interfere with an organ's normal function.

Another form of tumor, called a *malignant tumor*, is life-threatening. Malignant tumors are dangerous because the cells of the tumor do not remain in one area. They can migrate to and invade another tissue. Malignant breast tumors kill more than 20 000 women per year. Figure 8-11 illustrates some of the differences between benign and malignant tumors.

Malignant cells can enter the bloodstream and spread quickly throughout the body. Spreading can be delayed or prevented through the use of prescribed drugs or radiation treatments. Malignant tumors can be removed surgically, but their reappearance is unpredictable.

8-11 Cancer

Cancer is a condition in which malignant cells invade and destroy body tissues. Untreated, cancer is usually fatal. One in four people will develop cancer. More than 100 different kinds of cancer are recognized. Cancer cells do not necessarily divide faster than healthy cells, but they keep on dividing. A cancer cell growing in a petri dish divides well beyond the normal Hayflick limit of 50 divisions. Each type has a different cause and can affect the body in a different way. Curing all forms of cancer will not be easy.

Among the most common types of cancer are lung, breast, prostate, and colon-rectal cancer. Each of these diseases is stimulated by a cancer-causing agent, or **carcinogen**. Three major groups of carcinogens have been discovered: radiation, viruses, and chemicals. All these carcinogens attack the DNA. For example, excessive exposure to the ultraviolet radiation of the sun can break the DNA of skin cells. If these breaks disrupt a gene that controls cell division, the affected cells can become cancerous.

Certain viruses cause cancer by inserting their own DNA directly into that of a cell. Defective DNA does not respond to the normal regulators of cell growth and division. Cancer is frequently the result.

Research has shown that certain chemicals attack the base pairs in the DNA of many cells. These reactions slightly alter the structure of some base pairs. The next time the DNA replicates, new bases will not pair accurately to the old ones. If this occurs in a gene controlling cell division, cancer may result.

Cancer cells absorb nutrients at a faster rate than the normal cells from which they descend, and they secrete substances that

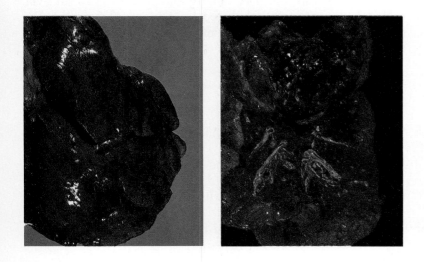

Figure 8-12 Cigarette smoke contains carcinogens that can cause lung cancer. These compounds alter the DNA in lung cells and cell division goes out of control. *Left:* normal lung; *Right:* cross section of lung tissue ravaged by cancer

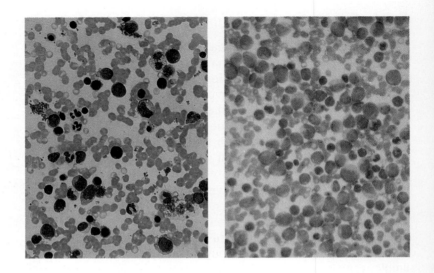

Figure 8-13 *Leukemia* is the name given to certain cancerous diseases of the cells that make white blood cells. When these cells divide uncontrollably, they produce abnormally large numbers of new white blood cells. *Left:* a normal blood sample; *Right:* An increase in the number and size of white blood cells is a symptom of leukemia. In both photos, the white blood cells are stained purple. The red blood cells appear gray.

promote blood vessel growth around them. Cancer cells thus nestle into healthy tissue and outcompete for space and nutrients with healthy tissue. Additionally, cancer cells do not stick to each other the way normal cells do. Cancer cells have the ability to break away from the main cluster. They are then carried in the blood stream where they continue to divide uncontrollably. Eventually these cancer cells become lodged in new tissue. Soon, unlimited cell division increases the total number of cancer cells within the healthy tissue. Eventually, normal cells die and are replaced by even more cancer cells. At this point, an entire organ often ceases to function properly.

There are other characteristics that separate cancer cells from normal cells. Cancer cells have irregular shapes and sizes, unusual numbers of nucleoli, and abnormal mitotic structures. The cells divide before they are mature and tend to grow all over each other, seemingly unaffected by contact inhibition. Much research is being done to learn more about the causes, prevention, and cures for cancer.

CHECKPOINT ◆

14. List several factors that influence the rate of mitosis and cell division.
15. What property do warts and cancers have in common?
16. What are the three major groups of carcinogens?
17. What property of cancer cells allows them to spread from one body part to another?
▶ 18. How would a knowledge of the processes of mitosis and cytokinesis aid cancer research?

▶ Denotes a question that involves *interpreting* and *applying* concepts.

LABORATORY ACTIVITY

HOW THE RATE OF DIFFUSION IN A CELL IS AFFECTED BY THE SURFACE-TO-VOLUME RATIO

Objectives and Skills

☐ *Describe* the relationship between cell size and the rate of diffusion.
☐ *Relate* the surface-to-volume ratio of a cell to mitosis and cell division.
☐ *Predict* the relationship between cell size and rate of diffusion.

Materials

250-mL beaker	block of agar-
clock or watch	phenolphthalein
metric ruler	100 mL of dilute sodium
plastic spoon	hydroxide solution
scalpel	safety goggles
paper towels	lab apron

Procedures and Observations

1. Read all instructions for this laboratory activity before you begin your work.
2. Put on safety goggles and a lab apron.
3. Obtain a large block of agar. Use a scalpel to cut the agar block into three cubes that measure 1 cm, 2 cm, and 3 cm on a side. **CAUTION: Use extreme care when using the scalpel. Cut in a direction that is away from yourself.**
4. Place the cubes in the beaker. Pour enough sodium hydroxide solution into the beaker to cover the cubes. Record the time. **CAUTION: Dilute sodium hydroxide is irritating to skin and eyes; it could damage clothing. Wear safety goggles and laboratory coat or apron. Wash off spills and splashes with plenty of water. Report to your teacher.**
5. Turn the blocks frequently with the plastic spoon for the next ten minutes.
6. Draw a data table like the one shown on

this page. Use the formulas from Figure 8-6 to calculate the values in the table.

DATA TABLE				
Cube Size	SA	V	SAV	Depth of Diffusion
1 cm				
2 cm				
3 cm				

7. After waiting 10 minutes, use the plastic spoon to remove the cubes from the beaker. Place the cubes on a paper towel. **CAUTION: Do not handle the cubes with your fingers.**
8. Use a scalpel to slice the first cube in half. Observe the cut surfaces. Measure the depth to which the sodium hydroxide has diffused. Record your results in the table. Rinse the scalpel and ruler.
9. Repeat step 7 with the other two cubes.
10. Discard your agar cubes and sodium hydroxide as directed.
11. Clean up your materials.

Analysis and Conclusions

1. What effect did sodium hydroxide have on the cubes?
2. Which cube has the largest surface-to-volume ratio? the smallest?
3. In which cube was the depth of diffusion greatest? smallest?
4. Based on this experiment, how would you predict cell size affects the rate of diffusion?
5. What effect does mitosis have upon the surface-to-volume ratio? How does mitosis help the cell maintain a chemical balance?

CUTTING EDGE

New Weapons to Fight Cancer

The challenge in vanquishing cancer is to destroy cancer cells while sparing healthy cells. The three standard cancer treatments—surgery, chemotherapy (drugs) and radiation—often harm healthy cells along with cancer cells. For this reason, researchers are seeking new approaches to taming tumors. Three promising alternative techniques use commonplace tools—heat, cold, and light.

Hyperthermia

Using heat to fight disease (hyperthermia) is an ancient art. A 5000-year-old Egyptian papyrus depicts a red-hot poker piercing a tumor.

Over the past decade, 10 000 patients have had tumors treated with heat, either externally with microwaves, or with tubes inserted into deeper tumors, through which microwave heat energy is sent. The absorbed energy causes the molecules in the targeted tissue to vibrate, generating heat that kills cancer cells.

Hyperthermia may be most effective when administered with a standard therapy. It works best in the interiors of tumors, whereas surgery and radiation work best on tumor edges. Hyperthermia can also be teamed with chemotherapy, because heat makes cancer cell membranes more fluid and therefore able to absorb more drug. The membranes of healthy cells, however, are more rigid. Heat also enables biological cancer fighters such as interferon to work better.

Cryotherapy

As with heat, using cold to kill abnormal cells isn't new. Freezing has been used to destroy growths of the skin, head, neck, urinary tract, and female reproductive system.

Now the technique is being turned to a very vital structure, the liver.

Many cancers that begin elsewhere in the body—the lungs, colon, or breasts, for example—spread to the liver, even if they are eliminated from the first site. Treating the liver tumors would be life-saving. This has been difficult, however, because the liver is both inaccessible and delicate, and destroying large portions of it can too severely impair its many functions. Gary Onik, M.D., of Allegheny Hospital in Pittsburgh has developed a way to freeze out liver tumors.

First surgery is performed to expose the liver. Then Dr. Onik uses an ultrasound scanner to locate the tumors, and

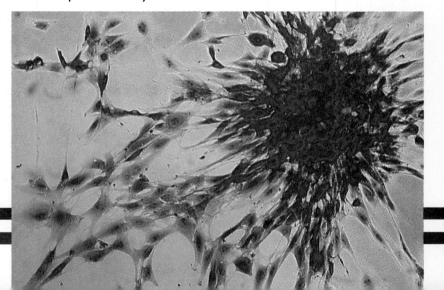

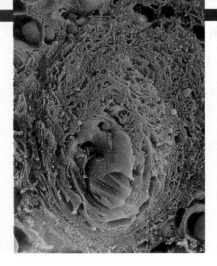

inserts fine hollow needles at the site. Tiny capsules containing liquid nitrogen are sent through the needles, and they freeze the targeted tumor cells to −323° F. Each tumor receives 3 freezes of 8 minutes each. The cancerous tissue dies immediately, but it takes about 6 months for it to be replaced by scar tissue. Also, the tumor cell surfaces are altered in a way that stimulates the immune system, perhaps guarding against a recurrence.

Photodynamic Therapy

In photodynamic therapy (PDT), a laser light (intense light of a single wavelength) is used to excite a drug that has been sent into cancerous tissue. The drug is a chemical cousin of porphyrin, which is part of hemoglobin, the molecule that carries oxygen in red blood cells. Next an argon laser is applied to the tumor site. Light from an argon laser is blue-green, and it is absorbed by tissues with the complementary colors red and orange. Blood would absorb the laser light.

When a molecule of the photosensitive drug absorbs the argon laser light, its oxygen atoms are boosted to a higher energy level. This starts a chain reaction of unstable molecules, called free radicals, which interact with neighboring cells, causing damage. Membranes both within and surrounding red blood cells unravel, and the cells die. Cancerous tumors have lush blood vessel networks to fuel their runaway growth, so they are particularly vulnerable to PDT which effectively cuts the tumor's source of fuel.

A patient receives an injection of the photosensitive drug two to three days before the laser is delivered through a fiber-optic endoscope, a narrow, lighted tube snaked through a natural body opening or surgically inserted. Care is taken to avoid healthy but bloody structures, such as the kidney, liver, or spleen. Afterward the patient must avoid sunlight for several weeks because the drug collects in small blood vessels at the skin's surface.

Like hyperthermia and cryosurgery, PDT is still experimental, but its seems to be very successful on cancers of the bladder, throat, lung, and colon and may help treat Kaposi's sarcoma, a cancer often seen in AIDS patients.

DISCUSSION & RESEARCH

1. How does each of these three cancer therapies attempt to target only the cancerous tissue?
2. How can each of the three new therapies be used along with existing treatments?
3. If you had cancer, would you prefer to be treated with surgery, radiation, or chemotherapy? Would you prefer to try a new treatment?

CHAPTER REVIEW

Summary

▶ Cells produce new cells through the processes of mitosis and cytokinesis. During mitosis the already duplicated DNA is equally distributed to opposite sides of the cell. During cytokinesis the contents of the cell are divided into two new cells.

▶ The stages of mitosis describe a continuous progression of changes in the cell that result in cell reproduction. These stages include prophase, metaphase, anaphase, and telophase. They are followed by interphase, which is a period of growth that precedes the next cell division.

▶ A cell must maintain an efficient surface-to-volume ratio in order to survive. When a cell reaches a certain size, it divides.

▶ To overcome the limits of surface-to-volume ratios, an organism must be multicellular.

▶ Mitosis and cytokinesis in unicellular organisms result in reproduction. Mitosis and cytokinesis in multicellular organisms are the mechanisms for growth, repair, replacement, and regeneration of new cells.

▶ Although every cell in an organism contains the same DNA, only a certain portion of that DNA is active in any one cell. Therefore, each type of cell makes a specific set of proteins. As a result, each cell type has a unique structure and function.

▶ Groups of similar cells compose tissues, groups of tissues compose organs, and organs working together form a system.

▶ Some cells lose the ability to regulate their rate of division and grow into tumors. Cancer tumors spread throughout the body and invade other tissues.

▶ Cancer therapy is based upon an understanding of the principles of mitosis and the nature of cell function.

Vocabulary

anaphase	metaphase
cancer	microfilament
carcinogen	mitosis
centromere	mitotic spindle
chromatids	organ
contact inhibition	organ system
cytokinesis	prophase
furrow	regeneration
interphase	spindle fiber
karyokinesis	telophase
kinetochore	tissue

Concept Mapping

Construct a concept map for cell reproduction. Include the following terms: mitosis, centrioles, furrow, chromosomes, cytokinesis, cell plate, and mitotic spindle. Add additional terms as you need them.

Review

Match the phase of mitosis with the proper description.

1. prophase
2. metaphase
3. anaphase
4. telophase

a. Chromatids line up at the equator.
b. Chromosomes reach opposite poles.
c. Chromosomes begin to move toward opposite poles.
d. The spindle forms.

5. How is the ratio of surface area to volume affected by an increase in cell size?
6. How do the processes of mitosis and cell division benefit unicellular organisms?
7. What role does kinesin play in mitosis?

8. How are the needs of a cell affected by an increase in the volume of a cell?
9. How do multicellular organisms benefit from mitosis and cell division?
10. List some factors that control growth in healthy cells.
11. In what ways does cytokinesis in plants differ from that in animals?
12. Explain how an increase in the volume of a cell affects the rate of diffusion.
13. How can so many different types of cells come from the same DNA code?
14. What is meant by contact inhibition?
15. Name three carcinogens. Explain how each one may affect DNA.
16. How do cancer cells differ from normal cells?
17. During what phase of mitosis does the nuclear envelope disintegrate and the mitotic spindle form?

Interpret and Apply

18. What factors influence the life span of a cell?
19. Microtubules and microfilaments are both part of the cytoskeleton. How does each function in the process of nuclear and cytoplasmic division?
20. The data below represent the growth in height of a stem of bamboo. Construct a growth curve for this plant by graphing the data in the table. Place *Age* on the x-axis and *Height* on the y-axis. Explain the trend indicated by the curve.

Age (weeks)	1	3	5	7	9
Height (meters)	0.7	2.5	6.2	10.2	13.2

21. Compare the rates of recovery from a broken leg in a young girl and in her grandmother. Explain your answer.

22. The most rapidly multiplying bacteria have a life span that lasts 11 minutes. How many cells could form from one cell in 4 hours?

Critical Thinking

23. If certain bacteria reproduce at a rapid rate, why is the world not overrun by these organisms?
24. Cancer is thought to result from a change in one cell. How can a change in one cell do so much damage?
25. What would happen if all the mitochondria in a cell ended up in only one of the two cells following cytokinesis?
26. If isolated from your body, could one of your skin cells live independently? Explain your answer.
27. Describe one event in mitosis and one in cytokinesis that illustrates the *fluid* nature of membranes.

DATA FAKED TO GET GRANT

Case Study 1

John Hendricks is a graduate student working on a thesis. He greatly admires his advisor, Dr. Marx. John's thesis is based on research Dr. Marx has been working on for over 25 years. It involves the study of how the drug ritalin affects the behavior of hyperactive children.

While going over the results of one of Dr. Marx's studies, John notices some odd data that do not seem to agree with other studies he has read. He checks other sources against Dr. Marx's data. He can see that Dr. Marx could not have such perfect results.

John also knows that Dr. Marx was given $100,000 from a private organization to run studies on ritalin. He thinks the data might have been faked because Dr. Marx needed more funding. Dr. Marx probably thought that with good results more grant money would be available.

The drug tests could affect when and how doctors prescribe ritalin to children because Dr. Marx's work is among the best in the field.

1. What should John do?
2. Since the study is already done, would it make any difference if John just forgot his discovery?
3. If you were on a committee investigating Dr. Marx, what would you advise? Why?
4. What effect would revealing this problem have on the scientific community and the public?

Case Study 2

Dr. Kenneth Pinkerton is a well-known plant researcher and has worked at a university for 24 years. He considers himself an expert on Dutch elm disease, which spreads from tree to tree quickly and kills thousands of elms every year.

Last year, Dr. Pinkerton used recombinant DNA (rDNA) techniques and created bacteria that produce an antibiotic (a drug) that is effective against the fungus that causes Dutch elm disease.

He perfected the bacteria in the lab and knew the rules for using rDNA in research. He wanted to try out the bacteria on real trees. The rules state that a permit from the Environmental Protection Agency (EPA) is needed to release an rDNA organism into the environment. EPA approval of a permit can take up to a year.

Two days before he applied for the EPA permit he tried his procedure on fourteen American elm trees. His experiment involved injecting the trees with Dutch elm disease and then with his altered bacteria. Before this time, the only diseased trees were four miles from the campus. Thirty days later he informed the university of his actions.

Although he had committed no crime, the university held a hearing to decide what to do with Dr. Pinkerton.

1. If you were on the board, what punishment would you have given Dr. Pinkerton? Why?
2. Would you feel differently if he had injected rDNA bacteria into a sick human being without permission? Why or why not?
3. Can you justify Dr. Pinkerton's decision not to wait for EPA approval?
4. Give two reasons in favor of having strong regulations on working with rDNA organisms and releasing them into the environment. List some rules that scientists should follow.

UNIT REVIEW I

Synthesis

1. The opening pages of this unit contain four photographs. These photographs illustrate a theme common to the chapters of the unit. Identify the theme and describe how it relates to what you studied in the chapters.

2. **Process of Science:** Suppose you are the scientist in charge of examining rocks from the planet Mars. On one of these rocks is a fuzzy green patch. Outline the procedures you would use to determine whether or not the material was alive. What precautions would you take with this rock?

3. **Homeostasis:** Many unicellular organisms that live in fresh water contain organelles called water vacuoles. Excess water from the cytoplasm of these organisms collects in the water vacuole and is then released from the cell. How does this organelle help these microorganisms maintain homeostasis? What would happen to these organisms if they did not have a water vacuole? Why is this organelle common in organisms that live in fresh water but not in those that live in salt water?

4. **Structure Is Related to Function:** Membranes are found throughout all cells. Describe the role of membranes in the following processes: (a) maintaining homeostasis, (b) respiration, (c) secretion, and (d) cell division.

5. **Structure Is Related to Function:**
   a. What elements are in a phosphate group?
   b. Name two kinds of molecules that contain phosphate groups. How does the structure of these molecules affect their function in the cell?
   c. Living things share certain characteristics. Identify two of these characteristics that involve molecules with phosphate groups.

Critical Thinking

6. **Process of Science:** Many newspapers and magazines have a section devoted to science and technology. The stories that appear in this section explain some of the developments and techniques used in scientific research. Such stories are often written by reporters with little background in science. Explain how it might be possible for you to judge if a particular story is accurate. How can you know whether or not the facts reported are correct?

7. **Structure Is Related to Function:** Some laundry detergents contain enzymes. Manufacturers of this product claim that enzymes remove grass and blood stains better than detergents without enzymes. Why might enzymes take out some stains that ordinary detergents cannot? Where do you think these enzymes might come from? Suggest reasons why these enzymes might not be as effective as the manufacturers claim.

Additional Reading

deDuve, C. *A Guided Tour of the Living Cell.* San Francisco: Freeman, 1985.

Doolittle, R.F. "Proteins," *Scientific American.* October 1985.

Harre, Rom. *Great Scientific Experiments.* New York: Oxford, 1983.

Medawar, P.B. *Advice to a Young Scientist.* New York: Harper, 1984.

Thomas, Lewis. *The Lives of a Cell: Notes of a Biology Watcher.* New York: Viking, 1974.

Watson, James D. *The Double Helix.* New York: Atheneum, 1968.

GENETICS AND EVOLUTION

Leopard

Protective spines on tree trunk

Cryptic moth on leaf litter

Mole emerging from burrow

Chapter 9 **Basis of Heredity**
Patterns of Inheritance
The Cellular Basis of Heredity

Chapter 10 **Chromosomes and Genes**
Chromosomes and Inheritance
Changes in Genetic Material

Chapter 11 **Human Inheritance**
Patterns of Inheritance
Human Disorders
Detecting Disorders
Treating Disorders

Chapter 12 **Applications of Genetics**
Controlled Breeding
Artificial Methods of Genetic Control

Chapter 13 **Population Genetics**
Variation in Populations
Changes in Populations

Chapter 14 **Evolution**
Evidence of Evolution
Theory of Evolution
Process of Evolution

Chapter 15 **History of Life**
Origin of Life
Multicellular Life

Chapter 16 **Human Evolution**
The Human as a Primate
Tracing Human Evolution

Chapter 17 **Classification of Life**
Systems of Classification
Identifying Organisms

BASIS OF HEREDITY

Overview

PATTERNS OF INHERITANCE

9-1   Mendel's Hybrid Peas
9-2   Dominant and Recessive Traits
9-3   The Principle of Segregation
9-4   Genotype and Phenotype
9-5   Solving Genetics Problems
9-6   Testcross
9-7   Principle of Independent Assortment
9-8   Codominance

THE CELLULAR BASIS OF HEREDITY

9-9   Chromosome Number
9-10 Asexual and Sexual Reproduction
9-11 Meiosis
9-12 The Chromosome Theory of Inheritance

Why are these young birds less colorful than their parents?

PATTERNS OF INHERITANCE

Fascination with the passage of traits probably dates back to the first humans. Farmers, in what is now Egypt, carefully bred wheat 10 000 years ago. Asian horse breeders kept detailed records of their animal's traits 4000 years ago. Even the Old Testament mentions the inheritance pattern of hemophilia.

The first scientist to correctly interpret patterns of inheritance was an Austrian monk named Gregor Mendel. He lived over 100 years ago in a monastery school near what is now Brno, Czechoslovakia. Mendel studied patterns of inheritance by breeding pea plants in his monastery garden. His study took over seven years and required him to collect data from over 30 000 individual plants. Although Mendel's work was ignored during his lifetime, it provided the basis for the modern study of heredity.

How could Mendel learn so much from a pea plant? How did he set up his experiments?

9-1 Mendel's Hybrid Peas

In the early 1800s, very little was known about how inherited characteristics, or **traits**, were transmitted from one generation to the next. During the later part of the century, it was found that reproductive cells called **gametes** carry genetic information. The information contained in one gamete is combined with another gamete in a process called **fertilization**.

Mendel studied patterns of inheritance by breeding pea plants in his monastery garden. Much of his success can be attributed to the fact that the flower of a pea plant has both male and female reproductive parts. Every flower can therefore produce both male gametes, called **sperm**, and female gametes, called **eggs**. Because the flowers of pea plants have both kinds of gametes, the plants are capable of self-fertilization. Yet, it was also possible for Mendel to cross-fertilize plants. As a result, he could mate, or breed, different plants in a controlled way.

Mendel bred plants that were distinctive for a particular trait. For example, he obtained tall pea plants and allowed them to self-fertilize for many generations. He noticed that the tall pea plants in the garden always produced seeds that grew into tall plants. Likewise, short plants always produced seeds that grew into short plants. The tall and short pea plants were two distinct varieties, or pure lines. All self-fertilized offspring of **pure lines** display the same trait as their parents. When parents of two different pure lines are crossed, the offspring are called **hybrids**.

Mendel studied the inheritance of pea traits by designing his experiments carefully. Initially, he studied one trait at a time.

Section Objectives

A *Explain* the difference between genotype and phenotype.

B *Distinguish* between a homozygous genotype and a heterozygous genotype.

C *State* and *give examples* for each of Mendel's principles.

D *Compare* complete dominance with codominance.

E *Construct* and *interpret* Punnett squares for monohybrid, dihybrid crosses, and testcrosses.

Figure 9-1   The seven pairs of pea plant characteristics that Mendel studied are all visible traits.

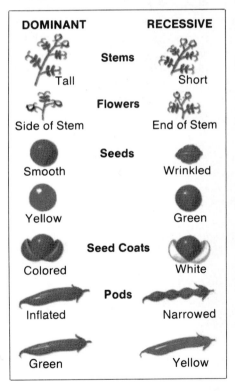

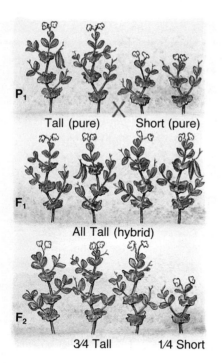

P₁

Tall (pure)   X   Short (pure)

F₁

All Tall (hybrid)

F₂

3/4 Tall   1/4 Short

Figure 9-2 When pure lines of tall and short pea plants are crossed, the offspring are all tall hybrids. Crossing the tall hybrids yields some tall and some short pea plants.

The traits he chose, such as plant height or seed texture, could be distinguished easily. Each trait appeared in two different forms. Just as a light switch is either on or off, the traits Mendel studied were in either one form or another. The texture of a seed was either smooth or wrinkled. The height of a plant was either tall or short. Mendel selected seven such contrasting characteristics, as pictured in Figure 9-1.

To understand what Mendel did, consider his study of plant height. Mendel began by crossing a pure line of tall pea plants with a pure line of short pea plants. He referred to this generation as the parental generation, or the **P₁ generation**. What would you expect the offspring to look like? Look at Figure 9-2. You might have expected the offspring from this cross to be a blend of their parents—to be of medium height. This was not the case. All the offspring were tall. Mendel called this generation the **F₁ generation**. (*F* stands for *filial*, which means "of an offspring.") There were no short or medium-sized plants in the F₁ generation. The trait for shortness seemed to have disappeared! Did the F₁ plants lose their ability to produce short plants?

To answer this question, Mendel produced the next generation of pea plants. Mendel did this by allowing plants from the F₁ generation to self-fertilize. The offspring are called the **F₂ generation**. Look again at Figure 9-2. Surprisingly, not all of the F₂ offspring were tall. One out of every four of the F₂ offspring was short. The trait for short pea plants had reappeared. Mendel repeated his experiment by crossing other F₁ plants and found similar results. He had discovered a significant pattern in the inheritance of traits in pea plants.

9-2 Dominant and Recessive Traits

Mendel explained the results of his crosses with a simple, yet brilliant hypothesis. He stated that distinct units of heredity, or factors, were responsible for the inherited traits. Furthermore, he thought that two factors controlled any single trait. For example, one factor produced tall plants and one produced short plants. In the F₁ plants, the tall factor appeared to be **dominant** over the short factor. In the F₂ generation, the hidden, or **recessive**, factor reappeared. The recessive factor seemed to *recede* into the background in the presence of the dominant factor.

Mendel experimented by crossing pea plants with other pairs of contrasting traits, such as seed texture and seed pod color. From the results, Mendel identified one factor in each pair as dominant and the other as recessive. In all of these crosses, only the dominant trait appeared in the F₁ generation. The recessive trait reappeared in the F₂ generation.

9-3 The Principle of Segregation

In analyzing his results, Mendel found that all recessive traits reappeared in the F_2 generation. Not only did the recessive traits reappear, but they reappeared in a constant proportion, or ratio. About three fourths of the plants showed the dominant trait. One fourth showed the recessive trait. In other words, for any pair of contrasting traits, the F_2 generation showed a ratio of about 3 dominant to 1 recessive, or 3:1. Mendel wondered why the ratio was 3 to 1 instead of 10 to 1 or 5 to 1.

Mendel proposed a principle that explained the results he observed. This explanation not only made sense out of the 3-to-1 ratio, but also correctly predicted the ratios for other crosses. This explanation is called the **principle of segregation**. The principle has three parts:

1. Hereditary characteristics are determined by distinct units or factors.
2. For each characteristic, an individual carries two factors, one inherited from each parent.
3. The two factors of each pair segregate from each other and end up in separate gametes.

Today these factors are called **genes** and are known to be specific portions of DNA molecules. Genes determine the characteristics of an organism. Alternate forms of a gene are called **alleles** [ə lēls′]. For example, a gene governs the seed color of peas. One allele of that gene produces green seeds and the other allele produces yellow seeds. Only one allele for each trait is passed on to the offspring from each parent.

■ BIOLOGY INSIGHT ────

Continuity of Life: A dominant trait is not necessarily better for the organism than a recessive one. In fact, it may be harmful. For example, Huntington disease, which causes brain degeneration affecting coordination, movement, and personality, is caused by a dominant gene.

9-4 Genotype and Phenotype

To make work in genetics simpler, letter symbols are used to represent alleles. A dominant allele is usually indicated by a capital letter. The matching recessive allele is indicated by the *same letter* in lowercase. For example, the allele for tallness is *T*, while the allele for shortness is *t*. Different letters are used to indicate other traits. For example, green pea pods are dominant over yellow pods. Thus, the capital letter *G* is used for green, whereas lower case *g* indicates yellow.

An organism inherits two alleles for each trait—one from each parent. Therefore, two letters are needed to describe each combination of alleles, or **genotype**, for that trait. Suppose a pea plant inherits an allele for tallness from each parent. The genotype of this pea plant would be expressed as *TT*.

Consider what other combinations of alleles are possible. A pea plant with the genotype *tt* has two alleles for shortness, whereas a plant with genotype *Tt* has one allele of each kind. Two of these three genotypes, *TT* and *tt*, have alleles that are identical. These genotypes are termed **homozygous**. A third genotype, *Tt*, has alleles that are different. This genotype is termed **heterozygous**.

An organism's genotype determines how a trait will be expressed. A plant with the genotype *TT* obviously will be tall. Since the allele for tallness is dominant over the allele for shortness, an organism with the genotype *Tt* will also appear tall. The way an organism's traits are expressed is called its **phenotype** [fē′ nə tīp]. The phenotype of an organism does not always reveal the combination of alleles in the organism. Organisms with the same phenotype, like *TT* and *Tt*, may have different genotypes.

Figure 9-4 The allele for green pod color in pea plants is dominant over yellow. The inheritance of pod color was one of many traits Mendel studied.

Genotype	GG	Gg	gg
Phenotype			
Pure or Hybrid?	Pure	Hybrid	Pure
Homozygous or Heterozygous?	Homozygous (dominant)	Heterozygous	Homozygous (recessive)

However, in the case of a recessive phenotype like shortness, the genotype of the pea plant must be *tt*. Can you see why this is so?

9-5 Solving Genetics Problems

If you know the genotype of the parents, it is possible to predict the likelihood of an offspring inheriting a particular phenotype. Prediction is important in the field of genetics. Predicting the likelihood of an offspring's phenotype involves the concept of probability. **Probability** simply means the chance that a given event will occur. It is usually expressed as either a fraction or a percent.

Calculating probabilities involves visualizing genetic crosses. Figure 9-5 will help you visualize a cross between parents who have the genotypes *TT* and *tt*. What is the probability that the offspring will be tall? According to the principle of segregation, each parent contributes one allele of a trait to an offspring. The tall parent plant, *TT*, can only contribute one kind of allele, *T*. The short parent plant, *tt*, also has only one kind of allele to contribute, *t*.

The genotype of the offspring are a combination of gametes from both parents. Thus, in Figure 9-6, all the offspring have the genotype *Tt*. Since tall is dominant over short, all the offspring will be tall. The probability of the offspring from this cross being tall is 100 percent.

Another helpful way to visualize the results of a genetic cross is by using a **Punnett square**, a chart that shows all possible genotypes of a cross. This chart was devised by the British mathematician and biologist R. C. Punnett. The Punnett squares in Figure 9-7 show the possible results of a cross between two pea plants, both are heterozygous for plant height. This cross is called a **monohybrid cross**.

There are four possible genotypes from this cross. Look at the Punnett square. There is one box with *TT*, two boxes with *Tt*, and one box with *tt*. This ratio can be written as 1 *TT*:2 *Tt*:1 *tt*,

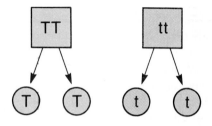

Figure 9-5 A tall pea plant, genotype *TT* can contribute only gametes with the tall allele, *T*. A short pea plant can only contribute gametes with the short allele, *t*.

Figure 9-6 During fertilization, the alleles combine to form offspring with both tall and short alleles, *Tt*.

Figure 9-7 This figure shows you how to construct a Punnett square for a monohybrid cross. The squares with circles represent gametes. Male gametes are shown with "tails." Letters inside the circles identify the allele carried by each gamete. Each box corresponds to the genotype of one kind of offspring.

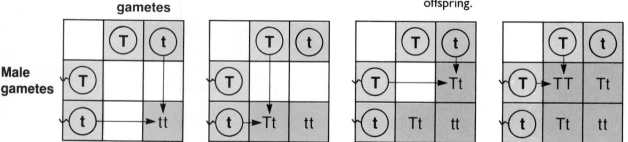

Female gametes

Male gametes

Figure 9-8 Mendel developed the testcross to determine the unknown genotype of pea plants. *Top:* Results if the unknown plant is heterozygous. *Bottom:* Results of the testcross if the unknown plant is homozygous dominant.

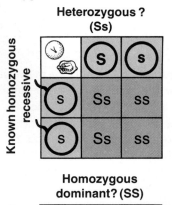

Heterozygous ?
(Ss)

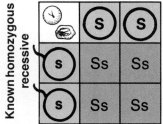

Homozygous
dominant? (SS)

or simply 1:2:1. Each offspring has a 1/4 chance of having the homozygous dominant genotype, *TT*, a 2/4 (1/2) chance of having the heterozygous genotype, *Tt*, and a 1/4 chance of having the homozygous recessive genotype, *tt*.

What ratio of offspring look tall or short? Remember that heterozygous individuals and individuals that are homozygous for the dominant allele exhibit the same phenotype. Therefore, the probable ratio of tall offspring to short offspring is the sum of the probabilities of the heterozygous genotype (*Tt*) and the homozygous dominant genotype (*TT*), or 3:1. This ratio is the one that Mendel found in his F_2 generation. This same ratio applies in monohybrid crosses where one allele is dominant over another.

9-6 Testcross

Is there a way to determine the genotype of an organism? If the organism shows the recessive trait, you know that the genotype of that individual is homozygous recessive. A short pea plant must have a genotype of *tt*. Any other combination will result in a tall plant. But what if, in fact, the plant is tall? How can you tell whether an organism showing a dominant phenotype is homozygous dominant (*TT*) or heterozygous (*Tt*)?

To determine such an unknown genotype, Mendel performed another type of cross as illustrated in Figure 9-8. Mendel obtained a pea plant that produced smooth seeds. Its genotype was unknown. The plant could have been *SS* or *Ss*. *S* represents the dominant smooth allele and *s* is for the recessive wrinkled allele. Mendel crossed this plant of an unknown genotype with a plant having a known genotype, the homozygous recessive (*ss*) plant. This type of cross is called a **testcross**. Mendel hypothesized the outcomes of both alternatives:

1. If the unknown plant was *SS*, crossing it with plants that were *ss* would yield offspring that were all of the genotype *Ss*. These plants would have smooth peas.
2. If the unknown plant had the genotype *Ss*, the probability was that half of the offspring would be *Ss* and half would be *ss*. Since these offspring would have different phenotypes, they would be easy to distinguish. Some would have smooth peas, and some would have wrinkled peas. The genotype of the unknown parent would become known.

The testcross is important to plant and animal breeders. They use the testcross to determine whether new varieties of organisms have established pure lines.

9-7 Principle of Independent Assortment

Organisms are a combination of many traits. So far, you have learned about crosses involving only a single trait. It is possible to study the inheritance of two traits such as pea color and plant height at the same time.

Mendel carried out thousands of dihybrid crosses with his pea plants. These crosses led him to describe a second pattern of inheritance called the principle of independent assortment.

The **principle of independent assortment** explains that the inheritance of alleles for one trait does not affect the inheritance of alleles for another trait. For example, whether a plant is short or tall has no effect on whether its seeds are smooth or wrinkled. All of the alleles segregate independently.

To test the principle of independent assortment, Mendel crossed plants that were homozygous dominant for height and pod color (*TTGG*) with plants that were homozygous recessive for height and pod color (*ttgg*). Can you predict what the offspring of this cross would look like? Remember that one parent can contribute only alleles for tallness and green pods. The other parent can contribute only alleles for shortness and yellow pods. As a result, every offspring inherits one dominant allele and one recessive allele for each trait. All the F_1 plants must be tall with green pods.

If a plant is heterozygous for both height and pod color, the possible parent contributions are different. In this case, a parent plant can contribute either one of *two* different alleles for each trait. Figure 9-9 illustrates the possible combinations of alleles that such a plant can contribute. Remember that only one allele of each pair is passed to any single offspring. Thus there are four possible combinations of alleles. Crossing two heterozygous plants yields many more combinations of traits. This type of cross is called a **dihybrid cross**.

The number of possible gene combinations in the offspring of a dihybrid cross are much greater than in a monohybrid cross. Look at the Punnett square in Figure 9-10. As predicted by the principle of independent assortment, individual plants may be dominant for one trait and recessive for another, dominant for both traits, or recessive for both traits. If you study this Punnett square, you will see that there is a 9-in-16 chance that the offspring will be dominant for both height and pod color. One out of every 16 plants (1/16) has a chance of being recessive for both characteristics. Although there are only four combinations of phenotypes possible from this dihybrid cross, there are many more combinations of genotypes. How many can you find?

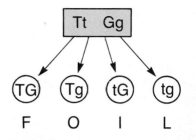

Figure 9-9 A parent can contribute one allele from each pair of alleles to an offspring. For a parent that is heterozygous for two separate traits, four possible combinations exist as shown above. *FOIL* is a memory device for figuring out the combinations: *F* is for the first two alleles of each trait; *O* is the outer two; *I* is the inner two; and *L* is the last two.

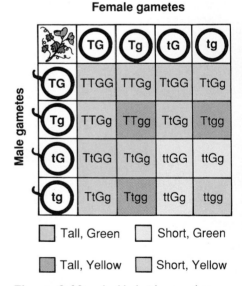

Figure 9-10 A dihybrid cross has 16 possible combinations of alleles for offspring. Which is the most common phenotype?

Figure 9-11 What is the genotype of this black Andalusian fowl?

9-8 Codominance

Up to this point, all of the characteristics you have studied are governed by dominance of one allele over the other. Mendel's pea plants were either tall or short, wrinkled or smooth, had green pods or yellow pods, and so on.

However for some genes neither allele is dominant over the other. This situation is called codominance. In **codominance**, heterozygous individuals express traits that are a blend of the phenotypes of two alleles. An example of codominance occurs in the Andalusian fowl, shown in Figure 9-11. The allele for feather color in this bird is either black or white. Birds that are homozygous are either black or white. However, in heterozygous birds, both the black allele and the white allele are expressed. Such a bird appears blue.

In writing genotypes for codominance, the lowercase initial letter of each allele is used. Thus a black fowl has the genotype *bb* and a white fowl has the genotype *ww*. This notation indicates that both alleles have equal influence in determining the phenotype of the offspring.

Crosses between heterozygous organisms that show codominance are similar to the monohybrid crosses you learned about in Section 9-5. The ratios of possible genotypes are the same. If two heterozygous fowl (blue:*bw*) are crossed, their offspring yield the monohybrid ratio of 1 homozygous dominant (*bb*): 2 heterozygotes (*bw*): 1 homozygous recessive (*ww*). In codominance, the phenotype of homozygous individuals is different from the phenotype of heterozygous individuals.

CHECKPOINT ◆

1. What term is used to describe the specific set of alleles an organism has for a trait?
2. What word describes an organism that carries two identical alleles?
3. What principle states that the inheritance of one characteristic does not affect the inheritance of another characteristic?
▶ 4. How would you determine whether a green-podded plant is homozygous or heterozygous?
▶ 5. A cross between a pure line of red-flowered snapdragons and a pure line of white-flowered snapdragons produced offspring with pink flowers. Is this an example of complete or codominance? Explain.

▶ Denotes a question that involves *interpreting* and *applying* concepts.

THE CELLULAR BASIS OF HEREDITY

Although Mendel's work was appreciated for the cleverness of his experiments and interpretations, his theories had no effect on the science of his time. Mendel's pairs of factors made sense, but their existence could not be demonstrated. No one had ever seen a factor. Nor were the scientists of Mendel's time aware of the existence of chromosomes or DNA.

9-9 Chromosome Number

Multicellular organisms are composed of two kinds of cells—reproductive cells and somatic cells. Reproductive cells contain a single set, or the **haploid** number of chromosomes. The haploid number of chromosomes is symbolized by the letter n. **Somatic cells**, or body cells, of most organisms contain two sets, or the **diploid** number of chromosomes. The diploid number is written as "$2n$."

The 46 chromosomes in your somatic cells actually are 23 matched pairs of chromosomes ($23 \times 2 = 46$). Matched pairs of chromosomes are called **homologous chromosomes**. You could think of homologous chromosomes as a pair of socks. Like socks, homologous chromosomes are the same size and shape. Unlike a pair of socks, however, homologous chromosomes are not identical. Because each member of the pair originated from a different parent, they do not carry exactly the same information.

9-10 Asexual and Sexual Reproduction

Living things reproduce in two ways. **Asexual reproduction** results in offspring that are identical to their single parent. Organisms employ a wide variety of methods of asexual reproduction. In all cases, however, the new individuals are the product of mitosis and thus are genetically identical to the parent.

In **sexual reproduction**, a new individual is formed after a female gamete is fertilized by a male gamete. The haploid gametes combine to form a diploid cell called a **zygote**. A zygote carries the combined genetic material of both gametes: two complete sets of chromosomes, one set from each parent. The zygote divides by mitosis and develops into a new organism. Since the zygote is a diploid cell, every somatic cell produced by mitosis also will be a diploid cell. Thus all the body, or somatic cells, of most organisms are diploid. Most cells in your body, except egg, sperm, and liver cells, are diploid.

Section Objectives

F *Explain* what is meant by homologous chromosomes.

G *Distinguish* between sexual and asexual reproduction.

H *Describe* the process of meiosis.

I *Compare* and *contrast* mitosis and meiosis.

J *Explain* how the chromosome theory accounts for the principles of segregation and independent assortment.

Figure 9-12 A pair of homologous chromosomes is shown. Usually the two chromosomes of a homologous pair are derived from two different parents. Exceptions do occur, as in the case of self-fertilizing plants.

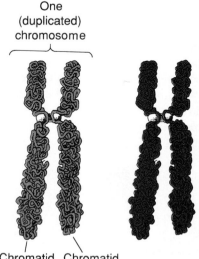

One (duplicated) chromosome

Chromatid Chromatid

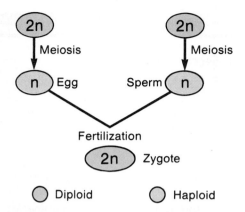

Meiosis

Meiosis

Egg   Sperm

Fertilization

Zygote

◯ Diploid   ◯ Haploid

Figure 9-13 Sexual reproduction begins with meiosis and ends at fertilization. In this process, meiosis precedes the formation of gametes, which are haploid sex cells. At fertilization, the nuclei of the two haploid cells fuse, restoring the diploid number of chromosomes in the zygote (a new individual).

Figure 9-14 The process of meiosis occurs in the nucleus of gamete-producing cells. Three pairs of homologous chromosomes are shown here. Meiosis requires two divisions, which proceed through stages having the same names as those in mitosis.

9-11 Meiosis

How does an organism with diploid body cells produce haploid gametes? The change occurs through a process called meiosis. During **meiosis** [mī ō' səs] cells are produced with chromosome numbers that have been *reduced* from diploid ($2n$) to haploid (n). Meiosis occurs in all organisms that reproduce sexually. In many complex plants and animals, meiosis occurs in specialized sex organs.

During meiosis, the chromosomes of a diploid cell replicate. The appearance of the chromosomes during meiosis is similar to their appearance in mitosis. Unlike mitosis, however, meiosis includes two cell divisions that yield four haploid cells. These two divisions are distinguished by the Roman numerals I and II. The stages of meiosis are shown in Figure 9-14.

Interphase Before meiosis begins, the chromosomes replicate much as they did at the start of mitosis. As a result, the nucleus now contains double the normal number of chromosomes. The chromosomes at this time are still in an uncoiled form, much like spaghetti on a plate.

Prophase I The chromosomes condense into short, thick rods that can be seen through a light microscope. Each chromosome is now double consisting of two chromatids. Homologous pairs of chromosomes come together on the spindle fibers. This pairing of homologous chromosomes is called **synapsis** [sə nap' səs]. In each synapsing group there are four chromatids—two chromatids composing each of the homologous chromosomes. Each group of four chromatids is called a **tetrad**.

Metaphase I The tetrads move along spindle fibers until they reach the equator of the cell.

Anaphase I The homologous chromosomes are pulled apart so that the pairs of chromatids from each tetrad move toward opposite poles of the cell. The pattern of chromatid distribution is random. What is important, however, is that homologous chromosomes segregate and move in opposite directions.

Telophase I The cell divides into two smaller cells. Each new

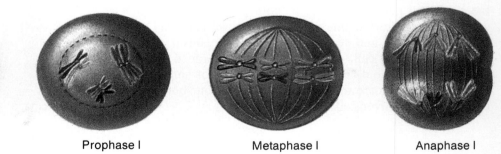

Interphase   Prophase I   Metaphase I   Anaphase I

cell contains one homologous chromosome from each original pair. The new cells are not identical since homologous chromosomes do not contain identical genetic information.

Interphase The chromatids do not replicate at this point. They uncoil and become invisible. Soon the two newly created cells enter into the second stage of meiosis.

The first cell division of meiosis is different from mitosis because number of chromosomes is reduced by one half. Thus meiosis is sometimes called a reduction division. The phases in the second meiotic division are similar to the phases of mitosis.

Prophase II The chromatid pairs condense and become visible.

Metaphase II Each chromatid pair moves along a spindle fiber until it reaches the equator.

Anaphase II The chromatids of each pair separate and move toward opposite poles of the cell. Each individual chromatid is now called a chromosome.

Telophase II Once the chromosomes reach their destinations, a nuclear envelope forms around each set of chromosomes.

At this point, each of the two cells divides to form two smaller cells. As a result of meiosis, one diploid cell undergoes two divisions to form four haploid cells. Thus each cell has only half as many chromosomes as the original diploid nucleus. But more important, each new cell contains a new combination of genetic material. The new combination makes offspring different from their parents. This is why siblings may resemble each other, but are not identical (unless they are identical twins).

The extent of genetic diversity possible because of meiosis is astounding. If an organism had only two pairs of chromosomes, they could line up in four (2^2) different ways during metaphase I to yield four different cells. However, human cells have 23 chromosome pairs. They can align more than eight million (2^{23}) different ways. However, even this number is exceeded because of a process called crossing over (Chapter 10).

| Telophase I | Interphase | Prophase II | Metaphase II | Anaphase II | Telophase II |

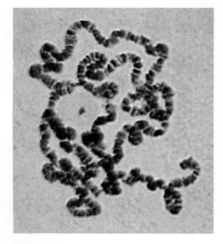

Figure 9-15 This is a light micrograph of chromosomes from the salivary gland of a fruit fly. Experiments with fruit flies were important to the development of the chromosome theory of inheritance.

9-12 The Chromosome Theory of Inheritance

In the spring of 1900 three botanists working in three different countries simultaneously rediscovered Mendel's work. After lying unread for 34 years, Mendel's work was suddenly recognized to contain the basic principles of heredity!

In 1902, two scientists pointed out that Mendel's results could be related to the movement of chromosomes during meiosis. These two men were Walter Sutton, an American graduate student, and Theodor Boveri, a German zoologist. Both Sutton and Boveri proposed that Mendel's "factors," were located on the chromosomes. One allele of each gene lay on one chromosome of each homologous pair. Different genes lay on different chromosomes. This explanation is called the **chromosome theory**.

The chromosome theory gives a cellular basis to Mendel's laws. According to the chromosome theory, genes occur in pairs because they are located on chromosomes, which also occur in pairs. One allele is derived from each parent because one chromosome comes from each parent.

The chromosome theory explains the law of segregation. Alleles segregate independently because they are located on homologous chromosomes. As you have learned, homologous chromosomes segregate during meiosis.

The law of independent assortment can also be explained by the chromosome theory. Genes on separate chromosomes assort independently because the chromosomes segregate randomly during meiosis. Not all genes assort independently, however. Genes on the same chromosome generally travel together.

With the announcement of the chromosome theory, the science of genetics began. Modern geneticists study and work with genes in ways that Mendel could never have imagined. They owe the foundations of their work to his pioneering experiments.

■ BIOLOGY INSIGHT

Continuity of Life: The chromosome theory explains the results of many experiments, and has been confirmed by the work of many scientists. It is one of the unifying principles of cellular biology and genetics.

CHECKPOINT ◆

6. Name the process and the type of reproduction in which two gametes fuse to form a zygote.
7. What is being reduced during the reduction division of meiosis?
8. Which cellular process produces two daughter cells identical to the parent cells?
9. During what stage of meiosis do the chromatids separate and move toward opposite poles?
10. What theory states that genes are located on chromosomes?

▶ Denotes a question that involves *interpreting* and *applying* concepts.

PROBABILITY AND HEREDITY

In this activity, you will simulate the chance formation and pairing of gametes and explore the effect of large numbers on the outcomes of random events.

Objectives and Skills

☐ *Simulate* Mendel's experiments by substituting coins for plant characteristics.
☐ *Compare* expected results with observed results.
☐ *Observe* the effects of the sample size on statistical results.

Materials

2 quarters
data sheets
pencil
paper

Procedure and Observations

1. Read all instructions for this laboratory activity before you begin your work.
2. On a separate piece of paper, draw a data table like the one shown on this page.

TOSS COMBINATIONS		
Result	**Count**	**Total**
Both heads HH		
One head, one tail HT		
Both tails TT		

3. Work in pairs. One person should flip the two coins at the same time. The other person records the outcome on the data table.
4. Repeat step 3 until you have completed four flips. What is your ratio of toss combinations for HH:HT:TT?

5. Repeat step 3 until you have completed a total of 50 flips. What is your ratio of toss combinations for HH:HT:TT?
6. Repeat step 3 until you have flipped the coins 100 times. What is your ratio of toss combinations for HH:HT:TT?

Analysis and Conclusions

1. Which combination of heads and tails did you expect to occur most frequently? Was your prediction correct?
2. What is the expected ratio of toss combinations for HH:HT:TT?
3. How did your actual ratio after 100 tosses compare with the expected ratio?
4. Were your actual results closer to the expected ratio after 4, 50, or 100 flips? Explain.
5. What biological processes are represented by flipping and pairing the two coins?
6. Apply the probabilities of a coin toss to that of two different alleles. How are the chances of getting two tails similar to getting a homozygous recessive genotype?

CHAPTER REVIEW

Summary

▸ Over 100 years ago, Mendel described the basic principles of genetics by carefully studying hybrid pea plants. His discoveries provided the foundations for modern genetics.

▸ The effects of genes reappear in hybrid crosses according to predictable ratios. In a hybrid cross of an F_1 generation, the expected ratio of dominant to recessive traits is 3:1. The ratio is explained by Mendel's principle of segregation.

▸ Genes on separate chromosomes are inherited independently. This principle of independent assortment leads to many different combinations of traits in offspring.

▸ Punnett squares can predict the probable outcome of a cross between parents of known genotypes. A testcross helps to determine an unknown genotype of an organism.

▸ Asexual reproduction results in offspring that are genetically identical to their single parent. Sexual reproduction occurs when two haploid gametes unite to form a diploid zygote.

▸ Meiosis is a process that reduces the diploid number of chromosomes to the haploid number.

▸ The chromosome theory of inheritance states that genes are located on chromosomes. This theory forms the basis for the science of genetics.

Vocabulary

allele
asexual reproduction
chromosome theory
codominance
dihybrid cross
diploid
dominant
egg
F_1 generation

F_2 generation
fertilization
gamete
gene
genetics
genotype
haploid
heterozygous

homologous chromosome
homozygous
hybrid
meiosis
monohybrid cross
P_1 generation
phenotype
principle of independent assortment
principle of segregation

probability
Punnett square
pure line
recessive
sexual reproduction
somatic cell
sperm
synapsis
testcross
tetrad
trait
zygote

Concept Mapping

Construct a concept map for cell reproduction. Include the following terms: somatic cells, gametes, zygote, number of chromosomes, asexual reproduction, sexual reproduction, mitosis, and meiosis. Use additional terms as you need them.

Review

1. What is a hybrid?
2. What is meant by the term *recessive allele*?
3. A mother has two alleles for a particular characteristic. How many does she give to an offspring?
4. What is the genotype of a pea plant with wrinkled seeds?
5. A white four-o'clock and a red four-o'clock produce offspring with pink flowers. This is an example of _____.
6. In which stage of meiosis does synapsis occur?
7. How many cells form from the process of meiosis?
8. What is the haploid chromosome number in humans? What is the diploid number?
9. The dihybrid cross illustrates which of Mendel's principles?

Interpret and Apply

10. Would cells in your bones be haploid or diploid? Explain.
11. Which kind of phenotype—dominant or recessive—can have more than one genotype? Give an example.
12. Is it possible to be heterozygous for a characteristic and show the recessive phenotype? Explain.
13. Does the height of a pea plant affect the color of the plant's flowers? Why or why not?
14. In a hybrid cross between homozygous dominant and homozygous recessive parents, there are 32 offspring in the F_2 generation. According to the Mendelian ratio, how many of the offspring should show the recessive trait?
15. The houseplant *Coleus* has curves on the edge of its leaves. Deep curves *(D)* are dominant over shallow curves *(d)*. Draw a Punnett square showing the possible offspring of a cross between a homozygous plant with deep-curved leaves and one with shallow-curved leaves. What are the possible phenotypes of the offspring?
16. An organism has two pairs of chromosomes.
    a. One of its cells undergoes mitosis. How many cells can result? How many chromosomes does each have?
    b. How many sperm cells can result from the meiosis of one of the organism's cells? How many chromosomes are in each?
17. Construct a Punnett square for the cross between two plants that are heterozygous for seed color and seed shape. Determine how many of each phenotype will be present among 16 offspring according to the Mendelian ratio.

18. One gene has alleles *E* and *e*; another gene has alleles *F* and *f*. For each of the following genotypes, determine the type(s) of gametes that will be produced.
    a. *EEFF*   c. *eeff*
    b. *Eeff*   d. *EeFf*

Critical Thinking

19. In dogs, short hair is dominant over long; dark hair is dominant over light. One dog is heterozygous for hair length and shows the recessive trait for hair color. Another dog is homozygous dominant for hair length and heterozygous for hair color. Construct a Punnett square showing a cross between these two animals. Identify the possible phenotypes.
20. Straight wings are dominant over curly wings in fruit flies. How would you determine whether a straight-winged fly is heterozygous or homozygous?
21. In guinea pigs, a black coat is dominant over a white coat. Can two white-coated parents produce an offspring with a black coat? Why or why not?
22. In certain cattle, the polled (hornless) trait is dominant over horns. A polled bull is mated to a cow with horns. Their calf is born and develops horns. The bull is then mated to another cow, which is polled. Their calf also develops horns. Identify the genotypes of all individuals.
23. Of all the chromosomes in one of your cells, half came from each of your parents. About what percentage of your chromosomes came from each of your grandparents? Your great-grandparents?

Chapter

10

CHROMOSOMES AND GENES

Overview

CHROMOSOMES AND INHERITANCE

10-1 Sex Determination

10-2 Sex Linkage and Linkage Groups

10-3 Sex Linkage in Humans

10-4 Crossing Over

CHANGES IN GENETIC MATERIAL

10-5 Mutagens

10-6 Nondisjunction: A Chromosomal Mutation

10-7 Other Chromosomal Mutations

10-8 Gene Mutations

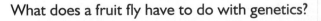

What does a fruit fly have to do with genetics?

CHROMOSOMES AND INHERITANCE

Mendel was able to demonstrate the principles of heredity by using pea plants. However, his experiments took seven years. These same principles can be demonstrated in just two or three months with a few bottles of fruit flies. As you will see, other important genetic principles have been discovered using these tiny organisms.

10-1 Sex Determination

When geneticists examined *Drosophila*, they found that each somatic, or body, cell had four pairs of chromosomes. As shown in Figure 10-1, three pairs of homologous chromosomes are the same in all the flies. The fourth pair, however, appears to be different in the female and male flies. In the female, both members of the fourth pair are straight—like rods. In the male, one chromosome is hooked on the end—like a cane.

The rod-shaped chromosome is called the X chromosome. The cane-shaped chromosome is called the Y chromosome. Because these chromosomes are related to the sex of an individual, they are called **sex chromosomes**. The other chromosomes are called **autosomes**.

In *Drosophila* sex depends on the number of X chromosomes that are present. A normal female has two X chromosomes. A normal male has only one X chromosome. Thus a normal male has one half the number of X chromosomes that a normal female has. The Y chromosome does not affect sex determination in fruit flies. A male fruit fly, however, needs a Y chromosome to produce fertile sperm.

Like the autosomes, the sex chromosomes segregate during meiosis. Thus each gamete receives one sex chromosome. When gametes combine during fertilization, offspring have a 50 percent chance of being either female or male. Female *Drosophila* can give only an X chromosome to a gamete. Male *Drosophila*, however, can give either an X or a Y chromosome. According to Mendel's principles, crossing a parent that is homozygous for a trait with a parent that is heterozygous for the trait should give homozygous and heterozygous offspring in a 1:1 ratio. This is just the case in sex determination. One half of the offspring are female (XX), and the other half are male (XY).

The discovery of sex determination in *Drosophila* gave support to the chromosome theory of inheritance. Geneticists were able to demonstrate that the phenotype of an organism—its sex, for example—is directly related to its chromosomes.

Section Objectives

A *Distinguish* between autosomes and sex chromosomes.
B *Explain* the chromosomal basis of sex determination.
C *Give* examples of sex-linked traits.
D *Discuss* the effect of linkage on independent assortment.
E *Describe* how crossing over affects linkage.

Figure 10-1   Male and female *Drosophila melanogaster*. There is no YY genotype because only the male can give a Y chromosome.

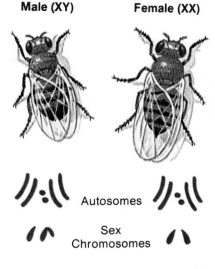

Male (XY)   Female (XX)

Autosomes

Sex Chromosomes

Figure 10-2 The pattern of sex determination varies in different organisms. In honeybees, females are diploid (XX). Males are haploid (X); they develop from unfertilized eggs.

Humans have 23 pairs of chromosomes. Twenty-two pairs are autosomes and one pair is sex chromosomes. Normally, women are XX and men are XY. Unlike fruit flies, however, maleness in humans does depend on the presence of a Y chromosome. At least one gene on the Y chromosome is known to "push" a developing human toward becoming a male. Many genes on the autosomes also contribute to the development of a male phenotype. Without the Y chromosome, a female usually develops. However, you will see in Chapter 11 that there are some other combinations.

10-2 Sex Linkage and Linkage Groups

Although the identification of the sex chromosomes supported the chromosome theory, it also raised another question. Did each characteristic have its own chromosome? Remember that *Drosophila* has only four pairs of chromosomes. But fruit flies have far more than just four characteristics. Surely there must be more than one gene on each chromosome.

Sutton had considered this problem when he proposed the chromosome theory. Sutton suggested that each chromosome carries many genes. The genes are linked together in a certain order on the chromosomes, like beads on a string. Genes on the same chromosome belong to the same **linkage group**.

Sutton further suggested that genes on a chromosome do not change position from generation to generation. In other words, the linkage groups are stable. Each gene occupies a specific position on a given chromosome. For geneticists at the beginning of this century, one question stood out: Where on the chromosomes are genes located?

Figure 10-3 Positions of genes on homologous chromosomes. Note that the position of an allele is the same on each homolog.

A pair of homologous chromosomes

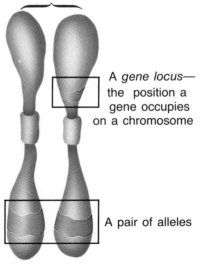

A *gene locus*— the position a gene occupies on a chromosome

A pair of alleles

The first opportunity to locate a gene on a chromosome came in 1909 at Columbia University, when the American geneticist Thomas Hunt Morgan discovered a white-eyed male in a colony of fruit flies. This was odd. *Drosophila* usually have red eyes.

To study this unusual trait, Morgan and his students crossed the white-eyed male with a normal red-eyed female. All the F_1 offspring had red eyes. From this Morgan concluded that the allele for white eyes was recessive.

Morgan and his students then crossed members of the F_1 generation. Again, the F_2 offspring conformed to the Mendelian ratio of phenotypes: 3/4 were dominant, with red eyes; and 1/4 were recessive, with white eyes. But there was something unexpected in the F_2 generation. All the white-eyed flies were male. None of the females had white eyes!

Morgan and his students interpreted this result according to the chromosome theory. They suggested that the gene for eye color in *Drosophila* must be on the same chromosome as the genes that determine sex. It is now known that this gene for eye color is located on the X chromosome. The Y chromosome does not carry a gene for eye color.

Remember from Chapter 9 that a dominant allele masks the phenotypic expression of a recessive allele. In most cases, an organism must have two recessive alleles to show a recessive phenotype. In male fruit flies, however, only one chromosome carries the gene for eye color. If that gene has the recessive allele, there will be no dominant allele to mask it. Thus one recessive allele is enough to make the male fly white-eyed. The female has two alleles for eye color because she has two X chromosomes. However, a female can have white eyes only if *both* X chromosomes carry alleles for the recessive trait.

Genes that are located on, or linked to, the X chromosome are called **sex-linked genes**. Traits determined by sex-linked genes are called **sex-linked traits**. White eye color in fruit flies is an example of a sex-linked trait.

Linkage of genes on the X chromosome is indicated by superscripts. A homozygous red-eyed female would be $X^R X^R$. A recessive male would be $X^r Y$. Because the Y chromosome carries no gene for eye color, it has no superscript.

As you can see in Figure 10-4, all the F_1 females have the genotype $X^R X^r$. They received X^R from their mother and X^r from their father. Study the Punnett square for the F_2 cross. Compare the genotypes of the offspring with those of the parents.

By 1915, Morgan and his group had investigated more than 100 genes. Each of these genes could be fit into one of four linkage groups. Since *Drosophila* has four pairs of homologous chromosomes, each of these four linkage groups could be related to one chromosome.

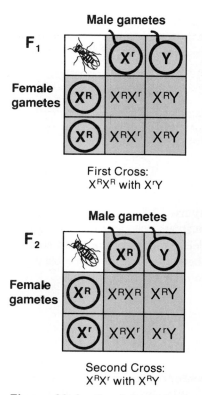

Figure 10-4 Sex-linked inheritance for red eyes in fruit flies.

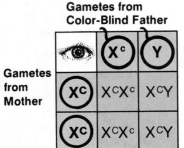

Gametes from Color-Blind Father

Gametes from Mother

	X^c	Y
X^C	$X^C X^c$	$X^C Y$
X^C	$X^C X^c$	$X^C Y$

Figure 10-5 All of this man's daughters will carry the recessive allele. Will any of the man's sons inherit the allele for color blindness from him?

10-3 Sex Linkage in Humans

The mechanism for inheritance of a sex-linked trait in humans is like that in *Drosophila*. Recall that human females have two X chromosomes, and human males have an X and a Y chromosome. Because a female has two X chromosomes, she must have two recessive alleles to express the recessive phenotype for a sex-linked trait. A male, with only one X chromosome, needs only one recessive allele to express the recessive phenotype.

An example of sex linkage in humans is red–green color vision. People who have the dominant allele for color vision can see all the colors in the visible spectrum. However, some people have **red–green color blindness**, the inability to distinguish red from green. Red–green color blindness is a recessive condition. The gene for red–green color vision is on the X chromosome. For a woman to be color-blind, both alleles for red–green color vision must be recessive. In men, however, one recessive allele on the X chromosome will result in color blindness because the Y chromosome does not carry the gene.

There are five possible genotypes for red–green color vision:

1. $X^C X^C$ — a woman with normal vision
2. $X^C X^c$ — a woman with normal vision who carries the allele for color blindness
3. $X^c X^c$ — a color-blind woman
4. $X^C Y$ — a man with normal vision
5. $X^c Y$ — a color-blind man

A woman with the genotype $X^C X^c$ can pass a recessive gene on to her offspring. She is described as a carrier. A **carrier** is an individual who is heterozygous for a recessive trait. Although the trait does not appear in the phenotype, the heterozygous individual carries the allele.

10-4 Crossing Over

Linkage groups are an important exception to the principle of independent assortment. Genes located on the same chromosome, or in linkage groups, do not assort independently. They usually will be transmitted to offspring as a group.

Traits that are linked together should follow the Mendelian ratio for a monohybrid cross. Imagine, for example, that a male *Drosophila* has three recessive alleles on its X chromosome— yellow body, white eyes, and miniature wings. If this male is bred with a female that is homozygous dominant for these genes, all F_1 offspring should display all three dominant traits. In the F_2 generation, half the males should display all three dominant traits and half the males should display all three recessive traits.

Morgan and his group carried out many crosses like the one just described. As they expected, in most cases the genes in a linkage group were inherited as a unit. Occasionally, though, Morgan found exceptions to these linkages. Sometimes males in the F_2 generation had yellow bodies and white eyes but normal wings. Other F_2 males had miniature wings and yellow bodies but normal red eyes. These results showed that sometimes the linkage groups break apart, or have **incomplete linkage**.

The cause of incomplete linkage can be found in meiosis. As you learned in Chapter 9, during prophase I the homologous chromosomes line up next to each other in synapsis. During synapsis two chromatids, one from each homologous chromosome, twist around each other. As they twist, the chromatids often break, and the broken ends may switch places. This exchange of genetic material is called **crossing over**.

Morgan noted an important fact about crossing over. Genes that are far apart on a chromosome will cross over more frequently than genes that are close together. Thus, genes that are far apart are more likely to end up on separate chromosomes.

By carefully analyzing the gene combinations of offspring in hybrid crosses, it is possible to measure how often genes in a linkage group are separated by crossing over. This information can be used to figure out the relative position of genes on the chromosome. This technique is called **chromosome mapping**.

Although most genes have a specific location on the chromosomes, a few genes can move about. Evidence of such movement was gathered by the American geneticist Barbara McClintock. McClintock showed that certain genes could move from one position to another, or even from chromosome to chromosome. McClintock called these genes "jumping genes." Scientists think that jumping genes probably occur in the DNA of all organisms. In recognition of her discovery, McClintock was awarded a Nobel Prize in 1983.

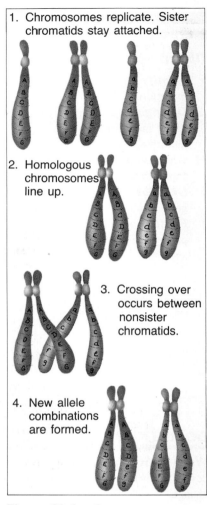

1. Chromosomes replicate. Sister chromatids stay attached.

2. Homologous chromosomes line up.

3. Crossing over occurs between nonsister chromatids.

4. New allele combinations are formed.

Figure 10-6 Crossing over is an equal trade that results in new combinations of alleles.

CHECKPOINT ◆

1. How do autosomes and sex chromosomes differ?
2. What chromosomes are characteristic of human males?
3. Name one trait that is sex-linked.
4. What causes incomplete linkage?
▶ 5. A white-eyed female fruit fly is crossed with a red-eyed male fruit fly. In what generation of offspring will both white-eyed and red-eyed males occur?
▶ 6. Suppose a female fruit fly is heterozygous for two traits (*AaBb*) found on the same chromosome. List all the combinations of alleles that could be found in her gametes.

▶ Denotes a question that involves *interpreting* and *applying* concepts.

Objectives

F *Identify* some causes of mutation.

G *Distinguish* between a chromosomal mutation and a gene mutation.

H *Give examples* of chromosomal mutations.

I *Describe* the three types of gene mutations.

J *Explain* how mutations are passed from one generation to another.

CONSUMER BIOLOGY

New varieties of plants are grown by culturing somatic tissue. If a cultured cell has a somatic mutation, a plant that regenerates from it will express the mutant phenotype. In this way, researchers have produced stringless celery, buttery corn, tastier carrots, and high-solids tomatoes.

Suppose that you had to type the same information 100 times. Chances are that you would make a mistake at some point. You might hit the wrong key, or a key might get stuck causing a mechanical error. The more often a task is repeated, the more likely it is that human or mechanical errors will occur.

Now consider the replication of DNA. Most genes pass from generation to generation unchanged. Occasionally, though, there is a change in the genetic information. Such a change is called a mutation. A **mutation** is an error in the replication of the genetic material that becomes part of the genotype of a cell and its descendants. How do these errors occur, and what is their effect upon an organism?

10-5 Mutagens

Geneticists estimate that an error in copying the genetic material occurs between 1 in 1000 and 1 in 100 000 replications. Thus the rate of mutation for any one gene is low. For a whole population, however, the rate of mutation is relatively high. It is estimated that each new person born will probably carry two new mutations.

Certain substances and conditions, called **mutagens**, can increase the rate of mutation. Extremely high temperature and some kinds of viruses have been found to cause mutations. Many industrial chemicals, such as benzene and formaldehyde, are mutagens. Some pesticides, weed killers, and food additives also have been found to increase mutation rates.

The best known mutagen is radiation. Radiation occurs naturally as ultraviolet light from the sun and as a result of the decay of certain elements found in rocks. Artificial radiation, such as X rays, also causes mutations.

Mutations are classified into two groups: chromosomal mutations and gene mutations. Chromosomal mutations affect whole chromosomes; gene mutations affect individual genes on a chromosome. Both kinds of mutations can occur in either somatic cells or reproductive cells, the cells that give rise to gametes. A mutation in a somatic cell may be passed on to descendants of the cell within the organism. Some cancers are caused by mutations in somatic cells. Mutations in these kinds of cells cannot be passed on to offspring. A mutation in a reproductive cell, however, can have far-reaching effects. Mutations in reproductive cells may be passed on to gametes and then to a zygote if any of the gametes are involved in fertilization. All of an organism's cells are descended from the zygote. Therefore, every cell of the offspring will carry the mutation.

10-6 Nondisjunction, a Chromosomal Mutation

Sometimes the separation of chromosomes during meiosis is impaired. When this happens, a gamete may end up with an unusual number of chromosomes.

Recall from Chapter 9 that during the first division in normal meiosis, the homologous chromosomes separate from each other. During the second meiotic division, the chromatids separate from each other. Sometimes, though, the chromatids or homologous chromosomes stick together instead of separating. These chromosomes do not disjoin, or come apart, and nondisjunction occurs. In **nondisjunction** two kinds of gametes form—one kind has an extra chromosome and the other kind lacks one chromosome.

What do you think would happen if one of these abnormal gametes were involved in fertilization? The resulting zygote also would be abnormal. It would have one or three of the nondisjoined chromosomes rather than the pair that is normally found in a diploid cell. All the cells descended from the zygote by mitosis also would have an abnormal number of chromosomes.

If a cell has one extra chromosome, the condition is called **trisomy**. If a cell is missing one chromosome, the condition is called **monosomy**. Either condition can be harmful. Organisms with either condition are often sterile, or unable to reproduce. Generally, monosomy is more harmful than trisomy because the organism lacks the genetic information carried on the missing chromosome. Monosomy is almost always lethal.

In humans, nondisjunction causes several serious disorders. You will learn more about these disorders in the next chapter.

10-7 Other Chromosomal Mutations

Polyploidy Sometimes a nucleus does not undergo the second meiotic division. When this happens, the gametes that result are diploid instead of haploid. The zygotes that result from such gametes have an extra set of chromosomes, so they are $3n$. Occasionally diploid gametes will fuse, forming zygotes that have a $4n$ set of chromosomes. An organism with extra sets of chromosomes is said to be **polyploid**. Polyploidy is lethal to most animals, but it is relatively common among plants. In fact, some polyploid plants are larger and healthier than their diploid relatives. Cultivated wheat and potatoes are polyploid.

Chromosomal Rearrangements Occasionally a piece of a chromosome will break off. When this occurs, the genetic information that the piece carried is lost. This kind of mutation is called a chromosomal **deletion**. Children with "cri du chat" syndrome

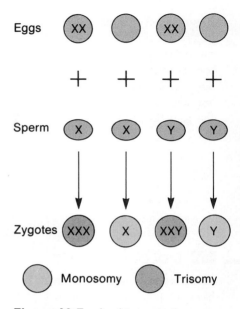

Figure 10-7 In this example, nondisjunction has occurred in the formation of eggs. Nondisjunction also can occur in the formation of sperm.

Figure 10-8 Polyploidy, although lethal in most animals, is common in plants such as wheat.

Chromosomes and Genes **171**

Figure 10-9 When translocation occurs in cells undergoing meiosis, the resulting gametes may carry too much or too little information. Some examples of such gametes are illustrated. What percentage of the gametes are normal?

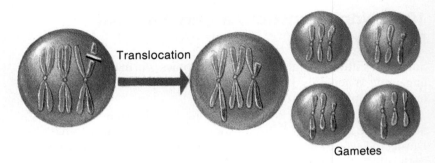

Translocation

Gametes

Adaptation and Evolution: Cells have complex mechanisms to repair their DNA which is constantly exposed to damaging chemicals and radiation.

Figure 10-10 In an inversion, no genetic material is lost. However, pieces of DNA do change position relative to the remainder of the chromosome.

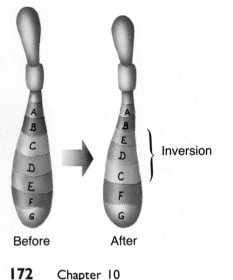

Before   After

have a deletion in the fifth largest chromosome. They are retarded and have an odd cry that sounds like a meow which gives the disorder its name.

As Figure 10-9 illustrates, a fragment from a chromosome also may become attached to another chromosome in the cell. This kind of rearrangement is called a translocation. In **translocation**, genes from one chromosome are transferred to another, non-homologous chromosome.

If a deletion occurs in a cell undergoing meiosis, the resulting gametes will lack genetic information. If translocation occurs during meiosis, some of the gametes may have too little or too much information. The effects of deletion and translocation can be like those of trisomy and monosomy. However, the effects of chromosomal rearrangements may be less severe than those of nondisjunction if fewer genes are involved.

Chromosomal Inversions Sometimes a segment of DNA in a chromosome will flip upside down, but remain in place, as shown in Figure 10-10. In this process, called an **inversion**, no genetic information is lost. A chromosomal inversion can, however, affect the organism in which it occurs. Genes that are located next to each other on a chromosome often participate in a common function. If the genes are separated by an inversion, they may not be able to function correctly. As in other chromosomal mutations, inversions may be passed on to offspring.

10-8 Gene Mutations

The word *mutation* most often refers to a change within a gene. To understand gene mutation, it is important to remember the structure of the genetic material presented in Chapter 7.

Recall that chromosomes contain long strands of DNA coiled into double helices. The sequence of the nucleotide bases in the DNA determines the structures of proteins. DNA triplets, which are groups of three bases, code for the mRNA codons that specify particular amino acids. Groups of triplets make up the genes that code for polypeptides and proteins, many of which are enzymes. Thus one chromosome may carry the genes that code for building thousands of proteins.

Point Mutations You could think of each gene as a message written in words of three letters. A short message might read, "The old dog ran and the fox did too."

Sometimes one base replaces another in a triplet. This kind of substitution is called a **point mutation**. Such a mutation changes only one nucleotide base in a gene. A substitution may change the meaning of the gene message. (The old *hog* ran and the fox did too.)

A point mutation may change the particular amino acid that the triplet represents. Recall that the order of amino acids in a protein determines its three-dimensional shape. In most proteins, the shape of the molecule controls its function. Therefore, if the sequence of amino acids is changed in a way that alters the protein's overall shape, its function may be changed.

How can a base substitution occur? Mutagens, for example, X rays or pesticides, can change the structure of a nucleotide base. When replication occurs, the altered base pairs with an incorrect base on the complementary strand. Recall from Chapter 7 that the complementary DNA strand acts as a blueprint for making additional DNA. When new DNA is made from an incorrect blueprint, it will be different from the original DNA. Indeed, every strand of DNA that descends from the altered strand will contain the same error. This explains how some genetic diseases are passed from one generation to the next.

Occasionally a point mutation has serious consequences. For example, a single amino acid substitution in the protein hemoglobin causes sickle-cell disease. You will learn more about this very painful disorder in Chapter 11.

Deletions and Insertions Sometimes a nucleotide is lost from the DNA sequence. This kind of mutation is called a **base deletion**. As Figure 10-12 illustrates, when a base deletion occurs, the entire message of the gene may be translated incorrectly. To understand why, consider what would happen if one letter was left out of the message about the dog and the fox—for example, the *a* in *ran*. If the triplet pattern was kept, the resulting message would be nonsense: "The old dog rna ndt hef oxd idt oo." In a similar way, base deletions often result in proteins that do not function correctly. The effect of a mutation on the organism depends upon the tissues and organs in which it is expressed.

The addition of an extra nucleotide base causes much the same problem as a deletion. Such a mutation is called a **base**

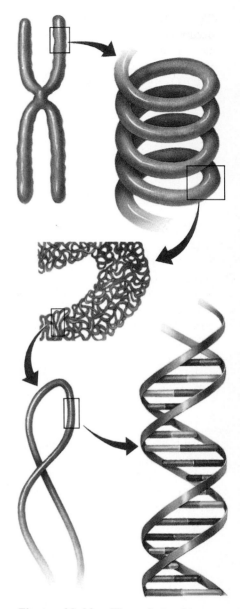

Figure 10-11 The relationship between a chromosome and a DNA helix.

Figure 10-12 Frame-shift and point mutations change the genetic information carried by a DNA segment.

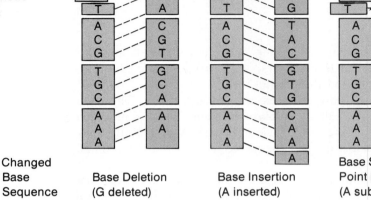

Original Base Sequence

Changed Base Sequence

Base Deletion (G deleted)

Base Insertion (A inserted)

Base Substitution— Point Mutation (A substitutes for T)

insertion. It distorts the translation of the entire message. Deletions and insertions are called **frame-shift mutations** because the reference point is changed for the entire message.

Since many genes usually affect the expression of a trait, most mutations have only a slight effect. However, even though the effects are slight, they are much more likely to be harmful than beneficial. Consider the complexity of metabolic pathways. These pathways are precisely balanced. A random change in the structure and function of an enzyme in the pathway is more likely to upset the system than to improve it. However, mutations are very important to life on Earth. They are the source of diversity among living things. You will learn in Chapter 14 how mutations and environmental conditions interact to produce new life forms.

CHECKPOINT ◆

7. What are mutagens?
8. State whether each of the following is a chromosomal or a gene mutation: polyploidy, base insertion, point mutation, nondisjunction.
9. What is the name of the condition in which a cell has one extra chromosome?
10. What kind of mutation involves a change in the translation of the DNA message?
▶ 11. In a population of red-eyed fruit flies, a brown-eyed fly is discovered. The brown-eyed fly is used to produce several generations of offspring. None of the offspring have brown eyes. In what kind of cell did the mutation causing brown eyes most likely occur? Explain your answer.

▶ Denotes a question that involves *interpreting* and *applying* concepts.

MAPPING GENES USING CROSSOVER FREQUENCY

Objectives and Skills

☐ *Examine* the relationship between allele position and crossover frequency.

☐ *Determine* how crossing over affects genotypic variation.

Materials

paper, pencil, one die

Procedure and Observations

1. On a separate sheet of paper, draw a data table like the one shown below.

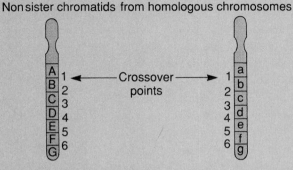

Non sister chromatids from homologous chromosomes

DATA TABLE

Number of times *a* is on the same chromosome as	Percentage of times *a* is on the same chromosome as
b	b
c	c
d	d
e	e
f	f
g	g

2. Study the figure, which represents a pair of chromosomes from a fruit fly. The fly is heterozygous for each of seven traits, *a* through *g*, found on each chromosome.

3. In the figure, numbers 1 through 6 represent points at which crossing over may occur, thus separating the alleles. For example, if a crossover occurred at point 3, the alleles on Chromosome 1 would be abcDEFG. The alleles on Chromosome 2 would be ABCdefg.

4. Roll the die. Using the number that comes up as a crossover point, note which alleles remain on the same chromosome as *a*. Record this information as a tally mark in your data table.

5. Repeat Step 4 another 99 times.

6. Calculate the percentage of the time each allele is found on the same chromosome as *a*. Record this information in your data table.

Analysis and Conclusions

1. Is the location of crossing over more or less random, or does it occur more frequently in any particular location?

2. Which recessive allele most often ends up on the same chromosome as *a*?

3. Which recessive allele is separated most often from *a*?

4. Assume a crossover occurs at point 2. What would be the order of alleles on the resulting chromosomes?

5. Suppose a fly containing the chromosomes in Question 4 was mated to a fly recessive for all seven characteristics. What would be the genotypes of the offspring?

6. How could the data you obtained have helped Morgan in determining the positions of genes on a chromosome?

Somatic Gene Therapy

Somatic gene therapy treats genetic illness at its source, correcting the problems in the cells that are directly responsible for the symptoms. Somatic gene therapy is conducted on body cells, not on the sperm or egg cells that would transmit the correction to the next generation. It has the potential of freeing the patient from painful treatments because his or her body will produce the missing substance. Not only will somatic gene therapy eventually help treat rare genetic diseases, but it can also be used to treat more common illnesses to which people

may have inherited susceptibilities, such as heart disease, emphysema, and diabetes.

Somatic gene therapy requires several steps. Isolating the gene that makes the desired substance and transferring it to the correct cells are the first two steps. Genes can be transferred by stitching them into viruses, which then ferry them into cells; or by exposing cells to brief electrical pulses to open pores and then bathing them in gene-containing solutions; and by packaging the therapeutic genes into tiny bubbles called liposomes. Once the curative genes are successfully introduced, they must be coerced into synthesizing their particular protein product when it is needed.

Introducing a "foreign" gene in precisely the right cells within a trillion-celled human is quite a challenge. Most early efforts focus on genetically engineering bone marrow because this tissue is easily removed, altered, and placed back in the body. But bone marrow transplants are excru-

ciatingly painful. Other somatic gene therapy targets will be easier to implement.

Endothelium—Gateway to the Bloodstream

Blood vessels are lined with a cell sheet, one-cell thick, which resembles bathroom tile and is called **endothelium**. Genetically altered endothelium can be grown in a laboratory and grafted into a person. A hemophiliac might receive a graft that releases clotting factor into the bloodstream. A dwarf might receive growth hormone. Engineered blood vessel linings might even secrete proteins that remove toxins from the blood. So far the procedure has been used to enable rabbit blood vessels to secrete the human protein that is missing in people suffering from severe combined immune deficiency. These people must live in huge plastic bubbles so that they do not come into contact with pathogens.

Skin-Deep Gene Therapy

Skin cells grow remarkably well outside the body. Researchers have engineered human skin cells to secrete growth hormone, then successfully grafted the skin onto mice. Genetically engineered skin grafts could serve as individualized living drug factories.

Preventing Emphysema

The destroyed air sacs (alveoli) of emphysema-stricken lungs result from absent or abnormal alpha-1-antitrypsin (AAT), a protein that normally prevents white blood cells from releasing an enzyme called elastase, which eats away at delicate lung linings. Connective tissue cells called fibroblasts can be engineered to produce AAT and then implanted into the lungs. So far this approach has worked in mice.

Treating Heart Disease via the Liver

The liver is an important target for gene therapy because this enormous gland is the metabolic headquarters of the body and therefore the source of hundreds of illnesses. Researchers have engineered liver cells to produce more of the cell surface receptor proteins that grab the artery-clogging form of cholesterol from the bloodstream. When these cells can be successfully implanted in a liver, they will be a lifesaver for the one in a million people who suffer from severe familial hypercholesterolemia. Their liver cells lack cholesterol receptors, and they die in childhood of massive heart failure.

RESEARCH & DISCUSSION

1. How can gene therapy for rare inherited disorders be applied to more common forms of those illnesses? Cite two examples.
2. Why won't people treated with somatic gene therapy pass their engineered abilities on to the next generation?
3. What type of chemical must be abnormal in a disease in order for somatic gene therapy to provide a possible treatment?

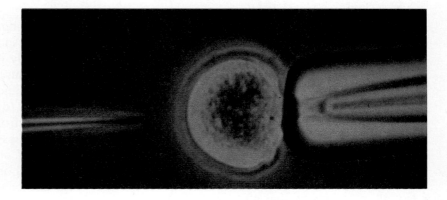

CHAPTER REVIEW

Summary

‣ The evidence collected by geneticists during the last century provides ample support for the chromosome theory of inheritance.

‣ Genes on autosomes and sex chromosomes influence the sex of an individual.

‣ Each gene has a particular location on a chromosome. Genes carried on the X chromosome are called sex-linked genes. Males carrying a recessive allele on their single X chromosome express a recessive phenotype. Females must carry recessive alleles on both X chromosomes to express a recessive phenotype.

‣ Because genes found on the same chromosome are linked, they do not segregate independently. However, linkage groups can be broken by crossing over. In crossing over, homologous chromosomes exchange alleles.

‣ Mutations can affect either chromosomes or individual genes. Chromosomal or gene mutations that occur in reproductive cells may be passed on to offspring.

‣ Nondisjunction of the chromosomes results in gametes that have either too few or too many chromosomes. In polyploidy, organisms have one or more extra sets of chromosomes.

‣ Deletion, translocation, and inversion are chromosomal mutations that involve changes in the chromosomes themselves rather than changes in chromosome number.

‣ Gene mutations are the result of changes in the sequence of nucleotides on the DNA. Gene mutations include deletions, insertions, and substitutions (or point mutations). A mutated gene does not correctly direct the synthesis of a protein, and so may be harmful to the organism.

‣ Not all mutations are harmful. Some mutations are beneficial. Mutation provides the ultimate source of variety among living things.

Vocabulary

autosome	mutagen
base deletion	mutation
base insertion	nondisjunction
carrier	point mutation
chromosome mapping	polyploid
crossing over	red–green color
deletion	blindness
frame-shift mutation	sex chromosome
incomplete linkage	sex-linked gene
inversion	sex-linked trait
linkage group	translocation
monosomy	trisomy

Concept Mapping

Construct a concept map for mutations. Include the following terms: chromosomal mutation, gene mutation, frame-shift mutation, inversion, nondisjunction, point mutation, and translocation. Add terms as you need them.

Review

Choose the best answer for each of the following questions.

1. Sex chromosomes can be distinguished from autosomes because (a) sex chromosomes occur only in females, (b) only sex chromosomes cause maleness, (c) the pair of sex chromosomes in females differs from those in males, (d) the autosomes in females are different from those in males.
2. In fruit flies and humans, females have (a) two Y chromosomes, (b) one X chromosome and one Y chromosome, (c) two X chromosomes, (d) only autosomes.
3. Genes located on the same chromosome are called (a) a linkage group, (b) alleles, (c) autosomes, (d) all of these.

4. *Drosophila* sperm cells can contain (a) only X chromosomes, (b) only Y chromosomes, (c) either an X or a Y chromosome, (d) only autosomes.
5. In *Drosophila*, the allele for white eyes is (a) recessive, (b) sex-linked, (c) located on the X chromosome, (d) all of these.
6. In humans, the gene for color vision is (a) located on the X chromosome, (b) located on the Y chromosome, (c) located on the twenty-third autosome, (d) a jumping gene.
7. A high frequency of crossing over between genes indicates that they are (a) far apart on the chromosome, (b) sex-linked, (c) dominant alleles, (d) close together on the chromosome.
8. The condition in which a zygote has one chromosome fewer than the diploid number is known as (a) trisomy, (b) monosomy, (c) monoploidy, (d) polyploidy.
9. Frame-shift mutations are caused by (a) base insertions, (b) base deletions, (c) both *a* and *b*, (d) neither *a* nor *b*.
10. Which of these is a mutagen? (a) water (b) oxygen (c) ATP (d) radiation

Interpret and Apply

11. In humans, which parent determines the sex of the offspring? Explain why.
12. The diagram below shows a section of a chromosome. The letters *A*, *B*, and *C* indicate the location of alleles.

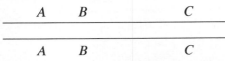

a. Between which two alleles would crossing over occur most often?
b. Which two of these alleles are least likely to assort independently?

13. Explain the difference between crossing over and translocation.
14. Would a mutation in a skin cell on your hand affect your offspring? Explain your answer.
15. How is a point mutation different from a frame-shift mutation?
16. Since any pair of chromatids can fail to separate during meiosis, theoretically there are 23 possible kinds of monosomy and trisomy. However, monosomies or trisomies for most of the 23 chromosome pairs are extremely rare—or unheard of—in live babies. Why do you think this is so?

Critical Thinking

17. While examining a population of fruit flies, you notice that a certain trait never appears in males. How can you account for this?
18. A couple has three sons and one daughter. What is the probability that a fifth child will be a girl? Explain your answer.
19. Three genes—*D*, *E*, and *F*—are located on the same chromosome. Crossovers occur between *D* and *E* 15 percent of the time. They occur between *E* and *F* 10 percent of the time. Between *D* and *F*, crossing over happens at a frequency of only 5 percent. Draw a chromosome showing the order in which these genes occur.
20. In general, a chromosomal mutation tends to affect the organism as a whole. A gene mutation, however, usually affects only one characteristic. Explain why this is so.
21. Part of a gene has the base sequence CAA CAT CTA GGG. Suppose the first adenine is deleted. Write the resulting triplets.
22. Which would be likely to produce a more severe distortion of a protein: a frame-shift mutation at the beginning of a gene, or one at the end of a gene? Why?

Chapter

11

HUMAN INHERITANCE

Overview

PATTERNS OF INHERITANCE

11-1 Traits Controlled by Multiple Alleles

11-2 Traits Determined by Multiple Genes

11-3 Sex-Limited and Sex-Influenced Traits

11-4 Genes and the Environment

HUMAN DISORDERS

11-5 Disorders Caused by Gene Mutations

11-6 Disorders Caused by Nondisjunction

DETECTING DISORDERS

11-7 Identifying Carriers

11-8 Finding Disorders before Birth

11-9 Genetic Counseling

TREATING DISORDERS

11-10 Treatment during Pregnancy

11-11 Treating Inborn Errors of Metabolism

Why do people look so different from each other?

PATTERNS OF INHERITANCE

In Chapter 9 you learned that Mendel studied traits that showed one of two possible forms. For example, Mendel's pea plants were either tall or short. Many traits, however, have a range of expression. If you look around your classroom, you can see that your classmates show a wide range of sizes—they are not just tall or short. Many traits in humans, such as height, do not follow the usual Mendelian pattern of inheritance. As you will learn in this lesson, simple dominant or recessive patterns are not the only ways in which traits are inherited.

11-1 Traits Controlled by Multiple Alleles

Recall from Chapter 9 that in humans and other diploid organisms, chromosomes occur in homologous pairs. The different alleles of a gene occupy corresponding positions on homologous chromosomes. In the examples considered so far, each gene had only two different alleles. Pea plants, for example, have alleles for smooth or wrinkled seed coats. It is possible, however, for a gene to occur in several different forms. A gene with more than two alleles is said to have **multiple alleles**. Multiple alleles result from different mutations of the same gene.

In traits governed by multiple alleles, each individual can carry only two of the several possible alleles, one on each of the homologous chromosomes. Human blood types are a good example of inheritance through multiple alleles. There is great variety in the chemistry of people's blood. To give a blood transfusion, it is necessary to match the blood type of the donor with the blood type of the person receiving the blood. People belong to different blood groups because their genes code for different carbohydrates on the surface of their red blood cells.

The best-known class of blood carbohydrates is the ABO group, determined by the alleles *A*, *B*, and *O*. Your blood type is determined by which two of these three alleles are found in your blood cells. The *A* and *B* alleles are both dominant over the *O* allele. They each mask the presence of *O* in the phenotype. However, when the *A* and *B* alleles are present together, each shows its effect completely in the phenotype. Neither one masks, nor even dilutes, the effects of the other. Thus there are four possible blood phenotypes: A, B, AB, and O. Note in Table 11-1 that each genotype consists of only two alleles for these blood carbohydrates, one on each homologous chromosome.

Consider an example of how blood type is inherited. The Punnett square in Figure 11-1 shows the possible offspring of a mother with type O blood and a father with type AB blood. What are the possible blood types of their children?

Section Objectives

A *Distinguish* between multiple alleles and multiple genes.
B *Give examples* of traits determined by multiple alleles and multiple genes.
C *Compare* sex-influenced and sex-limited inheritance.
D *Describe* the effect of environment on gene expression.

Table 11-1

BLOOD PHENOTYPES PRODUCED BY MULTIPLE ALLELES	
Genotype	Phenotype (Blood Type)
AA	A
BB	B
OO	O
AO	A
BO	B
AB	AB

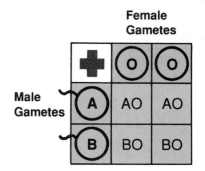

Figure 11-1   Would the result of this cross be any different if the father was type O and the mother was type AB?

HUMAN DISORDERS

E *Describe* several genetic disorders in humans.

F *State* the patterns of transmission for several genetic disorders.

Recall from Chapter 7 that many genes code for the production of proteins. Some of these proteins function as enzymes. Therefore, if the gene that codes for a particular enzyme is missing or defective, the reaction catalyzed by the enzyme will not occur. Such a condition is called an *inborn error of metabolism.*

Genes also code for proteins that have other important functions. For example, some proteins make up part of the structure of cells. Other proteins act as carrier molecules that transport substances across cell membranes. A defect in a gene that codes for these kinds of proteins can have medical effects as serious as those caused by missing or defective enzymes.

There are about 4000 known genetic-based disorders in humans. When people plan to have children, information about the inheritance of genetic disorders is sometimes needed. This lesson will familiarize you with a few well-known disorders.

11-5 Disorders Caused by Gene Mutations

Sickle-Cell Disease Sickle-cell disease is a disorder that occurs most often among people of tropical African descent. It is the result of a point mutation in the gene that codes for the protein **hemoglobin**. Hemoglobin in the red blood cells carries oxygen from the lungs to all the other cells of the body.

Normal red blood cells are circular but slightly uneven. In sickle-cell disease, the red blood cells are curved, or sickle-shaped. This shape is caused by a single base substitution in the gene for hemoglobin. In the normal gene, a particular base triplet codes for the amino acid glutamic acid. In the sickle-cell gene, this triplet codes for valine. Recall from Chapter 4 that the sequence of amino acids determines the shape of a protein molecule. The substitution of valine for glutamic acid changes the shape of the hemoglobin molecule. As a result, the shape of the blood cell is also changed. Refer to Table 7-1. Compare the sequence of base triplets that code for glutamic acid with those that code for valine. Can you tell what substitution caused the mutation?

The base substitution has many serious effects. Sickled cells are fragile and break apart easily. The body cannot produce new cells as fast as the defective ones break. This condition results in anemia, or a shortage of red blood cells. The sickled cells also clog small blood vessels, restricting blood flow. Reduced blood flow damages tissues and organs and causes severe pain in the affected areas.

People with sickle-cell disease are also very prone to infection, which can be life-threatening. It is important to realize, however,

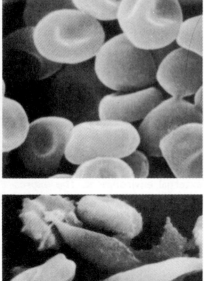

Figure 11-4 *Top:* Normal red blood cells. *Bottom:* Sickled red blood cells. How does the structure of the sickled cells affect their function of carrying oxygen swiftly through blood vessels?

that the severity of a particular genetic disease can vary greatly from person to person. One child with sickle-cell disease may be ill only once or twice a year, while another may be hospitalized very frequently. It has recently been found that when affected children are identified at birth, they can be treated with antibiotics for several years to prevent infection. In addition, they can be given special vaccinations. These types of treatments have enabled some affected children to live well into adulthood, which was not likely just a few years ago.

In people who are heterozygous for the sickle-cell allele, some of the hemoglobin is normal and some is abnormal. These people are said to have **sickle-cell trait**. They are generally healthy, but have a higher risk of heart attacks during very strenuous exercise. In malaria-infested areas, such as tropical Africa, it is an advantage to be heterozygous. Having sickle-cell trait lowers an individual's chances of developing malaria because the tiny organism that causes malaria cannot reproduce in the sickled cells.

Because of African ancestry, one out of ten children born to black families in North America is heterozygous for the sickle-cell gene. If a husband and wife both have the sickle-cell trait, they have a 25-percent chance of producing a child with sickle-cell disease. Arabic people are also at higher risk for sickle-cell disease.

Cystic Fibrosis Cystic fibrosis is the most common genetic disorder among North American caucasians. One in twenty white Americans is a carrier. In cystic fibrosis, thick mucus builds up in the lungs, allowing the growth of bacteria that cause severe respiratory infections. The disorder also causes a digestive enzyme deficiency, which prevents food from being digested and absorbed properly. This disorder leads to malnutrition.

Cystic fibrosis is now thought to be caused by a genetic defect that affects certain molecules in the plasma membrane of cells. Recall that some molecules help to regulate the movement of substances across membranes. In cystic fibrosis, this defect in regulation causes water to be excreted too quickly from the cells. The resulting imbalance causes mucus to accumulate.

Many exciting developments have recently taken place in understanding cystic fibrosis. The gene has been located, which means that people can be screened for the presence of the gene. Once the gene's function is identified, treatment may be possible. At present, antibiotics and respiratory therapy enable half of those with the disorder to reach age 21.

Huntington Disease Huntington disease is a lethal disorder caused by a dominant gene. Each child of a person with Huntington disease has a 50-percent chance of inheriting the dominant gene and developing the disease. It affects 1 in 25 000 people.

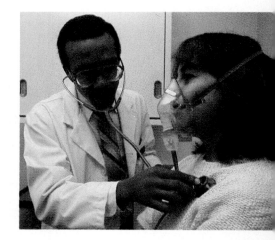

Figure 11-5 Physical therapy can help relieve some of the symptoms of cystic fibrosis, such as excess mucus clogging the lungs.

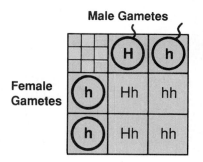

Figure 11-6 In a dominant-gene disorder such as Huntington disease, only one dominant allele is required for the abnormal phenotype to occur.

Although the gene for Huntington disease is present at birth, the symptoms of the disease do not appear until about age 40. These symptoms include loss of muscle coordination that makes a person's movements dancelike and uncontrollable. Mental deterioration can cause personality changes. A new test can tell members of a family with a history of Huntington disease whether or not they have inherited the disease-causing gene.

Hemophilia Gene mutations occur on sex chromosomes as well as on autosomes. Mutations on sex chromosomes give rise to sex-linked disorders. One well-known sex-linked disorder in humans is hemophilia, the inability of blood to clot. In most hemophilia victims, the body is not able to manufacture a certain protein needed for forming a blood clot. Hemophilia causes uncontrollable internal bleeding into the kidneys, brain, and other organs. Until recently, victims of hemophilia died at an early age. Now hemophilia can be treated with injections of clotting factor produced by recombinant DNA technology.

Hemophilia is caused by a recessive allele located on the X chromosome. Therefore, a man needs only one recessive allele to express the trait. A woman must have two recessive alleles.

Figure 11-7 The inheritance of hemophilia in the royal families of Europe. How many carriers are there in the pedigree? How many individuals are affected with the disorder?

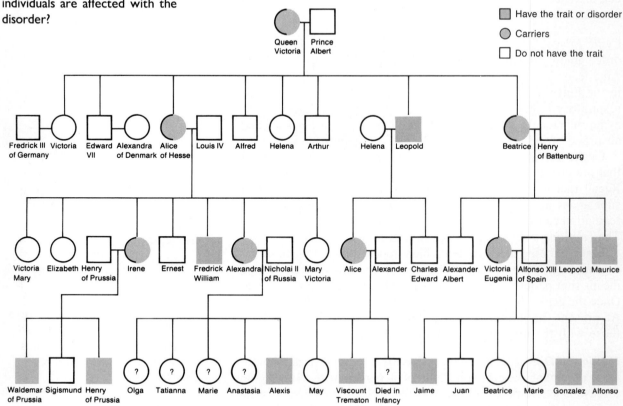

A woman who is a carrier of hemophilia has a 50-percent chance of passing the recessive allele on to each of her children.

The most famous carrier of hemophilia was Queen Victoria. She unknowingly passed the gene on to one of her sons and two of her daughters. To see how the gene for hemophilia was inherited in the royal families of Europe during the nineteenth century, refer to the pedigree in Figure 11-7.

A **pedigree** is a diagram that shows how a trait is inherited in a family. Notice in the pedigree that circles represent females and squares represent males. The filled-in spaces represent people who have the trait or disorder being followed. Half-filled spaces represent carriers, and unfilled spaces represent people who do not have the trait. A horizontal line between a circle and a square represents marriage. The children of a given marriage are shown with vertical lines. Can you explain why all the carriers in this pedigree are female?

Duchenne Muscular Dystrophy Another important sex-linked condition is Duchenne muscular dystrophy. This disorder causes deterioration of the muscles and then death by early adulthood. Males with muscular dystrophy do not live long enough to reproduce. Therefore, they never transmit the recessive allele to offspring.

Scientists recently located the gene responsible for Duchenne muscular dystrophy at a particular spot on the X chromosome and determined its DNA sequence. The protein it codes for is named *dystrophin*. Although dystrophin is normally present in only small amounts in muscles, its absence is devastating to muscle function, as seen in sufferers of Duchenne's muscular dystrophy. Now that the nature of the protein abnormality is known, a treatment is more likely to be developed.

11-6 Disorders Caused by Nondisjunction

As you learned in Chapter 10, chromosomes occasionally fail to separate properly during meiosis. When this occurs, the resulting egg or sperm will carry an abnormal number of chromosomes. If the egg or sperm is then involved in fertilization, the resulting zygote will also have an abnormal chromosome number. The disorders caused by abnormal chromosome numbers are often quite serious.

Geneticists can determine whether an individual has a normal set of chromosomes by making a karyotype [kar′ ē ə tīp]. A **karyotype** is a photograph of the chromosomes of a cell, which are arranged in order from the largest to the smallest.

To be prepared for a karyotype, a cell is treated chemically so that it will undergo mitosis. Recall that the individual chromosomes are visible only at this time. The cell is then stained and photographed through a microscope. The photograph is cut

Sex Chromosomes

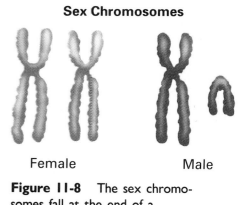

Female   Male

Figure 11-8 The sex chromosomes fall at the end of a karyotype.

CUTTING EDGE

Sequencing the Human Genome

When James Watson, along with Francis Crick, deciphered the structure of the genetic material DNA in 1953, he probably couldn't have imagined that today he would be heading an international effort to learn the sequence of the entire human genome— that is, all 3 billion DNA building blocks that comprise the 46 chromosomes in a human body cell. This genetic information is the equivalent of 13 sets of encyclopedias or 200 Manhattan telephone books.

The "human genome project" is being undertaken in two steps. The first is mapping, in which the 3 billion bases are cut into 100 000 fragments of approximately 40 000 bases each (some overlap) and each 40 000 base segment is assigned to its particular chromosome. In the second stage, sequencing, each 40 000 base piece is cut into 100 pieces of approximately 400 bases each. The precise order of the 4 DNA building blocks—the nitrogenous bases adenine (A), cytosine (C),

guanine (G), and thymine (T)— is determined for each 400-base sequence. These two steps have been compared to mapmaking. The major highways are indicated; then individual streets are marked.

The sequencing is complicated, although automated devices can process 30 000 bases a day. One technique is to break the 400-base fragment into a set of fragments of every possible size, all having an end in common and retaining the sequence. The end that varies is tagged with 1 of 4 chemicals, each representing 1 of the 4 bases. Then the DNA pieces are separated by size on a sheet of electrified gel, a technique called electrophoresis. Finally the sequence is read off by recording the base-identifying chemical at the end of each successively longer piece. For example, the sequence ATCG yields four fragments: A, AT, ATC, and ATCG. The 1-base piece would bear the tag for "A," the 2-base piece would be tagged for "T," the 3-base

piece for "C," and the 4-base piece for "G." The DNA sequence is therefore ATCG. If different 400-base pieces are sequenced, they can be aligned by where they overlap. In this way larger sequences will be put together.

What the Genome Project Can Tell You

It is difficult to imagine what you will accomplish by sequencing the genome. Certainly you will learn the biological bases of inherited diseases and disease susceptibilities. So

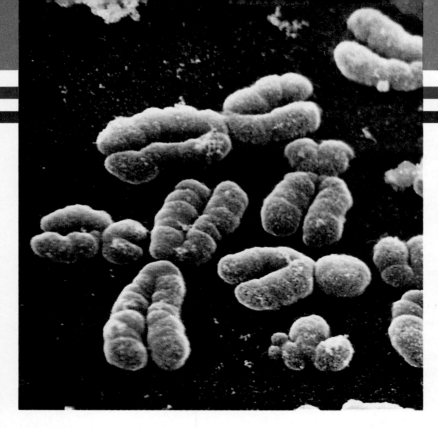

far only 4600 of the estimated 100 000 to 300 000 human genes have been identified. Of those, the sequences of only 600 are known.

Victor A. McKusick, M.D., a Johns Hopkins University geneticist who chronicles all known human genes in an annual volume titled *Mendelian Inheritance in Man*, calls the genome project a comprehensive sourcebook for biology and medicine. Along with revealing the mechanisms of many diseases, this knowledge will also clarify how many normal bodily processes are carried out.

What the Genome Project Cannot Tell You

Critics of the genome project question why so much needs to be known. It is estimated that only about 3 percent of the human genome codes for protein. Thirty percent consists of repeated sequences whose function is not known. 67 percent is DNA within genes, called intervening sequences or introns—with no known function. Why sequence material that may not be important?

Knowing the sequence of the genome will not shed light on some fundamental questions, such as how genes interact with each other and the environment and how cells become specialized by expressing only certain genes. Also, financing the project may divert funds from other worthwhile, if not as glamorous, endeavors.

DISCUSSION & RESEARCH

1. Do you think that the human genome should be sequenced? If so, who should provide the funding? How should the project be organized so that efforts are not duplicated?

2. Do you think that the genome should be sequenced from one end to the other (from chromosome 1 to chromosome 22) or should certain "important" genes be sequenced before others? What criteria should be used to specify which genes are important enough to be sequenced?

3. Go to a medical library and obtain a copy of McKusick's *Mendelian Inheritance in Man*. Make a list of ten traits or diseases that you never heard of before and think are very unusual or interesting. Can you find any traits in your family?

CHAPTER REVIEW

Summary

▸ Human genetics is governed by complex patterns of inheritance. Many human traits are governed by genes with multiple alleles. Other traits are governed by polygenic inheritance, in which several different genes combine to influence a single trait.

▸ A person's sex can influence the action of genes. Both sex-limited and sex-influenced genes act differently in males and females. The environment also affects the expression of genes. Different influences combine to produce an individual's phenotype.

▸ Many genetic disorders are recessive, requiring two recessive alleles for a harmful effect. Others, such as Huntington disease, are dominant. A person who is heterozygous for a recessive disorder will not have the disorder but can pass it on to the next generation.

▸ Several disorders are caused by nondisjunction of chromosomes. Specific syndromes result from nondisjunction of particular chromosomes. For example, Down syndrome results from a nondisjunction of the twenty-first pair of chromosomes. This condition is also called trisomy 21.

▸ Many genetic defects can be detected in carriers or diagnosed before birth by ultrasound, karyotyping, and various biochemical techniques. Sometimes a fetus can be treated before birth. Some genetic disorders can be treated after birth.

Vocabulary

amniocentesis
chorionic villus
  sampling
cystic fibrosis
Down syndrome
DNA probe
Duchenne muscular
  dystrophy
fetoscopy
fetus
genetic marker
hemoglobin
hemophilia
Huntington disease
karyotype
Klinefelter syndrome
melanin
multiple allele
pedigree
phenylketonuria
polygenic inheritance
sex-influenced trait
sex-limited gene
sickle-cell disease
sickle-cell trait
syndrome
Turner syndrome
ultrasound

Concept Mapping

Construct a concept map for genetic disorders. Include the following terms: amniocentesis, chorionic villus sampling, DNA probe, fetoscopy, fetus, karyotype, sickle-cell trait, and ultrasound. Use additional terms as you need them.

Review

1. Explain what is meant by *multiple alleles*.
2. Give an example of a trait that has multiple alleles.
3. What are two genotypes that produce blood type A?
4. An autosomal gene that is expressed in the phenotype of only one sex is said to be _____ .
5. A trait that is dominant in one sex and recessive in the other is called a _____ .
6. Identify two environmental factors that affect the development of the human phenotype.
7. What type of mutation originally caused the sickle-cell allele to appear?
8. Name a genetic disease in humans that is inherited through a dominant gene.
9. What is hemophilia? How is it inherited?
10. List two syndromes caused by disjunction.
11. Describe how a DNA probe can be used to identify a carrier of a genetic disorder.

12. What is amniocentesis? What can be learned from this procedure?
13. What is the purpose of genetic counseling?
14. Name one method used to treat disorders in fetuses.
15. Why must babies who have PKU not eat foods containing phenylalanine?

Interpret and Apply

16. A man with blood type B (genotype BO) marries a woman with blood type A (genotype AA). What blood types could their children have? Draw a Punnett square to illustrate this.
17. Suppose two people who were heterozygous for PKU married and had a child. What is the probability that their child would have PKU?
18. Explain the difference between the way in which ABO blood groups are inherited and the way in which skin color is inherited.
19. What is the difference between a sex-limited trait and a sex-influenced trait? Give an example of each.
20. Expectant parents want to learn whether the fetus the woman is carrying has sickle-cell disease. Could a genetic counselor determine this by looking at the fetus's karyotype? Explain.
21. Why might each of the following people want to consult a genetic counselor?
    a. a 37-year-old pregnant woman
    b. a couple whose nephew had cystic fibrosis
    c. a man whose mother has Huntington disease
22. Which type of test might the counselor recommend for each case in question 21?

Critical Thinking

23. Can an elderly person with a normal phenotype be a carrier of Huntington disease? Explain.

24. A woman having blood type A marries a man having blood type B. They have five children. Two sons have blood type O. One daughter has blood type AB; another daughter, type A; and a third, type B.
    a. Draw a pedigree showing the blood types of the parents and offspring. Use letters in the pedigree symbols to represent the individuals' blood types.
    b. Figure out the genotypes of the parents and children.
25. Suppose a characteristic is determined by two different genes. Each gene has three different alleles. How many phenotypes can there be?
26. Until the recent availability of DNA technology, information about human heredity could be obtained only slowly and over long periods of time. Explain why.
27. Suppose you collected data on foot size in a large group of people. The data are shown in the bar graph below. Based on the graph, what kind of inheritance do you think controls foot size? Explain.

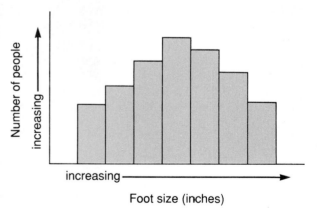

Chapter

12

APPLICATIONS OF GENETICS

Overview

CONTROLLED BREEDING

12-1 Selection
12-2 Inbreeding
12-3 Hybridization

ARTIFICIAL METHODS OF GENETIC CONTROL

12-4 Polyploidy
12-5 Cloning
12-6 Genetic Engineering
12-7 Manipulating Nature

What characteristics are desirable in breeding racehorses?

CONTROLLED BREEDING

Humans domesticated animals and plants long before the principles of genetics were known. Evidence indicates that animals were first domesticated around 11 000 years ago. Plants were domesticated over 1000 years later. Yet as you learned in Chapter 9, Mendel did not discover the principles that govern inheritance until the middle of the nineteenth century. How, then, did our distant ancestors succeed at breeding animals and plants?

The answer lies in controlled breeding. In **controlled breeding**, only those plants or animals with desired characteristics are allowed to reproduce. This technique is also called artificial selection, in contrast to Darwin's concept of natural selection, in which the environment determines which genetic variants are most likely to survive. Controlled breeding is widely practiced today, but with the benefit of an understanding of genetics.

12-1 Selection

The first step in breeding new varieties of plants or animals is to identify those organisms that have one or more desired traits. Only those organisms with desirable characteristics are then selected to reproduce. Their offspring stand a good chance of inheriting the desired characteristics.

Long ago, when there were fewer kinds of domesticated plants and animals to choose from, selection was carried out on a small scale. More recently, selection has been practiced with huge fields of crops and with enormous numbers of animals. Selection from a large number of organisms is called **mass selection**.

Mass selection was used frequently by Luther Burbank, an American horticulturist known for his success in plant breeding during the last century. Burbank planted huge fields of different flowers and vegetables. From these he would select individual plants that differed in certain ways from most of the others. For example, some of the plants he chose had unusually colored flowers or slightly different fruit. Burbank collected and planted the seeds from these unusual plants. Often the offspring had the same characteristics found in the parent plants. Using mass selection, Burbank developed hundreds of new varieties of fruits, flowers, vegetables, and grains. Some of the potatoes, plums, and apples that you eat were originally developed by Burbank.

Although mass selection can be used to develop a new variety of a plant or animal, it does not create new characteristics. An organism's characteristics—its phenotype—depend on its genotype. Selection does not create new genotypes for a given trait. Selection merely reshuffles alleles so that new combinations of various characteristics occur in offspring.

Section Objectives

A *Describe* the process of mass selection.

B *Explain* how inbreeding is used to maintain desired traits.

C *Discuss* the effects of inbreeding.

D *Contrast* inbreeding and hybridization.

1. Selection of Plant with Desired Trait

2. Collection and Planting of Seeds

3. Appearance of Additional Plants with the Desired Trait

4. Collection and Planting of Seeds

5. Appearance of More Plants with the Desired Trait

Figure 12-1   Mass selection

Applications of Genetics   **201**

12-2 Inbreeding

Once a variety of plant or animal has been developed by selection, breeders use another technique to ensure that succeeding
generations carry the desired traits. The technique, called **inbreeding**, is the crossing of two closely related individuals. In
animals, inbreeding may be done by matings between siblings.
In plants, inbreeding is done by self-pollination.

Since closely related individuals usually have a high percentage of genes in common, inbreeding makes it likely that the
desired genes will be passed on to offspring. After many generations of inbreeding, most of the offspring will be homozygous
for the desired traits. When this occurs, breeders are said to
have established pure lines. (Recall that Mendel worked with
pure lines of pea plants in his experiments.)

Because pure lines are homozygous for the selected traits, all
of the offspring will have those traits. Continued selection will
not produce any new variation within a breed. Thus pure lines
are said to "breed true." Selection and inbreeding have produced
many distinct breeds, such as the dogs shown in Figure 12-2.

As the offspring in a pure line continue to be inbred, it becomes more and more likely that individuals homozygous for
harmful alleles will arise. After many generations, a condition
called **inbreeding depression** may result. Inbreeding depression
is characterized by a decrease in the health or fertility of each
succeeding generation. For example, English sheepdogs tend to
develop severe joint problems because of extensive inbreeding.

Figure 12-2 This breed was developed for a specific purpose.
What do you think that purpose is?

The undesirable effects of inbreeding may be reduced by periodic **outcrossing**. In outcrossing, an inbred organism is crossed with a less closely related individual. Dog breeders often use the technique of outcrossing to prevent inbreeding depression. For example, an animal breeder may introduce new genes into a line by crossing one poodle of known ancestry with another, less closely related poodle.

12-3 Hybridization

Inbreeding preserves desirable characteristics within a breed. However, organisms selected for one trait often carry other, less desirable traits. For example, corn plants that are selected because they are hardy may not produce large kernels. Other breeds of corn may produce large kernels but not be hardy. Fortunately, there are ways to combine desirable traits.

To increase the number of desirable traits in plants or animals, breeders often use a technique called hybridization. In **hybridization**, two breeds are crossed to produce a variety with all the desirable characteristics of both parental breeds. The hybrid offspring have more of the favorable traits and fewer of the unfavorable traits than their parents do.

The superiority of F_1 hybrids is called **hybrid vigor**. The cause of hybrid vigor is not fully understood. It may be because different pure lines probably do not carry the same unfavorable recessive alleles. By combining favorable dominant alleles from one parent with unfavorable recessive alleles from another parent, it is possible to produce offspring that are heterozygous for the desired traits.

Hybridization can be used to develop a new breed. However, it is a painstaking, time-consuming process. Desirable traits are often linked on chromosomes with undesirable traits. With continued breeding, these traits may recombine through crossing over. (Recall from Chapter 10 that crossing over occurs often during meiosis.) Eventually some of the offspring will have all the desirable characteristics of both pure lines. But the process usually takes several generations.

Sometimes breeders make crosses from several different breeds to produce one line with all the desired traits. A Rhode Island Red hen, for example, contains genes from at least five different breeds: Red Malay, Shanghai, Chittagong, Brahma, and Leghorn. Other breeds of fowl and some breeds of cattle have also been produced by more than one hybridization.

The term *hybrid* may also refer to a cross between two different types of organisms. The mule is the best known animal hybrid of this sort. A mule is a cross between a female horse and a male donkey. The horse and the donkey are closely related animals. A mule combines the large size and strength of a horse

Figure 12-3 These hybrid lilies were produced by combining desirable characteristics of several varieties.

DO YOU KNOW?

Information: Reliance on a popular hybrid can be dangerous, however, if environmental conditions change. In 1970, the United States corn crop was decimated by a fungal disease called Southern leaf blight. Nearly all the plants were hybrids with genes making them susceptible to the illness.

Figure 12-4 At least five different breeds contributed genes to the Rhode Island Red.

CONSUMER BIOLOGY

Home gardeners often buy hybrid plants. To save money, they may use the seeds produced by these plants for the next crop. Since these seeds resulted from cross-pollination among hybrids, a variety of traits (some undesirable) would appear in the second crop.

with the hardiness of a donkey. Unfortunately, mules cannot reproduce.

Hybrids between different kinds of organisms usually are sterile, or unable to reproduce. Hybrid sterility is often caused by different numbers of chromosomes in the two parent types. The hybrid offspring, therefore, have unmatched sets of chromosomes. During meiosis, these unmatched chromosomes cannot form homologous pairs.

CHECKPOINT ◆

1. Name the first step in controlled breeding.
2. What method is used to preserve desirable traits in a breed?
3. What condition may result from generations of inbreeding?
4. Which of the following involves crossing unrelated individuals: inbreeding, outcrossing, or hybridization?
5. What beneficial condition results from hybridization?
▶ 6. A plant breeder finds that after many generations, one variety of daisy easily becomes infected with a virus. What should the plant breeder do to improve the health of the daisies?
▶ 7. Hybrid organisms usually are not used as parents. Based on your knowledge of Mendelian genetics, suggest an explanation for this.

▶ Denotes a question that involves *interpreting* and *applying* concepts.

ARTIFICIAL METHODS OF GENETIC CONTROL

Controlled breeding methods are based on trial and error. Often, many generations of plants or animals must be produced before the desired results are obtained. However, people now have a more detailed understanding of the function of genes. This understanding has allowed the development of techniques to change the genetic makeup of an organism. Many times these changes can then be bred into future generations. Thus new characteristics may be introduced into a breeding line in one generation.

As you will see in this lesson, these new techniques have many possible applications. They could lead to greatly improved plants and animals for agriculture.

12-4 Polyploidy

As you learned in Chapter 10, polyploidy is a condition in which the cells of an organism contain extra sets of chromosomes. Early in this century, biologists discovered that polyploid plants could be produced artificially by using a chemical called colchicine [kol′ chə sēn]. Colchicine applied to growing buds will prevent spindle formation during mitosis. Without a spindle, the chromatids cannot separate. As a result, cells treated with colchicine have double the normal number of chromosomes. A cell with four sets of chromosomes ($4n$) rather than two sets ($2n$) is called a *tetraploid* cell. Treatment with colchicine may also produce cells with more than four sets of chromosomes.

Polyploid plants often produce larger fruits and flowers than normal diploid forms. Polyploid plants may also be hardier than diploid plants, or they may mature earlier in the growing season.

Another way to produce polyploid plants uses special cells called protoplasts. **Protoplasts** are plant cells in which the cell wall has been removed chemically. The cells are induced to grow and divide. Protoplasts of two kinds of plants can be fused, or joined, and then treated to stimulate the development of a new cell wall. The process is called *protoplast fusion*. Protoplast fusion forms a polyploid hybrid between plants that normally would not be able to interbreed. The pomato plant, derived from fused potato and tomato protoplasts, is such a polyploid.

One possible use of protoplast fusion is in saving the American elm tree from Dutch elm disease. Researchers are trying to fuse protoplasts from the American elm with protoplasts from the Pioneer elm, which is not susceptible to Dutch elm disease. By fusing the two types of cells, it may be possible to grow American elms that are resistant to the disease.

Section Objectives

E *Explain* how polyploidy in plants can be produced artificially.

F *Describe* how plants and animals are produced by cloning.

G *Discuss* methods used to alter an organism's DNA.

H *Give examples* of the uses of genetic engineering.

I *Discuss* some of the concerns about genetic engineering.

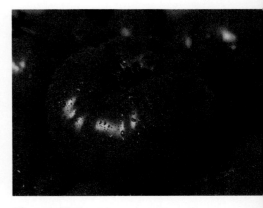

Figure 12-5 Many varieties of tomatoes are polyploid plants.

Figure 12-6 Researchers have had limited success in cloning animals such as mice. Cloned animals are genetically identical. Genetic identity is useful in some kinds of research.

12-5 Cloning

Recall from Chapter 9 that some organisms reproduce asexually by mitosis. This kind of reproduction yields offspring that are genetically identical to each other and to the parent. Offspring produced in this way are called **clones**. Large numbers of plants with desirable characteristics can be produced by cloning. This technique also can be used to produce offspring from hybrids that are unable to breed sexually.

Cloning animals is difficult because an unfertilized egg must be altered, and this cell is often quite small. The haploid nucleus of the egg is either inactivated by radiation or removed. A diploid nucleus from a somatic cell is then inserted. The egg divides and develops into a complete organism that is genetically identical to the donor of the somatic cell. So far, geneticists have been able to clone frogs, mice, and rats for use in experiments in which genetically identical animals can help control certain variables. Cloning a human would be very difficult because human egg cells are so small. Can you think of another reason why human cloning is not presently feasible?

Cloning also refers to the mass production of identical cells. These cells are grown in laboratories in large vats to which the appropriate hormones and nutrients are added. Microorganisms or somatic cells from multicellular organisms are grown this way. Useful substances can then be harvested from the cell cultures. For example, vats of genetically engineered *E. coli* bacteria produce human insulin that is extracted and provided to diabetics. The pancreas of a diabetic cannot produce insulin which is vital. Fungal cells are routinely cultured to produce substances that are used as antibiotic drugs to prevent or treat infections.

12-6 Genetic Engineering

Some of the most exciting research in genetics today is being done at the molecular level. New techniques, known collectively as **genetic engineering**, allow researchers to manipulate the genes of organisms. Genes also can be moved from one DNA molecule to another. The new DNA molecule that is created from two different DNA molecules is called **recombinant DNA**.

Recombinant DNA was made possible by the discovery of special enzymes called **restriction enzymes**. Each kind of restriction enzyme can cut a chain of DNA at a particular point in a sequence of nucleotides. For example, one restriction enzyme can cut a nucleotide sequence between two molecules of cytosine. This restriction enzyme would divide the nucleotide sequence ATGCCA into the pieces ATGC and CA. By using different restriction enzymes to cut overlapping pieces, a scientist can determine the sequence of nucleotides in a sample of DNA.

Restriction enzymes are used to remove a section of DNA containing a particular gene. This section can then be transferred to another DNA molecule. In bacteria, some of the DNA is located in rings called **plasmids**. A plasmid can be cut open with a restriction enzyme. The gene from another organism can be inserted, and the plasmid can be reconnected. Notice in Figure 12-7 that the reconnected plasmid carries the inserted gene.

When the plasmid replicates, it also copies the recombinant DNA. Thus all the offspring of the bacteria will also carry the recombinant DNA. The process of making extra copies of recombinant DNA is a form of cloning.

Bacteria containing recombinant DNA can be grown in huge vats. The bacteria reproduce quickly, making many copies of themselves in a short time. If the recombinant DNA carries the nucleotide sequence for a particular protein, these bacteria will produce large amounts of that protein. The protein can then be harvested.

Recombinant DNA in Medicine Through recombinant DNA technology, large quantities of proteins that are useful in medicine have been produced. Examples of these proteins are insulin to treat diabetes, human growth hormone to treat dwarfism, and a clotting factor to treat hemophilia.

Insulin regulates the amount of sugar in the bloodstream. People whose bodies do not produce enough insulin suffer from *diabetes* (dī ə bēt′ ēz). Until recently, people with diabetes were given insulin taken from cows and pigs. However, these insulins are slightly different in amino acid sequence from human insulin, and therefore sometimes cause allergic reactions in people. Insulin produced by genetically altered bacteria does not provoke an allergic reaction.

Figure 12-7 DNA spliced into a plasmid will be replicated each time the "host" DNA replicates.

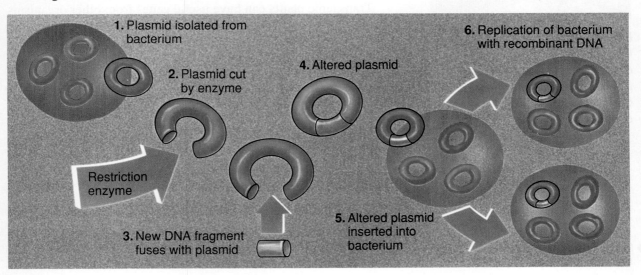

1. Plasmid isolated from bacterium

2. Plasmid cut by enzyme

Restriction enzyme

3. New DNA fragment fuses with plasmid

4. Altered plasmid

5. Altered plasmid inserted into bacterium

6. Replication of bacterium with recombinant DNA

Human growth hormone controls the growth of bones. Children who lack enough of this protein grow very slowly and never reach a normal size. Genetic engineering has made it possible to produce enough growth hormone to treat thousands of affected children worldwide. Another use for growth hormone is in the treatment of slow-healing bone fractures.

Hemophilia is the failure of blood to clot normally because of a missing clotting factor. Before recombinant DNA technology, clotting factor was pooled from many blood donors. This could transmit AIDS and other viral infections. Clotting factor made in recombinant bacteria is pure.

Recombinant DNA in Agriculture Geneticists are working to develop crops engineered for drought and salt resistance, higher yield, and improved nutrient value. For example, sunflowers have been engineered to produce seeds with a highly nutritious protein normally found in beans. Corn plants have been developed that have higher levels of tryptophan, an amino acid which increases the nutritional value of the corn seeds.

12-7 Manipulating Nature

The first recombinant organisms were bacteria. Now scientists can insert "foreign" DNA into fertilized eggs of multicellular organisms. The resulting organisms have the inserted gene in all their cells, and are called **transgenic**. Transgenic sheep are genetically engineered to secrete in their milk the human clotting factor needed by sufferers of hemophilia. This technique provides a less expensive and purer source of the clotting factor. Similarly, genetically engineered mice secrete a human heart drug in their milk called plasminogen activator.

Transgenic plants can have useful genes from other organisms inserted into their chromosomes. For example, a gene from the bacterium *Bacillus thuringiensis* allows plants to produce a substance that safely kills insect pests.

Figure 12-8 This transgenic hog looks like other hogs, yet it differs due to genetically engineered genes. Transgenic animals can become factories for the production of useful biochemicals.

CHECKPOINT ◆

8. What methods are used to produce polyploidy in plants?
9. What is cloning?
10. Name one product made by recombinant DNA.
11. Give one benefit and one risk of genetic engineering.
▶ 12. Suppose that restriction enzyme 1 cuts a DNA molecule after each GTT triplet. Restriction enzyme 2 cuts the molecule between all G and C bases. What fragments will be produced if a piece of DNA with the sequence GTTTAGAGCTA is treated with both enzymes?

▶ Denotes a question that involves *interpreting* and *applying* concepts.

PRODUCTION OF GENETICALLY IDENTICAL PLANTS BY VEGETATIVE PROPAGATION

Objectives and Skills

- ☐ *Produce* new plants by making cuttings.
- ☐ *Observe* growth of cuttings.
- ☐ *Explain* the causes of differential growth in cuttings.

Materials

6 small flower pots with damp potting soil
newspaper
scissors
metric ruler
2 clear plastic bags and ties
coleus and begonia plants

Procedure and Observations

1. Read all the instructions for this laboratory activity before you begin your work.
2. On a separate piece of paper, draw a data table like the one shown below.

DATA TABLE

Cutting	Number of leaves At start	Number of leaves At 3 weeks	Height At start	Height At 3 weeks
Coleus 4 leaves 2 leaves stem only				
Begonia 4 leaves 2 leaves stem only				

3. Spread out sheets of newspaper to keep your work area clean. Bring 6 flower pots with damp potting soil to your work area.

4. Using scissors, prepare the following cuttings from a coleus plant: stem and 4 leaves, stem and 2 leaves, stem only. Prepare the same type of cuttings from a begonia plant. **CAUTION: Be careful not to cut yourself when using the scissors.**
5. Measure the height of each cutting and record it in the data table.
6. Poke a hole with a pencil in the soil in each pot. Plant each of the cuttings to a depth of about 2 cm. Label each pot.
7. Place the flower pots in the clear plastic bags. Put 3 pots in each bag. Gently blow into each bag and then close it with the tie. The plastic bags will keep the plants from drying out.
8. Label the bags with your name and date. Place them in a sunny spot or under lights.
9. Clean up your work area and wash your hands thoroughly.
10. Check the plants periodically, add water if needed.
11. Three weeks after you make the cuttings, gently remove them from their pots. Rinse the roots with water to remove the soil. Record the number of leaves on each cutting. Record the height of each cutting.

Analysis and Conclusions

1. Did the number of leaves have any effect on the growth of the cuttings? Explain.
2. Which type of plant showed the greatest amount of growth? Explain why this is so.
3. How do plants compare to the parent plants both genotypically and phenotypically?
4. Suppose that after the cuttings have grown for several months, you take cuttings from them. How will the second set of cuttings compare with the original parent plants?

CUTTING EDGE

Deliberate Release of Genetically Engineered Microbes

April 24, 1987, was a landmark day for the field of genetic engineering. Early in the morning, researchers from a company called Advanced Genetic Sciences released an altered form of the bacterium *Pseudomonas syringae* onto 2400 strawberry plants growing in a patch near Brentwood, California. The bacteria normally bear a surface protein that serves as a nesting place in which ice crystals can begin growing. The altered microbe has the "ice-nucleating" gene deleted, and so it cannot prompt ice formation. When allowed to grow on crops, the deficient bacteria would prevent freezing of the plants. Laboratory and greenhouse experiments indicate that without the bacteria or with normal bacteria, strawberries freeze at 28° F; with the treated bacteria, the plants do not freeze until the mercury drops to 23° F. Avoiding frost damage could save billions of dollars a year.

By April 25, however, the experimental strawberry patch was in shambles, the work of vandals who objected to genetically engineered organisms being released into the environment. A similar public reaction occurred a month later farther north in the small town of Tulelake, where the very same "frostban" bacteria were sprayed onto potato seedlings.

Organisms with engineered traits that affect agricultural characteristics must ultimately be tested in the field. Here their interactions with other organisms can be observed. Will the altered organisms affect animals that might eat them? Will they transmit their advantageous traits to weeds?

People living near proposed test sites are understandably concerned about the safety of deliberate releases. This is why it is imperative that researchers comply with Environmental Protection Agency regulations.

Researcher Gary Strobel, without EPA approval, inoculated 14 elm trees with *Pseudomonas syringae*, engineered to produce biochemicals to resist Dutch elm disease. Part of the experiment was to test the vaccine by infecting the trees with the devastating Dutch elm disease fungus—an organism that is not normally present in that area.

The Strobel case, however, is very unusual. As the number of proposed deliberate release experiments has grown from a trickle to a torrent, scientists have developed quite rigorous safety measures. One approach is to booby-trap the engineered organism with a gene that kills it once the desired task has been accomplished. For example, bacteria that colonize crop plant roots, where they release an insecticide, can be altered to carry a gene for a chemical that kills them. The self-destruct mechanism isn't activated until the crop plant's roots have taken hold.

Another safeguard is to monitor the test site carefully. Consider the precautions taken by researchers at the Boyce Thompson Institute for Plant Research at Cornell University. In the summer of 1989, they released an altered form of a baculovirus, which naturally kills the cabbage looper, a foe of many crops. The virus has no effect on other animals. The baculovirus had the gene removed which normally allows it to manufacture a protective coat. This protective coat protects the virus in the environ-

ment for up to 12 years. Without its wrapping, the virus dies in a few days—a desirable characteristic if other genes are to be altered to enhance its killing effects on cabbage loopers and other pests.

The field test on a 2-acre plot in Geneva, New York, will show just how long the engineered virus can survive in plants infected with the loopers. The viruses were applied to 2500 plants in the center of the plot, with the remaining plants serving as a buffer zone. Plant and soil samples will be probed until 1991.

Results are in from that first deliberate release experiment of April 1987. Steven Lindow, who developed the frost-protecting bacteria when a graduate student in the 1970's, submitted a 400-page report on the release to the EPA. As expected from Lindow's extensive laboratory and greenhouse

experiments, the genetically engineered bacteria in the field stayed on or very near the plants where they were sprayed, and they indeed lowered the temperature at which frost forms on strawberries.

DISCUSSION & RESEARCH

1. Read the labels of some commercial pesticides used to protect garden plants. Do you think that using genetically engineered microbes as pesticides would be a safe alternative to chemical pesticides? What are the advantages and disadvantages of each type of pesticide?

2. Would you object if a deliberate release of a genetically engineered microbe was planned to take place in your community? Do you think nonscientists would be worried about deliberate releases if they understood more about genetic engineering? How can scientists educate the public on what they do?

3. If you were to carry out a deliberate release experiment, what precautions would you take?

CHAPTER REVIEW

Summary

▶ For thousands of years, humans have used controlled breeding to produce plants and animals that are desirable for agriculture. Controlled breeding begins with the selection of a few organisms with desirable characteristics. Only those organisms are allowed to reproduce. Selection today usually involves large numbers of organisms.

▶ Pure lines are established by inbreeding. After many generations, offspring produced by inbreeding may suffer from reduced health and fertility. Inbreeding depression can be prevented by periodic outcrossing with a less closely related individual.

▶ Crossing two or more pure lines often gives hybrid offspring that are superior to the parents. However, hybrid offspring from different kinds of organisms usually are sterile because they have unmatched sets of chromosomes.

▶ Modern genetics has led to many techniques for manipulating genes and chromosomes. These techniques promise great improvements in medicine and agriculture. Induced polyploidy, cloning, and genetic engineering are some of the most promising techniques.

▶ Genetic engineering also has certain risks. New developments must be evaluated continuously to ensure responsible use of the technology.

Vocabulary

clone
cloning
controlled breeding
genetic engineering
hybridization
hybrid vigor
inbreeding
inbreeding depression

mass selection
outcrossing
plasmid
protoplast
recombinant DNA
restriction enzyme
transgenic organisms

Concept Mapping

Construct a concept map for the techniques used in controlled breeding. Include the following terms: controlled breeding, hybridization, hybrid vigor, inbreeding, inbreeding depression, mass selection, outcrossing. Add additional terms as you need them.

Review

1. What is the purpose of mass selection?
2. What form of controlled breeding was practiced by Luther Burbank?
3. What is inbreeding?
4. What condition sometimes results from several generations of inbreeding? How can this result be avoided or reduced?
5. How is hybridization different from inbreeding?
6. What methods are used to produce polyploid plants artificially?
7. Describe the process of cloning.
8. What does a restriction enzyme do?
9. What name is given to the rings of DNA found in bacteria?
10. What is recombinant DNA? Explain how it is made.
11. Give two examples of how genetic engineering is used in medicine.
12. How might genetic engineering improve agriculture?
13. What are some of the concerns about the uses of genetic engineering?

Interpret and Apply

14. You have two snapdragon plants. One is much larger than the other. You know that one of the plants is tetraploid. Which one?
15. What could a blueberry grower do to get a bigger and better crop of berries?

16. You are working in your garden and discover a beautiful yellow daisy among all the white ones. You would like to have more yellow daisies in the future. What method of controlled breeding would you use to grow more yellow daisies? How would you employ this method?

17. What controlled breeding or genetic engineering technique is involved in each of the following?
    a. A cat has six kittens. Two of the kittens, a male and a female, are an unusually beautiful color. When the kittens mature, they are mated to each other in hopes of producing offspring with the same unusual color as the parents.
    b. Bacteria are used to produce clotting factor for hemophiliacs.
    c. A horticulturist uses colchicine to produce large, juicy blackberries.
    d. A breeder of toy poodles wants to avoid inbreeding depression by crossing one of his female poodles with an unrelated male poodle.
    e. You discover a four-leaf clover in a field of clover. You collect and plant seeds from that clover in hopes of one day having a whole field of four-leaf clover.

18. Hybrids are often large and strong. They exhibit hybrid vigor. Explain why crossing two hybrids usually does not produce offspring with greater hybrid vigor and more desirable traits.

19. Compare inbreeding depression and hybrid vigor.

20. A plant breeder has developed a tasty new vegetable by crossing a cauliflower plant with a cabbage plant. The new vegetable plant, however, is sterile. What method of reproduction could the plant breeder use to produce large numbers of hybrid offspring?

Critical Thinking

21. Why was the discovery of restriction enzymes necessary before scientists could produce recombinant DNA?

22. Genes that are next to each other on a chromosome often function as a unit. What do you think would happen if a transplanted gene was inserted in the middle of a unit in the host DNA?

23. Which are more genetically similar, mice produced by cloning or flowers produced by self-pollination? Why?

24. Use the graph below to answer the following questions.
    a. Which type of plants have the greatest genetic diversity?
    b. Suppose a lethal disease develops among the wheat plants. Which type of wheat is most likely to survive? Explain your answer.
    c. There are thousands of types of plants that could be edible. Modern agriculture, however, is based on just a few types of crops. Thus many scientists warn of a "crisis of uniformity." What do you think is meant by this warning?

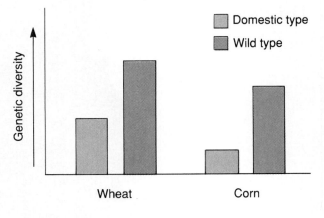

POPULATION GENETICS

Overview

VARIATION IN POPULATIONS

13-1 Definition of Species
13-2 Clines and Subspecies
13-3 Gene Pool
13-4 Hardy-Weinberg Principle

CHANGES IN POPULATIONS

13-5 Mutation
13-6 Small Populations
13-7 Nonrandom Mating
13-8 Migration
13-9 Harmful Genes

Why are cheetahs, the fastest land animals, in danger of extinction?

VARIATION IN POPULATIONS

If you went to a pet store to buy a turtle, you would not mistakenly bring home a bird or a fish instead. Each of these organisms is clearly different from the others. People have long been aware of the similarities and differences between living things. The Greek philosopher Aristotle thought living things existed in a number of distinct, unchanging types that he called "species." People believed that any organism could be identified by comparing its physical appearance with other known species. Close inspection of different kinds of plants and animals, however, shows that there can be enormous variation within a species.

13-1 Definition of Species

It is not always possible to identify living things simply by their physical appearance. To take into account the variations within a species, a more precise definition must be used. Biologists now define a **species** as a group of closely related organisms that can mate and produce fertile offspring.

The snow goose and the blue goose shown in Figure 13-1 were once placed in separate species. As you can see, they look quite different. Careful observation of these birds in the wild, however, reveals that they represent merely two colors of the same species. Both white and blue forms may hatch from eggs in a single nest. Snow geese are often found together with Canada geese. However, Canada geese are a separate species. Snow geese cannot mate with Canada geese and produce offspring.

Often it is not possible to determine whether organisms can breed and produce fertile offspring. This may be the case if the organisms being studied are separated geographically. The problem also exists if the organisms are no longer living. Botanists, for

Section Objectives

A *Describe* how organisms are grouped into species.

B *Distinguish* between a cline and a subspecies.

C *Explain* the concept of a gene pool.

D *State* how the Hardy-Weinberg principle explains genetic equilibrium in a population.

E *Identify* the five assumptions of the Hardy-Weinberg principle.

Figure 13-1 These blue geese (*left*) and the snow goose (*right*) were once considered separate species.

example, often study dried specimens of plants. In such work, they must depend greatly on physical characteristics to make a classification. However, they also must take into account the great variation that occurs within some species.

13-2 Clines and Subspecies

The organisms that make up a species are usually distributed over a wide geographic range. The smallest division of a species that can be identified and studied is a population. A **population** is all the members of a species that live in a particular location. For example, all the catfish that live in a lake make up a population of catfish.

Characteristics in a species vary both within a population and from one population to the next. Usually, the farther apart two populations are, the more they differ. Variation often follows a geographic pattern.

Figure 13-2 shows how the height of a wild flower called yarrow varies gradually with the location of the plant. Notice that yarrow plants growing at high altitudes are shorter than plants growing at low altitudes. However, the height differences are not due to the environment. When yarrow plants collected from different altitudes are grown under identical conditions in a greenhouse, the differences in height still persist. This experiment demonstrates that the height differences are hereditary. A gradual variation in a single trait from one population to the next that corresponds to changes in the environment is called a **cline**.

Clines occur in many different species of plants and animals. For example, whitetail deer are found over most of North America. Whitetail deer that are found in the North are far larger than those in the South. Northern males may have masses up to 180 kilograms. In the South, males may be as small as 23 kilograms.

Figure 13-2 A cline in the height of yarrow plants growing at different altitudes in the Sierra Nevada mountains of California.

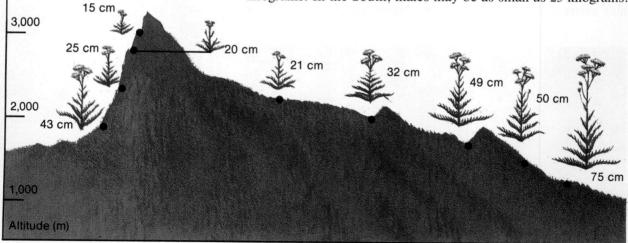

Figure 13-3 *Left:* The western red-shafted flicker; *Right:* The eastern yellow-shafted flicker. Both birds are classified as the same species, the common flicker.

If you compare the two ends of a cline, you will see that they are very different from each other. But because they are linked by gradual changes in neighboring populations, they cannot be divided easily into separate groups.

Variations among populations may involve a number of different traits. Also, variations do not necessarily correspond to gradual environmental changes. Consider the common flicker, a woodpecker that lives in woodlots, forests, and towns. The eastern flicker has yellow feathers under its wings and tail, so it is called a yellow-shafted flicker. The western flicker has red feathers under its wings and tail, so it is called a red-shafted flicker. In the central United States where the populations overlap, the birds sometimes interbreed and produce fertile offspring. (Hybrids may have orange underwings.) Thus the two varieties belong to the same species. Yellow-shafted and red-shafted flickers are subspecies of the common flicker. **Subspecies** are distinct populations of a species. Sometimes, different subspecies are separated by geographic barriers, such as a river or mountains.

13-3 Gene Pool

Recall from Chapter 9 that genes in individual organisms are mixed in new combinations during meiosis and sexual reproduction. Thus much of the variation in a species results from heredity. But how do patterns of variation such as clines or subspecies become established in whole populations? Answering such questions involves learning some principles of population genetics. **Population genetics** is the study of how genetic principles apply to entire populations.

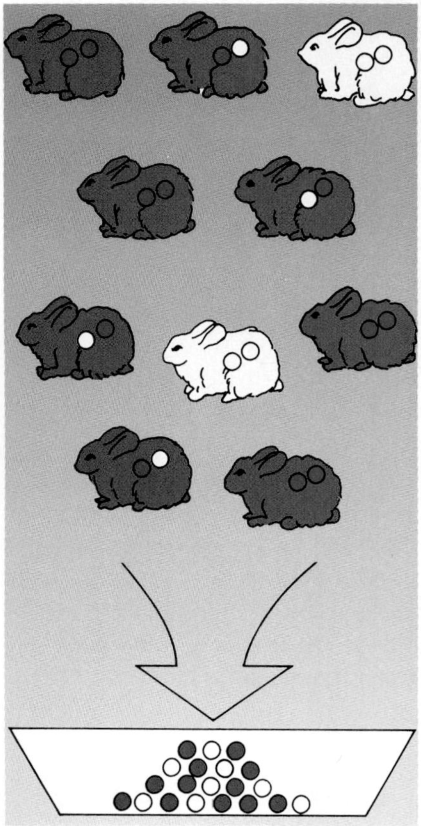

Figure 13-4 A gene pool for an imaginary rabbit population. Brown marbles represent the dominant allele for brown coat color (*B*). White marbles represent the recessive allele for white coat color (*b*).

Population genetics involves studying the frequency with which particular alleles occur in a population. Finding the frequency of an allele requires a method called population sampling. In **population sampling**, data from a small part of the population are assumed to be true for the whole population. Thus if a random sample of 100 rabbits in an area contains 50 rabbits with dark hair and 50 rabbits with light hair, it can be assumed that in the whole population, half the rabbits have dark hair and half have light hair.

The entire genetic content of a population is called the **gene pool**. The gene pool contains all of the genes for all of the characteristics of the population. For example, in a population made up of parakeets of various colors and sizes, all the genes in all the birds together make up the gene pool. As in Mendelian genetics, however, it is often convenient to consider only a single characteristic at one time.

Figure 13-4 illustrates a way of imagining the gene pool for coat color in a population of rabbits. Assume that there are only two alleles for coat color. (In a real gene pool, there would be multiple alleles for various traits.) The dominant allele, *B*, produces brown fur. The recessive allele, *b*, produces white fur. Each allele for fur in the rabbit population can be represented by a marble in the pan. A brown marble represents the allele for brown fur, and a white marble represents the allele for white fur. All the marbles in the pan represent the gene pool for coat color. If all the rabbits in the original population were homozygous for the brown allele, then all the marbles in the pan would be brown. If all the rabbits were white, then all the marbles would be white.

Suppose you determined what percent of the marbles are brown and what percent are white. These percents represent the frequency of each allele for fur color in the population. **Allele frequency** is the proportion, or percent, of an allele in the gene pool. The sum of all the allele frequencies for a gene within a population is equal to 1.0, or 100 percent.

In Figure 13-4, 40 percent of the marbles are white, and 60 percent of the marbles are brown. These numbers represent a rabbit population in which 40 percent of the alleles are for white fur and 60 percent are for brown fur.

BIOLOGY INSIGHT

Process of Science: Models that represent real situations in simplified form (often employing mathematical relationships) help to predict the behavior of complex real events.

13-4 Hardy-Weinberg Principle

In 1908, Godfrey Hardy, a British mathematician, and Wilhelm Weinberg, a German physician, each demonstrated how the frequency of alleles in a gene pool could be described by mathematical formulas. The **Hardy-Weinberg principle** states that under certain conditions, the frequency of dominant and recessive alleles remains the same from generation to generation.

To show how the principle can be applied, consider again the rabbit population represented in Figure 13-4. When these rabbits mate and produce offspring, each parent produces gametes with one allele for coat color. You can model the production of gametes in the rabbit population by imagining that you reach into the pan and randomly withdraw a pair of marbles. The pair of marbles represents a zygote formed by the fusion of a male and a female gamete. Each marble in the pair represents a gamete carrying an allele for coat color. (Just because two rabbits have an offspring, their alleles are not removed from the gene pool. The rabbits can have more than one offspring.)

The chance of choosing a marble of a particular color depends on the frequency of the different marbles in the gene pool. Because 60 percent of the marbles are brown, the chances are you would choose a brown marble about 60 percent of the time and a white marble about 40 percent of the time. In other words, on any draw, the probability that you will select a particular colored marble is equal to its frequency in the gene pool.

Each genotype is composed of two alleles. The probability of drawing a particular genotype is the product of the probabilities for drawing each of the two alleles separately. Thus the chance of drawing the genotype *BB* is 60 percent times 60 percent, or 36 percent (0.60 × 0.60 = 0.36).

The probabilities of drawing each genotype are shown in the table in Figure 13-5. This table, which works like a Punnett square, is called a **cross-multiplication table**. The frequency of each allele for the males in the population is listed across the top. The frequency of alleles for the females is listed on the left side. Frequencies are given as decimals rather than as percents. Notice that rabbits with the genotype *BB* make up 36 percent of the population and rabbits with the genotype *bb* make up 16 percent of the population. Two squares in the table show the genotype *Bb*. Recall from the crosses you learned to do in Chapter 9 that there are two kinds of combinations that produce heterozygous offspring. Similarly, the percentage of heterozygous rabbits in the population would be the sum of the values in these two squares, or 48 percent. Since the allele for brown coat is dominant over the allele for white coat, 84 percent (36 percent + 48 percent) will be brown, and 16 percent will be white.

How often will the genotype *bb* occur in the next generation? According to the Hardy-Weinberg principle, the allele frequencies will not change in the next generation. As long as a rabbit of any color is allowed to mate with a rabbit of any other color, the Hardy-Weinberg principle predicts that the probability of drawing each genotype will remain constant. After 15 or even 40 generations, there still will be 84 percent brown rabbits and 16 percent white rabbits. A population in which there is no

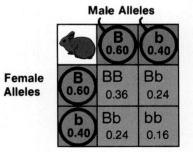

Figure 13-5 According to this cross-multiplication table, what is the probability of producing a *Bb* offspring?

Figure 13-6 According to the Hardy-Weinberg principle, allele frequencies remain the same from generation to generation, as shown by the similarities among these elephants.

change in allele frequency over a long period is said to be in **genetic equilibrium**.

According to the Hardy-Weinberg principle, a population must meet the following five conditions to be in genetic equilibrium.

1. No mutations occur.
2. The population is large.
3. Mating between males and females is random.
4. Individuals do not leave the population or enter from the outside.
5. No genotype is more likely to survive and have offspring than any other genotype.

Natural populations, however, rarely meet all of these conditions. If they did, allele frequencies would not change, and populations would stay the same over time. What use, then, is the Hardy-Weinberg principle? It is useful because it compares natural populations with an ideal situation. Such comparisons are a measure of change. In nature, allele frequencies are not constant, and populations do change over time, or *evolve*. You will learn more about these changes in Chapter 14.

The Hardy-Weinberg principle also shows that meiosis and sexual reproduction by themselves do not cause populations to change. Merely recombining genes does not change allele frequencies in a gene pool. Other factors must be at work. In other words, for change to occur, one or more of the conditions for genetic equilibrium must be violated. In the next part of this chapter, you will learn how some of these changes operate.

CHECKPOINT ◆

1. How do biologists identify a species?
2. Define the term *cline* and give one example.
3. The red-shafted flicker and the yellow-shafted flicker are examples of _____.
4. How is the frequency of an allele in a gene pool determined?
5. If 5 percent of a fruit fly population has white eyes and the other 95 percent has red eyes, what is the expected percentage of white-eyed flies in the next generation?
6. What conditions must exist for a population to be in genetic equilibrium?
▶ 7. How are the terms *species* and *population* related?
▶ 8. Suppose the frequency of *B* alleles (brown fur) in the gene pool of a rabbit population is 30 percent and the frequency of *b* alleles (white fur) is 70 percent. What percentage of rabbits in the next generation will have brown fur?

▶ Denotes a question that involves *interpreting* and *applying* concepts.

CHANGES IN POPULATIONS

Very few populations stay in genetic equilibrium. The existence of clines and subspecies shows that allele frequencies for particular characteristics can change in predictable ways within a population. Understanding how populations maintain genetic equilibrium, you can examine some of the conditions that can cause a population to depart from equilibrium. These departures enable populations to change over time with changing environments.

13-5 Mutation

Recall from Chapter 10 that mutations are changes in genetic material that may be passed on to offspring. These changes are the original source of genetic variation in a species. All genes are subject to mutation. Mutations change the frequency of alleles in a population. For example, mutations continually add genes for hemophilia to the human gene pool. Estimates indicate that mutations for the hemophilia gene occur in about 3 of every 100 000 gametes. While this may not seem like a large number, in a population with hundreds of millions of people, a significant number can carry this mutation.

Mutations occur at random and can occur in any gene. Some genes are more likely to mutate than others, for reasons not yet understood. About half of all genetic dwarfs, for example, owe their short stature to a newly-mutated gene.

In animals and many types of plants, a mutation cannot be passed to the next generation unless it is contained within the chromosomes of a gamete. In other plants, any cell has the potential to produce a new plant, and mutations can be passed on more easily.

Section Objectives

F *Describe* how mutations influence genetic equilibrium.

G *Explain* how small population size can affect genetic equilibrium.

H *Describe* how nonrandom mating and migration can affect allele frequencies.

I *Discuss* how interaction between genes and the environment over many generations can cause changes in allele frequencies.

BIOLOGY INSIGHT

Homeostasis: Mutations are strictly random events. Organisms do not anticipate the future to produce mutations that may be of later value.

Figure 13-7 Mutations are the original source of variation in populations as shown by the many varieties of roses available.

Figure 13-8 The 7-toed cat is an example of the founder effect.

13-6 Small Populations

When you flip a coin, your chance of getting either heads or tails is 50 percent. If you flip a coin 10 times, you would expect to get five heads and five tails. But in such a small number of tries, you might end up with all heads or all tails. Such a result is unlikely, but it is possible in such a small sample. If you flip a coin 1000 times, however, you would probably end up with close to 50 percent heads and 50 percent tails.

Recall that one assumption of the Hardy-Weinberg principle is that populations are large. This assumption is made because the laws of probability, on which the Hardy-Weinberg principle depends, are more accurate for large samples than small ones. In small samples, the results may vary from what is expected. Consider the following example.

In humans, male gametes carrying either X or Y chromosomes are produced in equal numbers. Thus there is a fifty-fifty chance that offspring will be either male or female. In fact, about half of the human population is male, and half is female. But as you know, some human families have all girls or all boys. Can you explain how this is possible?

More gametes are formed than are used in fertilization. Thus there is always a chance that some alleles (for example, those on the Y chromosome) will not occur in offspring. In a large population, the chances are great that most or all alleles will be found in offspring. In a small population, however, it is likely that some alleles will be lost and some will occur more often than in the previous generation. Allele frequencies in small populations can thus change from one generation to the next.

Other random events besides fertilization can affect allele frequencies in a small population. For example, a disease or a natural disaster could kill much of a population. The frequencies of various alleles in the remaining organisms would be different from those of the original population. A change in allele frequency in a small population due to random events is called **genetic drift**.

A vivid example of genetic drift is the **founder effect**, which is the change in gene frequencies that occurs when a population is founded on a few individuals. Huntington disease, which affects the nervous system is much more prevalent in southeast Indiana, northern Kentucky, and western Ohio than elsewhere in the United States. Settlements in these areas were founded by a few families, who carried the disease-causing gene. The founder effect also accounts for the large number of 7-toed cats in New England. These animals are all believed to have descended from a 7-toed female feline that arrived in colonial Boston, from England, in the 1700s.

13-7 Nonrandom Mating

The Hardy-Weinberg principle assumes that any male in a population is equally likely to mate with any female. In most populations, however, mating is not completely random. Many factors, such as courting behavior or appearance, influence the choice of a mate.

Some organisms are more likely to mate with similar organisms than with dissimilar organisms. For example, white rabbits may be more likely to mate with other white rabbits than with brown rabbits. Likewise, brown rabbits may be more likely to mate with other brown rabbits than with white rabbits. Over time, this kind of nonrandom mating causes the frequency of homozygous individuals to increase and the frequency of heterozygous individuals to decrease. Note that it is the frequency of the *genotypes* that changes. The frequency of alleles stays the same. However, because of the greater number of homozygous individuals, the frequency of the recessive allele appears to be higher than it is.

13-8 Migration

Genetic equilibrium will be altered if organisms can move into or out of a particular breeding population. This kind of movement is called **migration**. During the last 400 years, migration has changed the allele frequencies of the human population in North America. Every ethnic group that has come to this continent has brought with it a unique gene pool. The population today appears very different from both the original populations of American Indians and the population of European settlers who founded the American colonies.

13-9 Harmful Genes

The final assumption of the Hardy-Weinberg principle is that no genotype is more advantageous to an individual than any other genotype. As you already know, this is not always true. Genes for a disease such as hemophilia may be lethal. Organisms that are homozygous for harmful genes are less likely to survive and produce offspring than those that do not carry such genes. Over many generations harmful genes should disappear from a population. However, harmful genes continue to exist in a population at a certain frequency. Can you identify what factors would explain the persistence of such genes in a population over time? If not, reread Section 13-5 for one answer.

As you can see, natural conditions in the environment of an organism often make one genotype more likely to survive than another. Through this interaction of genes and the environment,

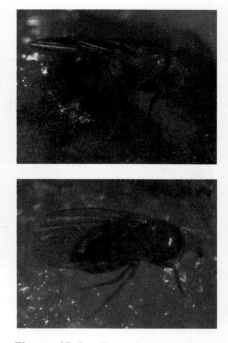

Figure 13-9 Experiments show that normal red-eyed fruit flies prefer red-eyed mates over flies with white eyes. Even in fruit flies, mating is not random. In what ways is human mating nonrandom?

Figure 13-10 Genes for camouflage help this dead-leaf butterfly (*left*) and pit viper (*right*) to blend with their surroundings. Such genes improve chances for survival and are an advantage in the organism's environment.

some alleles become common and others can disappear from a population.

The variation that results from this process apparently leads to the development of clines and subspecies. The variation also can lead to the development of new species. As different genes accumulate in populations in different geographical regions, the organisms become distinctly different and may no longer be able to interbreed. As you will see in the next chapter, the advantage of one allele over another in a particular environment is a major force behind the process of evolution.

CHECKPOINT ◆

9. What is the original source of most genetic variation in a population?
10. What is a change in the allele frequencies of a population due to small population size called?
11. Explain why mating in most populations is not random.
12. Movement of organisms into or out of a population is called _____.
13. Explain how the environment can favor the survival of organisms that carry a particular gene.
▶ 14. Why does choosing a mate with a similar phenotype produce more homozygous individuals in a population?
▶ 15. Which of the following can only *increase* the frequency of an allele in a population? mutation, migration, nonrandom mating, or genetic drift

▶ Denotes a question that involves *interpreting* and *applying* concepts.

UNDERSTANDING A GENE POOL

Objectives and Skills

☐ *Make a model* gene pool based on an initial assumed population.

☐ *Collect data* to test the Hardy-Weinberg principle.

☐ *Compare* the collected data to values predicted in a cross-multiplication table.

☐ *Use a model* gene pool to examine the change in allele frequencies caused by harmful genotypes in a given environment.

Materials

2 400-mL beakers   60 red beans
wax pencil   140 white beans

Procedure and Observations

1. On a separate sheet of paper, draw a data table like the one shown below.

DATA TABLE		
Two red	**One white, one red**	**Two white**
Pair tally		
Pair total		

2. Using a wax pencil, label a beaker "Male gametes." Label a second beaker "Female gametes."

3. Count out 30 red beans and 70 white beans and place them in one of the beakers. Place another 30 red beans and 70 white beans in the second beaker. The red beans represent the dominant allele for brown coat color (*B*)

in rabbits; the white beans represent the recessive allele for white coat color (*b*).

4. On another sheet of paper, draw a cross-multiplication table. Complete the table to calculate the expected frequency of red and white alleles in the population.

5. Without looking at the beans, reach into each beaker and draw out one bean. Record in your data table what combination of beans you drew from each beaker. Each pair of beans represents the genotype of one offspring from the population. After you record the result, place each bean back in the beaker from which it came. Mix the beans.

6. Repeat Step 5 another 49 times.

7. Combine your results with those of your class in a summary chart on the chalkboard.

8. Suppose that homozygous dominant individuals cannot survive to reproduce. Look at your data table to see how many homozygous dominant individuals you drew out. Remove one half that number of red beans from each beaker. Each beaker now represents the gene pool of the second generation.

9. Draw another data table and repeat Steps 5 and 6.

Analysis and Conclusions

1. How do the results of your first 50 draws compare with the frequencies predicted in your cross-multiplication table? How do the total results for the class compare with the frequencies predicted?

2. What happened to the allele frequencies in the second generation when homozygous brown rabbits were selected out of the population?

3. Do your results and the class's total results support the Hardy-Weinberg principle? Explain your answer.

CUTTING EDGE

Are Cheetahs on the Road to Extinction?

The cheetah is a sleek and powerful cat renowned for its ability to reach a running speed of 70 miles per hour. However, 5000 to 25 000 animals, all of one species *Acinonyx jubatus*, exist today, when 10 000 years ago 4 species roamed the plains of Europe, Asia, North America, and Africa. Today pockets of extinction are widening, as cheetah populations vanish from these regions. None have dwelled in India since the 1940's and none in Iran since the 1970's. Cheetahs are gone from Asia, and their numbers are plummeting in sub-Saharan and northeast Africa. Cheetahs in zoos are exhibiting high infertility and infant mortality rates. Nearly 70 percent of cheetah sperm is abnormal, and half of all cubs never reach adulthood.

When biologists took a closer look at cheetahs, they found evidence of profound genetic uniformity, which could explain the animals' reproductive problems. Stephen

O'Brien, a geneticist at the National Cancer Institute, examined proteins found in the red blood cells of 55 cheetahs which were from the wild, or descended from wild African cheetahs. Proteins are studied by placing them in an electric field (a technique called electrophoresis). Each protein travels in the electric field to a characteristic position, depending upon its size. In 250 animal species tested, 10 to 50 percent of individuals had variants for any one protein. But in the cheetahs, 200 different proteins were identical in all 55 animals. Because genes provide the biochemical instructions for making proteins, similarity in proteins reflects underlying genetic similarity.

Further molecular evidence for genetic uniformity comes from skin grafts between African cheetahs and zoo residents from Wildlife Safari in Oregon. Skin grafts, like any transplant, normally take only in very close relatives, but they were readily accepted from cheetah to cheetah. This result indicates that extremely similar immune systems exist in animals that come from diverse geographic regions. Beside being similar the immune systems of the cheetahs are not functioning normally. This is shown by the fact that cheetahs have become vulnerable to a disease called feline infectious peritonitis. Although this disorder kills only 5 percent of domestic cats that become infected, it is far more devastating to cheetahs, killing up to 50 percent of those infected.

Evolutionary success depends on genetic diversity. In the face of an environmental extreme, a species whose individuals are genetically dissimilar is likely to survive because some of them inherit genes that enable them to overcome the particular challenge. If all members of the species have the same genes, they also share vulnerabilities.

How might the cheetahs have become so genetically alike? One hypothesis is that they went through an event called a **population bottleneck**, in which some event kills most members of a species. In this case, it may have happened 10 000 years ago,

when many mammalian species became extinct. The survivors then founded a new population. Inbreeding (mating between blood relatives) occurred at first because there were few animals. Because the new population came from only a few individuals, its members share many of the same genes, inherited from common ancestors.

An alternate explanation is that cheetahs have become too well equipped as predators. In the course of evolving genes that help them hunt, they

somehow also accumulated genes that weakened their immune systems or damaged reproductive structures.

Perhaps the most compelling explanation for the cheetahs' problems is based on the perplexing fact that despite their genetic sameness, the cheetahs have survived, apparently for thousands of years. Cheetahs may indeed share many, many genes in common, but a few key genes remain diverse, and these have enabled this noble hunter to survive.

DISCUSSION & RESEARCH

1. How is the "founder effect" (page 222) similar to the current genetic situation among cheetahs?
2. How can electrophoresis of proteins be used to predict species that might become endangered?
3. What can be done to help increase the world population of cheetahs?

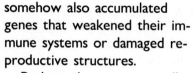

CHAPTER REVIEW

Summary

▶ A species is a group of organisms that can interbreed and produce fertile offspring. All species show variation. Some of this variation is caused by the environment and some is caused by heredity.

▶ A given species usually is made up of a number of populations spread out over a wide geographic area. A population is the smallest unit of a species that can undergo changes as a result of changes in its gene pool.

▶ Clines and subspecies are examples of the ways in which variation among populations is exhibited. Clines occur when populations show gradual variation in a single trait corresponding to changes in the environment. Subspecies occur when a group of populations shows variation in a number of traits. Subspecies are populations that are distinct from populations in other locations.

▶ In population genetics, genetic principles are applied to individual populations. Application of these principles allows geneticists to determine the frequency with which particular alleles occur in a population.

▶ The Hardy-Weinberg principle states that under certain conditions the allele frequencies in a population will remain constant from one generation to the next. The five assumptions of the Hardy-Weinberg principle are
1. no mutations,
2. a large population,
3. random mating,
4. no migration, and
5. no genotype is favored over another.

▶ Real populations are rarely in genetic equilibrium. Changes in allele frequency usually result when one or more of the Hardy-Weinberg assumptions are not met. Alleles may be added to or lost from the gene pool, or new combinations may occur on a nonrandom basis.

Vocabulary

allele frequency	migration
cline	population
cross-multiplication table	population
founder effect	genetics
gene pool	population
genetic drift	sampling
genetic equilibrium	species
Hardy-Weinberg principle	subspecies

Concept Mapping

Construct a concept map describing variation in populations. Include the following terms: allele frequency, cline, gene pool, genetic equilibrium, population, species, and subspecies. Add additional terms as you need them.

Review

Choose the best answer for each of the following questions.

1. The largest group of organisms that can mate among themselves and produce fertile offspring is called a (a) cline, (b) species, (c) gene pool, (d) race.
2. The Hardy-Weinberg principle assumes that (a) mating between males and females is random, (b) mating between males and females is restricted, (c) new individuals enter from outside, (d) mutations occur.
3. The difference between a cline and a subspecies is that a subspecies (a) cannot mate with members of another subspecies, (b) shows variation in only one trait, (c) shows variation in several traits, (d) will eventually become a cline.
4. All of the genetic content of a population of organisms is called a (a) genotype, (b) gene pool, (c) genetic equilibrium, (d) allele frequency.

5. In what kind of population is genetic drift likely to occur? (a) small population (b) large population (c) hybrid population (d) plant population
6. The movement of individuals into or out of a particular breeding population is called (a) genetic drift, (b) allele frequency, (c) migration, (d) variation.
7. Random mating is rare in most natural populations because (a) the choice of mates is affected by factors such as courting behavior and coloring, (b) genetic drift prevents it, (c) most populations are small, (d) subspecies cannot mate with one another.
8. Mutations (a) are rarely harmful, (b) can happen only to some genes, (c) rarely occur in subspecies, (d) are the original source of variation in populations.
9. A rabbit breeder purchases 100 heterozygous brown rabbits. The frequency of the allele for brown coat color (B) in the gene pool is (a) 100%, (b) 0%, (c) 25%, (d) 50%.
10. In a situation involving genetic drift, allele frequency for an allele can change due to (a) random events, (b) mutation, (c) inbreeding, (d) migration.
11. The difference in color between red-shafted and yellow-shafted flickers probably is a result of (a) mutation, (b) genetic drift, (c) genetic equilibrium, (d) migration.

Interpret and Apply

12. In the gene pool for a certain population of rabbits, there are two alleles for fur color, brown (B) and white (b). The allele frequency for brown fur is 63 percent. What is the allele frequency for white fur?
13. A male donkey and a female horse can mate, producing a mule. Why, then, are donkeys and horses not considered members of the same species?
14. How do mutation and meiosis work together to produce genetic variation in a population?
15. The frequency for the dominant allele for tongue rolling in a certain high school is 70 percent. Construct a cross-multiplication table for this gene. (a) What percentage of the student population is heterozygous for this trait? (b) What percentage is homozygous recessive?
16. Over many centuries, cows have been bred to produce larger amounts of milk than their wild ancestors produced. How is this breeding process similar to the process that occurs when the natural environment favors a certain genotype? How is it different?

Critical Thinking

17. Fifty heterozygous brown rabbits are placed with 100 homozygous white rabbits. What are the allele frequencies for brown fur (B) and for white fur (b)?
18. Two plants of the same species but from two different locations are grown in the same greenhouse under the same conditions. A difference in height is apparent and persists. What conclusions can you draw from this experiment? What is the experimental variable in this experiment?
19. Phenylketonuria (PKU) is a metabolic disease in which the body cannot break down the amino acid phenylalanine. In the United States, the gene for PKU has a frequency of 1 percent. What percentage of people in the United States carry the gene (are heterozygous)?
20. A farmer sprays a corn field with an insecticide to kill insect pests that damage the crop. Over time, fewer and fewer pests are killed by the insecticide. Explain what is happening in terms of the interaction between genotype and the environment.

14 EVOLUTION

Overview

EVIDENCE OF EVOLUTION

14-1 Evidence from Fossils

14-2 Determining the Age of Fossils

14-3 Evidence from Structure

14-4 Evidence from Development

14-5 Evidence from Molecular Biology

THEORY OF EVOLUTION

14-6 Early Evolutionary Theory

14-7 Darwin and Natural Selection

PROCESS OF EVOLUTION

14-8 Natural Selection Observed

14-9 Speciation

14-10 Adaptive Radiation

14-11 Convergent Evolution

14-12 Stabilizing Selection

14-13 The Pace of Evolution

Why do giraffes have long necks?

EVIDENCE OF EVOLUTION

You have probably noticed that there are many different species of organisms. You might have also noticed that certain species resemble each other. Eagles and hawks, for example, share certain characteristics, such as sharp, hooked beaks and claws. Other organisms resemble species that lived long ago. Elephants, for example, are very similar to woolly mammoths, which lived thousands of years ago and are now extinct. Similarities among past and present organisms can be explained by evolution. **Evolution** is a process by which existing species change or branch into new species. Thus eagles and hawks resemble each other because they both evolved from some preexisting hawklike species.

14-1 Evidence from Fossils

Evidence for evolution comes from many fields of science. Some evidence with which you might be familiar is the fossil record. **Fossils** are remains or traces of organisms that lived long ago. Fossils include seashells, bones, seeds, pollen grains, and impressions such as leafprints or footprints. Most fossils form in **sedimentary rock,** which is rock formed by the accumulation of many layers of sediment. Sediments include bits of broken rock, such as sand and gravel, and pieces of decayed organisms. As shown in Figure 14-2, sediments carried by water eventually settle and form layers. As many layers accumulate, the pressure squeezes the sediments together until they harden into rock.

A fossil forms when an organism dies and its body is trapped in a layer of sediment. The soft body parts decay, but hard parts like bones, teeth, or shells do not. Instead, these body parts become part of the sedimentary rock layer that forms. Water

Section Objectives

A *Describe* how fossils form.
B *State* how radioactive isotopes are used to date rocks and fossils.
C *List* and *explain* some of the supporting data for evolutionary theory.

Figure 14-1 These fossils are from organisms that lived about 85 million years ago.

Figure 14-2 Sediment layers are laid down very slowly and are very thin. Thus it takes millions of years, and millions of layers, to form sedimentary rock.

Organisms die

Sediment covers remains

Process continues as more layers form

Information: The sedimentary rock of the Grand Canyon was formed below sea level. The rim of the canyon is now 2000 meters above sea level.

seeping through the rock over time might eventually dissolve bones or shells. However, an impression, or mold, remains in the rock. New minerals might fill in the mold and create a cast, or exact copy of the original fossil.

The Grand Canyon in Arizona provides a good example of the nature of fossil records. The walls of the canyon consist of millions of layers of sedimentary rock that have been exposed by the cutting action of the Colorado River. Because of the way that sedimentary rock forms, the age of the layers can be determined in relation to each other. The oldest layers are the ones laid down first, and, therefore, are found at the bottom of the canyon. The younger layers, added later, are on top. If you were to hike down from the rim to the base of the canyon, it would be like walking back in time.

Since fossils form along with a given layer of sedimentary rock, the relative ages of fossils can also be determined. As with the rock, the oldest fossils are on the bottom and the youngest are on top. Thus the fossil record gives a view of the changes that have occurred in organisms over time. In the Grand Canyon, for example, rocks near the top contain fossils of land-dwelling reptiles, fern plants, and insects. A quarter of the way down, only fossils of marine organisms, including fish, are found. Deeper in the canyon, there are no fish fossils, only a few shells and traces of worms. Finally, at the bottom of the canyon, there are no fossils at all.

The pattern of fossils in the Grand Canyon is similar to that in other places where fossils have been found. This general pattern is illustrated in Figure 14-3. What can you conclude from

Figure 14-3 The fossil record shows important trends in evolution, such as increasing body size and complexity.

225 million years ago →

500 million years ago →

680 million years ago →

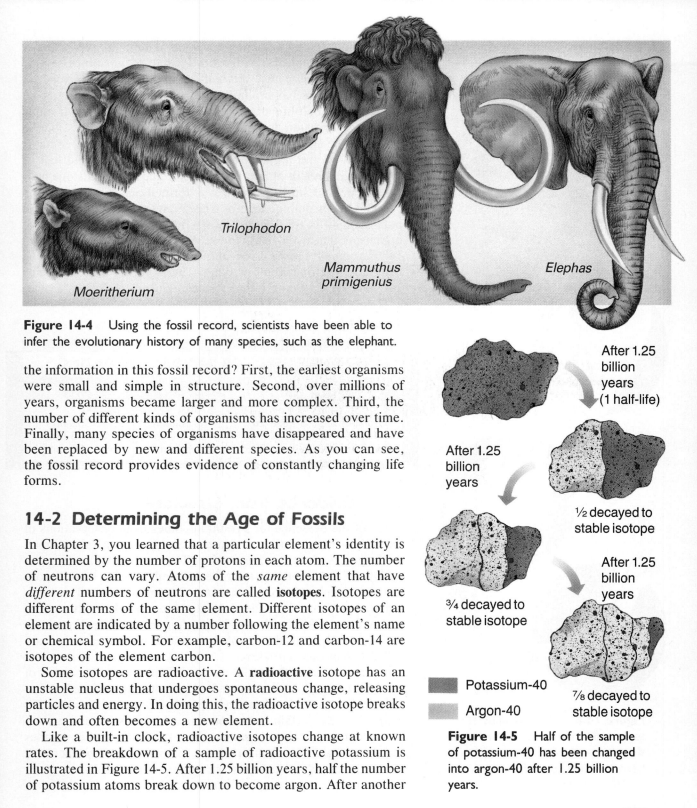

Figure 14-4 Using the fossil record, scientists have been able to infer the evolutionary history of many species, such as the elephant.

the information in this fossil record? First, the earliest organisms were small and simple in structure. Second, over millions of years, organisms became larger and more complex. Third, the number of different kinds of organisms has increased over time. Finally, many species of organisms have disappeared and have been replaced by new and different species. As you can see, the fossil record provides evidence of constantly changing life forms.

14-2 Determining the Age of Fossils

In Chapter 3, you learned that a particular element's identity is determined by the number of protons in each atom. The number of neutrons can vary. Atoms of the *same* element that have *different* numbers of neutrons are called **isotopes**. Isotopes are different forms of the same element. Different isotopes of an element are indicated by a number following the element's name or chemical symbol. For example, carbon-12 and carbon-14 are isotopes of the element carbon.

Some isotopes are radioactive. A **radioactive** isotope has an unstable nucleus that undergoes spontaneous change, releasing particles and energy. In doing this, the radioactive isotope breaks down and often becomes a new element.

Like a built-in clock, radioactive isotopes change at known rates. The breakdown of a sample of radioactive potassium is illustrated in Figure 14-5. After 1.25 billion years, half the number of potassium atoms break down to become argon. After another

After 1.25 billion years (1 half-life)

After 1.25 billion years

½ decayed to stable isotope

After 1.25 billion years

¾ decayed to stable isotope

⅞ decayed to stable isotope

■ Potassium-40
■ Argon-40

Figure 14-5 Half of the sample of potassium-40 has been changed into argon-40 after 1.25 billion years.

Evolution   **233**

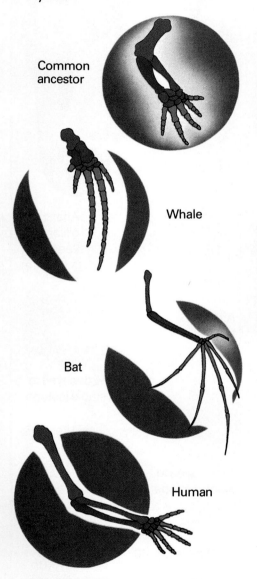

Common ancestor

Whale

Bat

Human

Figure 14-6 The forelimbs of several different organisms indicate that the same bone structure has been modified to perform a variety of different functions.

1.25 billion years, half the remaining potassium atoms break down. The amount of time it takes for half of an isotope sample to break down is called the **half-life** of the isotope. Every radioactive isotope has a unique half-life.

When the half-life of a radioactive isotope is known along with its proportion in a fossil-bearing rock, it is possible to calculate the age of the sample. For example, if a rock contains potassium-40 and argon-40 in equal amounts, then one half of the original amount of potassium-40 has decayed. Thus one half-life has passed since the rock was formed and it is 1.25 billion years old. For dating some organisms, however, the half-life of potassium-40 is too long to be useful. For example, fossils of organisms that lived relatively recently are dated using carbon-14. Carbon-14 can be used only to date fossils of once-living materials, such as wood or bone. The isotopes, listed in Table 14-1, are used to date different rocks and fossils.

Table 14-1

ISOTOPES USED FOR RADIOACTIVE DATING		
Isotope Pair	Half-life (yrs)	Useful range (yrs)
Carbon-14 to Nitrogen-14	5730	60 000
Uranium-235 to Lead-207	700 million	over 500 000
Potassium-40 to Argon-40	1.25 billion	over 500 000
Uranium-238 to Lead-206	4.5 billion	over 100 million

14-3 Evidence from Structure

Much of the evidence for evolution comes from observations of the body structures of existing organisms. Consider, for example, the forelimbs shown in Figure 14-6. The forelimb of a whale has a very different function than the forelimb of a bat or a human. Yet these limbs all share a common bone structure. This similarity of structure is evidence that these animals evolved from a common ancestor with a corresponding set of bones. Structures in different species that have the same evolutionary origin are called **homologous structures.**

Evidence for evolution is also provided by the existence of vestigial [ves tij' ē əl] organs. **Vestigial organs** are small or incomplete organs that have no apparent function. Snakes, for example, have certain small bones that have no useful function. These bones are homologous to bones found in other reptiles that have legs. The vestigial bones in snakes are evidence that the ancestor of snakes was a reptile with legs. During their evolution, however, snakes lost their legs.

14-4 Evidence from Development

Early stages in the development of some organisms also provide evidence of evolution and common ancestry. Organisms that share a common ancestor go through similar stages of development and therefore have embryos that look very much alike. An **embryo** is an organism in a very early stage of growth.

The embryos shown in Figure 14-7, for example, are difficult to tell apart. As you can see, they have certain structures in common, such as gill slits and a tail. In fish, the gill slits develop into gills. In humans, gill slits develop into the tube that connects the middle ear with the throat. This evidence indicates that the organisms shown in Figure 14-7 share a common ancestor whose embryo had gill slits.

14-5 Evidence from Molecular Biology

More direct evidence comes from studies involving the sequence of amino acids in the proteins of a wide variety of organisms. For example, cytochrome c is a protein in the electron transport chain of all aerobic organisms. Cytochrome c from chimpanzees is identical to cytochrome c from humans. However, human and fish cytochrome c differ by an average of 22 amino acids.

Comparisons of amino acid sequences for many different organisms (and for many different proteins) have been made. The similarity of protein structure reflects relationships among organisms that had been proposed long ago on the basis of other kinds of evidence. Why can the sequence of nucleotides in genes also be used to determine evolutionary relationships?

CHECKPOINT ◆

1. Most fossils are found in what kind of rock?
2. What is the name for the time required for half of a sample of a radioactive isotope to decay?
3. Describe how fossils form in sedimentary rock.
4. What are vestigial organs? Why are they significant?
5. What feature of radioactive isotopes allows scientists to determine the age of a particular fossil?
6. What are two kinds of molecules in cells that provide evidence supporting the idea of evolution?
▶ 7. Human proteins have more amino acids in common with gorilla proteins than they do with frog proteins. How is this observation consistent with the idea of evolution?
▶ 8. What general pattern in the fossil record supports the theory of evolution?

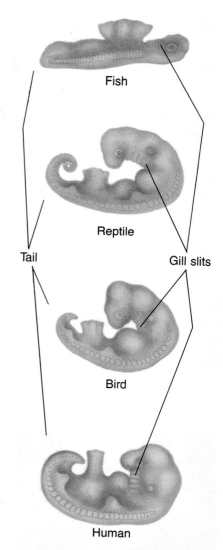

Fish

Reptile

Tail

Gill slits

Bird

Human

Figure 14-7 The evolutionary origin of certain structures can be inferred by comparing the embryological development of related organisms.

▶ Denotes a question that involves *interpreting* and *applying* concepts.

THEORY OF EVOLUTION

Section Objectives

D *Describe* Lamarck's contribution to evolutionary theory.

E *Identify* the role of variation and natural selection in Darwin's theory of evolution.

The idea that species change slowly over millions of years was once revolutionary. Until the early 1800s, most people believed that different species of organisms were fixed and unchanging. However, biological diversity, existence of vestigial structures, extinction, and other observations could not be explained by such beliefs. Why, for example, were there fossils of enormous dinosaurs and strange armored fish but no living representatives of those species? How could similarities and differences between extinct and living species be explained?

14-6 Early Evolutionary Theory

Probably the first scientist to challenge the idea of unchanging species was the French naturalist Jean Baptiste de Lamarck. In 1809, Lamarck proposed that over long periods of time, a species could evolve into new species. In proposing evolution, Lamarck was trying to solve one of the puzzles in the fossil record—that of extinction. Like other scientists of his time, Lamarck did not believe that species became extinct. He reasoned instead that extinct species had simply changed over time into new species.

Lamarck's explanation of evolution had two main parts. First, he believed all organisms had the ability to become more complex in structure. He considered this ability to be a law of nature that did not have to be explained. Second, Lamarck believed that organisms could change in response to changes in their environment. That is, by using some body parts more and other parts less, an organism could acquire needed adaptations. Recall from Chapter 2 that adaptations are structures or behaviors that enable an organism to survive in a given environment. The belief in acquired characteristics was common in Lamarck's time. Swimming birds, for example, need webbed feet. By using their feet more in a certain way, such birds would develop the needed webbing. If a characteristic was not needed, eventually it would be lost because it was not being used.

In addition, Lamarck believed that characteristics acquired by an organism would be passed to its offspring. However, he did not explain how the inheritance of acquired characteristics could happen. Recall, though, that an organism's characteristics are controlled by genes in each cell's nucleus. Except for mutations, genes are passed unchanged from generation to generation. An organism's use of a body part does not change the genes it carries. This statement represents an important fact to think about. If acquired characteristics were inherited, then the children of concert pianists would be born knowing how to play the piano.

Figure 14-8 How would Lamarck explain the characteristic long legs of this heron?

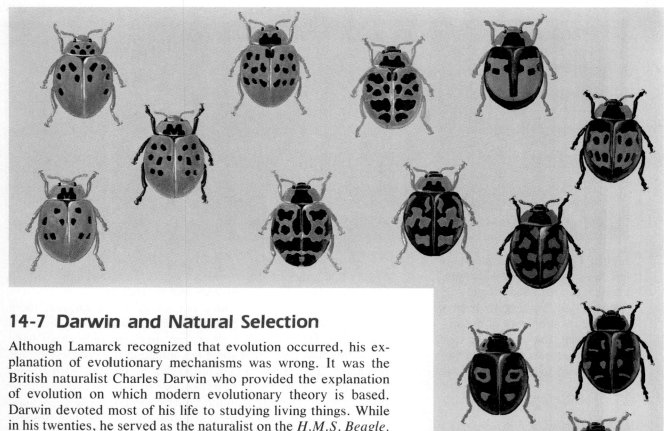

14-7 Darwin and Natural Selection

Although Lamarck recognized that evolution occurred, his explanation of evolutionary mechanisms was wrong. It was the British naturalist Charles Darwin who provided the explanation of evolution on which modern evolutionary theory is based. Darwin devoted most of his life to studying living things. While in his twenties, he served as the naturalist on the *H.M.S. Beagle*. During the ship's five-year expedition to South America and the South Pacific, Darwin observed and collected many specimens, examined fossils, and observed many geologic features. He wrote detailed notes of his observations and thoughts, which he then used over many years in developing his ideas.

Besides his experience on the *Beagle,* Darwin's thinking was influenced by readings in other fields. The book *Principles of Geology*, which he read during his voyage, led Darwin to think about the age of Earth and changes in landforms. Back in England, Darwin read an essay by economist Thomas Malthus that described human population growth and the fierce competition for resources that occurs among people trying to survive.

Darwin also drew on his observations of controlled breeding of domestic plants and animals. He recognized, for example, that no two individuals in a population are exactly alike. Organisms vary in such traits as size, coloration, behavior, and so on. Darwin realized that variations were the basis on which organisms were selected for breeding. He hypothesized that a similar kind of selection process occurred in nature.

Darwin observed, for example, that organisms produce more offspring than actually survive. Oak trees produce thousands of

Figure 14-9 These beetles are all members of the same species. Notice the great variation in color markings.

Figure 14-10 *Left:* Organisms like this treehopper have evolved camouflage adaptations. *Right:* Other animals are brightly colored, which warns predators of danger or bad-taste. The monarch butterfly shown here tastes terrible to birds, so they learn to avoid such insects.

▶ Denotes a question that involves *interpreting* and *applying* concepts.

acorns and frogs lay thousands of eggs. However, only a small fraction of the offspring survive and reproduce.

Darwin reasoned that since not all offspring survive, there must be competition for resources such as food, water, sunlight, and space. He reasoned further that surviving individuals have variations that give them some advantage in the competition for resources. Thus Darwin concluded that individuals with advantageous variations had a greater chance to survive and pass their traits to their offspring than individuals without those variations. Darwin used the term **natural selection** to describe this process by which organisms with favorable variations survive and reproduce at a greater rate.

Natural selection causes the number of individuals with a favorable variation to increase over many generations. And as many different favorable variations are accumulated, species change. Darwin concluded that evolution occurs as a result of natural selection. In 1859, after more than 20 years of collecting and analyzing data, Darwin published his findings in a book titled *On the Origin of Species by Means of Natural Selection*. Darwin's book is considered one of the greatest works in biology.

CHECKPOINT ◆

9. According to Lamarck, how do organisms acquire characteristics during their own lifetime?
10. Why is Darwin's theory more accepted than Lamarck's?
11. What mechanism did Darwin propose to explain the process of evolution?
▶12. How does Lamarck's hypothesis differ from Darwin's?
▶13. Give an example of an acquired characteristic among humans.

PROCESS OF EVOLUTION

In *On the Origin of Species,* Darwin presented a great deal of evidence to support his ideas. Remember, a scientific theory explains observations. If new evidence that contradicts the theory is discovered, the theory must change. In more than 100 years, Darwin's theory of natural selection continues to be the best explanation for most of the existing evidence for evolution.

Darwin had no knowledge of modern genetics. He could not explain how variations are produced. However, more information accumulated about how genes operate, and how populations change. This additional evidence supported and modified Darwin's theory. Thus Darwin's work became the basis of modern evolutionary theory. In this section, you will learn major concepts included in this modern theory.

14-8 Natural Selection Observed

Evolution occurs continuously. Major changes may not appear for thousands or even millions of years. Therefore, you might be tempted to conclude that it would be impossible to observe the process directly. However, there are several well-documented examples of evolution on a smaller scale.

One such case involves a color change in moths. Figure 14-11 shows two colors found in the peppered moth, a common inhabitant of the English countryside. In the early 1850s, most peppered moths in England were a light, speckled color. There were also a few dark-colored mutants. When the light-colored moths landed on light-colored tree trunks, they blended in with the background. Birds and other predators searching for food were more likely to find and capture the dark-colored moths.

By the early 1900s, industrial air pollution covered tree trunks with soot. The light-colored moths became easier to see. Birds then captured and ate a higher and higher proportion of light-colored moths. Dark-colored moths, once at a disadvantage, now blended in with their background. So darker moths survived and reproduced more frequently.

In recent years, pollution controls have resulted in trees once again having light-colored trunks. Natural selection now favors the light-colored moths, and they are again becoming more common in the English countryside.

In Chapter 13, you learned about the conditions of the Hardy-Weinberg principle. These conditions allow a population to maintain genetic equilibrium, or a state when there is no change in gene frequency over a period of time. You also learned that if any of those conditions change, the allele frequencies for certain

Section Objectives

F *Describe* the effects of natural selection on genetic equilibrium.

G *Explain* the role of isolation in the formation of new species.

H *Distinguish* between the processes of adaptive radiation and convergent evolution.

I *Explain* how selection can stabilize a species.

J *Distinguish* between gradual evolution and punctuated equilibrium.

Figure 14-11 Light and dark forms of the peppered moth are not equally visible on the trunk of a soot-covered tree.

Evolution   **239**

traits also may change. The peppered moth is a good example of this concept. Because of an environmental change, the allele (or alleles) for dark color became favored over those for light color. Natural selection caused the allele frequency for dark color to increase until dark moths became more common.

14-9 Speciation

When you look at a world globe, you recognize continents and oceans. It is hard to imagine that Earth has not always looked the same as it does now. However, evidence indicates that the continents gradually move. Until about 180 million years ago, Europe, Africa, North America, and South America formed a single, enormous landmass. As the continents moved apart, their climates changed. Great sheets of ice have covered much of the northern hemisphere at times. Tropical forests once grew on land that is now the frozen Antarctic.

Organisms with traits that are favored in a particular environment may not be as successful if that environment changes. Natural selection causes all species to adapt to changing conditions. Thus natural selection can lead to the formation of new species. This process is called **speciation** [spē′ shē ā shən].

Speciation often occurs when two groups in a population become isolated from each other. Since no two environments are identical, selection operates differently in each location. The gene pools of the two groups begin changing in different ways. Recall from Chapter 13 that members of the same species can mate to produce fertile offspring. If enough genetic changes occur in some members of a population, they may no longer be able to successfully reproduce with other members. The clines and subspecies described in the previous chapter can be the intermediate stages of speciation.

One way in which a population may be divided is by geographic boundaries. **Geographic isolation** occurs when a physical barrier cuts a single breeding population in two.

The Abert and Kaibab squirrels, shown on the next page in Figure 14-12, are examples of the effects of geographic isolation. These two species of ground squirrels live on opposite sides of the Grand Canyon. They show behavioral and structural similarities indicating that they share a common ancestor. How would the theory of evolution explain the development of the two species? They probably evolved from a single species that occupied northern Arizona over a million years ago. About that time, the Colorado River changed its course, splitting the squirrel population in two. The canyon carved by the river kept the two populations from breeding with each other.

If a population is divided, the distribution of alleles in the two groups may not be the same. For the squirrels, the forces of natural selection had different results on each side of the river. Each gene pool was subjected to different environments. Different traits were favored. After many years, genetic differences between the populations became so large that the two populations became two separate species.

Populations do not have to be physically isolated to split into new species. Many frog species live in the same area but breed at different times of the year. A population that breeds in May is genetically isolated from one that breeds in July. This kind of isolation is called **reproductive isolation.**

14-10 Adaptive Radiation

Sometimes new species evolve from a single, ancestral species. This type of evolution is called **adaptive radiation** and often occurs when a species enters a new environment.

A new environment may mean less competition for food. In the absence of competition, alleles that have been disadvantageous to an organism may now be favored. The population can evolve in many different directions resulting in different species.

An example of adaptive radiation is seen in the variety of finches on the Galápagos Islands. Darwin visited these islands and collected samples of the finches and sent them back to England. An ornithologist identified them as 13 different species.

The finches are similar in overall appearance, yet each species has a distinctive beak shape, feeding habits, and behavior. The different species are clearly related to each other. Thus they must have evolved from a common ancestor that was able to expand into many different environments.

Figure 14-12 The two species of ground squirrels have developed as a result of geographic isolation.

BIOLOGY INSIGHT

Adaptation and Evolution: The concept of adaptation is applicable not only at the organism level of organization, but at many other levels as well. Molecules, organelles, tissues, and organs can show adaptation. In later chapters you will see adaptation in communities of organisms.

Figure 14-13 Different species of finches in the Galápagos Islands evolved from a single species.

1. Small tree finch *Camarhynchus parvulus*
2. Medium tree finch *Camarhynchus pauper*
3. Mangrove finch *Camarhynchus heliobates*
4. Woodpecker finch *Camarhynchus pallidus*
5. Warbler finch *Certhidea olivacea* 6. Large tree finch *Camarhynchus psittacula* 7. Vegetarian finch *Platyspiza crassirostris* 8. Large cactus finch *Geospiza conitostris* 9. Cactus finch *Geospiza scandens* 10. Large ground finch *Geospiza magnirostris* 11. Medium ground finch *Geospiza fortis* 12. Small ground finch *Geospiza fuliginosa* 13. Sharp-beaked ground finch *Geospiza difficilis*

14-11 Convergent Evolution

Suppose several different kinds of populations live in similar environments. Can you predict what kinds of evolutionary changes might occur?

If the environments are similar, it is logical to assume that some of the same kinds of traits would be favored in the different populations. These different species may eventually develop some adaptations that are similar. For example, look at the general body shape of the organisms in Figure 14-14. A streamlined shape is an adaptation for rapid swimming. However, despite their outward similarity, these organisms are not closely related. **Convergent evolution** occurs when the environment selects similar adaptations in unrelated species.

The wings of birds, bats, and butterflies are another example of convergent evolution. In all three organisms, wings are used for flight, but in each case, the wings evolved independently. Another example is the similar eye structure of the human and the octopus. Sometimes examples of convergent evolution can be mistaken as an indication that organisms are closely related. Can you think of other examples of convergent evolution?

242

14-12 Stabilizing Selection

Natural selection does not always change the frequency of alleles in a population. In many situations, natural selection causes the characteristics of a population to stay the same. If a species is adapted to a particular environment and the environment does not change, then new variations will not be favored.

Mutations, which are the original source of variation, continue to occur. However, mutations that are harmful to the existing success of a population usually do not increase in frequency enough to cause further speciation.

Stabilizing selection maintains characteristics that enable an organism to be successful in its environment. Fossil evidence indicates, for example, that stabilizing selection has kept organisms such as sharks, turtles, and ferns virtually unchanged for many millions of years.

14-13 The Pace of Evolution

How fast does evolution occur? This question has caused intense debate among modern biologists. Some scientists describe speciation as the eventual outcome of gradually accumulating changes between different populations of ancestral species. In other words, as species form, they slowly become more genetically distinct.

Figure 14-14 None of these animals is closely related. The shark is a fish, the dolphin is a mammal, and the ichthyosaur is an extinct reptile. Their general similarity in shape is an adaptation for rapid swimming and is an example of convergent evolution.

Shark

Dolphin

Icthyosaurus

If this mechanism is correct, the fossil record would be expected to show organisms that are gradually different over time. There should be evidence of small changes in organisms leading to species that live now. But the fossil record is incomplete. Large numbers of fossils from many time periods exist for very few species.

Recent work suggests another explanation for the pace of evolution. Much of the fossil record shows that many types of organisms lived for very long periods without showing much change. Then "suddenly" a whole new set of different, but clearly related, species appeared. These species also lasted a long time relatively unchanged. (To anyone who deals with the history of life on Earth, a term like "sudden" is relative. A million years is a very short time when you consider the age of the Earth.)

This model of evolutionary change is called **punctuated equilibrium.** The term comes from the idea that species remain mostly the same (in equilibrium) for long periods of time. These periods are then punctuated by short periods of dramatic change. This theory may explain the sudden shifts in the fossil record at certain distinct times. It may also account for the lack of intermediate steps in the record that would be expected if evolution is always gradual.

There is considerable debate about whether evolution follows a gradual path or a path of punctuated equilibrium. The answer may be that both mechanisms contribute differently to the process of evolution. Support for and against these ideas will continue to build as more evidence is collected. Both theories are subject to refinement or change as new scientific evidence is collected. The theories used to explain evolution have always been subject to the criteria that define science as an endeavor.

CHECKPOINT ◆

14. Describe one way in which genetic equilibrium is affected by natural selection.
15. Physical separation of a population of organisms followed by selection of different characteristics in each population can result in _____ .
▶ 16. Five hundred million year-old fossils of a clamlike organism are almost identical to present-day clams. They would be a good example of what kind of selection?
▶ 17. Give an example of convergent evolution other than those given in this chapter.
▶ 18. What kind of evidence would be necessary to decide whether evolutionary change is gradual or occurs by punctuated equilibrium?

▶ Denotes a question that involves *interpreting* and *applying* concepts.

VARIATIONS AMONG INDIVIDUALS

Objectives and Skills

☐ *Draw conclusions* about the importance of sample size in studying variations among individuals of a species.

☐ *Observe, compare,* and *make predictions* about variations using graphs.

Materials

handful of peanuts (in shells)
5 preserved grasshoppers
metric ruler
plastic gloves
meter stick

Procedure and Observations

1. Obtain a handful of peanuts. Shell each and discard the shells.
2. Remove the thin, brown seed coat from each peanut. Split each peanut in half. Save the larger half, discard the smaller half.
3. Using a metric ruler, measure the length in millimeters of each of the halves in your sample. Make a data table to record your data and the class distribution data for peanut length.
4. Stretch out the fingers of your right hand so they lie flat on a table or desk top. Measure the distance in centimeters from the tip of your thumb to the tip of your little finger. Make a data table to record your measurements and class distribution data for hand spread.
5. Put on your plastic gloves. Obtain five preserved grasshoppers. Measure the upper part (femur) of each grasshopper's right jumping leg in millimeters. Make a data table to re-

cord your measurement and class distribution data for femur length.
6. Construct graphs of the class data for peanut length, hand spread, and femur length. Number of individuals should be your label for the *y* axis.
7. Dispose of the specimens as directed by your teacher. Before leaving the laboratory, wash your hands thoroughly with soap and water.

Analysis and Conclusions

1. How do the graphs for hand spread and grasshopper femur length compare to the peanut graph?
2. If you were to measure and plot the lengths of 500 grasshopper femurs, what shape would you expect the graph to be?
3. If you were to measure the hands of 300 students and plot the data, what shape would you expect the graph to be?
4. How can a scientist tell from looking at a graph if a sample is large enough to provide an accurate interpretation of results?
5. What do graphs of the general shape you observed in this activity indicate about the pattern of variation among individuals of a species?

CHAPTER REVIEW

Summary

▸ Fossils are evidence of living things that existed in the past. The most common fossils are found in sedimentary rock.

▸ Fossils can be dated using radioactive isotopes that occur in surrounding rock.

▸ Evidence supporting evolutionary theory includes adaptations to the environment, homologous and vestigial organs, similarity of embryonic development, and the similarity of nucleic acid and protein structure.

▸ Darwin's theory of evolution provides the foundation for modern theories of evolution. Modern theories include advances in population genetics.

▸ Speciation takes place over long periods of time and requires some kind of isolating mechanism. Adaptive radiation is the formation of many species from a single, ancestral species.

▸ Organisms that appear to have similar structures may be examples of convergent evolution.

▸ Stabilizing selection can keep a species genetically similar over long periods of time if the environment is stable.

▸ It is not clear whether evolution proceeds as a gradual accumulation of genetic differences or whether it involves periods of rapid change.

Vocabulary

adaptive radiation	natural selection
convergent evolution	punctuated
embryo	equilibrium
evolution	radioactive
fossil	reproductive isolation
geographic isolation	sedimentary rock
half-life	speciation
homologous structures	stabilizing selection
isotope	vestigial organ

Concept Mapping

Construct a concept map for the theory of evolution. Include the following terms: fossils, homologous, nucleic acid, protein, vestigial, natural selection, populations, molecular biology, structure, wings, development, and adaptation. Use additional terms as you need them.

Review

1. Briefly describe the pattern of fossils observed in a place like the Grand Canyon.
2. Name one pair of radioactive isotopes that is used to date ancient objects.
3. The webbed feet of swimming birds are an example of _____ .
4. Give an example of homologous structures.
5. Give an example of a vestigial structure.
6. The early developing stage of an animal is called a _____ .
7. According to Lamarck, organisms can inherit _____ .
8. What is the role of inheritance in Darwin's theory of evolution?
9. What one point would Darwin and Lamarck agree upon?
10. The moths of the English countryside are an example of _____ .
11. Give an example of geographic isolation.
12. _____ may result when a small population of organisms is introduced to a new location.
13. The wings of a butterfly, a bird, and a flying fish are examples of _____ .
14. An organism that has been the object of stabilizing selection is _____ .
15. The idea that evolution proceeds in rapid steps followed by long periods of stability is called _____ .

Interpret and Apply

16. What major question is implied by the statement that all living things come from other living things?

17. According to Lamarck, could children inherit large muscles from a parent who was a body builder? Explain.

18. Would an organism with greater resistance to disease tend to produce more offspring? Explain.

19. What kinds of processes expose fossils to view?

20. What can you tell about the age of a fossil from its location in the rock?

21. The cytochrome *c* molecule of a horse is more similar to your cytochrome *c* than it is to the cytochrome *c* of a fish. How would you interpret this information?

22. When does natural selection stabilize a population and when does it produce evolution?

23. Why is Darwin's theory of evolution more accepted than Lamarck's?

24. Turtles are thought to have evolved from lizardlike reptiles. How would Darwin explain the evolution of the turtle's shell?

25. Match the diagrams below with the process.
   a. punctuated equilibrium
   b. convergent evolution
   c. adaptive radiation
   d. gradual evolution

Critical Thinking

26. Suppose you examined a rock and found that it contained three times as much lead-207 as uranium-235. How old would you estimate the rock to be?

27. Explain how the adaptive radiation of the dinosaurs might have occurred.

28. How have the discoveries in genetics since the time of Darwin contributed to the theory of evolution?

29. What contribution does the Hardy-Weinberg principle make to our understanding of the mode of evolution?

30. How do you think Lamarck would explain the origin of the vestigial bones of snakes?

31. Good athletes tend to run in families. Explain this observation using concepts presented in this chapter.

32. Suppose two parts of a species became geographically isolated for a long time but were then rejoined while it was still possible for them to mate and produce fertile offspring. What would you predict would happen to the species?

33. Gradual evolution and punctuated equilibrium make different predictions about what should be found in the fossil record. What are these predictions? Does the existing fossil record provide evidence to support one of these predictions more than the other? Explain.

1.
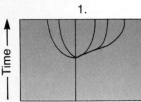

2.

3.
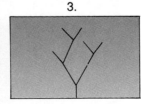

4.
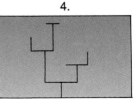

Time →

⸺ Range of variation ⟶

Chapter

15

HISTORY OF LIFE

Overview

ORIGIN OF LIFE

15-1 Chemical Evolution

15-2 First Cells

15-3 Origin of Eukaryotes

MULTICELLULAR LIFE

15-4 Precambrian Era

15-5 Paleozoic Era

15-6 Mesozoic Era: Age of Reptiles

15-7 Cenozoic Era: Age of Mammals

What were conditions like on Earth just after it formed?

ORIGIN OF LIFE

Earth is estimated to be about 4.5 billion years old. Life has existed on the planet for much of that time. Yet the organisms with which you are most familiar—birds and mammals, for example—have existed for only a tiny fraction of that time. To understand such a long timescale, imagine that the history of Earth is one year long. On this scale, Earth formed on January 1. The first living things, just single cells, appear during the first week of April. By early November, there are some marine worms and clams. Fish evolve around November 20, dinosaurs and small mammals around the middle of December, and most of the kinds of mammals living today by December 26. It is not until 11:45 P.M. on December 31 that the first humans appear. Humans are a relatively new species compared to the age of the Earth.

15-1 Chemical Evolution

As you can see, life on Earth has had an extremely long time to evolve. This evolution is consistent with another principle of biology that you studied earlier—biogenesis. Biogenesis is one of the most completely demonstrated principles in biology. Yet one critical question remains unanswered. Where did the first living things come from?

Scientists hypothesize that the first organisms were the result of a process of chemical evolution. This chemical evolution was possible under the conditions of early Earth, which were very different from those that currently exist. Early Earth had a surface much like the moon today—barren and rocky. It was bombarded constantly by meteorites. A hot, thick atmosphere of nitrogen, carbon dioxide, and small amounts of hydrogen, water vapor, and carbon monoxide blanketed the planet. Volcanoes spewed out hot lava and poisonous gases. Not long after it formed, the planet cooled enough so that water vapor condensed and fell as rain. Sometime about 4 billion years ago, enough water collected to form an ocean.

How could life have developed under such inhospitable conditions? In the 1920s, the Russian scientist A. I. Oparin and the British scientist J. B. S. Haldane independently developed the same hypothesis to explain the origin of life. These scientists proposed that energy from ultraviolet light, lightning, and volcanic heat caused chemical reactions to occur in the atmosphere. These reactions created small organic molecules that dissolved in the oceans. Over many millions of years, a large quantity of organic chemicals accumulated. According to Oparin and Haldane, the first life must have evolved from these organic compounds.

Section Objectives

A *Describe* the conditions on early Earth.

B *State* and *give evidence* supporting the heterotroph hypothesis.

C *Explain* the origin of the first autotrophs.

D *Compare* prokaryotic and eukaryotic cells.

E *Discuss* how eukaryotic cells might have evolved from prokaryotic cells.

Figure 15-1 Volcanic activity has been occurring continuously since Earth formed. This activity gives scientists information about the conditions early in Earth's history.

Figure 15-2 The repeating structure of kaolinite clay may represent the first self-replicating system.

Once a living thing evolved, it could use the organic chemicals in the ocean as a food source. Thus the first living thing was most likely a heterotroph. This idea is called the **heterotroph hypothesis.**

In the early 1950s, the Oparin–Haldane hypothesis received support from an experiment performed by the American scientist Stanley Miller. Miller tried to re-create conditions on Earth under which life may have formed. To represent the early oceans, he put water into a flask. The space above the water was filled with a mixture of gases thought to be similar to the early atmosphere. The gases were methane, ammonia, hydrogen, and water vapor. Electrical sparks represented lightning, one of many energy sources of early Earth.

After several days, the water in the flask changed color, indicating a chemical change had occurred. Analysis of the water showed that it contained numerous amino acids. Although amino acids are the building blocks of protein, Miller had not created life. He had however, shown that conditions like those on early Earth could produce some of the chemicals present in living things. Since then, Miller's experiments have been repeated and modified. Debates continue about the composition of the primitive atmosphere. Yet, whatever the experimental gas mixture or energy source used, the results are similar. Therefore the conditions of early Earth could have produced the building blocks of life.

How were biomolecules assembled into cells? Experiments have shown that structures similar to those in cells form under certain conditions. For example, when proteins are heated to temperatures above 100°C, dissolved in water, and then cooled, they clump together. The resulting spherelike structures have an outward resemblance to cells. Like cells, these structures are set off from their environment by a membranelike boundary. Some scientists hypothesize that the formation of membrane-bound structures was an intermediate step in the evolution of life.

Other scientists hypothesize that life began with "naked" self-replicating molecules. Recall that self-replication, or the ability to reproduce, is one of the major characteristics of living things. How might self-replicating molecules have evolved? One possibility comes from information about the properties of clay. It is known that minerals in clay crystallize in repeating patterns. Also, clay surfaces attract organic molecules. Thus the repeating pattern of mineral crystals could have acted as a mechanism to store and transmit coded information. Interactions between clay and organic molecules may have eventually led to the evolution of a self-replicating organic molecule, such as RNA.

Other experiments have shown how DNA, another self-replicating molecule, can become enclosed in a lipid membrane. Life may have begun with the evolution of a self-replicating system separated from the environment by a membrane. Different hypotheses about the origin of life each have some experimental support. However, no experiment has yet shown exactly how the first cells were assembled from biomolecules on early Earth.

15-2 First Cells

The first cells appear early in the fossil record. The oldest rocks that contain such fossils are about 3.5 billion years old. These

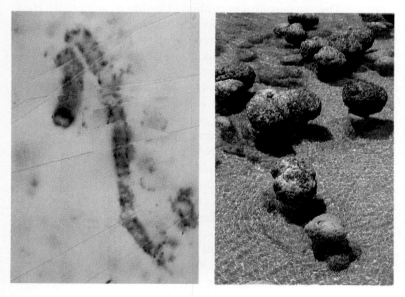

Figure 15-3 *Left:* A 3.5-billion-year-old prokaryote fossil from a stromatolite. *Right:* Modern stromatolites; these structures are made by lime-secreting bacteria.

fossils show no nuclear envelope. They differed from plant and animal cells. Cells without a membrane bound nucleus are called **prokaryotes.** The fossils resemble simple prokaryotes, like bacteria. How did the first cells live and survive?

According to the heterotroph hypothesis, the first living cells were dependent on dissolved organic molecules for food. Because the early atmosphere contained no oxygen, these first organisms must have been anaerobic.

As the first heterotrophs reproduced and spread throughout the oceans, the supply of dissolved organic molecules decreased. As food became scarce, autotrophic organisms (those that could manufacture their own food) had a distinct advantage. At this time, photosynthetic organisms may have evolved.

Photosynthetic organisms would have produced oxygen, which changed the composition of the atmosphere. Evidence indicates that oxygen produced by these organisms accumulated in the atmosphere about 2 billion years ago. With oxygen available, aerobic pathways may have evolved. As you learned in Chapter 6, aerobic respiration releases far more energy from food than does anaerobic respiration. Organisms with aerobic respiration would have a survival advantage.

15-3 Origin of Eukaryotes

Plant and animal cells are distinguished from prokaryotic cells in that the chromatin is contained in a nuclear envelope. Cells that contain such a nucleus are called **eukaryotes.** Eukaryotes have extensive internal membranes and membrane-bound organelles, such as mitochondria, vacuoles, Golgi bodies, and chloroplasts. The nucleus also is contained within a membrane. How did eukaryotic cells evolve? Recall from the previous chapter that one way to study past events is to examine clues from modern organisms. Modern eukaryotes are more complex and highly organized than prokaryotes.

Recent attention has focused on the chloroplasts and mitochondria of modern eukaryotic cells. These organelles resemble prokaryotic cells in several ways. Both organelles contain a circular molecule of DNA that more closely resembles bacterial DNA than it does nuclear DNA. Ribosomes within the mitochondria and chloroplast are more like bacterial ribosomes than they are like eukaryotic ribosomes. Many enzymes that are in mitochondria and chloroplasts are similar to bacterial enzymes. Look at Figure 15-4. A mitochondrion is shown in the process of division similar to that in bacteria. The life processes of bacteria are covered in more detail in Chapter 19.

These similarities provide evidence for the hypothesis that mitochondria and chloroplasts are descendants of an ancient

Figure 15-4 Mitochondria have many similarities to prokaryotes. Mitochondria contain their own DNA and ribosomes. As this photograph shows, they also replicate by division.

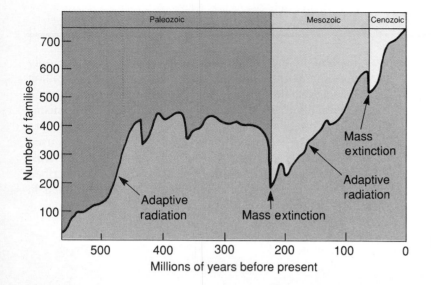

Figure 15-5 In addition to adaptive radiations, the transition from one era to another is marked by mass extinction.

"invasion" of one prokaryotic cell by another. Sometime, about 1.5 billion years ago, an anaerobic prokaryote was invaded by a smaller aerobic cell. The two cells eventually benefited from their association. The larger cell provided food for the smaller cell. The smaller cell provided energy in the form of ATP for both cells. According to the hypothesis, the smaller cell eventually evolved into today's mitochondrion.

At some later point, some of these new cells with mitochondria were invaded by a photosynthetic prokaryote. The new invader eventually evolved into the chloroplasts of modern-day plants. Most biologists agree that this explanation is a plausible one for chloroplasts and mitochondria. However, the evolution of other eukaryotic structures such as the endoplasmic reticulum and the nuclear envelope is much less clear. These structures may be formed by infolding of the cell membrane.

CHECKPOINT ◆

1. What kind of organic compound was produced in Miller's experiments?
2. How was the atmosphere of Earth changed by autotrophs?
3. List the major differences between prokaryotic cells and eukaryotic cells.
4. What two organelles of eukaryotes are thought to have evolved from the joining of prokaryotic cells?
▶ 5. Explain the selective pressure that resulted in the evolution of the first autotrophs.
▶ 6. Defend the statement that your cells carry clues to the evolutionary origin of eukaryotic organisms.

DO YOU KNOW?

Information: Many mass extinctions dot Earth's history. Recent evidence seems to indicate that a mass extinction occurs every 26 million years. The last major extinction occurred 13 million years ago.

▶ Denotes a question that involves *interpreting* and *applying* concepts.

History of Life   **253**

MULTICELLULAR LIFE

Section Objectives

F *Name* and *date* the four major eras in the history of life and briefly characterize each.

G *Describe* an explanation for the sudden appearance of multicellular organisms in the Paleozoic Era.

H *Evaluate* the explanations and evidence that explain past mass extinctions.

As you learned in the last lesson, prokaryotes were the only living things for about 2 billion years. Then, about 1.5 billion years ago, single-celled eukaryotes evolved. However, it took another several hundred million years for multicellular organisms to evolve. Such major changes in the kinds of living things are indicated by the fossil record. These changes have been used to divide the history of life into four time periods called **eras**. These four eras are illustrated in Figure 15-6 and are described below. Specific characteristics of each era will be outlined in the text that follows.

3.5 Billion Years Ago   570 Million Years Ago

PRECAMBRIAN ERA

- First cells
- Simple, many-celled animals in ocean

PALEOZOIC ERA

- Simple ocean plants
- First fish
- Plants invade land
- First land animals (ancestors of spiders and insects)

15-4 Precambrian Era

The time period from the origin of Earth to about 570 million years ago is known as the Precambrian Era. As you know, the living things that existed for the majority of this time were single-celled. In the late Precambrian, though, impressions of soft-bodied, multicellular organisms appear in rocks. The oldest animal fossils have been found in rocks dating from 580 to 680 million years ago. Given the rate of evolution, however, scientists hypothesize that multicellular organisms first evolved around 800 million years ago.

By the end of this era, the oceans were full of simple, multicellular animals. The fossil record shows that there were sponges, jellyfish, and worms. Fossil evidence of the ancestors of modern corals, clams, and starfish have also been found.

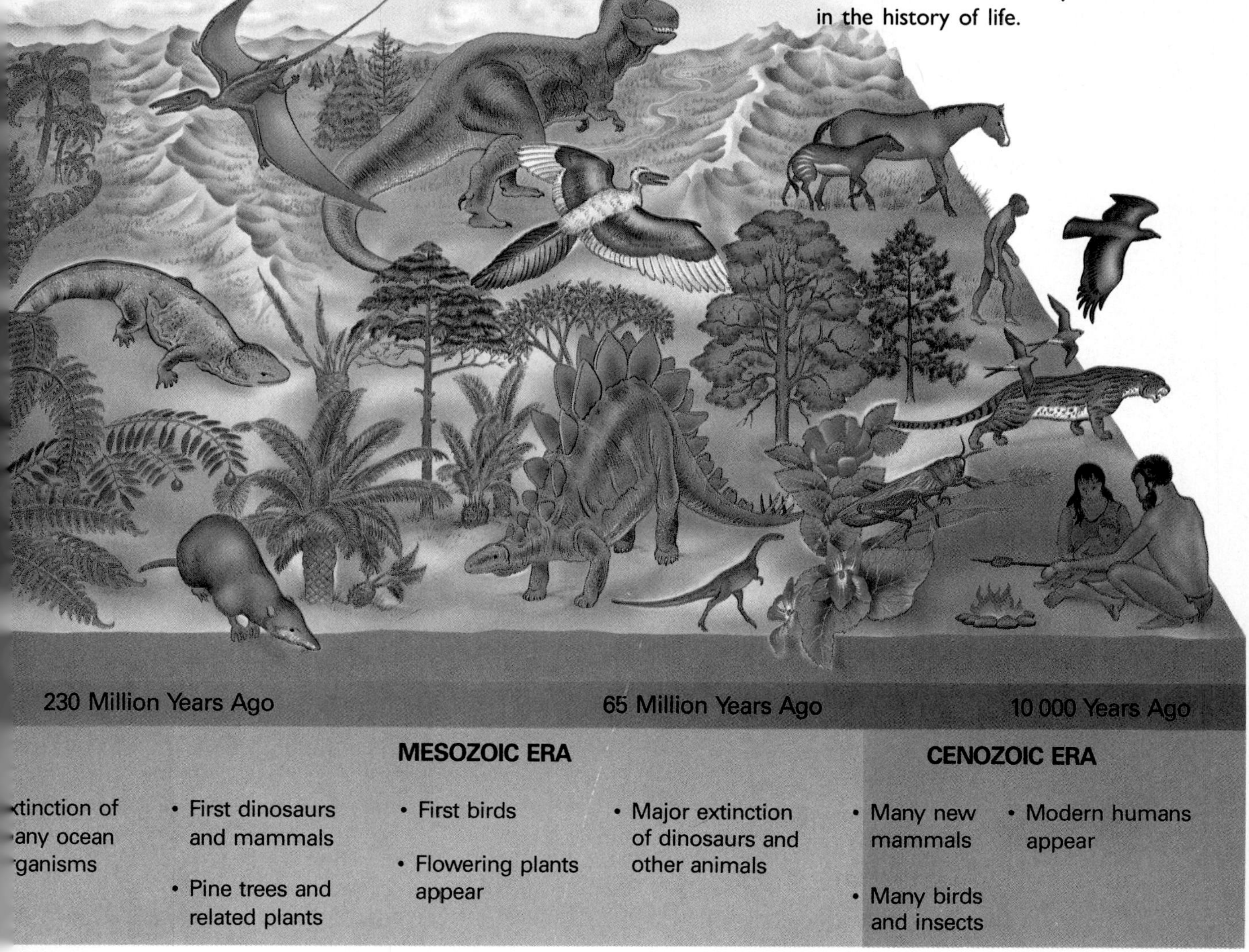

Figure 15-6 This geologic time-table summarizes the major events in the history of life.

230 Million Years Ago		65 Million Years Ago		10 000 Years Ago
MESOZOIC ERA				**CENOZOIC ERA**
xtinction of any ocean ganisms	• First dinosaurs and mammals • Pine trees and related plants	• First birds • Flowering plants appear	• Major extinction of dinosaurs and other animals	• Many new mammals • Many birds and insects • Modern humans appear

15-5 Paleozoic Era

The beginning of the Paleozoic Era, about 570 million years ago, was marked by a "sudden explosion" of animal populations. Fossils from this time represent most of the major groups of animals. The phrase *sudden explosion* describes the process of adaptive radiation that occurred over just a few million years. The appearance of so many different kinds of organisms in such a short time has been difficult to explain.

One clue that may explain the burst of adaptive radiation is contained in the fossil record. Fossils found in rocks formed before the Paleozoic Era come from organisms that did not have hard shells or skeletons. Soft-bodied organisms fossilize only under very unusual conditions. Paleozoic fossils, on the other hand, have protective outer shells or coverings that fossilize much more easily. Why would so many different kinds of organisms evolve hard shells during the same era? Under most conditions, natural selection favors organisms with a protective covering.

Recall from Chapter 14 the concept of punctuated equilibrium. It proposes that evolution is marked by brief periods of rapid adaptive radiation. The number of different kinds of fossils found in the early Paleozoic Era supports this concept.

Five other groups of organisms appeared during the Paleozoic Era. They are listed below.

1. *Fish* appeared about 520 million years ago. They were the first **vertebrates** [ver′ tə brāts], or animals with a backbone.
2. *Plants* were the first organisms to live on land. Many well-preserved fossils show they appeared about 420 million years ago.
3. *Insects* were the first major group of animals to inhabit land and appeared about 380 million years ago.
4. *Amphibians,* the first land vertebrates, evolved from one group of fish about 360 million years ago.
5. *Reptiles* appeared about 300 million years ago. Reptiles were the first vertebrates that were true land animals. Even today they do not have to return to water to reproduce as amphibians do.

The Paleozoic Era ended 230 million years ago with a mass extinction. Possibly 96 percent of all ocean-living species became extinct. Why did the extinction of so many organisms occur? Evidence indicates that by the end of the Paleozoic Era, all Earth's land was fused into one supercontinent called *Pangaea*. At the end of the Paleozoic Era, Pangaea broke up and the continents began a long, slow migration to their present positions. Climates and environments changed. If a species did not have adaptive traits to cope with these changes, it became extinct. While the breakup of Pangaea may have contributed to the Paleozoic extinctions, many scientists think other unknown factors were also involved.

15-6 Mesozoic Era: Age of Reptiles

The Mesozoic Era is marked by the appearance and radiation of several groups of organisms. Three major events characterize this time period.

1. The dominant group of animals were the reptiles. Some groups of reptiles became adapted to life in water. Other reptiles developed means to fly. The reptiles remaining on land, including the dinosaurs, were widespread and then disappeared according to the fossil record.
2. The first birds and mammals appeared about 200 million years ago.
3. Flowering plants appeared about 125 million years ago. Since about 80 to 90 million years ago, they have been the dominant land plants on Earth.

The extinction of the dinosaurs and many other species at the end of the Mesozoic Era has been one of the great puzzles of biology. It is not known whether dinosaurs died out in a single event or gradually.

One recent hypothesis concerning the sudden extinction of dinosaurs has some supporting evidence. Careful analysis of rocks 65 million years old shows an unusually high level of the element iridium. This element is very rare on Earth, but occurs in large amounts in meteorites. The discoverers of the high ir-

Figure 15-7 *Cynognathus* was a fierce, meat-eating reptile that is thought to be one of the ancestors of mammals. This animal lived about 225 million years ago.

Figure 15-8 The skeleton of a saber-toothed cat, *Smilodon*. This species became extinct about 10 000 years ago, along with many other huge mammals of the Cenozoic.

idium level have proposed that a very large meteorite or comet struck Earth 65 million years ago. The resulting explosion threw enormous quantities of dust into the atmosphere. The dust decreased the amount of sunlight reaching Earth's surface. Such a drastic and sudden change in the environment would put great selective pressures on organisms. Plants would no longer have as much solar energy to produce carbohydrates.

While this hypothesis has gained considerable popularity, several questions remained unanswered. Why were dinosaurs affected when certain kinds of plants left fossils in both Mesozoic and Cenozoic rocks? Why didn't early mammals die out? It is entirely possible that the extinction may have involved a number of independent factors, such as climatic changes, continental drift, or competition among species. Whether the cause is ever understood, the fossil record shows clearly where the Mesozoic ended and the Cenozoic began.

15-7 Cenozoic Era: Age of Mammals

The Cenozoic Era began about 65 million years ago. This era is often called the age of mammals. Mammals are animals that nurse and care for their young. They generally have a covering of hair, or fur, in contrast to the scales or feathers of other vertebrates.

The events that characterize the Cenozoic Era are the rapid evolution of mammals, birds, and flowering plants. Mammals evolved and assumed a dominance formerly held by reptiles. One particular group of mammals called primates appeared over 60 million years ago. About 3.5 million years ago, one group of African primates became able to walk upright on their rear legs. These mammals were the immediate ancestors of human beings.

CHECKPOINT ◆

7. What four major groups of organisms characterize the Mesozoic Era?
8. Describe one major reason for the radiation of organisms during the Precambrian Era.
9. What was the first group of organisms to invade land during the Paleozoic Era?
10. What event marks the end of one period of geologic time and the beginning of another?
▶ 11. Using the theory of natural selection, explain how a meteorite colliding with Earth could cause the extinction of a species.
▶ 12. The fossil record clearly shows that plants inhabited land before animals. How could you have predicted this?

▶ Denotes a question that involves **interpreting** and **applying** concepts.

COACERVATES—A MODEL FOR CELL EVOLUTION

In this activity you will see how particles called **coacervates** [kō as′ er vāts] display some of the properties of cells.

Objectives and Skills

☐ *Prepare* coacervates and *observe* them through the microscope.
☐ *Observe* coacervate formation under different environmental conditions.

Materials

safety goggles	slides
lab apron	coverslips
test tube	microscope
test-tube rack	gum arabic (stock
2 medicine droppers	solution)
10-mL graduated	gelatin (stock solution)
cylinder	dilute HCl in dropper
wide range pH paper	bottles

Procedure and Observations

1. Read all instructions for this laboratory activity before you begin your work.
2. Put on your safety goggles and lab apron.
3. In a test tube, pour 3 mL of gum arabic solution and 5 mL of gelatin solution. Gently shake the tube to mix the contents.
4. Measure the pH of the mixture using pH paper and record the result.
5. ☠ **CAUTION: Dilute hydrochloric acid is irritating to the skin and eyes; it could damage clothing. Wear safety goggles and lab apron. Wash off spills and splashes with plenty of water. Report to your teacher.** Add dilute HCl to the test tube one drop at a time. Swirl the test tube after each drop is added to mix the contents thoroughly. After several drops, the mixture in the tube

should become cloudy. When this happens, measure and record the pH.
6. Remove a drop from the tube and put it on a clean microscope slide. Place a coverslip on the drop.
7. Observe the slide under low power through the microscope. If you see coacervates, change to high power and observe closely. Do you observe any signs of movement, growth, joining, or breaking apart? On a data chart, draw a coacervate and record your observations.
8. Continue to add drops of acid to the test tube one drop at a time and mix. When the mixture becomes clear again, measure and record the pH.
9. Observe a drop of the clear mixture under the microscope. Are there any coacervates?
10. Before leaving the laboratory, clean up all materials and wash your hands thoroughly.

Analysis and Conclusions

1. If you had observed the mixture of gum arabic and gelatin before adding acid, what do you think you would have seen?
2. Compare coacervates to living cells.
3. What characteristics of life would you not observe if you watched coacervates for a longer period of time?
4. What does your pH data tell you about the sensitivity of coacervate existence to environmental conditions?
5. Do you think that a cell would also be sensitive to the pH of its surroundings? Why?
6. No one considers coacervates to be living, or even very close to it. Why?

CHAPTER REVIEW

Summary

▶ The heterotroph hypothesis states that the first living thing was a heterotroph that developed from organic molecules that accumulated in the early oceans. The first heterotrophs used the organic substances for food.

▶ Stanley Miller provided evidence that biologically important molecules could be produced under abiotic conditions thought to resemble early conditions on Earth.

▶ The earliest known fossils are of prokaryotic cells in rocks about 3.5 billion years old.

▶ Once the early heterotrophs used most of the organic material in the ocean, natural selection favored organisms that could produce their own food. The first autotrophs appeared and produced oxygen that accumulated in the atmosphere.

▶ Eukaryotic cells have more complex structures, such as mitochondria and chloroplasts, than prokaryotic cells. Eukaryotes may have evolved from early invasions of one cell type by another.

▶ The fossil record shows that eukaryotic cells appeared about 1.5 billion years ago.

▶ The end of each biological era is characterized by massive extinctions.

▶ In the Precambrian Era, fossils are generally of unicellular organisms.

▶ The Paleozoic Era is characterized by the rapid radiation of multicellular organisms. During this era, some plants and animals moved onto the land. The extinction ending the Paleozoic Era may have been related to the breakup of the supercontinent, Pangaea.

▶ Flowering plants, birds, mammals, and reptiles appeared during the Mesozoic Era. Reptiles dominated the land for 125 million years.

▶ The Cenozoic Era is characterized by the radiation of mammals, birds, and flowering plants.

Vocabulary

coacervate	heterotroph hypothesis
era	prokaryote
eukaryote	vertebrate

Concept Mapping

Construct a concept map for the history of life. Include the following terms: unicellular, Precambrian, Paleozoic, Mesozoic, Cenozoic, eras, mammals, reptiles, origin of life, multicellular, prokaryote, and eukaryote. Use additional terms as you need them.

Review

1. Who was the first to propose the heterotroph hypothesis?
2. According to the heterotroph hypothesis, what did the first living thing use as a source of food?
3. What are some of the energy sources thought to be present on early Earth that caused the formation of organic molecules?
4. What energy source did Miller use in his experiment?
5. How old are the rocks containing the oldest known fossil cells?
6. What gas in today's atmosphere was absent from Earth's original atmosphere?
7. What kinds of organisms were favored as the first heterotrophs used up their food sources?
8. Autotrophs use what energy source to produce food?
9. What kinds of organisms evolved after autotrophs?
10. What kinds of cells utilize meiosis during reproduction?
11. Most multicellular organisms are made of what kind of cells?
12. Give two pieces of evidence that mitochondria and chloroplasts evolved from prokaryotic ancestors.

13. What era encompasses most of Earth's history?
14. What group of vertebrates characterize the Cenozoic Era?
15. What term describes a group of organisms that appear in the fossil record but no longer exist?
16. What one general characteristic distinguishes Precambrian fossils from Paleozoic fossils?
17. List two factors that might explain the sudden appearance of fossils at the beginning of the Paleozoic Era.
18. What was the first major group of animals to occupy the land?
19. What were the first vertebrates to move onto the land?
20. What evidence indicates that a meteorite impact may have been responsible for the extinction of many animals at the end of the Mesozoic Era?
21. What is the name of the large supercontinent that existed at the end of the Paleozoic Era?

Interpret and Apply

22. Explain how each part of Miller's experiment was set up to model a particular condition present on early Earth.
23. Before Oparin and Haldane proposed the heterotroph hypothesis, most scientists assumed the first organisms were autotrophs. Why does an autotroph hypothesis make logical sense?
24. What is one of the major ''missing pieces'' of evidence in the sequence of events that led to the first living cell?
25. Give an evolutionary explanation for the origin of the first aerobic organisms.
26. If mitochondria resulted from the invasion of an early anaerobic prokaryote by an aerobic one, explain how this association benefited both organisms.

27. What advantages do multicellular organisms have over unicellular organisms? Can you think of any disadvantages?
28. How is the idea of punctuated equilibrium related to the appearance of fossils at the beginning of the Paleozoic Era?
29. Give a specific example of how a change in the environment has led to the extinction of a particular group of animals. Use evolution in your example.

Critical Thinking

30. Draw a line about 20 cm long on a piece of paper. Divide the line into equal segments, each representing 0.5 billion years. Locate the following events on the line: the origin of Earth, appearance of the first cells, appearance of first eukaryote, beginning of the four major eras in the history of Earth, first vertebrates, invasion of land by plants, insects, amphibians, and the first primates.
31. Explain why Miller's experiment did not prove the heterotroph hypothesis.
32. If it is true that mitochondria and chloroplasts resulted from combinations of different kinds of prokaryotic cells, what evidence can you give that the mitochondria evolved before chloroplasts?
33. Suggest an advantage that would apply to the first organisms that could leave the water and live temporarily (at first) on land. (The land is a hostile environment compared to water, and moving onto the land would have to be very advantageous.)

Chapter

16

HUMAN EVOLUTION

Overview

THE HUMAN AS A PRIMATE

16-1 Primate
     Characteristics
16-2 Apes and Humans

TRACING HUMAN EVOLUTION

16-3 Evidence of Human
     Evolution
16-4 Early Hominid Fossils
16-5 Later Hominid Forms
16-6 Culture and Human
     Brain Evolution
16-7 Modern Humans

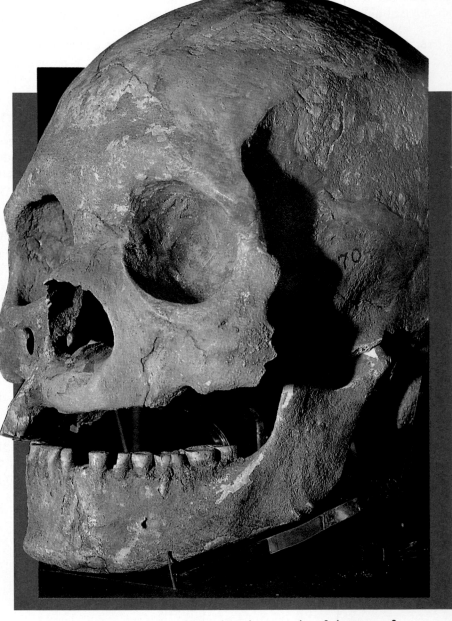

How do humans of today solve the puzzle of their past?

THE HUMAN AS A PRIMATE

In most every human society when a child is born someone asks the question, "who does she or he look like". The question of our origins has been one of intense concern before formal written records 6000 years ago. It may have been considered before the emergence of cave and rock art in Africa and Europe 35 000 years ago. Many people have tried to answer this question, yet there is no agreement among groups of people with different views. In this chapter, we shall learn that the question of our origins can be better answered from studying evolution and genetics. This knowledge enables us to better appreciate our connectedness to all of life.

With any discussion of human evolution many difficult questions arise. For example:

1. How do we distinguish among monkeys, apes, and humans, if all we have to go by are bones?
2. How, when, and why did apes and humans become different?

You may have heard someone say, "humans evolved from apes". This statement reflects a serious misunderstanding of the complex nature of evolution. It is not that we evolved from chimpanzees or gorillas, but that sometime in the past we shared a common ancestor. This chapter will deal with these and other questions you may have by examining three kinds of evidence—anatomical, genetic and behavioral similarities, and crucial differences between apes and humans.

16-1 Primate Characteristics

Humans belong to an order of animals known as **primates,** which include apes (chimpanzees, gorillas, orangutans, and gibbons), monkeys, lemurs, and tree shrews. Non-human primates are mainly found in rain forests in Africa, Asia, and parts of Central and South America.

Primates have a number of important common characteristics, such as large brains for their size, complex social behavior, hands with opposable thumbs. Their grasping fingers are backed with nails rather than claws and they have a flat face with forward-pointing eyes giving them stereoscopic vision. These and other evolved characteristics are of selective advantage to an animal living in rain forests. An **opposable thumb** can move so the tip of the thumb crosses the palm of the hand. Try to pick up a pen and write without using your thumb. The effort may give you an appreciation for the importance of an opposable thumb.

Section Objectives

A *Describe* the characteristics of primates and state how each was originally an adaptation for life in trees.

B *List* the similarities and differences between humans and apes.

C *State* how some of the differences between human and ape skeletons are related to bipedal walking in humans.

Figure 16-1 This primate depends on several specialized body structures to move freely through its environment.

Figure 16-2 The evolution of primates took place about 40 million years ago. There are at least four lines of evolution among primates. Prosimians have pointed faces and usually cannot make facial expressions. The monkeys include New World and the Old World monkeys. Humans and apes are thought to have evolved from a more recent common ancestor.

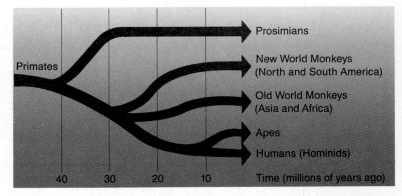

Prosimians

New World Monkeys (North and South America)

Old World Monkeys (Asia and Africa)

Apes

Humans (Hominids)

Primates

40   30   20   10   Time (millions of years ago)

Flexible shoulders and rotating arms are other adaptations that help primates move freely through trees, avoiding predators. Primates swinging through trees use the flexibility of their arms to grab branches at many different angles. A rotating arm makes it possible to change directions.

Primates live in highly organized stable societies. Primate social order is maintained through a complex interrelationship of five factors. The first factor is the mother-infant bond. The second factor is the age of the primate, which determines its role in the group as it grows older. The third factor is kinship—the ongoing relationship of an animal to a sister, brother, or its mother. The fourth factor is the adult male-female relationship. The fifth factor is dominance—how high each animal ranks socially in the group. This varied level of personal interchange creates a society where getting along with members of a group can be a daily challenge. For example, chimpanzees, like humans, make and break partnerships, bargain for social favors, and even try to deceive one another by using odd signals.

16-2 Apes and Humans

Modern humans are closely related to African apes. If you compare ape and human structures, you will observe many similarities. Like apes, humans have front-facing eyes, opposable thumbs, and flexible upper limbs. Skull features like the braincase, face, teeth, and jaw reveal additional similarities.

A closer look at ape and human skeletons reveals many differences too. The upright walk of the human accounts for many major skeletal differences. Upright walking on hindlimbs is called **bipedal** [bī ped′ əl] walking. Humans are completely bipedal. While some apes can walk upright for short distances, generally they lean forward and use their forelimbs and knuckles to support their weight.

The pelvic bones, or hipbones, of apes and humans reflect this difference in movement. A comparison of their skeletons

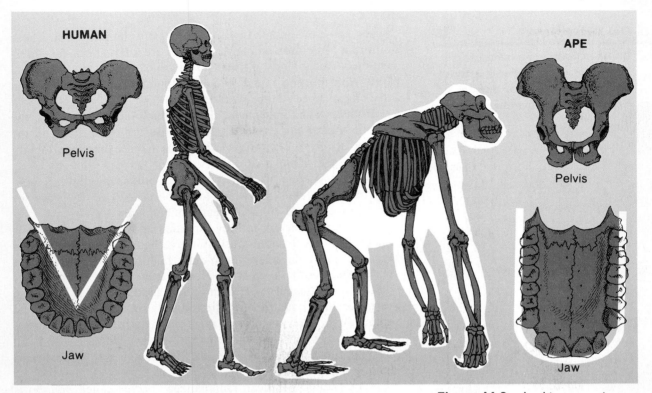

HUMAN

Pelvis

Jaw

APE

Pelvis

Jaw

shows that the human pelvis is broader than that of the ape. The flattened pelvic bones of humans provide a point of attachment for the muscles of the lower limbs. Sockets for the leg bones are positioned so that the legs can extend vertically downward. The position of the legs and pelvis helps humans to maintain their balance as they walk.

In humans, the spinal column supports the head during bipedal walking. The spinal column enters the skull at the bottom. In apes, the opening is toward, but not at, the bottom of the skull.

There are other differences between ape and human skulls. The most obvious difference is in the size of the brain cavity. The human brain volume is about 1300 cubic centimeters, whereas, the gorilla brain is about 500 cubic centimeters. The human forehead is almost vertical. The ape forehead, on the other hand, slopes back from the eyes.

When any mammal is born, its head must pass through the central opening of the mother's pelvis. The central opening in the human female pelvis is larger than in any other primate. The large size of this opening in humans allows for the birth of infants with large brains.

The shape of the jaw is different in humans and in apes. Notice in Figure 16-3 how the ape jaw is U-shaped. The human jaw, however, is V-shaped. Notice also that the teeth of the ape and human are shaped differently. In addition, there are spaces be-

Figure 16-3   In this comparison of ape and human skeletons, notice the following characteristics: arm length, foot size, pelvis width, and neck bones. In what ways is the human skeleton better adapted for bipedal posture?

DO YOU KNOW?

Information: The bones of a newborn's skull are not yet fused together. A baby's head shape must be somewhat flexible in order to exit through the pelvis. In the first six months to one year of life the brain doubles in size and continues to grow slowly until age six, when it stops growing.

BIOLOGY INSIGHT

Continuity of Life: The genetic information needed to construct your body is about 125 000 years old. Specific parts of human DNA are much older. For example, hair, eye color, and skin are constructed from genetic information many millions of years old.

tween some of the ape teeth, in contrast to human teeth. These different structures and arrangements are adaptations for different diets. What kinds of foods do you think ape teeth are adapted for? What do you notice about the number of ape and human teeth?

Both apes and humans have opposable thumbs. However, the human thumb can extend farther across the hand than can the thumb of any other primate. Humans have exceptional ability to grasp and manipulate objects.

Primates have a prolonged period of biological youth. Reaching maturity takes six years for baboons, 10 to 15 years for chimpanzees, and 20 to 28 years for humans.

Primates can learn both by imitation and teaching. Scientists have observed that the most imitative learning occurs between females and their offspring. Young baboons and chimpanzees watch their mothers select foods, peel fruits, and then copy their mothers' actions and sometimes share food. Chimpanzees learn to make tools, such as wooden sticks for termite fishing and eating meat. They use branches as clubs to threaten other members of the group in the same imitative way. Humans also learn by imitation, but teaching is also important and, probably, a unique human behavior.

A rare central African chimpanzee species called *bonobo* is thought to be the most humanlike of the great apes because of its physical appearance, learning capacity, and sexual behavior. Bonobos differ from their chimpanzee cousins in several important ways. They are smaller and seem to walk on two legs more easily than other apes. They enjoy singing in the rain, laughing and making faces—something other chimps never do. They seem to have a capacity for imagination because they like to play games such as blind man's bluff, covering their eyes with leaves or their fingers as they climb and swing. Like humans, bonobos kiss and hug, and are also able to resolve conflict and tension.

CHECKPOINT ◆

1. List two characteristics of primates that are adaptations for living in trees.
2. Compare ape and human periods of maturation.
3. Primates learn mainly by _____ .
4. The opening for the spinal column in humans is directly under the skull. How is the position and structure of the human pelvis related to bipedal walking?
▶ 5. What characteristics most reveal the close relationship between humans and chimpanzees?

▶ Denotes a question that involves *interpreting* and *applying* concepts.

TRACING HUMAN EVOLUTION

East Africa contains a complex network of habitats that preserves many evidences of early human evolution. Fossils found in sediments along East Africa's Rift Valley preserve a wealth of clues to the environment under which particular humanlike primates lived and died.

The number of human fossils available for study is extensive. More than 3000 specimens have been found. They often consist of small fragments of jaws, teeth, skulls, or other bones. Many of these fossils are dated between 2.5 and 7 million years old.

16-3 Evidence of Human Evolution

Anthropologists [an' thrə pol ə jists] study human cultures and human origins. Paleoanthropologists study prehistoric evidence of human life. They attempt to learn how, where, and when humans evolved. What evidence do they study?

Examining fossil skulls reveals different kinds of information. For example, by measuring the size of the brain cavity or the angle of the jaw, scientists try to determine if a skull is humanlike or apelike. The measurements indicate the degree of similarity to one or the other. Another helpful observation is the location of the opening for the spinal cord into the skull. What kind of information will this reveal?

Measurements of thigh and upper arm bones give an estimate of how tall the early human was. Comparisons of thigh and upper arm bones are useful too. Humans have upper arm bones that are about 70 to 75 percent as long as their thigh bones. The ape upper arm bone is about 95 percent as long as the thigh bone. The higher the ratio, the more apelike the fossil skeleton is.

Human bones are often found with other objects. Animal bones may indicate what early humans ate. Charcoal and burned animal bones may indicate that fire was used. Sometimes stone tools such as knives, axes, or scrapers are found near human bones. The number of different tools and the amount of skill required to make them tell how advanced the toolmakers were.

16-4 Early Hominid Fossils

In 1924 Raymond Dart, a South African anatomy professor, discovered an unusual skull in a limestone cave in South Africa. The skull has a small brain cavity much like that of an ape. However, the jaws are V-shaped and the teeth humanlike. The opening for the spinal cord is at the bottom of the skull, sug-

Section Objectives

D *Give examples* of evidence that reconstructs human history.

E *State* why *Australopithecus* is thought to be an early human ancestor.

F *Define* the term hominid.

G *Identify* the characteristics that distinguish *Homo habilis*, *Homo erectus*, and *Homo sapiens*.

H *Describe* the relationship between culture and brain evolution.

I *Compare* *Homo sapiens neanderthalensis* and *Homo sapiens sapiens*.

Figure 16-4 Through careful examination of fossils, anthropologists learn about hominid evolution.

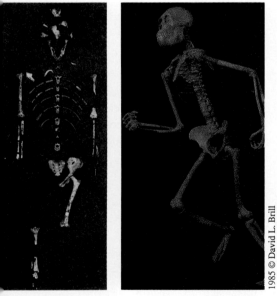

1985 © David L. Brill

Figure 16-5 *Top:* An *Australopithecus africanus* female searches for tubers with a stick. *Bottom:* This skeleton of Lucy was reconstructed based on the remains discovered in Ethiopia.

gesting that the animal walked upright. Dart named his discovery *Australopithecus* [os trā′ lə pith ə kəs] *africanus,* which means "southern ape from Africa." Radioactive dating techniques indicate that species of *Australopithecus africanus* lived between 1.2 and 3.6 million years ago.

Since 1924, many *Australopithecus* fossils have been discovered in Africa. Some of these fossils are different enough to be assigned to different species. All the *Australopithecus* fossils confirm that they were bipedal. In Ethiopia in 1974, an American anthropologist Donald Johanson, discovered an unusually complete skeleton of a small female that he named *Australopithecus afarensis,* nicknamed Lucy. Lucy was an adult that possessed a mixture of ape and humanlike characteristics. Yet the skull and the pelvis clearly show that Lucy was bipedal. A set of fossil footprints of approximately the same age confirm that bipedal primates existed in Africa about 3.8 million years ago.

All of the *Australopithecus* species, including Lucy, are hominids. **Hominids** [häm′ ə nədz] are humanlike, bipedal primates. A variety of hominids once lived. Africa has been a rich source of early hominid fossils. From this evidence, there is general agreement that humans initially evolved on the African continent.

16-5 Later Hominid Forms

Louis and Mary Leakey and their son Richard discovered a hominid fossil with a brain size of about 700 cubic centimeters— much larger than that of *Australopithecus.* The Leakeys named this fossil *Homo habilis. Homo habilis* is thought to be between 1.5 and 2 million years old. The Leakeys found simple stone tools near the fossil. These tools may have been made and used by *Homo habilis.* There is no definite evidence that any *Australopithecus* made stone tools.

Homo erectus is another species of hominid. Fossils of *Homo erectus* have been found in Africa, Europe, China, and the island of Java. *Homo erectus* first appeared in Africa and migrated to various parts of Asia and then Europe. *Homo erectus* fossils have been dated between 0.25 and 1.5 million years old. These larger-brained hominids made finely crafted stone tools, used fire, and probably lived in groups, and had more complex social activities.

16-6 Culture and Human Brain Evolution

Detailed studies of plaster casts of the interior surface of hominid skulls gives important clues to the nature of human brain evolution. The *Australopithecus* brain was about the same size as the chimpanzee brain, however, there were significant differences in shape and structure. With the emergence of the *Homo* species, there was a steady increase in cranial volume or brain size. This increase ranged from an average of 800 cubic centimeters for *Homo habilis,* to 1000 cubic centimeters for *Homo erectus,* to 1360 cubic centimeters for hominids like modern humans *Homo sapiens.*

As the fossil hominids show an increase in cranial volume, the archaeological record shows an increase in the range of stone tools and in the size and kinds of animals hunted. This evidence does not mean that there is a direct relationship between brain size and tool use or hunting habits. We do know that tools were used in a variety of different environments, and hominid cooperative social behavior was an important adaptation.

As more sharing and cooperation occurred between females and males, more time was available for males to associate for hunting, social interactions, and learning. As the maturation period for hominids increased, there were changes in the interactions among hormones which led to changes in male and female physiology and brain anatomy.

Hunting required an understanding of animal behavior, terrain, butchering, and perhaps storage. It also required more advanced behavioral development, bipedal motion, and communication which included symbolic language. Language development can lead to more complex social interaction. This type of interaction leads to further specialization of the human brain resulting in an increase of capabilities.

Complex written and symbolic languages are perhaps the most unique human activities. Gorillas, chimps and dolphins have been taught the meaning of several hundred words using sign languages. They can even construct simple sentences from their vocabulary and take action. Yet, they cannot pass on this learned behavior to succeeding generations. This exchange permits the existence of a very complex culture. **Culture** is the sum total of learned behavior patterns of a social group of human beings including objects invented for practical use and artworks.

16-7 Modern Humans

Hominid fossils that are similar to modern humans have been found throughout Africa. Many of these fossils are close to 400 000 years old. Crania of these fossils have characteristics of ancient *Homo erectus* and modern *Homo sapiens* and are generally termed archaic *Homo sapiens*. Archaic *Homo sapiens* later evolved into *Homo sapiens neanderthalensis* and *Homo sapiens sapiens*.

Figure 16-6 Neanderthals lived in ice-age Europe from 125 000 to about 32 000 years ago and abruptly disappeared. The activities of this Neanderthal social group involved the use of tools. A dead animal is skinned using stone tools, while others gather firewood and make flint spearpoints.

Human Evolution **269**

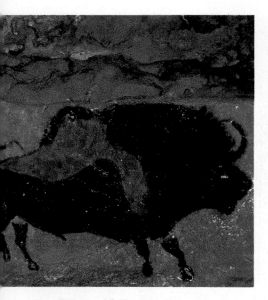

Figure 16-7 Between 35 000 and 10 000 years ago, Cro-Magnons decorated the walls of their caves with accurate representations of the animals they hunted.

Homo sapiens neanderthalensis are generally referred to as Neanderthals [nē an′ t(h)ŏl]. Study of Neanderthals' skeletons suggests they had short bulky bodies and limbs with larger heads than *Homo sapiens sapiens*. Their fossil remains have only been found in Europe and Asia and date from 130 000 to 32 000 years ago. Neanderthals developed more advanced tools to aid in killing and butchering large animals, such as wooly mammoths and rhinoceroses, and cave bears. They constructed shelters from the bones of these animals. These activities indicated this group had more highly developed thought processes.

Neanderthals engaged in rituals when burying their dead which included placing small objects in the graves and flower arrangements around the graves. Their complex culture suggests that they had a highly developed spoken language. Neanderthal people no longer exist. Many scientists theorize that they merged with *Homo sapiens sapiens* over time.

Homo sapiens sapiens or modern humans first evolved in Africa. Human fossils from Border cave in South Africa date between 115 000 and 80 000 years old and those from a cave in Qafzeh, Israel are 92 000 years old. However, research indicates that all modern human populations evolved from one or several central African females, around 200 000 years ago (actually between 140 000 and 290 000 years ago). This research is based on the study of DNA located in the mitochondria of a cell. In females this DNA shows a very slow mutation rate. Studies show that mitochondrial DNA in modern females closely matches that of early human females. It is hypothesized that *Homo sapiens sapiens* migrated out of Africa about 100 000 years ago. *Homo sapiens sapiens* appeared in Europe around 40 000 years ago and have been called Cro-Magnons after the caves in southern France where they were first found.

Homo sapiens sapiens people had a very complex social system, including a more sophisticated spoken language. Beautiful, interesting cave and rock art dated between 35 000 and 10 000 years old has been found in North Africa, Tanzania, South Africa, Europe, India and Brazil. Paintings include magnificently drawn animals, people, and strange symbols. There are stone and bone carvings which suggest that women developed lunar calendars during this period. This advance in human cognitive abilities made possible the development of agriculture and cities, the domestication of animals, written languages, more advanced tool technologies, and more complex systems of governance in the Nile and Tigris/Euphrates river valleys.

We have learned that the study of human origins is one that involves a number of scientific disciplines, such as ecology, embryology, geology, molecular biology, archaeology and paleoan-

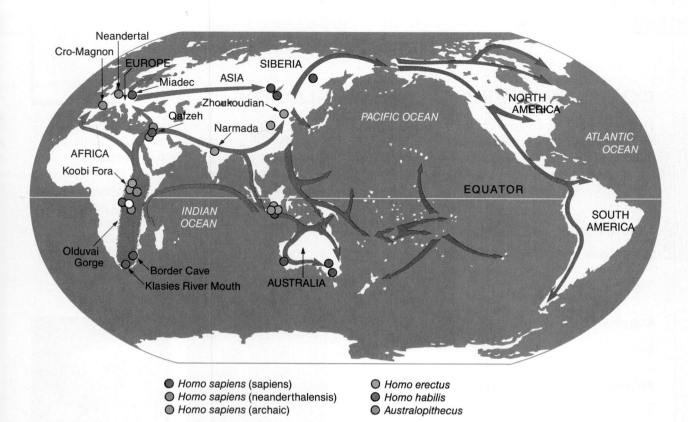

● Homo sapiens (sapiens)   ○ Homo erectus
● Homo sapiens (neanderthalensis) ● Homo habilis
○ Homo sapiens (archaic)   ○ Australopithecus

thropology. Scientists of these disciplines often passionately disagree over the meaning of the evidence they find. The questions about our origins have yet to be fully answered.

Figure 16-8 This map shows the movement of hominids from Africa throughout the world and major fossil finds.

CHECKPOINT ◆

6. What kind of evidence indicates that early humans used fire to cook meat?
7. Give two characteristics of *Australopithecus* that make it a candidate as an early human ancestor.
8. Name one characteristic shared by all hominids.
9. Which of the hominids was probably the first to use tools?
10. *Homo erectus* and *Homo sapiens* differ from each other in what major characteristic?
11. What two types of early humans are now considered to belong to the species, *Homo sapiens*?
▶ 12. Spoken language permits the existence of culture. Why do you think the rapid expansion of culture became possible only with the invention of written language?

▶ Denotes a question that involves *interpreting* and *applying* concepts.

COMPARING PRIMATE HEMOGLOBINS

Hemoglobin is the oxygen-carrying protein found in the red blood cells of many animals. The comparison of amino acid sequences of hemoglobins from different primates provides evidence of evolutionary relationships.

Objectives and Skills

☐ *Determine* and *correlate* the number of differences between human hemoglobin and hemoglobins from four other primates.

Materials

paper   pencil

Procedure and Observations

1. Read all instructions for this laboratory activity before you begin your work.
2. Look at the chart on the next page. At each amino acid position, count and record the number of differences between each primate's amino acid and the human amino acid.
3. Copy Figure 16-2, the primate "family tree". In the appropriate spot next to each type of primate, record the number of amino acid differences between that primate and human hemoglobin. Primate 1 is an old world monkey called a macaque. Primate 2 is a lemur (a prosimian). Primate 3 is a gorilla. Primate 4 is a new world spider monkey.

Analysis and Conclusions

1. Based on the amino acid data, which of the primates appears to be most closely related to humans? Which primate is most distantly related to humans?

2. The hemoglobin chain contains 146 amino acids. What percentage of amino acids are different in each of the four primates?
3. The primate "family tree" at the beginning of this chapter was produced largely on the basis of fossil evidence. Explain how the data you have collected here supports the conclusions presented in the "family tree."
4. What conclusion can you draw from the fact that 113 of the amino acids in the chain are identical in all five primates?

Macaque

Lemur

Gorilla

Spider monkey

Comparison of Hemoglobin of Five Primates

AMINO ACID POSITION											
	1	**2**	**4**	**5**	**8**	**9**	**10**	**12**	**13**	**21**	**22**
Human	VAL	HIS	THR	PRO	LYS	SER	ALA	THR	ALA	ASP	GLU
Primate 1	VAL	HIS	THR	PRO	LYS	ASN	ALA	THR	THR	ASP	GLU
Primate 2	THR	LEU	SER	ALA	ASP	ALA	HIS	THR	SER	GLU	LYS
Primate 3	VAL	HIS	THR	PRO	LYS	SER	ALA	THR	ALA	ASP	GLU
Primate 4	VAL	HIS	THR	GLY	LYS	SER	ALA	ALA	ALA	ASP	GLU
	33	**50**	**52**	**56**	**69**	**73**	**76**	**87**	**104**	**111**	**112**
Human	VAL	THR	ASP	GLY	GLY	ASP	ALA	THR	ARG	VAL	CYS
Primate 1	LEU	SER	ASP	GLY	GLY	ASP	ASN	GLN	LYS	VAL	CYS
Primate 2	VAL	SER	SER	SER	SER	GLU	HIS	GLN	LYS	SER	ALA
Primate 3	VAL	THR	ASP	GLY	GLY	ASP	ALA	THR	LYS	VAL	CYS
Primate 4	VAL	THR	ASP	SER	GLY	ASP	ALA	GLN	ARG	VAL	CYS
	113	**114**	**115**	**116**	**120**	**121**	**122**	**123**	**125**	**126**	**130**
Human	VAL	LEU	ALA	HIS	LYS	GLY	PHE	THR	PRO	VAL	TYR
Primate 1	VAL	LEU	ALA	HIS	LYS	GLY	PHE	THR	GLN	VAL	TYR
Primate 2	GLU	SER	GLU	LEU	HIS	ASP	LYS	SER	ALA	VAL	PHE
Primate 3	VAL	LEU	ALA	HIS	LYS	GLY	PHE	THR	PRO	VAL	TYR
Primate 4	VAL	LEU	ALA	HIS	LYS	GLY	PHE	THR	GLN	LEU	TYR

Abbreviations for amino acids:

ALA: Alanine
ARG: Arginine
ASN: Asparagine
ASP: Aspartic acid

CYS: Cysteine
GLN: Glutamine
GLU: Glutamic acid
GLY: Glycine

HIS: Histidine
LEU: Leucine
LYS: Lysine
PHE: Phenylalanine

PRO: Proline
SER: Serine
THR: Threonine
TYR: Tyrosine
VAL: Valine

CHAPTER REVIEW

Summary

▸ The first primates had forward-facing eyes, opposable thumbs, and rotating forelimbs, all characteristics suited for life in trees.

▸ Modern humans have physical features that distinguish them from the apes, their closest primate relatives. These features include a large brain, bipedal walk, fully opposable thumbs, and a large opening in the female pelvis.

▸ The human jaw is V-shaped with no spaces between the teeth, while the ape jaw is U-shaped and has spaces between some of the teeth.

▸ The large human brain has enabled the development of culture, the use of complex language, and the making of tools.

▸ Hominids are bipedal primates. The oldest fossil hominids are placed in a group called *Australopithecus*. They have ape-sized brains and human-like jaws. The oldest is estimated to be about 3.8 million years old.

▸ All hominids are closely related to humans. But not all are direct ancestors. Some became extinct.

▸ The first fossils that belong to the group called *Homo* are about 2 million years old. *Homo habilis* and *Homo erectus* have larger brains than *Australopithecus*.

▸ Modern humans, *Homo sapiens sapiens*, first evolved in Africa.

Vocabulary

anthropologist	*Homo habilis*
Australopithecus	*Homo sapiens*
bipedal	*neanderthalensis*
Cro-Magnon	*Homo sapiens sapiens*
culture	opposable thumb
hominid	*primate*
Homo erectus	

Concept Mapping

Construct a concept map for primate structure and evolution. Include the following terms: structure, movement, skull, jaw, brain case, opposable thumb, pelvic bones, apes, humans, and culture. Use additional terms as you need them.

Review

Choose the best answer for each of the following questions:

1. Humans belong to the group of animals called (a) carnivores, (b) marsupials, (c) primates, (d) apes.
2. Which of the following animals has a body structure most similar to that of a human? (a) chimpanzee (b) monkey (c) whale (d) seal
3. Which characteristic do scientists hypothesize was possessed by the original primates? (a) bipedal posture (b) the ability to make tools (c) three-dimensional vision (d) enlarged brain
4. In the human skull, where is the opening for the spinal cord located? (a) at the back (b) at the bottom (c) in the front (d) none of these
5. The human jaw (a) is U-shaped, (b) is V-shaped, (c) has more teeth than an ape, (d) has fewer teeth than an ape.
6. One bone that would be particularly useful to determine whether an animal was bipedal is the (a) pelvis, (b) rib, (c) upper arm bone, (d) jaw.
7. Information passed from one generation of human beings to another is (a) bipedalism, (b) education, (c) culture, (d) technology.
8. Which is not used to reconstruct human history up to the time of *Homo sapiens*? (a) stone tools (b) evidence of language (c) fossil bones (d) radioactive dating

9. Fossils of the earliest hominids are found in (a) Australia, (b) Europe, (c) Greece, (d) Africa.
10. *Australopithecus* was similar to an ape in (a) the size of its brain cavity, (b) its manner of walking, (c) the shape of its jaw, (d) the location where the spinal cord enters the skull.
11. All hominids (a) are bipedal, (b) have very large brains, (c) use tools, (d) use fire.
12. The oldest known hominid fossil is about how old? (a) 50 000 years (b) 100 000 years (c) 1.6 million years (d) 3.8 million years
13. Which of the following was most like human beings presently alive? (a) *Homo erectus* (b) Neanderthal (c) Cro-Magnon (d) *Homo habilis*

Interpret and Apply

14. Put the following events in order according to the time when they occurred. Number the earliest event one and the most recent five.
    a. evolution of bipedal walk
    b. creation of cave paintings
    c. existence of primate ancestors of apes and humans
    d. first use of tools
    e. existence of *Homo erectus*
15. Choose two differences between ape skulls and human skulls, and explain why the differences are significant.
16. In what ways did bipedal walking affect the skeleton of hominids?
17. Give an example of how one of the early primate adaptations for life in trees became an important adaptation for hominids.
18. Which is more like modern humans—*Australopithecus* or *Homo habilis*? Give evidence to support your answer.

19. In what way might the use of tools and the invention of language and culture be related?
20. One characteristic separates the hominids from all other primates. What is this characteristic and why is it so important in the evolution of *Homo sapiens*?
21. What is the significance of the observation that *Australopithecus* fossils occur only in Africa, but *Homo erectus* is found in Africa, Europe, and Asia?
22. Why are *Homo sapiens sapiens* unique?

Critical Thinking

23. Humans are sometimes called the toolmaking animal. Explain how a large brain, opposable thumbs, bipedal walk, and culture have resulted in this expression.
24. What stage in the life cycle would be most susceptible to evolutionary change?
25. You discover a fossil adult skull in the desert. The brain cavity is 480 cubic centimeters. The jaw is V-shaped. The opening into the skull for the spinal cord is located at the bottom. The fossil is about 2.5 million years old.
    a. Is this fossil a hominid? What evidence supports your conclusion?
    b. To what group might you assign this fossil?
26. One argument states that humans developed a large brain because they used tools. Another argument states that humans began to use tools after their brains became larger. Explain why each of these arguments is too simple.

CLASSIFICATION OF LIFE

Overview

SYSTEMS OF CLASSIFICATION

17-1 Binomial Nomenclature

17-2 Levels of Classification

17-3 Modern Techniques of Classification

17-4 Three-Kingdom System

17-5 Five-Kingdom System

IDENTIFYING ORGANISMS

17-6 How a Classification Key Works

17-7 How to Use a Classification Key

How would you begin to sort these shells for a collection?

SYSTEMS OF CLASSIFICATION

Classifying is a way of organizing information. To **classify** is to put objects or ideas into groups on the basis of similarity. The ancient Greek philosopher Aristotle made one of the first attempts at classifying living things. Aristotle classified all organisms as either plants or animals. He then classified each animal according to where it lived—on land, in water, or in the air. He classified each plant as an herb, a shrub, or a tree. Aristotle's system was a logical method of classification, but it is not very useful to modern biologists. Both bats and mosquitos fly, so under Aristotle's system they would both be air dwellers. Ants and mice live on the ground, so they would both be called ground dwellers. But scientists know now that a bat is really more closely related to a mouse than to a mosquito. An ant is more closely related to a mosquito than to a mouse.

Throughout history, biologists have used various systems of classification to identify order among organisms. What were some of these systems? Why are they no longer being used? What system of classification do scientists use today?

17-1 Binomial Nomenclature

When biologists study a particular organism, it is important to refer to that organism by a name that other scientists will understand. The use of local or common names for a species can be confusing. People who speak different languages give different names to the same species. Even within one country, one species may have many different names.

What would you call the fruit shown in Figure 17-1? In some regions of the United States, this fruit is called a mango. In other regions of the country, it is known as a bell pepper. In still other areas, it is known as a sweet pepper or a green pepper. Scientists call this plant *Capsicum frutescens*. To make matters even more confusing, the fruit of the plant *Mangifera indica* is also called a mango, and the seeds of the plant *Piper nigrum* are called pepper.

To avoid confusion, a system was developed in the seventeenth century for naming and classifying organisms. Latin was used in assigning the first scientific names to organisms.

Naturalists began to group similar species into larger groups called **genera** (singular, **genus**). For example, dogs and wolves belong to the genus *Canis*. Each species was given a long name called a **polynomial**. The polynomial consisted of the name of the genus and several descriptive words following it. The descriptive words made it possible for an organism's name to describe

Section Objectives

A *State* several reasons why systems of classification are important.

B *Explain* several advantages of using a system of binomial nomenclature.

C *List* the levels of classification developed by Linnaeus.

D *Describe* a modern technique used in classifying organisms.

E *Explain* why two- and three-kingdom classification systems were not adequate.

F *List* the criteria used in classifying organisms within a five-kingdom system.

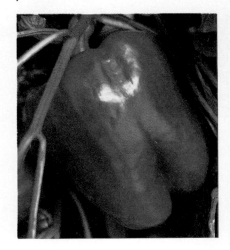

Figure 17-1 Scientists call this fruit *Capsicum frutescens*. What do you call it?

the organism in detail. But such names were awkward to use. The catnip plant, for example, was called *Nepeta floribus interrupte spicatus pedunculatis*. That's quite a mouthful!

During the eighteenth century, a Swedish naturalist named Carl von Linné established a simpler method of naming organisms. In keeping with the custom of that time, von Linné called himself by the Latin form of his name, *Carolus Linnaeus*.

In Linnaeus's system of naming, each species was identified by two names. The first name was the genus. The genus was often the Latin translation of the common name. The second name, called the **specific epithet**, was an adjective that described the species. In Latin, as in many other languages, it is common to place the adjective after the noun it describes. A human is known as *Homo sapiens*. *Homo*, the Latin name for humans, is followed by the specific epithet *sapiens*, which means knowing, or wise.

The specific epithet often describes the color of an organism, or where that organism is usually found. For example, *Betula alba* is the name of a white birch, and *Betula lutea* is the name of a yellow birch. *Peromyscus californicus* is the name of a mouse found primarily in California. In some cases, the specific epithet is actually the name of the person who originally described the species. *Gazella thompsonii* is the scientific name of an African antelope. The person who first described this animal was M.T. Thompson, a wildlife naturalist.

This two-part method of naming species is called **binomial nomenclature**. This system of naming things is still used by scientists today. Notice that in binomial nomenclature, the name of the genus always appears first and is capitalized. The specific epithet follows and is not capitalized. Both words should appear in italics. Italics may be indicated by underlining in handwritten or typed papers. Sometimes the genus name is abbreviated, so that *Drosophila melanogaster* may be written as *D. melanogaster*.

17-2 Levels of Classification

Suppose you were traveling in a foreign country and someone asked you where you live. If you simply said, "I live at 325 Spruce Street," without giving any more information, the stranger would have little idea of where you live. More likely you would first say what country you live in. Then you might mention your home state, your hometown, and maybe even your street address. By starting with the general and then moving to the specific, you would be using a system of classification.

Linnaeus also used the technique of classifying that started with the general and moved to the specific until he "zeroed in" on a particular species. He grouped together the organisms that

Figure 17-2 The common names of organisms can be misleading. *Top:* The starfish has very few characteristics in common with true fish. *Bottom:* The sea lion bears little resemblance to lions found on land.

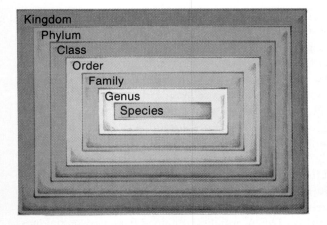

most closely resembled each other. Like Aristotle, Linnaeus divided all living things into two vast groups, which he called the plant and animal **kingdoms**. He then divided each kingdom into many smaller **phyla** (singular, **phylum**). Organisms that he placed in the same phylum not only shared the characteristics of their kingdom, but they also had in common additional characteristics that members of other phyla did not share. Linnaeus divided each phylum into classes, each **class** into orders, each **order** into families, each **family** into genera, and each genus into **species**. Figure 17-3 illustrates the relationship between levels of classification. Each organism fits into one group at each level of classification. If two organisms belong to the same species, you may also assume that they are in the same genus, family, order, class, phylum, and kingdom. (In plant classification, the word **division** is used instead of *phylum*.)

Linnaeus published his first work, *Species Plantarum*, in 1752. Because Linnaeus lived about 100 years before Darwin, he had no idea that new species could evolve from other species. He assumed that there was a fixed number of unchanging species that inhabited Earth. Linnaeus determined how closely related a group of species was by the degree of physical similarity among them.

17-3 Modern Techniques of Classification

Since the time of Linnaeus, scientists have learned much more about the evolutionary relationships between different organisms. **Taxonomists**, the scientists who study classification, attempt to arrange organisms into groups based on these relationships. The evolutionary history of a species is called its **phylogeny** [fī loj′ ə nē].

Modern taxonomists have many techniques available to them to help in their task of determining phylogenetic relationships.

BIOLOGY INSIGHT

Unity and Diversity: As new organisms and their relationships were discovered, new levels of classification were added. These include subkingdom, which is smaller than a kingdom but larger than a phylum; subphylum, which is smaller than a phylum but larger than a class; and subclass, which is smaller than a class but larger than an order.

DO YOU KNOW?

Word Root: Taxonomy is a branch of science that deals with the orderly arrangement of organisms based on phylogenetic relationships. The word *taxonomy* comes from the Greek *taxis,* meaning "an arrangement, order," and the Greek *nomos,* meaning "law; system."

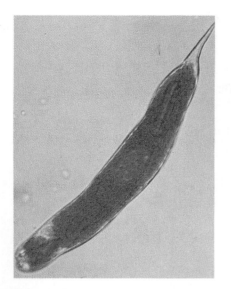

Figure 17-4   In which kingdom does *Euglena* belong? In which kingdom would Aristotle have classified this organism?

Figure 17-5   Coral is multicellular. Its cells have nuclei. It does not photosynthesize. In which kingdom does it belong?

Modern biochemical techniques provide new information that is helpful in classifying organisms.

Today it is possible to determine the amino-acid sequences of proteins. Differences in amino-acid sequences represent mutations. If two species have very similar sequences, scientists infer that the species are closely related. Human hemoglobin and baboon hemoglobin have more similar amino-acid sequences than human hemoglobin and horse hemoglobin. This observation confirms that humans and baboons are more closely related than humans and horses.

The theoretical basis of Linnaeus's scheme of classification was very different from that of modern taxonomy. Fortunately, though, Linnaeus's system was set up in such a way that scientists can still use it today. The information obtained from new techniques usually supports the relationships that taxonomists have hypothesized over the past several hundred years. The system of classification will certainly be updated as new information becomes available.

17-4 Three-Kingdom System

Before the use of the microscope, it seemed obvious to most people that living things were either plants or animals. The discovery of microorganisms, however, revealed many organisms that did not seem to fit neatly into either category. The euglena shown in Figure 17-4 is an example of one such troublesome organism. A euglena is a unicellular organism that contains chloroplasts and carries on photosynthesis. In this way, it resembles a plant. But it also swims by means of a flagellum and can ingest food. Both of these characteristics would seem to make *Euglena* an animal. So what is *Euglena*—plant or animal?

In 1866, the German scientist Ernst Haeckel proposed that a third kingdom be added to plants and animals. He called the third kingdom Protista. All one-celled organisms and others that were clearly neither plants nor animals were **protists.** Haeckel assumed that plants and animals had evolved from organisms in the protist kingdom. Haeckel's system was never widely accepted because, even within the protist kingdom, large differences existed between organisms.

One major difference among the organisms included in the protist kingdom was the presence or absence of a nucleus and membrane-bound organelles. Recall from Chapter 15 that organisms whose cells contain a nucleus and membrane-bound organelles are called eukaryotes. Organisms whose cells lack these structures are called prokaryotes. Many biologists thought that organisms with such fundamental differences should not be grouped into one kingdom.

17-5 Five-Kingdom System

Throughout the twentieth century, the science of taxonomy has evolved to fit new ideas and new information. In 1969, Robert Whittaker, a biologist at Cornell University, proposed a system of classification that included five kingdoms. Whittaker's system is based on three criteria: the number of cells in an organism; the presence or absence of a nucleus; and the mode of nutrition. The five kingdoms were identified as monerans, protists, fungi, plants, and animals. Although this system was not perfect, it gained wide acceptance.

Any system of classification is somewhat artificial. It is simply an attempt by humans to impose order on a vast, diverse group of organisms. So it is not surprising that a few organisms just do not fit neatly into one of the five kingdoms. For example, research has shown that water molds and slime molds, once considered fungi, have actually evolved from different protist groups. Research has also shown that red and brown algae evolved from unicellular ancestors rather than from ancestors of multi-cellular plants. The green algae, a group that includes unicellular and multicellular forms, no longer fits as neatly into a multicellular plant kingdom.

This book uses a five-kingdom system of classification. However, it is not identical to the system originally proposed by Whittaker. The Kingdom Protista has been expanded to include all eukaryotic microorganisms and their immediate descendants. This has been done in an effort to reflect the discoveries regarding evolutionary relationships. Water molds and slime molds and the red, brown, and green algae are now considered to be protists.

Descriptions for each of the five kingdoms can be found on pages 282 and 283. As more information becomes available, further modifications will probably be made to this system of classification.

BIOLOGY INSIGHT

Continuity of Life: Taxonomists attempt to classify extinct organisms as well as those alive today. Unfortunately, the only body parts that remain of many extinct organisms are their teeth and bones. Taxonomists use scanning electron microscopes to study patterns of wear on teeth. These patterns tell much about the diet and lifestyle of an organism. Many extinct organisms have been classified on the basis of a single tooth!

CHECKPOINT ◆

1. Why was Latin the language chosen for an international system of classification?
2. How are amino-acid sequences used in classification?
3. Why was *Euglena* a problem in the two-kingdom system of classification?
4. Which kingdom contains prokaryotic organisms?
▶ 5. Name a few differences between plants and animals.
▶ 6. If two organisms are in the same phylum, you can also assume that they are in the same _____.
▶ 7. Suggest a way to classify the cars in your school parking lot.

▶ Denotes a question that involves *interpreting* and *applying* concepts.

FIVE KINGDOMS OF LIVING THINGS

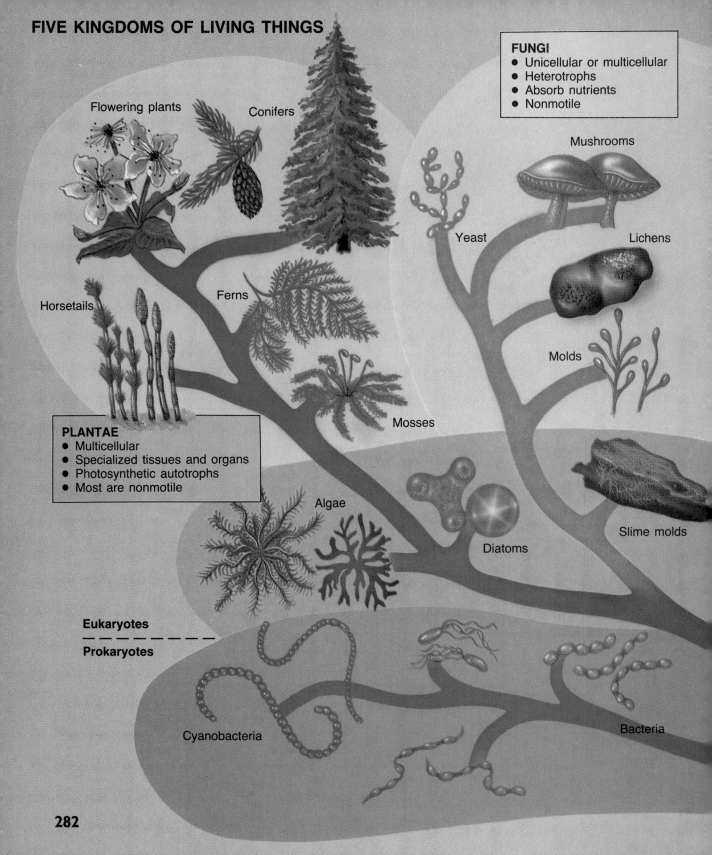

Flowering plants

Conifers

FUNGI
- Unicellular or multicellular
- Heterotrophs
- Absorb nutrients
- Nonmotile

Mushrooms

Yeast

Lichens

Horsetails

Ferns

Molds

PLANTAE
- Multicellular
- Specialized tissues and organs
- Photosynthetic autotrophs
- Most are nonmotile

Mosses

Algae

Diatoms

Slime molds

Eukaryotes

Prokaryotes

Cyanobacteria

Bacteria

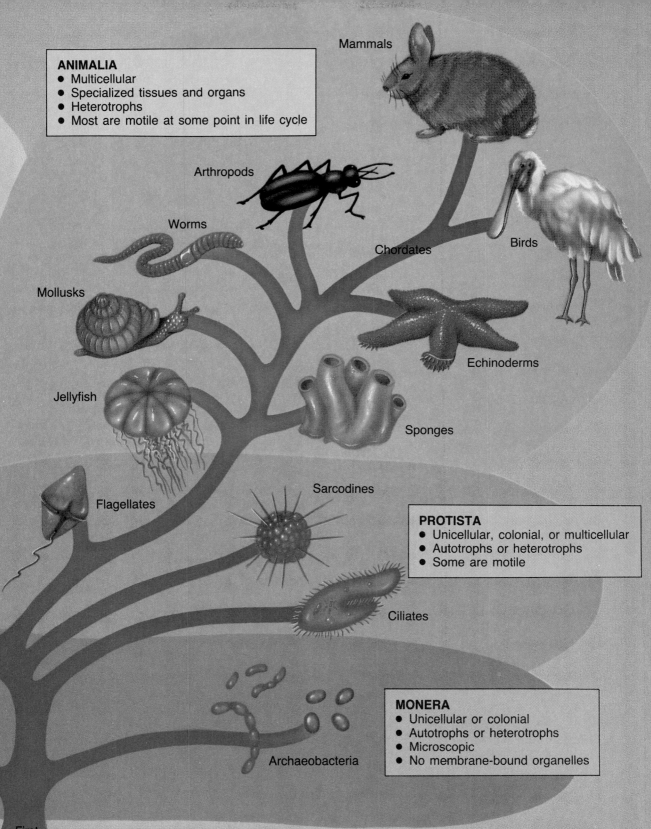

ANIMALIA
- Multicellular
- Specialized tissues and organs
- Heterotrophs
- Most are motile at some point in life cycle

Mammals

Arthropods

Worms

Chordates

Birds

Mollusks

Echinoderms

Jellyfish

Sponges

Flagellates

Sarcodines

PROTISTA
- Unicellular, colonial, or multicellular
- Autotrophs or heterotrophs
- Some are motile

Ciliates

MONERA
- Unicellular or colonial
- Autotrophs or heterotrophs
- Microscopic
- No membrane-bound organelles

Archaeobacteria

First cells

Section Objectives

G *Explain* how organisms can be identified.

H *Describe* how to use a classification key.

Have you ever seen a beautiful flower or brilliantly colored bird? Have you ever tried to describe what you saw to a friend? Chances are the only things you could remember were the size and color of each organism. You might have told your friend that the flower was short and pink, and the bird was small and yellow. At first, this description might seem adequate. Unfortunately there are over a hundred flowers and birds that would match these descriptions. If you knew the name of the organism, however, you and your friend could share the experience.

The best way to find the name of an organism is to use a classification key. The information in a classification key provides an efficient way of identifying organisms. What is a classification key? How can so much information be arranged in one key?

17-6 How a Classification Key Works

Classification keys are used in many branches of science as tools for identifying organisms. The purpose of a key is to help the user observe similarities and differences among organisms.

A classification key consists of many numbered steps. Each step presents a level of identification starting with general characteristics and moving to more specific features. The first few steps in a key help to direct the user's attention to gross external features. The steps that follow focus on the finer details of structure. Each step contains two or more statements. Only one of the statements in any given step can be true about a single organism. The true statement either directs the user to the next step or it identifies the organism. Identification keys are available for almost all living things.

17-7 How to Use a Classification Key

Look at the different shells in Figure 17-6 on the next page. Do you recognize any of these shells? You might be familiar with common names for one or more of them, but do you know their scientific names?

Use the classification key in Table 17-1 to identify each of the shells in Figure 17-6. Start by looking at the shell in the top right photograph. Note the shell's main characteristics. Then begin your identification by reading both statements in step 1. A quick visual inspection indicates that the shell is cone-shaped. The directions at the end of statement 1a tell you to go to step 2. Once you have read both parts of step 2, look closely at the outer surface of the shell to see which description best applies. Since the surface of the shell is ridged, you will skip over step 3 and go to step 4. The stripe of color on the shell means that you are looking at *Calliostoma annulatum*, the ringed-top shell. Use the key to identify the remaining six shells in the photographs. Remember to start each identification by reading step 1.

Table 17-1

SEASHELL IDENTIFICATION KEY	
1a Cone-shaped	Go to 2
1b Not cone-shaped	Go to 5
2a Outside surface smooth	Go to 3
2b Outside surface ridged	Go to 4
3a Surface solid color	*Conus californicus*
3b Surface spotted	*Conus spurius*
4a Surface one color	*Calliostoma supragranulosa*
4b Surface has contrasting stripe	*Calliostoma annulatum*
5a Holes along shell margin	*Haliotis rufescens*
5b No holes along shell margin	Go to 6
6a Purple in color	*Janthina janthina*
6b Not purple in color	*Littorina obtusata*

Figure 17-6   Notice how very different the seven seashells are from one another.

Figure 17-7 Characteristics including leaf shape, seed type, and appearance of bark are used to classify trees. Compare the characteristics of two trees shown. *Left:* A sugar maple displaying fall colors. *Right:* A blue spruce shows typical conifer features.

Classification keys are used by all types of scientists. Archaeologists use classification keys to identify the fossil remains of organisms. Microbiologists find classification especially useful for identifying unknown bacteria. Botanists use classification keys for identifying the variety of plants found in a forest. In what type of forest do you think a classification key would be most useful?

Consider the two types of plants shown in Figure 17-7. Each of these trees has its own familiar characteristics. Based on your knowledge of maple trees and spruce trees, which characteristics of trees would you use in constructing a tree identification key?

CHECKPOINT ◆

8. What is the purpose of a classification key?
9. Explain how a classification key is organized.
10. What information can be learned about an organism by using a classification key?
▶ 11. Write the scientific names of the shells in Figure 17-6.
▶ 12. Which of the shells named in question 11 is most closely related to the ringed-top shell? How did you determine your answer?
▶ 13. Construct a classification key for the following fruits: apple, orange, banana, plum, peach, watermelon, and grapefruit.

▶ Denotes a question that involves *interpreting* and *applying* concepts.

LABORATORY ACTIVITY

USING A CLASSIFICATION KEY TO IDENTIFY INSECTS

In this activity, you will study the external features of several insects and use a classification key to identify them.

Objectives and Skills

- ☐ *Practice* using a classification key.
- ☐ *Observe* the external structural characteristics of several insects.

Materials

magnifying glass
metric ruler
kit of insects

Procedure and Observations

1. Read all instructions for this laboratory activity before you begin your work.
2. On a separate piece of paper, draw a data table like the one shown below.

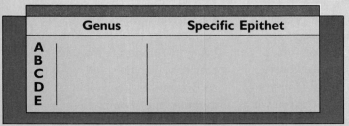

	Genus	Specific Epithet
A		
B		
C		
D		
E		

3. Assign letters to the insects in the kit provided. Carefully remove the *A* insect from the kit. Use care when handling these fragile specimens.
4. Use the magnifying glass to study the insect. Read each step in the classification key that follows to identify each insect. Write the scientific name of each insect next to the appropriate letter in the data table. Repeat this

INSECT IDENTIFICATION KEY		
1a	Longer than 15 mm	Go to 2
1b	Shorter than 15 mm	Go to 3
2a	Antennae longer than body	*Gryllus pennsylvanicus*
2b	Antennae shorter than body	*Odontotaenius disjunctus*
3a	Body hairy	Go to 4
3b	Body not hairy	Go to 5
4a	Antennae straight	*Acanthoscelides obtectus*
4b	Antennae bent	*Anthonomus grandis*
5a	Body long and slender	*Gerris remigis*
5b	Body broad	Go to 6
6a	Yellow spots on back	*Murgantia histrionica*
6b	No spots on back	*Pediculus humanus*

procedure until you have identified each insect.
5. When you have completed the lab, put all of the insects back into the kit. Before leaving the laboratory, clean up all your materials and wash your hands thoroughly.

Analysis and Conclusions

1. Which insects were most similar in their appearance?
2. Which characteristics were most useful in distinguishing one insect from another?
3. What characteristics were common to all of the insects?
4. Which insects are most likely to have similar amino-acid sequences in their proteins? How do you know?

CUTTING EDGE

The Number of Species on Earth

How many different types of organisms share Earth with you? About 1.5 million species have been directly identified and classified, but biologists suspect that there are many, many more. A major reason that the current catalog is sparse is that you are one species attempting to identify others. You spend much energy studying what one taxonomist called the furries and featheries, while paying less attention to marine worms, tropical mites, and parasites of insects, to name a few poorly studied types of organisms. Another problem is that some species are easier to find than others. The silver sword plant, for example, grows only in a single volcanic crater on the island of Maui. How many species go uncounted because you have not yet stumbled upon their homes?

Human biases complicate estimating the number of species because some biologists tend to focus on more differences between organisms than others in deciding what constitutes a separate species. For example, according to different sources, there are 200, 20, or just 2 species of English blackberry.

One approach to estimating the total number of species is to select a habitat of manageable size and count its resident species. However, habitats vary tremendously in how they are populated. A polluted environment or one that is recovering from a recent natural upheaval, such as a fire or storm generally has a few dominant species. Other species may have only a few members and could escape the scrutiny of a human census taker. An undisturbed natural habitat, in contrast, tends to have more equal representations of resident species.

Until recently, the accepted estimate of the number of total species was 3 to 5 million. This value is derived from the facts that most of the 1.5 million known species are insects living in temperate regions and that for mammals and birds, 2 to 3 times as many species dwell in the tropics than in temperate areas. Multiplying 1.5 million by 2 or 3 gives an extrapolation of about 3 to 5 million. However, field work conducted by Terry Lee Erwin of the National Museum of Natural History indicates that even 3 to 5 million species

may be a gross underestimate. He works in jungle treetops, where animal life is plentiful in response to the abundant plant food and sunshine.

Erwin's technique is simple in concept but difficult to carry out. He and his co-workers rope off areas of the jungle in South and Central America that measure 12 meters by 12 meters and suspend nets from the treetops. They then spray the area with an insecticidal fog and watch as thousands of insects fall into the nets. The nets are cone shaped and direct the dead insects into collecting bottles. As this happens, the scientists record which insects fall from which trees. The specimens are whisked to museums and laboratories, where entomologists (scientists who study insects) classify them. Back in the treetops, the insect population returns to normal within two weeks.

Erwin estimates the number of species from the diversity of captured insects. In a patch in Panama, for example, he cataloged approximately 1100 species of tree-dwelling beetles. For every species of tree in the area, roughly 160 species of beetle live only on that tree type. Taking into account the observation that beetles comprise 40 percent of known arthropods, the number of different insect species on each tree species is 400 ($0.4x = 160$). Erwin ups this estimate to "600" to account for insects that live on the portions of the trees closer to the ground. Finally the estimate of 600 insect species per tree species is multiplied by the 50 000 recognized species of tropical trees, giving an estimate of 30 million tropical arthropods. Using a conservative estimate of tropical arthropods comprising 60 percent of all insect species gives an estimate for the number of insect species as 50 million. The total number of species, then, must exceed 50 million.

DISCUSSION & RESEARCH

1. Make a list of as many different kinds of organisms as you can, excluding vertebrates.
2. How, do you think, can scientists agree on criteria for classifying different species?
3. What assumptions underlie Terry Erwin's estimate of the total number of species on Earth? How would the estimate be altered if there were only 300 insect species per tropical tree species?

CHAPTER REVIEW

Summary

▸ For thousands of years, humans have tried to classify and determine relationships among living things. Aristotle developed a classification scheme that separated organisms into two groups—plants and animals.

▸ Linnaeus established a system of naming organisms called binomial nomenclature. He also established the modern levels of classification.

▸ The levels of classification are species, genus, family, order, class, phylum, and kingdom. Plants are grouped into divisions rather than phyla.

▸ Modern taxonomy tries to establish classification on the basis of phylogeny rather than physical similarity. Modern genetics and biochemistry provide evidence of phylogeny.

▸ Systems of classification have been modified over the years as more information became available. The discovery of one-celled organisms made the two-kingdom system inadequate. The three-kingdom system was abandoned after the distinction was made between prokaryotic and eukaryotic organisms.

▸ This book classifies organisms in five kingdoms. These kingdoms are animals, plants, protists, fungi, and monerans.

▸ A classification key is used as an aid to identify organisms. It uses an organism's general characteristics and special features.

Vocabulary

binomial nomenclature
class
classify
division
family
genus
kingdom
order

phylogeny
phylum
polynomial
protist
species
specific epithet
taxonomist

Concept Mapping

Construct a concept map outlining the evolution of classification. Include the following terms: classify, five-kingdom system, taxonomists, three-kingdom system, and two-kingdom system. Use additional terms as you need them.

Review

1. How did Aristotle classify living things?
2. Why is binomial nomenclature preferable to the use of polynomials?
3. *Homo* is to genus as *sapiens* is to
   _____.
4. Why is it that scientists do not use regional or common names for species?
5. What are taxonomists?
6. What are the five kingdoms recognized in this book?
7. Describe one technique used by taxonomists to classify organisms.

For questions 8–12, determine whether the following descriptions refer to Linnaeus's classification system or to the modern classification system.

8. The evolutionary relationships of organisms are considered in classifying them.
9. The presence or absence of a nucleus is considered in the classification of organisms.
10. Two kingdoms are recognized.
11. This was the first system to use binomial nomenclature.
12. This system has a separate kingdom for fungi.
13. How are yellow birch and white birch related?
14. What is a classification key used for?
15. State one problem with the five-kingdom system currently in use.

	HUMAN	DAFFODIL	FROG	DOG	WOLF
Kingdom	Animalia	Plantae	Animalia	Animalia	Animalia
Phylum	Chordata	Anthophyta	Chordata	Chordata	Chordata
Class	Mammalia	Monocotyledonae	Amphibia	Mammalia	Mammalia
Order	Primates	Liliales	Salientia	Carnivora	Carnivora
Family	Hominidae	Amarylidaceae	Ranidae	Canidae	Canidae
Genus	Homo	Narcissus	Rana	Canis	Canis
Specific epithet	sapiens	pseudonarcissus	pipiens	familiaris	lupus

Interpret and Apply

16. *Panthera leo* (lion), *Canis latrans* (coyote), *Panthera tigris* (tiger), and *Procyon lotor* (raccoon) are all members of the order Carnivora. Which two are the most closely related? Explain.
17. If two animals are in the same class, what other categories must they have in common?
18. Why do many libraries have card catalogs?

Use the table above to answer questions 19–22.

19. What organism is *Rana pipiens*?
20. The dog is least closely related to what other organism?
21. The dog is most closely related to what other organism?
22. Write the Latin name of the wolf.
23. To which of the five kingdoms does each of the following belong?
    a. rose
    b. *Euglena*
    c. bald eagle
    d. bacterium
    e. mushroom
    f. fern
24. Two species have similar amino-acid sequences in many proteins. What does this tell you about the two species?

Critical Thinking

25. Arrange the following items in classification levels from general to specific.

    cake pans   muffin tin
    9-inch pie plate   baking equipment
    kitchen equipment   angelfood cake pan
    Bundt cake pan   pie plates
    sheet cake pan   10-inch pie plate

26. Why is the classification of all the living things on Earth (a) a job that could never be done by one person alone and (b) a job that will never be finished?
27. You examine two different organisms carefully. What evidence might you find to indicate that the organisms are closely related?
28. Suppose you were a microbiologist who had just discovered a new organism. The organism was unicellular, lacked chloroplasts, and had no cell wall. Which of the five kingdoms would you place the organism in? Explain why you eliminated each of the other four kingdoms.
29. In the construction of a classification key, words like large and small are not helpful. Why not?

ISSUES in Bioethics

GENETICIST REFUSES SCREENING

Case Study 1

Nancy Wexler is a doctor who specializes in genetic studies. She has been studying Huntington's disease for many years. She traveled to Venezuela to study the people in a town where the disease is widespread. Most of the adults over forty already have Huntington's. Dr. Wexler estimates that at least half of the remaining people have the dominant Huntington's gene (H) that will cause them to show the symptoms later in life.

Nancy has a special reason for being interested in Huntington's disease. Her mother died of Huntington's after many years in a wheelchair. Nancy's mother lost her memory and intelligence and had to be fed and cleaned by her father. Since the gene for Huntington's is dominant, there is a 50/50 chance that Nancy carries the fatal gene and could pass it on if she has children.

Nancy's research helped find a test for the Huntington's gene. It is now possible to test for the gene BEFORE any symptoms appear, but she is not sure whether she should take the test. She has tested many young people in Venezuela, but has not told them the results. The reason for her silence is that there is no cure or treatment for Huntington's. Knowing the results of the test will not stop the course of the disease.

1. Nancy also has a sister. Draw the pedigree for Nancy and her sister. Include her mother, father, and sister. Indicate which members of the family have the disease.
2. If you were Nancy or her sister, would you take the test? Why or why not?
3. Give three reasons to support your decision.
4. Give two reasons why someone might disagree.

Case Study 2

Gene therapy is used to replace "bad" genes with "good" genes. Gene therapy experiments are usually carried out with laboratory animals. Lesch-Nyhan syndrome is one candidate for gene therapy in humans. An enzyme, HPRT, is missing which causes a buildup of uric acid in the brain which results in the blocking of some biochemical reactions. This disorder can cause mental retardation, cerebral palsy, and an uncontrollable urge to mutilate one's own body.

Mike and June Smith's son, Mickey, was born with Lesch-Nyhan syndrome. Mickey is twelve and is confined to a wheelchair. He needs constant attention so he will not hurt himself. He understands what others say but he cannot speak very well. His care has been difficult for the Smiths, both emotionally and financially.

The Smith's have heard of a doctor who has had some success with gene therapy in animals. He injects a virus carrying the healthy gene into bone marrow and it spreads, via the blood, to other areas of the body. The body then starts making the missing enzyme.

Knowing that Mickey hasn't much longer to live and that the life he lives is so painful, his parents call the doctor and ask for a consultation.

1. If Mickey were your son, would you allow the doctor to test this new treatment on him?
2. What could happen to the doctor, Mickey, and the Smiths if they try this treatment?
3. Should Mickey be consulted about this possible treatment? Why or why not?
4. List two reasons supporting treatment for Mickey and two reasons against it.

UNIT REVIEW 2

Synthesis

1. The opening pages of this unit contain four photographs that were selected to illustrate a particular theme developed within the chapters of this unit. Describe the theme conveyed by these photos.

2. **Adaptation and Evolution:** What do genetic and chromosomal mutations have in common with the process of hybridization? How are all of these processes important to evolution?

3. **Structure Is Related to Function:** Most species reproduce sexually at some time during their life cycle. What are some of the advantages of sexual reproduction? Of asexual reproduction?

4. **Adaptation and Evolution:** A particular strain of roses has been inbred to produce large, yellow blooms. These plants remain healthy only if fertilized properly, watered often, and protected chemically from insects and fungi. Wild roses, with their smaller, red blossoms, are able to thrive without any of these artificial aids. Explain.

5. **Unity and Diversity:** How have modern medicine and science allowed harmful genes to accumulate and remain in the human gene pool?

6. **Process of Science:** Although modern taxonomists attempt to classify organisms on the basis of their evolutionary relationships, in practice organisms are more often classified on the basis of their structure. Why do you think this is true?

7. **Process of Science:** When Charles Darwin developed the theory of evolution, Mendel's principles of inheritance were unknown. How do the findings of modern genetics support the theory of evolution?

8. **Continuity of Life:** In a certain village, the population consists only of people descended from a small group that settled there several hundred years ago. No new people have moved into the village since then. What characteristics would you expect to find in the population?

9. **Adaptation and Evolution:** It has been said that natural selection does not act on genes but on phenotypes. Give an example that supports this statement.

Critical Thinking

10. **Process of Science:** Many people are born with small areas of differently colored skin called birthmarks. Some people believe that red-colored birthmarks are the result of mothers who eat too many strawberries when they are pregnant. How do you think such statements come to be believed by many people? How would you go about gathering evidence concerning the truth of such a statement?

11. **Process of Science:** Among groups of professional athletes, it is not uncommon to find members of the same family. A Lamarkian would explain this observation as the acquired characteristics of a parent are passed to their offspring. Based on your knowledge of genetics and evolution, how would you respond to this statement?

12. **Process of Science:** Evaluate the statement that human beings are no longer subject to the whims of natural selection and, therefore, will not evolve in the future. Does the conclusion follow from the first part of the statement? What evidence would you give to support your answer?

Additional Reading

Cairns-Smith, A.G. "The First Organisms." *Scientific American.* June, 1985.
Gould, Stephen Jay. *The Flamingo's Smile.* New York: Norton and Company, 1985.

MICROBIOLOGY

Fly agaric mushrooms, *Amanita muscaria*

Filaments of the cyanobacteria *Oscillatoria*

Didinium ingesting a paramecium

British soldier lichen

Chapter 18 Monerans and Viruses
  Kingdom Monera
  Viruses
Chapter 19 Protists
  Animallike Protists
  Plantlike Protists
  Funguslike Protists
Chapter 20 Fungi
  Characteristics of Fungi
  Variety of Fungi

MONERANS AND VIRUSES

Overview

KINGDOM MONERA

18-1   Moneran Cells
18-2   Classification of
       Monerans
18-3   Nutrition
18-4   Reproduction in
       Monerans
18-5   Exchange of Genetic
       Material
18-6   Importance of
       Bacteria

VIRUSES

18-7   Structure of Viruses
18-8   Replication of
       Viruses
18-9   Types of Viruses
18-10 AIDS Virus
18-11 Treatment of Viral
       Diseases
18-12 Viruses and Cancer
18-13 Origin of Viruses

What causes cavities?

KINGDOM MONERA

The smallest independent living things are prokaryotic cells. These organisms belong to the Kingdom Monera. As many as 10 000 moneran cells could lie end to end across your thumbnail. Why is it important to know about organisms you cannot even see? These organisms influence you in many ways. Some monerans cause disease; others produce substances that can cure disease. Some monerans are responsible for food spoilage; others make some of the foods you eat. You will see that organisms do not have to be large to be important.

18-1 Moneran Cells

Monerans are prokaryotes. In fact, prokaryotic cell structure is the major characteristic that defines the kingdom. Recall from Chapter 5 that unlike eukaryotes, prokaryotes do not have a membrane-bound nucleus. They have a single, circular DNA molecule in the cytoplasm. Prokaryotes also lack membrane-bound organelles such as mitochondria and chloroplasts.

Almost all monerans have a cell wall. The cell wall protects the cell and gives it shape. The cytoplasm of most moneran cells is very hypertonic to the environment. Without a cell wall, most moneran cells would absorb water by osmosis and explode. Unlike the cellulose cell wall of plants, however, the cell wall of monerans consists mainly of a nitrogen-containing polysaccharide called *peptidoglycan* [pep tid ō glī' kan]. Peptidoglycan is found only in monerans.

Some monerans have a layer outside the cell wall. This layer, called the *capsule*, is a sticky material that helps the cell cling to surfaces. Disease-causing cells often have a capsule, which may protect them from the host's immune system.

Monerans are extremely small. A typical bacterium, for example is about 2μm long. (The Greek letter μ, *mu*, is used to represent the prefix *micro-*, which means "one millionth." A micrometer is one millionth of a meter.) Yet each bacterium is a complete organism. Packaged into each cell are all the nucleic acids, enzymes, and other substances necessary to carry out the cell's life processes.

Many monerans have long, thin structures called **flagella** [flə-jel' lə] that allow them to move around. The flagella act like tiny propellers. They rotate and move the cell in response to chemical stimuli. Can you explain why flagella are useful structures? Some cells also have many short, hairlike protein strands called *pili*. Pili enable a cell to stick to a surface and obtain food.

Under harsh conditions, many bacteria form a protective structure called an endospore. An **endospore** consists of a thick

Section Objectives

A **List** the major differences between prokaryotic and eukaryotic cells.

B **Describe** how monerans are classified.

C **Explain** how monerans obtain nutrition.

D **Identify** the ways monerans obtain energy.

E **Describe** bacterial reproduction and **explain** two ways bacteria can exchange genetic information.

F **Discuss** the importance of monerans.

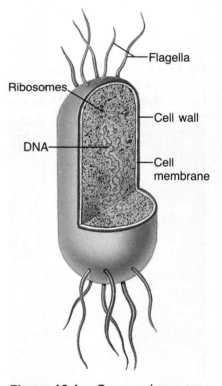

Figure 18-1 Compared to a typical eukaryotic cell, a typical prokaryotic cell has a much simpler structure.

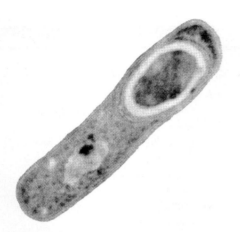

Figure 18-2 The large, round structure in the cytoplasm of this bacterial cell is an endospore in the process of forming.

Figure 18-3 Shape and grouping pattern are important characteristics for classifying bacteria.

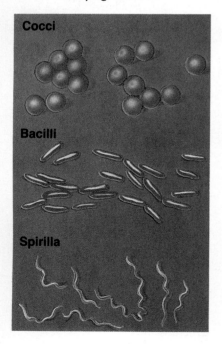

Cocci

Bacilli

Spirilla

wall surrounding the nuclear material and a small amount of cytoplasm. Endospores can withstand boiling water, drying out, or other extreme conditions. When the environment becomes favorable, cells emerge from the endospores and begin normal growth.

Many disease-causing bacteria can form endospores. Therefore, methods to kill spores are important in food preservation and in medicine. Endospores are usually killed by exposing them to pressurized steam at 121°C for ten to fifteen minutes—a procedure called *sterilization*.

18-2 Classification of Monerans

The classification of monerans is based on features such as cell shape, chemistry of the cell wall, and similarities in metabolism. Figure 18-3 shows some cell shapes that are useful in classifying these organisms. Spherical cells are called **cocci** [kok′ sī]. Rod-shaped cells are called **bacilli** [bə sil′ ī]. Spiral-shaped cells are called **spirilli** [spə ril′ ē]. In some species, cells stick together in small groups and this can be an identifying feature.

Another characteristic used for identification is the **Gram stain**. This method, developed in 1884 by the Danish doctor Hans Christian Gram, separates bacteria into two groups depending on whether or not they absorb a particular stain. *Gram-positive* bacteria absorb the stain and *gram-negative* bacteria do not. Absorbing the stain or not depends on the chemical structure and physical properties of the cell wall.

There are over 16 000 species of monerans. At present, there is still debate about the relationships among them. Recent work comparing the sequences of nucleic acids and important proteins is beginning to clarify some of the relationships. Table 18-1 shows some major groups of monerans.

18-3 Nutrition

Though they differ structurally, many prokaryotes share similar metabolic processes with eukaryotes. On the other hand, metabolism in some prokaryotes is more varied and has no counterpart among eukaryotes.

Autotrophs In Chapter 6, you learned that plants use the sun's energy to make food from carbon dioxide and water. Several groups of autotrophic monerans also carry out photosynthesis. **Cyanobacteria** [sī an ō bak tir′ ē ə], or blue-green bacteria, are one such group. The individual chemical steps of photosynthesis in cyanobacteria are essentially the same as eukaryotic cells. However, the chlorophyll in cyanobacteria is found on folded membranes in the cytoplasm rather than in chloroplasts.

CLASSIFICATION OF MONERANS			
Major Group	Nutrition	Energy	Role
Eubacteria Cyanobacteria	Photosynthetic	Aerobic	Carbon and nitrogen fixation
Gram-positive bacteria (actino-myetes, clostridia, mycoplasmas)	Heterotrophic	Aerobic and anaerobic species	Pathogens; normal residents of mouth, skin, and digestive tract; antibiotic producers; major soil bacteria
Spirochaetes	Heterotrophic	Anaerobic and a few aerobic species	Free-living in marine and fresh water; intestinal species; pathogens
Rickettsias	Heterotrophic	Anaerobic	Pathogens
Purple bacteria and relatives	Photosynthetic and heterotrophic species	Aerobic and anaerobic species	Free-living species; nitrogen fixers; intestinal bacteria; some pathogens
Green sulfur bacteria	Photosynthetic	Anaerobic	Carbon and nitrogen fixation
Myxobacteria	Heterotrophic	Aerobic	Decomposers
Chemoautotrophs	Chemosynthetic	Aerobic and anaerobic species	Cycle nitrogen, carbon, and sulfur
Archaeobacteria Methanogens	Heterotrophic	Anaerobic	Make methane from carbon dioxide; live in mud
Extreme halophiles	Heterotrophic	Aerobic	Live in very salty water
Thermoaci-dophiles	Heterotrophic	Anaerobic	Live in hot, acidic springs

Table 18-1

Cyanobacteria have additional photosynthetic pigments called *phycobilins*. Some of these pigments give cells the blue-green color for which they are named. Phycobilins allow cyanobacteria to use light of different wavelengths for photosynthesis.

In other groups of autotrophs, such as purple bacteria, the chlorophyll differs chemically from plant chlorophyll. Bacterial chlorophyll absorbs light of longer wavelengths. These bacteria, can carry on photosynthesis when there is very little light.

Purple and green sulfur bacteria have hydrogen sulfide rather than water as a source of electrons. The reaction gives off sulfur instead of oxygen, as shown in the overall equation below.

$$12H_2S + 6CO_2 \longrightarrow C_6H_{12}O_6 + 12S + 6H_2O$$

There are some autotrophic bacteria that are chemosynthetic. Like photosynthetic bacteria, **chemosynthetic bacteria** make their own food from carbon dioxide. However, they do not use light as a source of energy. Instead, they get energy from chemical reactions involving inorganic molecules.

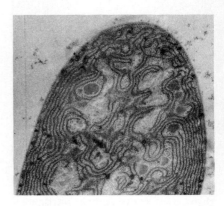

Figure 18-4 Cyanobacteria have internal folded membranes where chlorophyll is located and photosynthesis occurs.

Figure 18-5 In Yellowstone National Park, hot springs show bright coloring due to different species of monerans that survive in the hot, acidic water.

Figure 18-6 The swollen parts of these plant roots contain nitrogen-fixing bacteria. Plants like alfalfa with nitrogen fixers in their roots can grow in soil that most other plants could not tolerate.

Heterotrophs Many monerans are heterotrophs. They usually feed by secreting enzymes into their environment. These enzymes break down large food molecules. The resulting smaller molecules are absorbed through the cell membrane.

Many heterotrophic bacteria live in soil or water. These species are usually **saprobes** [sap′ rōbz], or organisms that feed on dead plants and animals. Saprobes convert this organic matter into simple chemicals which can then be taken in and used by other organisms. Because they break down decaying material, saprobes are also called *decomposers*. Can you imagine the environment without decomposers?

Other bacteria live on or in the bodies of living organisms and depend on their host for food. These bacteria often have little effect on their host. In some cases, they may even be beneficial. For example, bacteria live in the digestive tract of many large grazing animals. Without these bacteria, sheep and cows would not be able to digest cellulose in grass. The bacteria have a warm, moist environment and absorb food from the animal's digestive tract. Thus both organisms benefit from the association.

Sometimes bacteria harm their host. Organisms that harm their host are called **parasites**. Bacteria that cause diseases in humans are examples of parasites. These organisms are also called *pathogens*. You will learn more about pathogens in Chapter 41.

Nitrogen Fixers Living things require nitrogen to synthesize proteins and nucleic acids. Air is about 80 percent nitrogen gas, but most organisms cannot use the element in this form. Cyanobacteria and some other bacteria, however, can capture nitrogen from the air by a process called **nitrogen fixation**. Nitrogen fixers have enzymes that convert nitrogen gas into ammonia or other forms of nitrogen that plants can use.

Plants like clover, beans, and alfalfa have large numbers of nitrogen-fixing bacteria growing in swollen areas on their roots. The bacteria receive food from the plant, while the plant gets usable nitrogen from the bacteria. This association allows the plant to grow in nitrogen-poor soils. From year to year, farmers alternate nitrogen-fixing crops like soybeans with nitrogen-using ones like cotton. Why is this crop rotation a useful procedure?

You have read that bacteria have a number of ways of obtaining nutrients. How do bacteria extract energy from the nutrients they take in? You learned in Chapter 6 that cells obtain energy for metabolism by either respiration or fermentation. Bacteria that must have oxygen to carry out respiration are called **obligate aerobes** [ob′ li gət ar′ ōbz]. The chemistry of aerobic respiration in bacteria is similar to that in eukaryotes. Remember, though, that prokaryotes do not have mitochondria. The electron transport chain occurs on carrier molecules built into the cell membrane.

Some bacteria can live with or without oxygen. They are called **facultative** [fac′ əl tāt iv] **anaerobes** and generally obtain energy from fermentation. Other bacteria are actually poisoned by oxygen. These organisms are called **obligate anaerobes** and they are found in places where aerobic organisms cannot survive.

18-4 Reproduction in Monerans

Monerans do not divide by mitosis. Yet monerans do copy their genetic material and pass on copies to new generations. Moneran division is called **binary fission**. Unlike eukaryotic mitosis, binary fission does not involve condensing chromosomes and formation of spindle fibers. Moneran have a single, circular DNA molecule as illustrated in Figure 18-8. During binary fission, the DNA molecule attaches to the cell membrane and copies itself. Between the points where the DNA molecules are attached, the cell membrane begins to grow. The membrane then pulls the two DNA molecules apart. When the cell is about twice its original length, the cell membrane indents. The cytoplasm is divided into roughly equal parts. Each part has one DNA molecule. Cell walls then grow and completely divide the two cells.

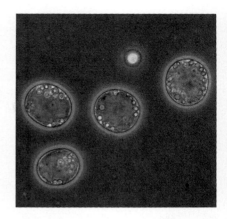

Figure 18-7 Species of *Thiobacillus* carry out anaerobic respiration using different forms of sulfur. These organisms are responsible for the sulfur deposits that form in sulfur hot springs. (160×)

18-5 Exchange of Genetic Material

Monerans do not reproduce sexually. There are several ways in which the genetic material of monerans can be recombined. Two of these methods are conjugation and transformation.

Figure 18-8 Monerans reproduce by binary fission.

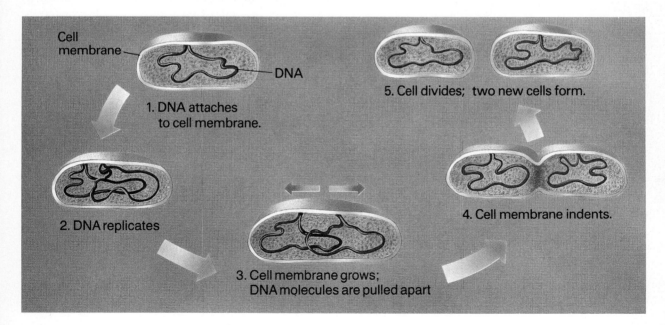

Cell membrane

DNA

1. DNA attaches to cell membrane.

2. DNA replicates

3. Cell membrane grows; DNA molecules are pulled apart

4. Cell membrane indents.

5. Cell divides; two new cells form.

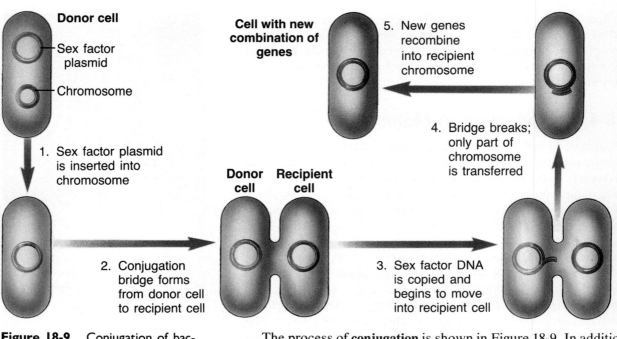

Donor cell
Sex factor plasmid
Chromosome

1. Sex factor plasmid is inserted into chromosome

2. Conjugation bridge forms from donor cell to recipient cell

Donor cell **Recipient cell**

3. Sex factor DNA is copied and begins to move into recipient cell

4. Bridge breaks; only part of chromosome is transferred

5. New genes recombine into recipient chromosome

Cell with new combination of genes

Figure 18-9 Conjugation of bacterial cells produces genetic variation by creating new combinations of genes.

The process of **conjugation** is shown in Figure 18-9. In addition to their large, single DNA molecule, some bacteria contain additional genetic information in the form of small circular molecules of DNA. These small molecules are called **plasmids**. In normal bacterial populations, plasmids carry genes not found on the primary DNA molecule. One of these genes is called a *sex factor*. Bacteria that carry the sex factor can conjugate with cells that do not carry the factor.

In conjugation, a bridge of cytoplasm forms between two cells. The cell that carries the sex factor makes a copy of its primary DNA molecule. The DNA copy then moves across the bridge into the second cell. Often the bridge breaks before the entire molecule is transferred, so the recipient cell gets only part of the donor cell's genes. The recipient cell then replaces some of its genes with the new genes from the donor cell. The genes removed from the recipient's DNA are destroyed by enzymes. Thus conjugation produces cells with new combinations of genes. However, the number of genes stays the same. Can you explain how this process resembles sexual reproduction in eukaryotes?

Another process by which bacteria can obtain new genes, called transformation, has been observed in laboratory experiments. In **transformation**, a bacterium takes in DNA released by another, broken cell.

Transformation of *Escherichia* [esh ə rik' ē ə] *coli* (*E. coli*) cells is shown in Figure 18-10. Most *E. coli* cells can make all the amino acids they need from simple chemicals they take in. However, some mutant *E. coli* cells lack the ability to make

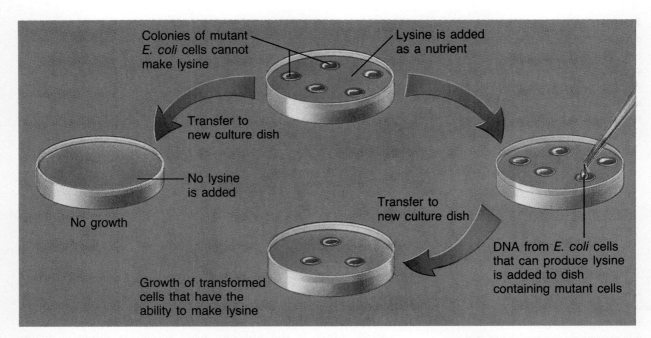

Colonies of mutant
E. coli cells cannot
make lysine

Lysine is added
as a nutrient

Transfer to
new culture dish

No lysine
is added

No growth

Transfer to
new culture dish

DNA from E. coli cells
that can produce lysine
is added to dish
containing mutant cells

Growth of transformed
cells that have the
ability to make lysine

certain amino acids. One mutant form of *E. coli* cannot make the amino acid lysine. These cells will not grow unless they are supplied with lysine. If DNA from *E. coli* that can make lysine is added to a culture of cells that cannot make it, then some of the cells will be transformed. These cells take the gene for lysine production into their DNA. Transformed cells can then grow in a culture without added lysine.

The processes of conjugation and transformation are used frequently in the study of bacterial genetics. Recombinant DNA techniques described in Chapter 12 use both of these processes to move genes from one organism into another.

18-6 Importance of Bacteria

Many human diseases are caused by bacteria. Food poisoning, strep throat, and wound infections are just a few examples. Farm animals and plants are also susceptible to bacterial diseases. Still other bacteria are responsible for spoiling large amounts of food. Billions of dollars are spent every year to preserve food. Canning, heating, salting, refrigerating, and adding chemicals are just some of the methods used to slow or stop the growth of bacteria on foods.

However, only a small percentage of bacterial species are actually harmful. A far greater number are both beneficial and necessary. Probably the most important role of bacteria is as decomposers. As you learned, saprobes break down the bodies of dead plants and animals. Without decomposers, important

Figure 18-10 Transformation is another way to move genes from one bacterial cell to another. Shown here is an experiment that transfers a gene for the ability to make the amino acid lysine.

CONSUMER BIOLOGY

The canning process preserves food by heating to kill all microorganisms and then sealing the food to cut off the supply of oxygen. If a can is damaged or dented, oxygen can reach the food providing an environment in which microorganisms can grow.

Figure 18-11 *Left:* Humans depend on bacteria in the large intestine for the production of certain vitamins. *Right:* Bacteria are grown in the laboratory on agar that is mixed with the nutrients needed for bacterial growth and reproduction.

nutrients would be unavailable to new generations of living things. Another important and related role of bacteria is nitrogen fixation. Most of the nitrogen used by living things is made available by nitrogen-fixing bacteria and cyanobacteria.

Bacteria contribute a great deal to human health and well-being. In the human intestine, bacteria produce vitamins needed by their host. Vinegar, yogurt, cheese, and other foods are made using bacteria. Some bacteria produce antibiotics. Other drugs have been produced using genetically engineered bacteria. The fuel methane is a waste product of some anaerobes. Certain bacteria species have been used as natural pesticides because they infect crop-destroying insects.

CHECKPOINT ◆

1. Name two structures found in prokaryotic cells that do not occur in eukaryotic cells.
2. What are two characteristics used to classify monerans?
3. How do cyanobacteria get food?
4. What is the difference between a saprobe and a parasite?
5. Describe one process by which monerans obtain energy from their food. What are these kinds of organisms called?
6. Identify two ways in which bacteria are useful to humans.
▶ 7. How do chemosynthetic autotrophs differ from photosynthetic autotrophs?
▶ 8. How does photosynthesis in a purple bacterium differ from photosynthesis in an oak tree?
▶ 9. In what ways are conjugation and transformation similar and in what ways are they different?

▶ Denotes a question that involves *interpreting* and *applying* concepts.

VIRUSES

When you have a cold, you know that the only "cure" is to rest while your body fights the infection. Unlike strep throat or other bacterial diseases, a cold cannot be treated with antibiotics. Antibiotics are effective only against living cells. A cold is not caused by a living cell; it is caused by a virus. A **virus** is a tiny particle made of nucleic acid and protein. The characteristics of viruses are such that they fall somewhere between true cells and nonliving things.

18-7 Structure of Viruses

Viruses were discovered in 1892 by a Russian biologist, Dmitri Ivanowski. The term *virus* was coined by a Dutch botanist, Martinus Willem Beijerinck, six years later. Ivanowski and Beijerinck each studied a disease of tobacco plants called mosaic disease, which caused brown spots on the leaves. They found that juice from the leaves of an infected plant would transmit the disease to a healthy plant. They assumed a bacteria caused the disease. However, attempts to prevent the disease by filtering juice from the leaves of an infected plant were unsuccessful. Even though the filter had pores small enough to trap any bacteria, the clear, filtered fluid would still cause the disease if rubbed on healthy tobacco plants.

The cause of mosaic disease, a virus, was too small to be seen with a light microscope. Only with the invention of the electron microscope were viruses finally observed directly. A large virus has about one tenth the volume of a small bacterium. The nucleic acid of a virus may be a molecule of single- or double-stranded DNA. Other viruses may have single- or double-stranded RNA as the nucleic acid. The amount of genetic information in any virus is small. Many viruses have fewer than 10 genes; large viruses may have as many as 100 genes. By comparison, an *E. coli* bacterium has about 2000 genes.

Section Objectives

G *Describe* the structure of a typical virus.

H *Explain* how a lytic virus replicates.

I *Distinguish* between a lytic cycle and a lysogenic cycle.

J *Compare* RNA viruses with DNA viruses.

K *Explain* how viruses can cause cancer.

L *Discuss* three explanations for the origin of viruses.

Figure 18-12 *Left:* A virus is very small in relation to other cells. *Right:* The tobacco mosaic virus is rod shaped and contains RNA as its genetic material. The protein coat is made up of repeating units.

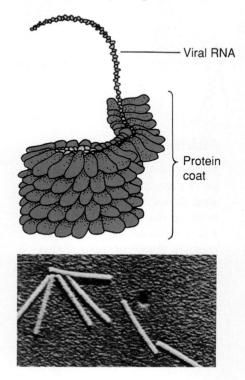

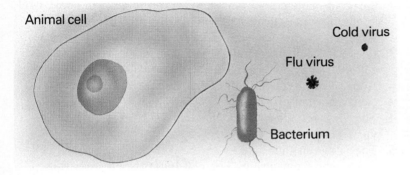

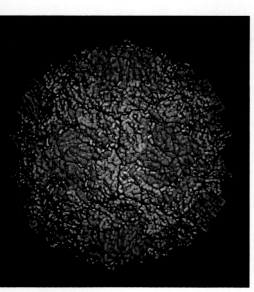

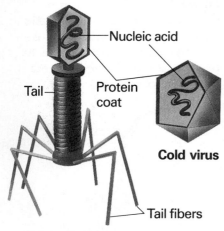

Nucleic acid

Tail

Protein coat

Cold virus

Tail fibers

Bacteria virus

Figure 18-13 *Top:* This computer generated model of a poliovirus shows the protein units that make up the virus shell. The three colors represent three different proteins. *Bottom:* A bacteriophage is an unusually complex virus. The cold virus looks simple by comparison.

The viral nucleic acid is surrounded by a protein coat called the **capsid**. The capsid is usually made of several hundred protein molecules packed together in a geometric pattern. Some larger viruses, such as the human influenza (flu) virus, have a complex envelope surrounding the capsid. The envelope has protein spikes that help the virus recognize and attach to a host cell.

Viral genes carry instructions for the production of new virus particles. However, the virus has no ribosomes or other cytoplasmic structures to carry out its genetic instructions. Viruses use the energy and protein-producing mechanisms of a host cell to make new virus particles. Viruses cannot live independently; they are all parasites of living cells.

Each type of virus infects a particular kind of cell in a host organism. The tobacco mosaic virus, for example, infects tobacco leaf cells. Cold viruses infect cells lining the human respiratory tract.

A virus that infects bacteria is called a **bacteriophage** [bak-tir′ ē ə fāj], or *phage* for short. The phage that infects *E. coli*, for example, has an unusual structure. It has a tail attached to its protein coat. At the base of the tail are long fibers that look like spider legs.

18-8 Replication of Viruses

Because viruses are not cells, the term **replication** is used instead of *reproduction* to describe the production of new virus particles. The replication cycle of the *E. coli* phage shown in Figure 18-14 is typical of many viruses. Refer to the figure as you read.

1. Initially, the phage attaches itself to the cell surface. Attachment occurs because proteins on the tail fibers of the virus have a shape that fits together with molecules on the host-cell surface. This molecular matching process explains why most viruses recognize and infect only one kind of host cell.
2. The phage tail releases an enzyme that breaks down the cell surface. The outer portion of the tail contracts, and the viral nucleic acid is injected into the cell. In some viral infections, the capsid is left outside. In others, the whole virus enters the cell, and then the capsid is destroyed.
3. Inside the cell, the viral nucleic acid takes over. The host cell's DNA is made inactive. Normal cellular metabolism stops. The host cell is directed to make copies of viral nucleic acid and proteins.
4. The viral protein and nucleic acids assemble into new viruses.
5. The host cell then makes an enzyme that digests the cell membrane from inside. The cell bursts open, releasing

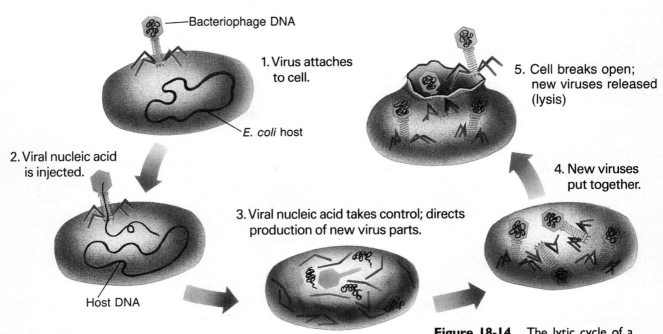

1. Virus attaches to cell.

—Bacteriophage DNA

E. coli host

2. Viral nucleic acid is injected.

Host DNA

3. Viral nucleic acid takes control; directs production of new virus parts.

4. New viruses put together.

5. Cell breaks open; new viruses released (lysis)

Figure 18-14 The lytic cycle of a bacteriophage is typical of many viruses.

hundreds of new viruses. This last step is called **lysis** [lī′ səs]. After lysis, the new viruses can go on to infect other cells. A replication cycle like that of the *E. coli* phage is called a **lytic** [lit′ ik] **cycle**.

Not all viruses cause rapid cell destruction. Some viruses enter a host cell but do not take over the cell's metabolism. Instead, the viral DNA combines with and becomes part of the host-cell's DNA. As part of the host's DNA, the viral DNA does not direct the production of new viruses. When the host cell copies its DNA, the viral genes are also duplicated. The viral DNA may be copied through many generations of the cell without harming the host. Introduction of viral DNA into the host cell's DNA in this way is called **lysogeny** [lī säj′ ə nē]. After several generations, the viral DNA in a lysogenic cell may become active. The viral DNA then directs the formation of new viruses which burst out of the cell as in the lytic cycle.

When lysogenic DNA becomes active, it breaks free of the host DNA. In doing so, the viral DNA may take several host genes with it. In the next infection cycle, the virus can carry genes from the previous host cell to the new host. The process of carrying genes from one cell to another by a lysogenic phage is called **transduction**. In addition to conjugation and transformation, transduction is a way that bacteria can increase their genetic variety. Scientists use lysogenic viruses in recombinant DNA research to transfer a desired gene from one organism into another.

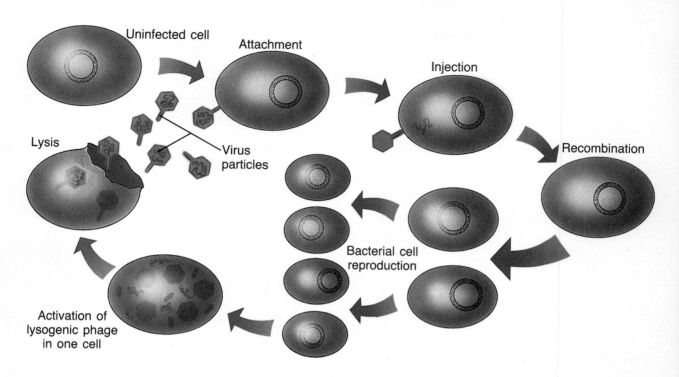

Uninfected cell

Attachment

Injection

Recombination

Lysis

Virus particles

Bacterial cell reproduction

Activation of lysogenic phage in one cell

Figure 18-15 Compare the lysogenic cycle of this virus with the lytic cycle shown in Figure 18-14.

18-9 Types of Viruses

Flu Viruses Viruses show remarkable diversity. The lytic and lysogenic cycles do not adequately describe replication for all viruses. For example, the human flu virus does not lyse its host cell, but exits by pushing out through the cell membrane. As a result, the outer envelope of the virus is made of host cell membrane. Embedded in that membrane are viral proteins that allow the virus to attach to another host cell and continue replicating.

Since flu viruses do not actually lyse the cell, the cell does not die. However, infected cells are disrupted, and you feel ill. Flu symptoms result from damage to infected cells and from your body's own response to fighting the infection. Other animal viruses, such as those causing mumps, measles, and rabies have a replication cycle similar to the flu virus.

The RNA viruses do not precisely follow the standard lytic or lysogenic cycles. Many of these viruses bring with them an enzyme that can use the viral RNA as a model from which to make messenger RNA molecules. (The host cell only has enzymes that make messenger RNA from DNA.) Once the viral messenger RNA is made, then the host cell can make viral proteins. All RNA viruses of this type are lytic viruses, since there is no way for viral RNA to become part of the host's DNA.

Retroviruses Another class of RNA viruses, called lysogenic retroviruses has received special attention in recent years. **Retro-**

Table 18-2

SOME TYPES OF VIRUSES		
Virus Type	**Nucleic Acid**	**Diseases**
Herpesviruses	DNA	One type causes cold sores. Another causes genital herpes infection.
Myxoviruses	RNA	Human influenza (flu). Influenza in other animals.
Papovaviruses	DNA	Warts in humans; cancer in other animals.
Paramyxoviruses	RNA	Human mumps; distemper in dogs.
Picornaviruses	RNA	In humans—polio and the common cold.
Poxviruses	DNA	Smallpox, cowpox in humans.
Retroviruses	RNA	Chicken tumors, mouse mammary tumors, cat leukemia, human leukemia, AIDS.
Rhabdoviruses	RNA	Rabies in mammals.
Togaviruses	RNA	Human rubella (measles), yellow fever, dengue fever. Horse encephalitis.

viruses carry a special enzyme called *reverse transcriptase*. When a retrovirus inserts its RNA into a host cell, reverse transcriptase makes a copy of DNA from the viral RNA. This process is the reverse of what normally happens in cells; DNA usually is the model for RNA. Viral DNA can then incorporate itself into the host's DNA and become lysogenic.

Retroviruses have been the subject of much attention because several have been identified as causing cancer in animals. A blood cancer in cats (feline leukemia), for example, is known to be transmitted by a retrovirus. In the early 1980's another retrovirus was identified as the cause of a rare type of human leukemia.

18-10 AIDS Virus

In the past decade another human disease has gained the attention of doctors and of the public—*acquired immune deficiency syndrome*, or AIDS. Patients with AIDS lose the ability to fight off pathogens. Patients die from unusual bacterial infections, normally harmless viruses, or sometimes a rare form of cancer. The cause of AIDS is now thought to be a retrovirus—one very similar to the human leukemia virus.

Retroviruses in general are difficult to deal with because they are lysogenic. When their genetic information is incorporated in the DNA of the host cell, the infected individual shows no symptoms at all. With AIDS, for example, some patients do not show disease symptoms for as long as seven or eight years after their original exposure to the virus. It is still not known what triggers the virus to leave its lysogenic phase, replicate, and begin the disease process.

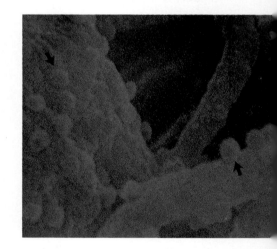

Figure 18-16 Retroviruses leave the host cell by budding. Notice that the host cell membrane forms part of the outer envelope of the virus after the virus breaks off.

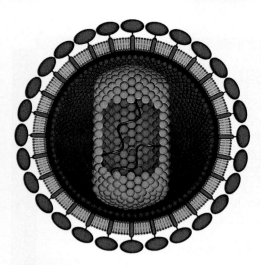

Figure 18-17 This artistic representation of the AIDS virus shows the outer proteins in green. RNA is depicted, in red, in the center of the virus. The enzyme, *reverse transcriptase*, is shown in yellow.

The AIDS virus, often referred to as *HIV* (which stands for *human immunodeficiency virus*) attacks a particular kind of blood cell that is an important part of the immune system. When these cells are finally destroyed by the virus, the body's defenses against pathogens are severely limited. Recent work has shown that the AIDS virus also attacks other kinds of cells, including brain cells. This finding may explain why some AIDS patients suffer mental losses in the later stages of their disease.

Unlike other viruses, the AIDS virus can pass from one cell to another directly through cell membranes. The virus can continue to infect cells without passing directly into the blood of the infected person. This property makes it very difficult to find a way to attack the virus. A further frustrating property of the AIDS virus is that it mutates easily. Mutations can change the shape of the proteins on its outer envelope. These changes keep the body's natural defenses from destroying the virus.

18-11 Treatment of Viral Diseases

Table 18-2 is only a partial list of the types of viruses and the kinds that infect virtually any species of organism. An enormous amount of research is going on to find ways to prevent and treat important plant, animal, and human viral diseases.

You will see in Chapter 41 that vaccines have been developed to prevent a number of viral diseases. But vaccines only prevent the initial infection. They cannot help once a host organism is infected. In fact, almost all medical treatments for viral diseases simply assist your body's own defenses, rather than directly attack the virus itself.

It is easier to understand why viruses are difficult to treat if you consider how bacterial diseases are treated. As prokaryotic cells, bacteria have many metabolic processes not found in eukaryotes. Antibiotics are substances that interfere with chemical reactions specific to prokaryotic cells. Therefore, they have few side-effects on your own cells and are safe to take.

But viruses use the metabolic mechanisms of their host cell. If a drug were used to try to interfere with the protein or nucleic acid synthesis of a virus, the host cell would also be destroyed.

In recent years, there has been some limited success with treatments for RNA viruses. These viruses have enzymes not found in the eukaryotic host to make copies of their RNA. Chemicals that interfere with these enzymes will disrupt virus replication without harming the host cell. A drug called acyclovir has been used to treat genital herpes virus and another drug called AZT has been used with some success against the AIDS retrovirus. However, the most successful approach to treating viral diseases is to mobilize the body's own defenses.

18-12 Viruses and Cancer

Not all cancers are caused by viruses. In fact, human cancers thought to have a viral origin are relatively rare. The viruses that cause cancer, however, carry genes into the host, or direct genes already in the host cell's DNA to trigger uncontrolled cell growth. Genes that turn cells cancerous are called **oncogenes** More than 30 viral oncogenes have been isolated.

One group of viruses that can cause cancer are the DNA tumor viruses. These viruses can infect cells and direct the synthesis of viral DNA and proteins. However, they do not complete replication and assemble new viruses. The DNA from a tumor virus becomes a permanent part of the host-cell DNA. The viral DNA then directs the constant synthesis of viral proteins that cause rapid cell growth and division. No new viruses are produced, so the infected cells never die. Instead, the viral oncogenes cause continuous growth and cell division—the characteristic of cancer.

As mentioned earlier, retroviruses are also known to cause cancer. Cancer-causing retroviruses work in different ways. Some of them carry oncogenes picked up from another host. When these genes are inserted into the DNA of a new host, they cause abnormal cell growth and division. Other retroviruses have genes that alter the function of host-cell genes. Normal genes in a host are transformed into oncogenes by the retrovirus.

Cancer viruses have many unusual characteristics. Little is known about how they are transmitted or why they cause cancer in some people but not in others. The Epstein-Barr virus (a member of the herpesvirus family) is a good example. This virus is known to be common among humans. People infected as children probably get a mild disease they may not even notice. Infection as a young adult results in a disease called *mononucleosis*. While "mono" can range from mild to unpleasant, and in some cases last several months, it is rarely fatal. It is easily treated by providing bed rest.

In certain parts of Africa and New Guinea, however, children infected with the Epstein-Barr virus have a high incidence of a kind of cancer seen nowhere else in the world. There is strong evidence that the virus has caused the cancer. Why should a virus that is basically common and harmless in most of the world, cause cancer in some populations? While the answers are not certain, it seems that several factors must be present for this virus to cause cancer. The situation is similar for other cancer viruses. Just having the virus does not produce the disease. It may take a specific mutation for the expression of an oncogene to be fatal. Much more remains to be learned about how environmental factors can trigger viral cancers in some people.

CONSUMER BIOLOGY

Studies indicate that diet can play an important role in preventing cancer. An ideal diet is low in fat, cholesterol, sugar, and salt; and high in fiber and starch.

18-13 Origin of Viruses

Like living things, viruses contain nucleic acids and proteins. The presence of these molecules might indicate that viruses are living things. Recall, though, that viruses by themselves can neither make nor use food, nor can they grow or reproduce. The host cell performs these functions for the virus. Would you say, then, that a virus is a living thing?

There are three current hypotheses concerning the origin of viruses. One hypothesis is that viruses are descendants of structures that developed in the early oceans before the first cells appeared. These structures then became parasites of the first living cells. According to this hypothesis viruses were never independently living organisms. A second hypothesis states that viruses evolved from monerans similar to the parasitic rickettsias and mycoplasmas. Through natural selection, these cells lost all structures except those necessary to transfer genes from one host to another.

A third hypothesis is that viruses are genes that have escaped from the chromosomes of living cells. At present, there is little evidence to support any of these ideas, and the question, like many others in science, remains unanswered.

The question has been further complicated by the discovery of viroids. **Viroids** are short pieces of RNA with no protein coat. Little is known about them except that they have a replication cycle similar to that of viruses. Viroids are very small. The shortest nucleic acid in any known virus is about 5000 bases long. Viroids are only about 350 bases long.

CHECKPOINT ◆

10. What two chemical substances are found in all viruses?
11. What happens to the host cell of a lytic virus?
12. What is lysogeny?
13. What kind of nucleic acid is found in retroviruses?
14. How does the replication of flu viruses differ from other viruses?
15. Name two diseases caused by retroviruses.
16. What is a viroid?
▶ 17. How would a disease caused by a lysogenic virus be different from a disease caused by a lytic virus?
▶ 18. Why must RNA viruses usually bring along their own enzyme for replication of viral RNA?
▶ 19. Would a retrovirus that could not direct reverse transcription be able to infect a host cell? Explain.
▶ 20. How are oncogenes in a DNA tumor virus different from oncogenes in a retrovirus?

▶ Denotes a question that involves *interpreting* and *applying* concepts.

GROWING BACTERIA IN THE LABORATORY

Objective and Skills

☐ *Observe* the effects of soap and hot water on the survival of certain bacteria.

Materials

safety goggles
wax pencil
paper towels
disinfectant solution
2 petri dishes of sterile
   nutrient agar

Procedure and Observations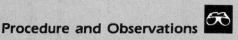

1. Read all instructions for this laboratory activity before you begin your work.
2. **Caution: Put your safety goggles on and wear them for the entire activity. Tie back long hair.**
3. Pour a small amount of disinfectant solution on the lab table in front of you. With a paper towel, wipe the disinfectant over your work area until the surface is almost dry.
4. Take two petri dishes of sterile nutrient agar. Notice that the agar is in the smaller, bottom half of the dish. *Note: Do not open the dishes*. Turn each dish upside down and use a wax pencil to write your name and date in small letters near the edge. Mark one dish *A* and the other *B*. Turn the dishes right side up.

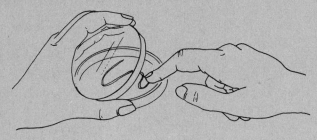

5. Quickly open dish *A* and rub your fingertip across the agar in a zigzag pattern as shown in the figure. *Note: Do this very gently or you will tear the delicate agar surface.* Replace the top of the dish.
6. Wash your hands thoroughly with soap and hot water.
7. Open dish *B* and rub a fingertip on the agar surface as you did in step 5. Close the dish.
8. Stack your dishes upside down and store them for 48 hours.
9. Clean up all your materials. Wash your hands thoroughly with soap and hot water.
10. After 48 hours, take out your dishes and observe the results. **CAUTION: Do not open any of the dishes.** None of the bacteria you are growing are likely to be harmful, yet even safe ones are treated carefully. When you are finished, the bacteria will be destroyed before they are discarded.
11. Record the number of colonies and the number of different kinds of colonies on plates *A* and *B*.
12. Return your plates to your teacher for proper disposal.

Analysis and Conclusions

1. What characteristics of the bacteria colonies growing on agar did you observe that might be used for classifying bacteria?
2. Which dish was the control and which dish was the experimental? Explain.
3. What conclusions can you make about the importance of using soap and hot water to wash your hands?

CHAPTER REVIEW

Summary

▸ Monerans are prokaryotic organisms. They are generally much smaller and simpler in cell structure than organisms in other kingdoms.

▸ The classification of monerans depends on such factors as cell shape, nutritional requirements, and cell chemistry.

▸ Monerans have many ways of obtaining and using energy. They may be photosynthetic or chemosynthetic, anaerobic or aerobic. The heterotrophic monerans can get their food from a variety of sources.

▸ Bacteria reproduce asexually, although there are numerous ways they can mix genes. Transformation, conjugation, and transduction all move genes from one bacterial cell to another.

▸ Bacteria affect humans in a variety of ways. Some cause disease or spoil foods. Many bacteria, however, have important roles. Some bacteria maintain soil fertility by decomposing dead organisms. Some foods are made with the help of bacteria. Certain species fix nitrogen. Other bacteria produce antibiotics, which can be used to control disease-causing species.

▸ Viruses are made of a nucleic acid core surrounded by a protein capsid. Some viruses have a membrane envelope surrounding the capsid. All viruses reproduce inside of living cells and use the cells' machinery to make new viral particles.

▸ Numerous types of viruses exist. There are DNA viruses and RNA viruses. Retroviruses are RNA viruses that incorporate their genetic information into the DNA of the host. AIDS is caused by a retrovirus.

▸ Some viruses cause cancer. DNA tumor viruses transform cells as a result of incomplete replication. Retroviruses transform cells by altering the function of host-cell genes or by carrying oncogenes from one host to another.

▸ The evolutionary origin of viruses is unknown. Therefore, it is difficult to classify viruses as living or nonliving things.

Vocabulary

bacilli	nitrogen fixation
bacteriophage	obligate aerobe
binary fission	obligate anaerobe
capsid	oncogene
chemosynthetic bacteria	parasite
cocci	plasmid
conjugation	replication
cyanobacteria	retrovirus
endospore	saprobe
facultative anaerobe	spirilli
flagella	transduction
Gram stain	transformation
lysis	viroid
lysogeny	virus
lytic cycle	

Concept Mapping

Construct a concept map describing monerans. Include the following terms in your map: bacilli, binary fission, chemosynthetic, cocci, conjugation, flagella, Gram stain, nitrogen fixation, plasmids, spirilli, and transformation. Add additional terms as you need them.

Review

1. Which of the following are found only in prokaryotes, only in eukaryotes, and which may be found in both: plasmids, cell membrane, chloroplasts, chlorophyll, DNA, ribosomes, nuclear membrane?
2. Name two groups of monerans that include disease-causing species.
3. Which moneran group carries out photosynthesis similarly to the way photosynthesis is carried out in eukaryotes?

4. How is an obligate anaerobe different from a facultative anaerobe?
5. What is the function of saprobes in the environment?
6. How does conjugation of bacteria differ from transformation?
7. What role do bacteria serve in the digestive system of a plant-eating animal?
8. What is a capsid?
9. What happens to the DNA of a lytic virus when it is injected into its host cell?
10. What happens to the DNA of a lysogenic virus when it is injected into its host cell?
11. What enzyme is found in retroviruses?
12. Explain how a DNA tumor virus causes cancerous cell growth.
13. Describe the structure of a viroid.

Interpret and Apply

14. *Chlorobium* is a green sulfur bacterium. *Thiocystis* is a purple sulfur bacterium. *Anabaena* is a cyanobacterium. Compare and contrast photosynthesis among these organisms.
15. A bacteria grows and reproduces in a test tube containing only water, glucose, and a few minerals. Why is it likely that this bacterium is a nitrogen fixer?
16. Why are decomposers important?
17. In diseases such as the flu, illness occurs within a day or two of exposure to the virus. AIDS patients sometimes do not show symptoms of disease for years after their initial infection with the virus. How can you explain this observation?
18. Lytic viruses generally kill their host cell, whereas retroviruses generally do not. Explain why.
19. What is the basis of the fact that each virus can infect only one kind of cell?
20. Explain why some viruses have an outer envelope made partly of host cell membrane.

Critical Thinking

21. You are given a test tube containing a liquid with bacteria growing in the liquid. If the species of bacteria growing in the tube is one that cannot synthesize guanine, what conclusion can you draw about the composition of the liquid in the tube?
22. Explain why lytic viruses have never been observed to carry out transduction of genes from one host cell to another.
23. Why is the evolution of cyanobacteria believed to have occurred before the evolution of eukaryotes?
24. Doctors hope that one day they will be able to cure some human genetic disorders by transplanting normal genes into enough of a patient's cells to replace their defective genes. The hope is that these patients will then be able to make enough normal gene product to restore health. Why do you think lysogenic viruses might play an important role in such a technique?

Chapter 19

PROTISTS

Overview

ANIMALLIKE PROTISTS

19-1 Sarcodines
19-2 Ciliates
19-3 Other Animallike
      Protists

PLANTLIKE PROTISTS

19-4 Unicellular Algae
19-5 Multicellular Algae
19-6 Reproduction in
      Multicellular Algae

FUNGUSLIKE PROTISTS

19-7 Acellular Slime Molds
19-8 Cellular Slime Molds
19-9 Mildew and Water
      Molds

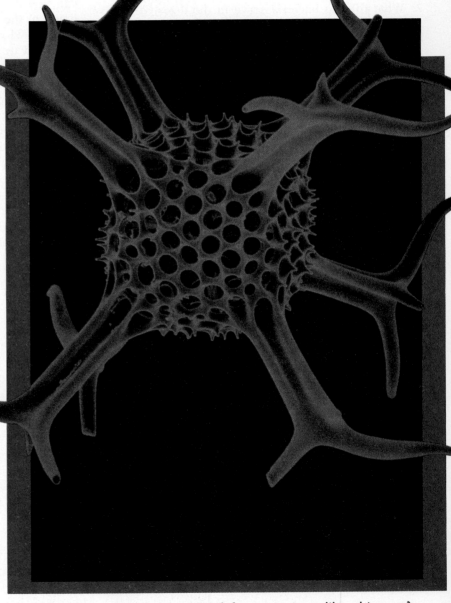

Why was a kingdom created for organisms like this one?

ANIMALLIKE PROTISTS

Members of the Kingdom Protista are eukaryotic. They have nuclei with a surrounding envelope, mitochondria, and other organelles. Many protists are single-celled, though several phyla are made up of large, multicellular forms. Asexual reproduction by mitosis is characteristic of protists. Many protists also reproduce sexually. The details of reproduction are important for classification.

Unfortunately, there are no characteristics that are unique to protists. As you will see, **protists** are most easily defined as organisms that do not belong to the other four kingdoms: monerans, fungi, plants, and animals.

19-1 Sarcodines

The **sarcodines** are protists that take in food by pseudopods [süd′ ə pädz]. **Pseudopods**, or "false feet," are temporary extensions of cytoplasm.

One of the best-known sarcodines is *Amoeba proteus*. This organism lives in ponds, lakes, and other bodies of fresh water. Figure 19-1 shows the general structure of an amoeba. Amoebas use pseudopods to move around. When an amoeba moves, some of its cytoplasm flows forward, thus extending the cell membrane. Amoebas also use pseudopods to feed, as other sarcodines do. The pseudopods trap bacteria and other small organisms by phagocytosis. Recall from Chapter 5 that in phagocytosis an organism surrounds its prey with its cell membrane, which then forms a food vacuole. Digestive enzymes released into the food vacuole break down the prey. Food molecules are then absorbed from the vacuole by the cell.

There are usually several food vacuoles within the cytoplasm. Each vacuole contains food in various stages of digestion.

Another structure common to amoebas and other protists is the contractile vacuole. The **contractile vacuole** controls the water balance of the cell. Water entering the cell by osmosis collects in the contractile vacuole. When filled, the vacuole contracts and pumps water out of the cell. The empty vacuole then begins to swell again as water continues to diffuse into the cell.

Amoebas reproduce asexually by mitotic cell division. Mitosis produces two nuclei containing exact copies of the DNA from the original cell nucleus. Cytokinesis follows mitosis and distributes cytoplasm and organelles between the two one-celled organisms. Other sarcodines reproduce sexually. In sexual reproduction, meiosis occurs. Gametes are produced, which fuse and develop into new organisms.

Section Objectives

A *Explain* why the protist kingdom contains a variety of seemingly unrelated organisms.

B *List* and *describe* the functions of some of the cell organelles found in protists.

C *Name* the major groups of animallike protists and *describe* the major characteristics of each group.

D *Describe* reproduction in animallike protists.

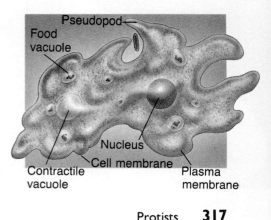

Figure 19-1 A typical amoeba. The front and rear of this protist are determined by the direction of motion at the time.

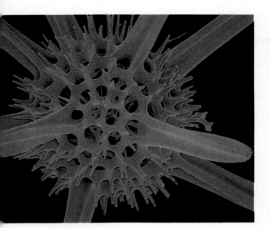

Figure 19-2 Many sarcodines, such as this radiolarian (1000×), have an external shell.

Many sarcodines have an external shell that gives them a distinctive shape. For example, *foraminiferans* [fôr ə min′ i fər rənz] secrete a shell made of calcium carbonate. Pseudopods poke out through holes in the shell to trap and digest prey. *Radiolarians* [rād ē ō lar′ ē ənz] have a glassy outer shell. These organisms also poke pseudopods out through holes in the shell. However, prey are drawn inside the shell to be digested. Radiolarians and most foraminiferans are marine organisms.

19-2 Ciliates

The **ciliates** are one-celled organisms that use cilia to swim and capture food. **Cilia** [sil′ ē ə] are short hairlike structures that extend from the cell. They are made up of bundles of protein fibers covered by an extension of the cell membrane. Cilia often cover the entire surface of the cell.

Most ciliates are free-living in fresh or salt water. A few species attach to a surface by a stalk and stay in one place. Other ciliates live in the bodies of host animals.

The most commonly studied ciliate is *Paramecium* [par ə mē′ sē əm]. This organism, which is illustrated in Figure 19-4, lives in freshwater ponds. Unlike amoebas, which have a variable shape, the slipper shape of paramecium is characteristic of the species. The shape of the cell is maintained by a flexible protein **pellicle** under the cell membrane.

Under the pellicle are flask-shaped capsules called **trichocysts** [trik′ ə sists]. Trichocysts can suddenly release a threadlike structure with a barb at the end. When approached by larger organisms, a paramecium releases its trichocysts, which seem to have a defensive function. In other ciliates, trichocysts may be used to capture prey or to anchor the organism in place.

Along the surface of the cell are parallel rows of cilia. These cilia function like the arms of a swimmer. When a cilium moves in one direction, it remains rigid. This movement has the same function as a swimmer's arm pulling through the water. On the return stroke, the cilia relax and slip along the side of the cell. For a paramecium to move, all the cilia must move in a coordinated pattern. The strokes occur in waves that travel along each row.

A paramecium can respond to stimuli. It swims toward food by detecting the presence of chemicals in the water. It can swim away from harmful chemicals such as acids. Such directed movement requires complex coordination of beating cilia. Just how this coordination is accomplished is not known, but it involves a network of fibers under the cell membrane.

Paramecia use their cilia to capture food. The cilia create currents that sweep food into an **oral groove** on the side of the cell. The oral groove leads to a narrow **gullet**. Cilia sweep food

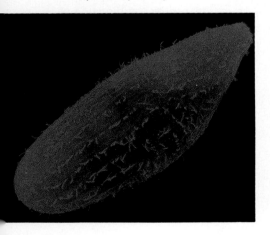

Figure 19-3 Most ciliates are free-swimming like the protist *Tetrahymena* (800×).

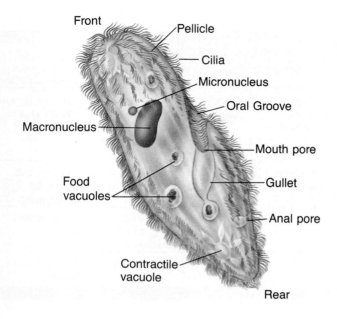

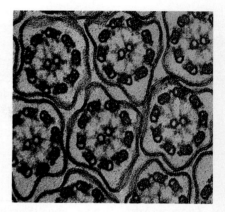

Figure 19-4 *Left:* The structure of a paramecium, a typical ciliate. *Right:* All eukaryotic cilia have nine double microtubules surrounding two single microtubules. The common structure suggests a common ancestor.

organisms down to the base of the gullet, where a food vacuole forms. The food vacuole then pinches off and moves into the cytoplasm. Food in the food vacuoles is digested by enzymes and absorbed into the cytoplasm. Undigested food is removed from the cell when the food vacuole fuses with the cell membrane at the **anal pore**.

Asexual reproduction in ciliates is by mitotic cell division. Sexual reproduction in ciliates is by conjugation. Recall from Chapter 18 that conjugation is a mechanism by which two individuals combine genetic information. Conjugation in paramecia is illustrated in Figure 19-5. Notice that the macronucleus disintegrates. Only the micronuclei are involved in conjugation. Each of the daughter cells receives a new combination of genetic material from the two original parent cells.

Figure 19-5 Conjugation in *Paramecium*. Sexual reproduction in these and other ciliates is unusual. These organisms have two kinds of nuclei. The **macronucleus** is similar in function to the nucleolus of other eukaryotes. RNA is manufactured in the macronucleus. The smaller nucleus, called the **micronucleus**, becomes active only during reproduction.

Two parent paramecia join at their oral grooves; micronuclei begin a series of divisions

One micronucleus from each moves to oral groove; macronuclei disintegrate

Micronuclei divide by mitosis

One from each pair transfers to the other paramecium

New pairs fuse; paramecia separate; new macronuclei reform

Table 19-1

CLASSIFICATION OF ANIMALLIKE PROTISTS						
Phylum	**Example**	**Method of locomotion**	**Skeleton or shell**	**Feeding**	**Lifestyle**	**Reproduction**
Sarcodina (sarcodines)	*Amoeba* *Difflugia* Heliozoans Radiolarians Foraminiferans	Pseudopods (amoebas only)	None, some silica, some calcium carbonate	Phagocytosis	Some free-living in marine and fresh water, some parasites	Asexual (amoebas only) and sexual
Ciliophora (ciliates)	*Paramecium*	Cilia	Pellicle under cell membrane	Food vacuole at end of gullet	Most free-living, some parasites	Asexual and sexual by conjugation
Zoomastigina (flagellates)	*Trypanosoma* *Trychonympha* *Codosiga*	Flagella	None	Absorption, phagocytosis	Some free-living, some parasites	Asexual and sexual
Sporozoa (sporozoans)	*Plasmodium*	None	None	Absorption	All parasites	Asexual and sexual

19-3 Other Animallike Protists

Flagellates are animallike protists that move by means of flagella. Flagella (singular: *flagellum*) occur at some time in the lives of most eukaryotes. Flagella have the same structure as cilia but are longer and less numerous. Species may have one, two, or several flagella. Some members of this phylum live in fresh or salt water, but most live in the bodies of other organisms.

An important flagellate is *Trypanosoma*. This protist is a parasite that causes sleeping sickness in humans. *Trypanosoma* also inhabits the blood of wild and domestic animals throughout much of Africa. The parasite is transmitted from one animal to another through the bite of the bloodsucking tsetse [set' sē] fly.

Other flagellates benefit their hosts. *Trichonympha*, for example, lives in the intestines of termites. The termite itself is incapable of digesting the wood that it eats. *Trychonympha* makes an enzyme that digests cellulose in the wood particles. Without flagellates in its intestine, the termite would eventually die of starvation.

Another important group of protists are the **sporozoans**. All members of this group are parasites. Sporozoans have no means of locomotion as adults. These organisms have complex life cycles that include reproduction and development in more than one host.

The best-known sporozoans are members of the genus *Plasmodium*. The life cycle of *Plasmodium vivax* is shown in Figure 19-6. This organism causes malaria. Malaria is carried from one host to another by mosquitoes. In tropical countries where malaria is common, one method of control is to kill the mosquitoes that

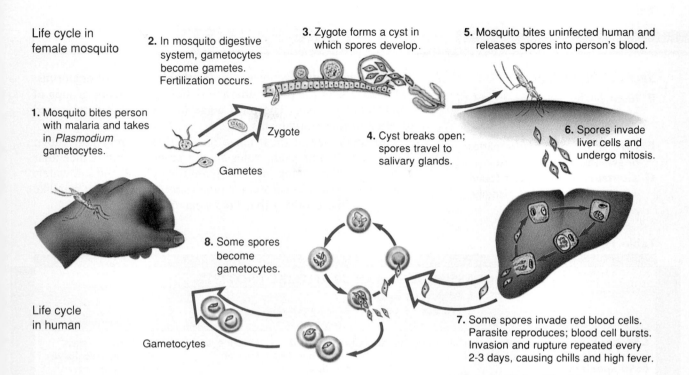

Life cycle in female mosquito

1. Mosquito bites person with malaria and takes in *Plasmodium* gametocytes.

2. In mosquito digestive system, gametocytes become gametes. Fertilization occurs.

Zygote

Gametes

3. Zygote forms a cyst in which spores develop.

4. Cyst breaks open; spores travel to salivary glands.

5. Mosquito bites uninfected human and releases spores into person's blood.

6. Spores invade liver cells and undergo mitosis.

7. Some spores invade red blood cells. Parasite reproduces; blood cell bursts. Invasion and rupture repeated every 2-3 days, causing chills and high fever.

8. Some spores become gametocytes.

Life cycle in human

Gametocytes

Figure 19-6 The life cycle of *Plasmodium vivax*.

transmit the disease. In the 1950s and 1960s, widespread spraying of pesticides reduced the incidence of malaria in many countries. Unfortunately, over the last decade, the malaria mosquito has developed partial resistance to pesticides. Today malaria continues to be a major human disease. It afflicts 200 million people a year.

CHECKPOINT ◆

1. Name one characteristic that all protists have in common.
2. What is the function of a contractile vacuole?
3. Name the primary method of locomotion used by each of the four groups of animallike protists.
4. What structural feature do cilia and flagella have in common?
5. What is the function of the micronucleus in *Paramecium*?
6. In which host does fertilization occur during the life cycle of *Plasmodium*?
▶ 7. Explain how the ability of paramecium to respond to stimuli would be useful to the organism in its natural environment.
▶ 8. You bring a jar of pond water into class to look for various protists. What phyla of animallike protists would you expect to find represented in the jar?

▶ Denotes a question that involves *interpreting* and *applying* concepts.

PLANTLIKE PROTISTS

Section Objectives

E **Identify** the six major groups of plantlike protists and **state** the major characteristics of each.

F **Give** an example of alternation of generations in a protist.

G **Contrast** the life cycles found in different groups of plantlike protists.

The plantlike protists represent a remarkable variety of organisms. Table 19-2 lists the major characteristics of six major groups of autotrophic protists. The term **algae** [al′ jē] is commonly used to refer to these organisms.

The small size of most algae makes them barely noticeable. Yet they play important roles in the environment. Unicellular algae are primary components of plankton in fresh and salt water. **Plankton** consists of microscopic organisms (most of them plantlike and animallike protists) that float near the surface.

Table 19-2

		CLASSIFICATION OF PLANTLIKE PROTISTS			
Division	**Example**	**Major components of cell wall**	**Photosynthetic pigments**	**Habitat**	**Comments**
Chrysophyta (golden algae–6650 species)	*Diatoma Aulacodiscus*	Silica and pectin	Chlorophyll *a* and *c*; other red and yellow pigments	Marine and fresh water	Patterned "glass" shells in two halves; major part of plankton
Dinoflagellata (fire algae–1100 species)	*Gonyaulax Gymnodinium Noctiluca*	Cellulose	Chlorophyll *a* and *c*; other red and yellow pigments	Most are marine	Most are single-celled. Some are bioluminescent. A few lack photosynthetic pigments and are heterotrophic.
Euglenophyta (euglenoids–800 species)	*Euglena*	No cell wall, flexible protein pellicle	Chlorophyll *a* and *c*; other red and yellow pigments	Fresh water, some marine	Some species are permanently lacking chloroplasts and are, therefore, heterotrophic; some parasites
Chlorophyta (green algae–7000 species)	*Volvox Spirogyra Oedogonium Ulva*	Cellulose and pectin like the wall of land plants	Chlorophyll *a* and *b*; other red and yellow pigments	Marine and fresh water	Both unicellular and multicellular forms; a major plankton component
Rhodophyta (red algae–4000 species)	*Chondrus Polysiphonia*	Cellulose	Chlorophyll *a* only; phycoerythrin	Most are marine	Most are large, multicellular organisms. Many form a hard crust of calcium carbonate.
Phaeophyta (brown algae–1500 species)	*Fucus*	Cellulose	Chlorophyll *a* and *c*; fucoxanthin	Marine, usually along rocky shorelines; some in open ocean	Large, multicellular with specialized parts; some reach a length of 100 m

19-4 Unicellular Algae

A major characteristic used to classify algae is the type of photosynthetic pigments they contain. Eukaryotic autotrophs all utilize chlorophyll to carry out photosynthesis. But there are several different kinds of chlorophyll that differ slightly in chemical structure. They are referred to in Table 19-2 as chlorophylls *a*, *b*, and *c*. In addition, various groups contain other colored pigments that sometimes mask the green color of chlorophyll.

Golden Algae The largest group of unicellular algae is the golden algae. Most members of this group are photosynthetic. However, their characteristic gold or brown color comes from the predominance of pigments other than chlorophyll. These protists are found in both the ocean and fresh water. Of the estimated 10 000 species, most are diatoms.

Diatoms are characterized by cell walls made of two overlapping halves. Instead of cellulose, the cell wall contains a gelatinous material called *pectin*. In most diatoms there is also silica in the cell wall. *Silica* is a glassy material rich in the element silicon.

Diatoms usually reproduce asexually. During mitosis, the two halves of the cell wall separate. The cytoplasm then divides, and each daughter cell gets half of the cell wall. Each daughter cell then produces a new half for the cell wall.

Occasionally diatoms reproduce sexually. The parent cell undergoes meiosis. Only one haploid nucleus survives meiosis; the other three degenerate. A flagellated gamete breaks out of the old cell wall and swims until it encounters another gamete of the same species. The cells fuse to form a diploid zygote. The zygote then develops an entirely new shell.

Figure 19-7 The diatom shell is something like a petri dish. One half is slightly larger than the other and fits over the smaller half. After mitosis, each daughter cell gets half of the old shell and must grow a new half (500×).

Figure 19-8 A typical dinoflagellate in its "armored" shell (2920 ×).

Fire Algae About 1100 species of single-celled protists make up the fire algae. The most common members of this group are the **dinoflagellates** [dī nō flaj′ ə ləts]. Much of the ocean's plankton is made up of dinoflagellates and diatoms.

The chloroplasts of dinoflagellates contain chlorophyll. However, abundant red and yellow pigments mask the green chlorophyll, giving the dinoflagellates a characteristic red or brown color. Most dinoflagellates have a cellulose cell wall made of many segments. The segments fit together like the pieces of a suit of armor.

Dinoflagellates usually have two flagella. One flagellum extends backward from the middle of the cell. This flagellum propels the organism forward. The second flagellum wraps around the middle of the cell in a groove. When this flagellum vibrates, the cell spins. For this reason, dinoflagellates rotate as they move through the water.

Some dinoflagellates do not have chloroplasts. These heterotrophic organisms feed on smaller protists and monerans. They are classified as dinoflagellates because of their similarity to the photosynthetic forms. Biologists assume that the heterotrophic dinoflagellates evolved from autotrophic forms.

The nucleus of dinoflagellates is unusual. Recall that in most eukaryotes, chromosomes are visible only during mitosis. In dinoflagellates, though, the chromosomes are always compact and visible. Because mitosis in dinoflagellates shows some similarities to prokaryotic cell division, some biologists think of dinoflagellates as being a link between prokaryotes and eukaryotes.

Many dinoflagellates can produce light. The ability to produce light is called *bioluminescence*. When boats, fish, or waves disturb such dinoflagellates at night, the water may glow with an eerie blue or green light.

Euglenoids One small group of single-celled algae consists of organisms with traits of both plantlike and animallike protists. These protists are the euglenoids. Figure 19-9 illustrates *Euglena*, a member of this group. The cell contains a large nucleus and nucleolus. Bright green chloroplasts are distributed throughout the cytoplasm. If a euglena is grown in the dark for several days, its chloroplasts disappear. Without chloroplasts, the cell can survive by absorbing nutrients through its cell membrane. When the euglena is exposed to light again, chloroplasts reappear and photosynthesis resumes.

Each euglena has two flagella, one long and one short. The long flagellum propels the cell through the water. The function of the smaller flagellum is not clear. Both flagella are attached at the **reservoir**, a depression at the front end of the cell. As in the animallike protists, the long flagellum emerges through the

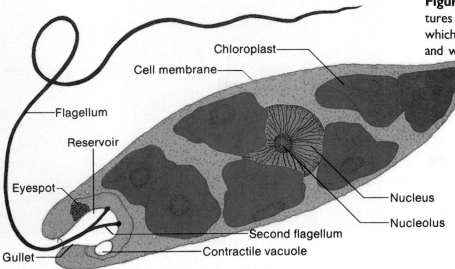

Figure 19-9 The structural features of a euglena. Can you identify which characteristics are plantlike and which are animallike?

Chloroplast

Cell membrane

Flagellum

Reservoir

Eyespot

Gullet

Second flagellum

Contractile vacuole

Nucleus

Nucleolus

gullet. In addition to moving by flagellum, euglenas can also crawl across a surface by euglenoid movement. This crawling motion occurs when the cell changes the shape of its flexible protein pellicle. Unlike other algae, euglenas do not have a cell wall.

Near the reservoir is a mass of red pigment called the **eyespot**. The eyespot directs the cell to swim toward light. This ability is a useful adaptation for a photosynthetic organism. In fact, many protists have eyespots.

Green Algae The green algae are the most diverse group of algae. Some green algae are single-celled, some are colonial, and some are multicellular. You will learn about the multicellular green algae in the next section. The major pigment in green algae is chlorophyll, but green algae also contain yellow carotenes. High concentrations of carotenes make some green algae appear yellow-green. Green algae are common in lakes and ponds. Some are marine.

Chlorella is an example of a unicellular green alga. Each cell contains a cell wall, a chloroplast, and a nucleus. *Chlorella* does not reproduce sexually. Asexual reproduction occurs by the formation of many nonmotile spores within the parent cell. A **spore** is a reproductive cell. When the cell wall disintegrates, the spores are released.

Some green algae have flagella and are motile. *Chlamydomonas* is a unicellular, flagellated alga that lives in fresh water. Each cell has a light-sensitive eyespot. The eyespot allows a *Chlamydomonas* cell to move towards the direction of light, thus aiding in photosynthesis.

Figure 19-10 The colonial green alga *Volvox*. The small green spheres are young colonies developing within the older parent colony.

Figure 19-11 *Chondrus crispus*, a multicellular red algae, is also called Irish moss. People who live on the coasts of Europe and North America eat Irish moss.

Volvox is an example of a colonial green alga. In colonial organisms, there is little or no specialization of cells or division of labor. *Volvox* colonies contain from 200 to 20 000 cells. Several colonies of *Volvox* are shown in Figure 19-10. Each *Volvox* colony is shaped like a hollow ball. Individual cells are enclosed in a gelatinlike material but are connected to each other by strands of cytoplasm. Each cell has two flagella and looks like a *Chlamydomonas* cell.

Sexual reproduction in *Volvox* is oogamous. In **oogamy**, two types of gametes are formed. Some cells produce large, nonmotile eggs. The eggs store food that can be used by the zygote for germination and growth. Other cells produce many small, motile sperm. The egg and sperm fuse in the center of the colony to form a zygote. When the parent colony disintegrates, it releases the zygote. The zygote undergoes a dormant period, then it begins to grow. Meiosis occurs, forming meiospores. A **meiospore** is a haploid spore that results from meiosis. Only one meiospore survives. This meiospore eventually produces a new colony. In the life cycle of *Volvox*, the only diploid cell is the zygote.

Red Algae Only a few species of red algae are single-celled or colonial. The majority are multicellular. One species occurs in patches on moist soil. Reproduction is by mitotic cell division.

19-5 Multicellular Algae

Multicellular algae are the largest protists. In contrast to the microscopic plankton, these algae are large, plantlike organisms. Some red algae, for example, can reach a length of 1 meter and have a complex branching shape. The brown algae are the giants of the protist kingdom, with some reaching a length of 100 meters.

Multicellular green algae include simple filamentous species and complex species with specialized structures. Compared to plants, however, these organisms have little or no division of labor among their cells.

Red Algae Red algae grow in tropical waters and along rocky coasts in colder waters. They attach to rocks by specialized cells called **holdfasts**. Red algae possess a photosynthetic pigment called phycoerythrin [fī kō ə rith′ rən] that allows them to grow in deep water. Phycoerythrin can capture the energy of blue light, which is the only wavelength of light that can penetrate deep water. The pigment then transfers this energy to chlorophyll. Some red algae are able to live more than 100 meters below the surface.

Many species of red algae withdraw calcium from ocean water, depositing it in their cell walls. When the cells die, they leave behind beds of calcium salts. In some cases, deposits from red algae have formed layers of limestone 300 meters thick.

Some red algae are important food plants in parts of Asia. Red algae are also the source of agar. Recall from Chapter 18 that agar is used to grow microorganisms in the laboratory.

Brown Algae There are about 1500 species of brown algae, most of them marine. They are common in coastal areas, especially cold water. Brown algae, also called *kelps*, are the largest and most complex marine protists. Their brown color is caused by the pigment fucoxanthin [fyü kō zan′ thən].

As shown in Figure 19-12, brown algae have many specialized structures. The branched plant body can have **air bladders** to keep the plant afloat. The broad, leaflike **blades** are connected to a tough stalk called a **stipe**. Multicellular holdfasts anchor the plant in place.

Brown algae such as rockweed, or *Fucus*, are common organisms along rocky, cold-water coastlines. In Asia, various brown algae are eaten as food. Many people anticipate that the brown and red algae may be an important human food source in the future. Algin, a compound found in brown algae, is often used in the manufacture of latex, ceramic glazes, cosmetics, and ice cream.

Green Algae As you learned in Section 19-4, the green algae are the most diverse of the plantlike protists. They are found both in fresh water and marine environments, and they show a variety of forms. It is thought that the green algae gave rise to plants. The cell walls of green algae are made of cellulose and pectin, the same chemicals found in the cell walls of plants. Green algae also use the same type of photosynthetic pigments as plants do. Like plants, green algae store food as starch.

Spirogyra, which lives in ponds and streams, is an example of a filamentous green alga. The cells of *Spirogyra* are attached

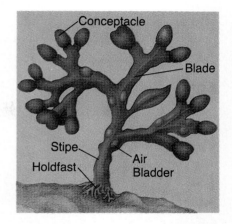

Figure 19-12 The brown algae *Fucus* is a common seaweed of rocky northern coasts. Quite plantlike in general appearance, the specialized structures are not related to similar looking structures in land plants. The general resemblance is due to convergent evolution.

DO YOU KNOW?

Information: The brown algae *Sargassum natans* reproduces by fragmenting into small pieces that grow and fragment again. This species lives in the open ocean, covering millions of square kilometers of the Atlantic between the Azores and the Bahamas. This area is called the Sargasso Sea.

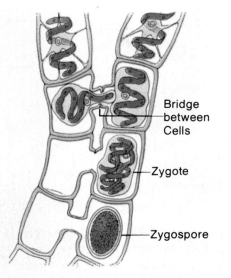

Bridge
between
Cells

Zygote

Zygospore

Figure 19-13 Conjugation in *Spirogyra*.

end to end in long threads, or **filaments**. Each cell of *Spirogyra* is a transparent cylinder. A ribbonlike chloroplast spirals through each cell. The cell contains a large vacuole. The nucleus is attached to the cell membrane by strands of cytoplasm.

Ulva, or sea lettuce, is a marine alga. The blades of this organism are two cells thick and may be as long as 1 meter. *Ulva* has specialized cells that enable it to cling to rocks.

19-6 Reproduction in Multicellular Algae

Reproduction in protists may be simple or it may be very complex. In the euglenoids, for example, reproduction is by mitosis. Multicellular algae undergo complex sexual reproduction.

Spirogyra, for example, is made up of haploid cells. It reproduces sexually by conjugation. The process in this alga has some similarities to bacterial conjugation described in the previous chapter. Two *Spirogyra* filaments touch each other and small bumps grow out from adjacent cells. The contents of the cells in one filament then enter the cells of the other filament. The transfer of cell contents from one strand to the other results in one filament of empty cells and one filament containing zygotes.

The zygotes form thick-walled zygospores. A **zygospore** is a diploid reproductive cell. When conditions are favorable, each zygospore undergoes meiosis. The resulting haploid cells grow into new filaments of *Spirogyra*.

A more complex life cycle occurs in the green alga *Oedogonium*. This organism can reproduce asexually or sexually. Sexual reproduction involves two kinds of specialized reproductive cells, the oogonium and the antheridium. An **oogonium** [ō ə gō′ nē əm] is a cell that produces an egg. An **antheridium** [an thə rid′ ē əm] is a cell that produces a sperm. Sperm swim to the oogonium and enter through a small pore. Once inside the oogonium, a sperm fertilizes the egg, thus forming a zygote.

When the zygote is released from the oogonium, it forms a thick wall and becomes a zygospore. The zygospore enters a period of dormancy that may last several months. It then undergoes meiosis, producing four flagellated reproductive cells called **zoospores**, each of which can start a new haploid filament.

The green alga *Ulva* shows a somewhat different life cycle. In this organism, an adult haploid plant produces gametes that are released into the water. The gametes fuse to form a zygote. The zygote then divides and forms another adult plant, which is diploid. The adult diploid and haploid plants look alike. Cells in the diploid plant undergo meiosis and produce haploid zoospores. The zoospores then divide and form an adult haploid plant.

Organisms that follow an orderly sequence of haploid and diploid generations are said to show **alternation of generations**.

Alternation of generations is characteristic of plants. The presence of this process in algae shows the evolutionary relationship between algae and plants.

In alternation of generations, the diploid phase is called a **sporophyte**. The multicellular haploid phase is called the **gametophyte**. In species like *Ulva*, the sporophyte and the gametophyte generation look alike. In other algae, the two generations can look completely different.

Alternation of generations is common in many green, red, and brown algae. Many red algae, for example, have very complex life cycles. The multicellular gametophytes produce two types of gametes—large eggs and smaller sperm. Thus reproduction is oogamous. Each egg is formed in a special flask-shaped oogonium. Sperm are produced in antheridia (plural of *antheridium*). Sperm lack flagella. Ocean currents carry the sperm to the egg.

In some species, the zygote remains attached to the oogonium and develops into a sporophyte. The sporophyte produces nonmotile spores. Currents carry the spores to new locations, where they begin a new gametophyte generation.

Sexual reproduction in brown algae also is oogamous. Reproductive organs called **conceptacles** are located at the ends of the blades. Each conceptacle contains a pore that opens to the outside. In gametophytes, a conceptacle may contain oogonia or antheridia. Eggs are large and nonmotile. Sperm are small and swim by means of two flagella.

Mature gametes are expelled from the conceptacle. Fertilization occurs in the water. The resulting zygote then develops into a multicellular sporophyte. The sporophyte reproduces by forming motile spores. These spores, in turn, grow into multicellular gametophytes. The familiar rockweed, *Fucus*, may also reproduce asexually by fragmentation.

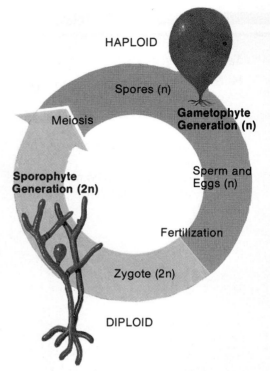

Figure 19-14 Alternation of generations is characteristic of many kinds of algae. The haploid part of the life cycle is shown in yellow and the diploid part in blue. Color will be used in the same way to show the life cycles of other organisms later in this chapter and in other chapters.

CHECKPOINT ◆

9. Which two groups of plantlike protists consist primarily of multicellular organisms?

10. Name one characteristic of the euglenophytes that is not found in any of the other plantlike protists.

11. In an organism that shows alternation of generations, what is the haploid organism called?

12. What group of plantlike protists has the simplest method of reproduction?

▶ 13. After several months, a greenish scum develops on the walls of your freshwater aquarium. You suspect it is some kind of plantlike protist. What steps would you take to identify this organism?

▶ Denotes a question that involves *interpreting* and *applying* concepts.

FUNGUSLIKE PROTISTS

Section Objectives

H **Name** the three major groups of funguslike protists and state the characteristics of each group.

I **Describe** the life cycle of a cellular slime mold.

J **Compare** the life cycles of acellular and cellular slime molds.

Have you ever had a problem that you wish would just go away? Taxonomists who like neat classification schemes must sometimes feel that way about the funguslike protists. These organisms do not fall easily into any of the traditional classifications. Table 19-3 shows three major phyla of funguslike protists. Because of their growth patterns, general appearance, and methods of feeding, these organisms resemble the fungi that you will study in the next chapter. Yet they are so different from fungi in other ways that they are placed in the protist kingdom.

19-7 Acellular Slime Molds

One group of funguslike protists are the Myxomycota [mix ō mī kō′ tə] or **acellular slime molds**. The life cycle of these organisms is shown in Figure 19-15. Sexual reproduction is common in these organisms. In the acellular slime molds, the feeding stage of the organism is a **plasmodium**, or a large mass of cytoplasm that contains many diploid nuclei. After a nucleus divides, the cytoplasm does not divide into separate cells. For this reason, these slime molds are described as being acellular.

As the cytoplasmic mass crawls over the forest floor, it engulfs pieces of leaves and decaying material. When it encounters unfavorable conditions, stalklike fruiting bodies form. These are similar in appearance to the spore cases of cellular slime molds. Meiosis occurs in the spores, however, and haploid flagellated gametes form. When two gametes meet, they fuse and form a zygote. The zygote grows into a new plasmodium. Thus acellular slime molds undergo sexual reproduction.

Table 19-3

CLASSIFICATION OF FUNGUSLIKE PROTISTS			
Division	**Example**	**Nutrition**	**Comments**
Myxomycota (acellular slime molds)	Physarum	Phagocytosis	Found on logs, bark, wet soils; feeding structures often yellow or orange
Acrasiomycota (cellular slime molds)	Dictyostelium	Phagocytosis	Found in damp soil and on rotting logs, feed on bacteria
Oomycota (downy mildew and water molds)	Saprolegnia Phytophthora	Parasites or saprobes	Feed by extending hyphae into tissues of host organism

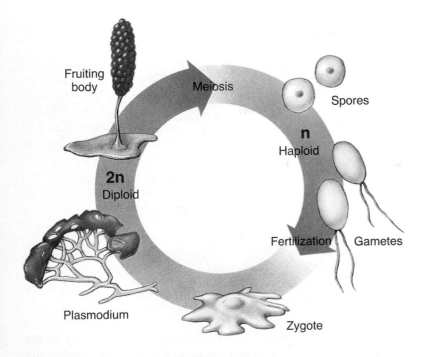

Fruiting body

Meiosis

Spores

n
Haploid

2n
Diploid

Plasmodium

Fertilization

Gametes

Zygote

Figure 19-15 The life cycle of an acellular slime mold. Compare the life cycle of this organism with that of the cellular slime mold that follows.

19-8 Cellular Slime Molds

Organisms in the division Acrasiomycota [ə krā zē ō mī kō′ tə] are usually called **cellular slime molds**. You have probably never seen one of these unusual organisms. They live in moist, decaying leaves and rotting logs.

At one stage in their life cycle, they exist as independent, single cells. Each cell feeds on decaying matter and bacteria. When food becomes scarce, the cells come together and form a single multicellular mass. This slug-shaped mass of cells migrates to a suitable location. When the slug stops moving, it rearranges its cells to form a stalk with a spore case at the top. When the spore case matures, it ruptures and releases haploid spores into the air. Each spore then develops into individual cells which begin the life cycle again. The spores are asexual and the entire life cycle consists of haploid cells.

19-9 Mildew and Water Molds

Organisms such as downy mildew and water molds are members of the division Oomycota [ō ə mī kō′ tə]. Downy mildew is parasitic on plants. Most water molds are saprobes. Recall that saprobes feed on dead organisms. A few water molds, such as *Saprolegnia*, are parasites of fish and fish eggs. Water molds are common in fresh water.

DO YOU KNOW?

Historical Note: An oomycote, *Phytophthora infestans*, causes a disease of potatoes called late blight. From 1846 to 1847, the entire potato crop of Ireland became infected. Over 1 million people starved to death. Many others left Ireland and emigrated to other countries.

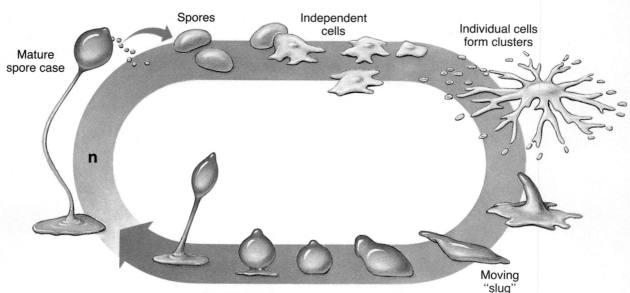

Spores

Independent cells

Individual cells form clusters

Mature spore case

n

Moving "slug"

Development of spore case

Figure 19-16 The life cycle of a cellular slime mold. Notice that the entire life cycle is haploid.

Saprolegnia and many other oomycotes are made up of numerous threadlike tubes called **hyphae** [hī′ fē]. The hyphae are not divided into individual cells, but nuclei are found at regular intervals in the cytoplasm.

Oomycotes produce asexual spores that have two flagella—one at each end of the spore. The spores are released and swim away to develop into new oomycote bodies.

Oomycotes also reproduce sexually. Haploid nuclei form in antheridia and oogonia. In *Saprolegnia*, however, gametes are not released into the water. Male and female nuclei fertilize after antheridia and oogonia come into contact. The male nucleus migrates through a bridge into the oogonium and fertilizes the female nucleus.

CHECKPOINT ◆

14. Which group of funguslike protists has many parasitic species?
15. In which group of funguslike protists does part of the life cycle consist of single, independently feeding cells?
16. What is the unusual feature of the feeding structure of the acellular slime molds?
17. Which group or groups of funguslike protists undergo sexual reproduction?
▶ 18. How is the life cycle of *Saprolegnia* similar to that of the green alga *Oedegonium*?

▶ Denotes a question that involves *interpreting* and *applying* concepts.

STRUCTURE AND POPULATION GROWTH OF *BLEPHARISMA*

Objectives and Skills

☐ *Observe* and *draw* the structure of the ciliate *Blepharisma*.
☐ *Measure* the growth of a population of *Blepharisma* started from an isolated individual.

Materials

compound microscope	rubber pipette bulb
microscope light source	dissecting microscope or hand lens
2 clean glass slides	
1 coverslip	2 small test tubes
medicine dropper	test tube rack
cotton	wax pencil
10-mL pipette	growth medium
micropipette	*Blepharisma* culture

Procedure and Observations

1. Read all the instructions for this laboratory activity before you begin your work.
2. Place a few cotton fibers on a clean glass slide. Put a small drop of water from the *Blepharisma* culture bottle on the cotton. Place a coverslip on top.
3. Set up the microscope and light source. Be sure the microscope has the low-power objective in place. *Note: Be sure not to tilt your microscope back. Keep the slide level.*
4. Put the slide on the stage and focus until you find actively swimming *Blepharisma*. The cotton fibers help to confine the *Blepharisma* so they cannot swim too far. Practice moving the slide so you can follow an individual organism.
5. When you can follow the organisms at low power, switch to a higher magnification and again try to follow them.

6. At high magnification, look for a contractile vacuole. It will grow in size and collapse. Time several cycles of the contractile vacuole and record your observations.
7. On a separate sheet of paper, draw a diagram of the organism and label the parts you see.
8. Using a 10-mL pipette, half fill the test tubes with *Blepharisma* culture medium.
9. Place a drop of the *Blepharisma* culture on a clean glass slide and observe under low magnification (10–15×) with a dissecting microscope or a hand lens. Using magnification, capture a single *Blepharisma* in the micropipette. Transfer this individual to a labeled test tube.
10. Transfer another individual into the second test tube. Plug each test tube with cotton and store them in a cool, dark place.
11. Clean up your materials and wash your hands thoroughly.
12. Each day for five successive school days, count and record the number of individuals in each tube.
13. For each test tube, make a graph of population size versus time.

Analysis and Conclusions

1. In what ways is *Blepharisma* similar to a paramecium? In what ways is it different?
2. How would you describe the shape of *Blepharisma*? Is the cell rigid in shape?
3. Would you expect *Blepharisma* to have a contractile vacuole? Explain.
4. From your graphs of population growth, was the growth rate in the two tubes similar? Estimate the amount of time between cell divisions.
5. Explain the shape of the population graphs.

CHAPTER REVIEW

Summary

▸ Kingdom Protista cannot be defined by a particular set of characteristics. It contains organisms that do not fit into the other four kingdoms. Thus it is convenient to group the protists according to their general resemblance to other organisms.

▸ Animallike protists are distinguished by their method of locomotion and by their feeding methods. Sarcodines feed by surrounding prey with pseudopods and engulfing them in vacuoles. Ciliates use cilia to swim and to push food into food vacuoles at the base of the gullet. Flagellates move by means of flagella and feed by phagocytosis or absorption. Sporozoans are all parasites. They have no method of independent movement and they feed by absorption.

▸ The structure of plantlike protists, or algae, varies from simple one-celled forms to very large multicellular organisms. Photosynthetic pigments and mode of reproduction are major characteristics used to classify these autotrophs.

▸ Multicellularity in the algae can be simple, as in the filamentous algae, or it can be more complex. Multicellular protists can be large and have specialized structures.

▸ Autotrophic plankton plays an important role in food production in oceans and fresh water. Plankton also produces large amounts of oxygen that enter the atmosphere. Some kinds of red and brown algae are used directly by humans as a food source.

▸ Reproduction in protists may be asexual or sexual. Many protists have very complex reproductive cycles.

▸ Some of the most unusual life cycles occur in the funguslike protists. In some slime molds, the organism consists of independent individual cells for part of its life cycle. Other slime molds exist as large, acellular, multinucleate feeding masses.

Vocabulary

acellular slime mold	macronucleus
air bladder	meiospore
algae	micronucleus
alternation of generations	oogamy
anal pore	oogonium
antheridium	oral groove
blade	pellicle
cellular slime mold	plankton
cilia	plasmodium
ciliate	protist
conceptacle	pseudopod
contractile vacuole	reservoir
diatom	sarcodine
dinoflagellate	spore
eyespot	sporophyte
filament	sporozoan
flagellate	stipe
gametophyte	trichocyst
gullet	zoospore
holdfast	zygospore
hyphae	

Concept Mapping

Construct a concept map for protist adaptations. Include the following terms: alternation of generations, anal pore, antheridium, cilia, eyespot, gametophyte, gullet, oogonium, oral groove, pellicle, pseudopod, spore, sporophyte, zoospore, and zygospore. Add additional terms as you need them.

Review

1. Movement of amoebas is accomplished by what structures?
2. Sexual reproduction in paramecium is called _____.
3. In *Plasmodium*, where does formation of sex cells take place?

4. How does *Trychonympha* help its host organism?
5. State at least one characteristic common to all the plantlike protists.
6. _____ is the material that makes up the cell wall of diatoms.
7. Name two major features used to classify the plantlike protists.
8. What is the arrangement of flagella in dinoflagellates?
9. Describe reproduction in diatoms.
10. At what stage in its life cycle is *Spirogyra* diploid?
11. Name a protist that exhibits alternation of generations.
12. The green alga *Ulva* has a life cycle that is characterized by _____ .
13. Funguslike protists that are commonly found growing in water belong to the group _____ .
14. Describe the feeding behavior of an acellular slime mold.
15. Describe the stages in the life cycle of a cellular slime mold.
16. Which group of slime molds reproduces asexually?

In the following list, match the protist group with the proper description.

17. dinoflagellates
18. sarcodines
19. diatoms
20. ciliates
21. flagellates
22. sporozoans
23. acellular slime molds
24. euglenoids
25. green algae
26. red algae

a. autotrophs with flagella and pellicle
b. have cilia
c. are all parasites
d. *Ulva* and *Volvox*
e. have pseudopods
f. organisms that cause red tide
g. contain phycoerythrin
h. heterotroph with flagella
i. have two-part, silica shell
j. funguslike

Interpret and Apply

27. If you observe a contractile vacuole in a protist, what is the most likely habitat of that organism?
28. All protists are eukaryotic. Why, then, is this trait not considered a characteristic that defines the group?
29. What characteristic is shared by flagellates and euglenoids, and why are these two groups not considered as a single phylum?
30. What are some of the similarities in the life cycles of *Trypanosoma* and *Plasmodium*?
31. Many red algae are adapted to growth in very deep water. Explain how this is an advantage for these deep-water species.
32. What is the advantage of sexual reproduction over asexual reproduction?

Critical Thinking

33. You bring home a jar of pond water to look for protists. The jar contains mud from the bottom and several water plants as well. Where would you take samples from if you were looking for sarcodines? Where would you look for ciliates?
34. Numerous studies have shown that acid rain kills most of the plankton in large lakes. (Acid rain is the result of raindrops falling to the ground through polluted air.) Explain how the loss of plankton affects other organisms in the lake.
35. Several species of euglenoids look identical to euglena except that they have no chloroplasts. One species of ciliate looks exactly like a paramecium except that its cytoplasm is filled with single-celled green algae. Why is the heterotroph classified as a euglenoid whereas the autotroph is classified as a ciliate?

FUNGI

Overview

CHARACTERISTICS OF FUNGI

20-1 Structure of Fungi
20-2 Nutrition in Fungi
20-3 Reproduction in Fungi

VARIETY OF FUNGI

20-4 Zygomycota
20-5 Ascomycota
20-6 Basidiomycota
20-7 Imperfect Fungi
20-8 Lichens

Are these mushrooms edible?

CHARACTERISTICS OF FUNGI

Have you ever opened a container of leftovers and found a colorful, velvety fuzz on the food surface? This fuzz is actually a fungus. How did the fungi get into the container? Why do fungi grow on food?

Fungi [fun' jī] have two major characteristics. First, fungi reproduce by spores. Recall that a spore is a unicellular reproductive cell that develops into a new individual. Fungal spores are very light and float in the air. Spores fell on the food before you placed it in a container and put it into the refrigerator. Second, fungi lack chlorophyll and cannot make their own food. Thus fungi obtain nutrition from your leftovers.

20-1 Structure of Fungi

Fungi are composed of threadlike structures called **hyphae**. Each hypha (singular for hyphae) is covered by a cell wall. The fungal cell wall is made primarily of a carbohydrate called **chitin** [kī' tin]. Chitin is the same material found in the hard shells of insects, lobsters, and spiders.

Within each hypha are cell structures like nuclei, cytoplasm, mitochondria, and ribosomes. As hyphae grow longer, nuclei in the cytoplasm divide. In some fungi, **cross walls** form between nuclei. In other fungi, cross walls are not formed and the cytoplasm becomes **multinucleate**.

Hyphae branch and rebranch to form an extensive network called a **mycelium** [mī sē' lē əm]. The velvety fuzz found on leftovers are the mycelia. Mycelial growth is another characteristic of fungi.

20-2 Nutrition in Fungi

All fungi are heterotrophic. Most fungi feed by secreting enzymes into their surroundings. The enzymes break food into small molecules. Fungal cells then absorb these molecules. This mode of nutrition is called **absorption**.

Most fungi are saprobes. Recall from Chapter 18 that a saprobe is an organism that absorbs its food from dead or decaying organic matter. Fungi are commonly found growing on rotting leaves, wood, or animal wastes. The enzymes that fungi secrete break down these organic materials. For this reason, fungi are very important in the decomposition of dead plants and animals.

Some fungi are parasites. The parasitic fungi usually grow on plants. They extend their hyphae between the cell walls of the

Section Objectives

A **Describe** the structure of a fungal hypha.

B **List** several different ways fungi obtain food from their environment.

C **State** the general characteristics of fungal reproduction.

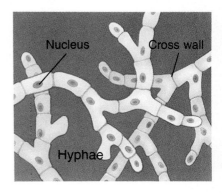

Figure 20-1 Fungi are composed of threadlike hyphae. The hyphae of some fungi do not have crosswalls.

Figure 20-2 All fungi reproduce by producing large numbers of spores. The "smoke" from this puffball is actually millions of spores being released. Spores are so light they can be carried for great distances by air currents.

host plant and absorb food from its cells. Such fungi attack important crops such as corn and wheat. A few parasitic fungi use animals as their hosts. Human conditions such as athlete's foot and ringworm are caused by parasitic fungi.

Another way some fungi obtain their nutrition is by forming an association with a plant. About 80 percent of land plants have fungi called **mycorrhizae** [mī′ kō rī zə] growing in close contact with their roots. The fungus absorbs mineral nutrients from the soil and passes them to the roots of the plant. The plant, in turn, provides the fungus with food. Most land plants cannot survive without their fungal partners.

20-3 Reproduction in Fungi

Many fungi reproduce asexually. The most important method of asexual reproduction is the production of spores. The tips of a hypha become specialized to produce spores. Many fungal spores are very small and are carried through the air or water over long distances. If a spore lands in an environment with adequate food and moisture, it can grow into a new mycelium. This ability to produce many airborne spores is an important factor in the wide distribution of fungi.

Most fungi also reproduce sexually. In fact, the parts of a fungus with which you are most familiar are reproductive structures. The visible portions of many fungi are reproductive structures called **fruiting bodies**. For example, mushrooms are fruiting bodies. Fruiting bodies release spores produced by sexual reproduction.

Typically, the life cycle of a fungus involves a haploid and a diploid stage. The diploid stage is usually very short. The nuclei of fungal mycelia are usually haploid. The life cycles of the different kinds of fungi are described in the next lesson.

CHECKPOINT ◆

1. A mycelium is made up of branching _____.
2. The cell walls of fungi contain the carbohydrate called
   _____.
3. In what way are saprobic fungi useful in the environment?
4. By what process do fungi obtain their nutrition?
5. What is a fruiting body?
▶ 6. Certain kinds of mushrooms grow only at the base of a particular species of tree. Explain why this happens.
▶ 7. Bracket fungi grow on the sides of trees. Where is the mycelium of these fungi?

▶ Denotes a question that involves *interpreting* and *applying* concepts.

VARIETY OF FUNGI

The organisms in the Kingdom Fungi show a wide range of form. Many different ways of classifying fungi are currently used. The classification of fungi in this text is based on their respective life cycles. All fungi are nonmotile throughout their life cycle, lacking cells with cilia or flagella.

The life cycle diagrams in this chapter are based on the pattern established in the previous chapter. The haploid part of the life cycle is shown in yellow and the diploid part in blue. This pattern will continue in later chapters.

20-4 Zygomycota

Most fungi in the division **Zygomycota** [zī′ gō mī cō tə] are terrestrial saprobes. The common bread mold, *Rhizopus* [rī′ zō pùs], is the best-known member of the group. In spite of its common name, *Rhizopus* can grow on many different foods. Its mycelium has several specialized types of hyphae. Horizontal hyphae grow across the surface of the food. In places where it contacts the surface, a branching network of hyphae grows into the food. These rootlike fibers are called **rhizoids** [rī′ zoidz]. Rhizoids anchor the fungus and absorb water and other substances. The horizontal hyphae and rhizoids do not have cross walls.

Rhizopus reproduces asexually by growing vertical hyphae, or stalks. Black spore cases form on top of these stalks. Each spore case contains millions of spores. Each spore may have one or more nuclei. The spores may be carried long distances by air currents.

Section Objectives

D *Diagram* the life cycle of a bread mold.

E *Describe* the characteristics of fungi in the division Ascomycota.

F *Give examples* showing how specific sac fungi and club fungi affect humans.

G *List* the characteristics that make fungi in the division Basidiomycota different from other fungi.

H *State* why some fungi are placed in a separate division.

I *Explain* why lichens are unique organisms.

Figure 20-3   All fungi are heterotrophs. The bread mold, *Rhizopus*, breaks down and absorbs carbohydrates from bread. *Inset:* Spore cases appear as black spheres in this magnified view.

Fungi   **339**

Figure 20-4 The life cycle of *Rhizopus* has an asexual and a sexual phase. Sexual reproduction occurs only between plus and minus mating types. When the two mating types are close to each other, they form outgrowths that come together and develop gametes. The gametes unite and form a zygospore.

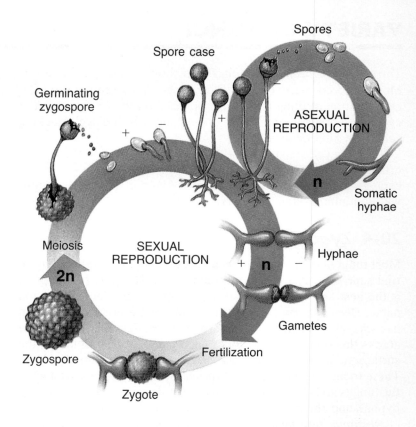

Sexual reproduction generally occurs when conditions become unfavorable for growth. Sexual reproduction in *Rhizopus* involves two genetically different hyphae. The two types of hyphae are called plus and minus mating types. The two mating types appear to be identical, but have slight chemical differences. When hyphae from plus and minus types touch, their nuclei fuse. This fusion results in a diploid structure called a **zygospore** [zī′ gō spor].

The zygospore remains dormant until conditions become favorable again. At that time the diploid zygote undergoes meiosis. A hypha with haploid nuclei grows from the zygospore, thus beginning a new generation.

20-5 Ascomycota

All members of the division **Ascomycota** [as′ kō mī cō tə] have a sacklike reproductive structure called an **ascus** [as′ kəs]. For this reason, these fungi are commonly called sac fungi.

The hyphae of sac fungi have partial cross walls. Each cross wall has a large hole that permits nuclei and cytoplasm to move from one cell to another. Nutrients absorbed into one cell can be transported to another.

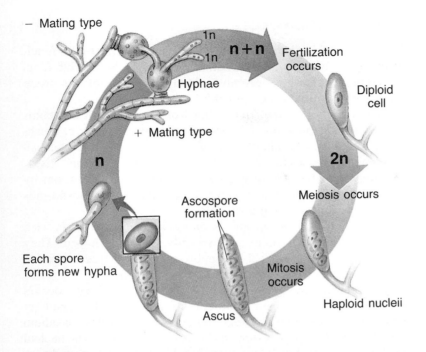

- Mating type

1n
1n
n + n Fertilization occurs

Hyphae

Diploid cell

+ Mating type

n

2n

Meiosis occurs

Ascospore formation

Mitosis occurs

Each spore forms new hypha

Haploid nucleii

Ascus

Figure 20-5 The sexual phase of a sac fungus involves the formation of spores in an ascus. The haploid spores are produced from diploid hyphae that undergo meiosis.

Figure 20-5 illustrates the life cycle of a typical sac fungus. Sexual reproduction begins as in the Zygomycota. Hyphae from two mating types touch. This forms a mycelium with two haploid nuclei per cell—one nucleus from each parent. In certain cells, the haploid nuclei fuse to form a diploid cell. The diploid stage is very short, with meiosis taking place immediately. The haploid nuclei then divide by mitosis and eventually become spores. When the spores break free from the ascus, they can develop into new mycelia to start the life cycle over again.

Many of the sac fungi are important to humans. *Neurospora* is a species used in many laboratories for genetic research. Truffles and morels are prized edible sac fungi. Yeasts also belong to this division. Only occasionally do they reproduce sexually and form an ascus. Asexually, yeast reproduce by **budding**, or pinching off part of the cell to form a new cell. Humans have used yeasts to produce bread and alcoholic beverages for thousands of years.

Not all the sac fungi are beneficial to humans. Some yeasts cause infections of the skin, lungs, and kidneys. Many are parasitic and cause considerable damage. American elm trees are parasitized by a sac fungus that causes Dutch elm disease. This disease is carried by beetles and enters the elms through wounds in the bark. The North American chestnut trees have been similarly damaged by a sac fungus disease. The disease of plants called ergot is caused by a parasite on rye. Ergot poisoning in humans causes nervous spasms and psychotic delusions. Biologists are working on ways to halt the spread of these diseases.

CONSUMER BIOLOGY

The distinctive flavors of many cheeses are caused by fungi. Some of these cheeses are Roquefort, Brie, Stilton, and Camembert.

Figure 20-6 The unicellular yeasts reproduce asexually by budding.

Many mushrooms make toxic poisons. Many cases of mushroom poisoning in humans occur each year. Most of the poisoning is caused by people who mistake members of the genus *Amanita* for edible species. The dangers of eating wild mushrooms cannot be stressed too much.

20-6 *Basidiomycota*

The division **Basidiomycota** [bə sid′ ē ō mī cō tə], or club fungi, includes mushrooms, shelf fungi, and puffballs. Some club fungi are edible; others are poisonous. Many members of this group are saprobes; others are parasites.

The mushroom is the fruiting body of the fungus. Mushrooms appear from a spreading network of underground hyphae. Mushrooms originate as a minute ball of interwoven hyphae. This ball of hyphae increases in size and develops into the "button" stage. The immature button stage grows rapidly into a mushroom by absorbing large amounts of water. This is the reason mushrooms are often seen following a rainfall.

The shape of a mushroom is one characteristic that is used to identify it. Mushrooms are typically umbrella-shaped. They usually consist of a stalk that supports a disclike structure called the cap. Beneath its cap are numerous thin **gills**.

The reproductive phase in the life cycle of the fungus occurs on the gill surface. Lining the gill surface are club-shaped reproductive cells called **basidia**. When two nuclei in a basidium fuse, a diploid nucleus is formed. Meiosis then occurs. The haploid nuclei move into four reproductive cells at the end of stalks on the basidium. These haploid cells are spores. Each mushroom can produce millions of spores.

An important group of club fungi are the parasitic **rusts**. Different rust species damage valuable crops such as wheat, corn, oats, and barley. Rusts have very complex life cycles. They are complex because rusts have more than one host. One part of the wheat rust life cycle for example, is in the wheat plant and another part is in the barberry bush. Destruction of the barberry bush is the best way to control wheat rust.

Figure 20-7 The fruiting bodies of two kinds of fungus are products of sexual reproduction. *Left:* Mushrooms sprout from an underground mycelium. *Right:* Bracket fungi grow from the side of sick or dead trees.

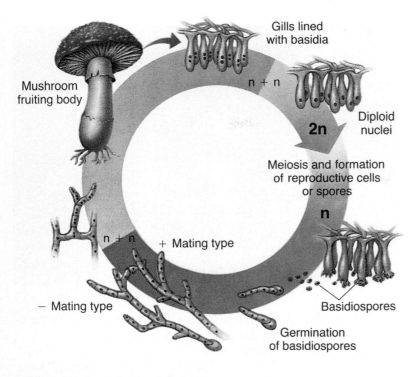

Gills lined
with basidia

n + n

2n

Diploid
nuclei

Mushroom
fruiting body

Meiosis and formation
of reproductive cells
or spores

n

n + n   + Mating type

− Mating type

Basidiospores

Germination
of basidiospores

Figure 20-8 A mushroom is a tightly interwoven mass of hyphae. It forms from the fusion of hyphae from two different mating types. Haploid spores are produced on the hyphae lining the gills of the mushroom. A mushroom may produce millions of spores.

20-7 Imperfect Fungi

Some organisms are very difficult to classify. The fungi that fit this description are placed in a group called the "Imperfect Fungi." This group contains the fungi in which sexual reproduction has never been observed. Although some species never reproduce sexually, others belong to this group only temporarily. Any of these species will be placed in another division when a sexual stage is observed. In fact, many species are moved out of this group each year.

Penicillium and *Aspergillis* are well-known members of this group. These are among the common blue and green molds you may have seen growing on food. These molds also help produce products like soy sauce and Roquefort cheese. *Penicillium* is the genus that produces the antibiotic penicillin.

20-8 Lichens

Another group that is difficult to classify are lichens. A **lichen** is not a single organism, but an association of two different organisms. Two organisms that live in close association are said to be **symbiotic** [sim bī ot′ ik]. Each lichen is a symbiotic association of a fungus and an autotrophic organism. The autotroph usually is a green alga, or a cyanobacterium. Both the fungus and the autotroph benefit from their association. The fungus keeps the

Figure 20-9 *Aspergillis* produces many asexual spores at the end of a long stalk. Some species of *Aspergillis* are harmful, whereas others are beneficial to humans.

lichen from drying out and attaches the organism to a surface. The autotroph supplies the lichen with food.

Lichens grow in places where few other organisms can live. They often grow on bare rocks and on tree bark. Lichens have been found in the coldest and driest valleys of Antarctica.

Lichens often are the first organisms to inhabit an area. As lichens grow on rocks, they secrete acids which break down the rock. Thus lichens change rock into small pockets of soil. Other plants are able to grow in these pockets.

CHECKPOINT ◆

8. The only diploid cell in the life cycle of bread mold is called a _____.
9. Are ascospores diploid or haploid?
10. To what division do yeasts belong and why?
11. Give an example of a parasitic sac fungus.
12. The membranes of a mushroom cap which produce spores are called _____.
13. What characteristic do all Imperfect Fungi have in common?
14. When two organisms are closely associated as in lichens, the association is called _____.
▶ 15. Suppose you have a mycelium growing in an agar dish. How would you determine if your mycelium is a plus or minus mating type?
▶ 16. Mushrooms often are seen growing in almost perfect circles called "fairy rings." Explain this observation.

▶ Denotes a question that involves *interpreting* and *applying* concepts.

FUNGI AND LICHENS

Objectives and Skills

☐ *Observe* and *draw* diagrams of yeast.
☐ *Observe* stages in the asexual reproduction of yeast cells.
☐ *Prepare* and *examine* microscope slides of *Aspergillis* hyphae and reproductive structures.

Materials

slides	suspension of yeast and
coverslips	water (fresh)
compound	suspension of yeast in a
microscope	6% aqueous solution of
forceps	molasses (24 hours
medicine	old)
droppers	culture of *Aspergillis*
methylene blue	several lichen species
stain	

Procedure and Observations

1. Read all instructions for this laboratory activity before you begin your work.
2. Put one drop of methylene blue stain on each of two slides. Set the slides aside at your desk while the drops dry completely. You will use these slides later.
3. Use forceps to remove some of the *Aspergillis* from its culture dish. Place it in a drop of water on a clean glass slide. Add a coverslip. Use low power to find hyphae and reproductive structures. Change to high power. On a separate piece of paper, draw several hyphae and reproductive structures.
4. Observe the two stock cultures of yeast. One was made up today with tap water. The other was made up 24 hours ago with a solution of 6% molasses. Pay close attention to differences in the stock solutions of yeast. Record your observations.

5. Take a drop of yeast and water suspension and put it on top of the dried methylene blue of one of the slides you prepared in Step 2. Add a coverslip. Observe the yeast cells under high power. Draw several typical cells.
6. Remove a drop of yeast/molasses suspension. Place it on top of the methylene blue stain of your second slide. Observe under high power. Look for signs of budding. Draw some cells in various stages of budding.
7. Place a small portion of a lichen in a drop of water on a clean glass slide. Use the point of your forceps to break the lichen into small pieces. Add a coverslip. Examine the slide using low power under the microscope. Locate the fungal hyphae. Draw a few typical threads. Also locate several cells or filaments that have a green pigment. Draw them.
8. Repeat Step 7 with other kinds of lichens.
9. Before leaving the laboratory, clean up all your materials and wash your hands thoroughly.

Analysis and Conclusions

1. What kind of reproduction is represented by the budding yeast cells?
2. Compare the number of budding yeast cells from the two different suspensions.
3. Explain the observations you made about the number of budding cells in each suspension.
4. How does the structure of yeast differ from the structure of *Aspergillis*?
5. Were there any cross walls in the *Aspergillis* hyphae?
6. *Aspergillis* is placed with the Imperfect Fungi. What conclusions can you draw about the nature of the reproductive structures in this fungus?
7. Where in the lichen structure are the fungal hyphae located?

CHAPTER REVIEW

Summary

‣ Fungi are spore-bearing, heterotrophic organisms. They have nonmotile cells throughout their life cycles. Fungi show mycelial growth.

‣ The fungal mycelium consists of a network of hyphae. In the Ascomycota and Basidiomycota, the hyphae have cross walls.

‣ Most fungi are saprobes, parasites, and mycorrhizae. They feed by secreting enzymes into their surroundings and absorbing the digested food.

‣ The method of reproduction is an important characteristic in classifying fungi. The division Zygomycota reproduce when hyphae with opposite mating types touch. A diploid zygospore is formed. Fungi in the division Ascomycota form a saclike fruiting body. Club fungi differ from other groups by having reproductive structures called basidia.

‣ Some fungi have never been observed to reproduce sexually. These fungi are placed in a group called Imperfect Fungi.

‣ Lichens are symbiotic organisms that consist of a fungus and an autotrophic alga or cynaobacterium that live together. The fungus keeps the lichen from drying out, and the autotroph supplies food to the entire organism.

Vocabulary

absorption	hyphae
Ascomycota	lichen
ascus	multinucleate
Basidiomycota	mycelium
basidium	mycorrhizae
budding	rhizoid
chitin	rust
cross walls	symbiotic
fruiting body	Zygomycota
fungi	zygospore
gill	

Concept Mapping

Construct a concept map for fungi structure and reproduction. Include the following terms: hyphae, mycelium, cell wall, cross wall, no cross wall, spores, fruiting body, chitin, partial cross wall, and multinucleate. Use additional terms as you need them.

Review

1. A _____ is a network of branching hyphae.
2. What is the most important difference between fungi and plants?
3. How would you describe the chromosome number of the nuclei in most fungal hyphae?
4. Give an example of a parasitic fungus.
5. With what kinds of organisms are mycorrhizae associated?
6. The asexual reproductive cells of fungi are called _____.
7. Give an example of a fruiting body.
8. What part of the life cycle of a bread mold is diploid?
9. _____ are the rootlike hyphae of bread molds.
10. How do the hyphae of sac fungi differ from those of bread molds?
11. Give an example of a harmful sac fungus.
12. In mushrooms, reproductive spores are produced by special cells called _____.
13. Name the club fungi that are economically important plant parasites.
14. In what group are fungi with no known sexual reproduction placed?
15. What two kinds of organisms make up lichens?
16. What effect do lichens have on the rocks where they grow?
17. What compounds do lichens make?

Complete the following analogies:

18. Fungus is to _____ as amoeba is to phagocytosis.
19. *Rhizopus* is to Zygomycota as _____ is to Basidiomycota.
20. Ascus is to morel as _____ is to mushroom.
21. _____ is to *Rhizopus* as parasite is to saprobe.
22. List the characteristics that distinguish fungi from plants and explain why a separate kingdom was created for fungi.
23. Explain the difference between a saprobe and a parasite.

Interpret and Apply

24. Why do you think fungi were once placed in the plant kingdom?
25. Explain the difference between absorption and phagocytosis.
26. In which fungus groups is contact between plus and minus mating types a regular feature of the life cycle?
27. Why are mycorrhizae not considered parasites?
28. Compare the life cycle of Rhizopus to the green alga, *Spirogyra*.
29. How is the production of dormant spores an adaptation for *Rhizopus*?
30. What characteristic of yeast makes it an unusual fungus?
31. Most mushroom mycelia grow in the soil. Why do mushroom fruiting bodies grow above ground?
32. How is it a disadvantage for some rust fungi to have two separate host organisms?
33. To a taxonomist, the Imperfect Fungi and the Protist Kingdom are similar. What do they have in common?

Critical Thinking

34. In what ways does an ascus differ from a basidium?
35. Other than lichens, find another example in this chapter in which the fungus and host organism benefit each other.
36. Lichens are called pioneer organisms in some environments. Based on what you know about these organisms, explain why the term *pioneer* may be appropriate.
37. When yeast cells absorb sugar as a food, how do they extract energy? Why does this process make them unusual among other eukaryotic organisms? (Hint: refer back to Chapter 6.)
38. What sort of chemical differences might explain how plus and minus mating types of hyphae would recognize each other?
39. A single puffball can produce millions of spores. Each spore is capable of growing into a new fungus. Why would an organism produce so many potential offspring?
40. Doctors have learned to use penicillin to control human diseases. What function could penicillin have for the fungus in its natural environment?
41. The classification system should reflect evolutionary relationships. Why do *Pennicilium* and lichens present a problem for taxonomists?
42. In most lichens, it is impossible to separate the fungus and the autotroph and grow them separately in the laboratory. Propose a hypothesis to explain this observation.

ISSUES in Bioethics

AIDS TESTING LAW PASSED

Case Study 1

Your state is about to pass a bill that makes it mandatory for couples applying for a marriage license to show that they have been tested with the HIV antibody test for AIDS. The test must be performed within 30 days of the application for a license. Couples may go to their own private doctor for the test. The doctor then provides a certificate stating they were tested. The certificate does not show the results of the test, but it does state that both parties have been informed of the results.

Doctors are required to report the HIV positive results and ask about previous sexual partners of the individuals that test positive. The law does not cover counseling and does not restrict any person who tests positive from getting married.

False positive test results can occur and a retest must be done in 3–6 months. Also, antibodies for the HIV virus may not show up for as long as a year or more after the AIDS virus enters the body.

1. List three problems you see with this law.
2. Write a letter to your congressional representative stating your opinion of the law and whether it should be supported.

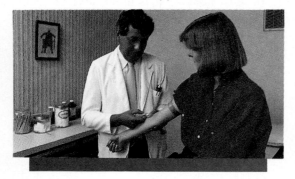

3. List three reasons why someone might not agree with your opinion.

Case Study 2

Biological warfare is the use of microorganisms to destroy people, animals, or crops. In 1925, the Geneva Convention prohibited the use of biological warfare. However, it is known that the United States government and governments of other countries have conducted research on biological warfare.

Recently, a biological research station developed a virus that could be released into the air using aerosol packages or artillery shells. The virus would make much of the population ill and many would die. Along with the virus, biologists have also developed a cure, or antidote. The problem is that they do not have a human test group on which they can try the antidote.

1. Assuming human testing were allowed, how would you select people to participate in the experiment?
2. Give two reasons supporting the need for biological warfare.
3. Give two reasons why biological warfare is wrong.
4. In 1971, the United States and the Soviet Union adopted an agreement to destroy all stored biological weapons, but the destruction has been slow. What problems do you see in destroying these weapons?
5. If an organism that was developed for biological warfare were accidentally released, who should be held responsible?

UNIT REVIEW 3

Synthesis

1. The opening pages of this unit contain four photographs. These photographs illustrate a common theme to the chapters of the unit. Identify the theme and describe how it relates to what you studied.

2. **Structures Is Related to Function:** Describe any similarities and differences in the reproduction of monerans and the reproduction of protists.

3. **Life Forms Are Interconnected:** Give an example from monerans, protists, and fungi of symbiosis that benefits both organisms involved in the relationship.

4. **Levels of Organization:** Which kingdoms in this unit have members that are autotrophic? Give an example of an autotroph from each kingdom.

5. **Levels of Organization:** Which kingdoms in this unit have members that are anaerobic? What do anaerobic organisms seem to have in common?

6. **Unity and Diversity:** What is the fundamental distinction between monerans and all other living things?

7. **Life Forms Are Interconnected:** Name a plant or animal disease that is caused by a moneran, a protist, and a fungus.

8. **Life Forms Are Interconnected:** Give an example of one organism that is beneficial to humans from each of the three kingdoms covered in this unit.

9. **Levels of Organization:** In single-celled organisms, each cell must carry out all of the functions necessary for life. In multicellular organisms, cells may be specialized to carry out particular functions. What are some of the advantages of cell specialization? Are there any disadvantages?

10. **Structure Is Related to Function:** List the ways organisms from the moneran, protist, and fungus kingdoms obtain food.

Critical Thinking

11. **Process of Science:** Chapter 2 describes the characteristics that distinguish living things from nonliving things. State which characteristics apply to viruses. Based on your analysis, are viruses alive? Explain.

12. **Adaptation and Evolution:** What evidence can you give to support the statement that monerans are more evolutionarily primitive than either protists or fungi?

13. **Adaptation and Evolution:** Some taxonomists argue that fungi evolved from plants and have lost the ability to carry on photosynthesis. Others argue that fungi and plants evolved from different ancestors. Plants probably evolved from a chlorophyte ancestor whereas fungi evolved from some nonphotosynthetic protist ancestor. What evidence from the text can you give to support either side of this controversy?

14. **Levels of Organization:** Ideally, a classification system should indicate evolutionary relationships among organisms. Cite evidence from this unit showing that the classification system as presently constructed succeeds in some ways and fails in others to meet the ideal.

15. **Process of Science:** Suppose someone proposed searching for a way to destroy all the prokaryotic organisms on Earth. In doing so, all diseases caused by these organisms would be totally eliminated. Using evidence from your reading, state why this might not be a very good idea.

Additional Reading

Gallo, Robert C., "The AIDS Virus." *Scientific American.* January 1987.

Scott, Andrew. *Pirates of the Cell: The Story of Viruses from Molecule to Microbe.* New York: Basil Blackwell, 1987.

PLANTS

Fruit stand in Bolivia

Logs transported to paper mills

Ruby-throated hummingbird

Sunlit leaves of
quaking aspen

Chapter 21 **Seed Plants**
Angiosperms
Flowers
Fruits and Dispersal
Gymnosperms

Chapter 22 **Plant Structure and**
Development
Development of the Plant Body
Plant Body Organization
Vegetative Reproduction

Chapter 23 **Roots and Stems**
Root Systems and Growth
Stem Structures and Functions
Conduction of Water and Food

Chapter 24 **Leaves**
Leaf Structure and Function
Leaf Modifications

Chapter 25 **Plant Growth and**
Response
Patterns of Plant Growth
Plant Response

Chapter 26 **Plant Diversity and**
Evolution
Plant Kingdom
Bryophytes
Spore-Bearing Vascular Plants

SEED PLANTS

Overview

ANGIOSPERMS

21-1   Characteristics of Angiosperms

21-2   Monocots and Dicots

FLOWERS

21-3   Flower Structure

21-4   Ovule and Pollen Formation

21-5   Pollination

21-6   Fertilization

FRUITS AND DISPERSAL

21-7   Fruit Development and Structure

21-8   Dispersal

GYMNOSPERMS

21-9   Conifers

21-10   Life Cycle of a Pine

21-11   Other Gymnosperms

Is a corn kernel a fruit?

ANGIOSPERMS

Consider a typical breakfast. Orange juice comes from oranges picked off a semitropical tree. Cereal is made from grains growing in expansive fields in the central part of North America. Milk comes from cows that eat grain. Oranges and grain are products of flowering plants, or **angiosperms** [an′ jē ə sperms]. Except for fish and other seafood, it is difficult to think of a type of food that did not come, directly or indirectly, from angiosperms.

21-1 Characteristics of Angiosperms

There are thousands of different kinds of flowering plants. They come in a variety of sizes, and are found in a number of different environments. They range from tiny pond-surface plants, which are less than a millimeter long, to trees 100 meters tall. You can find flowering plants in tropical rain forests, deserts, on mountainsides, and in windowboxes along city streets.

Despite the variety of angiosperms, they all have one feature in common. Angiosperms all produce seeds in reproductive structures called **flowers**. Then, as the seeds mature, the flower changes into a *fruit*. In fact, the name *angiosperm* means "covered seed." Mature seeds are scattered, or **dispersed**, along with the fruit.

21-2 Monocots and Dicots

How are so many different kinds of flowering plants classified? Do their flowers, fruit, or seeds show any similarities? Botanists

Section Objectives

A *Give examples* of the two groups of seed plants and their uses in your daily life.

B *List* several characteristics of angiosperms.

C *Distinguish* between monocots and dicots.

DO YOU KNOW?

Information: Duckweed is a common plant in ponds. This tiny angiosperm floats on the surface of the water. The entire plant is smaller than a dime.

Figure 21-1 Many breakfast foods are products of flowering plants.

Table 21-1

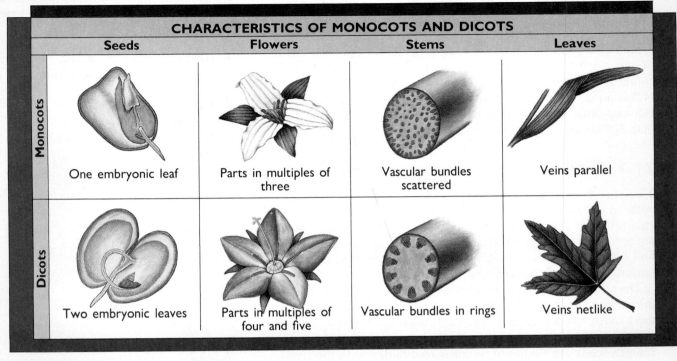

CHARACTERISTICS OF MONOCOTS AND DICOTS			
Seeds	**Flowers**	**Stems**	**Leaves**
Monocots One embryonic leaf	Parts in multiples of three	Vascular bundles scattered	Veins parallel
Dicots Two embryonic leaves	Parts in multiples of four and five	Vascular bundles in rings	Veins netlike

are able to divide the 235 000 species of angiosperms into two large groups based on the structure of their seeds.

Inside the seeds of angiosperms are tiny embryonic leaves called **cotyledons** [kot ə lē′ dunz]. The seeds of one group of angiosperms have one cotyledon. These angiosperms are called monocotyledons, or **monocots.** Other angiosperms have two cotyledons. These plants are called dicotyledons, or **dicots.** Differences between monocots and dicots are shown in Table 21-1.

CHECKPOINT ◆

1. Name some environments in which angiosperms are found.
2. What is the major characteristic of angiosperms?
3. Why was the flower an advantage to early angiosperms?
▶ 4. Is the lettuce plant a monocot or a dicot?
▶ 5. Explain why hamburgers would not exist without angiosperms.
▶ 6. List several angiosperm products found in your refrigerator.

▶ Denotes a question that involves *interpreting* and *applying* concepts.

FLOWERS

Flowers are among the most beautiful of nature's treasures. Their astounding array of colors dazzles the eyes, and their lovely fragrances perfume the air. The influence of flowers is everywhere. People give flowers on important occasions. Artists paint flowers; poets write about them. Flowers are used to make perfume and create gardens in a window box. In many places, the explosion of flowers in spring is delightful proof that winter has ended.

Flowers are very effective reproductive structures. Flowers produce gametes, and provide a place for them to unite and form a seed. Thus, the processes of meiosis and fertilization occur here. As you study the organization of a flower, note how its structure complements these functions.

21-3 Flower Structure

Flowers form at the end of a specialized branch of a plant. The tip of the branch is called the **receptacle**. Attached to the receptacle are four parts: sepals, petals, stamens and carpels. Figure 21-2 shows the arrangement of these parts.

The outermost part of the flower is made of the sepals and petals. Both of these kinds of structures appear leaflike. **Sepals** usually are green; **petals** are usually white or brightly colored. Sepals being the outermost part, commonly enclose the flower before it opens.

A **stamen** is the male reproductive part of a flower. It usually consists of a long filament topped with an **anther**. Inside the anther are numerous sacs in which **pollen** grains are produced.

In the middle of the flower is the female reproductive structure called the **carpel**. At the base of the carpel is the **ovary**. The ovary is sectioned into compartments that contain **ovules**. These are the structures that develop into **seeds**. Above the ovary is a tubular structure called the **style.** On top of the style is the **stigma**, the place where pollen first collects.

Flowers vary in the number, color, shape, and arrangement of their parts. Most flowers have both male and female parts. Such flowers are referred to as *perfect*. In contrast, some flowers have only male or only female parts and are termed *imperfect*. Some plants, like oak trees, have male and female flowers on the same plant. Other plant species have male and female flowers on separate plants.

The arrangement of flowers also varies among different kinds of plants. Some plants have flowers that occur singly, like tulips. Others have flowers in a cluster called an *inflorescence*.

Section Objectives

D *Name* and *state* the functions of the parts of a flower.

E *Explain* the formation of ovules and pollen.

F *Relate* several adaptations of flowers to their role in pollination.

G *Describe* the fertilization process in angiosperms.

Figure 21-2 The parts of a flower. Note how the parts are arranged. Flowers vary in size, shape, composition, and number of each part. A flower's structure is suited to its function in reproduction.

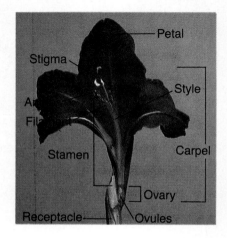

Information: Sperm-containing structures usually are not as large as egg-containing structures. A sperm-containing structure carries only a gamete, while an egg-containing structure must carry both gametes and food supply. Also, the number of sperm produced is always much larger than the number of eggs produced by a given species.

The characteristics of flowers are used to classify them. Monocots and dicots can be distinguished easily by differences in flower structure. Monocots usually have flower parts in multiples of three. For example, lilies usually have six sepals, six petals, and six stamens. Flower parts of dicots usually are in multiples of four and five. Look again at the photographs of flowering plants in this book. Can you distinguish between the monocots and dicots?

21-4 Ovule and Pollen Formation

The life cycle of a flowering plant consists of two distinct generations. The gametophyte generation is limited to the cells that produce ovules and pollen. The sporophyte generation consists of the structures you observe when you see a flowering plant.

The formation of eggs is diagramed in Figure 21-3. Within each newly formed ovule is a diploid cell. This diploid cell undergoes meiosis to form four haploid *megaspores*. Notice that of the four cells, three degenerate and only one remains. The remaining haploid cell undergoes three mitotic divisions in a row to form eight haploid nuclei. Three of the nuclei migrate to one end of the ovule, and three migrate to the opposite end. Each of these six nuclei are then surrounded by cell membranes and become separate cells. The middle cell of the three cells near the opening is the *egg cell*. The two nuclei left in the middle of the ovule are called *polar nuclei*.

Figure 21-3 The diagram shows the process of forming an egg cell within an ovule. The ovule is the female gametophyte in the life cycle of angiosperms.

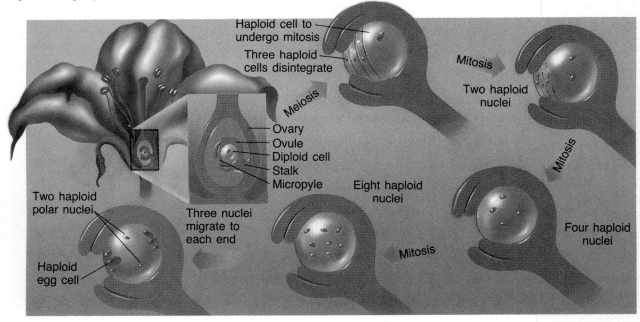

Recall from Chapter 19 that algae also have alternation of generations. Compared to algae, seed plants have a gametophyte generation that is very small. The mature ovule is the female gametophyte in angiosperms. When fully developed, the gametophyte consists of only two polar nuclei and the egg.

You can follow the process of pollen formation illustrated in Figure 21-5. Each anther contains large numbers of diploid cells, each of which undergoes meiosis to form four haploid *microspores*. Each microspore then undergoes mitosis once (in contrast to three times in the female), forming two cells within the spore wall. Thus each pollen grain contains two cells, the *tube cell* and the *generative cell*. The generative cell eventually produces sperm after it reaches the stigma. Pollen grains are released when the anther dries and splits open.

21-5 Pollination

Plants, unlike animals, cannot move from place to place to find food or shelter, or to reproduce. Flowering plants have adapted to their rooted condition by producing "moving" parts. One "moving" part is the sperm-producing pollen. Pollen moves from an anther to a stigma in a process called **pollination**. Plants use a variety of agents, or **pollinators**, to move pollen from one flower to another. Animals such as bees, bats, birds, and butterflies pollinate many different species of plants. Wind also disperses pollen. The structure of a flower is related to its method of pollination.

Flowering plants attract animal pollinators by supplying them with food. Many pollinators eat pollen or a sugary food, called *nectar*. As pollinators travel from flower to flower seeking food, some of the pollen from one flower is accidentally transferred

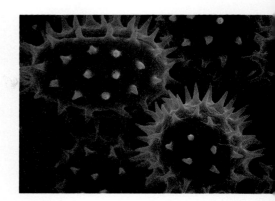

Figure 21-4 SEM photo of pollen grains. Their hard coat contains proteins that allow the stigma of a plant to recognize its own species and continue the process of fertilization.

Figure 21-5 Pollen grains are produced in anthers. Each haploid microspore divides to become a double-celled pollen grain. The generative cell is contained within the tube cell.

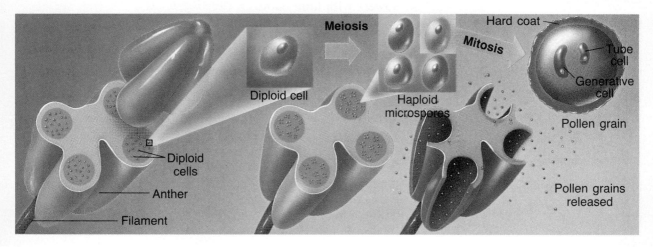

Diploid cell

Meiosis

Haploid microspores

Mitosis

Hard coat

Tube cell

Generative cell

Pollen grain

Diploid cells

Anther

Filament

Pollen grains released

Farmers and home gardeners rely on insect pollination for successful production of many fruit and vegetable crops. Bee colonies are often placed and maintained in artificial hives near orchards to serve as pollinators. The honey they produce is also harvested.

Figure 21-6 Flowers designed to be pollinated by bees often have special markings to help bees recognize them. The "honey guides" on the foxglove flower lead bees to the nectar. Bee flowers often have fused petals that serve as a landing platform.

to the stigma of another flower. Almost all pollinators are very specific, pollinating only certain species of plants. Thus it is more likely that pollen from one species of plant will land on the stigma of another plant of the same species.

A flower's color, odor, size, and shape are related to the specific pollinator of the plant. Many flowers have evolved structures that allow only certain kinds of insects to pollinate them. These insects, in turn, have evolved feeding structures adapted for particular plants. Butterflies and moths have long sucking mouthparts. Flowers that are pollinated by these insects often have petals that form a tube with nectar at the base. The parallel evolution of plants and pollinators was a major factor in the dominance of flowering plants on Earth.

In order for a pollinator to find its specific kind of plant, it must be able to distinguish the plant from many others. One way pollinators do this is by sighting the plant. The way we see flowers is not necessarily the ways bees and hummingbirds do. Many pollinators see colors differently from the way humans do. Bees, for example, cannot distinguish the color red, thus they are rarely found at red flowers. Bees easily distinguish and commonly pollinate blue or yellow flowers. Many flowers have patterns or stripes that direct the bees to the nectar in the center of the flower.

Another way pollinators find their way to a specific kind of plant is by detecting its odor. Many flowers produce sweet-smelling scents that advertise their pollen and nectar. However, not all insects are attracted to sweet-smelling flowers. Flies, for example, are attracted to flowers such as skunk cabbage which have the smell of decaying meat. This also is true for beetles, which usually pollinate white or dull-colored flowers with strong odors. The opposite is true for hummingbirds, which have a poorly developed sense of smell and therefore tend to pollinate flowers with little odor.

Wind is an inefficient means of pollination. To ensure that pollen reaches other plants, wind-pollinated plants produce enormous amounts of pollen. Nearly all of the pollen falls to the ground within 100 meters of the parent plant. Thus, wind pollination is successful only within a fairly large population of plants that grow close together.

Even though pollen is scattered randomly, plants pollinated by wind have evolved a number of structures that increase the chances of success. Grasses and trees such as oak, maple, and birch are examples of wind-pollinated plants. The flowers of these plants usually are small and grow in clusters. Since these plants do not attract animal pollinators, their flowers usually are drab-colored, odorless, and produce no nectar. The petals are small or absent. Wind-pollinated flowers usually have their stamens

Figure 21-7 *Left:* A different kind of "perfume" is produced by eastern skunk cabbage that lures insects to pollinate it. *Right:* Unlike most angiosperms, grass flowers are adapted for wind pollination. Grass flowers usually develop in clusters.

exposed so pollen can easily catch the wind. Grasses characteristically have anthers that hang down and feathery stigmas that increase the number of pollen grains caught by the wind.

Plants do not necessarily need a pollinator to reproduce. In some kinds of plants, pollen from an anther can fertilize eggs in the *same* flower. This is called **self-pollination**. Plants that use this method exclusively are uncommon, but some self-pollination occurs in many kinds of plants. In some plants, pollen grains and ovules mature at different times, making self-pollination impossible.

21-6 Fertilization

If the pollen grain lands on a stigma of the same plant species, a series of events begins. Chemicals in the stigma cause an extension of cytoplasm to grow out of the pollen grain. This extension becomes a structure called the **pollen tube**. As shown in Figure 21-8 on the next page, the tube grows through the cells of the style toward the ovary. The tube cell's nucleus is located at the front of the growing tube.

As the pollen tube grows, changes occur to the generative cell. The generative cell undergoes mitosis, forming two haploid **sperm nuclei**. When the pollen tube reaches the opening to the ovule, the end of the tube pushes through the ovule wall and breaks open. The tube cell's nucleus disintegrates and the two sperm nuclei fertilize the nuclei in the ovule.

CONSUMER BIOLOGY

The development of a single ear of corn depends on the successful fertilization of hundreds of ovules. Carried by wind, pollen grains land on the fine corn silk and pollen tubes grow through each strand to reach the ovules within the ear. Missing kernels in the mature ear are often a result of incomplete fertilization. Assuming the corn has been damaged by insects, people often throw it away.

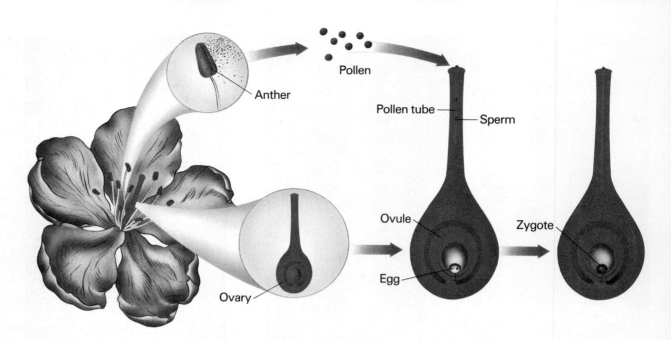

Pollen

Anther

Pollen tube — Sperm

Ovule

Zygote

Egg

Ovary

Figure 21-8 Fertilization in angiosperms occurs when a sperm cell produced in a pollen grain travels through a pollen tube to reach the egg cell in the ovary.

In flowering plants, fertilization involves the fusion of two pairs of nuclei. This type of fertilization is called **double fertilization**. One sperm nucleus fertilizes the egg cell. The resulting diploid zygote divides by mitosis forming an embryo. The second sperm nucleus joins with both polar nuclei to form a single triploid ($3n$) nucleus. Double fertilization is a unique characteristic of angiosperms.

The new triploid cell divides, forming a tissue called **endosperm**. The cells of the endosperm are rich in food—usually oil or starch. These foods nourish the embryo. The white part of popcorn is endosperm tissue. Coconut milk is liquid endosperm. The embryo and its triploid endosperm along with the ovule coverings form a seed.

CHECKPOINT ◆

7. Megaspore is to female as _____ is to male.
8. What is the name of the part of the pistil in which the ovules develop?
9. What structures compose the gametophyte generation? What structures compose the sporophyte generation?
10. Where does fertilization occur in the flower?
▶ 11. A beech tree has small, inconspicuous green flowers. Is it wind-pollinated or insect-pollinated? Explain.
▶ 12. Grasses usually grow in open areas forming vast fields. Explain.

▶ Denotes a question that involves *interpreting* and *applying* concepts.

FRUITS AND DISPERSAL

One of the pleasures of summer is the abundance of fruits available to please our tastes. Sweet strawberries, juicy peaches, and cool watermelons are just a few of nature's summer treats. What is a fruit? From what part of the plant do fruits develop? A tomato is a fruit to a botanist, but is not a fruit to a chef. To a botanist, a **fruit** is a mature ovary, a product of reproduction. To a chef, a fruit usually means a part of a plant that tastes sweet. To a botanist, pea pods, tomatoes, peppers, squashes, and corn are fruits; to a chef they are not.

21-7 Fruit Development and Structure

After fertilization, flower structures change to form fruits. While seeds mature within the ovary, the ovary walls themselves become modified to form the fruit. Fruits that develop from a single ovary in a single flower are called **simple fruits**. Tomatoes, plums, and pears are examples. **Aggregate fruits**, such as raspberries, develop from many different ovaries in a single flower. **Multiple fruits**, such as pineapples, develop from single ovaries of each flower in a cluster.

Section Objectives

H **Classify** various types of fruits on the basis of their structure.

I **Relate** the structural characteristics of several seed types to their modes of dispersal.

Figure 21-9 Flower parts become fruit parts. Ovules mature into seeds. Ovaries ripen into fruit. Different flowers produce different types of fruit.

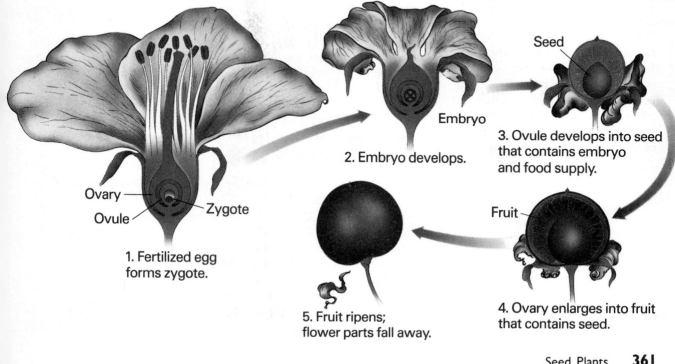

Ovary

Ovule

Zygote

1. Fertilized egg forms zygote.

Embryo

2. Embryo develops.

Seed

3. Ovule develops into seed that contains embryo and food supply.

Fruit

4. Ovary enlarges into fruit that contains seed.

5. Fruit ripens; flower parts fall away.

Figure 21-10 Burdock fruits attach themselves to passing animals or humans with small hooks on the end of each spine.

CONSUMER BIOLOGY

The inventor of velcro took his inspiration from the fruit of the burdock plant. These fruits, which you may know as "hitchhikers," are covered with barbed hooks that adhere to fur and clothing, aiding in their dispersal. The "hooked" side of velcro works the same way.

▶ Denotes a question that involves *interpreting* and *applying* concepts.

In fleshy fruits, the ovary wall thickens into a soft pulp. Once the fruit is ripe, it often has a high sugar content. Not all fruits are fleshy. Dry fruits often are mistaken for seeds.

21-8 Dispersal

Fruits and seeds are other parts of a plant that are "moving" parts. Seed-containing fruits are spread by wind, water, and animals. Fruits may be grouped according to how their seeds are dispersed.

Many plants produce light-weight fruits and seeds that are easily dispersed by wind. Dandelions and milkweed are perhaps the best-known examples. These plants produce fruits with a "parachute" of fibers that are so fine that even a slight breeze bears them aloft. Maple trees have winged fruits called samaras that are adapted for wind dispersal. In tumbleweeds, the entire adult plant breaks loose from its roots and is blown across the landscape. Seeds are jarred free as the plant rolls. In open country, a tumbleweed can travel for many miles.

The fruits and seeds of some plants are dispersed by water. The coconut discussed at the beginning of this chapter is an example. Some plants that live on hillsides and mountain slopes depend upon rain to disperse their seeds. Many seeds are washed downhill and begin to grow in valleys.

Many fruits and seeds are eaten and dispersed by animals. The soft, sweet, and fleshy fruits appeal to animals as much as they do to humans. Animals often carry fruits to a safe place to eat them. Sometimes they drop seeds as they eat the fruit. Many times seeds pass unharmed through an animal's digestive tract. These seeds are deposited in the animal's droppings, often a long way from the parent plant. Not only are the seeds dispersed, but they are left with a supply of fertilizer.

CHECKPOINT ◆

13. What kind of fruits develop from single ovaries in a flower cluster?
14. From what part of a flower are most fruits derived?
15. In addition to protecting the seeds, what is the major function of fruits?
16. Give an example of a fleshy fruit that develops from an enlarged receptacle.
▶ 17. What type of fruit is a plum?
▶ 18. The seeds of the brightly-colored grape are dispersed by _____ .

GYMNOSPERMS

If you ski, majestic pine and spruce trees, covered with snow, are a familiar sight. Chances are, part of the structure of your home and some of your furniture are made of pine. Lumber from fir trees is often used to build porches, decks, and wooden walks.

Pine, spruce, and fir trees are members of a large group of plants called gymnosperms. **Gymnosperms** represent all seed plants that do not form flowers. Plants in this group are not related by ancestry.

Members of this group do not develop flowers, thus they do not have seeds enclosed within a fruit. In fact, the name *gymnosperm* literally means "naked seed." You already know something about fertilization and pollination in flowering plants. Now you can learn how the same processes occur in other seed plants.

21-9 Conifers

By far the most numerous and widespread of the gymnosperms are **conifers**. They are cone-bearing woody trees and shrubs. The leaves are usually needlelike. This shape helps reduce water loss during dry seasons. Most conifers are evergreen, they do not drop their leaves in the autumn. However, conifers do shed their leaves, but not all at once. Most conifers replace their needles every two to four years.

Conifers grow in many different environments. They thrive in cool climates, poor soil, the moist air of the seashore, and the harsh conditions of mountains. Conifers form vast forests in northern Europe and North America. Among the 600 species of conifers are pines, firs, spruces, cedars, hemlocks, and sequoias.

Conifers produce many useful products. They are a major source of lumber, paper, and turpentine. The seeds of some pines, called pine nuts, are used in Middle Eastern and other Mediterranean cooking. They also are eaten by the Indians of the Southwest.

21-10 Life Cycle of a Pine

The life cycle of a pine is diagramed in Figure 21-12 on the next page. Pine trees produce two different kinds of cones. Male **pollen cones** and female **seed cones** are produced on the same tree, although usually on separate branches.

Pine seeds develop on the shelflike scales of a female seed cone. Inside the seed cones are *megasporangia*. Cells in the megasporangia undergo meiosis to produce megaspores. The megaspores then develop into female gametophytes. The female gametophytes produce eggs that are ready for fertilization.

Figure 21-11 Conifers like these spruce trees are adapted to snow-covered mountains. How are the angles of the branches an adaptation to heavy snow and ice?

Seed Plants **363**

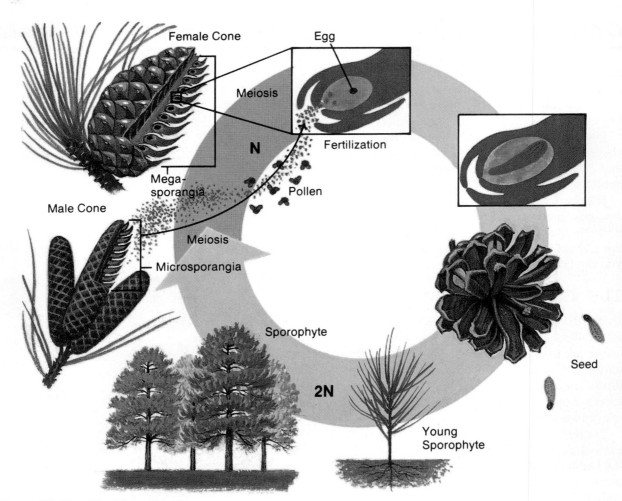

Figure 21-12 The life cycle of a pine occurs over two years. The pine tree, or adult sporophyte part of the life cycle grows cones that produce two different kinds of spores. The spores undergo meiosis, producing gametes. The sperm produced by germinating pollen grains reach the egg by a pollen tube. Thus, water is not necessary for fertilization. This is a major advantage of the seed plants.

Look at the male pollen cone diagramed in Figure 21-12. On the scales are pollen sacs called *microsporangia*. Inside the sacs reproductive cells undergo meiosis to produce microspores. The microspores develop into pollen grains.

Pollination occurs each spring as male cones release millions of pollen grains. Some grains land between the scales of the female cone directly on the ovule. When this occurs, the pollen grain then produces a pollen tube. Each pollen tube grows toward a female gametophyte. Within the tube, sperm are produced. A year may pass before the sperm fertilize the egg.

Inside the seed cone, a fertilized egg develops into a zygote. The zygote absorbs food from the female gametophyte, which develops as an initial food supply. The zygote develops into an embryo. A seed coat forms around the embryo and food supply. When the seeds are ripe, the woody cone opens. Each seed has papery wings, which help the wind to disperse it.

If a seed lands in a good location, it will begin to grow. An embryonic root pushes into the soil, and the young stem pushes upwards. A pine seedling absorbs the food stored by the female gametophyte until it is able to form leaves, make chlorophyll, and begin photosynthesis. If conditions are suitable, it will grow into the familiar pine tree.

21-11 Other Gymnosperms

The *Ginkgo*, or maidenhair tree, is the only surviving species of a once-large group. Ginkgoes grow to be tall trees, often reaching over 30 meters. Their leaves are shaped like fans. The veins in the leaves are parallel. Ginkgoes are **deciduous**, losing their leaves in the autumn.

Ginkgoes bear their pollen and ovules on separate trees. Wind transfers pollen from male trees to female trees. Ginkgo seeds resemble yellow cherries, but have an unpleasant odor.

DO YOU KNOW?

The oldest living things on Earth are bristlecone pines. These trees are found on the tops of mountains in California, Utah, and Nevada. These low-growing trees may live for 5000 years.

BIOLOGY INSIGHT

Adaptation and Evolution: In Jack pines, *Pinus banksiana,* the scales do not separate and release the seeds until the cones have been subjected to extreme heat. This species is one of the first to renew its population following a forest fire.

Seed Plants **365**

Figure 21-14 *Ginkgo biloba* is called the maidenhair tree. It is attractive, but slow-growing. Unlike other gymnosperms, *Ginkgo* is deciduous; its leaves change to a gold color in autumn.

CONSUMER BIOLOGY

Ginkgo trees are resistant to air pollution and are often planted in urban parks. Separate trees bear flowers containing male and female parts. Male trees are preferred because the fleshy fruit coats that develop in female flowers have a very rancid odor.

▶ Denotes a question that involves *interpreting* and *applying* concepts.

Table 21-2

REPRODUCTION IN SEED PLANTS		
	Angiosperms	**Gymnosperms**
Seed location	Within ovary	On scales
Reproductive structure	Flowers	Cones
Pollinators	Wind, water, animals	Wind and water
Site of pollination	On stigma; pollen tube grows to ovule	On ovule
Fertilization	Double	Single
Food storage tissue	Endosperm	Female gametophyte
Seed dispersal	Wind, animals	Wind

The *Gnetophytes* [nē′ tō fīts] also are gymnosperms. This small group includes a shrub called Ephedra, which is common in the southwestern deserts. The leaves of Ephedra plants are very tiny. Their green stems carry on photosynthesis.

Another interesting group of gymnosperms are the *Cycads*. They have unbranched stems that are crowned by long, leathery leaves. Like ginkgoes, cycads produce pollen and ovules on separate plants. The wind aids in pollination.

Cycads have a method of reproduction that represents, in abbreviated form, the process found in lower plants. You will learn more about this process in Chapter 26. The pollen grains produce large sperm. Each sperm is covered with cilia. The cycad egg is surrounded by a drop of water. The sperm must swim through the drop of water before it can unite with the egg.

This chapter has introduced you to the two groups of seed plants—angiosperms and gymnosperms. Together they have dominated the landscape for many millions of years. Table 21-2 summarizes their similarities and differences.

CHECKPOINT ◆

19. Name the four major groups of gymnosperms.
20. How do seeds of gymnosperms differ from those of angiosperms?
21. Of which generation, gametophyte or sporophyte, is the pollen of gymnosperms? The cones of gymnosperms?
▶ 22. What kind of angiosperm fruit is most similar to the papery wings of the gymnosperm seed?
▶ 23. Endosperm is to angiosperm embryo as _____ is to gymnosperm embryo.

GERMINATION OF POLLEN GRAINS

In this activity you will observe the germination of pollen grains. Germination occurs when a seed begins its initial growth.

Objectives and Skills

□ *Prepare* a hanging-drop slide.
□ *Illustrate* the structure of a pollen tube.
□ *Determine* the conditions necessary for pollen grain germination.
□ *State* the function of the pollen tube.

Materials

dropper pipette	microscope
depression slide	petroleum jelly
coverslip	10% sucrose solution
toothpick	pollen grains of lily, tulip,
dissecting needle	or daffodil

Procedure and Observations

1. Read all instructions for this laboratory activity before you begin your work.
2. Clean a slide and coverslip thoroughly.
3. Using the dropper pipette, place a drop of sucrose solution on the coverslip.
4. Using the dissecting needle, transfer some pollen from the anthers of the flower to the drop of sucrose.

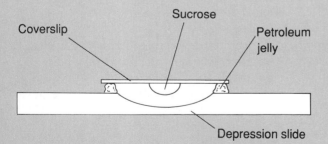

A diagram of hanging drop slide

5. Using the toothpick, apply a thin ring of petroleum jelly around the edge of the depression in the slide.
6. Carefully lay the slide over the drop of sucrose on the coverslip so that the petroleum jelly seals the pieces of glass together. (See diagram.)
7. Quickly invert the slide and coverslip, and examine under low power. The pollen tube should start to germinate after about 20 minutes.
8. Prepare a second hanging drop slide exactly like the first one, but replace the sucrose solution with water. Observe this slide under low power.
9. Before leaving the laboratory, clean up all your materials and wash your hands thoroughly.

1. On which part of the flower does pollen grain germination occur?
2. In which preparation, water or sucrose solution, does the pollen tube grow?
3. What purpose does the sucrose solution serve for the pollen grain?
4. From this lab activity, what two compounds are necessary for the growth of a pollen tube?
5. Are these two compounds found on the stigma of flowers?
6. Draw the germinated pollen tube, and label any parts that are visible in it.
7. What is the function of the pollen tube?

CHAPTER REVIEW

Summary

‣ The dominant plants of the landscape are the seed plants: angiosperms and gymnosperms. Angiosperms, the most recently-evolved plant group, produce flowers. Gymnosperms are seed plants that do not produce flowers.

‣ Two groups of angiosperms are monocots and dicots. Monocots have one cotyledon, parallel leaf veins, and floral parts in multiples of three. Dicots have two cotyledons, netlike leaf veins, and floral parts in multiples of four or five.

‣ A perfect flower is composed of a carpel and the surrounding stamens, sepals, and petals. The female carpel consists of a stigma, style, and ovary. Within the ovary, ovules develop into seeds. The male stamen consists of a filament and anther. Within the anther, pollen grains are produced.

‣ Pollination occurs when the pollen grains are transferred from the anther to the stigma. Some flowers are self-pollinated.

‣ When the pollen grain lands on the stigma, it develops a pollen tube, from which two sperm nuclei develop. One of the sperm nuclei fertilizes the egg; the other fertilizes the polar nuclei to form a food-storage tissue. Double fertilization occurs only in angiosperms

‣ After fertilization, each ovule develops into a seed. The surrounding ovary matures into a fruit. Some fruits are fleshy; others are hard and dry. Fruits protect seeds and also aid in their dispersal. Agents of seed dispersal include wind, water, and animals.

‣ Gymnosperms evolved earlier than the angiosperms. Gymnosperms do not produce fruits and flowers. Ovules are exposed on a cone's scales. The existing groups of gymnosperms include ginkgoes, gnetophytes, cycads, and conifers.

Vocabulary

aggregate fruits	ovule
angiosperms	petal
anther	pollen
carpel	pollen cones
conifer	pollen tube
cotyledons	pollinator
deciduous	pollination
dicots	receptacle
disperse	seed
double fertilization	seed cones
endosperm	self-pollination
flower	sepal
fruit	simple fruits
gymnosperm	sperm nuclei
monocots	stamen
multiple fruits	stigma
ovary	style

Concept Mapping

Construct a concept map for the structure and development of angiosperms. Include the following terms: flower, fruit, stamen, seeds, carpel, pollen, ovules, and dispersed. Use additional terms as you need them.

Review

1. Name three groups of gymnosperms.
2. What flower part may enclose the flower before it opens?
3. What feature do all angiosperms possess?
4. What term describes a flower with both male and female parts?
5. How many nuclei does the pollen tube have just prior to entering the ovule?
6. What is the female gametophyte of an angiosperm?

7. In double fertilization, which two nuclei fuse to form a diploid nucleus? Which two fuse to form a triploid nucleus?
8. What tissue stores food in the conifer seed?
9. What is the function of the anthers?
10. How are samaras usually dispersed?
11. What kind of fruit forms from many ovaries in a single flower?
12. Ovules mature into _____, and ovaries mature into _____.
13. List three ways seeds are dispersed.
14. What kind of pollinator is not attracted to red flowers?

Interpret and Apply

15. Place the following events in the correct order.
    a. Fertilization occurs.
    b. Sepals cover flower bud.
    c. Seeds and fruit mature.
    d. Pollen forms in the anther.
    e. The zygote develops into an embryo.
    f. Pollen lands on the stigma.
    g. The pollen grain has three nuclei.

Questions 16–24 refer to the photograph shown below.

16. How many stamens are shown?
17. How many petals are shown?
18. Is this flower "perfect"?
19. What color are the ovaries?
20. What kind of pollinator probably visits this flower?
21. How many styles does each carpel have?
22. How many carpels are shown?
23. What kind of fruit will develop?
24. How will the seeds be dispersed?

Critical Thinking

25. You have a brown bag lunch consisting of a cheese sandwich, an apple, and a can of tomato juice. Tell which plant, directly or indirectly, was the source of (a) the bag, (b) the bread, (c) the cheese, (d) the apple, and (e) the juice.

Questions 26–27 refer to the graph shown below.

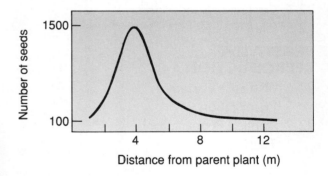

26. Describe the relationship between the number of seeds and the distance they are found from the parent plant.
27. Propose answers for the following:
    a. What kind of agent disperses the seeds?
    b. How tall is this plant?
    c. How large are the seeds from this plant?

Chapter

22

PLANT STRUCTURE AND DEVELOPMENT

Overview

DEVELOPMENT OF THE PLANT BODY

22-1 Seed Structure

22-2 Seed Dormancy

22-3 Germination and Establishment

PLANT BODY ORGANIZATION

22-4 Organs of Seed Plants

22-5 Plant Tissues

VEGETATIVE REPRODUCTION

22-6 Natural Vegetative Propagation

22-7 Applied Propagation Techniques

How do plants grow through rock or concrete?

DEVELOPMENT OF THE PLANT BODY

Have you ever eaten bean sprouts or alfalfa sprouts? It probably did not occur to you at the time that you were eating a mouthful of tiny plants, but that is what they are.

22-1 Seed Structure

After fertilization, the ovule of a plant begins to develop. A mature ovule becomes a seed. Each seed contains a young developing plant, or **embryo**. The embryo is surrounded by a food supply. The seed is enclosed by a tough covering.

The embryo is the first stage in the development of a seed plant. The cells at the tip of the embryo are called the **epicotyl**. These cells will form the leaves and upper stem of the plant. Cells on the other end of the embryo are called the **radicle**. The radicle will develop into the root system of the young plant. The epicotyl and radicle are connected by a tissue called the **hypocotyl**. The hypocotyl will become the lower part of the stem.

The food supply is an important part of the seed. When the embryo begins to grow, it can use these nutrients until it is capable of producing its own food by photosynthesis. In flowering plants, the food storage tissue is endosperm. The main food materials are carbohydrates, proteins, and lipids. This is one reason that seeds are an excellent source of nutrition in your diet.

Another source of nutrients for the embryo are the cotyledons. In monocots, the cotyledons nourish the embryo by digesting and absorbing food molecules from the surrounding endosperm. It then transports the food to the embryo. In dicots, the cotyledons serve as a storage tissue. Look at Figure 22-1. The cotyledons have absorbed the entire endosperm so that each half of the bean is primarily a large cotyledon.

The embryo and food supply are covered by a thick layer of tissue called the **seed coat**. It protects the enclosed embryo. The seed coat also controls germination by restricting water and oxygen to the embryo. On the surface of the seed coat is a scar called the **hilum**. This marking shows where the seed was once attached to the ovary.

22-2 Seed Dormancy

In the life cycles of most organisms, there is a stage of rest, or **dormancy**. This is a period when metabolism runs slowly. In humans and other large mammals, there is a daily sleep period, or a period of hibernation.

Section Objectives

A **Label** a diagram of a monocot and dicot seed.

B **Explain** the importance of dormancy.

C **Name** several factors that influence germination.

D **Compare** the process of germination in monocots with that in dicots.

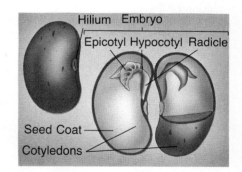

Figure 22-1 Seeds are composed of three main parts—a protective seed coat, a food supply, and an embryo. The embryo is further divided into the epicotyl, hypocotyl, and radicle.

Figure 22-2 The stages in the germination and establishment of a bean seed. They include the extension of the hypocotyl and the formation of leaves. Notice the shape and position of the cotyledons at each stage of development. Why do the cotyledons shrivel up as development proceeds?

In plants, the seed is the dormant part of the life cycle. Seeds are tolerant of unfavorable conditions, such as cold temperatures and drought. This adaptation ensures that seeds do not germinate at inappropriate times.

A seed is dispersed from the parent plant in a dormant condition. A seed that is capable of germinating is said to be **viable** [vī′ ə bəl]. Seeds remain viable under cool, dry conditions. The period of a seed's viability may last from a few weeks to many years. If it does not encounter the proper conditions for germination, it will eventually die.

22-3 Germination and Establishment

Viable seeds germinate if they encounter favorable growth conditions. This means there is sufficient moisture and oxygen in the soil. In addition to water and oxygen, other conditions are required to trigger germination. Many seeds require light for successful germination. Seeds of many northern plants will only germinate after they have been exposed to low temperatures. This ensures that seeds will not germinate during a warm period in the fall, only to be killed during the cold winter that follows.

The process of germination begins with the seed absorbing water. As water enters the seed, its enzymes become active. Digestive enzymes convert starch and fats into glucose. Recall from Chapter 6 that glucose is the primary fuel of cells. With the energy from cellular respiration, cells of the embryo begin to divide. The swelling tissues of the seed break open the seed coat. The seed is now called a seedling.

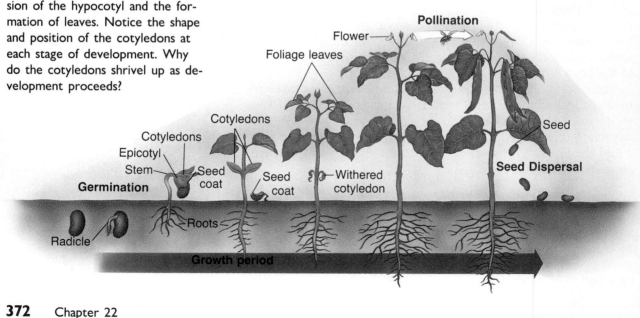

Once it has germinated, a seedling must *establish* itself as an independent organism. This is the most crucial part in the life of a plant. During this period, the plant is sensitive to a lack of water, parasitic fungi, and a wide variety of insect pests.

Dicot Germination The germination and establishment of a dicot is illustrated in Figure 22-2. The radicle, or embryonic root, usually emerges from the seed first. Root hairs quickly develop, enabling the plant to obtain water from the soil.

The hypocotyl then begins to grow. It is the first part of the seedling to appear above the soil. As the hypocotyl grows longer, it begins to straighten out. The growing hypocotyl pulls the cotyledons and epicotyl out of the soil. Eventually, the epicotyl develops into the upper stem and leaves of the plant.

Until its leaves are developed and it is able to make its own food by photosynthesis, the bean seedling obtains nutrients from its cotyledons. As the food in the cotyledons is digested and transported to the growing parts of the seedling, the cotyledons shrivel and fall off.

Monocot Germination The germination of a monocot seed, such as the corn seed, is different from that of a dicot. Look at Figure 22-3. The root from the radicle in the corn seedling is a temporary structure. Lateral roots soon branch from the primary root. Later, additional roots develop from the stem.

In monocots, the seedling's source of food is the endosperm. Unlike the cotyledons of the bean seed, the endosperm does not emerge from the soil. Instead, it remains buried throughout germination and establishment.

In grasses such as corn, the epicotyl is covered by a sheathlike structure called the **coleoptile** [kō lē op′ tīl]. The coleoptile protects the shoot as it pushes upward through the soil.

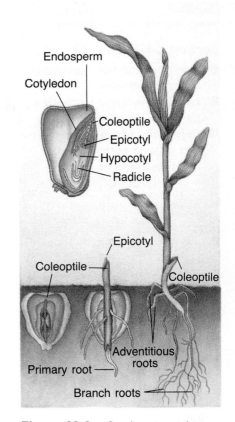

Figure 22-3 Seed parts and stages in the germination and establishment of corn, a monocot. Compare this series with Figure 22-2. What tells you that this stem carries on photosynthesis?

CHECKPOINT ◆

1. What is the inactive period called between seed formation and germination?
2. What is the food source of dicot seedlings? Of monocot seedlings?
3. What structure protects the shoot of the corn seedling?
4. What is the most crucial part of the life history of a seed plant?
5. How does the absorption of water stimulate germination?
▶ 6. How are the hypocotyl and the coleoptile similar?
▶ 7. Why do most seeds require oxygen to begin germination?

▶ Denotes a question that involves *interpreting* and *applying* concepts.

Plant Structure and Development   **373**

Section Objectives

E **Compare** the body organization of plants and animals.

F **List** and **state** the functions of the organs of seed plants.

G **Relate** the structures of the tissues of seed plants to their functions in the living plant.

Like the human body, plants contain many different types of cells, tissues, and organs. However, plants are structurally less complex than animals, thus they have fewer types of cells.

Plants are organized differently than animals. Like an apartment building or a condominium, a plant is composed of many repeating units. In seed plants, these units are *organs* such as leaves, roots, flowers, and stems. Each organ acts as a separate unit. In contrast, the repeating units of an animal are cells. An animal like a fruit fly or elephant is not composed of hundreds of hearts, lungs, or brains. It is a population of *cells*.

This type of organization allows plants a high degree of growth flexibility. A plant may react to stress by varying the number of its parts. For example, during a dry period, a plant may decrease the formation of new leaves. Yet the stress of starvation does not change the number of legs, hearts, or lungs of an animal.

Although you may never have thought about it, you use the organs of plants every day. Stems are used for building material. Fruits are an obvious source of food, but you also eat the leaves, stems, roots, and flowers of many plants.

22-4 Organs of Seed Plants

Seed plants have specialized organs for growth and reproduction. **Vegetative organs**—roots, stems, and leaves, function in the growth of the plant. The reproductive organs of seed plants include cones, flowers, and fruits. As you read about the organs of seed plants, look at Figure 22-4. Notice how the relative positions of the organs, as well as their structures, allow for interaction of the plant with its environment.

Roots are organs that are specialized to collect water and dissolved minerals. Water is necessary for photosynthesis and metabolism. Roots also anchor the plant and store food. Roots may extend deep into the ground, or far from the plant.

The parts of a plant above the soil surface make up the *shoot system*. A **stem** is an organ that conducts water and minerals from the roots to other parts of the plant. Another important stem function is to display the leaves of the plant to the light. The point on the stem where a leaf is attached is called a *node*. Many stems store food. In younger plants and those that live only for one year, the stem is also a photosynthetic organ. What aspect of the appearance of the stem in Figure 22-4 would indicate that the stem serves this function?

Leaves are the main food factories of seed plants. Leaves are somewhat flattened. This allows maximum collection of light

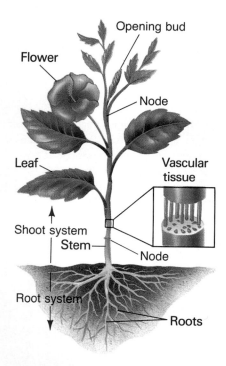

Figure 22-4 The organs of the seed plants. Every organ from the roots to the leaves is connected by continuous pipeline of vascular tissue.

energy. Leaves transport food to the stem to be used by the rest of the plant. Collectively the leaves are called the *canopy*. The canopy directly affects other plants in the environment.

22-5 Plant Tissues

Roots, stems, leaves, flowers, and cones are composed of tissues. Each type of tissue consists of cells with distinct structures and functions. Some tissues consist of dead cells, whereas other types are living and metabolizing.

All seed plants have common types of tissues. As you read about the various types of tissues, refer to the figures that illustrate them. Try to visualize how the structure of each type of tissue is suited to its function in the whole plant.

Meristematic Tissue Plants, unlike animals, continue to grow throughout their lives. All plant growth originates in meristems. A **meristem** is a growing point of a plant. It consists of unspecialized cells that are continually dividing and producing new cells. The cells in the meristem have thin walls and dense cytoplasm.

Meristems found at the tip (or apex) of a root or stem are called **apical meristems**. An apical meristem causes an increase in the length of the plant body. Another kind of meristem, called the **cambium,** causes a plant to grow in width.

Cells produced by meristematic tissues differentiate into other tissues. The walls of some cells become thickened. Other cells elongate. Each cell becomes specialized for a specific function, such as absorption, support, transport, reproduction, or storage. All of the following tissues develop from meristematic tissue.

Epidermis Epidermis is a tissue that covers the entire plant body. It is a living tissue that is specialized to reduce the loss of water. The epidermis is usually one cell thick and is covered by a waxy cuticle. The waxy cuticle acts like lip balm that you apply to your lips in the winter and summer. Do you think the epidermis of roots has a waxy cuticle?

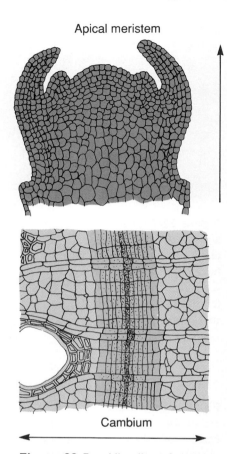

Apical meristem

Cambium

Figure 22-5 All cells and tissues originate from meristems. Cells farthest from meristems are the most mature and specialized. The apical meristem is shown cut lengthwise; the cambium is shown in cross section. Arrows indicate the direction of growth.

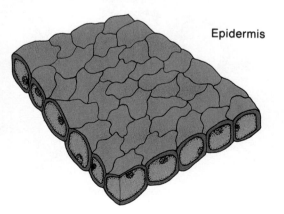

Epidermis

Figure 22-6 Epidermis is the plant tissue that contacts the environment. Cells are tightly packed together to minimize the loss of water and protect the plant from injury.

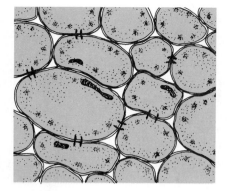

Figure 22-7 Parenchyma cells are the all-purpose cells of the plant, performing many different functions. They have thin cell walls. Cells are connected to each other for the transfer of stored substances.

Figure 22-8 Collenchyma cells are similar to parenchyma cells. The corners of collenchyma cells have a thickened cell wall. Sclerenchyma cells are usually long fibers with very thick walls for strength and support.

Parenchyma Parenchyma [pə ren′ kə mə] is tissue that is generally unspecialized. Depending upon its position in the plant, it serves a variety of functions. Commonly, parenchyma cells store sugars and starches. The cells of parenchyma are more or less spherical. They have thin walls and large vacuoles. Parenchyma cells have the ability to change their activities. When a plant is wounded, parenchyma cells begin to divide and heal the wound. In leaves, some types of parenchyma have chloroplasts and carry on photosynthesis.

Supportive Tissue There are two types of supportive tissue in plants. One type of living tissue that is strong and flexible is **collenchyma** [kə len′ kə mə]. Collenchyma cells are long and somewhat thickened near the corners. Collenchyma is often found in young stems and leaves. Another type of supportive tissue is **sclerenchyma** [sklə ren′ kə mə]. Long sclerenchyma cells give plants strength, support, and protection. Sclerenchyma cells have thick cell walls, often lack cytoplasm, and die at maturity. They give fruits like apples and pears a gritty texture. Would you expect roots to have an abundance of supportive tissue?

Vascular Tissue All seed plants contain vascular tissues. Vascular tissue supports the plant. This strength allows plants to grow to enormous sizes. However, vascular tissue serves a more important function. It conducts food, water, and dissolved minerals from one part of the plant to another. In general, the cells of vascular tissue are long and have thick cell walls. It serves as the plant's "plumbing system."

There are two major types of vascular tissues. **Phloem** [flō′ əm] is the tissue that transports sugars and starches from

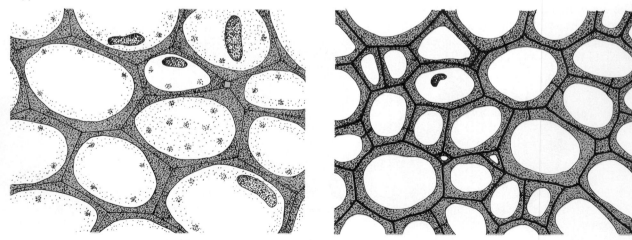

Collenchyma

Sclerenchyma

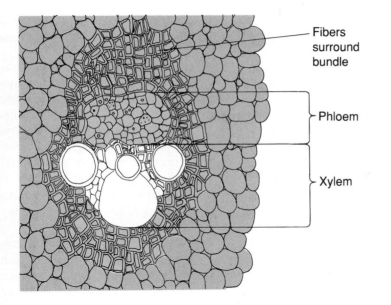

Fibers surround bundle

Phloem

Xylem

Figure 22-9 Vascular tissue connects the entire plant together. Water and food travels through vascular tissue from one part of a plant to another. This diagram is a cross section of a vascular bundle. The strings of celery are vascular bundles.

one part of a plant to another. Phloem cells are living. **Xylem** [zī′ ləm] is specialized for the transport of water and dissolved minerals. The cells of xylem are hollow and no longer living at maturity. Xylem and phloem often occur together in strands called *vascular bundles.*

Cork In older stems and roots of many plants, cork replaces the epidermis. Like epidermis, cork cells are specialized for conserving water and protecting the plant. Unlike epidermal cells, cork cells are dead at maturity. The bark of trees is composed of dead cork cells.

Homeostasis: In a normal healthy plant, there is a balance between the total surface area of the roots and the total surface area of the shoot. The root system supplies the shoot system with water and minerals. The shoot system must manufacture enough food for the growth and maintenance of the root system.

CHECKPOINT ◆

8. Distinguish between the structures and organization of a plant and an animal body.
9. What are the two types of vascular tissues?
10. Which tissues are living at maturity?
11. Compare epidermis and cork.
12. Which plant organs store food? Which tissue would you expect to observe in these organs?
13. Name three kinds of tissues that are specialized for support in vascular plants.
14. What plant organs have meristematic tissue?
▶ 15. Explain why hollow cells with thick walls are ideally suited to their function.
▶ 16. Would you expect roots to have cork tissue? Vascular tissue? Explain.

▶ Denotes a question that involves *interpreting* and *applying* concepts.

H *Cite* examples of naturally occurring vegetative propagation.

I *Describe* several techniques of
artificial vegetative propagation
as compared to sexual
reproduction.

In addition to reproducing sexually with flowers, many angiosperms
can also reproduce asexually. Recall from Chapter 9 that asexual
reproduction involves only one parent. Offspring are genetically
identical to their parent. Asexual reproduction in plants is called
vegetative propagation. Reproduction is accomplished by the vegetative organs—roots, stems, and leaves. Although this type of
reproduction allows for rapid increase in numbers of offspring,
it provides no genetic variety among them. From an evolutionary
standpoint, such a lack of genetic variety is a disadvantage because
an unfavorable change in conditions would have a negative effect
upon all the offspring.

You may have observed vegetative propagation. The spread
of crabgrass across a lawn is an example of vegetative propagation.
So is the spread of daffodils. Many of the fruits of modern
agriculture are also products of vegetative propagation.

22-6 Natural Vegetative Propagation

The strawberry plant is an example of a plant that reproduces
asexually by means of its stems. The parent plant sends out
horizontal stems called **stolons**, which grow along the ground.
Roots grow downward from the stolon's tip and into the soil.
Shoots grow upward into the air. The root and shoot form a new
plant that is independent of the parent plant.

Figure 22-10 Rarely do you find
a single cattail. Cattails form large
populations by vegetative reproduction. Each plant is connected to the
others by means of a rhizome.
Many other marsh plants reproduce
by rhizomes.

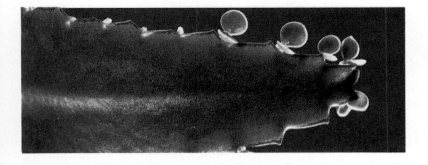

Another kind of horizontal stem, called a **rhizome**, grows underground. These stems are responsible for large populations, or stands, of trees and shrubs.

Sometimes horizontal roots form shoots that become independent plants. Milkweed, sumac, beech, elderberry, and lilac are examples of plants that reproduce by means of their roots. In a few cases, the leaves produce offspring. *Bryophyllum*, shown in Figure 22-11, is an example of propagation by leaves.

22-7 Applied Propagation Techniques

People involved in the production of agricultural and ornamental plants have developed many ways of using vegetative propagation. Plants produced by vegetative propagation often reach maturity more quickly than plants grown by seeds. Vegetative propagation allows the production of plants that are genetically identical to desirable plants, such as hybrids. As you know, the offspring of hybrids often do not resemble their parents.

Have you ever wondered how seedless fruits, such as navel oranges, reproduce? The original navel orange developed from a mutation in the bud of an orange tree that produced seeds. When this fruit was discovered, it was recognized as a desirable food. The branch of the tree containing the seedless oranges was propagated vegetatively to produce more seedless oranges. All navel oranges are descended from this single bud mutation.

One common method of vegetative propagation is to take **cuttings.** In this method, a leaf or stem is cut from a plant and placed in water or soil. The parenchyma cells of the stem change activity and begin to divide to form roots. Once a cutting establishes roots, it becomes an independent plant.

Other methods of vegetative propagation are shown in Figure 22-12. In the process of **layering,** roots are induced to grow from a stem that is still attached to the parent plant. In one method of layering, a branch of the plant is bent down to the ground and covered with soil except at the tip. Roots will grow from the buried part of the plant, and a shoot will rise from the

CONSUMER BIOLOGY

Some common foods are products of plants that can reproduce only asexually. Navel oranges, bananas, and pineapples are examples of such foods.

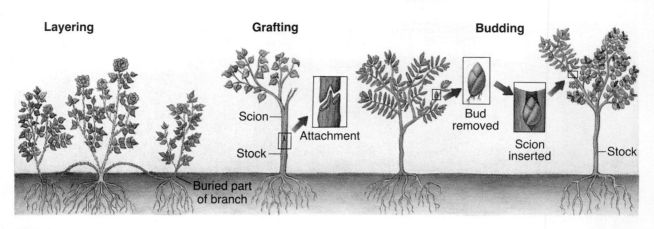

Layering   **Grafting**   **Budding**

Scion —

Stock — | — Attachment

Bud removed

Scion inserted

— Stock

Buried part of branch

Figure 22-12 Layering, grafting, and budding are artificial methods of plant propagation.

tip. Eventually, the new plant can be cut away from the parent plant. Layering is used with blackberries, raspberries, and roses.

In the technique of **grafting**, a part of one plant is attached to a healthy, rooted part of another plant. The rooted plant is called the *stock*. The part of the plant that is attached to the stock is called the *scion*. The scion does not form new organs, as in other forms of asexual reproduction. Rather, it becomes a part of the stock plant. The cambiums of the stock and scion must be placed carefully so that they touch. Thus the newly formed vascular tissue will form a continuous pipeline between the two branches.

The technique of **budding** is similar to that of grafting, but in budding the scion is a bud instead of a branch. A bud from one tree is slipped into a T-shaped slit in the bark of another tree. The year after the bud graft is made, the bud grows into a shoot. The part of the tree above the graft is cut off so that the budded portion becomes the apical meristem of the tree. Pears, plums, peaches, citrus fruits, and apples are produced by budding.

CHECKPOINT ◆

17. Strawberries reproduce asexually by means of horizontal stems called _____.
18. What two plant parts are joined in grafting?
▶ 19. Why would plants that reproduce vegetatively populate an area faster than plants that only reproduce sexually?
▶ 20. Your friend admires a lovely ivy plant on your windowsill. Which method could you use to provide your friend with a plant just like yours?
▶ 21. All of your strawberry plants are propagated from a single parent. If one of the plants is killed by a blight, what is the probable outcome for the other untreated plants?

▶ Denotes a question that involves *interpreting* and *applying* concepts.

LABORATORY ACTIVITY

THE EFFECT OF MOISTURE ON THE GERMINATION OF RADISH SEEDS

In this activity, you will observe the process of germination of radish seeds in different degrees of moisture.

Objectives and Skills

☐ *Demonstrate* the effect of moisture on radish seed germination.
☐ *Illustrate* the early stages of growth of a radish seedling.

Materials

15 radish seeds
3 petri dishes
3 pieces of filter paper

Procedure and Observations

1. Read all instructions for this laboratory activity before you begin your work.
2. Copy the data table like the one below onto a separate sheet of paper.
3. Cut three circles of filter paper so that each circle exactly covers the bottom of a petri dish.
4. Moisten one circle of filter paper with water and place it in the bottom of a petri dish. Label this dish A.

5. Place a dry piece of filter paper in the bottom of a second dish. Label this dish B.
6. In a third dish, place a piece of filter paper, and add water so that the petri dish is about half full of water. Label this dish C.
7. Place five radish seeds in each dish. Observe the seeds each day and record your observations on the table.
8. Before leaving the laboratory, clean up all your materials and wash your hands thoroughly.

Analysis and Conclusions

1. Under which conditions did the largest number of seeds germinate?
2. Which factors prevented germination in the other two conditions?
3. Which plant structure emerged first after germination?
4. What factor(s) will prevent the seedling from growing into a mature plant if kept in these conditions?
5. Draw and label the parts of a germinating radish seed.

DATA TABLE				
Dish	Day germination occurred	Day radicle emerged	Day shoot emerged	Percent seeds germinated
A				
B				
C				

Plant Structure and Development   **381**

CHAPTER REVIEW

Summary

- Many types of seeds require a period of dormancy before they can germinate. Dormancy increases the likelihood that germination will occur in conditions favorable to the survival and growth of the young plant.
- Moisture is a necessary condition for germination. Water absorbed by a seed activates enzymes that digest the seed's food supply. With nutrients made available to it, an embryo starts to grow.
- The first organ to develop in the seedling is the young root, or radicle. This allows absorption of additional water from the soil. The epicotyl develops into the shoot of the seedling. In some dicots, the growing hypocotyl pulls the shoot and cotyledons above the surface of the soil.
- A seed plant consists of vegetative and reproductive organs. They include roots, stems, leaves, fruits, flowers, and cones.
- Seed plants are composed of meristematic tissue that forms specialized tissues for protection, support, storage, and transport.
- Many angiosperms can reproduce vegetatively as well as sexually. Leaves, underground stems, and roots are plant parts that reproduce asexually under natural conditions.
- Artificial methods of vegetative propagation include cuttings, layering, grafting, and budding.

Vocabulary

apical meristem	embryo
budding	epicotyl
cambium	epidermis
coleoptile	grafting
collenchyma	hilum
cork	hypocotyl
cuttings	layering
dormancy	leaves

meristem	stem
parenchyma	stolon
phloem	vascular tissues
radicle	vegetative organs
rhizome	vegetative propagation
roots	viable
sclerenchyma	xylem
seed coat	

Concept Mapping

Construct a concept map for plant structure. Include the following terms: flower, fruit, radicle, roots, stem, shoot, leaves, endosperm, epicotyl, vegetative organs, reproductive organs, and seed. Use additional terms as your need them.

Review

1. If a seed is not viable, what happens when it is planted under favorable conditions?
2. Name four factors that influence germination.
3. What part of the seedling emerges from the bean seed first?
4. What part of a seed provides nutrients for dicot seedlings? For monocot seedlings?
5. What is the function of vascular tissue?

In the following list, match the tissue type to its function. Each tissue may have more than one function.

6.	xylem	a.	protection
7.	phloem	b.	photosynthesis
8.	epidermis	c.	conduction of food
9.	cork	d.	conduction of water
10.	parenchyma	e.	support
11.	sclerenchyma	f.	storage
12.	root	g.	growth
13.	meristem	h.	not a tissue

14. What are two advantages of vegetative propagation over sexual reproduction?
15. How might a plant respond to a stress differently than an animal?
16. The plant organ that produces most of a plant's food is the _____ .
17. Name a plant that produces vegetatively by its roots.

Interpret and Apply

18. Compare the germination of a bean seed with that of a corn seed.
19. Why is it important for root hairs to develop soon after germination?
20. Leaves grown in full sunlight often have thicker cuticles than those grown in shade. Why is this an advantage?
21. A seed lacks cotyledons. What will happen to it after it germinates? Explain.
22. Which of the following is *not* an organ? (a) root (b) stem (c) xylem (d) leaf
23. Which artificial method of vegetative propagation is similar to the natural vegetative propagation by stolons?
24. The word *dormancy* has the same derivation as the French word *dormir,* which means "to sleep." Explain why this word was chosen to describe the inactive period between seed formation and germination.
25. Stem is to support as _____ is to absorption.
26. Directions on some seed packages (beet seeds, for example) suggest soaking the seeds overnight in water before planting. What is the advantage of this procedure?

Critical Thinking

27. Seeds collected and grown in a temperate climate will not germinate in the tropics. Explain why not.

28. Your garden contains a healthy apple tree, but the apples do not taste good. Your neighbor has a tree with good-tasting apples. How can you improve the taste of the apples that your tree produces?
29. Recall the embryo transfer technique that you studied in Chapter 12. Explain how this technique of animal reproduction is similar to grafting, the plant reproduction technique described in this chapter.
30. In most environments, the number of dormant seeds in the soil vastly exceeds the number of growing plants. The store of seeds buried in the soil is called the seed bank. Explain how seeds are added to and removed from the seed bank.
31. Forty seeds of one species were planted. The graph below shows the total number of seeds that had germinated on each day.
    a. On which day was germination complete?
    b. What percentage of the 40 seeds were viable?

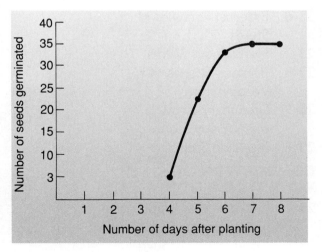

Chapter

23

ROOTS AND STEMS

Overview

ROOT SYSTEMS AND GROWTH

23-1   Root Systems
23-2   Primary Growth in Roots
23-3   Primary Root Tissues
23-4   Secondary Growth in Roots
23-5   Adventitious Roots

STEM STRUCTURE AND FUNCTION

23-6   External Features of Stems
23-7   Herbaceous Stems
23-8   Primary Tissues of a Woody Stem
23-9   Secondary Growth of a Woody Stem
23-10 Modified Stems

CONDUCTION OF WATER AND FOOD

23-11 Intake of Water and Nutrients
23-12 Conduction through the Xylem
23-13 Translocation of Food

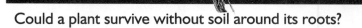

Could a plant survive without soil around its roots?

ROOT SYSTEMS AND GROWTH

Recall from Chapter 3 that cells require mineral elements such as sodium, calcium, and phosphorus to carry out their activities. The source of these minerals is the soil. Your body cells also require these minerals. How do these elements get from the soil to your body cells? You would not benefit by eating a handful of soil. Minerals essential to life enter land-dwelling organisms through roots of plants. You, in turn, eat plant cells that contain these minerals.

23-1 Root Systems

In many plants, more of the plant is located under the ground than above it. Massive root systems anchor the plant. The roots of alfalfa may extend to depths of 6 meters or more. Two common types of root systems are shown in Figure 23-1.

The roots of some plants consist of millions of branching roots, an arrangement called a **fibrous root system**. Grasses are an example. Why do plants have so many roots? Minerals are bound to soil particles. Thus new sources of minerals are found as plants extend their roots great distances. The roots of a single rye plant were measured and counted. The 6400 roots had 12.5 million root hairs with a total length of 250 kilometers! If you placed all the roots end to end, they would reach from Memphis, Tennessee, to Atlanta, Georgia.

Minerals are available to plants in very low concentrations. For example, the phosphorus taken up by roots is present at a concentration of about one part per million. Thus plants require a large surface area in which to absorb minerals. How much surface area do roots have? The roots of a single rye plant were found to have a surface area of 750 square meters!

Section Objectives

A *State* the functions of roots.
B *Distinguish* between taproots and fibrous roots.
C *Identify* the types of cells in a longitudinal root section.
D *Label* and *state* the function of tissues in a cross section of a mature root.
E *Contrast* primary and secondary growth in roots.
F *Describe* adventitious roots.

■ BIOLOGY INSIGHT ───

Adaptation and Evolution: The evolutionary tendency in land animals is to minimize surface area. The opposite is true of plants. Plants have extensive systems of surfaces both above ground and below it. This is an example of how the surface-to-volume ratio affects the organization of an organism.

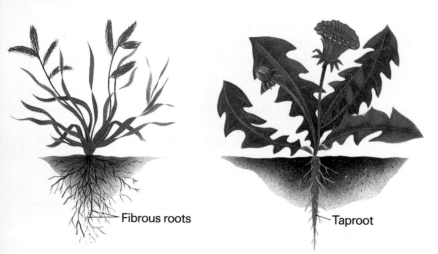

Fibrous roots   Taproot

Figure 23-1 Two common types of root systems.

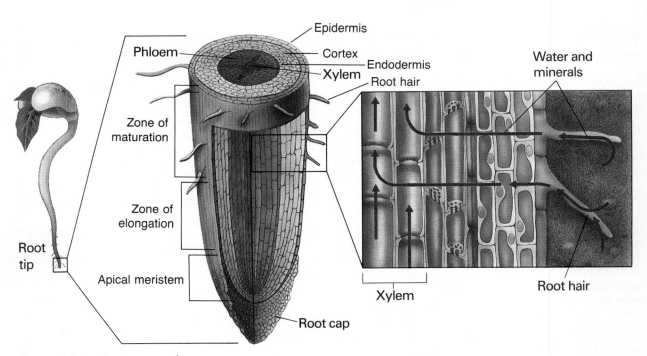

Phloem

Epidermis

Cortex

Endodermis

Xylem

Root hair

Water and minerals

Zone of maturation

Zone of elongation

Apical meristem

Root tip

Root cap

Xylem

Root hair

Figure 23-2 Roots grow from their tips. *Left:* This diagram of a root tip longitudinal section shows areas of cell division, growth, and specialization. *Right:* An enlarged view shows water and mineral absorption by root hairs and transport to xylem tissue.

In other plants, a single large **taproot** extends deep into the soil with other smaller roots branching from it. Dandelions have taproots. In some plants, taproots store food for the future growth of the plant. Without this stored food, many plants could not survive through the winter or during dry seasons. Carrots, parsnips, beets, turnips, and radishes all store food in fleshy taproots.

23-2 Primary Growth in Roots

Figure 23-2 illustrates a longitudinal section of a root tip. A root tip is divided into four different areas. From bottom to top, they are the root cap, the meristematic region, the zone of elongation, and the zone of maturation.

The **root cap** is a thimble-shaped group of cells covering the tip of the root. It protects the meristematic cells behind it from injury. As the root grows down into the soil, the cells of the root cap are constantly rubbed off.

The apical meristem is located just behind the root cap. It contains small, rapidly dividing cells. All of the tissues that arise from the meristem are called **primary tissues**.

Above the meristem is the **zone of elongation**. In this region, cell walls expand and vacuoles increase in size, making the cells longer. This growth has the effect of pushing the root deeper into the soil.

In the **zone of maturation**, the process of cell differentiation occurs. Cells develop into different kinds of tissues.

The outermost cells in the zone of maturation form tiny finger-like structures called **root hairs**. Each root hair grows from a single epidermal cell.

23-3 Primary Root Tissues

A cross section through the zone of maturation reveals the primary tissues of the root. As you read about the structure of the primary root, refer to Figures 23-2 and 23-3.

The outermost tissue of the young root is the epidermis. Inside the epidermis is a wide section of loosely packed parenchyma cells called the **cortex**. Food is stored in the cortex.

The innermost cells of the cortex form a ring called the **endodermis** [en' dō dėr məs]. The endodermal cell walls have a waxy layer that limits the movement of water and other materials. The endodermis is important in controlling movement of substances between the cortex and the interior root tissues.

Between the endodermis and the vascular tissues is a ring of parenchyma cells called the **pericycle**. Lateral roots grow from the pericycle, as shown in Figure 23-3. As lateral roots grow outward, they push aside the surrounding tissues, until finally they reach the soil.

Inside the pericycle is the central cylinder of vascular tissues. In dicots, the primary xylem is a star-shaped structure with arms that reach outward from the center of the root. Between the arms of the primary xylem are strands of primary phloem.

23-4 Secondary Growth in Roots

In dicots, after the primary tissues are mature, the root begins to grow in width. This widening of the root is called **secondary growth**. Secondary growth does not increase the length of the roots. In trees and shrubs that live for many years, most root cells are formed by secondary growth. Look at Figure 23-4 as you read about tissues produced by secondary growth.

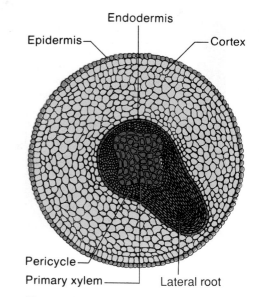

Figure 23-3   The cross section of a dicot root shows areas for absorption, food storage, and conduction. Lateral roots originate from the pericycle. The lateral root grows from the vascular cylinder so that xylem and phloem are continuous.

Figure 23-4   Secondary growth in roots occurs as a result of activity of the vascular cambium. The vascular cambium produces xylem to the inside and phloem to the outside.

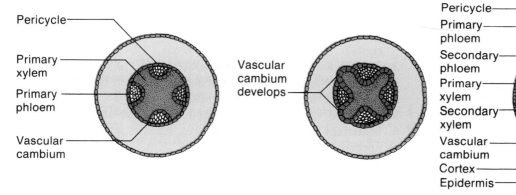

Figure 23-7 Herbaceous stems show different organizations of tissues. Compare them with the more complex woody stem. Can you find two differences between the monocot and dicot herbaceous stems?

23-7 Herbaceous Stems

Plants that do not contain woody tissue are called herbs. **Herbaceous** [hėr bā′ shəs] plants usually do not live for more than one year. Their stems are not specialized for protection or support. Thus the structure of herbaceous stems will differ from those of woody plant stems.

Like the root tip, all stems contain a meristem, a zone of elongation, and a zone of maturation. Unlike the root, however, there is no cap at the end of the stem. Why do you think there is no need for such a covering?

The stems of herbaceous dicots and monocots are somewhat different in structure. Cross sections of typical dicot and monocot stems are shown in Figure 23-7.

In the middle of most dicot stems is a region of parenchyma cells called the **pith**. A ring of vascular bundles surrounds the pith. Each vascular bundle consists of phloem cells on the outside, xylem cells on the inside, and cambium in the middle. The cambium cells divide so that they eventually produce an uninterrupted ring around the pith. The xylem and phloem bundles remain separate from each other. Outside the vascular bundles is the cortex. The cortex contains chloroplasts and carries on photosynthesis. There is a thin epidermis outside the cortex.

In the stem of a monocot, the vascular bundles are scattered rather than arranged in a ring. This arrangement makes it impossible to tell the pith from the cortex. The xylem is always on the inside of the vascular bundles, and the phloem is always on the outside. A band of sclerenchyma fibers often surrounds the entire bundle. In most monocots, there is no vascular cambium and, therefore, no secondary growth.

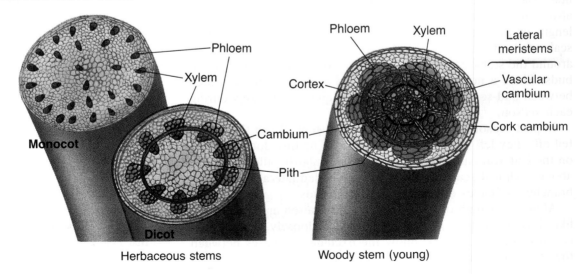

Herbaceous stems

Woody stem (young)

23-8 Primary Tissues of a Woody Stem

A cross section of a young woody stem is shown in Figure 23-7. Many of the tissues found in stems are similar to those in roots, but stems do not have a pericycle or an endodermis. The inner tissues of the young stem are protected by a single layer of epidermal tissue. Just inside the epidermis is a layer of cortex. Most of the cells of the cortex have thin walls and large vacuoles. They store food. Some of the cortex cells may have thick cell walls and serve to support the stem. In young woody stems, the cortex may contain chlorophyll and carry on photosynthesis.

Inside the cortex is the primary phloem. Directly inside the primary phloem is a ring of vascular cambium. Within the vascular cambium is a narrow ring of primary xylem. In the center of the stem are parenchyma cells that make up the pith. These are large, thin-walled cells that store food.

23-9 Secondary Growth of a Woody Stem

All of the primary growth of a stem occurs directly below the meristem, in the zone of elongation. For the stem to grow in width, meristematic tissues in the cambium must produce new tissues. As in the root, secondary tissues of the stem are produced by the cambium. Cells that form on the inside of the vascular cambium become part of the wood. Those that form on the outside become part of the bark.

Figure 23-8 Secondary growth of a woody stem over many years produces characteristic growth rings of xylem tissue formed during different times in the growing season.

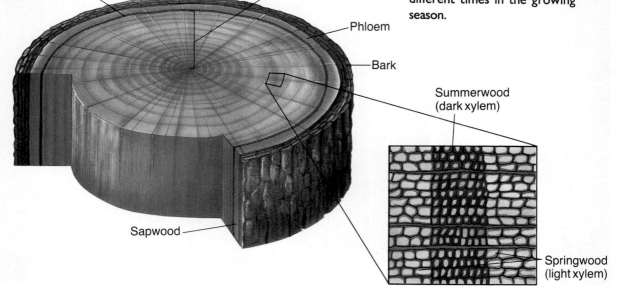

Vascular cambium

Xylem

Phloem

Bark

Sapwood

Summerwood (dark xylem)

Springwood (light xylem)

Information: A tree that is hollow, or missing its heartwood, can continue to live because its functional xylem is located in the sapwood. The loss of supporting tissue, however, makes the tree more likely to be knocked over.

Figure 23-9 *Left:* The familiar bark of a birch tree. *Middle:* The bark of slash pine is rough. *Right:* Smooth bark is characteristic of beech trees.

In a woody dicot, such as an oak tree, the main trunk is a stem, as is each branch of the tree. The cross section of a woody dicot stem in Figure 23-8 shows the arrangement of tissues.

Wood Xylem is the Greek word for "wood." Every year, the vascular cambium produces new xylem tissue, which you would recognize as the wood of the tree. If you examine a piece of wood, you will see alternating bands of dark and light xylem, one inside the other. Because the conditions for growth are usually more favorable in the spring than in the summer, wood cells that form in the spring are usually larger than those that form in the summer. The light xylem bands are composed of cells that formed in the spring. The dark xylem bands are composed of smaller cells that formed in the summer. The tree adds one light and one dark band each year. By counting the number of bands, called **growth rings**, you can determine the age of the tree.

As the years pass, new xylem forms, increasing the width of the trunk. At the same time, the pith and the older wood, which are closer to the center of the trunk, gradually become filled with resin and other materials. This prevents the passage of water through these cells. The clogged inner wood, called **heartwood**, appears darker than the newer **sapwood**.

Bark All tissues outside the vascular cambium are part of the bark. The phloem is the innermost of the bark tissues. Phloem formed by the cambium does not increase the width of the tree.

Instead, the new phloem pushes the existing phloem against the outer tissues, crushing the older phloem cells.

The cork cambium lies outside the cortex. When this meristematic tissue divides, it produces cork. The cork cells produce a waxy, water-resistant substance that separates the epidermis from its food and water supplies. This causes the epidermis to die and peel off. Eventually, the cork cells also die and become filled with air. The living tissues beneath the bark exchange gases through lenticels in the cork layer.

Cork has other important functions. It prevents water loss from the other stem tissues. Cork quickly forms over tree wounds, preventing fungi from entering the stem. The cork of some trees gives the bark a distinctive appearance. Often, you can identify a tree by its bark. Three kinds of bark are shown in Figure 23-9.

23-10 Modified Stems

Not all stems grow above the ground or are shaped like a cylinder. The stems of plants show a variety of structures and growth patterns that are modified to perform a variety of functions. A familiar example of an underground stem is the white potato. What makes it a stem rather than a root? A swollen underground stem such as the potato is called a **tuber**. The "eyes" of a white potato are *nodes*. Unlike roots, stems always have nodes. If you examine sweet potatoes or yams, you will see that they lack nodes. Thus sweet potatoes and yams are roots.

Corms are underground stems that are short, thick, and fleshy. They produce stems and store food to be used during early growth of the shoot. Crocuses and tuberous begonias have corms. **Bulbs** are similar to corms. Unlike corms, bulbs are composed of a short stem surrounded by numerous fleshy leaves. The leaves, which are full of food, store energy for growth the following spring. Onions and daffodils develop from bulbs.

Recall from Chapter 22 that rhizomes are stems that grow horizontally underground. Upright stems arise from the nodes of rhizomes. These stems are really branches of the main underground stem. Iris, water hyacinth, and some types of blueberries have rhizomes.

Stolons are horizontal stems that grow along the surface of the ground. New leaves and roots develop where a node touches the ground. When the stolon dies, the roots and stems become independent plants. Strawberries reproduce asexually by stolons. Stolons are often called runners.

A lawn becomes a thick mat by the spreading of rhizomes and stolons. Rhizomes and stolons allow a plant to move by growing over a horizontal surface.

CONSUMER BIOLOGY

Commercial cork, such as that from which bottle corks are made, is obtained from the cork oak, which grows in the Mediterranean area. Every 8–10 years, the cork cambium and cork are stripped off the tree. A new cork cambium then forms.

DO YOU KNOW?

Information: The skin of a potato is actually the cork. In a new potato, the cork layer is so thin that it can easily be rubbed off.

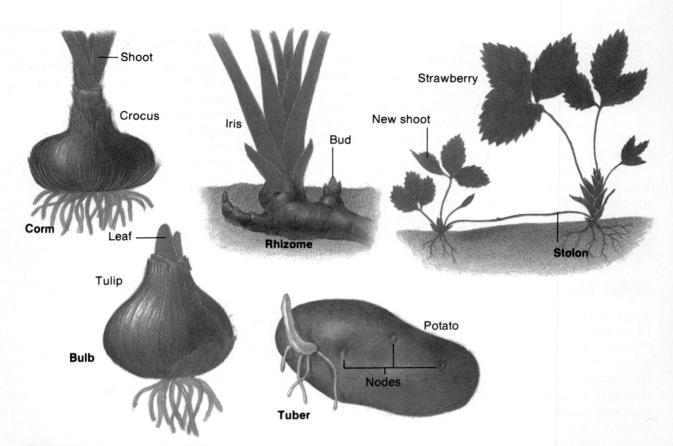

Shoot

Crocus

Corm

Leaf

Tulip

Bulb

Iris

Bud

Rhizome

Strawberry

New shoot

Stolon

Potato

Nodes

Tuber

Figure 23-10 Stems are modified to perform reproductive and food storage functions.

Many plants, especially shrubs, have sharp-pointed woody branches called thorns. Prickles are not entire branches, but are pointed outgrowths of a stem. Prickles are not connected to vascular tissue and may be dislodged by pushing them sideways. Rose prickles are a familiar example.

CHECKPOINT ◆

8. List four functions of stems.
9. How do the arrangements of vascular bundles of herbaceous monocots and dicots differ?
10. What type of underground stem is a white potato?
11. Name the three types of meristematic tissue in a woody stem.
12. What happens to the epidermis of the skin during secondary growth?
13. How are annual growth rings formed in woody stems? **(L)**
▶ 14. How many years' growth are shown on the twig in Figure 23-6?

▶ Denotes a question that involves *interpreting* and *applying* concepts.

CONDUCTION OF WATER AND FOOD

Redwoods, the tallest trees, can be over 100 meters tall. Water and dissolved minerals are absorbed in the soil far below. How are they transported to the tops of these huge trees? The method by which materials move from roots to leaves must also be explained for much smaller plants. Botanists have proposed several mechanisms for upward transport of materials in plants. Their explanations are based on knowledge of the structure and function of vascular tissues and the properties and behavior of water molecules. Experiments have shown that no simple, single method can be entirely responsible for the whole process.

23-11 Intake of Water and Nutrients

Water enters a plant through its root hairs, which extend between particles of soil. Many of the soil particles are surrounded by a thin layer of water called **capillary water**. Capillary water provides the roots with moisture during periods when there is no rain. Recall from Section 23-2 that each root hair grows from a single epidermal cell. Thousands of these structures on each root tip provide tremendous surface area for water absorption.

As you learned in Chapter 5, molecules move from an area of high concentration to an area of lower concentration. The cytoplasm of the root hairs contains a high concentration of organic compounds. Therefore, the concentration of water molecules in the root hairs is lower than the concentration of water molecules in the surrounding capillary water. As a result, water molecules in the soil move through the epidermal cell membrane into the cytoplasm of the root hairs. This movement of water molecules across a selectively permeable membrane is called osmosis. Thus water flows into root hairs by osmosis. After water enters the root hairs, it continues to pass by osmosis through the cells of the cortex. It eventually reaches the xylem through which it is carried upward to the rest of the plant.

The concentration of water ouside the root is always greater than that inside the root. Therefore, osmosis occurs continuously. The difference between water concentrations in root tissues and the soil results in a pushing of water into the root tissues. Since water enters the root faster than it leaves, pressure builds up in the root. The pressure exerted by the water is called **root pressure**. Root pressure pushes water upward through the stem. Experimental measurements have shown that root pressure alone could move water to a height of about 30 meters.

Section Objectives

M *Explain* movement of water and minerals into a plant in terms of osmosis and active transport.

N *Describe* and *relate* the structure of xylem and phloem to their functions.

O *State* the pressure-flow hypothesis of translocation.

P *Give an explanation* for the upward movement of water in a plant.

Figure 23-11 In some redwoods, water must travel over 100 meters from the soil to the leaves.

Roots and Stems **395**

Plants also obtain mineral nutrients from the soil. Nutrients such as nitrogen, calcium, and potassium are taken into the root in the form of ions. Unlike water molecules, mineral ions are more concentrated within the root cells than in the surrounding soil. Under these conditions, minerals would tend to move out of the root by diffusion. Therefore, the root cells must use active transport to take in minerals. This means that the cells must expend energy in the form of ATP to absorb essential minerals.

23-12 Conduction through the Xylem

Water and dissolved minerals are carried to the rest of the plant through the xylem. The two major types of conduction cells in the xylem are tracheids and vessel elements.

Tracheids [trā′ kē idz] are long, thick-walled cells with tapering ends. Tracheids are dead at maturity and are hollow. The ends of the tracheids overlap, allowing water to pass from one cell to the next.

Another type of conducting cell is found only in flowering plants. **Vessel elements** are larger in diameter than tracheids. Like tracheids, vessel elements are dead at maturity and contain no cytoplasm. Individual vessel elements are arranged end to end, much like barrels stacked on top of each other. The vessel elements form long tubes through the plant called *xylem vessels.* Each xylem vessel may be up to one meter long.

Once inside the xylem, water molecules travel upward toward the leaf. There are several hypotheses to explain this movement. The root pressure mechanism has already been described. Another possible explanation is based on a property of water known as **capillarity** [kap ə lar′ ət ē]—the ability to move upward (against the force of gravity) through narrow tubes. This movement is called capillary action.

Capillary action occurs as a result of the strong attraction that water molecules have for surfaces such as glass or the walls of a tracheid or xylem vessel. This attraction between substances of unlike molecules is called **adhesion** [ad hē′ zhən]. The water molecules adhere to the surfaces of the xylem vessels and are pulled up by capillary action. Experiments have shown that capillary action is a slow process and, like root pressure, cannot account for water transport in very tall plants.

Water molecules also have a strong attraction for each other. This attraction between like molecules is called **cohesion** [kō hē′ zhən]. A third explanation for upward movement of water in plants is the **cohesion-tension theory**. This mechanism involves a continuous column of water that stretches from the roots to the leaves. Water is constantly being lost from the leaves by evaporating during a process called **transpiration**. As water

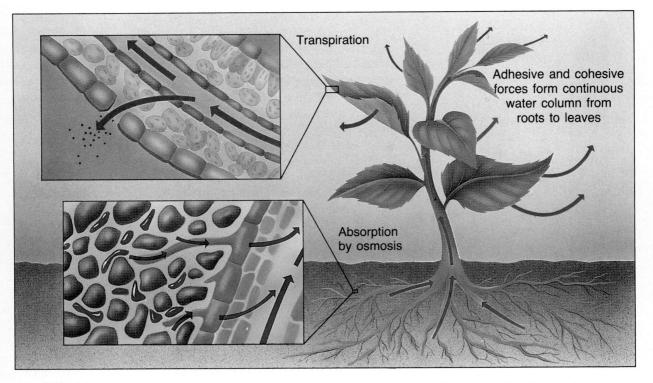

Transpiration

Adhesive and cohesive forces form continuous water column from roots to leaves

Absorption by osmosis

Figure 23-12 Water absorption and conduction in plants involves osmosis, adhesion, cohesive forces, and transpiration.

molecules leave, cohesive forces cause them to pull other water molecules after them. This pull or tension is transmitted down the entire length of the water column. In an unbroken chain, the water molecules move upward through the xylem from the root through the stem to the leaf. Water molecules in the soil replace those that are lost through the leaves. The high cohesive forces between the water molecules allow no air spaces in the xylem vessels, which are never empty.

Although no single process has been shown to account for upward movement of water in all plants, some combination of the forces described may provide an acceptable explanation. Root pressure, capillary action, adhesion, evaporation, cohesion, and tension should all be considered.

23-13 Translocation of Food

Sap containing dissolved sugars is transported through the plant by the phloem tissue. The movement of food from one part of a plant to another is called **translocation**.

Like xylem vessels, phloem cells form a continuous pipeline through the plant. In phloem, the pipelines are called *sieve tubes*. The cells of the sieve tubes, called **sieve tube elements**, are long and thick-walled. Their sloping ends contain many tiny holes,

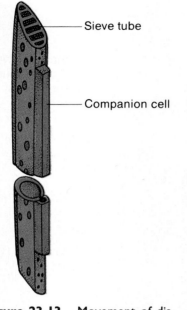

Figure 23-13 Movement of dissolved sugars occurs through sieve-like structures in the phloem.

giving them the appearance of sieves. The sieve tube elements are arranged end to end through the length of the plant.

Unlike the vessels of xylem, the sieve tubes are made up of living cells. Although sieve tube elements contain cytoplasm, as they mature they lose their nuclei. In flowering plants, sieve tube elements are connected to nearby cells, called **companion cells**, by thin strands of cytoplasm. The nuclei of the companion cells probably control the activities of the sieve tube elements. A sieve tube element and a companion cell are shown in Figure 23-13.

Although phloem has been studied for many years, botanists have not been able to determine exactly how translocation occurs. The hypothesis that has the most experimental support is the **pressure-flow hypothesis** which proposes that food is transported through the phloem as a result of differences in pressure.

When sugar molecules produced in a leaf enter a particular sieve tube element, the concentration of water in that element is lowered. Water enters from neighboring cells by osmosis and increases the pressure in the sieve tube. Eventually, the contents of the element are pushed out through the sieve at the end and into the next element. Evidence indicates that translocation is a process that requires energy.

Dissolved food moves downward from its point of manufacture in the leaf to other parts of the plant. There, it may nourish stem and root tissues, or it may be stored. In late winter, just before the growing season begins, food stored in the roots travels upward. This is when sap is collected for maple syrup. The food provides energy for the upper parts of the plant until the new leaves are able to manufacture food.

If you peel a ring of bark from a tree, a process called *girdling*, the phloem peels off with the cork. Without phloem, the tissues below the girdled area are cut off from their supply of food. Without food, the root tissues starve and the tree dies. Early American settlers used girdling as a method of clearing land.

CHECKPOINT ◆

15. What process causes water to enter root hairs?
16. What is the attraction between like molecules called?
17. What is a difference between xylem and phloem cells?
18. What characteristic of vessel elements makes them well suited for the transport of liquid?
19. Explain the pressure-flow hypothesis.
▶ 20. According to the cohesion theory, what would happen to the upward movement of water if the column of water in the xylem vessels broke?
▶ 21. Vessel elements are to xylem as _____ are to phloem.

▶ Denotes a question that involves *interpreting* and *applying* concepts.

EXAMINATION OF THE GROWING TIP OF A ROOT

In this activity you will look at the area of primary growth in a living root.

Objectives and Skills

☐ *Prepare* and *observe* a slide of living root tissue.
☐ *Locate* regions of the root tip.

Materials

slide and coverslip
medicine dropper
razor blade
microscope
iodine solution
radish or bean seedlings

Procedure and Observations

1. Read all instructions for this laboratory activity before you begin your work.
2. Observe the location of root hairs on the seedling.
3. Using the razor blade, cut off the top of the root, including some of the root hairs. **CAUTION: The blade is sharp. Take care not to cut your fingers.**
4. Make a longitudinal section of the root tip; that is, cut it lengthwise. Cut as thin a section as possible so that light can penetrate the section.
5. Make a wet mount slide of the root tip and stain it with a drop of iodine solution.
6. Examine the slide under low power, beginning at the tip and working upward. Look for differences in cell size and shape. Notice where cells are tightly packed.
7. Before leaving the laboratory, clean up all your materials and wash your hands thoroughly.

Grasses have a fibrous root system.

Analysis and Conclusions

1. The smallest cells are the newest. In which part of the root tip are new cells produced?
2. Describe the cells next to the smallest cells. What process has occurred in these cells?
3. Do any of the smallest cells have root hairs? Why or why not?
4. Draw a diagram of the root tip, labeling the three zones of primary growth.

CHAPTER REVIEW

Summary

‣ Roots and stems conduct materials within the plant. Roots also store food, absorb water, and anchor the plant. Stems also manufacture and store food and display leaves to light. Roots supply the plant with minerals and water. Stems connect the roots with leaves.

‣ Stems grow upward from their tips, and roots grow downward from their tips. Primary growth from rapid cell division occurs in the meristematic region. Newly-formed cells elongate and then become specialized for various functions.

‣ Secondary growth produced by the vascular cambium increases the width of a plant.

‣ The tissues of the root and stem include tissues for storage, conduction, protection, and reproduction.

‣ Branches of stems originate on the stem's surface, while lateral roots originate in the interior of the root.

‣ Herbaceous plants usually live for only one year and are limited in size. Woody stems may live for many years and increase their width each year. Herbaceous monocots and dicots have different arrangements of vascular tissue.

‣ Some types of stems are modified for storage and reproduction. Examples include tubers, stolons, and corms.

‣ Vascular tissues transport water, dissolved minerals, and food throughout the plant. Xylem is composed of hollow vessels and tracheids. Phloem contains sieve tubes.

‣ Water enters the root hairs by the process of osmosis. Adhesion to the sides of the xylem vessels and cohesion of molecules to each other allow water to rise in a plant.

‣ Phloem conducts sap containing dissolved sugars throughout the plant. The best explanation for this process is the pressure-flow hypothesis.

Vocabulary

adhesion	lenticel
adventitious root	pericycle
bud scale	pith
bud scale scar	pressure-flow
bulb	hypothesis
capillarity	primary tissues
capillary water	root cap
cohesion	root hair
cohesion-	root pressure
tension theory	sapwood
companion cell	secondary growth
cork cambium	sieve tube element
corm	taproot
cortex	terminal bud
endodermis	tracheid
fibrous root system	translocation
growth ring	transpiration
heartwood	tuber
herbaceous	vessel element
lateral bud	zone of elongation
leaf scar	zone of maturation

Concept Mapping

Construct a concept map for stems. Include the following terms: herbaceous, cortex, xylem, vascular cambium, primary tissues, epidermis, cork cambium, phloem, secondary tissues, and woody. Use additional terms as you need them.

Review

1. Name three functions of roots.
2. What is the function of the root cap?
3. What tissue is found in the center of a mature dicot root? In the center of a mature dicot stem?
4. Place the following tissues of a dicot root in the correct order, beginning with the innermost tissue. (a) cork (b) cork cambium (c) cortex

(d) endodermis (e) epidermis (f) pericycle
(g) phloem (h) primary xylem (i) secondary
xylem

In the following list, match the stem tissue with
its function.

5.	cork	a.	stores food in
6.	cork cambium		young plant
7.	cortex	b.	carries water
8.	phloem	c.	produces second-
9.	pith		ary xylem and phloem
10.	vascular	d.	absorbs water from
	cambium		soil
11.	xylem	e.	carries food
		f.	reduces water loss
			from stem
		g.	produces cork cells

12. What tissues are found in the bark? What tissues are found in the wood?
13. Where in the stem does primary growth occur?
14. Indicate which of the following types of cells are found in xylem and which are found in phloem. (a) companion cell (b) vessel element (c) sieve tube element (d) tracheid
15. What hypothesis explains the translocation of food in vascular plants?
16. A parsnip, which looks like a white carrot, is an example of a _____ root.
17. Roots that grow out of stems are called _____ roots.

Interpret and Apply

18. The epidermis of the root lacks the waterproof cuticle found on the epidermis of most stems and leaves. Why is this important to the function of the root?
19. Compare the formation of lateral roots with the formation of branches in the stem.

20. Name two ways in which tracheids are different from xylem vessels.
21. Name two tissues found in the root that are not found in the stem.
22. Which of the following tissues are composed of cells that are dead at maturity? (a) vascular cambium (b) cork (c) xylem (d) epidermis (e) phloem
23. For which of the following processes must the plant expend energy? (a) absorption of water (b) translocation of sugars (c) uptake of minerals
24. Why does stripping the bark off a tree eventually kill it?
25. Name two functions that roots and stems have in common.
26. Tuber is to _____ as stolon is to asexual reproduction.

Critical Thinking

27. You have twigs from two different trees of the same species. On one twig, the bud scale scars are much closer together than on the other. Explain why.
28. When houseplants are transplanted, many of the root hairs are accidentally broken off. For this reason, it is important to water transplanted houseplants frequently. Explain why this is necessary.
29. You are given a branch of a tree. Describe two methods you could use to determine the age of the branch.
30. You could think of the growing tips of the root and shoot as mirror images of each other. Label the six regions and explain why the two growing tips are mirror images.
31. Can you think of a situation in which water would flow from a tree into the soil? What might cause this to happen and what would be its effect on the tree?

Chapter

24

LEAVES

Overview

LEAF STRUCTURE AND FUNCTION

24-1 Leaf Shape and Arrangement

24-2 Structure of the Leaf

24-3 Leaf Venation

24-4 Photosynthesis in the Leaf

24-5 Gas Exchange

24-6 Transpiration

24-7 Wilting

LEAF MODIFICATIONS

24-8 Specialized Leaves

24-9 Insectivorous Plants

Why are most leaves very thin?

LEAF STRUCTURE AND FUNCTION

Whether you live in the city or country, you probably will find dozens of different leaves. Each leaf will be a different shade of green, a different size and shape, and the pattern of the veins will differ from leaf to leaf. However, most of the leaves you find will share a common function—photosynthesis.

24-1 Leaf Shape and Arrangement

Leaves grow out of meristematic tissue in the stem. You may recall that meristematic tissue is plant tissue which is still able to reproduce. The region of the stem where the leaf is attached is called the **node**.

Dicot leaves are usually composed of two parts, the blade and the petiole. The **blade** is the flattened portion of the leaf. The flattened leaf blade allows for maximum exposure of the leaf surface to sunlight. In addition, the arrangement of leaves on a plant gives maximum exposure to the sun. The **petiole** is the stemlike structure that connects the blade to the stem. There is always a bud at the base of each petiole. Monocot leaves typically consist of a blade surrounded by a sheath.

A leaf with a petiole that is attached to a single blade is called a **simple leaf**. Some leaves have many small blades, or **leaflets**, that are attached to one petiole. The leaflets all arise from one bud. The entire structure is a single leaf. Because it came from one bud, it is called a **compound leaf**. You can tell the difference between a group of simple leaves and a single compound leaf by looking for the buds. Simple leaves have a bud at the base of each petiole. Compound leaves have a bud located at the base of its single petiole.

Section Objectives

A **Describe** the external structure of a leaf.

B **Identify** the structures present in a leaf cross section and **state** the function of each.

C **Relate** the structure of the stomata to the processes of gas exchange and transpiration.

D **Discuss** the relationship of leaves to other plant parts and to the environment in transpiration.

DO YOU KNOW?

Information: A leaf has a life history. It is born from a meristem, dies, and falls to the ground. During its life, a leaf changes from being an importer and consumer of resources to being an exporter and supplier of carbohydrate.

Figure 24-1 A simple leaf arises from a node on a stem. *Left:* In dicots, a leaf commonly consists of a petiole and a blade. *Right:* Monocots typically have a long and narrow blade without a petiole.

Leaves **403**

Figure 24-2 In compound leaves, many leaflets are attached to one petiole, which is attached to the stem. Notice that there is a bud at the base of each petiole. There are *no* buds at the base of the leaflets of compound leaves.

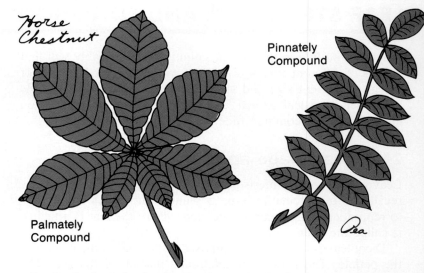

Horse Chestnut

Pinnately Compound

Palmately Compound

Pea

In the leaf of the horse chestnut, the leaflets come together at a central point. This is similar to the arrangement of your fingers which all join at your palm. Therefore, this leaf type is said to be **palmately compound**. In other plants, such as the pea, the leaflets attach to the petiole in a pattern resembling a feather. Such leaves are said to be **pinnately compound**.

24-2 Structure of the Leaf

Leaves are composed of the same types of tissues as roots and stems. Each type of tissue contributes to the process of photosynthesis. An amazing amount of photosynthetic machinery fits into a leaf. The arrangement of tissues in Figure 24-3 is typical of many familiar dicot leaves.

Epidermis The top and bottom layers of the leaf are called the epidermis. The epidermis protects the inner tissues from injury and drying out. The upper and lower epidermis form a sort of sandwich, with the inner tissues as filling.

Epidermal cells secrete a substance that forms the **cuticle**, a waxy covering on leaves. The cuticle prevents water escaping from the leaf. This is a critical function. In order to photosynthesize, leaves need both sunlight and water. The leaves of any plant have an enormous amount of surface area. This, of course, is ideal for water evaporation. Imagine a film of water as thin as a leaf. How quickly would it evaporate?

Epidermal hairs also decrease the rate of water evaporation. These fine hairs are extensions of epidermal cells and cover the leaves of many plants. They slow down the rate of evaporation by slowing down the rate of air movement near the leaf surface. This creates a layer of still, humid air next to the leaf.

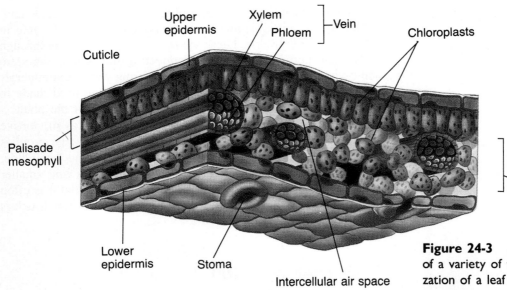

Upper epidermis
Xylem
Phloem
Vein
Chloroplasts
Cuticle
Palisade mesophyll
Spongy mesophyll
Lower epidermis
Stoma
Intercellular air space

Figure 24-3 A leaf is composed of a variety of tissues. The organization of a leaf centers around veins that conduct food away from, and water toward, the green mesophyll cells.

Guard Cells and Stomata Embedded in the epidermis, especially the lower epidermis, are crescent-shaped cells called **guard cells**. Unlike other cells of the epidermis, guard cells contain chloroplasts and carry out photosynthesis. Each pair of guard cells surrounds an opening called a **stoma** [stō′ mə]. The stoma (plural, stomata) is a pore that opens and closes, depending on the shape of the two guard cells around it. When the stomata are open, gases can move in and out of the leaf. The main gases moving through the stomata are carbon dioxide and water vapor. You may notice that greenhouses are kept very humid. This reduces water loss from the stomata. This is one of the reasons plants thrive in greenhouses. Many home gardeners mist their plants to achieve the same effect. Why do you think this would be effective?

Mesophyll Inside the epidermis are two layers of cells called **mesophyll** [mēz′ ō fil]. Most photosynthesis takes place in the mesophyll. Mesophyll cells near the upper epidermis are long and narrow. Because they resemble the palisades, or stakes, of a fence, these cells are called **palisade mesophyll**.

Below the palisade mesophyll are loosely packed cells with many air spaces between them. The air spaces give these cells the name **spongy mesophyll**. The cells of the spongy mesophyll contain fewer chloroplasts than those of the palisade mesophyll.

Look at the leaf cross section in Figure 24-3. Notice that the spaces in the spongy mesophyll are arranged so that all the palisade and mesophyll cells are in contact with air spaces inside the leaf. This organization allows mesophyll cells direct access to the carbon dioxide entering the leaf through the stomates.

BIOLOGY INSIGHT

Unity and Diversity: The plant leaf, like the human lung, can function only when it is able to exchange gases with the environment. As a result, the leaf, like the lung, is an organ that is sensitive to smog and air pollution.

DO YOU KNOW?

Information: The leaf of the black oak has about 100 000 stomata per centimeter on its lower epidermis. This accounts for less than 1 percent of the leaf's surface.

Information: If the large and small vascular bundles in a single elm leaf were placed end-to-end, they would measure more than 200 meters long.

Leaf Veins Throughout the mesophyll are vascular bundles containing xylem and phloem. Vascular bundles that are located in the leaf are called **veins**. These vascular bundles continue through the petiole and into the stem, connecting the leaf to the stem and eventually to the root. Xylem cells bring water and minerals from the root to the leaf. Phloem cells carry the food made in the leaf away from the mesophyll to other parts of the plant.

The veins are surrounded by fiber cells which act as supportive tissue and help support the leaf blade. Several vascular bundles enter the leaf blade through the petiole. Within the leaf blade, each bundle branches and rebranches into smaller and smaller groups of vessels. The branching becomes so fine that it is often difficult to see with the unaided eye. Thus no mesophyll cell is more than a few cells away from vascular tissue.

24-3 Leaf Venation

The mesophyll of a leaf is filled with numerous veins. The arrangement of veins in a leaf is called its **venation**. The veins are continuous with the vascular system of the stem. Look at Figure 24-4. In most monocots, leaf veins of similar size are nearly parallel to each other. This arrangement is called *parallel venation*.

In dicots, the veins of the leaves are branched in a network pattern. The arrangement of veins in a leaf that has one main vein from which other smaller veins branch off is known as *netted venation*.

24-4 Photosynthesis in the Leaf

Recall that chloroplasts require water, carbon dioxide, and light energy in order to carry on photosynthesis. Glucose and oxygen gas are produced. The plant uses the glucose and the oxygen diffuses into the atmosphere. The oxygen in the air you breathe comes almost entirely from the process of photosynthesis.

Water also travels to the mesophyll through the vascular bundles. Since the branching of the xylem is so fine, no mesophyll cell is more than a short distance from the water supply. Water can easily diffuse through the distance of a few cells.

Phloem, like xylem, branches out in the leaf so that no mesophyll cell is far from phloem. Glucose produced during photosynthesis is quickly loaded into the phloem. Some of the glucose is converted to starch, which may be stored in the mesophyll cells. Additional glucose is used by the leaf to make ATP for its own needs. Still more glucose is carried by the phloem to the stems and roots where it is used for storage, growth, and metabolism.

Figure 24-4 The arrangement of veins, or venation, varies in leaves of different species of plants. In most dicots, the veins are arranged in a branching pattern. By comparison, most monocots have veins arranged parallel to each other.

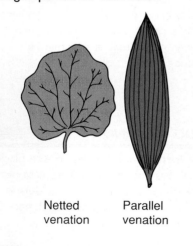

Netted
venation

Parallel
venation

Since roots are below the ground, they are not exposed to light and cannot photosynthesize. This means they get their glucose from mesophyll cells in the leaves. It is interesting to observe that if the leaves of a plant die, the roots and stems will eventually die also. The Irish potato famines of the 1850s were caused by a fungus which destroyed the leaves of the potato plant. Since the leaves could not photosynthesize, there was no glucose for the potato plants.

24-5 Gas Exchange

The guard cells and the stomata regulate the exchange of gases between the leaf and the atmosphere. Special adaptations of the guard cells allow them to control the rate at which water vapor leaves the leaf.

Because the guard cells contain chloroplasts, they are able to carry out photosynthesis. During photosynthesis, the guard cells become swollen with water, or *turgid*.

The walls of the guard cells next to the stomata are thick and relatively inflexible. The outer walls of the guard cells, the ones next to the epidermis, are thinner and more elastic. As the guard cells become turgid, the thinner, outer walls of the cells push outward into the epidermal cells. This change in shape pulls the thicker inner walls away from each other, opening the stomata.

On sunny days when photosynthesis is proceeding rapidly, the cells in the leaf require carbon dioxide. At that time, the stomata are usually open. When it is dark, of course, photosynthesis cannot occur. Then the guard cells lose water. The loss of water causes the guard cells to become limp, closing the stomata. When the stomata are closed, carbon dioxide does not enter the leaf, and water vapor does not leave. Since photosynthesis does not occur at night, there is no need for carbon dioxide. The closed stomata conserve water.

Many people wonder if the tissues of the leaf carry out cellular respiration as well as photosynthesis. They do. In respiration, sugars are broken down to provide energy (ATP) for the processes occurring in the plant. Leaves use the food they produce during photosynthesis for respiration. The cells of the leaf use some of the oxygen produced in photosynthesis for respiration. Photosynthesis occurs only while it is light, while respiration continues around the clock.

24-6 Transpiration

Recall from Chapter 23 that water from the soil enters the root by osmosis. Water molecules travel upward through the xylem vessels as a result of cohesion to each other and adhesion to the

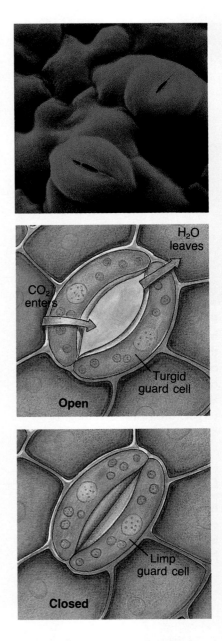

Figure 24-5 *Top:* This SEM shows the guard cells surrounding a stoma. *Middle:* When guard cells are turgid, the stoma is open. *Bottom:* When guard cells are limp, the stoma is closed.

Leaves   **407**

Figure 24-6 Plant cells usually have high concentrations of salts in their vacuoles. As a result, plant cells constantly absorb water and remain turgid. When a plant cannot absorb enough water to maintain turgor, the result is wilting, or drooping of the leaves and stem.

▶ Denotes a question that involves *interpreting* and *applying* concepts.

walls of the xylem vessels. Once in the leaf, some of the water is used for photosynthesis. Some is used in other metabolic processes. Most of the water evaporates through the stomata into the atmosphere. The evaporation of water from leaves is called *transpiration*.

As water evaporates from the stomata, cells close to the stomata absorb water from the neighboring cells by osmosis. Those cells, in turn, absorb water from more distant cells, until water is eventually absorbed from xylem in the veins of the leaf. In this way, water from the xylem is available to all the cells in the leaf.

24-7 Wilting

Water diffuses from the xylem vessels into the other cells of the plant. When a plant cell is full of water, its cytoplasm presses outward against the cell wall. A cell in this condition is said to be turgid. Turgor pressure provides the support that keeps the stems of herbaceous plants erect.

When a plant cell lacks water, its cytoplasm shrinks away from its cell wall, resulting in plasmolysis. If a plant's rate of water loss by transpiration is greater than its rate of water absorption, its cells suffer plasmolysis. You can see the result of this loss of turgor, or **wilting**, in the plant in Figure 24-6.

When plants wilt, the stomata close. With the stomata closed, the rate of transpiration decreases; therefore, closed stomata conserve water. When more water becomes available, the stomata open again. Therefore, wilting is a response that allows plants to regulate their water balance. If water deprivation is severe enough or occurs over enough time, plants can no longer recover from wilting. This is called the *permanent wilting point* of the plant.

CHECKPOINT ◆

1. Describe a simple leaf. What are the functions of each part?
2. Which tissue prevents the leaf from injury or drying out?
3. Which leaf structure provides water for photosynthesis?
4. How is wilting helpful to a plant?
5. Explain how each ingredient required for photosynthesis gets to the chloroplasts in the leaf.
▶ 6. How would covering a plant with clear plastic affect the rate of transpiration? Explain.
▶ 7. Which plant would require more water—one in the shade or one in direct sunlight? Explain.

LEAF MODIFICATIONS

When you think of a leaf, you probably picture the typical leaf, which is broad and flat. Not all leaves fit that description. Although different types of leaves share the same basic structure, there are many variations in this structure and, therefore, the function of leaves. Each type of modification allows the plant to thrive in situations where it otherwise might not survive. As you read about types of specialized leaves, try to determine the selective advantage given to the plant by its modification.

24-8 Specialized Leaves

The leaves of conifers are often modified into **needles**. In comparison to the leaves of angiosperms, needles have a small surface area. They are covered with a thick, water-resistant cuticle that is resistant to freezing. For these reasons, needles are able to remain on conifers during the cold winter months.

Some leaves, such as those of the grape shown in Figure 24-7, are modified into tendrils. **Tendrils** are long, slender, curling structures that wrap around branches or other objects. Tendrils support the plant as it climbs.

Some leaves are modified into sharp structures called **spines**. If you have ever grasped the stem of a plant with spines, you know its function. The spines of a cactus are actually modified leaves. (Cacti can be confusing. The fleshy pads of some cacti are not leaves, but actually modified stems.) Can you imagine how tasty a moist, juicy cactus would be to a thirsty desert animal? A cactus without spines would soon be eaten.

BIOLOGY INSIGHT

Structure Is Related to Function: Climbing roots and tendrils are distinguishable from each other because they contain different tissues. The identity of an organ is determined by the arrangement of its tissues.

Figure 24-7 *Left:* A pine needle is shown in cross section. Note that the vein is located in the middle of the leaf. *Right:* The tendrils of a grapevine are modified leaves.

Figure 24-8 Venus's Flytrap attracts insects with nectar on its leaf surface. The insect brushes against hairs that trigger the traplike closing of the leaf.

▶ Denotes a question that involves *interpreting* and *applying* concepts.

Some leaves also have hairs that serve as protection. Nettle leaves, for example, have cells that are modified into hairs. Each hair has a tiny vessel on its tip. When you brush against it, your skin stings for several minutes. Once you have touched a nettle, you are unlikely to touch another.

Many leaves also contain poisonous or protective chemicals. The nicotine in tobacco is a defensive compound that is toxic to many vertebrates. The leaves of poison ivy are also well protected, although some mammals, birds, and insects can eat them.

Sometimes leaves become thickened and may store food in their blades or petioles. **Succulents**, like the familiar jade plant store water in their thick, fleshy leaves. In what climate might this ability be useful?

24-9 Insectivorous Plants

Insectivorous, or insect-eating, plants have highly modified leaves. Insectivorous plants usually grow in bogs or other areas where there is little nitrogen in the soil. These plants capture and digest insects to obtain nitrogen and other nutrients.

The pitcher plant is an example of an insectivorous plant. In pitcher plants, the leaf is modified into a tube with an overhanging hood and hairs that point downward. This arrangement traps insects unfortunate enough to enter the leaf. Another insectivorous plant is the sundew. In the sundew, glands on the leaf margin secrete a gluey substance that traps insects that land on the leaf. In both cases, enzymes in the leaves digest the captured insects. The leaves of insectivorous plants are able to carry out photosynthesis, so they do not actually eat the insects. They use insects only as a source of nitrogen.

CHECKPOINT ◆

8. What are the leaves of a cactus called?
9. Which nutrient do insectivorous plants obtain from insects?
10. Give two reasons why the modifications in pine needles enable them to remain on a tree during winter.
▶ 11. Most forests in the United States are dominated by deciduous trees, whereas forests in Canada are dominated by evergreens. Explain.
▶ 12. The fleshy leaves of succulents are ιο water conservation as tendrils are to _____.
▶ 13. Are insectivorous plants autotrophs or heterotrophs? Support your answer.

THE OBSERVATION OF GUARD CELLS

In this activity you will observe the action of guard cells in response to their environment.

Objectives and Skills

☐ *Locate* stomata and guard cells on a leaf.
☐ *Observe* stomata and guard cells in different conditions.
☐ *Explain* how guard cells help plants maintain homeostasis in a changing environment.

Materials

paper towel	medicine dropper
water	microscope
2 slides	4% salt solution
2 coverslips	geranium leaf
scalpel	safety goggles

Procedure and Observations

1. Read all instructions for this laboratory activity before you begin your work.
2. Copy a data table like the one shown below onto a separate sheet of paper.
3. Remove a piece of the lower epidermis of a geranium leaf. Break the leaf with a snapping action. This will leave the two parts connected at the bottom by a transparent layer, which is the lower epidermis. Carefully peel away one half of the leaf from the epidermis attached to the other half of the leaf. **CAUTION: The scalpel is sharp. Use it with care.** Cut a piece of the epidermis and prepare a wet mount slide.
4. Observe the slide under the microscope. Locate the stomata and the guard cells surrounding them. Draw and label a single stoma and its surrounding guard cells. Note the structures present in the guard cells.
5. Put on safety goggles and lab apron.
6. Place a few drops of salt water at the edge of the coverslip of one of your slides. Use a paper towel to draw the salt water across the slide. Observe this slide under the microscope again. Draw the stoma and guard cells and note any changes in their appearance.
7. Before leaving the laboratory, clean up all your materials and wash your hands thoroughly.

Analysis and Conclusions

1. How does the structure of a guard cell aid the plant?
2. What would happen if too much water left the plant?
3. How do stomata prevent water from leaving the plant?
4. How did the addition of salt water change the concentration of water in the guard cells? How did the guard cells respond to this change?
5. How do the guard cells help the plant to maintain homeostasis?
6. After adding salt water to the slide, which way does water flow, into the guard cells or out of the guard cells? Explain.

DATA TABLE		
	Before salt water	**After salt water**
Drawing:		
Observations:		

CHAPTER REVIEW

Summary

▸ Leaves are the primary photosynthetic organs of the plant. Although leaves vary in outward appearance, they are all adapted to bring carbon dioxide, water, and light to the chloroplasts for photosynthesis.

▸ Leaves are adapted to conserve water. These adaptations are reflected in structures, such as a waxy noncellular cuticle, an upper and lower epidermis, veins, guard cells, and stomata.

▸ The internal structure of a leaf is adapted for maintaining photosynthesis. The process of photosynthesis occurs in mesophyll cells. Each type of tissue in a leaf has a specific function.

▸ The leaf veins contain xylem and phloem which are continuous with the xylem and phloem in the stem and the root. Therefore, the leaf veins complete the continuous pipeline that carries water from the soil to the leaf.

▸ Water exits the leaf through stomata. Guard cells regulate this process, thus aiding the plant in maintaining homeostasis.

▸ Sugar produced in the leaf enters the phloem of the veins and is carried to other parts of the plant. This sugar is used in the process of respiration, carried on by all cells of the plant.

▸ Some types of leaves are modified in structure and have functions other than photosynthesis. Some of these functions include protection, capturing insects, and climbing.

Vocabulary

blade	mesophyll
compound leaf	needle
cuticle	node
guard cells	palisade mesophyll
insectivorous	palmately compound
leaflet	petiole

pinnately compound	succulent
simple leaf	tendril
spine	vein
spongy mesophyll	venation
stoma	wilting

Concept Mapping

Construct a concept map for leaf structure and function. Include the following terms: sugar, mesophyll, stoma, carbon dioxide, vein, water, photosynthesis, and epidermis.

Review

1. Draw and completely label a diagram of a typical leaf cross section.
2. Name the two tissues found in leaf veins. Give the function of each.
3. Name two ways leaves are adapted to conserve water.
4. Name in order, from lower surface to upper, the tissues found in a leaf.
5. Where are the guard cells located?
6. In which tissues are the chloroplasts located?
7. What is a succulent?
8. A leaf in which many leaflets are attached to one petiole is called a _____ leaf.
9. A maple leaf has _____ venation.
10. What nutrient do insectivorous plants obtain from insects?

In the following list, match the leaf part with its function.

11. cuticle	**a.** conduction of food and water
12. epidermis	
13. mesophyll	**b.** protection
14. stomata	**c.** waterproofing
15. veins	**d.** exchange of gases
	e. photosynthesis

In the following list, match the leaf modification with its function.

16. fleshy leaves
17. tendril
18. spine
19. insect trap
20. needle

a. protection
b. water storage
c. prevention of water loss
d. obtaining nitrogen
e. climbing

Interpret and Apply

21. How are spongy and palisade mesophyll alike? How are they different?
22. How does the flat shape of many leaves aid in photosynthesis?
23. How do guard cells control the size of the stomata?

Choose the best answer for each of the following questions. Write your answers on a separate sheet of paper.

24. Which of the following is not contained in a vascular bundle?
(a) xylem   (b) phloem   (c) mesophyll
25. Which of the following does not belong with the others?
(a) bud   (b) compound   (c) petiole
(d) blade
26. Which of the following is not a leaf tissue?
(a) cork   (b) epidermis   (c) mesophyll
(d) phloem
27. Which cell type does not contain chlorophyll?
(a) guard cell   (b) spongy mesophyll
(c) xylem   (d) palisade mesophyll
28. Which of the following does not belong with the others?
(a) spine   (b) stoma   (c) tendril
(d) needle
29. How could tendrils aid a grapevine in survival?

30. What tissues would you expect to find in tendrils?
31. Why is water conservation important for a leaf?

Critical Thinking

32. If you watered a plant well, why would it still be helpful for the plant to be in a moist environment?
33. How are the veins in a leaf like the veins in your body? How are they different?
34. What would happen to the rate of photosynthesis if leaves were spherical instead of flat? Explain.
35. If the stomata were closed during the day, how would the rate of photosynthesis be affected? Explain.
36. Propose a reason for the term "guard cells."
37. Stomata open and close in response to sugar concentration and osmosis. Recall from Chapter 5 that the rate of diffusion increases with temperature. How would high temperatures affect the rate at which stomata open?
38. Name several factors that might speed up the flow of water into the roots, through the xylem, and out of the stomata.
39. Generally, how many cotyledons are contained in the seed of a plant that bears a leaf without a petiole?
40. Trace the path of a molecule of water from the time you water a plant until the water is used in photosynthesis.

Chapter

25

PLANT GROWTH AND RESPONSE

Overview

PATTERNS OF PLANT GROWTH

25-1 Time Patterns of Plants
25-2 Growth Patterns of Plants
25-3 Plant Hormones
25-4 Apical Dominance

PLANT RESPONSE

25-5 Tropisms
25-6 Control of Flowering
25-7 Leaf Senescence
25-8 Nastic Movements

How do commercial growers control the flowering of plants?

PATTERNS OF PLANT GROWTH

Growth is a fundamental process in living things. It represents the synthesis of new living material. In order to grow, plants require the basic building-block molecules to build new cell walls, cytoplasm, and other cell parts. The plant organs you studied in Chapters 23 and 24 function to supply the necessary ingredients and energy for growth. What controls the growth of a plant?

Individual plants of the same species have tremendous variations in growth and reproduction. You may have noticed the differences in size of vegetables at the supermarket. In nature, wide variations in weight or number of seeds can easily be found. What causes these differences?

Section Objectives

A *Place* the stages in the life of a seed plant in the correct order.

B *Give* examples of plants with different life spans.

C *List* four classes of plant hormones and *state* the function of each.

D *Explain* the cause of apical dominance.

25-1 Time Patterns of Plants

Plants pass through two phases of growth—vegetative and reproductive. Vegetative growth increases the size of the root and shoot of the plant. In the sexually reproducing phase, the flower, fruit, and seed are produced. Together, the two phases comprise the life history of a plant. Seed plants typically pass through the following stages of their life history diagramed in Figure 25-1.

Plants that pass through all of these stages in a single growing season are called **annuals**. The growing season may be many months or only a few weeks long. Many weeds, wildflowers, garden flowers, and vegetables are annuals. In general, annuals are herbaceous plants that produce many small seeds. The dormant seeds represent next year's crop of plants.

A **biennial** is a plant that lives for two growing seasons. The vegetative phase occurs during the first season as the seed germinates and produces leaves and roots. The reproductive phase occurs during the second season when the plant flowers and produces seeds. Biennials are mostly herbaceous. Often biennials store food from one growing season to the next in fleshy stems or roots. Carrots, beets, celery, and cabbage are biennials.

A **perennial** is a plant in which the vegetative structures live year after year. Perennials may be either woody or herbaceous. Herbaceous perennials often grow from bulbs or rhizomes. Some garden perennials are peonies, irises, and roses. Woody perennials like shrubs and trees flower only when they become adult plants.

Plant activities are timed to correspond to environmental cues. It may help to think of a play in which an actor listens for a cue to speak the correct line at the appropriate time. Without the cue, the play would not make sense. Similarly, stages in the life of a plant must occur at an appropriate time for the plant to grow and reproduce.

Figure 25-1 The stages in the life history of an annual are shown. Note the large proportion of time that a plant spends as a seed in the dormant phase.

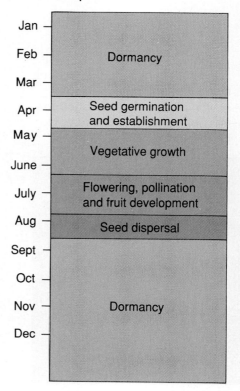

Jan —
Feb — Dormancy
Mar —
Apr — Seed germination and establishment
May —
June — Vegetative growth
July — Flowering, pollination and fruit development
Aug — Seed dispersal
Sept —
Oct —
Nov — Dormancy
Dec —

Adaptation and Evolution: The length of time a plant lives is an example of gene-environment interaction. Although the genes of a plant dictate a specific life span, many environmental factors have an effect. Variations in offspring of the same plant may increase the life span of some individuals. Those which are best adapted to the environment will survive longer.

DO YOU KNOW?

Information: The growth of tendrils may be very rapid. Tendrils produced by members of the gourd family (squash, pumpkin, and cucumber) can coil completely around a support object within ten minutes.

Figure 25-2 Pokeberry is a common perennial that flowers during summer. Much of the variation and many of its activities are controlled by hormones.

25-2 Growth Patterns of Plants

Plants have characteristic patterns of growth. They grow into the air and into the soil, forming various types of root systems, flowers, and leaves. A plant's form varies according to the amount of light and moisture it receives.

The overall form of a plant is the result of cell growth and development. Plant cells go through three fairly distinct growth phases. First, new cells are formed by mitosis and cell division. Second, the newly formed cells then increase in size. Many types of cells enlarge by getting longer, a process called *elongation*. The third phase consists of cells becoming specialized, or mature, by the process of differentiation. The same sequence of phases occurs in all growing parts of a plant.

25-3 Plant Hormones

What controls the activities of a plant? What causes a stem to grow straight or to branch? Botanists now know that plant activities are controlled by a combination of factors. One important factor is heredity. Recall from Chapter 9 that plant height, seed texture, and flower color were determined by hereditary factors.

Another factor that controls plant activities includes chemical substances called **hormones**. Hormones are active in very small quantities and are transported throughout the body of a plant. Each plant hormone has a different effect on the plant. Some hormones *stimulate* cells to divide, elongate, or mature. Others *inhibit* growth and cause dormancy. Sometimes the actions of several hormones combine to cause a particular plant response. The functions of many plant hormones are not fully understood. It is one of the most exciting areas of plant research today.

Auxins Auxins are a group of hormones that influence plant growth in a variety of ways. The effects of auxins depend on their concentration and the type of tissue in which they are found. Auxins are best known for their ability to increase plant growth by stimulating enlargement and elongation of stem cells. There also is evidence that auxins may act with other hormones to stimulate cell division.

Gibberellins Gibberellins, like auxins, are hormones that produce stem elongation. Plant stems that are treated with gibberellin become long and thin. Dwarf varieties of plants are often caused by mutations that result in an unusually low production of gibberellins. If gibberellins are applied to dwarf plants, the plants often grow to normal heights.

Cytokinins Another class of growth hormones is the cytokinins. This group of hormones stimulates cell division rather than cell

elongation. Cytokinins may be important in regulating the transport and storage of food in plant tissues. Cytokinins are produced in the meristems of the roots.

Ethylene Ethylene is a particularly interesting plant hormone because it is a gas. It is the hormone primarily responsible for fruit ripening. It also interacts with other chemicals to play a major role in a plant's loss of leaves, flowers, and fruits.

Did you ever leave unripe tomatoes in a paper bag and return a week later to find them ripe and delicious? This ripening was caused by ethylene. Ethylene gas produced by the unripe fruit is held in by the paper bag, and causes the fruit to ripen. Similarly, fruits on a plant will ripen because of the ethylene produced by the plant.

CONSUMER BIOLOGY

Commercial growers have to ship fruit over long distances. They pick the fruit while it is still unripe and treat it with ethylene gas in order to have it ripe, but not spoiled, when it reaches the market. Consumers who buy fruit that is still unripe may speed up the process by enclosing the fruit in a small bag. This traps the ethylene that is given off by the ripening fruit.

25-4 Apical Dominance

As you learned in Chapter 23, growth at the terminal bud makes a stem get longer. Growth of lateral buds makes the stem branch and become bushy. The terminal bud, or apical meristem, produces auxins. Auxins in high concentration inhibit lateral bud formation, or branching. As the auxins diffuse down the stem, their concentration decreases. The inhibition of branching also decreases. Therefore, branches begin to develop at a distance from the terminal bud. This influence of the terminal bud on the growth

Figure 25-4 The cone shape of these fir trees is the result of hormones called auxins. The terminal buds produce auxin in concentrations high enough to inhibit lateral buds.

of lateral buds is called **apical dominance**. Apical dominance is easily demonstrated by removing the apical meristem of a bean plant. The lateral buds begin to grow.

In many conifers, such as fir or spruce trees, apical dominance is responsible for a cone-shaped tree. Branches farthest from the terminal bud show the greatest growth. In other plants, such as maple trees, apical dominance is not as strong. Instead, the trunk divides into several branches, making the tree appear rounded.

CHECKPOINT ◆

1. How many growing seasons do biennial plants live?
2. What class of plant hormones stimulates cell division? What hormones stimulate cell elongation?
3. How does the production of auxins in the apical meristem influence the growth of lateral buds?
4. List the stages in the life of a seed plant.
5. What two factors control plant activities?
6. A herbaceous plant that produces many small seeds is probably a _____.
▶ 7. Which hormone would help heal a wound in the stem of a plant?
▶ 8. Carrot is to biennial as maple tree is to _____.

▶ Denotes a question that involves *interpreting* and *applying* concepts.

PLANT RESPONSE

One property of all living things is the ability to detect and respond to the environment. Many animals are able to detect changes and respond to their environment by moving from one place to another. For example, if you are too cold, you can move to another place. By contrast, a plant is rooted from the time it germinates, so it cannot pick up and move to a more comfortable location. However, plants do have the ability to detect and make adjustments to changes in the environment.

25-5 Tropisms

If you see a fast-moving object headed straight for you, you must either move out of the way or hold up your hand to block it. You respond to a stimulus by moving. Even though they are rooted, plants also have the ability to move. Unlike the movement of your arm or leg, a plant's movement is not caused by muscles. Rather, it is the result of growth. The growth of a plant in a particular direction in response to a stimulus is called a **tropism**.

Tropisms result from unequal stimulation on opposite sides of the plant. In tropisms, the movement of the plant is dependent on the direction from which the stimulus comes. Movement toward a stimulus is called *positive tropism*. Movement away from a stimulus is called *negative tropism*.

Phototropism The growth of the plant toward a source of light is called positive phototropism. Look at Figure 25-5. When light is more intense on one side of a plant than on the other, auxins in the stem migrate toward the darker side of the plant. This causes the side of the stem farther from the light to grow more quickly. The uneven growth causes the stem to curve toward the light.

Geotropism Geotropism is the growth of a plant in response to gravity. Positive geotropism, or movement toward gravity, occurs in roots. Negative geotropism, or movement away from gravity, occurs in stems and leaves.

Like phototropism, negative geotropism results from an unequal distribution of auxins in the stem. If you place a growing plant in a horizontal position, most of the auxins accumulate in the lower side of the stem. This causes the cells on the lower side of the stem to grow longer than the cells on the upper side of the stem. As a result, the stem curls upward.

Positive geotropism causes roots to grow down in the direction of gravity. It is now thought that this root response is *not* due to auxins. Rather, it appears to be due to another, not yet identified, growth regulator.

Figure 25-5 *Top:* An example of positive phototropism. *Bottom:* Auxin movement causes cell elongation.

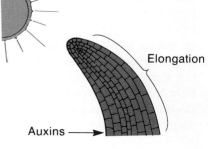

Elongation

Auxins

Plant Growth and Response **419**

Thigmotropism This tropism is the growth of a plant in response to touch. The tendrils of climbing plants show thigmotropism. When a tendril contacts a solid object, the side of the tendril away from the object grows faster than the side touching the object. The unequal rates of growth cause the tendril to curl around the object. There is some evidence that auxins play a role in this response.

25-6 Control of Flowering

Why do forsythias flower in the spring while chrysanthemums flower in the fall? Why do some species of dogwood or daylilies flower earlier or later than others? Clearly, the flowering of plants is somehow related to the time of year. **Photoperiodism** is a term used to describe plant processes that are influenced by the length of day or night. Photoperiodism affects flowering, seed germination, and leaf senescence.

After many years of research, it is now known that the time a particular plant flowers is related to the length of night. Some plants will flower only when the night is longer than a critical time. These are called short-day plants because they will flower during long nights and short days. Short-day plants include ragweed, goldenrod, and chrysanthemums. Notice that these plants tend to flower in the fall and winter.

Figure 25-6 This plant is responding to gravity. What kind of tropism is this called?

CONSUMER BIOLOGY

Florists often artificially vary the length of day to cause flowers to bloom in seasons when they would not naturally do so.

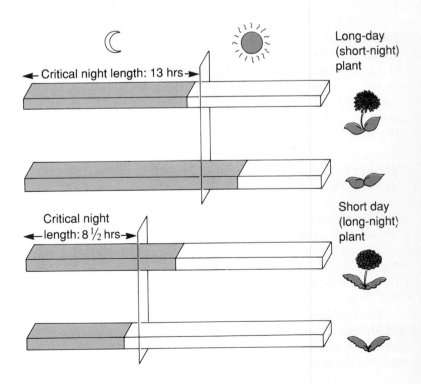

Figure 25-7 Flowering results from the combination of length of night (dark bar) and a plant's specific critical night length. The vertical marker shows the critical night length for two different plants. Notice that one plant has a critical night length of 13 hours, whereas the other plant has a critical night length of 8½ hours.

Other plants will flower only when night is shorter than a critical time. These are called long-day plants because they will flower during short nights and long days. Long-day plants include spinach, iris, and clover. These plants are typically spring bloomers —the long day indicates that winter is over. How do you think this is an adaptation that will help a plant survive?

Day-neutral plants appear to be unaffected by the length of night. Plants such as tomatoes, beans, and roses flower over a wide range of photoperiods.

The mechanism by which the length of night controls flowering is not fully understood. Evidence indicates that pigments in the leaves are sensitive to the amount of daylight. A proper photoperiod causes the leaves to produce a hormone that travels through the phloem to the flower buds. There it stimulates flowering. However, the hormone that controls flowering has not been isolated.

Finally, flowering is dependent on the general health of the plant. Plants require a lot of stored energy in order to flower. This is why a sickly house plant will not flower even if the length of night is appropriate.

25-7 Leaf Senescence

The processes leading to the death of a plant, or any of its parts, is called **senescence**. Recall from Chapter 22 that a plant is a population of parts. A plant may respond to seasonal changes or stress by changing the number of parts. Color changes and falling leaves are characteristic of many perennial plants.

During autumn, deciduous trees start the process of leaf senescence by halting the production of chlorophyll. This results in beautiful foliage colors every fall. Cytokinins are needed to maintain chlorophyll. For reasons not yet known, cytokinin production drops in the fall. The drop in cytokinin production causes the green chlorophyll molecule to break down. The magnesium ions in the chlorophyll are stored for new leaves in the next growing season.

Once nutrients have been withdrawn from the leaf, the process of leaf abscission begins. The separation of leaves from the stem is called **abscission**. Have you ever looked at a leaf that was about to fall from a plant? If so, you would notice a very thin layer of seemingly shriveled cells at the base of the petiole of the leaf. This layer is called the *abscission layer*. It actually is a layer of parenchyma cells which forms as the result of the interaction of several plant hormones.

Auxins inhibit abscission, whereas a hormone called ethylene promotes it. *Abscisic acid* speeds up the formation of the abscission layer. Later, enzymes destroy the walls of the cells in the abscission layer. When the cell walls are destroyed, only the

Figure 25-8 Weather can affect the color of fall foliage. Cool nights and sunny days give the leaves of maple and sumac trees a brilliant red color.

Figure 25-9 In many plants, the normal separation of the leaf from the stem is preceded by changes at the base of the petiole. These chemical and structural changes form an abscission layer indicated by the arrow below.

Plant Growth and Response **421**

Figure 25-10 The drooping of the leaves of the sensitive plant *Mimosa pudicum* is an example of a nastic movement.

vascular bundles remain to connect the leaf and stem. Thus each leaf is hanging by only threads of vascular tissue. Leaves in this condition are easily knocked from the plant by wind or rain. After the leaf falls, a layer of cork forms over the leaf scar. This cork protects the tissues of the stem.

25-8 Nastic Movements

Morning glories, as their name implies, open in the morning and close at night. What causes the petals to move? As the temperature of the air rises, changes in turgor pressure cause the morning glories to open their petals. The falling temperature of the evening causes their petals to close.

Some flowers open and close in response to light. These kinds of responses are called **nastic movements**. Unlike tropisms, nastic movements are independent of the direction from which the stimulus comes. Nastic movements usually occur as a result of changes in turgor pressure and are reversible.

Probably the best-known example of a nastic movement in response to contact is found in *Mimosa*, also called the sensitive plant. If you touch the leaflets of this plant, they fold upward, and the petiole droops. The response is immediate. As is true of all nastic movements, the reaction is reversible, and the leaflets soon assume their original, open position. The response of the mimosa leaf is the same if you touch the top or the bottom of the leaf. Unlike thigmotropism, nastic movement in response to touch is independent of the direction of contact.

The insect-trapping action of a Venus's-flytrap is another example of nastic movement. Hairs in the center of the leaves are stimulated when an insect lands on them. This stimulation causes the two sides of the leaf to snap together, trapping the insect.

CHECKPOINT ◆

9. What hormone stimulates the abscission of leaves?
10. A plant that flowers in the fall is probably a _____-day plant.
11. What term describes the growth of leaves toward the sun?
12. What plant organ has positive geotropism?
13. What changes occur in the leaf cells of *Mimosa* that cause it to respond rapidly to touch?
▶ 14. Do flowering plants that grow near the equator show photoperiodism? Explain.
▶ 15. Poinsettias are popular during winter, and irises are popular during spring. Why is the seasonal use of these plants unlikely to change?

▶ Denotes a question that involves *interpreting* and *applying* concepts.

THE EFFECT OF GIBBERELLIC ACID ON STEM GROWTH

In this activity, you will treat plants with a hormone and compare their growth to that of untreated plants.

Objectives and Skills

☐ *Perform* a controlled experiment.
☐ *Observe* stem growth under two conditions.
☐ *Compare* group and individual data.

Materials

ruler	2 plant misters
safety goggles	potting mixture
lab apron	gibberellic acid solution
2 plastic foam cups	2 bean seedlings

Procedure and Observations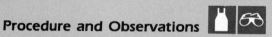

1. Read all instructions for this laboratory activity before you begin your work.
2. Copy the data sheet on this page onto a separate sheet of paper. Put on a lab apron.
3. Obtain two cups. Write your name on both cups. On one cup, write "treated." On the other cup, write "control." Fill each cup about 3/4 full of potting mixture. Place a bean seedling in each cup and cover its base with more mixture. Place the plants out of direct sunlight and keep them moist.
4. Before leaving the laboratory, clean up all materials and wash your hands thoroughly.
5. After three days, measure the height of each plant in centimeters and record the data.
6. Put on your safety goggles. Separate the two plants by several meters. Spray the plant in the cup labeled "treated" with the plant mister labeled "gibberellic acid." Continue to spray the stem and leaves until they are moist but *do not spray the soil*. Repeat the

procedure with the control plant, using the plant mister labeled "water."
7. Before leaving the laboratory, clean up all materials and wash your hands thoroughly.
8. For each of the next four days, measure each plant and record the data in your table. At the end of four days, determine how much each plant has grown since treatment with gibberellic acid. For each plant, divide the amount of growth in centimeters by the original height in centimeters to obtain the percentage of increase.
9. Select a classmate who will collect data on percentage-increase for the entire class. When all data have been collected, the data keeper should calculate the class averages for the group of plants treated with gibberellic acid and for the control group.

Analysis and Conclusions

1. Why did you separate the two plants when you applied gibberellic acid to one of them?
2. Which of your plants showed the greatest percentage increase in growth?
3. What factor caused the faster growth rate?
4. What is the advantage of pooling class data? Do your results agree with those of the class?

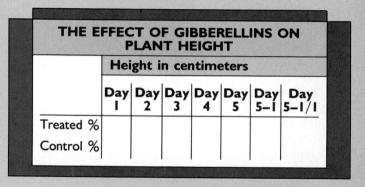

THE EFFECT OF GIBBERELLINS ON PLANT HEIGHT

	Height in centimeters						
	Day 1	Day 2	Day 3	Day 4	Day 5	Day 5–1	Day 5–1/1
Treated %							
Control %							

CHAPTER REVIEW

Summary

▸ Plants live in a particular space for a specific period of time. Although plants are stationary, they are active. Plant behavior is influenced by a variety of factors. Plant characteristics, such as life span and growth form, are under genetic and hormonal control. Some types of plants produce seeds and die in one growing season. Other types of plants complete their lives in two seasons, and still others live for many years.

▸ A plant's internal chemical environment also influences various plant functions. Chemical substances produced by the plant, called hormones, control plant growth, abscission of leaves and fruits, and the shape of the plant.

▸ The physical environment influences many plant activities. Plants have the ability to perceive changes in the environment. Activities such as leaf senescence, seed germination, and flowering time are determined by the length of darkness.

▸ The uneven accumulation of hormones called auxins is responsible for some types of plant movements, called tropisms. Tropisms can occur in response to many environmental stimuli and are irreversible.

Vocabulary

abscission	photoperiodism
annual	phototropism
apical dominance	senescence
auxin	thigmotropism
biennial	tropism
cytokinin	
ethylene	
geotropism	
gibberellin	
hormone	
nastic movement	
perennial	

Concept Mapping

Using the method of concept mapping described in the front of this book, complete a concept map for plant hormones. Copy the incomplete map and fill in the missing terms.

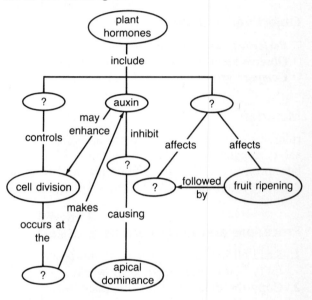

Review

1. What stimulus produces thigmotropism?
2. What is the difference between phototropism and photoperiodism?
3. Which of the following statements refer to tropisms and which refer to nastic movements? Some statements may refer to both.
   a. The movement is not reversible.
   b. The movement is due to changes in turgor pressure.
   c. The response is independent of the direction of stimulation.
   d. It can be a response to gravity.
   e. It can be a response to touch.
   f. It is caused by unequal distribution of auxins within the plant.
   g. It is reversible.

In the following list, match the hormone or class of hormones with the plant response or process that it controls. One hormone may control more than one process.

4. auxins
5. gibberellins
6. ethylene
7. cytokinins
8. unknown hormone

a. leaf abscission
b. flowering
c. cell elongation
d. cell division
e. phototropism
f. fruit ripening
g. apical dominance

9. What factors determine the life span of a plant?
10. Place the following stages in the life history of a seed plant in the correct order: death, germination, establishment, dormancy, senescence, flowering, seed dispersal, pollination, vegetative growth, and fruit development.
11. What hormone is responsible for the cone-shaped trees in a forest?

Interpret and Apply

12. Why is a plant tropism considered to be irreversible?
13. Give examples of plants with different life spans.
14. The roots of plants usually grow toward water. Is this a positive or negative tropism?
15. Most oak trees flower in the spring. Do you think they are long-day or short-day plants? Explain.
16. Which hormone is used on the roots of a plant that is about to be transplanted? Explain your choice
17. You have a tall, spindly plant. What could you do to the plant to make it fuller and more leafy?

18. Annual plants wither and die at the end of the growing season. How does this act as a dispersal mechanism?
19. Explain what may happen if an insect eats the apical meristem of a seedling.

Critical Thinking

20. Why can there be no nastic movement in response to gravity?
21. Why is it more efficient for color change to occur before leaf abscission rather than after?
22. What would happen if auxins were applied to the lateral buds of a pine tree?
23. Hydrotropism is a movement toward water. Which plant part, root or shoot, demonstrates hydrotropism?
24. Could the same plant demonstrate a tropism and a nastic movement? Explain.
25. Why could a tropism not be responsible for the closing of a Venus's flytrap?
26. Copy the incomplete graph below onto a separate piece of paper. Predict and label the continuation of the graph for the four groups of plant hormones.

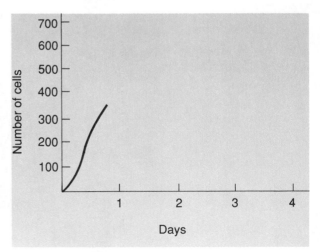

Chapter
26

PLANT DIVERSITY AND EVOLUTION

Overview

PLANT KINGDOM

26-1 Evolutionary Trends in Plants

26-2 Plant Classification

BRYOPHYTES

26-3 Characteristics of Bryophytes

26-4 Mosses

26-5 Liverworts

26-6 Adaptations to Life on Land

SPORE-BEARING VASCULAR PLANTS

26-7 Whiskferns

26-8 Club Mosses

26-9 Horsetails

26-10 Ferns

How many kinds of plants have scientists identified?

PLANT KINGDOM

Recall from Chapter 22 that the typical plant body consists of roots, stems, and leaves. In fact, you may think of these structures as important to plants as wheels are to a car. However, other kinds of plants do not have these structures. Plants are defined as multicellular, eukaryotic autotrophs. Other unfamiliar kinds of organisms fit this definition and are full-fledged members of the plant kingdom.

These plants include mosses, liverworts, and horsetails. Each kind of plant has a long evolutionary history. How are these plants related to each other?

26-1 Evolutionary Trends in Plants

Recall from Chapter 14 that all living things are thought to be related. Brothers and sisters are more closely related to each other than to their second cousins. Siblings have their parents in common, whereas second cousins have great-grandparents in common. The further back in time a common ancestor is, the fewer genes that are shared, and the less close the relationship is. This principle is used to determine evolutionary history.

Plants have origins dating from 450 million years ago. The fossil record only shows a broad outline of plant evolution. The relationships among different species are not clearly known. Figure 26-1 shows the evolutionary relationships among plant groups.

Section Objectives

A **Interpret** a drawing of the plant evolutionary tree.

B **Cite** instances of the evolutionary process occurring in the plant kingdom.

C **List** criteria used in plant classification.

Figure 26-1 One system of classification links together organisms based on shared ancestry.

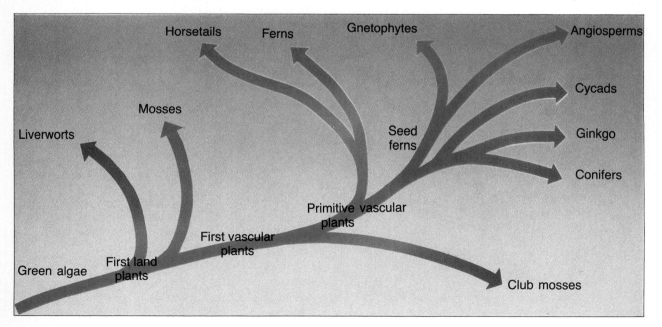

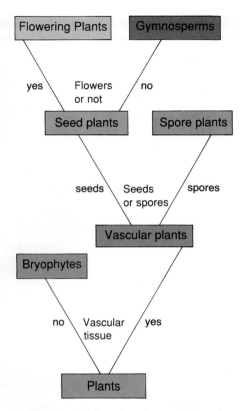

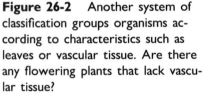

Figure 26-2 Another system of classification groups organisms according to characteristics such as leaves or vascular tissue. Are there any flowering plants that lack vascular tissue?

All plants have a common ancestor. Plants are thought to have evolved from an ancient group of green algae. Like green algae, plants have chlorophyll, produce starch as the carbohydrate food reserve, and have cellulose as the chief part of their cell walls.

For reasons not yet known, bryophytes, such as mosses, have undergone very little change over the past 400 million years. In contrast, groups like the angiosperms have undergone many "rapid" changes in the past 165 million years.

Finally, notice that the seed plants, particularly the angiosperms, form the most recently appearing branch of the tree. In this chapter, you will learn about some of the branches that evolved before the seed plants.

26-2 Plant Classification

Recall from Chapter 17 that organisms are classified into groups based on structural similarity. What structures are used to classify the thousands of different plants? Look at Figure 26-2. The presence or absence of specialized vascular tissue divides the plant kingdom into two main groups. One group, the *bryophytes*, lack this type of tissue. The other group, the **vascular plants**, have specialized conducting tissue—xylem and phloem.

There are two main groups of vascular plants. Some vascular plants like ferns, club mosses, and horsetails reproduce by spores. Others like conifers and flowering plants reproduce by seeds.

Plants with similar structures are thought to be closely related. This similarity presumably reflects common genetic material. The more specific the group, the closer the DNA of any two of its members, and the more recent a common ancestor is assumed to be. In fact, evolutionary relationships are being determined by new techniques comparing DNA. As with any classification system, there is not universal agreement about all the evolutionary relationships between groups.

CHECKPOINT ◆

1. Plants that are closely related share similar _____.
2. What group of plants lacks vascular tissue?
3. The algal ancestors of plants lacked vascular tissue. What group of modern plants shares this primitive characteristic?
▶ 4. Look at Figure 26-1. Which group of plants is most closely related to flowering plants?
▶ 5. According to Figure 26-2, did vascular plants evolve from bryophytes? Explain.

▶ Denotes a question that involves *interpreting* and *applying* concepts.

BRYOPHYTES

If you have ever gone camping in the woods, you know that finding a place to lay out your sleeping bag is sometimes a problem. If possible, you want a nice, soft cushion under you. If you are in a forest, a bed of moss is luxurious. These countless tiny, springy little green plants provide protection from the hard ground. The mossy patch feels like soft, thick velvet.

Mosses and liverworts make up the division called Bryophyta. The earliest bryophyte fossils are dated to be about 400 million years old. Until recently, the evolutionary relationships of bryophytes to other plant groups was unclear. Studies with DNA have shown that bryophytes evolved ''along the way'' from green algae to vascular plants.

26-3 Characteristics of Bryophytes

Bryophytes are usually small plants that grow close to the ground. Many are less than 2 centimeters long. They are usually abundant in moist areas, such as rain forests or woodlands. However, bryophytes are not found only in these areas. A number of moss species also are found in deserts. Despite the wide range of environments, all bryophytes require an environment that is moist for at least part of the year. Why?

Bryophytes lack the specialized tissue that transports water in vascular plants. Thus they cannot transport food or water over distances of more than a few centimeters. Water moves into these plants by osmosis. All movement of materials within the plant body is by diffusion. Since diffusion over great distances is inefficient and slow, these plants have not attained a large size. In addition, bryophytes lack the structural support of vascular tissue.

Bryophytes do not have true roots, true stems, or true leaves. They are anchored in the ground by delicate structures called **rhizoids**. Rhizoids are much simpler than true roots and do not channel water to other parts of the plant. Each leaflet is only one cell thick and can absorb water directly through its cell walls.

Bryophytes require water for sexual reproduction. For fertilization to occur, sperm must swim through water to reach the egg. Characteristically, bryophyte sperm have two flagella that propel them through the water.

Like some algae, bryophyte life cycles show an alternation of generations. The generation that makes up the major portion of all bryophyte life cycles is the *gametophyte* generation. Recall that the gametophyte produces haploid gametes. During sexual reproduction, gametes fuse, resulting in a diploid sporophyte.

Section Objectives

D *List* several bryophyte characteristics that limit these plants to a small size and a life in moist areas.

E *Explain* the life cycle of a moss.

F *Describe* reproduction in liverworts.

G *Relate* the requirements of land plants to their structures.

DO YOU KNOW?

Information: Not all plants called mosses are true mosses. Reindeer moss, for example, is a form of lichen. Spanish moss is an angiosperm, and club mosses are vascular plants.

Figure 26-3 This leafy liverwort is another example of a bryophyte. Like mosses, liverworts live in moist environments. The plant you see is the gametophyte generation.

26-4 Mosses

There are about 14 000 species of mosses. Like all bryophytes, mosses usually grow in moist, shady places, such as rocky ledges, along the sides of trees, or along the banks of streams. They tend to grow in large carpets composed of many plants.

Mature mosses consist of two distinct parts. Look at Figure 26-5. The familiar leafy green part is the gametophyte. Growing from the top of the gametophyte is the sporophyte. It appears as a stalk tipped with a spore-bearing **capsule**.

The life cycle of a moss plant begins when haploid spores are dispersed from the sporophyte capsule. The spore germinates and grows into a filament that resembles a green alga. This stage is called a **protonema**. The protonema develops into a small gametophyte. At maturity, multicellular sex organs are produced. The **archegonium** produces eggs, and the **antheridium** produces sperm. In some mosses, the gametophytes are unisexual, while in others, archegonia and antheridia are produced on the same plant.

Fertilization occurs after the sperm swim to the eggs through a thin film of water. The fertilized egg develops into the stalk of the sporophyte. The base of the sporophyte remains attached to the archegonium. The upper end of the sporophyte develops a capsule that produces spores.

Mosses are beneficial in the formation of soil. Since mosses need only a thin layer of soil, they can grow in places where other plants cannot, such as in the cracks between rocks. When mosses die, they add their organic material to the soil.

Figure 26-4 This SEM photo shows the spore capsule of a moss. Spores are dispersed when changes in moisture cause the "teeth" of the capsule to open.

Figure 26-5 The life cycle of a moss begins with the release of haploid spores. Spores that germinate begin cell division. This produces a filament that eventually forms a gametophyte.

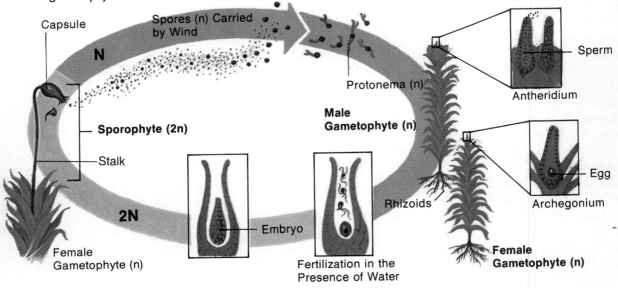

Capsule

Spores (n) Carried by Wind

N

Protonema (n)

Sperm

Antheridium

Sporophyte (2n)

Male Gametophyte (n)

Stalk

Egg

2N

Archegonium

Embryo

Rhizoids

Female Gametophyte (n)

Fertilization in the Presence of Water

Female Gametophyte (n)

Figure 26-6 *Left:* Liverworts undergo sexual reproduction by producing multicellular sex organs. Archegonia, the female sex organs are shown. *Right:* Gametophytes of *Marchantia* with cups containing gemmae

26-5 Liverworts

Liverworts are small plants that are less familiar than mosses. They are often found along streambanks. The body of the gametophyte may be ribbonlike or leaflike. Like mosses, liverworts commonly form green carpets consisting of thousands of plants. Unicellular rhizoids anchor them to the ground.

Look at Figure 26-6. Antheridia and archegonia grow on stalks that project above the gametophyte. Sperm are commonly carried to eggs by splashing raindrops or a thin film of water. The requirement of water for fertilization strongly suggests evolution from aquatic ancestors.

Liverworts also reproduce asexually. Some liverworts form cups that contain small flat structures called **gemmae**. When the gemmae are mature, raindrops can splash them out of the cups. If a gemma lands on a suitably moist spot, it develops rhizoids and grows into a new gametophyte.

26-6 Adaptations to Life on Land

As you read in Chapter 19, algae are primarily aquatic organisms. The algal ancestors of plants were well suited for their life in the oceans. The seas around them provided water and nutrients, support, and a medium for dispersing their gametes. The move onto land by the earliest plants required that all these needs be met in some other way.

Absorption Aquatic plants normally are able to absorb water and nutrients directly into their cells. However, land plants require special absorbing structures. Bryophytes obtain some water from the surface soil through their delicate rhizoids. Larger vascular plants develop complex root systems.

DO YOU KNOW?

Word Root: The name liverwort comes from the appearance of the plant. People once thought that it resembled a piece of liver. *Wort* is a British word meaning "herb."

Desiccation Land plants, unlike aquatic plants, are subjected to the drying effect of the air. Conserving the water the plant has absorbed is a function of a waxy material called cutin. Some bryophytes have a thin layer of cutin, whereas vascular plants have thicker layers.

Gas Exchange The exchange of gases is essential for photosynthesis and respiration. Aquatic plants absorb gases directly into their cells. Bryophytes and other land plants have stomates, or openings in the cuticle, for the exchange of gases with the air.

Support Lacking the buoyancy that the oceans gave the algae, the bryophytes are limited in size by their own weight. The evolution of vascular tissue provided internal support structures that compensated for the lack of support by the air. This factor allowed vascular plants to reach enormous sizes.

Conduction Vascular tissue provided a more efficient means of transporting water and dissolved food from one part of the plant to another. Large, sturdy, vascularized roots evolved, penetrating the soil and tapping its deep-water reserves.

Reproduction Algae sperm swim through water to reach an egg. However, land plants have a problem of gamete transport. The bryophytes were close enough to the ground so that a layer of dew provided sufficient water for the swimming sperm. In spore-bearing vascular plants, the gametophyte lies close to the soil, permitting sperm the necessary moisture in or on the soil. It was not until the development of seed plants that the independent gametophyte generation disappeared. With that advance, the wind, and eventually animals, carried the sperm to the eggs.

CHECKPOINT ◆

6. Name two adaptations that allow bryophytes to live on land.
7. Name two plant requirements that were met by the evolution of vascular tissue.
8. Liverworts produce _____ to reproduce asexually.
▶ 9. There are fewer bryophyte fossils than those of vascular plants. Explain why.
▶ 10. What is the sex of a moss plant that has a sporophyte attached to it? How can you tell?
▶ 11. Multicellular algae can attain large size without the presence of support tissue, while bryophytes cannot. Explain why.
▶ 12. If you choose to place your sleeping bag on a bed of moss, why would it be advisable to first spread out a sheet of plastic?

▶ Denotes a question that involves *interpreting* and *applying* concepts.

SPORE-BEARING VASCULAR PLANTS

Although bryophytes succeeded in colonizing land environments, their lack of specialized vascular tissue limited their size. The earliest vascular plants also were small, about 6 centimeters tall. Over millions of years, vascular plants evolved into enormous trees with trunks two meters in diameter. Today, their remains are used as coal and other fossil fuels.

There are four groups of spore-bearing vascular plants alive today—whiskferns, club mosses, horsetails, and ferns. In contrast to bryophytes, the dominant phase in the life cycle of these groups is the *sporophyte* generation. It is almost always larger and more complex than the gametophyte. Sporophytes often form rhizomes and may live for many years.

The gametophyte generation is a small structure, only a few millimeters long. It often reaches maturity in about a month. The reduction of the gametophyte generation relative to the sporophyte generation is a trend in plant evolution.

Reflecting their aquatic ancestry, all spore-bearing vascular plants alive today require water for fertilization. Because the gametophyte is small and grows close to the ground, the sperm usually can use dew and other temporary sources of water for fertilization.

26-7 Whiskferns

The simplest living vascular plants are members of the division Psilophyta. The whiskferns of Florida are the only North American representatives of this rare group.

Whiskferns are unique among living vascular plants because they lack both roots and leaves. These plants are rarely more than a meter tall. The branches of the sporophyte look like bundles of green forked sticks.

Some branches contain **sporangia**, which produce many small, wind-dispersed spores. Under suitable conditions, a spore develops into a **prothallium**. The prothallium, or gametophyte, grows underground. Rhizoids grow from the prothallus into the soil. Each prothallium is only a few millimeters in diameter and is covered by many antheridia and archegonia. Sperm from one prothallium swim through moisture in the soil to reach the eggs of other prothalli. Fertilization results in a simple embryo that eventually grows into a mature sporophyte.

Because the prothallium grows underground, it cannot photosynthesize. Instead, it relies on a symbiotic relationship with fungi that grow near it. The hyphae of the fungi in the soil penetrate the tissue of the prothallium.

Section Objectives

H *Compare* spore-bearing vascular plants to nonvascular plants and to seed plants.

I *Name* and *describe* several spore-bearing vascular plants that are alive today.

J *Describe* the life cycle of a fern.

CONSUMER BIOLOGY

Spores are often released during moist weather. People who suffer from hay fever are usually more sensitive to a specific type of airborne particle. Those who are allergic to spores will have more severe reactions after rainy weather. Those who react to dust or pollen will experience some relief as these particles are washed out of the air.

■ BIOLOGY INSIGHT

Adaptation and Evolution: One trend in plant evolution is the progressive reduction in size and complexity of the gametophyte. Another trend is from homospory to heterospory. All mosses, horsetails, and most ferns are homosporous. Seed plants are heterosporous.

26-8 Club Mosses

Despite their name, **club mosses** are not bryophytes. Instead, they are simple vascular plants that belong to the division Lycophyta. Club mosses such as *Selaginella* are common in the tropics. Other club mosses like "princess pine" live on the forest floor in cooler climates.

The sporophyte of all club mosses have many tiny, scalelike leaves called *microphylls*. Sporangia occur singly on the upper surface of some microphylls called *sporophylls*. Look at Figure 26-7. In this club moss, sporophylls are grouped into conelike structures. As in whiskferns, the club moss gametophyte is a prothallium that grows underground and obtains its food from fungi.

26-9 Horsetails

Like the other spore-bearing vascular plants, **horsetails** usually grow in moist or damp areas. Members of the genus *Equisetum* are the only living representatives of a once common division, the Sphenophyta. The word *Equisetum* means "horsetail" in Latin. *Equisetum* appears bushy like a horse's tail.

Look closely at Figure 26-7. Horsetails are easily recognized by jointed stems. At each joint, small leaves encircle the stem. Each stem arises from an underground rhizome and contains the element silicon, giving the stem a rough texture.

Cones develop at the tips of some stems. Inside the cones are sporangia. Spores germinate on the surface of wet soil. The resulting gametophyte, or prothallium, is about the size of a pinhead. It is green and either branched or lobed.

Figure 26-7 *Left:* Club mosses have scalelike leaves called microphylls. Modified microphylls called sporophylls produce spores. In this club moss, sporophylls form conelike structures at the top of the plant. *Right:* Horsetails are recognized by their bushy appearance.

26-10 Ferns

The **ferns** belong to the division Pterophyta. Ancestors of the ferns were abundant about 350 million years ago. Today, ferns are widely distributed from the tropics to the Arctic. Ferns also are aquatic, living on the surface of ponds and lakes. The 12 000 species of ferns range in size from tiny water ferns to tropical tree ferns, which may reach heights of 25 meters. However, most North American species do not exceed heights of 1 meter.

Ferns show a clear alternation of generations. As in all vascular plants, the sporophyte is much larger than the gametophyte.

The fern sporophyte consists of true stems, roots, and leaves. Stems usually are rhizomes that grow horizontally underground. Roots grow downward from rhizomes into the soil. Fern leaves called **fronds** grow upward from rhizomes. Although the fronds of the sporophyte may die each fall, the rhizomes may live for many years. Early in their development, fronds are tightly coiled into *fiddleheads*. In many places, the unfurling fiddleheads are a sure sign of spring. Although fiddleheads are cooked and eaten, it is now thought that they are mildly toxic.

The sporophyte produces thousands of spores within each sporangium. In some ferns, the sporangia appear as brown spots called **sori** on the lower surfaces of some fronds.

In a suitably moist, shady environment, the spore may germinate and form a heart-shaped gametophyte. As with the whiskferns, the gametophyte is called a prothallium. It is a flat green, sheet of cells about 3 millimeters wide. On the lower surface of the gametophyte, sex organs develop, gametes are produced, and fertilization occurs. The fertilized egg divides, grows, and develops into a new sporophyte.

Figure 26-8 Some ferns are "unfernlike." This aquatic fern *Azolla* floats on the surface of ponds.

Figure 26-9 *Left:* The leaves of ferns are called fronds, which are commonly divided into smaller leaflets. *Right:* Fronds in several stages of development.

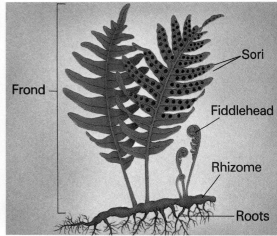

Frond

Sori

Fiddlehead

Rhizome

Roots

Plant Diversity and Evolution **435**

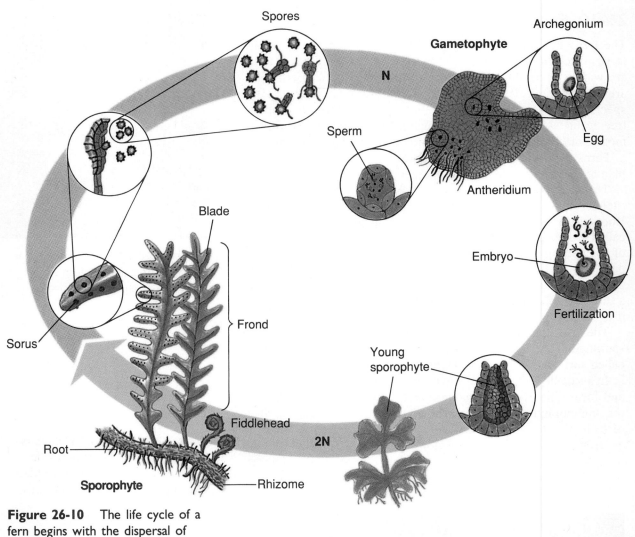

Figure 26-10 The life cycle of a fern begins with the dispersal of haploid spores.

CHECKPOINT ◆

13. Why are whiskferns considered the most primitive vascular plants?
14. Do club mosses have true leaves?
15. The fiddlehead fern is a member of which generation?
▶ 16. State one similarity and one difference between mosses and ferns.
▶ 17. State one similarity and one difference between seed plants and ferns.
▶ 18. Fiddleheads produce mildly toxic compounds. Explain how this is an adaptation for survival.

▶ Denotes a question that involves *interpreting* and *applying* concepts.

LABORATORY ACTIVITY

CHARACTERISTICS THAT DISTINGUISH DIFFERENT TYPES OF PLANTS

In this activity you will classify several different types of plants on the basis of their structure.

Objectives and Skills

☐ *Examine* representatives of several plant groups.
☐ *Classify* plants based upon observations.
☐ *Compare* structural features among groups.

Materials

Selaginella   Pteridium
Marchantia   African violet plant
Mnium

Procedure and Observations

1. Read all instructions for this laboratory activity before you begin your work.
2. Observe each specimen and record your observations in a table like the one below.
3. The plants that grow very close to the ground often lack vascular tissue. Use the size of the plant to determine whether or not vascular tissue is present. You can also use the appearance of veins to determine if vascular tissue is present. Reproductive struc-

tures may take the form of flowers, sporangia, or gemmae. A green color indicates the presence of chlorophyll.
4. When you have made all your observations, return your materials to their proper place. Consult Figure 26-2 to determine which type of plant each specimen is.
5. Before leaving the laboratory, clean up all your materials and wash your hands thoroughly.

Analysis and Conclusions

1. Which plants lack vascular tissue? Why do they tend to be small?
2. Which reproductive structures are used in sexual reproduction and which in asexual reproduction?
3. Which plants reproduce using seeds and which reproduce using spores?
4. In which plants are roots present?
5. Included in the specimens are a moss, a liverwort, a fern, and an angiosperm. On the basis of their characteristics, decide which is which and fill in the last column of the table.
6. In some systems of classification, green algae are considered to be plants. Explain why.

DATA TABLE				
OBSERVATIONS				
Plant	Vascular Tissue	Reproductive Structures	Chlorophyll	Other

CHAPTER REVIEW

Summary

▸ The plant kingdom contains a wide variety of forms, from tiny mosses to towering trees. All are eukaryotic, autotrophic, and multicellular, and are descendents of the green algae.

▸ Plants are classified into smaller groups on the basis of several characteristics, including the presence of vascular tissue, leaves, seeds, and flowers. In general, plants within a small group are thought to have a more recent common ancestor than plants outside that group.

▸ Bryophytes are represented by modern liverworts and mosses. Their size and environment are limited by the lack of vascular tissue for support and water transport. Fertilization depends on water, and dispersal occurs by spores.

▸ Vascular plants are larger than bryophytes. Some groups retain the characteristics of spore production, along with a requirement of water for fertilization. The sporophyte generation is dominant as in seed plants. Modern spore-bearing vascular plants include whiskferns, club mosses, horsetails, and ferns.

▸ The transition from the aqueous environment of the algal ancestors to a life on dry land was dependent on adaptations for absorption, conduction, support, gas exchange, and reproduction.

Vocabulary

antheridium	liverwort
archegonium	prothallium
bryophyte	protonema
capsule	rhizoid
club moss	sorus
fern	sporangium
frond	vascular plants
gemmae	whiskfern
horsetail	

Concept Mapping

Using the method of concept mapping described in the front of this book, copy and fill in missing terms to complete a concept map for bryophytes.

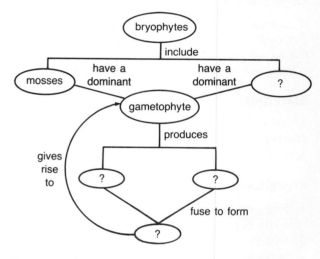

Review

1. From which division of algae did bryophytes evolve?
2. Distinguish between the life cycles of bryophytes and spore-bearing vascular plants.
3. What characteristics do green algae and plants have in common?
4. Which of the following is *not* found in bryophytes? (a) cuticle (b) stomata (c) roots (d) archegonium
5. Which characteristic distinguishes gymnosperms from ferns?
6. Are the spores dispersed by mosses haploid or diploid? Is this also true of ferns?
7. What group of organisms are thought to be the common ancestor of modern-day plants?
8. Name the groups of plants that are seed-producing vascular plants.

9. The male sex organ found in liverworts is called _____ .
10. How are liverwort sperm carried to the egg?
11. What process moves water into bryophytes?
12. Describe the appearance of the common horsetail.
13. You are asked to collect and measure the size of a fern gametophyte. Where would you look for it?

Interpret and Apply

14. Which evolutionary process is illustrated by the presence of chlorophyll throughout the plant kingdom?
15. In what way are land-living mosses still dependent on water?
16. Is a moss embryo haploid or diploid? Is the protonema haploid or diploid?
17. Name one characteristic present in ferns but not in mosses.
18. Name one characteristic present in angiosperms but not in ferns.
19. Which of the following characteristics represent earlier plants (E) and which represent more recently evolved plants (R)? (a) spores (b) seeds (c) gametophyte dominant (d) organs well developed (e) flowers (f) no vascular tissue
20. Roots are to angiosperms as _____ are to bryophytes.
21. A plant has vascular tissue but no leaves or roots. What kind of plant is it?
22. According to the family tree, which evolved more recently, horsetails or club mosses?
23. In liverworts, archegonia and antheridia are to sexual as _____ are to asexual.
24. How do the prothalli of whiskferns and club mosses differ from those of horsetails?

25. Place in the correct order the following stages in the life cycle of a fern: fiddlehead, embryo, mature sporophyte, spore, prothallium.

Critical Thinking

26. Why are stomata necessary in land plants but not in algae?
27. If scientists discover an ancestor of Chlorophyta, will it be more closely related to bryophytes or vascular plants? Explain.
28. Which climate would favor a very thick cuticle on the leaves?
29. Certain vascular plants, such as water lilies, live in water. Did these evolve before or after ferns?
30. Describe two other ways that the plant kingdom can be divided.

Use the graph to answer questions 31–33.

31. Match lines A, B, C, and D with moss, fern, horsetail and club moss.
32. What factors affect spore dispersal?
33. What affect does plant height have on distance?

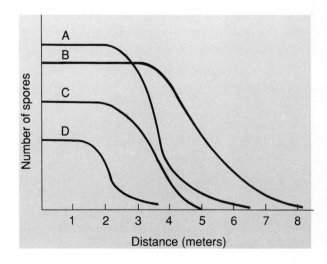

RAIN FOREST VANDALIZED

Case Study 1

Dr. Evan Nickols is a botanist working for a major university in Texas. When he obtained this teaching job he was thrilled because he would have time to do research on tropical rain forests. He found a number of colleagues at the university who were also interested in studying rain forests.

Dr. Nickols was given a grant to travel to Central America to study the rain forest directly. He and two of his fellow researchers, Dr. Franklin and Dr. Kurtz, were camped in the heaviest part of the forest studying plant and animal ecology. Dr. Franklin began a discussion of the possibility that there were still tribes of people living in the rain forest. He had read accounts of these tribes and their religions. Many tribes believe that the plants are gods, because of their healing powers.

Dr. Kurtz pointed out a plant that the tribes revered as holy. It was a plant that Dr. Nichols and Dr. Franklin had never seen before and might possibly be a new species. Dr. Franklin and Dr. Kurtz wanted to take samples back to the United States for study. Dr. Nickols thought removing the plant was wrong but he found it hard to argue.

1. State at least two arguments that Dr. Nickols could have used to keep his colleagues from removing the plant.
2. State at least two arguments that Dr. Kurtz and Dr. Franklin could have used to justify their removal of the plants.
3. The importance of the rain forest to global ecology is a subject of much current research. The world's supply of oxygen is affected by rain forest destruction. List other reasons for not destroying the rain forest.

Case Study 2

In northern California, vandals recently slipped past guards, climbed over a high fence, and spread rock salt and sprayed an herbicide (a plant-killing chemical) on a large strawberry field. The strawberry plants were destroyed and millions of dollars of research work was lost. The plants had been treated with genetically engineered bacteria. These bacteria were *Pseudomonas syringae* known as ice$^-$. When spread on the leaves of the plants, the bacteria inhibit ice formation.

The possible benefit of this treatment would be to extend the harvesting time of the strawberries and reduce the loss of plants by freezing.

The vandals were arrested and said they would do it again if they had the chance.

1. Why might these people want to destroy the strawberry fields?
2. If this type of bacteria could be helpful to farmers, should we encourage its use? Why?
3. Erwin Chargoff, a scientific writer, questions our right to change organisms that are products of millions of years of evolution. How does this relate to the use of recombinant DNA organisms in agriculture?

UNIT REVIEW 4

Synthesis

1. The opening pages of this unit contain four photographs. These photographs illustrate a common theme to the chapters of the unit. Identify the theme and describe how it relates to what you studied in the chapters.
2. **Structure Is Related to Function:** In a mature tree, many of the cells no longer contain living cytoplasm, although they continue to function as part of the living plant. Name two tissues of a mature tree that are composed of nonliving cells. What is the function of these tissues?
3. **Life Forms Are Interconnected:** Since plants are stationary, they must rely on other agents for fertilization of gametes. Describe the ways in which egg and sperm are brought together in mosses and ferns, conifers, and angiosperms with fragrant and colorful flowers.
4. **Unity and Diversity:** Angiosperms are classified as either monocotyledons or dicotyledons. Copy the following table onto a piece of paper and fill in the information.

	Monocots	Dicots
Number of cotyledons in a seed		
Pattern of leaf venation		
Arrangement of vascular bundles in herbaceous stems		
Number of petals and other floral parts		

Critical Thinking

5. **Levels of Organization:** In some systems of classification, algae are classified as the most primitive members of the plant kingdom. This book has classified algae as plantlike protists. Given the definition of plants as multicellular, autotrophic eukaryotes, give reasons for classifying algae as plants and reasons for classifying them as protists.
6. **Structure Is Related to Function:** The rhizoids of moss plants grow underground, help to anchor the plants, absorb water, and contain no chlorophyll; yet, they are not considered to be roots. What distinguishes rhizoids from roots?
7. **Process of Science:** Consider that all plants arose from algae, some of which are unicellular. The first plants were tiny mosses. Can you generalize that the more advanced a plant is, the bigger it is? If not, provide an example that refutes the generalization.

Additional Reading

Cronquist, Arthur. *How to Know the Seed Plants*. Dubuque, IA: William C. Brown, 1979.

Huxley, Anthony. *Plant and Planet*. New York: Viking, 1975.

Kourik, R. *Designing and Maintaining Your Edible Landscape Naturally*. Metamorphic Press, 1986.

Neiring, William, and Nancy Olmstead. *The Audubon Society Field Guide to North American Wildflowers*. New York: Knopf, 1979.

Newcombe, Lawrence. *Newcombe's Wildflower Guide*. Boston: Little, Brown, 1977.

Pohl, Richard W. *How to Know the Grasses*. Dubuque, IA: William C. Brown, 1978.

Slack, Adrian. *Carnivorous Plants*. Cambridge, MA: MIT Press, 1980.

Wohlrabe, Raymond A. *Exploring the World of Leaves*. New York: Thomas Y. Crowell, 1976.

INVERTEBRATES

Sea anemone

Sea nettle jellyfish

UNIT **5**

Gulf fritillary butterfly

Millipede

Chapter 27 Sponges and Cnidarians
            Characteristics of Animals
            Phylum Porifera
            Phylum Cnidaria
Chapter 28 Worms
            Phylum Platyhelminthes:
            Flatworms
            Phylum Nematoda: Roundworms
            Phylum Annelida: Segmented
            Worms

Chapter 29 Mollusks and
            Echinoderms
            Phylum Mollusca
            Phylum Echinodermata
Chapter 30 Arthropods
            Subphylum Chelicerata
            Subphylum Mandibulata
            Class Insecta
            Diversity of Insects

Chapter

27

SPONGES AND CNIDARIANS

Overview

CHARACTERISTICS OF ANIMALS

27-1 Subkingdoms Parazoa and Metazoa

27-2 Animal Development

27-3 Body Symmetry

PHYLUM PORIFERA

27-4 A Typical Sponge

27-5 Reproduction of Sponges

27-6 Sponge Diversity

PHYLUM CNIDARIA

27-7 Polyps and Medusae

27-8 The Hydra: A Typical Cnidarian

27-9 Jellyfish, Sea Anemones, and Corals

What makes these marine organisms so colorful?

CHARACTERISTICS OF ANIMALS

To many people, an animal is usually a furry creature with a head and four legs. In reality, many members of the Kingdom Animalia do not fit this description. Worms, insects, turtles, jellyfish, and sponges are all classified as animals.

All animals have two characteristics in common. First, all animals are multicellular organisms. The cells of these organisms are grouped together according to the function they perform. In all but the simplest animals, cells group together to form tissues. Likewise, tissues form organs and organs are organized into organ systems. Second, all animals are heterotrophic. They take in food and then digest it inside the body. Most animals are **motile** at some point in their lifetime. They must move from place to place to capture their food. Other animals are attached to a single spot and feed by capturing food that passes close to them. Animals that are attached to a single spot are **sessile**. Animals that are sessile as adults usually have a stage during their development when they are motile.

27-1 Subkingdoms Parazoa and Metazoa

Specialization of cells is a characteristic of the plant and animal kingdoms. Figure 27-1 shows some of the specialized animal cells that perform functions such as movement, support, digestion, and communication. Animal cells depend upon each other. For example, nerve cells that send messages depend on other cells to supply their food.

There are about 30 phyla of animals, which are divided into 2 subkingdoms. This division is based partly on the degree of interdependence among an animal's cells. One subkingdom, the **Parazoa**, contains only the sponges. Although sponges have specialized cell types, the cells are not so interdependent that they would die if separated from the organism as a whole. Experiments have shown if these cells are pulled apart, they will recombine over time to form a new sponge. Additional experiments have revealed that sponge cells are not permanently specialized. One cell type can be transformed into another type of cell depending on the needs of a sponge.

The second subkingdom, called the **Metazoa**, includes all animals except the sponges. In metazoans, cells are highly specialized and have little flexibility in function. In some metazoans, muscle cells are highly specialized for movement of body parts while certain blood cells transport oxygen to body cells. Neither specialized cell can do the other's job. In most cases, no metazoan cell would survive apart from the organism as a whole.

Section Objectives

A **List** some of the advantages of cell specialization in multicellular animals.

B **Identify** and **distinguish** the two subkingdoms of the animal kingdom.

C **Describe** the common features of development in the animal kingdom.

D **Explain** the difference between each type of symmetry found in animals.

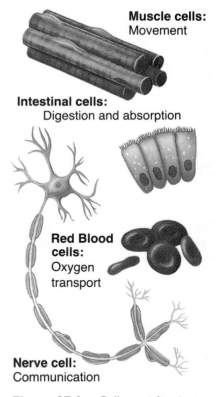

Muscle cells: Movement

Intestinal cells: Digestion and absorption

Red Blood cells: Oxygen transport

Nerve cell: Communication

Figure 27-1   Cell specialization and differentiation produce many different types of cells. The unique shape of each cell type determines the function of that cell.

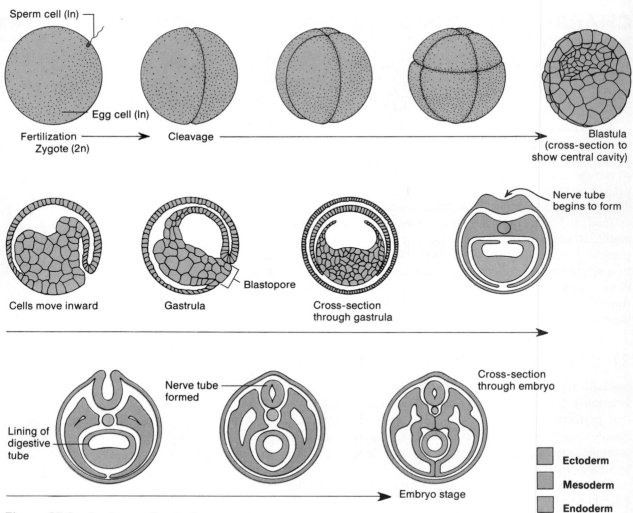

Figure 27-2 In almost all animals, development from a zygote follows a very similar pattern. Note that the gastrula is the same size as the zygote. Little cell growth occurs up to this point. After the gastrula forms, the cells and the organism begin to increase in size.

27-2 Animal Development

All members of the animal kingdom reproduce sexually, though many reproduce asexually as well. The development of an animal is different from the development of organisms in any other kingdom. Figure 27-2 illustrates the initial stages in the development of most animals.

All animal cells originally come from a zygote. The first cell divisions of the zygote are called **cleavages**. Several cleavages result in the production of a small, hollow ball of cells called a **blastula** [blas′ chə lə]. As the cells continue to divide, they push into the interior. The developing organism becomes a **gastrula** [gas′ trə lə]. The gastrula has an opening called the **blastopore** [blas′ tə pȯr]. Because each cleavage results in smaller and smaller

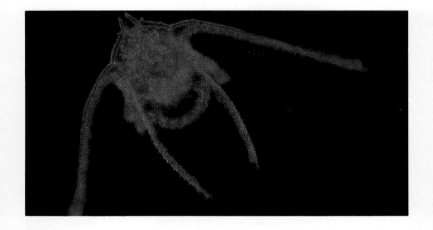

cells, the gastrula is usually about the same size as the original zygote.

During the later development of the gastrula, the cells undergo **differentiation**, developing different characteristics to suit their different functions. A single layer of cells, called the **endoderm** [en′ də derm], gives rise to the digestive tract. The outer layer of cells, called the **ectoderm** [ek′ tə derm], gives rise to the epidermis of the animal. In most animals, ectoderm also forms the nervous system. Many animals develop a third, middle layer of cells called the **mesoderm** [mez′ ə derm]. In some cases, the mesoderm gives rise to the circulatory, skeletal, and reproductive systems. All of the organs in an animal can be traced back to one of the three original cell layers. These three layers are called the **germ layers** of the developing organism.

By the time these germ layers form, the developing animal is called an **embryo**. In some animals, the embryo develops until it is a miniature version of the adult. In others, the embryo develops into an independent form that looks very different from the adult. This young stage is called a **larva** [lär və].

The developmental sequence illustrated in Figure 27-2 is typical of many animals, but the different groups of animals show variations. In fact, classification of animals depends in part on the details of their development.

Figure 27-3 The larval form and the adult form of an organism often are very different in appearance. Compare the starfish larva in the photograph on the left with the adult starfish on the right.

27-3 Body Symmetry

The bodies of most animals show some kind of symmetry. Three kinds of symmetry are illustrated in Figure 27-4. Organisms that lack symmetry are described as being **asymmetrical**.

An organism with **spherical symmetry** can be divided into equal halves by a plane passing in any direction through a central point. The only organisms with this kind of symmetry are protists. The

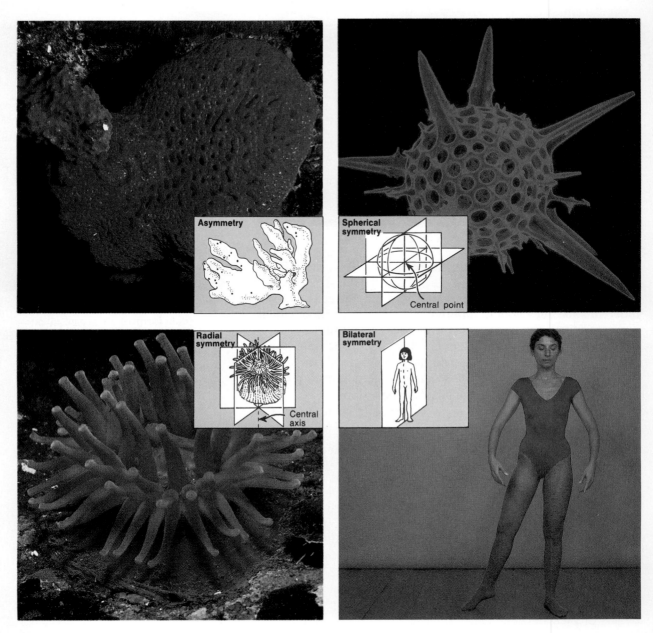

Figure 27-4 *Top left:* A sponge is asymmetrical. *Top right:* A radiolarian, a protist in the Sarcodine class, shows spherical symmetry. *Bottom left:* A sea anemone shows radial symmetry. *Bottom right:* A human shows bilateral symmetry.

radiolarian shown above is an example of an organism with spherical symmetry. **Radial symmetry** occurs in several animal phyla. An animal with radial symmetry can be divided into equal halves by passing a plane through the central axis of the animal in any direction. This type of symmetry allows an organism to receive stimuli equally from all directions of its environment. Animals with **bilateral symmetry** can be divided into equal halves only along a single plane. Most animals exhibit this type of symmetry.

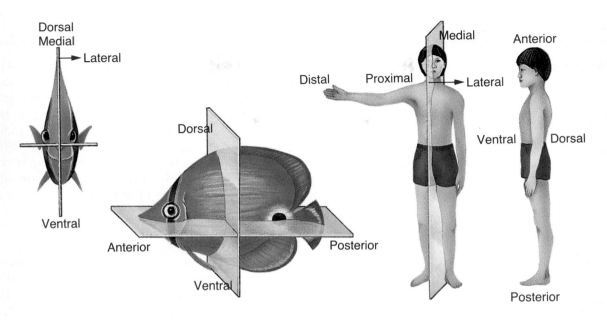

Several terms are used to describe the body of an organism that has bilateral symmetry. Refer to Figure 27-5 as you read about each term. The front region of the animal, or **anterior**, generally has a head. The opposite, or hind end, is the **posterior**. The underside is the **ventral** surface while the opposite surface, or back, is the **dorsal** side. **Lateral** structures are near the side of the animal. Notice that these terms can be applied to a human standing upright in the same way that they are applied to a horizontal animal.

CHECKPOINT ◆

1. What is the function of nerve cells? Of blood cells?
2. What are the two subkingdoms of the animal kingdom?
3. What is the difference between a blastula and a gastrula?
4. When a swimming larva settles in one spot, what term is used to describe the stationary adult?
5. What kind of symmetry has the fewest number of planes of symmetry?
▶ 6. In what ways are muscle cells dependent on other types of cells in an organism? How are other cells dependent on muscle cells?
▶ 7. List the following terms in the correct developmental sequence: cleavage, embryo, zygote, adult, meiosis, gastrula, fertilization, blastula, larva.

▶ Denotes a question that involves *interpreting* and *applying* concepts.

Section Objectives

E *Identify* the kinds of cells in sponges by type and function.
F *Describe* the structure of a typical sponge.
G *Explain* asexual and sexual reproduction in sponges.
H *Give* examples illustrating the diversity of sponges.

The phylum Porifera is made up exclusively of the sponges. The body of a sponge is riddled with interconnecting channels that open to the outside through many tiny pores. These pores give the phylum **Porifera** its name. Porifera is the only phylum in the subkingdom Parazoa. While a few simple sponges show radial symmetry, most are asymmetrical. Sponges have very primitive tissue development and no organs. They never develop a mesoderm. What does this physical description suggest about the position of sponges in the evolution of animals?

27-4 A Typical Sponge

The typical sponge has four basic types of specialized cells organized into two layers. Because these layers are composed of various types of cells, they are not considered to be tissues. The outer layer, called the **epidermis** [ep ə dər′ məs], is made of flattened cells. Penetrating the epidermis are cylindrical cells called **porocytes**, which permit water to enter the central cavity of the sponge. The porocytes are capable of doing this by opening or closing the pore. It is unlikely that they communicate with any other cells and they seem to act independently of what other porocytes are doing.

Just below the epidermis is a jellylike material which is called the **mesenchyme** [mez′ ən kīm]. Embedded in the mesenchyme are spiked structures called **spicules**. Spicules have two functions. First, they provide skeletal support for the cells. Second, they help protect the sponge from predators. Few fish enjoy a mouthful of needles.

Lining the interior cavity of the sponge is a layer that contains a number of flagellated **collar cells**. A close-up view of sponge cell layers is illustrated in Figure 27-6. The collar cells create currents that draw water through the pores and out the opening at the top of the sponge. The collar cells then withdraw food particles, such as algae or organic debris, from the water. In this way, the collar cells supply not only themselves but the rest of the cells with food.

A fourth type of cell found in sponges is a wandering cell that looks something like an *Amoeba*. These cells, called **amoebocytes**, move through the mesenchyme by means of pseudopods. Amoebocytes have several functions. They carry food particles from collar cells to epidermal cells and porocytes. Amoebocytes also make spicules in the mesenchyme. Amoebocytes are the least-specialized cells in the sponge and sometimes differentiate into another type of cell.

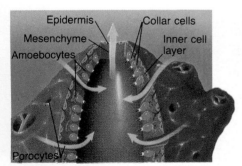

Figure 27-6 This cut-away view of a typical sponge reveals how each type of cell is positioned within the body wall.

27-5 Reproduction of Sponges

Sponges reproduce both sexually and asexually. **Budding** is one form of asexual reproduction. In budding, small groups of cells grow from the body wall of the adult. Eventually the bud breaks off and attaches elsewhere.

Another type of asexual reproduction occurs in many freshwater sponges. In late fall, they produce masses of amoebocytes that are surrounded by a tough wall. These structures are called **gemmules**. Gemmules can withstand winter freezing. In spring, the wall dissolves and the amoebocytes differentiate into a new sponge.

Most sponges are hermaphrodites. An organism that produces both eggs and sperm is a **hermaphrodite** [hər maf′ rə dīt]. Egg and sperm cells are produced either by amoebocytes or by collar cells that undergo meiosis. As illustrated in Figure 27-7, sperm are released into the water where they may enter a pore of another sponge of the same species. Once inside the other sponge, the sperm cell is surrounded by an amoebocyte and carried to an egg cell, where fertilization takes place. The zygote undergoes cleavage to form a flagellated larva. When the larva settles on a surface, it grows into a sessile adult.

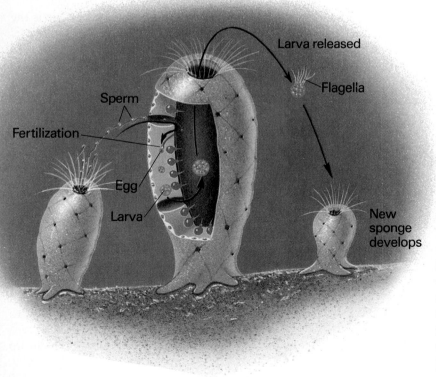

Sperm

Larva released

Flagella

Fertilization

Egg

Larva

New sponge develops

Figure 27-7 Fertilization and development of the zygote occur in the body wall of an adult sponge. Once the zygote reaches its larval form, it is released through a pore, and leaves the adult. Why is it important that the larva can swim?

Figure 27-8 The vertical tube sponge on the left and the vase sponge on the right give a sense of the variety of sponge shapes.

27-6 Sponge Diversity

There are about 10 000 species of sponges, most living in salt water. They show a remarkable variety of shapes, sizes, and colors.

The tremendous diversity among Porifera is due in part to years of evolutionary adaptations. Fossil sponges appear continuously in rocks up to 500 million years old. Some sponges have spicules made of calcium carbonate or silica. Since their mineral skeletons are easily preserved in rocks, fossil sponges are quite common.

Two primary features are used to classify sponges. One is the internal branching pattern of channels. The second characteristic is the material making up the skeleton. The most common sponges have mats of flexible fibers in the mesenchyme. The fibers are made of a protein called **spongin**. Spongin is chemically related to collagen, the protein that holds tissues together in all other kinds of animals.

CHECKPOINT ◆

8. Name four kinds of specialized cells found in sponges.
9. What are the two functions of spicules?
10. What is the name of an organism that can produce both sperm and eggs?
11. Why are sponges common in the fossil record?
12. Why are sponges classified as members of the animal kingdom?
▶ 13. Why is it advantageous that a sponge can reproduce both asexually and sexually?
▶ 14. What is the significance of the observation that spongin and collagen are chemically similar materials?

▶ Denotes a question that involves *interpreting* and *applying* concepts.

PHYLUM CNIDARIA

Some of the most beautiful animals on Earth belong to the metazoan phylum Cnidaria. The transparent jellyfish, flowerlike sea anemones, and lustrous corals all belong to this phylum. Most cnidarians are marine. Only a small percentage of the 10 000 species live in fresh water.

All **cnidarians** [nīd ar' e ənz] are radially symmetrical and have two distinct cell layers. Their cells are more highly specialized than those of sponges. As in sponges, the cell layers are not true tissues, since each layer is embedded with many different types of cells. Cnidarians have no mesoderm and they have no obvious head. What structural characteristics of a cnidarian resemble other animals? What specialized cell types make this resemblance possible?

27-7 Polyps and Medusae

Cnidarians exist in one of two body forms illustrated in Figure 27-9. One form is known as a **polyp** [päl' əp]. Polyps are vase-shaped, sessile animals that attach to a surface with their mouths facing up. The other body form of cnidarians, the bell-shaped **medusa** [mə dü' sə], is free swimming. A medusa is a bit like an upside-down polyp.

Many cnidarians have a life cycle that alternates between a medusa and a polyp stage. The life cycle of the jellyfish *Aurelia* is illustrated in Figure 27-10. Medusae reproduce sexually. In

Section Objectives

I **Compare** and **contrast** the polyp and medusa body forms.

J **Outline** the typical life cycle of a cnidarian.

K **Describe** the body structure of the hydra.

L **List** the major kinds of cnidarians and briefly describe the characteristics of each type.

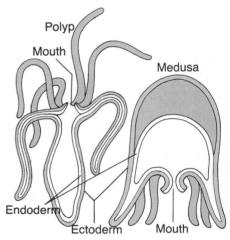

Figure 27-9 The structural differences between a polyp and a medusa are illustrated in these cross-sectional diagrams.

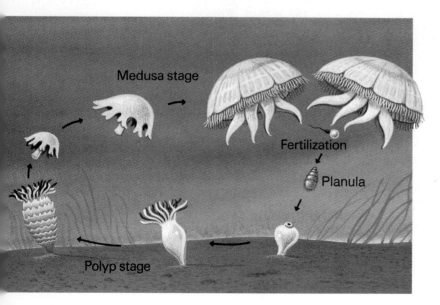

Medusa stage

Fertilization

Planula

Polyp stage

Figure 27-10 The life cycle of a typical jellyfish, such as an *Aurelia*, is more complex than that of a sponge. What parts of the jellyfish life cycle are haploid? What parts are diploid?

Sponges and Cnidarians   **453**

most medusae, sexes are separate with females producing eggs and males producing sperm. After fertilization, the zygote develops into a blastula, which elongates to form a ciliated larva called a **planula** [plan′ yə lə]. The planula eventually attaches itself to the bottom, where it grows into a polyp. The polyp reproduces asexually by forming medusae, which develop one on top of another. When the medusae form egg and sperm, the cycle is complete.

You may notice that the alternation of sexual and asexual stages in cnidarians appears similar to the alternation of generations seen in plants. In the cnidarians, however, there is no haploid generation. Both the medusa and the polyp are diploid. The only haploid cells are the sperm and eggs.

27-8 The Hydra: A Typical Cnidarian

With many groups of organisms, it is useful to study one member that illustrates the structures common to the group. The common, freshwater hydra is a typical cnidarian. Hydras are polyps with no medusa stage in their life cycle.

Hydras are small, only about 0.5 cm long. Their body is a cylinder with two cell layers. The inner layer is endoderm, and the outer layer is ectoderm. Between the two layers is a jellylike material called **mesoglea** [mez ə glē′ ə]. The cylindrical body attaches to surfaces by a **basal disk**.

Projecting from the top are a number of **tentacles** which trap food organisms that swim within reach. Food is pushed into the interior space or **gastrovascular** [gas trō vas′ kyə lər] **cavity** through a single opening, the mouth. Enzymes released by specialized cells in the endoderm digest the food. Digestion continues within endodermal cells that engulf particles by phagocytosis. Food moves within the gastrovascular cavity to all parts of the organism. The mouth serves as both an entrance for food and an opening from which indigestible wastes are expelled.

Organisms that come near a hydra's tentacles are stung by poisonous barbs called **nematocysts** [nem′ ət ə sists]. These stinging cells can paralyze relatively large organisms. Nematocysts are found in all cnidarians.

The hydra has no special transport system. It is able to survive without one because most of its cells are in direct contact with water. Oxygen moves into the hydra from the surrounding water and carbon dioxide moves out of the hydra into the environment by diffusion. Intercellular circulation also takes place by diffusion.

Hydra do not have a brain or spinal cord. Nerve cells found in the mesoglea carry messages from one part of the animal to another. The nerve cells coordinate the hydra's movements.

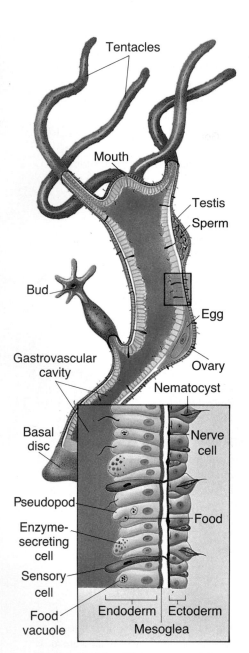

Figure 27-11 The structural features of a hydra can be identified by looking closely at the illustrations above.

During most of the year, hydras reproduce asexually by budding. But when winter approaches, hydras reproduce sexually. This seasonal pattern is common in metazoans. Asexual reproduction occurs when conditions are most favorable for the animal; harsh conditions trigger sexual reproduction.

Some species of *Hydra* are hermaphrodites, but most have two separate sexes. **Gonads**, organs in which cells for sexual reproduction are formed, develop from ectodermal cells. Male gonads are called **testes** while female gonads are called **ovaries**. Sperm released from the testes of one hydra swim to the ovaries of another, where fertilization occurs.

The developing zygote remains attached to the wall of the parent. A gastrula forms and is surrounded by a hard, protective coat. The encapsulated gastrula drops from the parent and survives winter. The following spring the coat dissolves and the young hydra emerges.

27-9 Jellyfish, Sea Anemones, and Corals

Most of the approximately 200 species of jellyfish are marine. They spend most of their life cycle as medusae. Jellyfish medusae may range in size from 2 cm to 2 m in diameter. A ring of muscles around the edge of the medusa contracts and pushes against the water. Such contractions move the jellyfish upward. When the muscles relax, the jellyfish slowly sinks. Like other cnidarians, jellyfish do not actively pursue prey. Jellyfish feed on anything from plankton to small fish.

The polyps of sea anemones have a more complex internal structure than that of the hydras. Study the illustration of a sea anemone in Figure 27-12. Notice how the gastrovascular cavity

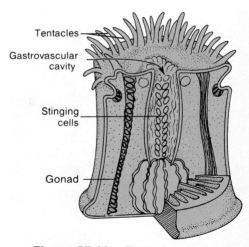

Figure 27-12 This cross-sectional illustration of a sea anemone reveals the organism's internal features.

■ *BIOLOGY INSIGHT* ────

Adaptation and Evolution: Nerve cells tend to be somewhat concentrated around the mouth of hydra. This concentration of nerves at the feeding end of the animal foreshadows the development of a head in animals discussed in later chapters.

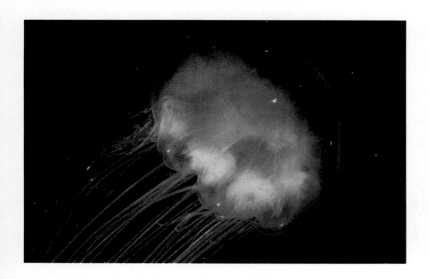

Figure 27-13 A jellyfish; despite varying degrees of mobility among cnidarians, all of them are carnivorous. Tentacles surrounding the mouth of a cnidarian trap food organisms and push them into the mouth. This special adaptation is one that has allowed cnidarians to become a successful phylum.

Sponges and Cnidarians   **455**

Figure 27-14 *Left:* The darkened band running parallel to the shoreline is referred to as a coral reef. This reef is made of the skeletal remains of generations of coral colonies. The presence of a coral reef changes the ecology along coastal waters. *Right:* Orange cup coral.

of sea anemones is divided into a number of compartments. Stinging cells line the inner walls of these compartments as well as the tentacles. Sea anemones feed on a variety of small animals, including fish.

Corals represent another major group of cnidarians. These polyps are unusual because they secrete a wall of calcium carbonate around themselves. Most corals are small, colonial animals, and their skeletons grow together into large masses. New generations of polyps build skeletons on top of old generations. Coral "houses" grow in a wide variety of colors and shapes.

In many coral species, dinoflagellates live with the polyps. Corals grow in clear shallow water where there is enough light for photosynthetic dinoflagellates. Coral animals sometimes occur in such large numbers that they form ridges, called coral reefs, around islands and near coastlines. The Great Barrier Reef off the coast of northeastern Australia is almost 2000 kilometers long.

CHECKPOINT ◆

15. What is the free-swimming form of a cnidarian called?
16. What is a planula?
17. Explain the function of nematocysts.
18. How does a sea anemone differ in structure from a hydra?
▶ 19. How does the gastrovascular cavity of cnidarians differ from the channels in a sponge?
▶ 20. How is sexual reproduction in hydra different from sexual reproduction in jellyfish?

▶ Denotes a question that involves *interpreting* and *applying* concepts.

MICROSCOPIC STRUCTURE OF SPONGES AND CNIDARIANS

In this activity, you will look at prepared slides of sponges and of hydra and identify specialized cell types in each organism.

Objectives and Skills

☐ *Locate* and *identify* the various cell types in a prepared slide of a portion of a sponge.
☐ *Observe* and *diagram* nematocysts.
☐ *Identify* the cell layers and different cell types in the wall of a hydra.

Materials

microscope and light source
prepared slides of a portion of a sponge
prepared slides of nematocysts
prepared slides of hydra
paper

Procedure and Observations

1. Read all directions for this laboratory activity before you begin your work.
2. Observe a prepared slide of sponge. Survey the slide at low magnification to get an idea of the overall structure of the sponge. Then identify the spaces that are inside the sponge and along its outside surface.
3. Observe the sponge under high power. Try to identify as many of the following structures in the sponge wall as possible: collar cells with flagella, porocytes, epidermal cells, amoebocytes, spicules or spongin fibers. Draw a diagram showing the arrangement of various cell types in the body wall of the sponge. Label each type of cell.
4. Observe a prepared slide of hydra under low power. On one part of the slide is a cross section and on the other part is a longitudinal section. Draw a simplified diagram of each section. Label the ectoderm, endoderm, mesoglea, and gastrovascular cavity. Do not show individual cell detail in this diagram.
5. Observe the hydra slide under high power. Draw a diagram showing a small section of the wall of the hydra showing several different types of cells. Find a cell containing a nematocyst. Draw a diagram of a nematocyst.
6. Before leaving the laboratory, clean up all your materials and wash your hands thoroughly.

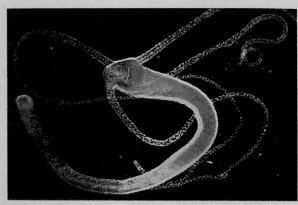

a brown hydra (40×).

Analysis and Conclusions

1. How many different kinds of cells did you observe in the sponge body wall?
2. How many different kinds of cells did you observe in the hydra body wall?
3. Do nematocysts seem to be located in greater numbers in any particular part of the hydra?
4. Describe the similarities and differences in the body walls of the two different organisms.
5. How does the location of the various kinds of cells you observed reflect the function of those cells?

CHAPTER REVIEW

Summary

▸ Animals are multicellular heterotrophs that show considerable cell specialization. Many animals have tissues organized into organs.

▸ Animals show a pattern of development different from that seen in any other kingdom. The zygote develops into a blastula and then becomes a gastrula. Some animals pass through a larval form that is different in appearance from the adult.

▸ The bodies of animals show symmetry. Other than asymmetric sponges, animals are either radially or bilaterally symmetric.

▸ Sponges are placed in their own subkingdom, the Parazoa. Sponge cells show less differentiation than the cells of other animals. Sponges do not have organs or true tissues and their bodies are usually asymmetric.

▸ Water circulates freely through a system of channels in the interior of the sponge. Porocytes allow water to enter the central channels.

▸ Cnidarians belong to the subkingdom Metazoa. Their bodies are made of two layers of cells that surround a central digestive cavity. Between the endoderm and the ectoderm is the jellylike mesoglea. Within the mesoglea, nerve cells carry messages from one part of the animal to another and coordinate movement. All cnidarians have special stinging cells.

▸ Cnidarians occur in two forms—sessile polyps and free-swimming medusae. Some have a life cycle with both forms.

▸ The hydra is a common freshwater cnidarian. Hydras are attached polyps that capture food with stinging cells in tentacles.

▸ Sea anemones, jellyfish, and corals are cnidarians. The polyps of corals secrete a hard outer skeleton of calcium carbonate. Large colonies of corals growing together may form reefs.

Vocabulary

amoebocyte	lateral
anterior	medusa
asymmetrical	mesenchyme
basal disk	mesoderm
bilateral symmetry	mesoglea
blastopore	Metazoa
blastula	motile
budding	nematocyst
cleavage	ovary
cnidarian	Parazoa
collar cell	planula
differentiation	polyp
dorsal	Porifera
ectoderm	porocyte
embryo	posterior
endoderm	radial symmetry
epidermis	sessile
gastrovascular cavity	spherical symmetry
gastrula	spicule
gemmule	spongin
germ layer	tentacles
gonad	testes
hermaphrodite	ventral
larva	

Concept Mapping

Construct a concept map for sponge reproduction. Include the following terms: sperm, gemmules, hermaphrodite, budding, eggs. Use additional terms as you need them.

Review

1. How are Parazoa different from Metazoa?
2. What are the three germ layers found in most animals?
3. Which of the three germ layers is absent in sponges and cnidarians?
4. What type of symmetry is found in all cnidarians?

5. What is the basic function of muscle cells?
6. What cell type in a sponge is responsible for taking in food?
7. What is the asexual reproductive structure of a sponge called?
8. What kind of symmetry is seen in most sponges?
9. What two characteristics are used to classify sponges?
10. What two types of body form are seen in cnidarians?
11. What part of the *Aurelia* life cycle produces eggs and sperm?
12. In what way do jellyfish differ from hydra?

Interpret and Apply

13. As the cells of organisms are specialized, what abilities are lost by these cells?
14. Name a major characteristic other than food supply that distinguishes plants from animals.
15. Why is it not adequate to define animals simply as multicellular heterotrophs?
16. Is your head anterior or posterior to your arms? Describe the location of your arms in relation to your shoulders.
17. What evidence can you give to support the statement that sponge cells still retain some independence?
18. Give three reasons for classifying sponges as animals rather than plants.
19. How does sponge reproduction by gemmules resemble sexual reproduction in hydra? How is it different?
20. Why are the cell layers of sponges and cnidarians not considered true tissues?
21. What are the two major functions of the gastrovascular cavity in cnidarians?
22. Why are sponges considered simpler organisms than cnidarians?

23. How are the functions of nematocysts and spicules similar?
24. Of the organisms described in this chapter, which would you expect to be most common in the fossil record and which the least common?

Critical Thinking

25. Two different species of sponge that differ in shape and color are pushed through a cloth into the same water. After several weeks, the cells have reassembled into sponges like the original two. What conclusions can you draw from this experiment about sponge cells?
26. What conclusions can be drawn from the observation that almost all animals undergo similar development from zygote to blastula to gastrula?
27. Of all the terms describing anatomical positions in Figure 27-5, which would be useful in describing an organism like hydra which has radial symmetry?
28. Several hydra species have green algae living within the cells of the endoderm and ectoderm. In the absence of light, these hydra grow more slowly than their counterparts growing in light. Explain how the hydra and green algae benefit from this association.
29. An entire fossilized coral reef has been discovered that extends from Ontario, Canada, into Ohio. This reef is thought to have formed over 400 million years ago. What inferences can you draw about this ancient environment?
30. How does the life cycle of *Aurelia* compare to the alternation of generation in plants? In what ways are they similar? In what ways are they different?

Chapter

28

WORMS

Overview

PHYLUM PLATYHELMINTHES: FLATWORMS

28-1 Flatworm Characteristics

28-2 Class Turbellaria: Free-Living Flatworms

28-3 Class Trematoda: Flukes

28-4 Class Cestoda: Tapeworms

PHYLUM NEMATODA: ROUNDWORMS

28-5 Nematode Characteristics

28-6 Parasitic Nematodes

PHYLUM ANNELIDA: SEGMENTED WORMS

28-7 Annelid Characteristics

28-8 Class Oligochaeta: Earthworms

28-9 Other Annelids

How many worms can you find in this picture?

PHYLUM PLATYHELMINTHES: FLATWORMS

What comes to mind when you hear the word *worm*? Your first thought is probably the common earthworm. Did you know, however, that there are over 20 000 wormlike organisms? There are so many different worms that they are classified into six or eight phyla depending on whose classification scheme you use. Despite their differences, all wormlike organisms have many features in common. They all have bilateral symmetry. Their bodies are made up of true tissues, organs, and organ systems. The tissues and organs of all worms are derived from three germ layers—ectoderm, mesoderm, and endoderm.

Three of the most important worm phyla are described in this chapter. These three groups include the flatworms, the round worms, and the segmented worms. Not only do these groups contain the largest number of species, they also have the greatest impact on humans.

Section Objectives
A **Describe** the basic body structure of flatworms.
B **List** the organ systems of flatworms and **describe** the function of each system.
C **State** how flukes differ in structure from free-living flatworms.
D **Outline** the life cycle of a fluke.
E **Explain** how tapeworms differ from other flatworms in structure and reproduction.

28-1 Flatworm Characteristics

The phylum **Platyhelminthes** [plat ē hel min′ thēs], or the flatworms, is divided into three classes—class Turbellaria, the free-living flatworms, class Trematoda, the flukes, and class Cestoda, the tapeworms. Within these classes, there are about 10 000 species. Members of this phylum are characterized by a very flat, thin body. The reason these worms are flat is that there are no spaces between the layers of tissue inside their bodies. Because of their shape, no cell is very far from the environment. As a result, oxygen from the environment diffuses directly into each cell. Similarly carbon dioxide diffuses from the body cells directly into the environment.

Flatworms are the most primitive animals to have a definite head. A head is a characteristic of animals with bilateral symmetry. Most bilaterally symmetrical animals, including flatworms, move actively throughout their environment. With senses concentrated at the anterior end of their bodies, flatworms can respond to the environment quickly. For example, with the senses of sight and smell located in the head, the flatworm can detect food and move toward it.

Nerve cells are concentrated near the sense organs. Nerve cells receive information from the sense organs and send information to other parts of the body. The **brain**, a collection of nerve cells located in the anterior end, acts as a control center. The tendency in animal evolution toward larger brains and more complex senses in the head is called **cephalization** [sef ə li zā′ shun].

Information: Planarians have two methods of moving. One method makes use of cells of the epidermis that secrete mucus. The ventral epidermal cells have cilia. As the cilia beat, the planarian glides over the mucus. The second form of movement involves three layers of muscle cells in the mesoderm. With these muscles, the worm can stretch or shorten its length as it crawls along.

Figure 28-1 Two organ systems of the planarian are illustrated below. Notice that the digestive system has only one opening. Food enters and wastes exit from the same opening. The nervous system is ladderlike with paired nerve cords extending back from the brain.

28-2 Class Turbellaria: Free-Living Flatworms

The class **Turbellaria** [tėr bə lār′ ē ə] consists of all free-living flatworms; that is, those flatworms that are not parasites. The most interesting members of this class are the planarians [plə nār′ ē əns]. Planarians are usually less than 1 or 2 cm long. While most turbellarians live in salt water, the planarians are primarily freshwater organisms.

The digestive system of planarians is illustrated in Figure 28-1. Like the digestive system of cnidarians, it has only a single opening. This opening, called the mouth, is on the ventral surface near the middle of the animal. The worm feeds by extending a muscular tube called the **pharynx** [far′ ingks] from its mouth. The pharynx connects to the digestive cavity, or **gut**. The gut has two posterior branches and a single anterior branch. Each major branch has many small side branches that increase the surface area and bring the gut cavity close to many body cells.

Most planarians are carnivorous. They eat protists and small animals which they trap in secretions from their mucous glands. The planarian grasps its prey with its mouth and wraps its body around the prey. The pharynx breaks food organisms into small pieces and pushes them into the gut. Cells lining the gut enclose

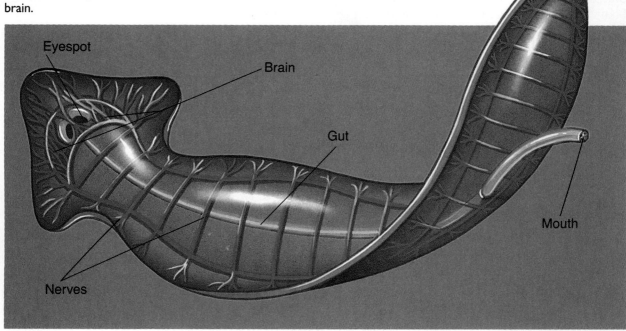

Eyespot

Brain

Gut

Mouth

Nerves

food particles in vacuoles. Food is then digested in these vacuoles, and the resulting molecules diffuse directly from gut cells to other body cells. Any undigested food is expelled through the pharynx and the mouth.

Like all flatworms, planarians have a nervous system. The nervous system, also illustrated in Figure 28-1, has a brain that coordinates information coming from the sense organs and directs the body's responses.

A planarian's head has two light-sensitive spots that resemble eyes. They sense the difference between light and dark. Projections at the side of the worm's head contain many cells that are sensitive to touch and to water currents. These cells may also be sensitive to chemicals in the water.

A water-regulating system is also found in planarians. The primary function of this system is similar to that of contractile vacuoles in protists. Freshwater turbellarians take in excess water by osmosis. Special ciliated **flame cells** help move excess water out of the body.

Planarians are hermaphrodites—each individual produces male and female gametes. During sexual reproduction, two planarians exchange sperm. Cross-fertilization occurs as the sperm from one worm fertilize the eggs of another worm. (Self-fertilization, by contrast, involves the union of male and female gametes produced by the same organism. Planarians do not normally self-fertilize.)

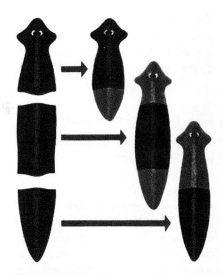

Figure 28-2 Planarians have a remarkable ability to regenerate. When a planarian is cut into pieces, each piece usually becomes a complete individual.

28-3 Class Trematoda: Flukes

Trematodes [trem′ ə tōds], also known as **flukes**, are parasitic flatworms. Flukes have organs and organ systems similar to those of planarians.

Many of the fluke's characteristics are typical adaptations to a parasitic way of life. For example, the surface of a fluke consists of tough, nonliving material called a **cuticle** [kü′ ti kəl]. The cuticle protects the fluke from the digestive enzymes of its host. In addition, most flukes have two suckerlike disks. One is on the worm's ventral surface, and the other surrounds the mouth. The suckers attach the worm to the host, generally in the host's digestive tract. The fluke absorbs digested food from the host's intestine.

The life cycle of the sheep liver fluke is illustrated on the next page in Figure 28-3. Flukes are hermaphroditic, and cross-fertilization is the rule. Adult worms release fertilized eggs in solid wastes from the sheep's intestine. If the eggs are deposited near a marsh or pond, they hatch into larvae. To survive, a larva must encounter a particular species of water snail within eight hours. The larva then burrows into the snail's body.

Figure 28-3 The life cycle of the sheep liver fluke involves two host organisms. Different developmental stages occur in each host.

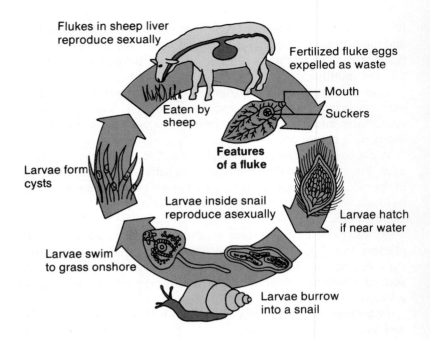

Flukes in sheep liver reproduce sexually

Fertilized fluke eggs expelled as waste

Mouth

Eaten by sheep

Suckers

Features of a fluke

Larvae form cysts

Larvae inside snail reproduce asexually

Larvae hatch if near water

Larvae swim to grass onshore

Larvae burrow into a snail

Figure 28-4 A tapeworm such as this one can live in the intestines of many animals, including humans.

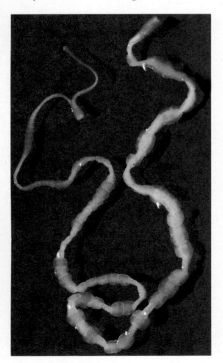

Within its host, the larva reproduces asexually. The resulting larvae are different in form from the original larva. After several weeks, these new larvae leave the snail. They swim until they reach a blade of grass near the edge of the water. On the grass, each larva forms a hard cyst. If a sheep eats the grass, the larva breaks out of its protective cyst. The fluke travels to the intestine of the sheep. From there, the fluke burrows into the liver, where it grows to full size and produces a new generation of eggs.

28-4 Class Cestoda: Tapeworms

All **cestodes** (ses' tōds), or **tapeworms**, are parasitic flatworms. Tapeworms are even more specialized than flukes. Unlike other flatworms, a tapeworm has a body divided into many sections, or **proglottids** [prō glot' ids]. A tapeworm continually makes new proglottids just behind its head. As each section is pushed away from the head, it grows in size. Species vary in length and number of proglottids. Some tapeworms have thousands of sections.

Look closely at the tapeworm proglottid illustrated in Figure 28-5. Notice that there is no digestive system. Tapeworms live in the intestine of a host animal. Food is absorbed directly from the intestine of the host into the cells of a tapeworm. Nerves run through each proglottid. Each section also has a flame cell system for removing excess water from the body.

Most of the space in each proglottid is filled with reproductive organs. Eggs are produced in ovaries; sperm is produced in

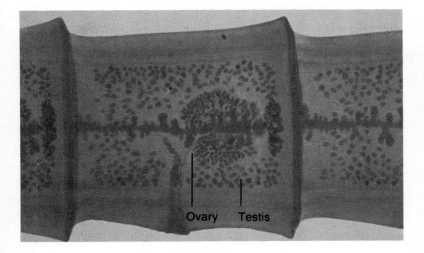

Ovary   Testis

Figure 28-5 *Left:* Each proglottid contains both male and female reproductive organs. *Right:* The head of a tapeworm may have suckers or hooks that attach the parasite to the wall of the host organism's intestine.

testes. Self-fertilization is possible. Cross-fertilization between different worms in the same host also occurs. Proglottids that are distant from the head are swollen with thousands of fertilized eggs. These proglottids break off and are excreted in the solid waste of the host. To survive, these eggs must reach another host for the next stage in the life cycle.

The life cycle of tapeworms is similar to that of flukes. It may involve one, two, or three different host organisms. Several human tapeworms are transmitted by infected pork, beef, or wild game that has not been thoroughly cooked. The meat contains a larva of the tapeworm in a cyst. Government meat inspection prevents most infected meat from reaching the market. However, it is still important to cook meat thoroughly.

CHECKPOINT ◆

1. What germ layers are found in flatworms?
2. What organ systems can be found in planarians?
3. List two adaptations that enable flukes to exist as parasites.
4. What host is required by the sheep liver fluke other than the sheep itself?
5. What organ system found in other flatworms is missing in tapeworms?
▶ 6. Summarize the differences between the two parasitic flatworm classes.
▶ 7. What organ system found in freshwater turbellarians would you expect to be reduced or absent in marine turbellarians? Explain.

▶ Denotes a question that involves *interpreting* and *applying* concepts.

PHYLUM NEMATODA: ROUNDWORMS

Section Objectives

F *Distinguish* the body plan of roundworms from that of flatworms.

G *Name* and *describe* two important parasitic roundworms.

Animals in the phylum **Nematoda** [nēm ə tōd′ ə] are characterized by their round tubelike shape. In fact, they are often called roundworms. You have probably never seen a roundworm, yet they are extremely common. There are over 10 000 species in the phylum. Most roundworms are small, usually less than a few millimeters in length. They live in the soil and in most bodies of water. Most of them are harmless, but some parasitic species can do great damage to plants, animals, and humans.

Why are nematodes round and not flat like turbellarians? Which nematodes are parasitic? How can parasites be avoided?

28-5 Nematode Characteristics

Two major features characterize the phylum Nematoda: a one-way digestive tract and a body cavity. All of the animals you have encountered so far have only one opening to the digestive cavity. This opening serves both as an entryway for food and an exit for wastes. Nematodes, however, have two openings. Food enters at the mouth and undigested wastes are expelled through a second opening, the **anus**.

Nematodes also have a body cavity between tissue layers. The fluid that fills the body cavity gives the organism its round shape much like air in a tire. The fluid also circulates material throughout the body.

Figure 28-6 The general body structure of roundworms is described as a tube within a tube. The digestive system forms a tube separated from the outer body wall tube by a fluid-filled cavity.

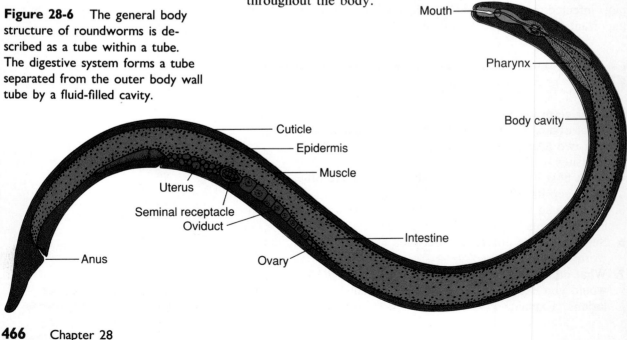

Mouth

Pharynx

Body cavity

Cuticle

Epidermis

Muscle

Uterus

Seminal receptacle

Oviduct

Anus

Ovary

Intestine

Figure 28-6 illustrates a typical roundworm. Beneath the cuticle is a layer of epidermal cells. Roundworms obtain oxygen and release carbon dioxide by diffusion through the epidermis. Under the epidermis is a single layer of muscle extending the length of the body. Below the muscle layer is the fluid-filled body cavity.

The digestive tract is inside the body cavity. Just posterior to the mouth is a muscular pharynx, which sucks food into the mouth. The pharynx joins the long **intestine**, where food is digested and absorbed. Undigested food is expelled at the anus.

The body cavity also houses the male or female sex organs. Most nematodes are not hermaphroditic; males and females are separate individuals.

28-6 Parasitic Nematodes

Hookworm is a common roundworm parasite of humans. It occurs in areas where sanitation is poor and where human wastes are used as fertilizer. Human wastes from an infected person contain hookworm eggs. If the eggs get into soil, they develop into larval worms. If the larval worms come in contact with human skin, they can pierce through the skin and burrow into the body. The larvae are carried by the bloodstream to various body parts. They burrow through tissues and cause severe damage. The adult worms attach to the intestine wall and feed on blood and tissue fluids. When the worms reproduce, eggs leave the host in wastes, and the life cycle begins again.

Trichina [tri kī′ nə] is another important roundworm parasite. At one stage in their life cycle, trichina worms may form cysts in the muscles of pigs and other mammals. If humans eat undercooked pork containing trichina cysts, the larvae will emerge from their cysts. These larvae mature quickly in the small intestine. The adult worms burrow into the intestinal wall and reproduce. These new larvae penetrate nearby blood vessels and are carried to muscle tissue where they form cysts.

Because of meat inspection, trichina infection is rare in the United States. However, for safety's sake, pork products and game meats should always be cooked thoroughly.

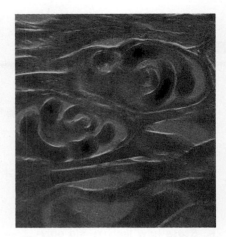

Figure 28-7 Trichinosis, caused by trichina larvae, is a painful disease that weakens its host. The larvae tear apart tissue as they bore deep into the muscles. They rob their host of nutrients and oxygen carried in the hosts' bloodstream. Trichina cysts, such as those illustrated above, can protect larvae from its hosts' defenses up to 20 years!

CHECKPOINT ◆

8. What feature of the nematode digestive system makes it different from the digestive system of flatworms?
9. What is the common name for nematodes?
10. Identify two common nematodes that are human parasites.
▶ 11. How are nematode and flatworm parasites similar?

▶ Denotes a question that involves *interpreting* and *applying* concepts.

PHYLUM ANNELIDA: SEGMENTED WORMS

Section Objectives

H **Compare** the structure of annelid worms with worms in other phyla.

I **Identify** the internal structures of the earthworm.

J **Describe** the function of the various organ systems of the earthworm.

K **State** how leeches and polychaetes differ from earthworms.

Have you ever started a garden early in the spring? Before you can plant anything, you have to get the soil ready. You dig in the garden, loosening large clumps of soil. What is the first sign of animal life you see? Earthworms—maybe hundreds of them. Earthworms help make soil suitable for plant growth.

The common earthworm represents a third worm phylum called the annelids. **Annelids** [an′ əl ids] are segmented worms. In what ways are annelids different from other worms? What other organisms beside the earthworm are classified as annelids? Why are earthworms important for plant growth?

28-7 Annelid Characteristics

One characteristic that separates annelids from the other worm phyla is the presence of a coelom. A **coelom** [sē′ ləm] is a fluid-filled body cavity surrounded by mesoderm. A coelom provides room in the body for complex internal organs. All organs in an annelid are suspended in the coelom by an attached membrane called the peritoneum. The **peritoneum** [per i ti nē′ əm] is a membrane that originates from the inner mesoderm. In addition to providing support, this membrane also holds the internal organs in place inside the coelom.

Figure 28-8 Comparisons among flatworms, roundworms, and segmented worms can be more easily made when looking at cross-sectional diagrams. Segmented worms are the only worms with a coelom and peritoneum.

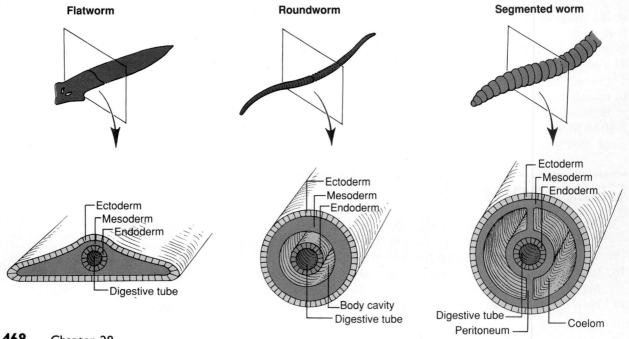

Flatworm	Roundworm	Segmented worm

Flatworm: Ectoderm, Mesoderm, Endoderm, Digestive tube

Roundworm: Ectoderm, Mesoderm, Endoderm, Body cavity, Digestive tube

Segmented worm: Ectoderm, Mesoderm, Endoderm, Digestive tube, Peritoneum, Coelom

The coelom is an important structural development. Animals with a coelom have muscle tissue around the body wall and also around the digestive tract. These two sets of muscles operate independently. Body wall muscles move the organism. Muscles around the digestive tract move food through the digestive system. By comparison, roundworms have only body wall muscles that carry out both functions.

The second major characteristic of annelids is **segmentation**, the division of the body into sections. Segmentation is important for two reasons. First, an animal can increase in size by adding more identical segments. Second, different segments can adapt to carry out special functions.

28-8 Class Oligochaeta: Earthworms

The earthworm is one of about 2500 species of **oligochaete** [ol′ i gō kēt] worms. The following sections describe how the earthworm carries out various life functions.

Gas Exchange and Circulation In flatworms and roundworms, gas exchange occurs by diffusion through the epidermis. Few flatworms or roundworms grow to be very large because oxygen cannot penetrate many layers of cells.

Earthworms have many more cell layers than flatworms or roundworms. In earthworms, a watery fluid called **blood** carries gases to and from body tissues. Oxygen diffuses through the epidermis and into nearby blood vessels. Oxygen is carried by the blood to cells deep in the body of the worm. Similarly, carbon dioxide is carried from body cells to the epidermis where it diffuses into the surroundings.

Blood also carries molecules of digested food to the body cells. The movement of blood through the body is called **circulation**. Earthworms have a circulatory system of blood vessels passing to all parts of the body.

The blood of earthworms contains a red protein called **hemoglobin** [hē′ mə glō bin]. Hemoglobin attracts oxygen molecules. Blood with hemoglobin carries 50 times more oxygen than blood without hemoglobin.

Near the anterior end of the worm, five pairs of muscle-lined vessels alternately squeeze and relax to move blood through the body. Blood moves from these simple pumps, or **hearts**, into a ventral vessel. This vessel takes blood toward the body cells. Blood returns to the hearts by a dorsal vessel. Between the ventral and dorsal vessels, blood travels through microscopic branches. Gases, food, wastes and other molecules enter and leave the blood by diffusion.

Digestion and Excretion The digestive system of earthworms is more complex than those of other worm phyla. As earthworms

CONSUMER BIOLOGY

Earthworms eliminate undigested food as wastes. Plants use these wastes as fertilizer. An earthworm may eliminate sand and plant material far from where the material was eaten. This movement of material renews and rotates the soil. The presence of earthworms in a garden is a good sign that the soil is fertile and aerated.

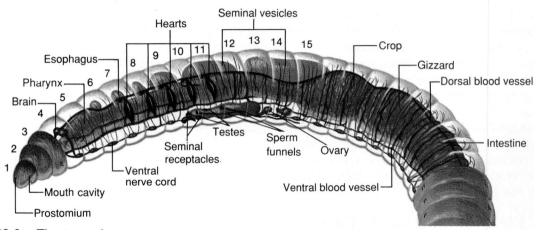

Figure 28-9 labels:
Seminal vesicles
Hearts
Esophagus
Pharynx
Brain
Crop
Gizzard
Dorsal blood vessel
Testes
Sperm funnels
Ovary
Intestine
Seminal receptacles
Ventral nerve cord
Mouth cavity
Prostomium
Ventral blood vessel

(segment numbers: 1, 2, 3, 4, 5, 6, 7, 8, 9, 10, 11, 12, 13, 14, 15)

Figure 28-9 The internal structure of an earthworm is very complex. Look closely at all of the labeled body parts. Do you know to which organ system each one belongs?

tunnel through the soil, they consume dirt. Dirt contains both food and sand particles. The food consists of material from plants and partially decomposed animals.

The earthworm takes food and sand in through its mouth. The mouth leads to a muscular pharynx. As illustrated in Figure 28-9, a short tube called the **esophagus** [i sof′ ə gəs] carries food from the pharynx to a large storage organ called the **crop**. The food and sand are stored in the crop before moving on to the gizzard. The **gizzard** is a muscular organ that grinds food. Sand particles in the dirt break organic material into small pieces. These pieces move on to the intestine. In the intestine, food is digested and absorbed into the blood.

Sand particles and undigested food move on to the end of the intestine. They are expelled through the anus. The expelled materials, called castings, fertilize the soil.

Earthworms also have an excretory system that gets rid of nitrogen wastes. Each segment, except the first three and the last one, has a pair of structures called **nephridia** [nə frid′ ē ə]. Nitrogen wastes from the blood diffuse into the nephridium and are excreted through an opening in the body wall.

Movement Earthworms move by using large muscle groups in each segment. Just beneath the epidermis is a layer of circular muscle. Below the circular muscle is a muscle layer, which extends the length of each segment. The earthworm moves by coordinated contraction and relaxation of the two layers. The process is illustrated in Figure 28-10.

Aiding movement are bristles called **setae** [sē′ tē]. Except for the first and last segments, each segment has four pairs of setae. They anchor each segment in the soil and minimize slippage.

Coordination and Senses The complex motion of the earthworm requires coordination from a well-developed nervous system.

Rear
setae
caught
in soil
Stretching
motion
Contraction to pull
worm forward
Front setae
caught in soil
Stretching
motion
Rear setae
caught in soil

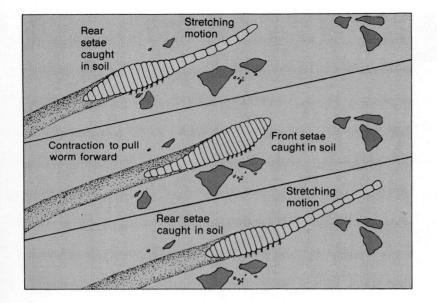

Figure 28-10 An earthworm moves by alternately contracting and stretching its body segments. Motion is aided by setae, which anchor the worm to the soil.

The brain is near the anterior end of the animal. The two brain halves send a nerve cord around each side of the pharynx. The two cords join to form one cord, which extends along the length of the worm.

The nerve cord is swollen in each segment. Each swelling, or **ganglion** [gang′ glē ən], is a grouping of nerve cells. These cells send messages up and down the nerve cord and along nerves that branch into each segment. Nerves in the epidermis detect touch and chemicals. Some also detect light.

Reproduction Earthworms reproduce sexually. Like many other worms, they are hermaphrodites. Eggs are produced in the ovaries, which are located in the thirteenth segment. The testes, which produce sperm, are found in the tenth and eleventh segments. During mating, two earthworms line up side by side. Sperm move from each earthworm to openings in the other's body, as illustrated in Figure 28-11 on the following page. The sperm are stored temporarily. After the worms part, each worm secretes a capsule. The capsule is secreted by the **clitellum** [kli tel′ əm]. Eggs move out of the worm's body into this capsule. The stored sperm are also released into the capsule. The gametes unite, and fertilization occurs. The capsule slips off the worm and is left in the soil. The eggs develop into small worms.

28-9 Other Annelids

The Class **Hirudinea** [hir ə din′ ē ə], or **leeches**, are best known as bloodsucking parasites. Many of the 300 or so species, however, are free-living. Nonparasitic leeches feed on worms, snails, and

DO YOU KNOW?

Information: Birds often have great difficulty pulling earthworms out of the ground because the worm's setae dig into the soil.

DO YOU KNOW?

Historical Note: Before the days of modern medicine, people believed that diseases could be cured by removing "bad blood" from the patient. Doctors routinely carried leeches with them for this purpose.

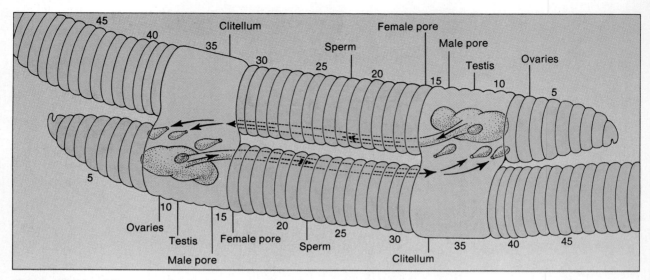

Figure 28-11 Mating earthworms exchange sperm, which travel from the male pore of one worm to the female pore of the other worm. Fertilization occurs later, within the capsule.

soft-bodied insect larvae. Parasitic leeches attach to the outer surface of animals such as fish. The leech sucks the host's blood, secreting a substance that keeps the blood from clotting. During a single feeding, a parasitic leech takes in many times its own weight in blood.

The class **Polychaeta** [pol′ i kēt ə] consists of over 6500 species of marine worms. These worms commonly hide in sand and mud along ocean coastlines. Polychaetes usually have a head with many sensory extensions. Each segment of the polychaetes has a limblike extension with many setae. These extensions are surfaces for gas exchange.

CHECKPOINT ◆

12. Explain how the coelom of annelids differs from the body cavity of roundworms.
13. List two major characteristics of annelids that separate them from the other worm phyla.
14. What substance in the blood of annelids helps carry oxygen?
15. What is the function of a gizzard?
16. Name three classes of annelids.
▶ 17. In what ways is the digestive system dependent on other body systems in the earthworm?
▶ 18. Annelids have a more complex nervous system than do roundworms or flatworms. Explain why this structural feature is necessary in annelids.

▶ Denotes a question that involves *interpreting* and *applying* concepts.

LABORATORY ACTIVITY

COMPARING FLATWORMS AND ROUNDWORMS

Objectives and Skills

☐ *Observe* prepared slides of a flatworm and a roundworm under a microscope. *Identify* internal structures in each worm.
☐ *Dissect* a roundworm and *identify* its internal structures.

Materials

microscope and light source
dissecting tray
dissecting equipment
safety goggles
lab apron
gloves
prepared slides of *Dipylidium* and *Turbatrix*
preserved specimen of *Ascaris*

Procedure and Observations

1. Read all instructions for this laboratory activity before you begin your work.
2. Use the low magnification on your microscope to observe a prepared slide of the

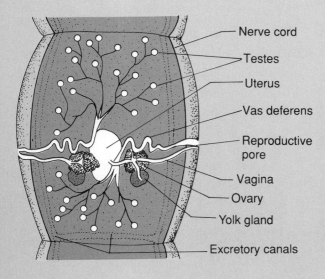

- Nerve cord
- Testes
- Uterus
- Vas deferens
- Reproductive pore
- Vagina
- Ovary
- Yolk gland
- Excretory canals

head of the dog tapeworm *Dipylidium*. On a separate piece of paper, draw a simple outline of the head and its hooks.
3. Also observe under low magnification a prepared slide of a tapeworm proglottid. Using the diagram, identify as many of the structures as possible.
4. Observe a prepared slide of the roundworm *Turbatrix* under low power. Draw a simple diagram comparing the general body structure of the tapeworm and roundworm. When you have finished, return your microscope and slides to their proper places.
5. Obtain a dissecting tray, dissecting pins, forceps, a scalpel, and a specimen of *Ascaris*. **CAUTION: Always use extreme care when handling dissecting equipment.**
6. Put on your safety goggles, lab apron, and gloves for this dissection. Place the specimen in the dissecting tray. Make an incision through the cuticle and muscle wall of the worm. Extend the incision along the entire length of the worm. Fold back the muscle wall and pin it to the wax in the dissecting pan. Use the diagram in Figure 28-6 on page 466 to identify as many organs as possible. Trade worms with a group that has a worm of the opposite sex and note the differences.
7. Before leaving the laboratory, clean up all your materials and wash your hands thoroughly.

Analysis and Conclusions

1. How is the structure of a tapeworm well adapted to its lifestyle as a parasite?
2. Contrast the general body structure of a tapeworm with that of a roundworm.
3. What is one major difference in the reproduction of the two types of worms?

CHAPTER REVIEW

Summary

▸ Worms make up a number of bilaterally symmetrical animal phyla that have three germ layers, organ systems, and show clear cephalization.

▸ Platyhelminthes are flat-bodied worms with simple nervous, reproductive, and digestive systems.

▸ Turbellarians are free-living flatworms. Planarians can regenerate lost body parts.

▸ Trematodes are parasitic flatworms. In the life cycle of the sheep liver fluke, two hosts are involved. Eggs produced by adult worms in a sheep are released in solid wastes. The eggs hatch into larvae, which enter the body of a water snail. New larvae leave the snail and form cysts. When a sheep eats grass containing these cysts, the worm's life cycle begins again.

▸ The tapeworm, a cestode, is an important flatworm parasite. Although more specialized than flukes, tapeworms exhibit a life cycle similar to flukes.

▸ Members of the nematode phylum have a body cavity and a complete digestive tract through which food moves in one direction. Nematodes have round, tubelike bodies.

▸ Hookworms and trichina are two important roundworm parasites of humans.

▸ Annelids are segmented worms. They have a coelom, which allows for the development and support of complex internal organs.

▸ Earthworms have a circulatory system in which blood transports materials between the body cells and the environment. An excretory system removes nitrogen-containing wastes. The earthworm's digestive, nervous, and reproductive systems are more complex than those of flatworms and roundworms.

▸ Most members of the class Hirudinea are blood-sucking leeches. The class Polychaeta includes the marine annelids.

Vocabulary

annelid	hemoglobin
anus	Hirudinea
blood	intestine
brain	leech
cephalization	nematode
cestode	nephridium
circulation	oligochaete
clitellum	peritoneum
coelom	pharynx
crop	Platyhelminthes
cuticle	Polychaeta
esophagus	proglottid
flame cell	segmentation
fluke	setae
ganglion	tapeworm
gizzard	trematode
gut	Turbellaria
heart	

Concept Mapping

Construct a concept map for flatworms. Include the following terms: cestode, fluke, parasite, planarian, Platyhelminthes, tapeworm, trematode, turbellarian. Use additional terms as you need them.

Review

Choose the answer that best completes each of the following questions.

1. The body cavity of earthworms is called a (a) coelom, (b) gastrovascular cavity, (c) gut, (d) peritoneum.
2. The nonliving protective covering of flukes and roundworms is called the (a) epidermis, (b) ectoderm, (c) cuticle, (d) skin.
3. Which of the following does *not* have a digestive system? (a) tapeworm (b) liver fluke (c) planaria (d) nematode

4. Which of the following is a parasitic round-worm? (a) leech (b) trichina (c) sheep liver fluke (d) planaria
5. In earthworms, the function of nephridia is to (a) excrete nitrogen wastes from the body, (b) excrete undigested food from the body, (c) absorb water from the surroundings, (d) sense light.
6. Which of the following has a circulatory system? (a) flatworm (b) roundworm (c) annelid (d) none of the above
7. Storage of food in the digestive system of the earthworm takes place in the (a) esoph-agus (b) crop (c) gizzard (d) intestine.
8. Which of the following terms best describes a major difference between leeches and earthworms? (a) parasite (b) segmented (c) circulatory system (d) annelid
9. Worms exhibit which kind of symmetry? (a) radial (b) spherical (c) bilateral (d) asymmetry
10. Which of the following does *not* have a body cavity of any kind? (a) planaria (b) trichina (c) earthworm (d) leech
11. How do the members of the phylum Platyhel-minthes obtain oxygen?
12. Briefly describe the life cycle of a sheep liver fluke.
13. What is the peritoneum?

Interpret and Apply

14. List the major features that distinguish worms from sponges and cnidarians.
15. What characteristics, if any, are common to all the parasitic worms from different phyla?
16. Give an explanation for the absence of a digestive system in tapeworms.
17. What are some of the structural specializa-tions of flukes that adapt them for life as parasites?

18. Why are flukes and hookworms placed in different phyla?
19. Explain why the digestive system of round-worms is an improvement over the digestive system of flatworms.
20. Why is the space between the body wall and the digestive system in roundworms not considered a true coelom?
21. Why is a circulatory system a useful adap-tation in annelids?

Critical Thinking

22. Describe a method that might be used to get rid of the sheep liver fluke from a given area.
23. Explain how flatworms and roundworms can survive without special structures for exchanging gases.
24. Many parasitic worms form cysts at some point in their life cycle. How do these cysts represent adaptive advantages to parasitic worms?
25. Why might it be an advantage for parasitic worms to be hermaphroditic?
26. Some organisms have circulatory systems with blood, but the blood contains no hemoglobin. What is the value of blood containing hemoglobin to annelids?
27. Parasites that kill their host are generally thought to have evolved more recently than those that do not kill their host. Explain why this might be true using natural selection to support your argument.
28. It is known that planaria move away from light. When given a choice, they will choose a dark area as opposed to a light one. What organ systems are involved in this response? Describe an experiment to test the hypothesis that planaria can distinguish various colors of light.

MOLLUSKS AND ECHINODERMS

Overview

PHYLUM MOLLUSCA

29-1 Class Gastropoda:
       Snails and Slugs
29-2 Class Pelecypoda:
       Bivalves
29-3 Class Cephalopoda:
       Squids and Octopuses

**PHYLUM
ECHINODERMATA**

29-4 Characteristics of
       Echinoderms
29-5 Class Asteroidea:
       Starfish

What is a live octopus really like?

PHYLUM MOLLUSCA

Perhaps more than any other group, the **mollusks** illustrate how a common body plan can be modified into a variety of forms. While most mollusk species are marine, there are also many freshwater and land-dwelling species. It is hard to believe that organisms as varied as clams, snails, and squid are actually members of the same phylum. Why are such varied organisms placed in the same phylum? What structural similarities does an oyster have in common with an octopus?

29-1 Class Gastropoda: Snails and Slugs

Gastropods are the largest mollusk group, with over 35 000 species. They show a wider variety of forms and live in more diverse environments than any other mollusk group. Many gastropods are aquatic; some are marine and others live in fresh water. Gastropods also include the only terrestrial mollusks. **Terrestrial** [tə res′ trē əl] organisms are those that live on land. The most common gastropods are snails and slugs.

Gastropods also show a variety of feeding habits. Snails and slugs are representative gastropods. The garden snail and slug eat plants and do extensive crop damage. Some gastropods eat meat while others feed on dead organisms. A few gastropods are parasites.

Section Objectives

A **Explain** the significance of the trochophore larva.

B **Identify** several typical gastropods and **describe** the characteristics of the class.

C **Describe** how bivalves differ from other mollusks.

D **Explain** how cephalopods are more highly specialized than other mollusk classes.

Figure 29-1 Most mollusks have soft bodies and some type of protective shell. This colorful marine snail is just one kind of mollusk. It is part of a group whose members show enormous variation of structure and lifestyle.

Mollusks and Echinoderms   **477**

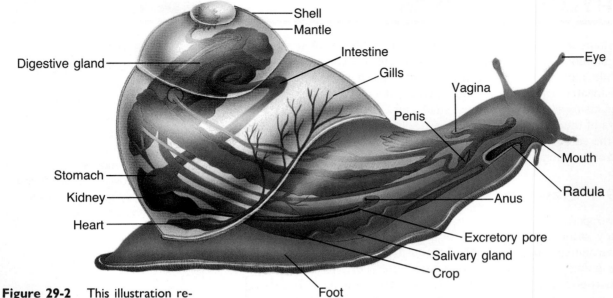

Shell
Mantle
Intestine
Gills
Vagina
Penis
Eye
Mouth
Radula
Anus
Digestive gland
Stomach
Kidney
Heart
Excretory pore
Salivary gland
Crop
Foot

Figure 29-2 This illustration reveals the internal structure of a typical gastropod. Notice the number of organs located in the head region. Why do you think the eyes are located on stalks?

The snail has a soft body without a skeleton. It is bilaterally symmetrical, and a coelom is present. Covering the body is a layer of cells called the **mantle**. The mantle secretes a hard material that forms a shell on the outside of the organism.

The snail's digestive system begins at the mouth. The **radula** (raj′ ù lə) is a feeding device found only in mollusks. It is a muscular structure with hard, toothlike projections. Like a file, the radula scrapes food from surfaces. Food travels to the stomach through the esophagus. Most digestion and absorption take place in the stomach and a nearby digestive gland. The intestine forms waste pellets which pass from the anus into the mantle cavity and out of the body.

In its search for food, the snail travels slowly on its large, muscular **foot**, a characteristic of all mollusks. Glands in the foot secrete mucus, which helps the snail slide along. The snail shows clear cephalization. The two eyes located on stalks as well as other chemical and touch sensors located in the head help a snail seek out food.

Aquatic gastropods exchange gases with the water environment using gills. **Gills** are thin, highly folded tissues that contain many microscopic blood vessels with a large surface area for gas exchange. The gills are located within the mantle cavity. Water flows into the mantle cavity and directly over the gills. Gills provide a large surface for gas exchange. They absorb oxygen from the water and release carbon dioxide into it.

Gastropods that live on land do not have gills. Instead, land snails have evolved a simple lung, an organ for gas exchange in air-breathing animals. Lungs are infoldings of the body wall with only a single, narrow opening to the outside. The small size of the opening prevents air from drying out the lung tissue. In the lung, gases diffuse between the air and the blood.

Blood circulation in mollusks is different from circulation in annelids. Recall that the circulatory system of an annelid is a **closed circulatory system** since blood is contained by vessels as it travels through the body. Most mollusks, however, have an **open circulatory system** in which blood is not confined to vessels after leaving the heart. A two-chambered heart pumps blood around the coelom. Blood also penetrates spaces between tissues and organs throughout the body. Mollusk blood has an oxygen-carrying molecule called **hemocyanin** [hē mə sī′ a nin]. Unlike red hemoglobin, hemocyanin is blue.

Many aquatic gastropods have separate sexes. Some species release eggs and sperm directly into the water. Fertilization occurs in water, not in the female's body. In other species, the two sexes mate, and fertilization occurs in the female's body. In a few species, development of the fertilized eggs also takes place within the female.

In most gastropods, a distinctive larva develops within the egg. This larva, which has its own digestive system, is known as a **trochophore** [träk ə fōr′] **larva**. This larva never leaves the egg. Inside the egg, the trochophore larva of some species develops into another form of larva while in others it becomes a tiny adult snail.

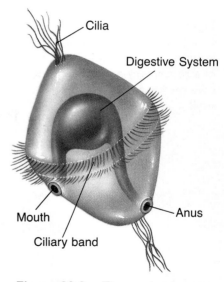

Figure 29-3 The trochophore larva is part of the life cycle of most mollusks.

29-2 Class Pelecypoda: Bivalves

The pelecypods are mollusks with two shells, or valves. Pelecypods are therefore called **bivalves**. The two valves are hinged so they open or close through the action of several large muscles. When closed, the valves protect the animal from predators. Oysters, clams, scallops, and mussels are bivalves.

The mantle and the shell extend out farther than the body. At the posterior end the overhang is so great that it forms a protected space called the **mantle cavity**.

The foot of most bivalves is specialized for burrowing in soft mud or sand. Extending out from between the valves, the leading edge of the foot fans into an anchor. Contraction of the foot then pulls the clam body deeper into the sand.

Bivalves do not have a radula. Instead, most bivalves use their gills for feeding as well as for respiration. A bivalve generally keeps its shells partly opened. Water, which carries food and oxygen, flows into the mantle cavity. Cilia on the gills create water currents within the cavity. Mucus on the gills traps plankton from the water. Cilia sweep the mucus and food particles toward

Figure 29-4 The internal anatomy of a clam shows the structural features of bivalves. Can you think of a reason why a clam does not have the same type of head as a snail?

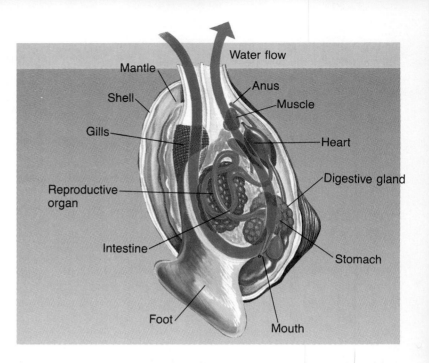

Water flow
Mantle
Anus
Shell
Muscle
Gills
Heart
Reproductive organ
Digestive gland
Intestine
Stomach
Foot
Mouth

Figure 29-5 The nautilus is free-swimming. It adjusts its depth in water by adding or removing gas from the shell chambers.

the mouth. In addition, oxygen from the water diffuses into the blood. Carbon dioxide diffuses from the blood into the water. Bivalves have an open circulatory system. Nephridia function in excretion, removing nitrogenous wastes and excess water.

Cephalization is not well developed in bivalves. The nervous system is bilaterally symmetrical, with two pairs of long nerve cords and three ganglia. The edge of the mantle contains sense organs that respond to light, chemicals, and touch.

The sexes are separate in most bivalves. Sperm and eggs are shed into the water, and fertilization occurs outside the body. The trochophore larva of bivalves differs from the snail trochophore because it swims freely for a time feeding on plankton. The larva settles to the bottom and develops into an adult.

29-3 Class Cephalopoda: Squids and Octopuses

Cephalopods [sef′ ə lə pods] are the most highly specialized mollusks. Squids and octopuses are typical cephalopods. Cephalopods have a well-developed nervous system with a large brain and complex sensory organs.

Ancient cephalopods had a large shell that protected their soft bodies. Only one type of living cephalopod, the nautilus, has retained an external shell. In the squid, the shell is reduced to an internal rod secreted by the mantle. The octopus has no shell at all.

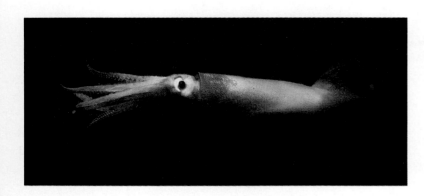

Figure 29-6 The squid actually has eight arms and two tentacles. Arms have fixed lengths, but tentacles can change in length.

In cephalopods, the foot has evolved into long arms that project from the head. The arms are equipped with suction disks. The cephalopod uses its arms to grasp prey and pull the food toward its mouth. All cephalopods are carnivorous. The mouth of cephalopods has a pair of hard, beaklike teeth used for biting and tearing prey.

Unlike most mollusks, cephalopods have a closed circulatory system. Closed circulation is usually an adaptation of rapidly moving animals. Of all the mollusks, the cephalopods are the most active movers. Such animals have greater metabolic requirements because they need energy for rapid swimming. With closed circulation, blood carrying oxygen and food is delivered efficiently to all parts of the body.

Movement in squids is unusual. They normally swim with graceful wavelike motions. In times of danger, they use a nozzlelike **siphon** on the ventral surface to move more rapidly. Rapid muscle contractions force water out of the mantle cavity through the siphon. Like a jet, the force of water moving out of the siphon propels the squid, helping it to escape.

DO YOU KNOW?

Information: Octopuses and squids can change color to match their background, to startle enemies, or to attract mates.

CHECKPOINT ◆

1. How does the mollusk larva differ from other larva you have studied?
2. Which mollusk class includes members with lungs?
3. Which mollusk class includes members that have two shells?
4. In what ways do cephalopods differ from other mollusks?
▶ 5. Compare the food getting structures for each class of mollusks.
▶ 6. How does the mantle cavity differ from a coelom?
▶ 7. Why is it not surprising that cephalopods are the only mollusk class to have a closed circulatory system?

▶ Denotes a question that involves *interpreting* and *applying* concepts.

Mollusks and Echinoderms   **481**

Section Objectives

E *List* the major characteristics of echinoderms.

F *Describe* the unique anatomical features of a starfish.

All **echinoderms** are marine organisms. There are over 5000 species in this phylum which includes starfish, sea urchins, sea cucumbers, and sand dollars. Like mollusks, echinoderms have a coelom and a one-way digestive system. You will see, however, that the echinoderms have several unique characteristics. What are echinoderms? What do they look like? Why are they classified in a phylum separate from mollusks?

29-4 Characteristics of Echinoderms

Most echinoderms exhibit **pentamerous radial symmetry**. An animal with this kind of symmetry can be divided into five equal parts from a central axis.

Radial symmetry has adaptive value in sessile and slow-moving animals. Recall that in bilateral animals, cephalization occurs at the end that moves first into the environment. In echinoderms, there is no real advantage for one body part to contact the environment sooner than another. As a result, those echinoderms that show radial symmetry do not show cephalization.

During development, echinoderms go through a **bipinnaria** [bī pin′ er ē ä] **larva** stage. The bipinnaria is bilaterally symmetrical. This suggests that echinoderms evolved from an ancestor with bilateral symmetry. The bipinnaria larva differs structurally from the trochophore larva of mollusks. Compare the larva illustrated in Figure 29-7 to that found in Figure 29-3. Two additional features are unique to echinoderms. One is their system of **tube feet**, a series of suction disks used in locomotion and getting food. Tube feet are powered by a unique system of water-pumping tubes. The other is an **endoskeleton**, or internal skeleton. The endoskeleton protects and supports the organism's soft tissues. It also provides a place to which muscles can attach. The endoskeleton is made of calcium compounds that form plates just below the epidermis. A number of spiny projections extend from these plates through the epidermis. Different spines are modified for different functions in the various classes of echinoderms. The name *echinoderm* means "spiny skin."

29-5 Class Asteroidea: Starfish

The starfish, also called seastars, are commonly classified as **asteroids**. These organisms demonstrate many features of echinoderms in general. A starfish has five arms, or rays, projecting from a central disk. Ciliated epidermal cells cover the endoskeleton. A network of nerve cells lies just below the epidermis. The plates

Figure 29-7 The bipinnaria larva is not unique to echinoderms. Members of the phylum Hemichordata and Chordata have the same or similar larval forms.

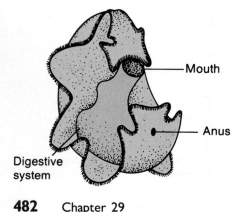

Mouth

Anus

Digestive system

Figure 29-8 *Left:* A starfish; *Right:* A sea urchin. Both exhibit radial symmetry.

Figure 29-9 A sea cucumber has spiny skin and radial symmetry characteristic of echinoderms.

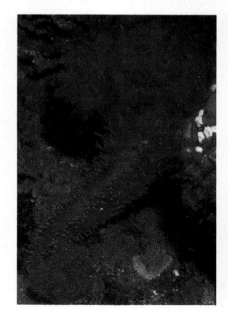

of the endoskeleton are flexible at their joints. A variety of spinelike projections emerge from the skeleton through the epidermis.

Starfish are primarily bottom dwellers. They usually move by using tube feet. The tube feet are located on the lower side of each of the five rays. The tube feet are part of a unique system called the **water vascular system**. Sea water enters the system through the **madreporite** [mad rə pōr′ ĭt] in the center of the starfish's upper surface. The water moves through a series of canals out into the tube feet. Each tube foot moves by a continuous filling and emptying of water. The mechanism of filling and emptying is not well understood.

Most starfish are carnivores. Food is taken into the mouth, located on the starfish's lower surface. From the mouth, food goes through the esophagus to the stomach, where digestion takes place. Many starfish can push the stomach outside of their body to surround a food organism. Digestive enzymes are produced by digestive glands in each arm. Undigested wastes are eliminated through the anus on the starfish's upper surface.

Digested food molecules are carried to the cells of the starfish by fluid in the coelom. (This fluid is separate from the water in the water vascular system.) Ciliated cells lining the coelom circulate this fluid. The circulation of coelomic fluid serves as a circulatory system.

Starfish have no excretory system. Wastes diffuse from cells into the coelomic fluid. They then diffuse out of the body through

Figure 29-10 This illustration identifies some of the external and internal features of a starfish.

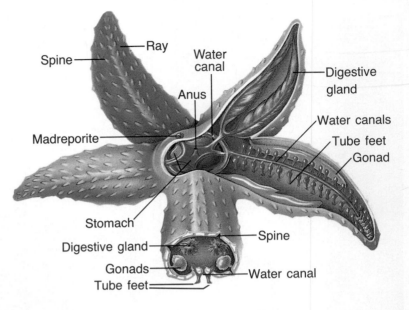

Spine — Ray

Water canal

Anus

Digestive gland

Water canals

Tube feet

Gonad

Madreporite

Stomach

Digestive gland

Gonads

Tube feet

Spine

Water canal

Figure 29-11 This starfish is feeding on an oyster. The starfish wraps around the oyster and pulls the shells apart. The oyster fights to keep closed but usually fails. One starfish can eat ten oysters each day.

▶ Denotes a question that involves *interpreting* and *applying* concepts.

the tube feet. Specialized spines function as gills. Gases are exchanged between the coelomic fluid and the exterior through these spines and through the tube feet.

Starfish have no obvious head. Their nervous system is a simple ring of nerve cells that branch into each of the arms.

Reproduction in starfish is usually sexual. Males and females generally shed egg and sperm cells into the water. Starfish also have remarkable powers of regeneration. If a starfish is broken into pieces, many of the pieces will regenerate. For example, a severed arm will regenerate into an entire animal as long as the arm has part of the central disk attached to it. A few species of starfish reproduce asexually by shedding arms.

CHECKPOINT ◆

8. What kind of symmetry is found in most echinoderms?
9. Describe an unusual characteristic of the stomach of a starfish.
10. Where are the respiratory surfaces of a starfish?
11. Tube feet are part of what system that is unique to echinoderms?
▶ 12. Explain why animals with radial symmetry do not show signs of cephalization.
▶ 13. Describe the differences between bipinnaria and trochophore larvae.

STRUCTURE OF A SQUID

Objectives and Skills

☐ *Identify* external structures of the squid.
☐ *Dissect* the squid and *identify* some of its internal structures.

Materials

dissecting tray	gloves
dissecting equipment	safety goggles
lab apron	preserved squid

Procedures and Observations

1. Read all the instructions for this laboratory activity before you begin your work.
2. Put on your safety goggles, lab apron, and gloves. **CAUTION: Be careful with sharp dissecting instruments.**
3. Place a squid in a dissecting tray. Rinse it thoroughly under running water. Use diagram A to help you identify the tentacles,

Diagram A

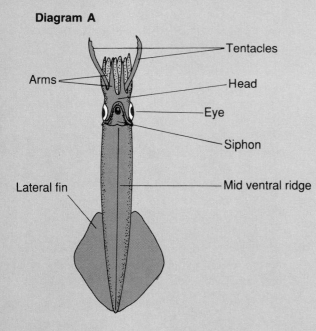

Diagram B

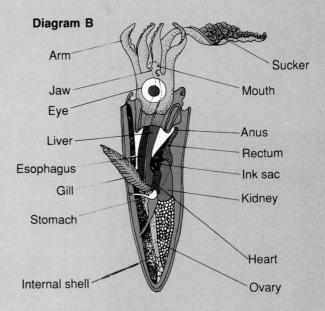

arms, head, eyes, siphon, midventral ridge, and lateral fins on your squid.

4. Use scissors to make an incision along the midventral ridge. Cut through the body wall beginning at the head and ending at the dorsal tip. Use pins to hold back both sides of the body wall. Use diagram **B** to help you identify the jaw, liver, esophagus, gill, stomach, internal shell, mouth, anus, ink sac, kidney, heart, and ovary.
5. Be sure to clean up the area around your desk and wash your hands thoroughly before leaving the lab.

Analysis and Conclusions

1. Determine the sex of your specimen.
2. Identify some of the external features of a squid that make this animal well adapted as a carnivorous hunter.
3. Describe how a squid uses its siphon and ink sac to escape from predators.

CHAPTER REVIEW

Summary

▸ Mollusks include such organisms as oysters, snails, and squids. Most mollusks pass through a trochophore larva stage. The structural characteristics shared by most mollusks include a shell, a mantle, a mantle cavity, gills, and an open circulatory system. Most mollusks also have a muscular foot used for movement and a radula used for feeding.

▸ Gastropods are the largest mollusk class. This group includes snails and slugs. Most gastropods are aquatic, but some are terrestrial. Terrestrial gastropods have a simple lung for respiration. Gastropods reproduce sexually. Some species are hermaphroditic, while in others the sexes are separate. The shell is absent in some gastropods.

▸ Pelecypods, or bivalves, are mollusks with two hinged shells. This group includes such organisms as clams and oysters. The foot of most bivalves is modified for burrowing in mud. Most bivalves use gills both for feeding and for respiration. The sexes are separate in most of these animals, and fertilization occurs outside of the body.

▸ Cephalopods are the most highly specialized mollusks. Included in this class are the squid, octopus, and the nautilus. The foot has evolved into tentacles. Cephalopods have a well-developed brain and sense organs, and a closed circulatory system.

▸ Echinoderms are marine organisms. Most exhibit pentamerous radial symmetry. The phylum includes animals such as starfish, sea urchins, sand dollars, and sea cucumbers. Echinoderms go through a bipinnaria larval stage. They have tube feet and an endoskeleton with spiny projections extending through the epidermis.

▸ Starfish belong to the Class Asteroidea. They move by means of tube feet, which are part of a water vascular system.

Vocabulary

asteroid	mantle
bipinnaria larva	mantle cavity
bivalve	mollusk
cephalopod	open circulatory system
closed circula-	pentamerous radial
tory system	symmetry
echinoderm	radula
endoskeleton	siphon
gastropod	terrestrial
gill	trochophore larva
hemocyanin	tube feet
madreporite	water vascular system

Concept Mapping

Construct a concept map for aquatic adaptations of mollusks. Include the following terms: cephalopod, pelecypod, radula, mantle, trochophore, siphon, and gastropod. Use additional terms as you need them.

Review

Choose the best answer for each of the following questions.

1. The larva that is characteristic of most mollusks is the (a) tornaria larva, (b) bipinnaria larva, (c) bilateral larva, (d) trochophore larva.
2. The group of mollusks with the largest number of species is the (a) gastropods, (b) pelecypods, (c) cephalopods, (d) asteroidea.
3. The foot of most bivalves is specialized for (a) burrowing, (b) crawling over surfaces, (c) swimming, (d) feeding.
4. The larva of echinoderms shows (a) pentamerous radial symmetry, (b) radial symmetry, (c) spherical symmetry, (d) bilateral symmetry.

5. For rapid escapes, cephalopods direct a jet of water through the (a) mantle cavity, (b) siphon, (c) mouth, (d) tentacles.
6. All echinoderms are (a) terrestrial, (b) freshwater, (c) marine, (d) marine and freshwater.
7. The tube feet of starfish are powered by (a) muscles, (b) coelomic fluid, (c) a water vascular system, (d) fluid from the mantle cavity.

Answer each of the following questions.

8. What kind of circulatory system is found in most mollusks?
9. What is the oxygen-carrying molecule in the blood of mollusks?
10. What is the respiratory structure of most land animals?
11. In bivalves, where does fertilization occur?

Interpret and Apply

12. The kind of symmetry shown by all mollusks is (a) radial symmetry, (b) bilateral symmetry, (c) pentamerous radial symmetry, (d) spherical symmetry.
13. Digestion and absorption of food in mollusks takes place in the (a) stomach and digestive glands, (b) crop, (c) intestine, (d) radula.
14. What is unusual about the trochophore larva of land snails? Why is this characteristic an adaptation to terrestrial life?
15. Explain how the gills of a clam perform two separate functions.
16. What is the advantage of a closed circulatory system to cephalopods?
17. Explain why cephalization would not be as advantageous to echinoderms as it is to animals such as annelids.
18. Describe some of the adaptations in starfish that make them well suited to life as bottom dwellers.

19. Explain how echinoderms survive without a circulatory system.
20. What evidence is used to support the claim that echinoderms evolved from animals with bilateral symmetry?
21. Give a possible explanation for the observation that cephalization has not been an important trend in the evolution of bivalves.
22. A starfish is cut into two pieces. One piece consists of four arms attached to the central disk. The other piece is the fifth arm without any of the central disk. Will either— or both—of these pieces regenerate? Explain.
23. Bivalves have paired shells that can open and close. Why is this type of shell a useful adaptation?
24. Make a list of the characteristics that could be used to classify an organism as a mollusk.

Critical Thinking

25. Most aquatic snails have separate sexes and shed their eggs and sperm into the surrounding water. Can you explain why the mating of terrestrial snails is a useful adaptation to land life?
26. Explain how the modifications of the foot in pelecypods, gastropods, and cephalopods are adaptations for different kinds of motion.
27. Slow-moving species, such as sea urchins, often go through a highly motile larval stage. How might a fast-moving larva be an advantage to such species?

ARTHROPODS

Overview

SUBPHYLUM CHELICERATA

30-1   General Arthropod Characteristics

30-2   Characteristics of Chelicerates

30-3   Class Arachnida: Spiders

30-4   Other Chelicerates

SUBPHYLUM MANDIBULATA

30-5   Class Crustacea

30-6   Classes Diplopoda and Chilopoda

CLASS INSECTA

30-7   Insect Body

30-8   Insect Development

30-9   Grasshopper

DIVERSITY OF INSECTS

30-10 Feeding Adaptations

30-11 Adaptations in Appearance

30-12 Reproductive Adaptations

30-13 Social Insects

Why are insects so common?

SUBPHYLUM CHELICERATA

The phylum Arthropoda contains about 800 000 species. **Arthropods** [är' thrō podz] make up about 80 percent of the known animal species. The phylum also includes extinct organisms such as trilobites. You may have seen trilobite fossils in pictures or at a museum.

Arthropods are divided into two subphyla, the chelicerates and the mandibulates. The **chelicerates** [kə lis' ər āts] include spiders, ticks, horseshoe crabs, and other related animals. The **mandibulates** [man dib' ye lāts] include organisms such as crayfish, centipedes, millipedes, and insects. What traits distinguish a chelicerate from a mandibulate? Which characteristics are used to identify an organism as an arthropod?

30-1 General Arthropod Characteristics

The most prominent characteristic of arthropods is their outside skeleton, or **exoskeleton**. Like any skeleton, an exoskeleton gives soft tissues support and protection. It also provides an anchoring place for muscles. The arthropod exoskeleton is made primarily of **chitin** [kī' tin], a strong, flexible polysaccharide.

If an animal is surrounded by a hard exoskeleton, how can it grow? All arthropods **molt**, or shed, their exoskeletons periodically. After an arthropod molts, there is a short time before the new exoskeleton hardens. During this time, the animal grows.

A skeleton that surrounds the body must have flexible joints to allow movement. All arthropods have joints between body sections. In addition, arthropods have jointed appendages. An **appendage** is a structure such as a leg that grows out from the main part of the body. To move the joints, arthropods have pairs of muscles. When one muscle contracts, the joint bends. When the other muscle contracts, the joint straightens.

Like annelids, all arthropods have segmented bodies. In arthropods, however, the segments are more highly specialized. Many arthropods have segments with appendages that function as jaws. In segments located just behind the head, paired appendages are adapted for locomotion.

The nervous system of arthropods is highly developed. Cephalization is more prominent than in annelids, with the brain and complex sense organs in the head region. Special organs sense touch, vibration, and chemicals. The eyes of many arthropods are particularly specialized.

All arthropods have an open circulatory system. The dorsal heart pumps blood from the posterior end of the animal to the anterior end.

Figure 30-1 Arthropods make up a vast majority of all animal species. Insects are by far the most common arthropods.

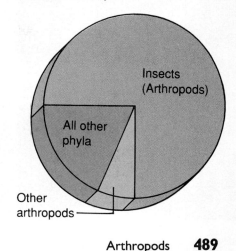

Arthropods **489**

Figure 30-2 Arthropods periodically molt their old exoskeletons. Before the new exoskeleton hardens, the animal grows. Why is this a dangerous time in the life of an arthropod?

Figure 30-3 The female black widow spider is appropriately named because she sometimes attacks and eats the much smaller male while the male is attempting to mate.

30-2 Characteristics of Chelicerates

The body of a chelicerate has two major parts. The **cephalothorax** [sef ə lō thōr′ aks] is a fused section composed of the head and any body segments that have legs attached. The **abdomen** consists of posterior segments that contain most of the internal organs.

Most chelicerates have six pairs of appendages. The four posterior pairs are walking legs. The two anterior pairs are highly specialized. The first pair, called *chelicera* [kə lis′ ər ə], are modified to aid in feeding. They function like the jaws of other animals. The second pair of appendages are called pedipalps. *Pedipalps* [ped′ ē palps] are modified in different chelicerates for a variety of functions. They are often sensory receptors, picking up sensations of touch, taste, and smell.

30-3 Class Arachnida: Spiders

Arachnids are a major class of chelicerates. The largest order of arachnids is the spiders. Like all chelicerates, spiders have a two-part body consisting of a cephalothorax and an abdomen. One pair of chelicerae, one pair of pedipalps, and four pairs of walking legs arise from the cephalothorax. All arachnids have eight walking legs.

Spiders' chelicerae are not modified for chewing. Rather they have piercing fangs with poison sacs used to kill prey. While all spiders have poison, only a few species are dangerous to humans. The black widow and the brown recluse are the most dangerous spiders in North America.

Digestion With no jaws to chew food, spiders digest food externally. They pump liquid from their digestive tract onto their prey. Enyzmes digest the food. The food is then pulled into the esophagus by muscular contractions of the pharynx. A series of tubes branching from the stomach absorb food into the blood. The digestive system and other internal organs of a spider are illustrated in Figure 30-4.

Silk Production All spiders have silk glands in the abdomen. Silk is released from the body through nozzlelike openings called **spinnerets**. Many spiders use their silk to make webs. Small animals, usually insects, become trapped in the sticky web. Not all spiders build webs, but they all make silk. Some spiders wrap excess food organisms in a silk cocoon. Females often wrap eggs in a protective silk case.

Respiration All spiders are terrestrial. Instead of gills, spiders have **book lungs** for gas exchange. Book lungs consist of folded membranes arranged in stacks, much like the pages in a book. This arrangement exposes a large surface area of lung tissue to

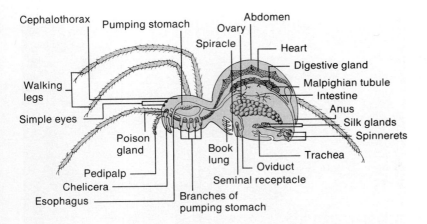

Cephalothorax — Pumping stomach
Abdomen
Ovary
Spiracle
Heart
Digestive gland
Malpighian tubule
Intestine
Anus
Silk glands
Spinnerets
Trachea
Walking legs
Simple eyes
Poison gland
Book lung
Oviduct
Seminal receptacle
Pedipalp
Chelicera
Esophagus
Branches of pumping stomach

Figure 30-4 The internal anatomy of the female spider illustrated here is similar to that found in most other chelicerates.

the air. Book lungs only open to the environment through a single small passage to the outside. This helps to keep the respiratory surfaces from drying out. The opening through the exoskeleton to the respiratory surface is called a **spiracle** [spī′ rə kəl].

In addition to book lungs, some spiders have tracheae. **Tracheae** [trā′ kē ə] are branching tubes that bring air close to the spider's cells and to the circulating blood. Air gets into tracheae through spiracles in the abdomen.

Circulation and Excretion In the spider's circulatory system, blood leaves the heart and moves through vessels to various parts of the body. It passes into open spaces around tissues and organs.

Malpighian [mal pig′ ē ən] **tubules** are the spider's major excretory organs. These tubules branch from the intestine and extend into the abdominal spaces. Nitrogen wastes from the blood pass through these tubes. The wastes then move into the intestine and out of the body.

Nervous System and Senses The nervous system of spiders consists of a rather large brain and a ventral nerve cord. Sensory organs are well developed in many spiders. Most spiders have eight simple eyes. A **simple eye** senses light and dark, but does not form images. These eyes are arranged in two rows of four.

Most spiders have sensory organs in their legs that detect vibrations. In web-builders, these organs detect trapped insects struggling in the web.

Reproduction The ovary of the female spider produces eggs. After a female mates with a male, the sperm cells are held in a small chamber called the **seminal receptacle**. Later, when the eggs are released, they are fertilized by sperm stored in the receptacle.

The male spider produces sperm in testes. The sperm are released from the body through an opening in the abdomen. The male has a suctionlike device on its pedipalps that draws sperm cells into the pedipalps. During mating, sperm are transferred from the pedipalp into the female's seminal receptacle.

BIOLOGY INSIGHT

Structure Is Related to Function: Folding is one way to increase the amount of surface area available in a confined space. Since gas exchange involves diffusion of gases across a surface, respiratory systems in organisms usually involve extensive folding of tissues.

DO YOU KNOW?

Information: Eyes are larger in spiders that stalk prey than in those that trap prey in webs.

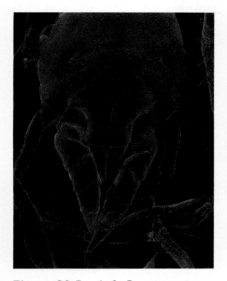 

Figure 30-5 *Left:* Because mites are so small, most people do not realize how common they are in the environment. *Right:* Horseshoe crabs, like the one illustrated here, are not really crabs. They are one of the few living members of an ancient chelicerate class. Most members of this class have been extinct for millions of years.

30-4 Other Chelicerates

There are several other groups of organisms that belong to the Class Arachnida. Scorpions, for example, are considered among the most primitive of the arachnids. The segments of the scorpion's abdomen are distinct, not fused together the way a spider's are. The sting and poison glands of the scorpion are located in the last abdominal segment. The pedipalps are modified into large pincers that grasp prey.

Mites are the most widespread of the arachnids. They are also the least obvious since most are less than a millimeter in length. The exoskeleton of mites shows few signs of segmentation. Mites are parasites of plants and animals, including humans.

Ticks are larger than mites but have a similar body form. They are parasites of many terrestrial animals. Like leeches, ticks attach to their host to feed on blood and then drop off. Ticks carry a number of human diseases, including Rocky Mountain spotted fever. People are generally more afraid of spiders and scorpions than mites and ticks, yet the latter do far greater damage.

CHECKPOINT ◆

1. List some characteristics of arthropods.
2. Name the two body divisions of chelicerates.
3. What is the function of chelicerae in spiders?
4. How do scorpions differ from spiders?
▶ 5. Why does the presence of an exoskeleton require jointed appendages?

▶ Denotes a question that involves *interpreting* and *applying* concepts.

SUBPHYLUM MANDIBULATA

The second subphylum of the arthropods is the mandibulates. Unlike chelicerates, mandibulates have *mandibles*, or jaws, for chewing food. They also have maxillae [mak sil′ ē] for holding food and passing it to the mandibles. All mandibulates have **antennae**—segmented sense organs on the head. Mandibulates also have three or more pairs of walking legs.

There are four major classes of mandibulates. The **crustaceans** [krus tā′ shənz] include such organisms as crabs, lobsters, and shrimp. The *diplopods* are better known as millipedes. The *chilopods* are the centipedes. Insects, the largest group of mandibulates, will be discussed in the next lesson. What do lobsters, millipedes, and flies have in common? What other organisms are classified as mandibulates?

Section Objectives

E *Identify* the characteristics of mandibulates and **explain** how they differ from chelicerates.

F *Name* the external and internal anatomical features of the crayfish and **describe** the function of each structure.

G *Compare* and **contrast** the structure of millipedes and centipedes.

30-5 Class Crustacea

With over 20 000 species, the crustaceans show tremendous diversity. Crustaceans include many animals such as lobsters, barnacles, and *Daphnia*, the water flea. Most crustaceans are marine, although some live in fresh water and on land.

The crayfish, a typical crustacean, is illustrated in Figure 30-6. The cephalothorax is covered by a single piece of exoskeleton called the **carapace** [kar′ ə pas]. The crustacean exoskeleton contains calcium and other minerals in addition to chitin. The minerals make the shell particularly hard and inflexible.

Appendages Crustaceans have paired appendages attached to each segment. The anterior-most appendages are two pairs of antennae. Just behind the antennae are the mandibles, or jaws. They crush, tear, and chew food before it enters the mouth. Following the mandibles are two pairs of maxillae. Behind the maxillae are three pairs of *maxillipeds* [mak sil′ ə peds], which serve as sense organs. They also help pass food toward the mouth.

The next appendages are the large, pincer-bearing *chelipeds* [kə′ li peds]. The crayfish uses its chelipeds to get food and protect itself from enemies. Behind the chelipeds are four pairs of walking legs. The abdominal segments bear appendages called *swimmerets*, which aid in swimming. At the posterior end, there are several flattened appendages called *uropods*. They lie on both sides of the flattened tail, or *telson*, and are used for swimming.

Feeding and Digestion In general, crayfish are scavengers. The mandibles shred food into small pieces. The esophagus, which leads to the stomach, has fine toothlike structures made of chitin

■ BIOLOGY INSIGHT

Adaptation and Evolution: A survey of the arachnids illustrates one very important trend of arthropod evolution: the reduction of body segmentation. The primitive scorpions show clear body segmentation. Segmentation is reduced in spiders. It is nearly absent in mites and ticks.

Figure 30-6 If you have ever eaten a lobster, the external and internal features of a crayfish should be familiar to you.

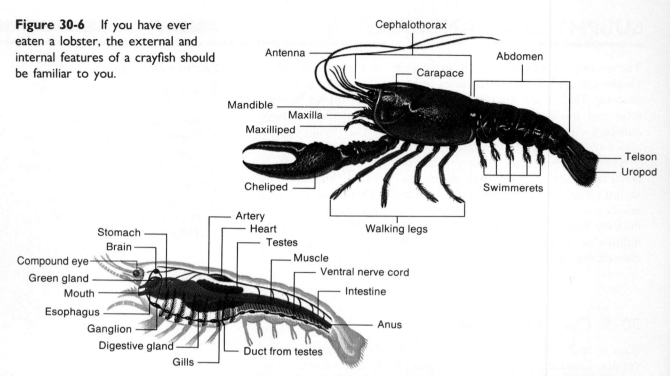

that grind food into fine particles. Final digestion and absorption of food occurs in large digestive glands located on both sides of the stomach.

Circulation, Respiration, and Excretion Gills are located at the base of the walking legs. As the crayfish moves, water flows over the gills. In the thin-walled gills, gases diffuse between the water and the blood.

Like all arthropods, crayfish have open circulation. Vessels carry blood from the heart to the various organs of the body. Blood then leaves these vessels and flows into spaces between the body organs. Blood returns from the organs and travels through the gills, where gases are exchanged. From the gills, blood moves to a space around the heart. Blood reenters the heart through slits called **ostia**.

Crayfish excrete nitrogen wastes from two green glands located in the head. These glands filter wastes from blood. Filtered wastes pass through pores to the outside.

Senses The crayfish brain receives stimuli from a variety of sense organs. The antennae are sensitive to touch and to chemicals in the water. The fine, hairlike projections that cover the body of a crayfish are sensitive to touch and to vibrations in the water. A crayfish can sense motion and can probably see crude images through its two large compound eyes. A **compound eye** is composed of many individual light-sensitive units.

Reproduction Crayfish reproduce sexually, and the sexes are separate. During mating, the male deposits sperm in the female's body where they are held until the eggs have matured. Later, as each egg leaves the ovary, sperm are released and fertilization occurs. The eggs stick to the swimmerets where they remain until they hatch.

30-6 Classes Diplopoda and Chilopoda

Turn over a pile of leaves and you are likely to see diplopods scurrying around. Diplopods are more commonly know as millipedes. Literally, *millipede* means "thousand feet." In reality, few millipedes have more than a few hundred feet. The strictly herbivorous millipedes range in length from 2 millimeters to 30 centimeters. The number of segments varies from about 10 to over 100.

A millipede's head has two groups of simple eyes, a pair of antennae, mandibles, and maxillae. The first four segments behind the head each have a single pair of legs. The abdominal segment is unique, however, since each external segment is actually two segments fused together.

The chilopods are generally referred to as centipedes, a name meaning "hundred feet." Centipedes may have between 15 and 150 pairs of legs, and are usually only a few centimeters long. Some tropical species, however, reach a length of 30 centimeters. Centipedes have simple, unfused body segments. Each segment has only one pair of legs.

Like millipedes, centipedes live under leaves and stones. However, centipedes are carnivores. A pair of anterior appendages is modified into poison claws. Centipedes use these claws to capture prey.

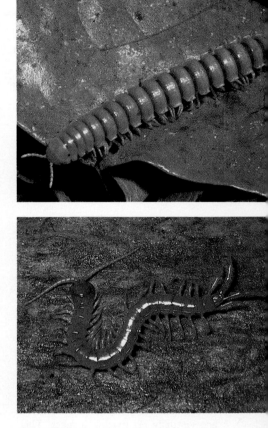

Figure 30-7 *Top:* A millipede; *Bottom:* A centipede. What is the main distinction between these organisms?

CHECKPOINT ◆

6. What are the major differences between mandibulates and chelicerates?
7. Chelipeds in a crayfish serve two functions. What are they?
8. Name three kinds of sensations a crayfish can detect with its sensory organs.
9. How do the feeding habits of a centipede differ from those of a millipede?
▶ 10. Pedipalps serve the same function in chelicerates as _____ do in mandibulates.
▶ 11. How do centipedes and millipedes differ from other classes of arthropods?

▶ Denotes a question that involves *interpreting* and *applying* concepts.

CLASS INSECTA

Section Objectives

H **List** the basic characteristics of an insect body.

I **Compare** the two types of metamorphosis observed in insects.

J **Identify** and **describe** the function of various parts of a grasshopper.

■ *BIOLOGY INSIGHT*

Unity and Diversity: In almost all of the major groups of primarily land-living animals, some members of the group have returned to partial or total aquatic existence. While many insects have evolved into freshwater organisms, there are virtually no marine insects. This is unusual for such a large group, particularly since many other arthropods live in the ocean.

Insects have had and will continue to have an enormous impact on humans. Some are incredibly destructive of plant crops and some carry disease. The next time a fly lands on your nose, or a cockroach speeds under a cabinet, you will be reminded that a lot of insects are just plain annoying. On the other hand, there are numerous beneficial insects. Many crops would not grow if insects did not pollinate flowers. Ladybird beetles are prized by gardeners who know that their larvae eat many harmful insects. Honeybees produce honey, silkworm moths produce silk, and butterflies can brighten up your day.

With 700 000 species, it should not be surprising that many insects affect humans. Their enormous success on Earth and their impact on humans make them a group well worth learning about. What factors have contributed to the tremendous diversity among insects? How have insects been able to adapt to so many environments?

30-7 Insect Body

Insects are typical arthropods. They have an exoskeleton, jointed legs, and segmented bodies. However, while most arthropods have two major body sections, insects have three. These are the anterior head, middle thorax, and posterior abdomen. Locate each segment in Figure 30-8.

The head of every insect has mouthparts, one pair of antennae, and eyes. There are usually a number of simple eyes as well as a pair of compound eyes.

Figure 30-8 Each of the structural features of an insect has contributed in part to the success of the class. Two features, however, have probably contributed the most to insect survival. Wings (not shown) and a three-part body increased the mobility of each individual, which increased the rates of survival and reproduction.

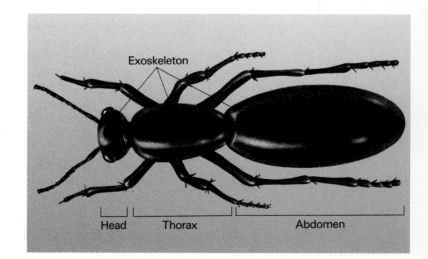

Exoskeleton

Head   Thorax   Abdomen

The **thorax**, or middle section, is specialized for locomotion. All insects have three pairs of legs attached to the thorax. In addition, there are usually two pairs of wings attached to the thorax. Within the thorax are the muscles which operate the legs and wings. Insects are the only arthropods with wings.

The abdomen is the third body section. Like other arthropods, the insect abdomen contains many of the internal organs. All insects show distinct male and female sexes. Segmentation of the thorax and abdomen is obvious in most insects.

30-8 Insect Development

Like all arthropods, insects must molt in order to grow. However, development among insects is unique. Insects generally go through several distinct stages during their development. **Metamorphosis** [met ə mōr' fə sis] is a process in which an animal develops into an adult by progressing through different structural stages.

Some species of insects, such as dragonflies, grasshoppers, and aphids, go through incomplete metamorphosis. Incomplete metamorphosis has three stages—egg, nymph, and adult. The immature form called a **nymph** hatches from the egg. Nymphs look much like small adults. However, they do not have wings or reproductive organs. After a series of molts, the nymph reaches adult size and form.

Other insects, such as butterflies and ants, undergo complete metamorphosis. Complete metamorphosis has four stages—egg, larva, pupa, and adult. A larva hatches from the egg. Larvae are wormlike and have no resemblance to the adult. They are specialized for eating. After several molts, the larva becomes a **pupa** [pü' pə]. During the pupal stage, the insect appears to be resting. In fact, though, the body of the larva is being broken down and transformed into the complex body of an adult.

30-9 Grasshopper

No single species of insect is typical of the entire group. Each species has adaptations for its specific way of life. The grasshopper, however, has characteristics common to many insects.

Figure 30-10 illustrates the external structure of a grasshopper. Located on the head region are three simple eyes, a pair of compound eyes, and a pair of antennae. Also located on the head are the specialized chewing mouthparts.

The thorax is divided into three segments. A pair of legs is attached to each thoracic segment. Two pairs of wings are also attached to the thorax. The first pair of wings is somewhat thickened. These wings protect the more delicate second set of wings underneath.

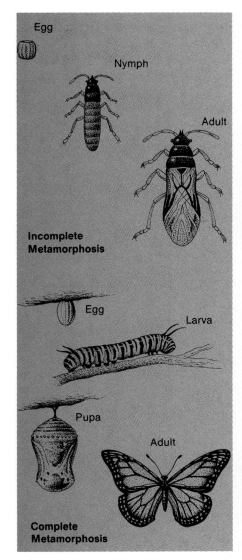

Figure 30-9 *Top:* The nymph stage of incomplete metamorphosis resembles the adult but does not have wings or reproductive organs. *Bottom:* Complete metamorphosis of a butterfly. How does this differ from the incomplete metamorphosis shown above?

Arthropods **497**

Figure 30-10 *Right:* Study the external anatomy of the grasshopper. Can you think of some advantages of having three movable body segments? *Below:* A close-up view of the structural features of a grasshopper's mouth reveal the complexity of this body part.

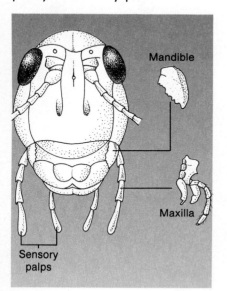

The abdomen of most grasshoppers is divided into ten segments. On the first abdominal segment is a round membrane called the **tympanum**, or hearing organ. Each abdominal segment has a pair of spiracles, as do the two posterior segments of the thorax. The spiracles open into the tracheae. Locate the tympanum and spiracles on Figure 30-10.

Feeding, Digestion, and Excretion The mouthparts of the grasshopper are adapted to a diet of grass. The mouthparts hold and manipulate food for biting and chewing by powerful mandibles. **Sensory palps** extend from the mouthparts and are the organs of taste.

Chewed food travels from the mouth through the esophagus and into the crop, where it is stored temporarily. Just behind the crop is a gizzard, where hard, chitinous teeth grind the food further. Food passes from the gizzard to the stomach or midgut. A number of blind pouches called **caeca** [sē′ kə] (singular, *caecum*) branch from the stomach and extend into the body space. The function of caeca in grasshoppers is not certain. In many insects, however, bacteria live in these pouches and supply the insect with vitamins.

Figure 30-11 This illustration of the internal anatomy of a grasshopper reveals a great deal about each body system. What characteristics of each system can you identify from the picture?

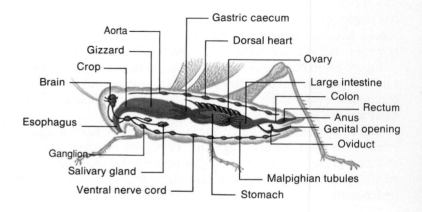

In the midgut, food is broken down by enzymes. Molecules of digested food are absorbed through the midgut wall and enter the bloodstream. Solid wastes are formed in the intestine.

Nitrogen wastes leave the blood and enter the Malpighian tubules. The wastes are excreted into the intestine. Later they are expelled with the solid wastes through the anus.

Nervous System, Senses, and Muscles The grasshopper's nervous system consists of a brain and a double, ventral nerve cord. Nerves branch from the brain and nerve cord ganglia into each segment of the body. All of the body muscles are operated by signals from these nerves. Many sense organs feed into the nervous system. In addition to the simple and compound eyes, antennae, sensory palps, and tympanum, the exoskeleton is covered with sensory hairs. These hairs are sensitive to the slightest touch.

Pairs of muscles bend joints of the exoskeleton in either direction. When one muscle contracts, the other relaxes. Figure 30-12 illustrates how the large flight muscles of the thorax cause the wings to beat up and down. The up-and-down movement of a grasshopper's wings, illustrated in Figure 30-12, is not enough to put it in flight. Instead, the up-and-down movement must be accompanied by a back-and-forth motion. For this reason, a single-wing beat pattern resembles somewhat of an oval shape.

A grasshopper's wings beat an average of 4 to 20 times per second. In comparison, a housefly or honeybee's wings beat an average of 190 times in one second.

Circulation and Respiration Like other arthropods, the grasshopper has an open circulatory system. The heart is located on the dorsal side of the abdomen. A vessel called the **aorta** [ā ȯr′ tə] extends forward from the heart into the head. Blood flows out of the aorta and into the body cavity. The blood moves back toward the posterior end of the grasshopper and finally back into the heart. The grasshopper's blood is a clear, watery fluid that transports food, waste molecules, and some gases.

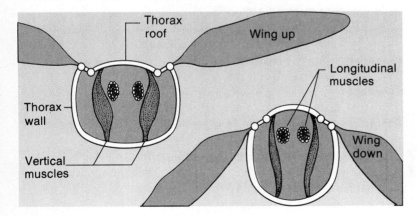

Figure 30-12 When the vertical flight muscles contract, the roof of the thorax comes down and the wings are pushed up. When the longitudinal muscles contract, the roof of the thorax is pushed up and the wings beat downward.

Arthropods **499**

Figure 30-13 The respiratory system of the grasshopper is highlighted here in light blue. During flight, spiracles open and close so that air is forced to circulate through the system of air sacs and tracheae. Why is this system an advantage for flying insects?

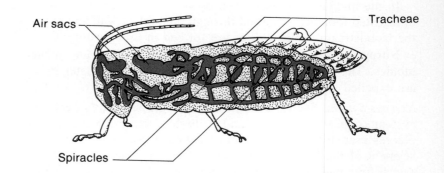

Air sacs

Tracheae

Spiracles

Insects obtain oxygen through a tracheal system. The tracheae of the grasshopper and many other insects open into balloonlike air sacs. Air sacs allow the grasshopper to move larger amounts of air through the tracheal system than would otherwise be possible. Increased gas exchange is an important adaptation in actively moving insects.

Reproduction Male grasshoppers produce sperm cells in a pair of testes. During mating, sperm cells travel through tubes to the **penis**, with which the male deposits sperm in the female's reproductive tract. The female stores sperm in seminal receptacles. In the female, eggs develop in the ovaries. The eggs travel from the ovaries through tubes called **oviducts** [ō′ vi dukts]. Before the eggs leave the body, they are fertilized by sperm cells from the seminal receptacles. Female grasshoppers have an external ovipositor. The **ovipositor** [ō vi poz′ i tər] is a structure through which fertilized eggs travel to the outside.

Most grasshoppers mate in the fall. The females deposit their eggs in a hole dug with the ovipositor. The following spring, the nymphs emerge from the eggs. Adults usually die shortly after the eggs are laid.

BIOLOGY INSIGHT

Adaptation and Evolution: The fertilization of insect eggs occurs inside the female's body. This process ensures that the sperm will not dry out before reaching the eggs. Internal fertilization is found in all the major classes of land animals, including reptiles, birds, and mammals.

CHECKPOINT ◆

12. What part of an insect's body is primarily responsible for locomotion?
13. What sensory structures are located on an insect's head?
14. How does a nymph differ from an adult insect?
15. In what two locations in a grasshopper is food broken into small pieces?
▶ 16. In what ways does a nymph differ from a larva?
▶ 17. The tympanum is a hearing organ. Most insects do not have such an organ. Why would a sense of hearing be valuable to a grasshopper?

▶ Denotes a question that involves *interpreting* and *applying* concepts.

DIVERSITY OF INSECTS

From large, brightly colored butterflies to tiny brown fleas, insects exhibit a variety of characteristics. Some differences among insects have to do with body structure. The number and structure of wings and the type of mouthparts are important anatomical characteristics. Another difference, as you have learned, involves the kind of metamorphosis an insect goes through. Insects also vary in the way they behave. For example, some insects live in groups, while others live as individuals. These and other characteristics are used to classify insects. Not all taxonomists agree on how insects should be divided into orders. Most classifications show between 20 and 26 orders.

Different characteristics allow insects to live under widely varying conditions. Specialized mouthparts and digestive systems enable different insects to eat everything from wood to other insects. Some adaptations protect insects from predators. Reproductive adaptations account in part for the large numbers of insects that exist. What are some examples of modified mouthparts in insects? How can some insects change their appearance?

30-10 Feeding Adaptations

Insect mouthparts are adapted to widely different functions. Mosquito mouthparts, for example, are modified into a pair of hollow tubes. These tubes puncture the skin of an animal and suck blood. Similar piercing and sucking mouthparts are found in aphids, which suck juices from plant stems. In some butterflies, the mouthparts are coiled into a very long tube. This tube unrolls to reach nectar deep within certain flowers.

Predatory insects use a variety of structures to help capture prey. In the dragonfly nymph, one mouthpart is modified into a hinged structure. The mouthpart unfolds to capture prey and

Section Objectives

K *Describe* some of the specific feeding adaptations of insects.
L *List* some of the ways color and shape adapt various insects to their environment.
M *Identify* some specific reproductive adaptations in insects.
N *Explain* how social insects differ from nonsocial species.

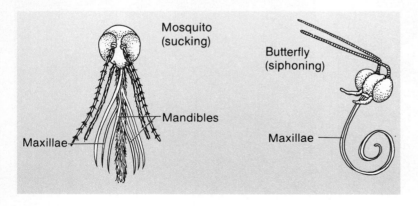

Mosquito (sucking)

Butterfly (siphoning)

Mandibles

Maxillae

Maxillae

Figure 30-14 The mouthparts of different insects are specialized for particular eating habits.

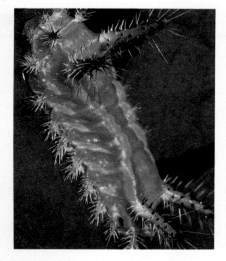

Figure 30-15 The bright colors and spines are a warning to predators that it would be a mistake to try to make a meal of this caterpillar.

Figure 30-16 *Left:* The monarch butterfly is distasteful to birds. *Right:* Birds avoid the viceroy butterfly since it resembles the monarch.

then pulls the victim back toward the mouth. The praying mantis has modified forelegs that reach out and capture insects. Wasps use poison glands and stingers in the abdomen to paralyze prey.

30-11 Adaptations in Appearance

Sometimes an animal has an advantage if it is not recognized for what it is. An animal can escape predators if it cannot be seen easily or if it resembles another animal. Similarly, if a predator goes unnoticed, it can take its victims by surprise.

Camouflage [kam′ ə fläzh] is a method by which an organism blends into its environment so that it cannot easily be seen. Many insect bodies are the same color as their background. Some praying mantises are the same shade of green as the plants they live on. Predatory birds have difficulty seeing the mantis as do insects on which the mantis preys.

In some cases an insect benefits by attracting attention. Insects that are brightly colored are often poisonous or otherwise harmful to predators. After one taste, predators learn to avoid the insect. Such body coloring is called warning coloration. Ladybird beetles, for example, are inedible. They are usually brightly colored and spotted.

A number of harmless insects have evolved bright coloration similar to that of poisonous or stinging species. Many nonstinging insects, such as certain beetles and flies, have coloring similar to bees and wasps. **Mimicry** is an adaptation in which one organism closely resembles another organism or an object in its natural environment. Predators avoid mimics because the mimics closely resemble harmful species.

30-12 Reproductive Adaptations

The enormous number of insects on this planet reflects their ability to reproduce successfully. Insects generally have a short life span, usually less than a year. During this short time, most species produce large numbers of offspring.

Insects have a number of adaptations that allow males and females of the same species to recognize and attract each other. Many female insects release a specific chemical into the air to attract males. A **pheromone** [fer′ ə mōn] is a chemical released by an animal that affects the behavior of others of the same species.

In some insects, fertilization of eggs is not always necessary. During most of the year, aphids reproduce asexually by laying eggs that are not fertilized. These eggs develop into adult aphids. The development of eggs without fertilization is called **parthenogenesis** [par thə nō jen′ i sis].

Reproduction is the primary function of adult insects. In the case of mayflies, the adult insect lives for only one day. During a few days in spring, adults emerge in large numbers. They mate, lay eggs, and die within a twenty-four hour period. Adult mayflies do not even have a digestive system.

Figure 30-17 The antennae of the male Cecropia moth sense pheromones released by females.

30-13 Social Insects

Certain kinds of insects exhibit a type of behavior that is unique among the invertebrates. Termites, ants, bees, and some wasp species live in societies. A society is a group of animals that live together and show division of labor. That is, different individuals within the colony perform different jobs. Some jobs of social insects include nest building, caring for the young, getting food, defending the colony, and reproducing. While humans live in societies by choice, social behavior in insects is inborn.

Honeybees are probably the best-known social insects. A typical honeybee colony has from 40 000 to 80 000 individuals. Each colony has three types of bees; the queen bee, the worker bees, and the drones. The queen bee is the only egg-laying female in the hive. Each hive has only one queen bee. Worker bees are nonreproducing females. They care for the young, gather food, and maintain the hive. The male bees, called drones, exist only to mate with a queen bee.

A honeybee colony starts when a queen bee leaves the hive and mates with a drone during flight. The sperm she receives during this single mating will fertilize all the eggs she lays during her lifetime. After her mating flight, the queen bee returns to the hive and begins laying eggs. Eventually all the members of the hive will be the offspring of this queen.

Figure 30-18 The cells of the honeycomb serve two functions in the beehive. Honey is stored in only some of the cells while in other cells, young bee larvae complete their life cycle.

The hive contains a comb made of six-sided chambers called cells. The queen lays a single egg in each cell. Each egg develops into a larva. After the pupal stage the new bee emerges from the cell and joins the colony.

The sex of the bee is determined by fertilization. Drones develop from unfertilized eggs. Females come from fertilized eggs. A queen bee develops from a female larva that is fed a substance called royal jelly, a food secreted by the worker's bodies. Female larvae not fed royal jelly become workers.

Some worker bees specialize in caring for the queen, making new hive cells, and feeding larvae. Others find and gather flower pollen and nectar. Bees communicate the location of food sources through special body movements. These movements, called a dance, are discussed in Chapter 46.

DO YOU KNOW?

Information: A queen bee may lay up to 200 000 eggs each day.

CHECKPOINT ◆

18. The mouthparts of a mosquito are adapted for what function?
19. What is the function of mimicry?
20. What is a pheromone?
21. What determines the sex of honeybees?
▶ 22. Explain how camouflage can benefit both predators and prey.
▶ 23. Mimics which taste good are usually present in much smaller numbers than the bad-tasting insects they resemble. Why is it important for the mimic to maintain a relatively small population?

▶ Denotes a question that involves *interpreting* and *applying* concepts.

OBSERVING INSECT BEHAVIOR

Objectives and Skills

☐ *Measure* and *record* the response of fruit flies to light and to gravity.
☐ *Determine* which response is stronger in the fruit flies.

Materials

two empty vials and stoppers   light source
masking tape   clock
black construction paper   fruit flies
scissors

Procedures and Observations

1. Read all instructions for this laboratory activity before you begin your work.
2. Transfer eight to ten fruit flies from the culture flask to a clean, glass vial. To do this, place the vial over the opening of the flask. Hold the two sideways until eight or ten flies have entered the vial. Quickly stopper both bottles.
3. Tap the vial until all of the flies fall to the bottom of the tube. Remove the stopper and place another vial over the opening. Tape the two vials together as illustrated below.
4. Make a sleeve out of black paper to cover one of the vials.
5. Place the taped vials horizontally on a table. Hold a bright light near the uncovered vial.

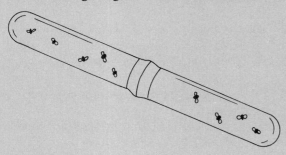

Wait two minutes. Quickly remove the sleeve and count the number of flies in each vial. Record your results.
6. Reverse the direction of the tube. Remove the sleeve from one vial and place it on the other. Repeat step 5. Perform this experiment several times, reversing the direction of the tube each time. Record your results.
7. Make a sleeve out of black paper to cover the other vial. Hold the taped vials vertically for two minutes. Remove both sleeves and quickly count the number of flies in the upper vial and in the lower vial. Record your results.
8. Invert the vials and repeat step 7. Repeat this procedure several times. Record your results.
9. Test the fruit flies' response to light and gravity by again holding the covered vials vertically. Uncover the vial opposite the one in which you would expect the flies to gather in response to gravity. Shine a light on this vial for two minutes. Remove the sleeve from the other end. Count the flies that collected in each end. Repeat this step several times. Record your results.

Analysis and Conclusions

1. What do your results show about the response of fruit flies to light? To gravity?
2. What was the purpose of reversing the direction of the tube after each repetition?
3. Based on your results, which behavior seems to dominate when both stimuli are present?
4. Would you expect other species of insects to respond in the same way as fruit flies? Explain.
5. How would these patterns of behavior benefit a fruit fly in the wild?

CHAPTER REVIEW

Summary

▸ There are more species of arthropods than of any other phylum. All arthropods have an exoskeleton, jointed legs, and segmented bodies. There are two major arthropod subphyla: the chelicerates and the mandibulates.

▸ Chelicerates do not have jaws. They usually have two body divisions and six pairs of appendages. The two anterior pairs of appendages are modified for sensory and feeding functions. The remaining four pairs are walking legs.

▸ Arachnids, a major class of chelicerates, includes spiders, scorpions, mites, and ticks.

▸ Mandibulates have mandibles for chewing food, antennae, and three or more pairs of walking legs. Insects, crustaceans, chilopods, and diplopods are the major classes of mandibulates.

▸ Crustaceans, such as the crayfish, are characterized by a great degree of specialization in various body segments.

▸ Diplopods and chilopods have many similar body segments. Diplopods have two pairs of legs on each abdominal segment and chilopods have only one pair on each segment.

▸ Insects differ from other classes of arthropods because they have three body sections—head, thorax, and abdomen. Attached to the thorax are always three pairs of legs. In most insects there are two pairs of wings attached to the thorax as well.

▸ During development, insects undergo either incomplete metamorphosis or complete metamorphosis.

▸ Insect adaptations show an enormous variety of structural, behavioral, and developmental differences which are used to classify this group.

▸ One remarkable behavioral adaptation is shown by the division of labor in honeybees which includes the queen bee, workers, and drones.

Vocabulary

abdomen	metamorphosis
antenna	mimicry
aorta	molt
appendage	nymph
arachnid	ostia
arthropod	oviduct
book lung	ovipositor
caecum	parthenogenesis
camouflage	penis
carapace	pheromone
cephalothorax	pupa
chelicerate	seminal receptacle
chitin	sensory palp
compound eye	simple eye
crustacean	spinneret
exoskeleton	spiracle
Malpighian	thorax
tubule	trachea
mandibulate	tympanum

Concept Mapping

Construct a concept map for the subphylum Mandibulata. Include the following terms: chilopods, crustaceans, diplods, mandibulates, and insects. Use additional terms as you need them.

Review

1. What material makes up the exoskeleton of an arthropod?
2. What is the process by which arthropods shed their old exoskeletons?
3. Spiders belong to which arthropod subphylum?
4. Name two gas exchange structures found in spiders.
5. Horseshoe crabs belong to what arthropod subphylum?

6. What is the function of a spider's spinnerets?

For questions 7 through 11, match the organism with the class.

7. chilopods   **a.** beetle
8. arachnids   **b.** crab
9. insects   **c.** millipede
10. crustaceans   **d.** tick
11. diplopods   **e.** centipede
12. How many pairs of appendages are found on the thorax of most insects?
13. Which type of metamorphosis has an immature stage in which the young resembles the parent? What is this stage called?
14. Which type of metamorphosis has a stage that is specialized for eating?
15. Describe the function of the mandibles and maxillae in grasshoppers.
16. What is a pheromone?
17. What is the function of swimmerets?
18. Describe the overall pattern of blood circulation in the grasshopper.
19. Why is warning coloration useful to some insects?
20. What is parthenogenesis?
21. What is a male honeybee called? What is its function?

Interpret and Apply

22. In what ways does the basic body plan of arthropods differ from your own body?
23. Why is it necessary for arthropods to molt?
24. How are the chelicerae of spiders different from the mandibles of a crayfish? How are they similar?
25. In what ways are book lungs and tracheae similar? In what ways are they different?
26. Compare and contrast complete and incomplete metamorphosis.

27. How would you describe the differences in the appendages of crayfish and of centipedes?
28. The flight muscles of a grasshopper are not attached directly to the wings of the insect. Explain how these muscles cause the wings to move.
29. Give an example of how the mouthparts of a specific insect are adapted for a particular kind of feeding.
30. Explain the difference between mimicry and camouflage. Give examples of each.
31. Explain how division of labor works in a honeybee society.

Critical Thinking

32. What is the major difference between the exoskeleton of arthropods and the various protective coverings of animals described in earlier chapters?
33. You discover a fossil organism which displays an exoskeleton, mandibles, maxillae, antennae, and abdominal segments with four legs on each segment. Into which phylum, subphylum, and class would you put the fossil?
34. Explain how the structure of each of the following organs is related to its function.
   a. antenna   **c.** spider chelicerae
   b. book lung   **d.** chelipeds
35. Compare the body plan of insects with the body plan of spiders. In what ways are they similar? In what ways are they different?
36. Why might a flying insect need a more efficient respiratory system than one that does not fly?
37. Explain how complete metamorphosis in insects is different from the process in which a human baby grows to become an adult.

Arthropods   **507**

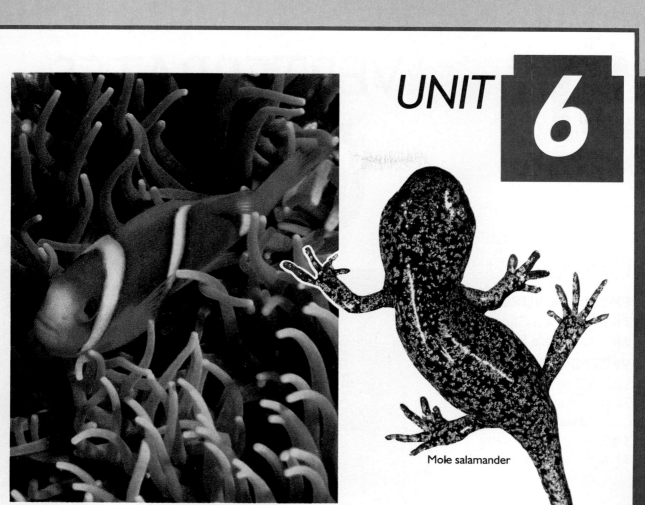

Clown fish

Mole salamander

Chapter 31 Vertebrates
   Phylum Chordata
   Vertebrates

Chapter 32 Fish
   Jawless Fish
   Cartilage Fish
   Bony Fish

Chapter 33 Amphibians
   Characteristics of Amphibians
   Other Amphibians

Chapter 34 Reptiles
   Characteristics of Reptiles
   Modern Reptiles
   Reptile Evolution

Chapter 35 Birds
   Characteristics of Birds
   Internal Features of Birds

Chapter 36 Mammals
   Characteristics of Mammals
   Monotremes and Marsupials
   Placental Mammals
   Mammal Evolution

UNIT 6

CHORDATES

Great horned owl

Koala

Chapter

31

VERTEBRATES

Overview

PHYLUM CHORDATA
31-1 What Is a Chordate?
31-2 Chordate Subphyla
VERTEBRATES
31-3 What Is a Vertebrate?
31-4 Vertebrate
       Classification
31-5 Fossil Vertebrates
31-6 Evolutionary Trends
       in Vertebrates

PHYLUM CHORDATA

To see how one animal is related to others, it is important to consider the animal's entire life cycle. Early development often reveals relationships that would be missed by looking only at the adults. Some of the organisms discussed in this chapter would be classified differently if the early stages in their life cycles were not noted.

31-1 What Is a Chordate?

Three basic characteristics distinguish Phylum **Chordata** [kȯr da′ tə] from all other animal phyla.

1. All chordates have a strong, flexible, rodlike structure called a **notochord** [not′ oh kord] at some time in their lives. The notochord runs the length of the organism near the dorsal surface. All chordate embryos have a notochord. However, in most chordate adults the notochord is replaced by a backbone.
2. The second characteristic structure of all chordates is the hollow **dorsal nerve cord**. It lies just above the notochord. The dorsal nerve cord begins to form in the embryo. Look again at Figure 27-2. You will see that the ectoderm of the embryo folds over to form a hollow tube. In time, this tube forms the brain and spinal cord of the adult.
3. Third, all chordates have **gill slits** at some time in their development. Gill slits are paired openings in the wall of the **pharynx**. The pharynx is the throat area just behind the mouth. Perhaps you are familiar with gill slits in fish. Water entering the mouth can pass through the gill slits and out of the body without going through the entire digestive system.

Section Objectives

A **List** the three characteristics common to all chordates.
B **Name** and **describe** the three subphyla of chordates.

BIOLOGY INSIGHT

Structure Is Related to Function: Every body plan in each of the animal phyla represents a different structural way to solve the same basic problems of movement, feeding, sensing the environment, and reproducing. No single body plan is necessarily superior to another—just different.

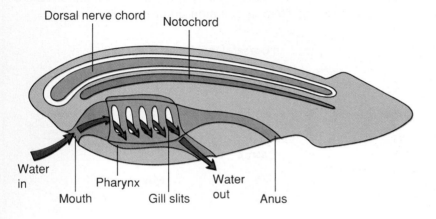

Dorsal nerve chord   Notochord

Water in   Mouth   Pharynx   Gill slits   Water out   Anus

Figure 31-1   The generalized body plan of a chordate. Why is the dorsal nerve cord described as hollow?

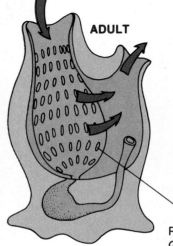

Figure 31-2 The sea squirt is a urochordate. What chordate characteristics present in the larva of this sea squirt are absent in the adult?

All chordate embryos have a notochord, a dorsal nerve cord, and gill slits. Most chordates, however, lose or modify one or more of these structures as they mature into adults.

Chordates also have many characteristics that are not unique to the group. They all have bilateral symmetry. Their muscle and nerve tissues show definite segmentation. This segmentation is most obvious in embryos. All the chordates have a true coelom.

31-2 Chordate Subphyla

The chordates are divided into three major subphyla: urochordates, cephalochordates, and vertebrates.

Subphylum Urochordate Of the approximately 2000 species in the subphylum **urochordates** [yùr ə kȯr′ dāts], all are marine and most are stationary, or sessile. Probably the most common members of this group are the sea squirts.

The chordate characteristics of the urochordates are apparent only in the larva. Figure 31-2 shows a typical sea squirt and its larva. The larva has all three of the typical chordate characteristics. The notochord and the dorsal nerve cord have disappeared in the adult.

The adult urochordate is so simple it even lacks a definite head. It also retains gill slits throughout its life. The gill slits are used in both respiration and feeding. Ciliated cells lining the pharynx sweep water into the mouth and out the gill slits. Here gases are exchanged between the water and the blood. At the same time, small organisms stick to the mucus on the pharynx wall. The ciliated cells sweep the food particles into the digestive tube. Straining water through gill slits in this way is called **filter feeding**.

Urochordates develop as free-swimming larvae. Most urochordate larvae become sessile adults. Others, however, remain free-swimming throughout their lives. Some species of sessile urochordates live as individuals. Others live in colonies, where many individuals share a common outer covering.

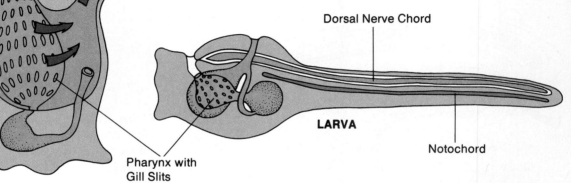

ADULT

Dorsal Nerve Chord

LARVA

Notochord

Pharynx with Gill Slits

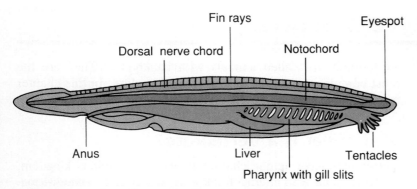

Fin rays

Dorsal nerve chord

Notochord

Eyespot

Anus

Liver

Tentacles

Pharynx with gill slits

Figure 31-3 *Left:* A diagram of the internal structure of *Amphioxus.* Compare this structure with Figures 31-1 and 31-2. *Right:* This lancelet belongs to the genus *Amphioxus.* They normally bury all but their head into the sand.

Subphylum Cephalochordata **Cephalochordates** [sef ə lō kȯr′ dāts] are a small group of about 200 species. They live in shallow water near seacoasts. The name cephalochordate means "chordate with a head." These animals retain all of the chordate characteristics throughout their life. They are commonly called lancelets.

Amphioxus is a typical cephalochordate. It has a notochord, which it retains as an adult. A hollow nerve cord runs the entire length of its body. As in urochordates, the gill slits of Amphioxus function in both respiration and filter feeding.

Unlike urochordates, Amphioxus has a definite head with sensory organs. It has sensitive "feelers" near the mouth opening. Amphioxus also shows clearly segmented muscles. In some ways the cephalochordates are intermediate between the urochordates and the third subphylum, the vertebrates.

Subphylum Vertebrata **Vertebrates** [vər′ tə brāts] derive their name from the large number of bones that surround and protect the nerve cord. These bones are called **vertebrae**. Vertebrae develop from and replace the notochord.

Vertebrates are by far the largest subphylum of chordates with over 40 000 species. Since humans fall into this category, people tend to divide animals into vertebrates and invertebrates. The division is not particularly logical. You have already seen that the animals are divided into many phyla. The vertebrates are a subphylum of the Phylum Chordata. Vertebrates represent a small segment of the animal kingdom.

DO YOU KNOW?

Information: There are only about 42 000 species of living vertebrates compared to over 1 150 000 species of living invertebrates.

CHECKPOINT ◆

1. What characteristics are common to all chordates?
2. Name the three chordate subphyla.
▶ 3. Sea squirts would probably not be classified as chordates unless their larval forms are taken into account. Why?
▶ 4. Why are bilateral symmetry, muscle segmentation, and the presence of a coelom not sufficient to define an organism as a chordate?

▶ Denotes a question that involves *interpreting* and *applying* concepts.

VERTEBRATES

Section Objectives

C **Identify** the major characteristics of vertebrates.

D **Name** and **describe** the major classes of vertebrates.

E **List** the major trends in the evolution of the vertebrates.

Vertebrates are called animals with backbones. They are the most complex organisms in the animal kingdom. In this chapter and those that follow, you will read about each class of vertebrates.

31-3 What Is a Vertebrate?

Vertebrates have unique characteristics in the animal kingdom. Vertebrates have an internal framework known as an **endoskeleton**. The endoskeleton may be made up of cartilage or bone. **Cartilage** is a tough, flexible material. **Bone** is a harder, inflexible material. The vertebrate endoskeleton has many of the same functions as the arthropod exoskeleton. It provides support and protection for soft internal organs. Muscles attach to the skeleton and move the body. However, an endoskeleton can grow with the organism, while arthropods must molt, or shed, their exoskeletons.

All vertebrate skeletons are built on a similar plan. The **skull** is a group of fused bones protecting the brain. The vertebrae protect the spinal cord. Ribs extend from some of the vertebrae and form the **rib cage**. The rib cage protects many internal organs. The skull, vertebral column, and rib cage form the **axial skeleton**.

In addition to the axial skeleton, most vertebrates have two pairs of limbs. The bones of the anterior limbs are attached to the axial skeleton by bones called the **pectoral** [pek′ tə rəl] **girdle**. The bones of the posterior limbs attach to the skeleton at the **pelvic girdle**. The two girdles and the limb bones form the **appendicular skeleton**. Study the illustration in Figure 31-4. Match each highlighted term with its corresponding body part.

In addition to skeletal differences, invertebrates and vertebrates are different in many other ways. The vertebrate's circulatory system is more developed than that of an invertebrate. The differences are striking when vertebrates are compared to arthropods, for example. Vertebrates have a closed circulatory system; arthropods have an open circulatory system. A vertebrate's heart is ventral and has specialized chambers; an arthropod's heart is dorsal and tubelike. Vertebrates have a dorsal nerve cord and highly developed brain; arthropods have a ventral nerve cord and a relatively small brain.

Figure 31-4 The endoskeleton of a salamander.

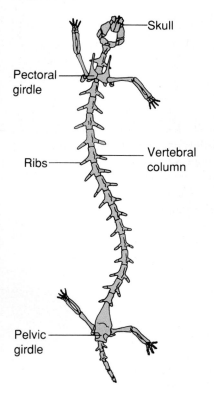

Skull

Pectoral girdle

Ribs

Vertebral column

Pelvic girdle

31-4 Vertebrate Classification

Most taxonomists divide living vertebrates into seven classes. These classes are listed in order of their appearance in the fossil record. Jawless fish are the most primitive vertebrates. Birds and mammals appeared most recently.

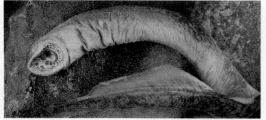

1. Class **Agnatha** [ag na′ thə]: the *jawless fish*. There are only a few living species in this class, such as the lamprey and the hagfish. These fish retain the notochord and have a minimal skeleton consisting of only a few cartilage plates in the skull.

2. Class **Chondrichthyes** [kon drick′ thēz]: the *cartilage fish*. Sharks, skates, and rays belong to this group. These fish have a movable jaw attached to the skull. Their skeleton is made entirely of cartilage.

3. Class **Osteichthyes** [os tē ik′ thēz]: the *bony fish*. Most fish belong to this group. Their skeleton is made largely of bone.

4. Class **Amphibia** [am fib′ ē ə]: the *amphibians*. Frogs, toads, and salamanders are amphibians. Most go through an aquatic larval stage and have gills. As adults, they have lungs and limbs adapted for life on land.

5. Class **Reptilia** [rep til′ ē ə]: the *reptiles*. Snakes, lizards, turtles, and alligators belong to this group. They reproduce on land by laying eggs.

6. Class **Aves** [ā′ vēz]: the *birds*. Birds have feathers and bodies adapted for flight. They reproduce by laying eggs.

Figure 31-5 The seven classes of living vertebrates are represented by the following organisms Agnatha: lamprey, Amphibia: toad, Aves: eagle, Chondrichthyes: shark, Osteichthyes: fish, Mammalia: raccoon, Reptilia: snake.

■ **BIOLOGY INSIGHT**

Evolution and Adaptation: Biologists often arrange groups of organisms to show evolutionary trends toward greater specialization and complexity. Yet every animal living today has specializations that suit its way of life. It is misleading to think of fish as incomplete amphibians, or of reptiles as unformed mammals.

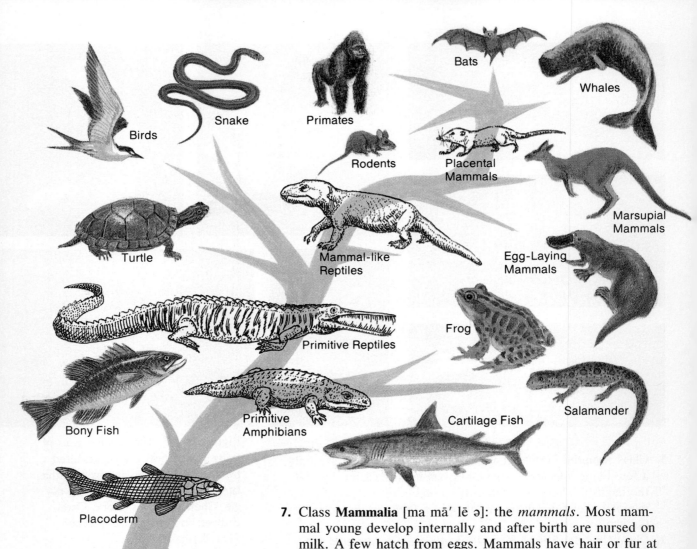

Birds

Snake

Primates

Bats

Whales

Rodents

Placental Mammals

Marsupial Mammals

Turtle

Mammal-like Reptiles

Egg-Laying Mammals

Primitive Reptiles

Frog

Bony Fish

Primitive Amphibians

Cartilage Fish

Salamander

Placoderm

Jawless Fish

Figure 31-6 A brief summary of vertebrate evolution showing representative examples of the seven vertebrate classes.

7. Class **Mammalia** [ma mā′ lē ə]: the *mammals*. Most mammal young develop internally and after birth are nursed on milk. A few hatch from eggs. Mammals have hair or fur at some time during their lives.

31-5 Fossil Vertebrates

Vertebrate classification would not be complete without mentioning one other group called the *placoderms*. The class Placodermi, now extinct, contained the first jawed fish. The fossil record indicates that they appeared after the jawless fish and before the cartilage fish. The name placoderm derives from their skin which was made of either thick scales or bony plates. They were heavily armored predators.

Even though placoderms became extinct toward the end of the Paleozoic Era, they contributed greatly to the development of vertebrates. Look at Figure 31-6 to see where placoderms fit within the history of vertebrate evolution.

31-6 Evolutionary Trends in Vertebrates

Many evolutionary trends can be traced in the fossil record of vertebrates. Among the more important of these trends are the following:

1. adaptations leading from total dependence on water to survival on land;
2. development of a more complex heart structure;
3. increase in cephalization;
4. increase in the size and complexity of the cerebrum.

One obvious trend in vertebrate history is the evolution of animals that can live on land. The agnathans, the cartilage fish, and the bony fish are aquatic. Amphibians are adapted to both water and land. The other classes are primarily terrestrial.

Vertebrates have evolved methods of locomotion appropriate to where they live. Fish are well adapted to swimming. Terrestrial animals walk or crawl on land or fly in the air. Adaptations of the basic body structure have allowed vertebrates to be successful in each of these environments. Recall the examples of homologous structures in Chapter 14 (Figure 14-6). In each case, the same basic bones of the forelimb are modified to function in different ways.

As vertebrates evolved, the heart became a more complex structure. Fish have two-chambered hearts. One chamber receives blood from the body. The other chamber pumps blood to the gills. Amphibians have three-chambered hearts. These hearts are slightly more efficient than that of a fish. Birds and mammals have even more efficient hearts with four chambers. This trend allows for better transport of oxygen and nutrients to the body's cells.

Another evolutionary trend among vertebrates is increasing **cephalization**. Cephalization is the concentration of nerve tissue in the anterior region of an organism. This trend can be traced through the chordate subphyla. Urochordate adults do not have a head at all. The cephalochordates have a brain and some sensory organs in the head. In the more recent vertebrate classes, the brain becomes larger. Also the number and complexity of sense organs in the head increases.

Another trend in vertebrate evolution is the increasing development of the anterior part of the brain. This part of the brain is called the **cerebrum**. The cerebrum has many functions, but primary among them is the control of learning and of complex behaviors. Most vertebrates can learn from experience. They can store events in their memory and use past experience to modify behavior. A dog can learn to roll over on command if it has been rewarded for this behavior in the past.

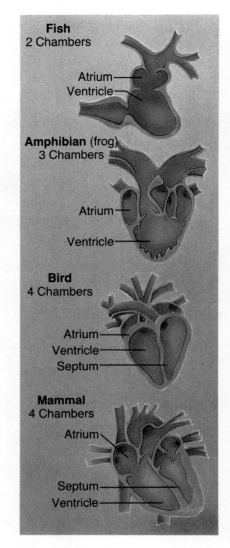

Fish
2 Chambers
Atrium
Ventricle

Amphibian (frog)
3 Chambers
Atrium
Ventricle

Bird
4 Chambers
Atrium
Ventricle
Septum

Mammal
4 Chambers
Atrium
Septum
Ventricle

Figure 31-7 These heart cross sections show the evolution of the complexity of heart structures.

Shark

Lizard

Bird

Ape (mammal)

Figure 31-8 An increase in the size of the cerebrum is a trend in vertebrate evolution. The tinted portion in each diagram highlights the cerebrum. Compare the relative size of the cerebrum in each case.

The invertebrates show relatively little learning ability. Among the vertebrates, on the other hand, learning is highly developed. The ability to learn seems to be related to the size of the cerebrum. Mammals have the largest cerebrum and the greatest learning capacity.

Among the mammals, human beings are capable of the most complex kinds of learning. The ability to solve problems never before encountered is considered the most complex behavior.

As you study the chapters in this unit, it is important to keep these evolutionary trends in mind. By doing this, you will better understand the relationships among all of the vertebrate classes.

In addition, you will find a summary of vertebrate evolution at the end of this unit, after Chapter 36. You can refer to the various evolutionary trees shown there as you study the chapters in this unit to get a clear picture of how vertebrate classes relate to each other and how they evolved through Earth's history.

CHECKPOINT ◆

5. List three functions of an endoskeleton.
6. Name the seven classes of vertebrates.
7. What are the four major trends of vertebrate evolution?
▶ 8. Which vertebrate class could be considered transitional between the other classes? Why?
▶ 9. Fossils of jawless fish have been found primarily in salt-water areas. Placoderm fossils have been found mainly in freshwater areas. How does this information relate to vertebrate development?

▶ Denotes a question that involves *interpreting* and *applying* concepts.

LABORATORY ACTIVITY

STRUCTURE OF A PRIMITIVE CHORDATE

Objectives and Skills

☐ *Identify* internal structures of *Amphioxus* by observing slides through the microscope.
☐ *Observe* and *identify* anatomical features of *Amphioxus* by dissecting a preserved specimen.

Materials

10X hand lens or dissecting microscope
compound microscope
whole-mount slide of *Amphioxus*
cross-section slides of *Amphioxus*
safety goggles and lab apron
dissecting tray and tools
preserved specimens of *Amphioxus*

Procedure and Observations

1. Read all instructions for this laboratory activity before you begin your work.
2. Use a low-power hand lens or microscope to examine a whole-mount slide of a lancelet. Identify the following structures on the slide: anus, eyespot, fin rays, gill slits, liver, dorsal nerve cord, notochord, tentacles. For help, refer to Figure 31-3.
3. Use the low power of a compound microscope to examine a slide showing a cross-sectional view of a lancelet. Compare what you see under the microscope with the diagram. Identify in your slide each of the labeled structures in the diagram.
4. Put on your safety goggles and lab apron. Collect dissecting equipment and a preserved lancelet specimen. **CAUTION: Wear safety goggles in the presence of preservative chemicals.**
5. Locate the eyespot, the anus, and the fins. Notice also the segmentation of muscle bundles along the lateral wall of the animal.

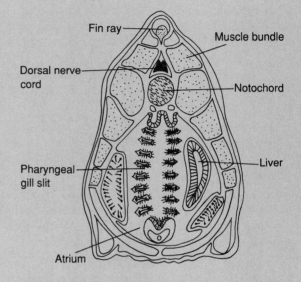

Fin ray — Muscle bundle — Dorsal nerve cord — Notochord — Pharyngeal gill slit — Liver — Atrium

6. Use dissecting tools to make an incision along the mid-ventral line from the mouth to the anus. **CAUTION: Be careful not to cut yourself when using dissecting tools.** Carefully separate the body walls to expose the internal structures. Examine your specimen carefully. Look for each labeled structure in Figure 31-3 and in the diagram above.

Analysis and Conclusions

1. What type of symmetry is shown by this animal?
2. What evidence can you give for cephalization in the lancelet?
3. Based on your observations of the anatomy of the lancelet, what is the function of the atrium?
4. While the lancelet can swim, it spends most of its time buried in sand and mud, with only its head exposed. Based on the anatomy, what do you think this animal eats?

Vertebrates   **521**

CHAPTER REVIEW

Summary

▸ Chordates are animals that have a notochord, a hollow dorsal nerve cord, and gill slits at some time during their development. Some chordates lose one or more of these traits as adults. It is important, therefore, to consider developmental stages when classifying organisms. There are three subphyla of chordates.

▸ Urochordates are sessile filter feeders. They are all marine organisms that lose their notochord and dorsal nerve cord as adults but maintain the pharynx and gill slits.

▸ The cephalochordates retain the three chordate characteristics throughout their life. These organisms, such as *Amphioxus*, are free-swimming filter feeders.

▸ Members of the third subphylum, the vertebrates, replace the notochord during early development with bones called vertebrae. They have an endoskeleton and are by far the largest group of chordates.

▸ The vertebrate endoskeleton consists of a central axial skeleton and an appendicular skeleton. The axial skeleton supports the head and major organs of the body. It includes the skull, spine, and ribs. The appendicular skeleton holds the limbs to the axial skeleton. It consists of the pectoral girdle, pelvic girdle, and limb bones.

▸ All vertebrates have a closed circulatory system and a ventral heart with specialized chambers.

▸ The seven vertebrate classes arranged in order of appearance in the fossil record show a transition from all aquatic organisms to organisms that are primarily terrestrial. They are the jawless fish, cartilage fish, bony fish, amphibia, reptiles, birds, and mammals.

▸ Some of the evolutionary trends apparent in vertebrates are adaptation to life on land, and increasing complexity of the heart and the brain.

Vocabulary

Agnatha	filter feeding
Amphibia	gill slits
appendicular skeleton	Mammalia
Aves	notochord
axial skeleton	Osteichthyes
bone	pectoral girdle
cartilage	pelvic girdle
cephalization	pharynx
cephalochordate	Reptilia
cerebrum	rib cage
Chondrichthyes	skull
Chordata	urochordate
dorsal nerve cord	vertebrae
endoskeleton	vertebrate

Concept Mapping

Construct a concept map for the framework of the vertebrate endoskeleton. Include the following terms: axial skeleton, appendicular skeleton, limbs, pectoral girdle, pelvic girdle. Use additional terms as you need them.

Review

For each of the following questions, select the best answer.

1. Which of the following is a characteristic found *only* in chordates? (a) bilateral symmetry (b) notochord (c) specialized organs
2. In the embryo, the chordate nervous system forms from (a) endoderm, (b) mesoderm, (c) ectoderm, (d) the blastopore.
3. What chordate characteristic is retained in adult urochordates? (a) gill slits (b) nerve cord (c) notochord (d) none of the above
4. The subphylum of chordates containing many sessile and colonial species is (a) urochordates, (b) cephalochordates, (c) vertebrates, (d) all of the above.

5. During development, what structure develops into vertebrae? (a) the dorsal nerve cord (b) the gill slits (c) the ventral nerve cord (d) the notochord

6. The skeleton of vertebrates is made from (a) cartilage, (b) bone, (c) both a and b, (d) neither a nor b.

7. Fish without a jaw belong to the vertebrate class (a) Amphibia, (b) Reptilia, (c) Agnatha, (d) Chondrichthyes.

8. In vertebrate skeletons, the pelvic girdle is (a) posterior to the pectoral girdle, (b) anterior to the pectoral girdle, (c) dorsal to the pectoral girdle, (d) ventral to the pectoral girdle.

9. Osteichthyes have a skeleton made primarily from (a) cartilage, (b) cellulose, (c) pectin, (d) bone.

10. One trend of vertebrate evolution involves (a) movement from land to water, (b) change to open circulation, (c) movement from water to land, (d) change to closed circulation.

Each of the following questions requires a short answer.

11. All chordates have _____ symmetry.

12. The chordate phylum with the fewest species is _____.

13. Segmentation of nerves and muscles is most obvious during what part of the life cycle of chordates?

14. Water is swept into the mouth of most urochordates by the action of _____.

15. Vertebrae support and protect the _____ of vertebrates.

16. What part of the vertebrate brain has shown considerable development over the course of evolution?

17. All vertebrates have a _____ circulatory system.

18. Mammals feed their young on _____.

19. The vertebrate group with an aquatic larva stage and a terrestrial adult stage is the _____.

Interpret and Apply

20. In what ways are vertebrates and arthropods different in structure?

21. In what ways are cephalochordates intermediate between urochordates and vertebrates?

22. What one chordate characteristic is still present in your body?

23. What two chordate characteristics are present in the body of an adult fish?

24. In urochordates and cephalochordates, the gill slits serve two functions. What function of the gill slits is lost in the vertebrates?

25. Compare the embryonic and adult characteristics of the subphyla of chordates.

Critical Thinking

26. Scientists sometimes refer to the invertebrate chordates. What group might qualify for this description and why?

27. Elephants and whales have much larger brains than humans. Yet humans are more intelligent than either of these animals. Why do you think this is the case?

28. Explain why it is important to study the development of embryos when classifying chordates.

29. Explain why gill slits are well suited to serve a dual function in some chordates.

30. In what way are vertebrae an advantage over a simple notochord?

31. Why is the practice of dividing all animals into invertebrates and vertebrates not particularly logical?

FISH

Overview

JAWLESS FISH

32-1   Primitive Fish

CARTILAGE FISH

32-2   Skeleton and
         Movement
         of the Shark

32-3   Shark Skin
         and Teeth

32-4   Gas Exchange

32-5   Temperature
         Regulation

32-6   Shark Reproduction

32-7   Rays and Skates

BONY FISH

32-8   External Anatomy

32-9   Digestion and
         Excretion

32-10 Circulation and Gas
         Exchange

32-11 The Nervous System
         of the Perch

32-12 Reproduction in the
         Perch

32-13 Adaptations of the
         Bony Fish

32-14 Fossil Osteichthyes

Why is it so easy for fish to swim?

JAWLESS FISH

Fish are not only the most common vertebrates, they also have the longest history. Fossil fish have been found in rocks as old as 520 million years. This is more than 160 million years before the first land-living vertebrates. The oldest fossil fish were unmistakably fish. Their bodies were fish-shaped, and they had scales and fins. Yet they were different from anything swimming in the oceans today. What did these ancient fish look like? Why were some of their adaptations lost over millions of years?

32-1 Primitive Fish

The earliest fish in the fossil record were members of the class Agnatha. *Agnatha* means "without a jaw." The most primitive of these jawless fish were the **ostracoderms**. Ostracoderms had a true endoskeleton with vertebrae surrounding their spinal cord. They were filter feeders that had no moving jaw. They used their pharynx and gill slits to strain food from the water. It is probable that these fish also used their gill slits to get oxygen from the water. In most modern fish, the gill slits are used entirely for gas exchange. Use of the gills for feeding has been abandoned.

Today there are only a few species of jawless fish remaining. They are the **cyclostomes** [sī′ klə stōms]. These fish are quite

Section Objectives

A Identify and describe the two types of jawless fish.
B List the principal characteristics of the jawless fish.

DO YOU KNOW?

Information: Ostracoderms became widely distributed over Earth's oceans before they all died out about 350 million years ago. Their extinction was speeded by the evolution of predatory jawed fish called placoderms. Placoderms took over the seas until they were, in turn, replaced by other forms.

Figure 32-1 This fossil ostracoderm is one of the earliest known fish that flourished during the Silurian and Devonian Periods about 360 to 280 million years ago. The organism is outlined in white. Notice the signs of segmentation in the posterior end of the animal. Most ostracoderms were less than one meter in length.

Figure 32-2 The circular mouth and individual gill slits identify the lamprey as an Agnathan.

▶ Denotes a question that involves *interpreting* and *applying* concepts.

different from the early ostracoderms. The jawless fish living today, like the lamprey and the hagfish, are parasites and scavengers. The lamprey illustrated in Figure 32-2 is a typical cyclostome. The lamprey's circular mouth is modified and serves as a suckerlike device. The lamprey attaches to the body of another fish. Its filelike tongue then cuts through the skin of the host fish. This allows the lamprey to feed on blood and tissues.

In addition to lacking a jaw, the lamprey has several other features that biologists consider primitive. For example, the lamprey does not have paired fins like those found in all other fish. Swimming is accomplished by snakelike movements of the body. Another primitive feature is the presence of multiple gill slits. Gill slits allow water that passes over the gills to leave the body.

The lamprey skeleton is also very primitive. The notochord remains in the adult. The only internal skeleton consists of the skull, which is made of cartilage.

Lampreys have moved into the Great Lakes and caused enormous damage to the trout-fishing industry. Hagfish are scavengers rather than parasites. They are a nuisance because they attack fish trapped in fishing nets.

CHECKPOINT ◆

1. What group of primitive agnathans are now all extinct?
2. What vertebrate characteristic is almost absent in the cyclostomes?
3. List the differences between the extinct agnathans and the modern cyclostomes.
▶ 4. Why is the jawless characteristic suited to life as a parasite?

CARTILAGE FISH

A fish with a movable jaw can grasp, chew, and crush; it can be a predator. The placoderms were the first fish with jaws. Now extinct, the placoderms were replaced by other fish. One group with placoderm ancestors is the Chondrichthyes, or cartilage fish. Sharks and rays are the best known members of this group. How much do you know about sharks?

32-2 Skeleton and Movement of the Shark

Every vertebrate has an endoskeleton made of cartilage at the beginning of its life. As most vertebrates mature into adults, the cartilage skeleton is replaced by bone. Adult Chondrichthyes, however, retain a cartilage skeleton all of their lives.

For sharks, a cartilage skeleton provides flexibility. Sharks have two sets of paired fins. The front pair are the **pectoral fins**. Posterior to the pectoral fins are the **pelvic fins**. These paired fins are found in most fish except the Agnatha. The paired fins allow the shark to turn or move up and down in the water. The large tail fin of the shark pushes from side to side and propels the fish forward. If a shark stops swimming, it will sink to the bottom. The shark's body is denser than water.

32-3 Shark Skin and Teeth

Shark skin feels like sandpaper. It is covered with small, spiny projections called **placoid** [plak′ oid] **scales**. Placoid scales are made of the same material as your teeth. In fact, shark teeth appear to be large versions of these scales. Evidence indicates that shark teeth evolved from placoid scales surrounding the jaw.

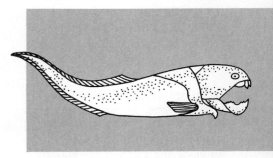

Lesson Objectives

C *Compare* the skeleton of a shark to the skeleton of other vertebrates.

D *Describe* the unique features of skin and teeth in sharks.

E *Explain* how sharks exchange gases with the environment.

F *State* how sharks regulate their body temperature.

G *Identify* the unusual features of shark reproduction.

H *Name* other members of the Chondrichthyes.

Figure 32-3 Placoderms were most common during the Devonian Period from about 325 to 280 million years ago. Many of these predators reached lengths of two to three meters.

Figure 32-4 The front pair of fins on the shark are pectoral fins; the rear pair are pelvic fins.

Figure 32-5 Notice the shape and the angle of teeth in the shark's jaw. What is the advantage of teeth that slant backward?

Figure 32-6 Water entering the mouth of the shark passes over the gills and out the individual gill slits on the side of the body.

Fish that had larger "scales" near the mouth might have been favored by selection. Shark teeth are triangular in shape and very sharp. The teeth tend to slant backward into the mouth. This helps to prevent food from slipping out once the shark bites into it. The teeth grow in rows. As new teeth grow, the teeth in the front row fall out and are replaced by others growing in from behind.

32-4 Gas Exchange

Sharks, like all cartilage fish, have **gills**. The gills remove oxygen from the surrounding water and release waste carbon dioxide into the water. Gills are composed of many folded tissues containing blood vessels. The folded structure of the gills provides a large surface area for gas exchange. Water enters the mouth of the shark and passes across the gills. Oxygen from the water passes into the blood in the gills. Carbon dioxide passes from the blood into the surrounding water. Each gill opens to the outside through a gill slit.

32-5 Temperature Regulation

Sharks, like fish, are **ectothermic**. Ectothermic animals do not maintain a constant body temperature. Therefore, as their surroundings get colder, their body temperature drops. Likewise, as their surroundings get warmer, their body temperature increases. Thus, fish are able to survive without the ability to maintain their body temperature. They simply must stay in water near a temperature where their bodies function best. If you have tropical fish, you know how closely their water temperature must be regulated to ensure their survival.

32-6 Shark Reproduction

The method of reproduction in sharks is somewhat unusual for fish. Sharks have internal fertilization. That is, sperm are deposited in the female's body by the male. In some shark species, the fertilized eggs are enclosed in a leathery egg case. The female deposits the egg cases into the water. In many shark species, however, the female retains the eggs inside her body until the embryos have developed. The eggs hatch and the young are born live. Newborn sharks receive no care from their mothers.

32-7 Rays and Skates

Rays—and their close relatives the skates—are also Chondrichthyes. They have the same general characteristics as sharks, but their bodies are greatly flattened. The pectoral fins are expanded and merge along the length of the body. Most rays and skates are adapted to living on the ocean bottom.

Bottom-dwelling rays have their mouths on the ventral surface, which is often buried in the sand. This makes it impossible to take water into the mouth for gas exchange at the gills. In these rays, water enters through two openings on top of the head. Water passes through the gills and out the gill slits on the bottom.

Figure 32-7 *Left:* A ray has a flattened body that is an adaptation for life at the ocean bottom. *Right:* Skates are closely related to rays.

DO YOU KNOW?

Information: Manta rays can have a "wingspan" of three or four meters. The large whale shark can reach lengths close to 20 meters. Interestingly, neither of these large species is carnivorous. Both filter microscopic plankton from the water.

CHECKPOINT ◆

5. The shark skeleton is made of _____.
6. What kinds of animals belong to the class Chondrichthyes?
7. Water exits the mouth of the shark through _____.
8. The body temperature of a shark depends on _____.
▶ 9. In most fish, eggs and sperm are deposited outside the body in the water. What is the advantage of internal fertilization?
▶ 10. Explain how shark teeth might have evolved from placoid scales.

▶ Denotes a question that involves *interpreting* and *applying* concepts.

Fish   **529**

Section Objectives

I *Compare* the external anatomy of bony fish to that of the shark.

J *Identify* the organs of digestion and excretion in bony fish.

K *Trace* the path of circulation in bony fish and show where gas exchange occurs.

L *Describe* the nervous system and senses of bony fish.

M *Compare* reproduction in bony fish with reproduction in sharks.

N *List* some adaptations of bony fish.

O *Name* the group of fish thought to be ancestors of terrestrial animals and *describe* their features.

Over ninety percent of all fish belong to the class Osteichthyes, the bony fish. Bony fish range in size from tiny guppies to 400-kilogram tuna. In shape, they range from the sleek barracuda to the elegant sea horse. Like all vertebrates, bony fish begin development by forming a skeleton of cartilage. While sharks retain cartilage throughout their life, bony fish and other vertebrates grow bone to replace the cartilage. The perch is a typical member of the class.

32-8 External Anatomy

The perch has overlapping scales arranged like shingles on a roof. The scales of different bony fish vary in size and shape. The primary functions of all scales are to protect the fish and to prevent water from entering or leaving the body.

A fish will have the same number of scales throughout its entire life. Adult fish do not grow new scales. Look at Figure 32-8. The scales' rate of growth varies with the seasons.

Have you ever felt a live fish? You probably noticed how slimy it felt. The perch has glands that secrete a slippery mucus, which covers the scales. The mucus protects against microorganisms. It also gives the fish a smooth surface that eases movement through the water.

The perch has several types of fins. The fins are made of thin membranes with supporting cartilage rays. The perch has a pair of **dorsal fins** along the back, a **caudal fin** on the tail, and a ventral **anal fin**. These fins are all located on the midline of the fish. Just as feathers on an arrow keep the arrow traveling in a straight line, these fins help the fish swim in a straight line.

There are two sets of lateral fins. On the sides are two pectoral fins, and just below these are the two pelvic fins. The caudal fin moves the fish forward through the water. The other fins maintain balance and change direction. In some bony fish the pectoral and pelvic fins aid the tail fin in producing forward motion.

32-9 Digestion and Excretion

The perch is carnivorous. Small sharp teeth help it grasp and hold prey. The mouth leads into a short tube called the **esophagus**. The esophagus leads to the stomach, where food is broken down into a soupy consistency. From the stomach, food enters the intestine. In the intestine, enzymes reduce the food to small molecules that can be absorbed into the blood. Also located near the junction of the stomach and intestine are several saclike

Figure 32-8 The annual lines on the scales of a fish can be used to determine the fish's age. How old is the fish from which this scale is taken?

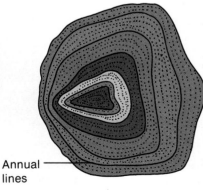

Annual lines

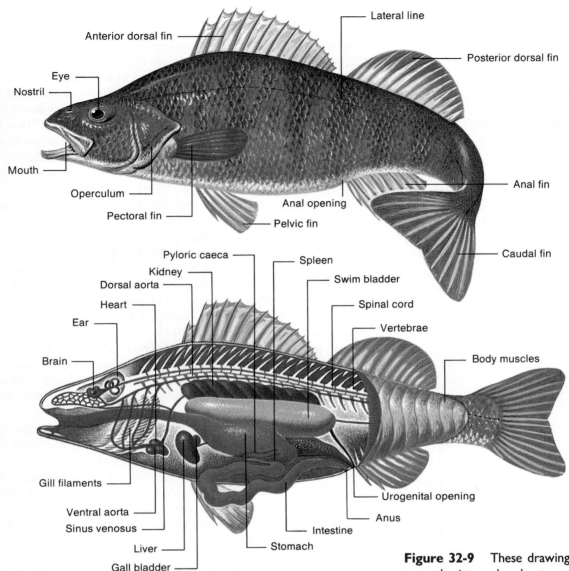

Anterior dorsal fin

Lateral line

Posterior dorsal fin

Eye

Nostril

Mouth

Operculum

Pectoral fin

Pelvic fin

Anal opening

Anal fin

Caudal fin

Pyloric caeca

Kidney

Dorsal aorta

Heart

Ear

Brain

Spleen

Swim bladder

Spinal cord

Vertebrae

Body muscles

Gill filaments

Ventral aorta

Sinus venosus

Liver

Gall bladder

Stomach

Intestine

Anus

Urogenital opening

Figure 32-9 These drawings illustrate the internal and external structures of a perch.

pouches called **pyloric caeca** [pī lȯr′ ik sē kə]. Digestion and absorption occur in these pouches as well. Food that cannot be digested is expelled from the body through the anus.

The **liver** is an organ with many functions. The liver produces **bile**, a substance that helps digestive enzymes break down fats. The liver also stores sugar for future energy needs.

The **kidneys** are a pair of long, thin organs that remove nitrogen wastes from the blood. The wastes leave the body as **urine** through an opening just behind the anus. The kidneys serve another function that is especially important to fish. They regulate the balance of water and salt in the fish's tissues.

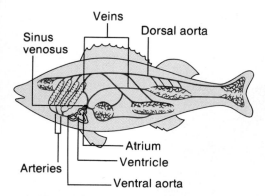

Figure 32-10 The many parts of the circulatory system of a perch.

32-10 Circulation and Gas Exchange

Figure 32-10 illustrates the circulatory system of the perch. Three kinds of vessels carry blood through the fish. **Arteries** carry blood away from the heart, and **veins** carry blood back to the heart. **Capillaries** are microscopic vessels that have very thin walls. Because their walls are so thin, nutrients and oxygen diffuse from the blood in the capillaries into the body cells. This fuel enables body cells to carry out cellular respiration. Carbon dioxide and nitrogen wastes diffuse out of cells and into capillaries.

Blood entering the heart from the body is depleted of oxygen and is rich in carbon dioxide. Veins returning blood from the body empty into a sac just behind the heart. This sac is called the **sinus venosus**. From here blood enters the heart itself.

The fish's heart is a muscular pump with two separate chambers. The first chamber of the heart is called the **atrium** [ā′ trē əm]. Blood is pushed by contractions of the atrium into the second chamber, called the **ventricle** [ven′ tri kəl]. The ventricle, in turn, pushes blood through a large blood vessel, the **ventral aorta**, to the gills. In the gill capillaries, blood picks up oxygen from the water and releases carbon dioxide. The blood then enters the **dorsal aorta** and travels to all parts of the body. As it passes through the various organs, the blood gives up its oxygen and nutrients to the body cells. It then carries off carbon dioxide and wastes. As in the earthworm, the circulatory system of fish and all other vertebrates is closed.

As in the shark, respiration occurs at the perch's gills. The perch takes water in through its mouth. Then, by raising the floor of its mouth, the perch forces water over its gills. The water leaves through a single slit on each side of the head. This single opening for gills is typical of bony fish, whereas the cyclostomes and Chondrichthyes have several gill slits. The **operculum** [ō pər′ kyə ləm] is a semicircular covering on the side of the head that protects the delicate gill tissue from damage. You can see the operculum move on a live fish as it breathes.

Figure 32-11 illustrates the detailed structure of the perch's gills. There are four **gill arches** on each side of the head. Each arch is supported by a piece of cartilage. On the front of each arch are folded tissues called **gill rakers**. These keep food particles from passing through the gills and damaging delicate tissue. The gills themselves contain capillaries which exchange gases when the water passes over each gill.

Gases also enter and leave the blood in another organ called the **swim bladder**. The swim bladder has no respiratory function. It acts as a gas bag, which functions to control the fish's depth. Changing the volume of gas in the bladder allows the fish to change its depth in the water.

Figure 32-11 Notice how many blood vessels surround each of the gills in a perch. Compare the direction of water flow to the direction of blood flow along a gill.

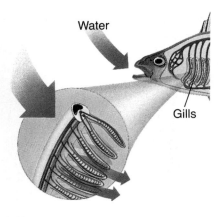

32-11 The Nervous System of the Perch

Perch have a well-developed brain and spinal cord. The brain, illustrated in Figure 32-12, has five major parts.

1. The **olfactory** [ol fak′ tō rē] **bulb** receives information about smell from the nose via the olfactory nerve.
2. The **cerebrum** [sə rē′ brəm] consists of the swollen areas behind the olfactory bulbs and is primarily involved in the interpretation of smell.
3. Behind each cerebrum are the **optic lobes**, which process visual information. These lobes also send impulses to muscles, so the fish responds to what it sees.
4. The **cerebellum** [ser ə bel′ əm] located behind the optic lobes is a structure that coordinates complex muscle movements.
5. Under the cerebellum is the **medulla**, which controls the internal organs of the fish.

The spinal cord continues from the medulla down the vertebral column. The spinal cord is the major pathway for information passing between the body and brain. Nerves branch from the brain and spinal cord. **Cranial nerves** branch from the brain itself, and **spinal nerves** branch from the spinal cord. As you will see in later chapters, the structures found in the fish brain are also found in the brains of other vertebrates. The structures of the fish brain are of great interest to evolutionary biologists.

The sense of smell is very important to the perch. Two olfactory sacs located internally near the mouth contain nerve endings. These endings are very sensitive to chemicals dissolved in the water. Cells sensitive to taste are also located in and around the mouth.

Despite having large eyes and large optic lobes, perch do not see very well. Most fish see only things that are quite close to them. At greater distances, the eyes serve primarily to detect movement.

Near the back of the brain, the fish has a pair of **semicircular canals**. These structures are involved in the fish's sense of balance and hearing. The perch does not have external ears. Sounds are probably carried through the body and the skull bones to the semicircular canals.

All fish, including cyclostomes and sharks, have a sense organ called the **lateral line**. The lateral line is different from any human sense organ. This sense organ extends along both sides of the fish's body. It is sensitive to pressure changes in the water. Fish use this sense to detect nearby movement. Fish that form schools use the lateral line to locate others in the school and to synchronize changes in direction.

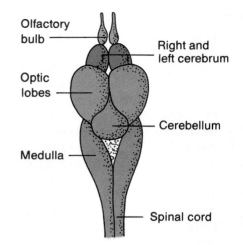

Figure 32-12 The structure of the brain of a perch shows increasing complexity. The human brain has most of the same structures but in much different proportions. For example, in the human brain the right and left cerebrum are by far the largest structures.

Figure 32-13 A lateral line is present in all fish and is used to detect pressure changes in the water.

Fish **533**

Evolution and Adaptation:
There are a number of evolutionary trends apparent in the reproduction of vertebrates. From fish to mammals, there is a trend from external to internal fertilization, and from external to internal development of young. There is also a trend toward increasing parental protection of the young, and fewer offspring. Since the chances of survival are increased, there is no need to waste energy producing numerous offspring.

Figure 32-14 Salmon swim from the ocean back to the same freshwater stream where they were born. When they reach that stream they reproduce.

32-12 Reproduction in the Perch

The female perch produces eggs in ovaries, and the male produces sperm cells in testes. In either case, the reproductive cells leave the body through an opening just behind the anus. Fertilization in the perch, unlike the shark, is external. The female lays several hundred eggs in the water. The male swims near the eggs and releases **milt** into the water. Milt is a fluid containing the sperm cells. Fertilization occurs in the open water, and the parents swim away without protecting the young.

This seems to be an inefficient way of reproducing. Many eggs are never fertilized. Those that are left are unprotected and eaten by predators. If it were not for the large number of eggs that are fertilized, survival of enough perch to continue the species would be doubtful.

32-13 Adaptations of the Bony Fish

Fish are adapted to their specialized environments in many ways. A few examples of the kinds of adaptations seen in fish are described in this section.

Saltwater Fish Some bony fish are adapted to fresh water while others are adapted to salt water. Saltwater and freshwater fish have opposite problems with maintaining the salt balance in their bodies. Salt water has a higher concentration of salts than is found in blood. Thus saltwater bony fish tend to lose water from their cells. Scales, which are impermeable to water, help prevent the loss. Also, the gills of saltwater fish actively transport salt *out* of the body. Their kidneys excrete only small amounts of highly concentrated urine. This helps the fish conserve water.

Freshwater Fish Freshwater fish have the opposite problem. They tend to absorb water from their surroundings by osmosis. The scales of freshwater fish, therefore, keep water out of the body. In addition, the gills of these fish actively transport what little salt there is in the water *into* the body. Kidneys help by excreting large volumes of excess water. Only a few bony fish, such as the salmon, can go from fresh water to salt water and back. The gills and kidneys of these fish can reverse their water and salt transport functions.

Life Cycles Salmon have an extraordinary life cycle. They hatch in freshwater streams, then swim to the sea. They live out most of their adult lives in the oceans. When they are mature, they exhibit a very strong homing instinct. Adult salmon leave the open oceans and return to the same freshwater stream of their birth. Here they reproduce and die. The new generation will return to the same stream to reproduce and die.

Feeding Other adaptations of bony fish are related to feeding. The sharp teeth of the barracuda are characteristic of predators. The barracuda's streamlined shape is an adaptation for swift pursuit of its prey. The hard, beaked tooth of the parrot fish is used to scrape algae from rocks. The strange wormlike appendage on the head of the angler fish attracts prey in the same way that a worm on a fishhook attracts fish.

Coloration Some bony fish are brilliantly colored. The distinctive coloring allows males and females of the same species to recognize one another. Distinctive coloration can also be a defensive adaptation. Potential enemies of the lion fish, for example, have learned to recognize its bright colors and, therefore, to avoid its poisonous spines. How does the flounder uses coloration for camouflage?

Deep Ocean Fish Some remarkable adaptations are seen in the bony fish of very deep seas. Very little light reaches depths below 150 meters. At these depths some fish generate their own lights that attract mates; others have lights that lure prey.

Reproductive Behavior The bony fish show many variations in reproductive structures and behavior. While most bony fish carry out external fertilization, some fertilize internally and bear live young. A number of these live-bearing fish, such as guppies, are popular in home aquariums. Some fish are mouth breeders. In these fish, eggs are fertilized externally. The female (or the male in some species) then takes the eggs into her mouth and holds them there until they hatch. A few fish even build nests for their eggs and guard them carefully until they hatch.

Lungfish There are several fish that have special adaptations for breathing air. The African lungfish lives in ponds that dry up completely for one season of the year. In the pond, the lungfish uses gills for respiration. Before the pond dries, the lungfish

BIOLOGY INSIGHT

Adaptation and Evolution: The body plan of an animal is a function of its life style and environment. Dolphins are mammals and penguins are birds, yet both these organisms have bodies shaped much like that of a fish. This shape is ideal for rapid movement in a water environment. This is an example of convergent evolution.

Figure 32-16 Color is used by some fish as a means of recognition or as a warning to predators.

Figure 32-17   The coelacanth is the only known lobe-finned fish alive today.

buries itself in the mud. It leaves a small passageway for air to enter the hole. The fish draws this air into a structure called a **lung**. A lung is an organ that is used to exchange oxygen and carbon dioxide with the atmosphere. The lungfish can survive in its mud hole until the next rainy season fills the pond.

32-14 Fossil Osteichthyes

The fossil record shows that ancestral Chondrichthyes and Osteichthyes evolved from placoderms about 380 million years ago. Soon after their appearance, the bony fish divided into three distinct groups. One group, quite common at that time, was the lungfish. The lungfish are represented today by only three genera. The second group successfully radiated into the many thousands of species that now occupy the waters of the world.

A third group, called the lobe-finned fish, also appears early in the fossil record. Scientists thought that these fish had become extinct about 70 million years ago. But in 1938, the crew of a fishing boat in the Indian Ocean found a strange looking fish in their nets. The fish was a **coelacanth** [sē′ lə kanth].

Scientists think of this fish as a "living fossil." They are especially interested in it for another reason. Notice in Figure 32-17 that the pectoral and pelvic fins of this fish are on the ends of fleshy stalks. Its structure indicates that this fish is descended from a common ancestor of the first vertebrates that walked on land with four legs.

CHECKPOINT ◆

11. What is the major difference between the Chondrichthyes and the Osteichthyes?
12. The saclike pouches in the perch's digestive system are called _____ .
13. The protective covering of the gills in bony fish is called a _____ .
14. _____ and _____ are the two muscular chambers of the perch's heart.
15. What is the largest part of the perch's brain?
16. What characteristic of the coelacanth is significant from an evolutionary point of view?
17. Give two functions of bright coloration in fish.
▶ 18. Explain why a freshwater fish would die if it were placed in salt water.
▶ 19. Contrast reproduction in bony fish with reproduction in sharks.
▶ 20. What is the function of the cartilage spines in fins?

▶ Denotes a question that involves *interpreting* and *applying* concepts.

THE RESPIRATORY RATE OF A GOLDFISH

Objectives and Skills

□ *Measure* the breathing rate of a goldfish at different water temperatures.
□ *Draw conclusions* about the respiration rate of a fish.

Materials

beakers (500-mL)	fishnet
nonmercury thermometer	ice
electric hot plate	aquarium water
large container for ice water	goldfish

Procedure and Observations

1. Read all instructions for this laboratory activity before you begin your work.
2. Divide the class into two groups. One group will test the response of the fish to colder temperatures and the other group will test the response to warmer temperatures. The high-temperature groups should place about 400 mL of aquarium water in a beaker and put the beaker on a hot plate. Warm the water to about 45°C. The cold-temperature group should place the same amount of aquarium water in a beaker that is in a large container of ice water. Cool the aquarium water to about 10°C.
3. While waiting for your water to warm (or cool), put about 200 mL of aquarium water into a second beaker. Use a fishnet to catch a goldfish and place it in the beaker.
4. Take and record the precise temperature of the water your fish is in. Now count the number of times the operculum of the fish moves in one minute. Record this information.
5. For the warm-water group: Slowly add and stir small amounts of warmed aquarium water to the beaker containing your fish. When the thermometer reads 2°C higher than the original temperature, record the number of operculum movements again.
6. For the cold-water group: Follow the directions described in step 4 using cold water. Add only enough water to lower the temperature in the beaker by 2°C.
7. Raise (or lower) the temperature slowly at 2°C intervals. Record the number of operculum movements per minute at each step. The temperature should *NOT* go above 30°C or below 14°C.
8. When you are finished, leave your fish in the beaker. Once the water temperature returns to normal, return the fish to the main aquarium.
9. Before leaving the laboratory, clean up all materials and wash your hands and fingernails thoroughly.
10. Compute class averages from the data table. Plot the average values as compared to temperature on a graph.

Analysis and Conclusions

1. What conclusions can you draw from your graph?
2. How do you think the body temperature of the fish was affected during this experiment?
3. At what temperatures would you expect the fish to use the most oxygen? Why? Is your answer consistent with your data?
4. Do different fish seem to give different results? Are there some variables that are not well controlled in this experiment?
5. As the temperature of water increases, the amount of oxygen that can dissolve in the water decreases. How does this fact affect your conclusions from this lab exercise?

CHAPTER REVIEW

Summary

▸ The first vertebrates to appear in the fossil record were the jawless fish. There are only a few members of the class Agnatha alive today. They are the lamprey and the hagfish. Without a movable jaw, these fish are parasites and scavengers.

▸ The placoderms evolved from Agnathan ancestors, and had a movable jaw. This kind of jaw allowed fish to become predators. The Chondrichthyes with a cartilage skeleton and the Osteichthyes with a bony skeleton evolved from the placoderms.

▸ All fish have gills for exchanging gases with the water environment. Another major characteristic of fish is the presence of paired pectoral and pelvic fins. Sharks, skates, and rays are the major living members of the Chondrichthyes.

▸ There are more species of bony fish than of any other vertebrate group. The anatomy of the perch is typical of all bony fish. The following systems are present in the perch:

1. a digestive system to break food down into small molecules that can travel to body cells through the blood;
2. a two-chambered heart that pumps blood in a closed loop—from the heart, to the body cells, and back to the heart;
3. four pairs of gills that take oxygen from the water and deposit carbon dioxide in the water;
4. a reproductive system that produces eggs or sperm cells for external fertilization.

▸ Within the many species of bony fish, there are various adaptations for specific environments, such as coloration, light generation, and lungs, and variations in feeding, life cycle, and reproduction.

▸ The bony fish have a long history in the fossil record. The coelacanth, a lobe-finned fish, is thought to be a descendant of the fish that gave rise to the first land-living vertebrates.

Vocabulary

anal fin	liver
artery	lung
atrium	medulla
bile	milt
capillary	olfactory bulb
caudal fin	operculum
cerebellum	optic lobe
cerebrum	ostracoderm
coelocanth	pectoral fin
cranial nerve	pelvic fin
cyclostome	placoid scale
dorsal aorta	pyloric caeca
dorsal fin	semicircular canal
ectothermic	sinus venosus
esophagus	spinal nerve
gill	swim bladder
gill arch	urine
gill raker	vein
kidney	ventral aorta
lateral line	ventricle

Concept Mapping

Construct a concept map for the structure and function of a perch's brain. Include the following terms: cerebrum, cerebellum, medulla, olfactory bulb, optic lobe. Use additional terms as you need them.

Review

1. _____ are the first fish in the fossil record.
2. _____ is the most distinguishing characteristic of the lamprey.
3. Give one example of a lamprey characteristic that is considered primitive.
4. How does the shark skeleton differ from that of cyclostomes?
5. From what structures did shark teeth probably evolve?

6. The respiratory structures of a shark are called _____.
7. A _____ animal is one whose temperature depends on the temperature of the surroundings.
8. Fertilization in sharks is _____.
9. Rays and _____ are other Chondrichthyes.
10. The posterior paired fins of a fish are called _____.
11. Nitrogen wastes are removed from fish by organs called _____.
12. _____ are blood vessels which carry blood away from the heart.
13. Coordination of muscle movements is the function of what part of the fish's brain?
14. What organs of the perch produce eggs?
15. Saltwater fish tend to lose water from their body cells by _____.
16. The only living lobe-finned fish is called the _____.

For questions 17–21, match the characteristic with the group. You may use an answer more than once.

17. first jawed fish
18. no paired fins
19. cartilage skeleton as adult
20. swim bladder
21. round mouth used as sucker

a. Chondrichthyes
b. placoderms
c. ostracoderms
d. Osteichthyes
e. cyclostomes
f. Agnatha

Interpret and Apply

22. What fish groups possess a jaw? Paired fins? Gills for respiration? Cartilage skeleton? Individual gill slits for each gill arch?
23. Explain the function of paired fins in the fish that have them.
24. Why are the first fish thought to have been filter feeders?

25. Why do gills have a large surface area?
26. What is unique about the way water enters the gills of a ray?
27. What are two functions of fish scales?
28. Explain how the kidneys of freshwater and of saltwater fish differ in function.
29. What is the function of blood capillaries?
30. Explain the function of the swim bladder in bony fish.
31. Sharks use their lateral line system to detect the presence of injured fish nearby. How might the lateral line system serve this function?
32. How do many fish overcome the problem of the inefficiency of external fertilization?
33. How are lungfish well adapted to their environment?
34. Describe an adaptation of deep sea fish and explain its function.
35. Describe the relationship of the circulatory system and the respiratory system in a fish.

Critical Thinking

36. How are the body shapes of rays and sharks similar, and how are they different?
37. Describe the path of a single blood cell on one trip around the circulatory system of a fish.
38. In what ways is the world sensed by fish similar to your own? In what ways is it different?
39. Explain how the gills, scales, and kidneys of a fish work together to help maintain water balance.
40. The mudskipper is a small fish that can crawl out of the water for extended periods of time. What advantages does this provide?

Chapter

33

AMPHIBIANS

Overview

CHARACTERISTICS OF AMPHIBIANS

33-1 Evolving from Water to Live on Land

33-2 A Typical Amphibian: The Frog

33-3 Frog's Skeleton

33-4 Frog Digestion and Excretion

33-5 Frog Circulation

33-6 Frog Respiration

33-7 Frog's Nervous System

33-8 Frog's Senses

33-9 Frog Reproduction and Development

OTHER AMPHIBIANS

33-10 Order Urodela: Salamanders

33-11 Order Apoda

33-12 Fossil Amphibians

How is this amphibian adapted for a dual life?

CHARACTERISTICS OF AMPHIBIANS

Amphibian [am fib' ē ən] means "dual life." Amphibians hatch from eggs as fishlike larvae. At some point in their lives, however, most amphibians undergo metamorphosis, changing into an adult form that can live on land. They move about on legs and breathe air. This transformation clearly illustrates the intermediate nature of these animals. How does an amphibian change from a fishlike larva to an organism capable of living on land? How do amphibians breathe on land?

33-1 Evolving from Water to Live on Land

Amphibians lay their eggs in water. The fishlike amphibian larva has fins for swimming, gills for gas exchange in water, and a circulatory system similiar to that of a fish. After metamorphosis, however, the adult has four legs for movement on land and lungs for gas exchange in the air. They also have a more complex circulatory system than that of the larvae.

All amphibians have smooth skin without scales. Their skin is often covered with mucus and must be kept moist. For all amphibians, the skin is an important respiratory surface.

Like fish, all amphibians are ectothermic. Since they cannot control their internal body temperature, most species of amphibians live in areas where the temperature shows little variation. Species that live where it is very hot or very cold have special adaptations that allow them to survive.

33-2 A Typical Amphibian: The Frog

Biologists divide amphibians into three orders. The order **Anura** [ə nür' ah] includes the frogs and toads. The order **Urodela** [yur' ə dē' lə] includes the salamanders—sometimes called newts.

Section Objectives

A *List* the basic characteristics of amphibians.

B *Identify* important external structures and adaptations of the frog.

C *Compare* and *contrast* the frog and the fish skeleton.

D *Identify* and *explain* the function of the digestive and excretory organs of the frog.

E *Describe* the structure and function of the frog's circulatory system.

F *Describe* the structure of the frog's respiratory system.

G *Identify* important parts of the frog's nervous system.

H *List* some of the sensory adaptations of the frog.

I *Describe* reproduction and development in frogs.

DO YOU KNOW?

Information: Embedded in the skin of most amphibians are special cells called chromatophores. These cells contain the colored pigments of the skin. In many species, they are capable of changing the color of the animal.

Figure 33-1 A salamander shows characteristics typical of amphibians. Notice the smooth skin of this animal. Many amphibians have bright, warning coloration because they secrete toxic materials onto the skin that make them distasteful to predators.

The order **Apoda** [a pō' də] is an uncommon group of legless amphibians that live in tropical regions. All modern amphibians live in or near fresh water.

The frog serves well as a typical amphibian. Frogs clearly show features common to the entire class and also illustrate specific adaptations of the anurans. Anurans do not have tails. They have broad, flat bodies with no distinct neck. They also have very large hind legs specialized for jumping.

Frog skin is smooth and very permeable to water. Frogs do not drink water because they absorb all they need through their skin. Because their skin is permeable, however, frogs can dry out when exposed to air. Frogs must occasionally moisten their skin, and they cannot stay in direct sunlight for long periods.

Glands secrete mucus onto the skin. Mucus slows the evaporation of water and also makes the frog slippery to predators. The frog's skin is only loosely attached, making it difficult for predators to hold on to frogs. Although frogs and toads are very similar, there are some differences. Toads live farther from water than frogs. Toads have drier skin, but they must live in humid places.

Figure 33-2 illustrates the external characteristics of a frog. At the front of the head, two nostrils open into nasal passages. These passages connect to the mouth cavity. Frog nostrils function both as organs of smell and as air passages. The frog can be submerged in water and breathe by exposing only the nostrils.

The two large eyes behind the nostrils can also stay above water when the body of the frog is submerged. Frogs have eyelids that protect the eyes. Another covering called the **nictitating** [nik' tə tāt ing] **membrane** protects the eyes from water and keeps them moist when the frog is out of the water.

Behind each eye is a round, flat membrane called the **tympanic** [tim pan' ik] **membrane**. These are the frog's ears.

Male frogs emit sounds to attract females. If you live near an area inhabited by frogs, you may have heard this sound in the spring or summer. In many frog species, the male frog pushes air from its mouth into vocal sacs under the chin. These vocal sacs help to amplify the sound.

The front legs of the frog are smaller than the rear legs. The "thumb" of the male frog often has an additional pad. The thumb pad helps to push eggs out of the female's body during mating. The rear legs of the frog are large and well adapted for leaping.

33-3 Frog's Skeleton

Look at the frog's skeleton in Figure 33-3. In some ways, this skeleton has features in common with that of a fish. Yet the frog's skeleton has adaptations for living on land. The skull consists

Figure 33-2 The external features of the frog.

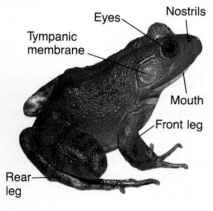

Eyes — Nostrils

Tympanic membrane

Mouth

Front leg

Rear leg

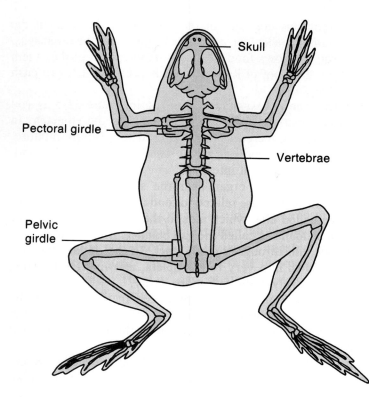

Skull

Pectoral girdle

Vertebrae

Pelvic girdle

of a low jawbone and a number of bones that surround the brain. Vertebrae surround the spinal cord, as in fish. In frogs the number of vertebrae is small, and there are no ribs. Adult frogs have no tail, but there is a long bone running from the end of the spine to the posterior point of the body.

The frog skeleton is most different from the fish skeleton in the bones that support the front and rear limbs. The **pectoral girdle** is a group of bones that almost surrounds the thorax and attaches the front limbs to the body. The rear limbs attach to the body by the **pelvic girdle.** In later chapters you will see that similar structures are found in all four-limbed vertebrates.

33-4 Frog Digestion and Excretion

Adult frogs are carnivores, and the structure of the mouth reflects their feeding habits. A number of small **maxillary teeth** line the margins of the upper jaw. Behind these teeth, near the internal openings of the nasal passages, are two small **vomerine** [vō' mə rīn] **teeth.** Frogs do not use their teeth to chew food, but to hold prey. The tongue of the frog is unusual. Instead of attaching at the back of the mouth, like a human tongue, the frog's tongue attaches at the front. This allows the frog to flick its tongue about and capture flying insects.

DO YOU KNOW?

Word Root: *Maxillary* derives from the Latin *maxilla,* meaning "jawbone, jaw."

Amphibians   **543**

Figure 33-6 illustrates the frog's heart in more detail. The heart has three chambers. Deoxygenated blood from the body cells returns to the heart through the **venae cavae.** These veins empty into a large collecting area in back of the heart called the **sinus venosus.** Blood then enters the **right atrium** of the heart. The right atrium is a chamber that pumps blood into the ventricle.

Amphibians   **545**

External nostril opening

Maxillary teeth

Internal nostril opening

Vomerine teeth

Eustachian tube

Gullet

Food organisms are immediately pushed to the back of the mouth toward the **gullet** [gəl′ ət], at the beginning of the esophagus. When a frog swallows food, it closes its eyes and pushes them down against the roof of its mouth. This pressure helps to push food into the gullet.

Trace the digestive system of the frog in Figure 33-5 as you read this explanation. The esophagus leads to the stomach. In the stomach, acid secretions reduce food to a soupy mixture. From the stomach, food enters the **duodenum** [dü ə dē′ nəm]

OTHER AMPHIBIANS

Section Objectives

J **Compare** the structure of urodeles and anurans.

K **Describe** the unique features of Apoda.

L **Explain** the significance of the amphibian fossil record.

While frogs and toads are probably the most familiar, they are not the only types of amphibian. Anyone who has spent time in the woods or around ponds has probably encountered members of the order Urodela. These are the salamanders. Some salamanders are only a few centimeters long. But one variety of Japanese salamander reaches a length of 1.5 meters! This species is the largest amphibian alive today. While amphibians are more common in tropical climates, a number of salamanders are found in colder regions of the world.

The third group of amphibians is the order Apoda. The apods, or legless amphibians, are a much rarer group. They are not found in North America.

33-10 Order Urodela: Salamanders

Salamanders have a body plan different from that of frogs. A salamander is long and slender. It has a neck between the head and body, and it has a long tail. Salamanders resemble lizards. However, as you will learn in the next chapter, lizards are reptiles. Unlike lizards, salamanders have the smooth, moist skin typical of amphibians.

Salamanders show more variation in body form and function than do frogs and toads. Some salamanders, for example, remain totally aquatic during their entire life. Other woodland species rarely return to the water. In fact, some woodland salamanders even lay eggs out of the water, in the humid areas of forests. The eggs of these species are surrounded by a gelatin capsule that prevents them from drying out. The young salamanders

Figure 33-11 *Left:* Notice that a salamander's body differs in structure from that of a frog. *Right:* an axolotl

undergo complete development to the adult, legged form within the egg capsules.

One species of Mexican salamander can remain in the larval form all its life. These larval salamanders are called **axolotls** [ak′ sə lot əls]. Axolotls do not develop lungs, yet they can still lay eggs. If, however, an axolotl's pond dries up, it can metamorphose into a land-living adult. Then it will move to a new pond and reproduce.

Some salamander species retain external gills throughout their life. The mud puppy is an example. This large salamander, up to 60 centimeters long, is found in streams in the mid-western United States. It has dark red, bushy gills on either side of its neck.

A number of species of salamanders have lost both lungs and gills, and depend on skin respiration for all its gas exchange needs. Several species of salamanders that are totally aquatic have very small limbs. The mud siren illustrated in Figure 33-13 has no hind limbs at all.

33-11 Order Apoda

The apods are the most unusual of the amphibians. These legless creatures live only in the tropical regions of Asia, Africa, Central America, and South America. There are only about 50 known species of this rare group of animals. The legless amphibians can be found burrowing under moist soils. If you look at Figure 33-13 you can see how an apod could easily be mistaken for an earthworm. Yet these amphibians are carnivorous and hunt for earthworms, insects, and insect larvae.

Figure 33-12 A mud puppy. Notice the exposed gills. Why do you think the gills are a different color than the body?

Figure 33-13 How is this salamander (*left*) different than the apod (*right*)?

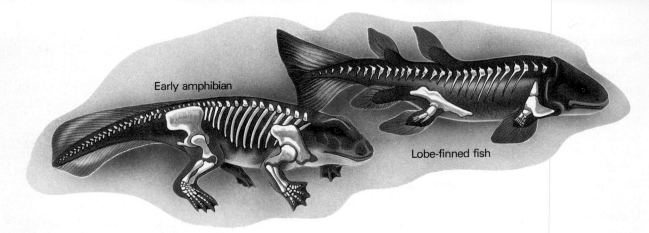

Early amphibian

Lobe-finned fish

Figure 33-14 Early amphibians, like *Diplovertebron* shown here, resembled modern salamanders and had to return to water to reproduce. Many amphibians became extinct as reptiles became more successful.

33-12 Fossil Amphibians

As you have seen, there are many ways that amphibians seem intermediate between fish and land-living animals. The modern amphibian body structure and life cycle support this idea. In fact, the fossil record also supports the hypothesis that amphibians were the first vertebrates to venture onto land. It shows also that other land-living vertebrates evolved from amphibians.

The oldest fossil amphibians have been dated at about 360 million years. They had four legs and looked much like modern salamanders. These legs possibly evolved from the stumplike fins of a lobe-finned fish, as shown in Figure 33-14.

Evidence found in rocks indicates that the period when the amphibians appeared was a time of worldwide droughts. As temperatures increased, many small bodies of water evaporated. This often happened as the seasons changed. In some cases, these conditions might have favored the selection of animals with amphibian characteristics. For example, any fish that had respiratory surfaces other than gills would have had an advantage.

DO YOU KNOW?

Information: Some of the early fossil amphibians reached lengths of more than three meters.

CHECKPOINT ◆

10. What larval structure is maintained in axolotls?
11. Fossil evidence suggests that the legs of *Diplovertebron* could have evolved from the _____ of a _____.
12. What are the two most obvious structural differences between salamanders and frogs?
13. What structural feature clearly distinguishes the apods from other amphibians?
▶ 14. What two major adaptations allowed the first amphibians to invade the land?
▶ 15. Of the three amphibian groups, it is likely that the apods evolved most recently. Explain why this theory seems logical.

▶ Denotes a question that involves *interpreting* and *applying* concepts.

FROG DEVELOPMENT

In this activity you will observe development of
the frog.

Objectives and Skills

☐ *Observe* the early divisions of a frog egg.
☐ *Describe* the stages of frog development.

Materials

aquarium   watch glass
beaker (1 L)   blank paper
pond water   fertilized frog eggs
fishnet
magnifying lens or dis-
  secting microscope

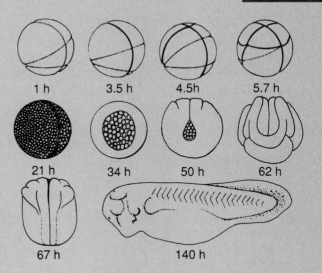

Procedure and Observations

1. Read all instructions for this laboratory activity before you begin your work.
2. Place about four or five centimeters of pond
   water or aged aquarium water in your
   beaker.
3. Obtain about 5 or 10 fertilized frog eggs
   from the main tank and place them in your
   beaker.
4. Place some water from your beaker into a
   watch glass. Using a fishnet, transfer the
   eggs to the watch glass. Look at the eggs
   under a magnifying glass or dissecting
   microscope.
5. Compare each of the eggs to the diagrams in
   the next column. Estimate how far along the
   eggs are in their development. On a separate
   piece of paper, make drawings of the eggs.
   Arrange the drawings in order of developmental stage. Indicate below your drawings
   the age of the egg.
6. Return your eggs to the beaker between observations. Occasionally during the next

week or two, make more observations and
drawings of the developing frogs.
7. Before leaving the laboratory, clean up all
   other materials and wash your hands
   thoroughly.
8. When the eggs hatch and the tadpoles begin
   to swim freely, feed them. Put the tadpoles
   into the main aquarium and continue to observe their development over the next several months.

Analysis and Conclusions

1. Perhaps some of the frog eggs never developed at all. What did those eggs look like
   compared to those that did develop?
2. How long did it take before the tadpoles
   hatched from their eggs?
3. Compared to the original egg, how large was
   the tadpole when it hatched? What does this
   observation imply about cell growth and cell
   division during this stage of frog
   development?
4. What fishlike characteristics can you observe
   in the young tadpoles?

CHAPTER REVIEW

Summary

▶ Most amphibians are terrestrial vertebrates with an aquatic larval stage. The larva undergoes metamorphosis into an adult with lungs, a more complex circulation, and four legs.

▶ Frogs have short bodies with no neck and no tail. The skin of a frog is moist. The front legs are small, and the rear legs are large and modified for jumping.

▶ The skeleton of a frog is similar to that of other four-legged vertebrates.

▶ Frogs are carnivores. The tongue and teeth are modified for capturing and holding prey. The digestive tract is divided into specialized organs, which have specific functions in the digestion and absorption of food.

▶ Frogs have a three-chambered heart and two circulation loops for the blood. Respiration takes place on the lung surfaces, the skin, and the inner lining of the mouth.

▶ The brain of a frog is divided into a number of specific areas with specific functions. As in other vertebrates, the nervous system of a frog can be divided into the central and peripheral nervous systems.

▶ Reproduction of frogs takes place in water. Fertilization and development are external. Eggs hatch into tadpoles, which undergo metamorphosis into adults.

▶ Salamanders belong to the order Urodela. This order of amphibians has a long body and tail. The four legs are usually about equal in size. Some retain gills throughout life, while others have lungs.

▶ The order Apoda includes some rare species of legless amphibians.

▶ The fossil record shows that the first amphibians appeared about 350 million years ago as the first land vertebrates.

Vocabulary

amphibian	pelvic girdle
Anura	peripheral nervous system
aorta	
Apoda	pituitary gland
axolotl	pulmonary artery
bile	pulmonary loop
bile duct	pulmonary vein
central nervous system	red blood cells
cloaca	renal artery
cranial nerve	renal vein
duodenum	right atrium
estivate	sinus venosus
eustachian tube	spinal nerve
fat body	systemic loop
gall bladder	tadpole
gullet	tympanic membrane
hibernate	ureter
larynx	urinary bladder
left atrium	Urodela
maxillary teeth	uterus
nictitating membrane	vasa efferentia
olfactory lobe	vena cava
oviduct	vocal cords
pancreas	vomerine teeth
pancreatic duct	white blood cells
pectoral girdle	

Concept Mapping

Construct a concept map for a frog's nervous system. Include the following terms: peripheral nervous system, optic lobe, spinal nerve, cerebellum, medulla, central nervous system, cranial nerve, cerebrum, olfactory lobe. Use additional terms as you need them.

Review

1. What is the function of teeth in frogs?
2. What are the two functions of the nasal passages in a frog?

3. To what amphibian order do the legless amphibians belong?
4. What organ produces sperm cells in the male frog? Egg cells in the female frog?
5. Name some bones that could be found in a frog skeleton that do not occur in a fish skeleton.
6. Which group of modern amphibians resembles the first fossil amphibians?
7. Where do most amphibians lay their eggs?
8. To what order of amphibians do salamanders belong?
9. What kinds of blood vessels exchange gases with the lungs and skin of the frog?
10. What is one function of mucus on the skin of amphibians?
11. What is the function of the cerebrum in the frog's brain?
12. What blood vessel in the frog carries blood from the ventricle of the heart to the body cells?

Interpret and Apply

13. If a red blood cell did not pick up oxygen in the lungs, where else might it do so?
14. What structural evidence can you give that the sense of vision is important to the frog?
15. In what major ways is a tadpole more like a fish than a frog?
16. Why is the three-chambered heart of the amphibian not as efficient as it might be?
17. Explain how the large hind legs of the frog might be a useful adaptation.
18. What are the three major problems presented by the terrestrial environment that are not encountered in the aquatic environment?
19. How do frogs deal with the problem of supplying sufficient surface area for gas exchange?

20. In what ways is the reproduction of apods and other amphibians similar?
21. Very few amphibians have externally visible gills like the mud puppy and the axolotl. In most larval amphibians, the gills are covered by an operculum. Explain why the external gills are absent in most species.
22. Explain why most amphibians are found in the tropical regions of the world.
23. The frog's tongue is covered with a rather thick mucus layer and is quite sticky. How is this a useful adaptation?

Critical Thinking

24. Suppose you are riding on a red blood cell in the vena cava of a frog. Describe the structures you will pass as you travel around the circulatory system, ending up back in the vena cava again.
25. Explain how using the skin as a respiratory surface is both an advantage and a disadvantage to the frog.
26. Explain how the pull of gravity is more of a factor in the terrestrial environment, and how gravity influenced the evolution of the first amphibians.
27. Certain sensory cells in the eyes of a frog have been shown to send signals to the brain whenever the general level of light entering the eyes drops rapidly. These signals are processed by the brain, which then sends signals to the rear legs causing the frog to jump. Can you explain the occurrence of such cells in a frog's eyes?
28. Experiments have shown that the element iodine is needed in the diet of amphibian larvae in order for them to undergo metamorphosis. Describe an experiment in which you could demonstrate the importance of iodine in amphibian development.

Chapter
34

REPTILES

Overview

CHARACTERISTICS OF REPTILES

34-1 Adaptations to Land
34-2 Reptile Eggs

MODERN REPTILES

34-3 Anatomy of the Snake
34-4 Variety of Snakes
34-5 Lizards
34-6 Order Chelonia: Turtles
34-7 Order Crocodilia
34-8 Order Rhynchocephalia: Tuataras

REPTILE EVOLUTION

34-9 Dinosaurs
34-10 Other Extinct Reptiles

Why are people afraid of snakes?

CHARACTERISTICS OF REPTILES

When reptiles first appear in the fossil record, the only other vertebrates on land were amphibians. Amphibians must stay close to water to keep their skin moist and to reproduce. But reptiles are much more independent of water; they are free to move inland. What characteristics gave them this independence? How were reptiles able to adapt to so many different environments? What enabled them to radiate into so many species?

34-1 Adaptations to Land

The skin of reptiles is thick, tough, and dry. It is covered with overlapping scales or flat plates. The scales or plates are made of a protein called **keratin** [ker′ ə tin]. Your fingernails are also made of keratin. Reptile skin is impermeable to water which keeps the reptile's body from drying out.

Reptiles are better adapted to movement on land than amphibians. Compare the limb position of the amphibian and reptile illustrated in Figure 34-1. Notice how the limbs of the amphibian project almost straight out from the body, whereas those of the reptile are directed downward. A reptile keeps its body higher off the ground which makes rapid movement over land much easier. A further distinguishing feature of reptile limbs is the presence of keratin claws on each toe.

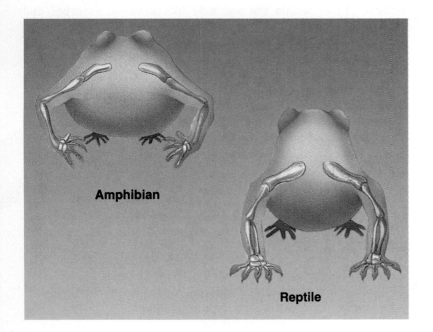

Amphibian

Reptile

Section Objectives

A *Compare* and *contrast* the characteristics of reptiles to those of amphibians.

B *Name* the various parts of a reptile egg and *explain* the function of each part.

DO YOU KNOW?

Information: The sea snake is the only totally aquatic reptile known. They bear live young in the open oceans. These snakes also have one of the most powerful poisons of any snake species.

Figure 34-1 Compared to the limbs of amphibians, the limbs of reptiles are better able to support the body on land.

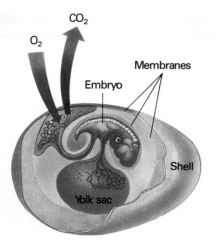

CO$_2$

O$_2$

Membranes

Embryo

Shell

Yolk sac

Figure 34-2 The embryonic membranes of a reptile egg function to support and protect the developing embryo.

▶ Denotes a question that involves *interpreting* and *applying* concepts.

Like fish and amphibians, modern reptiles are ectothermic. Life on the land, however, exposes reptiles to greater variations in temperature than does life in the water. Many reptiles are adapted to these extremes by specialized behaviors. One such behavior is **basking**. Lizards and snakes often bask in the morning sun. By basking, a reptile's body temperature is increased by the sun's energy.

A further adaptation to life on land is the reptile's method of reproduction. When amphibians mate, they release eggs and sperm into the water where fertilization takes place. Their eggs and sperm would dry out if exposed to air. Reptile reproduction is characterized by **internal fertilization**. When reptiles mate, the sperm cells of the male are deposited inside the body of the female where the sperm fertilize the egg cells.

34-2 Reptile Eggs

Reptiles lay very large eggs with leathery shells. The shell protects the contents of the egg and provides a barrier against evaporation.

Four membranes within the shell aid the developing reptile embryo. The internal structure of a typical reptile egg is illustrated in Figure 34-2. Just inside the shell is a thin membrane called the **chorion** [kôr' ē on]. The chorion holds the contents of the egg, yet it is permeable to gases. Oxygen and carbon dioxide are exchanged between the egg and its surroundings. The chorion also acts as a barrier that prevents microorganisms from entering the egg. The **amnion** [am' nē ən] is a sac that surrounds the embryo. Fluid within the sac acts like a shock absorber and protects the embryo.

The **allantois** [ə lan' tō is] is a membrane that contains many blood vessels. It is a respiratory surface for the embryo. Oxygen and carbon dioxide are exchanged between the blood vessels and the surrounding fluid. Nitrogen wastes accumulate within the allantois as the embryo increases in size. The last of the four membranes is the **yolk sac**. The yolk sac surrounds the yellow yolk, a protein which serves as food for the developing embryo. Blood vessels in the yolk sac carry food from the yolk to the growing embryo.

CHECKPOINT ◆

1. What is the special protein found in reptile skin?
2. What are the four membranes of a reptile egg?
▶ 3. What property of reptile skin makes these animals better adapted to terrestrial life than amphibians?
▶ 4. Why are reptile eggs larger than amphibian eggs?

MODERN REPTILES

The Class Reptilia consists of four orders. Snakes and lizards belong to the order of reptiles called the **Squamata** [skwə mäd′ ə]. The **Chelonia** [ke lō′ nē ə] are tortoises and turtles. The **Crocodilia** [kräk ə dil′ ē ə] include alligators and crocodiles. The **Rhynchocephalia** [ring kō sə fāl′ ē ə] consist of a single living species called the **tuatara** [tu ə tär′ ə]. There are about 6000 reptile species alive today.

Familiarity with a phylum is aided by learning about a typical member. Since snakes are probably among the most familiar reptiles, their characteristics will be discussed in this lesson. What are some of the characteristics unique to reptiles? Why is the class Reptilia divided into four separate orders?

34-3 Anatomy of the Snake

While snakes are typical reptiles in many ways, you will see that they have many unique adaptations related to their unusual lifestyle.

External Anatomy The most obvious feature of snakes is the absence of limbs. The entire body is covered with dry, overlapping scales. The scales on the ventral surface help a snake gain a hold on the ground and push itself forward.

The head of a snake has nostrils at the anterior end above the mouth. Snake eyes have no lids. Instead, the eyes are covered by a transparent, protective membrane. No snake has external ears, though it does have internal ears in the skull. The anus marks the boundary between the abdomen and the tail.

Skeleton The most unusual feature of a snake's skull is the way the jaws are hinged to the head. The photograph in Figure 34-3 illustrates how a snake opens its jaws to swallow large prey. The skeleton consists mostly of vertebrae and ribs. There are often more than 100 vertebrae with ribs attached to most of them. In most snakes, there is nothing that resembles a pectoral or pelvic girdle.

Digestion and Excretion Many of the internal structures of snakes reflect their unusual feeding behavior. All snakes are carnivores and eat infrequently. Some of the largest snakes of Africa and South America eat only once every few months. Some can live as long as a year between meals. When snakes do eat, they eat extremely large meals and swallow their prey whole. Just as the jaws unhinge to swallow large organisms, the ribs can also separate. Without pectoral or pelvic girdles in the way, large food organisms can pass along the digestive tract.

A snake's excretory system consists of a pair of long kidneys. One kidney is found on each side of the body. Instead of being

Section Objectives

C *Describe* the important anatomical features of snakes.

D *List* some adaptations of different snakes.

E *Compare* lizards with snakes.

F *State* some of the unique features of turtles.

G *Compare* and *contrast* alligators and crocodiles.

H *Explain* why the tuatara is considered a primitive reptile.

Figure 34-3 The jaws of a snake can open wide, thus allowing the snake to swallow large prey.

Reptiles **559**

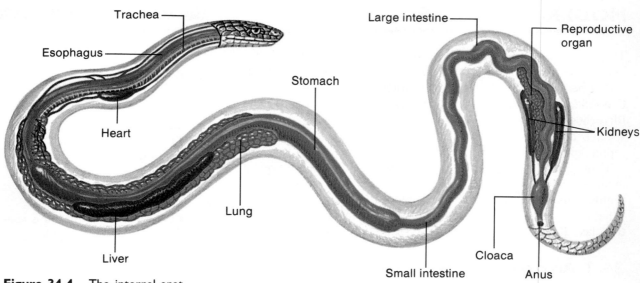

Figure 34-4   The internal anatomy of a snake reveals a number of unusual adaptations for its unique body plan. Elongated internal organs, a single lung, and the staggered position of the kidneys help to streamline a snake's body.

Figure 34-5   A snake's heart has an incomplete central wall that separates most of the blood in the right side of the heart from that in the left.

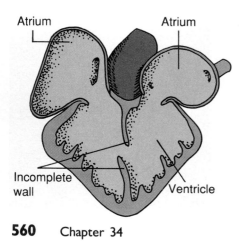

located opposite each other, the kidneys are staggered, so that one is in front of the other. As in amphibians, the ureter drains urine from the kidneys into the cloaca.

Circulation and Respiration   Recall that in amphibians, oxygenated and deoxygenated blood mix in the single ventricle of the three-chambered heart. This is not a critical problem, since amphibians add further oxygen to the blood by gas exchange through the skin. Reptile skin, however, is impermeable to water and gases. Reptiles cannot use their skin as a respiratory surface. A three-chambered heart would be a problem for them.

Most reptiles, including snakes, have a heart like the one illustrated in Figure 34-5. Note the wall that separates the right side of the ventricle from the left side. While a small amount of blood can mix, such mixing is minimal. The reptile heart keeps oxygenated and deoxygenated blood largely separate.

Without the skin as a respiratory surface, reptile lungs have to be more efficient gas exchange structures than amphibian lungs. The interior surfaces of reptile lungs are more highly folded and have a much greater surface area for gas exchange.

Snakes generally have only a single lung. The right lung is very long, but the left lung is tiny or completely absent. In snakes and other reptiles, air enters the lungs through a long tube called the **trachea** [tra′ kē ə].

The Nervous System and Sense Organs   The structure of the brain and nervous system in snakes, and in reptiles in general, is similar to that of frogs. Snakes, however, have a number of specific adaptations in their sense organs. Most snakes depend on the sense of smell to find prey. As an aid to the sense of smell, many snakes continually sample the surrounding air with flicks of their forked tongues. The tongue brings molecules from the air into the mouth. These molecules are sensed by the **Jacobson's organs** in the roof of the mouth.

Snakes have sensory organs in the skull that are similar in structure to the ears of other vertebrates. Although snakes are deaf to sound, they probably use their "ears" to detect vibrations from the ground, thus obtaining information about animals moving near them. Like the sense of hearing, a snake's sense of sight is not acute. With the sense of sight, snakes can only detect objects and movements close to them.

Pit vipers are snakes that have a small pair of pitlike structures located between the nostrils and the eyes. These pits are heat sensors. Pit vipers use them to detect and locate the warm bodies of nearby birds and mammals that are potential prey.

Reproduction Like other reptiles, snakes have internal fertilization and manufacture eggs in the female's body. Male reptiles have a structure that transfers sperm cells into the cloaca of the female during mating.

Many snakes lay shelled eggs and leave the eggs to hatch on their own. Other snakes hold the eggs internally until they hatch. In some of these species, the eggs never have shells. Reptiles that lay eggs are called **oviparous** [ō vip′ ər əs]. Reptiles that hold eggs internally and then bear live young are called **ovoviviparous** [ō vō vī vip′ ər əs].

34-4 Variety of Snakes

Some snake species are poisonous. In North America, the best known poisonous snakes are the 13 species of rattlesnakes. Rattlesnakes are pit vipers. They have hinged fangs that swing forward only when the snake is about to strike. The hollow fangs are like hypodermic needles. They inject poison into a prey that dies quickly and is then swallowed.

Rattlesnakes strike from a coiled position with incredible speed. The rattle at the end of the tail serves as a warning for any large animal to stay away. The venom not only kills prey but also deters predators.

Most snakes are nonpoisonous and subdue their prey in other ways. Some snakes are **constrictors**. Constrictors wrap quickly around their prey and squeeze. The prey cannot breathe and soon die. The large boa constrictors and pythons of South America and Africa are best known for this method of killing. The large pythons, which reach a length of six or eight meters, can kill pigs or small antelopes and swallow them whole. Many small common snakes use constriction as well. Snakes can eat meals that weigh as much as one fourth of their own weight.

Figure 34-6   Poison is stored in glands located at the mouth of some snakes. When a snake extends its fangs, this poison flows through a tube into the fangs. As the pointed fangs pierce the flesh of its prey, poison flows into the prey's bloodstream.

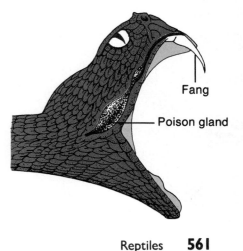

Fang

Poison gland

Reptiles   **561**

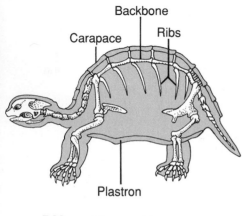

Figure 34-7 Lizards are a diverse group. *Top:* A gecko; *Bottom:* An iguana

Figure 34-8 The heavy dorsal shell of a turtle is supported by bone.

Backbone

Carapace

Ribs

Plastron

34-5 Lizards

Lizards and snakes belong to the order Squamata. Typically, lizards are four-legged terrestrial animals. The skeleton and internal anatomy of a lizard do not show the same specializations as do snakes. The limbs of a lizard are supported by a pectoral and pelvic girdle. The legs of a lizard are arranged to keep its body off the ground. Because of this adaptation, they can move rapidly. Both lungs in a lizard are well developed. Lizards also have external ears and eyelids.

The animals in Figure 34-7 are members of the lizard family. Geckos are small lizards with special pads on the ends of their toes. These pads allow geckos to climb vertically or upside down on very smooth surfaces. While most lizards are relatively small, the monitor lizards of Sumatra can be over three meters long. The Galápagos iguana is a marine lizard. Although most lizards are carnivorous, the Galápagos iguana is a herbivore. It feeds exclusively on marine algae. The Gila monster is one of only two species of poisonous lizards.

A few species of lizards are confused with snakes because they are legless. While this makes them appear like snakes, they have few of the anatomical specializations of snakes. Legless lizards live on forest floors and feed on insects and worms.

34-6 Order Chelonia: Turtles

While there are only about 200 species of chelonians, they are a group with an ancient fossil history. Forms clearly related to modern turtles have been found in rocks over 200 million years old.

As illustrated in Figure 34-8, the skeleton of a turtle is highly modified. Much of the body of a turtle is contained within two halves of a thick, resistant shell. The curved dorsal portion of the shell is called the **carapace** [kar′ ə pās]. Vertebrae are fused to the carapace, while the ribs are widened and flattened against it. The flattened ventral shell is called the **plastron** [plas′ trən]. It provides support and protection for the internal organs. Vertebrae in the neck bend into an S-shape when the head is withdrawn into the shell.

A terrestrial chelonian is called a **tortoise**. Although most tortoises are rather small, the Galápagos tortoise can have a mass of almost 200 kilograms.

Chelonians do not have teeth, and most are herbivores. Many turtles are aquatic. Freshwater turtles, or **terrapins**, are common inhabitants of ponds and lakes. The freshwater snapping turtles are carnivores, with very powerful jaws. Marine or sea turtles can be very large. They spend their adult lives at sea and only come on land to lay eggs.

34-7 Order Crocodilia

Like turtles, the fossil history of the order Crocodilia is ancient. Forms that look much like modern crocodiles and alligators have been found in rocks 225 million years old.

All members are adapted to living in shallow fresh water. They use their powerful tails to propel themselves in the water. Their eyes and nostrils are often the only things visible above the water's surface. All members of this order lay their eggs on land. A crocodilian heart has four chambers. Unlike other reptiles, the right and left ventricles are completely separated by a wall.

There are only about 25 living species in this order. Alligators have a much broader and more rounded snout than do crocodiles. Alligator teeth are hidden when the mouth is closed, while the teeth of a crocodile are visible. The Asian gavial [gā′ vē əl] and the tropical American caiman [kā′ mən] are also crocodilians. They differ from crocodiles and alligators in the shape of their snouts and the arrangement of scales on their skin.

34-8 Order Rhynchocephalia: Tuataras

Living on a few remote islands near New Zealand is the tuatara, the only surviving species of an ancient reptile order. Though the tuatara illustrated in Figure 34-9 looks like a lizard, its anatomy is more closely related to that of a reptile group called rhynchocephalians. They appeared in the fossil record 225 million years ago—at about the same time as the earliest crocodilians and chelonians.

The bony skull plates of this reptile are different from those of any other living group. The tuatara has a third "eye" in the middle of its forehead, called a **pineal** [pīn′ ē əl] **eye**. This small eye is covered by scales and cannot form images. Its function is not known, but there is some evidence that it is involved in temperature control. The pineal eye may once have been used for vision.

Figure 34-9   The tuatara is the only surviving species of the order Rhynchocephalia.

CHECKPOINT ◆

5. What is significant about the lungs of a snake?
6. What is the function of the sensory pit of a pit viper?
7. Name two methods used by snakes to subdue prey.
8. Other than snakes, what reptiles belong to the order Squamata?
9. What is the unique feature of a tuatara?
10. Explain how a turtle shell is a useful adaptation.
11. Why is the location of the eyes in a crocodile a useful adaptation?

▶ Denotes a question that involves *interpreting* and *applying* concepts.

Reptiles   **563**

REPTILE EVOLUTION

Section Objectives

I **Identify** the two major dinosaur groups.

J **List** and **describe** other types of extinct reptiles.

Reptiles have a long history which began over 300 million years ago in the Carboniferous Period. The first reptiles, called **cotylosaurs** [kät′ əl ō sȯ ərs], looked something like large, heavy lizards. These animals were sharp-toothed carnivores.

About 100 million years after the appearance of the first cotylosaurs, reptiles radiated into many orders. At that time, there were far more species of reptiles than there are today. In fact, there were 15 orders of reptiles, compared to only four today.

The fossil record and the anatomy of living animals give clues about how reptiles took over the land from amphibians. The fossil record also shows that reptiles were the ancestors of modern birds and mammals. How did reptiles come to be the dominant land animal? What evidence is there to support the theory that reptiles gave rise to birds and mammals?

34-9 Dinosaurs

The size and appearance of the extinct reptiles known as dinosaurs have made them a source of fascination for many people. Yet a number of misconceptions surround these reptiles. While some dinosaurs were the largest land animals ever to walk on Earth, many were little larger than a dog. While some were ferocious carnivores, most were harmless plant eaters.

The first dinosaurs appear in the fossil record about 200 million years ago. They fall into two distinct groups based on differences in the pelvic girdle, illustrated in Figure 34-10. The **saurischians** [sȯ risk′ ē ənz] had hip bones much like modern lizards. The **ornithischians** [ȯr na this′ kē ənz] were dinosaurs that had hip bones similar to those of modern birds. Some members

Figure 34-10 The structure of the hip bone divides dinosaurs into two distinct groups. *Left: Apatosaurus*, a saurischian: *Right: Iguanodon*, an ornithischian

of both dinosaur groups walked on two legs, while others walked on four.

For many years, scientists assumed that dinosaurs were ectothermic like modern reptiles. Recent evidence indicates that many, if not all dinosaurs may have been endothermic (able to regulate their own body temperature). This idea, however, is not universally accepted.

The last dinosaurs disappeared more than 60 million years before the first humans walked on Earth. One fascinating and unsolved question about Earth's history involves why dinosaurs disappeared so rapidly at the end of the Mesozoic Era.

There are two basic theories as to what may have happened to the dinosaurs. One theory focuses on a major change in climate. It is proposed that temperatures fell and dinosaurs could not survive the cold. The other theory focuses on an extraterrestrial event. Some scientists propose that a large asteroid hit Earth. The force of the collision may have sent out a huge dust cloud that blocked the sun or gave off poisonous gases. Evidence from the fossil record shows unusually high concentrations of certain elements found only in meteorites and asteroids.

34-10 Other Extinct Reptiles

Not all early reptiles were dinosaurs. Many of the creatures people assume were dinosaurs actually belonged to completely different reptilian orders. While the dinosaurs were the dominant land reptiles, two groups of marine reptiles dominated the oceans.

Two marine reptiles appeared in the fossil record about 225 million years ago. They are the **ichthyosaurs** [ik′ thē ō sȯ(ə)rz] and the **plesiosaurs** [plē′ zē ō sȯ(ə)rz]. Ichthyosaurs, like the one illustrated in Figure 34-11, bear a remarkable physical resemblance to modern-day porpoises. This resemblance is a good example of convergent evolution. The ichthyosaurs became extinct many millions of years before the plesiosaurs. Plesiosaurs were carnivores that became extinct about the same time as the dinosaurs.

A group of flying reptiles, or **pterosaurs** [ter′ ə sȯ(ə)rz] also appeared at about the same time as the dinosaurs. These bizarre creatures are not related to modern-day birds. Anatomical studies indicate that the pterosaurs were probably gliders. They do not seem to have had muscles strong enough to beat their wings and take off from the ground. Like ichthyosaurs, the pterosaurs became extinct before the dinosaurs disappeared.

Another group of early reptiles, the **therapsids** [thə rap′ sədz], are of considerable interest. The fossil record seems to indicate that they gave rise to modern-day mammals. Soon after the appearance of the dinosaurs, most therapsids became extinct, however, some descendants survived and appear in the fossil

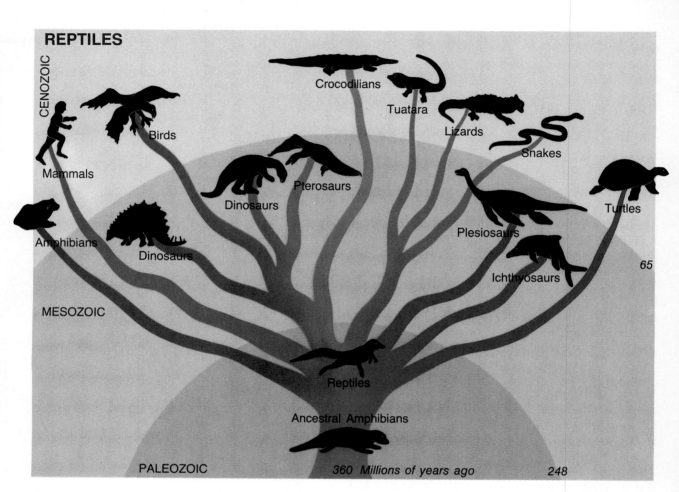

REPLITES

CENOZOIC

Birds

Mammals

Crocodilians

Tuatara

Lizards

Snakes

Pterosaurs

Dinosaurs

Amphibians

Plesiosaurs

Turtles

Dinosaurs

Ichthyosaurs

65

MESOZOIC

Reptiles

Ancestral Amphibians

PALEOZOIC   360 Millions of years ago   248

Figure 34-11 The diagram illustrates one theory of the evolutionary relationships among extinct and modern reptiles as well as modern birds and mammals.

record as bones of very small mammals that looked something like rats. With the unexplained disappearance of the dinosaurs, these therapsid descendants suddenly took over and became the dominant animals on Earth.

CHECKPOINT ◆

12. Name the two groups of dinosaurs.
13. What group of marine reptiles resembled modern-day porpoises?
▶ 14. What group of reptiles probably gave rise to modern birds? to modern mammals?
▶ 15. What evidence can you offer to support the theory that plesiosaurs and ichthyosaurs evolved from a terrestrial reptile ancestor?

▶ Denotes a question that involves *interpreting* and *applying* concepts.

COLOR CHANGE IN A CHAMELEON

Objectives and Skills

- *Observe* the effects of background color and light on the color of a chameleon.
- *Controlling variables* to determine a cause and effect relationship

Materials

2 small aquarium tanks
incandescent light sources
construction paper (various colors)
nonmercury thermometer
American chameleon (*Anolis carolinensis*)

Procedure and Observations

1. Read all of the instructions for this laboratory activity before you begin your work.
2. On a separate piece of paper, draw a data table like the one shown below.
3. Cover the bottom of one aquarium tank with white paper. Gently place the chameleon on the white paper and leave it for five minutes. Record the skin color of the lizard and the tank temperature in your data table. Try to keep the temperature constant throughout the experiment by moving the light sources closer. **CAUTION: Handle the lizard gently at all times. Do not make a lot of noise.**

4. Cover the bottom of the second tank with green paper. Remove the lizard from the first tank and place it into the second tank. Record the color of the paper and the lizard, and the temperature.
5. Repeat this procedure by covering the bottom of the first tank with brown paper and the second with black paper.
6. Using a white background, put the tank in a dark location for five minutes. At the end of the time, bring the lizard into the light. Note its color and record the temperature. Leave the animal in the light for five minutes. Note its color and record the temperature.
7. Before leaving the laboratory, clean up all your materials and wash your hands.

Analysis and Conclusions

1. What is the effect of color, darkness, and light on the skin color of a chameleon?
2. What was the purpose of recording the temperature in each situation?
3. What other variables do you think might be involved in triggering a color change in this animal?
4. Based on your observations, what might be the value of this ability to change color to a chameleon?

DATA TABLE		
Background Color	**Skin Color**	**Temperature**
White		
Green		
Brown		
Black		

CHAPTER REVIEW

Summary

▸ Reptiles are well adapted to life on land. They have impermeable skin, which keeps the animal from drying out. The position of the limbs keeps their body off the ground, making movement over land easier.

▸ Reptile reproduction is also well adapted to land life. Fertilization is internal, and reptiles lay large, shelled eggs. Reptile development occurs entirely within the egg after the egg is laid on land.

▸ A reptile egg is characterized by four membranes. These membranes are the chorion, amnion, allantois, and yolk sac.

▸ Since the skin of a reptile is impermeable, it is not available as a respiratory surface. Therefore, reptile lungs are internally highly folded. The ventricle of the heart is partially divided, which reduces the mixing of oxygenated and deoxygenated blood.

▸ The four orders of living reptiles are Squamata, which include the snakes and lizards; Chelonia, which include the turtles and tortoises; Crocodilia, which include the alligators and crocodiles; and Rhynchocephalia, which includes the tuatara.

▸ While snakes are typical reptiles, they also show a number of special adaptations that reflect their unusual body shape and feeding habits.

▸ There is evidence that all reptiles descended from a group of reptiles called cotylosaurs.

▸ The dinosaurs can be classified into two groups depending on the structure of their pelvic girdles.

▸ During the Mesozoic Era two reptile groups occupied the marine environment, while a group of flying reptiles dominated the air. The marine reptiles, flying reptiles, and dinosaurs became extinct during or at the end of the era.

▸ Some reptiles survived the extinctions of the Mesozoic Era. Among this small group were the therapsids which later gave rise to the mammals.

Vocabulary

allantois	oviparous
amnion	ovoviviparous
basking	pineal eye
carapace	plastron
Chelonia	plesiosaur
chorion	pterosaur
constrictor	Rhynchocephalia
cotylosaur	saurischians
Crocodilia	Squamata
ichthyosaur	terrapin
internal	therapsid
fertilization	tortoise
Jacobson's organ	trachea
keratin	tuatara
ornithischians	yolk sac

Concept Mapping

Construct a concept map for living reptiles. Include the following terms: alligator, Chelonia, Crocodilia, lizard, Rhynchocephalia, snake, Squamata, tortoise, tuatara. Use additional terms as you need them.

Review

1. How does the limb position of reptiles differ from that of amphibians?
2. What is the function of the chorion in a reptilian egg?
3. What function do the chorion and allantois have in common?
4. What reptile behavior assists in regulating body temperature?
5. Name two adaptations of a snake skeleton that allow this animal to swallow large food organisms.
6. What organ in the mouth of a snake aids the sense of smell?
7. How do poisonous snakes inject poison into their prey?

8. What are two anatomical features found in lizards that are not found in snakes?
9. What is unusual about the vertebrae of chelonians?
10. What kinds of organisms can be found in the order Crocodilia?
11. How does a reptile heart differ from an amphibian heart?
12. What primitive reptile group is ancestral to the tuataras?
13. What is the presumed function of the pineal eye of tuataras?
14. What characteristic separates the saurischian dinosaurs from the ornithischian dinosaurs?
15. What do the plesiosaurs and ichthyosaurs have in common?
16. What reptile group is probably ancestral to modern mammals?
17. Compare the snout of a crocodile and an alligator.

Interpret and Apply

18. How is the absence of a pectoral and pelvic girdle in snakes related to the feeding habits of these animals?
19. Describe how the feeding habits of snakes differ from other animals.
20. Why are legless lizards classified as lizards and not snakes?
21. What features distinguish alligators from crocodiles?
22. Tuataras closely resemble lizards. Why are they not placed in the same order?
23. Name three reptile groups that lived on Earth at the same time as the dinosaurs.
24. Most reptiles have claws on their toes. How might clawed toes have become an advantage over unclawed toes?
25. People who look at snakes in zoos often remark that the snake is staring at them. What anatomical feature explains this?

26. Explain how snake teeth are well adapted to their feeding habits.
27. What are two unique features of a Galápagos iguana?
28. What adaptation of chelonians explains their long existence on Earth?

Critical Thinking

29. Why is internal fertilization an important adaptation for terrestrial animals?
30. Snakes and lizards are quite different in many ways. Why do taxonomists consider them enough alike to put them in the same order?
31. Why might an ovoviviparous snake have an advantage over an oviparous snake?
32. What is the adaptive value of reptiles having partially or completely separated ventricles in the heart?
33. It is thought that the aquatic reptiles—both modern and extinct—share the same cotylosaur ancestor. The cotylosaur was a terrestrial animal. Give an explanation as to why some reptiles returned to the water.
34. Describe an example of convergent evolution in the bodies of reptiles and modern mammals.
35. Modern birds are thought to have evolved from reptile ancestors. What reptilian characteristic persists in birds today?
36. A rattlesnake's rattle warns large animals to stay away. What are other warning signs that a snake may be poisonous?
37. While all other members of the Order Rhynchocephalia have become extinct, members of the species tuatara still exist. Suggest possible hypotheses to explain this.

Chapter

35

BIRDS

Overview

CHARACTERISTICS OF BIRDS

35-1 Origin of Birds
35-2 Feathers
35-3 Structures of the Head
35-4 Other External Features

INTERNAL FEATURES OF BIRDS

35-5 Skeleton
35-6 Feeding and Digestion
35-7 Respiratory System
35-8 Circulatory System
35-9 Excretory System
35-10 Nervous System
35-11 Reproduction
35-12 Embryo Development

Why can birds fly?

CHARACTERISTICS OF BIRDS

Agile and graceful are adjectives frequently associated with birds. Birds, with their streamlined bodies, are able to set a course and maneuver around any obstacle. To learn how birds developed such skills, it is important to consider their evolutionary history.

Did you know that birds arose from reptiles? It may be even more surprising to know that many birds have retained some of the typical reptilelike structures.

35-1 Origin of Birds

Recently, scientists in western Texas found two sets of bones that strongly indicate that birds evolved from reptiles. The bones belong to a creature named *Protoavis*, which means "first bird."

Characteristic of reptiles, *Protoavis* had strong, heavy hind limbs, a bony tail, and a pelvis designed for running. The forward parts resembled a bird. It had a well-developed breastbone which was probably used to anchor flight muscles. It also had hollow bones and long forelimbs. *Protoavis* had well-developed ears. This indicates that, like most birds, it communicated by sounds. Reptiles of the time could not communicate vocally. It is not certain whether *Protoavis* had feathers since its fossils did not have feather impressions. Some bones did have small nodes to which feathers could have attached, however.

Protoavis seems to represent a transition between reptiles and birds. Its fossils are believed to be 225 million years old. Modern birds did not appear until 200 million years ago.

35-2 Feathers

Feathers, more than any other characteristic, distinguish birds from all other organisms. Except for their feet and beaks, the entire body of most birds is covered by feathers. Feathers are light yet very strong. This strength is due to the structure of a feather.

Like the scales of reptiles, feathers are made of keratin. However, feathers and scales differ in structure. Rather than having a flat shape as in the scales of reptiles, the keratin in a feather forms a hollow tube called the **shaft**. A hundred or more **barbs** attach to each side of the shaft. Each barb has a fringe of **barbules**. The barbules of one barb connect to those of another barb by means of tiny hooks. About 4 million hooks on a single feather strengthen the structure.

There are three main types of feathers: down feathers, contour feathers, and quill feathers. The feathers closest to the body are

Section Objectives

A *Compare* the features of *Protoavis* with those of birds and reptiles.

B *Describe* three types of feathers and *explain* how each one functions.

C *List* and *explain* the function of the external features of a bird.

D *Discuss* ways in which the structure of the feet and wings reflect a bird's way of life.

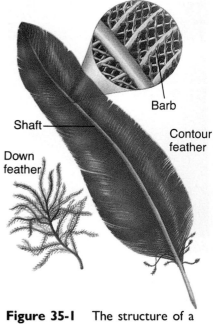

Barb

Shaft

Contour feather

Down feather

Figure 35-1 The structure of a quill feather is very elaborate. The barbules of one barb overlap the barbules of a nearby barb. If any of the barbs split, a bird will use its beak to rehook the barbules.

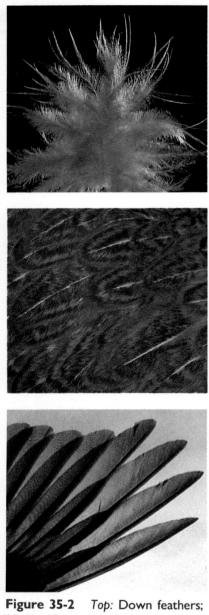

Figure 35-2 *Top:* Down feathers; *Middle:* Contour feathers; *Bottom:* Quill feathers. Each has a different function.

called **down feathers**. Down feathers are most obvious in newly hatched birds and in water birds. These feathers insulate the body against heat loss. Birds have body temperatures as high as 45°C, much higher than the surrounding air or water. Without down feathers, a bird would freeze to death.

Covering the down feathers are **contour feathers**. As their name implies, they give shape to a bird's body, making it streamlined for flight. Contour feathers also give a bird its coloration. Brown or gray contour feathers may help a bird blend in with its surroundings.

Colored feathers may act as a signaling device to other birds. A bird's color helps it to establish its territory and to attract a mate during mating season. Color is one feature that identifies one bird to another bird as a member of the same species.

The third group of feathers, **quill feathers**, grow on the wings and tail. Like the wings and tail of an airplane, the quill feathers help the bird to lift, balance, and steer while in the air.

Most birds have an oil gland at the base of the tail. With its beak, a bird spreads the oil over its feathers to waterproof them. This is especially important in water birds.

Many birds periodically lose feathers. The loss is gradual, with new feathers replacing those that are lost. This replacement of feathers is called **molting**.

35-3 Structures of the Head

A bird's beak is also made of keratin. Two **nares**, or nostrils, located on the beak function in breathing. The beak, unlike the reptilian mouth, is toothless. Birds use their beaks for scratching, cleaning, repairing feathers, collecting nesting materials, and as weapons to fight off enemies. Most importantly, birds use their beaks to obtain food.

The size and shape of a bird's beak are adapted to the type of food it eats. For example, a flamingo's beak contains a sieve that strains tiny crustaceans out of the water. The large, hooked beak of a parrot allows it to crack the shells of nuts, which is no small task. The beak of a sword-billed hummingbird is four times longer than the body of the bird. The hummingbird's food source is nectar that lies deep within flowers. A shorter beak would not allow the hummingbird to reach the nectar.

Birds have keen vision. They are able to see colors and discern objects at great distances. Such keen vision is useful to predatory birds, such as hawks, in searching for mice or other prey. It also allows other birds to watch for predators.

The eyes of most birds are located on the sides of the head. As a result, both eyes cannot look in the same direction at once.

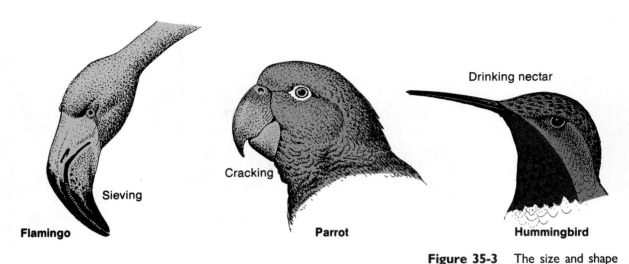

Sieving

Flamingo

Cracking

Parrot

Drinking nectar

Hummingbird

Figure 35-3 The size and shape of a bird's beak are adaptations to the type of food it eats.

A few birds, such as owls, have eyes located at the front of the head. This position allows owls to focus both eyes on a single object and to judge distances with great accuracy.

The ears of a bird are located directly behind the eyes. They are not obvious because feathers cover and protect them. A bird's hearing is acute. Canals starting at the outer ears lead to eardrums, or tympanic membranes, within the head. Eustachian tubes connect the mouth cavity with the eardrums and keep the pressure equal on both sides of the eardrum.

The senses of smell and taste are not well-developed in birds. Birds rely instead upon their senses of hearing and sight. A bird's tongue is used merely as a means of picking up food.

The neck is quite flexible. A bird can turn its head 180 degrees so that it can look directly behind itself. This movement is possible because there are many more vertebrae in the neck of a bird than in the necks of other vertebrates.

35-4 Other External Features

Unlike most vertebrates, birds stand on two legs. A bird's forelimbs are wings, rather than arms or fins. Its tail consists only of feathers, not of bones like the reptilian tail. Bones would be too heavy for efficient flight.

Like reptiles, birds' feet are clawed and covered with keratin scales. The feet vary with a bird's life-style. A typical bird's foot has four toes, three pointing forward and one pointing backward. This arrangement permits easy perching. Some birds, such as ducks, have webbed feet that allow them to swim. Others, such as hawks and eagles, have pointed talons that they use to kill their prey.

Figure 35-4 The major external features of a bird. Note the reptilian appearance of the feet and legs.

Eye

Ear

Beak

Wings

Breast

Scales on legs

Claws

Tail feathers

Birds **573**

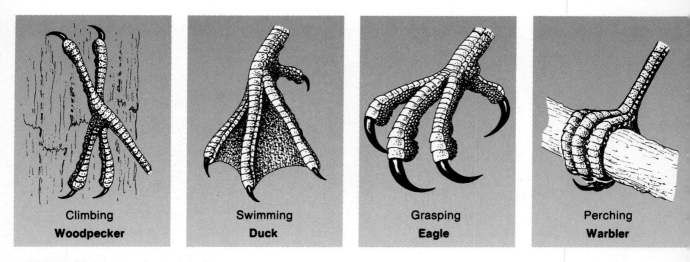

Climbing	Swimming	Grasping	Perching
Woodpecker	**Duck**	**Eagle**	**Warbler**

Figure 35-5 The structure of a bird's foot reflects its way of life.

Wings vary greatly in size and shape. Birds with long wings, such as swifts, falcons, and many sea birds, are long-distance fliers. They require wide-open spaces to accelerate, turn, glide, and brake. They rely upon their speed to escape from enemies.

Short-distance fliers live in woods, bushes, and reeds. Their short, wide wings do not permit long, swift flight but do allow them to turn easily in crowded areas. Blackbirds are examples of short-distance fliers.

Some birds, such as ostriches, penguins, and cassowaries, have lost the ability to fly. Many flightless birds have other protective adaptations. A cassowary, for example, can kick a large animal hard enough to rip its body open.

CHECKPOINT ◆

1. What similarities existed between *Protoavis* and reptiles? Between *Protoavis* and birds?
2. What structural adaptation is found in the feet of most swimming birds? In most grasping birds?
3. Name three types of feathers and describe how each one functions.
4. Compare the distance traveled by a bird with short wings and a bird with long wings.
5. What are two functions of the beak?
▶ 6. _____ feathers are to insulation as quill feathers are to balance.
▶ 7. Suppose that a mutation occurred, causing a bird's vertebrae to extend into a tail. Is it likely that such a mutation would be preserved by the environment? Explain.

▶ Denotes a question that involves *interpreting* and *applying* concepts.

INTERNAL FEATURES OF BIRDS

Have you ever watched an airplane taking off from an airport? It is truly an impressive sight. The airplane seems to rise up and cut through the air effortlessly. However, without certain design and structural features, an airplane would never get off the ground.

Engineers who design airplanes use birds as one of their models. The shape and internal structure of birds have provided engineers with a tremendous amount of insight into nature's ultimate flying machine. How are the structural features of a bird adapted for flight? What internal adaptations enable birds to fly?

35-5 Skeleton

A bird's skeleton is the heaviest part of its body. Compared to the skeletons of other vertebrates, though, the bird's skeleton is very light. The bones are hollow. Their strength is provided by cross struts, which add little weight. The bird's skeleton is composed of the pectoral and pelvic girdles, cranium, backbone, and limbs. Can you find each of these features in Figure 35-6?

The breastbone, or **keel**, is much larger than most of the bones in a bird's body. The keel provides a point of attachment for the powerful flight muscles. The other end of the muscles attach

Section Objectives

E *Explain* how a bird's skeleton is adapted for flight.

F *Relate* the energy requirements of a bird to the function of each of its body systems.

G *Describe* how the internal organs of a bird are adapted for flight.

H *Cite* examples of complex behavior in birds.

I *Discuss* reproduction and development in birds.

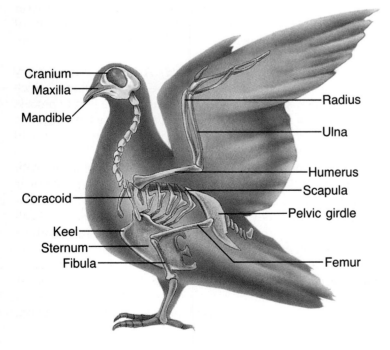

Figure 35-6 The skeletal features of a bird reveal a sleek, streamlined design.

to the bones in the upper part of the wing. A bird in flight moves its wings much as you move your arms when you row a boat. The wings go downward and backward, then upward and forward to their original position.

35-6 Feeding and Digestion

Flying requires an enormous amount of energy. A bird's body has many adaptations that help to provide the necessary energy. One adaptation is the maintenance of a high body temperature. To maintain a high body temperature, birds require large quantities of food. The foods of most birds, such as fish, nuts, fruit, nectar, and insects, are high in calories.

Because birds have no teeth, they cannot chew their food. Birds usually swallow their food whole. After a bird takes food into its beak, the food passes through the pharynx and down the esophagus. The **crop**, an enlargement at the base of the esophagus, stores the food and moistens it in preparation for digestion.

The stomach is divided into two parts. The first part is the pro-ventriculus. The walls of the **proventriculus** [prō ven trik′ yə ləs] secrete gastric fluid that mixes with the food. The gastric fluid contains digestive enzymes. The second division of the stomach, the **gizzard**, then receives the food. The gizzard is composed of two hard plates that rub against one another, crushing the food between them. Breaking the food into smaller pieces helps digest the food.

After leaving the gizzard, the partially digested food passes into the intestine. Usable food is absorbed through the walls of the intestine. Indigestible food passes into the rectum and finally out through the cloaca.

Digestion in birds proceeds rapidly. A bird can eat a berry and evacuate the seed from its body within 12 minutes. Such efficient digestion has two advantages. It allows the bird to process a large amount of food in a short time. Also, it eliminates unusable food quickly, so that the bird will not be carrying extra weight during flight.

The large quantities of food ingested by birds, combined with the insulation of the feathers, provide the means to regulate their body temperatures internally. This characteristic, called **endo-thermy**, is generally not found in reptiles or amphibians. Recall that most reptiles maintain their body temperatures by absorbing or releasing heat to the surrounding environment. Endothermy allows birds to remain active even in very cold temperatures.

Endothermy requires more food in order to fuel the higher rate of metabolism. Since they must have a large and constant supply of food, many birds **migrate**, or move to another location, when food is scarce. Migration among most birds occurs in late fall. The birds return in the spring when food is more plentiful.

Recall from Chapter 6 that animals obtain energy by the process of respiration. In respiration, molecules of digested food combine with oxygen in the mitochondria, forming ATP. Therefore, in addition to having a large food requirement, birds also require a large supply of oxygen. The respiratory and circulatory systems provide this oxygen.

35-7 Respiratory System

The respiratory system contains **air sacs** in addition to lungs and airways. The air sacs fill many spaces in the body cavity and even in some of the hollow bones. Air sacs allow a bird to inhale a large volume of air at one time.

Air enters the respiratory system through the nares in a bird's beak. It travels through the pharynx, larynx, trachea, and **syrinx**, or a bird's voice box. Below the syrinx, the trachea branches into two tubes called bronchi. Each **bronchus** passes through a lung and enters a posterior air sac. Smaller bronchi branch off the main bronchi in the lungs, leading to the anterior air sacs. Gas exchange occurs through the small bronchi. Use the illustration in Figure 35-7 to trace the path of air as it moves through the body of a bird.

Lungs

Air sacs

Air sacs

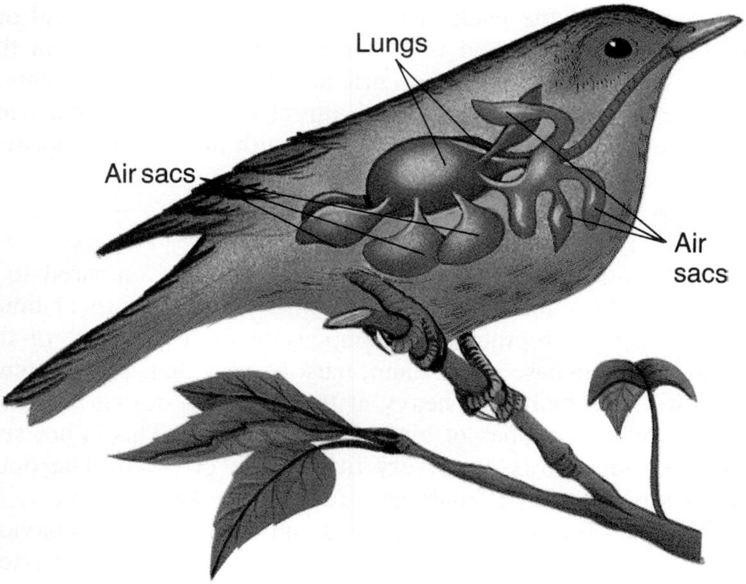

Figure 35-7 The internal anatomy of a bird is compact and highly efficient. Each of the internal organs function in a way that minimizes excess weight and energy consumption.

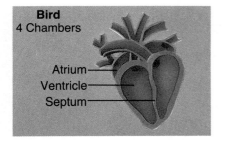

Figure 35-8 Birds have four-chambered hearts. Which is the last chamber through which blood passes before leaving the heart?

While air is traveling from the lungs to the anterior air sacs after inhaling, oxygen is entering the blood and carbon dioxide is entering the bronchi. When a bird exhales, the oxygen-rich air from the posterior air sacs enters the lungs through the small bronchi, and gas exchange occurs again. Thus, unlike other animals, a bird exchanges carbon dioxide for oxygen both while inhaling and exhaling.

35-8 Circulatory System

Once oxygen has entered the bloodstream, it must be pumped to all the tissues of the body. This task is accomplished by the heart. The heart of a bird, illustrated in Figure 35-8, contains four distinct chambers: two atria and two ventricles. The atria are thin-walled. The ventricles are thick-walled and muscular. Their function is to pump the blood.

The complete separation of the ventricles divides the heart into two separate pumps. The right side pumps deoxygenated blood from the body to the lungs, where it gains oxygen and loses carbon dioxide. The left side of the heart receives oxygenated blood from the lungs and pumps it through the aorta to the rest of the body. Thus the four-chambered heart does not allow oxygenated blood to mix with deoxygenated blood. The tissues of the body receive only blood that is rich in oxygen. This is especially important for an animal with a high oxygen requirement.

35-9 Excretory System

The excretory system of a bird is simple. The two kidneys, located toward the back of the bird's body, filter uric acid out of the blood. Uric acid is a waste product left over from the breakdown of proteins. When uric acid leaves a kidney, it enters a ureter. The two ureters empty directly into the cloaca, from which uric acid leaves the body along with the digestive wastes.

35-10 Nervous System

A bird's nervous system is highly developed. Compared to a reptile of the same body weight, a bird's brain is 6 to 11 times larger than the reptile's. To compensate for the weight of the brain, the brain case, or cranium, must be very thin. This prevents the bird from being too heavy at the head end during flight.

The olfactory lobes of birds are quite small. This is not surprising, since birds have very little sense of smell. The optic lobes are quite large, enabling birds to have keen vision.

The cerebrum is greatly enlarged, allowing complex behavior. In addition to being the seat of learned and unlearned behavior, the cerebrum is also the center for the controls that allow a bird to hop, fly, and swim. The cerebellum, which controls muscular coordination, is well-developed. The medulla controls functions such as breathing. It lies at the base of the brain and joins the upper end of the spinal cord.

35-11 Reproduction

The female bird has only one ovary. As birds evolved, the other ovary was probably lost as an adaptation for less weight during flight. Eggs develop in the ovary and leave through the oviduct.

The testes of the male bird lie above its kidneys. The sperm leave the testes through small tubes called the **vas deferens**, which lead to the cloaca.

When breeding season arrives, nest-building begins. Nests are usually inconspicuous because conspicuous nests would attract unwanted visitors. The type of nest a bird builds depends upon its species, where it lives, and the materials available. Tailor birds in India "sew" together the leaves of a tree, using plant fibers as thread. The male hornbill seals his mate and their eggs into a hole in a tree by covering the hole with mud. He leaves only a small opening, through which he passes food to his mate.

Once the nest has been built, the birds mate. When two birds mate, the male mounts the female so that their cloaca touch. Sperm from the male enters the female. The sperm can survive inside the female for long periods of time. One mating may be enough to fertilize many eggs.

Like reptiles, birds have internal fertilization. Fertilization occurs in the upper part of the oviduct. The newly fertilized egg consists of a yolk, on which rests the tiny embryo. The yolk contains fats and proteins that provide nutrients for the embryo.

Figure 35-9 Nesting behavior varies greatly among birds. Nesting in a tree is a behavior commonly associated with birds. The kingfisher builds its nest in the side of a riverbank.

CONSUMER BIOLOGY

Pores in an eggshell allow evaporation to occur from the egg. One can determine whether or not an egg is fresh by whether it sinks or floats when placed in water. A fresh egg has a small air pocket, making it heavy enough to sink. Over time the liquid inside evaporates, leaving a large air space which causes the egg to float in water.

DO YOU KNOW?

Word Root: The word *albumen* is derived from the Latin word *albus* which means "white."

First, the white, or **albumen**, is laid down. This contains protein and is another food source for the developing bird. Strands of stringy material called **chalaza** [kə la′ zə] suspend the embryo from the ends of the egg. This keeps the embryo from pressing against the wall of the egg. An outer membrane and a shell are secreted around the white by a gland. Additional glands deposit pigment on the shell.

A bird lays the fully formed egg less than two days after fertilization. A fertilized egg is illustrated in Figure 35-10. The shell protects the developing embryo without closing off the embryo from its environment. The shell has pores through which oxygen and carbon dioxide can pass.

Even as an embryo, a bird must maintain a high body temperature. Therefore, the parents must **incubate** the eggs, or keep them warm. In some species, only the mother sits on the eggs. In others, both parents share the brooding. A few species have developed alternatives to sitting on eggs, such as burying them in rotting plant matter or in volcanic ash. The North American cowbird lays its look-alike eggs in the nest of another species, tricking the foster parent into caring for the cowbird's young.

In preparation for incubation, a parent bird will loosen or pull a patch of feathers from the part of its chest that will contact the eggs. Beneath the skin of the **brood patch**, the blood vessels enlarge, bringing heat to the surface of the skin that is in contact with the eggs.

The period necessary for incubation varies with the size of the bird. The larger the bird, the longer the time required for incubation. Incubation times range from about two weeks to almost two months.

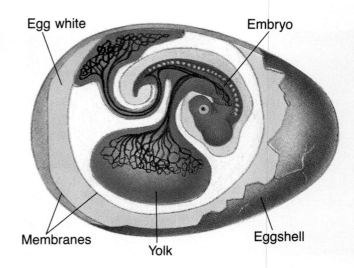

Figure 35-10 As a fertilized egg moves down the oviduct, layers of material are added to the egg which provide nutrition and protection.

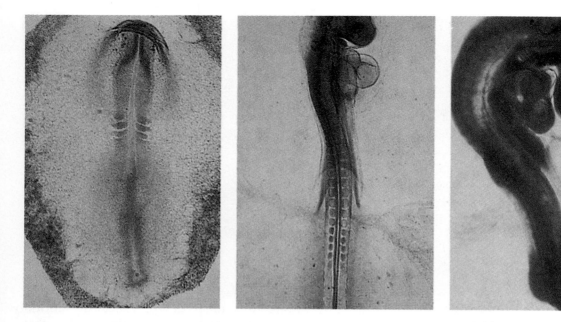

35-12 Embryo Development

When fertilization has occurred and the egg is warm enough, development proceeds. The zygote, which begins as a speck on the yolk, divides until the resulting cells cover the surface of the yolk. The cells develop into different types of tissues and organs.

A membrane grows out of the embryo's digestive system, enveloping the yolk. This membrane, called the yolk sac, produces digestive enzymes. The enzymes digest the food in the yolk. Blood vessels in the yolk sac deliver the digested food to the embryo. As the embryo grows, the yolk decreases in size. Like a reptilian egg, a bird's egg also contains three membranes besides the yolk sac. They are the amnion, the allantois, and the chorion.

The development of a chick embryo is illustrated in Figure 35-11. When the embryo has completed its growth within the shell, it pecks at the shell with a special structure called an **egg tooth**. The embryo eventually cracks the shell and continues pecking until the shell cracks enough for the young bird to emerge. The egg tooth disappears soon after hatching.

The number of eggs a bird species lays depends in part on how much care the newly hatched birds will require. If the young birds require much care, few eggs will be laid. If one or more eggs are lost before incubation begins, the female will lay more eggs to replace them. Even if the entire **clutch**, or group, of eggs is lost, the female will replace all of them if it is not too late in the breeding season. Cool temperatures do not harm the embryos during early stages of development. In most birds, incubation

DO YOU KNOW?

Information: If you remove an egg each time it is laid, the hen continues to lay eggs. It is not uncommon for domestic hens to lay 200 to 300 eggs in a year or over a thousand in a lifetime.

Figure 35-12 *Left:* Warblers are altricial birds that lay few eggs and produce young that are almost featherless. *Right:* Swans are precocial birds that lay large numbers of eggs and produce young that are downy and well developed.

does not begin until all the eggs have been laid. All the eggs hatch at about the same time.

Most birds belong to another group, called the **altricial** [al trish′ əl] birds. Altricial birds are quite helpless when they hatch. They are blind, often naked, and completely dependent upon their parents. The female of an altricial species lays fewer eggs than that of a precocial species. Blackbirds, nuthatches, and pigeons are examples of altricial birds.

Some birds, called **precocial** [pri kō′ shəl] birds, are quite advanced in their development when they hatch. They have down coats, can feed themselves, hop, and swim. Ducks, chickens, and swans are examples of precocial birds.

In altricial species, the parents feed the fast-growing young, bring them water, clean the nest, warm the young birds, and shield them from sun and rain. As you might expect, precocial birds take longer to develop in the egg than altricial birds do.

CHECKPOINT ◆

8. To which bone in a bird's skeleton are the flight muscles attached?
9. How is the excretory system of the bird adapted for flight?
10. What term is used to describe an organism's ability to regulate its body temperature?
11. Why does a bird pluck feathers from its brood patch?
12. What do scientists call birds that hatch in a helpless state?
▶ 13. People often say that someone with a small appetite "eats like a bird." Why is this expression inaccurate?

▶ Denotes a question that involves *interpreting* and *applying* concepts.

DENSITY OF BONES

In this activity, you will demonstrate how a bird's skeleton is adapted for flight.

Objectives and Skills

☐ *Determine* the density of bird and mammal bones.
☐ *Compare* the density of a bird bone to that of a mammal bone.
☐ *Relate* the density of a bird's bones to its ability to fly.

Materials

balance, centigram   hammer
graduated cylin-   blank paper
  der, 250-mL   chicken bone
safety goggles   beef bone

Procedure and Observations

1. Read all instructions for this laboratory activity before you begin your work.
2. On a separate piece of paper, draw a data table like the one shown below.
3. Use the balance to determine the mass of each bone. Record the data under the appropriate heading in your data table.
4. Use water displacement to determine the volume of each bone. Pour 100 mL of water into the graduated cylinder. (Remember that the volume of a liquid is read from the bottom of the meniscus.)
5. Tilt the graduated cylinder slightly. Place one of the bones on the edge of the cylinder and release it slowly. Read the new volume of water. Subtract the initial volume from the new volume of water. Record the difference in the data table. Repeat this procedure with the other bone.
6. Use the formula $D = M/V$ to determine the density of each bone. Record the values in the data table.
7. Put on your safety goggles. Observe the internal structure of each bone by breaking them open carefully with a hammer.
8. Draw a line down the middle of a blank sheet of paper. Label each side as either *Chicken* or *Beef*. Draw the internal structure of each bone on your paper.
9. Before leaving the laboratory, clean up all your materials and wash your hands thoroughly.

Analysis and Conclusions

1. Which bone had the higher density?
2. Describe how the internal structure of each bone contributes to its density.
3. Which structural feature adds strength to a bird's bones?
4. What aspects of the bones enable a bird to fly?

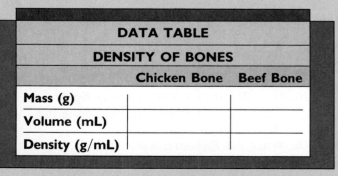

DATA TABLE		
DENSITY OF BONES		
	Chicken Bone	Beef Bone
Mass (g)		
Volume (mL)		
Density (g/mL)		

CHAPTER REVIEW

Summary

▶ *Protoavis* was a primitive creature that showed characteristics of reptiles and birds. Fossils of *Protoavis* appeared about 90 million years before fossils of modern birds. *Protoavis* is thought to have been the ancestor of modern birds.

▶ All birds have feathers. A body covering of feathers aids in flight, insulation, and communication with other birds. Other characteristics of birds include endothermy, development from amniotic eggs, and internal fertilization.

▶ Birds have a well-developed nervous system. Their senses of sight and hearing are acute, their movements are well-coordinated, and their behaviors are complex.

▶ Modifications in the structure of a bird's claws, wings, and beak reflect their way of life.

▶ Modifications for efficient flight include air sacs, a hollow skeleton, lack of teeth, absence of a urinary bladder, and a simple reproductive system. Other adaptations include rapid digestion and excretion to eliminate excess waste.

▶ A four-chambered heart and an efficient circulatory system deliver large amounts of oxygen to the flight muscles.

▶ Courtship, nestbuilding, and care of the young all involve behavior rituals that vary among species.

▶ All birds lay eggs after internal fertilization has occurred. These eggs are similar to those of reptiles.

▶ Upon hatching, precocial birds can regulate their body temperature, obtain their own food, and move about. Altricial birds are less developed at the time of hatching, and require much care from their parents.

Vocabulary

air sacs	gizzard
albumen	incubate
altricial	keel
barbs	migrate
barbules	molting
bronchus	nares
brood patch	precocial
chalaza	*Protoavis*
clutch	proventriculus
contour feathers	quill feathers
crop	shaft
down feathers	syrinx
egg tooth	vas deferens
endothermy	

Concept Mapping

Construct a concept map for bird development. Include the following terms: down, egg tooth, altricial, precocial, clutch. Use additional terms as you need them.

Review

1. Name three bird structures made of keratin.
2. Which two of the bird's senses are best developed?
3. Name a feature of a male bird that is used to attract a mate.
4. What features did *Protoavis* have that classify it as a bird?
5. What feature of a bird's skeleton makes it lighter than the skeletons of most other vertebrates?
6. How do air sacs help a bird in flight?
7. What is the first organ to develop in the chick embryo?
8. When did *Protoavis* live?

9. Which is *not* a function of feathers? (a) attracting a mate (b) balancing during flight (c) feeding of the young (d) signaling to other birds (e) maintaining high body temperature
10. The function of the chalaza is to (a) provide the embryo with food, (b) hold moisture, (c) camouflage the egg, (d) keep the embryo from pressing against the walls of the egg.
11. Which of the following is *not* a membrane in a bird's egg? (a) yolk (b) yolk sac (c) allantois (d) amnion
12. What function does each of the following perform?
    a. down feathers
    b. contour feathers
    c. quill feathers
    d. gizzard
    e. keel
    f. air sacs
    g. shell

Match the bird characteristics on the left with the correct statement on the right.

13. has webbed feet
14. long incubation
15. few eggs per clutch
16. has a long slender beak

    a. lives on or near water
    b. offspring are precocial
    c. offspring are altricial
    d. sucks nectar from flowers

Interpret and Apply

17. Compare altricial and precocial birds.
18. List several differences between birds and reptiles.
19. Name several structural features that lessen the weight of a bird for flight.

20. Name, in order, the parts of a bird's digestive system through which food passes.
21. Does the peacock share incubating duties with the peahen? Explain.
22. Place the following feather parts in order (from fewest to most plentiful) for a given bird: barbs, barbules, feathers, hooks.
23. Compare the functions of a bird's crop and gizzard with those of an earthworm.
24. How does its four-chambered heart aid a bird in flight?
25. Which of the following does not belong with the others? (a) four-chambered heart (b) high oxygen requirement (c) low metabolic rate (d) endothermy.
26. What effect would a damaged cerebellum have on a bird's ability to fly?

Critical Thinking

27. Name several structures that are found in birds but not in other types of vertebrates. How are these structures an advantage to a bird?
28. Which bird has a longer incubation period, a hummingbird or an ostrich?
29. What would happen to a bird whose feather barbules lacked hooks?
30. Make a table comparing the following characteristics of reptiles, *Protoavis*, and birds: bone structure, tail (if present), mouth, body covering, forelimbs.
31. How is endothermy an advantage to birds?
32. What is the advantage of starting the incubation of all eggs in a clutch at the same time?

Chapter
36

MAMMALS

Overview

CHARACTERISTICS OF MAMMALS
36-1 Common Features of Mammals
36-2 Mammalian Development

MONOTREMES AND MARSUPIALS
36-3 Characteristics of Monotremes
36-4 Characteristics of Marsupials
36-5 Representative Marsupials

PLACENTAL MAMMALS
36-6 Characteristics of Placental Mammals
36-7 Some Types of Placentals

MAMMAL EVOLUTION
36-8 Origin of Mammals
36-9 Rise of Modern Horses: An Example of Mammalian Evolution

Why can a polar bear be thought of as a "solar bear"?

CHARACTERISTICS OF MAMMALS

Have you ever felt beads of sweat running down your back after heavy exercise? Have you ever felt sticky at the end of the day? These two sensations make most people uncomfortable. However, without the ability to sweat, you could actually die by overheating.

Water is secreted on to the skin by sweat glands. The evaporation of sweat helps to cool the body. Sweat glands are found only in mammals. The glands are important in maintaining the body temperature within narrow limits.

Sweat glands are not the only characteristic unique to mammals. What other traits are unique among mammals?

36-1 Common Features of Mammals

Mammals have the most complex brains of all the vertebrates. The cerebrum is the largest structure of the mammalian brain. A large cerebrum allows mammals to perform complex types of behavior. The capacity of the mammalian brain is further increased because its surface is folded upon itself in ridges and grooves called **convolutions**. This folding fits more surface area into the unexpandable volume of the bony skull. The senses of hearing and smell are typically well developed.

Like birds, mammals are endothermic. Also, like birds, mammals have four-chambered hearts. Complete separation of oxygenated and deoxygenated blood ensures a good supply of oxygen to the body tissues. This oxygen supply is essential for the maintenance of endothermy.

Mammals breathe with well-developed lungs. Their intake of air is aided by a strong muscle located between the lungs and the abdomen called the **diaphragm**.

All mammals have some hair. The hair covering and the air layer trapped beneath the hair prevent mammals from losing body heat. This contributes to their success as warm-blooded animals. Many aquatic mammals have lost much of their hair as a streamlining adaptation. Their warmth comes from a thick layer of **blubber**, or fat, beneath their skin.

Mammalian skin contains four unique types of glands. The most important of these are the **mammary glands**. Milk secreted from these glands provides nourishment for the young. Sweat glands help to regulate the body temperature and rid the body of wastes. **Sebaceous** [si bā shəs] **glands** lubricate the hair and skin. Scent glands produce chemical substances that help mammals communicate with each other.

Most mammals have highly developed teeth. The diversity of mammalian teeth reflects the great variety of mammalian diets.

Section Objectives

A *List* and *describe* the structural characteristics of mammals.

B *Describe* the mammalian circulatory system.

C *Explain* the function of each of the four skin glands.

D *Discuss* the development of mammalian young.

Figure 36-1 This comparison shows the more highly developed teeth of a mammal versus a reptile.

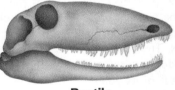

Reptile

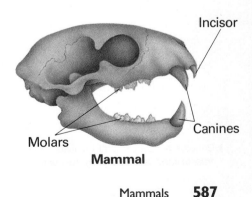

Incisor

Canines

Molars

Mammal

Figure 36-2 Mammals protect their young after birth and teach them survival techniques.

Structure Is Related to Function: The milk from most mammary glands is about 85% water. The remaining 15% is composed of carbohydrates, fats, proteins, vitamins, and minerals. Although the milk of all mammals contains the same nutrients, the proportions of nutrients vary from species to species. Thus, the milk of each species is ideally suited to the nutritional needs of its young.

36-2 Mammalian Development

Mammals, like reptiles and birds, reproduce by internal fertilization. With few exceptions, mammals do not lay eggs. Most mammals bear live young. In most mammals the embryo develops in a muscular organ called the **uterus.** Thus the developing embryo is protected by its mother's body.

After birth, the young continue to receive maternal care. They receive nutrition from the milk they obtain from their mother's mammary glands. In addition to providing their food, the mother protects them from natural enemies and teaches them to find their own food. Generally, the more complex behavior a mammal is capable of, the longer it associates with its mother after birth.

The period of maternal association reaches its extreme in humans. Born after nine months of development within the uterus, an infant is helpless and totally dependent at birth. For many years after birth, the young human learns amazingly complex social and intellectual behaviors from its parents.

CHECKPOINT ◆

1. Name five unique features of mammalian skin and body covering.
2. Explain how a mammal's circulatory system contributes to its endothermy.
3. What substance is produced in mammary glands?
▶ 4. A young mouse spends one month with its mother after birth, whereas an elephant spends several years. Which organism is more likely to show complex behavior?

▶ Denotes a question that involves *interpreting* and *applying* concepts.

MONOTREMES AND MARSUPIALS

Did you know that some mammals develop inside an egg? Did you know that other mammals develop in a pouch *outside* the mother's body? These methods of reproduction seem very different from the internal development you read about in the first lesson. All mammals share many characteristics. However, the mammal class is divided into three groups based on their different method of reproduction. These groups are the monotremes, the marsupials, and the placentals.

Monotremes, the most primitive of the living mammals, lay eggs and incubate them in a birdlike fashion. **Marsupials** are the pouched mammals. They bear tiny, premature young. These bee-sized young leave the mother's uterus and crawl up to the pouch. Here they attach to nipples and complete their development. These two groups are found mainly in Australia, New Guinea, New Zealand, and Tasmania. What other characteristics are unique to monotremes and marsupials? What characteristics set them apart from their distant relatives, humans?

36-3 Characteristics of Monotremes

Like all mammals, monotremes are covered with hair. They are warm-blooded and produce milk that nourishes their young. As in reptiles and birds, their cloaca serves excretory and reproductive functions. Fertilization is internal but the embryos develop externally in eggs. The eggs are incubated.

The heads of monotremes are remarkably birdlike in appearance. They have long, leathery, beaklike extensions of the face. The adults are toothless and lack external ears.

There are only three species of monotremes. The duck-billed platypus and two species of spiny anteaters are restricted to New Guinea, Australia, and Tasmania.

The duck-billed platypus is a small mammal about the size of a large squirrel. It is semiaquatic and has webbed feet tipped with claws. When swimming, the platypus paddles with its forefeet and steers with its hind feet. It uses its leathery bill to probe for crustaceans and plants that live at the bottom of the water. The claws are used for burrowing when on land.

After the female platypus mates, she digs a long burrow. At the end of the burrow she lays two eggs on a bed of moist leaves. The female platypus curls her body around the eggs during the 10-day incubation period. The platypus lacks nipples. Milk for the young is produced by sweat glands on the female's underside. When the young hatch, they get nourishment by licking milk from the mother's fur.

Section Objectives

E *Discuss* the geographic distribution of marsupials and monotremes.

F *Identify* and *describe* the three species of monotremes.

G *List* the characteristics of monotremes.

H *Describe* the characteristics of marsupials.

I *Explain* the developmental process in marsupials.

Figure 36-3 The duck-billed platypus was viewed with much skepticism when it was first discovered. Scientists at the time thought that the creature was a hoax. They believed that the bill and limbs of a duck had somehow been attached to the duck-billed platypus.

Mammals **589**

Figure 36-4 The spiny anteater is a monotreme. Other kinds of anteaters are placental mammals.

Figure 36-5 What evidence of underdevelopment do you notice in these newborn opossums?

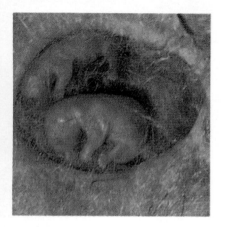

Both species of spiny anteater are covered with coarse hair and sturdy spines. Their masses range from 2 to 10 kilograms. Spiny anteaters have large, convoluted brains. Their powerful limbs are tipped with claws adapted for digging. They escape predators by burrowing rapidly into the ground. Spiny anteaters have long slender snouts. When foraging, they turn over stones and break into termite and ant nests. Anteaters capture their prey with their long, sticky tongues.

The female spiny anteater lays a single leathery egg, which she incubates in a pouch on her belly. The young are helpless when they hatch and remain in the pouch until their spines form.

36-4 Characteristics of Marsupials

Fertilization is internal in marsupials. Development of embryos begins in the mother's uterus. The embryos have tiny yolk sacs, which provide only a limited food supply. Therefore, the young are born very early in development.

At birth, the tiny marsupial young crawl from the mother's uterus, through her cloaca, across her fur, and into the pouch. There the young attach to the nipples of the mammary glands. The pouch protects the young. This pouch is the most striking characteristic of marsupial mammals. Milk from the nipples provides nourishment until the young are mature enough to be independent of the mother. The length of time spent in the pouch depends upon the species.

36-5 Representative Marsupials

Opossums are the only North American marsupials. They are active at night and live mostly in rural areas. They eat small birds and mammals, eggs, and insects. The opossum has the shortest period of **gestation**, or development within the mother's body, of any mammal known. The young are born only 12½ days after fertilization; 6 to 24 young are born at a time. They crawl through the mother's fur and into the pouch, where they attach to the nipples. After spending several weeks in the pouch, the young leave the pouch but still cling to their mother's fur.

There are many species of opossums in Central and South America. One type, called the water opossum, has a pouch with a muscle that can close the pouch the way that strings close a drawstring bag. The mother can then submerge herself, still keeping the young marsupials dry. They can remain in the pouch underwater for several minutes because they can tolerate high levels of carbon dioxide.

The marsupial mole is a rodentlike marsupial that lives in Australia. Since it is a burrowing animal, its pouch opens at the

Figure 36-6 Red kangaroos, which stand as tall as people, are the largest kangaroos.

posterior end of its body. This protects the young in the pouch when the mother burrows through the dirt.

The koala, a large, slow-moving marsupial, lives in eucalyptus trees. It eats the leaves of only a few species of eucalyptus trees. Only one koala is born at a time. It spends six months in its mother's pouch, and another six on her back.

Perhaps the best known of the marsupials are the kangaroos. Kangaroos are grass eaters. Smaller kangaroos are called wallabies. They have enormous, powerful hind legs. Their large tail helps them balance when they hop. They can hop along at speeds up to 60 kilometers per hour and can jump over fences nearly 3 meters high.

The red kangaroo's reproductive pattern is unusual. At any time in her adult life, the female may have three dependent young. One is an embryo in the uterus, one is a newborn in the pouch, and one is an older offspring that lives outside the pouch but returns to nurse.

■ BIOLOGY INSIGHT

Adaptation and Evolution: Many marsupial mammals in Australia are remarkably similar to placental mammals in North America. For example, there are marsupial wolves, mice, and moles. This similarity is the result of convergent evolution. Convergent evolution occurs when organisms are subjected to similar selective pressures.

CHECKPOINT ◆

5. Name the three species of monotremes.
6. In what parts of the world are monotremes found? Marsupials?
7. What reproductive characteristic classifies monotremes as primitive mammals?
8. What characteristic do all marsupials share?
▶ 9. Opossums can produce as many as 24 offspring at one time. Why are so many offspring born?
▶ 10. Compare the method of nutrition among young monotremes with that of young marsupials.

▶ Denotes a question that involves *interpreting* and *applying* concepts.

Mammals   **591**

PLACENTAL MAMMALS

Section Objectives

J *Explain* how young placental mammals differ from monotremes and marsupials.

K *List* the characteristics of placental mammals.

L *Discuss* the function of the placenta.

M *Name* and *describe* some of the major orders of placental mammals.

Placental mammals are the most successful and abundant group of living mammals. Both marsupials and placentals give birth to live young. The major difference between these two groups is the way the young are nourished before birth. The developing marsupials leave the uterus so early that they do not always survive the journey to the pouch. Placental young remain inside the uterus until they are much more developed. The amount of time an embryo spends in the uterus is related in part to the size of the animal. The gestation period for cats and dogs is about two months. The gestation period for the blue whale is eleven months.

Development inside the uterus accounts in part for the high survival rate among the young of placental mammals. What are the structural differences between placental mammals and other mammals? What kinds of animals share this structure?

36-6 Characteristics of Placental Mammals

A special structure allows the young of the placental mammals to remain inside their mothers' bodies until they develop enough to withstand environmental hazards. The structure is called the placenta. The **placenta** is a flattened organ that is rich in blood vessels. The placenta is connected to the unborn animal by an **umbilical cord**.

As you can see in Figure 36-7, the placenta lies next to the lining of the uterus. Notice that the surfaces of both the placenta and the uterus are convoluted. The convolutions greatly increase the surface area of the placenta and uterine wall that contact each other. Through these points of contact, materials are exchanged between the mother and the young. Blood does not cross the placenta, but oxygen and food diffuse from the mother's blood. There is also reverse traffic as carbon dioxide and nitrogen wastes from the embryo travel through the placenta, and into the mother's blood. The mother's blood removes the waste products from the uterus. Then the mother's kidneys filter out the waste products of the young along with those of her own body.

While the uterus contains developing young, the mother's body does not produce additional eggs. The placenta produces a chemical substance that prevents the release of more eggs. When the young are born, the placenta is also expelled from the mother's body as the afterbirth. Then the substances that prevented eggs from being released are no longer present, and the reproductive cycle begins again.

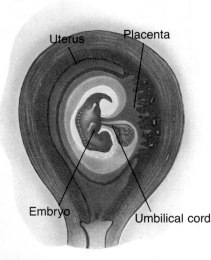

Figure 36-7 The structural features of the placenta are uniquely equipped to allow for the efficient exchange of nutrients and waste materials.

Uterus · Placenta · Embryo · Umbilical cord

36-7 Some Types of Placentals

There are 17 orders of placental mammals. Some are very large groups, containing hundreds of different species, while others contain relatively few species. Some are found all over the world, and others are limited to a few locations. Descriptions of some of the major orders of mammals follow.

Rodentia: Rodents With about 1700 species, the **rodents** make up the largest order of mammals. The mouse is a typical rodent. Rats and squirrels are other common rodents. Rodents live all over the world. Most of them eat plants, but some eat insects, fish, reptiles, small mammals, and birds. They can live in trees, on the ground, in burrows, and in water.

All rodents have a pair of **incisor** teeth on each jaw, as shown in Figure 36-8. The incisors grow continuously. Only the front tooth surface has enamel on it. When the upper teeth move against the lower teeth in gnawing, part of the back surface of the upper teeth wears off. This process results in sharp, chisel-shaped teeth. There is a distinct space between the incisors and the grinding teeth next to the cheeks.

One semiaquatic rodent, the beaver, is oustanding in its ability to modify its environment to suit its needs. Beavers can turn a meadow into a marsh. They use their sharp teeth to cut down trees and build dams across streams, thus forming deep pools. They build their homes in the water. Their large hind feet are webbed, and the openings to their eyes and ears can close when they submerge.

The largest rodents, the capybaras, live near marshes and streams in South America. They look like guinea pigs, but are as large as dogs.

Mice and rats spread many human diseases, such as typhus and bubonic plague. In some parts of the world, they compete strongly with humans for grain supplies.

Lagomorpha: Rodentlike Animals Rabbits, hares, and pikas are **lagomorphs**. Lagomorphs are found throughout much of the world. They have adapted to such diverse habitats as the Arctic and the desert. They inhabit forests as well as treeless mountains.

Many people mistakenly think that rabbits and hares are rodents. Lagomorphs are not considered rodents, however, due to the presence of an additional pair of incisors. Two small, peglike incisors are located behind the two larger ones. Like the incisors of rodents, the lagomorph incisors are ever-growing.

Jackrabbits have large hind legs and move by bounding across open spaces. They depend upon their speed, bursts of up to 70 kilometers per hour, for survival. This is important, since the deserts in which they live do not offer them places to hide from predators.

Figure 36-8 The beaver has a total of 20 teeth in its mouth. They use the 4 in the front for gnawing and the 16 in the back for chewing. It is hard to see the back teeth because a flap of skin folds behind the incisors. This flap prevents wood chips or water from entering the beaver's mouth while it is hard at work.

Figure 36-9 The jackrabbit has powerful hind legs that allow it to run as fast as a racehorse.

Mammals **593**

Figure 36-10 Bats are the only flying mammals. Their elongated finger bones act as supports for the wing membrane.

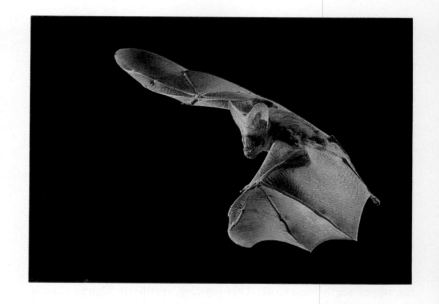

Chiroptera: Bats The second largest mammalian order is the order **Chiroptera**. It contains about 850 species of bats. Bats are the only group of mammals that can fly. They live everywhere except in the polar regions and on a few islands. The largest of all bats is the fruit bat. It has a wing span of 1.5 meters, which equals the wing span of many large birds.

Four fingers support the flying membrane of a bat's wing. The sternum has developed into a keel, to which the membrane attaches. The tailbones have been lost or have become very thin. The head is short and stubby, an adaptation that also reduces a bat's weight.

Most bats fly at night and guide themselves by using **echolocation**. They produce high-pitched sounds and listen for echos as sounds are reflected off objects. Bats use echolocation to avoid flying into obstacles in their path. Echolocation allows bats to capture flying insects, such as flies, mosquitoes, and moths.

Different types of bats have different diets. Food sources include insects, nectar, pollen, frogs, lizards, birds, and other bats. Vampire bats drink blood. A vampire bat's saliva contains a chemical that prevents its victim's blood from clotting. After a vampire bat has bitten an animal, such as a cow, it licks the free-flowing blood from the wound.

Young develop for a long time inside the mother bat. Since the mother must continue to fly during the gestation period, only one or two young are born at a time. A bat lives about 20 years, a long life span for such a small animal.

Mammals That Live in Water Members of many orders of mammals live in water. Most aquatic mammals are cigar-shaped, almost

hairless, and have a thick layer of blubber. The blubber insulates them from the cold. Their forelimbs are usually paddle-shaped and clawless. Often no hind limbs are visible.

The order **Cetacea** is one large group of aquatic mammals. It includes whales and dolphins. The blue whale, over 30 meters long and weighing as much as 25 elephants, is the largest animal that has ever lived. Surprisingly, it feeds on vast quantities of microscopic plankton, which it filters out of the water. In all cetaceans, the respiratory and digestive tracts are permanently separate. This prevents them from inhaling water.

Whales, like all mammals, are air-breathing. They can alternate breathing with periods of nonbreathing. A whale can remain submerged for as long as two hours. This is possible because it has about twice as many oxygen-carrying red blood cells for its weight as do land-dwelling mammals. A whale can also store oxygen in its muscles.

Carnivora: Flesh-Eating Mammals The order **Carnivora**, the flesh-eaters, contains about 280 species, most of which live on land. Carnivores include such familiar families of animals as cats, dogs, bears, raccoons, and weasels. Note the long pointed teeth in the mouth of the tiger in Figure 36-12. These teeth are characteristic of carnivores. They are used for shredding flesh. Despite their name, not all members of the order limit their diet to flesh. Bears are noted for eating a wide variety of foods, including berries and roots.

Some mammals of the order Carnivora also live in the water. Aquatic carnivores include seals, sea lions, and walruses. Although they are classified separately from animals such as whales, many similar structural characteristics permit them to follow an aquatic life.

Figure 36-12 The large incisor teeth in this Bengal tiger help to classify it as a carnivore.

Figure 36-13 A sea otter is also a carnivore. California sea otters are often seen floating on their backs while feeding on a variety of fish or shellfish.

Figure 36-14 The llama is a typical ungulate.

Ungulates: Hoofed Mammals Two orders of mammals compose a group of animals commonly called **ungulates**, or hoofed mammals. The **Perissodactyla**, or odd-toed hoofed mammals include the zebras, horses, and rhinoceroses. The **Artiodactyla**, or even-toed hoofed mammals, are a far larger group including goats, sheep, pigs, hippopotamuses, camels, llamas, deer, giraffes, and cattle.

Ungulates do not have claws. Instead, they walk on the tips of their toes. Their hooves are actually modified toenails. Ungulates have wide teeth with large grinding surfaces that are useful in chewing plant material. Most ungulates are large. Large size gives them an advantage in fighting or escaping from predators.

Plant matter is much harder to digest than animal matter because the cells of plants are surrounded by walls of cellulose. Mammals do not have the digestive enzymes necessary to break down cellulose. However, microorganisms living in the digestive tracts of ungulates can digest cellulose. The microorganisms obtain their nourishment from the cellulose and make the contents of the cells available to the ungulates.

Some ungulates, called **ruminants**, have several compartments to their stomachs. Food that is partially digested is regurgitated, rechewed, and then passed into another common compartment. When a cow "chews its cud," it is chewing regurgitated food so that it may be more fully digested.

Insectivora: Insect-Eating Animals The roughly 400 species of **insectivores** make up an ancient order of mammals dating from the Cretaceous period. These mammals live on all the continents but Australia and Antarctica. Insectivores are generally small mammals with long snouts. European hedgehogs, moles, and shrews are types of insectivores. Most insectivores have a well-developed sense of smell.

Moles live entirely underground, so there is no need for acute vision. While the mole's eyes are small, it does have sensory organs at both ends of its body. The nose provides its sense of smell. Bristles on its tail provide it with touch sensation. Moles dig long tunnels, which act as traps for worms and insects. The mole may eat such unfortunate animals immediately. However, it may just paralyze them by a bite, and haul them away to a special storage section of the tunnel for eating later.

The pygmy shrew, weighing only two grams, is the smallest living mammal. It can squeeze through tunnels as narrow as a pencil.

Edentata: Toothless Mammals The order **Edentata** includes about 30 species living in North and South America. One type, the anteater, has a long tongue covered with sticky saliva used to catch termites. The insects, swallowed whole, are ground up in the stomach.

Tree sloths are slow-moving and strictly plant-eating. Sloths live in the rain forests of South America, where they hang upside down. The sloth does not spend much time grooming itself. This may explain why algae grow in its long, coarse fur.

Armadillos are toothless animals covered with bony plates. They have sparse hair on their limbs and bellies between the bony plates. For protection, armadillos burrow into the ground or curl up so that only their bony armor is exposed.

Figure 36-15 The mole's long, sensitive snout has a keen sense of smell. Its powerful forelimbs are used for digging.

Figure 36-16 For protection, an armadillo will burrow or curl up so that only its bony armor is exposed.

Figure 36-17 Primates have the ability to grasp objects with their feet.

Primates The order Primates contains about 170 species of mammals. Primates have been most successful in tropical and subtropical regions. Primates include **prosimians** (lemurs, lorises, and tarsiers), monkeys, apes, and humans. Among the four existing types of apes are gorillas, orangutans, chimpanzees, and gibbons.

Of all the primates, only humans are fully bipedal, or walk only on two feet. Most other primates spend much of their time in the trees.

All primates show the influence of their present or past life in the trees. They have grasping hands, agility, and excellent coordination. Most have nails, not claws, and their fingers and toes have touch-sensitive pads on the ends. Most also have toes that are **opposable**, so that the thumb or big toe can touch the other digits. Opposable toes allow primates to grasp with their feet. As you can see in Figure 36-17, primates like the orangutan are able to use both their hands and their feet as they travel from tree to tree.

The primates' sense of smell is not as acute as that of other mammals, but their senses of hearing and vision are superior. Their eyes face forward, giving them excellent depth perception. Their eyes are also large in proportion to their bodies.

Perhaps the most striking characteristic of primates is their enlarged cerebrum and the high level of intelligence associated with it. Primates make and use tools, have complex social systems and methods of communication, and are capable of learning complicated tasks.

BIOLOGY INSIGHT

Adaptation and Evolution: Biologists think that the ancestors of the earliest primates may have been shrewlike insectivores.

CHECKPOINT ◆

11. What structure connects the embryo of a placental mammal to the placenta?
12. What is the source of food for embryos of placental mammals?
13. Which two orders of mammals have sharp, chisellike incisors?
14. Which order of mammals includes animals that are able to fly?
15. How does the placenta nourish and protect the developing embryo?
▶ 16. Which pair of animals is more closely related, a whale and a seal, or a raccoon and a seal? Explain your answer.
▶ 17. Describe the difference between a placental mammal and a marsupial at birth.

▶ Denotes a question that involves *interpreting* and *applying* concepts.

MAMMAL EVOLUTION

The Age of Reptiles lasted until the end of the Mesozoic era. Fossils indicate that many mammals existed at the same time as the dinosaurs but were overshadowed by them. The extinction of the dinosaurs was the opportunity for the mammals to begin their rise to power, a position they still hold. Today, mammals dominate the land. When did the first mammalian ancestors appear? What were they like?

36-8 Origin of Mammals

Even while the dinosaurs existed, some reptiles were becoming mammallike. Yet fossils do not show the remains of an animal that was definitely a mammal until the Jurassic period, about 180 million years ago. After the dinosaurs died out, mammals flourished.

The early mammals were limited in variety. Some were opossumlike marsupials. Others were placental insectivores. Most were about the size of a large dog. They had long bodies, short legs, and five-toed feet, on which they were able to run slowly. These early mammals had relatively small heads and long tails that were heavy at the base. Their teeth indicate that they ate both plants and animals. Yet even at that early date, mammals were somewhat specialized. Some ate more meat, while others ate more vegetable matter.

About 60 million years ago, the mammals had evolved into many different forms. There were many types of hoofed ungulates, some over one meter tall. There were also many types and sizes of carnivores and a few early rodents. There were even small animals that were probably the ancestors of monkeys. These species, and many more, gradually took over the environment.

36-9 Rise of Modern Horses: An Example of Mammalian Evolution

Although early mammals were recognizable as the ancestors of modern mammals, they were different from modern forms. Over millions of years, mammals have evolved from primitive types to more specialized ones. A classical example of mammalian evolution involves the horse.

The prehistoric *Hyracotherium* and the modern horse *Equus* are shown in Figure 36-18. *Hyracotherium*, which appeared about 55 million years ago, was only 20 to 25 centimeters high. It had four toes on each front foot and three on each hind foot. It walked on doglike feet. The head of *Hyracotherium* was small,

Section Objectives

N *Summarize* the events that gave rise to mammals.
O *Describe* the appearance of early mammals.
P *Compare* the modern horse, *Equus*, to its primitive ancestor, *Hyracotherium*.

DO YOU KNOW?

Information: Even the dinosaurs did not grow as large as the biggest whales. Their skeletons simply could not support that amount of weight. Whales can grow to their enormous size because the water helps to support their weight.

Mammals **599**

Hyracotherium

containing small teeth with small grinding surfaces suitable for eating soft vegetation but not for grazing on tough grass.

The modern horse *Equus* differs from *Hyracotherium* in many details. In *Equus* the number of toes on each foot has been reduced to one. The single toe has been modified into a hoof. This hard hoof aids the modern horse in running. The teeth of *Equus* are large with an increased grinding surface, permitting it to eat grass. Its eyes are set far back on the sides of the head. This adaptation allows horses to watch for predators while grazing. *Equus* is also several times larger than *Hyracotherium*.

Many fossils intermediate in form between *Hyracotherium* and *Equus* have been found. One way to interpret this evidence is to select several of the fossils and put them in order according to age, increasing size, and decreasing toe number. People do this to demonstrate changes that were gradual in one direction. However, most modern evolutionary biologists doubt that this was the case.

Actually, many of the intermediate fossil forms of horses are found in rocks of the same age. This indicates that they lived at the same time, and that one could not have evolved directly from the other. Rather, evolutionary biologists now interpret the evidence as showing that the family tree of horses was highly branched, with most branches now extinct. Changes were probably not gradual and constant but rapid and unpredictable. Only those horse ancestors with adaptations that were favorable to their environment were able to survive. The other forms eventually died out, leaving only their fossils behind.

Equus

Figure 36-18 *Hyracotherium* was much smaller than modern horses and had no hooves.

BIOLOGY INSIGHT

Adaptation and Evolution: Most of the early mammalian fossils are from the Rocky Mountain Region. Inferences are made based on this information about the age of rock in other parts of the United States.

CHECKPOINT ◆

18. What is the age of the earliest known mammal fossil?
19. What was the size of the early mammals?
20. How does the modern horse differ from *Hyracotherium?*
▶ 21. Does mammalian evolution always favor larger animals? Explain your answer.
▶ 22. Give two examples to support the theory that modern horses are better suited to their environment than were their ancestors.

▶ Denotes a question that involves *interpreting* and *applying* concepts.

EFFECT OF TEMPERATURE ON RESPIRATION

Objectives and Skills

☐ *Measure* the oxygen intake of a mammal at two different temperatures.
☐ *Construct a graph* relating time to volume of oxygen.

Materials

respirometer chamber	pipette
small mammal (mouse, hamster, etc.)	thermometer
	wire screen
beaker	shallow pan
soda lime	ice
cotton sheet	safety goggles
tape	lab apron and gloves

Procedure and Observations

1. Study the setup before beginning your work.
2. Put on your safety goggles, lab apron, and gloves. Place two tablespoons of soda lime in the sheet of cotton, then roll

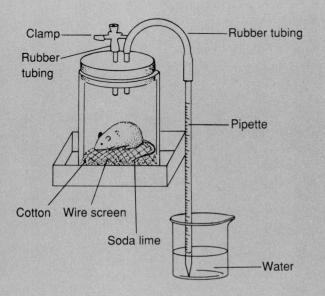

Clamp — Rubber tubing
Rubber tubing
Pipette
Cotton Wire screen
Soda lime
Water

the cotton and tape it shut. **CAUTION: Do not touch the soda lime.** Place the rolled cotton on the bottom of the chamber. The soda lime will absorb carbon dioxide exhaled by the mammal.

3. Next, place the screen above the cotton, then place the mammal in the jar. Cover the respirometer jar as shown in the diagram, and place it in the pan containing water at about 37°C. While the jar warms up, keep the pinch clamp open so that there is a supply of air in the jar. The pipette tip should be submerged in a beaker of water.
4. As the mammal takes in oxygen from the jar, the pressure will be reduced in the pipette and jar. Therefore, a change in the oxygen level of the jar/pipette should cause a change in the level of water in the pipette.
5. Close the clamp on the respirometer. Record the level of water in the pipette at time zero and take a new reading each minute for eight minutes. Then open the clamp.
6. Place the respirometer in a shallow pan containing ice water, and allow it to chill for five minutes. Repeat step 5.
7. Return the mammal to its cage. Clean up your materials and equipment. Wash your hands thoroughly before leaving the lab.

Analysis and Conclusions

1. By subtracting each value from the one before it, determine the volume of oxygen used per minute. Then calculate the average volume of oxygen used per minute in each trial.
2. Graph the data for each temperature condition. Label the *X* axis *minutes*. Label the *Y* axis *volume of oxygen used*.
3. At which temperature is more oxygen used?
4. What does the rate of oxygen used tell you about the animal's rate of respiration?

CHAPTER REVIEW

Summary

▸ Primitive mammals existed at the time of the dinosaurs. The extinction of the dinosaurs about 70 million years ago left mammals the dominant class of vertebrates on Earth.

▸ Several characteristics of mammals contributed to their evolutionary success. The large, convoluted brain allows for complex behavior. The four-chambered heart and diaphragm provide a rich supply of oxygen. Oxygen-rich blood enables mammals to maintain a constant body temperature. The body covering and sweat glands also contribute to homeostasis.

▸ The survival rate among young mammals is high because of extended parental contact. The young receive nourishment and learn patterns of behavior from their parents during this time.

▸ Mammals are divided into three groups based on their reproductive patterns. Monotremes lay eggs. Marsupials produce live but underdeveloped young, which stay in the mother's pouch for a period after birth. Placental mammals produce more highly developed young. Young placental mammals remain inside the mother for much of their development.

▸ Based upon their structure, the placental mammals are divided into 17 orders. Humans are members of the order Primates.

Vocabulary

Artiodactyla	gestation
blubber	incisor
Carnivora	insectivore
Cetacea	lagomorph
Chiroptera	mammary gland
convolution	marsupial
diaphragm	monotreme
echolocation	opposable
Edentata	Perissodactyla

placenta
placental mammal
prosimian
rodent
ruminant

sebaceous gland
umbilical cord
ungulate
uterus

Concept Mapping

Construct a concept map outlining the characteristics of mammals. Include the following terms: convolution, diaphragm, gestation, mammary gland, placenta, umbilical cord, uterus. Use additional terms as you need them.

Review

1. Name two characteristics that mammals share with birds. Name two characteristics of mammals that birds do not have.
2. How do bats locate their prey?
3. In what organ does the early development of marsupial embryos occur?
4. How long have mammals been the dominant form of life on Earth?
5. Which of the following mammals does *not* lay eggs? (a) duck-billed platypus (b) spiny anteater (c) sloth
6. Most marsupials live in (a) North America (b) South America (c) Asia (d) Australia

Match the order of mammals on the left with a characteristic on the right.

7. Chiroptera
8. Rodentia
9. Primates
10. Artiodactyla
11. Carnivora
12. Cetacea

a. able to fly
b. have hoofed feet
c. have large eyes in front of face
d. have sharp teeth useful for shredding flesh
e. is the largest order of mammals
f. live in water
g. have no teeth

13. Describe the characteristics of early mammals.
14. What is the genus of the ancestor of modern horses?
15. Which gland lubricates the skin? Aids in communication?

Interpret and Apply

16. Compare the teeth of a carnivore with those of an ungulate. How are these teeth adapted for each kind of diet?
17. How is a marsupial's method of reproduction like that of placental mammals? How is it different?
18. Which two groups of placental mammals have teeth that grow continuously?
19. Name three orders of placental mammals that have aquatic or semiaquatic members.
20. Name three adaptations of mammals that contribute to the maintenance of a high body temperature.
21. In the following list, indicate whether the phrase describes monotremes, marsupials, or placental mammals. Some phrases may describe more that one group.
    a. lay eggs
    b. young develop in pouch
    c. young develop attached to placenta
    d. endothermy not well developed
    e. only one type lives in North America
    f. group to which most species of mammals belong
    g. nourish young with milk
    h. contains species *Homo sapiens*
    i. only three species exist
    j. embryos rely on yolk for food inside the mother's uterus
    k. all members lack teeth as adults
    l. cloaca serves excretory and reproductive functions

22. Explain how the body of a female mammal is suited to provide food and shelter to its developing young.
23. Rabbits are classified as lagomorphs. Why are they not classified as rodents?
24. What structural features of early mammals may have been responsible for their rise to power after the dinosaurs became extinct?
25. Compare the circulatory system of mammals with that of birds.
26. Describe how the many life processes of placental mammals are performed during gestation.

Critical Thinking

27. Certain aspects of an animal's brain structure are associated with its intelligence. What do you think the human brain looks like? Describe its size, the relative size of the cerebrum, and the appearance of the surface of the cerebrum.
28. Apes are known to be capable of complex learning. That is, they are intelligent. Would you expect their period of dependence on their parents after birth to be long or short?
29. You discover a new type of fossil. The fossil shows that the animal was a large mammal that ate grass. In which group would you classify this new species? Explain.
30. Give two possible explanations for the fact that only one marsupial, the opossum, is found in North America.
31. What evolutionary principle is illustrated by the rise of mammals from small, similar creatures to a variety of organisms in different environments?

EVOLUTION OF LIFE

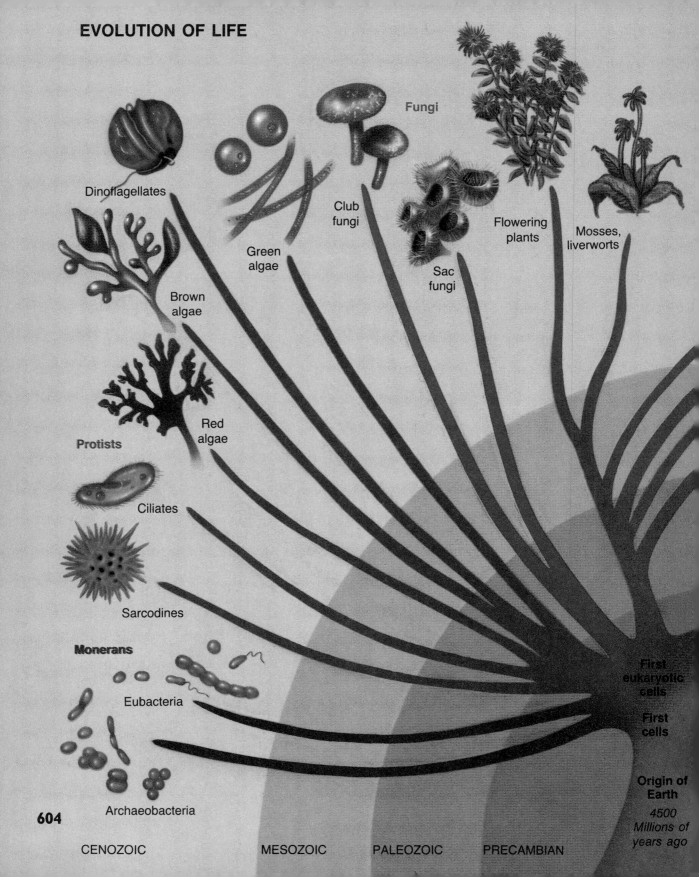

Dinoflagellates

Fungi

Club fungi

Green algae

Brown algae

Flowering plants

Sac fungi

Mosses, liverworts

Red algae

Protists

Ciliates

Sarcodines

Monerans

Eubacteria

Archaeobacteria

First eukaryotic cells

First cells

Origin of Earth

4500 Millions of years ago

604

CENOZOIC   MESOZOIC   PALEOZOIC   PRECAMBIAN

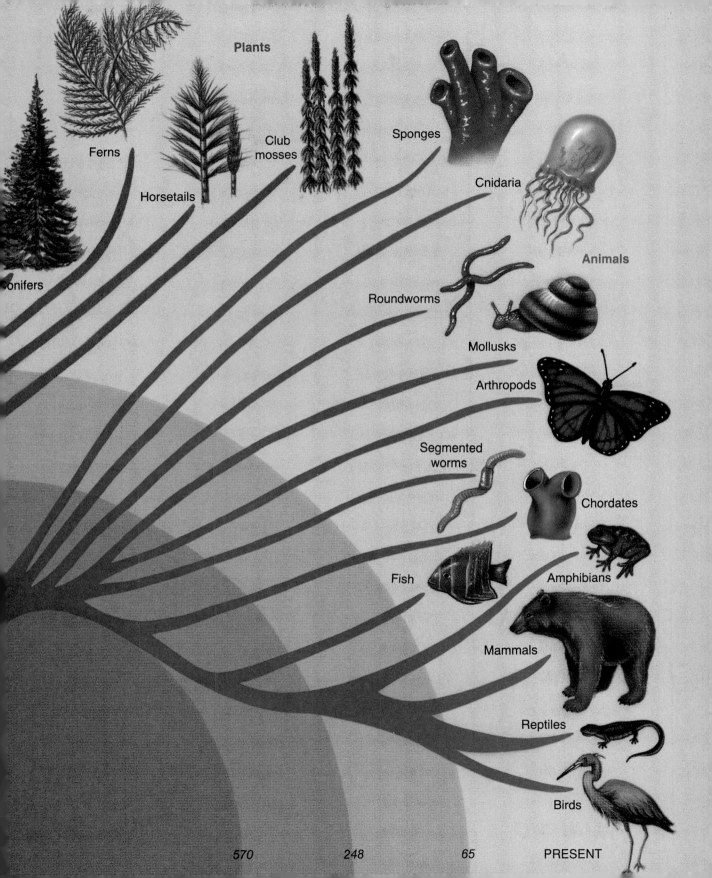

Plants

Ferns

Club mosses

Horsetails

Sponges

Cnidaria

Conifers

Animals

Roundworms

Mollusks

Arthropods

Segmented worms

Chordates

Fish

Amphibians

Mammals

Reptiles

Birds

570   *248*   *65*   PRESENT

VERTEBRATE EVOLUTION

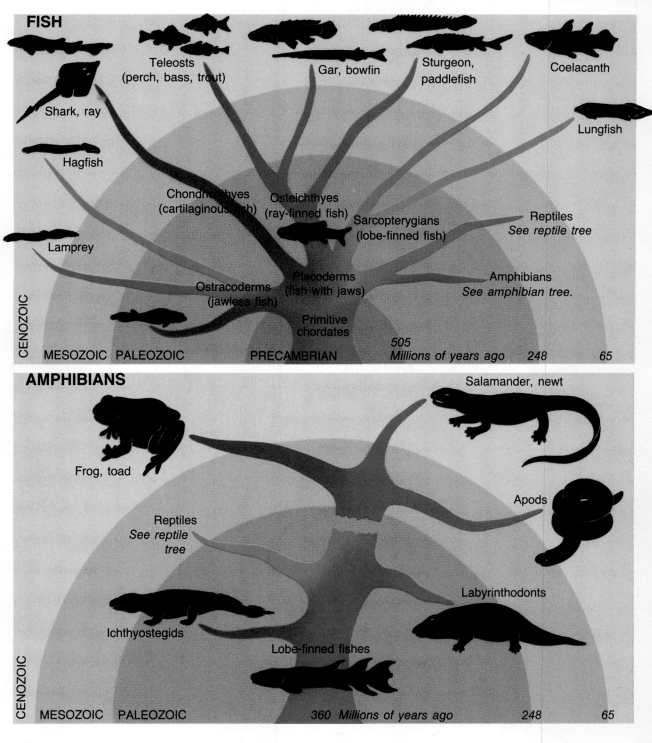

FISH

Teleosts (perch, bass, trout)

Gar, bowfin

Sturgeon, paddlefish

Coelacanth

Shark, ray

Lungfish

Hagfish

Chondrichthyes (cartilaginous fish)

Osteichthyes (ray-finned fish)

Sarcopterygians (lobe-finned fish)

Reptiles
See reptile tree

Lamprey

Ostracoderms (jawless fish)

Placoderms (fish with jaws)

Amphibians
See amphibian tree.

Primitive chordates

505

Millions of years ago   248   65

CENOZOIC

MESOZOIC   PALEOZOIC   PRECAMBRIAN

AMPHIBIANS

Salamander, newt

Frog, toad

Apods

Reptiles
See reptile tree

Labyrinthodonts

Ichthyostegids

Lobe-finned fishes

CENOZOIC

MESOZOIC   PALEOZOIC   360 *Millions of years ago*   248   65

The first animals with a backbone appeared during the Precambrian Era and are represented on the fish evolutionary tree (*top left*). Fish represent a very diverse group of aquatic vertebrates. Their unique body features are primarily adaptations for swimming. Teleosts are the most advanced ray-finned fish and the dominant order today. Times of drought are thought to have selected for the development of lungs. Lobed fins are the forerunners of limbs in amphibians and reptiles.

Amphibian evolution (*bottom left*) shows a link to lobe-finned fish and is marked by the emergence of vertebrates from water. There is a gap in the fossil record near the end of the Paleozioc Era that links Paleozoic amphibians to modern amphibians.

The reptile evolutionary tree (*bottom*) is most notably characterized by the presence of dinosaurs. This tree also shows the links to be bird and mammal trees on the next two pages.

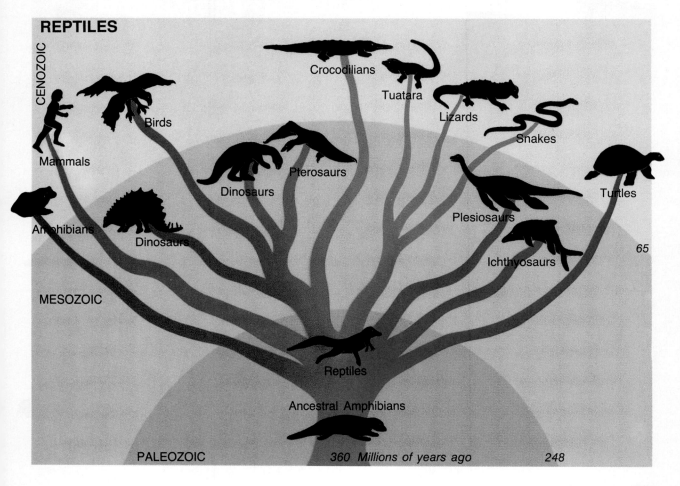

REPTILES

CENOZOIC

Crocodilians

Tuatara

Birds

Lizards

Snakes

Mammals

Pterosaurs

Dinosaurs

Turtles

Plesiosaurs

Amphibians

Dinosaurs

65

Ichthyosaurs

MESOZOIC

Reptiles

Ancestral Amphibians

PALEOZOIC   *360 Millions of years ago*   248

VERTEBRATE EVOLUTION

Birds appear to have evolved from thecodonts which were small, bipedal, carnivorous dinosaurs (*below*). Endothermy, hollow bones, feathers, and forelimbs generally adapted for flight are some characteristics of modern birds.

Mammals appear to have evolved from therapsids which were probably endothermic (*top right*).

The most advanced vertebrates are humans. *Australopithecus* is considered by most to be the forerunner of modern humans (bottom right). The sequence shown here is described in detail in Chapter 16.

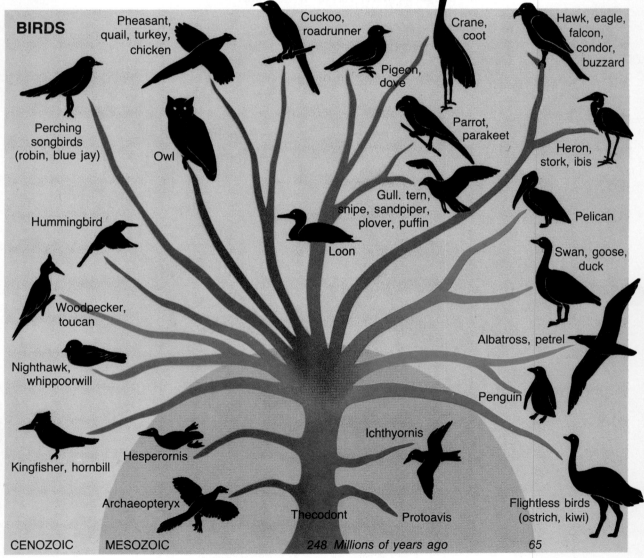

BIRDS

Pheasant, quail, turkey, chicken

Cuckoo, roadrunner

Crane, coot

Hawk, eagle, falcon, condor, buzzard

Pigeon, dove

Parrot, parakeet

Perching songbirds (robin, blue jay)

Owl

Heron, stork, ibis

Gull, tern, snipe, sandpiper, plover, puffin

Pelican

Hummingbird

Loon

Swan, goose, duck

Woodpecker, toucan

Albatross, petrel

Nighthawk, whippoorwill

Penguin

Kingfisher, hornbill

Hesperornis

Ichthyornis

Archaeopteryx

Thecodont

Protoavis

Flightless birds (ostrich, kiwi)

CENOZOIC   MESOZOIC   248 *Millions of years ago*   65

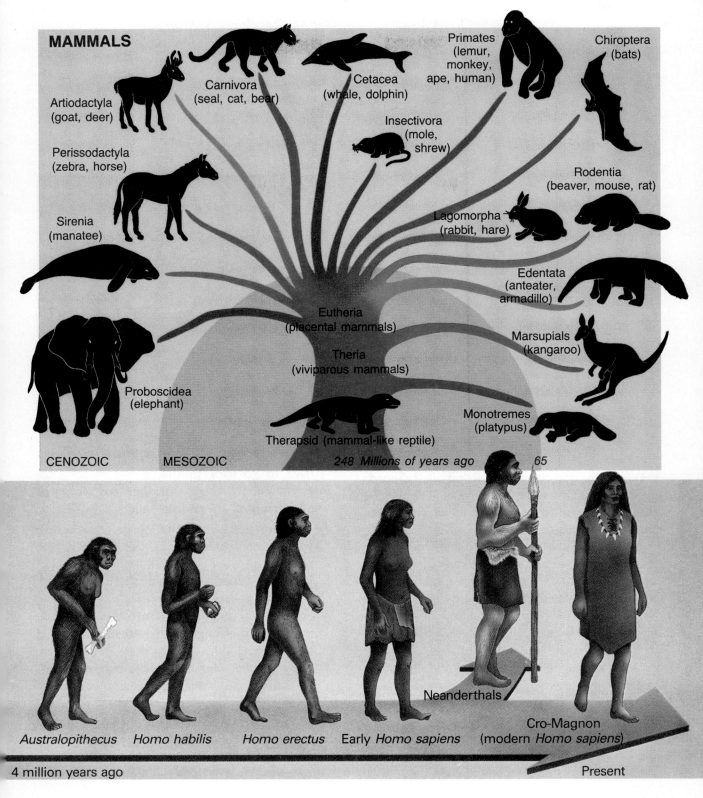

MAMMALS

Artiodactyla (goat, deer)

Carnivora (seal, cat, bear)

Cetacea (whale, dolphin)

Primates (lemur, monkey, ape, human)

Chiroptera (bats)

Perissodactyla (zebra, horse)

Insectivora (mole, shrew)

Rodentia (beaver, mouse, rat)

Sirenia (manatee)

Lagomorpha (rabbit, hare)

Edentata (anteater, armadillo)

Eutheria (placental mammals)

Marsupials (kangaroo)

Theria (viviparous mammals)

Proboscidea (elephant)

Monotremes (platypus)

Therapsid (mammal-like reptile)

CENOZOIC   MESOZOIC   *248 Millions of years ago*   *65*

Australopithecus   *Homo habilis*   *Homo erectus*   Early *Homo sapiens*   Neanderthals   Cro-Magnon (modern *Homo sapiens*)

4 million years ago   Present

Vertebrate Evolution   **609**

ISSUES in Bioethics

TEENS DEBATE ANIMAL RIGHTS

Case Study

LaShonda Liberg is a sixteen-year-old girl with diabetes. She has had the disease for as long as she can remember. Her diet is regulated and she takes insulin shots every day. She doesn't like it but has come to realize that there isn't anything she can do about it. She hopes that when she is older, doctors will have found a way to give her a new pancreas and she can stop the shots.

At Irvins High School, where LaShonda is a junior, there are many student organizations. One is an activist group whose goal is to stop all experimentation on animals. LaShonda went to one of their meetings and thought the subject was interesting. She wanted to learn more about it. At the meeting, the students talked about how cruel some researchers were to animals and how they should stop all experimentation. LaShonda has a dog and thought about what it would be like for her pet to be locked up in a cage and used in experiments. It seemed cruel.

When she went home she spoke to her mother about it. Her mother said there might be another side to the issue. "If they didn't experiment on animals, how would they find out anything about how drugs work?" her mother asked. "Should they try them out on people?"

"I don't know," said LaShonda.

"Wait a minute," her mother said. "I have a book I bought when you first got diabetes. It explains how they discovered that insulin could be injected for treatment."

LaShonda waited while her mother went to find the book. When she came back, LaShonda read the section her mother pointed out. It was true!

Dogs had been used in the experiments that led to the discovery and use of insulin. Before that people often died of diabetes!

"That could have been me," LaShonda thought. "I have to go back to that group meeting tomorrow and tell them that they are wrong to want to stop *all* animal experiments."

1. List several arguments LaShonda could use to support her position when she goes to the meeting.
2. List other actions she could take if she doesn't go to the meeting.
3. Some researchers use mice, rabbits, or monkeys instead of dogs. Do you think that makes a difference? Why or why not?
4. Many people who are against animal experimentation have rallies and picket in front of university labs and doctor's offices. They show pictures of monkeys and dogs being "tortured" in laboratories. Do you think this is a good way to get public support for their cause? Why or why not?

610   Issues in Bioethics

UNIT REVIEW 6

Synthesis

1. The opening pages of this unit contain four photographs. These photographs illustrate a common theme to the chapters of the unit. Identify the theme and describe how it relates to what you studied in the chapters.

2. **Adaptation and Evolution:** Explain how the pectoral and pelvic girdles of vertebrates have been modified as adaptations to different life-styles. Compare a perch, a bird, and a reptile.

3. **Adaptation and Evolution:** Compare the body covering, or integumentary system, of bony fish, amphibians, reptiles, birds, and mammals. State how each characteristic covering is an advantage to that group.

4. **Adaptation and Evolution:** Compare the structure of the heart and the flow of blood in a fish, a reptile, and a mammal.

5. **Adaptation and Evolution:** A female fish may spawn as many as one million eggs at a time. In contrast, most mammals bear only a few offspring at a time. Yet the populations of some mammals are as large as those of some fish. What adaptations allow mammals to maintain large populations while producing fewer young? Why is mammalian reproduction said to be more efficient than fish reproduction?

6. **Homeostasis:** Endothermy is believed to have evolved independently in birds and in mammals. Some dinosaurs may also have been endothermic. Describe how the circulatory system, respiratory system, and body covering of birds and mammals contribute to the maintenance of a constant body temperature.

7. **Adaptation and Evolution:** Each of the animals in the unit opener represents a class of vertebrates. Which evolutionary advance of each class is represented by the photo-

graphs? a. jaws b. ability to breathe air c. amniote egg d. endothermy

Critical Thinking

8. **Adaptation and Evolution:** Endothermy never arose among fish. It did arise among birds and mammals, which are terrestrial animals. Considering that their respective environments are the ocean and air, explain why selection would have favored endothermy in birds and mammals, but not in fish.

9. **Process of Science:** A report from an expedition to a remote island describes mating in a species of birds. The report states that the female lays the eggs, which are then fertilized in the nest by the male. Evaluate the report.

10. **Adaptation and Evolution:** Based on information about all the animals you have studied thus far, make a statement about the relationship between the life span of an animal and the number of offspring it produces at one time.

Additional Reading

Attenborough, David, *Life on Earth*. Boston: Little, Brown, 1987.

Smith, Hobart M. *Amphibians of North America*. (Golden Field Guide Series) New York: Western, 1978.

Wheeler, Alwyn. *Fishes of the World*. New York: Macmillan, 1975.

THE HUMAN BODY

Ultrasound of human fetus (color added)

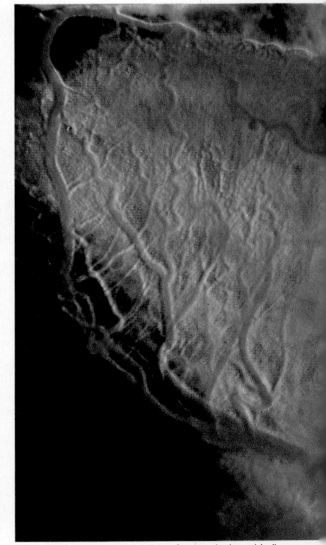

Angiograph showing narrowing of artery (color added)

UNIT 7

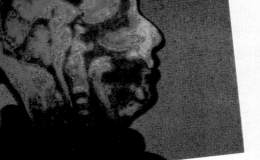

PET scan of axial section of human brain

Nuclear Magnetic Resonance image of adult head

Chapter 37 Bones, Muscles, and Skin
Human Skeleton
Muscles and Skin

Chapter 38 Digestion and Nutrition
Upper Alimentary Canal
Lower Alimentary Canal
Nutrition

Chapter 39 Respiration and Excretion
Respiration
Excretory System

Chapter 40 Circulation
The Heart and Blood Vessels
Blood and Lymph

Chapter 41 Disease and Immunity
Infectious Disease
The Body's Defenses
Treating Disease

Chapter 42 The Nervous System
Transmission of Information
Central and Peripheral Nervous Systems
The Senses

Chapter 43 Chemical Regulators
A Delicate Balance
Endocrine Glands at Work

Chapter 44 Substance Abuse
Drugs and Abuse
Alcohol and Tobacco

Chapter 45 Human Reproduction
The Structures of Reproduction
The Process of Reproduction

613

Chapter

37

BONES, MUSCLES, AND SKIN

Overview

HUMAN SKELETON

37-1 Bone and Cartilage
37-2 Joints of the Human Skeleton

MUSCLES AND SKIN

37-3 Skeletal Muscle
37-4 Chemistry of Contraction
37-5 Movement of Joints
37-6 Cardiac Muscle and Smooth Muscle
37-7 Structure and Function of Skin

How do muscles make the body move?

HUMAN SKELETON

The internal skeleton of all vertebrates serves many functions. It supports the body and protects internal organs. Working with muscles, the skeleton enables the body to move. Within many bones, millions of blood cells are made every second of every day. In addition, bone cells store and release important minerals.

Like all parts of the body, the skeleton is made up of tissues. In fact, your entire body is made up of the four basic types of tissue illustrated in Figure 37-1. **Epithelial** [ep ə thē′ lē əl] **tissue** covers interior and exterior body surfaces. **Muscle tissue** is responsible for movement. **Connective tissues** attach and support each part of the body. Some types of connective tissue are bone, cartilage, fat, and blood. **Nerve tissue** forms the communication system of the body. This type of tissue makes up the brain, spinal cord, and nerves.

Section Objectives

A *Name* the four basic types of human body tissue.

B *Compare* and *contrast* the structure and function of cartilage and bone.

C *Identify* the types of joints in the body and *describe* the range of motion in each type.

Figure 37-1 The structure of tissues in the human body varies tremendously. Compare and contrast the structure and function of each tissue illustrated below.

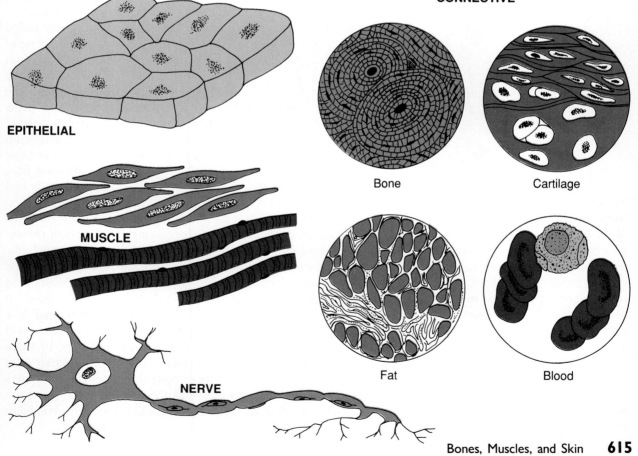

CONNECTIVE

EPITHELIAL

MUSCLE

NERVE

Bone

Cartilage

Fat

Blood

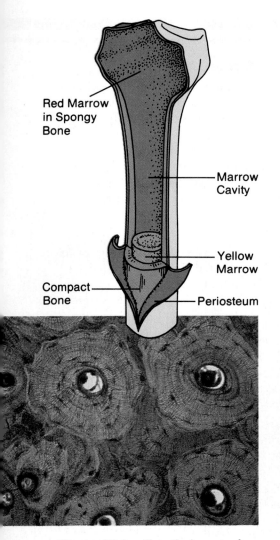

Red Marrow in Spongy Bone

Marrow Cavity

Yellow Marrow

Compact Bone

Periosteum

Figure 37-2 *Top:* Each part of a human long bone is vital to the life of the bone. The periosteum contains blood vessels that supply food and oxygen to other bone cells. Cells in compact bone store and release important minerals for use by the bone and other tissues. The marrow produces millions of blood cells. These blood cells carry oxygen and fight disease-causing organisms throughout the body. *Bottom:* This photomicrograph of a compact bone reveals a cross-sectional view of the Haversian canal system.

37-1 Bone and Cartilage

The human skeleton is made up mainly of bone. Figure 37-2 illustrates the internal structure of a long bone from an adult human. A tough membrane called the **periosteum** [per ē os' tē əm] surrounds and protects bones. Muscles attach to the periosteum. Cells responsible for bone growth are also found in the periosteum.

Beneath the periosteum is a hard, dense material called compact bone. Below the compact bone, particularly at the knobby ends, is more loosely packed spongy bone. Within the hollow spaces of spongy bone is a substance called **marrow**. Red marrow usually fills the spaces of spongy bone. Most blood cells are made in the red marrow. Certain bones, such as the long bones of the arms and legs, have a central cavity filled with yellow marrow, blood vessels, and nerves. Yellow marrow is primarily fat tissue.

Figure 37-2 shows the microscopic structure of compact bone. Bone cells called **osteocytes** [os' tē ə sīts] are found throughout this bone. These cells are surrounded by a nonliving material called **matrix**, which they secrete. Osteocytes are arranged in concentric rings centered on channels called **Haversian** [hə vėr' zhən] **canals**. Small blood vessels run through each canal.

Bone matrix contains large amounts of a fiberlike protein called **collagen** [kol' ə jen]. Collagen gives bone matrix its strength. Osteocytes deposit crystals of calcium phosphate and calcium carbonate around the collagen fibers. These crystals give bone its hardness. Osteocytes and bone matrix are involved in the storage and release of calcium and phosphorus. These two elements are necessary for the functioning of many body tissues.

Cartilage is another kind of connective tissue that makes up parts of your skeleton. You can feel cartilage at the tip of your nose. Notice how flexible it is. Cartilage gives the skeleton flexibility. Pads of cartilage between your vertebrae and at the end of many bones prevent bones from rubbing together.

In the early developmental stages of a human embryo, most of the skeleton is made of cartilage. Some cartilage will remain for the person's entire life. However, most of the cartilage gradually is replaced by bone. As the developing human grows, the cartilage cells are replaced by osteocytes. The process of bone formation is called **ossification** [os ə fə kā' shən]. Young people build up more bone than they break down. A person in their mid 20's builds up as much bone as is broken down. An older person will break down more bone compared to what is built up. In some people, a condition known as **osteoporosis** [ös tē ō pə rō' səs] exists that causes excessive loss of bone tissue, leaving the bones porous. As a result, bones are weakened and may fracture from normal activities such as coughing or bending over. This condition most often affects middle-aged, small-framed, females.

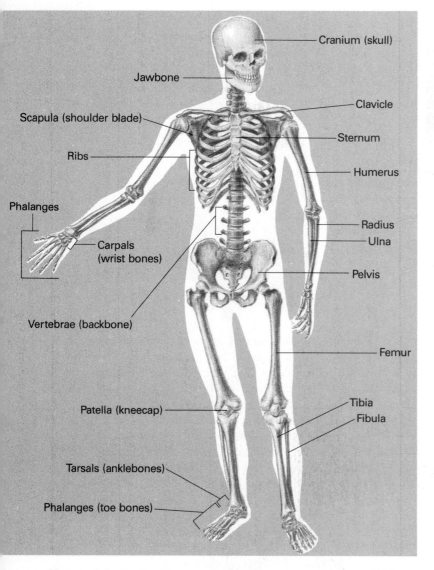

Cranium (skull)

Jawbone

Clavicle

Scapula (shoulder blade)

Sternum

Ribs

Humerus

Phalanges

Radius

Ulna

Carpals (wrist bones)

Pelvis

Vertebrae (backbone)

Femur

Patella (kneecap)

Tibia

Fibula

Tarsals (anklebones)

Phalanges (toe bones)

Figure 37-3 The central column of the human skeleton is made up of the skull, vertebral column, and rib cage. The remaining bones, including those of the arms and legs, are attached to this central skeleton. There are a total of 206 individual bones in the human skeleton.

Figure 37-4 An osteoporotic vertebra; osteoporotic bone is much more porous than normal bone. As a result, osteoporotic bone is weaker and breaks much easier.

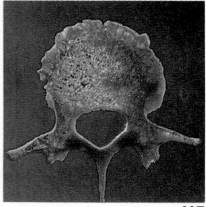

Research indicates, however, that there are a number of things that can be done during the growth years to stimulate ossification. Eating a diet of calcium-rich foods—such as cheese and broccoli—is one. Another is doing some type of exercise such as walking or bicycling. Bone produced this way may increase the bone mass and therefore guard against osteoporosis later in life.

37-2 Joints of the Human Skeleton

Joints occur where two or more bones come together. Most joints allow a certain range of motion. Figure 37-5 illustrates a cross-sectional view of a movable joint. In such joints, the bones are generally held together by tough, fibrous connective tissues

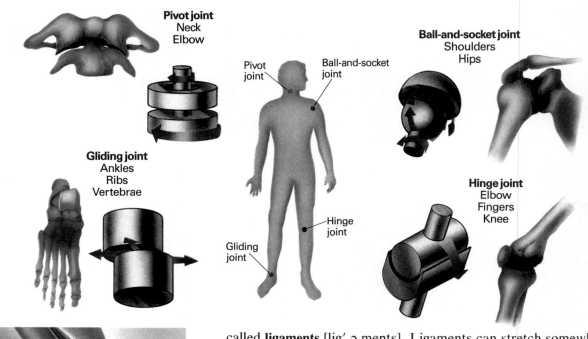

Pivot joint
Neck
Elbow

Gliding joint
Ankles
Ribs
Vertebrae

Pivot joint

Ball-and-socket joint

Hinge joint

Gliding joint

Ball-and-socket joint
Shoulders
Hips

Hinge joint
Elbow
Fingers
Knee

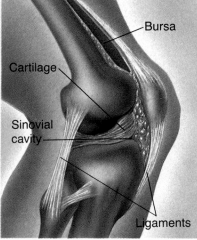

Bursa

Cartilage

Sinovial cavity

Ligaments

Figure 37-5 Joints are classified by the kind of motion that they permit. Some typical joints are illustrated here.

called **ligaments** [lig′ ə ments]. Ligaments can stretch somewhat. This allows the bones to move but not separate. Ends of bones in a movable joint have a thin layer of cartilage. This provides a smooth surface of contact. A lubricating liquid called **synovial** [sə nō′ vē əl] **fluid** reduces friction and keeps the joint ends from wearing out. Without cartilage and synovial fluid, the pain and swelling caused by bone-to-bone contact could immobilize a joint.

Joints are classified according to the kind of movement they allow. Several types of joints are illustrated in Figure 37-5. A **ball-and-socket joint**, like the hip or shoulder, allows movement in many directions. They allow the widest range of movement of any joint. The joints between vertebrae are examples of **gliding joints**. Pads of cartilage called **vertebral disks** allow limited twisting, turning, and sliding between vertebrae. **Hinge joints** can bend in only one direction. The knee is such a joint.

Some joints, called **immovable joints**, fit together so tightly that movement is prevented. Most of the skull bones are fused together at such joints.

CHECKPOINT ◆

1. List four types of tissue found in the human body.
2. Identify the tough membrane that covers bones.
3. What is the lubricating fluid of joints?
▶ 4. Explain the relationship of ligaments to bones.

▶ Denotes a question that involves *interpreting* and *applying* concepts.

MUSCLES AND SKIN

A skeletal system would be useless for movement without muscles. Your muscles and bones work together to allow you to walk, run, bend, and perform other actions. Your muscles also work alone to aid the functioning of some of your internal organs.

Your muscles and other body tissues are covered and protected by a double layer of skin. The skin helps the body regulate its internal temperature. This is important because the temperature in the human body must remain within narrow limits in order for most chemical reactions to occur. How does skin assist in temperature regulation? In what other ways does skin benefit the body?

37-3 Skeletal Muscle

Most of the muscle in your body is **skeletal muscle**. In fact, this type of muscle makes up about half of your entire weight. As its name suggests, skeletal muscle is attached to bones and makes them move. Skeletal muscle has a striped appearance when viewed through a microscope, as illustrated in Figure 37-6. Because of its stripes, skeletal muscle is often called **striated muscle**.

A muscle contracts when it receives impulses from nerves. Skeletal muscle receives some impulses from parts of the brain that are under your conscious control. Muscles under conscious control are called **voluntary muscles**.

Section Objectives

D *Describe* the structure of striated muscle.

E *Explain* the mechanism of contraction in skeletal muscle.

F *Identify* the energy source for muscle contraction.

G *Explain* how antagonist muscle pairs function.

H *Compare* and *contrast* smooth muscle, cardiac muscle, and striated muscle.

I *Describe* the structure and function of human skin.

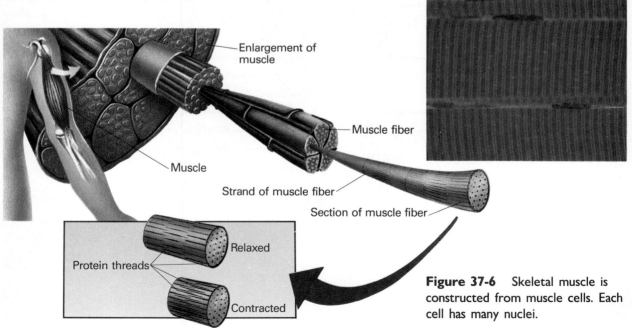

Enlargement of muscle

Muscle fiber

Muscle

Strand of muscle fiber

Section of muscle fiber

Relaxed

Protein threads

Contracted

Figure 37-6 Skeletal muscle is constructed from muscle cells. Each cell has many nuclei.

Figure 37-7 It is hard to imagine how many muscles are required to move the human skeleton.

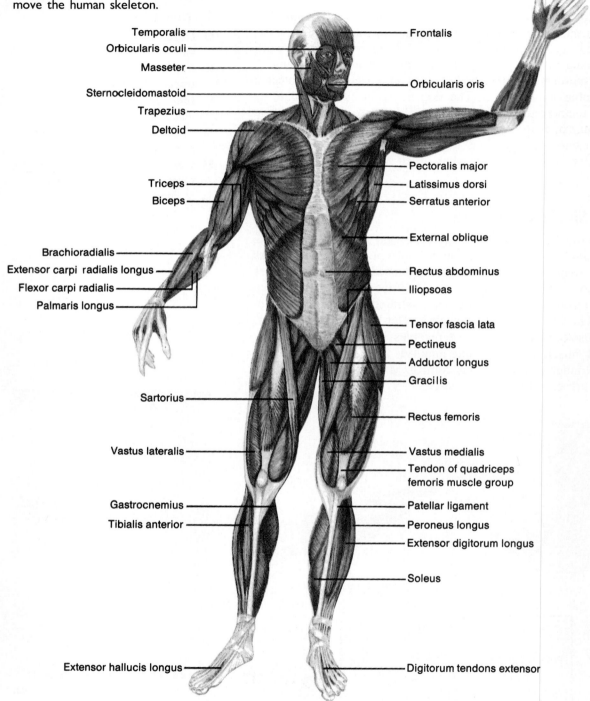

Temporalis

Orbicularis oculi

Masseter

Sternocleidomastoid

Trapezius

Deltoid

Triceps

Biceps

Brachioradialis

Extensor carpi radialis longus

Flexor carpi radialis

Palmaris longus

Sartorius

Vastus lateralis

Gastrocnemius

Tibialis anterior

Extensor hallucis longus

Frontalis

Orbicularis oris

Pectoralis major

Latissimus dorsi

Serratus anterior

External oblique

Rectus abdominus

Iliopsoas

Tensor fascia lata

Pectineus

Adductor longus

Gracilis

Rectus femoris

Vastus medialis

Tendon of quadriceps femoris muscle group

Patellar ligament

Peroneus longus

Extensor digitorum longus

Soleus

Digitorum tendons extensor

Muscle cells are often called fibers. Within each fiber are many smaller units called **myofibrils** [mī ō fī' brils]. Each myofibril contains many threadlike protein filaments that are lined up in a highly organized way. The appearance of myofibrils in the electron microscope is illustrated in Figure 37-8. Dark lines called Z-bands separate each myofibril into a number of identical units called **sarcomeres** [sar' kə mērs].

Figure 37-9 illustrates sarcomeres in a relaxed muscle and in a contracted muscle. Compare the two carefully. The central filaments in each sarcomere are thicker than the filaments attached to the Z-band. The thick filaments are made of a protein called **myosin** [mī' ə sin]. **Actin** is the major protein making up the thin filaments.

Each myosin molecule forms a bridge across to an actin molecule in a thin filament. Using the energy of ATP molecules, myosin bridges can pull the thin filaments toward the center of the sarcomere. This pulls the Z-bands closer together and shortens the entire sarcomere. The shortening of each sarcomere makes the fiber contract.

A muscle fiber either contracts fully or does not contract at all. This type of reaction is known as an all-or-none response. A whole muscle, however, does not have an all-or-none response. It can contract at different strengths. The intensity of a whole muscle's contraction is determined by the number of fibers that contract. The more fibers involved, the stronger the contraction of the whole muscle.

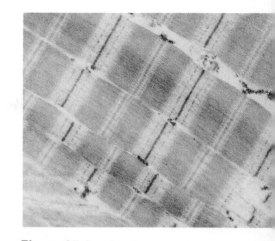

Figure 37-8 An electron micrograph of myofibrils. The Z-bands (dark lines) separate the myofibrils into sarcomeres.

Figure 37-9 When muscle contracts, the actin filaments of each sarcomere are pulled toward the middle, and the entire sarcomere shortens. Notice that the length of the actin and myosin filaments remains the same.

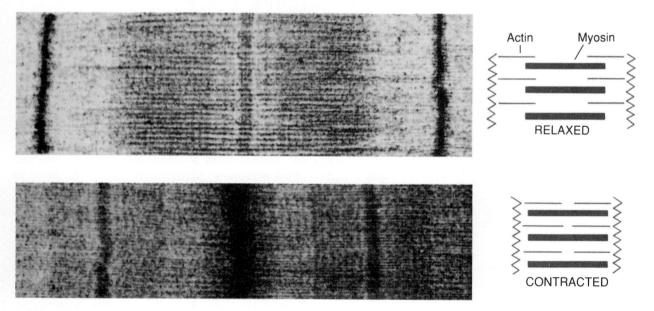

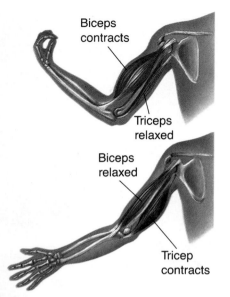

Biceps
contracts

Triceps
relaxed

Biceps
relaxed

Tricep
contracts

Figure 37-10 Bones are set in motion by the action of antagonistic muscle pairs. When one of the muscles contracts, the other usually relaxes. Can you think of a reason why standing can be more tiring than walking?

37-4 Chemistry of Contraction

The movement of actin and myosin filaments requires the breakdown of ATP. Normal respiration in muscle cell mitochondria supplies enough ATP for moderate activity. During strenuous exercise, however, muscles need far more ATP. To support increased work, the mitochondria need more glucose and oxygen. The heart and breathing rates speed up. It may take as long as a minute for the extra fuel and oxygen to get to the muscles.

Immediate fuel is provided by glucose. Stored glycogen can be quickly broken down into glucose to provide energy for ATP synthesis. Normally, cells need oxygen to break down glucose and synthesize ATP. However, muscle cells can release energy from glucose without oxygen present. This anaerobic process is called lactic acid fermentation. Therefore, during heavy exercise, lactic acid accumulates in muscle tissue.

When the heartbeat and breathing become stronger, muscle cells receive more oxygen. When you stop exercising, you continue to breathe hard for a while. The extra oxygen is used to convert accumulated lactic acid back to glycogen.

37-5 Movement of Joints

Muscles are attached to bones by **tendons**. Most skeletal muscles are attached to two bones. During contraction, only one of these bones usually moves. The **origin** of the muscle is the place where it attaches to the nonmoving bone. The **insertion** is the place where it attaches to the moving bone.

Figure 37-10 illustrates how muscles move the lower arm. When you bend your elbow, it is the biceps muscle that does the work. The origin of the biceps is the top of the upper arm bone. The insertion is on a bone of the lower arm. When your biceps contracts, your lower arm is brought up. To straighten your arm, you use the triceps muscle. The biceps then relaxes. Two muscles are necessary because a muscle can only exert a force when it contracts, not when it relaxes. Bending a joint is called flexion; straightening a joint is called extension.

The biceps and triceps form an **antagonist pair** of muscles. Each member of an antagonist pair usually moves the bone in a direction opposite to that of the other member. Most skeletal muscles are members of antagonist pairs. Complex motions require many sets of such muscles at each joint.

37-6 Cardiac Muscle and Smooth Muscle

The heart is made of **cardiac muscle**. Cardiac muscle cells are much shorter than skeletal muscle cells and they have many more mitochondria.

Cardiac muscle is involuntary. **Involuntary muscle** is under the control of automatic signals produced by the brain. You cannot control cardiac muscle as you control most skeletal muscle movements. However some skeletal muscle control is also involuntary.

Cardiac muscle does not tire as easily as skeletal muscle. If you open and close your fist 70 times a minute, your muscles will fatigue quickly. Yet cardiac muscle contracts and relaxes at this rate all the time. This requires a constant supply of ATP. Large numbers of mitochondria provides the necessary ATP.

Smooth muscle, illustrated in Figure 37-11, is a third type of muscle tissue. Each cell has a single nucleus. The cell is thin and tapered at both ends. Actin and myosin fibers are present in the cytoplasm. However, the fibers are not arranged in repeating units as they are in sarcomeres.

Smooth muscle occurs primarily in internal organs. For example, contractions of smooth muscle move food through the digestive system. The walls of many blood vessels contain smooth muscle. They regulate the flow of blood. Most smooth muscle is not under voluntary control.

37-7 Structure and Function of Skin

Human skin is composed of two basic layers of tissue. The outermost tissue, called **epidermis**, lies on top of the thicker **dermis**. Figure 37-12 illustrates a cross section of human skin.

Epidermis is made of layers of epithelial cells. Cells in the lowest layer undergo constant mitosis. New cells that result are pushed toward the surface. The uppermost layer consists of dead cells. These cells form a protective barrier that prevents harmful chemicals and microorganisms from entering the body. Epidermis also protects the body from harmful ultraviolet radiation. Recently, there has been an increase in the amount of ultraviolet radiation penetrating Earth's atmosphere. A greater number of skin cancer cases has accompanied this increase. More than ever, it is important to avoid over-exposure to the sun and other sources of this harmful radiation to protect your skin from potentially harmful rays.

The dermis contains several types of connective tissue. One type, **adipose** [ad′ ə pōs] **tissue**, includes fat-storing cells. Also located within the dermis are **hair follicles**. Each follicle produces a single hair. Next to every hair follicle is a **sebaceous** [sə bā′ shəs] **gland**. Oil from these glands helps prevent the skin's outer layer from drying and cracking. The dermis also contains **sweat glands**. When the body becomes heated, sweat glands secrete water onto the skin. The evaporation of sweat helps to cool the body. The skin helps maintain homeostasis by regulating heat loss.

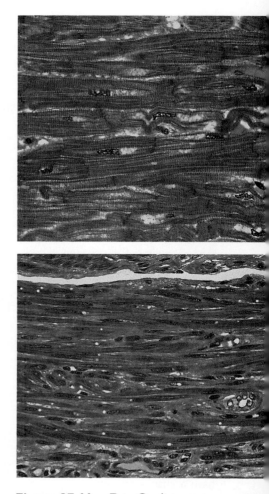

Figure 37-11 *Top:* Cardiac muscle tissue contracts at an average rate of 70 times per minute. The only time this tissue rests is in between contractions. *Bottom:* Smooth muscle moves by wavelike contractions that often go unnoticed.

CONSUMER BIOLOGY

Collagen in skin creams cannot make your skin appear younger by filling in wrinkles, because it cannot be absorbed by the skin. Injected collagen temporarily plumps sagging skin. However, the collagen is reabsorbed by the body and the wrinkles return.

DO YOU KNOW?

Information: Medical scientists have developed artificial skin for use with burn patients. This material is used to provide a barrier against infection but allows gases to diffuse. Artificial skin is used only temporarily while new skin grafts have a chance to take.

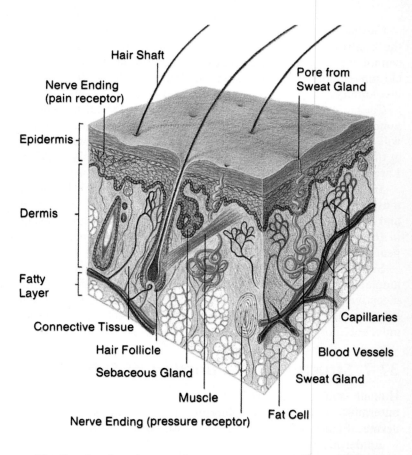

Hair Shaft

Nerve Ending (pain receptor)

Pore from Sweat Gland

Epidermis

Dermis

Fatty Layer

Connective Tissue

Hair Follicle

Sebaceous Gland

Muscle

Nerve Ending (pressure receptor)

Capillaries

Blood Vessels

Sweat Gland

Fat Cell

Finally the dermis contains many nerve endings. These are sensitive to pressure, touch, heat, cold, and pain. Through these senses your brain receives information from the environment.

CHECKPOINT ◆

5. What are the two major proteins found in sarcomeres?
6. What compound accumulates in skeletal muscle during exercise?
7. What term describes muscles that move a joint in opposite directions?
8. During vigorous exercise, the breakdown of what substance provides the energy needed for ATP synthesis?
9. Name the three types of muscle tissue in your body.
10. What are the two basic layers of the skin?
▶ 11. What property of muscle makes antagonist pairs necessary?
▶ 12. Explain why it is important that skeletal muscle is able to operate without oxygen for short periods of time.

▶ Denotes a question that involves *interpreting* and *applying* concepts.

A SURVEY OF HUMAN BODY TISSUES

In this lab you will compare and contrast various types of body tissues.

Objectives and Skills

☐ *Observe* and *recognize* the microscopic appearance of some basic human tissues.
☐ *Compare* the features of cardiac and striated muscle.

Materials

compound microscope
light source
prepared slides of:
   striated muscle
   cardiac muscle
   smooth muscle
   compact bone
   cartilage
   blood
   nerve
   skin

Procedure and Observations

1. Read all instructions for this laboratory activity before you begin your work.
2. Observe each of the three kinds of muscle tissue through a microscope. As always, begin by focusing on the slide with low power, then carefully switch the magnification to high power. Be careful not to touch the slide with the objective while focusing under high power.
3. Find a single muscle fiber or muscle cell on your slide. On a separate piece of paper, make a drawing of that cell as it appears under high power. Repeat this procedure with the other two types of muscle tissue.
4. Observe a slide of bone tissue under low power. Focus on a single Haversian canal

system and make a drawing of it. Label the Haversian canal itself, a few bone cells, and the matrix.
5. Observe a slide of cartilage. Locate the cartilage cells under high power and identify the matrix. Draw a typical cell.
6. Observe a slide of blood. There are two kinds of cells on this slide. The cells without nuclei are red blood cells. The cells with darkly stained nuclei are white blood cells. Draw a typical red cell and a white cell as seen under high power.
7. Observe a slide of nerve cells. Find one nerve cell under high power and make a drawing of it.
8. Finally observe a slide of skin. Compare what you see on the slide to Figure 37-12 in the chapter. Identify as many of the structures on the slide as you can.

Analysis and Conclusions

1. In all of the cells you observed, were there any common features?
2. In what ways was cardiac muscle similar to striated muscle? In what ways was it different?
3. Which of the kinds of cells you observed are classified as connective tissue?
4. Choose one type of cell from all those you observed and explain how its structure is suited to its particular function.

CHAPTER REVIEW

Summary

▶ The entire human body is made up of only four basic types of tissue: epithelial, nerve, muscle, and connective.

▶ Bone and cartilage are two types of connective tissue that make up the human skeleton. Bone is a living tissue made by osteocytes, which secrete a matrix around themselves. Collagen and minerals give the bone strength and hardness.

▶ The process of ossification replaces most of the cartilage in the human skeleton with bone. A diet containing both vitamins and minerals is necessary for proper bone growth and repair.

▶ Bones come together at joints. Joints are classified according to the kind of motion they allow.

▶ Muscle tissue exerts a force when it contracts. It is responsible for all body movements—both voluntary and involuntary.

▶ Skeletal or striated muscle is responsible for the voluntary movements of a human skeleton.

▶ Individual muscle fibers contain filaments of actin and myosin which are responsible for the contraction of a muscle.

▶ Under normal conditions, ATP for muscle contraction is produced by mitochondria in the muscle tissue. During strenuous exercise, ATP is produced by lactic acid fermentation.

▶ Since muscles can only exert force when contracting, joints move by the action of antagonist pairs. Tendons attach muscles to bones.

▶ Cardiac muscle is found only in the heart. It has a large number of mitochondria.

▶ Smooth muscle occurs primarily in internal organs. It is generally involuntary muscle.

▶ Skin consists of two basic layers, the epidermis and the dermis. Skin protects the body, regulates body temperature and picks up information from the environment.

Vocabulary

actin	matrix
adipose tissue	muscle tissue
antagonist pair	myofibril
ball-and-socket joint	myosin
cardiac muscle	nerve tissue
collagen	origin
connective tissue	ossification
dermis	osteocyte
epidermis	osteoporosis
epithelial tissue	periosteum
gliding joint	sarcomere
hair follicle	sebaceous gland
Haversian canal	skeletal muscle
hinge joint	smooth muscle
immovable joint	striated muscle
insertion	sweat gland
involuntary muscle	synovial fluid
ligament	tendon
marrow	vertebral disk
	voluntary muscle

Concept Mapping

Construct a concept map for muscle tissue. Include the following terms: bone, cardiac muscle, involuntary muscle, skeletal muscle, smooth muscle, striated muscle, voluntary muscle. Use additional terms as you need them.

Review

1. To which of the four basic tissue types do bone and cartilage belong?
2. Which of the four basic types of tissue can contract?
3. What kind of joint is most common in the skull? What kind of joint is the shoulder?
4. What two important elements are stored and released by bone cells?
5. How does cartilage change to bone?

In items 6 through 10, state the function of each of the structures.

6. ligament
7. sebaceous gland
8. glycogen
9. sarcomere
10. myosin
11. What kind of muscle tissue has the most mitochondria?
12. What is the insertion of a muscle?
13. Muscles produce lactic acid under what conditions?

Interpret and Apply

14. What properties of bone and cartilage suit them for different functions?
15. Which of the four types of tissue can be found in skin?
16. Given the all-or-none response of muscle fibers, explain how a muscle can exert different amounts of force.
17. What is the significance of the large number of mitochondria in cardiac muscle cells?
18. Why would a ball-and-socket joint be inappropriate as a knee joint?
19. Arrange the following terms in increasing order of size: sarcomere, muscle, myofibril, muscle fiber, actin.
20. What is the source of ATP for muscle fibers under normal conditions?
21. The muscles that open and close your jaw are an antagonist pair. One member of the pair is much larger and more powerful than the other. Which muscle is larger and why?
22. In what way is smooth muscle similar to striated muscle?
23. How does sweating help maintain homeostasis?

Critical Thinking

24. Ligaments contain a great deal of elastin, a protein that can stretch and return to its original length. Tendons have mostly collagen and very little elastin. How does the composition of these two types of connective tissue reflect their function?
25. Explain why the rate of your breathing and heartbeat does not decrease until several minutes after you stop exercising.
26. Suppose the nerve connections to the biceps muscle were damaged. How would this affect movement of the arm?
27. A structure called the iris controls the amount of light entering your eyes. The iris is controlled by muscles. Are these muscles skeletal, smooth, or cardiac? Are they voluntary or involuntary? Explain.
28. Suppose that your skin was not sensitive to pressure or pain. What might happen to the muscles and internal organs beneath the skin?
29. By the time you are 20 years old, most of your bones will have stopped growing. However, you will continue to need calcium. Why do you think this is so?
30. Why are immovable joints important in some parts of the skeleton?
31. How would you arrange a pair of antagonist muscles to turn your head from side to side?
32. There is concern because the ozone layer in the upper atmosphere of Earth is getting thinner. Ozone prevents some of the sun's ultraviolet radiation from reaching the surface of Earth. Why might this be a problem for humans?
33. Sharks have skeletons made entirely of cartilage. Why would such a skeleton not be practical for a human being?

DIGESTION AND NUTRITION

Overview

UPPER ALIMENTARY CANAL

38-1 The Digestive Process

38-2 The Mouth

38-3 The Esophagus

38-4 Stomach Structure and Function

LOWER ALIMENTARY CANAL

38-5 The Pancreas and Liver

38-6 Small Intestine: Structure

38-7 Small Intestine: Function

38-8 The Large Intestine

NUTRITION

38-9 Measuring Energy in Food

38-10 Carbohydrates and Fats in the Diet

38-11 Proteins in the Diet

38-12 Vitamins, Minerals, and Water

38-13 The Importance of a Balanced Diet

38-14 Eating Disorders

How do you know which kinds of foods are nutritious?

UPPER ALIMENTARY CANAL

The food you eat comes from organisms that were once living. Therefore, food is an extremely complex mixture of proteins, carbohydrates, lipids, and other substances. To supply your cells with these necessary substances, they first must be broken down into small molecules. This process is called **digestion**. Small molecules can diffuse through cell membranes and be absorbed into the body.

Food is digested in the alimentary canal. The **alimentary** [al ə ment′ ə rē] **canal** is a continuous tube beginning at the mouth and ending at the anus. Different parts of the alimentary canal are modified into specialized organs. In this lesson, you will learn about the functions of the upper part of the alimentary canal.

38-1 The Digestive Process

The digestion of food involves both chemical and mechanical processes. **Chemical digestion** is the chemical breakdown of large molecules into small ones. Remember that protein, carbohydrate, and fat molecules can be broken down by combining them with water. This process is known as hydrolysis. Proteins are hydrolyzed into amino acids. Polysaccharides are hydrolyzed into simple sugars, usually glucose. Triglycerides are hydrolyzed into fatty acids and glycerol. Many specialized digestive enzymes are secreted into the alimentary canal to hydrolyze each of these large molecules.

Mechanical digestion is the physical breakdown of food into small particles. Chewing and muscular churning help physically break apart food. Consider a cube of food like a piece of cheese. Only the molecules on the surface are exposed to digestive enzymes. However, if the cube of cheese is cut repeatedly, more surface area would be created. Digestive enzymes come into contact with greater numbers of food molecules. Therefore, by exposing more surface area of food to digestive enzymes, mechanical digestion speeds up chemical digestion.

38-2 The Mouth

Mechanical digestion begins in the mouth. Figure 38-1 is a diagram of the mouth. Jaw muscles contract, causing teeth to cut, tear, and grind food. The front four teeth are called **incisors** [in sī′ zers]. These sharp teeth cut food into smaller pieces. The pointed **canine teeth** also tear food. The **premolars** and **molars** have flat surfaces adapted for grinding. The variety of teeth

Section Objectives

A *Compare* and *contrast* chemical digestion and mechanical digestion.

B *Explain* how structures in the mouth help prepare food for the rest of the digestive system.

C *Describe* the structure and function of the esophagus.

D *Identify* several functions of the stomach.

Figure 38-1 Digestion begins in the mouth. Here, food is broken down into smaller pieces by the teeth and acted upon by enzymes from the salivary glands. The uvula helps prevent food from entering the upper part of the pharynx.

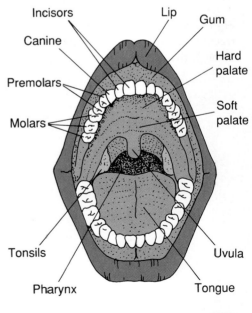

Digestion and Nutrition **629**

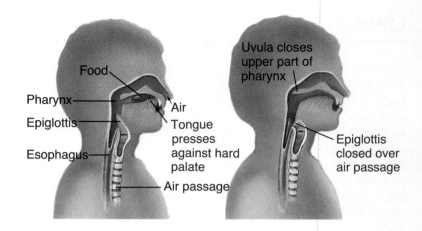

Figure 38-2 The process of swallowing consists of two main steps. The first step, which is voluntary, involves movement of food from the mouth to the pharynx. The second step, which is involuntary, is the movement of food from the pharynx into the esophagus. This involves closing the mouth, the upper pharynx, and the breathing tube.

Figure 38-3 The muscular contractions of peristalsis move food through the digestive system.

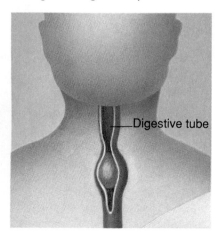

Digestive tube

indicates that you are adapted to eat a diet of both plant and animal sources.

Several secretions are added to food as it is chewed. **Mucus** comes from cells lining the mouth. Mucus makes food easier to swallow. Three pairs of salivary glands add **saliva** to food. Like mucus, saliva lubricates food. In addition, saliva contains the enzyme **amylase** [am′ ə lās]. Amylase breaks down long chains of polysaccharide starch into shorter chain polysaccharides and into the disaccharide maltose.

The tongue is a muscular organ. It keeps food where it can be chewed by the teeth. It also pushes food to the back of the mouth when you swallow. In addition, your sense of taste is located primarily on the tongue.

Swallowing involves complex muscle actions. It is illustrated in Figure 38-2. First, food is forced into the large area at the back of the mouth called the **pharynx** [far′ ingks]. From the pharynx, food then passes the point where air passes to the lungs. Food and liquids are prevented from entering the lungs by a structure called the **epiglottis** [ep ə glot′ əs]. The epiglottis closes over the air passage each time you swallow.

38-3 The Esophagus

After food is swallowed, it passes from the pharynx into the **esophagus** [i sof′ ə gəs]. The esophagus carries food from the mouth to the stomach. In some ways, the structure of the esophagus is typical of the entire alimentary canal. The hollow interior space of the esophagus is the **lumen** [lū′ men]. The layers of cells that line the lumen secrete mucus and are called the **mucosa** [myü kō′ sə]. The mucus helps ease the passage of food.

Beneath the mucosa are two layers of muscle. In the innermost layer, muscle fibers wrap around the esophagus. The fibers of the outermost layer, however, line up along the length of the esophagus. These muscle layers alternately relax and contract. This action causes waves of constriction to move along the esophagus. Food is pushed ahead of these waves. This rhythmic muscular action is called **peristalsis** [per ə stòl′ səs]. Beginning in the esophagus, peristalsis moves food through the entire alimentary canal.

38-4 Stomach Structure and Function

When food reaches the end of the esophagus it enters the **stomach**. The opening to the stomach is controlled by a sphincter muscle. Like the opening to a duffle bag, a **sphincter** [sfingk′ ter] muscle opens and closes a tube. Look at Figure 38-4. The stomach is a large J-shaped organ. One of the major functions of the stomach is food storage. It can hold about 2 liters of food. Without a stomach, you would have to eat many small meals each day.

Like the esophagus, the stomach is lined with a layer of cells called the mucosa. There are three kinds of cells in the stomach mucosa. One kind secretes mucus. Another kind secretes enzymes. The third secretes hydrochloric acid and water. The enzymes, water, and hydrochloric acid combine to form **gastric juice**. Hydrochloric acid is a strong acid. The pH of gastric juice is about 1.0. It helps break up connective tissue and cell membranes in food. The acid also kills many harmful bacteria.

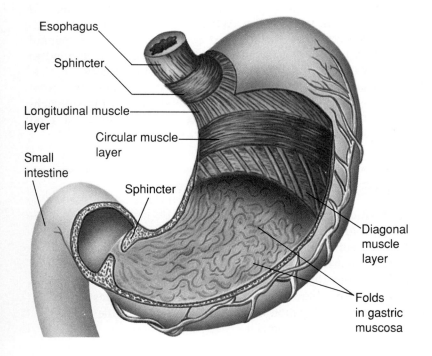

Esophagus

Sphincter

Longitudinal muscle layer

Small intestine

Circular muscle layer

Sphincter

Diagonal muscle layer

Folds in gastric muscosa

Figure 38-4 Mechanical digestion and movement are accomplished by the stomach's three muscle layers. Gastric glands secrete mucus, acid, and the enzyme pepsin. The stomach normally stores food for about four hours before moving it into the small intestine.

Table 38-1

DIGESTIVE ENZYMES		
Enzyme	**Origin**	**Function**
Amylase	Salivary glands, pancreas	Starch breakdown
Pepsin	Stomach	Protein breakdown
Trypsin	Pancreas	Further breakdown of protein
Lipase	Pancreas	Fat breakdown
Peptidase	Intestinal epithelium	Breakdown of short polypeptides
Maltase	Intestinal epithelium	Maltose breakdown

The enzymes produced by the stomach are mostly **proteases** [prō′ tē ā zez]. Proteases hydrolyze proteins. The principal stomach protease is called *pepsin*. Under acidic conditions, it breaks down protein into polypeptides.

Chemical digestion by gastric juice is aided by mechanical digestion. Peristalsis of the stomach walls churns food for several hours. After this, most food is the consistency of a thick soup.

Why are stomach cells not destroyed by gastric juice? Self-digestion is prevented by several factors. One is mucus. Mucus is resistant to attack by gastric juice and protects the delicate stomach cells. Sheets of fat molecules in the stomach resist digestion because fat digests more slowly than carbohydrate or protein. Finally, digestive enzymes are only activated by an acid environment in the stomach. When these factors are out of balance, stomach cells are attacked by gastric juice. This painful condition is known as an **ulcer**. Mild ulcers usually respond to changes in diet, but severe ulcers can require surgery.

A second sphincter muscle is located at the end of the stomach. Together, the two muscles keep food within the stomach. When the second sphincter relaxes, partially digested food moves into the small intestine.

BIOLOGY INSIGHT

Structure Is Related to Function: The shape of an enzyme is a function of how its amino acid side groups interact with each other and with the environment. The pH of the environment can affect the shape, and therefore the function, of an enzyme. Each enzyme has a pH at which it functions best. Amylase functions best in nearly neutral pH, and pepsin functions best in the acidic pH of the stomach.

CHECKPOINT ◆

1. What are the two types of digestion?
2. What are the four kinds of teeth in humans?
3. What substance is broken down by amylase?
4. How many muscle layers are found in the esophagus?
▶ 5. How does the combined action of sphincter muscles and peristalsis in the stomach aid in mechanical digestion?
▶ 6. Identify the location of chemical digestion in the mouth, esophagus, and stomach.

▶ Denotes a question that involves *interpreting* and *applying* concepts.

LOWER ALIMENTARY CANAL

The stomach prepares food for the **small intestine**, the most important organ of the digestive tract. If the small intestine was stretched out, it would be about six meters long. You will see that the small intestine is the site of most chemical digestion, and it is where food molecules are absorbed into the blood.

After leaving the small intestine, undigested wastes pass on to the **large intestine** where water is recovered. The remaining solid wastes are expelled from the body.

38-5 The Pancreas and Liver

The location of the pancreas and liver is shown in Figure 38-5. While they are not a part of the alimentary canal, these two organs play important roles in digestion.

The **pancreas** [pan' krē əs] has two principal functions. First, it produces hormones that regulate the homeostasis of blood glucose. You will learn more about this function in Chapter 43. Second, it produces **pancreatic juice**. Pancreatic juice neutralizes the acidic stomach contents before they move into the rest of the small intestine. Pancreatic juice also contains a number of digestive enzymes. Among them are several different proteases. They continue the protein digestion begun in the stomach, breaking down polypeptides into shorter chains.

The pancreas also secretes a **lipase**. This type of enzyme breaks fat molecules, or triglycerides, into fatty acids and glycerol. An amylase similar to the one produced in the salivary glands is also produced by the pancreas. Pancreatic juice reaches the small intestine through the pancreatic duct.

The liver has many functions, and several are related to digestion. If glucose is absorbed into the blood from a meal, liver cells take the glucose and convert it to glycogen, a polysaccharide. The liver stores this glycogen until it is needed by the body.

The liver also produces a complex fluid called **bile**. Bile contains no enzymes. It does, however, aid in the digestion of lipids. Recall that lipids do not dissolve in water; thus the lipids in your diet do not dissolve in watery gastric juice. An *emulsifier* is a chemical that breaks fats and oils into extremely tiny droplets. Emulsifiers in bile act on fats and oils in the intestine. Pancreatic lipase can then digest the lipids much faster since the small droplets have more surface area.

Bile travels through ducts to the **gallbladder**, where it is stored. During digestion, the gallbladder releases bile into the small intestine through the **common bile duct**. These structures and their relationship to the pancreatic duct are shown in Figure 38-5.

Section Objectives

E *List* the functions of the pancreas and the liver in digestion.

F *Describe* the structure and function of the small intestine.

G *Explain* the function of the large intestine.

DO YOU KNOW?

Information: One component of bile is a chemical left over from the destruction of old red blood cells. This chemical gives bile a brilliant yellow color.

BIOLOGY INSIGHT

Unity and Diversity: Repetitive, rhythmic muscle contraction is observed in all the animal phyla. Jellyfish use such contractions to swim weakly in the water. Earthworms move by body-wall contractions similar to peristalsis. There is peristaltic movement in the digestive systems of all animals that have such a system.

Digestion and Nutrition **633**

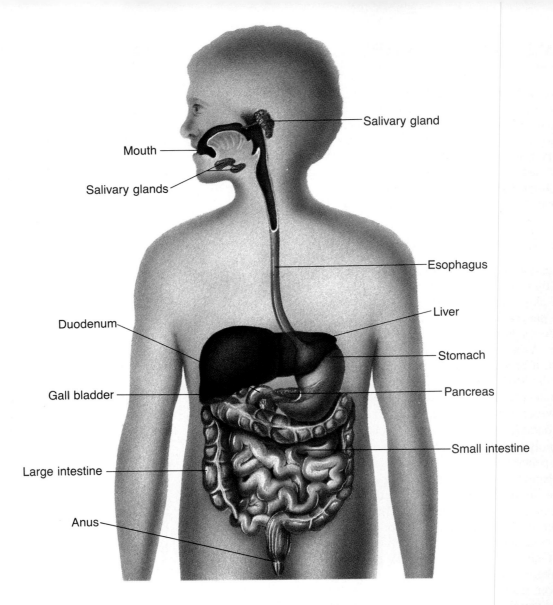

Mouth

Salivary glands

Salivary gland

Esophagus

Duodenum

Liver

Gall bladder

Stomach

Pancreas

Small intestine

Large intestine

Anus

Figure 38-5 The human digestive system is a long tube. Organs such as the salivary glands, the pancreas, and liver secrete substances into the tube that help digest and absorb nutrients.

You may know someone who has had gallstones. These stone-like deposits develop from insoluble materials in the bile. They can block the bile duct and cause bile to accumulate in the gallbladder. In serious cases, the gallbladder can be surgically removed. Removal has no serious lasting effects on an individual.

38-6 Small Intestine: Structure

The interior of the small intestine has an enormous surface area. This adaptation permits the absorption of a very large amount of food molecules. The mucosa of the small intestine is folded.

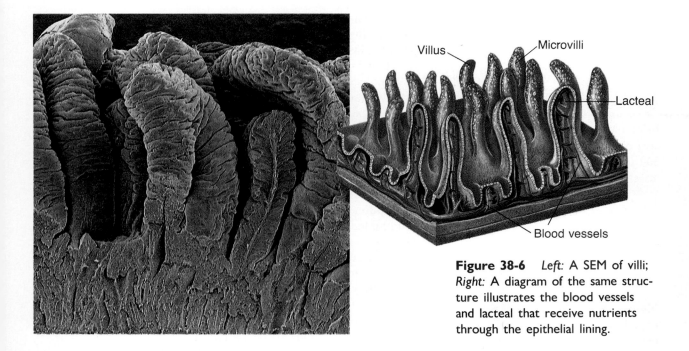

Figure 38-6 *Left:* A SEM of villi; *Right:* A diagram of the same structure illustrates the blood vessels and lacteal that receive nutrients through the epithelial lining.

These folds increase the surface area of the small intestine by a factor of two. The tiny fingerlike projections from these folds are called **villi** [vil′ ī]. The villi increase the surface area by another factor of ten.

Figure 38-6 is a diagram and a micrograph of a villus. There are vessels within the villus. Most of the vessels are blood capillaries. In addition to capillaries, there is a lacteal. The **lacteal** [lak′ tē əl] absorbs fats from the lumen of the intestine. Lacteals are part of the lymphatic system which is discussed in more detail in Chapter 40.

The villus is covered by a single layer of epithelial cells. Small food molecules from the lumen must pass through this layer of cells to reach the vessels. Note the cell membrane that faces the lumen of the intestine. This membrane is folded into many tiny projections. These are microvilli. They increase the total surface area of the small intestine even further.

38-7 Small Intestine: Function

Food from the stomach enters the first 30 centimeters of the small intestine called the **duodenum** [dü ō dē′ nəm]. Bile and pancreatic juice enter the small intestine here.

Cells of the intestinal epithelium also produce a number of digestive enzymes. These enzymes, unlike those of the pancreas, are not released into the lumen. Rather, they are embedded in

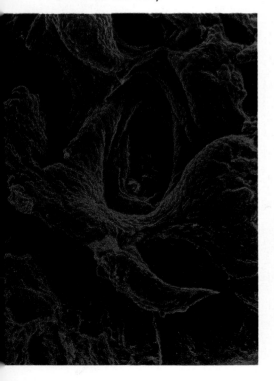

Figure 38-7 The lining of the large intestine contains many tunnels and crevices. Here, glands secrete mucus that helps to bind together waste materials for their exit from the body.

the epithelial cell membranes. Among these enzymes are **peptidases** [pep′ tə dā ses]. They break the short polypeptides into individual amino acids. Several other epithelial enzymes break disaccharides into monosaccharides. Maltase, for example, breaks maltose into two molecules of glucose. Maltose is produced when amylase digests starch.

Look again at Figure 38-5. After the duodenum, the next several meters of small intestine are called the **jejunum** [ji jü′ nəm]. In the jejunum, many small molecules are absorbed through the villi into blood vessels. By the time food reaches the last half of the small intestine, called the **ileum** [il′ ē əm], most chemical digestion has been completed. The process of absorption predominates in this part of the small intestine. Some food molecules move through the epithelium by simple diffusion. Other molecules, such as glucose and amino acids, are actively transported across the epithelial cell membranes.

Once simple sugars and amino acids cross the epithelial cell layer, they move into the bloodstream. Blood leaves the small intestine and moves directly to the liver. The liver removes excess glucose from the blood and stores it as glycogen. The liver also removes amino acids from the blood.

Fatty acids and glycerol follow a different path. These molecules pass into the intestinal epithelial cells. They are immediately converted back to triglycerides. The triglycerides are absorbed into the lacteals. Lacteals are part of a system of vessels that bypasses the liver and dumps the triglycerides directly into the bloodstream.

38-8 The Large Intestine

The large intestine gets its name from its diameter rather than from its length. The large intestine is only about two meters long. However, it is approximately twice as wide as the small intestine. The large intestine is also known as the **colon** [kō′ lən].

Where the small and large intestine join, there is a small projection called the **appendix**. Its exact functions are unclear, however, in some plant-eating animals like rabbits, it helps digest cellulose. Occasionally, bacteria can lodge in the appendix where they grow and secrete toxic waste products. The result is a painful inflammation called appendicitis. In such cases, the appendix is surgically removed. Appendicitis is more common in children than in adults because the opening to the appendix is larger in children.

The major function of the colon is to absorb water from the lumen. The amount of water in the body must remain reasonably constant. A great deal of water is pumped into the stomach as gastric juice. Cells of the colon mucosa actively transport ions

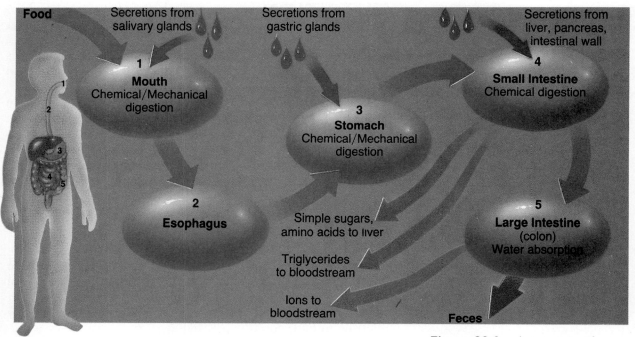

Food — Secretions from salivary glands

1 Mouth Chemical/Mechanical digestion

Secretions from gastric glands

Secretions from liver, pancreas, intestinal wall

4 Small Intestine Chemical digestion

3 Stomach Chemical/Mechanical digestion

2 Esophagus

Simple sugars, amino acids to liver

Triglycerides to bloodstream

Ions to bloodstream

5 Large Intestine (colon) Water absorption

Feces

Figure 38-8 A summary of digestive system activity is illustrated. Activities involve chemical digestion, secretion, movement, and absorption.

from the lumen into the blood. Water follows the ions by osmosis. The only residue of food at the end of the colon is indigestible waste, called **feces**.

Feces is about 75 percent water and 25 percent solid matter. The solid matter is composed of about 30 percent dead bacteria, 10–20 percent inorganic matter, 2–3 percent protein, and 30 percent undigested fiber of the food. In addition, feces contains epithelial cells and bile pigments.

The last 20 or 30 centimeters of the colon are called the **rectum**. Feces are stored there until they are eliminated from the body through the anus.

DO YOU KNOW?

Information: The brown color of feces is caused by bile pigments, which are derived from the breakdown of hemoglobin.

CHECKPOINT ◆

7. What enzymes are produced by the pancreas?
8. What is the function of bile?
9. What are villi?
10. What is another name for the large intestine?
▶ 11. If necessary, it is possible to remove most or all of the esophagus, the stomach, or the large intestine. Removal of most or all of the small intestine, however, is not possible. Explain why this is the case.
▶ 12. Why is it possible to live normally with your gallbladder removed?

▶ Denotes a question that involves *interpreting* and *applying* concepts.

NUTRITION

Section Objectives

H *Describe* the unit measuring the energy content of food.

I *Explain* the role of carbohydrates and fats in the diet.

J *List* several functions of proteins in your diet.

K *List* some important vitamins and minerals in the diet and *identify* their functions.

L *Explain* what is meant by a balanced diet and why such a diet is important.

M *Compare* two kinds of eating disorders.

CONSUMER BIOLOGY

Some artificial sweeteners taste like sugar because they are shaped like sugar and fit the taste receptors on the tongue for sweet taste.

Food supplies your body with energy. It also provides materials for growth, maintenance, and replacement of tissues. **Nutrition** is the process by which organisms obtain and use food.

The chemical substances that you consume to grow and remain healthy are called **nutrients**. There are two classes of nutrients: those that can provide energy and those that cannot. Energy-supplying nutrients include carbohydrates, fats, and proteins. Vitamins, minerals, and water are the nutrients that do not provide energy but serve equally important functions.

38-9 Measuring the Energy in Food

The energy content of food is measured in **food calories**, or kilocalories. A calorie is the amount of energy necessary to raise the temperature of one gram of water one degree Celsius. One thousand calories are equal to one kilocalorie, or one food calorie. When nutritionists list the calories in foods, they are actually referring to kilocalories.

Food molecules, like all other molecules, are composed of chemical bonds. The easiest way to measure the amount of energy in those bonds is to release it all at once as heat. This is done simply by burning a piece of food. The amount of heat released from the burning food can be measured as it heats a known amount of water.

38-10 Carbohydrates and Fats in the Diet

The primary function of carbohydrates in your body is to supply energy. As you will see, the simple sugar glucose is by far the most common carbohydrate in your diet. Your body cells use glucose in the process of cellular respiration, in which glucose combines with oxygen to produce carbon dioxide and water. ATP is produced which provides cells with usable energy.

Simple sugars other than glucose, such as fructose and galactose, also are a part of your diet. These molecules do not have to be digested in order to be absorbed by the small intestine. Disaccharides such as sucrose (table sugar) and lactose (milk sugar) are also common substances in the diet. These disaccharides must be hydrolyzed before they can be absorbed.

The majority of your carbohydrate intake is in the form of polysaccharides. Three plant seeds—rice, wheat, and corn—are rich in starch. Potato is also rich in starch. How much of your diet consists of these substances? Remember that wheat flour is the base of all breads, pastas, and related foods. As you have seen, starch is digested to glucose by amylases and maltase in the mouth and in the small intestine.

Another polysaccharide is cellulose, which forms the cell wall of all plant cells. Humans cannot digest cellulose. However, cellulose is an important part of a normal diet. It provides fiber, against which the intestinal muscles push. Food with high fiber content moves more quickly through the alimentary canal. There is some evidence that people with high-fiber diets have a lower incidence of colon cancer.

If you consume more carbohydrates than your body requires for day-to-day activity, the carbohydrate can be chemically converted to fat and stored.

The fats you consume are primarily triglycerides. Like carbohydrates, fats can provide the body with energy. However, fats contain far more food calories per unit of mass than do carbohydrates. Therefore, fat stores a lot of energy in a small volume and is available for use when food is not available on a constant basis.

The body uses fat for other things besides energy. Recall that fats form part of the cell membrane. Fat is necessary for the conduction of nerve impulses. Also, certain vitamins are found only in fatty foods. Foods that are rich in fats include margarine, butter, salad oils, cheeses, and many meats.

You may recall that saturated fats have no double bonds in the fatty acid molecules. Saturated fats, and another lipid called *cholesterol*, are associated with deposits on the inner wall of blood vessels. Such deposits can create serious problems with the circulatory system and are described in more detail in Chapter 40. Saturated fats are commonly found in fats of animal origin. Some of the foods rich in cholesterol are egg yolks, whole milk, and red meats.

■■ BIOLOGY INSIGHT ■

Life Forms Are Interconnected: The lumen of the large intestine is populated by an enormous number of *E. coli* bacteria. They are present in all normal, healthy individuals. It is thought that these bacteria are a major source of vitamin K for the body. Humans benefit by obtaining a necessary vitamin. The bacteria benefit by having a place with a constant warm temperature, constant food supply arriving from the small intestine, and a sufficient water supply. This is an ideal environment for bacterial growth.

CONSUMER BIOLOGY

Olives and avocadoes are pure fat.

Figure 38-9 Energy to fuel body processes is derived from the breakdown of chemical bonds in carbohydrates and fats. Each gram of carbohydrate yields four calories; each gram of fat yields nine calories. Current research indicates that Americans consume 60 percent of their calories as carbohydrate and 30 percent or less as fat.

Figure 38-10 Protein sources such as these are common in the American diet. Like carbohydrate, a gram of protein yields about four calories. It has been recommended that adults receive 10–15 percent of their calories from protein sources. Many Americans consume more than this.

CONSUMER BIOLOGY

Some vegetarians eat dairy products and eggs. They are getting complete proteins in these foods. Strict vegetarians, however, eat no animal products. Since plant proteins are incomplete, strict vegetarians must combine foods to obtain complete protein.

38-11 Proteins in the Diet

Proteins are the third group of nutrients that can provide energy. Their primary use, however, is not to supply the body with energy. They make up much of the structure of cells. Thus, they are needed for cell growth and repair. As enzymes, proteins also have a major role in governing cell metabolism.

Proteins are digested to amino acids in the small intestine and absorbed into the blood. When these amino acids reach body cells, they are reassembled to make new protein according to your own genetic instructions.

Recall that there are 20 amino acids found in protein. Of these, your cells can make 12; the other 8 must be obtained from food. These eight amino acids are called *essential amino acids*.

Unless the body has all the essential amino acids at the same time, it cannot make proteins. Certain foods, sometimes called complete protein foods, contain all the essential amino acids. If you eat one of these foods, you will have all the essential amino acids at one time. Meat, milk, poultry, fish, cheese, and eggs are complete foods.

Other foods contain some, but not all, of the essential amino acids. Soybeans, for example, lack valine and methionine. Rice does not have isoleucine or lysine. If you eat soybeans and rice together, they supply all the essential amino acids.

38-12 Vitamins, Minerals, and Water

Vitamins, minerals, and water are nutrients that do not supply the body with energy. Instead, they perform other functions.

Vitamins often act as coenzymes. Such molecules are necessary for various chemical reactions to occur in the body. The functions and food sources of various vitamins are described in Table 38-2.

If vitamins are missing from the diet, serious problems can result. These conditions are called **deficiency diseases**. For example, people develop scurvy when they do not have enough vitamin C for a long time. Their gums swell and bleed. Their teeth fall out, and their joints become sore. Vitamin-D deficiency produces a disorder called rickets. In rickets, the bones become soft, and bone deformities result.

Vitamins can be divided into two groups on the basis of their solubility. The water-soluble vitamins include vitamin C and the members of the vitamin-B complex. Water-soluble vitamins can be lost from foods if they are exposed to water for too long. Overcooking also destroys many vitamins.

The other group contains the fat-soluble vitamins. Vitamins A, D, E, and K belong to this group. As you might expect, these vitamins tend to occur in fatty foods.

If you take vitamin pills, can you be less careful about your choice of foods? Nutritionists think not. Nutrients you need should be obtained from food rather than supplements.

CONSUMER BIOLOGY

Avoid vitamin supplements labeled as "high potency." Exceeding the recommended dietary allowances for a vitamin does not provide better nutrition. Misuse of vitamin supplements could result in a toxic overdose.

Table 38-2

DIETARY VITAMINS			
Vitamin	**Source**	**Function**	**Deficiency Symptoms**
A	Egg yolks, butter, green and yellow vegetables, organ meats, fish liver oils	Growth, healthy skin and eyes	Night blindness, changes in epithelial cells, retarded growth
B$_1$ (thiamin)	Seafood, poultry, meats, grains, green vegetables, milk, soybeans	Carbohydrate metabolism; growth; heart, muscle, and nerve function	Retarded growth, beri-beri, nerve disorders, fatigue
B$_2$ (riboflavin)	Milk, eggs, poultry, yeast, meats, soybeans, green vegetables	Carbohydrate metabolism, growth	Retarded growth, premature aging
Niacin	Leafy vegetables, peanut butter, potatoes, whole or enriched grain, fish, poultry, meats, tomatoes	Growth, carbohydrate metabolism, digestion, nerve function	Digestive and nervous disturbances
B$_{12}$	Green vegetables, liver	Production of red blood cells, nerve function	Anemia
C (ascorbic acid)	Citrus fruit, tomatoes, leafy vegetables	Growth, healthy gums	Sore gums, susceptibility to bruising
D	Milk, liver, eggs, fish liver oils	Growth, calcium and phosphate metabolism	Poor tooth development, rickets
E (tocopherol)	Vegetable oils, butter, milk, leafy vegetables	Protects cell membranes, reproductive function	Unknown
K	Green vegetables, tomatoes, soybean oil	Blood clotting, liver function	Hemorrhaging

DIETARY MINERALS

Mineral	Source	Function	Symptoms of Deficiency
Calcium	Milk and other dairy products, bean curd, green vegetables	Tooth and bone formation, nerve transmission, muscle contraction	Rickets, osteoporosis
Phosphorous	Most foods	Bone development, transfer of energy in cells	Unknown
Sodium	Meats, dairy products, salt	Nerve transmission, muscle contraction	Dehydration, shock
Chlorine	Salt	Formation of HCl	Abnormal contraction of muscles
Potassium	Fruits	Regulation of heartbeat, maintenance of water balance, nerve transmission	Heart dysfunction
Magnesium	Nuts, grains, green vegetables, seafood, chocolate	Catalyst for ATP formation	Weakness, mental confusion
Iodine	Seafood, iodized salt	Thyroid activity	Goiter
Iron	Meats, green vegetables, dried fruits	Hemoglobin formation	Anemia

Table 38-3

CONSUMER BIOLOGY

Most calcium that is eaten is not absorbed but is excreted in the feces. Vitamin D increases the amount of calcium that can be absorbed. Milk is fortified with vitamin D to facilitate calcium absorption. In older adults, calcium deficiency causes osteoporosis, a disintegration of bones. This condition is responsible for the frequent breakage of bones in the elderly.

Minerals are inorganic substances, generally found in the form of ions. The minerals in your diet have many functions. For example, they maintain the acid-base balance in the body fluids. They are important parts of many body structures, such as bone and red blood cells. The functions of various minerals are outlined in Table 38-3.

You obtain water by drinking it. It is also present in many foods. Water has many functions in the body. Most are related to water's role as a solvent. It dissolves food materials, so that they can pass into the bloodstream. Most of the body's chemical reactions occur in water solutions. The importance of water to all living things has been stressed in many other chapters.

38-13 The Importance of a Balanced Diet

Solon, a Greek philosopher who lived thousands of years ago, said, "Nothing in excess." His advice, applied to food, still makes a great deal of sense.

One way that nutritionists divide sources of nutrients is to place them into four groups. These are the meat group, the milk group, the fruit and vegetable group, and the cereal-grain group. Foods in the meat group include meat, fish, poultry, eggs, and legumes. The legumes, often called meat substitutes, include beans, peas, and peanuts. Besides milk itself, the milk group contains milk-based products like cheeses and yogurt.

The fruit and vegetable group, as the name implies, includes all fruits and vegetables. They may be fresh, frozen, canned, or dried. The cereal group includes grains and grain products. Among these are bread, cereal, rice, pasta, and tortillas. To achieve a balanced diet, you should eat foods from each group every day. A wide variety of foods is the best way to ensure that your body's cells get a sufficient supply of all the nutrients they require.

People who do not eat a balanced diet can develop health problems. The most serious of these is **malnutrition**. In malnutrition, an individual may get sufficient calories, but certain kinds of nutrients are deficient.

Undernourished people are more likely to contract diseases. Iron deficiency leads to anemias and reduced brain function. Poor diets also harm the growth and development of children. For example, a protein-poor diet in the first five years of a child's life will result in permanent brain damage.

Obesity is a condition characterized by excessive body fat. While usually not as serious as undernourishment, obesity is also unhealthy. Overweight people frequently have health problems. Among them are diabetes and heart disease.

To lose weight, people often go on diets. A well-planned, nutritionally balanced diet with a program of exercise can be very helpful. However, many fad diets lack important nutrients. In addition, it is very dangerous to lose a lot of weight over a short period of time. Early establishment of proper nutrition combined with regular exercise will go a long way toward ensuring a healthy body and a long life.

CONSUMER BIOLOGY

Nutritionists have calculated recommended daily allowances (RDAs) for various nutrients that an average person needs. Individual requirements differ, of course. For example, to prevent osteoporosis an elderly person needs more calcium than a young adult.

Figure 38-11 The vegetarian obtains the necessary nutrients from fewer food groups. A vegetarian meal shown includes brown rice, melon, tofu, carrots, broccoli, beans, and spinach. A meal such as this one provides a balanced diet without meat. Some vegetarians also exclude dairy products or fish from their diets.

38-14 Eating Disorders

Even more dangerous than fad diets and poor nutrition are the serious conditions known as eating disorders. Two such disorders have received much public concern and attention in recent years.

Anorexia nervosa is a condition in which patients see themselves as overweight and almost completely stop eating. Food, in fact, becomes distasteful to them. They never feel hungry, they deny their condition, and remain unconcerned for themselves. In severe cases, death from malnourishment can occur.

For reasons that are not clear, most anorexia patients are women in their teens and twenties. To achieve a cure, the patient must agree to seek counseling. With the support of professionals and family, a greater number of anorexia patients may be able to overcome their disease.

A somewhat different, but related eating disorder is *bulimia*. Again, most bulimics are young, well-educated women. These individuals maintain a relatively normal weight, unlike anorectics. When around people, bulimics eat normal meals. When alone, however, they eat enormous quantities. Their craving for food is uncontrollable and they may consume many thousands of calories in less than an hour. Immediately after such an eating binge, however, bulimics will vomit what they have eaten. At the next opportunity, they will repeat the cycle. Among the serious effects of this behavior are the possibility of drastically altered blood chemistry or serious water loss. In severe cases, the stomach itself can rupture.

Bulimia is a psychological condition and the patients who suffer from it are generally depressed, anxious, and have a very poor self-image. Like anorexia, bulimia can be cured if patients can be convinced that they have a problem and if they are willing to help themselves reach a cure.

CHECKPOINT ◆

13. What is a calorie?
14. What are the three classes of nutrients that can provide energy?
15. What is scurvy?
16. What are the four basic food groups?
▶ 17. Explain why anorexic patients lose weight while a bulimic patient can maintain relatively normal weight.
▶ 18. Starch can provide enough energy to supply the demands of your body. Why could you not survive for an extended period on a diet of bread and water?

▶ Denotes a question that involves *interpreting* and *applying* concepts.

MEASURING FOOD ENERGY

Objectives and Skills

☐ *Measure* the heat released from a sample of food.
☐ *Calculate* the number of kilocalories per gram of food.

Materials

safety goggles
lab apron
test tube (about 20-mL capacity)
tin can calorimeter
cork with pin
nonmercury thermometer

wire stirrer
graduate cylinder
triple-beam balance
test tube holder
matches
shelled peanuts

Procedure and Observations

1. Read all instructions for this laboratory activity before you begin your work.
2. Put on your safety goggles and lab apron.
3. Break off a small piece of a peanut that is about one eighth of the nut. Find the mass of the piece and record your measurement.
4. Gently push the nut onto a pin which has been inserted in a cork. Do not push too hard or the nut will break.
5. Place the cork and nut under the tin can as shown by your teacher. Push the test tube into the top of the can until it is about one centimeter from the nut. Using the graduate cylinder, place 15 mL of water in the test tube.
6. Measure the temperature of the water and record it in a data table.
7. Lift the can and tube away from the nut. Hold a lighted match to the peanut until the nut begins to burn on its own. **CAUTION: Do not let the match burn your fingers. Extinguish the match completely before discarding it.**

8. Quickly place the can and test tube of water over the burning nut. Gently stir the water with the wire stirrer and watch the temperature. The temperature will rise, reach a maximum, and then begin to fall after the nut has burned out. Note the maximum temperature reached and record the value as the final temperature.
9. Use a test tube holder to remove the tube and discard the contents. **CAUTION: The test tube may still be very hot at this point.** Repeat steps 3 through 8 two more times.
10. Before leaving the laboratory, clean up all your materials and wash your hands.
11. Determine the temperature change (final temperature minus initial temperature) for each trial. Multiply the temperature change times the mass of water used (15 g). This value is the number of calories absorbed by the water. Record this number.
12. Divide the calories given off by each piece by the mass of the piece. This will give you the number of calories given off by one gram of peanuts. Record your results.
13. Convert the number of calories to food calories or kilocalories. Record these results and determine the average of the trials.

Analysis and Conclusions

1. Look up the food calorie content of peanuts in a reference book. How does this value compare with the value you have determined?
2. Why do nutritionists use food calories (kilocalories) rather than small calories when measuring the energy content of food?
3. How could you improve the design of the experiment?
4. How would you measure the calorie content of something like milk?

CHAPTER REVIEW

Summary

▸ Both mechanical and chemical digestion are required to reduce food to small molecules that can move across cell membranes.

▸ In the mouth, the teeth and tongue begin mechanical digestion. Amylase begins the chemical digestion of starch. Food moves from the mouth to the stomach through the esophagus. In the stomach, proteases begin the digestion of protein. Food in a semiliquid form moves into the small intestine.

▸ Accessory organs secrete substances into the small intestine. The pancreas secretes digestive enzymes, and the liver produces bile.

▸ Folds of the intestine wall, villi, and microvilli are adaptations of the small intestine that provide a large surface area for the absorption of food molecules. Cells in the intestinal epithelium contain enzymes that function in the final stages of chemical digestion.

▸ The large intestine absorbs water from the material remaining after digestion is complete. Undigested food is expelled from the body as feces.

▸ Nutrients are substances that you require to grow and remain healthy. Food energy is measured in food calories, which are equal to kilocalories. Excess calories are stored as fat.

▸ Energy-supplying foods include carbohydrates, fats, and proteins. Carbohydrates and fats are primarily used to supply energy. Proteins are used primarily for growth and repair of cells.

▸ Vitamins, minerals, and water do not supply energy. However, they are necessary for many life processes.

▸ A balanced diet includes foods from four main groups. These are meats and related foods, dairy products, fruits and vegetables, and cereal and grains. Vegetarians receive a balanced diet without meat.

Vocabulary

alimentary canal	malnutrition
amylase	mechanical digestion
appendix	mineral
bile	molar
canine teeth	mucosa
chemical digestion	mucus
colon	nutrient
common bile duct	nutrition
deficiency disease	pancreas
digestion	pancreatic juice
duodenum	peptidase
epiglottis	peristalsis
esophagus	pharynx
feces	premolar
food calorie	protease
gallbladder	rectum
gastric juice	saliva
ileum	small intestine
incisor	sphincter
jejunum	stomach
lacteal	ulcer
large intestine	villi
lipase	vitamin
lumen	

Concept Mapping

Construct a concept map for digestive activities. Include the following terms: enzyme secretion, absorption, chemical digestion, pepsin, mechanical digestion, muscles, chewing, and peristalsis. Use additional terms as you need them.

Review

1. Which type of digestion is carried out by teeth—mechanical or chemical? How do teeth do this?
2. What is the function of the mucosa in the esophagus?

3. What substance undergoes chemical digestion in the stomach?
4. What is the function of lipase?
5. What organ stores bile?
6. Name the three sections of the small intestine.
7. Name two enzymes produced by intestinal epithelial cells.
8. What is the final section of the large intestine where solid wastes are held before they are expelled?
9. How many calories are in a food calorie?
10. What is the major source of starch in the human diet?
11. What is the function of fat in your body?
12. Which eating disorder does not necessarily result in loss of weight?
13. What can happen to the amino acids taken in by cells from the blood?
14. What happens when your diet is missing a particular vitamin?
15. What is the primary function of calcium in the body?
16. What does nutrient mean?
17. To which food group do eggs belong?

Interpret and Apply

18. Explain how the structure of different kinds of teeth are adapted for eating different kinds of food.
19. How are mechanical and chemical digestion related?
20. Which process occurs in the small intestine —mechanical or chemical digestion? Explain.
21. What kind of muscle tissue is found in the wall of the alimentary canal? Why is this type of muscle best suited for this function?
22. What would happen if the stomach did not have sphincter muscles?

23. Describe the difference in movement of fats, amino acids, and carbohydrates after they are absorbed into the capillaries of the small intestine.
24. When the gallbladder is removed, the common bile duct is left intact. Why?
25. What is the importance of the large surface area of the small intestine?
26. A common symptom of many diseases is diarrhea when the large intestine ceases to perform its function. What is done until the colon regains normal function?
27. Why is malnutrition a complication of anorexia nervosa?
28. How much energy would be required to heat 10 grams of water from 19°C to 20°C? How much would be required to heat 10 grams of water from 5°C to 15°C?
29. Why is fat the preferred substance for long-term energy storage in your body?
30. What could be dangerous about a fad diet?
31. Corn has a fairly high amount of protein, but the protein is deficient in lysine. Could you survive on a diet of corn products as long as you also had rice in your diet?

Critical Thinking

32. A person can survive without a gallbladder but not without a liver. Explain.
33. Most plant proteins are incomplete. Strict vegetarians will not eat meat or animal products, such as milk, eggs, or cheese. How do they obtain complete protein?
34. People can survive for many weeks without food, but they can survive only a few days without water. Why is this the case?
35. Many people assume that gravity helps move food from the mouth to the stomach. Yet astronauts in a completely weightless environment have no trouble eating and drinking. Why?

Chapter

39

RESPIRATION AND EXCRETION

Overview

RESPIRATION

39-1   External and Internal Respiration
39-2   The Human Respiratory System
39-3   Gas Exchange
39-4   The Mechanism of Breathing
39-5   Control of Breathing Rate

EXCRETORY SYSTEM

39-6   The Organs of Excretion
39-7   The Nephron: Structure
39-8   The Nephron: Function
39-9   Homeostasis of Body Fluids
39-10 Kidney Failure

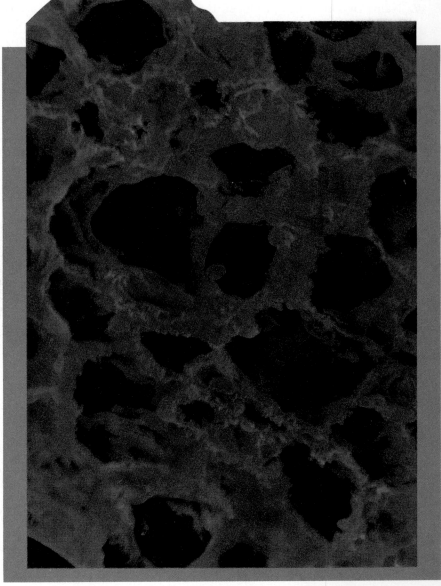

How is the lung's internal structure adapted for gas exchange?

RESPIRATION

Most people know that they cannot live for more than a few minutes without oxygen. In Chapter 6, you learned that oxygen is essential to provide energy for your cells. The function of the respiratory system is to obtain and transport oxygen to every cell in your body. In addition, the respiratory system removes carbon dioxide as a waste product.

39-1 External and Internal Respiration

The term **respiration** has many different meanings. Commonly, it may refer only to breathing or the moving of air into and out of the lungs. However, respiration has other, more specific meanings.

Respiration can be divided into three general processes. *External respiration* is the exchange of gases between the atmosphere and the blood. This takes place in the lungs, where oxygen diffuses from the air into the blood, and carbon dioxide diffuses from the blood into the air.

Gas exchange between the blood and the body cells is called *internal respiration*. Oxygen diffuses from the blood into the cells. Carbon dioxide, on the other hand, diffuses out of the cells and into the blood.

Recall that *cellular respiration* is the chemical process that takes place in the mitochondria of your cells. In this process, oxygen and molecules derived from food react and produce energy in the form of ATP. Carbon dioxide and water are produced as waste products.

Section Objectives

A **Compare** and **contrast** external, internal, and cellular respiration.

B **Identify** the structures of the human respiratory system and **state** the function of each structure.

C **Trace** the path of oxygen and carbon dioxide throughout the body.

D **Describe** how air enters and leaves the lungs.

E **Explain** the mechanism that controls breathing rate.

Figure 39-1 The function of the respiratory system is to deliver oxygen to cells for cellular respiration and to remove the carbon dioxide produced by cells.

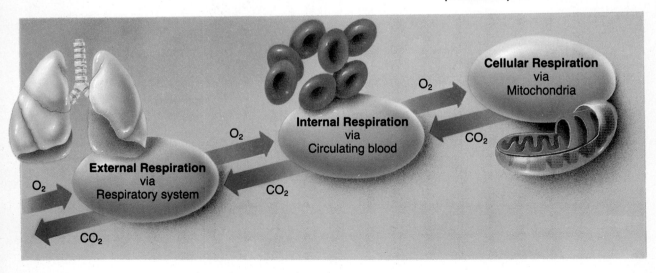

External Respiration
via
Respiratory system

Internal Respiration
via
Circulating blood

Cellular Respiration
via
Mitochondria

O_2 O_2 O_2

CO_2 CO_2 CO_2

39-2 The Human Respiratory System

Figure 39-2 is a diagram of the respiratory system. Air entering the lungs travels primarily through the nose. The nasal cavity contains many bony projections that create a large surface area. Soft epithelial tissue covers these projections. The epithelium contains many blood capillaries and cells that secrete mucus.

Both the nasal passage and the mouth open into the pharynx. If the nasal passages are blocked, air can reach the lungs through the mouth. However, with much less surface area than the nasal passages, the mouth is not as effective in cleaning and warming air.

From the pharynx, air moves into the **trachea** [trā′ kē ə], or windpipe. Recall that the epiglottis prevents food from entering

Figure 39-2 Air travels into the human respiratory system through nasal cavities, the trachea, bronchi, bronchioles, and alveoli.

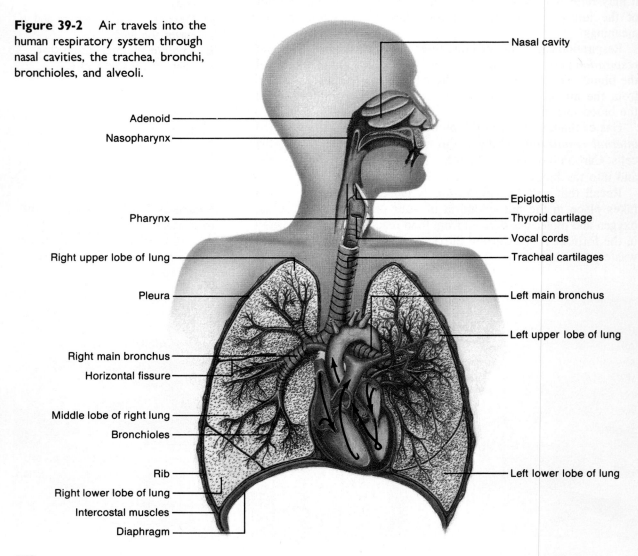

Nasal cavity

Adenoid

Nasopharynx

Epiglottis

Pharynx

Thyroid cartilage

Vocal cords

Right upper lobe of lung

Tracheal cartilages

Pleura

Left main bronchus

Left upper lobe of lung

Right main bronchus

Horizontal fissure

Middle lobe of right lung

Bronchioles

Rib

Left lower lobe of lung

Right lower lobe of lung

Intercostal muscles

Diaphragm

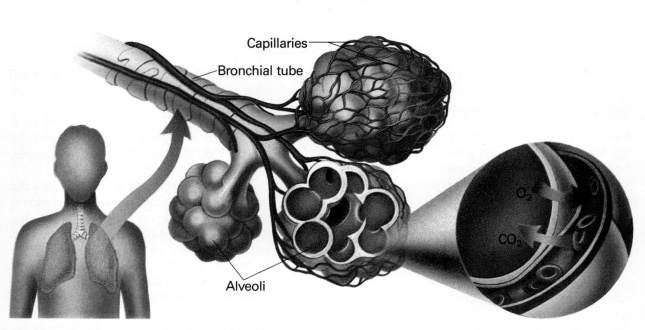

Capillaries

Bronchial tube

Alveoli

O_2

CO_2

Figure 39-3 Each alveolus is surrounded by a network of thin-walled capillaries. The exchange of gases between the internal environment and the atmosphere occurs here.

the trachea when you swallow. Just below the epiglottis is the **larynx** [lar′ ingks], or voice box. Here a pair of **vocal cords** stretches across the trachea. The vocal cords are made of tough connective tissue. When air is forced past the vocal cords, they vibrate and create sound.

The trachea carries air into the right and left **bronchi** [brong′ kī] (singular, bronchus). Within the lungs, the bronchi branch into finer tubes called **bronchioles** [brong′ kē ōls]. All of the air tubes have cartilage rings that keep the tubes open. Look at Figure 39-3. At the end of each bronchiole is a cluster of microscopic, balloonlike air sacs. These are called **alveoli** [al vē′ ō lī] (singular, alveolus).

Like the nasal cavity, the lining of the air passages contains cilia and cells that secrete mucus. Any particles that get past the nasal passages usually stick to the mucus. Cilia sweep the mucus out of the lungs. Nicotine in cigarette smoke inhibits the sweeping motion of the cilia for several hours. Also, tars from the smoke particles enter the lungs faster than the cilia can remove them. Similar to a clogged filter, the cilia are less effective in cleaning air entering the lungs. In addition, coughing helps to remove large objects from the lungs. Thus many adaptations ensure that only clean air finally reaches the alveoli.

The **lungs** are the large saclike organs in which external respiration takes place. Each lung is surrounded by a double membrane called the **pleura** [ploo′ rə]. The outer pleura is attached to the chest wall. The inner pleura is attached to the lungs. The space between the two membranes contains a lubricating fluid permitting free movement of the lungs.

■ BIOLOGY INSIGHT

Structure Is Related to Function: As you have seen in many other organisms, very large surface areas can be made to occupy a small space by folding surfaces. Both the nasal passages and the alveoli are folded surfaces in the respiratory system.

CONSUMER BIOLOGY

If viruses or bacteria become established in the air passages pneumonia can result. The alveoli secrete a watery fluid that partly fills the alveolar space and interferes with the diffusion of gases.

Respiration and Excretion   **651**

39-3 Gas Exchange

The alveoli are surrounded by capillaries. The walls of the alveoli are thin and moist. Gases can easily diffuse across the alveolar membrane.

Air is a mixture of gases. Approximately 80 percent of air is nitrogen, and about 20 percent is oxygen. Very small amounts of other gases are also present. Carbon dioxide, for example, makes up about 0.03 percent of air.

In external respiration, oxygen from the air moves into the respiratory system ending at the alveolus. Here, oxygen moves into the blood and carbon dioxide moves from the blood into the alveolus. Why does this happen? Look at Figure 39-4. The level of oxygen is higher in alveolar air than in the blood, so oxygen diffuses from the air into the blood. The blood then transports oxygen to the body cells. Cells constantly use oxygen, thus lowering its concentration. Therefore the concentration of oxygen is always less in the cytoplasm of body cells than in the blood. As a result, oxygen diffuses from the blood into the cells. Then the concentration of oxygen in the blood is low, or **deoxygenated** [dē ok′ sə jə nā ted].

Carbon dioxide accumulates in cell cytoplasm from cellular respiration. There is a greater concentration of carbon dioxide in the cytoplasm than there is in the blood. Carbon dioxide diffuses out of the cells and into the blood. There is more carbon dioxide in this blood than in alveolar air. Therefore, carbon dioxide diffuses out of the blood and into the alveoli. Blood leaving the lungs is low in carbon dioxide and rich in oxygen. This oxygen-rich blood is **oxygenated**.

How are gases carried in the blood? A small amount of oxygen dissolves in the blood plasma. However, most oxygen molecules

Figure 39-4 Oxygen and carbon dioxide move by diffusion. The concentration of oxygen in the alveolus is higher than that in the blood. The two gases move in opposite directions from an area of high concentration to an area of lower concentration.

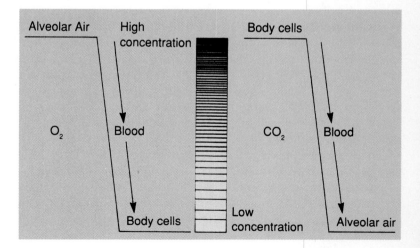

bind to **hemoglobin** [hē′ mə glō bən]. Hemoglobin is a protein located in the red cells. Hemoglobin with oxygen attached gives blood a bright red color. In contrast, deoxygenated blood is a dull purplish red.

Like oxygen, a small amount of carbon dioxide dissolves in the blood plasma. Some carbon dioxide attaches to hemoglobin. However, most of the carbon dioxide reacts with water in the cytoplasm of red blood cells. An enzyme speeds the formation of carbonic acid, or H_2CO_3, in the cytoplasm.

Like all acids, carbonic acid forms hydrogen ions in water. As shown in the following equation, it also forms HCO_3^-, or bicarbonate ions.

$$CO_2 + H_2O \rightarrow H_2CO_3 \rightarrow H^+ + HCO_3^-$$

H^+ and HCO_3^- ions accumulate in the red cells and diffuse into the plasma. In the lungs, bicarbonate ions change back to carbon dioxide.

39-4 The Mechanism of Breathing

To supply body cells with a fresh supply of oxygen, air in the lungs must be constantly replaced. Air in the lungs is replaced by the process of breathing. **Inspiration**, or inhaling, is the phase of breathing that takes air into the lungs. During **expiration**, or exhaling, air is expelled from the lungs.

Figure 39-5 shows a model of how the lungs work. An elastic sheet covers the bottom of a glass jar. Two balloons are attached to a Y-tube that opens to the outside air. When the elastic sheet is pulled down, air pressure decreases in the space around the balloons. Reduced pressure causes outside air to rush into the

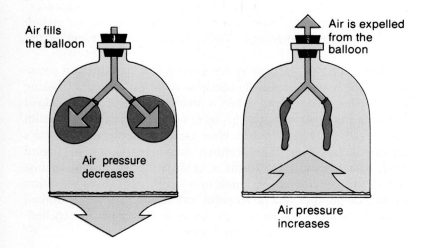

Air fills
the balloon

Air pressure
decreases

Air is expelled
from the
balloon

Air pressure
increases

Figure 39-5 Air is pumped in and out of the lungs by the action of the diaphragm. The diaphragm is a sheet of skeletal muscle. *Left:* When the diaphragm contracts, air pressure decreases, causing the lungs to fill with air and expand. *Right:* When the diaphragm relaxes, increased air pressure causes the lungs to deflate.

Figure 39-6 *Left:* During inspiration, the rib muscles contract moving the rib cage upward and outward. The diaphragm contracts and moves downward. *Right:* During expiration, the rib muscles relax. The diaphragm relaxes and moves upward.

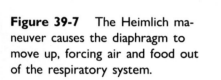

Inhaling

Trachea

Lung

Ribs

Diaphragm contracts

Rib muscles contract

Exhaling

Diaphragm relaxes

Rib muscles relax

Figure 39-7 The Heimlich maneuver causes the diaphragm to move up, forcing air and food out of the respiratory system.

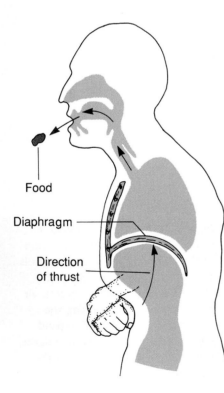

Food

Diaphragm

Direction of thrust

balloons. Pushing the elastic sheet up increases the air pressure in the space. Increased pressure forces air out of the balloons.

Your lungs work in a similar way. Lungs are like the balloons. The **diaphragm** [dī′ ə fram] is like the elastic sheet. It is a large, dome-shaped muscle between the chest cavity and the abdomen.

When you inhale, the diaphragm contracts. During contraction, the diaphragm flattens out. At the same time, muscles move the ribs up and out. Both of these muscle actions increase the volume of the chest cavity. As in the model, increased volume reduces pressure on the lungs, and air rushes in. Inspiration stretches the alveolar walls.

During expiration, the diaphragm relaxes. It returns to its dome shape. Rib muscles also relax. Both movements reduce the volume of the chest cavity. Pressure on the lungs increases. Like the rubber of a stretched balloon, the walls of the alveoli return to their smaller size. These actions force air out of the lungs.

Obstruction of the airway for even a few minutes can cause death. The brain is especially sensitive to lack of oxygen. Choking often occurs at mealtime when a piece of food becomes lodged between the epiglottis and the sides of the pharynx. The victim cannot talk and begins to turn blue. One way to clear the victim's airway is by using the Heimlich maneuver. Look at Figure 39-7. The rescuer's fist forms a knob, which is placed against the victim's abdomen. A quick upward thrust causes elevation of the diaphragm and a forceful expiration. As air is forced through the trachea, the foreign object in the airway is expelled, restoring the flow of air to the lungs.

39-5 Control of Breathing Rate

The rib muscles and the diaphragm are striated muscles. As such, they can be under voluntary control. You can choose to take deep breaths or shallow breaths. You can even choose to stop breathing for a short time. Eventually, however, your automatic controls take over, forcing you to gasp for air. The rib muscles and diaphragm are automatically stimulated by several nerves. These nerves bring impulses from a *breathing center* deep in the brain.

The breathing rate depends on your activity level. When you sleep, your breathing slows. When you exercise, your breathing speeds up. These changes in rate are logical. During sleep, your cells use less oxygen and produce less carbon dioxide than when you are awake and active.

Control of the breathing rate is complex. A special group of cells connected to the breathing center constantly monitor the pH of the blood. When the amount of carbon dioxide in the blood increases, for example, the blood's pH increases and these cells send messages to the breathing center. The breathing center, in turn, sends a signal to the diaphragm to contract, thus causing an increase in the rate of breathing. The increased breathing rate removes carbon dioxide from the blood and returns the pH to normal. What effects would too much oxygen have on the breathing rate?

CONSUMER BIOLOGY

Aging affects all body parts. Lung capacity can decrease up to 50 percent as a person grows older. Routinely engaging in aerobic exercise can reduce the effects of aging on the lungs.

CHECKPOINT ◆

1. What term describes gas exchange between alveolar air and the blood?
2. The trachea branches into two air passages. What are they called?
3. What is another name for the voice box? How is sound produced?
4. Where in the blood is hemoglobin found?
5. What muscles are involved in breathing? How are they stimulated?
6. What happens to the breathing rate when the level of carbon dioxide increases in the blood?
7. Compare the structure of your lungs to the structure of gills.
8. Explain why oxygen diffuses into the blood at the alveoli and out of the blood at the body cells.
▶ 9. Compare the mechanism of oxygen transport in the blood with the mechanism of carbon dioxide transport.

▶ Denotes a question that involves *interpreting* and *applying* concepts.

EXCRETORY SYSTEM

F *Describe* the location and function of the kidneys.

G *Identify* the various parts of a nephron.

H *Explain* the function of the nephron.

I *State* how the kidneys serve a role in maintaining homeostasis of body fluids.

J *Explain* the methods used to treat kidney failure.

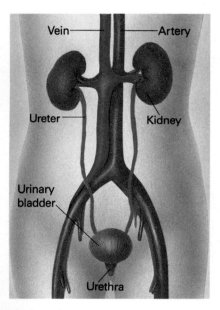

Figure 39-8 Humans have two kidneys. About 20 percent of your blood is processed by the kidneys each minute. The tissue masses on top of each kidney are the adrenal glands about which you will learn in Chapter 43.

Cell respiration produces carbon dioxide as one of its wastes. Other metabolic processes produce chemicals that are of no use to the cell. In fact, these wastes can be toxic if they accumulate. **Excretion** is the process of getting harmful or useless molecules out of cells and out of the organism.

39-6 The Organs of Excretion

The lungs are excretory organs that remove carbon dioxide from the body. The liver is an excretory organ too. The liver excretes materials in bile, which contains products of the breakdown of red blood cells. The liver is also the major organ in which amino acids are broken down. When the liver metabolizes amino acids, it produces the molecule **urea** [ü rē′ ə], which contains nitrogen. In high concentration, urea is very toxic to cells.

The **kidneys** remove urea and excess salts from the blood. They are the main excretory organs of your body. Every day, the kidneys filter about 180 liters of fluid from the blood.

Your kidneys excrete wastes in **urine**. Urine is mostly water. It contains small amounts of dissolved urea, salts, and traces of other substances. By controlling the volume of urine, the kidneys also help to maintain proper water balance in the body.

Figure 39-8 shows the kidneys to be a pair of bean-shaped organs. They flank the lower part of the vertebral column. The **renal arteries** carry blood into the kidneys. Purified blood leaves the kidneys through the **renal veins**. Blood leaving the kidneys has less urea and slightly less water than when it entered.

Urine produced by the kidneys flows through the **ureter** [ür′ ət ′er]. Ureters carry urine to a storage organ called the **bladder**. The bladder empties to the outside of the body through a single tube, the **urethra** [ü rē′ thrə].

Figure 39-9 shows the internal structure of the kidney. The outermost layer is called the **renal cortex**. Inside the cortex is the **renal medulla**. The filtration of blood and the formation of urine take place in the cortex and medulla. Urine collects in a large cavity called the **renal pelvis**. The ureter drains urine from the renal pelvis.

On occasion, minerals can come out of solution and form rocklike particles called *kidney stones* that gather in the renal pelvis. These stones vary from the size of a sand grain to larger than a golf ball. Kidney stones can be removed surgically or by several new techniques that use sound waves or even laser light to break them up.

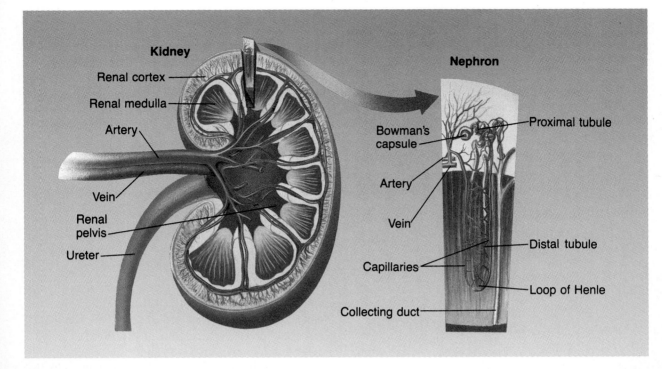

Kidney

Renal cortex
Renal medulla
Artery
Vein
Renal pelvis
Ureter

Nephron

Bowman's capsule
Artery
Vein
Capillaries
Collecting duct
Proximal tubule
Distal tubule
Loop of Henle

39-7 The Nephron: Structure

The renal cortex and medulla are made of over a million microscopic units called **nephrons** [nef′ rons]. Figure 39-9 shows a single nephron.

In the kidneys, the renal artery branches into many smaller vessels. Each of these ends in a group of capillaries called a **glomerulus** [glō mėr′ yə ləs]. The glomerulus sits inside a cuplike structure called a **Bowman's capsule**. All the Bowman's capsules and glomeruli of the kidney are located in the renal cortex.

Each Bowman's capsule is at the beginning of a long, continuous tube. Sections of this tube differ in structure and function. Just behind the Bowman's capsule is the twisted **proximal tubule**. This leads into the **loop of Henle** [hen′ lē]. The loop of Henle dips into the medulla and then returns to the cortex. There it becomes the **distal tubule**. The distal tubule drains into the **collecting duct**. The collecting duct goes through the medulla and opens into the renal pelvis.

Notice that the space in the tube beginning with Bowman's capsule eventually leads to the outside of the body. Also notice how the blood capillaries in the glomerulus merge into vessels which then surround the proximal tube, loop of Henle, and distal tubule before joining and leaving the kidney as the renal vein.

Figure 39-9 The kidney is a major excretory organ. The inside of a kidney contains many blood vessels. Blood is processed by the functional unit of the kidney—the nephron.

39-8 The Nephron: Function

The nephron controls the composition of blood and urine. Look at Figure 39-10. The membranes of the glomeruli and Bowman's capsules are permeable to small molecules and ions. Water, ions, sugar, amino acids, and urea move from the blood into the Bowman's capsules. This process is called **filtration**. In fact, of the 180 liters of water filtered into the Bowman's capsules every day, only 1 liter of water is excreted as urine. What happens to the other 179 liters of water?

As the fluid travels from Bowman's capsule to the collecting duct, its composition changes. This change occurs by two processes: **reabsorption** and **tubular secretion**. Materials that the body conserves, like water, glucose, and other important substances, are reabsorbed from the tubules back to the bloodstream. Cells in the proximal tubule, distal tubule, and collecting ducts pump sodium ions back into the blood capillaries. Water molecules follow the sodium ions by osmosis. In this way, the body recovers over 99 percent of the water and sodium that is filtered into the Bowman's capsules. Substances that are excreted by the body, like urea, are not reabsorbed and remain in the tubules.

Other substances such as hydrogen ions and foreign chemicals are secreted by active transport from the bloodstream into the tubules for exit from the body. The remaining fluid reaches the kidney pelvis. It is now urine, which consists mainly of the water that has not been reabsorbed, some salts, and urea.

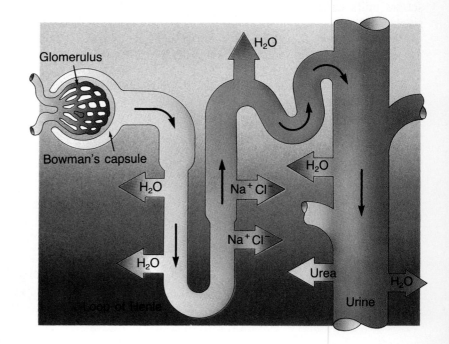

Figure 39-10 The nephron processes blood plasma by filtration, secretion, and reabsorption. The fluid that remains is excreted by the body as urine.

39-9 Homeostasis of Body Fluids

All the cells of your body are surrounded by a watery tissue fluid. This fluid contains dissolved salts. For cells to function properly, the concentration of salts in this fluid must always be about the same. If your body loses or takes in too much water, the salt concentration of tissue fluid can change. Salt in the diet or loss of salt through excretion can also affect the tissue fluid. However, homeostatic mechanisms keep the composition of tissue fluid more or less constant. The kidneys are an important part of this process.

There are four principal ways your body loses water each day. Air entering the lungs is moistened. About one liter of this moisture is lost by expiration. Another 100 milliliters of water are lost daily in feces. Between 0 and 10 000 milliliters of water evaporate as perspiration each day. The kidneys excrete about another liter of water.

Within limits, the kidneys can control the amount of water that reaches the bladder. For example, consider what happens when you perspire a lot. Under these conditions, membranes of the kidney tubules become very permeable to water. Most of the water in the tubules is reabsorbed into the blood. There is little water for urine formation. Therefore, the volume of urine is low. The color is darker than usual because the dissolved materials are more highly concentrated.

On the other hand, what happens when you drink excess water? The cells of the distal tubule and the collecting duct become impermeable to water. Water stays within these tubules. The resulting urine is high in volume and pale in color.

Another complex and poorly understood mechanism controls the amount of sodium pumped out of the tubules. The kidneys can change the amount of salt excreted in the urine. By this means, they help to control the salt balance of the tissue fluid.

39-10 Kidney Failure

The location of the kidneys makes them vulnerable to physical injury. Many bacterial infections can damage the kidneys as well. Should one kidney stop functioning, the other kidney can take on the job of filtering the entire bloodstream. Many individuals function quite normally with a single kidney. Should both kidneys stop functioning, however, there are far more serious consequences. Urea accumulates in the body fluids and urea poisoning will result in death within a week.

Such patients have two options: kidney transplant or dialysis. *Dialysis* [dī al′ ə sis] involves a machine that takes blood from a vessel in a patient's arm and passes it over a filtering membrane.

Urea diffuses through the membrane and out of the blood. The cleaned blood is returned to the patient. These treatments must be repeated at least weekly.

Peritoneal [per ə tə nē′ əl] *dialysis* is an alternate method that can be used where expensive dialysis machinery is not readily available. In this treatment, large quantities of liquid are dripped into the patient's abdominal cavity and the fluid is removed from the other side of the abdomen through another tube. Diffusion of urea takes place from the patient's blood into the abdominal fluid which leaves the body through the tube. Obviously, dialysis patients must stay near the locations where the procedures are carried out. Neither form of dialysis is a replacement for healthy kidneys, but these methods can keep people alive for many years.

Dialysis is generally used on a patient until a transplant is possible. In transplant surgery, a single kidney from a donor is placed into the recipient. The surgery is relatively simple and involves attaching the renal artery, renal vein, and the ureter of the donor to the comparable structures of the recipient. The success of a transplant depends primarily on the genetic similarity of transplanted tissue to the recipient's tissue. Many times, it is possible to find a family member who is willing to donate one kidney and who is likely to have similar tissue. If there are no suitable family members, an individual must wait for a donor organ from an accident victim. In such a case, doctors try to match the tissues as closely as possible.

You will see in Chapter 41 that foreign tissue is rejected by your body's defense system. Even genetically similar tissue can be rejected. Modern drugs that minimize rejection have made kidney transplantation a procedure that has saved many lives and freed people from the necessity of weekly dialysis treatments.

CONSUMER BIOLOGY

Some recent fad diets recommend an increase in high-protein foods while cutting down on carbohydrates. Such diets always recommend drinking about eight glasses of water a day. With increased protein in the diet, the liver makes far more urea than usual. The kidneys must remove the extra urea, and more water is needed to make the excess urine.

CONSUMER BIOLOGY

In order for small molecules to filter into a Bowman's capsule, blood must be under significant pressure. Kidney failure will occur if the blood pressure drops too low.

CHECKPOINT ◆

10. What are the tubes called that carry urine from the kidneys to the bladder?
11. Into what part of the nephron do small molecules diffuse from the capillaries of the glomerulus?
12. List some of the molecules that leave the glomerulus and move into the nephron.
13. Under what conditions would you produce small amounts of concentrated urine?
14. What technique is used to clean urea out of the blood mechanically if both kidneys have failed?
▶ 15. Describe the role of reabsorption in kidney function.

▶ Denotes a question that involves *interpreting* and *applying* concepts.

LUNG AND KIDNEY STRUCTURE

In this activity you will observe the microscopic structure of a lung and kidney. You will also examine an animal kidney.

Objectives and Skills

☐ *Observe* the microscopic structure of a lung and kidney.
☐ *Dissect* an animal kidney.

Materials

compound microscope	preserved animal
safety goggles	kidney
lab apron	prepared slides of:
dissecting materials	lung sections
magnifying glass	kidney sections
gloves	

Procedure and Observations

1. Read all instructions for this laboratory activity before you begin your work.
2. Set up a microscope. Observe a prepared slide of lung tissue at low magnification. Identify the alveoli, epithelial cells of the alveoli, and blood capillaries. Draw and label what you see.
3. Observe the slide under high power. Draw several epithelial cells as you observe them under the microscope.
4. Obtain a prepared slide of kidney sections. Observe the slide under low power. Find a glomerulus and Bowman's capsule in the cortex and observe it under high power. Draw the glomerulus and Bowman's capsule. What other parts of the nephron can you see in your slide?
5. Obtain dissecting equipment and put on your safety goggles, lab apron and gloves. Bring a preserved kidney to your station.
6. Observe the external structure of the kidney. Identify the renal artery and the renal vein that carry blood in and out of the kidney. The renal artery has thicker walls than the renal vein. Identify the ureter which transports urine out of the kidney. Draw and label the kidney.
7. Using a scalpel, carefully cut the kidney in half to expose the interior of the kidney as shown in Figure 39-9. **CAUTION: Be careful with sharp dissecting tools.** Identify the renal cortex, renal medulla, renal artery and vein, ureter, and pelvis. Use a magnifying glass to observe the cortex and the medulla. What differences do you observe?
8. Before leaving the laboratory, clean up all materials and wash your hands thoroughly.

Analysis and Conclusions

1. Describe the appearance of epithelial cells in an alveolus. How does their structure reflect their function?
2. Did you observe any muscle tissue in the slide of the lung? What is the significance of your observation?
3. What is the function of the renal pelvis?
4. In what part of the kidney are the Bowman's capsules located?
5. From your observations under the microscope, what difference do you see in the structure of the renal cortex and the renal medulla?

CHAPTER REVIEW

Summary

▸ External respiration takes place in the lungs and is the exchange of gases between the blood and the body cells. This process is required to deliver oxygen to and remove carbon dioxide from cells.

▸ The human nasal passages are adapted to clean, moisten, and warm air before it enters the lungs. The trachea and bronchi also clean and remove foreign particles from the lungs.

▸ A cluster of microscopic alveoli are at the end of each bronchiole. The exchange of gases between the lungs and the blood occur here. Hemoglobin in red blood cells carries most of the oxygen.

▸ Breathing involves many muscles. When you inhale, the ribs move up and out, and the diaphragm contracts and flattens. Breathing rate is controlled by nerves originating in the brain.

▸ The lungs remove carbon dioxide from the body. The liver excretes wastes produced by the destruction of red blood cells.

▸ The kidneys remove urea from the blood and excrete it in urine. Urine flows through the ureters and is stored in the bladder. It leaves the body through the urethra.

▸ The kidneys are made up of millions of nephrons. Nephrons filter, reabsorb, and secrete substances that form urine.

Vocabulary

alveoli	nephron
bladder	oxygenated
Bowman's capsule	pleura
bronchi	proximal tubule
bronchioles	reabsorption
collecting duct	renal artery
deoxygenated	renal cortex
diaphragm	renal medulla
distal tubule	renal pelvis
excretion	renal vein
expiration	respiration
filtration	tubular secretion
glomerulus	trachea
hemoglobin	urea
inspiration	ureter
kidney	urethra
larynx	urine
loop of Henle	vocal cords
lung	

Concept Mapping

Construct a concept map for kidney structure and function. Include the following terms: secretion, loop of Henle, reabsorption, Bowman's capsule, cortex, medulla, proximal tubule, nephron, and filtration. Use additional terms as you need them.

Review

1. Describe the movement of oxygen during internal respiration.
2. What is the function of mucus in the nasal passages?
3. What structures prevent the trachea and bronchi from collapsing?
4. After kidney failure, what method uses the abdominal fluids to remove urea from a patient?
5. What gas diffuses from the blood to the air in the alveoli?
6. What is the primary gas carried by hemoglobin in red blood cells?
7. What happens to the ribs when the diaphragm contracts during inspiration?
8. What happens to the size of the alveoli during expiration?
9. What organ controls the breathing rate?
10. Urea is produced from the metabolism of what kind of molecule?

11. What is the primary component of urine?
12. In what region of the kidney are glomeruli located?
13. Name the tube through which urine leaves the body.
14. What substances move from the nephron tubules back into the blood?
15. Identify four ways water is lost from your body.

Interpret and Apply

16. List the following structures in the order that a carbon dioxide molecule would pass on its way from the blood to the outside of the body.
    a. bronchiole   d. alveolus
    b. nasal passage   e. bronchus
    c. trachea   f. pharynx
17. How does cellular respiration ensure that oxygen and carbon dioxide will diffuse in the appropriate direction?
18. What is the function of the large surface area of the nasal passages?
19. Explain the role of the diaphragm in breathing.
20. In pneumonia, watery fluid partly fills the alveoli. Why does this fluid interfere with external respiration?
21. Other than the amount of oxygen, in what ways do oxygenated and deoxygenated blood differ?
22. List the following structures in the order that a urea molecule would pass through them on its way from the blood to the outside of the body.
    a. renal pelvis   f. urethra
    b. loop of Henle   g. ureter
    c. bladder   h. Bowman's capsule
    d. proximal tubule   i. distal tubule
    e. collecting duct

23. What is the relationship between the level of body activity and the rate of breathing?
24. Describe the process by which water returns from the kidney tubules to the blood.
25. What function of normal kidneys is not performed by dialysis machines?
26. In what ways are the kidneys involved in maintaining a constant internal environment for cells?
27. What is wrong with considering the kidneys as simple blood filters?

Critical Thinking

28. If you go to sleep when your nasal passages are completely blocked because of a cold, you may wake up to find your mouth very dry. Why do you think this happens?
29. Sneezing is an involuntary response. What function might sneezing have for the respiratory system?
30. Describe the protective mechanisms that make it unlikely for a bacterial cell to reach an alveolus.
31. Unlike gills through which water goes by in one direction and then out of the body, lungs have a single opening to the outside. Air must go in and out of the same opening. What would be the advantage of lungs having this structure?
32. What is the role of thirst in maintaining homeostasis of the water in the body?
33. How is active transport important in the functioning of a nephron?
34. In what ways is blood leaving a nephron different in composition from the blood entering a nephron?
35. How many cell membranes must a molecule of oxygen cross when it moves from the air of an alveolus to its point of attachment on a hemoglobin molecule?

Chapter

40

CIRCULATION

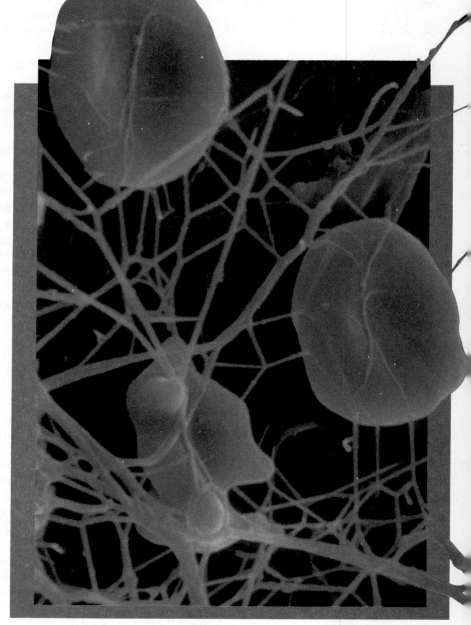

Overview

**THE HEART AND
BLOOD VESSELS**

40-1 The Heart
40-2 Heart Rate
40-3 Heart Disorders
40-4 The Pattern of
Circulation
40-5 Blood Vessels
40-6 Blood Pressure

BLOOD AND LYMPH

40-7 Blood Plasma and
Clotting
40-8 Red Blood Cells and
Blood Types
40-9 White Blood Cells
40-10 The Lymphatic
System
40-11 Circulation and the
Liver

What causes blood clots to form?

THE HEART AND BLOOD VESSELS

Recall that the digestive, respiratory, and excretory systems work closely with the circulatory system. This is because the primary role of the circulatory system is transport. It is one of the systems that provides direct communication from one part of the body to another.

As the word *circulation* indicates, blood travels in repeating loops. Blood passes through the heart on each loop. The heart is the pump that keeps blood moving in one direction through a system of vessels.

40-1 The Heart

Figure 40-1 is a diagram of the human heart. The heart is located between the lungs and above the diaphragm. It is surrounded by a protective membrane called the **pericardium** [per ə kär′ dē əm]. Recall that the heart is made of cardiac muscle, a type of muscle specialized to make repeated contractions without fatigue.

The human heart, like that of other mammals, consists of four chambers. These are the left **atrium** [ā′ trē əm], right atrium, left **ventricle** [ven′ tri kəl], and right ventricle. The atria are collecting chambers. They receive blood from the lungs and body. Atria then pump blood into the ventricles. The ventricles with thick, muscular walls, are the pumping chambers.

The flow of blood through the heart begins in the right atrium. Here, deoxygenated blood returns from all parts of the body. Contraction of this chamber moves blood past the **tricuspid valve** into the relaxed right ventricle. Then the right ventricle contracts, forcing blood up and out of the ventricle. This causes the tricuspid to close and the **pulmonary semilunar** [pul′ mə ner ē sem′ ē lü ner] **valve** to open. From the right ventricle, blood travels to the lungs.

From the lungs, oxygenated blood returns to the heart. It enters the left atrium. From the left atrium, blood moves past the **bicuspid valve** and enters the left ventricle. When the left ventricle contracts, blood opens the **aortic semilunar valve**. The bicuspid valve closes. Oxygenated blood now travels to the body. It will return to the right side of the heart as deoxygenated blood. Thus blood on the right side of the heart is deoxygenated; blood on the left side is oxygenated.

Just above the aortic semilunar valve is the opening of a vessel that carries blood to nourish the heart muscle. The muscular walls of the heart are too thick to get oxygen and food directly from the blood in the heart chambers. The system of vessels that supply the heart muscle is called the **coronary** [kor′ ə ner ē] **circulation**.

DO YOU KNOW?

Information: During an average lifetime, the heart beats more than two and a half billion times. In this time, it pumps enough blood to fill about 2000 swimming pools.

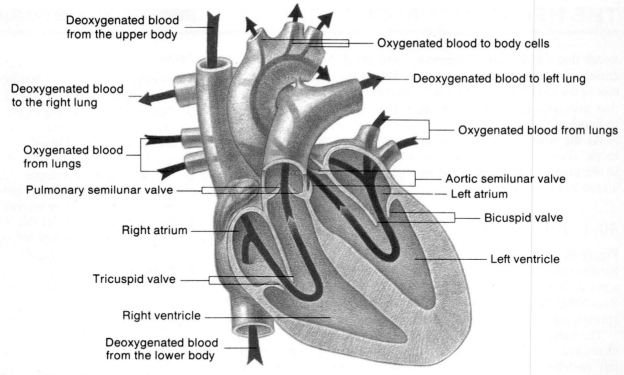

Deoxygenated blood
from the upper body

Oxygenated blood to body cells

Deoxygenated blood
to the right lung

Deoxygenated blood to left lung

Oxygenated blood from lungs

Oxygenated blood
from lungs

Aortic semilunar valve

Pulmonary semilunar valve

Left atrium

Bicuspid valve

Right atrium

Left ventricle

Tricuspid valve

Right ventricle

Deoxygenated blood
from the lower body

Figure 40-1 The human heart is a muscular pump. If the terms right and left seem reversed to you as you look at this diagram, remember that when you face someone, their left hand is on your right side.

40-2 Heart Rate

What causes the heart to beat? Buried in the wall of the right atrium is a group of specialized cardiac muscle cells called the *pacemaker*. These cells generate electrical impulses that cause the heart muscle to contract. The basic heartbeat rate depends on how often the pacemaker generates its signals.

Nerves from the brain connect to the pacemaker. One of these nerves increases the rate of the pacemaker; the other slows down the rate. When you rest, your heart rate slows; and when you exercise, your heart rate speeds up. The change in the heart rate corresponds to changes in the energy demands of body cells. Changes in breathing rate correspond to changes in heartbeat rate.

Sometimes the heart beats irregularly or stops beating because of a defective pacemaker. Doctors can implant an electronic pacemaker that performs the function of the defective tissue.

40-3 Heart Disorders

Heart disease is a leading cause of death in developed nations. Disorders of the heart muscle arise from a variety of sources. For example, when the heart valves close, they make characteristic sounds. Doctors listen to these sounds as an indication of the heart's state of health. Unusual or muffled sounds may indicate defects in the heart valves. If a valve does not close completely or at the right time, blood moves backward. This causes the heart to beat faster. Such increased work over a long time may fatigue the heart muscle and lead to a heart attack.

A second class of heart attacks results from a blockage in the coronary circulation. The blockage decreases or cuts off the flow of blood to the heart muscle. Without sufficient amounts of oxygen and glucose, the heart muscle cells die. Depending on the amount of heart muscle involved, the heart may or may not survive such damage.

Several kinds of heart defects can be treated. For example, faulty valves can be replaced by open heart surgery. In this procedure, a machine acts as a temporary replacement for the heart and the lungs. The patient's heart can then be opened, and valves can be repaired or replaced.

An individual with a severely damaged heart may be a candidate for a heart transplant. The healthy heart is taken from a donor who has died of some cause unrelated to heart disorders. Donors are often accident victims whose brains have ceased functioning. With such an operation, the recipient can usually look forward to several years of normal life. The most common complication is that the recipient's body rejects the donated heart as foreign tissue. This topic is covered in more detail in the next chapter.

Another solution to a severely damaged heart is the artificial heart. Such devices are still in the experimental stages of development. These plastic and metal pumps solve some of the problems of transplants. For example, they are not rejected by the body and are always available. However, the power source for these devices must be carried outside the body because it is about the size of a suitcase. Currently, artificial hearts are used only to keep people alive until a donor heart becomes available.

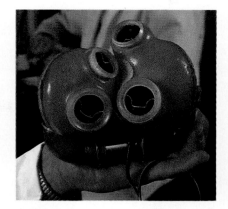

Figure 40-2 The artificial heart has been developed to replace an individual's damaged heart. The power source for such a device is located outside of the body.

40-4 The Pattern of Circulation

Blood flow in the circulatory system follows a path from the heart through vessels of differing sizes and back to the heart (see Figure 40-3). Upon leaving the heart, blood first enters an artery. An **artery** carries blood *away* from the heart and toward the body tissues. Arteries branch into smaller vessels called **arterioles** [är tir′ ē ōls]. Blood flows from arterioles into **capillaries**. These are the smallest vessels of the circulatory system. Exchange of materials between the blood and tissues takes place across capillaries. From capillaries, blood enters **venules** [vən′ ūls]. These tiny vessels join to form veins. **Veins** are vessels that carry blood back *toward* the heart.

Figure 40-3 The heart pumps blood under high pressure into arteries. Blood then travels into smaller arterioles, then into capillaries and returns to the heart through venules and veins. All vertebrates have this basic circulation pattern.

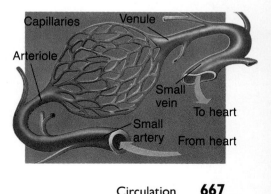

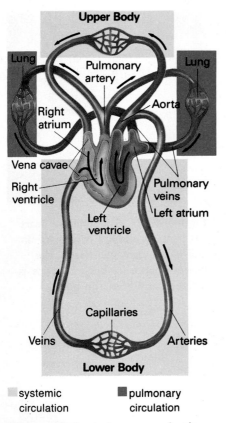

Lung

Lung

Pulmonary artery

Aorta

Right atrium

Vena cavae

Right ventricle

Pulmonary veins

Left atrium

Left ventricle

Capillaries

Veins

Arteries

Lower Body

■ systemic circulation

■ pulmonary circulation

Figure 40-4 In humans and other mammals, blood flows in two major pathways—systemic and pulmonary circulation. How does the blood in the pulmonary artery differ from blood in the aorta?

Figure 40-4 shows the path of circulation in humans: Blood flow to the upper and lower body and back to the heart is called **systemic circulation**. Blood flow between the lungs and heart is called **pulmonary circulation**. This pattern of blood flow is common to all mammals.

Deoxygenated blood is carried into the right side of the heart by the largest veins, the **venae cavae** [vē′ nə kā və]. The right ventricle pumps blood through the pulmonary artery to the lungs. Oxygenated blood returns to the heart through the pulmonary veins. It is then pumped to the body capillaries through the **aorta**, the largest artery in the body.

40-5 Blood Vessels

There are three kinds of blood vessels. The structure of arteries, capillaries, and veins is shown in Figure 40-5. Notice that arteries and veins have the same number of tissue layers. However, arteries have thicker layers of muscle and a thicker outer coat to withstand blood flowing through them at high pressure. A person can bleed to death in a few minutes from a cut artery. Fortunately, an artery's thick walls make it more resistant to injury. Also arteries tend to be buried deep within the body.

Capillaries consist of a single layer of cells. Small molecules easily diffuse through them. It is in the capillaries that the exchange of materials between the blood and tissue fluid takes place.

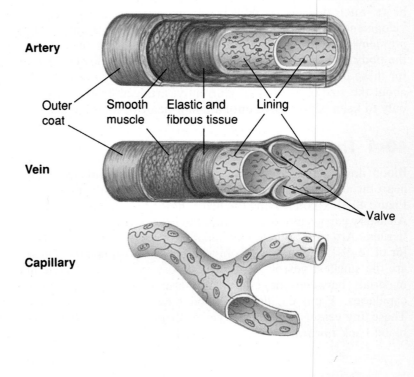

Artery

Outer coat

Smooth muscle

Elastic and fibrous tissue

Lining

Vein

Valve

Capillary

Figure 40-5 Capillaries are living tubes composed of a single layer of cells. Arteries and veins have additional layers of tough connective tissue and muscle.

Veins serve as collectors of blood. Blood in veins is under very little pressure. Valves occur every few centimeters in most veins. The valves are arranged so they open only when blood flows toward the heart. If blood starts to go backward, the valves close. Skeletal muscle activity in the surrounding muscles helps squeeze veins. Such squeezing, plus one-way valves, keeps blood moving back toward the heart. This is shown in Figure 40-6.

A number of diseases affect the blood vessels. One common disease is **arteriosclerosis** [är tir ē ō sklə rō səs]. In this disease, artery walls become less elastic. **Atherosclerosis** [ath ə rō sklə ro′ səs] occurs when deposits of cholesterol build up on the inner wall. The heart must work harder to pump blood, and over many years, fatigue from such work may cause a heart attack.

Cholesterol deposits in coronary arteries can limit the blood flow to heart muscle. Chest pains that result from this partial blockage are called *angina*. The heart's ability to pump blood during exercise is limited, and patients often tire easily. As the coronary arteries become narrower, the risk of a serious heart attack increases. Bypass surgery is sometimes helpful in these cases. In this surgery, another vessel, usually a vein taken from the leg, is sewn in above and below the point of blockage in the artery, and blood bypasses the blocked spot. Double, triple, and quadruple bypasses can be done if there is more than one narrowed artery.

Cholesterol deposits can also trigger the formation of a blood clot. Such a clot in a coronary artery can cause a heart attack as described earlier. Fortunately, many heart attacks involve only a small part of the heart muscle, and an individual can survive such an attack.

Evidence collected over many years suggests that arteriosclerosis is associated with a diet rich in cholesterol and saturated fats. Cholesterol is a necessary substance with many functions in the body. But your cells can synthesize cholesterol, and there is no need to get extra amounts from your diet. One lifestyle change that can significantly lower your chances of having heart disease is to lower your intake of cholesterol and saturated fats.

40-6 Blood Pressure

Blood pressure is the force that blood exerts against the wall of a blood vessel. It results from the force the heart applies to the blood at any given time. Pressure is highest in arteries when the ventricles contract. Pressure drops in arteries when the ventricles relax. Contraction of the ventricles is called **systole** [sis′ tə lē]. The relaxation phase is called **diastole** [dī as′ tə lē]. Artery walls stretch when blood enters them during systole. The pulse you feel in your wrist is this expansion of the artery wall.

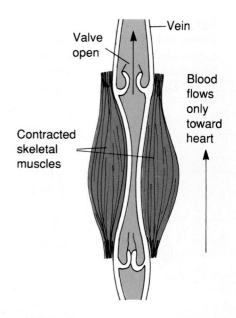

Figure 40-6 Valves in veins allow blood to move only in a direction toward the heart.

Figure 40-7 The difference between the thickness of muscle tissue between the right and left ventricles is shown in this cross section of the heart (viewed from the top). *Left:* During diastole, the diameter of the ventricles enlarges. *Right:* During systole, the diameter decreases, thus blood is pumped into arteries.

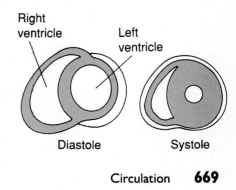

Figure 40-8 Blood pressure increases and decreases with each contraction of the heart. As blood flows away from the heart, the overall blood pressure decreases.

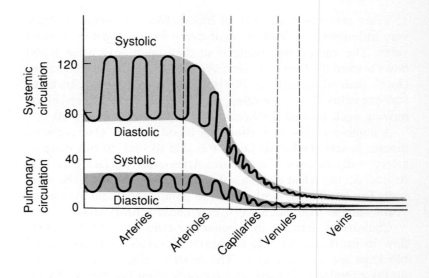

■ *BIOLOGY INSIGHT*

Homeostasis: Sphincter muscles control blood flow through arterioles. By increasing and decreasing the amount of blood flow near the skin, your body regulates the amount of heat lost to the environment and, therefore, your body temperature.

Blood pressure is usually measured in your upper arm. Pressure is given as two numbers, for example, 120/80. The larger number, the systolic pressure, is the pressure at the peak of systole. Under this pressure the blood moves fastest. The lower number, called diastolic pressure, is the pressure during diastole.

High blood pressure, or **hypertension**, can have many different causes. Atherosclerosis, for example, produces hypertension because the heart works harder moving blood through restricted arteries. Being overweight can lead to hypertension. The heart pumps harder to move blood through additional capillaries in adipose tissue. Some people inherit a tendency toward hypertension. In any case, hypertension is a signal that the heart must work hard to pump sufficient blood through the body. Such prolonged hard work leads to heart attacks. Medication, weight loss, and low-salt diets can generally control the problem.

CHECKPOINT ◆

1. Which two valves keep blood from flowing back into the ventricles?
2. What kind of vessel connects arteries with capillaries?
3. In what kind of vessels is blood pressure highest?
4. What is the term for contraction of the ventricles?
5. What is the function of the pacemaker?
6. What are the two basic causes of heart attacks?
▶ 7. Explain why the left ventricle has thicker walls than the right ventricle.
▶ 8. What is the only artery in the body that carries deoxygenated blood?

▶ Denotes a question that involves *interpreting* and *applying* concepts.

BLOOD AND LYMPH

Blood is a very complex fluid. Every cell depends on blood to deliver needed substances and to carry away waste materials. About 55 percent of the blood's volume is a clear golden fluid called **plasma**. The other 45 percent consists of cells. Some liquid and cells from the blood escape from the capillaries. These are returned to the circulation via the lymphatic system.

40-7 Blood Plasma and Clotting

Small molecules and ions are dissolved and transported in blood plasma. Among them are glucose, amino acids, calcium, carbonic acid, and urea. Some of these molecules are necessary for normal cell function; others are wastes.

Approximately six to eight percent of plasma is protein. Some of this protein consists of antibodies. **Antibodies** attack and neutralize substances that are foreign to the body. These foreign substances are usually molecules from some other living thing. Plasma also contains proteins involved in blood clotting. Blood clots stop the potentially dangerous flow of blood from damaged vessels.

Blood clotting is a complex process. It is usually triggered by structures in the plasma called **platelets** [plāt' lets]. Platelets are cell fragments that have broken off from special cells in the bone marrow. There are about 250 million platelets per cubic centimeter of blood. When platelets encounter damaged blood vessels,

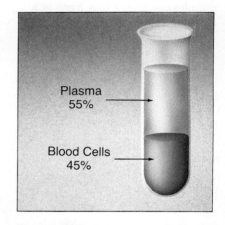

Figure 40-9 *Above:* Whole blood is about 55% liquid and 45% solid. The liquid portion is approximately 90% water, 8% protein, and 2% dissolved substances.

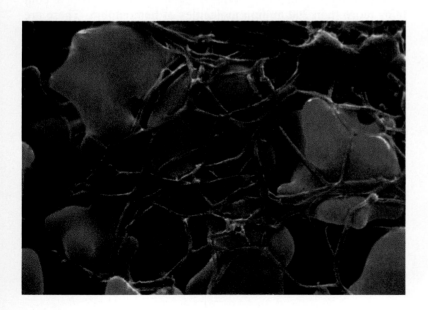

Figure 40-10 *Left:* This colorized electron micrograph shows strands of fibrin trapping several red cells (shown here in green). This network forms a clot that stops blood from leaving cut vessels.

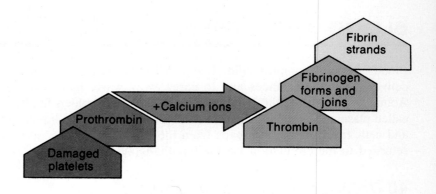

Figure 40-11 Blood clotting is a complex sequence of reactions where each step must occur in proper sequence. Every step is controlled by enzymes. Such a chain of events is much like a row of falling dominoes.

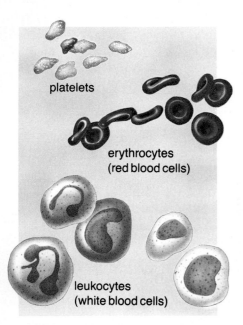

Figure 40-12 Human blood contains platelets, red blood cells (erythrocytes), and several types of white blood cells (leucocytes).

they break open. The broken platelets release a chemical into the plasma. This chemical converts a plasma protein called *prothrombin* into an enzyme called *thrombin*. Calcium ions must also be present for prothrombin to change to thrombin.

Thrombin causes changes in another blood protein, *fibrinogen*. In the presence of thrombin, many molecules of fibrinogen join together. They form a long, strandlike molecule called *fibrin*. Many strands of fibrin gather at the ends of cut vessels. They trap blood cells in a tangled mesh, or clot. This sequence of events is summarized in Figure 40-11.

40-8 Red Blood Cells and Blood Types

Red blood cells are also called **erythrocytes** [i rith′ rə sīts]. Mature red blood cells lack nuclei. The cytoplasm of erythrocytes consists of a water solution of hemoglobin.

Recall that hemoglobin carries oxygen. Each erythrocyte contains more than 200 million molecules of hemoglobin. There are usually between 4.5 and 5.5 billion red blood cells per cubic centimeter of blood. The total surface area of all your red cells combined is greater than that of a football field. Thus, the oxygen carrying capacity of the blood is enormous.

Anemia [ə nē′ mē ə] occurs when there is a shortage of hemoglobin in the blood. The shortage may result from too few red cells or from too little hemoglobin in each cell. The cause can range from defects in the red cell production system to a lack of sufficient iron in the diet.

Erythrocytes carry carbohydrates that determine blood type. In the early 1900s, Karl Landsteiner, an American physician, discovered four major blood types: A, B, O, and AB. He found that whenever different types of blood were mixed, the red cells in the different blood samples usually clumped together. This clumping is called **agglutination** [ə glüt n ā′ shən].

Agglutination occurs because of antigen carbohydrates on the red cell membranes. An **antigen** [an′ ti jen] is any molecule that

Blood Type	Antigens Present in Red Cells	Antibodies Present in Plasma
A	A	Anti-B
B	B	Anti-A
AB	A and B	none
O	none	Anti-A and Anti-B

Table 40-1

causes the synthesis of an antibody when injected into another organism. Table 40-1 shows which antigens and antibodies are found in each of the four basic blood types.

Anti-A antibody reacts with A antigen; anti-B antibody reacts with B antigen. Notice the antibodies found in the plasma of blood types A, B, and O. Suppose a person with blood type B receives a transfusion of type A blood. What would happen? The anti-A antibodies in the person's plasma will react with the A antigens on the donated red blood cells. This reaction will make the cells agglutinate.

You might conclude from the chart that no blood type can mix with another. In fact, a person with type O blood is known as a universal donor. Since type O blood has no antigens, it will not react with antibodies. Therefore, moderate amounts of it can be transfused into people of all blood types. People with type AB blood, on the other hand, are universal recipients. This blood type has no blood-type antibodies. People with blood type AB can therefore receive a moderate amount of any blood type.

Rh factors are other antigens that may be present on red blood cells. Most people have these antigens, and they are said to be Rh positive. People who lack these antigens are Rh negative.

Rh factors may cause problems when a developing embryo has Rh positive blood and the mother is Rh negative. The mother's circulatory system and the embryo's are separate. However, a few blood cells from the embryo occasionally pass into the mother's bloodstream. Once there, the mother produces anti-Rh antibodies. These antibodies can then pass into the baby's blood.

Usually these anti-Rh antibodies do not form until late in pregnancy, if they are produced at all. Therefore, the first baby of an Rh-negative woman is generally unharmed. Once the woman has anti-Rh antibodies in her blood, though, there may be problems with later babies. These antibodies may make the baby's red blood cells agglutinate.

Fortunately, scientists have developed a way to prevent or lessen Rh problems. After a pregnancy, an Rh-negative woman is given an injection. A substance in the injection destroys any anti-Rh antibodies she may have produced. They will not be present to harm future babies.

CONSUMER BIOLOGY

Absorption of dietary iron, which is important for producing hemoglobin in red cells, can be increased by consuming iron-rich foods with a good source of vitamin C, such as orange juice. Too much iron in the blood, however, can also be dangerous because it encourages the growth of bacteria.

DO YOU KNOW?

Word Root: Rh is short for *rhesus*. The Rh factor was first discovered in rhesus monkeys.

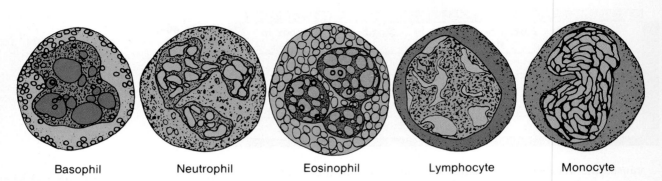

Basophil   Neutrophil   Eosinophil   Lymphocyte   Monocyte

Figure 40-13 There are many different kinds of white blood cells. They are distinguished primarily by the way in which they absorb certain stains.

40-9 White Blood Cells

White blood cells, or **leucocytes** [lü′ kə sīts], are less numerous than red blood cells. There are generally between 5 and 9 million white blood cells per cubic centimeter of blood. Like red blood cells, many leucocytes are made in bone marrow. Figure 40-13 shows some of the different kinds of leucocytes. Notice that they have a large nucleus.

Leucocytes protect the body against infection. They can be divided into two major groups. The first group are called **macrophages** [mak′ rə fäj]. They move and digest foreign materials similar to the way amoebas do. The second group are called **lymphocytes** [lim′ fə sīts]. They manufacture antibodies that help to combat disease organisms. Leucocytes can leave the bloodstream through tiny spaces in the capillary walls. They then move over and around your body cells, destroying foreign materials.

Leukemia [lü kē′ mē ə] is a cancer of white blood cells. In this disease, leucocytes continue to divide out of control. Enormous numbers of leucocytes accumulate in the circulatory system. Although leukemia was once considered incurable, new methods have been developed to treat this disease. Certain forms of leukemia are now among the most curable forms of cancer.

40-10 The Lymphatic System

All body cells are surrounded by **tissue fluid**. This fluid consists primarily of water and small molecules that have moved out of capillaries. In addition, it also contains larger molecules, such as plasma proteins. White blood cells also move from capillaries into tissue fluid. By diffusing through tissue fluid, many materials pass between the blood and body cells.

Look at Figure 40-14. Blood plasma, consisting mostly of water, enters the capillaries under pressure and moves into the tissue fluid. Towards the venous end of the capillary, water moves back into the capillary by osmosis. Overall, slightly more water leaves the capillary than reenters the blood.

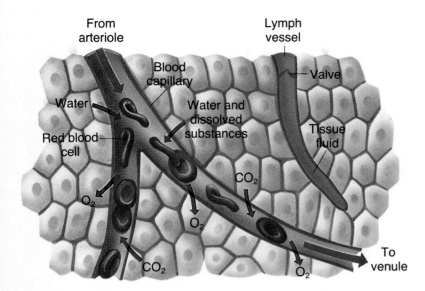

DO YOU KNOW?

Information: Tonsils and adenoids are lymph nodes that are located at the back of the mouth and the upper throat. When swollen, they can interfere with breathing and swallowing.

The excess tissue fluid is collected and drained away through a system of **lymph vessels**. Lymph vessels have thin walls. Tissue fluid readily passes into these vessels, which form a network throughout the body, the **lymphatic system**. Once the tissue fluid is in the lymph vessels, it is called **lymph**. Excess tissue fluid returns to the blood circulation through the lymphatic system.

Figure 40-15 shows the entire lymphatic system. The largest lymph vessels join with two large veins near the heart. Here, lymph drains back into the circulatory system. The lymphatic system has no pump. Therefore, the system depends on one-way valves to move tissue fluid upward from the arms and legs. In what other vessels does this occur?

As you learned in Chapter 38, the lymphatic system is also involved in the absorption of fats. Another major function of the lymphatic system is combating disease. This occurs in swellings in the lymph vessels called **lymph nodes**. Disease-causing organisms are attacked there by white blood cells. In the next chapter, you will learn more about how white cells and the lymph system work to protect your body from invasion by viruses and foreign organisms.

40-11 Circulation and the Liver

The composition of blood is constantly changing. As the blood travels through the circulatory system, it picks up and delivers materials as needed. Oxygen is picked up, and carbon dioxide is released in the lungs. As it passes the digestive system, the blood delivers oxygen and picks up nutrients for distribution elsewhere. All blood leaving the digestive system travels to the

Figure 40-15 The lymphatic system is a network of lymph vessels that drain into the vein at the right side of the heart.

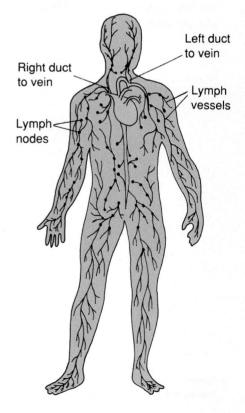

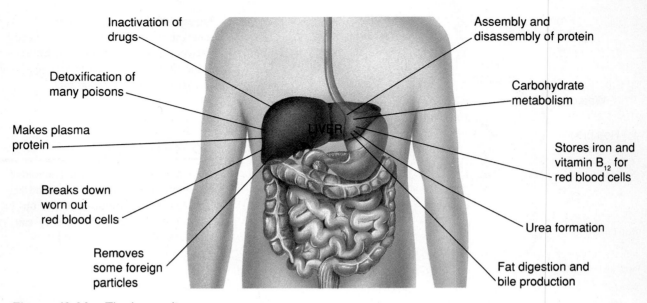

Inactivation of drugs

Detoxification of many poisons

Makes plasma protein

Breaks down worn out red blood cells

Removes some foreign particles

Assembly and disassembly of protein

Carbohydrate metabolism

Stores iron and vitamin B$_{12}$ for red blood cells

Urea formation

Fat digestion and bile production

Figure 40-16 The human liver has an important role in many different body activities. Nutrients entering the blood are processed in the liver before circulating throughout the body.

liver, which has the function of changing the composition of blood to make it better suited for use by other tissues.

The liver processes the carbohydrates, fats, proteins, vitamins, and minerals you eat. Excess sugar is stored as starch. Fats and proteins are dismantled and reassembled. The liver also stores many fat-soluble vitamins and iron. Poisons, such as nicotine, caffeine, and other drugs would be deadly unless they first were inactivated by liver cells. Without plasma proteins produced by the liver, blood would not clot properly, and the distribution of water in the body would be unequal, causing bloating.

CHECKPOINT ◆

9. What is a blood clot composed of?
10. What is another name for red blood cells?
11. Which blood type has no major antigens on the red cells?
12. What are the two major types of white blood cells?
13. What food substance is absorbed by the lymphatic system from the small intestine?
▶ 14. Which function of the liver helps regulate the amount of tissue fluid draining into lymphatic vessels?
▶ 15. The term *closed circulatory system* does not fully apply to white blood cells. Explain why.
▶ 16. In some cases, people who know they are going to have surgery several months in advance can have several pints of blood removed ahead of time and stored until their surgery. What is the advantage of this procedure?

▶ Denotes a question that involves *interpreting* and *applying* concepts.

LABORATORY ACTIVITY

THE STRUCTURE OF THE HEART

Objectives and Skills

☐ *Dissect* a mammalian heart and identify its parts.
☐ *Explain* the function of the chambers, valves, and vessels of the heart.

Materials

safety goggles
lab apron
disposable plastic or
   rubber gloves

dissecting pan
scalpel
metal probe
preserved sheep heart

Procedure and Observations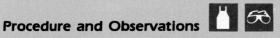

1. Read all instructions for this laboratory activity before you begin your work.
2. Put on safety goggles, lab apron, and gloves. Obtain a dissecting pan, scalpel, and several blunt metal probes.
3. Obtain a preserved sheep heart. **CAUTION: Exert special care with sharp dissecting instruments and avoid splashing preservative.** Examine the external appearance of the heart. Generally locate the vessels on top of the heart, the two atria, and the walls of the ventricles.
4. Identify the ventricles as follows. Look for a fat deposit on the lower two thirds of the heart that extends diagonally across the muscle surface. A coronary artery in the middle of this fat deposit marks the line separating the right and left ventricles.
5. Now identify the right and left atrium. These chambers lie on top of the two ventricles.
6. Identify the major vessels entering and leaving the heart. You may or may not have vessels entering the two atria, depending on the preparation. If the vessels are not there, you will see the opening in the atria where they once entered. Identify the

venae cavae (or where they enter the right atrium). Identify the pulmonary veins (or where they enter the left atrium).
7. With a scalpel, cut through the ventricle walls and expose the interior of these chambers. Do not cut the upper third of the heart at this time. Also notice the large muscular wall that separates the two ventricles.
8. Use a metal probe to trace the path of blood. Insert it into the right atrium and observe how it enters the right ventricle. Identify the tricuspid valve between these two chambers. Notice the cords of connective tissue that attach the valve to the ventricle wall. Now use the probe to follow the path of blood from the ventricle out through the pulmonary arteries. Using the scalpel, cut the upper part of the heart to expose the semilunar valve at the top of the right ventricle where the pulmonary artery emerges.
9. Repeat the procedure outlined in step 8 on the left side of the heart. Locate and identify the valves.
10. Before leaving the laboratory, clean up all your materials and wash your hands thoroughly.

Analysis and Conclusions

1. What external structure shows the boundary between the two sides of the heart?
2. Compare the size and muscle of the right and left sides of the heart.
3. Why is there not a similar difference in the size of the two atria?
4. Explain how the valves of the heart keep blood moving in one direction.
5. In what way are the pulmonary arteries and veins unusual?

CHAPTER REVIEW

Summary

▸ The heart is a muscular, four-chambered pump. It moves blood by means of rhythmic, alternating contractions of atria and ventricles. The basic heart rate is determined by the pacemaker. Nerves from the brain also influence the rate.

▸ Heart attacks result from situations in which the heart muscle fatigues over a long period of time. Blocked blood flow in the coronary arteries can also produce a heart attack.

▸ Blood circulates in humans through two separate loops. The pulmonary loop takes blood from the heart to the lungs, then back to the heart. The systemic loop carries blood from the heart to the body and back to the heart.

▸ Blood moves away from the heart through thick-walled arteries. Materials are exchanged between body cells and the blood at capillaries. Veins have thinner walls than arteries. Valves in veins assist in returning low pressure blood to the heart.

▸ Blood is a complex fluid that is about half cells and half plasma. Plasma contains water and a number of proteins. Antibodies are the plasma proteins which neutralize foreign organisms. Other plasma proteins are involved in blood clotting. Platelets are also part of this complex process.

▸ Red blood cells are the oxygen carriers of the blood. They are produced in the bone marrow. Antigen molecules determine blood type and are found on the membranes of red cells. The four major blood types are, A, B, AB, and O.

▸ White cells are present in much smaller numbers than red cells. White cells are involved in protecting the body against disease.

▸ The lymphatic system drains excess tissue fluid back to the circulatory system. The lymph nodes contain many white blood cells, which destroy harmful microorganisms.

Vocabulary

agglutination	lymph node
anemia	lymph vessels
antibodies	lymphatic system
antigen	lymphocyte
aorta	macrophage
aortic semilunar	pericardium
valve	plasma
arteriole	platelet
arteriosclerosis	pulmonary circulation
atherosclerosis	pulmonary semilunar
artery	valve
atrium	Rh factor
bicuspid valve	systemic circulation
capillary	systole
coronary circulation	tissue fluid
diastole	tricuspid valve
erythrocyte	vein
hypertension	vena cava
leucocytes	ventricle
leukemia	venule
lymph	

Concept Mapping

Construct a concept map for the circulatory system. Include the following terms: antibodies, thrombin, cells, plasma, blood, blood vessels, protein, platelets, erythrocytes, water, heart, and leucocytes. Use additional terms as you need them.

Review

Choose the best answer for questions 1–14.

1. Deoxygenated blood leaving the heart must come from what chamber? (a) right ventricle (b) right atrium (c) left ventricle (d) left atrium
2. Which of the following carries oxygenated blood to the body? (a) vena cava (b) pulmonary artery (c) pulmonary vein (d) aorta

3. Blood leaving capillaries enters (a) an arteriole, (b) a vein, (c) a venule, (d) the heart.
4. Which of the following are made of a single layer of cells? (a) veins (b) arteries (c) arterioles (d) capillaries
5. In which of the following would you expect to find the highest blood pressure? (a) veins (b) venules (c) arteries (d) arterioles
6. What part of the heart determines normal heart rate? (a) valves (b) ventricles (c) pacemaker (d) atria
7. The enzyme in blood plasma that directly causes fibrinogen to form fibrin is (a) prothrombin, (b) thrombin, (c) platelets, (d) calcium.
8. What disorder is characterized by too few red blood cells? (a) anemia (b) leukemia (c) cancer (d) arteriosclerosis
9. What antigen is found in type A blood? (a) A (b) B (c) O (d) anti-A
10. Which of the following cell types can produce antibodies? (a) macrophages (b) lymphocytes (c) erythrocytes (d) platelets
11. Cancer of the white blood cells is called (a) anemia, (b) leukemia, (c) arteriosclerosis, (d) hypertension.
12. What structure do lymph vessels and veins have in common? (a) thick walls (b) three tissue layers in the wall (c) valves (d) connections to arteries
13. Which organ produces plasma proteins that are used to clot blood?
14. Which organ destroys worn-out erythrocytes?

Interpret and Apply

15. Heart sounds indicate damage to what part of the heart?
16. What are the advantages of an artificial heart over a heart transplant? What are the disadvantages?

17. How does the blood in the pulmonary artery differ from blood in all the other arteries of the body?
18. Explain how arteriosclerosis can result in high blood pressure.
19. How can the basic heart rate set by the pacemaker be modified?
20. What would happen if a person with type A blood received a transfusion of type B blood?
21. In what ways are some white cells similar to an amoeba?
22. Why is it significant that arteries are generally located far below the body's surface?
23. How does tissue fluid return to the blood?
24. The earliest artificial pacemakers could generate impulses at only one speed. What would be the disadvantages of such a device?
25. What is the approximate ratio of white cells to red cells in normal human blood?

Critical Thinking

26. Suppose a person's plasma lacked the materials necessary to convert prothrombin to thrombin. What might happen if that person cut a blood vessel?
27. Agglutination problems may occur when an Rh-negative woman is pregnant with an Rh-positive fetus. Why is there generally no problem when an Rh-positive woman carries an Rh-negative fetus?
28. Occasionally a child is born with an opening in the heart wall between the right and left ventricles. Explain how such a defect might affect the child.
29. Choose two body systems and explain how they depend on the circulatory system for proper functioning.
30. Explain the relationship between diet and heart disease.

DISEASE AND IMMUNITY

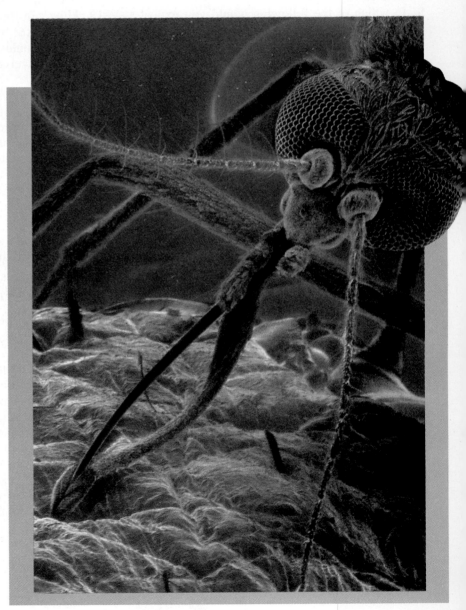

Overview

INFECTIOUS DISEASE
41-1   Agents of Disease
41-2   Disease
        Transmission

**THE BODY'S
DEFENSES**
41-3   Restricting Access
41-4   The Immune System
41-5   Recognizing Invaders
41-6   T cells, B cells, and
        Immunity
41-7   AIDS Virus and the
        Immune System

TREATING DISEASE
41-8   Vaccines
41-9   Antibacterial Drugs
41-10   Immune System
        Malfunctions and
        Control
41-11   Hope for the Future:
        Lymphokines and
        Monoclonal
        Antibodies

Why do mosquito bites itch?

INFECTIOUS DISEASE

The bite of a mosquito is one way foreign microorganisms can gain entry into the body. Mosquitoes, infected with *Plasmodium* parasites, are carriers of an infectious disease. **Infectious diseases** are body disorders caused by microorganisms or viruses that can be transmitted from one person to another. Any disease-producing organism or virus is called a **pathogen**. When pathogens cause a disease to spread rapidly and uncontrollably an epidemic occurs. You often hear of influenza or flu epidemics. In 1918 and 1919, an influenza epidemic killed more people than were killed in World War I.

41-1 Agents of Disease

Long ago, people believed that evil spirits and the night air caused disease. In fact, the name *malaria* comes from the Italian words meaning "bad air." These beliefs changed when Louis Pasteur developed what is referred to as the germ theory of disease. This theory states that microorganisms cause many diseases.

In 1876, the German doctor Robert Koch discovered a way to determine the identity of pathogens that caused a particular disease. His earliest work involved a disease of sheep called anthrax. He used a series of procedures now known as Koch's postulates to prove that a particular microorganism causes a disease.

1. The microorganism must be found in all animals (or plants) affected by the disease.
2. The microorganism must be removed from the host and grown in a pure culture.
3. When some of the microorganisms are injected into healthy hosts, they must produce symptoms of the disease.
4. The microorganisms must be found in the body of the newly infected hosts.

Bacterial Disease Most pathogenic bacteria cause disease by producing toxins. A **toxin** is a substance that interferes with the normal functioning of body cells. Diphtheria and tetanus are caused by bacterial toxins. Diphtheria bacilli grow and multiply in the throat. The toxin they produce is very poisonous, causing sore throat and respiratory difficulties. Untreated, diphtheria bacilli can release enough toxin to cause death.

Tetanus is caused by bacteria that enter deep puncture wounds. These bacteria release a powerful neurotoxin. A **neurotoxin** attacks nerve cells. In tetanus, nerve damage can cause rigid muscle

Section Objectives

A *Explain* Robert Koch's contribution to bacteriology.
B *Explain* how bacteria and viruses cause disease when they enter the human body.
C *List* several ways that disease can be transmitted from one person to another.

CONSUMER BIOLOGY

A potent neurotoxin is found in puffer fish, a delicacy in Japan. Specially-trained chefs remove portions of the fish containing the toxin, leaving behind just enough to cause a pleasant warmth when the fish is eaten. A few unlucky diners die each year from improperly prepared puffer fish.

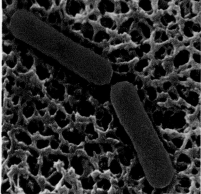

Figure 41-1 *Top:* The bacteria that cause strep infections. Shown here are *Streptococcus* bacteria growing in small colonies on an agar plate. *Bottom:* The bacterium that causes botulism can grow without oxygen in a sealed can.

CONSUMER BIOLOGY

Antibiotic drugs kill bacteria, but not viruses. A sore throat caused by bacteria, such as strep, will be cured by antibiotics, but a sore throat caused by a virus will not.

contractions. The jaw muscles are often affected. For this reason, tetanus is commonly called lockjaw.

Some bacteria can produce toxins before they enter the body. For example, spores of botulism-causing bacteria are sometimes present in foods being canned. If the food is not sterilized properly, the spores survive. The bacteria then multiply inside the can and produce the botulism neurotoxin which is extremely powerful. The presence of very small amounts in the body can cause death. The growth of these bacteria produces a gas that may make the can swell. Food from swollen cans should never be eaten.

Not all bacterial diseases are caused by toxins. Some bacteria invade and damage body tissues. Tuberculosis is a disease caused by bacteria that destroy lung tissue.

Viral Disease Viruses are smaller than bacteria. Most are not visible with light microscopes. Recall from Chapter 18 that viruses are parasites that infect living cells. The viruses use the machinery of their host cells to reproduce. New virus particles are released when the host cell bursts or the viruses split off from the cytoplasm. The free virus particles then infect other cells. Each type of virus infects only a specific kind of cell.

The most familiar human infectious disease, the common cold, is caused by a virus. Common cold viruses are classified as rhinoviruses. A rhinovirus contains RNA rather than DNA. Influenza, or flu, is another common viral disease. Its symptoms include fever, muscle aches, and respiratory congestion. The virus that causes poliomyelitis, or polio, destroys cells of the nervous system. Because of nerve cell damage, polio can cause paralysis and death. Mumps, measles, and chicken pox are also caused by viruses.

41-2 Disease Transmission

For a disease to be infectious, pathogens must pass from one person to another. There are three principal transmission paths for bacteria and viruses. First, pathogens may be carried through the environment by air, water, or some object such as food or silverware. Second, disease organisms can be transmitted by direct bodily contact between an infected and a noninfected person. Third, independent organisms, like mosquitoes, can carry pathogens from one person to another.

Pathogens are dispersed into the air when an infected individual sneezes or coughs. Moisture droplets can carry bacteria and viruses into the respiratory tract of a healthy person. Flu is a viral illness that is transmitted in this way. Pneumonia, strep throat, diphtheria, and tuberculosis are diseases caused by bacteria that spread through the air.

Pathogens can also leave an infected person's body in solid wastes. Untreated sewage that filters into lakes, wells, or rivers can contaminate a water supply. Bacterial diseases transmitted this way include typhoid fever and cholera. Hepatitis, a viral disease of the liver, is also spread through contaminated water.

Venereal [və nir′ ē əl] **diseases** are spread by sexual contact. Syphilis and gonorrhea are venereal diseases caused by bacteria. One other type of venereal disease is caused by the herpes virus. The primary modes of transmission for the AIDS (acquired immune deficiency syndrome) virus are sexual contact, the transfusion of infected blood, and the use of contaminated needles for injecting drugs. The effects of the AIDS virus will be discussed in Section 41-7.

The transmission of the AIDS virus is through very specific mechanisms. The AIDS virus is not an airborne pathogen, thus it is not transmitted by casual contact like cold and flu viruses. You cannot get AIDS by shaking hands, or hugging an infected person.

Diseases can be carried from one human to another by a third organism as in the case of malaria. The bacteria that cause bubonic plague are passed to a person by the bite of a flea. The flea picks up the bacteria by biting an infected rat. Shellfish in contaminated waters can be carriers of hepatitis.

Pathogens are very specific in their attack on the body. If a pathogen of a certain disease does not reach the appropriate part of the body to reproduce and grow, disease does not occur. For example, if food is contaminated with pneumonia bacteria, the person eating the food gets the disease only if the bacteria get into the respiratory system.

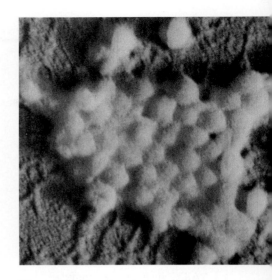

Figure 41-2 An electron micrograph of a group of flu viruses.

CHECKPOINT ◆

1. What scientific contribution do Koch's postulates represent?
2. Name one disease caused by a bacterial poison that affects nerve cells.
3. Name three viral diseases.
▶ 4. The mosquito that carries the malaria parasite is found in the United States, but malaria is rare in this country. Why?
▶ 5. Why might Koch's postulates be difficult to apply in the case of human disease?
▶ 6. What is the principal difference between the way bacteria cause disease and the way viruses cause disease?
▶ 7. How does the transmission medium for the AIDS virus differ from that of a cold virus?

▶ Denotes a question that involves *interpreting* and *applying* concepts.

THE BODY'S DEFENSES

Section Objectives

D *Identify* your body's primary barriers to invasion by pathogens.

E *Describe* the major parts of the human immune system.

F *Explain* the role of antibodies in fighting disease organisms.

G *State* how the various leuco-cytes of the immune system defend against disease and establishing immunity.

H *Describe* the effects of the AIDS virus on the immune system.

You coexist on this planet with a great variety of living things. Many are large enough for you to see, while most are invisible to the naked eye. Bacteria and viruses are in the air, soil, and water. The surface of your skin is a home to millions of bacteria. Along with the bacteria *Escherichia coli* in your intestine, many other microscopic organisms would find your body a suitable home. After all, it affords them a warm environment to reproduce with an inexhaustible food supply. How do you keep from being taken over by invaders you cannot even see? How does the body keep out disease-producing organisms, or pathogens? How does it deal with pathogens that do get in? Why are the effects of a disease like AIDS so devastating?

41-3 Restricting Access

Your skin is effective in preventing a large number of micro-organisms from entering the body. Figure 41-3 shows the effectiveness of skin as a protective layer. As new skin cells are being produced in the dermis, old, dead cells at the surface are being shed along with microorganisms residing there. The skin surface not only shields the body from microorganisms, its replenishment aids in keeping microorganisms from gaining a stronghold. However, if the skin surface is broken such as from a cut, microorganisms now have an entryway into the body. The protective effects of skin are further shown in the case of burn victims. Stripped of skin, burn victims can fall prey to a variety of infections.

In addition to the outer covering of skin, the body is lined internally by the membranes of the respiratory and digestive tracts. These linings provide another barrier to some pathogens.

Figure 41-3 *Left:* Your body has physical barriers to stop the entry of microorganisms. *Right:* A colorized SEM of bacteria (green spheres) occupying a pore on human skin.

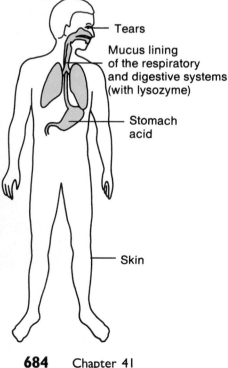

- Tears
- Mucus lining of the respiratory and digestive systems (with lysozyme)
- Stomach acid
- Skin

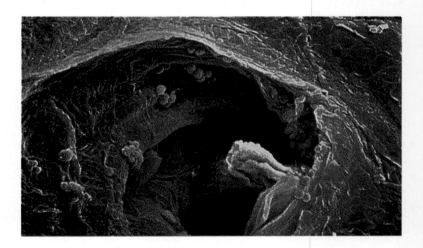

The mucus lining these membranes serves to trap foreign substances. Then cilia in the lungs move the trapped debris to a point where it can be coughed out or swallowed. Mucous-secreting cells and the tear ducts produce an enzyme called **lysozyme** [lī′ sə zīm]. Lysozyme destroys many bacteria by breaking down their cell walls before they can enter the bloodstream. If a pathogen does make its way to the digestive system, the gastric juice in the stomach could destroy it. In spite of the variety of protections in the respiratory and digestive tracts, most disease organisms that do gain entry do so through the mucus barrier.

What happens to a pathogen once it has made it past the body's structural barriers?

41-4 The Immune System

The **immune system** is a collection of cells and tissues that defend your body against pathogens that gain entry. The immune system differs from some other body systems in that it is not a closed system. It has cells throughout the body ready to take on a pathogen at any point of entry. The lymphatic system that you studied in Chapter 40 provides the connecting network among the parts of the immune system shown in Figure 41-4.

White blood cells, leucocytes, are basic to the immune system. These cells are found in the blood, tissue fluid, and lymph. You learned in Chapter 40 that there are two classes of leucocytes that protect the body against infection—lymphocytes and macrophages. Lymphocytes are produced in the thymus and bone marrow and are stored in the spleen, lymph nodes, tonsils, adenoids, appendix, and tissues embedded in the small intestine.

Macrophages are another class of leucocytes that protect you from foreign invaders. Their function is to consume invaders by engulfing them. Macrophages are produced in bone marrow. Once released by the marrow, they travel through the body by way of the circulatory system.

Now you will look at how the immune system works when you get a cut. Bacteria entering the cut will begin to multiply crowding healthy cells until a macrophage comes on the scene. Damaged body cells release several chemicals that cause the damaged tissue to become swollen, red, and sore. This response is called **inflammation**. One of the released chemicals is **histamine** [his′ tə mēn] which increases the diameter of the capillaries allowing for greater blood flow. Histamine also makes the capillaries more porous to release more tissue fluid than normal. Many leucocytes escape the capillaries and collect at the site of the inflammation.

If the inflammation response at the site of the cut is insufficient in dealing with the foreign invaders, lymph nodes nearest the

Figure 41-4 The lymphatic system is a major part of the immune system.

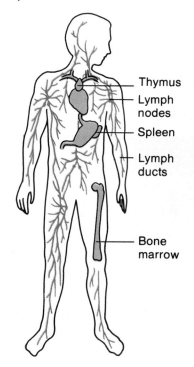

Thymus

Lymph nodes

Spleen

Lymph ducts

Bone marrow

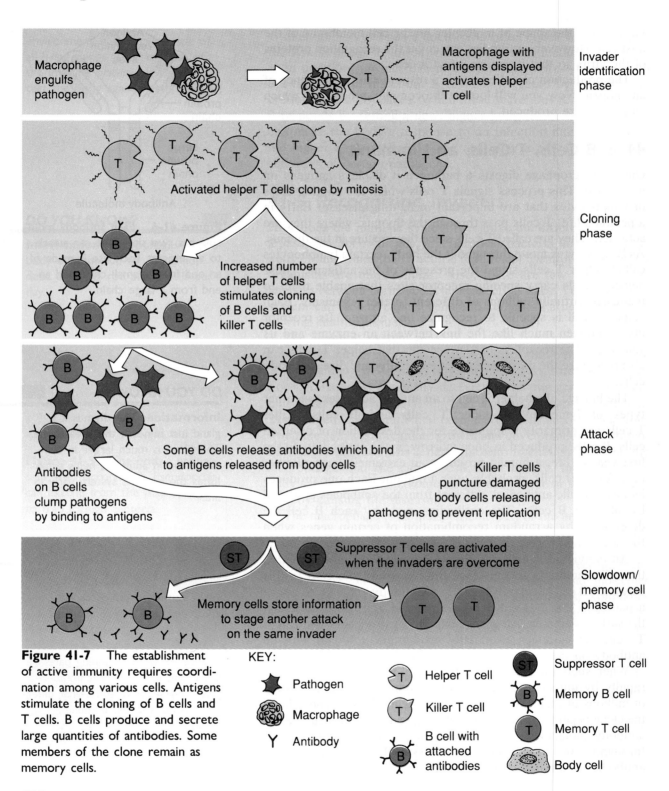

Macrophage engulfs pathogen

Macrophage with antigens displayed activates helper T cell

Invader identification phase

Activated helper T cells clone by mitosis

Increased number of helper T cells stimulates cloning of B cells and killer T cells

Cloning phase

Antibodies on B cells clump pathogens by binding to antigens

Some B cells release antibodies which bind to antigens released from body cells

Killer T cells puncture damaged body cells releasing pathogens to prevent replication

Attack phase

Suppressor T cells are activated when the invaders are overcome

Memory cells store information to stage another attack on the same invader

Slowdown/ memory cell phase

Figure 41-7 The establishment of active immunity requires coordination among various cells. Antigens stimulate the cloning of B cells and T cells. B cells produce and secrete large quantities of antibodies. Some members of the clone remain as memory cells.

KEY:

Pathogen

Macrophage

Antibody

Helper T cell

Killer T cell

B cell with attached antibodies

Suppressor T cell

Memory B cell

Memory T cell

Body cell

All B cells in the clone make only one kind of antibody. If a B cell in the clone contacts a different type of antigen, nothing happens.

Meanwhile killer T cells are destroying those body cells infected by pathogens. As pathogens are released from the destroyed body cells, they are neutralized by the massive number of available antibodies.

Once the pathogens are neutralized, suppressor T cells limit the activities of B cells and other T cells. In other words, when the battle is over, suppressor T cells call off the troops. Special B cells and T cells remain in the body after the attack. These are called memory cells. If the same type of antigen gets into the body again, memory B cells secrete a large number of antibodies to destroy the invading antigens. Specific **memory cells** give you immunity to recurrences of diseases such as chicken pox or mumps. **Immunity** is the ability to resist a particular disease. The existence of memory cells explains why you feel the effects of certain diseases only once in your lifetime. Through the activation of the immune response you have acquired an **active immunity** to the disease.

Both B cells and T cells respond to the presence of specific antigens and undergo cloning. However, T cells differ from B cells in several ways. T cells never release antibodies into the plasma. While B cells respond to individual molecules, T cells respond to whole cells. For example, T cells will react to your own cells if those cells are infected with viruses. B cells, on the other hand, react to free viruses in the plasma. T cells will usually attack cancer cells and cells of transplanted organs. They also stimulate the production of antibodies and macrophages.

To kill pathogens, T cells release toxic chemicals. They can also release chemicals that attract macrophages which will then engulf the pathogens.

Early in life, before the immune system is established, antibodies are passed to a fetus through the placenta. Once the child is born, the delivery of these antibodies can continue if the infant is given mother's milk. As a result, the infant acquires a **passive immunity** to some diseases. The term *passive* refers to antigens in the baby's body that are neutralized by the mother's antibodies rather than its own. Passive immunity is short term.

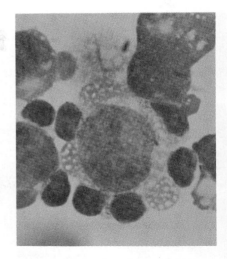

Figure 41-8 It is killer T cells that wage the fight against cancer cells. In the photograph, killer T cells are attacking a cancer cell. The killer T cells are stained deep red.

41-7 AIDS Virus and the Immune System

AIDS (acquired immune deficiency syndrome) is a relatively new disease. The origin of the virus, human immunodeficiency virus (HIV), is not known although it resembles viruses that infect monkeys in Central Africa. Although AIDS symptoms in humans were described earlier, HIV was isolated and identified in 1984.

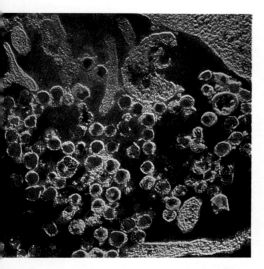

Figure 41-9 This false-color TEM shows AIDS virus particles (small yellow circles) inside a T cell (pink). The RNA in the virus is shown in red (8800×).

The AIDS virus is classified as a retrovirus. Recall from Chapter 18 that a retrovirus has RNA as its nucleic acid. The enzyme reverse transcriptase makes a DNA copy of the viral genetic material. This DNA is then incorporated into the host cell's DNA where it may remain for a long time without showing any sign of its presence.

Recall from Section 41-2 that AIDS is a sexually-transmitted disease. However, AIDS can also be spread by direct contact with body fluids, such as semen and blood, from an infected person. The sharing of hypodermic needles by intravenous drug users also spreads the disease. The virus is able to take hold when given direct access to the bloodstream.

The host cell of the AIDS virus is a helper T cell which regulates other cells of the immune system. Without helper T cells, the entire immune system becomes deficient in its ability to fight off infections. AIDS patients usually die of infections or rare forms of cancer. The immune system of a normal individual would prevent these infections from spreading in the body. The virus also can fuse helper T cells, thereby enabling it to move from cell to cell without entering the bloodstream. Thus, the virus is safe from antibodies in the blood.

An infected individual can carry the virus for as long as eight to ten years before showing symptoms of the disease. This disease is spreading at an alarming rate because individuals can infect others during the period when they appear to be healthy. Generally, these individuals are unaware that they carry the virus. A baby infected with the virus has either contracted the disease from its mother before birth or by a blood transfusion. The spread of the disease can be checked by using a condom during sexual intercourse (though this is not 100 percent effective). How else can the spread of the disease be prevented?

CHECKPOINT ◆

8. Name two surface barriers to pathogens.
9. Red, swollen skin is the sign of what immune response?
10. How does histamine function in fighting pathogens?
11. What name is used for foreign substances that trigger the formation of antibodies?
12. How does the immune system prevent reinfection by the same antigen?
13. What immune cells are most seriously affected by the AIDS virus?
▶ 14. Compare the role of B cells and T cells.
▶ 15. Why would patients with serious burns be kept in germ-free rooms?

▶ Denotes a question that involves *interpreting* and *applying* concepts.

TREATING DISEASE

There are thousands of people across the world who are engaged in disease research. Finding the cure for cancer, and AIDS, as well as isolating and reducing the instances of genetic diseases are among the goals of this research. Genetic engineering plays a key role in the hopes that we may someday artificially stimulate the immune system to build its defenses before any bacteria or virus has the chance to take hold.

Though there are many diseases which have no cure at present, the fight has been won against others. In this lesson you will look at some of the medical advances that have helped conquer some diseases.

41-8 Vaccines

Once the cause of a disease is understood, researchers can focus on effective methods of treatment and prevention. Polio is a viral disease in which the virus attacks nerve cells. The most successful method of dealing with a virus like polio involves boosting the body's defense system. **Vaccines** prepare the body's defenses against a particular pathogen before it strikes. A vaccine usually consists of dead or damaged pathogens that can no longer cause the disease. The Salk vaccine for polio contained killed viruses. The Sabin vaccine for polio, which was developed later, uses polio viruses that have been altered to weaken the pathogen. Even though the pathogen is weakened, its antigens still trigger the production of antibodies. When the immune response is stimulated by the use of vaccines, an individual acquires an active immunity to the disease. The immune system has been actively stimulated to produce memory cells programmed to respond to the disease antigens.

Vaccines now exist for many diseases. Children are routinely immunized against diphtheria, tetanus, whooping cough, mumps, rubella, measles, and polio. As a result of a widespread immunization program, polio is now very rare in North America. In addition, there has not been a case of smallpox anywhere in the world for a number of years.

Some diseases are not easily controlled by vaccines. The common cold is an example. Colds are caused by more than 600 different but related viruses. Antibodies you make for one kind of cold virus do not neutralize other cold viruses. Thus you can continue to get colds even though your body becomes actively immune to a particular cold virus. It is impractical to give people vaccines for each cold virus. However, vaccines have been developed to prevent some flu epidemics.

Section Objectives

I **Explain** how vaccines function.

J **Describe** how chemicals can sometimes help treat disease.

K **Describe** two types of immune system malfunctions.

L **List** reasons why drugs might be used to alter the activities of the immune system.

M **Describe** the potential uses of lymphokines and monoclonal antibodies.

DO YOU KNOW?

Word Root: *Vaccinia* is another word for "cowpox." Jenner called his procedure *vaccination* because he used material from cowpox sores.

The search for an AIDS vaccine poses some of the same problems as the common cold. Besides being able to elude antibodies by hiding in T cells, the AIDS virus appears to be constantly changing its antigens through mutation. It is not known whether a single vaccine can be developed to protect the body against all mutant forms of the virus.

41-9 Antibacterial Drugs

Chemotherapy is the use of chemicals to treat disease. In the early 1900s, a German chemist, Paul Ehrlich, was the first to find a chemical effective against a bacterial disease. He discovered an arsenic compound that destroyed syphilis bacteria. Unfortunately, since arsenic is a poison, Ehrlich's chemical had harmful side effects. However, Ehrlich's discovery is important in that it led the search for better chemicals to fight bacteria.

In 1928, Alexander Fleming discovered the antibiotic, penicillin. An **antibiotic** [ant i bī ät′ ik] is a bacteria-killing substance produced in living organisms. Antibiotics are usually very effective in fighting bacterial diseases. Penicillin and its derivatives are still in use today to kill bacteria. In addition, many other antibiotics have been discovered to fight bacterial infections.

The number of available antibiotics is enormous. No single antibiotic is useful in killing all types of bacteria. To prescribe an effective antibiotic, a doctor must identify the bacteria causing the infection. Also, bacteria undergo constant mutation. Therefore, as bacteria evolve, they can develop a resistance to the antibiotic. Penicillin is now ineffective in killing some strains of bacteria.

Antibiotics are not effective against viral infections. Remember that viruses reproduce using the chemical machinery of your own cells. Any substance that interferes with this chemistry would kill your own cells along with the virus.

There have been a few drugs developed in recent years that interfere with enzymes made by certain viruses. While these drugs show some promise in reducing the severity of viral infections, they do not cure the disease.

41-10 Immune System Malfunctions and Control

The malfunction of the immune system can be the cause of disease. Diseases like rheumatoid arthritis and multiple sclerosis are called **autoimmune diseases**, which means that the immune system attacks the body's own healthy cells. For rheumatoid arthritis, the attack is staged on bone and tissue in the joints. For multiple sclerosis, the attack is mounted on the myelin covering of nerve fibers.

Figure 41-10 *Top:* The mold from which penicillin is derived. *Bottom:* The use of an antibiotic causes this bacterial cell to explode.

692 Chapter 41

Allergies are the result of another type of immune malfunction. In the case of hayfever, the ingestion of pollen launches a full scale attack on the pollen as if it were a foreign antigen. The same pollen would have no effect on an individual who does not have a hay fever allergy. The use of antihistamines for hay fever does not cure the allergy but chemically suppresses the immune response to the pollen.

Organ transplants are another area where chemicals are used to suppress the immune system. When a nonfunctioning or diseased organ threatens life, the only hope for survival may be an organ transplant. The success of the transplant depends on the body's acceptance of foreign tissue. The drug, cyclosporin, is used to chemically suppress the function of helper T cells. As a result, the threat of rejection of the foreign tissue is minimized. However, altering the immune response leaves the patient vulnerable to many types of infections. That is why you often hear of transplant patients dying from infections like pneumonia.

41-11 Hope for the Future: Lymphokines and Monoclonal Antibodies

Lymphokines In Section 41-6, you studied how various cells in the immune system are coordinated to fight disease. It is through chemicals called **lymphokines** [lim′ fō kīnz], which are proteins, that immune cells communicate with each other. Interleukin-1 (Il-1) is the lymphokine that stimulates the fever response. Interleukin-2 (Il-2) is secreted by helper T cells and stimulates the cloning of killer T cells and B cells. Interferon is another lymphokine that was widely researched a few years ago. Interferon is a protein produced by cells that have been infected by viruses. Interferon makes healthy cells resistant to viral attack by causing them to produce a protein that prevents the virus from reproducing once it enters a healthy cell.

Interleukin-2 has shown some promise in the treatment of cancer. Though still in the experimental stage, killer T cells produced using large quantities of interleukin-2 seem to be more powerful than those produced naturally. These T cells may be more effective in killing cancerous cells.

Monoclonal Antibodies The ability to produce a specific antibody to focus an attack on a particular pathogen or cancer cell is a goal of monoclonal antibody research. **Monoclonal antibodies** are artificially cloned outside the body using the rapid cell division capabilities of cancer cells. At present, biologists have been unable to clone B cells outside the body.

The production process is shown in Figure 41-12. A mouse or other suitable mammal is injected with the antigen that will

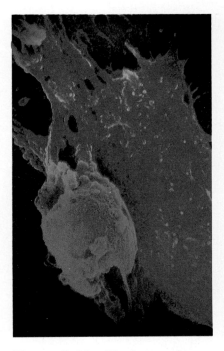

Figure 41-11 The key to the monoclonal antibody process is the production of a hybridoma. In this SEM of a hybridoma, the cancer portion of the hybrid is the larger of the two parts.

Disease and Immunity **693**

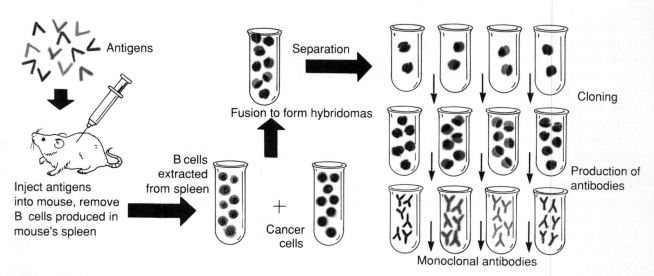

Antigens

Inject antigens into mouse, remove B cells produced in mouse's spleen

B cells extracted from spleen

Fusion to form hybridomas

+

Cancer cells

Separation

Cloning

Production of antibodies

Monoclonal antibodies

Figure 41-12 The process used to mass produce antibodies.

produce the needed antibody. The B cells that naturally produce the antibody are extracted from the spleen of the mouse. The B cells are then fused with cancer cells to start the cloning process. This fused hybrid of the B cell and cancer cell is called a **hybridoma** [hī brə dō′ mə]. The hybridoma has the rapid reproduction characteristics of a cancer cell. As a result, mass quantities of a particular antibody, a monoclonal antibody, can be produced.

Monoclonal antibody research is seen as having some potential in diagnosing cancers. Since an antibody is specific, it can be used as a tracking device to note the presence of a specific type of tumor. If the antibody can be loaded with a substance that is toxic to cancer cells, it could be used to seek and destroy those cells without disturbing healthy cells.

CHECKPOINT ◆

16. Name a viral disease that is not easily controlled by vaccination.
17. What is the term for the use of chemicals to treat diseases?
▶ 18. Once you get a disease, why is it too late to be vaccinated?
▶ 19. Why is a positive throat culture a requirement for prescribing antibiotics for strep throat?
▶ 20. How does an allergen differ from a pathogen?
▶ 21. How does the function of lymphokines differ from that of B cells and T cells?
▶ 22. How have the characteristics of a cancer cell been used in a positive way to fight disease?

▶ Denotes a question that involves *interpreting* and *applying* concepts.

MICROORGANISMS IN THE ENVIRONMENT

Objectives and Skills

☐ *Collect* bacteria from the environment and grow them in cultures.
☐ *Determine* the effect of cleaning agents on the number of bacteria in your environment.

Materials

sterile cotton swabs
wax marking pencil
sterile petri dishes with nutrient agar
hand soap
various household cleaners
pond water

Procedure and Observations

1. Read all instructions for this laboratory activity before beginning your work.
2. On the bottom of each agar dish, use the wax marking pencil and draw a line dividing the dish in half. Put a letter *C* on one side and a letter *E* on the other side (for *Control* and *Experimental*).
3. On the first dish, you will compare the number of bacteria on your hands before and after washing them. On the front of the first dish, write the label: #1—hands. Open the dish and quickly rub the tip of your finger back and forth on the *C*-side of the agar surface. Touch the agar surface lightly or it will tear. Close the dish immediately.
4. Wash your hands thoroughly with soap and hot water. Now open the same dish and rub your fingertip back and forth on the *E*-side of the agar. Close the dish immediately.
5. Label another dish: #2—table. Take the foil off a cotton swab. Do not touch the cotton. Rub the cotton on the surface of the lab table. Now open the petri dish and

lightly rub the swab on the *C*-side of the agar. Throw the cotton swab away.
6. Now use a household cleaner to clean the tabletop. Use a second cotton swab to sample the tabletop after it has been cleaned. Rub the cotton swab on the experimental side of the agar in dish 2.
7. Use the cotton swab method to test other surfaces in your environment before and after cleaning. Label each dish by number and location.
8. Use the same method to test the difference between tap water and pond water.
9. Store the dishes upside-down in a warm, dark location for at least 48 hours. Clean all your laboratory equipment. Wash your hands thoroughly.
10. **CAUTION: Do not open any of the dishes.** After 48 hours, look at your dishes. Count or estimate the number of microorganism colonies growing on each half of the dish. Make a chart to record your observations. Return the dishes to your instructor for disposal.

Analysis and Conclusions

1. Based on your results, what conclusions can you draw about the effectiveness of washing your hands?
2. What conclusions can you draw about the effectiveness of household cleaners in reducing the number of bacteria on surfaces? Which were most effective?
3. Are some microorganisms more common in some locations than in others?
4. Not all microorganisms grow on the kind of agar you used in this experiment. How does this influence the results of your experiment?

New Diseases

The spread of AIDS is more than enough evidence that new diseases can arise. The fact that bacteria and viruses reproduce very often enables you to see the effects of mutations that render them pathogenic. Described here are four disorders that have been identified since 1970.

Lyme Disease

In the fall of 1974, the Murray family of Lyme, Connecticut, suddenly came down with

swollen, painful joints. Local doctors were puzzled. It looked like rheumatoid arthritis, a disease that is not transmissible. Then another family reported similar symptoms, and then another. About all that the 30 neighbors had in common was a peculiar mark that looked like a red bull's-eye.

It was this mark that led Yale researcher Allen Steere, M.D., to the tiny deer tick, *Ixodes dammini*, and later its parasite, the spirochete bacterium *Borrelia burgdorferi*, which causes what is now called Lyme disease. Recalls Dr. Steere, "The people from Lyme told me about an unusual skin lesion, occurring before the onset of the arthritis. I went to the dermatology texts and found such a skin lesion associated with a tick bite. So I began looking for people with skin lesions and followed their progress—and some indeed developed arthritis." He was also alerted by the rural setting of the Connecticut town; the onset of the illness in early summer through fall, when

ticks are plentiful; and the fact that many family members were affected. The ticks are carried on deer and mice.

Lyme disease has spread along the East Coast and is also in Wisconsin, Minnesota, California, and Oregon. Thousands have been affected. In addition to the rash and arthritis, symptoms include flulike aches and pains, fatigue, and in some patients nervous problems such as memory loss and facial twitching. Fortunately Lyme disease is treatable with antibiotics.

Reye's Syndrome

Reye's syndrome strikes a few days after a child or adolescent has recovered from flu or chicken pox. The first symptom is a day of violent vomiting. The person becomes

WARNING: Children and teenagers should not use this medicine for chicken pox or flu symptoms before a doctor is consulted about REYE'S SYNDROME, a rare but serious illness reported to be associated with aspirin.

groggy, confused, and disinterested in the surroundings. Sometimes he or she shouts and thrashes about, goes into a coma, and dies. Physicians noted early on that these are also symptoms of aspirin poisoning—an important clue.

Throughout the 1980's, study after study linked Reye's syndrome to aspirin use following a viral infection. Although it is still not known exactly how Reye's syndrome occurs, widespread publicity has resulted in the replacement of aspirin by acetaminophen for pain relief and fever reduction in the young. This change has sharply reduced the incidence of Reye's syndrome.

Legionnaire's Disease

A bacterial pneumonia called Legionnaires' disease appeared in July 1976 at an American Legion convention to celebrate the nation's bicentennial at a hotel in Philadelphia. In the days following the meeting, several conventioneers came down with what looked like severe flu. Within days, 100 Legionnaires reported the illness, and 20 of them died. Medical detectives from the

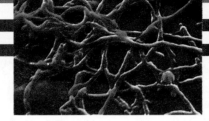

Legionella pneumophila

Centers for Disease Control finally isolated an apparently new bacterium, *Legionella pneumophila* ("little army that loves lungs"), the first new bacterium identified in 25 years. Further outbreaks allowed researchers to trace the source of the bacteria to cooling towers in large buildings. Legionnaires' disease is treatable with antibiotics.

Toxic Shock Syndrome

In 1978, Dr. James Todd of Denver's Childrens Hospital reported seven children with severe headache, high fever, confusion, and a sunburnlike rash. Within a few days, the children vomited, had diarrhea, and went into shock, following a sudden plunge in blood pressure. Finally their kidneys failed, bodies swelled, and the skin on their palms and soles peeled. One child died.

In 1980, reports of similar cases began to trickle into the CDC. All of the patients were women who were menstruating during or shortly before

the onset of symptoms. Most of them were infected with *Staphylococcus aureus*, a common bacterium not known to bring on such severe symptoms.

Eventually the illness was traced to a particular brand of superabsorbent tampon. If kept in the body for more than a few hours, organic chemicals in the tampon prompted *Staphylococcus aureus* already present to produce a toxin, which caused the symptoms. The offending tampon was quickly removed from the market, and new, safer products have made toxic shock syndrome a rarity.

DISCUSSION & RESEARCH

1. How might a new infectious disease arise?
2. If several of your classmates suddenly developed a rash, sore throat, and headache, how would you identify the cause of their symptoms?
3. The diseases described here are all preventable or treatable. What signs and symptoms should you be aware of to help your doctor reach a swift diagnosis should you contract one of these illnesses?

CHAPTER REVIEW

Summary

▸ Pasteur's germ theory of disease and Koch's postulates gave scientists a procedure to help determine the causes of some infectious diseases.

▸ Bacteria cause disease by producing toxins or damaging body tissues.

▸ Viruses cause disease by reproducing in cells and then destroying these cells.

▸ Pathogens can be transmitted through: air, water, or contaminated objects; direct contact with an infected person; other organisms such as insects that can carry pathogens from one individual to another.

▸ The skin and mucus lining of the respiratory and digestive tracts provide the primary body barriers against infection by pathogens.

▸ B cells are lymphocytes that make antibodies against any antigens encountered. Antibodies work by clumping antigens together and by covering the recognition sites of viruses. Killer T cells secrete toxins that destroy whole cells. Helper T cells secrete chemicals that attract macrophages and stimulate the cloning of B cells. Suppressor T cells halt the attack.

▸ AIDS is caused by a retrovirus that infects helper T cells.

▸ A vaccine is a damaged or weakened pathogen that can no longer cause disease but will cause formation of antibodies. Chemotherapy is the use of chemical substances to fight disease. Antibiotics are bacteria-killing substances produced by living organisms.

▸ Regulation of the immune process is seen as the key to conquering autoimmune diseases. The success of organ transplants and relief from the effects of allergies depend on the use of chemicals to suppress the immune response.

▸ The use of lymphokines and monoclonal antibodies are being considered to combat disease.

Vocabulary

active immunity	lymphokine
antibiotic	lysozyme
autoimmune disease	memory cell
B cell	monoclonal antibody
chemotherapy	neurotoxin
histamine	passive immunity
hybridoma	pathogen
immune system	T cell
immunity	toxin
infectious disease	vaccine
inflammation	venereal disease

Concept Mapping

Construct a concept map for immunity. Include the following terms: pathogen, vaccine, B cell, T cell, inflammation, lysozyme, histamine, immune system, infectious disease. Use additional terms as you need them.

Review

1. What is the first step in determining what microorganism causes a particular disease?
2. Name a disease that results from the production of a neurotoxin by the bacteria.
3. For each of the following diseases, write **B** if it is caused by bacteria and **V** if it is caused by viruses.
   - **a.** tetanus
   - **b.** diphtheria
   - **c.** gonorrhea
   - **d.** cold
   - **e.** measles
   - **f.** polio
   - **g.** tuberculosis
   - **h.** influenza
4. Name one disease which is transmitted in each of the following ways:
   - **a.** through the air
   - **b.** by direct contact
   - **c.** by insect bite
5. What is the enzyme secreted into mucus and tears that helps destroy bacteria?

6. What gland must T cells pass through in order to be activated?
7. What kind of lymphocyte responds to viruses that are outside cells?
8. What type of cell provides a person with an active immunity to a disease?
9. To what family of viruses does the AIDS virus belong?
10. What family of antibacterial substances is produced by living organisms?
11. Name an autoimmune disease and describe its effect on the body.
12. What family of drugs is used to suppress the immune response to an allergen like pollen?
13. What types of cells are used to make a hybridoma?
14. To what macromolecule class do lymphokines belong?

Interpret and Apply

15. Explain why Koch's postulates might be difficult to apply to a viral disease.
16. Why should you discard food contained in a bulging can?
17. Suppose you catch the flu. Where are you more likely to have picked up the virus— the air or the water? Explain.
18. A virus causing a digestive-tract illness is carried by air into the lungs. Is it likely to cause sickness? Explain.
19. Why are sewage treatment plants so important in the control of infectious diseases?
20. Why are transplanted organs often rejected by the body?
21. How does a virus find and infect a specific kind of host cell?
22. Explain what happens when an antigen new to the body encounters a B cell with the corresponding antibody on its surface.

23. Why is it currently not possible to develop a vaccine for the common cold?
24. Years ago, penicillin was effective against a wider variety of bacteria than it is today. Why?
25. Once people have measles, they will not get the disease again, even if they are exposed to the measles virus. Explain why this is true.
26. Name two ways an individual can become actively immune to a disease.
27. Name a disease that suppresses the immune system.
28. Why is it inappropriate for a doctor to prescribe antibiotics for a simple cold?
29. Doctors often do not prescribe an antibiotic until they have grown a culture of the bacteria that are causing the disease. Why?

Critical Thinking

30. Malaria was once common in some parts of the United States. An intensive program of mosquito control has essentially gotten rid of malaria in this country. The mosquito species that carries malaria is now fairly common again. Why has malaria not returned?
31. Why are organ transplant patients more susceptible to cancer that normal?
32. Since the massive vaccination programs for polio, instances of the disease have been rare. As a result, some parents do not feel the need to have their children vaccinated against the disease since it rarely occurs. What is wrong with this argument?
33. What digestive side effect would you expect to occur after taking antibiotics for an extended period of time?
34. Make a list of preventive measures you should observe to protect yourself from the AIDS virus.

Chapter

42

THE NERVOUS SYSTEM

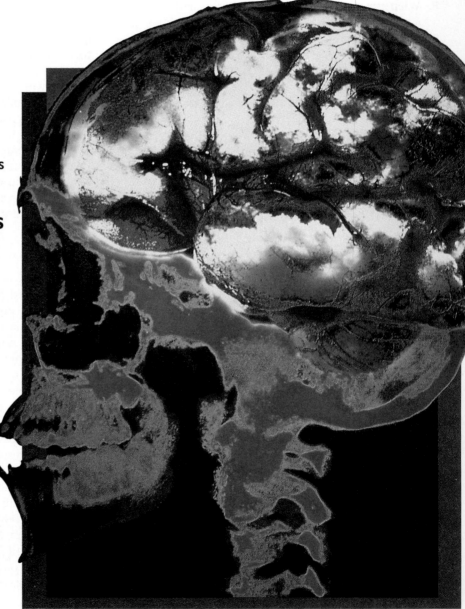

Overview

TRANSMISSION OF INFORMATION

42-1   Neurons and Nerves
42-2   The Nerve Impulse

CENTRAL AND PERIPHERAL NERVOUS SYSTEMS

42-3   The Central Nervous System
42-4   The Cerebrum
42-5   Other Structures of the Brain
42-6   The Spinal Cord
42-7   The Peripheral Nervous System

THE SENSES

42-8   The Skin Senses
42-9   Taste
42-10   Smell
42-11   Hearing and Balance
42-12   Vision

What parts of your brain are used to solve a problem?

TRANSMISSION OF INFORMATION

Your nervous system is an intricate communications network fueled by electrical and chemical energy. Tiny jolts of energy, or impulses, travel along this network at tremendous speeds.

The number of routes that connect different parts of the network is astronomical. These routes make it possible for messages to travel to and from the cells in your body. From your cells, messages that contain information about things happening inside and outside the body travel to your brain and spinal cord, the central relay stations of your nervous system. This communication is accomplished through structures called **receptors**. Messages are then sent out from the brain and spinal cord telling the body how to react. Parts of the body that carry out the orders of the central relay station are called **effectors** because they effect a change in the environment.

42-1 Neurons and Nerves

The basic unit of structure and function in the nervous system is the **neuron** [nü' ron], or nerve cell. A neuron carries information from one location to another. **Sensory neurons** pick up information from the environment. **Motor neurons** carry information to muscles or glands, causing them to act. **Interneurons**, also called associative neurons, carry information between two other neurons.

Look at Figure 42-1. Notice the structures that make up a typical neuron. The cell body contains the nucleus and most of the cytoplasm. Many threadlike **dendrites** branch from the cell body. A long, thin fiber called an **axon** also extends from the cell body. The axon often has a discontinuous coating of myelin, a white, fatty material. Myelin prevents signals from one neuron from interfering with signals in a neighboring neuron. Axons are sometimes called nerve fibers. These fibers occur in bundles called **nerves**.

The dendrites receive stimulation from the external environment or from within the body. If this stimulation is strong enough, a nerve **impulse**, or message, is generated in and travels along the axon. From the end of the axon, a signal passes to a muscle, a gland, the dendrites of another neuron, or another axon.

A **synapse** is the junction of an axon and the structure with which it communicates. Figure 42-1 illustrates a neuromuscular junction, the synapse between a neuron and a muscle cell. As you can see, the axon of the neuron does not actually touch the muscle (or in other types of synapses, the gland or dendrites) with which it communicates. There is a space of about 0.00002 millimeter between the axon and the adjacent structure.

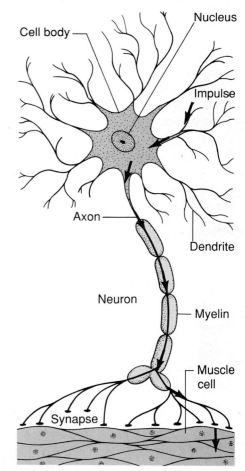

Figure 42-1 An impulse travels from the dendrites to the cell body to the axon, then crosses the synapse to the muscle.

The Nervous System   **701**

42-2 The Nerve Impulse

What starts a nerve impulse? What makes it travel along a nerve fiber? Electric charges are involved in the generation and conduction of nerve impulses. A nerve impulse is not, however, an electric current.

Remember from Chapter 3 that an ion is an electrically charged atom. Some ions carry positive charges; others are negatively charged. All cells contain dissolved ions, as does the tissue fluid outside cells. Like all cells, the neuron has a plasma membrane that is selectively permeable. In other words, only certain materials can pass through the membrane.

When there is no impulse, a neuron is described as being in a resting state. At such times, the membrane is not permeable to sodium ions. It is, however, somewhat permeable to potassium ions. As a result, the concentration of potassium ions is higher inside the membrane and the concentration of sodium ions is higher outside the membrane. The outside of the membrane is slightly positive compared to the inside. The membrane is said to be *polarized* because of the difference in charge between the two sides.

When a neuron is stimulated strongly enough by information from the senses or from other neurons, the permeability of the membrane changes. At the site of stimulation, the membrane becomes highly permeable to sodium ions, causing them to rush into the cell. Then, potassium ions move out of the cell due to an increase in permeability of the plasma membrane to these ions. The polarity of the membrane momentarily changes, triggering a nerve impulse. As you can see in Figure 42-2, once the polarization is reversed in a particular location, the membrane of the neighboring portion becomes permeable to sodium ions. The process of polarity reversal is repeated, causing a chain reaction so that the impulse travels along the length of the axon. The nerve impulse travels several meters per second. After the impulse passes, the membrane restores itself. During this time, no nerve impulses can be generated within the membrane. This time is called the **refractory period**.

How is the resting state of a neuron restored? In Chapter 5, you studied active transport by carrier proteins. A similar process is involved in the restoration of ion concentration of the resting state. After the impulse has passed, millions of tiny protein structures, called **sodium-potassium pumps**, move the ions back to their original locations. These protein structures are embedded in the plasma membrane and are powered by ATP.

Once an impulse reaches the end of an axon, it must cross the synapse to a muscle, gland, or another neuron.

Neurotransmitters are chemicals, produced at the ends of the axons, that diffuse across the synapse. As the impulse

Figure 42-2 The nerve impulse travels as the change in polarity moves down the axon in a wave-like motion.

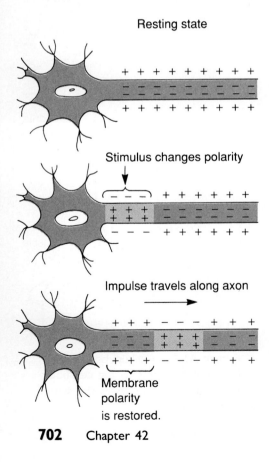

Resting state

Stimulus changes polarity

Impulse travels along axon

Membrane polarity is restored.

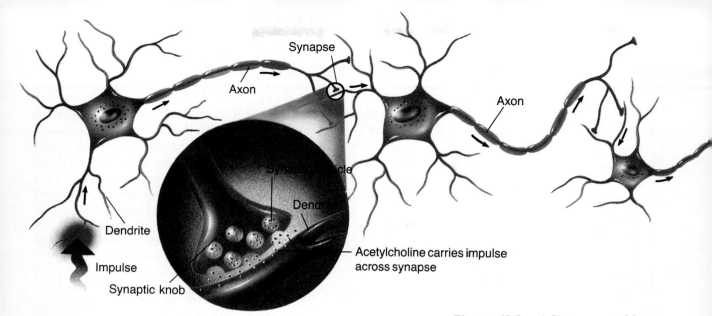

Synapse

Axon

Axon

Synaptic Vesicle

Dendrite

Acetylcholine carries impulse across synapse

Dendrite

Impulse

Synaptic knob

reaches the end of an axon, tiny vesicles in the synaptic knobs (Figure 42-3) secrete a neurotransmitter, such as **acetylcholine** [ə sēt əl kō′ lēn], or ACh. ACh attaches to receptor molecules on the next cell's membrane, causing a change in the membrane's permeability to ions. The polarity of the membrane then changes, which begins the impulse in the next cell.

ACh does not remain active for long. Cells make an enzyme called **acetylcholinesterase**, or AChE, that inactivates the ACh. Another impulse starts if additional ACh is released by the axon.

Acetylcholine is called an *excitatory* neurotransmitter because it increases the likelihood that there will be a response in the adjacent cell. There are several types of excitatory neurotransmitters, each found in a different type of neuron. There are also *inhibitory* transmitters, which decrease the likelihood that there will be a response in the adjacent cell. In other words, excitatory neurotransmitters cause nerve impulses to occur, while inhibitory neurotransmitters prevent nerve impulses from occurring.

Figure 42-3 ACh is secreted by synaptic vesicles in the knoblike ends of the axons. Receptors in the dendrites on the second cell bind to ACh, causing the impulse to continue.

CHECKPOINT ◆

1. What type of neuron picks up information from the environment?
2. In which part of the neuron is the nucleus located?
3. How does the nerve impulse cross the space between two adjacent neurons?
4. How is the ionic composition in a neuron affected at the start of a nerve impulse?
▶ 5. What would happen to a contracted muscle in the absence of acetylcholinesterase?

▶ Denotes a question that involves *interpreting* and *applying* concepts.

CENTRAL AND PERIPHERAL NERVOUS SYSTEMS

Section Objectives

F *Describe* the structure and function of the cerebrum.

G *Name* several brain structures and their functions.

H *State* two functions of the spinal cord.

I *Distinguish* the parts of the peripheral nervous system from each other.

J *Identify* some nervous system disorders.

DO YOU KNOW?

Information: Inflammation of the meninges, called meningitis, can be caused by several pathogenic agents. It may be fatal.

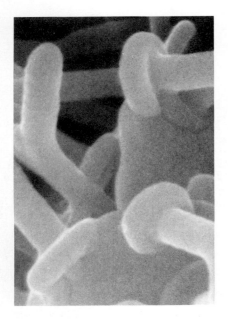

Figure 42-4 A SEM of the ends of an axon show the enlarged synaptic knobs.

Recall from Chapter 17 that a classification system categorizes the vast array of organisms found on Earth. The nervous system contains billions of neurons distributed throughout the body. Like the countless number of living things, the nervous system would be very difficult to understand unless some order were imposed upon its jumble of nerves. For this reason, scientists divide the nervous system into two major parts, the **central nervous system** and the **peripheral nervous system**. Each part is then further subdivided. What does each part of the nervous system do and how are the parts related to each other?

42-3 The Central Nervous System

The central nervous system contains the brain and spinal cord. Both of these organs are covered by three protective membranes called **meninges**. The space between the two inner meninges is filled with **cerebrospinal** [sə rē brō spīn′ əl] **fluid**, which is produced in cavities within the brain. From these cavities, the fluid drains into blood vessels in the brain. Cerebrospinal fluid cushions the brain and spinal cord against shock. It also removes waste materials from the brain.

The nervous tissue of the brain and spinal cord lies under the meninges. The outer portion of the brain tissue is gray. Beneath the gray layer, the brain is white. In contrast, the spinal cord appears white on the outside and gray on the inside.

42-4 The Cerebrum

The human brain contains about 12 billion neurons. Of the 12 billion, about 9 billion neurons are in the **cerebrum** [sə rē′ brəm], the large upper region of the human brain. Remember from Chapter 16 that as human evolution progressed, the brain became larger. In particular, the cerebrum became larger and more folded compared to the rest of the brain. The surface of the cerebrum, called the cerebral cortex, is folded into ridges and depressions called convolutions. This arrangement greatly increases the surface area of the cerebral cortex. The cerebral cortex controls many functions that are associated with intelligence, including memory, creativity, and reasoning.

The cerebrum is divided into right and left halves called cerebral hemispheres. The hemispheres are connected to each other by bundles of axons. Through these axons, one side of the brain can communicate with the other. Deep folds in the cortex divide each hemisphere into four lobes. These lobes are shown in Figure 42-6.

Part of the cerebrum receives information about the environment from the sensory neurons. The cerebrum can send information to muscles and glands by means of motor neurons. Look at the brain map in Figure 42-6 and find the area of the cerebrum that controls the striated muscles. If this part of the brain is damaged, a condition called cerebral palsy may result. Cerebral palsy is a disturbance in motor function.

Messages that originate in the left hemisphere of the brain cross over to neurons that control movement on the right side of the body. Messages from the right hemisphere control the left side of the body. Similarly, the left part of your brain gets information from the right side of your body and vice versa.

The left hemisphere of the brain is usually dominant over the right. Left-hemisphere dominance is associated with right-handedness. Left-handed people usually have a dominant right hemisphere. In most people, an area in the left hemisphere controls speech. The left side of the brain is also specialized for mathematics and logic. The right side is usually specialized for art and music.

42-5 Other Structures of the Brain

The **cerebellum** [ser ə bel′ əm] lies beneath the back of the cerebrum. It also is convoluted. Signals from the motor neurons that control skeletal muscles pass from the cerebrum through the cerebellum. Here impulses from these nerves are coordinated to produce smooth motions. Without the cerebellum, only unrefined jerky movements would be possible. The cerebellum also helps maintain the balance of your body.

Locate the **thalamus** [thal′ ə məs] in Figure 42-7. Note that it lies beneath the cerebrum. The thalamus is a sensory relay station. It receives impulses from most sensory neurons entering the brain. Through synapses with other neurons, the thalamus directs the impulses to the parts of the cortex where they will be interpreted. In addition, the thalamus screens out less significant stimuli. How often do you think about the pressure on the soles of your feet when you are standing or the pressure on your wrist from your watch? Do you feel the weight and texture of your clothing all day long?

You are not constantly aware of the pressure on the soles of your feet or of the presence of your watch and clothes. Neither are you constantly aware of everything within your field of vision. If your cerebrum had to sort out all these stimuli, it would be needlessly overworked. The thalamus prevents sensory overload by sending only those stimuli that are important for responding to the environment.

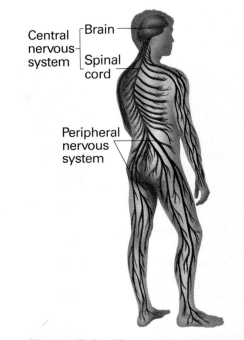

Figure 42-5 The central and peripheral nervous systems

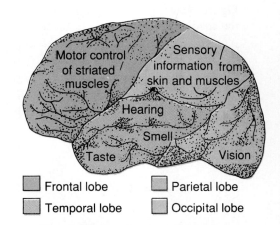

Figure 42-6 A map of the cerebrum indicates the locations of certain functions in the brain.

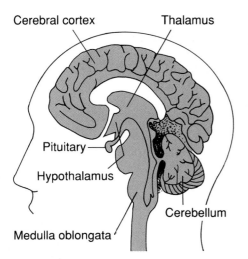

Cerebral cortex   Thalamus

Pituitary

Hypothalamus

Cerebellum

Medulla oblongata

Figure 42-7 Notice the location of the indicated parts of the human brain. State the function of each.

CONSUMER BIOLOGY

It takes about 20 minutes for the hypothalamus to realize that the stomach is not empty after eating. Eating soup or salad prior to a main course can help keep you from overeating.

Figure 42-8 A cross section of the spinal cord

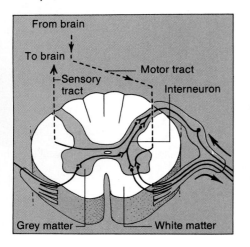

From brain

To brain

Sensory tract

Motor tract

Interneuron

Grey matter   White matter

The **hypothalamus** lies beneath the thalamus. The hypothalamus controls important sensations involved in maintaining homeostasis, such as hunger and thirst. Temperature maintenance, water balance, and blood pressure are also controlled by the hypothalamus. In addition, the hypothalamus plays a crucial role in the regulation and release of many hormones. You will read more about the work of the hypothalamus in Chapter 43.

The **medulla oblongata** [mə dəl′ ə äb lòn gät′ ə] extends downward from the central brain and connects to the spinal cord. Basic life functions such as heartbeat rate and breathing are controlled by the medulla oblongata. Even if a person's cerebrum and cerebellum are damaged, the medulla oblongata may enable life to continue.

As you may guess, the brain is richly supplied with blood vessels, which deliver oxygen and nutrients to the brain cells. A blockage or rupture of a large vessel results in a stroke. Brain tissue is damaged, and the function for which that brain part was responsible is affected.

42-6 The Spinal Cord

The spinal cord extends downward from the medulla. Through the spinal cord, sensory and motor information passes between the brain and the other parts of the body. All sensory and motor nerves located below the neck must pass through the spinal cord on the way to the brain. A cross section of the spinal cord is shown in Figure 42-8. Note the pathways shown for sensory impulses to the brain and for motor impulses to the body.

Your spinal cord passes through holes in your vertebrae. In this way, your backbone provides protection for your spinal cord. Sometimes the protection of the backbone is not enough to prevent injury. Perhaps you have heard of someone who had a serious accident that crushed the spinal cord. In such a case, the ability to move parts of the body located below the injury is frequently lost. An injured person has little or no sensation in those body parts.

Have you ever touched a hot frying pan by accident or been poked by a pin? Your response to both of these situations was probably a quick movement away from what hurt you. A **reflex** is an automatic, unthinking response to a stimulus. Most of your reflexes are controlled by your spinal cord, rather than your brain.

Consider what happens when you experience a painful skin stimulation. Suppose you are walking barefoot on the beach and you step on a broken shell. Within an instant of touching the shell, your foot springs up and away. The sharp edge of the shell activates certain dendrites in a sensory neuron. An impulse travels

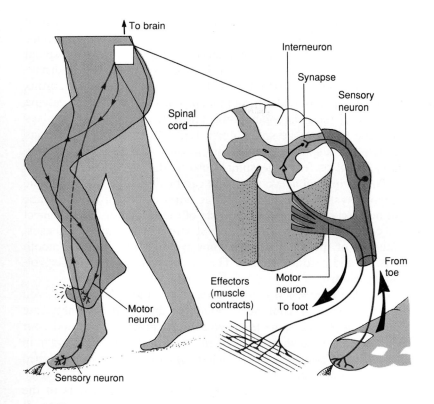

To brain

Interneuron

Synapse

Sensory
neuron

Spinal
cord

Motor
neuron

From
toe

Effectors
(muscle
contracts)

Motor
neuron

To foot

Motor
neuron

Sensory neuron

Figure 42-9 A spinal reflex pulls the foot away from the stimulus. An impulse also travels to the cerebrum. You become aware of the pain only after you have moved your foot.

along the sensory neuron to the spinal cord. There the sensory neuron synapses with an interneuron. The interneuron, in turn, synapses with a motor neuron that sends an impulse to a muscle in your leg. The muscle contracts, and your leg pulls away from the sharp object.

Meanwhile, another impulse travels upward through your spinal cord to the cerebral cortex. Your brain will interpret the impulse as pain. However, this impulse does not reach your brain as quickly as the reflex action takes place. You do not feel pain until after you have removed your foot!

Reflexes serve an important protective function. What would happen if you left your hand on a hot stovetop until you felt it burn? If your body could not react quickly enough to painful or threatening stimuli, you would be in much more danger of injury.

42-7 The Peripheral Nervous System

All parts of the nervous system except the brain and spinal cord are included in the peripheral nervous system. This division of the nervous system includes the cranial and spinal nerves. **Cranial nerves** are 12 pairs of nerves that emerge from the brain. For the most part, they connect with areas in the head and the face.

■ BIOLOGY INSIGHT

Homeostasis: It has recently been found that permanent damage from spinal injuries often results from a lack of blood supply to the injured part of the cord immediately after the accident. New techniques are being developed to maintain the blood supply to the spine following the injury. Researchers hope that someday they may be able to prevent most of the paralysis that now follows injuries to the spinal cord.

DO YOU KNOW? ■

Information: Your brain uses one fifth of the body's energy supply.

BIOLOGY INSIGHT

Levels of Organization: Flatworms possess nervous systems that demonstrate the true beginning of a differentiation into a peripheral nervous system and a central nervous system.

Figure 42-10 The structural features of a spinal nerve

Muscles that move the eyes and tongue are activated by cranial nerves. These nerves also carry sensory information to the brain.

There are 31 pairs of **spinal nerves** that branch from the spinal cord. Each branch contains both sensory and motor neurons. Notice in Figure 42-10 that the cell bodies of the sensory neurons are located just outside the spinal cord in swellings called **ganglia** [gan′ glē ə] (singular, ganglion). These neurons carry impulses from the body to the spinal cord. Cell bodies of motor neurons lie within the spinal cord and not in the ganglia. These neurons carry impulses from the spinal cord to the body.

The peripheral nervous system can be divided into the somatic nervous system and the autonomic nervous system. The **somatic** [sō mat′ ik] **nervous system** consists of motor neurons that connect the central nervous system to the striated, or voluntary, muscles. Neurons of the **autonomic nervous system** go to glands, smooth muscle, and cardiac muscle. These structures are not under voluntary control.

Recall a time when you were running a race. As you ran, you became aware of your heart pounding and your breathing rate increasing. At the same time, your blood pressure rose and your liver released its stored glycogen, raising the level of sugar in your blood. Soon after you completed the race, your body returned to its normal state.

The **sympathetic nervous system**, one of the divisions of the autonomic nervous system, was in control during the race. It enabled you to run as fast as you could. This part of your nervous system is dominant during times of great stress.

The **parasympathetic nervous system** is the other division of the autonomic nervous system. It counteracts the effects of the

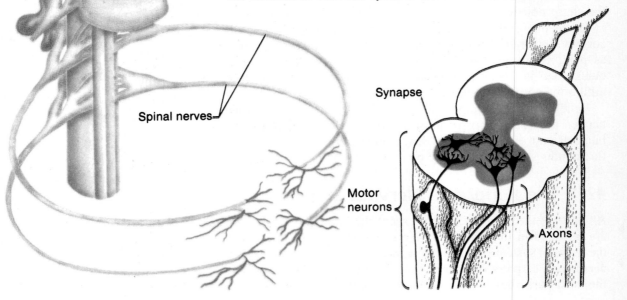

Ganglia

Spinal nerves

Synapse

Motor neurons

Axons

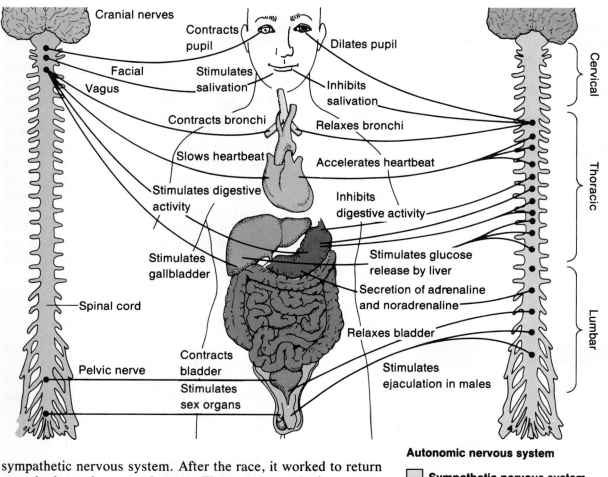

Cranial nerves

Contracts pupil

Dilates pupil

Facial

Stimulates salivation

Vagus

Inhibits salivation

Contracts bronchi

Relaxes bronchi

Slows heartbeat

Accelerates heartbeat

Stimulates digestive activity

Inhibits digestive activity

Stimulates gallbladder

Stimulates glucose release by liver

Spinal cord

Secretion of adrenaline and noradrenaline

Relaxes bladder

Pelvic nerve

Contracts bladder

Stimulates ejaculation in males

Stimulates sex organs

Cervical

Thoracic

Lumbar

sympathetic nervous system. After the race, it worked to return your body to its normal state. The parasympathetic nervous system will remain dominant under normal conditions.

The vagus nerve, a cranial nerve, is the main nerve in the parasympathetic nervous system. It branches to the heart, respiratory system, and parts of the digestive tract. It plays a role in vital functions such as control of heartbeat rate.

Autonomic nervous system

Sympathetic nervous system

Parasympathetic nervous system

Figure 42-11 Each organ is contacted by both sympathetic and parasympathetic nerves, which have opposite effects.

CHECKPOINT ◆

6. What is the largest part of the human brain?
7. In a reflex, which occurs first, your response to a stimulus or your awareness of the stimulus?
8. What is cerebral palsy?
▶ 9. Hypothalamus is to temperature regulation as _____ is to muscle coordination.
▶ 10. Which part of the peripheral nervous system is involved in throwing a ball?

▶ Denotes a question that involves *interpreting* and *applying* concepts.

THE SENSES

Section Objectives

K *Name* the types of sense receptors located in the skin.

L *Explain* why taste and smell are called "chemical senses."

M *Relate* the structure of the ear to the sense of hearing.

N *Describe* the structure of the eye.

You begin to cross a street, and the driver of a rapidly approaching car beeps the horn. Your eyes and ears send information to your brain informing you that a car is coming. As a result, your brain directs your feet to move you out of the way.

Your body has other senses of which you are not aware. For example, there are receptors that tell your brain how much salt is in your bloodstream. Others make your brain aware of your blood pressure. In each case, your brain directs parts of the body, such as the kidneys or the smooth muscles of the blood vessels, to correct deviations from the normal range.

How does information about the environment arrive at your brain? How is the image of a tree, the sound of music, or the feel of velvet transformed into nerve impulses? The information comes from your senses.

42-8 The Skin Senses

Your skin contains receptors for touch, pain, pressure, heat, and cold. Each of these sensations has a different kind of receptor. For example, touch receptors inform the brain of the lightest touch. Pressure receptors are buried deeper in the skin than the touch receptors. A gentle touch will not activate the pressure receptors, but firm pressure will.

Pain is one of the most important skin senses. It serves as a warning against tissue injury and potentially dangerous environmental conditions. Some pain receptors detect pricking sensations while others detect burning or aching pain. The source of pricking pain can be precisely located; burning and aching pain can only be felt in a general area, however.

If you have ever received a tetanus shot, you may remember the pricking sensation in your skin's outer layer. At that time, you could feel the precise location of penetration. A burning sensation that originated deep in the skin could later be felt. This sensation could be felt in the general location of the injection.

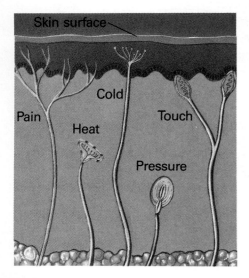

Figure 42-12 Each type of receptor in your skin has a different structure.

42-9 Taste

Taste is a chemical sense, or one that is stimulated directly by chemicals. Receptors for taste are located in structures called **taste buds**, which cover the top and sides of your tongue and some of the skin of your throat. Food molecules activate receptors in the taste buds. Nerve impulses are sent to the brain, which interprets these impulses as tastes.

There are different types of taste receptors. Each type senses a different taste. Four major tastes are sweet, sour, bitter, and salty. Most foods have a blend of several different tastes. Each food stimulates more than one type of receptor.

When you have a cold, your sense of taste does not function as well as usual. The reason for this is that much of your ability to taste actually depends on the sense of smell. When your nose is blocked, your sense of smell does not work well.

42-10 Smell

Like the sense of taste, smell is a chemical sense. Unlike taste receptors, however, the olfactory, or smell, receptors respond to molecules in the gaseous state. When you smell a substance, at least some of its molecules must be in the form of gases.

Smell receptors are neurons embedded in the lining of the nose. The axons of these neurons compose the olfactory nerve, a sensory cranial nerve. Impulses travel along the olfactory nerve to the olfactory region of the cerebral cortex, where they are interpreted as smells.

Smells evoke strong memories. Just the thought of your favorite food can bring to mind vivid imaginary aromas. You may associate a person with the scent of a particular cologne or remember a place you have visited if you smell a similar scent somewhere else. Have you ever encountered a skunk? Do you remember the scent of a rose or of salt water near an ocean? Could you identify these things using only your sense of smell?

42-11 Hearing and Balance

Imagine that you are at a party with many other people. Everyone in the room is involved in conversation but, suddenly amidst all the chatter, you hear your name. Your ears are constantly monitoring all the sounds around you. As you learned earlier in this chapter, the thalamus screens stimuli. In this case, your thalamus worked with your ears to detect the mention of your name.

The ear is a complex organ. It is responsible for both hearing and balance. The ear is divided into three main areas—the outer ear, middle ear, and inner ear.

The outer ear is composed of the ear flap and the **auditory canal**. The auditory canal ends at the **tympanic** [tim pan′ ik] **membrane**, or eardrum. On the other side of the tympanic membrane is the middle ear. Connecting the middle ear to the pharynx is the Eustachian tube. This tube contains air that helps to equalize the pressure between the outer and middle ear.

In the middle ear, there are three tiny bones in a row—the hammer, anvil, and stirrup. These bones connect the tympanic

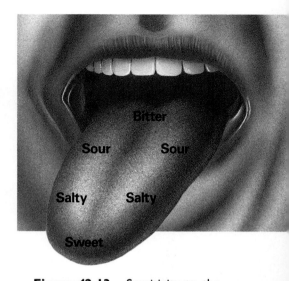

Figure 42-13 Sensitivity to the four major tastes are on different areas of the tongue. Each area has many taste receptors, or buds, embedded in the tongue's surface.

CONSUMER BIOLOGY

Long term exposure to loud sounds damages the hairs in the inner ear that transmit sounds. Rock stars are susceptible to this type of hearing loss.

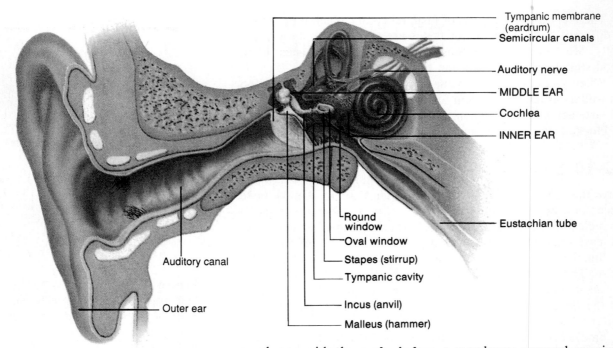

Tympanic membrane (eardrum)
Semicircular canals
Auditory nerve
MIDDLE EAR
Cochlea
INNER EAR
Eustachian tube
Round window
Oval window
Stapes (stirrup)
Tympanic cavity
Incus (anvil)
Malleus (hammer)
Auditory canal
Outer ear

Figure 42-14 Each structure of the ear is related in some way to either the sense of hearing or balance.

■ *BIOLOGY INSIGHT*

Structure Is Related to Function: The round window of the ear is located near the oval window. The round window acts as a pressure release. Each time the vibrations strike the oval window, they cause the membrane to vibrate inward toward the inner ear. This, in turn, causes the fluid in the cochlea to vibrate. If there was no flexible element beyond the cochlea, the incompressible fluid might cause a rupture.

membrane with the **oval window**, a membrane-covered opening between the middle and inner ear.

A coiled structure, the **cochlea** [kō′ klē ə], is located in the inner ear. This structure is filled with fluid. Receptor cells in the cochlea contain nerve endings that transmit impulses to the brain. The **semicircular canals**, which are involved in the senses of balance and motion, are also in the inner ear.

Sound travels through air as waves of vibrating air molecules. When these vibrations reach the outer ear, they travel through the auditory canal and make the tympanic membrane vibrate too. Next, these vibrations pass to the bones in the middle ear behind the tympanic membrane. One after another, these bones start vibrating. The stirrup, the last of these bones, touches the oval window. Vibration of the stirrup makes the membrane of the oval window vibrate. Then this vibration moves on to the fluid in the cochlea. The motion of the fluid stimulates the receptor cells. Sensory neurons that compose the auditory nerve send impulses to the brain, where these impulses are interpreted as sound.

In addition to hearing, your ears are involved in your sense of balance. The three semicircular canals of the inner ear are at right angles to one another, like the floor and two walls that meet at a corner of a room. This arrangement allows you to sense motion in three dimensions.

The semicircular canals are filled with fluid. In addition, they contain sensory hair cells. When your head changes position, the fluid puts pressure on the hairs. Sensory neurons detect the relative strength of the pressure on each hair. Impulses sent to the brain from these neurons communicate the position of the head.

42-12 Vision

Have you ever tried to understand someone who was speaking softly? If so, you may have found that it was easier to understand what the person was saying when you could see his or her lips. Humans rely heavily on vision, and the human eye is well-adapted for receiving light. Your eye is covered by a tough outer layer. The front of this covering, the **cornea** [kȯr′ nē ə], is transparent. The cornea is more curved than the eye as a whole. This curved surface bends incoming light rays.

Behind the cornea is the **iris**, the colored area of the eye. The iris contains smooth muscles that can make the iris more closed or open. This adjustment of the iris changes the size of the **pupil**, an opening in the middle of the iris. In strong light, the pupil becomes smaller, admitting less light to the eye. In dim light, the pupil becomes larger.

The **lens**, the eye's primary light-focusing structure, is behind the pupil. Muscles attach to it. When these muscles contract, the lens changes shape enabling the lens to focus light.

Light rays are focused on the **retina**, a thin membrane on the back of the eye that contains light-sensitive receptors. These

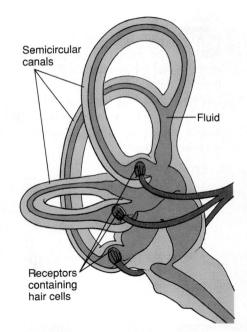

Figure 42-15 Changes in the position of the head are detected by pressure exerted on the receptors in the semicircular canals.

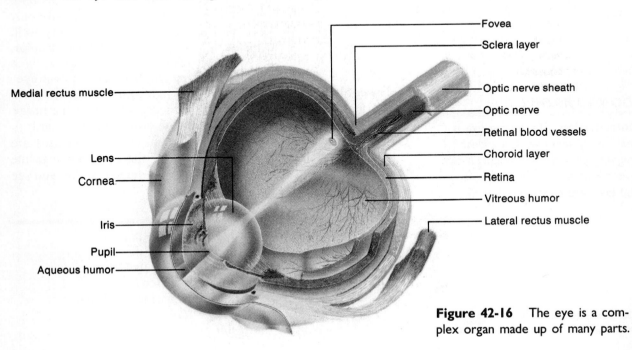

Figure 42-16 The eye is a complex organ made up of many parts.

Figure 42-17 *Top:* Light rays strike the rods and cones in the retina. Nerve impulses are then sent via the optic nerve to the brain. *Bottom:* The image of an object focused on the retina is reversed. When visual impulses are interpreted by the brain, the image is reversed again.

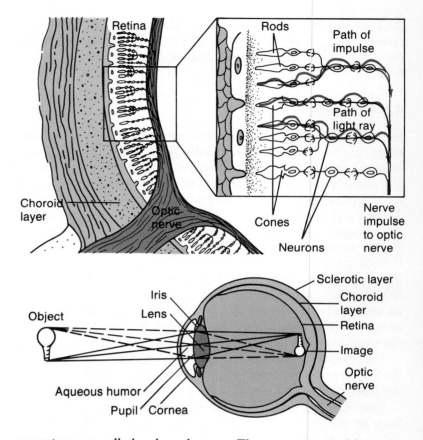

receptors are called rods and cones. The **cones** are sensitive only in bright light. They can distinguish form and color very well. The **rods** are sensitive in dim light. They cannot distinguish color. Therefore, in dim light, you can see only shades of gray.

You see when light reflected from an object enters your eye. The cornea and lens bend the light rays together. The rays cross and focus on the retina. Notice in Figure 42-17 that the image formed on the retina is actually upside down and backward.

When light strikes the rods and cones, nerve impulses are created. Those impulses are carried by the optic nerve to the brain. In the brain, the retinal image is reversed so that you see the object right side up.

CHECKPOINT ◆

11. What five types of receptors are located in the skin?
12. Where are the taste receptors located?
▶ 13. What would be the result of a missing anvil, hammer, or stirrup?
▶ 14. What would be the result of a lack of cones?

▶ Denotes a question that involves *interpreting* and *applying* concepts.

SKIN SENSITIVITY TO TOUCH

Objectives and Skills

- *Observe* the distribution of touch receptors in various skin surfaces.
- *Explain* the adaptive significance of the differential distribution of touch receptors.

Materials

6 paper clips   1 millimeter ruler   tape

Procedure and Observations

1. Working with a partner, construct skin sensitivity testers using paper clips. Bend each clip into a U. Using a ruler, adjust the 2 points of each U so that the distances between the points measure 1 mm, 2 mm, 4 mm, 8 mm, and 16 mm, respectively. After adjusting the distances, wrap cellophane tape around each U to keep the distances fixed.
2. Have your partner sit before you with eyes closed. Touch the points of each tester to your partner's fingertips, palms, forearms, and nape of the neck, one part at a time. Occasionally, touch only one point to the skin so that your partner will not assume that there will always be two points.
3. Ask your partner to report the number of points touching the skin. If your partner can feel two points, put a (+) in the appropriate place in the table. If your partner cannot feel two points, put a (−) in the table. Do not record anything for the one-point trials.
4. When you have tested each body part listed, switch roles and repeat the experiment.
5. Before leaving the laboratory, clean up all your materials and wash your hands thoroughly.

Analysis and Conclusions

1. In which skin area did you record the most sensitivity? the least sensitivity?
2. If the touch receptors are close together, it is easier to distinguish two points that are close together. Which skin areas have the highest density of touch receptors?
3. Correlate the density of touch receptors in an area with the function of that area.
4. Would you expect the soles of your feet or the skin on your knees to have a higher density of touch receptors? Explain.

SKIN SENSITIVITY					
Distance	Lip	Fingertip	Palm	Forearm	Nape of the Neck
1 mm					
2 mm					
4 mm					
8 mm					
16 mm					

CHAPTER REVIEW

Summary

▸ The basic units of structure and function of the nervous system are neurons. Their structure allows electrochemical signals to travel along their length. Each electrochemical signal is then transmitted across a synapse, activating a muscle, a gland, or another neuron.

▸ The nervous system is divided into two parts. One part, the central nervous system, includes the neurons of the brain and spinal cord. The peripheral nervous system includes all other neurons.

▸ Most parts of the human brain are known to have specific functions. The most highly developed part, the cerebral cortex, is the seat of higher intellectual function.

▸ The spinal cord, which connects the brain to the peripheral nervous system, also governs much reflex behavior.

▸ The somatic nervous system activates striated muscle, which is voluntarily controlled. Glands and muscles of internal organs are governed by the autonomic nervous system. Each gland and organ receives two sets of neural controls. One set, called sympathetic neurons, is dominant during a crisis. The other set, the parasympathetic neurons, takes over when the body is in a resting state.

▸ The brain does not act in a vacuum. The directions it gives to the body by way of the peripheral nervous system are based on the information it receives from the environment. This information reaches the brain through messages sent from the sense organs.

▸ Receptors in sense organs send information along sensory neurons to the central nervous system via nerve impulses. Within the central nervous system, interneurons relay the chemical signals to motor neurons, which cause parts of the body to respond to the incoming stimuli.

Vocabulary

acetylcholine (ACh)
acetylcholinesterase
auditory canal
autonomic nervous
   system
axon
central nervous
   system
cerebellum
cerebrospinal fluid
cerebrum
cochlea
cone
cornea
cranial nerve
dendrite
effector
ganglia
hypothalamus
impulse
interneuron
iris
lens
medulla oblongata
meninges
motor neuron

nerve
neuron
neurotransmitter
oval window
parasympathetic ner-
   vous system
peripheral nervous
   system
pupil
receptor
reflex
refractory period
retina
rod
semicircular canals
sensory neuron
sodium-potassium pump
somatic nervous
   system
spinal nerve
sympathetic nervous
   system
synapse
taste bud
thalamus
tympanic membrane

Concept Mapping

Construct a concept map for the nervous system. Include the following terms: sensory neurons, thalamus, hypothalamus, cerebrum, interneurons, motor neurons, central nervous system, peripheral nervous system. Use additional terms as you need them.

Review

1. Identify the three types of neurons.
2. Identify the structures with which a neuron may synapse.

3. Which structure in the central nervous system is associated with creativity?
4. Which brain structure screens stimuli that reach the cerebrum?
5. What parts of the body are controlled by the autonomic nervous system?
6. What do the senses of smell and taste have in common?
7. What parts of the eye bend incoming light rays?

Interpret and Apply

8. What is the difference in function between acetylcholine and acetylcholinesterase?
9. Which branch of your autonomic nervous system is active when you are doing each of the following?
   a. sleeping peacefully
   b. putting out a grease fire in your kitchen
10. In the process of hearing, all the following structures are set to vibrating. Write them in the order in which they begin to vibrate.
    a. oval window   d. tympanic membrane
    b. anvil   e. stirrup
    c. cochlear fluid f. hammer
11. If you blow a breath of air over your skin, you can feel the moving air. Which type or types of receptors detect this sensation?
12. When your eyes see, light passes through some, but not all of the following structures. Which of the following structures does light pass through?
    a. retina   d. lens
    b. cornea   e. optic nerve
    c. iris muscles f. pupil
13. If a person's spinal cord was crushed at the neck, resulting in paralysis, what parts of the body would be affected?
14. How is the spinal cord like the trunk of a tree?

15. You accidentally touch a hot iron. Your hand quickly moves away from the iron.
    a. What is the name for this type of action?
    b. Do you feel pain before you pull your hand away? Explain.
    c. Describe what happens in the central nervous system to allow you to react so quickly.
16. How is the membrane potential of the resting state restored after a nerve impulse has passed?
17. During a nerve impulse how do the charges inside and outside the neuron's membrane compare?
18. Which part of a neuron is found closest to a sense organ—the dendrite, axon, or cell body?
19. A person has a stroke, resulting in paralysis on the left side. Which area and side of the brain were damaged by the stroke?

Critical Thinking

20. You feel hungry and remember that there are apples in the fruit bowl. You remove an apple from the bowl and eat it.
    a. Identify the part of the brain that directs each of the following actions or feelings: feeling of hunger; memory of where you put the apples; movement of arm muscles.
    b. Describe the paths of the nerve impulses involved in the following: seeing the apple in the bowl; moving your arm to pick up the apple.
21. You could think of two adjacent neurons as two parts of a trail on opposite sides of a river. Which structure serves as the bridge that connects the two parts of the trail? Explain.
22. There are only a limited number of different taste receptors, yet humans can sense a great variety of tastes. Explain.

Chapter

43

CHEMICAL REGULATORS

Overview

A DELICATE BALANCE

43-1 Nervous vs. Chemical
Controls

43-2 A Summary of Body
Hormones

43-3 Target Cells and
Receptors

**ENDOCRINE GLANDS
AT WORK**

43-4 The Hypothalamus-
Pituitary Connection

43-5 Negative Feedback
Mechanisms

43-6 The Sex Hormones

43-7 Insulin and Glucagon:
Hormones Keeping a
Balance

43-8 Other Endocrine
Sources

43-9 New Developments
in Endocrinology

What mechanisms work together to balance this athlete's body?

A DELICATE BALANCE

A delicate balance exists in your body. Every hour of your life conditions are monitored and adjusted to maintain an internal environment that keeps your cells healthy and functioning. You should recognize this description as *homeostasis*. Earlier in this course (Chapter 5), you learned that homeostasis is a state of balance within a cell. You learned how a single cell responds to changes in its internal and external environments in order to survive. Similarly, as a multicellular organism, your body maintains homeostasis. An intricate pattern of communication helps to control such things as water balance, protein and carbohydrate metabolism, growth, sexual maturity, response to stress, and more.

43-1 Nervous vs. Chemical Controls

Recall from Chapter 42 that the nervous system coordinates activities in your body by way of messages sent between neurons. Neural pathways in your brain, spinal cord, and body organs carry impulses, which may activate a muscle, a gland, or another neuron. For the most part, impulses in the nervous system travel to their effector sites quickly and result in rapid responses.

Another mechanism for coordination of reponses comes from glands. You have more than one kind of gland in your body. **Exocrine** [ek′ sə krən] **glands** such as your salivary glands secrete their products locally through ducts, and have only local effects. **Endocrine** [en′ də krən] **glands** secrete chemicals directly into the bloodstream. These chemicals, known as **hormones**, serve as messengers and can affect several body systems at once. Unlike the impulses of the nervous system, which follow specific routes along neurons, hormones travel throughout the body in a generalized way. Hormones move more slowly than nerve impulses, but their effects can last for a longer time.

Your nervous system and your endocrine glands work together. Nerve impulses can activate certain glands to secrete their hormones, and the effects of some hormones can influence behavior through the nervous system. The feeling of butterflies in your stomach is an example of nervous and endocrine interactions.

In a stressful situation, impulses of your sympathetic nervous system cause immediate changes in, among other things, your heart rate, blood pressure, respiration rate, and blood-sugar level, preparing you to cope with whatever may happen. The sympathetic nervous system also carries impulses to your **adrenal** [ə drēn′ əl] **glands**, located on top of your kidneys. The impulses stimulate the glands to secrete **adrenaline** [ə dren′ əl ən]. This hormone, also known as epinephrine, circulates in the blood-

Section Objectives

A *State* how hormones contribute to maintaining homeostasis.

B *Distinguish* between the ways the nervous and endocrine systems coordinate activities in the body.

C *Describe* the significance of target cells and receptors.

D *Compare* the actions of two types of hormones on their target cells.

E *Name* several hormones and *state* their sources and functions.

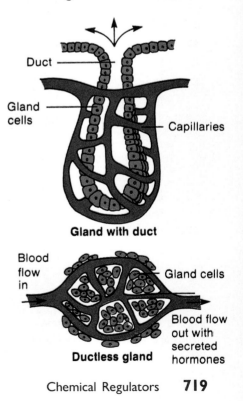

Figure 43-1 Exocrine glands such as salivary glands and sweat glands have ducts through which secretions move to their place of action. Endocrine glands have no ducts.

Duct

Gland cells

Capillaries

Gland with duct

Blood flow in

Gland cells

Blood flow out with secreted hormones

Ductless gland

Information: The pituitary has often been called the "master gland." If you look at Table 43-1, you will probably see why. However, it would be more accurate to give that name to the hypothalamus.

BIOLOGY INSIGHT

Homeostasis: The endocrine system is not a system in the same sense as a system like the digestive system. The functions of hormones from different glands can be completely unrelated. However, the overall effect of their actions is to maintain homeostasis. Their similarity of operation and interdependency of some hormones lead people to describe them collectively as a system.

stream and prolongs the effects begun by the sympathetic nervous system. When the stressful situation is over, the effects of the hormone linger. Adrenaline is sometimes called the fight-or-flight hormone. You can probably guess why.

43-2 A Summary of Body Hormones

The adrenal glands are just one part of the group of glands known collectively as the endocrine system. Figure 43-2 shows the major glands of this system and where they are located. Use the diagram to familiarize yourself with their names and locations as you read more about how they work.

Your endocrine glands secrete a wide variety of hormones that influence many body functions. Table 43-1 lists the major endocrine glands, the particular hormone or hormones each gland secretes, and the effects that these hormones produce. Occasionally the function of a gland may be disturbed due to such factors as disease, dietary deficiencies, genetic abnormalities, surgery, and so on. Disruption can result in an abnormal amount of hormone

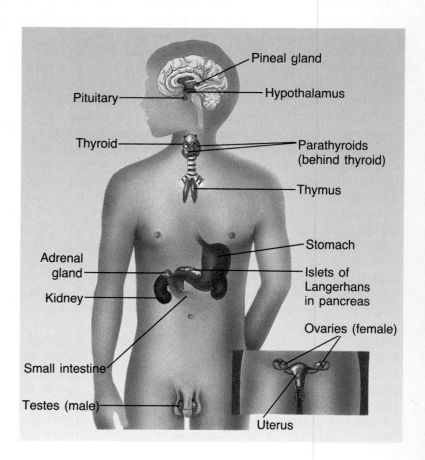

Figure 43-2 The endocrine glands are scattered throughout the body.

Table 43-1

MAJOR ENDOCRINE GLANDS AND THEIR HORMONES		
Gland	**Hormone**	**Influence**
Anterior Pituitary	Growth hormone (somatotropin)	Body growth and nutrient metabolism; imbalances may result in dwarfism or gigantism.
	ACTH (adreno-corticotropic hormone)	Stimulates adrenal cortex to secrete the corticoids
	TSH (thyroid-stimulating hormone)	Secretion of thyroid hormones
	FSH (follicle-stimulating hormone)	Maturation of eggs and production of sperm
	LH (lutenizing hormone)	Secretion of sex hormones by ovaries and testes
	Prolactin	Mammary gland growth and milk production
Posterior Pituitary (from hypothalamus)	Oxytocin	Milk release; contractions of uterus
	ADH* (antidiuretic hormone)	Water resorption by kidneys; prevention of dehydration; too little hormone causes diabetes insipidus, characterized by large volumes of dilute urine
Hypothalamus	Releasing factors	Stimulate anterior pituitary
	Oxytocin	See posterior pituitary.
	ADH	See posterior pituitary.
Adrenal cortex	Corticoids	Metabolism of protein, carbohydrates, and fats
	Aldosterone	Retention by kidneys of sodium and potassium
Adrenal medulla	Adrenaline**	Response to stress; dilation of blood vessels, increase in blood pressure, blood sugar
	Noradrenaline	Same as adrenaline; also is a neurotransmitter
Thyroid	Thyroxine	Growth and metabolism; inadequate dietary iodine causes hypothyroidism (slow metabolism, reduced body temperature, overweight)
	Calcitonin	Decrease of calcium in blood plasma
Parathyroid	Parathormone	Increase of calcium in blood plasma
Pancreas	Insulin	Decreases blood sugar; deficiency causes diabetes mellitus
	Glucagon	Increases blood sugar
Thymus	Thymosin	Development and action of lymphocytes
Kidney	Erythropoetin	Production of red blood cells
	Angiotensin	Blood pressure regulation
Pineal	Melatonin	Sexual maturity
Ovaries	Estrogens	Female sexual maturity
	Progestrone	
Testes	Testosterone	Male sexual maturity

being secreted. Some of the disorders caused by abnormal hormone levels are listed in the table.

Notice that the table includes the hypothalamus. Do you remember reading about this structure in Chapter 42? Although

* ADH is also known as vasopressin.
** Adrenaline is also known as epinephrine; noradrenaline is also known as norepinephrine.

the hypothalamus is part of the nervous system, it also secretes hormones and plays an important role in regulating some endocrine glands. You will read more about the relationship between the hypothalamus and the endocrine glands later.

43-3 Target Cells and Receptors

If you connect a battery to a flashlight, a light comes on. If you hook the same battery to a radio, music can be heard. If you hook the battery to a pan of scrambled eggs, nothing happens at all.

Something similar occurs with the action of hormones. For any hormone, certain organs respond to it and others do not. And different organs may respond differently to the same hormone. For example, note in Table 43-1 that **FSH**, a pituitary hormone, stimulates the maturation of eggs in the ovary. In the testes, FSH stimulates sperm production.

How do the body's cells "know" how to react? If you guessed that the process has to do with a cell's DNA, you would be right. Cells do what they are genetically programmed to do. The effect of a hormone is to set into motion a sequence of events already established in a cell's DNA code. How, then, does a hormone trigger such a sequence? The answer is related to the chemistry of hormones and how they work at the cellular level.

Most of the hormones produced by the endocrine glands can be divided into two major chemical groups. One group is the steroids, which are lipid-soluble and can enter a cell through its plasma membrane. Examples of steroid hormones include the sex hormones—*testosterone*, *progesterone*, and the *estrogens*—plus the adrenal hormones—*aldosterone* and the *corticoids*.

Protein hormones include the *releasing factors* of the hypothalamus, *insulin*, *glucagon*, *thyroxine*, and the pituitary hormones. Unlike steroids, protein hormones cannot pass through the plasma membrane. Instead, they interact with other proteins, called **receptors**, that are embedded in the membrane.

Cells that are affected by a particular hormone are called **target cells**. These cells contain receptors for the hormone and can thus bind to it, leading to a response. The cells of the ovaries and testes are target cells of FSH. Cells in your elbow are not. The target cells of steroids also contain receptors, but they are located within the cell rather than on the plasma membrane.

Figure 43-3 (left) illustrates the action of a protein hormone on a target cell. When a hormone molecule binds to its receptor in the plasma membrane, an enzyme, called adenylate cyclase, is activated inside the cell. Located on the inner surface of the membrane, adenylate cyclase catalyses the conversion of ATP to **cyclic AMP** (adenosine monophosphate). Cyclic AMP is often

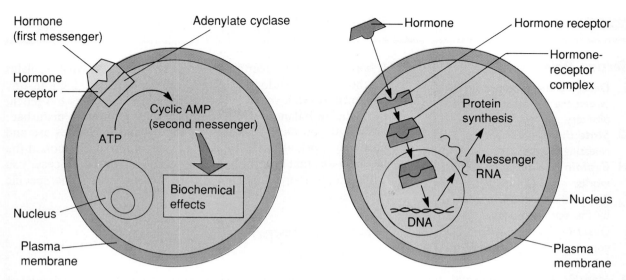

Figure 43-3 *Left:* Protein hormones do not enter their target cells. They bind to receptors in the plasma membrane, which results in chemical changes in the cell. *Right:* A steroid hormone penetrates the plasma membrane and binds to a receptor within the cell. The complex can activate a segment of a chromosome to begin steps for the synthesis of specific proteins.

called a "second messenger." It causes the response inside the cell that the hormone (the first messenger) began.

The presence of cyclic AMP sets in motion the response already coded for in the cell's DNA. Since the DNA of a woman is different from that of a man, the response to FSH differs.

Steroid hormones work in a different way. Notice from the diagram in Figure 43-3 (right) that these lipid-soluble hormones pass through the plasma membrane. Once inside the cell, the hormone combines with a receptor in the cytoplasm. The hormone-receptor complex moves into the nucleus and attaches at a particular location on a chromosome. This event activates one or more genes that then cause the synthesis of new proteins that are related to the cell's specific function.

CHECKPOINT ◆

1. List several conditions of the body that are controlled, in part, by hormones.
2. How is the effect of a hormone different from the effect of a nerve impulse?
3. What is a target cell?
4. What is the role of cyclic AMP in a target cell?
5. List five endocrine glands and their hormones.
6. Which kind of hormone, protein or steroid, has its effect directly within a cell?
▶ 7. Are estrogen receptors within a cell or on the plasma membrane? Support your answer.
▶ 8. If a cell cannot produce adenylate cyclase, how will the cell's response to a protein hormone be affected?

Section Objectives

F *Describe* the relationship between the hypothalamus and pituitary.

G *State* the role of hypothalmic releasing factors.

H *Explain* how negative feedback works.

I *Name* the functions regulated by the sex hormones.

J *Describe* how insulin and glucagon work as regulators of the same body condition.

K *Identify* the endocrine roles of other body structures.

L *List* some recent developments in the field of endocrinology.

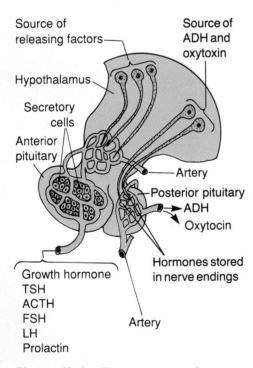

Source of releasing factors

Source of ADH and oxytoxin

Hypothalamus

Secretory cells

Anterior pituitary

Artery

Posterior pituitary

ADH

Oxytocin

Growth hormone
TSH
ACTH
FSH
LH
Prolactin

Hormones stored in nerve endings

Artery

Figure 43-4 The structures of the pituitary and hypothalamus reflect their close functional relationship.

If hormones regulate certain conditions in the body, what regulates the hormones? Endocrine glands secrete their products in tiny amounts. If the level of even one hormone fluctuates too much, the delicate balance within the body may be greatly disturbed. Now that you have a basic idea about what hormones are and how they work at the cellular level, you are ready to look at the mechanisms that control hormone secretion. In the process, you will become more familiar with the functions of some specific hormones.

43-4 The Hypothalamus-Pituitary Connection

Recall from Section 43-1 that the adrenal glands can be stimulated to secrete adrenaline by an impulse from the sympathetic nervous system. A more common form of regulation depends on the interactions of hormones with each other and with the glands themselves. Both forms of regulation can be seen in the relationship between the hypothalamus and the rest of the endocrine system.

In Chapter 42, you learned that the hypothalamus receives input about the levels of various chemicals in the bloodstream. It also receives messages from other parts of the brain. Just beneath the hypothalamus is a pea-sized structure called the **pituitary** [pə t(y)ū′ ə terē] **gland**. Like other endocrine glands, the pituitary secretes its products directly into the bloodstream. The hypothalamus and the pituitary are directly linked by both neurons and blood vessels. In a sense, these two structures act as a bridge between the nervous system and the endocrine system.

Look at Figure 43-4. Notice that the pituitary gland is actually two structures. The *anterior* pituitary is connected to the hypothalamus by blood vessels. At times, the hypothalamus functions as a gland, secreting hormones called **releasing factors** through these vessels into the anterior pituitary. The releasing factors influence the activity of the pituitary by stimulating or inhibiting its secretions.

The *posterior* pituitary is connected to the hypothalamus via neurons. Hormones (*ADH* and *oxytocin*) produced in the cell bodies in the hypothalamus are transported down the axons to the posterior pituitary where they are stored. From there, the hormones are released by nerve impulses from the hypothalamus, and are carried into the bloodstream. ADH regulates water balance. Oxytocin influences smooth muscle contractions, especially in the uterus during labor and in the mammary glands to let down milk as a baby nurses.

43-5 Negative Feedback Mechanisms

How do the chemicals of the hypothalamus and the pituitary, as well as the hormones produced by other glands, regulate each other? One mechanism closely resembles something with which you are probably familiar—the working of a furnace.

Suppose the temperature in a room drops below the setting on the thermostat. Immediately the furnace is activated, producing heat to warm up the room. When the temperature reaches the setting on the thermostat, the furnace shuts off. The *increase in heat* acts as a signal that subsequently *turns off the heat*. This type of event is called **negative feedback**—a cycle in which the last step in a sequence inhibits the first step in the sequence.

Negative feedback is a key mechanism for controlling the activity of an endocrine gland. Figure 43-5 illustrates the similarities between the furnace operation and a simple biological example of negative feedback.

Looking back to Table 43-1 you will see that the **thyroid gland** secretes the hormone **thyroxine** [thī rok′ sēn], which helps regulate growth and metabolism. Stimulation of the thyroid gland to secrete its hormone is regulated by TSH (thyroid-stimulating hormone) from the pituitary. Notice in the diagram that as TSH acts on the thyroid, the resulting increase in thyroxine affects the pituitary. Negative feedback inhibits TSH secretion, and therefore stimulation of the thyroid gland is reduced.

Feedback mechanisms that involve the hypothalmic releasing factors demonstrate the more elaborate interactions of the glands. The adrenal cortex produces a group of hormones known as the **corticoids** [kort′ ə koids]. These hormones are involved in regulating the metabolism of proteins and carbohydrates. Stimulation of the

Figure 43-5 A simple negative feedback mechanism operates like a thermostat-driven furnace. In this example, the pituitary stimulates the thyroid to produce a hormone, just as the thermostat signals the furnace to produce heat. The thermostat turns off the furnace once the room is warm enough. Similarly the pituitary's decrease of TSH, in response to a rising level of thyroxine, causes a decrease in activity of the thyroid.

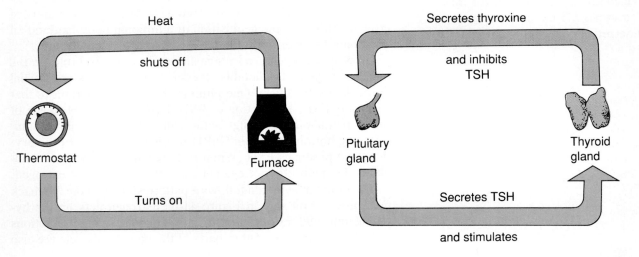

Heat shuts off

Thermostat

Furnace

Turns on

Secretes thyroxine and inhibits TSH

Pituitary gland

Thyroid gland

Secretes TSH and stimulates

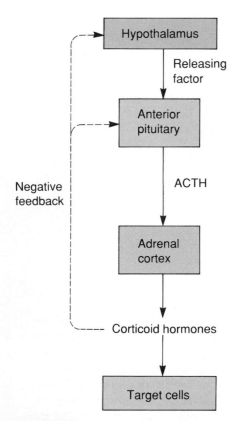

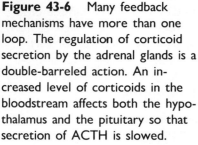

Figure 43-6 Many feedback mechanisms have more than one loop. The regulation of corticoid secretion by the adrenal glands is a double-barreled action. An increased level of corticoids in the bloodstream affects both the hypothalamus and the pituitary so that secretion of ACTH is slowed.

adrenal cortex begins with the hypothalamus. It secretes a releasing factor to the pituitary, which in turn secretes adrenocorticotropic hormone, or **ACTH**. As ACTH reaches the adrenal cortex, it causes the secretion of the corticoid hormones. You can follow this scheme in Figure 43-6. The bloodstream delivers corticoids to cells throughout the body, including those of the pituitary gland and hypothalamus. Notice in the figure that there are two feedback "loops". Eventually the level of the corticoids is high enough to cause the hypothalamus to decrease its output of ACTH releasing factor. At the same time, the increased level of the corticoids also has a negative feedback effect on the pituitary. The gland cells become less responsive to the hypothalmic releasing factors, and therefore produce less ACTH.

On the other hand, as soon as the level of ACTH reaching the adrenal glands falls, they decrease their secretion of corticoids. When the level of these hormones in the bloodstream decreases enough, the cycle will begin again. The interaction between the hypothalamus, ACTH, and the corticoids represents a self-contained system in which a product controls the rate of its production.

43-6 The Sex Hormones

The ovaries and testes are among the many glands that produce their hormones in response to signals from the hypothalamus and pituitary. In addition to the production of sex cells, these glands secrete the sex hormones. These steroid hormones are responsible for the enhancement of the secondary sex characteristics during puberty (usually the early teenage years).

The female sex hormones include **progesterone** [prō jes′ tə rōn] and a group of substances known collectively as the **estrogens** [es′ trō jənz]. The latter group causes changes associated with sexual maturity, such as enlargement of the breasts (due to development of the mammary glands), widening of the hips, a growth spurt, and the acquisition of additional body hair and an additional layer of body fat.

Both the estrogens and progesterone have central roles in the menstrual cycle. Predictably, feedback mechanisms are crucial in regulating the cycle. One pituitary hormone important to that pattern is FSH. Production of FSH depends on the presence of the hypothalmic releasing factor called GnRH (gonadotropin-releasing hormone). When GnRH reaches the anterior pituitary, the gland produces FSH. When FSH reaches the ovary, it stimulates the maturation of egg cells and the secretion of estrogen.

The effect of estrogen follows a pattern similar to the feedback mechanisms you saw in Figure 43-6. Estrogen acts on the hypothalamus and the pituitary to cause decreases in the secretions of FSH-RF and FSH. Other parts of the menstrual cycle are also affected by the changing levels of these hormones. You will learn more about the cycle in Chapter 45.

In males, the major sex hormone is **testosterone** [te stos′ tə rōn]. During puberty, testosterone causes deepening of the voice, increased growth of body hair, and a rapid spurt of skeletal growth. Like the female sex hormones, the secretion of testosterone is regulated in a feedback mechanism with the hypothalamus and the pituitary.

43-7 Insulin and Glucagon: Hormones Keeping a Balance

The level of glucose in your blood is very important. Your brain cells, major consumers of glucose, function poorly when the glucose level is too high or too low. Two different hormones regulate blood glucose. They are **insulin** and **glucagon**, which are both produced by the pancreas.

As you learned in Chapter 38, the pancreas secretes digestive enzymes through a duct directly into the small intestine. In this respect, the pancreas acts as an exocrine gland. However, insulin and glucagon are endocrine hormones that are secreted into the bloodstream. These two hormones have opposite effects. Insulin causes a decrease in blood sugar, and glucagon causes an increase. Since both are protein hormones, both work via membrane receptors.

Look at Figure 43-8. Glucagon is secreted by the pancreas when blood glucose is too low. Glucagon receptors are located

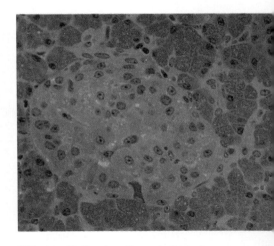

Figure 43-7 Insulin and glucagon are produced in specialized groupings of pancreatic cells called Islets of Langerhans (visible here as the lighter pink oval).

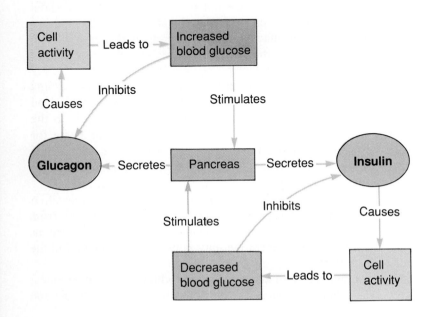

Figure 43-8 The secretions of insulin and glucagon act independently of each other to maintain a healthy level of blood glucose. In each case, follow the different colored arrows to see how each hormone is regulated. When you eat a meal high in carbohydrates, the insulin level is elevated quickly, leading to absorption of glucose by cells in the body. As the level of blood glucose drops, so does the level of insulin.

Chemical Regulators   **727**

in the membranes of liver and muscle cells. When glucagon attaches to its receptors, it promotes the formation of cyclic AMP. After several intermediate steps, an enzyme called phosphorylase is activated. It catalyzes the breakdown of glycogen to glucose, which then quickly enters the bloodstream. As the level of glucose in the bloodstream rises, the secretion of glucagon by the pancreas is halted.

The pancreas secretes insulin when the level of glucose in the blood rises too high. Scientists think that insulin works by increasing the permeability of the cell membrane to glucose molecules. Recall from Chapter 5 that specific carrier proteins in the membrane greatly increase the rate at which their corresponding substances diffuse across the membrane. Vesicles containing glucose carrier proteins are located just inside the plasma membrane. When insulin binds to its receptors on the membrane, two things happen. First, the vesicles fuse with the membrane, greatly increasing the number of carrier proteins embedded there. This change allows for the rapid uptake of glucose by the cell. Second, a chain of chemical reactions occurs, leading to the activation of the enzyme glycogen synthase. The cell can now begin to synthesize glycogen from glucose. The resulting decrease in the level of blood glucose inhibits further insulin secretion.

43-8 Other Endocrine Sources

Recent research has provided information about other sources of hormones. Their production has been discovered in individual body cells and organs that are not usually described as glands. *Gastrin*, for example, is produced by the stomach and stimulates gland cells in the stomach lining to secrete hydrochloric acid. *Secretin*, produced by the small intestine, causes the pancreas to secrete its digestive juices.

Among the organs whose functions are the subject of ongoing research are the thymus gland, pineal gland, and kidney. You learned in Chapter 41 that the thymus gland plays a role in the body's defense against disease. In addition to being a site for production of specialized lymphocytes, the thymus gland also secretes a hormone, called *thymosin*. This hormone is thought to stimulate lymphocytes into action when the need arises.

The function of the pineal gland is not clearly understood. A hormone, named *melatonin*, has been identified as coming from the pineal gland. Its action in some mammals inhibits the secretions of FSH and LH. The hormone may play a role in regulating the onset of puberty.

The kidney has been identified as a producer of two hormones, *angiotensin* and *erythropoetin*. Angiotensin stimulates production

CONSUMER BIOLOGY

Erythropoetin is now available through genetic engineering technology. It is used to treat anemia, to bolster blood supplies of kidney patients who must have their blood cleansed by a dialysis machine, and to help people who have lost blood in an injury or surgery.

of aldosterone by the adrenal cortex. Together these two hormones regulate the amount of salt retained by the kidneys. As a result, the hormones affect water balance and blood pressure. Erythropoetin stimulates the bone marrow to produce increased numbers of red blood cells.

A group of hormonelike substances called **prostaglandins** has received much attention. Prostaglandins are continuously secreted by most body cells, and rapidly destroyed by enzymes in body fluids. The hormones have several effects. They contribute to the contraction of smooth muscle like that in the uterus, making them important in childbirth. Some prostaglandins cause aggregation of platelets and may be involved in the healing of wounds. Prostaglandins are used in medicine to treat such problems as ulcers and asthma, and to cause the start of labor.

43-9 New Developments in Endocrinology

The field of endocrinology has changed much in the last few decades. When your parents studied biology, their knowledge of the endocrine system was probably limited to a list of glands and their hormones. As the fields of genetics and cell biology develop, the emphasis continues to shift steadily to how hormones work and new ways of correcting endocrine disorders.

In Chapter 12, you read about one example of the applications of new research. A deficiency of insulin causes **diabetes mellitus**, a disease in which glucose is restricted from entering the cells. Therefore, the cells metabolize other food sources, with harmful biochemical effects. Also, glucose accumulates in the blood and is excreted in the urine. Long-term effects of this disorder include blindness, circulatory problems, and death. Recombinant DNA techniques have made possible the mass production of human insulin by bacteria. Since this insulin is identical to insulin produced by humans, diabetics have an accessible supply that avoids the adverse side effects of the animal insulin.

Another hormone that has been mass-produced using genetic engineering is human growth hormone, or **somatotropin**. Somatotropin is normally secreted by the anterior pituitary. When the hormone reaches the liver, it causes the secretion of somatomedin, which regulates the rate of growth in bone and skeletal muscle. A somatotropin deficiency in childhood causes dwarfism. The traditional approach to treating a deficiency was to administer somatotropin extracted from the pituitary glands of deceased humans. Over time, the extract often promoted growth.

Because the supply of somatotropin was severely limited, an alternative was to use recombinant DNA technology to synthesize somatotropin in quantity. Interestingly, the change comes at a

DO YOU KNOW?

Information: With its complications, all forms of diabetes collectively are the third leading cause of death by disease in the United States. There are over one million Americans known to have diabetes mellitus and more who do but don't know it. People with diabetes are at risk for blindness, heart disease, and stroke, and 17 times more prone to kidney disease.

Figure 43-9 An overproduction of growth hormone during childhood can result in a condition called gigantism. Different kinds of dwarfism can result from the underproduction of growth hormone.

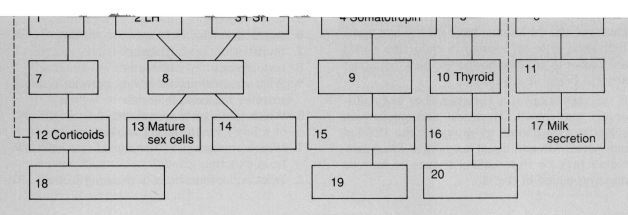

DO YOU KNOW?

Information: The tallest person on record was over three meters tall.

time when the older source of growth hormone has become suspect. Many people who received the traditional pituitary extract therapy are now suffering from a deadly virus that attacks the nervous system. The virus is a "slow virus," which takes years to develop after it enters the body. Doctors think the virus may have been present in the pituitaries from which the extracts were obtained. Individuals treated 20 years ago are only now showing signs of the viral disease. The use of bacteria-produced somatotropin should decrease the spread of the virus.

Some recent research has shown that the effects of the bone disease osteoporosis can be lessened by treatment with estrogen. Recall from Chapter 37 that osteoporosis mainly affects women who are beyond middle age. By that time, the level of estrogen in their bodies is significantly reduced. Treatment with estrogen

Chapter

44

SUBSTANCE ABUSE

Overview

DRUGS AND ABUSE

44-1 Dependence on Drugs

44-2 Some Drugs That Are Abused

44-3 Endorphins— Natural Opiates

ALCOHOL AND TOBACCO

44-4 Immediate Effects of Alcohol Consumption

44-5 Effects of Long-Term Drinking

44-6 Effects of Smoking and Tobacco Use

44-7 Effects of Smoking on Others

44-8 Using Prescription Drugs

What are you risking by getting involved in drug abuse?

DRUGS AND ABUSE

A **drug** is a chemical substance that alters the function of the mind or body. The use of drugs is probably more common than you imagine. For example, if you have ever had surgery, you know how helpful painkillers can be in getting through the first painful days. Perhaps a parent or grandparent takes blood pressure medication to prevent the occurrence of a potentially fatal stroke. An antibiotic may have hastened your recovery from bronchitis or some other bacterial disease. Maybe you know a diabetic who depends on daily injections of insulin to regulate blood glucose level. Clearly, the good health most of us enjoy is partly due to the existence of these and other helpful drugs.

44-1 Dependence on Drugs

The chemical nature of some abused drugs creates a **psychological dependence** in the user. The user feels a strong emotional need for the drug and will go to great lengths to obtain it.

In addition, some drugs cause **physical dependence**. The body's metabolism actually adapts itself to the presence of a drug in the bloodstream, thus establishing a physical dependence. Without the drug, the body suffers unpleasant effects called **withdrawal symptoms**. Depending on the drug, these symptoms might include fever, nausea and vomiting, or convulsions. There might be hallucinations, such as the belief that one is covered with crawling bugs. Withdrawal symptoms can be so severe that the sudden withdrawal from certain drugs can cause death.

Sometimes the body becomes so adapted to a drug's presence that increasing amounts are required to prevent withdrawal symptoms. Drug users who habitually use a particular drug are said to have an **addiction** to the drug.

44-2 Some Drugs That Are Abused

Narcotics are drugs that are often abused. Because these drugs are derived from the opium poppy, **narcotics** are often called opiates. Morphine, codeine, and heroin are opiates. Morphine and codeine are prescribed for relief of pain. Codeine can be found in prescription cough medicines as it reduces the severity of a cough. Heroin is not used for medicinal purposes.

All narcotics are **depressants**, drugs that decrease the activity of the nervous system. To understand how narcotics work, recall from Chapter 43 that neurons transmit messages to each other using chemical neurotransmitters. A neurotransmitter affects the

Section Objectives

A *List* the effects of several drugs that are abused.
B *Distinguish* between psychological and physical dependence.
C *Distinguish* among stimulants, depressants, natural, and synthetic drugs.
D *Explain* how the function of endorphins is tied to the action of narcotics.

Figure 44-1 Since the actions of many drugs are not clearly understood, their availability is controlled by the Food and Drug Administration. This is why many drugs can only be obtained with a doctor's prescription through a licensed pharmacist.

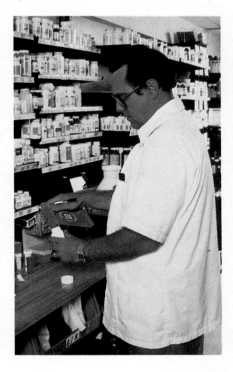

neuron following it by binding to receptors in that neuron, thus activating it. Narcotics bind to these receptors, prohibiting the neurotransmitters from doing so. As a result, the neuron is not stimulated, and it does not transmit information. If neurons carrying pain messages are depressed in this manner, no pain is felt. That is why codeine and morphine are prescribed for pain relief. Along with absence of pain, the patient experiences a sense of euphoria.

All narcotics are addictive. Heroin is so addictive that it is illegal in the United States. The sale of codeine and morphine is strictly controlled by law. Therefore, an addict must obtain drugs illegally in order to avoid withdrawal symptoms. Narcotics use also poses the risk of AIDS infection since addicts often share needles. The number of AIDS-infected addicts is growing rapidly because of this practice.

Marijuana The most common source of **marijuana** is *Cannabis sativa*, a species of the plant that seems to grow almost anywhere. It is the most widely abused illegal drug. Like narcotics, marijuana is a depressant and may cause euphoria. People may develop a psychological dependence on marijuana, but the drug is not physically addictive.

Until recently, it was believed that long-term marijuana use was not dangerous. That belief, however, has changed. THC (tetrahydrocannabinol), the active substance in marijuana, is not water-soluble. Therefore, it is stored in the lipid portions of cells for as long as a month after smoking. Due to selective breeding techniques, the concentration of THC in today's marijuana is about ten times higher than it was ten years ago. More THC is now being stored in the tissues when the user smokes.

Long-term use of marijuana interferes with the production of male and female sex hormones. It results in a lowered sperm count in males and disruption of the menstrual cycle in females.

There are more carcinogens in marijuana smoke than in cigarette smoke. Thus there is strong suspicion that long-term use of marijuana may cause lung cancer. In addition, smoking marijuana destroys disease-fighting white blood cells, causing reduced immunity to diseases.

The effects of marijuana on the nervous system include impaired perception, concentration, memory, and judgment. Driving while under the influence of marijuana is responsible for thousands of teenage auto accidents, many of them fatal.

THC, in a pure, synthetic form, is used legally to relieve the nausea accompanying cancer therapy. It is not a cure for cancer but a way of reducing a side effect of cancer treatment.

Tranquilizers Drugs that are used to depress the central nervous system for the purpose of reducing anxiety are called **tranquilizers.** A class of drugs called barbiturates were once prescribed as

Figure 44-2 The opium poppies from which narcotics are derived.

Figure 44-3 *Cannabis sativa*, the source of marijuana.

tranquilizers. Now barbiturates are generally used as sleep aids. Barbiturates are no longer prescribed as tranquilizers because of their highly-addictive properties.

Today, most tranquilizers come from the benzodiazeprine family of drugs. *Valium* is the trade name for a common benzodiazeprine tranquilizer. Drugs like *Valium* are considered relatively safe when used as directed. Misuse can lead to addiction and withdrawal symptoms. Other side effects include excitability and insomnia which are baffling due to the depressant action of tranquilizers.

Cocaine Cocaine, obtained from the leaves of the coca plant of South America, is another euphoria-producing drug. Its mode of action is different from that of the depressants. Cocaine is a **stimulant** which means it increases the activity of the nervous system. It works by preventing neurotransmitter molecules from being reabsorbed by the neuron that produced them. The synapse is then flooded with neurotransmitter molecules, causing a state of excitement in the nervous system. This excited condition can have serious, and even fatal effects.

All forms of cocaine can cause psychological dependence with serious physical effects. In its newest form, crack, cocaine is even more addictive than heroin. The user could have a seizure which affects the brain's respiration center, causing suffocation. Heart attacks have resulted from just a single use of crack, even in otherwise healthy teenagers and athletes. Also from only a single use, the blood pressure may rise high enough to cause a stroke even in healthy young people. The psychological effects include hallucinations, sleeplessness, memory lapses, and depression.

Amphetamines Amphetamines, commonly known as speed or uppers, are synthetic drugs. They, like cocaine, are stimulants. People often use amphetamines in order to stay awake. Amphetamines also depress the appetite and are an ingredient in many prescription diet pills. Although they usually do not cause physical dependence, amphetamines may cause psychological dependence.

For unknown reasons, amphetamines affect young children differently than adults. Thus, these drugs are sometimes prescribed in the treatment of hyperactive children. Amphetamines have a calming effect on these children.

Hallucinogens Use of **hallucinogens** causes the abuser to see, feel, or hear things that are not there. LSD (lysergic acid diethylamide) and PCP (phencyclidine, also known as angel dust) are two illegally used hallucinogens. Both drugs can cause intense fear and anxiety for the user as a result of the hallucinogens. Prolonged use can lead to mental breakdown and murder or suicide due to an impaired

Figure 44-4 Crack is a form of cocaine. It is smoked, so it reaches the circulatory system by being inhaled into the lungs. The drug can produce an intense high in about 6 seconds.

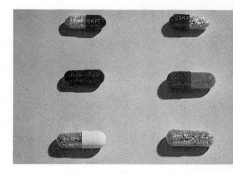

Figure 44-5 Amphetamines are synthetic drugs that act as stimulants on the central nervous system.

Figure 44-6 Large muscles that result from taking steroids come at the cost of serious and sometimes fatal side effects.

BIOLOGY INSIGHT

Homeostasis: Mind-altering drugs exert their actions on the central nervous system by altering the release of neurotransmitters from certain neurons. In general, stimulants increase excitatory neurotransmitters, and depressants have the opposite effect.

▶ Denotes a question that involves *interpreting* and *applying* concepts.

mental condition. How these drugs cause their hallucinogenic effects is not known and they have no medical use.

Steroids Recall from Chapter 43 that hormones are classified as steroids. Synthetic steroids were first developed to build body tissue and prevent its breakdown from some diseases. Because of their effects on the body, steroids have become a target of abuse among athletes who think their use is the key to increased ability in sports such as football and weight lifting.

The side effects of steroid abuse are extensive. They include: acne, cancer, heart disease, liver disease, jaundice, abnormal growth of breasts and the penis in males, and sterility in both sexes. Young athletes have died from complications due to the side effects of steroids. Abuse of steroids also appears to affect the mind by causing severe depression that often leads to the abuse of other drugs.

Studies now show that the body-building effects of steroids are limited and short-term in nature. The health risks far outweigh any of the short-term gains.

44-3 Endorphins—Natural Opiates

Perhaps you know someone who claims to be "addicted to running." You may assume that this is just a figure of speech, but there is evidence that such addiction really can occur. The brain produces polypeptides called **endorphins**. These are secreted in large amounts in times of great physical stress, such as running long distances. When endorphins bind to their receptors in the brain, a feeling of euphoria occurs. These same receptors also bind opiates such as morphine. Narcotics produce a sense of euphoria because their molecules are shaped somewhat like those of the naturally occurring endorphins.

CHECKPOINT ◆

1. How do some drugs stop pain?
2. Distinguish between physical dependence and psychological dependence on drugs.
▶ 3. If someone told you that naturally occurring drugs were safer than synthetic drugs, what evidence to the contrary could you offer?
▶ 4. Predict the effects of taking a stimulant and a depressant at the same time.
▶ 5. Levels of endorphins are increased during the labor that precedes childbirth. Explain why.

ALCOHOL AND TOBACCO

Ninety-three percent of all high school seniors have experimented with alcohol, the most-abused drug in our society. Unlike ''harder'' drugs such as heroin, alcohol is accepted by many segments of society. Many people are unaware of its destructive powers.

Ten million Americans admit that they are alcoholics. It is possible that a similar number of people have a drinking problem but have never admitted it. What are the problems associated with excessive alcohol use?

Do you smoke cigarettes? If you do, you are part of a group that is getting smaller each year. In the past two decades, the percentage of Americans who smoke has been cut in half. As knowledge of the health risks of tobacco usage grows, smoking becomes less acceptable to society. Even among teenagers, the rate of smoking is leveling off. Only about one in five teenagers smokes. Yet, for a large group of teenagers, smoking is still "the thing to do." It may bring acceptance by a group of peers and a false feeling of belonging.

Why do you, or people you know, continue to smoke despite knowledge of its dangers? Some smokers simply say that they enjoy smoking and do not wish to give up the habit. But many smokers, particularly females, say that they are unable to stop smoking. Why is smoking so difficult to give up? Why should you stop smoking?

44-4 Immediate Effects of Alcohol Consumption

Alcoholic beverages contain ethanol, C_2H_5OH. The ethanol molecule is quite small; therefore, it enters the bloodstream quickly from the small intestine. This process can take less than two minutes. The liver metabolizes, or processes, alcohol. What happens if a person drinks more than the liver can process? Some of the excess alcohol in the bloodstream is excreted by the kidneys. The lungs also excrete some, accounting for the characteristic breath of a person who has been drinking heavily. However, most of the alcohol circulates in the blood until the liver can process it.

It takes a 70-kilogram person about 1.5 hours to metabolize a drink. A drink consists of a 12-ounce can of beer, a 4-ounce glass of wine, or a 1-ounce shot of liquor. If a person drinks more than one drink every 1.5 hours, the alcohol level in the blood will rise. The smaller the person, the more slowly that person's liver metabolizes alcohol. If a person's blood alcohol

Section Objectives

E *Describe* the immediate action of alcohol on the body.

F *Explain* why driving under the influence of alcohol is illegal.

G *Describe* the long-term effects of alcohol on the body.

H *Describe* the hazards and diseases associated with smoking, tobacco, and smoke.

I *List* practices that reflect a responsible use of drugs.

Figure 44-7 Alcoholic beverages differ in their ethanol concentrations. However, the volume of each beverage shown delivers about the same amount of ethanol to the body.

Beer 12 oz.   Wine 4 oz.   Liquor 1 oz.

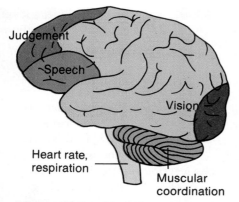

Figure 44-8 Alcohol progressively depresses different areas of the brain. Excessive amounts of alcohol can cause unconsciousness, and even death.

level goes higher than a certain point, that person becomes intoxicated. Consuming large quantities of alcohol quickly, such as chug-a-lugging, is extremely dangerous and can even be fatal. When you see how alcohol works, you will understand why.

Alcohol is a depressant that affects just about every organ in the body. Look at Figure 44-8. Alcohol first depresses the part of the cerebral cortex that controls judgment and inhibitions. The loss of inhibition may make a person feel happy and lively. However, it may also cause uncontrolled, unthinking behavior that may later be embarrassing. Driving a car during this period of decreased judgment is an invitation to disaster. Operating a car requires that the driver be able to make split-second decisions at any time. As the blood alcohol level rises, the speech and vision parts of the brain become depressed. This causes blurred vision and slurred speech. In addition, the part of the brain that controls voluntary muscles is also affected causing a lack of coordination. In over 60 percent of fatal automobile accidents, the driver has been using alcohol. There are about 7000 such deaths among teenagers each year in the United States. In fact, alcohol-related accidents are the number one cause of death among teenagers.

Scientists estimate that 10 000 brain cells are destroyed each time a drink is consumed. At a very high blood alcohol level, the brain's respiratory center is depressed, resulting in death. Teenagers lucky enough to recover from near-fatal experiences with alcohol have shown some brain and nerve damage. The alcohol in your small intestine continues to enter the bloodstream even after you stop drinking and even if you pass out. If you drink a large quantity of alcohol slowly, death is not likely, although vomiting, passing out, and hangovers are the short-term effects.

44-5 Effects of Long-Term Drinking

Generally, people who drink occasionally and moderately have no problem with alcohol. However, some people become physically and psychologically dependent upon alcohol. This condition is called **alcoholism**.

Scientific evidence indicates that a tendency toward alcoholism may be genetic. Children of alcoholics are 2–4 times more likely to become alcoholics than children of nonalcoholics. Half of all alcoholics have at least one close blood relative who is an alcoholic. This does not mean that if one of your parents is an alcoholic, you will be too. But knowledge of alcoholism in the family acts as a red flag, urging caution.

Of the teenagers who drink, one in fifteen will become an alcoholic. There are 3.5 million teenage alcoholics in the United

States. Dependence does not necessarily take years to establish. Within a matter of months, alcohol can become the focus of life for an abuser. To satisfy the urge for alcohol, some people have been poisoned by ingesting isopropyl alcohol or wood alcohol. Both substances can have fatal effects in limited quantities.

Alcoholism is a disease that can be controlled but not cured. Addiction to alcohol is a permanent condition. Remember that alcohol quickly dulls one's judgment. Just one drink can undermine an alcoholic's determination not to abuse alcohol. For this reason, alcoholics are unable to regulate the amount of alcohol they consume. Therefore, they must totally avoid drinking.

On the average, alcoholism shortens a normal life span by about 12 years. Alcoholics risk many health problems. The esophagus, stomach, and intestines may become irritated. Teenagers who drink heavily experience frequent digestive problems. The pancreas and brain may be harmed. The metabolic action of the liver may be impaired, affecting many chemical reactions in the body. Alcoholics often do not eat a balanced diet because a high percentage of their caloric needs is fulfilled by alcohol. Vitamin deficiencies and malnutrition may result. Poor nutrition can lower an alcoholic's resistance to disease.

Cirrhosis of the liver is one possible long-term effect of drinking. Scar tissue gradually replaces healthy liver cells. As a result, the liver becomes less able to function. Eventually, cirrhosis can result in death.

An alcoholic may develop a severe mental condition called alcohol psychosis. Hallucinations and serious memory failure are characteristic of alcohol psychosis. This condition may be partly caused by brain damage and partly by a deficiency of B vitamins.

Figure 44-9 One important function of the liver is to detoxify the body. You can see the prolonged effects of alcohol on the liver shown at the left. Compare this picture to the healthy liver on the right. A diseased liver can no longer regulate homeostasis of body fluids and can no longer control body processes.

44-6 Effects of Smoking and Tobacco Use

Two factors make the tobacco habit hard to give up. First, tobacco causes psychological dependence. Second, **nicotine**, one of the many harmful substances in cigarette smoke, also causes physical dependence. Cigarettes, therefore, cause both physical and psychological dependence.

In addition to nicotine, cigarette smoke consists of gases and tiny particles. These substances harm the cilia and mucous membranes that line the breathing passages. Healthy cilia sweep foreign particles upward, keeping the lungs clean. When the cilia are damaged, tar particles accumulate in the breathing passages. Smoker's cough results from attempting to clear the breathing passages of the accumulated particles.

Smoke also damages the structure of the lungs. Long-term smoking can cause the walls of the alveoli to rupture. As you

DO YOU KNOW?

Historical Note: In 1492, Columbus was the first European to discover tobacco. By 1614, there were 7000 tobacco shops in London.

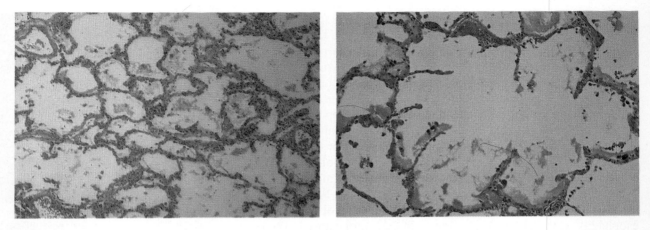

Figure 44-10 The alveoli in normal lung tissue are small. Heavy smoking ruptures alveoli, decreasing the surface area for gas exchange.

Figure 44-11 Each time smokers look at a package of cigarettes, they see one of these warnings. This long-standing campaign has begun to have an effect. In twenty years, it has halved the incidence of smoking in the American population.

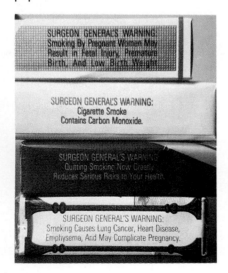

can see in Figure 44-10, this damage greatly decreases the surface area for gas exchange. This condition, called emphysema, reduces the amount of oxygen the lungs can take in and may be fatal.

The best-known result of heavy smoking is lung cancer. Chemicals in smoke cause changes within the cells of the lungs. These changes may lead to cancer. Death from lung cancer is about ten times more frequent for smokers than for nonsmokers.

In the lungs, nicotine passes into the bloodstream. In the blood, nicotine travels to all parts of the body. Nicotine causes the blood vessels to constrict, or become narrow. When blood has to move through narrower vessels, blood pressure goes up. This increased pressure puts the smoker at high risk for such problems as strokes and heart attacks. Cigarette smoking is also a factor in coronary-artery disease and atherosclerosis.

The respiratory and circulatory systems are not the only parts of the body harmed by smoking. Cigarette smoking has been associated with ulcers in the digestive tract. Cancers of the larynx, mouth, esophagus, bladder, and pancreas have also been linked to smoking.

Perhaps, like many people your age, you are not especially worried about what may happen to you 40 years from now. You may even assume that by the time you are old enough to develop heart disease or lung cancer, scientists will have found a cure for them. Even if that happens (and there is no guarantee), smoking causes other problems with more immediate effects. What are some of these effects?

If you are an athlete, you will become winded more easily when you smoke, impairing your performance. Nicotine stains your teeth. Tobacco gives your breath a foul odor. Consider that heart disease is the number one killer in America and cancer is number two. These diseases contribute to 350 000 deaths, or over half the deaths in the United States per year. Since smoking is a factor in all these diseases and since it is addictive, it makes sense not to smoke. It makes sense to quit if you already smoke.

In an effort to minimize lung damage, some former smokers have switched to chewing tobacco, or "smokeless" tobacco. However, current research has shown that the use of chewing tobacco can cause gum disease and tooth loss. Chewing tobacco is also associated with a high incidence of mouth cancer. The skin on the gums, lips, and inner cheeks develops leathery white patches from contact with acidic tobacco juice. This condition, if unchecked, may lead to mouth cancer. The treatment of mouth cancer often involves disfiguring facial surgery, such as removing part of a jaw. Sometimes, it is not treatable at all. Mouth cancer is a particularly dangerous type of cancer called squamous cell carcinoma. It is known for the speed at which it spreads through the body. Death from the spread of mouth cancer associated with smokeless tobacco has occurred in people as young as 18 years of age.

44-7 Effects of Smoking on Others

There is much evidence that smoke from other people's cigarettes affects nonsmokers. This smoke, called **sidestream smoke**, contains higher levels of many harmful chemicals than does the smoke that is inhaled directly by the smoker. Even if you do not smoke, if you are in a room with smokers, smoke from their cigarettes will affect your health. If you have an allergy, asthma, or other lung problems, smoke will aggravate them.

Thirty million Americans have diseases involving the heart and lungs. These problems are worsened by other people's cigarette smoke. Babies whose parents smoke are more likely to have pneumonia or bronchitis during their first year than babies in smoke-free homes. The mounting evidence that smoking is a hazard even to nonsmokers has prompted the attempts to limit smoking in public places. Nonsmoking ordinances are gaining in popularity as are treatment programs for those who want to "kick the habit."

The damage caused by cigarette smoking is not always permanent. If a person stops smoking, the lungs may return to a healthier, more normal condition. The damaged cilia resume their sweeping role, and the lungs gradually become clear of tars.

44-8 Using Prescription Drugs

Some of the drugs discussed in this chapter have legal medical uses and can be beneficial if used as directed. However, there is a certain level of risk in using any drug. Not every individual

Figure 44-12 As the population becomes less accepting of cigarette smoke, antismoking messages are becoming more prevalent.

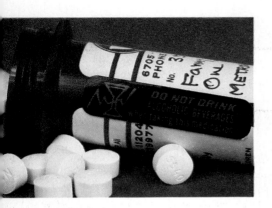

Figure 44-13 Since the action of many drugs is unknown, mixtures of drugs can be extremely harmful to the body. Always read the labels and warnings for any medicine you take.

CONSUMER BIOLOGY

The Food and Drug Administration requires that any over-the-counter or prescription drug sold in the United States be accompanied by information about the ingredients and possible side effects, as well as what activities and other drugs should be avoided when taking the medication.

▶ Denotes a question that involves *interpreting* and *applying* concepts.

responds to the same drug in the same way. In addition, the actions of many drugs are poorly understood. All drugs can be harmful if used improperly.

When a drug is prescribed, it should be used exactly as directed. Changing the dosage, timing, or other conditions can have unexpected side effects.

When taking any medicine, it is important to find out how that drug interacts with other drugs if you are taking more than one medicine at a time. For example, certain antibiotics are not effective if they are mixed with alcohol. Antihistamines, found in cold remedies, can cause severe drowsiness if taken with alcohol. Such drowsiness may lead to accidents. The combination of barbiturates, found in sleeping pills, and alcohol can be deadly. If you read the labels on prescription and nonprescription drugs, you will find warnings about unsafe drug combinations.

Among people who knowingly abuse drugs, mixing drugs to heighten the effects is a common practice. This practice is particularly dangerous, as the liver can break down only a limited amount of a drug in a given time. The more rapidly a particular drug is metabolized, the less impact it has on the body. If more than one drug is used at a time, the drugs affect the liver's ability to metabolize them, and their effect is prolonged. If alcohol and another depressant drug are used at the same time, their combined depressive effect on the brain can cause unconsciousness or even death.

CHECKPOINT ◆

6. Name one way in which long-term drinking can be fatal. Name one way in which short-term drinking can be fatal.
7. What are the effects of an alcohol overdose?
▶ 8. Your biology class consists of 35 students and 93 percent of them drink alcohol. How many students are likely to become alcoholics?
▶ 9. How is the body's normal functioning affected by a liver disease such as cirrhosis?
▶ 10. Why is a drinking habit difficult to give up?
11. What chemical in tobacco causes physical dependence?
12. Name three diseases caused by smoking cigarettes.
13. How does smoking affect the alveoli?
▶ 14. In what two ways can a person who does not smoke be harmed by tobacco?
15. What precautions should be taken when using a prescription drug?

LABORATORY ACTIVITY

EFFECT OF DRUGS ON THE HEART RATE

Objective and Skills

☐ *Determine* how different drugs affect the heart-beat rate in *Daphnia*.

Materials

Daphnia	timing device (watch)
microscope	0.5% alcohol
microscope slides	tea
and coverslips	coffee
droppers	cola with caffeine
cotton fibers	cola without caffeine

Heart

Procedure and Observations

1. Read all instructions for this laboratory activity before you begin your work.
2. Copy the table format on separate paper.
3. Study the photograph of the tiny, transparent crustacean *Daphnia* and locate the heart.
4. Use the dropper to obtain one or two *Daphnia* specimens from the culture and place them on a slide. Withdraw excess water from the slide, leaving only enough to cover the *Daphnia*. Place a few cotton fibers on the slide to slow the movement of the *Daphnia* and then cover with a coverslip. Under low power of the microscope, locate the heart of the *Daphnia*. Reducing the amount of light will help you to see better and will protect the *Daphnia* from overheating.

5. While one partner keeps time, the other partner should count the number of heartbeats per minute. Take three different counts, which will be averaged. Record this resting heartbeat rate in the table.
6. Place a drop of alcohol on the slide. After a minute or two, observe and record the heartbeat rate of the *Daphnia*. Again, three trials should be recorded. Use the dropper to place the *Daphnia* into a second culture.
7. Using a new *Daphnia* each time, repeat steps 5 and 6, replacing alcohol with coffee, tea, regular cola, and decaffeinated cola.
8. Before leaving the laboratory, clean up your materials and wash your hands thoroughly.

Analysis and Conclusion

1. Why did you place the *Daphnia* into a second culture after use, rather than replacing them in the original culture?
2. What was the average baseline heartbeat rate of your *Daphnia*? How did this value compare to the class data?
3. How did each chemical substance affect the baseline heartbeat rate?
4. Using class data, prepare a bar graph illustrating your results. Plot intervals of heartbeat rate on the x-axis. Plot the number of *Daphnia* falling within each interval on the y-axis.

DAPHNIA HEART RATE				
Trials	I	2	3	Average
Baseline Control				
Alcohol				

Substance Abuse **745**

CHAPTER REVIEW

Summary

▸ Modern medicine relies heavily on the use of drugs to treat, cure, and prevent illnesses. Some chemical substances, including certain drugs, can be abused, causing harm to both the user and society.

▸ Long-term smoking of marijuana can have serious effects on the lungs, the brain, the reproductive system, and the body's immune system.

▸ Long-term use of any drug can cause harmful reactions in the body. Overdosing on certain drugs and using certain combinations of drugs may cause death.

▸ Use of the newest illegal form of cocaine, crack, can be fatal even for the first-time user.

▸ Alcohol, a depressant, is the most commonly abused drug in American society. Its immediate effects include loss of inhibition, dulling of speech and vision, and lack of coordination. An alcohol overdose can cause brain and nerve damage. In extreme cases, the effects are fatal.

▸ Alcoholism can result from long-term use of alcohol. Alcohol is damaging to interpersonal relationships and may cause serious and even fatal diseases.

▸ Cigarette smoke contains nicotine, a substance that causes psychological and physical dependence in the user. It can cause cancer of the lungs and other organs, heart disease, and emphysema, as well as chronic respiratory disorders.

▸ There is growing evidence that cigarette smoke is harmful to nonsmokers who inhale it.

Vocabulary

addiction	depressant
alcoholism	drug
amphetamine	endorphins
cocaine	hallucinogen
marijuana	sidestream smoke
narcotics	stimulant
nicotine	tranquilizer
physical dependence	withdrawal symptoms
psychological dependence	

Concept Mapping

Construct a concept map for drug abuse. Include the following terms: stimulant, addiction, alcohol, amphetamine, tranquilizer, physical dependence, depressant. Add additional terms as you need them.

Review

Choose the best answer for each of the following.

1. The chief preventable cause of illness and early death in American society is (a) overeating, (b) smoking, (c) use of heroin, (d) use of tranquilizers.
2. Emphysema consists of damage to the (a) lungs, (b) nose, (c) liver, (d) brain.
3. Narcotics are produced (a) from alcohol, (b) from marijuana, (c) from the opium poppy, (d) in cigarette smoke.
4. Which of the following is not a risk associated with cigarette smoking? (a) cirrhosis of the liver (b) lung cancer (c) high blood pressure (d) heart attack
5. The plant *Cannabis sativa* is the source of (a) barbiturates, (b) tranquilizers, (c) marijuana, (d) all of these.
6. The chemical in cigarette smoke that can cause physical dependence is (a) tar, (b) carbon, (c) nicotine, (d) all of these.
7. Which of the following is not a natural drug? (a) marijuana (b) nicotine (c) cocaine (d) an amphetamine
8. Alcohol is metabolized in the (a) stomach, (b) lungs, (c) kidneys, (d) liver.

9. Which of the following does not normally create a physical dependence in the user? (a) amphetamines (b) barbiturates (c) cigarettes (d) alcohol

10. Which of the following is not a risk associated with marijuana use? (a) lung damage (b) physical dependence (c) psychological dependence (d) lowered sperm count

11. Automobile drivers who have been drinking alcohol (a) are usually very careful, (b) do not drive as well as they would if they had not been drinking, (c) are rarely involved in accidents, (d) never take risks while driving.

12. Prolonged use of alcohol can result in (a) dietary deficiencies, (b) cirrhosis of the liver, (c) irritation of the stomach, (d) all of these.

13. Using which of the following drugs is illegal in the United States? (a) alcohol (b) nicotine (c) heroin (d) morphine

14. A drug that reduces anxiety is called a (a) stimulant, (b) depressant, (c) psychosis, (d) tranquilizer.

15. State two hazards of using smokeless tobacco.

16. On what evidence is current antismoking legislation based?

17. What drug do endorphins resemble in structure?

Interpret and Apply

18. A person drinks a glass of orange juice each morning. One morning there is no juice in the refrigerator, and the person feels unhappy and deprived. What kind of dependence is this?

19. In what ways are the effects of marijuana similar to those of narcotics? How are the effects of marijuana different from those of narcotics?

20. Morphine, codeine, and heroin all relieve pain. Morphine and codeine may be prescribed for pain relief, but use of heroin is totally illegal. Explain.

21. Amphetamine is to _____ as narcotic is to depressant.

22. Suppose you are trying to convince a friend not to start smoking. List at least three arguments you would use.

23. List three harmful effects of long-term marijuana smoking.

24. Why do victims of advanced emphysema often have to wear portable oxygen tanks while doing everyday activities?

25. Why is crack more dangerous than amphetamines to the drug addict?

26. A person with a drinking problem joins Alcoholics Anonymous and stops drinking for a year. The person now feels that one glass of wine with dinner each night would not be a problem. Do you agree? Explain.

27. A friend of yours is taking a prescription antibiotic for a bacterial infection. Your friend thinks that taking twice the dose will cure the disease faster. Do you agree? Explain.

Critical Thinking

28. A person with a mass of 70 kilograms and another with a mass of 100 kilograms each drink alcohol at the same rate. Which person will become intoxicated faster? Explain.

29. An alcoholic's liver function has been affected by alcoholism. If this person uses another drug, such as a barbiturate, will its effect on the body last longer or shorter than normal? Explain.

30. There is a saying that giving coffee to an intoxicated person does not make that person sober. The coffee just produces a wide-awake drunk. Explain why this is true.

Chapter

45

HUMAN REPRODUCTION

Overview

THE STRUCTURES OF REPRODUCTION

45-1 Male Reproductive System

45-2 Female Reproductive System

45-3 The Menstrual Cycle

THE PROCESS OF REPRODUCTION

45-4 Fertilization

45-5 Implantation and Early Development

45-6 Differentiation

45-7 Harmful Effects on the Fetus

45-8 Birth

45-9 Formation of Twins

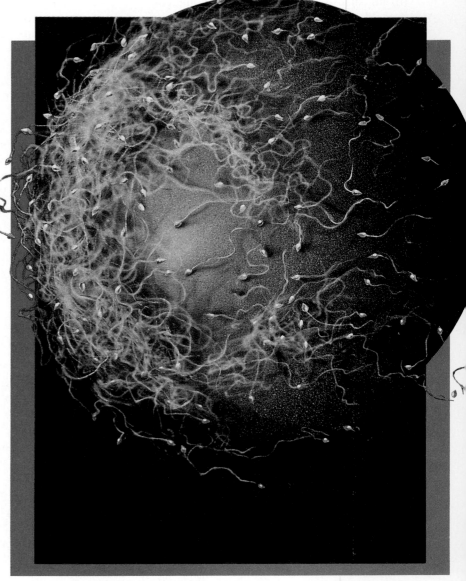

748

How does a single egg cell become a complete human being?

THE STRUCTURES OF REPRODUCTION

Most human organs and organ systems are similar in the male and female. For example, only the trained eye could distinguish the thigh bone of a man from that of a woman. The structure and function of the male and female reproductive systems, however, are quite different. These differences provide the basis for sexual reproduction and the development of the young inside the mother until birth.

45-1 Male Reproductive System

In Chapter 43, you learned that the two male gonads, the testes, produce testosterone and other male sex hormones. The testes have another important function, which is the production of the male gametes, sperm.

The testes are located in a pouch called the **scrotum**, which hangs outside the body cavity. This arrangement allows the scrotum to be cooled by outside air. The temperature inside the scrotum is 1.5°C lower than that within the body cavity. Sperm require this slightly lower temperature for development.

Before a boy is born, his testes develop within his abdominal cavity. Several weeks before birth, the testes normally descend into the scrotum.

Section Objectives

A *List* the parts of the male and female reproductive systems and their functions.

B *Compare* the production of sperm and eggs.

C *Trace* the paths of sperm and eggs from their points of origin to the point at which they meet.

D *Relate* the levels of hormones to changes in the ovary and uterine lining during the menstrual cycle.

Figure 45-1 The male reproductive system. The seminal vesicles, prostate, and Cowper's gland add secretions as sperm move toward the urethra. Arrows indicate the path sperm follow out of the body.

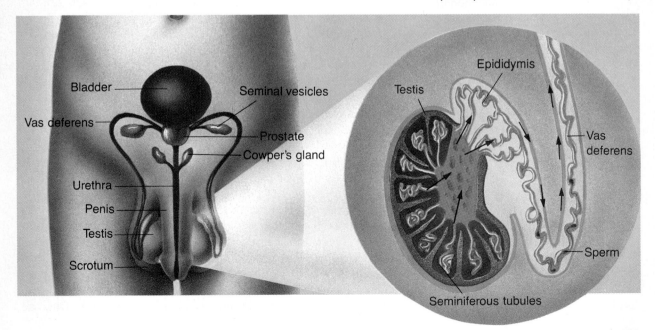

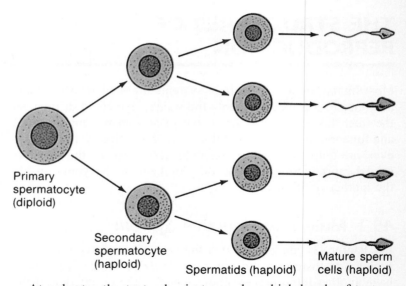

Primary spermatocyte (diploid)

Secondary spermatocyte (haploid)

Spermatids (haploid)

Mature sperm cells (haploid)

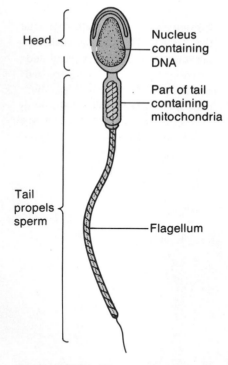

Head

Nucleus containing DNA

Part of tail containing mitochondria

Tail propels sperm

Flagellum

Figure 45-3 The structural features of a sperm cell. Which part of the sperm actually participates in fertilization?

At puberty, the testes begin to produce high levels of testosterone in response to hormone signals from the hypothalamus and pituitary gland. Under the influence of testosterone, the testes produce sperm. As you know, the sperm are haploid cells produced by meiosis. Since diploid human cells contain 46 chromosomes, human sperm contain 23.

The testes contain many diploid cells that are specialized for the production of sperm. As you read about the process, refer to Figure 45-2. In the first step of sperm formation, specialized diploid cells develop into **primary spermatocytes**. These cells undergo the first meiotic division, during which each primary spermatocyte develops into two **secondary spermatocytes**. In the second meiotic division, each secondary spermatocyte divides into two haploid cells. Each haploid cell sheds most of its cytoplasm, develops a flagellum, and becomes a sperm cell.

Look again at Figure 45-1 and find the coiled tube called the **epididymis** [ep ə did′ ə məs]. The epididymis stores sperm produced in the testis. One end of the epididymis is attached to the testis, and the other end is attached to a second tube called the **vas deferens** [vas def renz]. The vas deferens extends upward into the abdominal cavity, where it joins the urethra. Together the epididymis, vas deferens, and urethra form a continuous passageway that exits the body through the penis. In the male, both urine and sperm leave the body through the urethra.

As sperm cells travel from the epididymis to the urethra, several glands add secretions that together are known as seminal fluid. Seminal fluid carries the sperm and lubricates the passageway through which sperm travel. It also gives the sperm chemical protection from the acidic environment of the female reproductive tract. In addition, seminal fluid contains fructose, which the sperm use for energy. The seminal fluid and the sperm are collectively called **semen**.

As illustrated in Figure 45-3, the head of the sperm contains the haploid nucleus. The sperm's long, thin tail is a flagellum. The anterior part of the tail contains many mitochondria. Sperm cells absorb fructose from the seminal fluid, and the mitochondria quickly convert the fructose into usable energy stored in ATP. Sperm use that energy to move their flagella, which propel them through the female reproductive tract.

45-2 Female Reproductive System

The two female gonads, the ovaries, lie within the abdominal cavity. Like the testes, they have a dual function: they produce female hormones and female gametes. Each female gamete is called an egg, or **ovum** (plural, ova). Since it contains a large amount of cytoplasm, an ovum is huge compared to a sperm.

Like sperm, ova are produced by meiosis. Egg production begins in the ovaries of a girl before she is born, as the egg-producing cells become **primary oocytes**. At birth, a girl has about a million diploid primary oocytes, her lifetime supply. The primary oocytes begin the first meiotic division but do not complete it. Ovum development ceases until a girl reaches puberty.

When a girl becomes sexually mature, the development of primary oocytes resumes. About every 28 days, a primary oocyte completes the first meiotic division. This division produces 2 cells of unequal size. As Figure 45-5 illustrates, the larger cell, the **secondary oocyte**, receives most of the cytoplasm. The smaller cell is called the first polar body. A **polar body** is a small cell resulting from the unequal division of cytoplasm during ovum formation. Polar bodies are discarded and soon disintegrate.

The secondary oocyte is released from the ovary as an ovum. The second meiotic division is not actually completed until a

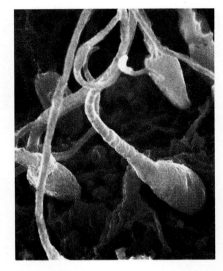

Figure 45-4 Sperm are produced continually during a male's adult lifetime. The rate of sperm production and the numbers of healthy sperm vary among individuals.

■ **BIOLOGY INSIGHT**

Structure Is Related to Function: In sexually reproducing organisms, the male gametes are generally small and motile, while the female gametes are larger and nonmotile.

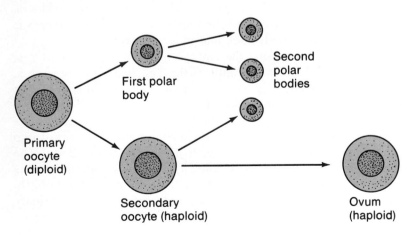

Primary oocyte (diploid)

First polar body

Second polar bodies

Secondary oocyte (haploid)

Ovum (haploid)

Figure 45-5 In the production of ova, each primary oocyte produces only one ovum.

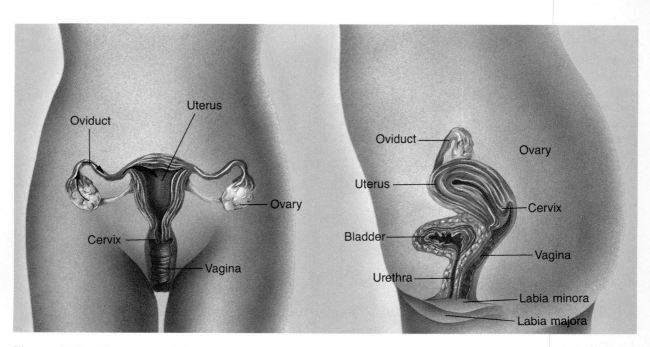

Figure 45-6 The structural features of the female reproductive system. The arrows indicate the path of the ovum from its point of origin to the uterus.

sperm enters the ovum. After this second meiotic division, another polar body is released. The mature, haploid ovum contains almost all the cytoplasm once found in the primary oocyte. This cytoplasm will provide nourishment for the zygote.

Often, the first polar body undergoes a second meiotic division, producing two cells. None of the polar bodies produced during ovum formation, however, live long. Only one ovum develops from each primary oocyte. In contrast, as you read in Section 45-1, a total of four sperm develop from each primary spermatocyte.

When an ovum leaves an ovary, it enters the abdominal cavity. It is soon drawn into the open end of a tube called an **oviduct**, which in humans is also called a Fallopian tube. Two oviducts, one on each side, lead into the uterus, or womb. The **uterus** is a fist-sized organ with thick and muscular walls.

If fertilization occurs, the embryo implants inside the uterus, growing and developing, until birth. The lining of the uterus, called the **endometrium**, is well supplied with blood vessels that nourish the developing embryo.

The narrow lower end of the uterus is called the **cervix**. As you can see in Figure 45-6, the cervix extends downward into the **vagina**, or birth canal, which leads out of the body. The vagina has two functions. It allows the entry of sperm into the female's body, and it allows the exit of the baby during birth. Unlike the male, the female has separate openings for the urinary and reproductive functions.

45-3 The Menstrual Cycle

Many parts of a woman's reproductive system undergo periodic changes that are controlled by hormones. These changes are known as the **menstrual cycle**. The coordination among all the parts of the system is exquisitely fine-tuned. Refer to Figures 45-7 and 45-8 as you read about the changes during the cycle.

Each primary oocyte is enclosed in a structure called a **follicle**. At the beginning of the cycle, **follicle-stimulating hormone**, (FSH) and **luteinizing hormone** (LH) are secreted by the pituitary gland. (Recall from Chapter 43 that the pituitary secretions occur in response to the releasing factor GnRH from the hypothalamus.) When FSH and LH reach the ovary, they cause several follicles to grow. One follicle usually grows faster, and the others stop developing.

The growing follicle fills with fluid and protrudes from the surface of the ovary. It also secretes estrogen, which causes the endometrium to thicken and its blood supply to increase, preparing the uterus for pregnancy.

The growth of the follicle and the thickening of the endometrium continue for 10 to 14 days. Just before the fourteenth day of the cycle (on average), the pituitary gland secretes a burst of additional LH. The sudden rise of LH in the bloodstream causes the follicle to rupture, and the ovum is released from the follicle into the abdominal cavity. This release of the egg is called **ovulation**.

After ovulation, LH converts the follicle into a yellow structure called the **corpus luteum**. The corpus luteum secretes the hormone progesterone. The progesterone further prepares the endometrium for pregnancy. If fertilization occurs, the corpus luteum remains active, continuing to secrete progesterone for several weeks.

Sequence in the ovary	Development of the follicle	Ovulation	Corpus luteum

| Changes in uterine lining | Endometrium | | |

| Time sequence | 2 4 6 8 10 12 14 16 18 20 22 24 26 28 2 | | |
| | Flow phase 4–6 days | Fertile period | Flow phase |

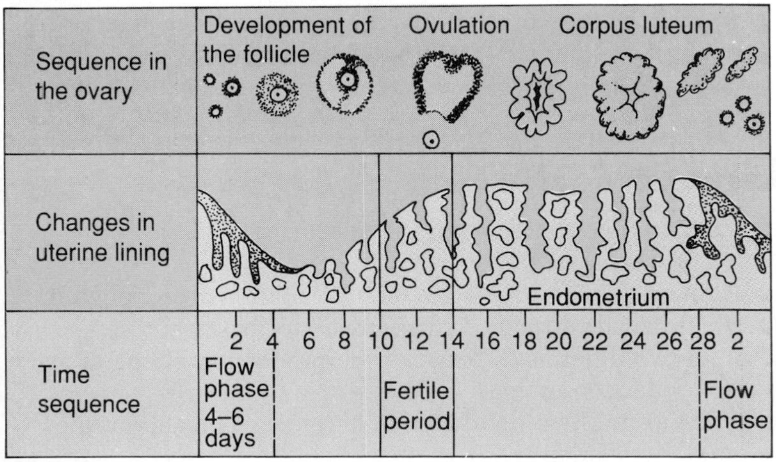

Figure 45-7 The sequence of events in the ovary and the changes in the uterine lining are interrelated. Note the most fertile period in the cycle.

Figure 45-8 In the menstrual cycle, note the relationship between the levels of pituitary and reproductive hormones. The sudden rise in LH triggers ovulation.

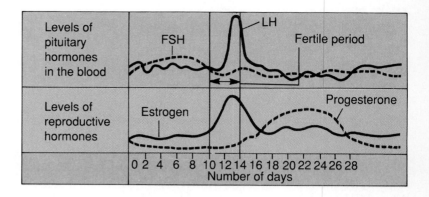

If fertilization does not occur, the ovum begins to disintegrate after about a day. As you can see in Figure 45-7, the corpus luteum also begins to break down. About 11 days after ovulation, the progesterone level falls. This causes the endometrium to break down. Blood and some endometrial tissue then leave the body through the vagina. This process, called **menstruation**, lasts a few days.

While progesterone levels are high, FSH is suppressed. When progesterone levels fall, the pituitary again begins to produce FSH and a new cycle begins. Each cycle lasts about 28 days. But the length of the cycle varies among women. Also, the length of the cycle may vary from month to month in the same woman. Usually, a woman's body stops producing eggs when she is between 40 and 50 years old. This time is referred to as **menopause**.

Hormonal changes in the menstrual cycle can be artificially altered. Note in Figure 45-8 that the level of estrogen is lowest at the beginning of the cycle when the follicle begins to develop. A high level of estrogen inhibits the release of FSH and, therefore, follicle development. Oral contraceptives, or birth control pills, work on this principle. By keeping the level of estrogen artificially high, the pills suppress FSH secretion. If no follicle develops, then no egg is released and fertilization will not occur.

CHECKPOINT ◆

1. What are two functions of the testes?
2. What is contained in semen?
3. Through which opening do sperm leave a male's body?
▶4. Which female structure corresponds to the male testes?
▶5. State two differences between the production of sperm and the production of eggs.
▶6. Which of the two reproductive hormones is higher at the time of ovulation?

▶ Denotes a question that involves *interpreting* and *applying* concepts.

THE PROCESS OF REPRODUCTION

Fertilization happens when the egg nucleus and the sperm nucleus join. If the egg is fertilized, the menstrual cycle is interrupted, and a series of changes occurs within the female to sustain pregnancy. The fertilized egg attaches to the wall of the uterus where it will grow and develop over a 38-week period until birth.

45-4 Fertilization

When ovulation occurs, tiny cilia at the ends of the oviducts create currents that draw the egg into an oviduct. Then the egg is carried down the oviduct. Fertilization, if it occurs, usually takes place within 24 hours and occurs in the upper third of the oviduct. As you noted in Figure 45-8, the fertile period is typically near the midpoint of the menstrual cycle. In many women, however, the fertile period may vary considerably.

Millions of sperm may enter a woman's reproductive tract during intercourse. Although most sperm do not survive long, a substantial number may live for a few days within the woman's body. Only one of these sperm will be necessary to complete fertilization if an egg becomes available.

When one sperm does penetrate the ovum, the ovum immediately undergoes its second meiotic division, producing a haploid nucleus. The sperm discharges its DNA into the ovum. There the sperm's DNA unites with the DNA in the nucleus of the egg. The union of two haploid nuclei produces a diploid cell called a zygote. Immediately, electrical and chemical properties of the ovum's membrane change, preventing the entry of additional sperm.

In some cases, the natural fertilization process is unsuccessful. About one in six couples in the United States is infertile, or unable to have children. There are many causes of infertility. Some, such as a low sperm count, occur in the male. Others, such as failure to ovulate, occur in the female. One cause of infertility is the inability of the egg or sperm to travel through the oviduct. Damaged oviducts can prevent sperm and egg from meeting. The technique of *in vitro* **fertilization** was developed to solve this problem.

In this technique, a woman's menstrual cycle is carefully monitored. Hormones are administered to ensure precise timing of ovulation. Within hours of ovulation, one or more eggs are surgically removed from the ovary and placed in culture in a petri dish (see Figure 45-10 on the next page). Sperm from the prospective father are added, and fertilization occurs in the dish. (*In vitro* is Latin for "in glass.") The fertilized eggs are allowed

Section Objectives

E *Identify* the fertile period in the menstrual cycle.

F *Describe* the process of fertilization.

G *List* the stages that occur between zygote and fetus.

H *State* the origins and function of the embryonic membranes.

I *Contrast* the development of identical and fraternal twins.

J *Name* several factors that can harm an embryo.

K *Describe* the changes that occur in the mother and baby immediately before, during, and after birth.

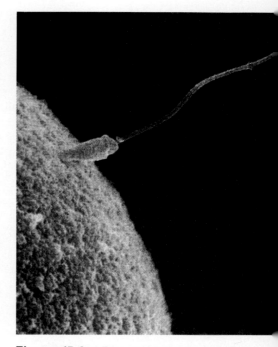

Figure 45-9 Enzymes from the sperm aid its penetration through the egg's protective outer layers.

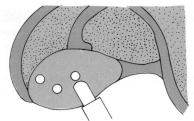

1. Removal of eggs from ovary

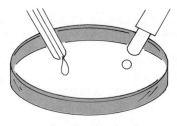

2. Fertilization *in vitro*

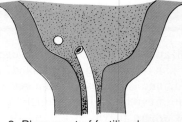

3. Placement of fertilized eggs
into uterus

Figure 45-10 In *in vitro* fertilization, the events that ordinarily happen in the oviduct are made to happen in a culture dish. If the procedure is successful, the result is identical: a healthy baby.

to go through several divisions in the dish. They are then placed in the uterus of the woman. If the procedure is successful, the fertilized egg or eggs follow the same sequence of development that occurs if fertilization happens in the oviducts.

If sperm are prevented from contacting the ovum, fertilization will not occur. This condition is the basis for many forms of contraception. Use of a sheath, or condom, by males reduces the likelihood that sperm will enter the vagina. If sperm are allowed to enter the vagina, the use of a diaphragm by the female can prevent fertilization. A diaphragm is a rubber, dome-shaped cover that fits snugly over the cervix, blocking the passage of sperm into the uterus. Since condoms and diaphragms block the transfer of sperm, they are referred to as mechanical barriers.

In addition to mechanical barriers, chemical barriers also may prevent fertilization. These sperm-killing substances, or spermicides, include contraceptive foams and jellies, which are applied inside the vagina before intercourse. When used along with a mechanical barrier method, they are effective contraceptives.

45-5 Implantation and Early Development

For a few days after the egg and sperm nuclei unite, the zygote undergoes a series of rapid mitotic divisions. Growth does not occur between divisions, and the resulting ball of tiny diploid cells is no bigger than the original fertilized egg. As it divides, the ball of cells travels down the oviduct, arriving in the uterus about four days after fertilization.

The ball of cells remains unattached in the uterus for three or four days while the cells continue to divide. A structure called a blastocyst forms. The **blastocyst** [blas′ tə sist], as illustrated in Figure 45-11, consists of a hollow, fluid-filled cavity surrounded by cells. A group of cells in one area of the blastocyst becomes the **inner cell mass**. The inner cell mass will become the embryo, or developing human organism. The layer of cells surrounding the cavity is called the **trophoblast** [tro′ fə blast], which will become the membranes that protect and support the embryo.

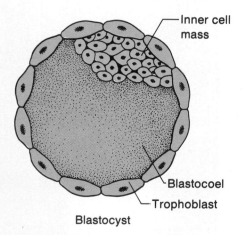

Blastocyst

Figure 45-11 The blastocyst contains an inner cell mass and a trophoblast. What will each become?

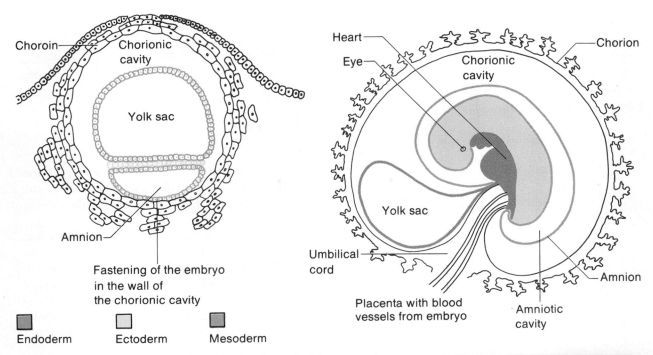

Choroin — Chorionic cavity

Yolk sac

Amnion —

Fastening of the embryo in the wall of the chorionic cavity

Heart — Chorion

Eye — Chorionic cavity

Yolk sac

Umbilical cord

Placenta with blood vessels from embryo

Amnion

Amniotic cavity

■ Endoderm ☐ Ectoderm ■ Mesoderm

About six or seven days after fertilization, the blastocyst buries itself in the endometrium. Part of the trophoblast develops into a membrane called the **amnion** [am′ nē ən]. During the entire time that it is in the uterus, the embryo is enclosed in the amnion. The amnion contains amniotic fluid, which cushions the embryo, protecting it against external shocks. It also prevents the embryo from sticking to the uterine wall.

Another membrane, the **chorion** [kōr′ ē ən], also develops from the trophoblast. The chorion surrounds the amnion and has fingerlike projections called chorionic villi. Recall from Chapter 11 that tissue samples taken from the chorionic villi are used in prenatal diagnosis. Chemicals secreted by the chorionic villi destroy endometrial tissue, making more room in the uterus for the embryo. The chemicals also open capillaries in the endometrium. Blood from the mother oozes into the spaces around the chorionic villi. After a time, the **placenta** forms where the chorionic villi embedded in the endometrium. A small part of the placenta comes from the mother, but most of it is derived from the chorion. (See Figure 45-12.)

The embryo is attached to the placenta by the **umbilical cord**. Arteries from the embryo reach through the umbilical cord to the placenta. In the villi of the chorion, capillaries branch from these arteries (Figure 45-13). Materials pass from the blood in these capillaries into the mother's blood. Also, substances diffuse from the mother's blood into the capillaries in the villi. Umbilical veins carry the blood back to the embryo.

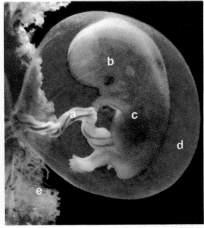

Figure 45-12 *Above left and right:* The developing extraembryonic membranes are diagrammed. Notice how the various tissues become distributed in the early embryo. *Below right:* The photograph identifies some of these structures in a 10-week-old embryo: *a)* umbilical cord; *b)* eye; *c)* heart; *d)* amnionic sac; *e)* placenta.

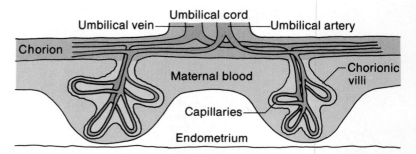

Figure 45-13 The structural features of the placenta separate the blood supplies of the mother and embryo. Substances diffuse across the membranes when traveling from one blood supply to another.

The embryo's circulatory system is separate from that of the mother. The embryo's blood stays within the capillaries of the chorionic villi, as shown in Figure 45-13. The blood of the mother and the embryo do not mix.

The placenta carries out many functions for the embryo that other organs take care of after birth. It serves as lungs by absorbing oxygen from the mother's blood and by passing carbon dioxide back. It acts like a digestive system, bringing dissolved food from the mother's blood to the embryo. It also serves as kidneys, removing nitrogen-containing wastes from the embryo's blood. The mother's excretory system then eliminates these wastes.

45-6 Differentiation

The cells of an embryo start out genetically and structurally alike. These identical cells become specialized as a result of the activation of different genes in different cells. The specialization process, called differentiation, is responsible for the development of the many varied types of tissues in the body.

The process of differentiation is not completely understood. Experiments suggest that biochemical controls affect which genes in a specific cell are active and which are not. The fate of the cell and its descendants depends on which genes become functional.

In Chapter 27, you learned about the process of gastrulation, in which three **germ layers** are formed in the embryo. Gastrulation occurs by the tenth day after fertilization, after the blastocyst has implanted in the endometrium. The three germ layers are the **endoderm**, **mesoderm**, and **ectoderm**. Each germ layer gives rise to certain types of tissues and organs. (See Table 45-1.)

By the fourth week, the embryo has taken the form of a bent cylinder. During the fourth and fifth weeks, the arms and legs begin to form. By the eighth week, fingers and toes have become distinct.

During the second month, the facial features develop. By the end of the second month, the major body structures have been established. The remainder of development within the uterus

Table 45-1

TYPES OF TISSUES PRODUCED FROM GERM LAYERS	
Cell Layer	**Tissue Produced**
Ectoderm	Brain Spinal cord Nerves Outer layer of skin Some parts of the eye Nose Ears
Mesoderm	Skeleton Muscles Gonads Excretory system Inner layer of skin
Endoderm	Pancreas Liver Lining of digestive system Lungs

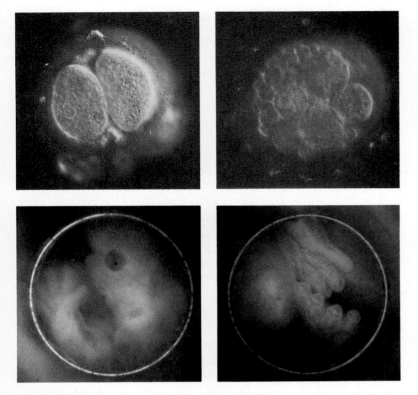

Figure 45-14 Successive mitotic divisions of the fertilized egg repeatedly double its number of cells (*upper left and right*). Continued growth and development produce recognizable features by five weeks (*lower left*) and eight weeks (*lower right*).

consists of growth and refinement of these structures. Initially the embryo's skeleton is composed entirely of cartilage. After the second month, bone begins to replace the cartilage. At this point, the embryo is called a **fetus**.

Figure 45-15 Growth and differentiation continue in the fourth and fifth months. Shown here are a 16-week-old fetus (*left*) and a 22-week-old fetus (*right*).

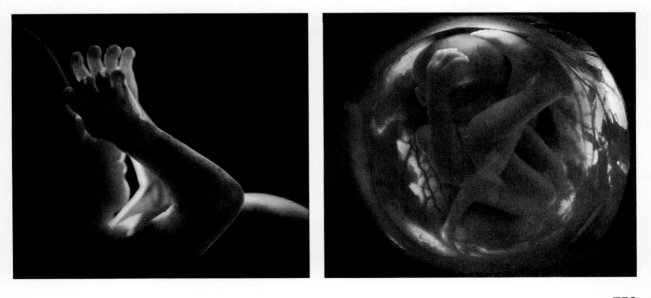

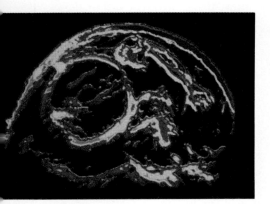

Figure 45-16 Sonograms produced using ultrasound techniques reveal much about the developing fetus, but the harmful effects of substance abuse during pregnancy do not usually become known until after the baby is born.

 BIOLOGY INSIGHT ——

Homeostasis: Diethylstilbestrol (DES), a substance that has been in the news in recent years, is a chemical that can harm the fetus without harming the mother. It was given to women in the 1950's to prevent miscarriage. Daughters of these women may have problems with their own reproductive system. Some are sterile, some are fertile but cannot carry a child to term, and some develop cancer of their reproductive organs.

DO YOU KNOW?

Information: Your navel is the spot where your umbilical cord was attached to your body.

45-7 Harmful Effects on the Fetus

People used to think that the placenta prevented harmful substances from passing through the uterus into the embryo. However, scientists now know that the placenta does not act as a barrier. Viruses, for example, can move from the mother into the embryo and in some cases cause harm. For example, if the German-measles virus infects an embryo, it may cause deafness, blindness, or mental retardation. The AIDS virus can also be passed through the placenta, infecting the fetus.

The effects of substance abuse during pregnancy have been widely studied. If a pregnant woman drinks alcohol, her baby may be born with a condition called fetal alcohol syndrome. This defect includes misshapen facial features and mental retardation. Smoking marijuana during pregnancy may have a similar effect. If a pregnant woman uses a drug such as heroin or cocaine, her baby may be born addicted to the drug. Even caffeine is suspected of causing damage to the fetus. There is no way of knowing how much of a drug is necessary to harm a fetus, so pregnant women are cautioned to avoid all unnecessary drugs.

Smoking cigarettes also can cause problems during pregnancy. Nicotine causes the blood vessels of the endometrium to become narrower, decreasing the blood supply to the placenta and resulting in a decrease in the amount of food delivered to the fetus. The baby's birth weight may be lowered too, threatening its health and development.

45-8 Birth

During the last weeks of pregnancy, hormonal changes occur in the mother's body. For example, the level of estrogen rises. Estrogen increases the ability of the uterine muscle to contract. Oxytocin, a hormone secreted by the posterior pituitary gland, also causes contractions of the uterus. Around the thirty-eighth week after fertilization, the uterus begins to contract over and over. These repeated contractions are called **labor**.

Throughout pregnancy, the muscular cervix remains tightly closed, supporting the weight of the fetus and the surrounding fluid, about seven kilograms in all. Labor contractions push the baby's head against the cervix. Eventually the cervix becomes stretched enough to permit the baby to pass through it. The subsequent contractions push the baby through the vagina and out of the mother's body.

The baby emerges from the mother's body still attached to the placenta by the umbilical cord. When the umbilical cord is cut, the baby becomes an independent organism. Additional contractions soon expel the placenta from the mother's body. The placental material is commonly referred to as afterbirth.

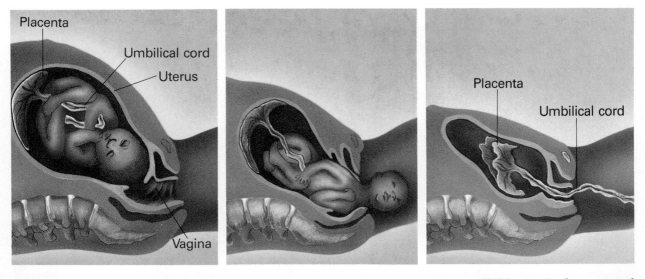

Placenta
Umbilical cord
Uterus
Vagina
Placenta
Umbilical cord

A newborn adjusts rapidly to the dramatic change in its living environment. While in the uterus, the fetus had no need to breathe, and its lungs were filled with amniotic fluid. At birth, the baby's first cries rid the lungs of fluid and fill them with air.

As soon as a baby takes that first breath, its circulatory system changes too. While the fetus is in the uterus, most of its blood bypasses the lungs by traveling from the right ventricle through a duct into the aorta. However, this specialized duct closes at birth. As a result, the right ventricle begins pumping blood to the baby's lungs.

Another circulatory adjustment occurs in a newborn baby's heart. Before birth, an opening exists between the right and left atria of the heart. Normally this opening closes shortly after birth. The closing prevents oxygenated and deoxygenated blood from mixing in the heart.

Once a baby's umbilical cord has been cut, it requires a new food supply. During pregnancy, the hormone prolactin caused milk to develop in the mother's breasts. A baby is born with the ability to suck and can usually nurse right after birth.

45-9 Formation of Twins

About once in 88 births, two babies are born instead of one. Twins usually occur in one of two ways. **Identical twins** come from one embryo that splits into two separate embryos. This splitting occurs very early in development, probably during the blastocyst stage. Since identical twins come from the same zygote, they each have the same genes. Therefore, they are always the same sex. Identical twins resemble each other very strongly.

Figure 45-17 In the first stage of labor, the baby's head presses against the cervix. The cervix eventually dilates and allows the baby to pass through the birth canal. The placenta and the remains of the amnion and umbilical cord are expelled in the third stage.

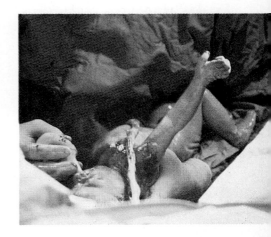

Figure 45-18 A newborn is still attached to the placenta by the umbilical cord.

Human Reproduction   **761**

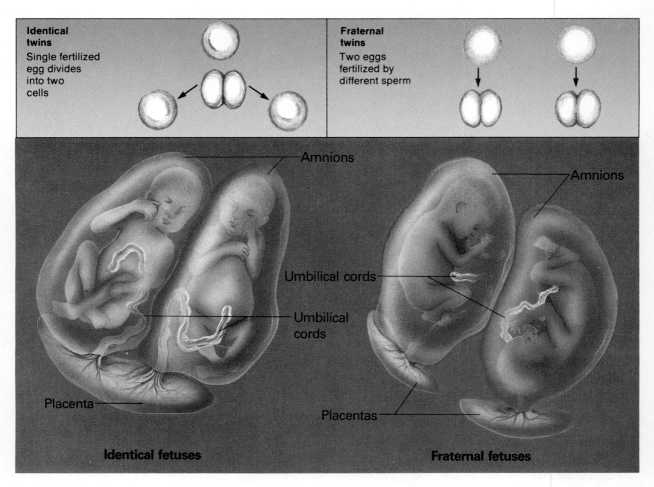

Identical twins
Single fertilized egg divides into two cells

Fraternal twins
Two eggs fertilized by different sperm

Amnions

Amnions

Umbilical cords

Umbilical cords

Placenta

Placentas

Identical fetuses

Fraternal fetuses

Figure 45-19 Two ways in which twins form are pictured. Identical twins usually share one placenta and may or may not share an amnionic sac. Fraternal twins do not share either.

If two eggs are released from the ovary during the same cycle, each may be fertilized by a separate sperm. Each resulting zygote is the product of a different egg-and-sperm combination. Two babies produced this way are called **fraternal twins** and are not genetically identical.

CHECKPOINT ◆

7. At which stage of its development does the embryo attach to the endometrium?
8. What is the fertile period during the menstrual cycle?
9. What structure attaches an embryo to the placenta?
10. From how many eggs do identical twins arise?
11. Where does fertilization occur?
▶ 12. Nicotine is to low birth weight as alcohol is to _____.
▶ 13. How does synthetic oxytocin shorten labor?

▶ Denotes a question that involves *interpreting* and *applying* concepts.

LABORATORY ACTIVITY

THE DEVELOPMENT OF A FERTILIZED EGG

Although there are differences in embryonic development among different organisms, there also are many similarities. In this activity, starfish embryos are used to illustrate some of the developmental changes that occur in embryos of multicellular animals.

Objectives and Skills

☐ *Examine* the stages of development of a starfish embryo.
☐ *Compare* the development of a starfish embryo to the development of a human embryo.

Materials

prepared slides of starfish cleavage
  (unfertilized eggs, 2-cell stage, 4-cell stage, 8-cell stage, 16-cell stage, morula, blastula, gastrula)
microscope
drawing paper
pencil

Procedure and Observations

1. Read all instructions for this laboratory activity before you begin your work.
2. Using the low-power objective of your microscope, examine a prepared slide of an unfertilized starfish egg. On your drawing paper, draw a diagram of what you see on the slide.
3. Repeat this step with slides that show fertilized eggs divided into 2 cells, 4 cells, 8 cells, and 16 cells respectively. Be sure to include a title with each diagram for identification. (You may find it helpful to review the information in Chapter 27 about the development of animal embryos.)
4. As a starfish embryo divided beyond the 16-cell stage, it develops into a solid ball of cells called a morula. Examine a prepared

slide of this stage of the starfish and sketch what you see.
5. Continue work by looking at and sketching the blastula and gastrula stages of a starfish.
6. Before leaving the laboratory, clean up all of your materials and wash your hands thoroughly.

Analysis and Conclusions

1. During cleavage, what happens to the size of the individual cells in the embryo?
2. What happens to the total size of the embryo?
3. The blastula stage of the starfish is comparable to the blastocyst stage of human embryos. What characteristics do these two stages have in common? How are they different?
4. In a human blastocyst, what are the functions of the trophoblast and the inner cell mass?
5. Prepare a data table that compares body tissues of the human embryo and the invertebrate embryo. List the body tissues that eventually are produced from the endoderm, mesoderm, and ectoderm layers of a human embryo. How does your answer compare with the development of these layers in an invertebrate embryo as described in Chapter 27?

DATA TABLE		
	Human Embryo	Invertebrate Embryo
Endoderm		
Mesoderm		
Ectoderm		

CHAPTER REVIEW

Summary

▸ Both male and female reproductive systems contain gonads. Testes produce sperm and male hormones; ovaries produce eggs and female hormones. The male testes produce huge numbers of haploid sperm by meiosis. The ovaries function in a cyclic way, producing one haploid egg each month.

▸ The menstrual cycle is a monthly preparation for pregnancy. Under the control of hormones, an egg develops in the ovary and the uterine lining thickens. The egg is released from the ovary at mid-cycle. If the egg is not fertilized, the uterine lining disintegrates and is shed, and menstruation occurs. A new cycle begins following menstruation.

▸ If fertilization occurs, the cycle is interrupted. Fertilization takes place in the oviduct, forming a diploid zygote. As it travels toward the uterus, the zygote undergoes several mitotic divisions.

▸ The inner cell mass of the blastocyst becomes the embryo. Other cells become the surrounding membranes. One membrane forms part of the placenta, through which materials are exchanged between mother and embryo.

▸ Implantation of the blastocyst in the uterus lining is followed by the development of three germ layers. These give rise to the various tissues and organs of the embryo.

▸ Occasionally, harmful substances pass across the placenta from mother to embryo, resulting in damage to the embryo.

▸ Development within the mother ends about 38 weeks after fertilization. At that time, uterine contractions push the baby out of the mother's body, and the baby begins an independent life. Even after birth, the baby receives nourishment from the mother in the form of milk.

▸ Sometimes two babies are born at once. They may be identical twins or fraternal twins.

Vocabulary

amnion
blastocyst
cervix
chorion
corpus luteum
ectoderm
endoderm
endometrium
epididymis
fetus
follicle
follicle-stimulating
   hormone
fraternal twins
germ layers
identical twins
inner cell mass
in vitro fertilization
labor
luteinizing hormone

menopause
menstrual cycle
menstruation
mesoderm
oviduct
ovulation
ovum
placenta
polar body
primary oocyte
primary spermatocyte
scrotum
secondary oocyte
secondary spermatocyte
semen
trophoblast
umbilical cord
uterus
vagina
vas deferens

Concept Mapping

Construct a concept map for the effects of female reproductive hormones. Include the following terms: corpus luteum, FSH, LH, menstruation, ovulation. Use additional terms as you need them.

Review

1. What hormone stimulates the testes to produce sperm?
2. What is the function of a sperm's flagellum?
3. What happens to the polar bodies produced in the formation of an ovum?
4. Sperm contain mitochondria. For what process do these mitochondria provide energy?
5. About how often is an ovum produced?
6. How many sperm result from the division of one primary spermatocyte? How many ova are produced from one primary oocyte?

7. Which hormone causes the development of follicles?
8. During the menstrual cycle, what is usually the fertile period?
9. What causes the follicle to burst and ovulation to occur?
10. What happens to the corpus luteum if fertilization occurs? What happens to it if pregnancy does not occur?
11. Once fertilization takes place, what prevents other sperm from entering an egg?
12. From what part of the blastocyst will the embryo develop? From what part will the embryonic membranes develop?
13. How does an embryo get oxygen?
14. Explain how identical twins form.
15. What is meant by differentiation?
16. What are germ layers? Name the germ layers of a human embryo.
17. Identify three things that can harm a developing embryo.
18. At what point in development does an embryo become a fetus?

Interpret and Apply

19. Explain why testes that have not descended into the scrotum cannot normally produce sperm.
20. Which sex produces more gametes in a lifetime?
21. Maria and Pedro are twins. What kind of twins are they, identical or fraternal? Explain.
22. Why does menstruation not occur if the ovum is fertilized?
23. Write the following structures in the order in which a sperm travels through them.
    a. epididymis   **c.** urethra
    b. testes   **d.** vas deferens
24. Identify two ways in which meiosis is different in men and women.

25. Identify the functions of estrogen in the menstrual cycle and in the birth process.
26. How is a baby's circulatory system different from an embryo's?
27. Which part of the female corresponds to the vas deferens in the male?
28. Why is it a good idea for girls to be vaccinated against German measles before they reach childbearing age?

Critical Thinking

29. If a blastocyst separated into four equal parts and each developed independently, what would be the result?
30. What would happen if each vas deferens in a man's body was blocked?
31. Suppose a woman's oviducts were blocked. Would she produce ova? Could she become pregnant? Explain.
32. What would happen if the corpus luteum disintegrated after an ovulation that resulted in a pregnancy?
33. Explain how negative feedback works in regulating the level of FSH during different stages of the menstrual cycle.
34. How are the chorionic villi in humans similar to the root hairs in plants: (a) structurally and (b) functionally?
35. Why would a low sperm count be a possible cause of infertility?
36. The incidence of multiple births is nine times greater than average among couples who have used *in vitro* fertilization. Explain why.

EARLY TREATMENT PROVED HARMFUL

Case Study 1

Sue had just had her tonsils removed and she was recuperating at home. Her throat felt very uncomfortable. She was reading the newspaper and found an interesting article. It discussed doctors who had been looking for a cure for tonsilitis 25 years ago. These doctors didn't prefer surgery for young children and teenagers so they found a way to shrink their tonsils without removing them.

The method involved exposing the patient's tonsils to X rays for three seconds. It was painless and sounded like a better alternative to Sue's operation. As she read on, Sue learned that some of these people developed cancer of the thyroid 20–30 years after being x-rayed.

"That's right," she thought. "The thyroid gland is near the tonsils in the throat." The X rays weren't a better treatment than surgery.

She showed the article to her father and he read it several times.

"I think I was one of the children whose tonsils were x-rayed," he said. "Oh, Dad!" Sue cried. "You'd better have your thyroid checked!"

"It was a long time ago. If something had happened to my thyroid, I'd already be sick," he answered. "Don't worry about me."

1. What would you do if you were Sue?
2. Should you try to force someone to go for medical tests or treatment? Why or why not?
3. List several reasons Sue's father might have for not wanting to go and several arguments Sue could use to try to change his mind.
4. If Sue's father had thyroid cancer, do you think he could sue the doctors who x-rayed his tonsils? Why or why not?

Case Study 2

Jane and Mark Irving, both in their late 30's, were expecting a baby. As a precaution, Dr. Nolan, Jane's gynecologist, decided to perform a simple test called an ultrasound. During this test, sound waves were sent into Jane's uterus from a microphone passed over her abdomen. A picture of the fetus was projected on a screen in the doctor's office. Jane was excited about seeing the baby and watching it move but, as the test progressed, Jane knew from Dr. Nolan's expression that something was wrong.

After the test, Jane and Mark spoke with Dr. Nolan and he explained what he had seen. The baby's head was very small and he suspected it had anencephaly, an underdeveloped brain. If they are not stillborn, babies with this condition rarely live longer than a week. The Irvings were stunned.

A few days later, Jane read an article about a couple who had donated the organs of their baby born with anencephaly. She called Dr. Nolan to ask him if they could do the same thing when their baby was born. He said that if the baby were born alive it could be kept alive by a respirator until the organs were donated to babies or children who needed them.

1. Why do you think the Irvings wanted to do this?
2. Would you do the same? Why or why not?
3. Give several reasons why someone would disagree with Jane and Mark's decision to keep their baby alive long enough to donate the organs.
4. Should the Irvings be told whose children are given their baby's organs? Why or why not?

UNIT REVIEW 7

Synthesis

1. The opening pages of this unit contain four photographs. These photographs illustrate a common theme to the chapters of the unit. Identify the theme and describe how it relates to what you studied in the chapters.

2. **Adaptation and Evolution:** List the characteristics that make humans different from other animals. How have these characteristics allowed humans to become such a successful species?

3. **Structure Is Related to Function:** Describe the fate of a bacon, lettuce, and tomato sandwich as it travels through your digestive system. What ultimately happens to the substances in the sandwich as they are digested?

4. **Structure Is Related to Function:** Name three categories of substances in the human diet that are necessary for life but that do not provide calories. Describe why each group is necessary.

5. **Structure Is Related to Function:** Using your knowledge of the respiratory system, trace the path that an oxygen molecule would travel from the atmosphere outside your body to reach the mitochondrion of a muscle cell.

6. **Structure Is Related to Function:** What is the relationship between protein in the diet and the function of human kidneys?

7. **Homeostasis:** Explain how the circulatory system helps maintain the functions of the other body systems.

8. **Structure Is Related to Function:** Explain how the fight-or-flight response involves both the nervous system and the endocrine system.

9. **Structure Is Related to Function:** Describe how the human endocrine system and reproductive system are related.

10. **Structure Is Related to Function:** Describe the two-loop pattern of blood circulation in the human body. How does this pattern compare to the pattern of circulation in a human fetus? What happens to a baby's circulatory system at birth?

11. **Structure Is Related to Function:** Explain how the agglutination that occurs when different blood types are mixed is similar to the process by which pathogens are neutralized within your body.

Critical Thinking

12. **Structure Is Related to Function:** Several lifestyle factors have been shown to increase the risk of heart disease. These include smoking, a diet high in saturated fats, lack of exercise, and emotional stress. Use this information to demonstrate the interrelatedness of the body systems.

13. **Adaptation and Evolution:** Recall what you know about vertebrate evolution. If another species of vertebrates were to evolve from humans in the future, speculate about the following aspects of the species: size of cerebral cortex, life span, ability to adapt to a changing environment. Also, explain how these three characteristics might be related to each other.

14. **Structure Is Related to Function:** A hypothetical machine contains the following parts: filter, computer, pump, insulation, steel struts, moving parts, radiator, plug (energy input), exhaust opening. Choose from the following list the parts that perform the corresponding function in the human body: brain, kidney, fat, muscles, skin, skeleton, anus, mouth, heart.

ECOLOGY

Sunlight filtering through trees

Mouse eating a grasshopper

Woman harvesting rice

UNIT 8

Caterpillar eating a leaf

Chapter 46 Behavior
Instinct and Learning
Patterns of Behavior

Chapter 47 Distribution of Life
Biomes on Land
Aquatic Biomes

Chapter 48 Ecosystems and Communities
Living Communities
Changes in Communities
Cycles in the Biosphere

Chapter 49 Population Dynamics
Population Growth Patterns
Environmental Resistance
The Human Population

Chapter 50 Human Impact on the Biosphere
Natural Resources
Energy Resources
Pollution

BEHAVIOR

Overview

INSTINCT AND LEARNING

46-1 Behavior and Natural Selection

46-2 Innate Behavior

46-3 Learning

46-4 Types of Learning

PATTERNS OF BEHAVIOR

46-5 Orientation

46-6 Courtship

46-7 Territoriality and Aggression

46-8 Social Behavior

46-9 Communication

How do leaf cutter ants find their way to their farms?

INSTINCT AND LEARNING

People sometimes say a good athlete was born knowing how to play ball. Of course, no one is born with such highly developed skills. Playing ball is a behavior that must be learned. Yet some behaviors are present at birth. What are some of these inherited behaviors? How do they differ from learned behaviors?

46-1 Behavior and Natural Selection

You learned in earlier chapters that genes provide the blueprint for an organism's physical makeup. These physical traits are acted on by the forces of natural selection. Beneficial traits will be preserved in a population; harmful traits will not be preserved.

Like physical traits, **behavior**, or what an animal does, contributes to its survival and reproductive success. There are three main ways by which natural selection acts on behavior.

1. An animal's behavior must allow it to survive. For example, it must be able to find food when it is hungry. It also must be able to escape or hide from predators.
2. An animal's behavior must allow it to reproduce. It must be able to find a mate and prepare a nesting site. In many species, successful reproductive behavior also involves care of offspring while they are young.
3. An animal's behavior must allow it to determine which stimuli are important for survival and reproduction. There are many sights, sounds, and smells in the environment. It is not necessary, nor is it possible, to respond to everything.

46-2 Innate Behavior

Animal behavior falls into two broad categories: innate behavior and learning. **Innate behavior** is behavior that is done perfectly the first time it occurs. It is genetically programed. The organism is born knowing how to do it.

Consider, for example, the digger wasp. By the time a female digger wasp emerges from her underground pupa, her parents have been dead for several months. The newly emerged wasp will live for only a few weeks. During this brief time, she must dig a hole for a nest, construct the nest, mate, hunt prey to place in the nest to nourish her young, and lay her eggs. There is little time for her to learn these tasks. Furthermore, there is no one to teach her. She is born knowing how to complete the tasks. Such complex behaviors that are performed perfectly without learning are called **instincts**.

Section Objectives

A **Explain** how natural selection acts on behavior.
B **Give examples** of innate behavior.
C **Distinguish** between innate and learned behavior.
D **State** the advantages of innate and learned behavior.
E **Name** several types of learning and give examples of each.

BIOLOGY INSIGHT

Continuity of Life: Behavioral characteristics can be inherited in the same way that physical characteristics can. One example is the complex nests built by weaverbirds, which, under the proper conditions, are built perfectly on the first attempt.

Figure 46-1 The digger wasp builds her nest which is an instinctive behavior.

Figure 46-2 Hibernation is one way for animals to avoid extreme temperatures and limited resources.

Instinctive behavior patterns are often repeated in response to changes in the environment. Behavior that is based on a 24-hour cycle is called a **circadian rhythm**. Circadian rhythms are related to the lengths of daylight and darkness. Some animals, such as bluejays and ground squirrels, are active during the day. These organisms are said to be *diurnal*. Other animals, such as flying squirrels and bats, are active at night. They are *nocturnal*.

Rhythmic behaviors also occur over long periods of time. *Hibernation*, a period of dormancy, occurs in some animals in response to cold winter temperatures and limited food supplies. During hibernation, an animal's metabolism slows down dramatically. Its body temperature drops to near that of its surroundings and its breathing rate is greatly reduced.

Many animals in hot, arid environments also become dormant when conditions are harsh. This is usually during the hottest, driest months. *Estivation*, like hibernation, is a period of dormancy in which an animal's metabolism slows down greatly. Can you think of a reason why this behavior is advantageous?

Dormancy does not occur in all animals. Many birds and mammals, for example, move to new locations as the seasons change. This behavior, called *migration*, enables animals to find new breeding and feeding grounds. Migrating animals usually follow the same routes year after year.

46-3 Learning

In contrast to instinctive behaviors, certain behaviors are obviously learned. No one is born knowing how to solve algebra problems. **Learning** occurs when an animal's experience results in a change of behavior. Learned behavior is not determined by an organism's genes. Because it permits behavior that is flexible, learning allows an animal to adapt to changes in its environment.

Figure 46-3 Lions teach their cubs to hunt. Hunting is a learned behavior for lions.

Learned behavior is characteristic of organisms with complex nervous systems. In general, the more advanced the brain, the more elaborate the patterns of learned behavior.

Learning is also related to the amount of time a developing animal spends with its parents. In animals that develop without parental care, behaviors are more likely to be innate. The longer the developmental period, the more learning (and the less innate behavior) there is. Humans, who have the longest period of parent–young attachment, have the highest level of learning and the fewest innate behaviors of all animals. The reason is that the human brain takes several years to develop completely. During the entire period of brain development, a baby depends on its parents to provide it with food, shelter, protection, and anything else it needs. But during this time of dependence, an enormous amount of learning takes place. By the time the baby becomes an adult, he or she is capable of complex behavior.

Learning, unlike instinct, offers great potential for changing behaviors as conditions in the environment change. For example, if an animal innately knows how to build a certain type of nest, it is at a loss if the specific building materials are not available. However, if nest building is a learned behavior and new building material becomes available, an animal can learn a new type of nest building. Learning ability is related to the life span of an animal. If an animal lives for only a few weeks, as the digger wasp does, the ability to meet a changing environment may not be necessary. On the other hand, in animals that live for many years, such as primates, the ability to change behavior as the environment changes is extremely valuable.

▪ BIOLOGY INSIGHT

Continuity of Life: Between the two extremes of innate and learned behavior lie many types of behavior that have elements of both. For example, young felines spend much of their time at play, stalking imaginary prey. Their play is actually practice, during which they are learning to be good hunters. But the tendency to play is not learned; it is innate.

Figure 46-4 These young cygnets have imprinted on their mother.

DO YOU KNOW?

Historical Note: Imprinting was first documented by the Austrian scientist Konrad Lorenz. In one of many studies, he removed the mother duck and substituted himself at the critical period. The ducklings imprinted on him.

Figure 46-5 Primates are able to use reasoning to solve problems in unfamiliar situations.

46-4 Types of Learning

One of the simplest types of learning, called imprinting, occurs among very young animals. **Imprinting** is a form of learning in which an animal forms a social attachment to an organism soon after hatching or birth. This kind of learning is rapid and irreversible. Imprinting was first observed in ducklings, who will follow their mother soon after they hatch. Ducklings exposed to a female of another species instead of their mother will follow the substitute mother.

Imprinting occurs during a *critical period* in which a duckling learns to identify its mother. This critical period occurs between 13 and 16 hours after hatching. If a substitute mother is available before or after this critical period, imprinting is not as likely to occur.

Habituation is a form of learning in which an animal learns not to respond to a repeated stimulus. Imagine that you are working in a quiet place and suddenly there is a loud noise. You may be startled to the point of jumping out of your seat. If the same noise is repeated several times during a short period, though, your response will be reduced each time. Over time, you will probably not respond to the noise at all.

Habituation allows an organism to focus its energy on new stimuli rather than on old, repeated stimuli that are not important. Can you explain how this type of learning might be useful to young animals?

Insight learning, or reasoning, is a type of behavior that occurs only in primates and other higher vertebrates. **Insight learning** is the ability to solve an unfamiliar problem without the benefit of trial and error. (Trial-and-error learning is described in Table 46-1.)

774 Chapter 46

Table 46-1

DIFFERENT TYPES OF LEARNING BEHAVIOR		
Type	**Behavioral Characteristic**	**Example**
Associative learning* Habituation	Animal learns not to respond to repeated stimulus.	A dog learns not to bark at a frequent visitor.
Conditioned reflex	Animal learns to respond to stimulus that would not normally cause a response.	Dogs normally salivate when they see food. They can be conditioned to salivate when a bell is rung, even if no food is given.
Trial-and-error learning	Animal's behavior by chance produces a reward; the animal learns to repeat the behavior (practice).	A young lion chases rodents and eventually catches one. It perfects its prey-catching movements.
Latent learning	Occurs without obvious reward or punishment; often occurs when animal is exploring a new area	A mouse that has recently eaten seems not to notice a pile of grain. The mouse returns later to eat the grain when it is hungry.
Insight learning	Depends on results of past experiences to find a solution to a new problem	A girl who has taken a carpentry class fixes a broken drawer on her desk.

* Reinforcement (a reward or punishment) is important in associative learning. This kind of learning occurs best when the stimulus, response behavior, and reinforcement happen close together.

A classic study of reasoning involved a chimpanzee closed in a room with a bunch of bananas and some boxes. The fruit was hanging from the ceiling. The chimpanzee could not reach the bananas by jumping. Eventually the chimp figured out that by piling boxes on top of each other, it could climb high enough to reach the bananas. Although the chimpanzee had had no experience with this type of problem, it was able to use knowledge gained in other situations and apply it to this one.

CHECKPOINT ◆

1. Natural selection favors behaviors that allow an organism to _____ and _____.
2. What term describes complex patterns of innate behavior?
3. What types of behaviors are usually associated with longer life spans?
4. What is habituation?
▶ 5. When you feel yourself falling forward, you reach out to break your fall. What type of behavior is this?
▶ 6. Kittiwakes are sea birds that nest on narrow ledges. When kittiwake chicks hatch, they immediately stand still. How is this behavior adaptive?
▶ 7. How is imprinting adaptive for an animal's survival?

▶ Denotes a question that involves *interpreting* and *applying* concepts.

Section Objectives

F **Name** three types of orientation behavior.

G **State** the adaptive significance of courtship.

H **Explain** the functions of territoriality and aggression.

I **List** the advantages of social behavior.

J **Give examples** of communication among animals.

Figure 46-6 Which form of orientation is illustrated by the red-winged blackbirds (*top*) and green turtle (*bottom*)?

When you want to transmit information to another person, you may speak, write, or use hand signals. Communication is one of several categories of behavior that appear throughout the animal kingdom. In this lesson, you will learn about the different kinds of behavior that allow animals to survive and reproduce. As you read, remember that natural selection is responsible for many complex behavior patterns. Animals with certain behavior patterns are better adapted for survival than animals that lack those behaviors.

46-5 Orientation

To find food, shelter, protection from predators, or mates, animals must position, or orient, themselves in their environment. The simplest type of **orientation** is kinesis. **Kinesis** is moving about without direction. For example, a wood louse increases its rate of motion when placed in an environment of low humidity. The animal's movement is nondirectional. However, it needs an atmosphere of high humidity to survive. Kinesis increases the probability that the wood louse will eventually end up in an area of higher humidity. Once this condition is met, the wood louse will stop moving.

Another type of orientation is called **taxis**, a movement directly toward or away from a source of stimulation. Moths move toward a source of light. Bloodsuckers move toward warm-blooded animals. Green turtles move toward the sea.

Compass orientation is the most complex type of orientation. It involves several elements. Some frogs, for example, find their home ponds by using the location of the pond relative to the sun, moon, and stars. But these objects are not always in the same position; their positions change with time of day, month, and year. The frog's brain has an internal clock, a mechanism that allows it to compensate for the regular movements of the planets and stars. The frog can therefore find its home even though the "landmarks" have moved.

Animals that migrate, particularly birds, use compass orientation. Some species of birds fly thousands of miles each year, using only the stars and their internal clocks as pathfinders.

46-6 Courtship

Courtship is a specialized behavior pattern that allows the male and the female of a species to recognize each other and get close enough for mating to occur. It also ensures that mating occurs only among members of the same species. If an animal mated with a member of another species, it would not produce fertile offspring. It would have wasted its genes, an evolutionary disadvantage. Courtship prevents such a waste of genes.

Courtship often involves a complex series of actions, usually carried out by the male of the species. For example, the male bowerbird of New Guinea builds an elaborate nestlike structure called a bower to attract a mate. The male decorates the bower with colorful objects, such as shells, rocks, flowers, bottlecaps, and bits of plastic. The more colorful the bower, the greater the chance of attracting a female.

46-7 Territoriality and Aggression

Territoriality, the defense of a certain amount of space, is widespread in the animal kingdom. Male birds singing their glorious songs in the spring are announcing to other males that they are in possession of a certain territory. Territorial animals use threatening postures and noises to warn other animals away.

You have probably seen male dogs urinating on objects. They are marking their territory. The urine contains chemicals called **pheromones**. The scent of the pheromones informs other dogs that the territory has been claimed.

Territoriality has several functions. A given amount of space will provide enough food and resources for only a limited number of breeding animals. By establishing a territory, an organism is securing adequate food for its offspring. Only those animals that can secure the minimum amount of space required are able to breed successfully. Territoriality also lowers the amount of predation and disease in an area and keeps mating pairs together.

Most animals occasionally engage in **aggression**, or fighting behavior. Its function may be to defend young or a territory. Aggressive behavior is meant to deliver a message. If you approach a dog in its yard, the dog may bark loudly, indicating that you are trespassing. Bared fangs and flattened ears confirm the threatening message.

46-8 Social Behavior

Some animals spend almost their whole lives alone. They interact with others of their species only to mate. Many organisms, however, live together in groups, such as flocks of birds or colonies of ants. An organized group of animals is called a **society**.

Social behavior evolves when animals are better able to survive and reproduce in a group than when they are alone. The greatest selection pressure on animals to form groups is predation. An animal that is part of a group is usually safer than a lone animal

Figure 46-7 Territorial behavior varies from one species to another. *Top:* These bighorn sheep clash over territory. *Bottom:* This indigo bunting sings to announce his territory.

■ *BIOLOGY INSIGHT* ━━━

Unity and Diversity: Aggressive postures usually tend to make the aggressive animal look bigger than it is. Some examples other than the dog include the cat, whose hair stands up on an arched back, and the fish, which lifts its dorsal fins when angry.

Figure 46-8 The leaping Thomson's gazelle alerts other members of its herd to a potential threat, possibly a predator.

is. A group animal has the benefit of many eyes watching for predators. In some groups, the members act together to defend themselves against attack.

Defense against predators and other activities often involves cooperation. **Cooperation** occurs when animals work together for a common purpose. Wolves are very cooperative animals. A lone wolf cannot subdue a large prey, such as a moose, but a pack of wolves can. It is to the advantage of every wolf in the pack to cooperate in the hunt.

Societies are often organized into different levels of authority called a **dominance hierarchy**. Among baboons, for example, one male in the troop is at the top of the hierarchy. He has first choice of safe places to sleep, food to eat, and females with whom he can mate. Each baboon has his place in the hierarchy. An individual's rank may change because of fighting, injury, or old age. Females also form hierarchies. This reduces aggression and competition for resources within the society.

46-9 Communication

Animals living in groups must be able to exchange information, or **communicate**. The location of food is a message frequently communicated to one or more members of the society. Communication depends on a variety of signals that can be seen, heard, felt, or smelled. A dolphin in distress, for example, will emit a series of whistles that signal its need for help to other dolphins. An antelope will signal the approach of a predator to other antelopes by lifting its tail and displaying a white patch.

Honeybees, which have complex societies, use an elaborate dance to communicate the location of a food source. The bee moves along the wall of the hive and shakes, or waggles, its whole body. The waggle dance indicates the direction, distance, and amount of available food.

CHECKPOINT ◆

8. Distinguish between taxis and kinesis.
9. What kind of behavior prevents animals from wasting their genes by mating with inappropriate animals?
10. Give an example of communication among animals.
▶ 11. Studies with rats allowed to reproduce in a limited space indicate that when the space becomes too crowded, the rats begin to fight with one another. This results in a decrease in reproduction. How is this adaptive?
▶ 12. All the bees in a hive contribute to feeding and protecting the young of that hive. What type of behavior is this?

▶ Denotes a question that involves *interpreting* and *applying* concepts.

LEARNING BY TRIAL-AND-ERROR

Objectives and Skills

□ *Observe* the effect of practice on the rate of learning.
□ *Prepare* a graph of the data.

Materials

small puzzle or portion of a large puzzle
stopwatch
graph paper
metric ruler

Procedure and Observations

1. Read all instructions for this laboratory activity before you begin your work.
2. On a separate piece of paper, draw a data table like the one shown below.
3. Working alone or with a partner, mix up the pieces of the puzzle. Then attempt to complete the puzzle as quickly as possible. Record your time.
4. Perform three more trials and record the time for each trial in the data table.
5. When each partner has completed all four trials, place the puzzle pieces in their container and return the container as directed.
6. If time allows, repeat steps 3–5 with a second puzzle.

Analysis and Conclusions

1. What effect did practice have on the time needed to do the puzzle?
2. Is doing a puzzle learned or innate behavior? Explain.
3. If you tried a second puzzle, how did your results compare to those for the first puzzle? Did your work with the first puzzle have any effect on your performance on the second puzzle? Why or why not?
4. Graph your results using a different color pen for each puzzle you used. Label the horizontal axis "Trial." Label the vertical axis "Time to complete puzzle (minutes.)"
5. How does your graph compare with those of your classmates? Explain any differences.

DATA TABLE	
Trial	**Time to complete puzzle (min)**
1	
2	
3	
4	

CHAPTER REVIEW

Summary

▸ Natural selection acts on behavior as well as on physical characteristics. Thus animals behave in ways that enhance their individual survival and that favor long-term survival of their genes in future generations.

▸ Some behaviors are innate. They are genetically programmed and require no learning. However, they also allow no flexibility and may not be useful if the environment changes.

▸ Learned behaviors require longer to develop, but they allow flexibility if the demands of the environment change. Learning requires a long association with parents. In general, animals that spend more time with their parents have a greater capacity for learned behavior.

▸ There are many different learning processes. Some of these are imprinting, habituation, and insight learning. Different skills are learned by different processes. Reinforcement, which increases the incidence of the behavior with which it is paired, is important in learning.

▸ Certain categories of behavior are present in much of the animal kingdom. Their widespread existence indicates that evolution has selected them. Types of behavior that are found in a wide range of animals include the ability to orient in the environment, courtship, aggressive and territorial behavior, social behavior, and communication. All of these are important in the interactions of organisms with each other and with the environment.

Vocabulary

aggression	courtship
behavior	dominance
circadian rhythm	hierarchy
communicate	habituation
cooperation	imprinting

innate behavior	orientation
insight learning	pheromone
instinct	society
kinesis	taxis
learning	territoriality

Concept Mapping

Construct a concept map to describe various patterns of behavior. Include the following terms: orientation, courtship, territoriality, cooperation, communicate, society, taxis, and kinesis. Add additional terms as you need them.

Review

1. Define instinctive behavior and give an example in animals.
2. Name an advantage of innate behavior over learned behavior.
3. What is the main advantage of learning over instinct?
4. What is migration?
5. Give an example of taxis.
6. What type of learning occurs only in primates and higher vertebrates?
7. Give an example of a rhythmic behavior.
8. Why do animals have courtship behavior?
9. Name one advantage of living in a social group.
10. How do bees communicate the location of food sources?
11. Bared fangs are common in _____ behavior.
12. Name several advantages to having fixed territories.
13. Name three species of animals that exhibit cooperation.
14. What mechanism do frogs use to orient themselves in their environment?

15. Indicate whether each of the following is characteristic of innate or learned behavior.
    a. most often present in lower animals
    b. most often present in animals with short life spans
    c. requires practice to develop
    d. often requires a teacher
    e. is rigid and unchanging
    f. includes reflexes
    g. is the most common type of behavior in humans
    h. may not be apparent at birth but requires no practice
    i. allows for adaptation and change
    j. may be influenced by rewards
    k. is genetically determined

Interpret and Apply

16. Name the general type of behavior represented by each of the following.
    a. salmon swimming upstream to spawn
    b. thousands of termites building an enormous nest together
    c. a peacock strutting past a peahen, with his tail magnificently displayed
    d. a fish assuming a threatening posture toward its reflection in an aquarium
    e. a cat arching its back, with its tail and hair erect
17. As winter approaches, Canada geese fly south along the Atlantic coast to warmer areas. When the weather warms up, they fly north to their original nesting grounds. What two behaviors are involved in this process?
18. A dominant baboon snarls at a lower ranking baboon. The subordinate responds with a submissive gesture. How is this behavior adaptive?

19. For each of the following examples, name the type of learning described.
    a. The first time a baby pets a dog, the dog snaps at the baby. The baby is afraid of dogs after that.
    b. A dog wags its tail when its owner comes home each night. The owner buys a new car. The dog learns to recognize the sound of the car. Now the dog wags its tail when it hears the car.
    c. You move into a new house. It is close to a fire station, and you are awakened by sirens several times during the first few nights that you live in the house. After about a week, you stop waking up even though the sirens continue.

Critical Thinking

20. Animals are genetically programmed to learn the behavior patterns of their own species. Explain why this is so.
21. Name the members of a dominance hierarchy in a human society. Some ideas may be governing bodies, military officers, or employees of a factory.
22. Many courtship behaviors are actually modified aggressive behavior. Suggest an explanation for the relationship between these behaviors.
23. Explain why genetic programming will not enable a crab to locate its burrow on a sandy beach that is full of holes.
24. In some animal groups, one male mates with many females; therefore, most males do not mate. Would this make the gene pool more or less diverse?
25. The term *mouth-watering* is often used to describe appetizing food. Explain in terms of conditioning how this expression came to be.

Chapter

47

DISTRIBUTION OF LIFE

Overview

BIOMES ON LAND

47-1   The Biosphere
47-2   Biomes and Climate
47-3   Tundra
47-4   Taiga
47-5   Temperate Deciduous Forests
47-6   Temperate Rain Forests
47-7   Tropical Rain Forests
47-8   Grasslands
47-9   Deserts
47-10   Mountains

AQUATIC BIOMES

47-11   The Marine Biome
47-12   Freshwater Biomes
47-13   Estuaries

How is the camel adapted for life in the desert?

BIOMES ON LAND

If you have traveled to different regions, you have probably noticed variations in dress, food, and climate. All these variations are related. Dress depends partially on the climate. The plant foods that people eat are often grown nearby and, therefore, also depend on the climate. For example, mango trees grow in Florida, but not in Alaska. It makes sense then, that Floridians eat more mangoes than do Alaskans. Why do mangoes grow in Florida but not in Alaska? The answer to this question is important in understanding why different organisms are found in particular regions.

47-1 The Biosphere

Life on Earth exists in a thin layer of soil, water, and air known as the **biosphere**. The biosphere extends from about 8 km deep in the oceans to about 8 km high in the atmosphere. The biosphere has all the materials and conditions needed to support life.

Nonliving aspects of the biosphere are called **abiotic factors**. Temperature, rainfall, wind, and soil characteristics are abiotic factors. The pH of soil and water and the salinity, or saltiness, of water are also abiotic factors. Some living things can tolerate a broad range of abiotic conditions. Certain fish, for example, can live in either salt or fresh water. Other organisms require very specific conditions. A frost would kill tropical plants. In any case, the characteristics of the physical environment limit which life-forms it will support.

The biosphere can be divided into units called biomes. A **biome** is a geographical region with a characteristic group of plants and animals. Usually a biome is named for the dominant vegetation it contains. A grassland biome, for example, contains mainly grasses.

There are several major terrestrial biomes that you will study in this lesson: tundra, taiga, temperate deciduous forest, temperate rain forest, grassland, desert, and tropical rain forest. Although named for its plant communities, a biome also includes many kinds of animals. The animals found in a given biome are determined mainly by the vegetation.

Aquatic biomes are bodies of water such as lakes, rivers, and oceans. These biomes are identified by their dominant animal populations.

The extreme northern and southern areas of Earth are the **polar regions**. For most of the year, these regions are solid ice up to 30 m thick. During a brief summer, some of the ice melts and patches of open water occur.

Section Objectives

A *Describe* how biomes are determined by climate.

B *Identify* the major terrestrial biomes and *describe* the main characteristics of each.

C *Give examples* of plant and animal adaptations to climate.

D *Compare* the effects of latitude and altitude on the sequence of biomes.

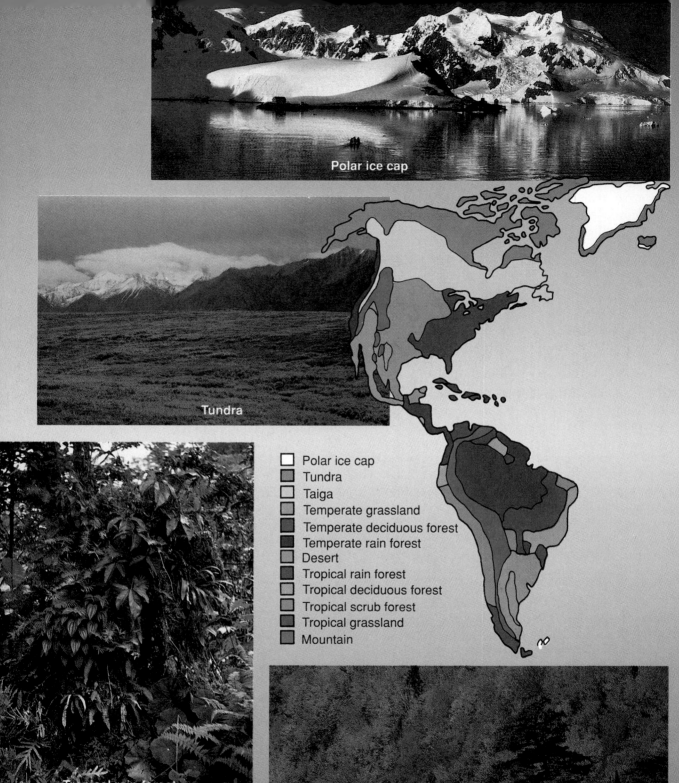

Polar ice cap

Tundra

Tropical rain forest

Temperate deciduous forest

☐ Polar ice cap
☐ Tundra
☐ Taiga
☐ Temperate grassland
☐ Temperate deciduous forest
☐ Temperate rain forest
☐ Desert
☐ Tropical rain forest
☐ Tropical deciduous forest
☐ Tropical scrub forest
☐ Tropical grassland
☐ Mountain

Temperate
rain forest

Desert

Taiga

Grassland

47-2 Biomes and Climate

The type of biome that develops depends to a large extent on climate. Climate, in turn, depends mainly on temperature and precipitation. These factors vary with latitude, or distance from the equator, and altitude, or height above sea level. Upon moving from the equator toward the poles, average temperature decreases. Upon moving from sea level up into the mountains, temperature also decreases.

Precipitation is influenced by mountains and other landforms and by large bodies of water. Air circulating over water picks up moisture. Therefore, coastal areas have more humid air and more precipitation than do inland regions. On the other hand, the temperature of coastal regions tends to vary less than the temperature inland. Large bodies of water have a moderating effect on temperature.

The same types of biomes exist in different geographical locations with similar climates. Deserts, for example, are found on all the continents, except Antarctica. Locate these areas on the map shown on the previous two pages. Although the type of biome is the same, all deserts do not contain exactly the same species of plants and animals. But the species in each desert are similarly adapted to their environments. For example, the sand adder snake of North Africa and the sidewinder rattlesnake of North America are different species. However, they have similar adaptations. Each snake moves along shifting desert sands by slithering sideways. This is an example of convergent evolution, which you studied in Chapter 14.

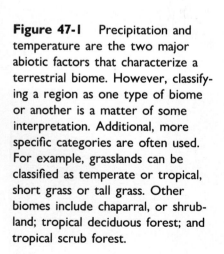
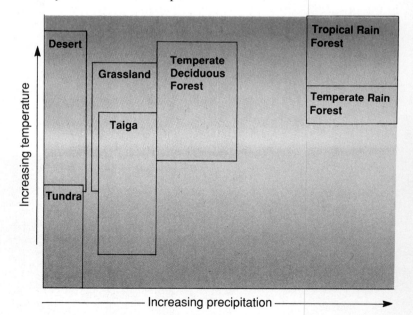

Figure 47-1 Precipitation and temperature are the two major abiotic factors that characterize a terrestrial biome. However, classifying a region as one type of biome or another is a matter of some interpretation. Additional, more specific categories are often used. For example, grasslands can be classified as temperate or tropical, short grass or tall grass. Other biomes include chaparral, or shrubland; tropical deciduous forest; and tropical scrub forest.

47-3 Tundra

Just south of the Arctic, in the northern parts of North America, Europe, and Asia, is a treeless region called the **tundra**. Winter on the tundra lasts 6 to 9 months. Temperatures are usually below freezing, and the skies are dark. Only during the brief summer does the snow melt. Sunlight is available 24 hours a day.

The top layer of tundra soil thaws during the brief summer, but the ground beneath the top meter is permanently frozen. This permanently frozen ground is called **permafrost**. Because of the permafrost, melting snow cannot drain into the ground. Instead, it forms many shallow bogs and streams.

Plants on the tundra rarely grow more than 10 centimeters high because the permafrost prevents the development of deep roots. Small root systems do not generally support large plants. Therefore, the dominant vegetation consists of lichens, grasses, mosses, herbs, and low-growing woody plants.

Few animals are able to live on the tundra through the harsh winter. Most animals migrate south and return during the summer to breed. Ducks, geese, sandpipers, gulls, and songbirds nest all over the tundra. Herds of caribou and reindeer, musk oxen, and rodents such as lemmings are common. Wolves and arctic foxes prey on the smaller mammals and on birds. Bloodsucking insects such as mosquitoes and midges descend in clouds. They are the most abundant animals on the tundra during the short summer. Most insects survive the winter as eggs or pupa. They emerge when the weather becomes warmer.

There is no tundra in the Southern Hemisphere. Antarctica, in the polar region, is always frozen. Sparse growth of mosses, lichens, and a few flowering plants occurs at the edge of the continent. Migrating animals such as penguins, dolphins, whales, seals, and sea birds depend on the ocean for food.

47-4 Taiga

South of the tundra lies a continuous band of forest made up mostly of conifers. This biome is the **taiga** [tī′ gə], or coniferous forest. Like the tundra, the taiga has long, cold winters. Most precipitation is in the form of snow. However, summers are longer and warmer than those in the tundra. The longer summers allow the acidic soil to thaw completely, which permits the growth of trees. Like the tundra, though, the taiga has many bogs.

Spruce, pine, and fir trees are the dominant vegetation. These conifers are well adapted to the snowy winters of the taiga. Their flexible branches bend easily, allowing them to shed heavy snow without breaking. Conifer leaves have a thick cuticle and needlelike shape that reduces evaporation. The trees retain their leaves all

Figure 47-2 *Top:* Like many tundra animals, this Arctic fox has a white coat that blends with its surroundings. *Bottom:* Delicate-looking flowering plants are well adapted to harsh tundra conditions.

Canopy

Understory

Shrub
layer

Herb layer
Forest floor
Soil

Figure 47-3 Differences in the amount of available light lead to vertical stratification in a temperate deciduous forest. Where are the most shade-tolerant plants found?

year. Thus they are ready to carry out photosynthesis whenever the conditions are favorable.

The trees of the taiga provide food and shelter for many animals. Year-round residents include moose, lynx, porcupines, red squirrels, and many small rodents. Many of these animals hibernate during the winter, living off supplies of stored body fat. Many migratory birds spend the summer in the taiga, living on the numerous insects. Flocks of seed-eating birds, such as finches, spend all year in the taiga.

47-5 Temperate Deciduous Forests

In regions where summers are long and warm and rainfall is plentiful, **temperate deciduous forests** occur. The dominant vegetation in these regions are deciduous trees, which lose their leaves seasonally. Deciduous forests are found south of the taiga in North America, Europe, and Asia. In the Southern Hemisphere, deciduous forests are found in Australia and New Zealand.

Plants in a deciduous forest grow in a series of layers. The tallest trees make up the **canopy**, or leafy covering of the forest. Canopy trees, such as oak, maple, beech, and hickory, may reach heights of 30 meters.

Sunlight filters through the thin leaves of the canopy to the plants below. This light allows smaller trees to form a layer called the **understory**. Redbuds and dogwoods are understory trees. Beneath the understory is the **shrub layer**. Shade-tolerant herbs and ferns occupy the shady **herb layer** close to the forest floor. Covering the forest floor is a layer of decomposing leaves called **litter**. The leaves that fall every year decompose slowly, making the soil rich in nutrients.

The layering in the forest, called *vertical stratification*, provides food and shelter for a variety of animals. Gray squirrels, whitetail deer, black bears, raccoons, and opossums are found on the ground. Many insects and birds live in the upper layers.

47-6 Temperate Rain Forests

Along the Pacific coast of northern California, Oregon, and Washington, the climate is cool and moist all year. Abundant winter rainfall and summer fog rolling off the ocean provide an ideal climate for **temperate rain forests**. Temperate rain forests also occur in Chile, New Zealand, and eastern Australia. A few temperate rain forests grow in some tropical mountain regions.

Most of the trees in the temperate rain forest are conifers. These trees reach impressive heights of 60 to 90 m because of the warm temperatures and unlimited moisture. Some trees, such as California redwoods, can reach heights of over 100 m.

Numerous birds, insects, and mammals live in temperate rain forests. Most of these animals are found on or near the ground.

47-7 Tropical Rain Forests

As their name suggests, **tropical rain forests** are found in the tropics, close to the equator. Large tropical rain forests are located in the Amazon Basin in South America, the Malaysian Islands, and the Congo Basin in Africa. These regions are marked by year-round warm temperatures, strong sunlight, and abundant rainfall (more than 200 cm annually). Such conditions are ideal for plant growth. Thus rain forests contain the greatest diversity of living organisms of any biome. Two thirds of all the world's species of organisms are thought to live in tropical rain forests.

The trees of the rain forest are broad-leaved evergreens. The tallest trees may reach 80 m, but most are closer to 50 m. A few very tall trees, called **emergents**, tower above the other trees of the canopy. Unlike trees in other biomes, tropical rain forest trees have shallow roots. The trees are anchored in the soil by a spreading, or *buttressed*, base.

Hanging from boughs in the canopy are many ferns and orchids. These plants are called **epiphytes** [ep′ ə fīts]. Anchored by their roots to tree branches, epiphytes are able to take in water and minerals from falling rain.

Because of the dense covering of the canopy, the floor of the rain forest is dark and has few shrubs or herbs. Many woody vines climb up the tall trunks, thrusting their leaves toward the light. When leaves and fruit fall to the forest floor, they are rapidly decomposed by bacteria, fungi, and insects. Nutrients are immediately reabsorbed by the trees. Therefore, there is very little accumulation of organic material in the soil.

Most of the animal life in the rain forest is found in the canopy. Brightly colored parrots, hummingbirds, eagles, sloths, and monkeys are some of the animals that spend their lives high above the forest floor. A great variety of snakes, frogs, lizards, and insects also live in the trees, as well as on the ground. Big cats, such as leopards and jaguars, are the predators of the rain forest.

The tropical rain forest is a fragile environment. Unfortunately, a number of human activities threaten its existence. Vast areas are being cut for wood. Other areas are being cleared for farming, even though the soil is not suited for this use. Once the vegetation is cut down, the soil quickly loses its fertility. In just a few years, the land must be abandoned. However, the forest and the animals that lived in it do not usually recover. At the present rate of destruction, many rain forests and uncountable numbers of organisms will disappear within the next 50 years. In Chapter 50, you will read more about the importance of forests.

Figure 47-4 *Top:* Orchids and other epiphytes are common plants in the rain forest canopy. *Bottom:* Tropical animals are often brilliantly colored.

Figure 47-5 Trampling and churning of prairie soil by bison clear away dead plants. New grass and herbs are thus able to grow.

Figure 47-6 Snow may fall on a cold desert in winter.

47-8 Grasslands

Grasses are the dominant form of vegetation in areas that are too dry to support trees. There are **grasslands** in both temperate and tropical regions. The *steppes* of Asia, the *pampas* of South America, the *veldts* of South Africa, and the *savannas* of Africa are all grasslands. In North America, *prairie* covers a huge area that extends south from central Canada to the Gulf of Mexico, and west from the Mississippi River to the Rocky Mountains.

Grasslands usually receive between 25 and 75 cm of rain a year. This low amount of precipitation is the main reason that trees cannot grow well in this biome. Strong, drying winds and frequent fires caused by lightning also make it difficult for trees to grow. Grassland plants have extensive root systems that allow them to survive these drying conditions. Often, more than half of a plant consists of roots buried in the soil. Many grassland plants also have underground stems. In this way, they can survive fires. After the top growth is burned away, the underground stem sends out new shoots.

Grassland animals on different continents have similar adaptations. Some animals move around by hopping or jumping to see over tall grass. To avoid predators, many animals have long, powerful legs to run quickly. Herding behavior also is common. Can you explain how this behavior is adaptive?

47-9 Deserts

Deserts are the driest biomes, having an annual rainfall of less than 25 cm. The rainfall in deserts is so sparse that not even grasses can thrive. Deserts are subject to the most extreme daily temperature changes of any of the world's biomes. In the daytime, the air temperature may reach 40°C. At night, the temperature may drop below freezing.

Water in the desert is usually available during a brief, but heavy rainy season. Surprisingly, a large number of plants and animals are adapted to the harsh desert conditions. Organisms either have features to help them withstand the heat and dryness or they avoid these conditions altogether.

One way plants survive in the desert is by storing water for long periods of drought. **Succulents** are plants that store water in their leaves or stems. These plants have extensive root systems that enable them to soak up large amounts of water rapidly during seasonal rains. Modified leaves that have either a reduced surface area (the spines of a cactus, for example) or a thick cuticle reduce water losses due to evaporation.

Other kinds of plants survive in the desert by remaining dormant for long periods. Many small, fast-growing herbs germinate only

Figure 47-7 In drought-stricken parts of Africa, livestock often die of starvation after their grazing lands have been stripped bare.

after a heavy rain. These plants then grow, flower, and produce seeds within a brief period, sometimes just a few days or weeks.

Desert animals also survive by avoiding or resisting drought conditions. Many animals are active only at night, early morning, or late afternoon when it is cooler. During the heat of the day, these animals burrow underground or hide in the shade of plants. Jackrabbits and foxes have oversized ears that radiate body heat. Other animals cool themselves by panting or sweating.

To conserve water, many animals excrete highly concentrated urine. Snakes and lizards have watertight skins that reduce water loss. Most desert animals can also take in water from the food they eat. Many go their whole lives without ever drinking.

In many parts of the world, the desert is spreading. The process of *desertification* is a result partly of natural changes. More often, however, desertification is caused by human activities. In developing countries, people need firewood for fuel and grazing land for animals. With rapidly increasing human populations, more land is being stripped bare as people struggle to survive. Without the roots of plants to hold it in place, the soil is blown away by the wind or carried away by rain. An unproductive wasteland is left in the place of productive land. It is estimated that 15 million acres of useful land are destroyed each year by desertification.

47-10 Mountains

If you were to travel north from the southern United States up into Canada, you would encounter a variety of biomes: deciduous forest, taiga, and tundra. These changes reflect decreasing temperatures and reduced precipitation. If you were to climb a tall

■ BIOLOGY INSIGHT

Adaptation and Evolution: Endothermic animals tend to be much larger in cold climates than in warm climates. A moose is larger than a gazelle. Larger animals have a smaller surface-to-volume ratio, and retain heat more efficiently than smaller animals. This is not true of ectothermic animals. Many equatorial insects, such as the legendary tropical cockroach, are famous for their size.

Figure 47-8 Changes in vegetation are affected by both latitude and altitude.

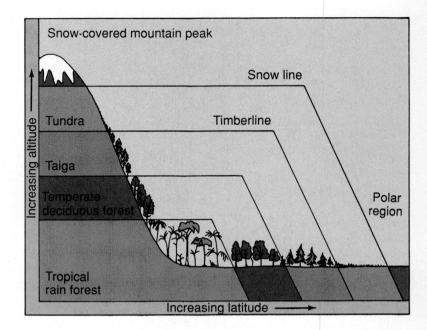

Snow-covered mountain peak

Snow line

Timberline

Increasing altitude

Tundra

Taiga

Temperate deciduous forest

Polar region

Tropical rain forest

Increasing latitude ⟶

mountain, you would encounter similar changes in the sequence of life zones. With increasing altitude, the climate becomes colder and drier.

Figure 47-8 shows the vegetation zones on a mountain. At the beginning of your climb, you might encounter deciduous trees. After climbing for awhile, you would enter a forest of firs and spruce trees similar to those in the taiga. Eventually you would reach a part of the mountain where it is too cold and windy for trees to survive. Here the vegetation resembles the low, scrubby plants of the tundra. The point at which trees can no longer grow is called the **timberline**.

The very top of a mountain, with its high winds and scant soil, may be covered with bare rocks and snow. Can you think of a region at a lower altitude where such conditions occur?

CHECKPOINT ◆

1. What kind of biome is found in a region that receives more than 200 cm of rain a year?
2. What features characterize the tundra?
3. In which biome are spruce trees most common?
4. Explain how desert plants survive long periods of drought.
▶ 5. What biomes would you expect to see on a mountain-climbing trip at the equator?
▶ 6. You buy a small cactus from a plant shop. What conditions must you provide for the plant to enable it to survive?

▶ Denotes a question that involves *interpreting* and *applying* concepts.

AQUATIC BIOMES

Life in the water, like life on land, depends on various environmental conditions. Aquatic biomes, however, do not have dominant plant communities by which they are identified. Instead, aquatic biomes are classified on the basis of salinity. The level of salt is the principal abiotic factor influencing the type of organisms that will be present.

The ocean, or marine biome, is between 3 and 3.7 percent salt. Freshwater biomes, such as lakes, streams, and ponds, are less than 0.005 percent salt. Estuaries, which are a mixture of salt and fresh water, have a variable salinity. In this lesson, you will learn how abiotic factors different from those on land affect the distribution of life in the water.

47-11 The Marine Biome

Oceans cover over 70 percent of Earth's surface. The distribution of organisms in this vast environment depends on physical and chemical factors such as salinity, temperature, light, and available nutrients. These factors vary from seashore to open water and from the surface to the seafloor.

With increasing depth, temperature and available light decrease. Water pressure increases and salinity becomes more uniform. There are fewer dissolved nutrients in the water.

Ocean water mixes locally and globally. Mixing occurs even at great depths, although the process may take thousands of years. In some coastal regions, wind causes warm surface water to move out to sea. Cold, nutrient-rich water moves up from below to replace it. These *nutrient upwellings* are the sites of abundant sea life.

Littoral Zone The seashore is an area that is alternately underwater or exposed to the air. This region is the littoral zone. The littoral zone is the most variable region in the ocean because of the rise and fall of the tides. Inhabitants of this region must be able to tolerate temperature extremes, the pounding action of waves, and periodic exposure to air.

During low tide, some organisms, such as crabs and clams, burrow into the moist sand. Mussels, attached to rocks by suction or threads, close themselves tightly in their shells. Some worms retreat into tubes. Algae, anchored firmly to rocks by their holdfasts, secrete a protective gelatinous coating that keeps them from drying out. Smaller organisms, such as limpets and snails, often take shelter among the blades of the moist seaweed.

Sublittoral Zone The shallow waters between the littoral zone and the edge of the continental shelf make up the sublittoral

Section Objectives

E *Identify* the abiotic factors that influence the distribution of aquatic organisms.

F *Describe* the major life zones of the ocean and *give* the characteristics of each.

G *Distinguish* between standing water and running water biomes.

H *Explain* how an estuary differs from other aquatic biomes.

Figure 47-9 These intertidal organisms are able to withstand the force of waves and exposure to air for long periods.

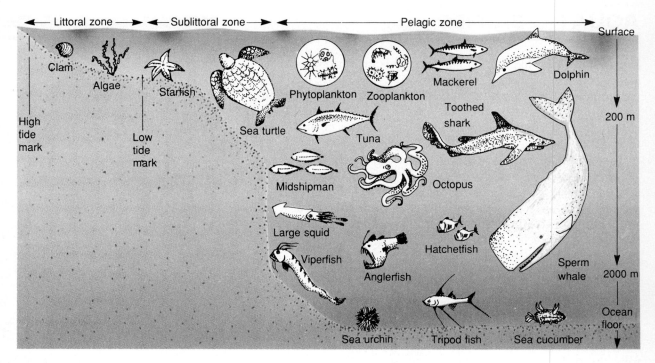

Littoral zone → ← Sublittoral zone → ← Pelagic zone →

Surface

Clam

Algae

Starfish

Sea turtle

Phytoplankton Zooplankton

Mackerel

Dolphin

High tide mark

Low tide mark

Toothed shark

200 m

Tuna

Midshipman

Octopus

Large squid

Viperfish

Anglerfish

Hatchetfish

Sperm whale

2000 m

Sea urchin Tripod fish Sea cucumber

Ocean floor

Figure 47-10 The marine biome shows vertical and horizontal stratification. Some movement of organisms from one layer to another does occur.

zone. The sublittoral zone is a more stable environment than the littoral zone. There is less variation in temperature, and organisms are not exposed to the air. Light penetrates to the depths, allowing the growth of both free-floating and bottom-anchored algae. These algae support a diverse group of animals, including many fish.

Free-swimming organisms, such as fish and turtles, make up the **nekton**. Bottom-dwelling organisms, for example, crabs and starfish, are called **benthos**. In tropical areas, benthos may include coral reefs.

Pelagic Zone The open waters beyond the sublittoral zone are called the pelagic [pə laj′ ik] zone. This region can be divided vertically based on the depth of light penetration. From the surface of the ocean to about 200 m is the *photic zone*. **Phytoplankton**, or floating photosynthetic organisms, are plentiful in the photic zone. Phytoplankton include diatoms, green algae, and dinoflagellates. These organisms are food for crustaceans and other tiny floating heterotrophs called **zooplankton**. Fish, whales, and other nekton feed on the plankton.

Little light penetrates the ocean below 200 m. The region from 200 to 2000 m is known as the *bathyal* [bath′ əl] *zone*. Organisms in this zone are heterotrophs since there is not enough light for photosynthesis. Food comes in the form of dead and decaying organic matter falling from the photic zone.

The depths of the sea below 2000 m are called the *abyssal* [ə bis′ əl] *zone*. This region is permanently cold and dark, and pressure here is hundreds of times greater than at the surface. Organisms have various adaptations to survive in the deep sea. Some depend on bioluminescent structures to lure prey and attract mates. Since food is so scarce, fish often have huge teeth, extendable jaws, and expandable stomachs. These adaptations enable them to seize prey much larger than themselves. Other organisms move up from the depths to feed. Small size, slow growth, and a long life span are common features of deep-sea creatures.

In parts of the abyssal zone, cracks in the ocean floor allow heat to seep up from Earth's interior and warm the surrounding water. The hot water combines with chemicals in the Earth's crust, producing hydrogen sulfide (H_2S) gas. Bacteria living near the cracks use H_2S as an energy source in chemosynthesis, much as plants use sunlight. Chemosynthetic bacteria provide food for other animals of the deep, including clams, mussels, crabs, and giant tube worms.

47-12 Freshwater Biomes

There are two types of freshwater biomes: standing water, such as ponds and lakes, and running water, such as rivers. The types of organisms that will be found in each of these biomes depends on several conditions, or **limiting factors**. Important limiting factors include temperature, turbidity, current, and dissolved oxygen.

Water temperature varies less than air temperature. Therefore, most aquatic organisms can survive only in a narrow range of temperatures. Terrestrial organisms, by contrast, often experience drastic changes in temperature ranging from freezing cold to intense heat.

Turbidity is the amount of suspended material in water. Since the amount of light that can penetrate water depends on whether it is cloudy or clear, turbidity determines the amount of photosynthesis that can occur. The number of phytoplankton in a lake or pond thus depends on turbidity. This in turn determines what zooplankton and higher organisms will occur.

Current is a major limiting factor determining the distribution of organisms in running water. Fast currents limit plant and animal life to those organisms that can hold on to rocks and gravel in the streambed. Many types of insect larvae, for example, have hooks and suckers. Aquatic mosses and algae also cling to the rocks. There are no plankton in fast-moving water. Fast currents also remove dead organisms before they can decompose, so the water tends to have few nutrients.

In streams with slower currents, there is a greater variety of life-forms. These include snails, crayfish, catfish, and bass. Clams

Figure 47-11 Physical conditions limit the kinds of organisms that will be found in freshwater biomes.

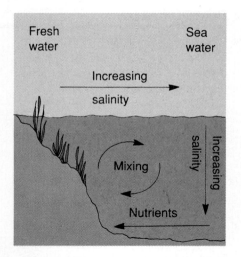

Figure 47-12 Nutrients brought in by ocean currents are trapped in an estuary. The constant high level of nutrients accounts for the high productivity.

and worms are able to burrow into the muddy bottom, and rooted plants grow along the banks.

Current also affects the amount of dissolved oxygen in the water. Because of tumbling and mixing with air, rapidly moving water has more oxygen than does slowly moving or standing water. A brook trout adapted to a high-oxygen environment would not survive in a lake's low-oxygen environment.

Deep lakes are stratified much like the marine biome. The littoral, or near-shore, zone contains rooted plants, phytoplankton, and many animals. The upper open water supports various phytoplankton and zooplankton. Nekton consists mostly of fish. In the deep water, where there is not enough light for photosynthesis, only heterotrophs are found. These organisms feed on material sinking from the upper waters. Benthos includes worms, small clams, and some insect larvae. Bacteria and fungi in the bottom sediment are decomposers.

47-13 Estuaries

Estuaries form where fresh and salt water meet, for example, the mouth of a river or a salt marsh. The mixing of fresh water and salt water causes salinity to vary horizontally and vertically.

Estuaries are more productive biomes than either the ocean or fresh water. The water is shallow, allowing light to penetrate to the bottom. Plant life is abundant and varied. Marsh grasses and other rooted vegetation ring the shore. Algae coat the rocks. Plankton thrive in the open water. The tidal action of the ocean creates strong currents. Constant mixing of the water keeps nutrients in the estuary and quickly removes wastes from it.

Estuaries support many types of animals. Oysters, clams, and mussels are the most common animals. Snails live among the marsh grasses. Bottom-dwellers include sponges and worms. Many types of fish use the estuary as a nursery. When the young are large enough, they leave the estuary for the ocean.

CHECKPOINT ◆

7. Which zone in the marine biome shows the least variation in abiotic factors?
8. In what kind of biome is turbidity an important factor?
9. Why is the depth of an estuary important to plants?
▶ 10. Would you expect to find phytoplankton at a depth of 350 m in the ocean? Explain.
▶ 11. Would you expect to find large populations of bacteria, fungi, and worms in the bed of a swiftly flowing stream? Explain.

▶ Denotes a question that involves *interpreting* and *applying* concepts.

LABORATORY ACTIVITY

SOIL PROPERTIES AND PLANT GROWTH

Objectives and Skills

☐ *Compare* water holding properties of various soils.
☐ *Determine* how soil characteristics affect plant growth.

Materials

250-mL beaker	timing device
funnel with filter paper	spatula
100-mL graduated cylinder	clay
ringstand and ring	garden soil
safety goggles	sand

Procedure and Observations

Part I
1. Put on your safety goggles and wear them throughout this activity.
2. Read all instructions for this laboratory activity before you begin your work.
3. On a separate piece of paper, draw a data table as shown by your teacher.
4. Set up the apparatus as shown below.
5. Fold a piece of filter paper into quarters, open it to a cone, and place it in the funnel. Fill the funnel with clay to about 1 cm

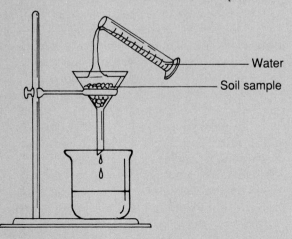

Water
Soil sample

from the top of the filter paper or funnel, whichever is lower. Tap the funnel gently to settle and level the clay.
6. Position the funnel so that its stem reaches into a beaker placed under the ring.
7. Fill a graduated cylinder with 100 mL of water. Slowly and carefully, pour the water into the clay in the funnel. Do not splash the water or allow it to flow over the sides of the funnel or filter paper. Record how much time it takes for the water to drain out of the sample into the beaker.
8. Use the graduated cylinder to measure the amount of runoff water from the sample.
9. Dispose of the clay and runoff water as directed by your teacher.
10. Repeat steps 5–9 using sand as the sample.
11. Repeat steps 5–9 using garden soil.

Part II
12. Fill the graduated cylinder with 100 mL of water and place it under the ring.
13. Repeat step 5.
14. Place the packed funnel in the ring. The stem should be immersed several millimeters in the water. Record how long it takes for water to rise into the sample.
15. Repeat steps 12–14 using sand.
16. Repeat steps 12–14 using garden soil.
17. Clean up your materials. Wash your hands with soap and water before leaving.

Analysis and Conclusions

1. Compare the water-holding capacities of the three samples.
2. How does the water-holding capacity of soil affect the types of plants in a region?
3. What kind of root development would you expect to find in a plant that grows in soil that does not retain water well? Name a biome in which such a plant might be found.

CHAPTER REVIEW

Summary

‣ Life on Earth exists in a thin layer known as the biosphere. A dominant type of vegetation and associated animals make up a unit of the biosphere called a biome.

‣ Terrestrial biomes are determined mainly by climate. Climate is the result of temperature, precipitation, altitude, and latitude.

‣ The coldest biomes are the tundra and the taiga. Each of these regions is characterized by long, cold winters and a brief summer growing season.

‣ At middle latitudes, the growing season lasts several months of the year. Precipitation is the major factor determining the kind of biome that develops. Temperate deciduous forests receive the most rainfall and deserts receive the least. Grasslands are intermediate between the two.

‣ At the equator, year-round warm temperatures and abundant water give rise to the tropical rain forest biome. Tropical rain forests have the greatest species diversity of any biome.

‣ From the base to the top of a mountain, the sequence of biomes is like that seen moving from the equator to the poles.

‣ Aquatic biomes are classified as either fresh water or marine, depending on their salinity. The largest aquatic biome, the ocean, is about 3 percent salt. Fresh water contains almost no salt.

‣ The various zones of the marine biome reflect differences in depth, temperature, and light intensity.

‣ Fresh water may be either still or running. Some abiotic factors that vary in the freshwater biome include depth, turbidity, dissolved oxygen content, and current.

‣ Estuaries are mixtures of salt and fresh water. They are more protected than the ocean, but more nutrient-rich than rivers. They support a great variety of species.

Vocabulary

abiotic factor	pelagic zone
benthos	permafrost
biome	phytoplankton
biosphere	polar region
canopy	shrub layer
desert	sublittoral zone
emergent	succulent
epiphyte	taiga
estuary	temperate deciduous forest
grassland	temperate rain forest
herb layer	tropical rain forest
limiting factor	timberline
litter	tundra
littoral zone	understory
nekton	zooplankton

Concept Mapping

Construct a concept map for biomes. Include the following terms: aquatic, marine, fresh water, estuary, zones, standing water, terrestrial, desert, tundra, grassland, permafrost, and running water. Use additional terms as you need them.

Review

1. List three abiotic factors that determine the distribution of biomes.
2. What term describes the depths of the ocean where no light can penetrate?
3. List the following biomes in order from highest to lowest average annual temperature: tundra, temperate forest, taiga, tropical rain forest.
4. Which terrestrial biome contains the greatest diversity of species?
5. Name an adaptation that allows plants to live in the desert.
6. Name an adaptation that allows animals to live on grasslands.

7. In which biome would you expect to find a timberline?
8. Why are there no trees on a prairie?
9. Name two physical conditions that affect the distribution of organisms in the ocean.
10. Name two ways in which a stream differs from a lake.

In the following list, match the biome with the characteristic form of vegetation.

11. tundra
12. taiga
13. temperate deciduous forest
14. tropical rain forest
15. grassland
16. desert

a. broad-leaved evergreens, vines, and epiphytes
b. scattered shrubs and succulents
c. conifers
d. lichens, mosses, and low plants
e. continuous grasses
f. broad-leaved deciduous trees

Interpret and Apply

17. How is the soil of the tundra different from that of the taiga?
18. Compare the soil of the grasslands to the soil of a rain forest.
19. A kangaroo rat gets water for metabolism from the food it eats. In which biome would you expect to find this animal?
20. Compare vertical stratification in a temperate deciduous forest with that in a tropical rain forest.
21. Place the following layers in the proper sequence: (a) canopy, (b) herb layer, (c) understory, (d) litter, (e) shrub layer.
22. Why are there no phytoplankton in the abyssal zone of the ocean?
23. Compare the distribution of organisms in a deep lake with that in the ocean.

Critical Thinking

24. While hiking in the woods, you pass a dam built by a beaver on a small stream. Describe the effects the dam will have on organisms in the stream.
25. Fungi, which are decomposers, live in association with the roots of many trees in the tropical rain forest. What benefit do you think the trees get from this relationship?
26. Some mountains do not have a tundra zone. On other mountains, the tundra zone extends farther down on one side than on the other. Suggest an explanation for these differences.
27. In one sense, deserts and the littoral zone of the ocean are alike. Tropical rain forests and the ocean's abyssal zone also are alike. Explain.
28. A climatogram is a graph that represents the average monthly precipitation (bar graph) and temperature (line graph) in a region. What kind of biome is represented by the climatogram below?

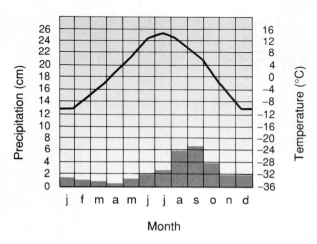

Month

Chapter

48

ECOSYSTEMS AND COMMUNITIES

Overview

LIVING COMMUNITIES
48-1 Ecosystems
48-2 Organisms in the Environment
48-3 Flow of Energy
48-4 Energy Pyramids
48-5 Symbiosis

CHANGES IN COMMUNITIES
48-6 Primary Succession
48-7 Secondary Succession

CYCLES IN THE BIOSPHERE
48-8 Water Cycle
48-9 Carbon Cycle
48-10 Nitrogen Cycle
48-11 Oxygen Cycle

How are these organisms dependent on each other?

LIVING COMMUNITIES

In a classic demonstration in biology, three test tubes are filled with water from the same source. A snail is placed in one tube, and a sprig of *Elodea* is placed in the second. Both a snail and *Elodea* are placed in the third tube. All three test tubes are capped. Before long, the organisms in the first two tubes die. Those in the third tube, however, remain healthy.

The water in all three test tubes is identical at the start of the experiment. Some factor, however, must be different. As the snail in the first tube carries out respiration, it uses up the oxygen in the tube. Without oxygen, it dies. The *Elodea* in the second tube uses up carbon dioxide as it carries out photosynthesis. It, too, eventually dies. In the third tube, however, both organisms are able to survive. As you can see, the interaction between these organisms and their environment determines their fate.

The study of interactions between organisms and their environment is called **ecology**. This lesson introduces you to some of the important concepts in ecology.

48-1 Ecosystems

You learned in the last chapter that the biosphere can be divided into units called biomes. When ecologists study organisms and the environment, they find it useful to divide the biosphere into even smaller units, known as ecosystems. An **ecosystem** is a unit of the biosphere where matter and energy are transferred as organisms interact with each other and with the environment.

Usually an ecosystem has some sort of natural boundary. For example, a single tidal pool that forms on a beach at low tide is an ecosystem. A rotting log in a forest and a meadow in the grassland biome are also ecosystems. Ecosystems may be large, like a forest, or small, like the rotting log. Even a small puddle of water filled with microorganisms and insect larvae can be considered an ecosystem.

Section Objectives

A *Describe* the characteristics of an ecosystem.

B *Identify* the role of organisms in an ecosystem.

C *Diagram* the feeding levels in food chains and food webs.

D *Explain* how a pyramid can be used to represent energy flow in a food web.

E *Give examples* of symbiosis.

■ BIOLOGY INSIGHT

Life Forms Are Interconnected: One ecosystem may overlap another. For example, birds may fly from a nearby meadow ecosystem to feed on pond insects; seeds may be blown from the edge of the pond to a nearby marsh.

Figure 48-1 Which levels of organization of living things include more than an ecosystem? Which include less?

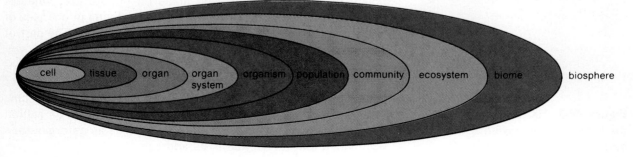

cell   tissue   organ   organ system   organism   population   community   ecosystem   biome   biosphere

Within an ecosystem are many populations of organisms. Recall that a population is composed of all the members of a given species in a particular area. All the different populations of organisms in an area make up a **community**. For example, all the plants, animals, fungi, and microorganisms in a meadow make up the community of that meadow.

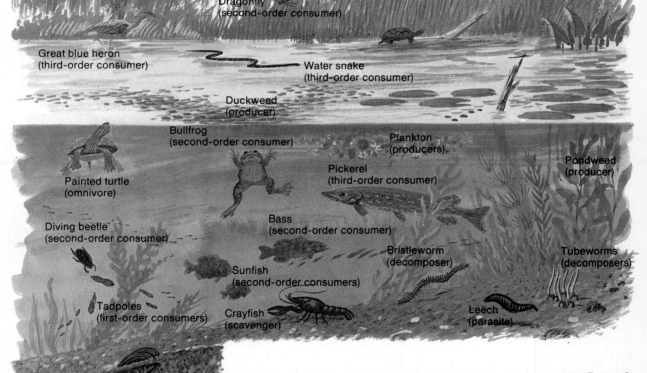

Dragonfly
(second-order consumer)

Great blue heron
(third-order consumer)

Water snake
(third-order consumer)

Duckweed
(producer)

Bullfrog
(second-order consumer)

Plankton
(producers)

Pickerel
(third-order consumer)

Pondweed
(producer)

Painted turtle
(omnivore)

Diving beetle
(second-order consumer)

Bass
(second-order consumer)

Bristleworm
(decomposer)

Tubeworms
(decomposers)

Sunfish
(second-order consumers)

Tadpoles
(first-order consumers)

Crayfish
(scavenger)

Leech
(parasite)

Mussel
(first-order consumer)

Bacteria
(decomposers)

Figure 48-2 In this ecosystem, the habitat of the crayfish is the bottom of the pond.

The pond illustrated in Figure 48-2 is an ecosystem. Rooted and floating plants, phytoplankton, fish, turtles, frogs, and small crustaceans are among the members of the pond community. Notice in the figure that each organism is found in a particular region of the pond. Duckweed floats on the surface, whereas crayfish crawl along the bottom. Organisms living in one part of an ecosystem are not normally found in other parts. The part of the ecosystem in which an organism lives is its **habitat**. As you can see in the figure, an ecosystem has many habitats.

Within its habitat, each organism has a specific role. Water lilies photosynthesize and produce food. Water snakes consume small animals. The role each organism carries out in its habitat is called its **niche**. You could think of a niche as an organism's occupation and its habitat as its address.

48-2 Organisms in the Environment

All organisms require energy for metabolism. In most ecosystems, the original source of energy is the sun. Autotrophs are able to use the sun's energy to produce their own food by the process of photosynthesis. These kinds of organisms are called **producers**. Trees and shrubs are producers. Can you identify the producers in an aquatic ecosystem?

Besides making their own food, producers provide food for all the other organisms in the ecosystem. For example, the leaves of trees are eaten by insects such as caterpillars. Organisms that get food by eating other organisms are called **consumers**.

Consumers that eat only plants are called **herbivores**. Most insects, such mammals as deer and giraffes, and some zooplankton are examples of herbivores. Many herbivores, in turn, are eaten by other animals. A caterpillar, for example, may be consumed by a bird. Animals that eat other animals are called **carnivores**. Some carnivores are *predators;* they actively hunt and kill their food. The animals that are hunted are called *prey.* Other carnivores—vultures and hyenas, for example—are *scavengers.* Scavengers feed on dead and dying animals. Some consumers, such as raccoons and bears, are **omnivores**. These animals eat both plants and animals. Humans are omnivores.

Fungi and bacteria make up a third group of organisms in the ecosystem called **decomposers**. Recall from Chapter 18 that decomposers, or saprobes, feed on dead organisms and on the wastes of living organisms. Nutrients that were tied up in living tissue are thus released into the soil, where they are again available to producers.

Figure 48-3 Nudibranchs are carnivorous mollusks. They feed on sessile organisms such as soft corals, sponges, and barnacles.

Ecosystems and Communities   **803**

Duckweed

Duckling

Snapping turtle

Figure 48-4 In a food chain, all organisms above the level of producer are consumers.

48-3 Flow of Energy

Suppose the duckweed in a pond is eaten by a duckling. The duckling is then eaten by a snapping turtle. As one organism eats another, energy is transferred. The transfer of energy from the sun through a series of organisms in an ecosystem is called a **food chain**.

Figure 48-4 illustrates the food chain just described. Notice the food chain begins with a producer, the duckweed. All succeeding levels in the food chain are made up of consumers. The duckling is a *first-order consumer*. The snapping turtle is a *second-order consumer*. What would you call an animal that eats the snapping turtle? The food chain ends when the last consumer dies and is decomposed by saprobes.

Ecosystems contain many food chains. Usually the organisms in one food chain are part of other chains as well. Consider a meadow ecosystem. One food chain might be *grass—mouse—snake—hawk*. Another food chain might be *grass—grasshopper—frog—snake*. Several interconnected food chains, such as those shown in Figure 48-5, are called a **food web**.

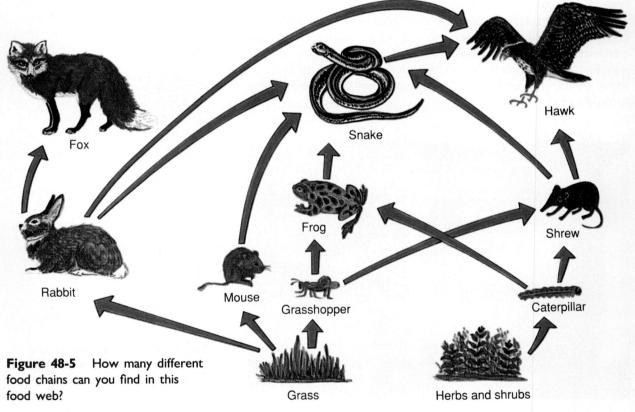

Fox

Snake

Hawk

Frog

Shrew

Rabbit

Mouse

Grasshopper

Caterpillar

Grass

Herbs and shrubs

Figure 48-5 How many different food chains can you find in this food web?

48-4 Energy Pyramids

Each time energy is transferred from one organism to another, a large fraction of the total amount is lost. An **energy pyramid**, such as the one shown in Figure 48-6, can be used to represent the transfer of energy in a food chain.

Producers (grass, for example) trap less than 2 percent of the sun's incoming energy for photosynthesis. Most of this energy is used by the plants for their metabolism. Only a small fraction is available for a first-order consumer such as a mouse. In each feeding level, most energy is lost as heat during metabolism. Only about 10 percent of the energy taken in by an organism is stored in its body. A hawk feeding at the top of the food chain, therefore, might receive only 0.1 percent of the energy stored in the grass at the bottom of the food chain.

In most ecosystems, producers are the most plentiful organisms. First-order consumers are less numerous because these organisms must eat many producers to obtain enough energy. Consumers at the top of the pyramid are fewest in number. These relationships can be represented by a *pyramid of numbers*.

Energy transfer in a food chain can also be shown by a *pyramid of biomass*. **Biomass** is a measure of the total mass of dry organic matter produced in a given area. The mass of producers is usually greater than the mass of consumers. Can you explain why this is so?

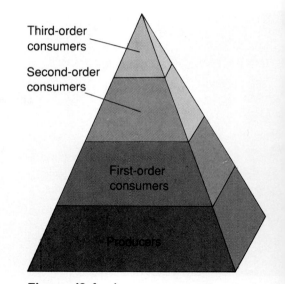

Figure 48-6 In an energy pyramid, there are fewer organisms at the top than at the bottom.

Figure 48-7 This clownfish lives among the tentacles of a sea anemone. Both organisms benefit from the association.

48-5 Symbiosis

Organisms in an ecosystem depend on other organisms for survival. Many times, the relationship between two types of organisms is very specific and permanent. Long-term interactions between two species are called **symbiosis**. Symbiosis [sim bē ō′ səs] is a Greek word meaning "living together." There are several types of symbioses.

Parasitism is a symbiotic relationship that benefits one organism and harms another. Recall that a parasite is an organism that gets its nutrition from the tissues of another organism, or host. Some parasites, such as tapeworms, live inside their host. Others, such as fleas, live on the surface of their host. Although parasites usually do not kill their hosts, they often weaken them.

Mutualism is a symbiotic relationship that is beneficial to both organisms. Lichens, which you studied in Chapter 20, are a well-known example of mutualism. Other examples of mutualism can be found in coral reef communities. Figure 48-7 shows two coral reef inhabitants—a clown fish and a sea anemone. In their mutualistic relationship, the brightly colored clown fish attracts prey to the stinging tentacles of the anemone. In return, the clownfish,

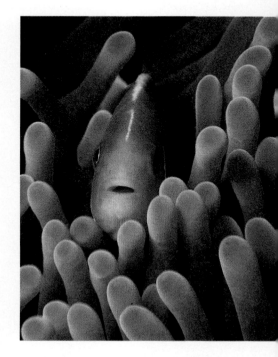

Figure 48-8 These ants will vigorously defend the acacia on which they live against any intruders. The large spikes on the acacia protect it from herbivores like giraffes.

which is immune to the anemone's deadly sting, receives shelter from its predators.

One of the most complex examples of mutualism involves a species of ant and the thorn acacia in the tropical rain forests of South America. When vines grow near the acacia, the ants cut through the stems and kill them. This prevents other plants from competing with the acacia. The ants also bite and sting intruding insects that could harm the acacia.

Acacia leaves secrete a rich solution that the ants drink. The tips of some leaves grow structures that are rich in proteins and vitamins. Adult ants collect these structures and feed them to their larvae. In the hollow thorns of the acacia, the ants lay their eggs and rear their young. The relationship between these two organisms has evolved to the point that neither could survive without the other.

Commensalism is a symbiotic relationship in which one organism benefits and the other is unaffected. Epiphytes that grow on trees in tropical rain forests are examples of commensals. Because of the lush vegetation, the rain forest floor is too dark for most plants. By growing high on the branches of trees, epiphytes can obtain enough sunlight to carry out photosynthesis. Thus the epiphyte benefits, while the host tree is neither helped nor harmed.

A second example of commensalism involves oysters and a particular species of tiny crabs. As a larva, the crab enters the mantle cavity of the oyster. The crab grows while inside the cavity until it is too large to escape. It spends its entire life sheltered by the shell of the oyster, apparently doing no significant harm to the oyster.

The relationship between sharks and remoras is another example of commensalism. A remora is a small fish that attaches itself to the underside of a shark. There it feeds on pieces of food from the shark's meals. The shark is unaffected by the presence of the remora.

CHECKPOINT ◆

1. What two things are transferred in an ecosystem?
2. What is the role of an autotroph in an ecosystem?
3. An organism that eats a producer is called a _____.
4. Which accounts for more biomass, producers or third-order consumers?
5. In which type of symbiosis do both organisms benefit?
▶ 6. Would you expect a meadow ecosystem to be able to support a fourth-order consumer? Explain.
▶ 7. A wolf that lives in the coniferous forest eats caribou and moose. Identify the wolf's niche and habitat.

▶ Denotes a question that involves *interpreting* and *applying* concepts.

CHANGES IN COMMUNITIES

Do you live near a pond or wooded area? Although it may look the same to you now as it did when you were a child, it is slowly and constantly changing. If your grandparents grew up in the same town, they may remember the area as being different.

Organisms that live in an area change the environment by their very presence. An environment that was favorable to them when they arrived may become more favorable to other life forms. Thus one type of organism may pave the way for another. The orderly change in the makeup of a community over time is called **succession**. How does succession occur? What effect does it have on the environment in a particular area?

48-6 Primary Succession

Succession occurs both on land and in the water. Figure 48-9 illustrates succession in a newly formed pond. At first, there are no living things in the pond. Eventually, algal protists and cyanobacteria invade and reproduce. These first inhabitants make up the **pioneer community**.

Heterotrophic protists and small invertebrates follow the pioneers, and small food chains begin. Organic matter builds up on the bottom of the pond. Rain carries in sediment from surrounding land, making the pond more shallow. Rooted floating plants such as pondweed and water lilies become established.

As material accumulates and the pond fills in, cattails and bullrushes replace floating plants. Larger, more complex animals become part of the pond community. Over time, the edges, and then the middle, of the pond become a marsh. The marsh may eventually fill in completely, allowing shrubs and trees to grow. Thus a terrestrial ecosystem replaces an aquatic one.

Eventually, the community in an ecosystem stops changing. The final stage of succession is called the **climax community**. A climax community has a diversity of species and complex food chains. Unlike earlier successional stages, a climax community can tolerate the environmental conditions it brings about.

The species that make up the climax community differ from one biome to another. In the temperate deciduous forest, the climax community may contain oak and hickory trees. In the taiga, spruce and fir trees may make up the climax community.

Succession in a newly formed area is called **primary succession**. Primary succession occurs in new lakes and ponds, as well as on cooled lava and bare rocks. Lichens are the first to colonize rocks. They excrete acids that help dissolve the rock. Dead lichens add organic matter. Mosses and small animals follow the

Section Objectives

F *Give examples* of the changes that occur during succession.

G *Distinguish* between primary and secondary succession.

H *Contrast* a pioneer community with a climax community.

Figure 48-9 A terrestrial ecosystem may form from succession in a pond.

Figure 48-10 Secondary succession occurred in this area after it was damaged by fire.

lichens. As soil develops, more plants grow. The community changes as succession continues.

48-7 Secondary Succession

Sometimes a storm or fire will destroy the species growing in a climax community. When this happens, succession will resume until there is a climax community again. Succession that occurs where an area has been disturbed is called **secondary succession**. For example, if a fire kills the spruce and fir trees in a coniferous forest, aspen trees will soon spring up. Later, spruce and fir trees will grow in the shade of the aspens.

Human activities often cause secondary succession to occur. Cutting forests for timber, farming, and construction destroy climax communities. If the places where these activities have taken place are then abandoned, native species usually recolonize.

Climax communities and other successional stages may be disturbed by introducing a foreign species. Human travelers bring species from one ecosystem to another, sometimes deliberately and sometimes accidentally. A species introduced to a region may become part of the existing community. Many times, though, a new species causes serious disruption, as described in Table 48-1.

Table 48-1

EFFECTS OF FOREIGN SPECIES BROUGHT TO UNITED STATES		
Species	Introduction	Result
Chestnut blight fungus	Accidental, on plant imports from Asia	Most eastern American chestnut trees destroyed
Japanese beetle	Accidental, on plants imported from Japan	Mass destruction of trees and shrubs
Sea lamprey	Accidental, through ship canal from Canada	Lake trout and whitefish in Great Lakes destroyed
Starling	Intentional, from Europe	Crop damage; replace native songbirds; form large noisy flocks

CHECKPOINT ◆

8. What organisms are found in a pond's pioneer stage?
9. Succession on a recently plowed field is called _____.
▶ 10. Which of the following would you expect to find in a climax community: cyanobacteria, duckweed, deer, prairie chickens, oak trees?
▶ 11. Why might a grassland be considered an earlier stage in succession, rather than a climax community?

▶ Denotes a question that involves *interpreting* and *applying* concepts.

CYCLES IN THE BIOSPHERE

Have you ever watched the continuous flow of water in a fountain? There seems to be an endless supply. In reality, though, the volume of water is not large. The same water is used again and again, or *recycled*.

The same situation exists on a much larger scale throughout the biosphere. Water and other substances essential to life are constantly recycled. What materials are recycled in an ecosystem? What forms do they take? The answers to these questions are important in understanding the close relationships between living things and their environment.

48-8 Water Cycle

Less than 3 percent of the water on Earth is fresh. Most of this water is frozen in the polar ice caps. Only a tiny fraction of all water is available to land organisms for metabolism. This limited supply is replenished constantly by the water cycle. This is important because water is used to combine chemically with other substances to carry out life's functions. It is more abundant in the bodies of organisms than any other compound. The **water cycle** is the movement of water between the atmosphere and Earth.

Figure 48-11 illustrates the water cycle. As with any cycle, it has no beginning or end. However, it is helpful to choose a

Figure 48-11 Without the water cycle, living things would not have a continuous supply of fresh water.

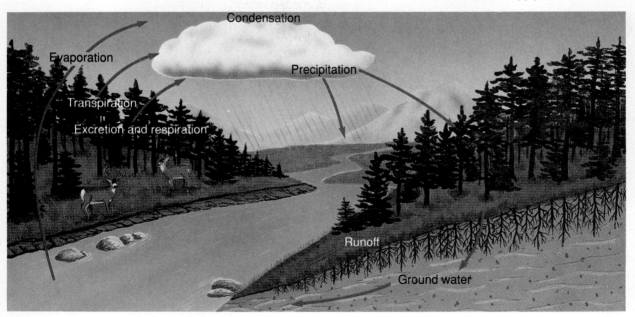
Condensation · Evaporation · Transpiration · Excretion and respiration · Precipitation · Runoff · Ground water

starting point, such as precipitation. Precipitation includes rain, snow, sleet, hail, and fog.

Some precipitation falls directly into lakes or streams. Some runs off the surface of the land into rivers. Water also filters down through the soil and flows underground. Much of the underground water eventually empties into the oceans.

Plants take water up from the ground through their roots. Some of this water is eventually returned to the air by evaporation. Recall that evaporation from the leaves of plants is called transpiration. Water is drunk by animals and then released by respiration and excretion. This water, along with water from lakes, oceans, and other bodies, also returns to the atmosphere by evaporation. Water vapor in the air condenses into clouds, and the cycle continues with precipitation.

48-9 Carbon Cycle

Carbon is a key element in organic molecules. In its inorganic form, carbon exists mainly as carbon dioxide (CO_2) gas in the air. Carbon dioxide is also dissolved in sea water. Carbon is cycled between carbon dioxide and organic molecules in living tissues by means of the **carbon cycle**, shown in Figure 48-12.

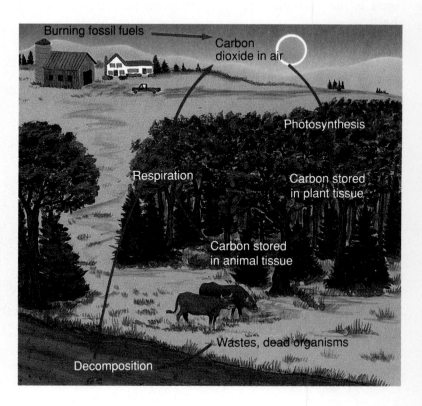

Figure 48-12 Respiration and photosynthesis are biological processes that contribute to the cycling of carbon.

Photosynthesis takes carbon from its inorganic state and transforms it into organic molecules. Some of these molecules become bound up in cells and tissues and are passed from one organism to another through food chains.

Carbon is returned to its inorganic state when organisms break down complex compounds during respiration. Decomposition of wastes and dead organisms also releases carbon dioxide.

Sometimes carbon becomes involved in longer pathways. Not all dead plants and animals decompose. Some are compressed underground for long periods. There they are converted to fossil fuels such as coal, oil, and gas. Carbon trapped in these forms is removed from circulation in the carbon cycle for a long time—as long as millions of years. When humans burn fossil fuels, they return these carbon atoms to the active carbon cycle.

48-10 Nitrogen Cycle

Nitrogen is an essential element in proteins and nucleic acids. However, nitrogen gas (N_2), which makes up 78 percent of the atmosphere, is not a form of nitrogen that is usable by most organisms. How, then, does nitrogen become part of living things?

Nitrogen for biological processes becomes available by nitrogen fixation. Nitrogen fixation may be considered the first step in the **nitrogen cycle**. Lightning causes some nitrogen fixation. Recall

Figure 48-13 Nitrogen is found in different forms in the nitrogen cycle. In what form is nitrogen found in living things?

Nitrogen gas in atmosphere (N_2)

Animals eat plants

Nitrogen fixation by lightning

Nitrogen fixation by monerans

Denitrifying bacteria release N

Plants use nitrate

Ammonification of wastes and dead organisms

Ammonium (NH_4^+)

Nitrifying bacteria

Nitrate (NO_3^-) ⟵ Nitrite (NO_2^-)

Information: Legumes often are planted to introduce ammonia into nitrogen-poor soils.

from Chapter 18, however, that most nitrogen fixation is done by monerans. Cyanobacteria, some free-living soil bacteria, and bacteria living symbiotically with certain plants convert nitrogen gas into ammonium ions (NH_4^+). Free-living nitrogen fixers release ammonium ions into soil or water. Symbiotic bacteria release ammonium ions into the roots of their host plants.

Ammonium ions are also produced by ammonification. In *ammonification*, amino acids from animal wastes and dead organisms are converted by bacteria into ammonium ions.

Although some plants can use ammonium ions directly, others can use nitrogen only in the form of nitrates (NO_3^-). *Nitrifying bacteria* convert ammonium ions into nitrate ions, which are released into the soil. Nitrification occurs in two steps. One group of bacteria converts NH_4^+ into nitrite (NO_2^-). A second group converts NO_2^- into NO_3^-. Plants then use nitrates to synthesize amino acids and proteins. Animals take in usable nitrogen by eating plants or animals that have eaten plants.

Some ammonium ions released through ammonification are used again by plants. Some is converted to nitrate. *Denitrifying bacteria* convert some nitrate into nitrogen gas, which is released into the air.

48-11 Oxygen Cycle

Like carbon and nitrogen, oxygen is cycled between the atmosphere and living things. Oxygen is used in cellular respiration. As you learned in Chapter 6, glucose reacts with oxygen to form carbon dioxide, water, and energy during this process. Water generated by this process is released as vapor. Water vapor enters the water cycle and is taken in by autotrophs for photosynthesis. During photosynthesis, carbon dioxide and water react in the presence of solar energy to yield glucose and oxygen. The release of oxygen gas to the air completes the **oxygen cycle**.

CHECKPOINT ◆

12. By what process does water in the oceans return to the atmosphere?
13. How does inorganic carbon become available to living things?
14. How does oxygen in the air become part of biological processes?
15. In what form do decomposers release nitrogen?
▶ 16. In the carbon cycle, what process can be thought of as the reverse of photosynthesis?

▶ Denotes a question that involves *interpreting* and *applying* concepts.

EXAMINATION OF NITROGEN-FIXING BACTERIA

Objective and Skill

□ *Prepare* and *observe* slides of nitrogen-fixing bacteria.

Materials

coverslip
medicine dropper
microscope
scalpel
slides
methylene blue

leguminous plant with
  roots intact
lab apron
safety goggles
mortar and pestle

Procedure and Observations

1. Read all instructions for this laboratory activity before you begin your work.
2. Put on safety goggles and lab apron. Then, place a drop of methylene blue on a microscope slide and allow it to dry.
3. Obtain a portion of the root system of a leguminous plant (clover, bean, pea, etc.) Locate the swellings, or nodules, which contain nitrogen-fixing bacteria.
4. Use the scalpel to cut off a nodule. **CAUTION: The blade of the scalpel is sharp. Be very careful when using this tool.**
5. Crush the nodule using a mortar and pestle. Then add a few drops of water and continue crushing the nodule. This makes a wet smear of the bacteria from the nodule.
6. Use the medicine dropper to obtain some of the material from the smear. Place one drop of the material on the slide containing dried methylene blue. Seal with a coverslip. Observe the slide under the microscope. As the methylene blue diffuses into the water, the bacteria should become visible. Draw the organisms you observe.

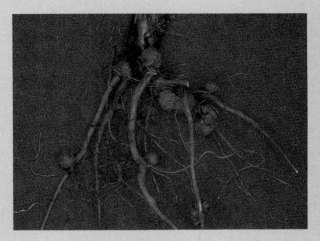

Soybean roots with nodules

7. Before leaving the laboratory, clean up all materials and wash your hands thoroughly.

Analysis and Conclusions

1. Describe the shape of the bacteria you observed. Refer to Chapter 18 to identify the type of bacteria you found.
2. The roots of the plant provide a place for the bacteria to live. What do the bacteria provide for the plant?
3. Of which type of symbiotic relationship are the bacteria and plant an example?
4. Farmers have long known that clover increases the productivity of the land on which it is grown. Modern farmers often add chemical fertilizer to the soil to increase productivity. What is one of the major components of commercial fertilizer?
5. Legumes are a good source of dietary protein. Explain why these, much more than other plants, help to meet your body's protein requirements.

Ecosystems and Communities **813**

CHAPTER REVIEW

Summary

▶ The biosphere contains many smaller units, called ecosystems, in which materials and energy are exchanged as organisms interact with each other and with the environment.

▶ Each organism has a specific habitat, or place to live, in the ecosystem. Organisms also have specific roles, or niches.

▶ The relationships among organisms in an ecosystem may be represented by food chains and food webs. The transfer of energy through food chains and webs often is represented by pyramids.

▶ Most energy is lost during the transfer from one organism to another. Therefore, each animal usually must eat many others to fulfill its energy requirement. Organisms lower in a food chain are usually far more numerous than those higher in the food chain.

▶ Organisms in an ecosystem often have specific relationships that enhance survival. These relationships are known as symbioses. In some forms of symbiosis, both species benefit. In others, one species benefits and the other is unaffected. Sometimes, one species benefits while the other is harmed.

▶ Over time, the community in an ecosystem undergoes change, or succession. Succession occurs in newly formed areas and in areas where the existing community is disturbed. Natural events, such as fires and storms, and human activities, such as construction, cause succession to occur. The final stage of succession is the climax community.

▶ Energy must be supplied to an ecosystem continuously. It cannot be reused. Matter, however, is recycled. Water, carbon, nitrogen, and oxygen are among the important materials that are recycled. These materials alternate between an inorganic state in the environment and an organic state in living things.

Vocabulary

biomass	herbivore
carbon cycle	mutualism
carnivore	niche
climax community	nitrogen cycle
commensalism	omnivore
community	oxygen cycle
consumer	parasitism
decomposer	pioneer community
ecology	primary succession
ecosystem	producer
energy pyramid	succession
food chain	secondary succession
food web	symbiosis
habitat	water cycle

Concept Mapping

Construct a concept map that illustrates the relationships among organisms in an ecosystem. Include the following terms: carnivore, community, consumer, omnivore, herbivore, producer. Add additional terms as you need them.

Review

1. By what process does energy enter a food chain?
2. By what process is organic carbon returned to the atmosphere?
3. Which organisms convert nitrogen (N_2) into a form that is biologically usable?
4. To what can a habitat and a niche be compared?
5. Approximately what percentage of the energy consumed by an animal is stored in body tissue?
6. Give an example of two organisms in a mutualistic relationship.
7. Name two ways in which water enters the atmosphere.

8. Give an example of a change that may occur during succession.
9. What form of symbiosis benefits one organism and harms the other?
10. Where are nitrogen-fixing bacteria found?
11. How does primary succession differ from secondary succession?
12. What are some of the characteristics of a climax community?

Interpret and Apply

13. How is a second-order consumer such as a fox dependent upon the energy of the sun?
14. Both mosses and bacteria live in a rotting log. Do they have the same habitat or the same niche? Explain.
15. Place the following in order from most general to most specific: consumer, heterotroph, second-order consumer, wolf.
16. List three ways in which energy is lost from an ecosystem.
17. What is the difference between a predator and a parasite?
18. Compare the carbon cycle to the flow of energy through an ecosystem. How are they related? How are they different?
19. Mistletoe is a flowering plant that grows on the branches of trees. Mistletoe must rely on its host plant for food and water. Occasionally a large number of mistletoe plants may harm their host tree. What term describes this relationship?

In the following questions, select the letter of the answer that best completes the question.

20. Which of the following processes returns carbon to the atmosphere most quickly?
    a. decomposition of dead animals
    b. formation of oil
    c. photosynthesis
    d. respiration

21. Which of the following is not the same as the others?
    a. herbivore
    b. first-order consumer
    c. second-order consumer
    d. cow

22. Which of the following would decrease the amount of CO_2 in the atmosphere?
    a. increasing the number of plants
    b. decreasing the number of plants
    c. burning of fossil fuels
    d. increasing the number of animals

23. Draw a food web showing the relationships of the following organisms: grasshopper, mouse, hawk, fox, grass, sparrow.
24. Which process in the water cycle occurs as a direct result of the sun's energy?

Critical Thinking

25. How would a food web in the tundra be similar to a food web in a rain forest? How would it be different?
26. Minnows are herbivores. Bass are carnivorous fish that often feed on minnows. Which kind of fish would you expect to be more numerous in a pond? Explain.
27. What is the basis of ocean food chains?
28. Draw a simple diagram of the oxygen cycle.
29. The first law of thermodynamics states that energy can neither be created nor destroyed. The second law of thermodynamics states that in every conversion of energy, some energy is lost as heat. Explain how these laws relate to the functioning of ecosystems.
30. Growing nonleguminous crops on the same land year after year results in plants that are less vigorous each year. Resting the land for a year by planting clover, then plowing it into the ground, improves future crops. Explain why.

Chapter

49

POPULATION DYNAMICS

Overview

POPULATION GROWTH PATTERNS
49-1 Biotic Potential
49-2 Population Growth
49-3 Population Size

ENVIRONMENTAL RESISTANCE
49-4 Density-Independent Factors
49-5 Density-Dependent Factors

THE HUMAN POPULATION
49-6 Changes in the Human Population
49-7 Predictions for the Future

Why is the giant panda disappearing from the wild?

POPULATION GROWTH PATTERNS

In many species, far more offspring are produced than can survive. Why does this occur? Simple logic reveals that any two parents could reproduce themselves with just two offspring. For many organisms, however, environmental factors prevent most offspring from surviving to a reproductive age. Thus species whose offspring are not likely to survive produce large numbers of offspring.

What factors prevent offspring from surviving? What would happen to population size if all offspring survived? As you will see, many factors affect the growth and size of populations.

49-1 Biotic Potential

Consider the following situation. A female housefly lays, on the average, 100 eggs at a time. About half of these are female. A housefly can reproduce when it is slightly less than a month old. Several generations are possible within a year.

Suppose one female fly produces 50 female offspring, each of which dies after producing her own 50 female offspring. After seven generations, the existing number of flies descended from the original female would be over 15 billion. If all the females survived to reproduce during each generation, the resulting number of flies after a year would be 4.88×10^{18}. Such runaway reproduction illustrates the biotic potential of the housefly. **Biotic potential** is the highest rate of reproduction possible for a population under ideal conditions.

Fortunately, flies do not achieve their biotic potential for any length of time, nor do other organisms. Biotic potential is kept in check by limiting factors in the environment. One limiting factor is the amount of food that is available for the flies in the environment. The amount of available living space is another factor that limits population size. The sum of all the limiting factors in the environment that prevent a population from reaching its biotic potential is called **environmental resistance**.

49-2 Population Growth

The pattern of growth of the houseflies is represented in Figure 49-1. Such growth is said to be exponential because the population grows rapidly to an infinitely high number of individuals. However, the growth of this fly population does not represent a realistic situation. It is assumed that every fly produced lives to reproduce. It is also assumed that each female lives for only one generation. These assumptions, however, do not describe real-life circumstances.

Section Objectives

A **Explain** why populations do not reach their biotic potential.

B **Discuss** the relationship between growth rate and carrying capacity.

C **List** several factors that affect population size.

Figure 49-1   The exponential growth curve is also known as a J-shaped curve. It illustrates that, if unchecked, a population would increase to an infinitely high number.

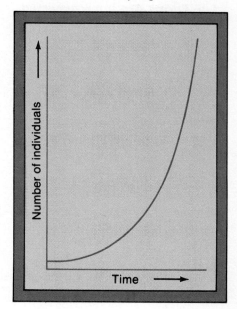

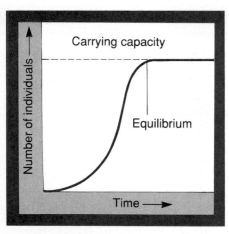

Figure 49-2 A population levels out when its numbers reach the carrying capacity of its environment. At this point, the population has reached equilibrium. How might the carrying capacity be raised?

▶ Denotes a question that involves *interpreting* and *applying* concepts.

Real populations can grow exponentially only for short periods of time. Environmental resistance sets limits on growth. Real population growth often resembles the pattern shown in Figure 49-2. Notice that the curve is *S*-shaped. Growth begins at a slow rate and then increases rapidly. The rate then slows again until the curve becomes level. This leveling of the curve means that the population has stopped growing. At this point, the population has reached the carrying capacity of its environment. **Carrying capacity** is the number of individuals of a given population that the environment can support indefinitely. At the carrying capacity, the population is gaining and losing individuals at the same rate. Thus the population has reached a state of **equilibrium**.

49-3 Population Size

The size of a population at any time depends on the balance between the rate at which individuals are added to the population and the rate at which they are removed. Population size is increased by the addition of new individuals by reproduction. The rate at which reproduction adds new individuals to the population is called the **birth rate**. This rate is usually expressed as a percentage. For example, if 300 births occur among 10 000 deer in a year, the birth rate would be 300/10 000 × 100 percent, or 3 percent.

Immigration also increases the size of a population. **Immigration** is the movement of organisms into a new area. You should recall from your history courses how the human population of North America changed as a result of immigration.

Deaths and emigration reduce the size of a population. The **death rate** is the rate at which individuals in the population die. Like the birth rate, the death rate is expressed as a percentage. **Emigration** is the movement of organisms out of an area.

If the birth rate and immigration are greater than the death rate and emigration, the population is growing. The rate at which the population is changing size is called the **growth rate**. If the rates of addition and loss are the same, the population's size is not changing. Its growth rate is zero. Can you determine what would happen to a population with a negative growth rate?

CHECKPOINT ◆

1. What is environmental resistance?
2. How does carrying capacity affect growth rate?
3. Name two factors that increase population size.
▶ 4. Suppose a population is in equilibrium and a new food source enters the environment. How might carrying capacity for the population be affected?

ENVIRONMENTAL RESISTANCE

If you have ever planted a garden, you know that the plants should be thinned after they reach a certain size. Without thinning, the plants will be crowded together and may not grow to normal size.

Each type of organism requires a certain amount of space. Some species can tolerate much more crowding than others. However, each species has its limit.

What factors limit the number of organisms in a population? In this lesson, you will learn how population growth is affected by changes in environmental conditions.

49-4 Density-Independent Factors

Many factors affect the growth rate and size of populations. Some of these factors operate whether there are a few or many individuals in the population. For example, a flood may destroy the habitat of a population of burrowing rodents. Without nesting places, the growth rate of the rodents is reduced. The effect on the population is the same whether there are 25 or 50 rodents.

The number of individuals in a population per unit area is the **population density**. Environmental conditions that affect a population regardless of its density are called **density-independent factors**. Density-independent factors are usually abiotic. Seasonal weather cycles and natural disasters such as earthquakes are examples of density-independent factors. Many human activities, such as clearing forests for agriculture, function as density-independent factors.

49-5 Density-Dependent Factors

As a population increases in size, its density begins to affect its growth rate. For example, diatoms grown in a laboratory culture increase in number very quickly until crowding decreases the light available for photosynthesis. At the same time, their waste products accumulate and interfere with metabolism. As a result, the growth rate of the population is reduced. If sessile animals are so crowded that they do not receive enough food, their reproductive rate is reduced. Factors that affect population growth as a result of density are called **density-dependent factors**.

Density-dependent factors usually affect populations that are close to or over the carrying capacity for their environment. However, these factors also affect some populations with a low density. Oysters are an example of this type of population. Young oysters must spend part of their development attached to a hard

Section Objectives

D **Name** several density-independent factors that limit population growth.

E **Give examples** of factors that are density-dependent.

F **Explain** how prey-predator relationships help to regulate population growth.

G **Distinguish** between interspecific and intraspecific competition.

Figure 49-3 A high population density is a problem for sessile organisms such as mussels and barnacles which cannot move around in search of food and other resources.

object, usually another oyster. If oysters are scarce, younger oysters cannot develop.

Other populations, such as whales, require a certain minimum population density to support a normal rate of reproduction. If the population is too small, individuals have a difficult time finding mates.

Disease At high densities, physical contact between individuals increases. Close physical contact makes it easier for pathogens and parasites to spread from one host to another. You have probably noticed, for example, that colds and the flu spread easily during the winter. These diseases spread because people are crowded together indoors. While colds are not usually serious, different flu epidemics have killed millions of people.

Stress Animals crowded together show increased levels of stress. As a result, they may behave abnormally. For example, crowding among mice causes them to neglect their young. This neglect causes the death rate to increase.

In some animal populations, stress causes increased aggression. Stress also causes hormonal changes that decrease fertility. Thus growth rate is reduced.

Predation Population growth is also limited by interactions between predators and prey. Consider, for example, the relationship between the snowshoe hare and its predator, the Canada lynx. As you can see in Figure 49-4, the growth of these populations shows a cyclic pattern. The hare population increases, and after a brief lag, the lynx population also increases since more food is available. The carrying capacity for the lynx population has been increased.

With increased predation, the prey population decreases. This, in turn, limits the predator population since less food is available. With reduced predation, the prey population begins to grow and the cycle is repeated.

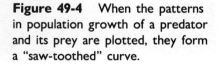

BIOLOGY INSIGHT

Life Forms Are Interconnected: When one animal eats another, the prey is killed. When an animal eats a plant, however, part of the plant usually survives and grows new parts, such as leaves. Thus predation on plants does not necessarily remove individuals from the population.

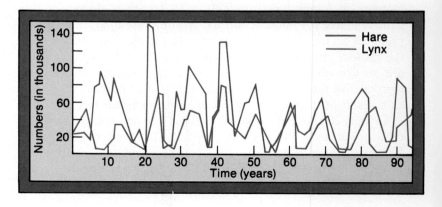

Figure 49-4 When the patterns in population growth of a predator and its prey are plotted, they form a "saw-toothed" curve.

Although predation is a limiting factor, it is not the only one that keeps a prey population below its carrying capacity. In the example of the lynx and hare, recent studies have shown that the hare population also rises and falls in regions where the lynx is not present. Why does this happen? The size of the hare population depends mainly on the amount of available food. It has been found that some of the plants eaten by hares will produce toxic substances when the plants are overgrazed. Therefore, when the hares exceed the carrying capacity, they die of starvation or are poisoned by their food source. The size of the population then decreases.

Competition Often two types of organisms require similar resources from the environment, such as food, water, or space. When two species require the same resources, they are competing with each other to meet their needs. Competition between different species is called **interspecific competition**.

Recall from Chapter 48 that each species has a particular niche. No two species can occupy exactly the same niche. One of the two competitors will be better adapted and will survive. The less successful species will die out. This is known as the **competitive exclusion principle**.

Competition for resources can also occur within a population. This situation is known as **intraspecific competition**. Intraspecific competition is usually more intense than interspecific competition. Can you explain why this is so? Intraspecific competition may cause some members of a population to emigrate. In other populations, intraspecific competition causes stress and reduced health. As a result, the reproductive rate declines. Recall that in some species, territoriality and dominance hierarchies reduce intraspecific competition. Only individuals with territories or in a dominant position have access to limited resources. Can you explain what effect this has on population size?

Figure 49-5 Several species cannot exist in the same habitat using exactly the same limiting resources. The three species of warblers shown here are adapted to obtain food at a different level on the tree. Close examination of species that appear to be using the same resources usually shows there are slight structural, physiological, or behavioral differences among them.

CHECKPOINT ◆

5. Give an example of a density-independent factor that limits population growth.
6. Name two factors that limit population growth in response to density.
7. In a small meadow, toads and birds prey on some of the same insects. What type of competition is this?
▶ 8. In many areas, humans have eliminated predators such as wolves or mountain lions. What do you think happened to the populations of prey species, such as deer, in these areas?

▶ Denotes a question that involves *interpreting* and *applying* concepts.

Section Objectives

H *Give reasons* for the high growth rate of the human population.

I *Contrast* the growth rates of populations that have undergone demographic transition with those of populations that have not.

J *Discuss* the importance of uncontrolled population growth in terms of carrying capacity.

DO YOU KNOW?

Information: Changes in the environment can change the carrying capacity and, therefore, the point of equilibrium in the growth curve. An example of an environmental change might be the accumulation of toxic wastes.

BIOLOGY INSIGHT

Adaptation and Evolution: Traditionally, a high birth rate has been necessary to ensure the survival of at least a few offspring. With the advent of modern hygiene, agriculture, and medicine, the odds for survival have been increased. Thus fewer children are necessary to ensure the survival of the species.

Although *Homo sapiens* appeared only about 50 000 years ago, the number of humans on Earth numbered 5.3 million by 8000 B.C. The population reached about 200 million during the Roman Empire. Today there are over 5 billion humans on Earth.

The fact that the population grew to such high numbers is impressive. Even more impressive, though, is the rate of increase. It took all of prehistory and the period of history up until 1832 before there were 1 billion humans on Earth. Yet little more than 150 years were needed to add another 4 billion people to the human population.

How have humans managed to achieve such high rates of growth? How much longer can growth continue before the carrying capacity of Earth is reached? The answers to these questions are important to the quality of human life now and in the future.

49-6 Changes in the Human Population

Early human societies survived by hunting and gathering. Limited food resources, disease, and other environmental factors kept population growth at a low level. With the development of agriculture and the domestication of animals, though, food became abundant. Thus the carrying capacity was increased. The human population began to grow rapidly.

Rapid growth of the human population can be explained by the process of demographic transition. In **demographic transition**, the growth rate changes in relation to social and economic progress. There are three identifiable stages in the transition. In the first stage, birth rate and death rate are high so the population grows very slowly or not at all. This stage is typical of early hunting and gathering societies.

Societies move into the second stage with improvements in living conditions. Increased food production, advances in medicine, and improved sanitation, for example, allow more children to survive into adulthood. Thus the second stage has a greatly reduced death rate. However, the birth rate is still high so the population grows rapidly.

A higher standard of living and a reduced infant death rate usually lead families to have fewer children. This is the third stage of demographic transition. Birth rate and death rate become balanced at a lower level. Population size becomes stable.

Over the last 100 years, most industrialized nations have undergone a transition to the third stage. In nonindustrialized, or developing, countries, however, the situation is different. The use of vaccines and antibiotics brought about a decline in the death rate. Medicine and other improvements allowed many developing nations to move into the second stage. Unfortunately, the economic gains needed for transition to the third stage have not occurred. Thus nonindustrialized countries have become stuck in the second stage. This "demographic trap" has serious consequences for population growth.

49-7 Predictions for the Future

At present, the average yearly rate of population growth is 2 percent. This means that 20 people are born each year for every 1000 already alive. At this rate, the population will double in just 35 years. This time period is called the **doubling time**. The value for doubling time is not fixed. Over the last 150 years, the doubling time has steadily decreased. If the current growth rate continues, by the year 2000 there will be over 6 billion humans on Earth.

There is some disagreement over how many people Earth can support. Most scientists agree, however, that there is an upper limit. Industrialized nations have used technology to raise the carrying capacity of their environments. But technology cannot extend carrying capacity indefinitely. Look at Figure 49-6. When will humans reach the carrying capacity of Earth?

Many developing countries have already reached or exceeded the carrying capacity of their environments. Water, soil, and other resources on which life depends are being destroyed by rapidly growing populations. Great numbers of people in India and Latin America, for example, have become trapped in a cycle of poverty, population growth, and environmental destruction.

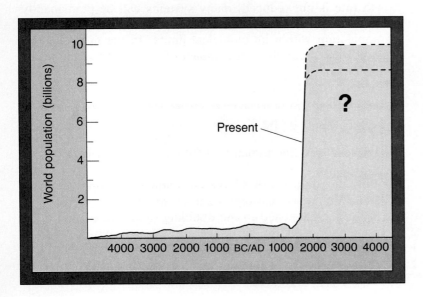

Figure 49-6 The exponential growth of the human population is shown. It is estimated that there were only 10 million people worldwide 10 000 years ago. Note the slight dip after 1000 A.D. This represents the loss of 75 million Europeans to the bubonic plague, or Black Death, between 1347 and 1351. What does the future hold? The question mark indicates that the size of human population may level off at 9 or 10 billion.

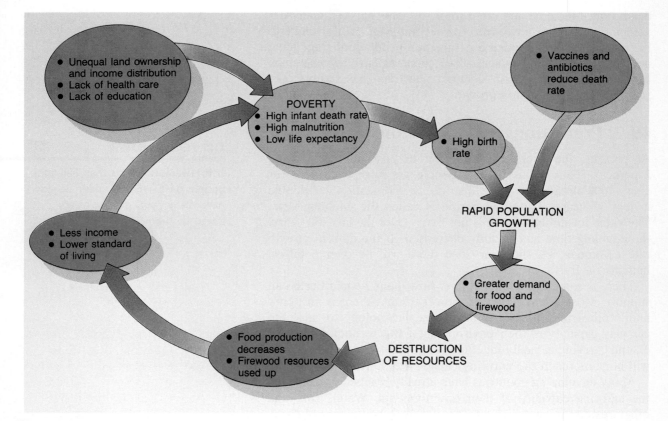

- Unequal land ownership and income distribution
- Lack of health care
- Lack of education

POVERTY
- High infant death rate
- High malnutrition
- Low life expectancy

- High birth rate

- Vaccines and antibiotics reduce death rate

RAPID POPULATION GROWTH

- Greater demand for food and firewood

DESTRUCTION OF RESOURCES

- Food production decreases
- Firewood resources used up

- Less income
- Lower standard of living

Figure 49-7 In developing countries, the infant death rate is high, family farming and other survival activities require much labor, and parents depend on their children for support during old age. From this viewpoint, large families are considered advantageous.

Population growth in both industrialized and developing nations is greatly stressing environmental life-support systems. If the growth rate is not reduced, many systems will be permanently destroyed. At that point, only an increased death rate will keep the population within its biological limits. In the next chapter, you will learn more about the impact of human activities on the environment.

CHECKPOINT ◆

9. Explain why the human population has such a high growth rate.
10. Why do countries that have not completed demographic transition have such high rates of growth?
11. What has happened to the doubling time of the human population over the past several thousand years?
▶ 12. In which countries is doubling time shortest?
▶ 13. Has the human population reached Earth's carrying capacity yet? Explain.

▶ Denotes a question that involves *interpreting* and *applying* concepts.

LABORATORY ACTIVITY

EFFECT OF DIFFERENT REPRODUCTIVE PATTERNS ON POPULATION SIZE

Objective and Skill

□ *Demonstrate mathematically* the effect of early reproduction on population size.

Materials

white beans
black beans
1 250-mL beaker

Procedure and Observations

1. Read all the instructions for this laboratory activity before you begin your work.
2. On a separate sheet of paper, draw a data table.
3. Consider a situation in which two species have different reproductive patterns. In one species, each female produces ten offspring when she is a year old and does not reproduce again. Half of the offspring are female and half are male. In the second species, each female reproduces yearly until she is five. Each year she produces two offspring, one of which is female.
4. Use the white beans to represent females and the black beans to represent males. Place one white bean and one black bean in the beaker. Then add another five white beans and five black beans. These represent the parents and first generation of offspring of species 1.
5. Remove beans that represent the parents and all the male offspring. Record the remaining number of individuals under year 1 in your data.
6. For each female, add ten offspring (half female, half male) to the beaker. Remove beans that represent the original females

and all the male offspring. Record the remaining number of individuals under year 2.
7. Repeat step 6 to obtain population data for a third generation.
8. Return the beans to their containers. You will use them again to simulate population growth of species 2.
9. Place one white bean and one black bean in the beaker to represent the first set of parents. To represent the first generation of offspring, add one white bean and one black bean to the beaker. Remove the males and record the remaining number under year 1. Do not remove the original female, who will continue to produce for four more years.
10. For each of the two females in the beaker, add two offspring, one female and one male. Again remove the males, but not the female parents. Record the population under year 2.
11. Repeat step 10 to obtain population data for a third generation.

Analysis and Conclusions

1. What is the pattern of increase for each species?
2. Calculate what the population size of each species will be after five years.
3. For each of these species, a given female has ten offspring. Yet the two species do not have the same population size even though they each started with a single set of parents. Explain why this is so.
4. Over a century ago, the English economist Thomas Malthus stated that the overpopulation problem could be solved by late marriage and childbearing. Was he correct? Explain.

CHAPTER REVIEW

Summary

▸ Each species has certain reproductive characteristics. These include how often reproduction occurs, how long the reproductive life of an individual lasts, and how many young are produced at a time. Not all the young of a species survive long enough to reproduce.

▸ Real populations grow exponentially for short periods due to environmental resistance. Exponential growth stops when a population reaches the carrying capacity of its environment.

▸ The size of a population at a given time is determined by its growth rate. Growth rate is determined by four factors: birth rate, immigration, death rate, and emigration.

▸ Many factors, such as natural disasters, limit population growth. These factors act independently of the population density.

▸ Environmental resistance often depends on population density. Crowding of organisms can reduce available nutrients, allow the spread of disease, and interfere with reproduction.

▸ Predator–prey relationships regulate population growth and size. The size of one population influences the size of the other.

▸ Competition for an environment's limited resources occurs between members of a population and between different species in an area. Competition also limits population size.

▸ Humans are unique in their ability to modify the carrying capacity of their environment in their favor. Human population growth is currently exponential. The doubling time for the human population is still decreasing.

▸ Most scientists agree that it is only a matter of time before humans will be unable to increase Earth's carrying capacity any further. At that point, either the birth rate must fall, or the death rate must rise.

Vocabulary

biotic potential
birth rate
carrying capacity
competitive exclusion principle
death rate
demographic transition
density-dependent factor
density-independent factor
doubling time
emigration
environmental resistance
equilibrium
growth rate
immigration
interspecific competition
intraspecific competition
population density

Concept Mapping

Construct a concept map for populations. Include the following terms: biotic potential, birth rate, death rate, density-dependent factor, density-independent factor, emigration, environmental resistance, growth rate, and immigration. Use additional terms as you need them.

Review

1. What is the name given to the environmental forces that prevent organisms from reaching their biotic potential?
2. What is the point of the growth curve at which the population gains individuals at the same rate as it loses individuals?
3. What effect does a high birth rate have upon population size?
4. What four components determine the growth rate of a population?
5. Name two density-independent factors
6. How does the size of a prey population affect the carrying capacity of a predator?
7. How does a low density of whales in an area affect whale population growth?

8. Name two density-dependent factors that limit a population.
9. Name three factors that have minimized traditional controls on the size of the human population.
10. Which part of the demographic transition has not yet occurred in nonindustrial countries?
11. When is the human population expected to double in size?
12. How is parasitism affected by population density?

Interpret and Apply

13. What factors prevent a population from growing exponentially for any length of time?
14. How are population equilibrium and carrying capacity related?
15. What is the relationship between carrying capacity and the number of different populations in the same environment?
16. How does an exponential growth curve differ from a real growth curve?
17. What is the relationship between interspecific competition and the competitive exclusion principle?
18. The timber wolf, once plentiful in the United States, is now quite rare as a result of extermination by humans. What kind of growth-limiting factor was involved?
19. If the sum of immigration and birth rate is greater than the sum of emigration and death rate, what happens to the rate of population growth?
20. Suppose that a deadly, highly contagious disease breaks out worldwide. There are no cures or preventive measures available. What will happen to the growth rate of the human population?

Critical Thinking

21. Suppose a single female rabbit produces six offspring. These six rabbits are the second generation. If half of the rabbits produced in each generation are female and go on to produce six offspring, how many rabbits will be in the population by the fourth generation? Each female reproduces for one generation only.
22. How might an increase in the lynx population affect the population of plants on which snowshoe hares feed?
23. Suppose there are 500 blackbirds living in a marsh. The population is growing at a rate of 10 percent per year. What will the size of the population be after 5 years?
24. The three diagrams below represent hypothetical populations. In which population will the growth rate increase? In which will the growth rate decrease? In which is the population in equilibrium?

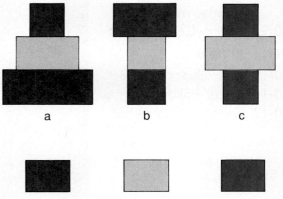

a   b   c

Postreproductive   Reproductive   Prereproductive

Chapter

50

HUMAN IMPACT ON THE BIOSPHERE

Overview

NATURAL RESOURCES

50-1   Soil
50-2   Water
50-3   Wildlife
50-4   Forests

ENERGY RESOURCES

50-5   Nuclear Energy
50-6   Solar Energy
50-7   Biomass Energy
50-8   Wind, Water, and
       Geothermal Energy
50-9   Energy Conservation

POLLUTION

50-10 Air Pollution
50-11 Water Pollution
50-12 Other Pollutants

Can energy needs be met while preserving the environment?

NATURAL RESOURCES

Throughout history, humans have depended on Earth for all the raw materials needed to survive. Materials that are necessary for life or that are used to make other products are called **natural resources**. Some natural resources are **renewable**, that is, they are replaced over time by natural processes. Fish are an example of a renewable resource. As long as the size of the breeding population does not become too small, the supply of fish available for consumption will be constant.

Other natural resources, such as metal ores, are **nonrenewable**. Once these resources have been removed from the ground, they cannot be replaced. However, some nonrenewable resources, such as aluminum, can be recycled.

Until recently, natural resources were relatively abundant. Lumber and fuel came in seemingly endless supplies from vast forests. Lakes and rivers provided clean drinking water and energy. Large populations of game animals roamed freely on fertile grasslands that, in turn, could be used to grow crops.

Now, however, the supply of natural resources is shrinking. Some of these resources are in danger of disappearing completely. A rapidly expanding population is one cause of diminishing supplies. Another cause is the way in which humans use resources. In this lesson, you will become familiar with some of the natural resources on which social and economic systems depend. You will also examine how the current uses of these resources affect their availability.

50-1 Soil

Soil is a complex mixture of tiny particles of rock, decaying organic materials, and microorganisms. The size of the rock particles and the amount of decaying materials determine the properties of the soil. These include how rich in nutrients the soil is, how much water it holds, and how much air space it contains. The properties of soil determine what can grow in it.

Soil is formed over centuries. Rock is worn away, forming the inorganic portion of the soil. The action of decomposers gradually adds organic matter, making the soil more able to support plant life. Although soil forms very slowly, it is a renewable resource.

Soil is threatened by activities that speed up **erosion**, or wearing away by wind or water. Careful farming practices can help protect soil from erosion. Contour plowing, strip cropping, planting cover crops, and terracing are techniques farmers use to reduce or prevent erosion.

Section Objectives

A **Identify** important natural resources.

B **Distinguish** between renewable and nonrenewable resources.

C **Explain** how human activities endanger natural resources.

D **Give examples** of methods to preserve natural resources.

BIOLOGY INSIGHT

Life Forms Are Interconnected: An estimated 4 billion tons of eroded soil enter streams in the United States each year. By volume, sediment is the largest water pollutant. Sediment makes water cloudy, decreasing the amount of light available for photosynthesis. Sediment also makes it difficult for aquatic animals to breathe.

Impact on the Biosphere **829**

Figure 50-1 Plowing and planting patterns are important in preventing erosion.

DO YOU KNOW?

Word Root: *Aquifer* derives from the Latin *aqua*, meaning "water," and the Latin *ferre*, meaning "to carry or bear."

DO YOU KNOW?

Information: A running faucet allows up to 20 liters of water to flow down the drain in a minute.

In **contour plowing**, rows are plowed at right angles to the slope of the land. Each row thus acts as a miniature dam. Runoff water is trapped in shallow grooves, or furrows, between the rows. With less water washing across the land, less soil is carried away.

In **strip cropping**, rows of grasses, such as hay, are alternated with rows of other crops, such as vegetables. Runoff from vegetable rows is caught by the rows of grasses. Often, strip cropping and contour plowing are done together.

After harvesting their crops, farmers often plant **cover crops** to protect the soil from the impact of rain. The roots of cover crops help to hold the soil in place. (Bare soil is more vulnerable to erosion than is soil covered with plants.) Cover crops are not harvested. They are plowed under, thus adding nutrients to the soil.

On hilly land, which would erode more quickly than flat land, farmers practice terracing. **Terracing** is the building of steps in the hillside. Grass is planted on the slopes between the steps, and crops are grown on the leveled surfaces. This practice is common in the hilly regions of the Far East.

When a piece of land is planted with the same crop year after year, nutrients in the soil are used up. To maintain soil fertility, farmers practice crop rotation. In **crop rotation**, farmers alternate plantings of crops that take a lot of nitrogen from the soil with plants that add nitrogen to the soil. Legumes such as soybeans, alfalfa, and clover are particularly important in crop rotation. The nitrogen-fixing bacteria in their roots add usable nitrogen to the soil and increase its fertility.

50-2 Water

Recall from Chapter 48 that fresh water is supplied through the water cycle. Thus water is a renewable resource. Water for domestic and industrial uses comes either from surface water, such as lakes and rivers, or from aquifers. An **aquifer** is a deep, underground water supply that has accumulated over a long period.

Humans use water for drinking, washing, waste disposal, irrigation of crops, and the manufacture of many products. As long as the amount of water used does not exceed the amount generated by natural processes, the water supply will remain renewable. Unfortunately, human activities seriously threaten this resource.

In the United States, for example, far more water is drawn from aquifers than can be replaced by the water cycle each day. In addition, the quality of water supplies is being reduced. Salt from icy highways, sediment from erosion, and farm and lawn chemicals contaminate water supplies. Many industries release toxic chemical wastes into rivers and streams. Cities and towns dump sewage into bodies of water. Contamination of water resources is discussed later in this chapter.

There are ways, however, to protect and conserve water resources. One way is *gray-water recycling*, in which water from bathing and laundering is reused in toilets. (The flush toilet is the single largest use of water in the home.) Clean water would not have to be used in flushing. Limiting the amount of wastes released by industries would also protect water supplies. And improvements in sewage treatment processes can reduce the amount of poisonous chemicals used to disinfect wastewater. In many cities, the solid part of sewage is extracted and recycled for fertilizer.

50-3 Wildlife

At one time, humans depended completely on wild plants and animals for food and clothing. Today, wildlife still represents an important natural resource. Wildlife provides food, hides, and other products. Wildlife also has recreational and artistic value.

Beyond their value to humans, wild plants and animals are parts of ecosystems. They have complex relationships with each other and the environment. Each species also contributes to the genetic diversity of the biosphere.

Human activities, however, have brought many species close to extinction. **Extinction**, or the disappearance of species from Earth, is a continuously occurring process. Species have been evolving and becoming extinct since life began. But humans have increased the rate at which extinction occurs.

The largest cause of extinction is habitat destruction. Habitat destruction occurs when people clear land for agriculture, construction, and other purposes. Plants and animals cannot survive when their habitats have been destroyed. When a species becomes extinct, its genes and the potential resources they represent are lost forever.

There are many approaches that can be taken to save a species from extinction. One is the establishment of **refuges**, areas in which wildlife is legally protected. The establishment of refuges has saved the whooping crane from extinction. Once plentiful in much of North America, these marsh birds became rare as their habitats were destroyed for farming. By the 1960s, there were only 50 whooping cranes left. Whooping cranes now nest in the Wood Buffalo National Park in northwestern Canada. They winter in the Arkansas National Wildlife Refuge in Texas. The governments of Canada and the United States have cooperated in saving this bird.

Captive breeding programs have also been successful in saving endangered species. Captive breeding programs are often carried

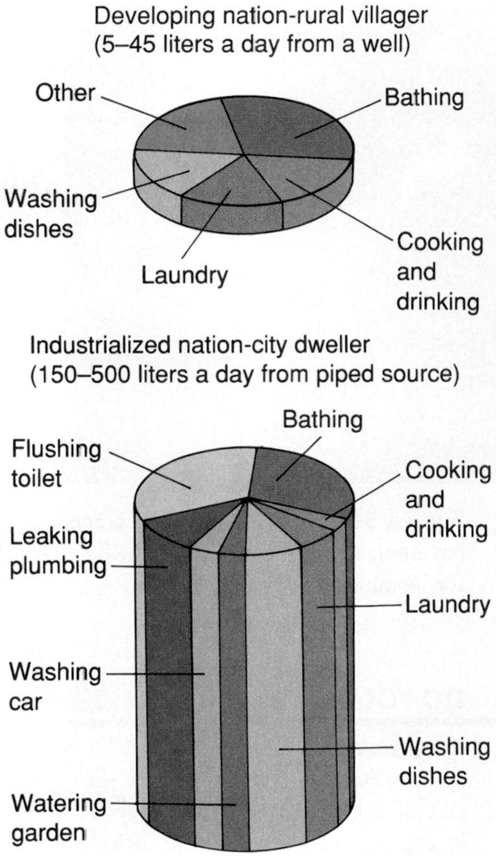

Developing nation-rural villager
(5–45 liters a day from a well)

Other / Bathing / Washing dishes / Laundry / Cooking and drinking

Industrialized nation-city dweller
(150–500 liters a day from piped source)

Flushing toilet / Bathing / Cooking and drinking / Leaking plumbing / Laundry / Washing car / Washing dishes / Watering garden

Figure 50-2 Water use is much higher in countries that have piped water than in countries that do not. In some developing countries, people may walk as far as 2 km to get water each day.

■ **BIOLOGY INSIGHT**

Continuity of Life: The genetic resources in wildlife are like a well-stocked library. Billions of different traits are represented by all the different organisms on Earth. This genetic library contains the information needed for survival in response to changing environmental conditions.

Figure 50-3 The whooping crane has been saved from extinction by the establishment of refuges.

out in zoos and aquariums. Animals born in captivity may eventually be released in their native habitats. Endangered plants may be protected and bred in botanical gardens. In some places, survival centers have been set up to preserve endangered and rare breeds of farm animals.

Restrictions on hunting and on the trade in wildlife products also protect animals and plants from extinction. For example, many species of whales have been hunted almost into nonexistence. International pressure has forced many whaling nations to reduce or stop their whale harvest. Cheap substitutes for whale oil have also helped reduce the threat to different whale species. Unfortunately, a few countries have refused to give up the hunt.

50-4 Forests

Forests are spread over about 30 percent of Earth's land surface. Compared with other ecological zones, forests have more biomass and support the greatest number of plant and animal species. Thus forests contain the greatest amount of genetic diversity. They are the main sites where new species develop. Forests also play a major role in the cycling of carbon, nitrogen, and oxygen.

Wood is the primary resource taken from forests. It is used as a raw material for many products, such as paper and construction materials. In many parts of the world, wood is a major fuel.

As the human population grows, forest resources become increasingly threatened. In poor tropical countries, demand for farmland is the chief cause of forest destruction. In other developing countries, destruction of forests is caused mainly by the need for firewood. Recall from Chapter 47 that destruction of forests causes desertification.

Fortunately, many people have begun to recognize the value of forests. In North America, new trees are planted to replace the ones taken for lumber and other products. Recycling paper products can save thousands of trees. In developing countries, programs to help local people plant trees are being set up. However, other methods that address the needs of a growing population must also be used to relieve the stress on forests.

CHECKPOINT ◆

1. Name three natural resources.
2. Which of the following are renewable resources: soil, aluminum, wood, water, iron?
3. What effects do human activities have on water supplies?
4. Describe two practices used by farmers to preserve soil.
▶ 5. Is air a renewable resource? Explain.

ENERGY RESOURCES

Economic and cultural activities depend on energy as well as on raw materials. Each time you switch on a light or the television, you use energy. All the machines and electronic devices used by industrial societies need an energy source to work. Modern agriculture also uses huge amounts of energy to produce farm chemicals and to power farm equipment.

In industrialized nations, the majority of energy comes from fossil fuels. **Fossil fuels** are the remains of organisms compressed underground for millions of years. Oil, coal, and natural gas are fossil fuels.

Fossil fuels, which are nonrenewable resources, are being consumed rapidly. As a result, supplies of these materials are being depleted. What other sources of energy are available? Why is it important to develop alternatives to fossil fuels? As you read about the answers to these questions, think of the ways in which your life would change without a reliable source of energy.

50-5 Nuclear Energy

As fossil fuel supplies are used up, interest in alternative energy sources grows. For many years, it was thought that much of society's energy needs would be met by nuclear fission. In **nuclear fission**, heat energy is released from the splitting of atoms. The heat is then used to produce hot water or steam, which runs turbines connected to electrical generators.

Although there are abundant supplies of uranium for fuel, many countries have decided to reduce or eliminate their nuclear energy programs. The fission process creates wastes that are dangerously radioactive for thousands of years. No permanent, safe method of disposal for nuclear wastes has yet been developed.

The safety of nuclear reactors is also in doubt. In 1986, an explosion and fire occurred at one of the reactors at Chernobyl in the Soviet Union. This led to the worst accident in the history of nuclear power. Many deaths and injuries resulted. Over 100 000 people had to be evacuated from their homes. Winds carried radioactive fallout over much of Europe.

Public opposition, high costs, and technical problems also have led to a decline in the demand for nuclear power.

50-6 Solar Energy

The sun's energy reaches Earth continuously. This energy can be captured and converted into electrical energy by **photovoltaic cells**. When light strikes a photovoltaic cell, electrons are released,

DO YOU KNOW?

Information: The United States makes up just one twentieth of the world's population but uses one third of the world's energy resources.

Figure 50-4 The nuclear industry has a relatively short but troubled history.

Figure 50-5 This commercial power plant is fueled by solar energy. In the years to come, solar energy will become a more commonly used energy source.

producing an electric current. These devices are still too expensive for widespread use. However, scientists predict that production of electricity using photovoltaic cells eventually will be competitive with traditional energy production.

Solar energy can be used to heat homes. You may have seen solar panels on the roofs of some houses. The panels concentrate diffuse solar energy, using it to heat water. The hot water flows through pipes in the walls and gives off heat to different rooms in the house. Hot water for washing is also generated by the system. Naturally, solar heating is more efficient in warmer climates than in colder ones.

50-7 Biomass Energy

Over two billion people, most of them in developing countries, depend on biomass as their main energy source. **Biomass energy** is the energy stored in organic matter as a result of photosynthesis. Biomass energy sources include wood, animal wastes, and plant wastes left after harvest.

Developing countries are faced with a serious shortage of firewood for cooking food, purifying water, and heating homes. Fortunately, wood is a renewable resource. Both China and South Korea, for example, have begun successful reforesting programs. Other countries are experimenting with fuelwood plantations to produce fast-growing trees. A new approach to reforesting is the development of village woodlots. Trees planted on community or private land provide wood products for village use.

Biomass energy can be generated by fermenting farm animal, human, and plant wastes. The fermentation process yields methane gas that can be burned to produce heat, light, or electricity. Leftover solid material can be used as fertilizer. Ethanol, another fuel, can be made by fermenting plant wastes.

50-8 Wind, Water, and Geothermal Energy

In open areas with moderate to strong winds, energy can be generated using windmills. Wind energy is converted into mechanical and electrical energy in the turbine of a windmill. Clusters of windmills are called wind farms. Windmills are also used to do mechanical work, such as pumping water for agriculture.

Electricity can be generated from flowing or falling water. You are probably aware of large hydroelectric plants like the one at Hoover dam on the Colorado river. Energy in ocean currents and tides can also be used to produce electricity.

Geothermal energy takes advantage of the heat in Earth's interior. Geothermal plants use this heat to produce hot water or steam for direct use or to power turbines for electrical generation. Over 130 geothermal plants are in operation around the world.

50-9 Energy Conservation

Developing new sources of energy is one way to meet the world's energy needs. **Conservation**, or managing existing resources, is another way to make sure energy supplies will be available.

New technologies have greatly improved energy efficiency over the last decade. Modern household appliances use much less energy than do similar, older appliances. Today's cars are smaller, lighter, and more fuel efficient than earlier models. The use of plastics and ceramics in cars will further improve fuel efficiency. Insulation is built into most new buildings and homes, reducing the amount of fuel needed for heating and cooling.

Cogeneration is another way to conserve energy. In **cogeneration**, waste heat or electricity from one process is used in another process. For example, electrical generation produces waste heat in the form of steam. The steam can be used by nearby industries for manufacturing or to heat buildings. On the other hand, some industries create waste electricity when they generate steam for certain processes. The electricity can be used as a power source. Increased use of cogeneration could save thousands of barrels of oil a day.

Recycling materials saves huge amounts of energy. The amount of energy saved by recycling is shown in Table 50-1.

Figure 50-6 Windmills generate both electrical and mechanical energy.

Table 50-1

ENERGY SAVED BY RECYCLING	
Material	**Energy Saved (%)**
Aluminum	90–97
Glass	4–32
Paper	23–74
Steel	47–74

CHECKPOINT ◆

6. Name three ways to generate electricity.
7. Is methane gas a renewable or nonrenewable energy source?
8. Give two examples of energy conservation practices.
▶ 9. Can energy be recycled? Explain.

▶ Denotes a question that involves *interpreting* and *applying* concepts.

POLLUTION

DO YOU KNOW?

Information: Smog has decreased about 10 percent in the last decade, as a result of pollution-control practices.

Figure 50-7 Motor vehicles are a major source of air pollution. Improved mass transportation systems would reduce dependence on personal vehicles and cut down on smog and other pollution.

Today you may have driven rather than walked five blocks to the store. You may have eaten a fast-food hamburger served in a foam package. In either case, it probably did not occur to you that you were contributing to **pollution**, an unfavorable change in the environment. Such activities and so many other things you do each day are potentially harmful to your surroundings. Imagine the combined effects of millions of people doing the same harmful activities that you do.

What are some of the ways in which humans pollute the environment? What steps can be taken to reduce the amount of pollution?

50-10 Air Pollution

Harmful solid particles and gases are released into the air as a result of many different human activities. These harmful materials cause air pollution. The main source of air pollution is the burning of fossil fuels.

Complete burning of fossil fuels yields carbon dioxide and water as waste products. However, fossil fuels do not usually burn completely because of the inefficiency of most engines and furnaces. The incomplete burning of fossil fuels releases carbon dioxide, carbon monoxide, hydrocarbons, and oxides of nitrogen and sulfur. When coal is burned, small solid particles called soot are also released.

Photochemical Smog Hydrocarbons and nitrogen oxides react in the presence of strong sunlight to form **photochemical smog**. Smog is extremely harmful to plants and is a serious health hazard for humans. It makes breathing difficult for people with respiratory disorders and heart disease. Smog is a problem in many large cities. The use of catalytic converters on cars helps to reduce the release of pollutants that cause smog.

The Greenhouse Effect Carbon dioxide normally found in Earth's atmosphere is important in regulating climate. Carbon dioxide absorbs solar energy reflected off Earth that would otherwise be lost to outer space. The burning of fossil fuels has greatly increased the amount of carbon dioxide in the atmosphere. Thus more heat is being trapped and atmospheric temperature is gradually rising. This process is called the **greenhouse effect**.

Scientists estimate that increasing carbon dioxide levels could cause a significant rise in the temperature of the atmosphere in a few hundred years. This rise in temperature could change atmospheric moisture patterns. Some areas would become drier and others would become wetter. Agriculture would be disrupted

Figure 50-8 *Left:* Industrial scrubbers on smokestacks reduce the amount of pollutants released into the air. *Right:* The damage caused by acid rain to ecosystems and outdoor structures like this statue is of international concern.

in many regions. Increasing air temperature could also cause the polar ice caps to melt, leading to flooding of coastal cities.

Acid Rain One of the most serious forms of air pollution caused by burning fossil fuels is acid rain. **Acid rain** forms when nitrogen and sulfur oxides dissolve in water vapor in the atmosphere. The dissolved oxides form nitric acid and sulfuric acid, which fall to Earth in rain. The burning of high-sulfur coal is a major source of acid rain.

Acid rain causes extensive damage to trees. Lowered pH causes important minerals to seep out of the soil. Acid rain also lowers the pH of lakes and rivers, killing fish and other organisms. Many building materials, such as marble and limestone, are dissolved by acid rain. Metal structures such as bridges are corroded.

The production of acid rain is an international problem. Sulfur and nitrogen oxides produced in one country may be carried by winds many miles away and fall as acid rain in another country. For example, some of the acid rain falling on Canada's lakes is caused by the burning of coal in the United States. International agreements and stronger antipollution laws are needed to combat the problem.

50-11 Water Pollution

Many of the pollutants that contaminate air affect water as well. Acid rain falling into lakes and rivers is one example of this problem. Water pollution is also caused by runoff and dumping of wastes. Runoff from farms carries animal wastes and fertilizers

■ *BIOLOGY INSIGHT*

Homeostasis: Many air pollutants have synergistic effects with each other; that is, the effect of being exposed to two of the pollutants at one time may be greater than the sum of being exposed to the two effects separately. The EPA establishes standards for the types and allowable amounts of pollutants that can be released into the air.

Figure 50-9 Algal blooms reduce the dissolved oxygen concentration in lakes and ponds. In turn, the ability of the water to support different forms of life is reduced.

into rivers and lakes. Fertilizers used by homeowners on their lawns also are washed by rain into bodies of water. Many communities have treatment plants that dump poorly treated sewage into the nearest body of water.

Fertilizers and sewage contain nitrogen and phosphorus, which are nutrients. Adding nutrients to water causes rapid population growth of cyanobacteria and algae. This explosive growth is called an **algal bloom**. Eventually the algal bloom dies and is decomposed by bacteria. Decomposition uses up the dissolved oxygen in the water. Species that require a high level of oxygen, such as trout, die. They are replaced by species that can tolerate a low level of oxygen in the water, such as carp.

Runoff from farms and lawns also contains pesticides. **Pesticides** are toxic chemicals used to kill weeds and insect pests. Unfortunately, these chemicals also kill nonpest species.

Some pesticides accumulate in fatty tissue. As one organism eats another, the chemicals become more concentrated. Thus organisms high in the food chain may take in dangerous amounts of pesticides. This process is called **biological magnification**. Biological magnification of the pesticide DDT caused bald eagles to lay eggs with weak shells. The eggs would break when the birds tried to incubate them. The use of DDT brought bald eagles and several other predatory birds almost to extinction. DDT was also found in the blood and fatty tissues of many people. Therefore, the use of DDT in the United States was banned in 1972.

Many pesticides besides DDT have been banned in recent years. However, some companies still produce large amounts of DDT and other pesticides for export to developing countries.

50-12 Other Pollutants

Solid Waste Americans use vast amounts of disposable products, including bottles, plates, cups, diapers, containers, and packaging materials. Such conveniences cut down on work. However, they also add to the expense of products, require energy for production, and create disposal problems.

All societies generate waste. However, industrial societies with high incomes produce more waste per person than do poor, developing societies. As people earn more money, they use more convenience products. Take-out foods and canned, frozen, and vacuum-packed foods for home preparation come heavily packaged. Fresh foods from local sources, on the other hand, need little packaging.

The average American throws away about 300 kilograms of packaging materials a year. Most of this waste is paper, followed by glass, metal, and plastic. With the exception of plastic, all these materials can be easily recycled.

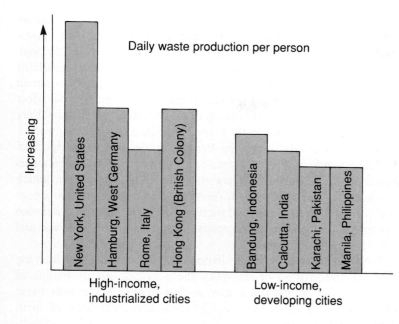

Daily waste production per person

Increasing

New York, United States
Hamburg, West Germany
Rome, Italy
Hong Kong (British Colony)

High-income,
industrialized cities

Bandung, Indonesia
Calcutta, India
Karachi, Pakistan
Manila, Philippines

Low-income,
developing cities

Figure 50-10 The amount of waste produced per person is much higher in urban areas than in rural, undeveloped areas. Much of the waste produced in urban areas comes from packaging used to ship food and keep it fresh and attractive.

In the United States, the majority of solid waste is buried in landfills. Unfortunately, many cities are finding that they are rapidly running out of landfill space. More than half the cities in the country will run out of space in existing landfills in several years.

One proposed solution to the garbage crisis is to burn the wastes. A number of cities already use this approach. Many others have plans for huge incinerators on the drawing board. However, burning certain materials produces toxic compounds. Plastic and bleached paper, for example, contain chlorine compounds that form dioxins when burned. Some dioxins are among the most toxic substances known. Incineration of municipal waste has been shown to release dioxins and other toxic chemicals into the air. Heavy metals such as lead are also released. The ash left behind after burning also contains toxins.

Recycling would eliminate much of the need for incineration and landfill space. Recycling reduces the need for raw materials, saves energy, and cuts down on air and water pollution.

Toxic Chemicals One of the most serious causes of both air and water pollution is the manufacture, use, and disposal of toxic chemicals. Many common products, such as detergent, household cleansers, and plastic containers, are made using toxic chemicals. Toxic chemicals are generated as waste in industrial production processes. Toxins are also produced by some waste disposal methods, such as burning.

It is estimated that industrial nations produce 70 000 different chemicals. The vast majority of these chemicals have not been

CONSUMER BIOLOGY

Foam cups, plates, and containers are made using a group of gaseous compounds called chlorofluorocarbons. These compounds drift into the upper atmosphere, where they break down ozone. The use of chlorofluorocarbons is considered to be a major threat to the ozone layer that protects organisms from harmful solar radiation.

DO YOU KNOW?

Information: Large incinerator plants that burn trash can add as much lead to the air as has been removed by taking the lead out of gasoline.

Figure 50-11 In the United States, thousands of toxic waste dumps have been found. Most of these sites existed before federal regulations were developed to prevent unsafe disposal practices. The Environmental Protection Agency has a list of hundreds of priority sites that are a threat to human health or the environment.

DO YOU KNOW?

Information: The government estimates that the United States produces 40 billion kilograms of toxic waste each year.

▶ Denotes a question that involves *interpreting* and *applying* concepts.

tested to determine their long-term environmental and health effects. Of the chemicals that have been studied, it is known that many cannot be broken down by microbial decomposition. These types of chemicals are said to be **nonbiodegradable** [non bī ō di grād′ ə bəl]. Such chemicals remain in the environment for long periods, where they cause ecological damage and affect human health. Even if chemicals do eventually break down, they may be dangerous while they are loose in air, water, or soil.

Toxic chemicals, including heavy metals, often undergo biological magnification. At certain concentrations, these substances cause serious disorders in humans. Pesticides and PCBs, which are used in electrical transformers, have been linked to cancer and other illnesses. Lead and mercury damage the central nervous system. Other heavy metals cause lung and kidney damage and can lead to heart disease.

Until recently, industries disposed of toxic wastes by burying them in the ground or dumping them in landfills or bodies of water. There is growing evidence that people living near toxic chemical dump sites have a higher-than-average rate of birth defects and cancer.

New technology to destroy the chemicals is being developed by environmental engineers. For example, at Love Canal in New York, toxic chemicals are burned with superheated gases. In Florida, soil contaminated with PCBs is being detoxified by exposure to infrared heat in special truck-sized ovens. Some of the chemicals in toxic wastes can be recycled.

Technology can often find ways to solve environmental problems created by human actions. Technology alone, though, cannot solve all pollution problems. Environmental legislation has begun to force industries to find ways to reduce or destroy toxic wastes. However, individuals are also responsible for pollution. Much of what industry produces is in response to consumer demands. People must be willing to make certain lifestyle changes if they want to protect the environment and enjoy good health.

CHECKPOINT ◆

10. What kinds of pollutants are associated with a high standard of living?
11. What causes an algal bloom?
12. Which pollutant causes the greenhouse effect?
13. Name three health effects of pollution.
14. How can the solid waste problem be reduced?
▶ 15. Most laundry detergents are now made without phosphorus. How does this improve water quality?

LABORATORY ACTIVITY

EFFECTS OF ACID RAIN

Objectives and Skills

□ *Demonstrate* the effect of acid on metal.
□ *Observe* the effect of acid on seeds.

Materials

safety goggles	cotton
lab apron	100 mustard seeds
dilute sulfuric acid	steel wool
4 50-mL beakers	graduated cylinder
2 petri dishes	pH paper
filter paper	wax pencil

Procedure and Observations

Part I

1. Read all instructions for this activity.
2. Put on your safety goggles and lab apron.
3. ☠ Label one 50-mL beaker *water* and another beaker *acid*. Using a graduated cylinder, pour 25 mL of water into the first beaker and 25 mL of dilute sulfuric acid into the second beaker. **CAUTION: If acid gets on your skin, immediately wash the affected area with water.**
4. Dip a piece of pH paper into the water. Find the pH of the water by comparing the color of the pH paper to the color chart on the pH paper container. A pH between 1 and 6 is acidic; a pH of 7 is neutral. Above 7, the pH is basic. Then measure the pH of the sulfuric acid.
5. To each of the beakers, add a small piece of steel wool. *Do not splash the liquid when you add the steel wool.* Leave the steel wool in the beakers overnight.
6. Repeat step 3.
7. To each of the beakers, add 50 mustard seeds and leave them overnight.
8. After 24 hours, check the steel wool in both beakers. Note any changes.

Part II

9. Spread a thin layer of cotton in the bottom of two petri dishes and cover the cotton with filter paper. Pour the contents of each of the beakers containing the seeds into one of the petri dishes. Cover each dish and label it. Leave the petri dishes overnight.
10. After 24 hours, check the seeds in both petri dishes. Count the number of seeds that have germinated in each dish. Seeds that have germinated may have roots over 1 cm long, or they may have just a small, white point poking out. Record the number of seeds that have germinated. Calculate the percentage of seeds that have germinated in each petri dish and record the results in the table below.
11. Before leaving the laboratory, clean up all your materials and wash your hands.

DATA TABLE			
		Seeds germinated	
Substance	**pH**	**Number**	**Percent**
Water			
Sulfuric Acid			

Analysis and Conclusions

1. What is the purpose of studying the effect of acid on steel wool and seeds?
2. Based on your observations, how would you expect the pH of normal rain water to compare to the pH of acid rain?
3. What effect does acid have on steel? When is this important to people?
4. What effect does acid have on seeds? Why is this important?

CHAPTER REVIEW

Summary

▸ Natural resources are necessary for human survival and for the manufacture of useful products. Some natural resources are water, soil, wildlife, and forests. Increasing population and careless use have caused depletion of natural resources. Some related problems are soil erosion, species extinction, desertification, and water shortages.

▸ Efforts to reverse environmental damage and to conserve remaining resources for the future include reforesting, captive breeding, and efficient plowing and planting methods.

▸ Fossil fuels are being used up rapidly. Therefore, many scientists are exploring alternative energy resources.

▸ Nuclear fission is a nonrenewable alternative energy source. Problems with disposal of radioactive wastes and concerns about reactor safety have led to a decline in the demand for nuclear power plants.

▸ Such renewable resources as solar, biomass, and wind energy show promise for helping to meet future energy needs. All of these are currently in use on a small scale. Cogeneration is a process in which heat lost in energy conversion is recaptured and used. Its use will probably increase in the future. Energy conservation practices account for a decrease in energy demand.

▸ Pollution causes damage to ecosystems and is harmful to human health. Air, water, soil, and food resources are affected by pollution. Some of the many pollutants include automobile exhaust, fertilizers, pesticides, industrial wastes, radioactive wastes, and household trash. Growing populations and increasing use of convenience products contribute greatly to pollution.

▸ Government regulations, community efforts, and changes in the habits of industries and individuals are necessary to solve pollution problems.

Vocabulary

acid rain
algal bloom
aquifer
biological
  magnification
biomass energy
cogeneration
conservation
contour plowing
cover crop
crop rotation
erosion
extinction
fossil fuel

geothermal energy
greenhouse effect
natural resource
nonbiodegradable
nonrenewable resource
nuclear fission
pesticide
photochemical smog
photovoltaic cell
pollution
refuge
renewable resource
strip cropping
terracing

Concept Mapping

Construct a concept map for conservation. Use the following terms: cogeneration, conservation, contour plowing, crop rotation, fossil fuel, nonrenewable resource, renewable resource, strip cropping, terracing. Add terms as you need them.

Review

1. How does algal growth affect the amount of dissolved oxygen in water?
2. Give two examples of a renewable resource.
3. How does contour plowing protect soil from erosion?
4. Are shrimp a renewable or nonrenewable resource? Explain.
5. Explain why forests are a threatened resource.
6. Which of the following energy resources is renewable? (a) coal (b) oil (c) natural gas (d) wind
7. What fuel is used in nuclear fission?

8. What two acids are found in acid rain?
9. What are two possible long-range consequences of the greenhouse effect?
10. Name three substances that undergo biological magnification.

Match each conservation practice with the resource it is meant to preserve.

11. air
12. soil
13. water
14. wildlife
15. fossil fuels

a. flow restrictors for showerheads
b. exhaust emission controls on cars
c. smaller, lighter cars
d. crop rotation
e. breeding programs for whooping cranes

Interpret and Apply

16. What is the relationship between pollution and human population density?
17. How are aquifers, fertile topsoil, and oil reserves similar?
18. Which natural resources are important for food production?
19. Which natural resources are endangered by desertification?
20. What resources are conserved by taking a shorter hot shower?
21. Compare the use of paper products with the use of plastic for similar purposes in terms of environmental impact.

Critical Thinking

22. Which is more likely to suffer erosion, flat land or hilly land? Explain.
23. You have a choice between bicycling and riding in a car to school. Name all the advantages of each transportation method.

24. The use of pesticides results in the development of pesticide resistance among target organisms. Thus increasingly higher doses of pesticides are needed to get the desired results. In terms of natural selection, explain why this happens.
25. A grassy area now occupies several acres uphill from a stream. There are plans to replace the grassy area with a parking lot. How would a parking lot change the stream? How could the parking lot be built in a way that would cause less damage to the stream?
26. Discuss the pros and cons of laws requiring that soft-drink bottles be returned and reused.
27. How is a photovoltaic cell like a leaf?
28. The graph below shows the population growth of two insect species. One species is a pest that feeds on the leaves of trees. The other species is a carnivorous insect that eats the pest. Suppose these species are found on trees in a commercial forest. Pesticides are used to eliminate the pest. What effect does the pesticide have on the two populations? Is the effect beneficial? Explain your answer.

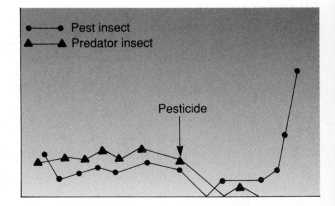

ISSUES in Bioethics

MEDICAL WASTE POLLUTES BEACH

Case Study 1

Esther Calder, a retired widow, had decided to buy a home on the coast. She called a realtor who found her dream house with its own ocean beach. While negotiating with the realtor, Esther asked if there were any water pollution problems. The realtor never provided an answer to her question. Esther did not pursue it because she was happy with the property and was busy moving.

Several weeks later, Esther was walking along her beach and saw a plastic bag. In the bag were two hypodermic needles and cotton. She had read about medical waste that had washed ashore in other states. She was very careful when she picked it up. She called the regional Environmental Protection Agency (EPA) to investigate.

While on the beach again Esther's dog ran into the water and came out with another plastic bag in his mouth. The needles in this bag had blood on them and while trying to get him to let go of the bag, Esther and her dog were both cut by the needles.

Three months later the dog became ill, was diagnosed with canine cancer, and died. Five months after her pet's death, Esther went for a blood test and found, as she feared, that she was HIV positive (infected with the AIDS virus).

The EPA found that a waste removal company hired by a local hospital was secretly dumping into the ocean—an offense for which they had been fined once before.

1. If you were Esther, how would you feel?
2. List all people who you think are at fault. Why should they be held responsible?
3. Give several arguments on both sides of the issue of dumping wastes in the ocean.

Case Study 2

The people in a small African town are facing a serious problem. Cattle raising is an important part of the economy. Cattle provide the people with milk, meat, and hides for clothing. Cattle are also sold or traded for other necessities.

Because they are slow-moving and sometimes fenced-in, the cows are easy prey for lions that live nearby. The town's citizens formed a group to guard the cattle. One night, a lion that was stalking a large cow was shot and killed by a guard.

The next day, game wardens came and were angry with the townspeople. Killing a lion was against the law. The people didn't understand why the man who shot the lion was arrested.

1. What arguments would you use to defend the man who killed the lion?
2. List several ways to resolve the conflict between protecting domesticated and endangered animals.
3. Why do we need to save endangered species?

UNIT REVIEW 8

Synthesis

1. The opening pages of this unit contain four photographs. These photographs illustrate a common theme to the chapters of the unit. Identify the theme and describe how it relates to what you studied in the chapters.
2. **Adaptation and Evolution:** Would you expect to find more kinds of plants at the top of a mountain or at the bottom? Explain your answer.
3. **Levels of Organization:** How is the flow of energy through an ecosystem related to the flow of nutrients in that ecosystem? What is the major difference between the flow of energy and the flow of nutrients?
4. **Homeostasis:** Describe two ways in which the high growth rate of human populations is related to current problems of pollution.
5. **Adaptation and Evolution:** Describe the process by which the behavior of a predator, such as a fox, can influence the evolution of its prey, such as a rabbit.
6. **Levels of Organization:** Tropical and temperate forests exhibit vertical stratification, or layering. What limiting factors cause these layers? Does vertical stratification occur in the oceans? If so, what limiting factors cause stratification in the oceans?
7. **Levels of Organization:** How does vertical stratification in an ecosystem affect interspecific competition?

Critical Thinking

8. **Life Forms Are Interconnected:** One type of biomass energy is ethanol. Ethanol is a liquid fuel produced by the fermentation of sugarcane. The production of ethanol involves processes that normally occur in most ecosystems. What are these processes and what kinds of organisms (consumers, etc.) carry them out?

9. **Homeostasis:** In many developing countries, people eat little or no meat. Their diets consist of various combinations of grains, legumes, fruits, vegetables, fish, and dairy products. By contrast, people in industrial countries eat large amounts of meat. Compare and contrast a vegetarian diet with a meat diet in terms of resource use and energy flow. Which type of diet would be more likely to meet the needs of a growing human population? Explain.
10. **Life Forms Are Interconnected:** Choose one biome and discuss how its carrying capacity may be affected by human activities. In your example, state whether the size of the human population influences the extent of the impact.

Additional Reading

Attenborough, David. *The Living Planet.* Boston: Little, Brown, 1986.

Begon, Michael *et al. Ecology: Individuals, Populations and Communities.* Sunderland, MA: Sinauer Assoc., 1986.

Brown, Lester R. *et al. State of the World 1987: A Worldwatch Institute Report on Progress toward a Sustainable Society.* New York: W. W. Norton, 1987.

Carson, Rachel. *The Silent Spring.* Boston: Houghton-Mifflin, 1962.

Healy, Timothy and Paul Houle. *Energy and Society.* Boston: Boyd & Fraser, 1983.

Lederer, Roger J. *Ecology and Field Biology.* Menlo Park, CA: Benjamin-Cummings, 1984.

Milne, Louis and Margery Milne. *A Shovelful of Earth.* New York: Holt, 1987.

Myers, Norman (ed.). *Gaia: An Atlas of Planet Management.* Garden City, NY: Anchor Books, 1984.

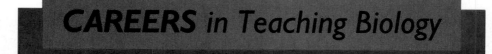
Are you interested in the study of living things? Do you like helping others learn? Are you good at explaining how things work? If you enjoy these activities, consider a teaching career in biology. *Biology teachers* have a fascination with living things and a desire to communicate their enthusiasm to others.

High school biology teachers do many things as part of their jobs. One day a biology teacher may make a difficult concept clear by discussing it and giving several examples of how it works. The next day might be spent supervising a laboratory investigation; the teacher helps students set up equipment, make observations, and evaluate data. Biology teachers also enrich and expand on the information presented in their students' textbooks. They may do this by showing films, working with computers, suggesting additional reading, and helping students with special projects. These teachers also help students relate what they are learning in biology to other subjects, such as math, chemistry, or even history.

College biology teachers usually specialize in one area of biology. Two such specialized subjects are botany (plant life) and anatomy (the structure of living things). In addition, college professors generally do research. They perform experiments in their areas of specialization.

All biology teachers need to read magazines, books, and newspapers to learn about new scientific developments. Each year scientists learn a vast amount of new information about living things. Concepts that are taught this year may be changed or even replaced next year because of new experimental data. Biology teachers need to be able to answer students' questions about scientific discoveries.

Requirements: For high school biology teachers, requirements vary from state to state. In all cases, however, a person must prepare to teach biology by attending college. In addition to biology, courses in chemistry, mathematics, and physics are usually

required. A future biology teacher may also study other sciences. These might include geology, anthropology, and psychology. Generally a student planning to become a teacher will also learn effective teaching methods and will do some practice teaching. College biology teachers usually need a Ph.D. degree. This involves several years of study beyond the four years of undergraduate college.

Well-trained science teachers are needed in many parts of the country. If you like biology and if you enjoy working with people, perhaps someday you will be teaching a course like the one you are taking now.

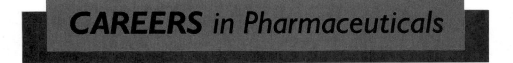

Antibiotics are substances produced largely by molds, yeasts, and bacteria. These substances can either destroy or inhibit the growth of disease-causing microorganisms. Many pharmaceutical companies develop and market antibiotics.

Before an antibiotic is put on the market, much research is necessary to determine whether it is safe and effective. Initial tests are performed on animals such as mice, guinea pigs, and monkeys. In the final stages of research, the antibiotic is administered to humans.

Most of the tests for antibiotic activity in animals are performed by *lab technicians*. They measure the animals' physiological responses before, during, and after the antibiotic is given. They then record such data as behavior patterns, blood pressure, heart action, and respiration. Lab technicians are usually required to have a college degree in biology.

A *biochemist* analyzes the changes that have occurred in tissues and body fluids due to the presence of an antibiotic. *Pharmacologists* analyze how the antibiotic acts in the body. Both of these careers require additional education beyond a college degree.

After extensive testing has been completed, the antibiotic moves on to the development stage. Developing the product requires determining a suitable dosage, the stability of it, and the potential side effects of the antibiotic. These tests are often performed by lab technicians. The results are analyzed by both biochemists and pharmacologists. A new antibiotic is ready for marketing when sufficient data have been accumulated.

Pharmaceutical companies produce millions of tons of antibiotics annually. A variety of different jobs are required for the production process. In one production process, a large quantity of microbial broth is allowed to ferment in a large tank. While in the tank, the liquid is stirred, aerated, and provided with growth nutrients. The antibiotic broth must be purified by filtration and further cleansed by the use of solvents. This process must be carefully

monitored by workers who have a knowledge of the life-sustaining requirements of microorganisms.

Quality control of medicines is vital. Many different types of analytical procedures are used to ensure the stability and uniformity of antibiotic preparations. Lab technicians perform many of these tasks. The size of particles and their crystalline structure are checked using a microscope to assure product uniformity. Each tablet and ointment batch must be uniform in shape, color, weight, taste, odor, stability, and purity.

Pharmaceutical sales representatives present information about their company's vaccines, drugs, or medicines to health care specialists. Using this information, for example, a doctor may choose to recommend a specific product.

There are many positions in a pharmaceutical company that require only a few weeks of on-the-job training. For example, workers are needed to perform inventory management, manufacturing, and packaging of products.

CAREERS *in Botany*

Humans could not exist without plants. Our food comes directly or indirectly from plants. Plants also provide us with such products as furniture, drugs, paper, and clothing. There are many career opportunities in the field of botany.

Florists sell cut flowers and potted plants. They help customers choose the appropriate flower or plant for various occasions. In many cases, they prepare ornamental flower arrangements. Some florists grow many of the flowers and plants sold in their shops. There are no specific requirements for this job. Many florists offer apprenticeships to interested workers. There are schools, however, that offer courses in floriculture, the science of growing and caring for ornamental plants.

A nursery is a place where plants are grown and maintained. *Nursery workers* fertilize, feed, and water young plants. They must have knowledge of plant germination, the growth habits of plants, and plant nutrition. In addition, they must know how to control diseases caused by insects and weeds. Nurseries sell trees, shrubs, flowers, and seedlings. These plants are transplanted in fields, orchards, homes, gardens, and landscaped areas. Federal and state nurseries provide saplings to reforest public lands. Commercial nurseries sell to the public. Many high schools offer vocational training programs in plant management.

Landscape architects plan the use of land for conservation and human enjoyment. They study soil composition, water supply, and local vegetation to plan appropriate land development. They recommend designs for parks and gardens. Landscape architects are responsible for trees, shrubs, and flowers lining city streets. They work with planners on highway development to conserve farmland and forested areas. A college degree in landscape architecture is required for this profession.

Agronomy is an agricultural science dealing with food and fiber crops, and the soil in which they grow. *Agronomists* conduct research on crop rotation, irrigation, drainage, plant breeding, and soil

fertility. They also develop ways to control weeds, diseases, and insect pests. The results of their work often lead to more efficient crop production, higher yields, and an improvement in the quality of the crop. A college degree is required for this profession.

Plant pathologists study the causes and methods of controlling plant diseases. After isolating disease-causing agents, these scientists find ways to destroy the agent. Then they perform studies on healthy and diseased plants to test their findings. They also study the spread of the disease under different environmental conditions. Plant pathologists have often completed degree programs beyond the college level.

Foresters protect woodlands from fire, insects, and disease. They make sure that trees are harvested properly. Additional aspects of forestry include logging engineering, and the manufacture and sale of forest products. Foresters usually have a college degree from a school of forestry.

CAREERS in Medicine

Professionals in the field of medical care devote their lives to healing those who are sick. Therefore, most careers in the medical field require specialized training. In addition to doctors and nurses, there are many other professionals in medicine. There are 23 major specialty fields in the medical profession. The length of the training program varies for each field.

Emergency medical technicians (EMT) must complete a 12-week course. These people are trained to perform cardiopulmonary resuscitation, remove obstructions from airways, and administer other emergency procedures until the patient can be given hospital care. A *paramedic* has had a year of experience as an EMT and has completed a one-year course. A paramedic has more responsibilities than an EMT and can, under certain conditions, take the place of a physician.

Medical illustration requires two years of training. *Medical illustrators* combine a knowledge of anatomy and physiology with artistic ability. They are needed to provide diagrams of surgical instruments and procedures for textbooks and surgical supply companies. Many art schools offer a major in medical illustration.

A technician is a specialist in the mechanical or scientific details of a particular field. *Radiology technicians* have completed two years of training. They prepare patients for X rays and operate X-ray equipment. They also assist in treating specific diseases by exposing the patient to concentrated amounts of X rays. *Medical technologists* have completed a four-year program. A medical technology program of study combines a knowledge of biology with specific laboratory procedures. They perform tests of a chemical, microscopic, or bacteriologic nature. This information is used in the treatment and diagnosis of diseases.

Therapy is a branch of medicine that deals with treatment or rehabilitation of diseases without the use of drugs or surgery. Registered *respiratory therapists* have completed a five-year program.

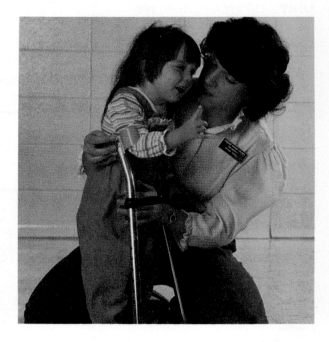

They help people with breathing problems. They work to restore the heart and lungs following complications such as cardiac failure, asthma, or emphysema. *Physical therapists* have completed a four-year program. They plan and administer physical therapy treatment programs for patients. The purpose of such therapy is to restore function, relieve pain, and prevent disability following disease, injury, or loss of body parts. *Occupational therapists* must complete a four-year program. They are responsible for planning, organizing, and conducting activity programs. These programs rehabilitate mentally, physically, or emotionally handicapped people.

The medical profession relieves human suffering and saves lives. When an epidemic or disaster strikes, the medical team is there. Medical care is provided in hospitals, clinics, private practices, nursing homes, and private homes. There are tremendous opportunities and rewards in the medical field.

APPENDIX A

Measurements Used in Biology

UNITS OF MEASUREMENT

Quantity	Name	Symbol
length	meter	m
mass	kilogram	kg
volume	cubic centimeter (liter*)	cm^3 (mL or L)
temperature	Celsius**	°C

* Though used with SI, liter is not technically an SI unit.
** Kelvin is the SI base unit for temperature

SI PREFIXES

Prefix	Symbol	Multiple
kilo	k	1000
centi	c	0.01 (1/100)
milli	m	0.001 (1/1000)

EXAMPLES USING THE METER

Name	Symbol	Equivalent
kilometer	km	1000 m
meter	m	1 m
centimeter	cm	0.01 m
millimeter	mm	0.001 m

Periodic Table of the Elements

(based on $^{12}_{6}C = 12.0000$)

Key example:
14 — Atomic number
Si — Symbol
Silicon — Name
28.0855 — Atomic mass

Element	Atomic Number	Atomic Mass
H Hydrogen	1	1.007
He Helium	2	4.0026
Li Lithium	3	6.941
Be Beryllium	4	9.012
B Boron	5	10.81
C Carbon	6	12.0111
N Nitrogen	7	14.0067
O Oxygen	8	15.9994
F Fluorine	9	18.998
Ne Neon	10	20.179
Na Sodium	11	22.98977
Mg Magnesium	12	24.305
Al Aluminum	13	26.9815
Si Silicon	14	28.0855
P Phosphorus	15	30.973
S Sulfur	16	32.06
Cl Chlorine	17	35.453
Ar Argon	18	39.94
K Potassium	19	39.098
Ca Calcium	20	40.08
Sc Scandium	21	44.955
Ti Titanium	22	47.88
V Vanadium	23	50.9415
Cr Chromium	24	51.996
Mn Manganese	25	54.938
Fe Iron	26	55.847
Co Cobalt	27	58.933
Ni Nickel	28	58.69
Cu Copper	29	63.546
Zn Zinc	30	65.39
Ga Gallium	31	69.72
Ge Germanium	32	72.59
As Arsenic	33	74.92
Se Selenium	34	78.96
Br Bromine	35	79.904
Kr Krypton	36	83.80
Rb Rubidium	37	85.467
Sr Strontium	38	87.62
Y Yttrium	39	88.905
Zr Zirconium	40	91.224
Nb Niobium	41	92.906
Mo Molybdenum	42	95.94
Tc Technetium	43	(98)
Ru Ruthenium	44	101.07
Rh Rhodium	45	102.906
Pd Palladium	46	106.42
Ag Silver	47	107.868
Cd Cadmium	48	112.41
In Indium	49	114.82
Sn Tin	50	118.71
Sb Antimony	51	121.75
Te Tellurium	52	127.60
I Iodine	53	126.905
Xe Xenon	54	131.29
Cs Cesium	55	132.905
Ba Barium	56	137.3
La Lanthanum	57	138.906
Hf Hafnium	72	178.49
Ta Tantalum	73	180.948
W Tungsten	74	183.85
Re Rhenium	75	186.207
Os Osmium	76	190.2
Ir Iridium	77	192.22
Pt Platinum	78	195.08
Au Gold	79	196.967
Hg Mercury	80	200.59
Tl Thallium	81	204.383
Pb Lead	82	207.2
Bi Bismuth	83	208.980
Po Polonium	84	(209)
At Astatine	85	(210)
Rn Radon	86	(222)
Fr Francium	87	(223)†
Ra Radium	88	(226.0)
Ac Actinium	89	227.028
104	104	(261)
105*	105	(262)
106	106	(263)
107	107	(262)
108	108	
109	109	(266)

TRANSITION METALS

INNER TRANSITION METALS

Lanthanide series

Element	Atomic Number	Atomic Mass
Ce Cerium	58	140.12
Pr Praseodymium	59	140.908
Nd Neodymium	60	144.24
Pm Promethium	61	(145)
Sm Samarium	62	150.36
Eu Europium	63	151.96
Gd Gadolinium	64	157.25
Tb Terbium	65	158.925
Dy Dysprosium	66	162.50
Ho Holmium	67	164.930
Er Erbium	68	167.26
Tm Thulium	69	168.934
Yb Ytterbium	70	173.04
Lu Lutetium	71	174.96

Actinide series

Element	Atomic Number	Atomic Mass
Th Thorium	90	232.038
Pa Protactinium	91	231.036
U Uranium	92	238.029
Np Neptunium	93	(244)
Pu Plutonium	94	(244)
Am Americium	95	(243)
Cm Curium	96	(247)
Bk Berkelium	97	(247)
Cf Californium	98	(251)
Es Einsteinium	99	(252)
Fm Fermium	100	(257)
Md Mendelevium	101	(258)
No Nobelium	102	(259)
Lr Lawrencium	103	(260)

*The numbers heading each column represent group numbers recommended by the American Chemical Society Committee on nomenclature.
† Masses in parentheses are the mass numbers of the most stable isotope.

Eyepiece
Contains the magnifying lens

Low-power objective
Contains the low power magnifying lens

High-power objective
Contains the high power magnifying lens

Stage clips
Hold the microscope slide in place

Stage
Supports the microscope slide

Stage opening
Allows for the passage of light through the slide and into the lenses

Diaphragm
Controls the amount of light that enters the lenses

Light source
Directs light through the object being viewed and into the lenses

Turret
Attachment point for the objectives; can be turned to move a particular objective into viewing position

Arm
Supports the barrel

Coarse adjustment
Focuses the image under low power

Fine adjustment
Sharpens the image under high and low power

Base
Supports the microscope

Care and Use of the Microscope

1. Carry the microscope to your lab table by holding the microscope arm with one hand and the base with the other hand.
2. Place the microscope on the lab table with the microscope arm facing you. Be sure the microscope is not near the edge of the table.
3. Refer to the labeled diagram to identify the parts of the microscope. Use lens paper to clean off the lenses. Lens paper will not scratch the lenses. Do not use any other kinds of paper.
4. The two lenses of the microscope are located at opposite ends of the **barrel.** You look at objects by placing your eye near the **eyepiece**, or **ocular.** This lens usually has a magnification of 10 times. The magnification is written on the ocular as *10×*.

5. The lens at the bottom of the barrel is called the **objective**. The objective generally magnifies between 5 and 43 times. Check the magnification that is written on this lens. In most microscopes, there are two or three objectives located on a rotating **turret**. The turret turns to bring a different objective in line with the eyepiece. When changing objectives, listen for a click as the objective locks into position over the hole in the stage.

6. The total magnification of a microscope is determined by multiplying the magnification of the eyepiece with that of the objective. For example, an objective and eyepiece with respective magnifications of 43 and 10 give a total magnification of 430.

7. Look through the eyepiece. The white circle that you see is referred to as the field of view. Adjust the diaphragm so that the maximum amount of light from the light source enters the lens.

8. Using the stage clips, fasten a prepared slide to the microscope stage. Center the object on the slide over the opening of the stage.

9. Now use the coarse adjustment to move the barrel as close to the specimen as possible. Look from the side to make sure the objective does not actually touch the specimen slide. Now look through the eyepiece and slowly move the coarse adjustment so the barrel moves up and away from the slide. As a general rule, you should always try to focus upward when first locating a specimen. The specimen should soon come into focus. Use the fine adjustment to make small adjustments.

10. If higher magnification is necessary, move the slide to center what you want to see in the field of view. Rotate the turret and bring the higher magnification objective into place. As you do, watch carefully from the side to make sure the objective does not touch the slide.

11. Now look in the eyepiece. You should see the subject at higher magnification. You may have to make some adjustments with the fine focus. If the field is too dark, adjust the diaphragm. When you change slides, always return to low magnification first.

12. When you are finished using the microscope, remove the slide from the stage and put the slide away. Move the low-power objective into position over the stage opening. Clean the lenses and the stage. Return the microscope to its storage cabinet.

Laboratory Safety

At the beginning of the year, your teacher will acquaint you with the safety equipment in the room. You should know the location of items such as fire exits, fire blankets, fire extinguishers, eye-wash fountains, and emergency showers. Know where to locate brooms, dustpans, and other cleanup equipment.

The first priority in any laboratory is safety. In all of the activities suggested in this text, uniform safety symbols are used to alert you to materials, procedures, or situations that could be potentially dangerous or harmful. Positive learning and enjoyment of the activity are possible only in an environment where you are in control of what you are doing. It is essential, therefore, that you read all procedures *before* coming into the lab.

Lab Apron: When chemicals are used that could damage skin or clothing, a lab apron is required.

Safety Goggles: In any laboratory activity involving chemicals, flames, or the possibility of broken glassware, eye protection is essential at all times. Even if you wear glasses, you must also wear safety goggles. Safety goggles protect the side of the eye and are unbreakable.

Sharp Instruments: In numerous activities you will use scalpels, scissors, probes, or other sharp instruments. Treat them with great respect. Always direct the sharp edge or point away from you and other people. Do not use too much force when cutting. Use an appropriate instrument. For example, do not use a scalpel if scissors will do the job. Inspect glassware before you use it for chips or cracks. Do not use chipped or cracked glassware. If glassware breaks, be sure to clean the glass up immediately and dispose of it in a separate waste container. Broken glass should not be placed in the wastebasket.

Fire Hazard: Whenever possible, use electric hot plates for heating. In situations where burners are necessary, your teacher will show you how to light the burner safely. If matches are used for lighting, they should be extinguished in water before disposal. When burners are used in the lab, long hair should be tied back and loose-fitting sleeves rolled up. In no case should organic solvents be used in the same room as burners. The burners should be shut off completely when you have finished using them. When heating a test tube, always point the open end of the tube away from people. Sudden bubbles in the tube can cause the contents to blow out at a high velocity.

Hazardous Chemicals: The hazards associated with chemicals can range from mild to severe. Chemicals may be corrosive, flammable, or toxic. Make a habit of treating *all* chemicals as though they were dangerous. Never smell or taste chemicals in the laboratory. Acids and bases require particular caution. Never pour water into a strong acid; splattering can result. Know where the sinks are in the room so that you can immediately wash off spills with a large amount of water. Never dispose of organic chemicals in the sink. These should go into a toxic-waste container for special disposal. Flammable materials should never be stored in a refrigerator. Sparks from the electrical parts of the refrigerator present a potential hazard.

Biohazard: The symbol for a biohazard is used when dangerous organisms are manipulated. In no case will dangerous organisms be intentionally used. In microbiology labs, however, it is possible that a dangerous organism from the environment might grow in the nutrient medium. While this is extremely unlikely, it is standard practice to assume that all microorganisms are potentially dangerous.

APPENDIX C

FIVE-KINGDOM CLASSIFICATION

The classification presented here is not intended to be exhaustive. Groups of organisms described in the text are included. Very small phyla with few species are omitted, since it is unlikely that students will ever encounter these organisms.

Kingdom Monera

Prokaryotes; unicellular or in filaments or colonies; no membrane-bound organelles.

Subkingdom Archaeobacteria

Unusual lipids in cell membrane; unique biochemical pathways; mostly anaerobic organisms adapted to extreme environments; includes methanogens, halophiles, and thermophiles.

Subkingdom Eubacteria

True bacteria with peptidoglycan cell walls.

Phylum Cyanophyta
Blue-green bacteria or algae; photosynthetic autotrophs containing chlorophyll but no chloroplasts; includes some nitrogen fixers.

Phylum Schizophyta
Mostly heterotrophs; some photosynthetic and chemosynthetic species; some free-living and some parasites; includes bacteria, spirochetes, rickettsias, and others.

Phylum Prochlorophyta
Photosynthetic autotrophs with chlorophyll; thought to be related to organisms that became chloroplasts of modern eukaryotes through symbiosis.

Kingdom Protista

Eukaryotes; unicellular, colonial, and multicellular; heterotrophs and autotrophs.

Subkingdom Protozoa (animallike)

Heterotrophs; unicellular; phyla based on means of locomotion.

Phylum Sarcodina
Pseudopods for movement (amoebas only) and feeding; some secrete shells of silica or calcium carbonate; includes amoebas, radiolarians, foraminiferans, and heliozoans.

Phylum Ciliophora
Cilia for movement and feeding; sexual reproduction by conjugation; *Paramecium*.

Phylum Zoomastigina
One or more flagella for movement; *Trypanosoma*.

Phylum Sporozoa
No means of locomotion; all are parasitic with complex life cycles; *Plasmodium*.

Subkingdom Protophyta (plantlike)

Unicellular; mostly autotrophs.

Phylum Chrysophyta
Chlorophylls a and c; golden algae, diatoms with silica shells, and chrysophytes.

Phylum Dinoflagellata
Chlorophylls a and c; propelled and rotated by two flagella; platelike cell wall made of cellulose; dinoflagellates.

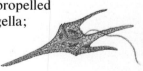

Phylum Euglenophyta
Chlorophylls a and c; move by means of flagella and euglenoid movement; protein pellicle, no cell wall; *Euglena*.

Phylum Chlorophyta
Chlorophylls a and b; unicellular and multicellular; considered to be ancestors of the modern plant kingdom; green algae.

Phylum Rhodophyta
Chlorophyll a and phycoerythrin; most are multicellular; some secrete a hard calcium carbonate crust; red algae.

Phylum Phaeophyta
Chlorophylls a and c plus fucoxanthin; multicellular; apparent tissue specialization; kelp or brown algae.

Subkingdom Gymnomycota (funguslike)
Heterotrophs; some multicellular stages.

Phylum Myxomycota
Large, multinucleate feeding plasmodium; haploid plasmodium with short diploid part of life cycle; acellular slime molds.

Phylum Acrasiomycota
Independent, amoebalike cells in one stage of life cycle; cells unite to form multicellular reproductive structure; cellular slime molds.

Phylum Oomycota
Diploid during most of life cycle; sexual reproduction involves oogamy; white rusts, downy mildew, and water molds.

Kingdom Fungi

Eukaryotes; nonmotile throughout life cycle; cells lacking cilia or flagella; body consists of a network of hyphae forming a mycelium; all are heterotrophs; obtain nutrients by saprobic or parasitic means.

Phylum Zygomycota
Sexual reproduction involving zygospores; bread molds; *Rhizopus*.

Phylum Ascomycota
Ascospores formed by sexual reproduction in asci; ascomycetes or sac fungi, yeasts, morels, and truffles; lichens sometimes classified in this group, since fungal partner in most lichens is an ascomycete.

Phylum Basidiomycota
Basidiospores formed by sexual reproduction in club-shaped basidia; basidiomycetes or club fungi, rusts, and mushrooms.

Phylum Deuteromycota
No known sexual stage; known as "imperfect fungi"; *Aspergillis* and *Penicillium*.

Kingdom Plantae

Eukaryotes; photosynthetic with chlorophyll in chloroplasts; multicellular; nonmotile; cell walls made of cellulose; haploid gametophyte generation alternates with diploid sporophyte.

Botanists have traditionally divided the plant kingdom into divisions rather than phyla—the term preferred by zoologists.

Division Bryophyta
Amphibious; found in damp places on land; nonvascular; no true roots; attach by means of rhizoids; oogamous sexual reproduction; flagellated sperm require water to achieve fertilization; spores develop in a sporangium; gametophyte is dominant generation.

Class Musci: Mosses; asexual reproduction often by fragmentation; leafy gametophyte; sporophyte is parasitic on gametophyte but performs some photosynthesis; *Polytrichum* (haircap moss) and *Bryum* (silver moss).

Class Hepaticae: Liverworts; asexual reproduction involves gemmae; stalky sporophyte produces haploid spores; *Marchantia*.

Division Psilophyta

Whiskferns; oldest vascular plants; no true roots; unicellular rhizoids act as roots; no true leaves; photosynthesis takes place in stems; some vascular tissue; gametophyte has both antheridia and archegonia; only two living genera: *Psilotum* and *Tmesipteris*.

Division Lycophyta

Club mosses; true roots, stems, and leaves; most have tiny leaves that act as sporangia; some species produce both microspores and megaspores; independent gametophyte; biflagellate sperm; *Isoetes, Lycopodium, Selaginella*.

Division Sphenophyta

Horsetails; stems jointed and hollow; scalelike leaves in whorls; dominant sporophyte; independent gametophyte; water required for fertilization of egg by flagellated sperm; one genus: *Equisetum*.

Division Pterophyta

Ferns and tree ferns; well-developed vascular system; sporangia develop on undersides of leaves or on specialized leaves; sporophyte dominant; independent gametophyte; flagellated sperm require water for fertilization; *Azolla* (water fern), *Polypodium, Botrychium*.

Division Coniferophyta

Nonflowering seed plants; leaves are needles or scales; seed not enclosed in fruit; mostly cone-bearing trees; most produce two kinds of spores; male microspores give rise to pollen; pollen wind-carried to female megaspores; *Cedrus* (cedar), *Tsuga* (hemlock), *Pinus* (pines).

Division Ginkgophyta

Trees with fanlike leaves; one living species: *Gingko biloba* (maidenhair tree).

Division Cycadophyta

Palmlike leaves; woody, vascular stem; *Cycas* (sago palm), *Stangeria*.

Division Gnetophyta

Cone-bearing plants; cones lack tough covering; usually found in deserts; three living genera: *Ephedra, Gnetum, Welwitschia*.

Division Anthophyta

Flowering plants; sex organs in flowers; dominant sporophyte produces two kinds of spores; seeds contained in fruit developed from the ovaries.

Class Monocotyledonae: Monocots; one cotyledon in embryo; parallel veins in leaves; vascular bundles scattered throughout stems; flower parts in multiples of three; grasses, wheat, corn, lilies, tulips.

Class Dicotyledonae: Dicots; two cotyledons in embryo; leaves with petioles and branched veins; most have stems with vascular cambium and show secondary growth; vascular bundles form a circle and are sometimes fused; flower parts in multiples of four or five; oak, maple, rose, bean, tomato, dandelion.

Kingdom Animalia

Eukaryotes; multicellular; heterotrophs; most have tissue, organ, and organ system levels of development; reproduction in most involves union of flagellated sperm and nonmotile egg to form a zygote.

Subkingdom Parazoa
Phylum Porifera
Sponges; sessile adults; no tissues or organs; specialized cells; porous body with cells in direct contact with environment; filter feeders; skeletal elements of calcium carbonate, silica, or spongin.

Subkingdom Metazoa
Phylum Cnidaria
Body with two cell layers; digestive system with one opening; tentacles with nematocysts bring food into gastrovascular cavity; radial symmetry; most are marine.
Class Hydrozoa: Many colonial forms; gonads found only on epidermal layer; may reproduce by budding; no nematocysts in gastrodermis; *Hydra, Obelia,* and *Physalia.*

Class Scyphozoa: Jellyfish; marine; medusa stage predominates in life cycle.
Class Anthozoa: Sea anemones and corals; polyp stage predominates; complex gastrovascular cavity.

Phylum Platyhelminthes
Flatworms; three body layers with tissues and simple organs; single opening to digestive system; bilateral symmetry.
Class Turbellaria: Free-living; planaria.
Class Trematoda: Parasitic flukes.
Class Cestoda: Tapeworms.

Phylum Nematoda
Roundworms; free-living or parasitic; two openings to digestive tract.

Phylum Rotifera
"Wheel animals"; ring of cilia brings food into digestive system; microscopic; mostly freshwater forms.

Phylum Annelida
Segmented worms; true coelom; closed circulatory system.
Class Oligochaeta: Common earthworms.
Class Polychaeta: Marine; sandworms.
Class Hirudinea: Parasitic leeches.

Phylum Mollusca
Mollusks; body covered by mantle that secretes a shell in most species; usually show cephalization; muscular foot; trochophore larva in many species.
Class Gastropoda: Snails and slugs; most species aquatic, some terrestrial.
Class Pelecypoda: Clams, oysters, scallops; two shells close by means of muscles.
Class Cephalopoda: Squids and octopuses; shell internal, external, or absent; free-swimming; tentacles with suction disks.

Phylum Echinodermata
Pentamerous radial symmetry; spiny skin; water vascular system; all are marine.
Class Crinoidea: Sea lilies and crinoids; many fossil forms.
Class Asteroidea: Starfish and brittle stars.
Class Echinoidea: Sea urchins and sand dollars.
Class Holothuroidea: Sea cucumbers.

Phylum Onychophora
Segmented body externally resembling annelid body; clawed legs on each segment; antennae; possibly an intermediate form between annelids and arthropods.

Phylum Arthropoda
Segmented body; exoskeleton made of chiton; jointed appendages; largest animal phylum.

Subphylum Trilobita
Trilobites; all extinct; very common fossils; relatively undifferentiated appendages.

Subphylum Chelicerata
Specially modified mouthparts; two body segments: cephalothorax and abdomen.
Class Merostomata: Horseshoe crabs.
Class Arachnida: Scorpions, spiders, mites, and ticks; four pairs of walking legs.

Subphylum Mandibulata
Specially modified mouthparts; antennae on the head.
Class Crustacea: Crabs, crayfish, lobster, shrimp; two pairs of antennae; most are marine.
Class Diplopoda: Millipedes; two pair of legs on each abdominal segment; many internal organs are paired in abdominal segments.

Class Chilopoda: Centipedes; many body segments; one pair of legs per segment; poison sacs in mouthparts.
Class Insecta: Three body sections; three pairs of walking legs; usually two pairs of wings.
Order Thysanura: Silverfish and bristletails.
Order Ephemeroptera: Mayflies; reduced chewing mouthparts and no digestive system in adults.
Order Odonata: Dragonflies and damselflies.
Order Orthoptera: Grasshoppers, locusts, and crickets.
Order Blatteria: Cockroaches.
Order Isoptera: Termites.
Order Dermaptera: Earwigs.
Order Plecoptera: Stoneflies.
Order Psocoptera: Book lice.
Order Mallophaga: Chewing lice.
Order Anoplura: Sucking lice.
Order Thysanoptera: Thrips.

Order Hemiptera: True bugs with piercing, sucking mouthparts.
Order Homoptera: Aphids, scale insects, and cicadas.
Order Neuroptera: Dobsonflies, alderflies, and lacewings.
Order Coleoptera: Beetles.
Order Siphonaptera: Fleas.
Order Trichoptera: Caddisflies.
Order Diptera: Flies and mosquitoes.
Order Hymenoptera: Ants, bees, and wasps.
Order Lepidoptera: Moths and butterflies.

Phylum Chordata
Animals with notochord, dorsal hollow nerve cord, and gill slits at some point during life.

Subphylum Urochordata
Tunicates and seasquirts; adults with reduced nervous system and lost notochord.

Subphylum Cephalochordata
Small, fishlike filter feeders; retain notochord as adults; Amphioxus.

Subphylum Vertebrata
Notochord replaced by cartilage or bone to form vertebral column.
Class Agnatha: Jawless fish; reduced skeleton of cartilage; retain notochord as adults; lampreys and hagfish.
Class Chondrichthyes: Fish with cartilage skeleton; separate gill openings; sharks, skates, and rays.
Class Osteichthyes: Bony fish; bone-derived scales; perch.
Class Amphibia: Four-legged vertebrates; eggs shed in water; aquatic larval stage with gills; adults with lungs; use skin as respiratory surface.
Order Anura: Frogs and toads.

Order Urodela: Salamanders and newts.
Order Apoda: Legless amphibians.
Class Reptilia: Waterproof skin; shelled eggs with extra-embryonic membranes.

Order Chelonis: Turtles and tortoises.
Order Rhynchocephalia: Tuatara.
Order Squamata: Snakes and lizards.
Order Crocodilia: Alligators, crocodiles, and caimans.

Class Aves: Birds; feathers and shelled eggs; endothermic.
Class Mammalia: Young nourished by milk produced by female mammary glands; most are viviparous; most have body hair; endothermic.

Order Monotremata: Egg-laying; duck-billed platypus and spiny anteater.

Order Marsupalia: Bear young after short gestation; young raised in pouch; kangaroos, possum, koala.
Order Insectivora: Insect-eaters; moles, shrews.
Order Chiroptera: Flying mammals; bats.
Order Edentata: Sloths, anteaters, armadillos.
Order Lagomorpha: Rabbits, hares.
Order Rodentia: Rodents.
Order Cetacea: Whales, dolphins, porpoises.
Order Carnivora: Bears, dogs, cats, hyenas.
Order Proboscidea: Elephants.
Order Sirenia: Manatees.
Order Perissodactyla: Odd-toed ungulates; horses, tapirs, rhinoceroses.
Order Artiodactyla: Even-toed ungulates; pigs, hippos, camels, giraffes, buffalo, cows.
Order Primates: Lemurs, monkeys, gibbons, orangutans, gorillas, humans.

GLOSSARY

A

abdomen: the body region posterior to the thorax of arthropods; a region in vertebrates between the thorax and pelvis containing many internal organs (p. 490)

abiotic factor: a physical or nonliving aspect of the environment that affects an organism (p. 783)

abscission: the separation of a leaf, flower, seed, or fruit from a stem (p. 421)

abscission layer: a thin layer of cells at the base of a petiole that forms at the end of a growing season and causes abscission to occur (p. 421)

absorption: the process by which substances such as nutrients and oxygen pass through a body membrane (p. 77)

abyssal zone: deepest part of the ocean where light never penetrates, with depths generally greater than 1000 meters (p. 795)

acellular slime mold: a group of funguslike protists that exists as a large, acellular, multinucleate feeding mass at one stage of its life cycle (p. 330)

acetylcholine: a compound with the formula $C_7H_{17}O_3N$ that functions in the transmission of nerve impulses (p. 703)

acetylcholinesterase: an enzyme that blocks the function of acetylcholine (p. 703)

acid: a substance that releases hydrogen ions when mixed with water (p. 45)

acid rain: a type of pollution caused by the combination of sulfur oxides and nitrogen oxides with water vapor in the atmosphere to produce dilute acid solutions that fall to Earth as precipitation (p. 837)

acquired characteristics: traits that an organism develops during its lifetime (p. 236)

ACTH: a hormone secreted from the pituitary to the adrenal cortex that causes the secretion of corticoid hormones (p. 726)

actin: a protein that is the main component of the thin filaments in a muscle myofibril (p. 621)

activation energy: the initial energy required to begin a chemical reaction (p. 61)

active immunity: immunity to a disease acquired through the activation of memory cells (p. 689)

active site: the portion of an enzyme molecule that reacts with a substrate (p. 61)

active transport: the movement of particles across a membrane that requires cellular energy (p. 83)

adaptation: an inherited trait that promotes survival and reproduction for a species; the process of becoming better suited to the environment (p. 31)

adaptive radiation: evolution of many diverse species from a single, ancestral species (p. 241)

addiction: a strong physical or psychological dependence on a drug (p. 735)

adenine: a nitrogen base with the formula $C_5H_5N_5$ found in DNA and RNA (p. 109)

adhesion: an attraction between unlike molecules due to intermolecular forces (p. 397)

adipose tissue: connective tissue specialized to store fat (p. 623)

ADP (adenosine diphosphate): a coenzyme composed of adenine, ribose, and two molecules of phosphoric acid that is found in all cells and can be converted to ATP (p. 92)

adrenal gland: an endocrine gland located above each kidney that secretes corticoid hormones and adrenalin (p. 719)

adrenalin: a hormone secreted by the adrenal gland that acts to increase blood pressure by stimulating heart action and constriction of some blood vessels; also called epinephrine (p. 719)

adventitious root: any root that grows from a part of the plant that is not the primary root (p. 388)

aerobic: requiring oxygen to extract energy from glucose (p. 92)

agglutination: the clumping of an antigen (p. 672)

aggregate fruit: a type of fruit that develops from many different ovaries in a single flower (p. 361)

aggression: dominant or fighting behavior (p. 777)

Agnatha: the living vertebrates class composed of jawless fish (p. 517)

air bladder: a broad, leaflike blade that helps keep brown algae afloat (p. 327)

air sac: an organ of gas exchange that opens off the trachea (p. 577)

albumen: a protein-rich substance laid down around the yolk in a bird's egg (p. 580)

alcohol: a class of compounds having an –OH group attached to one or more carbon atoms; any intoxicating substance derived from ethanol C_2H_5OH (p. 52)

alcoholic fermentation: the anaerobic decomposition of glucose to produce an alcohol and carbon dioxide (p. 93)

alcoholism: a condition characterized by physical and psychological dependence on alcohol (p. 740)

algae: group of autotrophic protists (p. 322)

algal bloom: rapid population growth of cyanobacteria and algae caused by the addition of nutrients to water (p. 838)

alimentary canal: the tube through which food passes; in humans it includes the mouth, pharynx, esophagus, stomach, and intestine (p. 629)

allantois: an extraembryonic membrane that aids in respiration and excretion for embryos of birds, reptiles, and some mammals (p. 558)

allele frequency: the proportion, or percent, of an allele in a gene pool (p. 218)

alleles: pairs of the alternate forms of a gene that occupy corresponding positions on homologous chromosomes (p. 151)

alternation of generations: a life cycle that shows an orderly sequence of haploid and diploid generations (p. 328)

altricial: a group of birds that are not developmentally advanced and are helpless when hatched (p. 582)

alveoli: microscopic air sacs at the end of each bronchiole in the lungs (p. 651)

amino acid: one of 20 organic acids with one or more attached amino groups ($-NH_2$) that are the building blocks of proteins (p. 59)

amino group: a functional group having the formula $-NH_2$ (p. 52)

amniocentesis: a procedure by which a small amount of amniotic fluid is withdrawn during pregnancy to detect genetic defects (p. 191)

amnion: a fluid-filled sac that encloses an embryo and protects it (p. 558)

amoebocyte: an unspecialized wandering cell type in sponges having several functions (p. 450)

amphetamine: a class of drugs that act as stimulants on the central nervous system (p. 737)

Amphibia: the living vertebrates class composed of amphibians (p. 517)

amphibian: any cold-blooded vertebrate belonging to the class Amphibia; they hatch as fishlike eggs and transform into an adult that can live on land (p. 541)

amylase: an enzyme that breaks down starch, carbohydrates, and glycogen (p. 630)

anaerobic: not requiring oxygen energy from glucose (p. 92)

anal fin: a single fin located ventrally near the tail of bony fish (p. 530)

anal pore: the structure in paramecia through which undigested material is expelled from the cell (p. 319)

anaphase: the third stage of mitosis in which the chromatids move to opposite poles of the cell (p. 126)

anemia: a condition caused by a shortage of hemoglobin in the blood (p. 672)

angiosperm: a flowering plant (p. 353)

annelid: a segmented worm that has a coelum; earthworm (p. 468)

annual: a plant that lives for only one growing season (p. 415)

antagonist pair: two muscles working in opposition so that as one contracts, the other relaxes (p. 622)

antenna: a sensory appendage in mandibulate arthropods (p. 493)

anterior: the front of an animal (p. 449)

anther: the part of a flower stamen that bears the pollen (p. 355)

antheridium: a sperm-producing structure found in some plants (p. 328)

anthropologist: a scientist who studies human cultures and human origins (p. 267)

antibiotic: a substance produced synthetically and in living organisms that inhibits the growth of or destroys bacteria and other microorganisms (p. 692)

antibody: a specific protein formed in response to a virus or other foreign substance in the blood or tissues (p. 671)

anticodon: three nucleotide bases found at one end of each transfer RNA that determines which amino acid the transfer RNA will carry (p. 117)

antigen: any substance that causes the formation of antibodies in the body (p. 672)

antisense strand: the side of the DNA double helix that is not transcribed during protein synthesis; may be involved in silencing or stopping the sense strand (p. 115)

Anura: an order of amphibians that includes frogs and toads (p. 541)

anus: the posterior opening of the alimentary canal through which waste and undigested food is expelled from the body (p. 466)

aorta: a large artery leading from the heart (p. 499)

aortic semilunar valve: a valve in the heart at the base of the aorta (p. 665)

apical dominance: the retardation of lateral bud growth caused by the presence of the terminal bud (p. 418)

apical meristem: unspecialized cells that divide to produce new cells at root or stem tips (p. 375)

Apoda: an order of amphibians that are legless and live in tropical regions (p. 542)

appendage: any structure that grows out from the main part of the body (p. 489)

appendicular skeleton: the pelvic and pectoral girdles and limb bones in vertebrates (p. 516)

appendix: a small projection from the large intestine that helps digest cellulose in some animals but has no function in humans (p. 636)

aquifer: permeable rock yielding an underground water supply (p. 830)

arachnids: a major class of chelicerates that includes spiders, scorpions, mites, and ticks (p. 490)

archegonium: an egg-producing reproductive structure in plants (p. 430)

arteriole: a small artery (p. 667)

arteriosclerosis: a disease in which the walls of the blood vessels thicken and harden (p. 669)

artery: a blood vessel that carries blood away from the heart (p. 532)

arthropod: any member of the phylum Arthropoda, which contains 80 percent of known animal species; all arthropods have exoskeleton, jointed legs, and segmented bodies (p. 489)

Artiodactyla: the order of even-toed, hoofed mammals; it includes goats, sheep, and pigs (p. 596)

Ascomycota: a division of fungi in which the members have a saclike reproductive structure, or ascus (p. 340)

ascus: a saclike reproductive structure that produces spores in certain fungi (p. 340)

asexual reproduction: a method of producing offspring without the joining of two gametes, resulting in offspring identical to their single parent (p. 157)

asteroid: an echinoderm with five arms projecting from a central disk; a starfish (p. 482)

asymmetrical: lacking any regular shape (p. 447)

atherosclerosis: disease that results when deposits of cholesterol build up on inner walls of arteries (p. 669)

atom: the smallest particle of an element that retains the characteristics of that element (p. 38)

ATP (adenosine triphosphate): a compound that stores the energy needed for all cellular activities (p. 91)

atrium: the heart chamber that receives blood from veins in vertebrates (p. 532)

auditory canal: the outer ear canal leading to the eardrum (p. 711)

Australopithecus: the oldest known species of hominids, characterized by apelike brains and humanlike jaws (p. 268)

autoimmune disease: a disease caused by a malfunction of the immune system, which attacks the body's own healthy cells (p. 692)

autonomic nervous system: motor neurons that connect the central nervous system to smooth muscles, cardiac muscles, and glands (p. 708)

autosome: any chromosome other than the sex chromosomes (p. 165)

autotroph: an organism that can manufacture its own food from simple inorganic substances (p. 27)

auxin: a plant hormone that stimulates plant growth (p. 416)

Aves: the living vertebrate class composed of birds (p. 517)

axial skeleton: the skull, vertebral column, and rib cage in vertebrates (p. 516)

axolotl: a type of larval salamander capable of reproducing (p. 551)

axon: a long, thin branch of a neuron that carries impulses away from the cell body (p. 701)

B

bacilli: rod-shaped bacteria (p. 298)

bacteriophage: a virus that infects bacteria (p. 306)

bacterium: a very small, unicellular moneran (p. 297)

ball-and-socket joint: a type of joint allowing movement in many different directions (p. 618)

barb: a branch from the central shaft of a feather (p. 571)

barbiturate: any of a group of depressant drugs used to induce sleep or relaxation (p. 736)

barbules: tiny hooks that connect the barbs of a feather (p. 571)

bark: all the tissue outside the vascular cambium in a woody stem (p. 392)

basal disk: a specialized area of a sessile organism where a polyp attaches to a surface (p. 454)

base: any substance that combines with hydrogen ions when mixed to form water (p. 46)

base deletion: a mutation in which a nucleotide base is lost from the DNA sequence (p. 173)

base insertion: a mutation in which an extra nucleotide base is added to the DNA sequence (p. 173)

basidiomycota: a division of fungi that includes mushrooms, shelf fungi, and puffballs; also called club fungi (p. 342)

basidium: a club-shaped reproductive structure that forms spores in certain fungi (p. 342)

basking: being out in the sun to increase the body temperature by the sun's energy (p. 558)

B cell: an antibody-producing lymphocyte (p. 687)

behavior: all the activities of an organism (p. 771)

benthos: organisms that live on the ocean floor (p. 794)

bicuspid valve: a valve in the heart between the left atrium and left ventricle (p. 665)

biennial: a plant that lives for two growing seasons (p. 415)

bilateral symmetry: symmetry in which an organism can be divided into equal halves only along a single plane (p. 448)

bile: a substance produced by the liver that aids in the digestion of fat (p. 531)

bile duct: a tube that transports bile from the gall bladder to the duodenum (p. 544)

binary fission: cell division in bacteria in which there is no formation of spindle fibers and no chromosomal condensation (p. 301)

binomial nomenclature: a two-name system of naming organisms (p. 278)

biogenesis: the idea that all living things arise only from other living things of the same type (p. 29)

biological magnification: the steady accumulation of a substance in the tissues of organisms with increasing feeding level in a food chain (p. 838)

biology: the study of living things (p. 3)

bioluminescence: the ability of a living organism to produce light (p. 324)

biomass: a measure of the total mass of dry organic matter produced in a given area (p. 783)

biomass energy: energy stored in organic matter as a result of photosynthesis (p. 834)

biome: a large geographical area with a characteristic form of dominant vegetation (p. 783)

biosphere: the thin layer of Earth's surface where life exists (p. 783)

biosynthesis: a chemical reaction from which more complex molecules are made from simple ones (p. 53)

biotic potential: the highest rate of reproduction for a population under ideal conditions (p. 817)

bipedal: the characteristic of walking on two limbs (p. 264)

bipinnaria larva: a larval stage in echinoderms (p. 482)

birth rate: the rate at which new individuals are added to a population by reproduction (p. 818)

bivalve: a mollusk having two shells hinged together; pelecypods (p. 479)

bladder: an organ that stores urine before emptying it to the outside of the body (p. 656)

blade: a leaflike part of nonvascular plants (p. 327); the flattened portion of a vascular leaf (p. 403)

blastocyst: a hollow ball of cells (p. 756)

blastopore: the opening into the gastrula stage of a developing embryo (p. 446)

blastula: a small, fluid-filled ball of cells that is an early stage in the development of an embryo (p. 446)

blood: a liquid that functions as an exchange medium between an organism and its environment (p. 469)

blubber: a thick layer of fat in some aquatic mammals (p. 587)

bone: a hard, inflexible material that makes up the endoskeleton of most vertebrates (p. 516)

book lung: an organ of gas exchange found in many arachnids (p. 490)

Bowman's capsule: a cuplike part of a nephron (p. 657)

brain: a collection of neurons located anteriorly that acts as a control center for body processes (p. 461)

breathing center: a portion of the medulla oblongata that controls breathing (p. 655)

bronchi: two large tubes branching from the trachea (p. 651)

bronchioles: tiny branches of the bronchi in the lungs (p. 389)

bronchus: one of two large tubes branching from the trachea (p. 577)

brood patch: an area of enlarged blood vessels in a bird's chest that brings body heat to the surface, used in incubation (p. 580)

bryophyte: a small nonvascular plant anchored to the ground by rhizoids (p. 429)

budding: a type of asexual reproduction in which a small group of cells grows from the body of an adult to become another individual (p. 341); a type of grafting in which the scion is a bud (p. 380)

bud scale: a small, thick, modified leaf that protects a bud (p. 389)

bud-scale scars: rings left around a stem that mark the location of past terminal buds (p. 389)

bulb: a short, underground stem surrounded by numerous fleshy leaves (p. 393)

C

caeca: blind pouches branching from the stomach of insects (p. 498)

Calvin cycle: second phase of photosynthesis during which carbon atoms from CO_2 are combined to form sugars; light is not the energy source for these reactions (p. 102)

cambium: unspecialized cells that divide to produce new cells, which cause a plant to grow in width (p. 375)

camouflage: any means of blending with the environment (p. 502)

cancer: a condition in which malignant cells invade and destroy body tissues (p. 137)

canine tooth: a pointed tooth used for tearing and piercing (p. 629)

canopy: the leafy covering of a forest (p. 788)

capillaries: microscopic blood vessels having thin walls through which gas and nutrient exchange occurs (p. 532)

capillarity: ability of a liquid to move upward against the force of gravity due to molecular adhesion to surface of the surrounding vessel (p. 396)

capillary water: a loose film of water around soil particles (p. 395)

capsid: a protein coat surrounding viral nucleic acid (p. 306)

capsule: a layer of sticky material outside the cell wall of some monerans (p. 297); a spore-producing structure in mosses (p. 430)

carapace: a section of exoskeleton covering the cephalothorax in crustaceans (p. 493); the upper, or dorsal, shell in a turtle (p. 562)

carbohydrate: an organic compound made of carbon, hydrogen, and oxygen (p. 53)

carbon cycle: the movement of carbon between inorganic and organic states, mainly through the processes of photosynthesis and respiration (p. 810)

carbon fixation: the second stage of photosynthesis in which carbon dioxide is assembled into carbohydrate molecules (p. 99)

carcinogen: a cancer-causing agent (p. 137)

cardiac muscle: the muscle that makes up the heart (p. 622)

Carnivora: the order of flesh-eating mammals that have long, pointed teeth for shredding flesh (p. 595)

carnivore: an animal that consumes other animals for food (p. 803)

carpel: female reproductive structure of flowering plants; contains ovules (p. 355)

carrier: an individual who is heterozygous for a recessive trait (p. 168)

carrier protein: a protein embedded in the plasma membrane that aids the entry of a specific substance into the cell (p. 84)

carrying capacity: the number of individuals of a population that the environment can support indefinitely (p. 818)

cartilage: a strong, flexible material that makes up some part of the endoskeleton in all vertebrates (p. 516)

catalyst: a substance that changes the rate of a chemical reaction without being used up or changed in the reaction (p. 61)

caudal fin: a single fin located on the tail of bony fish (p. 530)

cell: the basic structural and functional unit of a living organism (p. 29)

cell plate: a structure formed at the equator of a dividing plant cell during cytokinesis (p. 128)

cell theory: the theory that all cells come from other cells and all organisms are composed, or are by-products, of cells (p. 29)

cellular respiration: the process of converting food energy into a form of energy usable by cells that takes place in the mitochondria (p. 94)

cellular slime mold: a type of slime mold that consists of independent single cells at one stage of its life cycle (p. 331)

cellulose: a polysaccharide that makes up most of a cell wall (p. 54)

cell wall: a rigid structure lying outside the plasma membrane in plant cells (p. 75)

central nervous system: the brain and spinal cord (p. 547)

centrifuge: an instrument that applies very high forces to small objects by spinning them rapidly, separating their different parts into layers (p. 16)

centriole: a cylindrical organelle just outside the nucleus that functions in cell division (p. 74)

centromere: the region that ensures proper pairing of sister chromatids during metaphase (p. 126)

cephalization: a tendency in animal evolution toward larger brains and more complex senses in the head (p. 461)

cephalochorate: a free-swimming, filter-feeding chorate that lives in shallow water (p. 515)

cephalopod: a mollusk that has a well-developed nervous system with a large brain and complex sensory organs (p. 480)

cephalothorax: one of two main body parts in some arthropods made up of fused head and thorax (p. 490)

cerebellum: the region of the brain controlling muscular coordination and balance (p. 533)

cerebrospinal fluid: a fluid in the brain and spinal cord that cushions against shock (p. 704)

cerebrum: the largest part of the human brain; the control area for reasoning, memory, and voluntary nervous activity (p. 519)

cervix: a muscular ring of tissue at the junction of the uterus and vagina (p. 752)

cestode: a parasitic flatworm that has a body divided into many sections; tapeworm (p. 464)

Cetacea: the order of aquatic mammals; it includes whales and dolphins (p. 595)

chalaza: strands of a protein material that suspend the yolk from the ends of an eggshell (p. 580)

chalone: a protein produced in normal, healthy cells; when present, a cell does not undergo mitosis (p. 133)

chelicerate: an arthropod that does not have jaws and usually has two body divisions and six pairs of appendages, four of which are for walking and the remaining two for sensory and feeding functions (p. 489)

chemical digestion: the breakdown of food through the action of enzymes and emulsifiers (p. 629)

chemical formula: chemical symbols and numbers used to represent the composition of a substance (p. 39)

chemical reaction: a reaction where chemical bonds between atoms are broken or formed (p. 43)

chemical symbol: a one- or two-letter abbreviation used to represent each element (p. 37)

chemosynthetic: autotrophic bacteria that receive energy from chemical reactions involving inorganic molecules (p. 299)

chemotherapy: the use of chemicals to treat disease (p. 692)

Chiroptera: the only order of mammals that can fly; it contains about 850 species of bats (p. 594)

chitin: a hard carbohydrate material found in the exoskeletons of arthropods and also in the cell walls of some fungi (p. 337)

chlorophyll: a green pigment in plants required for photosynthesis (p. 100)

chloroplast: a plastid containing chlorophyll (p. 73)

Chordata: a phylum made up of organisms with a notochord, a dorsal nerve cord, and gill slits (p. 513)

chorion: a fetal membrane lying outside of the amnion that becomes the fetal portion of the placenta (p. 757); a thin membrane inside the shell of a land egg (p. 558)

chorionic villus sampling: a procedure by which a small piece of membrane surrounding the fetus is removed to detect genetic defects (p. 191)

chromatid: a single chromosomal strand (p. 126)

chromatin: a complex of protein and DNA that make up the chromosomes (p. 70)

chromoplast: a plastid containing red, orange, or yellow pigments (p. 73)

chromosomal rearrangement: types of mutations in which chromosomal pieces are moved from their original locations (p. 171)

chromosome mapping: a method of determining the relative position of genes on a chromosome using information on crossover frequency (p. 169)

chromosomes: long coiled strands in the nucleus that contain the genetic material (p. 70)

chromosome theory: the idea that genes are located on the chromosomes (p. 160)

cilia: short, hairlike projections used for locomotion in some protists; present in some tissues of multicellular organisms (p. 318)

ciliate: a one-celled organism that uses cilia to swim and capture food (p. 318)

circadian rhythm: cyclic behavior patterns with a period of 24 hours (p. 772)

circulation: the movement of blood through the body's blood vessels (p. 469)

cirrhosis of the liver: a condition in which scar tissue gradually replaces healthy liver cells (p. 840)

citric acid cycle: a series of reactions in the aerobic phase of cellular respiration that breaks down acetyl CoA, releasing energy (p. 95)

class: a group of related taxonomic orders (p. 279)

classify: to put objects or ideas into groups on the basis of similarity (p. 277)

cleavage: one of the first cell divisions in a zygote (p. 446)

climax community: the final stage of succession in a particular area (p. 807)

cline: a gradual variation in a single trait from one population to the next that corresponds to changes in the environment (p. 216)

clitellum: a secretory area of the earthworm's body that produces the capsule during reproduction (p. 471)

cloaca: a common chamber that receives materials from the digestive, excretory, and reproductive systems (p. 545)

clone: an organism reproduced asexually by mitosis, thus being genetically identical to other offspring and to the parent (p. 206)

cloning: a method of asexual reproduction in which a single somatic cell produces large numbers of identical cells (p. 206)

closed circulatory system: a circulatory system in which blood is enclosed in vessels throughout the body (p. 479)

club moss: a spore-bearing vascular plant that lives in moist areas and belongs to the division Lycophyta (p. 434)

clutch: a group of bird eggs laid at one time (p. 581)

cnidarian: a radially symmetrical organism that has two distinct cell layers and no distinct head (p. 453)

coacervate: a particle that displays some of the properties of cells (p. 259)

cocaine: a euphoria-producing drug that acts as a stimulant on the central nervous system (p. 737)

cocci: spherical-shaped bacteria (p. 298)

cochlea: a fluid-filled coiled tube in the middle ear receiving vibrations that stimulate the auditory nerve (p. 712)

codominance: genetic situation in which heterozygous individuals express traits as a blend of phenotypes of two alleles (p. 156)

codon: a sequence of three nucleotide bases in an RNA molecule that codes for one amino acid in a protein (p. 116)

coelocanth: a primitive lobe-finned fish (p. 536)

coelom: a fluid-filled body cavity surrounded by mesoderm (p. 468)

coenzyme: an organic molecule that works with an enzyme to catalyze a reaction (p. 60)

cofactor: a coenzyme or a metal ion that works with an enzyme to catalyze a reaction (p. 62)

cogeneration: a method of energy conservation in which waste heat or electricity from one process is used in another process (p. 835)

cohesion: the attraction between like molecules (p. 396)

cohesion-tension theory: explains upward movement of water in plants; continuous water column, joined by cohesive forces, transmits tension from leaves to roots (p. 396)

coleoptile: the first leaf of a monocot that forms a protective sheath around the growing shoot (p. 373)

collagen: a fibrous protein that acts as a connective tissue (p. 616)

collar cell: a flagellated cell lining the internal cavities of a sponge (p. 450)

collecting duct: a tubule that drains urine from the nephron into the renal pelvis (p. 657)

collenchyma: a plant tissue specialized for strength and support (p. 376)

colon: the large intestine (p. 636)

commensalism: a symbiotic relationship in which one organism benefits and the other is unaffected (p. 806)

common bile duct: a tube that transports bile from the gall bladder into the small intestine (p. 633)

communication: the exchange of information (p. 778)

community: all the populations of organisms living in a specific area (p. 802)

companion cell: a type of phloem cell found in association with sieve tube elements (p. 398)

compass orientation: a form of orientation by which animals move from place to place using the relative positions of the sun, moon, and stars (p. 776)

competition: the interaction between individuals that use one or more of the same resources (p. 821)

competition exclusion principle: the statement that two species cannot exist in the same habitat using exactly the same limiting resources (p. 821)

complementary: a characteristic of DNA nucleotides in which adenine always pairs with thymine and cystosine always pairs with guanine (p. 111)

complete metamorphosis: a type of metamorphosis with egg, larva, pupa, and adult stages (p. 497)

compound: a substance made of two or more chemically-bonded elements (p. 39)

compound eye: an eye made up of many individual light sensitive units (p. 494)

compound leaf: a type of leaf in which many small leaflets are attached to the same petiole (p. 403)

compound microscope: a magnifying device having two lenses (p. 13)

conceptacles: reproductive organs in brown algae (p. 329)

cone: a light-sensitive cell of the retina that responds only in bright light and can distinguish forms and colors (p. 714)

conifer: a cone-bearing woody tree or shrub, usually with needlelike leaves (p. 363)

conjugation: a primitive type of sexual reproduction in which the contents of two cells unite; an exchange of nuclear material in paramecia (p. 302)

connective tissue: a specialized group of cells that connect and support parts of the body (p. 615)

conservation: the management of existing resources (p. 835)

constrictor: a snake that kills its prey by wrapping around and suffocating it (p. 561)

consumer: an organism that gets its food from another organism (p. 803)

contact inhibition: the cessation of cell division of healthy cells upon contact with other cells (p. 135)

contour feathers: feathers that streamline a bird's body for flight (p. 572)

contour plowing: a method of erosion prevention in which plowing is done across a slope (p. 830)

contractile vacuole: an organelle that controls the water balance of a protist by expelling excess water from the protist (p. 317)

control: the part of an experiment that is used as a standard of comparison for experimental observations (p. 8)

controlled breeding: the allowance of only the organisms with a selected trait to reproduce (p. 201)

controlled experiment: an experiment in which only one factor is varied at a time (p. 8)

convergent evolution: a type of evolution in which unrelated species produce descendants with similar traits (p. 242)

convolution: a fold of brain tissue (p. 587)

cooperation: working toward a common purpose (p. 778)

cork: a water resistant outer layer of cells around plant roots and stems (p. 377)

cork cambium: a meristematic layer of cells that produces water-resistant cork cells (p. 386)

corm: a short, thick fleshy underground stem (p. 383)

cornea: the transparent covering of the eye (p. 713)

coronary circulation: the system of blood vessels that supply blood to the heart (p. 665)

corpus luteum: tissue that forms from a ruptured ovarian follicle and that produces progesterone (p. 753)

cortex: a food storage area in plants (p. 744)

corticoid: a hormone secreted by the adrenal cortex that helps regulate the metabolism of proteins and carbohydrates in the body (p. 725)

cotyledon: an embryonic leaf of a seed plant that provides food for the young plant (p. 368)

courtship: a specialized pattern that occurs before mating can take place (p. 776)

covalent bond: a bond formed when two atoms share a pair of electrons (p. 41)

cover crop: grass or other vegetation planted on bare fields to protect the soil from erosion (p. 830)

cranial nerve: a nerve that branches from the brain (p. 533)

critical period: a short period of time following hatching or birth during which imprinting can occur (p. 774)

Crocodilia: the order of reptiles in which alligators and crocodiles belong (p. 559)

Cro-Magnon: a group of early *Homo sapiens* with skeletons almost identical to those of modern humans (p. 269)

crop: an enlargement at the base of the esophagus in birds that stores food (p. 576); a storage organ in the digestive system of most segmented worms (p. 470)

crop rotation: planting different crops on a given piece of land to allow the replenishing of soil nutrients (p. 830)

crossing over: exchange of parts between two homologous chromosomes (p. 169)

cross-multiplication table: a Punnett square used to determine the frequency of any genetic combination in a population (p. 219)

cross wall: a wall that grows between nuclei in some fungi (p. 337)

crustacean: a mandibulate with a great degree of specialization in various body segments (p. 493)

culture: all the information and ways of living built up over generations by a group of human beings (p. 266)

cuticle: a tough outer surface that protects the bodies of parasitic flatworms from the digestive action of their hosts (p. 463); a waxy covering on the epidermis of plants (p. 404)

cutting: a leaf or piece of a stem cut from a parent plant (p. 379)

cyanobacteria: a group of autotrophic monerans that carries out photosynthesis; also called blue-green bacteria (p. 298)

cyclic AMP: a chemical produced in a cell that mediates hormonal action (p. 722)

cyclostomes: the only remaining jawless fish; they are parasites and scavengers (p. 525)

cyst: a resting stage with a hard protective covering that is part of the life cycle of certain parasitic flatworms (p. 465)

cystic fibrosis: a genetic disorder in which thick mucus builds up in lungs, leading to severe respiratory infections (p. 185)

cytokinesis: the process of cytoplasmic division in a cell (p. 128)

cytokinin: a plant hormone that stimulates cell division (p. 416)

cytoplasm: all organelles and materials within a cell between the plasma membrane and nuclear envelope (p. 70)

cytosine: a nitrogen base found in DNA and RNA (p. 109)

cytoskeleton: a system of microtubules and other proteins in the cytoplasm that provides internal support for the cell (p. 73)

cytosol: protein-rich, semifluid substance in which cell organelles are suspended (p. 70)

D

data: the measurements, observations, and information collected from a controlled experiment (p. 9)

death rate: the rate at which individuals in a population die (p. 818)

deciduous: woody plants that shed their leaves annually (p. 365)

decomposer: an organism that breaks down dead organisms for its food; saprobe (p. 803)

deficiency disease: a disorder caused by the lack of one or more vitamins in the diet (p. 641)

deletion: a mutation in which a chromosomal piece breaks off and is lost (p. 171)

demographic transition: a shift in birth and death rates that affects the size of a population (p. 822)

dendrites: finely divided branches of a neuron that carry impulses toward the cell body (p. 701)

denitrifying bacteria: bacteria that convert ammonium ions to nitrogen gas (p. 812)

density-dependent factor: a condition affecting population growth that is a result of density (p. 819)

density-independent factor: an environmental condition affecting a population that is not related to its density (p. 819)

deoxygenated: blood low in oxygen content (p. 652)

depressant: a drug that slows the functioning of the central nervous system (p. 735)

dermis: the layer of tissue directly under the epidermis (p. 623)

desert: a biome characterized by little rainfall and extremes in daily temperatures (p. 790)

development: the process of orderly change an organism goes through from the moment it begins life, until it reaches maturity (p. 30)

diabetes mellitus: a disease caused by insulin deficiency, restricting glucose from entering the cells (p. 729)

diaphragm: a large muscular sheet that separates the lungs from the abdomen and is important in breathing (p. 587)

diastole: the relaxation period between heart contractions (p. 669)

diatom: an autotrophic unicellular protist having a cell wall with two overlapping halves (p. 323)

dicot: a seed plant with two seed leaves, or cotyledons (p. 354)

differentiation: the process of cell specialization (p. 447)

diffusion: the movement of molecules from an area of higher concentration to an area of lower concentration (p. 77)

digestion: the process of reducing food to small molecules that can be absorbed by the body (p. 55)

dihybrid cross: a genetic cross involving two sets of traits (p. 155)

dinoflagellate: an autotrophic protist, having a segmented cell wall and two flagella for locomotion (p. 324)

diploid: having two of each type of chromosome (p. 157)

disaccharide: a sugar formed by combining two monosaccharides (p. 53)

disperse: to scatter (p. 353)

distal tubule: a thin tube leading from the loop of Henle in a nephron (p. 657)

division: a group of related taxonomic classes in plant classification (p. 279)

DNA (deoxyribonucleic acid): a nucleic acid found in the nucleus that contains the genetic information of a cell (p. 70)

DNA probe: a short strand of radioactively labeled, synthetic DNA that has a base sequence complementary to that of a defective gene (p. 189)

dominance hierarchy: the organization of a society into different levels of authority (p. 778)

dominant: a term used to describe a gene or trait that prevents the expression of a recessive trait (p. 150)

dormancy: a period of inactivity in a seed or spore before germination (p. 371)

dorsal: the top or the back of an animal (p. 449)

dorsal aorta: a large vessel receiving blood from the gills in fish (p. 532)

dorsal fins: a pair of fins located along the back of bony fish (p. 530)

dorsal nerve cord: a major nerve that lies above the notochord and becomes the brain and spinal cord in chordates (p. 513)

double bond: a covalent bond involving two pairs of electrons (p. 41)

double fertilization: in angiosperms, a type of fertilization in which one sperm nucleus fertilizes the egg and the other fertilizes the polar nuclei (p. 360)

double helix: the "twisted ladder" structure of DNA (p. 111)

doubling time: the time it takes for a population to double in size (p. 823)

down feathers: small feathers that insulate a body against heat loss (p. 572)

Down syndrome: a group of symptoms including abnormal facial features and mental retardation resulting from an extra copy of the twenty-first chromosome (p. 188)

drug: any chemical that alters the functioning of the mind or body (p. 735)

Duchenne muscular dystrophy: a sex-linked disorder that causes deterioration of the muscles and then death by early adulthood (p. 187)

duodenum: the portion of the small intestine closest to the stomach (p. 544)

E

echinoderm: a marine organism having tube feet and an endoskeleton that has spiny projections extending through the epidermis (p. 482)

echolocation: a method of detecting prey and obstacles using reflected sound waves (p. 594)

ecology: the study of the relationship between organisms and their environment (p. 801)

ecosystem: a unit of the biosphere in which matter and energy are transferred as organisms interact with their environment; a small part of a biome (p. 801)

ectoderm: the outer layer of cells in an embryo or mature animal (p. 447)

ectothermic: describes organisms that do not maintain constant body temperature; body temperature depends on the temperature of their surroundings (p. 528)

Edentata: the order of toothless mammals, which includes the anteater, the tree sloth, and the armadillo (p. 597)

effector: part of the body that responds to messages sent out from the brain and spinal cord and effects a change in the environment (p. 701)

egg: the female reproductive cell or gamete (p. 149)

egg tooth: a small structure on the end of a hatching bird's beak used in pecking through the eggshell (p. 581)

electron: a very small, negatively charged particle spinning around the nucleus of an atom (p. 38)

electron microscope: a microscope that uses a beam of electrons instead of light as its source of illumination (p. 14)

electron transport chain: a series of reactions in the aerobic phase of cellular respiration in which a large amount of energy is used to produce ATP (p. 96)

element: a substance that cannot be broken down into simpler substances; a substance made of only one kind of atom (p. 37)

embryo: an organism in the early stages of development (p. 235)

emergent: a very tall tree that extends above the canopy of a tropical rain forest (p. 789)

emigration: the movement of organisms out of an area (p. 818)

emphysema: a condition in which the alveoli in the lungs are ruptured; interferes with oxygen intake (p. 742)

endocrine gland: a ductless gland that secretes chemicals directly into the bloodstream (p. 719)

endocytosis: the transport of molecules into cells through vesicles (p. 85)

endoderm: the inner layer of cells in an embryo or mature animal (p. 447)

endodermis: the innermost ring of cortex cells in a plant root (p. 386)

endometrium: the lining of the uterus in humans (p. 752)

endoplasmic reticulum: a network of channels in the cytoplasm of a cell (p. 71)

endorphins: polypeptides secreted from the brain in large amounts during times of great physical stress that can cause a feeling of euphoria (p. 738)

endoskeleton: an internal framework of bones and/or cartilage (p. 482)

endosperm: a triploid tissue containing stored food for the embryonic plant within a seed (p. 360)

endospore: a thick-walled cell formed by bacteria during unfavorable conditions (p. 297)

endothermy: the ability of some organisms to maintain a constant internal body temperature (p. 576)

energy: the ability to do work (p. 27)

energy pyramid: a representation of the loss of energy as it is transferred through levels of a food chain (p. 805)

environment: all the living and nonliving factors that make up the surroundings of an organism (p. 27)

environmental resistance: the sum of all the limiting environmental factors that prevent a population from reaching its biotic potential (p. 817)

enzyme: a protein molecule that acts as a catalyst to speed up biochemical reaction rates and regulate a cell's metabolism (p. 61)

epicotyl: the part of an embryonic plant that will become the leaves and stem (p. 371)

epidemic: the rapid and uncontrollable spread of a disease (p. 681)

epidermis: a specialized outer layer of cells in an organism that protects and covers surfaces (p. 375)

epididymis: a coiled tube leading from the testis where sperm is stored (p. 750)

epiglottis: a flap of cartilage that closes over the trachea when a person swallows (p. 630)

epiphyte: a plant that lives supported by the boughs of a tree (p. 789)

epithelial tissue: a specialized group of cells covering exterior and interior body surfaces (p. 615)

equilibrium: a state where the rate of molecules or organisms entering and leaving an area is equal (p. 80)

era: a large division of time used by geologists to divide Earth's history (p. 254)

erosion: the wearing away of soil by wind and water (p. 829)

erythrocyte: a red blood cell that transports oxygen throughout the body (p. 672)

esophagus: a tube that connects the mouth and the stomach (p. 470)

establishment: the period of a plant's life history between germination and the development of leaves (p. 372)

estivation: period of inactivity and reduced metabolism (p. 549)

estrogen: a female sex hormone secreted by the ovaries that prepares the uterine lining for a pregnancy and causes the development of secondary sex characteristics (p. 726)

estuary: a region in which fresh water and salt water mix (p. 796)

ethylene: a hormone produced seasonally by plants that causes leaf abscission and plant ripening (p. 417)

eukaryote: any cell with a membrane-bound nucleus (p. 252)

eustachian tube: a canal that connects the space behind the tympanic membrane to the pharynx (p. 548)

evolution: the process of change that produces new species from preexisting species over time (p. 231)

excretion: the process of eliminating chemical waste from an organism by the breakdown of foods (p. 28)

exocrine gland: a gland having ducts through which secretions move to a local place of action and have only local effects (p. 719)

exocytosis: the transport of molecules out of a cell by means of vesicles (p. 85)

exoskeleton: an external skeleton (p. 489)

experiment: a procedure carried out under certain conditions in order to test a hypothesis (p. 8)

expiration: the phase of breathing during which air is expelled from the lungs (p. 653)

external respiration: the exchange of gases between the atmosphere and the blood (p. 649)

extinct: a term used for a species that no longer exists on Earth (p. 231)

extinction: the disappearance of a species from Earth (p. 831)

eyespot: a small, pigmented area sensitive to light (p. 325)

F

facilitated diffusion: a mechanism that accelerates the rate of diffusion across the plasma membrane when demand for materials inside a cell is high (p. 89)

facultative anaerobes: anaerobic bacteria that are not poisoned by oxygen (p. 301)

family: a group of related taxonomic genera (p. 279)

fat: a triglyceride that is solid at room temperature (p. 57)

fat body: a large group of fat cells (p. 545)

fatty acid: a lipid molecule made of a long chain of carbon and hydrogen atoms with COOH (carboxyl) group at the end (p. 55)

feces: solid, indigestible waste (p. 637)

fermentation: an anaerobic process of glucose breakdown forming lactic acid or ethanol (ethyl alcohol) (p. 93)

fern: a spore-bearing vascular plant that belongs to the division Pterophyta (p. 435)

fertilization: the union of a male gamete, or sperm, and a female gamete, or egg (p. 149)

fetoscopy: a technique of viewing the fetus directly by inserting a slender tube with a light on the end into the womb (p. 191)

fetus: an embryo in its later stages of development (p. 190)

F_1 generation: the first generation of offspring in a genetic cross (p. 150)

F_2 generation: the second generation of offspring in a genetic cross (p. 150)

fibrous root system: a type of highly branched root system in vascular plants (p. 385)

fiddlehead: a new, tightly coiled fern frond (p. 435)

filament: a group of cells joined end to end (p. 328)

filter feeding: the process of straining water to obtain food (p. 514)

filtration: the process in which water, ions, sugar, amino acids, and urea move from the blood into the Bowman's capsules (p. 658)

first-order consumer: an animal that feeds directly on producers; a herbivore (p. 804)

fission: a process in which one cell divides in two (p. 129); the splitting of atoms to produce energy (p. 833)

flagella: long, whiplike projections from a cell that are used for locomotion (p. 297)

flagellate: an animallike protist that moves by means of flagella (p. 320)

flame cell: a ciliated cell that helps remove excess water from a turbellarian flatworm (p. 463)

flower: the reproductive structure of angiosperms (p. 353)

fluke: a parasitic flatworm with organs and organ systems similar to those of planarians; trematode (p. 463)

follicle: a small hollow in the ovary where an egg develops (p. 753)

follicle-stimulating hormone (FSH): a pituitary hormone that stimulates the growth of ovarian follicles and the ripening of an egg (p. 722)

food calorie: a unit of measure to indicate the energy content of food (p. 638)

food chain: the transfer of energy and nutrients through a series of organisms in an ecosystem (p. 804)

food web: a series of interrelated food chains in an ecosystem (p. 804)

foot: a large muscular organ used for locomotion in most mollusks (p. 478)

fossil: an imprint or part of an organism that lived long ago (p. 231)

fossil fuel: combustible materials that are the remains of ancient, fossilized plants and animals (p. 833)

founder effect: change in gene frequency that occurs when a population is founded on a few individuals (p. 222)

frame-shift mutation: a mutation in which a base deletion or insertion causes the gene's message to be translated incorrectly (p. 174)

fraternal twins: the offspring resulting from two eggs being fertilized by two different sperm (p. 762)

frond: a highly branched leaf (p. 435)

fruit: a structure that develops from the ovary of a plant and surrounds the seeds (p. 361)

fruiting body: a spore-containing capsule in myxobacteria and slime molds (p. 338)

functional group: a group of atoms that gives an organic molecule or a family of organic molecules distinctive properties (p. 52)

fungi: plantlike, heterotrophic organisms (p. 337)

furrow: a curve formed around the equator of an animal cell by the tightening of the plasma membrane during cytokinesis (p. 128)

G

gallbladder: the organ in which bile is stored (p. 544)

gamete: a male or female reproductive cell that carries genetic information (p. 149)

gametophyte: the haploid stage of a plant in alternation of generations that produces gametes (p. 329)

ganglion: a group of nerve cell bodies outside of the brain or spinal cord (p. 471)

gastric juice: a fluid in the stomach made of enzymes, water, and hydrochloric acid (p. 631)

gastropod: a member of the largest mollusk group, with over 35 000 species, including snails and slugs (p. 477)

gastrovascular cavity: the interior space of a cnidarian where digestion occurs (p. 454)

gastrula: the stage following the blastual stage during which germ layers are formed (p. 446)

gemmae: asexual reproductive structures in liverworts (p. 431)

gemmule: a type of asexual reproductive structure in sponges made of a tough walled group of amoebocytes (p. 451)

gene: a piece of DNA that codes for a particular trait; the basic unit of heredity (p. 151)

gene pool: all the genes present in a population (p. 218)

genetic drift: a change in allele frequency in a small population due to random events (p. 222)

genetic engineering: the use of recombinant DNA and cloning techniques to manipulate the genes of organisms (p. 206)

genetic equilibrium: a state achieved in a population when there is no change in allele frequency over a long time (p. 220)

genetic marker: a known DNA sequence that lies close to a disease-causing gene, indicating the presence of this gene (p. 189)

genetics: the study of heredity (p. 160)

genotype: the combination of two alleles that an organism inherits for a certain trait (p. 152)

genus: a group of similar species (p. 277)

geographic isolation: the division or separation of a single breeding population by a physical barrier, such as a mountain range (p. 240)

geothermal energy: heat from Earth's interior (p. 835)

geotropism: the growth response of a plant to gravity (p. 419)

germinate: to sprout or to begin development into a plant (p. 372)

germ layer: one of three original layers of cells in a developing embryo that forms the ectoderm, mesoderm, or endoderm (p. 447)

gestation: the period of development inside the mother's body (p. 590)

gibberellin: a plant hormone that promotes cell elongation (p. 416)

gill: an organ that functions in gas exchange in most aquatic animals (p. 478); a spokelike structure beneath the cap of a mushroom (p. 342)

gill arches: the structures that support the gill filaments in fish (p. 532)

gill rakers: structures that keep particles from passing through the gills in fish (p. 532)

gill slit: an opening that leads to the gills in fish; paired opening in the wall of the pharynx of chordates (p. 513)

girdling: the process of removing a ring of bark from a tree (p. 398)

gizzard: a muscular grinding organ that is part of the digestive system in segmented worms and birds (p. 470)

gliding joint: a type of joint allowing limited movement between bones (p. 618)

glomerulus: a tuft of capillaries inside the Bowman's capsule of a nephron (p. 657)

glucagon: a hormone secreted by endocrine cells within the pancreas that converts glycogen to glucose causing an increase in blood sugar (p. 727)

glucose: the most common simple sugar and primary cellular fuel of most organisms, having the formula $C_6H_{12}O_6$ (p. 53)

glycerol: a three-carbon alcohol molecule (p. 56)

glycogen: a carbohydrate made of glucose molecules; used as a food storage molecule by animals (p. 54)

glycolysis: the anaerobic stage of cellular respiration in which glucose is broken down into pyruvic acid producing two ATP molecules (p. 95)

Golgi apparatus: an organelle that prepares and stores proteins for secretion (p. 71)

gonads: the sex organs; the ovaries or testes (p. 455)

grafting: a type of vegetative propagation in which a part of one plant is attached to a rooted part of another (p. 380)

Gram stain: moneran classification in which bacteria are either Gram-positive or Gram-negative (p. 298)

grassland: a biome in which grasses are the dominant forms of vegetation (p. 790)

greenhouse effect: the process by which carbon dioxide in the atmosphere absorbs heat energy causing the temperature of the atmosphere to rise (p. 836)

growth hormone: a hormone secreted by the anterior pituitary that controls the growth of bones (p. 729)

growth rate: the rate at which the population is changing size (p. 818)

growth ring: a band of xylem cells formed in one season (p. 392)

guanine: a nitrogen base found in DNA and RNA (p. 109)

guard cells: crescent-shaped epidermal cells around the stoma of vascular plants regulating the movement of gases (p. 405)

gullet: an extension of the oral groove in paramecia that forms food vacuoles (p. 318); the beginning of the esophagus (p. 544)

gut: the digestive cavity (p. 462)

gymnosperm: a type of seed plant in which seeds develop unprotected on the scales of cones (p. 363)

H

habitat: the part of an ecosystem in which an organism lives (p. 802)

habituation: a form of learning in which an animal learns to ignore a stimulus upon repeated exposure to it (p. 774)

hair follicle: a small pocket in the dermis from which hair grows (p. 623)

half-life: the amount of time it takes for one half of a radioactive isotope sample to break down (p. 234)

hallucinogen: a drug that causes the abuser to see, feel, or hear things that are not there (p. 737)

haploid: having only one of each type of chromosome (p. 167)

Hardy-Weinberg principle: a principle stating that under certain conditions, the frequencies of alleles in a population will remain constant from generation to generation (p. 218)

Haversian canal: a channel running through bone that contains blood vessels and nerves (p. 616)

heart: a muscular organ that pumps blood through an organism (p. 469)

heartwood: the central portion of an older woody stem that no longer conducts water (p. 392)

hemocyanin: a blood protein that transports oxygen in mollusks (p. 479)

hemoglobin: a protein in red blood cells responsible for oxygen transport (p. 184)

hemophilia: a sex-linked disorder in humans in which blood cannot clot (p. 186)

herbaceous: having no woody stem tissue; soft, green stem tissue that lives for only one season (p. 390)

herbivore: a consumer that eats only plants (p. 803)

herb layer: a layer of shade-loving plants and ferns in a deciduous forest (p. 788)

heredity: the passing of traits from one generation to another (p. 148)

hermaphrodite: an organism that produces both eggs and sperm (p. 451)

heterotroph: an organism that cannot make its own food and must take in nourishment from its environment (p. 27)

heterotroph hypothesis: an idea proposed by A.I. Oparin that the first living thing was a heterotroph (p. 250)

heterozygous: a term used to describe a genotype having unlike alleles (p. 152)

hibernation: a period of winter inactivity and reduced metabolism in certain animals (p. 549)

hilum: a scar on a seed where it was attached to the ovary (p. 371)

hinge joint: a type of joint allowing movement in only one direction (p. 618)

Hirudinea: a class of bloodsucking parasites, including leeches (p. 471)

histamine: a substance that dilates blood vessels and increases their permeability (p. 685)

holdfast: a specialized cell of an alga that anchors it to a substrate (p. 327)

homeostasis: the process of maintaining a constant internal environment despite changing external conditions (p. 83)

hominid: modern humans and their ancestors (p. 268)

Homo erectus: a species of larger hominids that made tools, used fire, and probably lived in groups, whose earliest fossils appear in rock layers about 1.5 million years old (p. 269)

Homo habilis: a hominid fossil much larger than that of *Australopithecus* that is thought to be between 1.5 and 2 million years old (p. 269)

homologous chromosomes: the chromosomes of a matching pair (p. 157)

homologous structure: a structure having a common ancestry but with different uses in various species (p. 234)

Homo sapiens: a species name for humans (p. 266)

homozygous: a term used to describe a genotype with two identical alleles (p. 152)

hormone: any chemical regulator secreted by the endocrine glands that is transported to an area of the body where it causes a response (p. 416)

horsetail: a spore-bearing vascular plant that lives in damp areas and belongs to the genus *Equisteum* (p. 434)

host: an organism on or in which a parasite lives (p. 805)

Huntington's disease: a fatal genetic disorder caused by a dominant gene, the symptoms of the disease being loss of muscle coordination and mental deterioration (p. 185)

hybrid: an offspring produced by crossing two pure lines (p. 149)

hybridization: the crossing of two breeds to obtain an offspring with characteristics of both (p. 203)

hybridoma: a fused hybrid of a B cell and a cancer cell in the monoclonal antibody process that reproduces a monoclonal antibody rapidly (p. 693)

hybrid vigor: the superiority of hybrids resulting from the cross of two inbred lines (p. 203)

hydrocarbon: any one of a group of molecules made of hydrogen and carbon (p. 51)

hydrolysis: a chemical reaction in which a large molecule is split into two smaller molecules by the addition of a molecule of water (p. 54)

hypertension: high blood pressure (p. 670)

hypertonic solution: a solution having a higher concentration of dissolved substances, or solutes, than the solution to which it is being compared (p. 80)

hyphae: filamentous strands filled with cytoplasm and many nuclei that make up the bodies of most true fungi (p. 332)

hypocotyl: a part of the embryonic plant that connects the epicotyl and the radicle (p. 371)

hypothalamus: a region of the brain that controls many of the body's internal activities, such as maintaining homeostasis and regulating the release of many hormones (p. 706)

hypothesis: a possible explanation for a set of observations (p. 7)

hypotonic solution: a solution having a lower concentration of dissolved substances, or solutes, than the solution to which it is being compared (p. 80)

I

identical twins: the offspring resulting from a fertilized egg splitting into two separate embryos (p. 762)

ileum: the last half of the small intestine (p. 636)

immigration: the movement of organisms into a new area (p. 818)

immovable joint: a type of joint allowing no movement of the jointed bones (p. 618)

immune system: a collection of cells and tissues that defends the body against pathogens (p. 685)

immunity: the ability to resist a particular disease (p. 689)

imprinting: a type of learning in which an animal forms a social attachment to another organism soon after hatching or birth (p. 774)

impulse: a nerve message generated by reversing polarity at the nerve cell membrane (p. 701)

inbreeding: the technique of crossing two closely related individuals (p. 202)

inbreeding depression: a condition of decreased health or fertility after many generations of inbreeding (p. 202)

incisor: a sharp, chisel-shaped tooth used for cutting (p. 593)

incomplete linkage: the breaking apart of genes in the same linkage group through the crossing over of chromosomal material (p. 169)

incomplete metamorphosis: a type of metamorphosis with egg, nymph, and adult stages (p. 497)

incubate: to keep eggs warm so they can mature to hatching (p. 580)

infectious disease: any body disorder caused by microorganisms or viruses that can be transmitted from one person to another (p. 681)

inflammation: a response by damaged tissue that includes becoming swollen, red, and sore (p. 685)

inflorescence: a group of flowers occurring together in a definite arrangement. (p. 355)

inheritance: characteristics passed from generation to generation through the genetic material (p. 30)

innate behavior: unlearned behavior that is genetically controlled; instinct (p. 771)

inner cell mass: a group of cells in the blastocyst that develops into the embryo (p. 756)

insectivores: insect-eating organisms (p. 596)

insight learning: the ability to solve an unfamiliar problem without the benefit of trial and error; reasoning (p. 774)

insoluble: a term used to describe a substance that does not dissolve in a solvent (p. 45)

inspiration: the phase of breathing during which air is taken into the lungs (p. 653)

instinct: an innate behavior involving complex responses to a stimulus (p. 771)

insulin: a hormone secreted by endocrine cells within the pancreas that converts glucose into glycogen causing a decrease in blood sugar (p. 207)

interferon: a blood protein thought to be effective in making some cells resistant to viral attack (p. 693)

internal fertilization: a type of reproduction in which sperm is deposited directly into the female's body (p. 558)

internal respiration: the exchange of gases between the blood and the body cells (p. 649)

interneuron: a nerve cell that transmits information between two other neurons; associative neuron (p. 701)

interphase: the period of cell growth and DNA replication occurring between divisions (p. 158)

interspecific competition: competition between members of different species for the same resource (p. 821)

intestine: an organ that functions in the digestion and absorption of food (p. 633)

intraspecific competition: competition between members of a population for the same resource (p. 821)

inversion: a mutation in which a segment of DNA in a chromosome flips upside down, but remains in place (p. 172)

***in vitro* fertilization:** a technique in which one or more eggs are removed from the ovary and placed in culture in a petri dish, to which sperm are added (p. 755)

involuntary muscle: muscle that is not under conscious control (p. 623)

ion: an electrically charged atom or group of atoms, positive or negative (p. 40)

ionic bond: a chemical bond between oppositely charged ions resulting from the transfer of electrons (p. 42)

iris: the colored area of the eye that regulates the amount of light admitted to the pupil (p. 713)

islets of Langerhans: endocrine cells within the pancreas that secrete insulin and glucagon (p. 727)

isotonic: the characteristic of having the same concentration of dissolved substances, or solutes, as the solution to which it is being compared (p. 81)

isotope: one of two or more atoms of the same element that has a different number of neutrons (p. 233)

J

Jacobson's organs: tiny pits inside a snake's mouth that contain odor-sensing nerve endings (p. 561)

jejunum: section of the small intestine between the duodenum and the ileum (p. 636)

K

karyotype: a photograph of a cell's chromosomes, arranged in order from largest to smallest (p. 187)

keel: the enlarged breastbone in birds to which the flight muscles are attached (p. 575)

keratin: a fibrous protein of which hair, horns, and feathers are made (p. 557)

kidney: an organ that removes nitrogen wastes from the blood and forms urine (p. 531)

kinesis: a simple behavior involving undirected movement in response to a stimulus (p. 776)

kinetic energy: the energy a moving object possesses; the energy of motion (p. 77)

kinetochore: a structure on chromatids where microtubules connect from the mitotic spindle; ensures the proper movement of chromatids during anaphase (p. 126)

kingdom: the broadest division in taxonomic classification (p. 279)

Klinefelter syndrome: a condition in males that includes abnormal sexual development resulting from the presence of an extra X chromosome (p. 188)

Koch's postulates: a series of procedures developed by Robert Koch to determine whether a particular microorganism caused a disease (p. 681)

L

labor: a period of uterine contractions that eventually push the baby out of the vagina at birth (p. 760)

lacteal: lymph vessels found in villi (p. 635)

lactic acid fermentation: an anaerobic process of glucose breakdown that produces lactic acid (p. 93)

lagomorphs: rodentlike animals distinguished from rodents by an additional pair of incisors (p. 593)

large intestine: a part of the digestive system between the small intestine and rectum that absorbs water from indigestible materials (p. 633)

larva: the immature stage in the life of certain animals (p. 447)

larynx: the voice box (p. 547)

lateral: the sides of a bilaterally symmetrical organism (p. 449)

lateral bud: a small side bud above each leaf scar that develops into new growth on a twig (p. 389)

lateral line: a sense organ found in all fish that is sensitive to pressure changes caused by movement (p. 533)

layering: a type of vegetation propagation in which roots are induced to form from a stem (p. 379)

leaf: the chief photosynthetic organ of a plant (p. 374)

leaflet: small blade attached to a compound leaf (p. 403)

leaf scar: a mark left on a twig that indicates the attachment of a leaf in a previous season (p. 389)

learning: a change in behavior that results from experience (p. 772)

leech: a bloodsucking parasite; a member of the class of Hirudinea (p. 471)

left atrium: the heart chamber that receives oxygenated blood from the lungs (p. 546)

lens: a protein structure behind the pupil that focuses light on the retina (p. 713)

lenticel: a group of loosely spaced cells on a stem surface that functions in gas exchange (p. 389)

leucocyte: a white blood cell (p. 674)

leucoplast: a colorless plastid in which starch molecules are synthesized from sugar molecules (p. 73)

leukemia: a cancer of white blood cells in which leucocytes divide out of control (p. 673)

lichen: a symbiotic association of a fungus and a photosynthetic organism (p. 343)

ligament: a tough, fibrous connective tissue joining bones at a joint (p. 618)

light reactions: the first stage of photosynthesis in which energy from the sun is captured as chemical energy (p. 99)

limiting factors: certain conditions that determine the types of organisms that reside in a freshwater biome (p. 795)

linkage group: genes that occur together on the same chromosome (p. 166)

lipase: an enzyme that breaks down fats (p. 633)

lipid: a nonpolar organic molecule that will not dissolve in water, made of carbon, hydrogen, and oxygen (p. 55)

litter: the layer of decomposing plant material on a forest floor (p. 788)

littoral zone: the area of the shore between high tide and low tide marks; intertidal zone (p. 793)

liver: an organ that produces bile, destroys old red blood cells, and stores glycogen (p. 531)

liverworts: small bryophytes often found along streambanks or other moist environments (p. 431)

loop of Henle: a section of tubule between the proximal and distal tubules of a nephron (p. 657)

lumen: a hollow interior space, such as the inside of a tube (p. 630)

lung: an organ that functions in gas exchange with the atmosphere (p. 536)

luteinizing hormone (LH): a pituitary hormone that causes a follicle to rupture and then become the corpus luteum (p. 753)

lymph: tissue fluid in the lymphatic vessels; exchanges materials with body cells (p. 675)

lymphatic system: the network of lymph vessels and lymph nodes (p. 675)

lymph node: a swelling in a lymph vessel where disease organisms are removed by white blood cells (p. 675)

lymphocyte: a type of white blood cell that manufactures antibodies (p. 674)

lymphokines: proteins through which immune cells communicate to each other, so that they are coordinated to fight disease (p. 693)

lymph vessels: a network of thin-walled vessels in which excess tissue fluid is collected and drained away (p. 675)

lysis: the final step of viral replication, where the host cell bursts open, releasing hundreds of new viruses (p. 307)

lysogenic virus: a type of virus that remains inactive in a cell for several generations (p. 307)

lysogeny: a process in which viral DNA is attached to and carried by the DNA of a host cell (p. 307)

lysosome: a membrane-bound organelle that stores digestive enzymes (p. 73)

lysozyme: an enzyme produced by mucous-secreting cells and tear glands that destroys bacteria (p. 705)

lytic cycle: a viral replication cycle in which the host cell lyses after producing new virus particles (p. 307)

M

macromolecule: an organic molecule made of a very large number of atoms (p. 54)

macronucleus: an organelle in paramecia that manufactures RNA (p. 319)

macrophage: a type of moving white blood cell that digests foreign materials (p. 674)

madreporite: sievelike intake opening for the water vascular system of echinoderms (p. 483)

malnutrition: a condition that occurs when a person does not eat an adequate or balanced diet (p. 643)

Malpighian tubules: a group of small tubes branching from the intestine of terrestrial arthropods that absorb nitrogenous wastes (p. 491)

maltose: a disaccharide made of two glucose molecules (p. 54)

Mammalia: the living vertebrates class composed of mammals (p. 518)

mammary gland: a gland in female mammals that secretes milk (p. 587)

mandibulate: an arthropod that has mandibles for chewing food, antennae, and three or more pairs of walking legs (p. 489)

mantle: a layer of tissue over a mollusk body that secretes the shell (p. 478)

mantle cavity: a protected space formed by the mantle hanging down over the body of a mollusk (p. 479)

marijuana: a depressant that may cause euphoria and a psychological dependence (p. 736)

marrow: tissue in the hollows of some bones that produces blood cells or stores fat (p. 616)

marsupial: a pouched mammal (p. 589)

mass: the quantity of matter in an object (p. 37)

mass selection: the selection of organisms with desired traits from a large group (p. 201)

matrix: a nonliving material secreted by osteocytes (p. 616); the dense fluid inside a mitochondrion

matter: anything that has mass and occupies space (p. 37)

maxillary teeth: small teeth that line the margins of the upper jaw of frogs (p. 543)

mechanical digestion: the physical breakdown of food by chewing and by the muscular churning of the stomach (p. 629)

medulla oblongata: a region of the brain controlling involuntary body processes (p. 533)

medusa: a bell-shaped, free-swimming body form found in cnidarians (p. 453)

megasporangium: a female reproductive structure of the conifers that produces haploid megaspores (p. 363)

megaspore: a haploid cell giving rise to the female gametophyte in gymnosperms and angiosperms (p. 356)

meiosis: a process of cellular division in which the number of chromosomes is reduced by half (p. 158)

meiospore: a haploid spore that results from meiosis (p. 326)

melanin: a dark pigment (p. 182)

memory cell: a type of B cell that remains in the body after infection (p. 689)

meninges: protective membranes covering the brain and spinal cord (p. 704)

menopause: the time when a woman's body stops producing eggs permanently (p. 754)

menstrual cycle: monthly hormonal changes causing ovulation and preparation of the uterus for a possible pregnancy (p. 753)

menstruation: a period in the menstrual cycle in which the uterine lining breaks down and is expelled from the body along with blood and the unfertilized egg (p. 754)

meristem: a plant tissue made up of unspecialized rapidly dividing cells (p. 375)

mesenchyme: a jellylike material underneath the epidermis of a sponge (p. 450)

mesoderm: the middle layer of cells in an embryo or mature animal (p. 447)

mesoglea: a jellylike material separating the two cell layers in a cnidarian (p. 454)

mesophyll: two layers of cells inside the epidermis of leaves where most photosynthesis takes place (p. 405)

messenger RNA (mRNA): a type of RNA that carries the instructions for protein synthesis from the DNA to the ribosome where it acts as a blueprint (p. 115)

metabolism: the sum of the chemical and physical processes of getting energy from food and using it to maintain the structure and function of a cell or an organism (p. 30)

metamorphosis: a series of changes in form during development of an immature form to an adult (p. 497)

metaphase: the second stage of mitosis during which the chromatid pairs align at the cell's equator (p. 126)

Metazoa: the animal subkingdom that includes all animals except the sponges (p. 445)

microdissection: the process of dividing cells into their various components (p. 16)

microfilament: a protein structure that forms a ring around the equator of an animal cell during cytokinesis (p. 128)

micronucleus: an organelle in paramecia that contains the chromosomes (p. 319)

microorganism: a microscopic living thing (p. 10)

microscope: an instrument consisting of a lens or combination of lenses that produces an enlarged image (p. 13)

microsporangium: a male reproductive structure of the conifers that produces haploid microspores (p. 364)

microspore: a haploid cell giving rise to the male gametophyte or pollen grain in gymnosperms and angiosperms (p. 357)

microtubule: long, cylindrical protein structures in the cytoplasm that give support to the cell (p. 74)

middle lamella: a layer of intercellular material separating the primary cell walls of neighboring cells (p. 76)

migrate: to move seasonally from one environment to another (p. 576)

migration: movement of individuals from one geographic area to another (p. 223)

milt: in fish, a sperm-containing fluid made by the testes (p. 534)

mimicry: a protective adaptation in which one species of insect resembles another poisonous or harmful species (p. 502)

mineral: any inorganic substance necessary for the proper functioning of the body (p. 642)

mitochondrion: an organelle in which energy production for the cell occurs (p. 72)

mitosis: the process in which a cell's chromosomes are divided prior to cytoplasmic division (p. 125)

mitotic spindle: fibrils that form between the poles of a cell during mitosis (p. 126)

mixture: a combination of substances involving no chemical changes where each substance retains its own characteristics (p. 44)

molar: a flat tooth located next to the premolars that is used for grinding (p. 629)

molecule: the smallest unit of a compound that still has the properties of that compound (p. 40)

mollusk: a phylum that includes such varied organisms as oysters, snails, and squids (p. 477)

molt: to shed the outer layer as a periodic part of growth (p. 489)

Monera: kingdom of organisms characterized by prokaryotic cell structure (p. 297)

moneran: member of Kingdom Monera (p. 297)

monoclonal antibody: an artificial antibody cloned outside the body (p. 693)

monocot: a seed plant with one seed leaf, or cotyledon (p. 354)

monohybrid cross: a genetic cross involving only one pair of alleles (p. 153)

monosaccharide: a simple sugar (p. 53)

monosomy: the condition of missing a chromosome (p. 171)

monotreme: an egg-laying mammal (p. 589)

motile: moving from place to place to capture food (p. 445)

motorneuron: a nerve cell that transmits information to a muscle or gland from the brain or spinal cord (p. 701)

mucosa: layers of cells lining the alimentary canal that secrete mucus (p. 630)

mucus: a lubricating substance secreted by mucous glands that makes food easier to swallow (p. 630)

multicellular: made of more than one cell (p. 29)

multinucleate: having many nuclei in one cell (p. 337)

multiple alleles: three or more different alleles for a given trait (p. 181)

multiple fruit: a type of fruit that develops from a single ovary of each flower in a cluster (p. 361)

muscle tissue: a specialized group of contractile cells responsible for movement (p. 615)

mutagen: any agent that can increase the rate of mutation (p. 170)

mutation: a change in the genetic material that results from an error in replication of DNA (p. 170)

mutualism: a symbiotic relationship that is beneficial to both organisms (p. 805)

mycelium: a network of filamentous hyphae in fungi (p. 337)

mycorrhizae: a fungus that absorbs mineral nutrients from soil and passes them to the roots of plants (p. 338)

myofibril: small fibers that make up each muscle cell (p. 621)

myosin: the protein making up the thick filaments in a muscle myofibril (p. 621)

N

narcotic: a pain-killing drug (p. 735)

nares: nostrils (p. 572)

nastic movement: a plant response that is independent of the stimulus direction (p. 422)

natural resource: a raw material necessary for human life or that is used to make other products (p. 829)

natural selection: the process by which the environment allows only the better adapted organisms to survive and reproduce (p. 238)

Neanderthal: a group of early *Homo sapiens* with thick, massive bones (p. 269)

needle: the leaf of a conifer (p. 409)

negative feedback: a cycle of actions in which the final event inhibits the first event (p. 725)

negative tropism: a growth response away from a stimulus (p. 419)

nekton: free-swimming organisms (p. 794)

nematocyst: a stinging cell in cnidarians (p. 454)

nematode: a worm characterized by its round, tubelike shape; roundworm (p. 466)

nephridium: an excretory structure in segmented worms (p. 470)

nephron: the tiny excretory unit of the kidney (p. 657)

nerve: a bundle of neuron fibers (p. 701)

nerve tissue: a specialized group of cells capable of conducting electrical impulses and forming the communication system of the body (p. 615)

neuron: a nerve cell; a cell specialized to carry information (p. 701)

neurotoxin: a substance that interferes with the normal functioning of neurons (p. 681)

neurotransmitter: a chemical stored and released at the end of an axon that transmits impulses across a synapse (p. 703)

neutron: an uncharged particle found in the nucleus of an atom (p. 38)

niche: the role an organism carries out in habitat (p. 802)

nicotine: a physically addictive drug found in tobacco (p. 741)

nictitating membrane: a thin covering over a frog's eye that protects it and keeps it moist (p. 542)

nitrifying bacteria: bacteria that convert ammonium ions into nitrite ions (p. 812)

nitrogen cycle: the cycling of nitrogen between inorganic forms in the environment and organic forms in living things (p. 812)

nitrogen fixation: a process by which certain bacteria and cyanobacteria convert atmospheric nitrogen into nitrates (p. 300)

nitrogen-fixing bacteria: bacteria that convert atmospheric nitrogen into ammonium ions (p. 300)

node: the region of the stem where the leaf is attached (p. 403)

nonbiodegradable: not capable of being broken down by biological decomposition (p. 840)

nondisjunction: the failure of homologous chromosomes to segregate during meiosis (p. 171)

nonrenewable resource: a natural resource that is in limited supply and cannot be replenished by natural processes (p. 829)

notochord: in lower chordates and in embryos of higher vertebrates, a flexible supportive rod running the length of the dorsal side (p. 513)

nuclear envelope: a double membrane surrounding the nucleus of a cell (p. 70)

nuclear fission: the release of heat energy through the splitting of atoms (p. 833)

nucleic acid: any of several organic acids made of nucleotides. Nucleic acids control all the activities of the cell. (p. 109)

nucleolus: an organelle within the nucleus composed of multiple copies of ribosomal RNA (p. 70)

nucleotide: an organic molecule made of a five-carbon sugar, a phosphate group, and a nitrogen base (p. 109)

nucleus: a membrane-bound organelle (p. 36); containing the chromosome (p. 70); the center of an atom containing the protons and neutrons (p. 38)

nutrient: a chemical substance that is consumed for growth and good health (p. 638)

nutrition: the process by which an organism obtains and uses food (p. 638)

nymph: an immature stage in metamorphosis in which the organism resembles an adult (p. 497)

O

obesity: a condition characterized by excessive body fat (p. 643)

obligate aerobes: bacteria that require oxygen to carry out respiration (p. 300)

obligate anaerobes: anaerobic bacteria that are poisoned by oxygen (p. 301)

oil: a triglyceride that remains in liquid form at room temperature (p. 57)

olfactory bulb: a part of the brain in fish that processes information about smell (p. 533)

olfactory lobe: the most anterior part of the brain, which receives input from the nose for the sense of smell (p. 547)

oligochaete: a class of worms containing 2 500 species, including the earthworm (p. 469)

omnivore: a consumer that eats both plants and animals (p. 803)

oncogene: a gene that causes cancer (p. 311)

oogamy: sexual reproduction in which the male gamete is flagellated and the female gamete is a larger, nonmotile egg cell (p. 326)

oogonium: an egg-producing structure found in some plantlike protists (p. 328)

open circulatory system: a circulatory system in which blood is not entirely contained in vessels (p. 479)

operculum: the gill cover in fish (p. 532)

opposable: the characteristic of a toe or a thumb that can move so it can touch the other digits, making it possible to grasp objects (p. 264)

optic lobes: the parts of the brain that process visual information (p. 533)

oral groove: an opening in a paramecium through which food is ingested (p. 318)

order: a group of related taxonomic families (p. 279)

organ: a structure composed of several tissues working together to perform a function (p. 132)

organelle: an organized structure within a cell that has a specific function (p. 67)

organic acid: a class of organic compounds having a functional group with the formula –COOH (p. 52)

organic chemistry: the study of carbon-containing compounds in living organisms (p. 51)

organic compound: a unique chemical compound made by living things and containing carbon (p. 30)

organism: any living thing (p. 27)

organ system: a group of organs working together to perform a function (p. 132)

orientation: the ability of an organism to position itself in the environment in order to find food, shelter, protection, or a mate (p. 776)

origin: the end of a muscle attached to a nonmoving bone (p. 622)

ornithischians: dinosaurs with hip bones like those of modern birds (p. 564)

osmosis: the movement of water molecules across a membrane from an area of higher concentration to an area of lower concentration (p. 79)

osmotic pressure: the pressure created against the cell membrane by the movement of water molecules in osmosis (p. 80)

ossification: the process of bone formation in which cartilage is replaced by bone (p. 616)

Osteichthyes: the living vertebrates class composed of bony fish (p. 517)

osteocyte: a bone cell (p. 616)

osteoporosis: a condition in which there is an excessive loss of bone tissue, leaving the bones porous and weakened (p. 616)

ostia: small openings through which blood enters the heart of crustaceans and insects (p. 494)

ostracoderm: the most primitive jawless fish—the earliest fish in the fossil record (p. 525)

outcrossing: the crossing of an inbred individual with a less closely related individual (p. 203)

oval window: a membrane-covered opening between the middle and inner ear (p. 712)

ovary: the female reproductive organ (p. 355)

oviduct: a tube that carries eggs from the ovary (p. 500)

oviparous: egg-laying (p. 561)

ovipositor: a structure in female insects through which fertilized eggs travel to the outside of the body (p. 500)

ovoviviparous: giving birth to live young (p. 561)

ovulation: the release of an egg from the ovary (p. 753)

ovule: a structure in the ovary of a flower that becomes a seed after fertilization (p. 355)

ovum: the female gamete, or egg (p. 751)

oxygenated blood: blood rich in oxygen content (p. 652)

oxygen cycle: the movement of oxygen between the atmosphere and living things by means of respiration, evaporation, and photosynthesis (p. 812)

oxytocin: a hormone produced by the hypothalamus that causes uterine contraction during labor and promotes milk flow from the mammary glands (p. 724)

P

P₁ generation: the first parental generation in a genetic cross (p. 150)

pacemaker: a group of specialized cardiac muscle cells that generate the electrical impulses causing heart muscle to contract (p. 666)

palisade mesophyll: a layer of long, narrow cells under the upper epidermis of a leaf (p. 405)

palmately compound: a type of leaf in which the leaflets join together before attaching to the petiole (p. 404)

pancreas: an organ that secretes enzymes for intestinal digestion as well as the hormones insulin and glucagon (p. 544)

pancreatic duct: a tube that transports digestive enzymes from the pancreas to the duodenum (p. 544)

pancreatic juice: a substance produced by the pancreas that contains digestive enzymes and that neutralizes stomach acid in the duodenum (p. 633)

parasite: an organism that lives on or in another organism and gets nourishment from it; an organism than harms its host (p. 300)

parasitism: a symbiotic relationship in which one organism lives on or in another organism, usually harming the host (p. 805)

parasympathetic nervous system: a part of the autonomic nervous system that returns the body to normal after an emergency and maintains homeostasis (p. 708)

parathormone: a hormone secreted by the parathyroid glands that regulates the levels of calcium and phosphate ions in the blood (p. 721)

parathyroid glands: four small endocrine glands on the surface of the thyroid that produce parathyroid hormone (p. 721)

Parazoa: the animal subkingdom that contains only the sponges (p. 445)

parenchyma: a plant tissue specialized for storage of food (p. 376)

parthenogenesis: the development of eggs without fertilization (p. 503)

passive immunity: the ability to resist a particular disease by means of antibodies passed on to a fetus through the placenta or to an infant through mother's milk (p. 689)

passive transport: the movement of molecules across a membrane without the use of cellular energy (p. 83)

pathogen: disease-producing organism or virus (p. 681)

pectoral fins: a pair of fins located laterally near the gill openings in all jawed fish (p. 527)

pectoral girdle: the part of the skeleton to which the anterior limbs are attached (p. 516)

pedigree: a diagram showing how a trait is inherited in a family (p. 187)

pelagic zone: the open ocean (p. 794)

pellicle: a flexible protein layer under the cell membrane of a paramecium (p. 318)

pelvic fins: pair of fins located posterior to pectoral fins (p. 527)

pelvic girdle: the part of the skeleton to which the posterior limbs are attached (p. 516)

penicillin: a chemical that kills certain bacteria without harming the body (p. 11)

penis: a male reproductive organ in animals that have internal fertilization (p. 500)

pentamerous radial symmetry: a type of body plan that can be divided into five equal parts from a central axis (p. 482)

pepsin: the principal protease in the stomach (p. 632)

peptidase: an enzyme that breaks short polypeptides into individual amino acids (p. 636)

peptide bond: a covalent bond that forms between an organic acid group of one amino acid and an amino group of another amino acid (p. 59)

perennial: a plant that lives for more than two growing seasons (p. 415)

perfect flower: a flower having both stamens and a pistil (p. 355)

pericardium: a protective membrane that surrounds the heart in humans (p. 665)

pericycle: a layer of cells around the vascular tissues from which branch roots grow (p. 386)

periosteum: a tough membrane that surrounds all bones (p. 616)

peripheral nervous system: all of the neurons lying outside of the brain and spinal cord (p. 547)

Perissodactyla: the order of odd-toed, hoofed mammals that includes the zebra, the horse, and the rhinoceros (p. 596)

peristalsis: a rhythmic, muscular action that moves food along the digestive tract (p. 631)

peritoneum: a membrane that suspends the internal organs in the coelom (p. 468)

permafrost: a layer of ground in the tundra that is always frozen (p. 787)

permeable: the characteristic of allowing to pass through (p. 78)

pesticide: a toxic chemical used to kill weeds and insect pests (p. 838)

petals: brightly colored, modified leaves that surround the reproductive organs of a flower (p. 355)

petiole: the stemlike structure that connects the blade of the leaf to the stem (p. 403)

PGAL (phosphoglyceraldehyde): a three-carbon sugar that is an intermediate product of photosynthesis (p. 102)

phagocytosis: the process in which large, solid particles are actively engulfed by a cell (p. 85)

pharynx: an extendable muscular tube used for feeding in turbellarian flatworms (p. 462); an area of the throat between the mouth and esophagus (p. 513)

phenotype: the expression of an organism's traits as a result of its genetic makeup (p. 152)

phenylketonuria (PKU): a genetic disease in which the absence of an enzyme causes a buildup of the amino acid phenylalanine causing severe retardation (p. 194)

pheromone: a chemical released by an animal that affects the behavior of others of the same species (p. 503)

phloem: a vascular tissue that transports sugars and starches throughout a plant (p. 376)

phosphate group: a functional group with the formula $-PO_3$ (p. 91)

phospholipid: a molecule composed of a lipid group and a phosphate group (p. 74)

photochemical smog: air pollution that is the result of hydrocarbons and nitrogen oxides reacting in the presence of strong sunlight (p. 836)

photoperiodism: the response of a plant to varying periods of light and darkness (p. 420)

photosynthesis: a process by which plants, using chlorophyll and energy from the sun, manufacture carbohydrates from carbon dioxide and water (p. 27)

phototropism: the growth response of a plant to light (p. 419)

photovoltaic cell: a cell that captures the sun's energy and converts it into electrical energy (p. 833)

pH scale: a logarithmic measure of the number of hydrogen ions in a solution; level of acidity (p. 46)

phycobillin: a blue photosynthetic pigment found in cyanobacteria (p. 299)

phycoerythrin: a red photosynthetic pigment found in cyanobacteria and red algae (p. 327)

phylogeny: the evolutionary history of a species (p. 279)

phylum: a large group of related taxonomic classes in animal classification (p. 279)

physical dependence: a drug-related condition in which a person suffers physical problems when a drug is withdrawn; addiction (p. 735)

phytoplankton: tiny photosynthetic organisms that float on or near the surface of a body of water (p. 794)

pigment: any substance that absorbs light (p. 99)

pili: short, hairlike protein strands that enable a bacterial cell to stick to a surface to obtain food (p. 297)

pineal eye: a vestigial eye in one species of reptile (p. 563)

pinnately compound: a type of leaf in which the leaflets attach to the petiole in a pattern resembling a feather (p. 404)

pinocytosis: the process in which a small particle or liquid droplet enters a cell through the plasma membrane (p. 85)

pioneer community: the first organisms to inhabit a specific environment (p. 807)

pith: the central part of a stem (p. 390)

pituitary gland: a small endocrine gland at the base of the brain that secretes hormones affecting all other endocrine glands (p. 547)

placenta: an organ in the uterus that exchanges materials between the mother and fetus (p. 592)

placental mammal: a mammal that nourishes its developing young through the placenta (p. 592)

placoid scale: a small, spiny type of scale found in sharks (p. 527)

plankton: free-floating, mostly microscopic, aquatic organisms (p. 322)

planula: a ciliated larval type found in cnidarians (p. 454)

Plantae: a kingdom of multicellular, eukaryotic autotrophs (p. 427)

plasma: the fluid portion of the blood that carries the blood cells (p. 671)

plasma membrane: the protective barrier that surrounds a cell; the cell membrane (p. 74)

plasmid: a small, circular piece of DNA found in bacteria (p. 207)

plasmodium: a large mass of multinucleate cytoplasm found in acellular slime molds (p. 330)

plasmolysis: loss of turgor pressure in plant cells (p. 82)

plastid: an organelle in plants that functions in photosynthesis or food storage (p. 73)

platelet: a blood cell fragment involved in clotting (p. 671)

Platyhelminthes: flat-bodied worms with simple nervous systems, reproductive systems, and digestive systems; flatworms (p. 461)

pleura: a double membrane surrounding the lungs (p. 651)

point mutation: a mutation in which one base replaces another in the DNA chain (p. 173)

polar body: a small cell resulting from unequal cytoplasmic division (p. 751)

polar molecule: a molecule with an unbalanced charge distribution (p. 45)

polar region: the areas around the north and south poles; the Arctic and Antarctic (p. 783)

pollen: grains that contain the male reproductive cells of a seed plant (p. 355)

pollen cone: a male reproductive structure of the conifers containing pollen-producing microsporangia (p. 363)

pollen tube: an extension of the pollen grain through which sperm nuclei travel to the egg (p. 360)

pollination: the transfer of pollen to the female reproductive structures (p. 357)

pollution: any unfavorable change in the environment caused partly or wholly by the actions of humans (p. 836)

Polychaeta: the class of over 6 500 species of marine worms (p. 472)

polygenic inheritance: a condition in which characteristics are governed by more than one gene (p. 182)

polynomial: a long name of a species consisting of the name of the genus plus several descriptive words (p. 277)

polyp: a vase-shaped sessile body form found in cnidarians (p. 453)

polypeptide: a molecule made of three or more amino acids (p. 59)

polyploid: a condition of having extra sets of chromosomes (p. 171)

polysaccharide: a large carbohydrate molecule made of three or more monosaccharides or simple sugars (p. 54)

polysome: a group of ribosomes bound to the same molecule of messenger RNA (p. 118)

polyunsaturated: a term used to describe lipid molecules having more than two double bonds between carbon atoms and having less than the maximum number of hydrogen atoms (p. 57)

population: all the members of a species that live in a particular location (p. 216)

population density: the number of individuals per unit of space (p. 819)

population genetics: the study of how genetic principles apply to an entire population (p. 217)

population sampling: a method in which data obtained from part of a population is assumed to be true for the entire population (p. 218)

Porifera: the only phylum in the subkingdom Parazoa; it is made up exclusively of the sponges (p. 450)

porocyte: a cylindrical cell through which water enters in some sponges (p. 450)

positive tropism: a growth response toward a stimulus (p. 419)

posterior: the back of an animal (p. 449)

precocial: a group of birds that are developmentally advanced when they hatch (p. 582)

predator: an organism that actively seeks out its prey (p. 535)

premolar: a flat tooth located next to the canines that is used for grinding (p. 629)

pressure-flow hypothesis: the concept that food is transported through the phloem as a result of differences in pressure (p. 398)

primary cell wall: the part of a cell wall that is laid down when the cell is formed and expands as it grows (p. 75)

primary oocyte: cell that divides in meiosis to produce the secondary oocyte and the first polar body (p. 751)

primary growth: the proliferation of meristematic tissue that adds length to a root or stem (p. 386)

primary spermatocyte: cell that divides in meiosis I to produce two secondary spermatocytes (p. 750)

primary succession: ecological succession occurring in an area not previously colonized (p. 807)

primary tissue: any of the tissues in a plant that arise from the meristem (p. 386)

primate: a mammal having an enlarged brain and a complex social system (p. 263)

principle of independent assortment: the principle that states that the inheritance of alleles for one trait does not affect the inheritance of alleles for another trait (p. 155)

principle of segregation: the principle that states that for any pair of contrasting traits, the F_2 generation shows a ratio of 3 dominant to 1 recessive trait (p. 151)

probability: the chance that a given event will occur (p. 153)

producer: an organism that manufactures its own food (p. 803)

product: a substance resulting from a chemical reaction (p. 43)

progesterone: a female sex hormone that maintains the uterus in a prepared state for pregnancy and causes the development of secondary sex characteristics (p. 726)

proglottid: a segment of a tapeworm (p. 464)

prokaryote: cell without a membrane-bound nucleus (p. 252)

prolactin: a hormone secreted by the anterior pituitary that stimulates the secretion of milk from the mammary glands (p. 762)

prophase: the first stage of mitosis in which the chromosomes contract and the mitotic spindle forms (p. 125)

prosimian: any of a group of primitive primates including lorises, lemurs, and tarsiers (p. 598)

prostaglandin: a chemical produced in a cell that mediates hormonal action (p. 729)

protease: any of a group of enzymes that break down protein (p. 632)

protein: a macromolecule made of amino acids held together by peptide bonds (p. 58)

prothallium: a small algaelike gametophyte in psilopsids and ferns (p. 433)

protist: a member of Kingdom Protista (p. 280)

Protista: a kingdom of eukaryotic organisms, including unicellular and multicellular forms, autotrophs and heterotrophs, with various forms of locomotion; organisms that do not fit into the other four kingdoms (p. 317)

Protoavis: a primitive creature that showed characteristics of both reptiles and birds (p. 571)

proton: a positively charged particle found in the nucleus of an atom (p. 38)

protonema: a filamentous stage that develops into the gametophyte in mosses (p. 430)

protoplast: a plant cell whose cell wall has been removed chemically (p. 205)

proventriculus: the first part of a bird's stomach that secretes gastric juices (p. 576)

proximal tubule: a thin tube connected to Bowman's capsule in a nephron (p. 657)

pseudopod: "false foot"; temporary extensions of the cytoplasm in amoeboid cells that are used for locomotion or food-getting (p. 317)

psychological dependence: a strong emotional need for a drug (p. 735)

puberty: a time, usually in the early teenage years, when the sex hormones cause the release of eggs from the ovary, sperm production in the testes, and the development of secondary sex characteristics (p. 726)

pulmonary artery: a large artery that carries blood from the heart to the lungs (p. 546)

pulmonary circulation: the passage of blood between the heart and the lungs (p. 668)

pulmonary loop: the circulation of blood between the heart and the lungs (p. 545)

pulmonary semilunar valve: a valve in the heart at the base of the pulmonary artery (p. 665)

pulmonary vein: a large vein that carries blood from the lungs to the heart (p. 546)

punctuated equilibrium: the evolutionary process in which species remain relatively unchanged for long periods of time punctuated by short periods of dramatic change in organisms (p. 244)

Punnett square: a chart used to visualize all possible genotypes of a genetic cross (p. 153)

pupa: an insect in the immature stage in insect metamorphosis during which the tissues of the organism are completely reorganized (p. 497)

pupil: an opening in the middle of the iris that admits light into the eyeball (p. 713)

pure line: a breed of plant or animal that produces offspring with the same traits as the parents (p. 149)

pyloric caeca: pouches extending from the upper end of the intestine in fish (p. 531)

pyruvic acid: a three-carbon compound that is the end product of glycolysis (p. 93)

Q

quill feathers: feathers on the wings and tail that help to stabilize a bird in flight (p. 572)

R

R group: any functional group that gives an amino acid its chemical properties (p. 59)

radial symmetry: a type of symmetry in which an organism can be divided into equal halves by passing a plane through the central axis of the animal in any direction (p. 448)

radicle: the part of an embryonic plant that will become the root (p. 371)

radioactive: a term used to describe unstable atomic nuclei that break down, releasing particles and energy (p. 233)

radula: a feeding device in mollusks having toothlike projections for scraping (p. 478)

reabsorption: the process of bringing substances from tubules back into the bloodstream (p. 658)

reactant: a substance entering into a chemical reaction (p. 43)

receptacle: the enlarged tip of a stem that supports the flower (p. 355)

receptor: a structure of the central nervous system responsible for receiving stimuli from inside and outside the body (p. 701); a protein hormone embedded in the plasma membrane that interacts with other proteins (p. 722)

recessive: a term used to describe a gene or trait that is hidden by a dominant gene (p. 150)

recombinant DNA: the new DNA that results from combining two or more types of DNA (p. 206)

rectum: the end of the large intestine (p. 637)

red blood cells: hemoglobin-containing cells that transport oxygen throughout the body (p. 545)

red-green color blindness: the inability to distinguish red from green (p. 168)

reflex: an automatic response to a stimulus (p. 706)

refractory period: the time after a nerve impulse is completed during which the plasma membrane restores itself and no new nerve impulses can be generated (p. 702)

refuge: an area in which wildlife is legally protected (p. 831)

regeneration: the cell replacement of an entire body part (p. 133)

reinforcement: a reward used in learning situations (p. 775)

releasing factor: any of a group of hormones produced by the hypothalamus that stimulates the pituitary to secrete specific hormones (p. 724)

renal artery: an artery bringing blood to the kidneys (p. 545)

renal cortex: the outer layer of the kidney (p. 656)

renal medulla: the inner portion of the kidney (p. 656)

renal pelvis: a cavity in the kidney in which urine collects (p. 656)

renal vein: veins taking blood from the kidneys (p. 545)

renewable resource: a resource unlimited in supply that is replaced over time by natural processes (p. 829)

replication: a process in which a strand of DNA is reproduced; process by which new viral particles are produced (p. 112)

reproduction: the process by which organisms produce more organisms of the same kind (p. 30)

reproductive isolation: a barrier to interbreeding caused by varied breeding times (p. 241)

Reptilia: the vertebrate class composed of reptiles (p. 517)

research method: an organized procedure for investigating problems that includes experimentation (p. 9)

resolution: the ability to distinguish between two objects next to each other (p. 14)

respiration: the process of converting food energy into a form of energy usable by cells; the exchange of oxygen and carbon dioxide between cells and their environment (p. 649)

response: the reaction of an organism to a stimulus (p. 27)

restriction enzyme: an enzyme capable of cutting DNA into fragments at specific points in the nucleotide sequence (p. 206)

retina: a thin area on the back of the eyeball containing light-sensitive receptor cells (p. 713)

retrovirus: a cancer-causing virus that transforms cells by altering the function of host-cell genes or by carrying oncogenes from one host to another (p. 308)

Rh factor: a type of antigen on red blood cells (p. 673)

rhizoid: rootlike structures in fungi and bryophytes (p. 339)

rhizome: a horizontal underground stem (p. 379)

ribosomal RNA (rRNA): a type of RNA that makes up the ribosomes (p. 115)

ribosome: tiny organelles scattered throughout the cytoplasm and attached to the endoplasmic reticulum that are the sites of protein synthesis (p. 71)

right atrium: the heart chamber that pumps blood into the ventricle (p. 545)

RNA (ribonucleic acid): a single-strand nucleic acid that carries the code for protein synthesis out of the nucleus (p. 114)

rod: a light-sensitive cell of the retina that responds in dim light; cannot distinguish colors (p. 714)

rodent: the largest order of mammals; it includes mice, rats, and squirrels (p. 593)

root: a plant organ specialized to absorb water and minerals from the soil (p. 374)

root cap: a group of protective cells covering the growing tip of a root tip (p. 386)

root hair: a small, fingerlike extension of a root epidermal cell in the zone of maturation (p. 386)

root pressure: pressure exerted by water in the root that helps move water up the plant (p. 396)

RuBP (ribulose biphosphate): a five carbon sugar found in the chloroplasts that functions in carbon fixation (p. 102)

ruminant: an ungulate having several compartments to its stomach (p. 596)

rust: a parasitic fungus with two different hosts that infects many kinds of plants, causing crop damage (p. 342)

S

saliva: a fluid produced by the salivary glands (p. 630)

salivary gland: a group of secretory cells that produce saliva (p. 634)

saprobe: an organism that feeds on dead organic matter; decomposer (p. 300)

sapwood: the younger portion of a woody stem that can conduct water (p. 392)

sarcodine: a protist that takes in food by pseudopods (p. 317)

sarcomere: the region of a myofibril from one Z band to the next; the contractile unit of a muscle cell (p. 621)

saturated: a term used to describe an organic molecule with single bonds between carbon atoms and has the maximum number of hydrogen atoms bonded to each carbon (p. 56)

scales: small, hard, overlapping structures covering the surface of bony fish (p. 530)

scanning electron microscope: an electron microscope that takes pictures of an object's surface (p. 15)

scavenger: an animal that feeds on dead organisms (p. 803)

scientific theory: a hypothesis that is supported by experimental evidence (p. 10)

scion: the part of a plant attached to the rooted stock in grafting (p. 380)

sclerenchyma: a plant tissue specialized for strength, support, and protection (p. 376)

scrotum: external sac that surrounds the testes of a mammal (p. 749)

sebaceous gland: oil-producing gland in the epidermis (p. 587)

secondary cell wall: the portion of a cell wall that is laid down after a cell reaches its full size (p. 75)

secondary growth: the proliferation of cambium tissue that adds width to a root (p. 387)

secondary oocyte: a cell that undergoes meiosis II to produce the ovum and a second polar body (p. 751)

secondary spermatocyte: a cell that divides in meiosis II to produce sperm cells (p. 750)

secondary succession: ecological succession occurring in an area stripped of its previous community (p. 808)

second-order consumer: an animal that eats a first-order consumer (p. 804)

secretion: a process of releasing a material; the material released (p. 71)

sedimentary rock: a type of rock made of compressed layers of sediment from beneath a body of water (p. 231)

seed: a multicellular structure containing a diploid embryonic plant and a food supply protected by a seed coat (p. 355)

seed coat: a waterproof covering around a seed (p. 371)

seed cone: a female reproductive structure of the conifers containing spore-producing megasporangia (p. 363)

segmentation: the division of the body into sections (p. 469)

selection: choosing the individuals with a desired trait as the first step in controlled breeding (p. 201)

selectively permeable: the characteristic of only allowing certain substances to pass through (p. 78)

self-pollination: pollen that fertilizes eggs in the same flower in which it is produced (p. 360)

semen: a liquid made up of seminal fluid and sperm (p. 751)

semicircular canals: organs that function in balance and hearing in vertebrates (p. 533)

seminal receptacle: a chamber that stores sperm in many female invertebrates (p. 490)

senescence: any process that leads to the death of a plant or any of its parts (p. 421)

sense strand: the side of the DNA double helix that is transcribed during protein synthesis (p. 115)

sensory neuron: nerve cell that transmits information from the environment to the brain or spinal cord (p. 701)

sensory palp: a slender organ of taste that extends from the mouth part of an insect (p. 498)

sepal: one of the outermost flower structures; a modified leaf that encloses the flower before it opens (p. 355)

sessile: living permanently attached to the substrate (p. 445)

setae: bristles on each segment of segmented worms that function in locomotion (p. 470)

sex chromosomes: one of a pair of chromosomes related to the sex of an individual (p. 165)

sex-influenced traits: characteristic that is dominant in one sex and recessive in the other (p. 183)

sex-limited gene: a gene that is expressed only in individuals of a certain sex (p. 182)

sex-linked gene: a gene located on, or linked to, the X chromosome (p. 167)

sex-linked trait: a characteristic determined by genes on the X chromosome (p. 167)

sexual reproduction: a method of producing offspring in which two haploid gametes join to form a diploid zygote (p. 157)

shaft: a hollow tube that forms the central part of a feather (p. 571)

shrub layer: a layer of bushes in a deciduous forest (p. 788)

sickle-cell disease: a hereditary disease in which hemoglobin is abnormal and red blood cells are sickle-shaped (p. 184)

sickle-cell trait: the condition of being heterozygous for sickle-cell disease (p. 185)

sidestream smoke: cigarette smoke affecting nonsmokers that contains higher levels of many harmful chemicals than does the smoke that is inhaled directly by the smoker (p. 743)

sieve tube element: a long, thick-walled phloem cell (p. 397)

simple eye: a light-sensitive organ in invertebrates (p. 491)

simple fruit: a type of fruit that develops from a single ovary in a single flower (p. 361)

simple leaf: a type of leaf in which only one blade is attached to the petiole (p. 403)

single bond: a covalent bond involving a single pair of electrons (p. 41)

sinus venosus: a sac just behind the heart in fish and frogs that collects blood as it returns to the heart (p. 532)

siphon: a nozzlelike structure of cephalopod mollusks used for rapid locomotion (p. 481)

skeletal muscle: voluntary muscle that moves bones; striated muscle (p. 619)

skull: a group of fused, bony plates protecting the brain (p. 516)

small intestine: a part of the digestive system between the stomach and the colon in which most chemical digestion occurs (p. 633)

smooth muscle: nonstriated muscle found in many internal organs like the stomach, intestine, and blood vessels (p. 623)

society: a group of animals that live together and show a division of labor (p. 777)

sodium-potassium pump: a protein structure located in the plasma membrane of neurons and powered by ATP that is responsible for the restoration of ion concentration within the cell (p. 702)

soluble: a term used to describe a substance that dissolves in a solvent (p. 45)

solute: the substance dissolved in a solvent in a solution (p. 44)

solution: a mixture in which the individual molecules or ions of a solute are uniformly distributed (p. 44)

solvent: the medium in which some substance is dissolved (p. 44)

somatic cell: all body cells except germ cells (p. 157)

somatic nervous system: motor neurons that connect the central nervous system to striated, or skeletal, muscles (p. 708)

somatotropin: a human growth hormone secreted by the anterior pituitary to the liver that causes the secretion of somatomedin (p. 729)

sorus: a cluster of sporangia found on the underside of fern fronds (p. 435)

speciation: the formation of a new species due to natural selection (p. 240)

species: a group of closely related organisms capable of mating and producing fertile offspring (p. 215)

specific epithet: the second part of binomial nomenclature; it describes a species (p. 278)

sperm: male reproductive cells, made in the testes (p. 149)

sperm nuclei: two haploid nuclei produced from the generative nucleus in the pollen tube (p. 360)

spherical symmetry: a type of symmetry in which an organism can be divided into equal halves by passing a plane in any direction through a central point (p. 447)

sphincter: a circular, smooth muscle that closes a tube when it contracts (p. 631)

spicule: a needlelike structure that provides support and protection in sponges (p. 450)

spinal nerve: a nerve that branches from the spinal cord (p. 533)

spindle fibers: microtubule tracks on which chromatid pairs are pulled to the cell's equator during metaphase (p. 126)

spine: a type of modified leaf that is very sharp and is used for protection (p. 409)

spinneret: a nozzlelike opening in the abdomen of spiders that releases silk (p. 490)

spiracle: a small opening through which air enters a terrestrial arthropod; the external opening to the trachea (p. 491)

spirilli: spiral-shaped bacteria (p. 298)

spongin: a flexible protein fiber that makes up the skeleton in some sponges (p. 452)

spongy mesophyll: a layer of loosely packed cells beneath the palisade mesophyll that carry out photosynthesis (p. 405)

spontaneous generation: the idea that living things can arise directly from nonliving material; abiogenesis (p. 21)

sporangium: a spore-producing organ (p. 433)

spore: reproductive cells that originate from asexual division (p. 325)

sporophyte: the diploid stage of a plant in alternation of generations that produces spores (p. 329)

sporozoans: a group of protists made up of parasites, having no means of locomotion as adults (p. 320)

stabilizing selection: a process that maintains traits that are successful for an organism in its environment (p. 333)

stamen: the male reproductive structure of a flower (p. 355)

starch: a carbohydrate made of hundreds to thousands of glucose molecules; used as a food storage molecule by plants (p. 54)

stem: a plant organ specialized for conducting water and minerals up from the roots and food down from the leaves (p. 374)

stigma: the tip of the pistil, where pollen first collects (p. 355)

stimulant: a drug that increases the activity of the central nervous system (p. 737)

stimulus: change in the environment that causes a reaction in an organism (p. 27)

stock: the rooted plant used in grafting (p. 380)

stolon: a horizontal stem that grows along the surface of the ground (p. 378)

stoma: a pore found in the leaves of vascular plants (p. 405)

stomach: a hollow organ that receives food and where the process of digestion begins (p. 631)

striated muscle: voluntary muscle that moves bones; skeletal muscle (p. 618)

strip cropping: an erosion prevention technique in which rows of grasses are alternated with rows of other crops (p. 830)

stroma: the enzyme-containing fluid filling chloroplasts (p. 100)

structural formula: a graphic method of showing the bonds between atoms and the arrangement of the atoms within a molecule (p. 51)

style: the long, tubular part of a pistil that supports the stigma (p. 355)

sublittoral zone: an area of shallow water from below the low tide mark to the edge of the continental shelf (p. 793)

subspecies: a distinct population of a species; a race (p. 217)

substrate: the molecule on which an enzyme acts (p. 62)

succession: an orderly change in the community of an area over time (p. 807)

succulent: a fleshy plant that stores water in its stems or leaves (p. 410)

sweat gland: a gland in the dermis that releases water and minerals when the body becomes overheated (p. 623)

swim bladder: a gas-filled organ that functions in depth control in fish (p. 532)

symbiosis: a long-term, specific association between two species (p. 805)

symbiotic: the term used to describe two organisms living in close association with one another (p. 343)

sympathetic nervous system: a part of the autonomic nervous system that initiates responses to prepare the body for an emergency (p. 708)

synapse: the gap between an axon and the structure with which it communicates (p. 701)

synapsis: the pairing of homologous chromosomes during meiosis (p. 158)

syndrome: a group of symptoms with a single underlying cause (p. 188)

synovial fluid: a lubricating liquid found in movable joints (p. 618)

systemic circulation: the passage of blood from the heart to body cells and back to the heart (p. 668)

systole: the contraction of the heart ventricles (p. 669)

T

taiga: a biome characterized by coniferous forests (p. 787)

tapeworm: a parasitic flatworm; cestode (p. 464)

taproot: a single large root that often functions in food storage (p. 386)

target cell: a specific cell type that responds to a particular hormone (p. 722)

taste bud: a taste receptor on the tongue (p. 710)

taxis: a movement away from or toward a stimulus (p. 776)

taxonomist: a scientist who studies classification of organisms (p. 279)

taxonomy: the science of classifying organisms (p. 279)

T cell: a type of lymphocyte that signals the presence of antigens, attacks infected cells, and suppresses the immune response (p. 687)

telophase: the fourth stage of mitosis in which chromosomes uncoil and new nuclear membranes form (p. 126)

temperate deciduous forest: a biome having long, warm summers, plentiful rainfall, and deciduous trees (p. 788)

temperate rain forest: a biome characterized by a cool climate, plentiful rain, and conifers (p. 788)

tendon: a strong, fibrous connective tissue attaching muscles to bones (p. 622)

tendril: a type of modified leaf that is long and slender and wraps around supports as a plant climbs (p. 409)

tentacle: one of many long appendages that function in food-getting in cnidarians and cephalopod mollusks (p. 454)

terminal bud: an area of undeveloped tissues at the tip of a woody stem (p. 400)

terracing: a method of erosion prevention in which steps are built in a hillside to plant crops on level surfaces (p. 830)

terrapin: a freshwater turtle (p. 562)

terrestrial: living on land (p. 477)

territoriality: the defense of a certain amount of space by an organism (p. 777)

testcross: a genetic cross using a homozygous recessive type to determine whether an individual is homozygous or heterozygous dominant (p. 154)

testes: the male gonads that produce sperm and the male sex hormones (p. 455)

testosterone: an androgen produced by the testes that causes the development of male secondary sex characteristics (p. 727)

tetrad: the group of four chromatids in a replicated set of homologous chromosomes (p. 158)

tetraploid: a cell with four sets of chromosomes (p. 205)

thalamus: a region of the brain that relays and screens sensory stimuli (p. 705)

theory: a hypothesis that is supported by experimental evidence (p. 10)

thigmotropism: the growth response of a plant to touch (p. 420)

thorax: the middle section of an insect body, which is specialized for locomotion (p. 497)

thylakoid: a tiny membrane-bound sac containing the chlorophyll in a chloroplast (p. 100)

thymine: a nitrogen base found only in DNA (p. 109)

thymus: a gland located beneath the breastbone that helps establish the immune system in juveniles (p. 687)

thyroid gland: an endocrine gland on the trachea that secretes thyroxine (p. 725)

thyroxine: a hormone secreted by the thyroid gland that controls the body's metabolic rate (p. 725)

timberline: the point on a mountain slope above which trees cannot grow (p. 792)

tissue: a group of similar cells that work together to perform a function (p. 132)

tissue fluid: a liquid similar to plasma that escapes from the capillaries and bathes the body cells (p. 674)

tortoise: a land-living turtle (p. 562)

toxin: any substance that interferes with the normal functioning of body cells (p. 681)

trachea: the windpipe, a tube leading from the mouth to the bronchi (p. 560); a tube that opens to the outside for gas exchange in insects and spiders (p. 491)

tracheid: a long, thick-walled hollow xylem cell (p. 396)

trait: an inherited characteristic (p. 149)

tranquilizer: a drug used to reduce anxiety (p. 736)

transcription: the process of copying the DNA code onto a strand of RNA (p. 115)

transduction: a process in which a bacteriophage injects a portion of one bacterial chromosome into another bacterium (p. 307)

transfer RNA (tRNA): a type of RNA that delivers amino acids to the messenger RNA blueprint at the ribosomes (p. 115)

transformation: a process by which some bacteria can absorb and incorporate DNA from their surroundings (p. 302)

transgenic: describes multicellular organisms with "foreign" genes in all cells; developed from fertilized eggs into which genes from other organisms were inserted (p. 208)

translation: the process of assembling amino acids into proteins at the ribosomes according to the code in messenger RNA (p. 117)

translocation: a mutation in which a chromosomal piece becomes attached to another chromosome (p. 172); the transport of food through the phloem of a vascular plant (p. 397)

transmission electron microscope: a microscope that directs a beam of electrons through an object (p. 14)

transpiration: the loss of water from a plant by evaporation (p. 388)

trematode: a parasitic flatworm with organs and organ systems similar to those of planarians; fluke (p. 463)

trichocyst: a flask-shaped cell under the pellicle of a paramecium that can release a threadlike structure for defense or for food-getting (p. 318)

tricuspid valve: a valve in the heart between the right atrium and right ventricle (p. 665)

triglyceride: an organic molecule made of three fatty acid molecules bonded to glycerol (p. 56)

triplet: a series of three nucleotides on a DNA molecule that codes for one amino acid (p. 112)

trisomy: the condition of having an extra chromosome (p. 171)

trochophore larva: a larva developed within the egg of mollusks and some annelids (p. 479)

trophoblast: a layer of cells in the blastocyst that will develop into the embryonic membranes (p. 756)

tropical rain forest: a biome characterized by heavy rainfall, constant warm temperatures, and dense growth of many plant species (p. 789)

tropism: a directional growth response of a plant to an environmental stimulus (p. 419)

tube feet: a series of small suction disks used for locomotion and food getting in echinoderms (p. 482)

tuber: a swollen underground stem (p. 393)

tubular secretion: the process of secreting substances from the bloodstream into tubules for exit from the body (p. 658)

tundra: a biome having a short growing season, little precipitation, permafrost, and low-growing vegetation (p. 787)

Turbellaria: the class of free-living flatworms (p. 462)

turgid: the state of being swollen with water (p. 82)

turgor pressure: osmotic pressure exerted by the contents of a plant cell against the cell wall (p. 82)

Turner syndrome: a condition in females that includes abnormal sexual development, resulting from the absence of the X chromosome (p. 188)

tympanic membrane: the ear of a frog (p. 542); the eardrum (p. 711)

tympanum: the hearing organ of insects (p. 498)

U

ulcer: a painful condition that results from gastric juices attacking the stomach cells (p. 632)

ultrasound: a technique using sound waves to locate and view a fetus in the uterus (p. 190)

umbilical cord: a long cord that connects the fetus to the placenta (p. 592)

understory: a layer of smaller trees and plants in a deciduous forest (p. 788)

ungulate: a hoofed mammal (p. 596)

unicellular: made of only one cell (p. 29)

unsaturated: a term used to describe an organic molecule with double bonds between carbon atoms and fewer than the maximum number of hydrogen atoms bonded to each carbon (p. 56)

uracil: a nitrogen base found in RNA (p. 114)

urea: a nitrogenous waste product from the digestion of protein, the main component of urine (p. 656)

ureter: a tube that carries urine from the kidney to the bladder or cloaca (p. 545)

urethra: a tube that carries urine from the bladder and, in males, transports sperm (p. 656)

urinary bladder: a hollow organ that stores urine (p. 545)

urochordate: a sessile, filter-feeding, marine chordate that loses its notochord and dorsal nerve cord as an adult (p. 514)

Urodela: an order of amphibians that includes salamanders; newts (p. 541)

uterus: muscular organ in which the embryo develops (p. 588); in many less complex animals, a long tube where eggs are stored (p. 548)

V

vaccine: a solution of weakened or killed microorganisms administered to produce immunity to a disease (p. 691)

vacuole: membrane-bound, fluid-filled spaces in the cytoplasm of a cell (p. 73)

vagina: the canal that leads to the uterus in female mammals; the birth canal (p. 752)

variable: condition in an experiment that can be changed or varied in an experiment while the other conditions remain the same (p. 8)

vasa efferentia: several fine tubes carrying sperm from the testes to the vas deferens (p. 547)

vascular bundle: a strand of xylem and phloem cells (p. 377)

vascular cambium: a layer of meristematic cells that give rise to secondary xylem and secondary phloem (p. 387)

vascular plant: a plant that has specialized tissues for the transport of food and water (p. 428)

vascular tissue: plant tissue specialized for transport of food, water, and minerals; also for support (p. 376)

vas deferens: a tube leading from the testes, through which sperm travel (p. 579)

vasopressin: a hormone produced by the hypothalamus that regulates the reabsorption of water in the kidney; also called antidiuretic hormone (ADH) (p. 724)

vegetative organs: organs—roots, stems, and leaves—that accomplish reproduction of a seed plant (p. 374)

vegetative propagation: asexual reproduction in plants (p. 378)

vein: a blood vessel that carries blood back to the heart (p. 532); a vascular bundle in a leaf (p. 406)

vena cava: a large vein that returns blood to the heart (p. 545)

venation: the arrangement of veins in a leaf (p. 406)

venereal disease: any sexually transmitted disease (p. 683)

ventral: the underneath of an animal; in humans, the front (p. 449)

ventral aorta: a large blood vessel carrying blood from the ventricle to the gills in fish (p. 532)

ventricle: the chamber that pumps blood away from the heart (p. 532); a cavity within the brain (p. 665)

venule: a blood vessel that receives blood from capillaries; joins to form veins (p. 667)

vertebrae: the bony parts of the spinal column in vertebrates (p. 515)

vertebral disk: a pad of cartilage between vertebrae (p. 618)

vertebrate: an animal with a backbone (p. 256)

vesicle: a tiny, membrane-bound sack within the cytoplasm of a cell (p. 71)

vessel element: a long, wide xylem cell (p. 396)

vestigial organ: a body part that is no longer fully developed or useful (p. 234)

viable: having the capability of growth (p. 372)

villi: small, fingerlike projections of tissue that function to increase surface area (p. 635)

viroid: short piece of RNA, with no protein coat, that cause several plant diseases (p. 312)

virus: particles consisting of a single molecule of DNA or RNA surrounded by a protein coat; reproduces only in a host cell (p. 305)

vitamins: organic nutrients that are necessary for many chemical reactions in the body (p. 640)

vocal cords: the structures within the larynx that vibrate to produce sound (p. 547)

voluntary muscle: skeletal muscles under conscious control (p. 619)

vomerine teeth: two very small teeth behind the maxillary teeth in the upper jaw in frogs (p. 543)

W

water cycle: the movement of water between the atmosphere and Earth (p. 809)

water vascular system: a series of water-filled canals in an echinoderm that functions in locomotion (p. 483)

whiskfern: the simplest living vascular plant lacking both true roots and leaves (p. 433)

white blood cells: any of several colorless cells that function in protecting an organism against infection (p. 545)

wilting: the loss of turgor by a plant (p. 408)

withdrawal symptoms: a characteristic group of symptoms that occurs after use of a drug has been stopped by a person who is physically dependent on that drug (p. 735)

X

xylem: a vascular tissue that transports water and minerals throughout a plant (p. 377)

xylem vessel: a vertical column of vessel cells (p. 396)

Y

yolk sac: a membrane that surrounds the yolk of an egg in birds, reptiles, and mammals (p. 558)

Z

zone of elongation: an area of a root or stem where plant cells grow in length (p. 386)

zone of maturation: an area where the process of differentiation is completed and plant cells develop into other kinds of tissues (p. 386)

zooplankton: tiny heterotrophic organisms that float on or near the surface of a body of water (p. 794)

zoospore: flagellated reproductive cells (p. 328)

Zygomycota: a division of fungi that contains terrestrial saprobes, of which common bread mold is a member (p. 339)

zygospore: a diploid zygote with a thick outer layer (p. 328)

zygote: a fertilized egg that results from the joining of two haploid gametes (p. 157)

INDEX

Abdomen, 490, 497
Abiotic factor, 783
ABO blood group, 180; *table,* 180
Abscissic acid, 421
Abscission, 421–422; *illus.,* 421
Absorption, intestinal, 636–637; in plants, 431; *illus.,* 637
Abyssal zone, 795
Acetic acid, 45–46, 95–96
Acetylcholine, 703; *illus.,* 703
Acetylcholinesterase, 703; *illus.,* 703
Acid, 45–46
Acid rain, 46, 837; *illus.,* 837
Acquired characteristic, 236
Acrasiomycota, 331; *table,* 330
ACTH, *See* Adrenocorticotropic hormone
Actin, 621; *illus.,* 621
Activation energy, 61; *illus.,* 61
Active site, 61–62; *illus.,* 61
Active transport, 396; *illus.,* 83
Adaptation, 31, 236; of bony fish, 534–536; of plants to land, 431–432; of reptiles to land, 557–558; *illus.,* 31, 236
Adaptive radiation, 241; *illus.,* 242
Addiction, 735
Adenine, 91, 109
Adenoids, 675
Adenosine diphosphate, *See* ADP
Adenosine triphosphate, *See* ATP
Adhesion, 397
Adipose tissue, 623
ADP, 92
Adrenal gland, 719, 725–726; *illus.,* 656, 726; *table,* 721
Adrenalin, 719; *table,* 721
Adrenocorticotropic hormone (ACTH), 726; *illus.,* 726; *table,* 721
Adventitious root, 388; *illus.,* 388
Aerobe, fermentation in, 92–93; obligate, 300; *table,* 299
Aerobic reaction, 92
Aestivation, 549
Agar, 304, 327; *illus.,* 304
Agglutination, 672–673
Aggression, 777
Agnatha, 517, 525–526; *illus.,* 526
AIDS, 309–310, 348, 664, 674, 683, 689–690, 692, 760, 844; *illus.,* 310, 690

Air, dispersal of pathogens, 682; pollution of, 836–837; *illus.,* 836, 837
Air bladder, 327
Air sac, 577; *illus.,* 577
Albumen, 580
Alcohol, 52, 744, 760; immediate effects of, 739–740; long-term effects of, 740–741; *illus.,* 52, 739–740
Alcoholic fermentation, 93
Alcoholism, 740–741
Aldosterone, 722; *table,* 721
Algae, 281, 322–329, 428, 793–795; algal bloom, 838; multicellular, 326–329; reproduction in, 328–329; unicellular, 323–326; *illus.,* 838; *table,* 322
Alimentary canal, lower, 633–637; upper, 629–632
Allantois, 558, 581
Allele, 151–152, 160; independent assortment of, 155, 160; multiple, 181; *illus.,* 152
Allele frequency, 218–220, 222–223; *illus.,* 218, 220
Allergy, 693
Alligator, 517, 559, 563; *illus.,* 166
Alternation of generations, 328–329, 356–357, 429; *illus.,* 329
Altitude, 786, 792; *illus.,* 792
Altricial bird, 582; *illus.,* 582
Alveoli, 651; *illus.,* 650, 651
Amino acid, 58–59, 640; codons for, 116; essential, 640; structure of, 59; *illus.,* 59; *table,* 116
Amino group, 52
Ammonification, 812
Amniocentesis, 191; *illus.,* 191
Amnion, 558, 581, 756–757
Amniotic fluid, 757
Amoeba, 317; *illus.,* 317; *table,* 320
Amoebocyte, 450
Amphetamine, 737; *illus.,* 737
Amphibian, 517, *See also* Frog; characteristics of, 541; evolution of, 256, 552
Amphioxus, 515; *illus.,* 515
Amylase, 62, 630, 633; *table,* 632
Anaerobe, facultative, 301; obligate, 301; *table,* 299
Anaerobic reaction, 92–93

Anaerobic respiration, 301; *illus.,* 301
Anal fin, 530
Anal pore, 319
Anaphase, meiotic, 158–159; mitotic, 126; *illus.,* 127
Anemia, 672–673
Angina, 669
Angiosperm, 353–354, 366; *illus.,* 353, 354; *table,* 366
Angiotensin, 728–729; *table,* 721
Angler fish, 535
Animal, body symmetry, 447–449; characteristics of, 445–449; development in, 446–447; dispersal of fruits and seeds, 362; experimentation, 610
Animallike protist, 317–321
Annelida, 468–472; *illus.,* 468–472
Annual plant, 415; *illus.,* 415
Anorexia nervosa, 644
Ant, 497, 503, 770, 806; *illus.,* 770, 806
Anteater, 597
Antelope, 778; *illus.,* 778
Antenna, 494
Anterior surface, 449
Anther, 355; *illus.,* 357
Antheridium, 328–329, 430–431, 433
Antibacterial drug, 692
Antibiotic, 692; *illus.,* 692
Antibody, 671, 686–689; monoclonal, 693–694; *illus.,* 687, 688, 693, 694; *table,* 673
Anticodon, 117–118
Antigen, 672–673, 686–689; *illus.,* 687, 688; *table,* 673
Antisense strand, 115, 120
Anura, 541–542
Anus, 466, 637; *illus.,* 466
Aorta, 499, 546; dorsal, 532; ventral, 532
Aortic semilunar valve, 665
Ape, 263–266, 598; *illus.,* 263, 267
Aphid, 497, 501, 503
Apical dominance, 417–418; *illus.,* 418
Apical meristem, 375, 386; *illus.,* 375
Apoda, 542, 551–552
Appendage, of arthropod, 489; of crustacean, 493
Appendicular skeleton, 516

Appendix, 636
Aquifer, 830
Arachnida, 490–491
Archaeobacteria, *table*, 299
Archegonium, 430–431, 433; *illus.*, 431
Aristotle, 21
Armadillo, 597; *illus.*, 597
Arteriole, 667; *illus.*, 667
Arteriosclerosis, 669
Artery, 532, 667–669; *illus.*, 667, 668
Arthropod, 488–507; *illus.*, 489
Artificial heart, 667; *illus.*, 667
Artiodactyla, 596
Ascomycota, 340–341; *illus.*, 341
Ascorbic acid, *See* Vitamin C
Ascus, 340–341; *illus.*, 341
Asexual reproduction, 157
Aspartame, *illus.*, 194
Aspergillus, 343; *illus.*, 343
Associative learning, *table*, 775
Aster, 126
Asteroidea, 482–484
Asymmetrical animal, *illus.*, 448
Atherosclerosis, 669
Atom, definition of, 38; in elements, 38; *illus.*, 38
ATP, 91–92; production in cellular respiration, 93–97; production in electron transport chain, 96–97; production in fermentation, 92–93; production in glycolysis, 95–96; production in photosynthesis, 99–101; structure of, 91; use in muscle contraction, 622–623; use in nerve impulse transmission, 702; *illus.*, 91, 92, 93, 99, 101, 102
Atrium, 532, 545–546, 665; *illus.*, 666
Auditory canal, 711–712
Aurelia, 453–454; *illus.*, 453
Australopithecus, 268, 271; *illus.*, 268, 271
Autoimmune disease, 692
Autonomic nervous system, 708–709
Autosome, 165
Autotroph, 27, 104, 252, 298–299, 803; *illus.*, 28
Auxin, 416–417, 419, 421; *illus.*, 418, 419
Aves, 517
Axial skeleton, 516
Axolotl, 551; *illus.*, 550

Axon, 701; *illus.*, 701
Azolla, 435

Baboon, 778
Bacilli, 298; *illus.*, 298
Bacteria, *See also* Moneran; denitrifying, 812; disease-causing, 298; Gram staining of, 298; importance of, 303–304; intestinal, 304; laboratory culture of, 304; in mouth, 296; nitrifying, 812; pathogenic, 681–682; *table*, 299
Bacteriophage, 306; *illus.*, 307
Balance, 711–713; *illus.*, 712, 713
Baldness, 183; *illus.*, 183
Barb, 571; *illus.*, 571
Barbiturate, 736–737, 744
Barbule, 571; *illus.*, 571
Bark, 391–393; *illus.*, 392
Barnacle, 493; *illus.*, 819
Barracuda, 535
Basal disk, 545
Base, 45–46
Base pairing, complementary, 111; *illus.*, 114
Basidia, 342
Basidiomycota, 342; *illus.*, 342, 343
Basking, 558
Bat, 594; *illus.*, 594
Bathyal zone, 794
B cells, 687–689; *illus.*, 688
Beak, 572; *illus.*, 573
Bear, 586, 595; *illus.*, 586
Beaver, 593; *illus.*, 593
Bee, 358, 503–504, 778; communication among, 504; *illus.*, 358
Behavior, 770–781; innate, 771–772; natural selection and, 771; patterns of, 776–778; social, 777–778; *illus.*, 777
Beijerinck, Martinus Willem, 305
Benthos, 794, 796
Bicuspid valve, 665
Biennial plant, 415
Bighorn sheep, *illus.*, 777
Bilateral symmetry, 448–449; *illus.*, 448, 449
Bile, 531, 544, 633
Bile duct, 544
Binary fission, 301, 317, 319; *illus.*, 301
Binomial nomenclature, 277–278
Biogenesis, 29, 30
Biological magnification, 838, 840
Biological warfare, 348
Biology, branches of, 3

Bioluminescence, 324
Biomass, 805
Biomass energy, 834
Biome, aquatic, 793–796; climate and, 786; on land, 782–792
Biosphere, 783–785; cycles in, 809–812; human impact on, 828–843
Biosynthesis, 53
Biotic potential, 817; *illus.*, 817
Bipedal walking, 265–266; *illus.*, 266
Bipinnaria larva, 482; *illus.*, 482
Bird, 517, 570; altricial, 582; circulatory system of, 578; digestion in, 576–577; embryonic development in, 581–582; evolution of, 236, 566, 571; excretory system of, 578; external features of, 573–574; feathers of, 571–572; feeding in, 576–577; flightless, 574; head of, 572–573; nervous system of, 578–579; precocial, 582; reproduction in, 579–580; respiratory system of, 577–578; sense organs of, 572–573; skeleton of, 575–576; songs of, 777; *illus.*, 570
Birth, 760–762; *illus.*, 761
Birth rate, 818, 822
Bivalve, 479–480; *illus.*, 480
Black widow spider, *illus.*, 490
Bladder, swim, 532; urinary, 545, 656; *illus.*, 656
Blade, algal, 327; leaf, 403; *illus.*, 403
Blastocyst, 756; *illus.*, 756
Blastopore, 446
Blastula, 446
Blood, 545, 671–674; alcohol level, 740; composition of, 658; deoxygenated, 652; in earthworm, 469; oxygenated, 652; plasma, 671–672; whole, 671; *illus.*, 667, 671
Blood bank, 664; *illus.*, 664
Blood clot, 669, 671–672; *illus.*, 671, 672
Blood pressure, 669–670; *illus.*, 669, 670
Blood transfusion, 673
Blood type, 181, 672–673; *table*, 181, 673
Blood vessel, 668–669
Blubber, 587, 595
Boa constrictor, 561
Body cavity, 466–467; *illus.*, 466, 468

Body fluid, homeostasis of, 659
Body symmetry, 447–449
Bond, covalent, 41; double, 41; ionic, 41–42; peptide, 59; single, 41; *illus.,* 41, 42
Bone, 516, 616–617; *illus.,* 616, 617
Bony fish, 517, 530–536
Book lung, 490–491
Botany, career in, 848
Botulism, 682; *illus.,* 682
Boveri, Theodor, 160
Bowman's capsule, 657; *illus.,* 658
Bracket fungi, *illus.,* 342
Brain, 700, 704; of bird, 578–579; convolutions of, 587; development of, 773; evolution of, 266, 461; of fish, 533; of frog, 547; of mammal, 587; size of, 265, 269; *illus.,* 269, 533, 579, 587, 705
Bread mold, *illus.,* 339
Breathing, 93–94, 648; mechanism of, 653–654; rate of, 655; *illus.,* 648
Breathing center, 655
Breeding, controlled, 201–204
Bronchiole, 651; *illus.,* 650
Bronchus, 577, 651; *illus.,* 577, 650
Brontosaurus, *illus.,* 564
Brood patch, 580
Brown algae, 326–327, 329; *illus.,* 327; *table,* 322
Bryophyllum, 379; *illus.,* 379
Bryophyte, 429–432; *illus.,* 429
Bubonic plague, 683; *illus.,* 823
Bud, lateral, 389, 417; terminal, 389, 417; *illus.,* 418
Budding, 341; plant propagation by, 380; sponge, 451; *illus.,* 341, 380
Bud scale, 389
Bud-scale scar, 389
Bulb (plant), 393
Bulimia, 644
Bumblebee, *illus.,* 358
Burbank, Luther, 201
Burdock, *illus.,* 362
Butterfly, 358, 497, 501; dead leaf, 224; monarch, 502; viceroy, 502; *illus.,* 224, 238, 497, 502
Bypass surgery, 669

Cactus, 409, 790
Caeca, 498
Caiman, 563
Calcitonin, *table,* 721

Calcium, 616–617; *table,* 642
Calorie, 638
Calvin cycle, 102; *illus.,* 102
Cambium, 375; cork, 387, 393; vascular, 387, 391; *illus.,* 375, 387, 391
Camel, 782; *illus.,* 782
Camouflage, 502; *illus.,* 224, 239
Cancer, 124, 137–138, 170, 686, 689, 694; lung, 742; skin, 623; treatment, 140–141; viruses and, 311; *illus.,* 137, 689
Canine teeth, 629
Canopy, forest, 788–789; plant, 375
Capillarity, 396
Capillary, 532, 667–669; *illus.,* 667, 668
Capillary water, 392
Capsid, 306; *illus.,* 306
Capsule, moneran, 297; moss, 430
Captive breeding program, 831–832
Carapace, 493, 562
Carbohydrate, 53–55; in diet, 638–639; *illus.,* 639
Carbon, 38, 39; chemistry of, 51–52; fixation of, 99, 102; *illus.,* 51, 95; *table,* 39
Carbon-14, *table,* 234
Carbon cycle, 810–811; *illus.,* 810
Carbon dioxide, 41, 93, 94, 95–96; greenhouse effect, 836–837; in lung, 652; *illus.,* 41, 652; *table,* 39
Carbonic acid, 653
Carbonic anhydrase, 653
Carboniferous Period, 564
Carboxyl group, 52
Carcinogen, 137; *illus.,* 137
Cardiac muscle, 622–623; *illus.,* 623
Career, in botany, 848; in medicine, 849; in pharmaceuticals, 847; in teaching, 846
Carnivore, 595–596, 599, 803; *illus.,* 595, 596, 803
Carpel, 355; *illus.,* 355
Carrier, 168, 186–187; identification of, 189–190; *illus.,* 186
Carrying capacity, 818, 823; *illus.,* 818
Cartilage, 516, 616–617
Cartilage fish, 517, 527–529
Carybaras, 593
Catalyst, 61

Caterpillar, *illus.,* 502
Cattail, *illus.,* 378
Caudal fin, 530
Cave art, 270; *illus.,* 270
Cavity (dental), 296; *illus.,* 296
Cell, 28–29; animal, 29, 68; differentiation, 445; first, 251–252; function of, 67–68; growth of, 129–130; interaction with environment, 77–82; lifespan of, 134; plant, 29, 69, 75; regulation of, 109–118; replacement of, 133; shape of, 131; size of, 129–131; somatic, 157; specialized, 445; structure of, 69–70; surface area of, 129–130; volume of, 129–130; *illus.,* 28, 29, 68, 69; *table,* 67
Cell division, 125–127; abnormal, 135–138; regulation of, 134–138; significance of, 129–133; *illus.,* 137
Cell plate, 128; *illus.,* 128
Cell theory, 29; *illus.,* 30
Cellular respiration, 93–97; aerobic phase of, 95–98; glycolysis, 95–96
Cellulose, 54–55, 75, 596, 639
Cellulose membrane, 78; *illus.,* 79, 80
Cell wall, 75–76, 81, 128; moneran, 297–298; primary, 75–76; secondary, 75; *illus.,* 75; *table,* 322
Cenozoic Era, 258, 599; *illus.,* 254–255, 258
Centipede, 494–495; *illus.,* 495
Central nervous system, 547, 704; *illus.,* 704
Centrifuge, 16
Centriole, 74, 126; *illus.,* 74
Centromere, 126; *illus.,* 126
Cephalization, 461, 489, 519
Cephalochordate, 515
Cephalopoda, 480–481; *illus.,* 480
Cephalothorax, 490
Cerebellum, 533, 547, 704
Cerebral cortex, 704
Cerebral palsy, 705
Cerebrospinal fluid, 704
Cerebrum, 519–520, 533, 547, 578–579, 587, 598, 704–705; *illus.,* 520, 579, 705, 707
Cervix, 752, 760
Cestoda, 461, 464–465; *illus.,* 464, 465

Cetacea, 595
Chalaza, 580
Chalone, 133
Chaparral, *illus.*, 786
Cheetah, 226–227; *illus.*, 214
Chelicerata, 489–492
Cheliped, 493
Chelonia, 559, 562; *illus.*, 562
Chemical communication, 770;
 illus., 770
Chemical control, 719–720
Chemical formula, 39; *table*, 39
Chemical reaction, 43–44; *illus.*, 43
Chemical regulator, 718–733
Chemical symbol, 37
Chemoautotroph, *table*, 299
Chemosynthetic bacteria, 299;
 table, 299
Chemotherapy, 692
Chestnut blight fungus, *table*, 808
Chewing, 629–630
Chewing tobacco, 743
Chicken pox, 682
Chilopoda, 494–495; *illus.*, 495
Chiroptera, 594
Chitin, 337, 489
Chlamydomonas, 325
Chlorella, 325
Chlorine, 40; *table*, 40, 642
Chlorophyll, 73, 100–101, 322–329,
 421; *illus.*, 100, 101; *table*, 322
Chlorophyta, *table*, 322
Chloroplast, 73, 100–101; origin of,
 252–253; *illus.*, 73
Choking, 654
Cholera, 683
Cholesterol, 639, 669
Chondrichthyes, 517, 527–529
Chordate, definition of, 513–514;
 subphyla of, 514–515; *illus.*, 482,
 513
Chorion, 558, 581, 757; *illus.*, 758
Chorionic gonadotropin, *table*, 721
Chorionic villus sampling, 191
Chromatid, 126, 158–159; crossing
 over of, 168–169 *illus.*, 126
Chromoplast, 73
Chromosome, 70; genes and, 164–
 175, 178–179; homologous, 157–
 158, 160; inheritance and, 165–
 169; linkage groups on, 166–167;
 mapping of, 169; mutation, 170–
 172; number of, 157; rearrangement, 171; sex, 165–166; theory
 of inheritance, 160; *illus.*, 160,
 171–173

Chrysophyta, *table*, 322
Cigarette smoke, *illus.*, 137
Cilia, 318–319, 651; *illus.*, 319;
 table, 320
Ciliate, 318–319; *illus.*, 318, 319;
 table, 320
Ciliophora, *table*, 320
Circadian rhythm, 772
Circulation, 665; in birds, 578;
 coronary, 665, 667; in crayfish,
 494; in earthworm, 469; in frog,
 545–546; in grasshopper, 499;
 liver and, 675–676; in mollusks,
 479; pattern of, 667–668; in
 perch, 532; pulmonary, 545, 668;
 in snake, 560; in spider, 491; systemic, 545, 668; *illus.*, 532, 546,
 667, 668, 676
Circulatory system, closed, 479;
 open, 479
Citric acid cycle, 95–96; *illus.*, 95
Clam, 479, 793, 795–796; *illus.*,
 480
Class, 279
Classification, 276; binomial nomenclature, 277–278; five-kingdom system, 281–283; levels of,
 278–279; modern techniques of,
 279–280; of monerans, 298; of
 plants, 427–428; of protists, 320,
 322, 330; three-kingdom system,
 280; of vertebrates, 516–518;
 illus., 279, 298, 427, 428, 517;
 table, 299, 320, 322, 330
Classification key, 284–286; *illus.*,
 286; *table*, 285
Claw, 557
Cleavage, of zygote, 446
Climate, 786
Climax community, 807
Cline, 216–217, 224, 240; *illus.*,
 216
Clitellum, 471
Cloaca, 545
Clone, 206
Cloning, 206; *illus.*, 206
Clownfish, 805; *illus.*, 805
Club fungi, 342
Club moss, 433–434; *illus.*, 434
Clutch, 581
Cnidaria, 453–456
Cocaine, 737, 760; *illus.*, 737
Cocci, 298; *illus.*, 298
Cochlea, 712
Codeine, 735–736
Codominance, 156; *illus.*, 156

Codon, 116, 173; initiation, 117–
 118; termination, 116; *table*, 116
Codosiga, *table*, 320
Coelocanth, 536; *illus.*, 536
Coelom, 468–469; *illus.*, 468
Coenzyme, 62, 640–641
Cofactor, 62
Cogeneration, 835
Cohesion, 396; *illus.*, 397
Cohesion-tension theory, 396; *illus.*,
 397
Colchicine, 205
Coleoptile, 373
Collagen, 616
Collar cell, 450; *illus.*, 450
Collecting duct, 657
Collenchyma, 376; *illus.*, 376
Colon, *See* Large intestine
Colony, green algae, 326; *illus.*,
 326
Coloration, in fish, 535; warning,
 502; *illus.*, 502, 535
Color blindness, red-green, 168;
 illus., 168
Commensalism, 806
Common ancestor, *illus.*, 235
Common bile duct, 633–634; *illus.*,
 634
Common cold, 682, 691
Common name, *illus.*, 278
Communication, 776, 778; among
 bees, 504; chemical, 770; *illus.*,
 770
Community, 801–806; changes in,
 807–808; climax, 807; definition
 of, 802; pioneer, 807
Compact bone, 616; *illus.*, 616
Companion cell, 398
Compass orientation, 776
Competition, interspecific, 821;
 intraspecific, 821; *illus.*, 821
Competitive exclusion principle, 821
Complementary base pairing, 111;
 illus., 114
Compound, definition of, 39; from
 elements, 39–40; organic, 51–52
Compound microscope, 13–14;
 illus., 851
Computed tomography scanner,
 illus., 16
Computer, *illus.*, 16
Conceptacle, 329
Conditioned reflex, *table*, 775
Cone (plant), pollen, 363–364;
 seed, 363–364; *illus.*, 365
Cones (eye), 714; *illus.*, 714

Conifer, 363, 409, 787–788; *illus.,* 363

Conjugation, 301–303, 319; *illus.,* 302, 319, 328

Connective tissue, 615; *illus.,* 615

Conservation, 835; *illus.,* 835

Constrictor, 561

Consumer, 803, 805; first-order, 804; second-order, 804; *illus.,* 804

Contact inhibition, 135

Contour feather, 572; *illus.,* 572

Contour plowing, 830

Contraception, 754, 756

Contractile vacuole, 317

Contraction, of muscle, 621–622, 703; *illus.,* 621

Controlled experiment, 8–9; *illus.,* 9

Convergent evolution, 242, 591; *illus.,* 243

Cooperation, 778

Coordination, in earthworm, 470–471

Copper, 62

Coral, 455–456; *illus.,* 280, 456

Coral reef, 456, 794; *illus.,* 456

Cork, 377, 393

Cork cambium, 387, 393; *illus.,* 391

Corm, 393

Cornea, 713

Coronary artery, 669

Coronary circulation, 665, 667

Corpus luteum, 753

Cortex, 386, 391

Corticoid, 722, 725–726; *illus.,* 726; *table,* 721

Cotyledon, 354, 371; *illus.,* 372

Cotylosaur, 564

Courtship, 776–771

Covalent bond, 41; *illus.,* 41

Cover crop, 830

Crab, 494, 793–794, 806

Crack, 737; *illus.,* 737

Cranial nerve, 533, 547, 707

Crayfish, 493–495, 795; *illus.,* 494, 802

Crick, Francis, 111–112

Crocodile, 559, 563

Crocodilia, 559, 563

Cro-Magnons, 269–271; *illus.,* 270

Crop (animal), of bird, 576; of earthworm, 470

Crop (plant), cover, 830; rotation of, 830

Crossing over, 168–169; *illus.,* 169

Cross-multiplication table, 219; *illus.,* 219

Cross wall, 337; *illus.,* 337

Crustacea, 493–495; *illus.,* 494

Cud, 596

Culture, 266, 270

Cuticle, of fluke, 463; of plant, 375, 404, 409

Cuttings, plant, 379

Cyanobacteria, 298–299, 300, 343; *illus.,* 299; *table,* 299

Cycad, 366

Cycles, in biosphere, 809–812

Cyclic AMP, 722–723, 728

Cyclosporin, 693

Cyclostome, 525–526

Cystic fibrosis, 185; *illus.,* 185; *table,* 189

Cytochrome *c*, 235

Cytokinesis, 128; *illus.,* 128

Cytokinin, 416–417, 421

Cytoplasm, 70–74; *illus.,* 68–69

Cytosine, 109

Cytoskeleton, 126

Cytosol, 70; *illus.,* 68–69

Dart, Raymond, 267

Darwin, Charles, 237–238; *illus.,* 237, 238

Data, 9

DDT, 610, 838

Death rate, 818, 822; *illus.,* 823, 824

Decay, 800; *illus.,* 800

Deciduous tree, 365, 788; *illus.,* 366

Decomposer, 300, 303–304, 800, 803; *illus.,* 800

Deep ocean fish, 535

Deep sea, 795

Deer, 216

Defenses, body, 684–690

Deficiency disease, 641; *table,* 641, 642

Deletion, 171, 173–174

Demographic transition, 822

Dendrite, 701; *illus.,* 701

Denitrifying bacteria, 812

Density-dependent factors, 819–820

Density-independent factors, 819

Deoxyribonucleic acid, *See* DNA

Deoxyribose, 109

Depressant, 735

Dermis, 623

Desert, 782, 786, 790–791; *illus.,* 790, 791

Desertification, 791; *illus.,* 791

Dessication, of plant, 432

Development, 30; of animal, 446–447; as evidence of evolution, 235; of fruit, 361–362; of human, 756–759; of insect, 497; of mammal, 588; *illus.,* 235, 446

Devonian Period, *illus.,* 527

Diabetes, 207, 610, 729

Dialysis, 659–660; peritoneal, 660

Diaphragm, 587, 654; *illus.,* 653, 654

Diastole, 669; *illus.,* 669

Diatom, 323, 794; *illus.,* 323

Dicot, 353–354, 356; germination of, 373; leaves of, 403, 406; root of, 387; *illus.,* 354, 372, 387, 390, 403, 4064

Diet, balanced, 642–643; carbohydrates in, 638–639; fats in, 638–639; minerals in, 640–642; protein in, 640; vitamins in, 640–642; water in, 640–642

Differentiation, 445, 759; *illus.,* 759

Diffusion, 77–78, 83; facilitated, 83–84; *illus.,* 78, 84

Digestion, 55, 629–637; in birds, 576–577; chemical, 629; in crayfish, 493–494; in earthworm, 469–470; enzymes in, 632; in frog, 543–545; in grasshopper, 498–499; mechanical, 629; in perch, 530–531; in planarian, 462–463; in snake, 559; in spider, 491; *illus.,* 462, 491, 544, 629, 631, 637; *table,* 632

Digestive system, as barrier to pathogens, 684–685

Digger wasp, 771; *illus.,* 772

Dihybrid cross, 155; *illus.,* 155

Dinoflagellate, 324, 456; *illus.,* 324; *table,* 322

Dinosaur, 257–258, 564–565, 599; *illus.,* 255, 564

Dipeptide, 59; *illus.,* 59

Diphtheria, 681–682, 691

Diploid, 157; *illus.,* 158

Diplopoda, 494–495; *illus.,* 495

Diplovertebron, illus., 552

Disaccharide, 53, 638; *illus.,* 54

Disease, autoimmune, 692; infectious, 681–683, 691–694, 696–697; population density and, 820; venereal, 683

Distal tubule, 657

Diurnal animal, 772

Division, 279

DNA, 70; changes in, 170–174; coding properties of, 112; damage to, 137, 172–174; function of, 110–111; recombinant, 206–207, 303; replication of, 112–113; structure of, 111; transcription of, 115–116; *illus.,* 109–113, 137, 173

DNA probe, 189; *illus.,* 190; *table,* 189

Dog, 777

Dolphin, 31, 595, 778

Dominance, apical, 417–418

Dominance hierarchy, 778

Dominant trait, 150–152; incomplete, 156; *illus.,* 151, 156

Dormancy, seed, 371–372

Dorsal aorta, 532

Dorsal fin, 530

Dorsal nerve cord, 513–514; *illus.,* 513

Dorsal surface, 449

Double bond, 41

Double fertilization, 360

Double helix, 111; *illus.,* 111

Doubling time, 823

Down feather, 572; *illus.,* 572

Down syndrome, 188; *illus.,* 188

Dragonfly, 497, 501–502; *illus.,* 488

Drinking water, 681

Drosophila, See Fruit fly

Drug, abuse of, 734–747; addiction to, 735; antibacterial, 692; career in pharmaceutical industry, 843; definition of, 735; mixture of, 744; physical dependence on, 735; prescription, 735; psychological dependence on, 735; responsible use of, 743–744; *illus.,* 735, 744

Duchenne muscular dystrophy, 187; *table,* 189

Duck-billed platypus, 589; *illus.,* 589

Duckling, 774; *illus.,* 774

Dujardin, Felix, 29

Duodenum, 544, 635–636

Dutch elm disease, 144, 341

Dwarfism, 729; *illus.,* 729

Ear, 711–713, 716; *illus.,* 712, 713

Earth, primitive, 249–251; *illus.,* 248, 249

Earthworm, 460, 469–471; *illus.,* 460, 470–472

Eating disorder, 644

Echinodermata, 482–484; *illus.,* 482–484

Echolocation, 594

Ecology, 801

Ecosystem, 801–802; *illus.,* 801, 802

Ectoderm, 447, 759; *table,* 759

Ectothermic animal, 528, 541, 546, 558, 791

Edentata, 597; *illus.,* 597

Effector, 701

Egg, 149; of bird, 579–582, 838; of human, 751; incubation of, 580–582; of insect, 497; of mammal, 589–590; of reptile, 558; of snake, 561; *illus.,* 558, 580, 582

Egg cell, plant, 356

Egg protein, *illus.,* 58

Egg tooth, 581

Electron, 38; *illus.,* 38

Electron microscope, 14–16; scanning, 15–16; transmission, 14–16; *illus.,* 14

Electron transport chain, 96–97; in photosynthesis, 100–101; in respiration, 96–97; *illus.,* 96, 97, 101

Element, compounds from, 39–40; definition of, 39; in earth, 38; in human body, 38; *illus.,* 38

Elodea, illus., 82

Elongation, 416; zone of, 386

Embryo, 235, 447, 748, 756, 758; development of, 581–582; plant, 371; *illus.,* 235, 371, 581, 758, 759

Emergent, 789

Emigration, 818

Emphysema, 177, 742

Emulsifier, 633

Endangered Species Act, 832

Endocrine gland, 719, 724–730; *illus.,* 719, 720; *table,* 721

Endocytosis, 85

Endoderm, 447, 759; *table,* 759

Endodermis, plant, 386

Endometrium, 752, 754

Endoplasmic reticulum, 71; rough, 71; smooth, 71; *illus.,* 71; *table,* 67

Endorphin, 738

Endoskeleton, of echinoderm, 482; of vertebrate, 516; *illus.,* 516

Endosperm, 360, 371, 373

Endospore, 297–298; *illus.,* 298

Endothermic animal, 576, 587, 791

Energy, biomass, 834; in chemical reaction, 43–44; conservation of, 835; content of food, 638; conversions in monerans, 300–301; flow in environment, 804; from food, 91–98; geothermal, 835; kinetic, 77; nuclear, 833; production in cell, 90–104; requirement of living things, 27; resources, 833–835; solar, 99–101, 833–834; water, 835; wind, 835; *illus.,* 43, 639, 833–835

Energy pyramid, 805; *illus.,* 805

Environment, 27; energy flow in, 804; in evolution, 240; genes and, 183; interaction of cell with, 77–82

Enzyme, 60–62; in digestion, 632; *illus.,* 61

Ephedra, 366

Epicotyl, 371, 373; *illus.,* 371

Epidemic, 681

Epidermal hair, 404

Epidermis, of plant, 375, 386, 391, 404; of skin, 623; of sponge, 450; *illus.,* 375

Epididymis, 750

Epiglottis, 630, 651

Epiphyte, 789, 806; *illus.,* 789

Epithelial tissue, 615; *illus.,* 615

Equilibrium, genetic, 220, 239; population, 818; punctuated, 244; *illus.,* 818

Equisetum, 434

Era, 254

Ergot, 341

Erlich, Paul, 692

Erwin, Terry, 288–289

Erosion, 829–830; *illus.,* 830

Erythrocyte, *See* Red blood cells

Erythropoetin, 728–729; *table,* 721

Esophagus, 470, 530, 630, 631; *illus.,* 630

Establishment of plant, 372–373; *illus.,* 372, 373

Estivation, 772

Estrogen, 722, 726, 730, 753, 760; *table,* 721

Estuary, 793, 796; *illus.,* 796

Ethanol, 52, 93, *See also* Alcohol; *illus.,* 93; *table,* 52

Ethylene, in plants, 417, 421; *illus.,* 417

Eubacteria, *table,* 299

Euglena, 280, 324; *illus.,* 280, 325

Euglenoid, 324–325; *illus.,* 325; *table,* 322

Euglenophyta, *table,* 322

Eukaryote, origin of, 252–253; *illus.*, 252

Eustachian tube, 548, 711

Evergreen, 789

Evolution, 220, 223–224; of amphibians, 552; of birds, 566, 571; of brain, 461; convergent, 242, 591; definition of, 231; evidence from development, 235; evidence from fossils, 231–233; evidence from molecular biology, 235; evidence from structure, 234; of fish, 512; of humans, 262–275; of mammals, 258, 566, 599–600; pace of, 243–244; of plants, 427–428, 431–432; of primates, 258, 263; process of, 239–244; of reptiles, 564–566, 571; of sponges, 452; theory of, 236–238; of vertebrates, 518–520; of viruses, 312; *illus.*, 427, 518, 566

Evolutionary tree, *illus.*, 427, 604–609

Excretion, 28; in birds, 578; in crayfish, 494; in earthworm, 469–470; in grasshopper, 498–499; organs of, 656–660; in perch, 530–531; in planarian, 463; in snake, 559–560; in spider, 491; *illus.*, 463, 544

Exocrine gland, 719; *illus.*, 719

Exocytosis, 85

Exon, 116

Exoskeleton, 489–490

Experiment, 8; controlled, 8–9; variables in, 8; *illus.*, 8, 9

Expiration, 653; *illus.*, 654

Exponential growth curve, *illus.*, 817

External fertilization, 548

Extinction, 214, 226–227, 831; mass, 248, 256–257

Eye, 713–714; color of, 182; compound, 494; evolution of, 264; pineal, 563; simple, 491; *illus.*, 182, 713, 714

Eyespot, protist, 325

F₁ generation, 150

F₂ generation, 150–151

Facilitated diffusion, 83–84; *illus.*, 84

Facultative anaerobe, 301

Fallopian tube, 752

Family, 279

Fang, 561; *illus.*, 561

Fat, 57; in diet, 638–639; *illus.*, 57, 639

Fat body, 545

Fatty acid, 55–57; polyunsaturated, 57; saturated, 56, 639, 669; unsaturated, 57; *illus.*, 57

Feather, 571–572; contour, 572; down, 572; quill, 572; *illus.*, 58, 571, 572

Feces, 637

Feedback, negative, 725–726; *illus.*, 725, 726

Feeding, in birds, 576–577; in crayfish, 493–494; filter, 514; in fish, 535; in grasshopper, 498–499, in insects, 501–502

Female reproductive system, 751–752; *illus.*, 751, 752

Fermentation, 92–93; in aerobic organism, 98; alcoholic, 93; lactic acid, 93, 98, 622; *illus.*, 92, 93, 98

Fern, 433, 435–436; *illus.*, 435, 436

Fertilization, 149, 748, 755–756; double, 360; external, 548; internal, 558, 579, 588; *in vitro,* 755; plant, 360, 364; randomness of, 222–223; *illus.*, 153, 158, 222, 360, 548, 755

Fertilizer, 838

Fetal alcohol syndrome, 760

Fetoscopy, 191

Fetus, 759; finding genetic disorders in, 190–192; harmful effects on, 760; treatment of genetic disorder in, 193–194

Fever, 686

Fiber, 55, 639

Fibrin, 672; *illus.*, 671

Fibrinogen, 672

Fiddlehead, 435

Fight-or-flight hormone, 720

Filament, algal, 328

Filter feeding, 514

Filtration, in nephron, 658; *illus.*, 658

Fin, anal, 530; caudal, 530; dorsal, 530; pectoral, 527, 530; pelvic, 527, 530; *illus.*, 527

Finch, 241; *illus.*, 242

Fingerprint, 614; *illus.*, 614

Fire algae, 324; *illus.*, 324; *table,* 322

Fish, 524, 794–796, *See also* Perch; bony, 517, 530–536; cartilage, 517, 527–529; color of, 531;

deep ocean, 535; evolution of, 256, 512; feeding in, 535; fossil, 536; freshwater, 534; jawless, 517, 525–526; lobe-finned, 536; primitive, 525–526; reproduction in, 535; saltwater, 534; *illus.*, 524

Fission, 129; *illus.*, 129

Five-kingdom classification system, 281–283, *illus.*, 282–283

Flagella, 297, 320; *illus.*, 297; *table,* 320

Flagellate, 320; *table,* 320

Flame cell, 463–474

Flatworm, 461–465; free-living, 462–463; parasitic, 463–465; *illus.*, 462, 463, 468

Fleming, Alexander, 11, 692

Flicker, 217; *illus.*, 217

Flight, 570

Flight muscle, 499; *illus.*, 499

Flower, 352–353; fertilization of, 360; imperfect, 355; ovule, 356–357; perfect, 355; pollen formation in, 356–357; pollination in, 357–360; structure of, 355–356; *illus.*, 355, 357–360; *table,* 366

Flowering, control of, 414, 420–421

Fluke, 461, 463–464; *illus.*, 464

***FOIL* memory device,** *illus.*, 155

Follicle, 753

Follicle-stimulating hormone (FSH), 726–727, 753–754; *table,* 721

Food, energy from, 91–98, 638; spoilage of, 21–23, 303; translocation in plants, 397–398; *illus.*, 22

Food calorie, 638

Food chain, 804–805; *illus.*, 804

Food groups, 642–643

Food vacuole, 319

Food web, 804; *illus.*, 804

Foot, of bird, 573; of snail, 478; tube, 482; *illus.*, 574

Foraminiferan, 318; *table,* 320

Foreign species, 808; *table,* 808

Forelimb, 234; *illus.*, 234

Forest, destruction of, 832; temperate deciduous, 788; temperate rain, 788–789; tropical rain, 789; *illus.*, 786, 788, 789

Fossil, 231–233, 512; amphibian, 552; determining age of, 233–234; fish, 525, 536; hominid, 267–271; horse, 599–600; reptile, 564–566;

vertebrate, 518; *illus.*, 231, 232, 512, 525, 552
Fossil fuel, 833, 836–837
Founder effect, 222, 227
Fox, 791; *illus.*, 787
Frame-shift mutation, 174; *illus.*, 174
Franklin, Rosalind, 111, 113
Freshwater biome, 795–796; *illus.*, 795
Freshwater fish, 534
Frog, 517, 540–542, 776; circulation in, 545–546; digestion in, 543–545; external characteristics of, 542; nervous system of, 547; reproduction in, 548–549; respiration in, 546–547; senses of, 547–548; skeleton of, 542–543; *illus.*, 540, 542–549
Frond, 435; *illus.*, 435
Fructose, *illus.*, 53
Fruit, aggregate, 361; definition of, 361; development of, 361–362; dispersal of, 362; dry, 362; fleshy, 362; multiple, 361–362; ripening of, 417; seedless, 379; simple, 361; structure of, 361–362; *illus.*, 352, 361, 362, 417
Fruit fly, 164, 167; *illus.*, 160, 165, 223
Fruiting body, 338, 342; *illus.*, 342
FSH, *See* Follicle-stimulating hormone
Fucoxanthin, 327
Fucus, 327, 329; *illus.*, 327
Functional group, 52; *illus.*, 52
Fungi, 281; imperfect, 343; nutrition in, 337–338; reproduction in, 338; variety of, 339–344; *illus.*, 337, 800
Funguslike protist, 330–332
Furrow, 128; *illus.*, 128

Galactose, 53; *illus.*, 53
Galápagos Islands, 241; *illus.*, 241
Gallbladder, 544, 633–634; *illus.*, 634
Gamete, 149, 153; *illus.*, 153, 158
Gametophyte, 329, 356–357, 429–430, 433, 435; *illus.*, 356, 357, 429, 431
Ganglion, 471, 708
Garbage, 828, 838–839; *illus.*, 828, 839
Gas, *illus.*, 37
Gas exchange, 649; in earthworm,

469; in leaf, 407; in lung, 652–653; in perch, 532; in plants, 432; in shark, 528; *illus.*, 652
Gasteroneus, *illus.*, 512
Gastric gland, *illus.*, 631
Gastric juice, 631–632; *illus.*, 631
Gastropoda, 477–479; *illus.*, 477–479
Gastrovascular cavity, 454
Gastrula, 446–447, 759; *illus.*, 446
Gavial, 563
Gecko, 562; *illus.*, 562
Geese, 215; *illus.*, 215
Gemmae, 431; *illus.*, 431
Gemmule, 451
Gene, 151, 160; chromosomes and, 164–175, 178–180; environment and, 183; harmful, 223–224; jumping, 169; linkage of, 166–167; moneran, 301–303; with multiple alleles, 181; position of, 166–167, 196–197; sex-linked, 167; silencing, 120–121; *illus.*, 166
Gene mutation, 170, 172–174; genetic disorders caused by, 184–187; *illus.*, 174
Gene pool, 217–220; *illus.*, 218
Generations, alternation of, 328–329, 356–357, 429; *illus.*, 329
Generative cell, 357
Genetic control, artificial methods of, 205–208, 210–211
Genetic counseling, 192; *illus.*, 192
Genetic cross, 153; *illus.*, 153
Genetic disorder, 184–188, 292; caused by gene mutation, 184–187; caused by nondisjunction, 187–188; detection of, 189–192, 292; finding before birth, 191–192; treatment of, 176–177, 193–194, 292
Genetic drift, 222
Genetic engineering, 206–208, 210–211, 440; *illus.*, 207
Genetic equilibrium, 220, 239–240
Genetic marker, 189–190
Genetic material, changes in, 170–174
Genetics, applications of, 201–208, 210–211; population, 214–225, 228–229; problem solving in, 153–154
Genotype, 152–153, 181, 223; determination of, 154; *illus.*, 153
Genus, 277–278

Geographic isolation, 240; *illus.*, 241
Geothermal energy, 835
Geotropism, 419; *illus.*, 420
Germination, 372–373; *illus.*, 372, 373
Germ layer, 447, 759; *table,* 759
Germ theory of disease, 681
Gestation, 590, 592
Gibberellin, 416
Gigantism, *illus.*, 729
Gila monster, 562
Gill arch, 532
Gill raker, 532
Gills, of fish, 528, 532; of gastropod, 478; of mushroom, 342; *illus.*, 528, 532
Gill slit, 513–514
Ginkgo, 365; *illus.*, 366
Girdling, 398
Gizzard, of bird, 576; of earthworm, 470
Glomerulus, 657; *illus.*, 658
Glucagon, 722, 727–728; *illus.*, 727; *table,* 721
Glucose, 53, 638; blood level of, 727–728; entry into cells, 83–84; production in photosynthesis, 102; *illus.*, 53, 727
Glycerol, 56; *illus.*, 56
Glycogen, 54
Glycolysis, 95–97, 98
Gnetophyte, 366
Golden algae, 323; *illus.*, 323; *table,* 322
Golgi apparatus, 71–72; *illus.*, 72; *table,* 67
Gonad, hydra, 455
Gonorrhea, 683
Grafting, plant, 380; *illus.*, 380
Gram, Christian, 298
Gram stain, 298; *table,* 299
Grand Canyon, 232–233, 240; *illus.*, 232
Grass, 359, 373, 790; *illus.*, 359, 790
Grasshopper, 497–500; *illus.*, 498–500
Grassland, 790; *illus.*, 786, 790
Gray-water recycling, 831
Green algae, 325–328, 343; *illus.*, 326; *table,* 322
Greenhouse effect, 836–837
Green sulfur bacteria, 299; *table,* 299
Griffith, Frederick, 110–111

Ground squirrel, 240–241; *illus.,* 241
Growth, *See also* Population growth; patterns in plant, 415–418; rate of, 818; regulator of, 135
Growth hormone, 729–730; *illus.,* 729; *table,* 721
Growth ring, 392
Guanine, 109
Guard cell, 405, 407; *illus.,* 407
Gullet, 318–319, 544
Gut, 462
Gymnosperm, 363–366; *table,* 366

Habitat, 802–803; destruction of, 831
Habituation, 774; *table,* 775
Haeckel, Ernst, 280
Hagfish, 517, 526
Hair, 587
Hair follicle, 623
Half-life, of isotope, 233–234; *illus.,* 233
Hallucinogen, 737–738
Halophile, *table,* 299
Handedness, 705
Haploid, 157–158
Hardy, Godfrey, 218
Hardy-Weinberg principle, 218–220, 222–223, 239–240; *illus.,* 219, 220
Hare, 593, 820–821; *illus.,* 820
Hatching, 581; *illus.,* 581
Haversian canal, 616; *illus.,* 616
Hearing, 711–713, 716; *illus.,* 712
Heart, 665; artificial, 667; of bird, 578; disorders of, 666–667; of earthworm, 469; of fish, 532; of frog, 545–546; of mammal, 587; of snake, 560; transplant of, 667; of vertebrate, 519; *illus.,* 546, 560, 578, 666, 667
Heart attack, 672
Heart rate, 666
Heartwood, 392
Hedgehog, 596
Heimlich maneuver, 654
Heliozoan, *table,* 320
Hematocyst, 454
Hemichordata, *illus.,* 482
Hemocyanin, 479
Hemoglobin, 184–185, 469, 653, 672
Hemophilia, 186–187, 208, 221; *illus.,* 186

Hepatitis, 683
Herbivore, 803
Herb layer, 788
Heredity, 148–163
Hermaphrodite, 451
Heroin, 735–736, 760
Heterotroph, 27–28, 104, 300; *illus.,* 28
Heterotroph hypothesis, 249–251, 252
Heterozygosity, 152
Hibernation, 549, 772; *illus.,* 772
Hilum, 371
Hirudinea, 471–472
Histamine, 685
Holdfast, 327
Homeostasis, 83, 659, 719
Hominid, fossil, 267–271
Homo erectus, 269; *illus.,* 269
Homo habilis, 269
Homo sapiens, See Human being
Homologous chromosomes, 157–158, 160; *illus.,* 157, 158
Homologous structures, 234; *illus.,* 234
Homozygosity, 152
Honeybee, 503–504, 778; *illus.,* 166, 504
Hooke, Robert, 28–29; *illus.,* 28, 30
Hormone, animal, 719–722; plant, 416–417; *illus.,* 416, 723; *table,* 721
Horse, evolution of, 599–600; *illus.,* 600
Horseshoe crab, *illus.,* 492
Horsetail, 433–434; *illus.,* 434
Hot springs, *illus.,* 300
Human being, composition of, 38, 50; evolution of, 262–275; genetic disorders of, 184–188, 193–194, 292; growth curve of, 135; impact on biosphere, 835–843; inheritance in, 181–194, 196–197; karyotype of, 187–188; population, 822–824; relationship to apes, 264–266; reproduction in, 748–765; respiratory system of, 650–651; skeleton of, 615–619; tracing evolution of, 267–271; *illus.,* 823–824
Human growth hormone, 207
Hunger, 628
Huntington disease, 185–186, 189–190, 292
Huxley, Thomas Henry, 26

Hybrid, 147, 203–204; *illus.,* 203
Hybridization, 203–204; *illus.,* 203
Hybridoma, 694; *illus.,* 693
Hybrid vigor, 203
Hydra, 454–455; *illus.,* 454
Hydrocarbon, 51
Hydrochloric acid, 631; *illus.,* 631
Hydrogen, 40; *illus.,* 40, 41; *table,* 39
Hydrogen ion, 45
Hydrogen peroxide, *illus.,* 40
Hydrolysis, 54–55, 61, 629; *illus.,* 55, 61
Hydroxide ion, 42, 46
Hydroxyl group, 52
Hypertension, 670
Hypertonic solution, 80–81; *illus.,* 81
Hyphae, fungal, 337; slime mold, 332; *illus.,* 337
Hypocotyl, 371–373; *illus.,* 371
Hypothalamus, 706, 721, 724–726; *illus.,* 724, 726; *table,* 721
Hypothesis, 7
Hypotonic solution, 80–81; *illus.,* 81
Hyracotherium, 599–600; *illus.,* 600

Ichthyosaur, 575; *illus.,* 243, 575
Iguana, 562; *illus.,* 562
Iguanodon, illus., 564
Ileum, 636
Immigration, 818
Immune system, 685–691; control of, 692–693; malfunction of, 692–693; *illus.,* 685
Immunity, 687–689; active, 689; passive, 689; *illus.,* 688
Imperfect fungi, 343; *illus.,* 343
Implantation, 748, 756–759
Imprinting, 774; *illus.,* 774
Inborn error of metabolism, 184, 194
Inbreeding, 202–203, 214; *illus.,* 202
Inbreeding depression, 202–203
Incisor, 593, 629; *illus.,* 593, 595
Incomplete linkage, 169
Incubation, of eggs, 580–582
Independent assortment, 155, 160
Indigo bunting, *illus.,* 777
Infectious disease, 681–682; agents of, 681–682; bacterial, 681–682; transmission of, 682–683; treatment of, 691–694; viral, 682
Inflammation, 685
Inflorescence, 355

Influenza, 682; *illus.,* 683
Inheritance, 30; chromosomes and, 165–169; chromosome theory of, 160; human, 181–194, 196–197; patterns of, 149–156, 181–183; polygenic, 182
Initiation codon, 116
Innate behavior, 771–772; *illus.,* 772
Inner cell mass, 756; *illus.,* 756
Insect, 488, 496–500; appearance of, 502; as biological controls, 508; body of, 496–497; development of, 497; evolution of, 256; feeding adaptations of, 501–502; in pollination, 357–359; populations, 288–289; reproductive adaptations in, 503; social, 503; transmission of pathogens, 683; *illus.,* 358, 488, 489, 496–500
Insectivore, 596–597, 599; *illus.,* 597
Insectivorous plant, 410; *illus.,* 410
Insertion, 173–174
Insight learning, 774; *table,* 775
Insoluble substance, 45; *illus.,* 44
Inspiration, 653; *illus.,* 654
Instinct, 771–775
Insulin, 207, 722, 727–729; *illus.,* 727; *table,* 721
Internal fertilization, 558, 579, 588
Interneuron, 701
Interphase, meiotic, 158–159
Intestine, large, 633, 636–637; nematode, 467; small, 633–636; *illus.,* 304, 635, 636; *table,* 632
Intron, 116
Inversion, 172; *illus.,* 172
Iodine, *table,* 642
Ion, 40, 41–42
Ionic bond, 41–42; *illus.,* 42
Iris (eye), 713
Iron, 62; *table,* 642
Islets of Langerhans, *illus.,* 727
Isotonic solution, 81; *illus.,* 81
Isotope, 233; radioactive, 233–234; *illus.,* 233; *table,* 234
Itching, 680
Ivanowski, Dmitri, 305

Jackrabbit, 791
Jacobson's organ, 561
Japanese beetle, *table,* 808
Jaw, 265, 494, 559; *illus.,* 559
Jawless fish, 517, 525–526
Jejunum, 636

Jellyfish, 453–456; *illus.,* 453, 455
Jenner, Edward, 7
Johanson, Donald, 268
Joint, 617–618; ball-and-socket, 610; gliding, 618; hinge, 618; immovable, 618; movement of, 622; *illus.,* 618
J-shaped curve, *illus.,* 817
Jumping gene, 169
Jurassic Period, 599

Kangaroo, 591; *illus.,* 591
Karyotype, 187–188; *illus.,* 187
Keel, 575
Kelp, 327
Keratin, 557, 571
Kidney, 531, 545, 648, 656–658, 728; failure of, 659–660; transplant of, 660; *illus.,* 560, 656, 657
Kidney stone, 656
Kinesin, 126
Kinesis, 776
Kinetic energy, 77
Kinetochore, 126; *illus.,* 126
Kingdom, 279; *illus.,* 280, 282, 283
Klinefelter syndrome, 188
Knee, *illus.,* 618
Koala, 591
Koch, Robert, 681
Koch's postulates, 681

Labor, 760
Lacteal, 635–636
Lactic acid, 98
Lactic acid fermentation, 93, 98, 622; *illus.,* 98
Lactose, 54
Ladybird beetle, 502
Lagomorph, 593
Lake, 793, 795
Lamarck's hypothesis, 236; *illus.,* 236
Lamprey, 517, 526; *illus.,* 526
Lancelet, *illus.,* 515
Landfill, 839–840; *illus.,* 828
Landsteiner, Karl, 672
Large intestine, 633, 636–637; *illus.,* 636
Larva, 447, 454; amphibian, 541; bipinnaria, 482; insect, 497; sea squirt, 514; trochophore, 479; *illus.,* 447, 451, 479, 482
Larynx, 547, 651
Latent learning, *table,* 775
Lateral line, 533; *illus.,* 533
Lateral surface, 449

Latitude, 786
Law of independent assortment, 160
Law of segregation, 160
Layering, 379–380; *illus.,* 380
Lead, 840
Leaf, 374–375, 402; abscission of, 421–422; arrangement of, 403–404; color changes in, 421–422; compound, 403–404; function of, 403–408; gas exchange in, 407; palmately compound, 404; photosynthesis in, 406–407; pinnately compound, 404; respiration in, 407; senescence of, 421–422; shape of, 403–404; simple, 403; specialized, 409–410; structure of, 354, 404–406; transpiration in, 407–408; wilting of, 408; *illus.,* 354, 372, 402, 403, 405
Leaflet, 403
Leaf scar, 389
Leaf vein, 397; *illus.,* 397
Leakey, Louis, 268
Leakey, Mary, 268
Leakey, Richard, 268
Learning, 771–775; associative, 775; insight, 774–775; latent, 775; trial-and-error, 775; *illus.,* 773, 774; *table,* 775
Leech, 471–472
Leeuwenhoek, Anton von, 13, 23
Legionnaire's disease, 697
Lemur, 263
Lens (eye), 713
Lenticel, 389
Le Système International d'unités, 12
Leucocytes, *See* White blood cells
Leucoplast, 73
Leukemia, 674; *illus.,* 138
LH, *See* Luteinizing hormone
Lichen, 343–344, 805; *illus.,* 344
Life, characteristics of, 27–31; early, 249–253; origin of, 21–26, 249–253
Lifespan, of cell, 134; *illus.,* 135
Ligament, 618
Light, wavelength of, 99–100; *illus.,* 100
Lightning, *illus.,* 240
Light microscope, 14
Light reactions, 99–101; *illus.,* 99, 101
Limb, of amphibians, 557; of reptiles, 557; *illus.,* 557

Limiting factor, 795
Limpet, 793
Linkage, incomplete, 169; sex, 166–168
Linkage group, 166–167
Linnaeus, Carolus, 278–279; *illus.*, 278
Lion fish, 535
Lipase, 633; *table*, 632
Lipid, 55–57
Liquid, *illus.*, 37
Litter, forest, 788
Littoral zone, 793; *illus.*, 793
Liver, 531, 544, 633–634, 656, 741; circulation and, 675–676; *illus.*, 634, 676, 741
Liverwort, 429, 431; *illus.*, 429, 431
Lizard, 517, 558–559, 562, 791; *illus.*, 562
Llama, *illus.*, 597
Lobe-finned fish, 536; *illus.*, 536
Lobster, 494
Lockjaw, 682
Locust, *illus.*, 816
Loop of Henle, 657
LSD, 737–738
Lucy (fossil), 268; *illus.*, 268, 271
Lumen, 630
Lung, 649–655; book, 490–491; cancer of, 137; of frog, 546–547; of lungfish, 536; smoking and, 741–743; of snake, 560; *illus.*, 137, 547, 560, 742
Lungfish, 533–536
Luteinizing hormone (LH), 753; *table*, 721
Lycophyta, 434
Lyme disease, 696
Lymph, 675
Lymphatic system, 674–675; *illus.*, 675, 685
Lymph node, 675, 685–686; *illus.*, 675
Lymphocytes, 674, 685, 687–689
Lymphokine, 693–694
Lymph vessel, 675; *illus.*, 675
Lynx, 820–821; *illus.*, 820
Lysogenic cycle, 308; *illus.*, 308
Lysosome, 73; *table*, 67
Lysozyme, 685
Lytic cycle, 306–307, 308; *illus.*, 307

Macromolecule, 54
Macronucleus, 319; *illus.*, 319

Macrophages, 674, 685–687, 689; *illus.*, 686
Madreporite, 483; *illus.*, 484
Magnesium, *illus.*, 38, 642
Magnetic resonance imaging, *illus.*, 613
Maidenhair tree, 365; *illus.*, 366
Malaria, 320–321, 680–681, 683
Male reproductive system, 749–751; *illus.*, 749–750
Malignant cell, *illus.*, 136
Malnutrition, 643
Malpighian tubule, 491
Maltase, 61–62; *illus.*, 61
Maltose, 54; *illus.*, 55
Mammal, 518, 586; aquatic, 594–595; common features of, 587; development of, 588; egg-laying, 589–590; evolution of, 257–258, 566, 599–600; flesh-eating, 595–596; hoofed, 596; placental, 592–598; pouched, 590–591; toothless, 597; *illus.*, 258
Mammary gland, 587–588
Manatee, *illus.*, 595
Mandible, 494
Mandibulata, 489, 493–495; *illus.*, 494–495
Mantle, 478
Mantle cavity, 479
Maple syrup, 384
Mapping, chromosome, 169
Marchantia, illus., 431
Marijuana, 736, 760; *illus.*, 736
Marine animals, evolution of, 255–256; *illus.*, 243
Marine biome, 793–795; *illus.*, 793–794
Marine worm, 472
Marrow, 616, 674; *illus.*, 616
Marsupial, 589–591, 599; *illus.*, 590, 591
Mass extinction, 253, 256–257; *illus.*, 253
Mass selection, 201; *illus.*, 201
Maternal care, 588; *illus.*, 588
Mating, nonrandom, 223; *illus.*, 223
Matrix, bone, 616
Matter, definition of, 37
Maturation, zone of, 386
Maxillae, 494
Maxillary teeth, 543
Maxilliped, 493
Mayfly, 503
McClintock, Barbara, 169

Measles, 682, 691
Measurement, 12
Medicine, career in, 849
Medulla, 533, 547
Medulla oblongata, 706
Medusa, 453–454; *illus.*, 453
Megasporangia, 363
Megaspore, 356
Meiosis, 158–160; errors in, 171; *illus.*, 158
Meiospore, 326
Melanin, 182; *illus.*, 182
Melatonin, 728; *table*, 721
Membrane, polarized, 702
Memory cells, 689, 691; *illus.*, 688
Mendel, Gregor, 149–150, 154; *illus.*, 154
Mendel's hybrid peas, 149–150; *illus.*, 149, 150
Meninges, 704
Meningitis, 705
Menopause, 754
Menstrual cycle, 726–727, 753–754, *illus.*, 753, 754
Menstruation, 754
Mercury, 840
Meristem, 375, 403; apical, 375, 386; *illus.*, 375, 391
Mesenchyme, 450
Mesoderm, 447, 468, 759; *illus.*, 468; *table*, 759
Mesoglea, 454
Mesophyll, 405; palisade, 405; spongy, 405; *illus.*, 405
Mesozoic Era, 257–258, 565; *illus.*, 255
Messenger RNA, *See* mRNA
Metabolism, 30; inborn error of, 184, 194
Metamorphosis, in amphibian, 541; in frog, 548–549; in insect, 497; *illus.*, 497, 549
Metaphase, meiotic, 158–159; mitotic, 126; *illus.*, 127
Metazoa, 445
Methane, 51; *illus.*, 51
Methanogen, *table*, 299
Methanol, 52
Microdissection, 16; *illus.*, 16
Microfilament, 128
Microfossil, *illus.*, 251
Micronucleus, 319; *illus.*, 319
Microorganism, 10; classification of, 280; in disease, 10–11; in food spoilage, 23–24
Microphyll, 434; *illus.*, 434

Microscope, 13–14; compound, 13–14; electron, 14–16; light, 14; resolving power of, 14; simple, 13; *illus.,* 14

Microsporangia, 364

Microspore, 357

Microtubule, 74, 124, 126; *illus.,* 319

Middle lamella, 76

Migration, 223, 576–577, 772, 776

Mildew, 331–332; *table,* 330

Miller, Stanley, 250

Millipede, 494–495; *illus.,* 495

Milt, 534

Mimicry, 502; *illus.,* 502

Mimosa, 422; *illus.,* 422

Mineral, 640–642; *table,* 642

Mite, 492; *illus.,* 492

Mitochondrion, 72, 94–98; origin of, 252–253; *illus.,* 72, 97, 252; *table,* 67

Mitosis, 125–127; regulation of, 134–138; significance of, 129–133; *illus.,* 126, 127

Mitotic spindle, 126

Mixture, 44–45

Molar, 629

Mole, 590–591, 596; *illus.,* 597

Molecule, definition of, 40; neutral, 40; polar, 45

Mollusk, 477–481; *illus.,* 477–481, 803

Molting, in arthropods, 489–490, 497; in birds, 572; *illus.,* 490

Moneran, 281; cell structure of, 297–298; classification of, 298; energy conversion in, 298–301; exchange of genetic material in, 301–303; importance of, 303–304; nutrition in, 298–301; reproduction in, 301; *illus.,* 298; *table,* 299

Monkey, 263; *illus.,* 263

Monoclonal antibody, 693–694; *illus.,* 693, 694

Monocot, 353–354, 356; germination of, 373; leaves of, 403, 406; *illus.,* 354, 373, 390, 403, 406

Monohybrid cross, 153–154; *illus.,* 153

Monosaccharide, 53; *illus.,* 53

Monosomy, 171

Monotreme, 589–590; *illus.,* 589, 590

Morel, 341

Morgan, Thomas Hunt, 167–169

Morphine, 735–736

Moschops, illus., 566

Mosquito, 501, 680; *illus.,* 680

Moss, 426, 429–430, 795; *illus.,* 426, 430

Moth, 358, 776; peppered, 239–240; *illus.,* 239

Motor neuron, 701

Motor vehicle, 836; *illus.,* 836

Mountains, 791–792; *illus.,* 792

Mouse, 593

Mouth, 629–630, 651; insect, 501–502; *illus.,* 501, 629, 630

Movement, 27; of earthworm, 470; of joints, 622; of shark, 527; of vertebrates, 519; *illus.,* 471

mRNA, 115; synthesis of, 115–116; translation into protein, 117–118; *illus.,* 114, 115, 118

Mucosa, 630–631

Mucus, 630–632, 651, 685; *illus.,* 631, 636

Mud puppy, 551; *illus.,* 551

Mud siren, 551; *illus.,* 551

Multicellular algae, 326–329

Multicellular organism, 29; cell specialization in, 130–131; origin of, 254–255; *illus.,* 131

Multinucleate fungi, 337

Multiple alleles, 181; *table,* 181

Mumps, 682, 691

Muscle, 132; antagonist pair of, 622; cardiac, 622–623; contraction of, 621–622, 703; energy requirement for, 98; of grasshopper, 499; insertion of, 622; involuntary, 623; origin of, 622; skeletal, 619–621; smooth, 622–623; striated, 619; voluntary, 619; *illus.,* 98, 499, 619–623, 703

Muscle tissue, 615; *illus.,* 615

Muscular dystrophy, 187; *table,* 189

Mushroom, 336, 342; *illus.,* 336, 342, 343

Mussel, 479, 793, 796; *illus.,* 819

Mutagen, 170, 173

Mutation, 170–174, 221, 236; chromosomal, 170–172; gene, 170; *illus.,* 171–174, 221

Mutualism, 805–806; *illus.,* 85, 806

Mycorrhizae, 338

Myofibril, 621; *illus.,* 621

Myosin, 621; *illus.,* 621

Myxobacteria, *table,* 299

Myxomycota, 330–331; *illus.,* 331; *table,* 330

Narcotic, 735–736; *illus.,* 736

Nares, 572

Nasal cavity, 650–651, 711; *illus.,* 650

Nastic movement, 422; *illus.,* 422

Natural resource, 829–832; nonrenewable, 829; renewable, 829

Natural selection, 237–238; behavior and, 771; observation of, 239–240; *illus.,* 237–239

Nautilus, 480; *illus.,* 480

Neanderthals, 269–271; *illus.,* 270

Nectar, 357–358

Needham, John, 23; *illus.,* 24

Needle, conifer, 409; *illus.,* 409

Negative feedback, 725–726; *illus.,* 725, 726

Nekton, 794, 796

Nematode, 466–467; parasitic, 467; *illus.,* 466, 467

Nephridia, 470

Nephron, 657–658; *illus.,* 657, 658

Nerve, 132, 701; cranial, 533, 547, 707; spinal, 533, 547, 708; *illus.,* 131, 708

Nerve cord, dorsal, 513–514; *illus.,* 513

Nerve impulse, 701–703; *illus.,* 701, 702

Nerve tissue, 615; *illus.,* 615

Nervous control, 719–720

Nervous system, 701–703, *See also* Central nervous system; Peripheral nervous system; of birds, 578–579; of frog, 547; of grasshopper, 499; of perch, 533; of planarian, 463; of snake, 560–561; of spider, 491; *illus.,* 463, 547

Nesting behavior, 579; *illus.,* 579

Nettle, 410

Neuron, 701; motor, 701; sensory, 701; *illus.,* 701

Neurospora, 341

Neurotoxin, 681–682

Neurotransmitter, 703, 735–736; excitatory, 703; inhibitory, 703; *illus.,* 703

Neutron, 38, 233; *illus.,* 38

Newborn, 761; *illus.,* 761

Niacin, *table,* 641

Niche, 802–803; *illus.,* 802

Nicotine, 741–742

Nictitating membrane, 542

Nirenberg, Marshall, 112

Nitrification, 812

Nitrifying bacteria, 812

Nitrogen, *table,* 38
Nitrogen cycle, 811–812; *illus.,* 811
Nitrogen fixation, 300, 304, 811–812; *illus.,* 300
Nocturnal animal, 772
Node, lymph, 675, 685–686; plant, 374, 393, 403
Nonbiodegradable, 840
Nondisjunction, 171; genetic disorders caused by, 187–188; *illus.,* 171
Nonrandom mating, 223; *illus.,* 223
Noradrenalin, *table,* 721
Notochord, 513–514
Nuclear energy, 833; *illus.,* 833
Nuclear envelope, 70, 76
Nuclear fission, 833
Nuclear pore, *illus.,* 115
Nuclear waste, 833
Nucleic acid, 109–110, *See also* DNA; RNA
Nucleolus, 70; *illus.,* 70
Nucleotide, 109; *illus.,* 109
Nucleus, 126; atomic, 38; cell, 70; *illus.,* 38, 70, 115; *table,* 67
Nudibranch, *illus.,* 803
Nutrient, 638; uptake by plants, 395–396; upwelling, 793
Nutrition, 638–644; in fungi, 337–338; in moneran, 298–301
Nymph, 497; *illus.,* 497

Obesity, 643
Obligate aerobe, 300
Obligate anaerobe, 301
Ocean, 793–795; *illus.,* 793, 794
Octopus, 476, 480–481; *illus.,* 476
Odor, flower, 358–359; *illus.,* 359
Oedogonium, 328
Oil, 57
Olfactory bulb, 533
Olfactory lobe, 547, 578; *illus.,* 579
Oligochaeta, 469–471
Omnivore, 803
Oncogene, 311
Oocyte, primary, 751–752; secondary, 751–752; *illus.,* 751
Oogamy, 326
Oogonium, 328–329
Oomycota, 331–332; *table,* 330
Oparin, A.I., 249
Operculum, 532
Opossum, 590; *illus.,* 590
Opposable thumb, 264, 266; *illus.,* 264
Opposable toe, 598; *illus.,* 598

Optic lobe, 533, 547
Oral contraceptive, 754
Oral groove, 318
Orangutan, 262; *illus.,* 262
Orchid, 789; *illus.,* 789
Order, 279
Organ, 131–132, 445; plant, 374–375; vegetative, 374; vestigial, 234; *illus.,* 132, 374
Organ donation, 766
Organ system, 131–132, 445; *illus.,* 132
Organelle, 67, 70–74; *illus.,* 69; *table,* 67
Organic compound, 30, 51–52; *illus.,* 51
Orientation, 776; *illus.,* 776
Ornithischian, 564; *illus.,* 564
Osmosis, 78–81, 83, 395–396; *illus.,* 395, 397
Osmotic pressure, 80, 82; *illus.,* 79
Ossification, 616
Osteichthyes, 517, 530–536
Osteocyte, 616
Osteoporosis, 616, 730; *illus.,* 617
Ostia, 494
Ostracoderm, 525; *illus.,* 525
Outcrossing, 203
Oval window, 712
Ovary, 726, 751–753; flower, 355; hydra, 455; *illus.,* 361, 754
Oviduct, 500, 548, 752, 755
Oviparous animal, 561
Ovipositor, 500
Ovoviviparous animal, 561
Ovulation, 753
Ovule, 355–357; *illus.,* 356, 361
Ovum, 751, *illus.,* 751
Oxygen, 37, 40; in cellular respiration, 93–94; in lung, 652; transport in blood, 652–653; *illus.,* 652; *table,* 39
Oxygen cycle, 812
Oxytocin, 724, 760; *table,* 721
Oyster, 479, 796, 806, 819–820

P₁ generation, 150
Pacemaker, 666
Pain, 707, 710–711; *illus.,* 707
Paleozoic Era, 256–257; *illus.,* 254–255
Palp, sensory, 498
Pampas, 790
Pancreas, 544, 633–634, 727–728; *illus.,* 634, 727; *table,* 632, 721
Pancreatic duct, 544

Pancreatic juice, 633
Paramecium, 318–319; *illus.,* 129, 319; *table,* 320
Parasite, 805; arthropod, 492; flatworm, 463–465; leech, 471–472; moneran, 300; nematode, 467
Parasympathetic nervous system, 708–709; *illus.,* 709
Parathormone, *table,* 721
Parathyroid gland, *table,* 721
Parazoa, 445
Parenchyma, 376; *illus.,* 376
Parental care, 773; *illus.,* 773
Parrot fish, 535; *illus.,* 535
Parthenogenesis, 503
Passive transport, 83; *illus.,* 83
Pasteur, Louis, 10, 25–26, 681; *illus.,* 25–26
Pasteurization, 26
Pathogen, 300, 681–682; defenses against, 684–690; *illus.,* 682
PCB, 840
PCP, 737–738
Pectin, 323
Pectoral fin, 527, 530; *illus.,* 527
Pectoral girdle, 516, 543
Pedigree, 187; *illus.,* 186
Pedipalp, 490
Pelagic zone, 794–795
Pelecypoda, 479–480; *illus.,* 480
Pellicle, of *Paramecium,* 318
Pelvic fin, 527, 530; *illus.,* 527
Pelvic girdle, 516, 543
Pelvis, 265–266
Penicillin, 11, 692; *illus.,* 692
Penicillium, 343
Penis, 500
Pepsin, 632; *illus.,* 631; *table,* 632
Peptidase, 636; *table,* 632
Peptide bond, 59; *illus.,* 59
Peptidoglycan, 297
Perch, anatomy of, 530; circulation in, 532; digestion in, 530–531; excretion in, 530–531; gas exchange in, 532; nervous system of, 533; reproduction in, 534; *illus.,* 531–533
Perennial plant, 415; *illus.,* 416
Pericardium, 665
Pericycle, 386–387; *illus.,* 387
Periosteum, 616; *illus.,* 616
Peripheral nervous system, 547, 704, 707–709; *illus.,* 547, 704
Perissodactyla, 596
Peristalsis, 631–632, 634; *illus.,* 630

Peritoneal dialysis, 660
Peritoneum, 468; *illus.*, 468
Permafrost, 787
Permanent wilting point, 408
Permeability, 78–81; *illus.*, 78
Pesticide, 508, 838, 840
Petiole, 403; *illus.*, 403
Phaeophyta, *table*, 322
Phage, 306
Phagocytosis, 85, 317; *illus.*, 85
Pharynx, 462, 513, 630, 651; *illus.*, 630
Phenotype, 152–153, 181
Phenylalanine, 194
Phenylketonuria, 194; *illus.*, 194; *table*, 189
Pheromone, 503, 777
Phloem, 376–377, 381, 390–393, 397–398, 406; *illus.*, 377, 387, 398
Phosphate, 91
Phosphoglyceraldehyde, 102
Phosphoglyceric acid, 102
Phospholipid, 74–75; *illus.*, 75
Phosphorus, *table*, 642
Photic zone, 794
Photochemical smog, 836; *illus.*, 836
Photoperiodism, 420–421; *illus.*, 420, 421
Photosynthesis, 27, 42–43, 99–101; in algae, 322–329; in carbon cycle, 810–811; carbon-fixation reactions in, 102–103; comparison with respiration, 103–104; evolution and, 252; in leaf, 406–407; light reactions of, 99–101; in monerans, 298–299; in oxygen cycle, 812; in protists, 322–329; *illus.*, 99, 101, 299, 810; *table*, 299, 322
Phototropism, 419; *illus.*, 419
Photovoltaic cell, 833–834
pH scale, 46; *illus.*, 45
Phycobilin, 299
Phycoerythrin, 327
Phylogeny, 279
Phylum, 279
Phytoplankton, 794–795
Pigment, 100, 299, 322–329; *illus.*, 100; *table*, 322
Pika, 593
Pili, 297
Pine, 363–365; *illus.*, 364, 365
Pineal eye, 563
Pineal gland, 728; *table*, 721
Pinocytosis, 85
Pioneer community, 807

Pitcher plant, 410
Pith, 390–391
Pituitary gland, 547, 722, 724–725, 729; anterior, 724; posterior, 724; *illus.*, 724–726; *table*, 721
Pit viper, 561; *illus.*, 224
Placenta, 592–598, 757–759, 761; *illus.*, 592, 758, 761; *table*, 721
Placoderm, 518, 527; *illus.*, 518, 527
Placoid scale, 527
Planarian, 462; *illus.*, 462, 463
Plankton, 322
Plannula, 454
Plant, adaptation to land, 431–432; classification of, 427–428; day-neutral, 421; evolution of, 256–257, 427–428, 431–432; genetic engineering of, 208, 210–211; growth patterns of, 415–418; hormones of, 416–417; insectivorous, 410; long-day, 421; organs of, 374–375; reproduction in, 432; responses of, 414, 419–422; seed, 352–369; short-day, 420; spore-bearing vascular, 433–436; time patterns of, 415; tissues of, 375–377; uptake of water and nutrients, 395–396; vascular, 428; vegetative propagation of, 378–380
Plantlike protist, 322–329
Plasma, 671–672
Plasma membrane, 74–75, 722; *illus.*, 75, 723; *table*, 67
Plasmid, 207, 302; *illus.*, 207
Plasmodium, 320–321, 330, 680; *illus.*, 321; *table*, 320
Plasmolysis, 81–82, 408; *illus.*, 82
Plastid, 73
Plastron, 562
Platelets, 671–672
Platyhelminthes, 461–465
Plesiosaur, 565; *illus.*, 565
Pleura, 651
Pneumonia, 682
Point mutation, 173; *illus.*, 174
Pokeberry, *illus.*, 416
Polar body, 751–752
Polar molecule, 45; *illus.*, 44
Polar nucleus, 356
Polar region, of earth, 783
Poles, of cell, 126
Polio, 682, 691
Pollen, 355–357, 693; *illus.*, 357, 364

Pollen cone, 363–364
Pollen tube, 360, 364; *illus.*, 360, 364
Pollination, 357–360, 364; *illus.*, 358, 359; *table*, 366
Pollinator, 357–359; *illus.*, 358; *table*, 366
Pollution, air, 836–837; water, 837–838; *illus.*, 836–838
Polychaeta, 472
Polygenic inheritance, 182; *illus.*, 182
Polynomial, 277–278
Polyp, 453–454; *illus.*, 453
Polypeptide, 59
Polyploidy, 171, 205; *illus.*, 171, 205
Polysaccharide, 54, 638–639; *illus.*, 54
Polysome, 118; *illus.*, 118
Polyunsaturated fatty acid, 57
Pond, 793, 795, 802, 807; *illus.*, 802, 807
Population, changes in, 221–224; definition of, 216; density of, 819–820; dynamics of, 816–827; human, 822–824; sampling of, 218; size of, 818; small, 221–222; variation in, 215–220; *illus.*, 819, 820
Population genetics, 214–225, 228–229
Population growth, 817–818; density-dependent factors in, 819–820; density-independent factors in, 819; *illus.*, 817–819
Porifera, 450–452
Porocyte, 450
Potassium, *table*, 642
Potassium-40, *illus.*, 233; *table*, 234
Potato, 393
Prairie, 790; *illus.*, 790
Precambian Era, 255; *illus.*, 254–255
Precipitation, 786; *illus.*, 786
Precocial bird, 582; *illus.*, 582
Predation, 820–821
Predator, 535, 803, 820–821; *illus.*, 820
Pregnancy, treatment of genetic disorder during, 193
Premolar, 629
Pressure-flow hypothesis, 398
Pressure receptor, 710
Prey, 803, 820–821; *illus.*, 820
Prickle, 394

Primate, 598; characteristics of, 263–264; evolution of, 258; *illus.,* 254–255, 598
Princess pine, 434
Principle of independent assortment, 155
Principle of segregation, 151
Probability, 153
Problem solving, 7–8
Producer, 803–805; *illus.,* 804
Product of reaction, 43–44; *illus.,* 43
Progesterone, 722, 726, 753–754; *table,* 721
Proglottid, 464; *illus.,* 465
Prokaryote, 251–253; *illus.,* 251, 297
Prolactin, 762; *table,* 721
Prophase, meiotic, 158–159; mitotic, 125–126
Prop root, 388
Prosimian, 598; *illus.,* 263
Prostaglandin, 729
Protease, 632–633
Protein, carrier, 84; in diet, 640; function of, 58–60; in nitrogen cycle, 811–812; sequence relationships of, 235; shape of, 60; structure of, 58–59; synthesis of, 71, 114–118; *illus.,* 58, 60, 640
Prothallium, 433–435
Prothrombin, 672
Protist, 280–281; animallike, 317–321; classification of, 320, 322, 330; funguslike, 330–332; plantlike, 322–329; *table,* 320, 322, 330
Protoavis, 571
Proton, 38; *illus.,* 38
Protonema, 430
Protoplast, 205
Protoplast fusion, 205
Proventriculus, 576
Proximal tubule, 657
Pseudopod, 317–318; *table,* 320
Psilophyta, 433
Pteranodon, illus., 566
Pterophyta, 435–436
Pterosaur, 565–566; *illus.,* 566
Puffball, 342; *illus.,* 338
Pulmonary artery, 546
Pulmonary circulation, 545, 668; *illus.,* 668
Pulmonary semilunar valve, 665
Pulmonary vein, 546
Punctuated equilibrium, 244
Punnett, R.C., 153

Punnett square, 153–155; *illus.,* 153, 155
Pupa, 497
Pupil, 713
Pure line, 149, 154, 202; *illus.,* 150
Purple bacteria, 299; *table,* 299
Pyloric caeca, 531
Pyramid of biomass, 805
Pyramid of numbers, 805
Pyruvic acid, 93, 95, 96, 98; *illus.,* 95
Python, 561

Quill feather, 572; *illus.,* 572

Rabbit, 593; *illus.,* 593
Radial symmetry, 448; pentamerous, 482; *illus.,* 448, 483
Radiation damage, 170
Radicle, 371, 373; *illus.,* 371
Radioactive isotope, 233–234; *illus.,* 233; *table,* 234
Radiolarian, 318, 448; *illus.,* 318; *table,* 320
Radula, 478
Rain, acid, 46, 837; *illus.,* 837
Rain forest, 440, 788–789; *illus.,* 789
Rat, 593
Rattlesnake, 561
Ray (animal), 517, 529; *illus.,* 529
Reabsorption, 658; *illus.,* 658
Reactant, 43; *illus.,* 43
Receptacle (flower), 355
Receptor, 701, 722–723, 728; *illus.,* 723
Recessive trait, 150–152; *illus.,* 151
Recombinant DNA, 206–208, 303; in agriculture, 144, 208; in medicine, 207–208; *illus.,* 207
Rectum, 637
Recycling, 809, 829, 838–839; graywater, 831; *table,* 835
Red algae, 326–327, 329, 795; *table,* 322
Red blood cells, 81, 184–185, 545, 653, 672–673; *illus.,* 58, 81, 184, 671; *table,* 673
Redi, Francesco, 21–23; *illus.,* 22
Red-winged blackbird, *illus.,* 776
Reflex, 706–707; conditioned, 775; *illus.,* 707; *table,* 775
Refractory period, 702
Refuge, 831; *illus.,* 832
Regeneration, 133, 484; *illus.,* 133
Regulation, 109–118

Releasing factors, 722, 724–726; *table,* 721
Renal artery, 545, 656
Renal cortex, 656
Renal medulla, 656
Renal pelvis, 656
Renal tubule, 657–658; *illus.,* 658
Renal vein, 545, 656–657
Replication, of DNA, 112–113; of virus, 306–307; *illus.,* 113
Replication fork, 112; *illus.,* 113
Reproduction, 30; in algae, 328–329; asexual, 157; in birds, 579–580; in crayfish, 495; in earthworms, 471; in fish, 534–535; in frogs, 548–549; in fungi, 338; in grasshoppers, 500; in humans, 748–765; in insects, 503; in monerans, 301; in plants, 366, 432; in reptiles, 558; sexual, 157–158; in sharks, 529; in snakes, 561; in spiders, 491; in sponges, 451; *illus.,* 158, 471, 548
Reproductive cell, 157
Reproductive isolation, 241
Reproductive system, female, 751–752; male, 749–751; *illus.,* 749–751
Reptile, 517, *See also* Snake; adaptation to land, 557–558; eggs of, 558; evolution of, 256–258, 564–566, 571; reproduction in, 558; *illus.,* 257
Research method, 9–10
Reservoir (euglenoid), 324
Resolution, 14; *illus.,* 14
Resource, energy, 833–835; natural, *See* Natural resource
Respiration, 648–655; anaerobic, 300; in birds, 577–578; in carbon cycle, 810–811; cellular, 93–97, 649; comparison with photosynthesis, 103–104; in crayfish, 494; external, 649; in frogs, 546–547; in grasshoppers, 499; in humans, 650–651; internal, 649; in leaves, 407; in oxygen cycle, 812; in snakes, 560; in spiders, 490–491; *illus.,* 94, 301, 500, 649, 810
Respiratory system, 132; as barrier to pathogens, 684–685
Response, 27
Restriction enzyme, 206
Retina, 713–714; *illus.,* 714
Retrovirus, 308–309, 690; *illus.,* 309; *table,* 309

Reyes syndrome, 696
Rh factor, 673
Rhinovirus, 682
Rhizoid, 339, 429, 431, 433
Rhizome, 379, 393, 435; *illus., 378*
Rhizopus, 339; *illus., 339–340*
Rhodophyta, *table,* 322
Rhynchocephalia, 559, 563; *illus.,* 563
Rib cage, 516, 654; *illus.,* 617, 654
Riboflavin, *See* Vitamin B-complex
Ribonucleic acid, *See* RNA
Ribose, 91, 114; *illus.,* 114
Ribosomal RNA (rRNA), 115
Ribosome, 117–118; *illus.,* 117, 118
Ribulose biphosphate (RuBP), 102
Rickets, 641; *table,* 641
Rickettsiae, *table,* 299
Ripening, 417; *illus.,* 417
River, 795
RNA, function of, 114–115; processing of, 115–116; structure of, 114–115
Rockweed, 327, 329; *illus.,* 327
Rodent, 593, 599
Rods (eye), 714; *illus.,* 714
Root, 374, 384; adventitious, 388; development of, 373; fibrous system, 385; nitrogen fixers in, 300; primary growth in, 386; primary tissues of, 386–387; prop, 388; secondary growth in, 387; structure of, 385–386; *illus.,* 300, 385, 386, 388, 395
Root cap, 386
Root hair, 386, 395–396
Root pressure, 396
Root tip, *illus.,* 386
Roundworm, 466–467; *illus.,* 466–468
rRNA, 115
Rubella, 691
RuBP, 102
Ruminant, 596
Runner (plant), 393
Rusts (plant), 342

Sac fungi, 340–341; *illus.,* 341
Salamander, 517, 541, 550–551; *illus.,* 516, 541, 550
Salinity, 793
Saliva, 630
Salivary gland, *illus.,* 629, 634, 719; *table,* 632
Salmon, 534; *illus.,* 534
Salt, 40; *table,* 39

Salt marsh, 796
Salt water, 793–795; *illus.,* 42
Saltwater fish, 534
Sand dollar, 482
Sap, 384, 397–398; *illus.,* 384
Saprobe, 300
Saprolegnia, 331–332
Sapwood, 392
Sarcodine, 317–318; *illus.,* 317, 318; *table,* 320
Sarcomere, 621; *illus.,* 621
Sargassum, 327
Saturated fatty acid, 56
Saurischian, 564; *illus.,* 564
Savanna, 790
Scale, fish, 530; placoid, 527; *illus.,* 530
Scallop, 479
Scanning electron microscope, 15–16; *illus.,* 14
Scavenger, 803
Scent gland, 587
Schleiden, Matthais, 29
Schwann, Theodor, 29
Scientific theory, 10
Scion, 380
Sclerenchyma, 376; *illus.,* 376
Scorpion, 492
Scrotum, 749
Scurvy, 641; *table,* 641
Sea anemone, 455–456, 805; *illus.,* 448, 455, 805
Sea cucumber, 482
Seal, 595
Sea lamprey, *table,* 808
Sea lettuce, 328
Sea lion, 595
Sea otter, *illus.,* 596
Seashell, identification of, 284–285; *illus.,* 285; *table,* 285
Seashore, 793
Sea squirt, 514
Sea urchin, 482; *illus.,* 483
Sebaceous gland, 587, 623
Second messenger, 723
Secretion, 71–72, 658
Sediment, 231–232; *illus.,* 231
Sedimentary rock, 231
Seed, 352, 355, 364; dispersal of, 353, 362; dormant, 371–372; germination of, 372–373; structure of, 354, 371; viable, 372; *illus.,* 352, 354, 361, 365, 371; *table,* 366
Seed coat, 371; *illus.,* 371
Seed cone, 363–364; *illus.,* 365

Seedling, 372–373
Seed plant, 352–369
Segmentation, 469, 489; *illus.,* 525
Segmented worm, 468–472; *illus.,* 468–472
Segregation, genetic, 151; law of, 160
Selaginella, 434
Selection, controlled, 201; mass, 201; natural, *See* Natural selection; stabilizing, 243; *illus.,* 201
Self-pollination, 360
Semen, 751
Semicircular canal, 533, 712–713; *illus.,* 713
Seminal fluid, 750–751
Seminal receptacle, 491
Semmelweis, Ignaz, 10–11
Senescence (leaf), 421–422; *illus.,* 421
Sense organ, *See also* specific senses; of bird, 572–573, 578–579; of crayfish, 494; of earthworm, 470–471; of frog, 547–548; of grasshopper, 499; of snake, 560–561; of spider, 491
Sense strand, 115, 120
Sensitive plant, 422
Sensory neuron, 701
Sensory palp, 498
Sepal, 355
Sessile animal, 445, 819; *illus.,* 819
Setae, 470; *illus.,* 471
Sewage, 683, 831, 838
Sex chromosome, 165–166
Sex determination, 165–166; *illus.,* 165, 166
Sex factor, 302
Sex hormone, 722, 726–727
Sex-influenced trait, 182–183; *illus.,* 183
Sex-limited trait, 182–183
Sex linkage, 166–168; *illus.,* 167
Sex-linked gene, 167
Sex-linked trait, 167
Sexual reproduction, 157–158; *illus.,* 158
Shaft, of feather, 571
Shark, 517, 806; gas exchange in, 528; movement of, 527; reproduction in, 529; skeleton of, 527; skin of, 527–528; teeth of, 527–528; temperature regulation in, 528; *illus.,* 243, 528
Shelf fungi, 342
Shell, egg, 580; turtle, 562

Shoot system, 374
Shrew, 597
Shrimp, 494
Shrubland, *illus.*, 786
Shrub layer, 788
Sickle-cell anemia, *table,* 189
Sickle-cell disease, 173, 184–185; *illus.*, 184
Sickle-cell trait, 185
Sidestream smoke, 743
Sieve tube, 397–398
Sieve tube element, 397–398
Silica, 323
Silicon, *illus.*, 38
Silk, spider, 491
Simple microscope, 13
Single bond, 41
Sinus venosus, 532, 545
Siphon (squid), 481
Sirenia, *illus.*, 594
SI units, 12
Skate, 517, 529; *illus.*, 529
Skeletal muscle, 619–621; *illus.*, 131, 619
Skeleton, appendicular, 516; axial, 516; of bird, 575–576; evolution of, 264–265; of frog, 542–543; of human, 615–619; of shark, 527; of snake, 559; of turtle, 562; *illus.*, 265, 543, 575
Skin, 132, 614; as barrier to pathogens, 684; color of, 182; function of, 623–624; of reptile, 557; sense organs on, 710; of shark, 527–528; structure of, 623–624; *illus.*, 29, 131, 684, 710
Skull, 516; *illus.*, 617
Sleeping sickness, 320
Slime mold, acellular, 330–331; cellular, 331; *illus.*, 331, 332; *table,* 330
Sloth, 597
Slug, 477–479
Small intestine, 633–636; *illus.*, 635
Smallpox, 7–8, 691
Smell, 711
Smog, 836; *illus.*, 836
Smokeless tobacco, 743
Smoking, 651, 741–743, 760; *illus.*, 742, 743
Smooth muscle, 622–623; *illus.*, 623
Snail, 477–479, 793, 795–796; *illus.*, 477, 478
Snake, 517, 556, 558, 791; anatomy of, 559–561; circulation in, 560; digestion in, 559; excretion in, 559–560; nervous system of, 560–561; poisonous, 561; reproduction in, 561; respiration in, 560; sense organs of, 560–561; skeleton of, 559; variety of, 561; *illus.*, 556, 559–561
Social behavior, 777–778; *illus.*, 778
Social insect, 503
Society, 777, 822
Sodium, 42; *illus.*, 38, 42
Sodium chloride, *illus.*, 42; *table,* 39
Sodium hydroxide, 46
Sodium-potassium pump, 702
Soil, 829–830; *illus.*, 830
Solar energy, 99–101, 833–834; *illus.*, 834
Solid, *illus.*, 37
Solid waste, 838–839; *illus.*, 839
Soluble substance, 45
Solute, 44
Solution, 44–45; hypertonic, 80–81; hypotonic, 80–81; isotonic, 81; *illus.*, 44, 81
Solvent, 44
Somatic cell, 157
Somatic nervous system, 708
Somatomedin, 729
Somatotropin, *See* Growth hormone
Sori, 435
Spallanzani, Lazzaro, 23–24; *illus.*, 24
Speciation, 240–241; *illus.*, 241
Species, 279; definition of, 215–216; foreign, 808; number of, 288–289; *illus.*, 215
Specific epithet, 278
Sperm, 149, 749–751; *illus.*, 749, 750
Spermatocyte, primary, 750; secondary, 750; *illus.*, 750
Sperm nucleus, 360
Sphenophyta, 434
Spherical symmetry, *illus.*, 448
Sphincter, 631–632
Spicule, 450
Spider, 490–491; *illus.*, 490, 491
Spinal cord, 533, 704, 706–707; *illus.*, 706, 707
Spinal nerve, 533, 547, 708; *illus.*, 708
Spindle fiber, 126
Spine (plant), 409
Spinneret, 491
Spiny anteater, 589–590; *illus.*, 590
Spiracle, 491, 498
Spirilli, 298; *illus.*, 298
Spirochaete, *table,* 299
Spirogyra, 327–329; *illus.*, 328
Sponge, 444–445, 796; diversity among, 452; evolution of, 452; reproduction in, 451; structure of, 450; *illus.*, 444, 448, 450–452
Spongin, 452
Spongy bone, 616
Spontaneous generation, 21–23; *illus.*, 21–22
Sporangia, 433–434
Spore, algal, 325; fungal, 337–338, 343; moss, 430; *illus.*, 338, 343, 364, 430
Spore-bearing vascular plant, 433–436
Sporophyll, 434; *illus.*, 434
Sporophyte, 329, 356–357, 429–430, 433, 435; *illus.*, 364
Sporozoan, 320–321; *table,* 320
Spruce, *illus.*, 363
Squamata, 559
Squid, 480–481; *illus.*, 481
Squirrel, 593
S-shaped curve, 818; *illus.*, 818
Stabilizing selection, 243
Stamen, 355
Starch, 54, 638–639; *illus.*, 54
Starfish, 482–484, 794; *illus.*, 133, 447, 483–484
Starling, *table,* 808
Stem, 374, 384; external features of, 389; herbaceous, 390; modified, 393–394; primary tissues of, 391; secondary growth in, 391–393; woody, 391–393; *illus.*, 389–391, 394
Steppe, 790
Steroid, 722–723; abuse of, 738; *illus.*, 723
Stigma, 355; *illus.*, 357
Stimulant, 737
Stipe, 327
Stock, 380
Stolon, 378, 393
Stomach, 631–632; *illus.*, 631; *table,* 632
Stomata, 405, 407–408; *illus.*, 407
Stratification, horizontal, 794; vertical, 794; *illus.*, 794
Stream, 793, 795–796
Strep throat, 682

Streptococcus, illus., 682
Stress, 718–719; population density and, 820
Striated muscle, 619
Strip cropping, 830
Stroke, 672, 706
Stroma, 100
Style, 355
Sublittoral zone, 793–794
Subspecies, 216–217, 224, 240; *illus.,* 217
Substance abuse, 734–747; *illus.,* 734
Substrate, 62
Succession, primary, 807–808; secondary, 808; *illus.,* 807, 808
Succulent, 410, 790
Sucrose, 53
Sugar, 638–639; *illus.,* 42
Sulfur, *illus.,* 34, 38
Sunflower, 414; *illus.,* 414
Supportive tissue, plant, 376
Sutton, Walter, 160
Swallowing, 630; *illus.,* 630
Swan, *illus.,* 582
Sweat gland, 587, 623; *illus.,* 719
Swim bladder, 532
Swimmeret, 493
Symbiosis, 343–344, 805–806; *illus.,* 805, 806
Symmetry, body, 447–449; radial, 482; *illus.,* 448, 483
Sympathetic nervous system, 708; *illus.,* 709
Synapse, 701–703; *illus.,* 701
Synapsis, 158
Syndrome, 188
Synovial fluid, 618
Syphilis, 683
Syrinx, 577; *illus.,* 577
Systemic circulation, 545, 668; *illus.,* 668
Systole, 669; *illus.,* 669

Tadpole, 548; *illus.,* 549
Taiga, 787–788
Tapeworm, 461, 464–465; *illus.,* 464, 465
Taproot, 386; *illus.,* 385
Target cells, 722–723; *illus.,* 723
Taste, 710–711
Taste bud, 710
Taxis, 776
Taxonomist, 279–281
Tay-Sachs disease, 189
T cells, 687–690; *illus.,* 688–690

Teaching career, 846
Teeth, 587, 597, 629; cavities in, 296; egg, 581; incisor, 593; maxillary, 543; of shark, 527–528; vomerine, 543; *illus.,* 296, 528, 593, 595, 629
Telophase, meiotic, 159; mitotic, 126; *illus.,* 127
Telson, 493
Temperate deciduous forest, 788; *illus.,* 788
Temperate rain forest, 788–789
Temperature, 528, 786; *illus.,* 786
Tendon, 622
Tendril, 409, 420, 422; *illus.,* 409
Tentacle, 454; *illus.,* 455
Termination codon, 116, 118
Terminator, 116
Termite, 320, 503
Terracing, 830
Terrapin, 562
Territoriality, 777; *illus.,* 777
Testcross, 154; *illus.,* 154
Testis, 455, 726, 749–751
Testosterone, 722, 727, 750
Tetanus, 681–682, 691
Tetrad, 158
Tetrahymena, illus., 318
Tetraploid, 205
Thalamus, 705
THC, 736
Theory, scientific, 10
Therapsid, 566; *illus.,* 566
Thermoacidophile, *table,* 299
Thiamin, *See* Vitamin B-complex
Thigmotropism, 420
Thiobacillus, illus., 301
Thorax, 497
Thorn, 394
Thorn acacia, 806; *illus.,* 806
Three-kingdom classification system, 280
Thrombin, 672
Thumb, opposable, 264, 266; *illus.,* 264
Thylakoid, 100
Thymine, 109
Thymosin, 728; *table,* 721
Thymus, 687, 728; *table,* 721
Thyroid gland, 725, 766 *illus.,* 725; *table,* 721
Thyroid-stimulating hormone (TSH), 725; *illus.,* 725; *table,* 721
Thyroxine, 722, 725; *illus.,* 725; *table,* 721
Tick, 492

Tiger, 595; *illus.,* 595
Timberline, 792
Tissue, 131–132, 445; *illus.,* 132, 375, 376, 615
Tissue fluid, 674–675; *illus.,* 675
Toad, 517, 541
Tobacco, 741–743; smokeless, 743
Tobacco mosaic virus, 305–306; *illus.,* 305
Tocopherol, *See* Vitamin E
Toe, opposable, 598; *illus.,* 598
Tongue, 544, 630, 710; *illus.,* 544
Tonsils, 675, 766
Tortoise, 559, 562
Touch receptor, 710; *illus.,* 710
Toxic shock syndrome, 697
Toxic waste, 839–840, 844; non-biodegradable, 840; *illus.,* 840
Toxin, 681–682
Trachea, 560, 651; *illus.,* 650
Tracheae, 491
Tracheid, 396–397
Trait, 149; controlled by multiple alleles, 181; controlled by multiple genes, 182; dominant, 150–152, 156; recessive, 150–152; sex-influenced, 182–183; sex-limited, 182–183; sex-linked, 167; sickle-cell, 184–185; *illus.,* 151
Tranquilizer, 736–737
Transcription, 115–116; reverse, 309; *illus.,* 115
Transduction, 307
Transfer RNA, *See* tRNA
Transformation, 302; *illus.,* 303
Transgenic organism, 208; *illus.,* 208
Translation, 117–118; *illus.,* 117
Translocation, 172; of food in plants, 397–398; *illus.,* 172
Transmission electron microscope, 14; *illus.,* 15
Transpiration, 396, 407–408; *illus.,* 397
Transplant, 693; of heart, 667; of kidney, 660
Transport, active, 83–85, 396; passive, 83; *illus.,* 83
Transport vesicle, *table,* 67
Tree, deciduous, 365, 788; identification of, 286; *illus.,* 286
Trematoda, 461, 463–464; *illus.,* 464
Trial-and-error learning, *table,* 775
Trichinosis, 467; *illus.,* 467
Trichocyst, 318

Tricuspid valve, 665
Triglyceride, 56–57, 639; *illus.*, 56
Triplet code, 112
Trisomy, 171
tRNA, 115, 117–118; *illus.*, 114
Trochophore larva, 479; *illus.*, 479
Trophoblast, 756; *illus.*, 756
Tropical deciduous forest, *illus.*, 786
Tropical rain forest, 789; *illus.*, 789
Tropism, 414, 419–420; negative, 419; positive, 419; *illus.*, 414, 419, 420
Truffle, 341
Trychonympha, *table*, 320
Trypanosoma, 320; *table*, 320
Trypsin, *table*, 632
TSH, *See* Thyroid-stimulating hormone
Tuatara, 559, 563; *illus.*, 563
Tube cell, 357
Tube feet, 482
Tuber, 393
Tuberculosis, 682
Tubular secretion, 658
Tumor, 136; benign, 136; malignant, 136; *illus.*, 136
Tundra, 787; *illus.*, 787
Turbellaria, 461–463; *illus.*, 462, 463
Turbidity, 795
Turgid cell, 82
Turgor pressure, 81–82, 407–408, 414, 422
Turner syndrome, 188
Turtle, 517, 559, 562, 776, 794; *illus.*, 562, 776
Twins, 183; fraternal, 762; identical, 762; *illus.*, 762
Tympanic membrane, 542, 547–548, 711–712
Tympanum, 498
Typhoid fever, 683

Ulcer, 632
Ultrasound, 190–191; *illus.*, 191
Ulva, 328–329
Umbilical cord, 592, 758, 760–761; *illus.*, 761
Understory, 788
Ungulate, 596, 599; *illus.*, 597
Unicellular algae, 323–326
Unicellular organism, 29; cell division in, 129
Unsaturated fatty acid, 56; *illus.*, 56
Uracil, 115

Uranium-235, *table*, 234
Uranium-238, *table*, 234
Urea, 656, 659–660
Ureter, 545, 656; *illus.*, 656
Urethra, 656, 750
Urinary bladder, 545
Urine, 531, 656–659; *illus.*, 658
Urochordate, 514; *illus.*, 514
Urodela, 541, 550–551
Uropod, 493
Uterus, 548, 588, 592, 748, 752; *illus.*, 754
Uvula, *illus.*, 629

Vaccine, 691–692
Vacuole, 73; contractile, 317; food, 319; *table*, 67
Vagina, 752
Valium, 737
Vampire bat, 594
Variable, 8
Vasa efferentia, 548
Vascular bundle, 377, 390; *illus.*, 377, 405
Vascular cambium, 387, 391; *illus.*, 391
Vascular cylinder, *illus.*, 387
Vascular plant, 428
Vascular tissue, plant, 376–377, 428, 432; *illus.*, 377
Vas deferens, 579, 750
Vasopressin, 724; *table*, 721
Vegetarian, *illus.*, 643
Vegetative organ, 374
Vegetative propagation, 378–380; applied, 379–380; natural, 378–379; *illus.*, 378, 379
Vein, 532, 667–669; leaf, 406; valves in, 669; *illus.*, 406, 667, 668, 669
Veldt, 790
Venae cavae, 545, 668
Venation, 406; netted, 406; parallel, 406; *illus.*, 406
Venereal disease, 683
Ventral aorta, 532
Ventral surface, 449
Ventricle, 532, 665; *illus.*, 666, 669
Venule, 667; *illus.*, 667
Venus's-flytrap, 422; *illus.*, 410
Vertebrae, 515–516
Vertebral column, *illus.*, 617
Vertebral disk, 618
Vertebrate, 515; classification of, 516–518; definition of, 516; evolution of, 518–520; *illus.*, 517

Vesicle, 71, 85; *illus.*, 85; *table*, 67
Vessel element, 396–397
Vestigial organ, 234
Villi, 635; *illus.*, 635
Virchow, Rudolph, 29
Viroid, 312
Virus, 305, 682; cancer and, 311; evolution of, 312; replication of, 306–307; structure of, 305–306; *illus.*, 305, 306, 310, 683; *table*, 309
Vision, 713–714; *illus.*, 713, 714
Vitamin, 62, 640–642; *illus.*, 304; *table*, 641
Vitamin A, 641; *table*, 641
Vitamin B-complex, 641; *table*, 641
Vitamin C, *table*, 641
Vitamin D, 641; *table*, 641
Vitamin E, 641; *table*, 641
Vitamin K, 641; *table*, 641
Vocal cords, 547, 651
Volvox, 326; *illus.*, 326
Vomerine teeth, 543

Waggle dance, 778
Walking, bipedal, 265–266; *illus.*, 266
Wallaby, 591
Wallace, Alfred, 238
Walrus, 595
Warbler, *illus.*, 582
Wasp, 503
Water, balance in body, 659; capillary, 395; chemistry of, 40; dispersal of fruits and seeds, 362; energy from, 835; intake of, 640–642; as natural resource, 830–831; pollution of, 837–838; as solvent, 44–45; uptake by plants, 395–396; within cells, 30; *illus.*, 40, 41, 44, 831, 838; *table*, 39
Water cycle, 809–810; *illus.*, 809
Water flea, 493
Water mold, 331–332; *table*, 330
Water vascular system, 483
Watson, James, 111
Web (spider), 491
Weinberg, Wilhelm, 218
Whale, 124, 595, 599, 820, 832
Whiskfern, 433
White blood cells, 545, 674–675, 685; *illus.*, 138, 674
Whittaker, Robert, 281
Whooping cough, 691
Whooping crane, 831; *illus.*, 832
Wildlife resources, 831–832

Wilkins, Maurice, 111
Wilting, 408; *illus.,* 408
Wilting point, permanent, 408
Wind, dispersal of fruits and seeds, 362; energy from, 835; pollination by, 359; *illus.,* 359, 835
Wing, of bat, 594; of bird, 574; of insect, 499; *illus.,* 496, 499, 594
Withdrawal symptoms, 735
Wolf, 778
Wood, 95, 392, 834; *illus.,* 95
Worm, 796; segmented, 468–472
Wound, *illus.,* 58

X chromosome, 165–168, 182
Xylem, 377, 387, 390, 392, 406; conduction through, 396–397; *illus.,* 377, 387
Xylem vessel, 396

Yarrow, 216; *illus.,* 216
Y chromosome, 165–168
Yeast, 336, 341; fermentation by, 93; *illus.,* 93, 341
Yolk, 579–580
Yolk sac, 558, 581

Z-band, 621; *illus.,* 621
Zinc, 62
Zone of elongation, 386
Zone of maturation, 386
Zoomastigina, *table,* 320
Zooplankton, 794
Zoospore, 328
Zygomycota, 339–340; *illus.,* 339
Zygospore, 328, 340
Zygote, 157, 748, 755–756; *illus.,* 446, 757

ACKNOWLEDGMENTS

Illustration Credits

Alexander & Turner: 60, 127, 132, 271, 282–283, 356, 357, 450, 451, 453, 462, 463, 479, 496, 566, 604–605, 606, 607, 608, 609, 637, 649, 695, 703. Sally J. Bensusen: 237, 257. Ka Botzis: 234, 235, 587. Nancy Kaplan: 617. George Kelvin, "The Aids Virus", © 1987 by *Scientific American, Inc.,* all rights reserved: 310. Joe LeMonnier: 38, 46, 78, 79, 80, 91, 92, 93, 94, 95, 96, 99, 130, 166, 169, 172, 427, 658, 671, 824. Paul Metcalfe: 263, 374. Precision Graphics: 172, 187. Brenda Robinson: 56, 71, 75, 297, 298, 302, 303, 308, 319, 445, 449, 478, 484, 519, 545, 557, 575, 618, 619, 622, 630, 634, 635, 651, 654, 656, 657, 705, 710, 711, 720, 749, 752, 761, 762. Rossi & Associates: 5, 9, 22, 24, 25, 28, 32, 37, 75, 83, 104, 125, 126, 231, 232, 233, 301, 305, 308, 327, 337, 385, 389, 390, 391, 405, 454, 520, 558, 571, 577, 581, 592, 667, 668, 672. Wendy Smith-Griswold: 373, 380. Krystyna Srodulski: 173, 331, 332, 340, 341, 343. Edgar Stewart: 242, 243. James Teason: 480. Sarah F. Woodward: 72, 73, 98, 233, 254, 256, 317, 319, 354, 360, 361, 371, 372, 435, 854–859. Amy Bartlett Wright: 148, 286, 403, 407.

Photo Credits

Picture Research: Connie Komack, Linda Finigan

Front Matter: iv: Francis Leroy, Biocosmos/SPL (Photo Researchers). v: Philippe Plailly/SPL (Photo Researchers). vi: *t* © David Scharf; *b* E.R. Degginger. vii: *t* E.R. Degginger. viii: M.P.L. Fogden (Bruce Coleman, Inc.). x: *r* Runk/Schoenberger (Grant Heilman Photography); *l* Martin Miller (Positive Images). xi: Gary Bell (Ellis Wildlife Collection). xii: Zig Leszczynski (Animals Animals). xiii: *r* Peter B. Kaplan (Photo Researchers); *l* Alex Kerstitch. xiv: *r* James H. Carmichael, Jr (Bruce Coleman, Inc.); *l* Leonard Lee Rue III (Animals Animals). xv: C. Rentmeester (FPG International). xvi: *l* Prof. Luc Montagnier, Institut Pasteur (Photo Researchers); *r* Bill Longcore (Photo Researchers). xvii: Dave Black (Sportschrome). xviii: *r* Tom Hollyman (Photo Researchers); *l* Fred Bavendam (Peter Arnold, Inc.). xix: *t* Bildarchiv Okapia (Photo Researchers); *b* Peter Menzel (Stock Boston).

Unit One: xxiv: *l* Cecil Fox (Photo Researchers); *r* Nathan Benn (Woodfin Camp, D.C.). **1:** *l* Rainbow; *r* Herbert Wagner (Phototake). **2:** Petit Format, J.P. Mornon, C. Edelman (Photo Researchers). **4:** Hank Morgan (Photo Researchers). **6:** *tl* Breck Kent (Animals Animals); *tl inset* Bruce Iverson; *tr* Valerie Hodgson (Photo/Nats); *tr inset* Bruce Iverson; *b* E.R. Degginger. **8:** Eric Grave (Phototake). **9:** Bruce Iverson. **10:** Paul Conklin. **13:** David Scharf (Peter Arnold, Inc.). **14:** Lawrence Migdale (Photo Researchers). **15:** *t&bl* N.J. Lang, University of California, Davis (BPS); *br* J.N.A. Lott, McMaster University (BPS). **16:** *t* Malcolm Kirk (Peter Arnold, Inc.); *b* Dan McCoy (Rainbow). **20:** Robert Lee (Photo Researchers). **21:** James Simon (Bruce Coleman, Inc.). **26:** Institut Pasteur. **27:** Jerry Howard (Positive Images). **28:** *t* Countway Medical Library. **29:** *t* Bruce Iverson; *b* SIU (Photo Researchers). **31:** *tl&tr* E.R. Degginger; *b* Russ Kinne (Photo Researchers). **36:** Richard Megna (Fundamental Photos). **37:** *l&c* Bruce Iverson; *r* Norman Owen Tomalin (Bruce Coleman, Inc.). **42:** *l&r* Ken O'Donoghue (D.C. Heath). **44:** *t&m* Tom Magno (D.C. Heath); *b* Ken O'Donoghue (D.C. Heath). **45:** William Leatherman (D.C. Heath). **50:** Lonnie Major (Allsport). **51,52,57:** Ken O'Donoghue (D.C. Heath). **66:** Francis Leroy, Biocosmos/SPL (Photo Researchers). **70:** *t* Harry Przekop (Medichrome); *m* Dwight Kuhn; *b* K.G. Murti (Visuals Unlimited). **71:** D.W. Fawcett (Photo Researchers). **72:** *t* G.T. Cole, University of Texas, Austin (BPS); *b* K. Porter (Photo Researchers). **73:** Biophoto Associates (Photo Researchers). **74:** D.W. Fawcett (Photo Researchers). **77:** Tom Magno (D.C. Heath). **81:** *all* Biophoto Associates (Photo Researchers). **82:** *both* A. Owczarzak (Taurus Photos). **90:** Jerry Howard (Positive Images). **92:** © David Scharf. **95:** Martin Kuhnigk (Valan Photos). **98:** Brian Parker (Tom Stack & Associates). **100:** Grant Heilman Photography. **108:** Philippe Plailly/SPL (Photo Researchers). **118:** J. Somers (Taurus Photos). **121:** Ann Reilly (Photo/Nats). **124:** CNRI/SPL (Photo Researchers). **128:** *t* A. Owczarzak (Taurus Photos); *b* M.I. Walker (Photo Researchers). **129:** Eric Grave (Visuals Unlimited). **131:** *l* Ed Reschke (Peter Arnold, Inc.); *c* Biophoto Associates (Photo Researchers); *r* Dwight Kuhn. **133:** Breck Kent (Animals Animals). **137:** *l* Martin Rotker (Phototake); *r* C. Overton FHMC (Phototake). **138:** *l* Manfred Kage (Peter Arnold, Inc.); *r* SIU (Bruce Coleman, Inc.). **140:** Cecil Fox (Photo Researchers). **141:** Manfred Kage (Peter Arnold, Inc.).

Unit Two: 146: *l* Wayne Lynch (DRK Photo); *r* George Musil (Visuals Unlimited). **147:** *l* G.I. Bernard (Animals Animals); *r* Leonard Lee Rue III (Animals Animals). **148:** G.C. Kelley (Photo Researchers). **151:** E. Rao (Photo Researchers). **156:** Dave Schaeffer. **160:** E.R. Degginger. **164:** © David Scharf. **166:** Norman Lightfoot (Photo Researchers). **171:** Jon Feingersh (Tom Stack & Associates). **176:** *l* Dan McCoy (Rainbow); *r* NASA (Photo Researchers). **177:** Hank Morgan (Photo Researchers). **180:** Will McIntyre (Photo Researchers). **182:** Tom Magno (D.C. Heath). **184:** *t* Biophoto Associates (Photo Researchers); *b* G. Grimes (Taurus Photos). **185:** Yoav Levy (Phototake). **188:** *t* Gary Bublitz (Marvin Dembinsky Photo Associates); *b* Phototake. **191:** Dr. Jason Birnholz, Brigham & Women's Hospital, Boston. **192:** Arthur Sirdofsky (Medichrome). **193:** Courtesy of Dr. Michael Harrison, University of California, San Francisco Medical Center. **194:** *l* Daniel Pashko (Envision); *r* Dan McCoy (Rainbow). **196:** Sinclair Stammers/SPL (Photo Researchers). **197:** Biophoto Associates (Photo Researchers). **200:** E.R. Degginger. **202:** J. Gajda (FPG International). **203:** Park Seed Co. **204:** Spencer Grant (Stock Boston). **205:** Roy Morsch (Bruce Coleman, Inc.). **206:** Dave Schaeffer. **208:** Courtesy of the Agricultural Research Service, USDA. **210:** Larry Lefever (Grant Heilman Photography). **211:** Chris Hildreth (Cornell University). **214:** E.R. Degginger. **215:** *both* E.R. Degginger. **220:** E.R. Degginger. **221:** Frank Curran (Picture Cube). **222:** *both* Nancy Sheehan (D.C. Heath). **223:** *both* Oxford Scientific Films (Animals Animals). **224:** *l* Breck Kent (Animals Animals); *r* Peter Dombrovskis (Envision). **226:** M.P. Kahl (Bruce Coleman, Inc.). **227:** E.R. Degginger. **230:** Zig Leszczynski (Animals Animals). **231:** A.J. Copley (Visuals Unlimited). **236:** Mark Warner. **238:** *l* K.G. Preston-Mafham (Animals Animals); *r* Townsend Dickinson (Photo Researchers). **239:** Kim Taylor (Bruce Coleman, Inc.). **241:** *l&r* Pat & Tom Leeson (Photo Researchers); *c* Breck Kent. **248:** © Thomas Ives. **249:** © William E. Ferguson. **250:** Courtesy of Glenn M. Mason, Western Research Institute, University of Wyoming. **251:** *l* S.M. Awramik, University of California (BPS); *r* © William E. Ferguson. **252:** Don Fawcett (Photo Researchers). **258:** Tom McHugh/Natural History Museum of Los Angeles County (Photo Researchers). **262:** Tom McHugh (Photo Researchers). **267:** Robert Frerck (Odyssey, Chicago). **268:** *t&b* Cleveland Museum of Natural History. **270:** French Government Tourist Office. **272:** *tl&tr* Gary Milburn (Tom Stack & Associates); *bl* Robert Comport (Animals Animals); *br* Gary Milburn (Tom Stack & Associates). **276:** George Holton (Photo Researchers). **277:** Grant Heilman Photography. **278:** *t* Zig Leszczynski (Animals Animals); *b* E.R. Degginger. **280:** *t* Runk/Schoenberger (Grant Heilman Photography); *b* Jeff Rotman. **285:** *t* Gary Robinson (Visuals Unlimited); *ml* Runk/Schoenberger (Grant Heilman Photography); *mc* Keith Gillett (Animals Animals); *mr* E.R. Degginger; *bl* Bill Tronca (Tom Stack & Associates); *bc* Ken Brate (Photo Researchers); *br* E.R. Degginger. **286:** *l* Jerry Howard (Positive Images); *r* Grant Heilman Photography. **288:** Camera Hawaii, Inc. **289:** *t* Scott Camazine (Photo Researchers); *b* M.P.L. Fogden (Bruce Coleman, Inc.).

Unit Three: 294: *l* Ray Coleman (Photo Researchers); *r* T.E. Adams (Visuals Unlimited). **295:** *l* Eric Grave (Photo Researchers); *r* Don Johnston (Photo/Nats). **296:** David Scharf (Peter Arnold, Inc.). **298:** Drs. Chapman & Costa, Georgetown University. **299:** Norma J. Lang, University of California, Davis (BPS). **300:** *t* D. Jorgenson (Tom Stack & Associates); *b* Runk/Schoenberger (Grant Heilman Photography). **301:** P.W. Johnson & J. McN Sieburth, University of Rhode Island (BPS). **304:** *l* David Phillips (Visuals Unlimited); *r* Michael Gabridge (Visuals Unlimited). **306:** Computer graphics modeling and photography, Arthur J. Olson, Ph.D., Research Institute of Scripps Clinic, La Jolla, CA © 1989. **309:** Visuals Unlimited. **316:** Manfred Kage (Peter Arnold, Inc.). **318:** *t* Manfred Kage (Peter Arnold, Inc.); *b* David Phillips (Visuals Unlimited). **319:** Omikron (Photo Researchers). **323:** Manfred Kage (Peter Arnold, Inc.). **324:** P.W. Johnson & J. McN Sieburth, University of Rhode Island (BPS). **326:** *t* Manfred Kage (Peter Arnold, Inc.); *b* W.H. Hodge (Peter Arnold, Inc.). **336:** R.M. Meadows (Peter Arnold, Inc.). **338:** Ray Kamal (Earth Scenes). **339:** Bruce Coleman, Inc.; *inset* Breck Kent (Earth Scenes). **341:** Science Photo Library (Photo Researchers). **342:** *l* S. Runnels (Grant Heilman Photography); *r* E.R. Degginger. **343:** John Cunningham (Visuals Unlimited). **344:** Cy Furlan (Berg & Associates). **348:** Steven Ogilvy (Bruce Coleman, Inc.).

Unit Four: 350: *l* G.I. Bernard (Animals Animals); *r* Thomas Kitchin (Tom Stack & Associates). **351:** *l* Wayne Lankinen (DRK Photo); *r* John Shaw (Tom Stack & Associates). **352:** Larry Lefever (Grant Heilman Photography). **353:** Envision. **355:** Paul Johnson (D.C. Heath). **357:** Manfred Kage (Peter Arnold, Inc.). **358:** Larry West. **359:** *both* W.H. Hodge (Peter Arnold, Inc.). **362:** M.L. Dembinsky Photo Associates. **363:** Grant Heilman Photography. **365:** *t* John Cunningham (Visuals Unlimited); *b* John MacGregor (Peter Arnold, Inc.). **366:** Joy Spurr (Bruce Coleman, Inc.). **370:** Grant Heilman Photography. **378:** Envision. **379:** Runk/Schoenberger (Grant Heilman Photography). **384:** Runk/Schoenberger (Grant Heilman Photography). **388:** Grant Heilman Photography. **392:** *l* W.H. Hodge (Peter Arnold, Inc.); *c* Walter Dawn; *r* Jerry Howard (Positive Images). **395:** Spencer Swanger (Tom Stack & Associates). **399:** John Cunningham (Visuals Unlimited). **402:** Martin Miller (Positive Images). **403:** D. Newman (Visuals Unlimited). **407:** Dr. Jeremy Burgess/SPL (Photo Researchers). **408:** C. Shuman (Grant Heilman Photography). **409:** *l* John Cunningham (Visuals Unlimited); *r* J. Colwell (Grant Heilman Photography). **410:** Kerry Givens (Tom Stack & Associates). **414:** Muriel Orans. **416:** Ken Brate (Photo Researchers). **417:** Robert Pettit (M.L. Dembinsky Photo Associates). **418:** Imagery. **419:** Grant Heilman Photography. **420:** John Cunningham (Visuals Unlimited). **421:** *t* Clyde Smith (Stock Shop); *b* Bruce Iverson. **422:** Richard Trump (Photo Researchers). **426:** Lefever/Grushow (Grant Heilman Photography). **429:** Larry West (Photo Researchers). **430:** Biophoto Associates (Photo Researchers). **431:** *l* Richard Carlton (Photo Researchers); *r* © William Ferguson. **434:** *l* Doug Wechsler; *r* Imagery. **435:** *t* K.G. Preston-Mafham (AA/Earth Scenes); *b* Stephen Kraseman (DRK Photo). **440:** W.H. Hodge (Peter Arnold, Inc.).

Acknowledgments

903

Unit Five: **442:** *l* Robert Holland (DRK Photo); *r* Runk/Schoenberger (Grant Heilman Photography). **443:** *l* Stephen Dalton (Animals Animals); *r* Robert Simpson (Tom Stack & Associates). **444:** Gary Bell (Ellis Wildlife Collection). **447:** *l* Bob Evans (Peter Arnold, Inc.); *r* McLove (Peter Arnold, Inc.). **448:** *tl* D. Woodward (Taurus Photos); *tr* Manfred Kage (Peter Arnold, Inc.); *bl* Ralph Oberlander (Stock Boston); *br* Tom Magno (D.C. Heath). **452:** *l* Ronald Sefton (Bruce Coleman, Inc.); *r* D. Woodward (Taurus Photos). **455:** Jeff Rotman. **456:** *l* Nicholas Devore III (Bruce Coleman, Inc.); *r* Ashod Francis (Animals Animals). **457:** James Bell (Photo Researchers). **460:** Zig Leszczynski (Animals Animals). **464:** Russ Kinne (Photo Researchers). **465:** *both* Biophoto Associates (Photo Researchers). **467:** Jerome Metzner (Peter Arnold, Inc.). **476:** Alex Kerstitch. **477:** E. Robinson (Tom Stack & Associates). **480:** James Carmichael (Bruce Coleman, Inc.). **481:** Jeff Rotman. **483:** *tl&tr* Christopher Newbert (Bruce Coleman, Inc.); *b* Jeff Foott (Bruce Coleman, Inc.). **484:** Zig Leszczynski (Animals Animals). **488:** William H. Calvert (E.R. Degginger). **490:** *t* Jane Burton (Bruce Coleman, Inc.); *b* Joe McDonald (Bruce Coleman, Inc.). **492:** *l* © David Scharf; *r* Doug Wechsler. **495:** *t* Peter Ward (Bruce Coleman, Inc.); *b* Jack Dermid (Bruce Coleman, Inc.). **502:** *t* M.P.L. Fogden (Bruce Coleman, Inc.); *bl&br* David Overcash (Bruce Coleman, Inc.). **503:** Don Riepe (Peter Arnold, Inc.); *inset* Peter G. Aitken (Photo Researchers). **504:** A.J. Deane (Bruce Coleman, Inc.). **508:** E.R. Degginger.

Unit Six: **510:** *l* Leonard Lee Rue III (Photo Researchers); *r* Hartman De Wit (Comstock). **511:** *l* R. Myers (Visuals Unlimited); *r* Jeff Lepore (Photo Researchers). **512:** Peter B. Kaplan (Photo Researchers). **514:** Douglas Faulkner (Photo Researchers). **515:** Runk/Schoenberger (Grant Heilman Photography). **517:** *tl* Runk/Schoenberger (Grant Heilman Photography); *tc* Grant Heilman Photography; *tr* W. Perry Conway; *m* Phil Degginger; *bl* Jeff Rotman; *bc&br* J.H. Robinson. **524:** Alex Kerstitch. **525:** David Schwimmer (Bruce Coleman, Inc.). **526:** *l* Runk/Schoenberger (Grant Heilman Photography); *r* Oxford Scientific Films (Animals Animals). **527:** Miriam Austerman (Animals Animals). **528:** *t* Ron Taylor (Bruce Coleman, Inc.); *b* Taurus Photos. **529:** *l* Zig Leszczynski (Animals Animals); *r* Miriam Austerman (Animals Animals). **533:** Grant Heilman Photography. **534:** U.S. Fish & Wildlife Service. **535:** *both* Carl Roessler (Animals Animals). **536:** Source Unknown. **540,541:** Zig Leszczynski (Animals Animals). **542:** Joseph T. Collins (Photo Researchers). **548:** M. Fogden, Oxford Scientific Films (Animals Animals). **550:** *both* Zig Leszczynski (Animals Animals). **551:** *t* E.R. Degginger (Animals Animals); *bl* Zig Leszczynski (Animals Animals); *br* Oxford Scientific Films (Animals Animals). **556:** James H. Carmichael, Jr. (Bruce Coleman, Inc.). **559:** M. Phillip Kahl (Photo Researchers). **562:** *t* Moira & Rod Borland (Bruce Coleman, Inc.); *b* Gunter Ziesler (Peter Arnold, Inc.). **563:** Norman Owen Tomalin (Bruce Coleman, Inc.). **570:** Richard R. Hansen (Photo Researchers). **572:** *t* Jerome Wexler (Photo Researchers); *m&b* Terry Domico (Earth Images). **573:** Wardene Weisser (Bruce Coleman, Inc.). **579:** J. Gerlach (Tom Stack & Associates). **581:** *all* Carolina Biological Supply Co. **582:** *l* H. Harrison (Grant Heilman Photography); *r* Margo Conte (Animals Animals). **586:** Leonard Lee Rue III (Animals Animals). **588:** *l* Zig Leszczynski (Animals Animals); *r* Warren Garst (Tom Stack & Associates). **589:** Tom McHugh (Photo Researchers). **590:** *t* G.R. Roberts; *b* Leonard Lee Rue III (Tom Stack & Associates). **591:** Dr. Nigel Smith (Animals Animals). **593:** *t* Des & Jen Bartlett (Bruce Coleman, Inc.); *b* Stefan Myers (Animals Animals). **594:** Stephen Dalton (Animals Animals). **595:** *t* M.T. O'Keefe (Tom Stack & Associates); *b* N. Orabona (Tom Stack & Associates). **596:** *t* Tom Walker (Stock Boston); *b* E.R. Degginger (Bruce Coleman, Inc.). **597:** *t* Michael Habicht (Animals Animals); *b* William Weber (Visuals Unlimited). **598:** Tom McHugh (Photo Researchers). **610:** Michael Kienitz (Picture Group).

Unit Seven: **612:** *l* CNRI/SPL (Photo Researchers); *r* Science Photo Library (Photo Researchers). **613:** *l* CNRI/SPL (Photo Researchers); *r* Steiner (Photo Researchers). **614:** C. Rentmeester (FPG International). **616,617:** Manfred Kage (Peter Arnold, Inc.). **619:** Ed Reschke (Peter Arnold, Inc.). **621:** *t* J. Dennis (Phototake); *m&b* Dr. H.E. Huxley, MRC Lab of Molecular Biology, U.K. **623:** *both* G.W. Willis (BPS). **628:** Barry L. Runk (Grant Heilman Photography). **635:** © David Scharf. **636:** © Lennart Nilsson, *The Incredible Machine*, Boehringer Ingelheim Intl. GmbH (Bonnier Fakta). **639,640:** Imagery. **643:** Daniel Tessier. **648:** CNRI/SPL (Photo Researchers). **664:** Manfred Kage (Peter Arnold, Inc.). **667:** Hank Morgan (Photo Researchers). **671:** David Phillips (Visuals Unlimited). **680:** © Lennart Nilsson. **682:** *t* Michael Abbey (Photo Researchers); *b* Science Photo Library (Photo Researchers). **683:** J. Somers (Taurus Photos). **684:** Lennart Nilsson, *Behold Man*, 1974, Little, Brown & Co., used by permission (Bonnier Fakta). **686:** Boehringer Ingelheim Intl. GmbH (Bonnier Fakta). **689:** Dan McCoy (Rainbow). **690:** Prof. Luc Montagnier, Institut Pasteur (Photo Researchers). **692:** *t* Carolina Biological Supply Co.; *b* Dr. Victor Lorian, Bronx Lebanon Hospital. **693:** Phillip A. Harrington, courtesy of the Schering-Plough Corporation. **696:** Alfred Pasieka (Bruce Coleman, Inc.). **697:** CNRI/SPL (Photo Researchers). **700:** Bill Longcore (Photo Researchers). **704:** E.R. Lewis, Y.Y. Zeevi, T.E. Everhart, University of California (BPS). **718:** Dave Black (Sportschrome). **727:** M.I. Walker (Photo Researchers). **729:** The Bettmann Archive. **734:** Terry E. Eiler (Stock Boston). **735:** SIU (Peter Arnold, Inc.). **736:** *t* Farrell Grehan (Photo Researchers); *b* E.R. Degginger (AA/Earth Scenes). **737:** *t* Wesley Bocxe (Photo Researchers); *m* J. Somers (Taurus Photos). **741:** A. Glauberman (Photo Researchers). **742:** *tl&tr* Phototake; *b* Envision. **743:** Suzanne Arms (Jeroboam). **744:** Envision. **745:** Oxford Scientific Films (Animals Animals). **748:** Francis Leroy, Biocosmos/SPL (Photo Researchers). **751,755:** © Lennart Nilsson, *The Incredible Machine*, National Geographic Society (Bonnier Fakta). **757:** © Lennart Nilsson, *Behold Man*, Little, Brown & Co. **759:** *tl&tr* © Lennart Nilsson, *Being Born* (Bonnier Fakta); *ml&mr* A. Tsiaras (Photo Researchers); *bl* © Lennart Nilsson, *Behold Man*, Little, Brown & Co. (Bonnier Fakta); *br* © Lennart Nilsson, *The Incredible Machine*, National Geographic Society (Bonnier Fakta). **760:** Howard Sochurek (Woodfin Camp, N.Y.). **761:** N. Mason (FPG International).

Unit Eight: **768:** *l* Sylvia Martin (Photo Researchers); *r* William Weber (Visuals Unlimited). **769:** *l* F. Stuart Westmoreland (Tom Stack & Associates); *r* Dave Spier (Tom Stack & Associates). **770:** J.A.L. Cooke/OSF (Animals Animals). **772:** *t* Oxford Scientific Films (Animals Animals); *b* Breck Kent (Animals Animals). **773:** Michael & Barbara Reed (Animals Animals). **774:** Boulton-Wilson (Jeroboam). **776:** *l* Bates Littlehales (Animals Animals); *r* Michael Murphy (Photo Researchers). **777:** *t* David Fritts (Animals Animals); *b* K. Maslowski (Visuals Unlimited). **778:** Peter Pickford (DRK Photo). **782:** Tom Hollyman (Photo Researchers). **784:** *t&m* R. McIntyre (Tom Stack & Associates); *bl* Robert & Linda Mitchell; *br* R. McIntyre (Tom Stack & Associates). **785:** *t* Pat O'Hara (DRK Photo); *m* C. Allan Morgan (Peter Arnold, Inc.); *bl* S.J. Kraseman (Peter Arnold, Inc.); *br* Rod Planck (Tom Stack & Associates). **787:** *t* Robert Dunne (Bruce Coleman, Inc.); *b* Stephen Kraseman (DRK Photo). **789:** *t* AA/Earth Scenes; *b* C. Allan Morgan (Peter Arnold, Inc.). **790:** *t* Tom Bean (DRK Photo); *b* Emil Muench (Photo Researchers). **791:** Mark Boulton (Photo Researchers). **793:** E.R. Degginger (Animals Animals). **795:** *t* Michael Gadomski (Photo Researchers); *b* Pat O'Hara (DRK Photo). **800:** Fred Bavendam (Peter Arnold, Inc.). **803:** W. Gregory Brown (Animals Animals). **805:** Tim Rock (Animals Animals). **806:** B.G. Murray, Jr. (Animals Animals). **808:** Grant Heilman Photography. **813:** W.H. Hodge (Peter Arnold, Inc.). **816:** Bildarchiv Okapia (Photo Researchers). **819:** Jeff Foott (Bruce Coleman, Inc.). **828:** Peter Menzel (Stock Boston). **830:** Cary Wolinsky (Stock Boston). **832:** C. Allan Morgan (Peter Arnold, Inc.). **833:** Kathy Tarantola (Picture Cube). **834:** Jeff March (Tom Stack & Associates). **835:** Dan McCoy (Rainbow). **836:** David Doody (Tom Stack & Associates). **837:** *l* John Earle (Stock Market); *r* Gary Milburn (Tom Stack & Associates). **838:** Vic Cox (Peter Arnold, Inc.). **840:** Gary Milburn (Tom Stack & Associates). **844:** Mark Sherman (Bruce Coleman, Inc.). **851:** Ken O'Donoghue (D.C. Heath).